ASHE Reader on The History of Higher Education

Edited by
Lester F. Goodchild
Loyola University of Chicago
and
Harold S. Wechsler
Northwestern University

ASHE Reader Series
Barbara Townsend, Series Editor

10 9 8 7 6 5 4

Cover Illustration:
Margaret Drake Penfield (?)—Oberlin student, 1841-1846, did not graduate—oil on board, Tappan Hall (one of the other buildings, especially the one on the left, may be Ladres Hall), c. 1838-1841.

ISBN 0–536–57566–5

BA 3025

 GINN PRESS

160 Gould Street/Needham Heights, MA 02194
Simon & Schuster Higher Education Publishing Group

Copyright Acknowledgments

Association for the Study of Higher Education Reader on the History of Higher Education

Edited by
Lester F. Goodchild, Iowa State University
Harold S. Wechsler, National Education Association

TABLE OF CONTENTS

Part II. Higher Education during the Antebellum Period (1790-1860)

Part III. The Rise of American Universities During the Nineteenth and Twentieth Centuries

A. Introduction

B. State and Land-Grant Universities

Preface

This *Reader* comprehensively covers the history of American higher education. We assume students have some exposure to American history, but no work in the history of education.[1]

Historical analysis is not an antiquarian exercise. It illuminates, instructs, and occasionally prescribes. Knowing where we've come from is crucial to understanding where we're going. Every individual, institution, educational and social movement has a history. Every professor and administrator works in an institution with distinctive and shared traditions, values, and practices. The faculty or staff member must adjust to conditions that arise from this history—just as the institution and its other employees must adjust to the individual's personal history. The history of an immediate work environment, a profession, an institution, and the larger academic world affect daily performance.

The history course also makes higher education scholars aware that their research topics have histories, and that their findings are historical data for future researchers. But, not all scholars or practitioners recognize the discipline's centrality.

Many books invoke history without drawing upon its analytical resources. Justificatory and ornamental histories abound. C. James Quinn's handbook on college admissions practices, for example, traces the history of the "profession" (Quinn's word) back to the medieval period and the creation of the bursar's office. Along the way, Quinn makes the obligatory reference to Hastings Rashdall's classic history of early universities.[2] The discussion is not integrated with the remainder of the volume.[3] Its purpose is to justify the registrar as a professional with specialized knowledge, perquisites, values, and ethics. This approach ignores the relevance of history to contemporary issues.

This *Reader* gives professors of higher education, who share the historian's concerns about continuity and change, a rich vein of material from which to draw scholarly and policy implications. The last section of this *Reader* shows it is not necessary to end the historical analysis of a topic in 1945. An understanding of previous curricular reform movements, for example, sheds light upon the motivations, goals, and values of the current generation of reformers.

Where does a history course fit into a higher education program? Those who study, teach, or administer at a college or university will profit from understanding the history of higher education and of their particular institution. Without such understanding, new students, faculty, administrators, or trustees orient themselves with greater difficulty. Older hands find it harder to navigate through their institutions' norms and expectations. And scholars may ask the wrong questions of their data.

An historical approach performs several functions within a higher education program. Graduate students in higher education should be exposed to documentary analysis: the key analytical tool of the historian. Students who become academic administrators will themselves generate documents that become the grist for future generations of historians. The history course permits students to confront the meaning and nature of a document, learn how to dissect it, and understand that no document is "neutral." All documents have intended (as well as unintended) readers and "messages." Learning the circumstances behind a "report" and then reading that report should alert the potential administrator to the ways in which "reports" may be used. Similarly, a memo in a file may serve multiple functions, including "covering" the memo writer by presenting that writer's version of an event.

Having learned the basics of documentary analysis, the student may work with "case studies" in a disciplined fashion. Higher education programs that rely upon the "case method" can construct a "casebook" comprised of contemporary documents, from which students can reconstruct events and personalities. Students will learn the purpose(s) of a document, methods of analysis and of validation, and the constellation of forces that result in a major decision.

Students may trace an institutional decision by examining external correspondence, internal memoranda, committee, faculty, and trustee minutes, official materials such as reports, accreditation materials and catalogues—a most maligned resource, unofficial publications, such as newspapers and magazines, and quantitative material. Such materials enable students to analyze a decision, and to trace the development of policy over time and in the context of an institution's history.

There are few better introductions to the study of higher education than an exploration of an academic archive. Archival material facilitates sophisticated analyses of events and personalities. Rather than fitting events into preconceived categories, such as "collegial," "bureaucratic," and "political" models of decision-making, historical reconstructions allow students to understand actors and their motives, and events and their intended and unintended consequences in their full complexity.[4]

Multidisciplinary approaches to higher education that include historical analysis may greatly enrich our understanding of important events, actors, and trends. How does a sociological "snapshot" fit in with the long term evolution of an institution? How does one interpret the financial status of an institution? Can one count on various revenue sources? Are tuition increases "out of line" with those of comparable institutions or with an institution's long-term practice? Students will learn that certain social and economic variables—some of which may not be immediately apparent—are historically more subject to change than others.

Historiography challenges students who search for a "proven" method that prescribes action under a specific set of circumstances. Disagreements about the past make unanimous prescriptions about the future unlikely.

Many observers posit three generations of American historians of higher education—especially historians of antebellum institutions.[5] These observers characterize the first generation as "progressive," the second, "consensus," the third, "revisionist." Each generation reflected the preoccupations of their contemporaries: Progressives celebrated the triumph of universal education over hostile forces, and read that triumph back into past events. Consensus historians looked at a relatively placid post-World War II America and sought out continuities—not conflict—in American history. They also decried anti-intellectual features of American education. Revisionists, influenced by the campus demonstrations of the late 1960s, raised questions about the role of the university in modern society. As the university's stock declined, historians, for example, reassessed antebellum institutions that offered community, but eschewed bureaucracy.

Two generations ago, progressive historians emphasized the gradual response of colleges to the pressures of nineteenth century egalitarian American and their eventual triumph over the legacy of aristocratic eighteenth-century institutions. These historians examined modifications of an admittedly stale and prescribed antebellum undergraduate curriculum. Applauding advances, such as the introduction of scientific courses parallel to the dominant classical course, these historians painted an essentially optimistic picture of increased convergence between college and society.[6]

Scholarship of the 1950s and 1960s seriously challenged this approach. Richard Hofstadter, Walter Metzger, and others emphasized the nineteenth-century dominance of educational conservatives and argued that the typical old-time college had in fact retrogressed from its eighteenth century predecessors. Its faults, Hofstadter said, did not result from its concentration on the classics *per se*, "for just such a curriculum had long contributed enormously to the rearing of the best minds of Western society." The real problem, continued Hofstadter, was "that it trained no good classicists, reduced the study of classics to grammar and linguistics, that it usually failed to convey the spirit of the cultures of antiquity, that it often failed, indeed, even to teach very much Latin." The instructional method compounded these curricular shortcomings. The recitation system, in which students memorized a text or translation while the instructor merely checked on the correctness of the student's verbal regurgitation, "dulled the minds of students and blunted the edge of faculty scholarship; and such well-educated students as the colleges turned out were usually triumphs of the human spirit over bad methods."[7]

Reform would await the rise of universities at the end of the century. Lectures and seminars rather than recitations, knowledge creation rather than knowledge dissemination, secularization of governance, faculty, and curriculum, and incorporation of professional education made universities discontinuous with their antebellum predecessors.

The revisionist historians of the 1970s and 1980s pronounced a less clear-cut verdict. David Allmendinger, Colin Burke, and W. Bruce Leslie suggest that old-time colleges may not have been drab, isolated places. Students and colleges were integrated into the cultural and economic life of the surrounding community. David Allmendinger sees these colleges as an alternative for socially mobile students who wanted neither to move west, nor to remain on the farm.[8]

Historians of twentieth century higher education differ over the centrality of higher education to modern America, the importance of professional education within the university structure, the role of philanthropy in effecting academic and social change, and the relationship between higher education and the economy, the military, and the family.

Dividing historians of higher education into these three generations is a convenient first cut at a more complex scholarly array. Contemporary historians investigate: groups of institutions, for example, women's colleges, Southern colleges, Black colleges, in addition to histories of single institutions,[9] disciplines and professions, and academic and professional societies,[10] and concepts, such as "research," "professionalization," or "democratization."[11] Lawrence Cremin, for example, places the history of schools and colleges into the broader context of formal and informal educational configurations that individuals employ to educate themselves.[12] Quantitative approaches to the history of higher education complement traditional methods.[13] We are learning who went to college, where, and why. Some historians are investigating career paths of graduates. Historians of women in higher education investigate the effect of college attendance on marriage and birth rates, and on propensity to enter the work force. New studies also explore: the relationship between higher education and other social institutions, such as religion, the economy, the polity, and philanthropy,[14] the role of students in academic and campus life,[15] and minority groups and women. These investigations redefine familiar territory and place familiar academic figures in different, often unbecoming, light.[16] Historians also return to the personal questions such as the history of the undergraduate curriculum.[17]

We have sophisticated historical studies of many facets of American higher education, but we have no synthesis that is less then a generation old.[18] Contemporary calls for synthesis are a sign of the field's success since many building blocks exist. This *Reader's* selection offers the "latest" interpretation (along with a few "classics"), but the "latest" is neither the "only" nor the "correct" interpretation. Nor do the articles in the *Reader* add up to a consistent synthesis.

The *Reader's* historiographic eclecticism encourages students to generate their own syntheses and outlooks. Historical analysis allows for the complexity and uncertainty of human existence, and for multiple approaches to the same phenomenon. It informs students—as well as policy makers and administrators—but does not dictate to them.

In editing this *Reader*, we confronted several key decisions: the role of primary and secondary sources, the importance of articles that emphasized a single individual or institution versus more comprehensive articles, and the role of the historiography of higher education. The *Reader* emphasizes secondary readings, but primary sources—including the 1828 Yale Report, the Morrill Act, and the GI Bill—were inescapable. We have included at least one primary reading in each section.[19] We opted for comprehensive articles whenever possible, and for articles that include historiographic discussions. We are painfully aware of this *Reader's* omissions but hope that students will gain a working historical knowledge of the opportunities and problems that confront American higher education. We expect the bibliography to launch many discussions, papers, and theses. We hope this *Reader* conveys the enthusiasm we share for the role of history in the study of higher education.

Harold S. Wechsler
Washington, D.C. and Evanston, Illinios

Notes

1 The *Reader* may be supplemented with Richard Morris, ed., *Encyclopedia of American History*; the *International Encyclopedia of Higher Education*; the *Encyclopedia of Educational Research*; and Edward A. Krug, *Salient Dates in American Education* (New York: Harper, 1966). The *Dictionary of American Biography* and *Notable American Women* include sketches of prominent college presidents and faculty members. See also Mark Beach, ed., *A Bibliographic Guide to American Colleges and Universities from Colonial Times to the Present* (Westport, Conn.: Greenwood Press, 1975), and *A Subject Bibliography of the History of American Higher Education* (Westport, Conn.: Greenwood Press 1984). The bibliography at the end of this volume contains further references.

2 Hastings Rashdall, *The Universities of Europe in the Middle Ages*, 3 vols. (Oxford: Clarendon Press, 1895).

3 C. James Quinn and associates, *Admissions Academic Records, and Registrar Services: A Handbook of Policies and Procedures* (San Francisco: Jossey-Bass Publishers, 1979), chapter 1.

4 Increased academic interaction with other social institutions means that substantial archival records exist in collections other than university archives. Foundation archives are rich resources. Federal and state records aid historial reconstruction of many educational events and movements. Academic freedom, federal funding of higher education, and the university's research function are extensively addressed in public records. Corporate archives yield information on the relationships between business and higher education. There are about 30 well-established corporate archives in the New York City area, and many others in gestation.

5 For historiographic essays on higher education, see Ernest E. Bayles, "History of Education," *Encyclopedia of Educational Research*, 4th ed.; Robert L. Church, "History of Education as a Field of Study," *Encyclopedia of Education* (1970); Michael Sedlak, "Higher Education" in *American Educational History: A Guide to Information Sources* (New York: Garland Press, 1981), pp. 93-95; Wayne Urban, "Historiography," *Encyclopedia of Educational Research*, 5th ed., v. 2, 791-794; Geraldine Clifford, "Education: Its History and Historiography," *Review of Research in Education* 4 (1976), 210-267; Douglas Sloan, "Historiography and the History of Education," *Review of Research in Education* 1 (1973), 239-269; James McLachlan, "The American College in the Nineteenth Century: Toward a Reappraisal," *Teachers College Record* 80 (1978), 287-306; Donald Warren, "Higher Education, History," *Encyclopedia of Educational Research*, 5th ed.; and John Thelin, "Colleges and Universities: Peculiar Institutions," in *Higher Education and Its Useful Past* (Rochester, Vt.: Schenkman Books, Inc., 1982).

6 See for example, R. Freeman Butts, *The College Charts Its Course: Historical Conceptions and Current Proposals* (New York: McGraw-Hill Book Co, 1939).

7 Richard Hofstadter, *Academic Freedom in the Age of the College* (New York: Columbia University Press, 1961 [1955]), 228-229. This book and its companion, Walter P. Metzger, *Academic Freedom in the Age of the University* (New York: Columbia University Press, 1961 [1955]), along with Frederick Rudolph, *The American College and University: A History* (New York: Vintage Books, 1962), are often cited as exemplars of this school. See also Laurence Veysey, *The Emergence of the American University* (Chicago: University of Chicago Press, 1965).

8 See, for example, David F. Allmendinger, Jr., *Paupers and Scholars: The Transformation of Student Life in Nineteenth Century New England* (New York: St. Martin's Press, 1975); Colin R. Burke, *American Collegiate Populations: A Test of the Traditional View* (New York: New York University Press, 1982); Jurgen Herbst, "American College History: Reexamination Underway," *History of Education Quarterly*, 14 (Summer, 1984); Konrad Jarausch, ed., *The Transformation of Higher Learning, 1860-1930* (Chicago: University of Chicago Press, 1983); and Wilson Smith's essay, "Apologia Pro Alma Mater" in this volume.

9 See, for example, W. Bruce Leslie, "Localism, Denominationalism, and Institutional Strategies in Urbanizing America: Three Pennsylvania Colleges, 1870-1915," *History of Education Quarterly* 17 (1977), 235-256.

10 See Alexandra Oleson and John Voss, eds., *The Organization of Knowledge in Modern America, 1860-1920* (Baltimore, Md.: Johns Hopkins University Press, 1979).

11 Burton Bledstein, *The Culture of Professionalism* (New York: W. W. Norton & Co., 1976), and Roger L. Geiger, *To Advance Knowledge: The Growth of American Research Universities, 1900-1940* (New York: Oxford University Press, 1986).

12 Lawrence Cremin, *American Education: The Metropolitian Experience* (New York: Harper & Row, 1988). See also James McLachlan, "Lawrence Cremin on American Higher Education: A Review Essay," *History of Higher Education Annual* 8 (1988), 113-124.

13 David Allmendinger, Jr., "Mount Holyoke Students Encounter the Need for Life-Planning, 1837-1850," *History of Education Quarterly* 19 (Spring, 1979), 27-46, and Colin Burke, *American Collegiate Populations: A Test of the Traditional View* (New York: New York University, 1982).

14 The classic study is Merle Curti, *Philanthropy in the Shaping of American Higher Education* (New Brunswick, N.J.: Rutgers University Press, 1965). See also Ellen C. Lagemann, *Private Power for the Public Good: A History of the Carnegie Foundation for the Advancement of Teaching* (Middletown, Conn.: Wesleyan University Press, 1983), Steven Schlossman, Michael Sedlak, and Harold Wechsler, *The New Look: The Ford Foundation and the Revolution in Business Education* (Los Angeles: Graduate Management Admissions Council, 1988), and Steven C. Wheatley, *The Politics of Philanthropy: Abraham Flexner and Medical Education* (Madison, Wisc.: University of Wisconsin Press, 1988).

15 See Frederick Rudolph, "Neglect of Students as a Historical Tradition," in Lawrence E. Dennis and Joseph Kaufman, eds., *The College and the Student* (Washington, D.C.: American Council on Education, 1966), and Paula Fass, *The Damned and the Beautiful: American Youth in the 1920s* (New York: Oxford University Press, 1977).

16 See Part VI in this volume, and Frederick Chambers, ed., *Black Higher Education in the United States: A Selected Bibliography on Negro Higher Education and Historically Black Colleges and Universities* (Westport, Conn.: Greenwood Press, 1978). See also Joyce Antler, "Culture, Service, and Work: Changing Ideas of Higher Education for Women," in Pamela Perun, ed., *The Undergraduate Woman: Issues in Educational Equity* (Lexington, Mass.: Lexington Books, 1982), and Harold Wechsler, *The Qualified Student: A History of Selective College Admission in America 1870-1970* (New York: Wiley-Interscience, 1977).

17 Benchmarks include: R. Freeman Butts, *The College Charts Its Course*; the historical chapters of Daniel Bell, *The Reforming of General Education: The Columbia College Experience in the National Setting* (New York: Columbia University Press, 1966); and Frederick Rudolph, *Curriculum: A History of the American Undergraduate Course of Study Since 1636* (San Francisco: Jossey-Bass Publishers, 1977).

18 Partial exceptions include: Lawrence Cremin, *American Education*; Frederick Rudolph, *Curriculum*; Helen L. Horowitz, *Campus Life: Undergraduate Cultures from the End of the Eighteenth Century to the Present* (New York: Knopf, 1987); and Barbara Solomon, *In the Company of Educated Women: A History of Women and Higher Education in America* (New Haven, Conn.: Yale University Press, 1985).

19 Richard Hofstadter and Wilson Smith, *American Higher Education: A Documentary History*, 2 vols. (Chicago: University of Chicago Press, 1961) is out of print. There are other collections of documents on education, although none as comprehensive for the history of American higher education. See, for example, Sol Cohen, ed., *Education in the United States: A Documentary History*, 5 vols. (New York: Random House, 1974); Arthur Levine, ed., *Handbook on Undergraduate Curriculum* (San Francisco: Jossey-Bass Publishers, 1978); and Thomas Woody, *A History of Women's Education in the United States* (Lancaster, Pa.: Science Press, 1929).

A Note to the Reader

This long-awaited volume fills a special and important place in the Reader Series. The content of the volume reflects the strong efforts of the Volume Editors and Reader Series Editor to respond affirmatively to the emphasis of the ASHE Board on recognizing the diversity of voices, faces, and perspectives within higher education. Thus, the volume includes both coverage of foundational periods, events, and issues in the history of higher education, as well as articles pertaining to the history of minority as well as majority groups.

The reader will notice the volume is unique in its format. In order to include as much content as possible, guided by our desire to be inclusive in the volume's coverage of history, and commited to avoiding the cost to students of two volumes, the Series Editor and Volume Editors agreed that, where possible, space would be saved by printing two reduced size columns on a page. In such cases, the first page of the article reads vertically, but subsequent pages run horizontally. This decision was made after wide consultation with various ASHE members as well as students. We hope that the inconvenience caused to the reader by the atypical format is more than outweighed by the inclusiveness of the volume's coverage and the savings to students.

This first edition of the *ASHE Reader on the History of Higher Education* is expected to be in print for approximately three years, beginning January, 1990. Typically, the readings included in each *Reader* are reviewed and updated every few years.

A revised edition of this *Reader* is anticipated. Thus, we would appreciate your comments on the current *Reader* and suggestions for improvement. In particular, we would like to know which articles, documents, and book chapters you found especially helpful, thought-provoking, or informative. Also, we ask your help in identifying literature which might be included in future editions of this *Reader*.

Please send your comments and suggestions regarding this *ASHE Reader* to either of its editors:

Lester F. Goodchild
25 Dover Avenue
LaGrange, Illinois 60525

Harold Wechsler
School of Education and Social Policy
Northwestern University
Evanston, Illinois 60208

Suggestions regarding other topics which could be addressed through the *ASHE Reader* Series should be sent to:

Barbara Townsend
College of Education
Memphis State University
Memphis, TN 38152

We hope you will find this *Reader*, as well as others in the Series, to be useful in your study of higher education.

Acknowledgements

We began working on the *ASHE Reader on the History of Higher Education* two years ago when the ASHE publications board issued a call for a course text to be published by Ginn Press. We wish to thank the individuals who contributed their knowledge and time to create and produce a work that will provide an historical overview to future higher education practitioners and researchers. Our special gratitude goes to the *Reader's* own Advisory Board. The following educational and intellectual historians sent us their suggestions and evaluated our choices for the *Reader*:

Joyce Antler	Brandeis University
Robert Blackburn	University of Michigan—Ann Arbor
Joan Burstyn	Syracuse University
Clifton Conrad	University of Wisconsin—Madison
Steven Diner	George Mason University
E.D. Duryea	State University of New York—Buffalo
Roger Geiger	Pennsylvania State University
Lynn Gordon	University of Rochester
Elizabeth Hawthorne	University of Toledo
Allan Karp	Teachers College—Columbia University
Bruce Kimball	University of Rochester
Bruce Leslie	State University of New York—Brockport
James McLachlan	Princeton, New Jersey
John Thelin	College of William and Mary
Paul Vogt	State University of New York—Albany
Jennings Wagoner, Jr.	University of Virginia
Donald Warren	University of Maryland

Kathryn M. Moore of Michigan State University and Michael Olivas of the University of Houston commented on the appropriateness of our selections for higher education programs. Over 40 other professional colleagues contributed their syllabi, articles, and books for this publication.

The staff and doctoral students at Iowa State University handled many practical details associated with the *Reader*. Marva Ruther coordinated our work with the Advisory Board and typed the *Reader's* editorial elements. Daphanne Thomas's research in Parks Library produced an accurate bibliography. Barbara Plakans provided us with a list of land-grant institutions. Richard Warren, director of the Research Institute for Studies in Education at Iowa State University's College of Education, approved a mini-grant for our editorial work.

Wynn E. Goodchild and Lynn D. Gordon contributed insightful comments improving the text's quality and readability.

A special thanks to the National Education Association for providing the support and resources necessary to write this book.

Introduction

The History of American Higher Education:
An Overview and a Commentary

The 1838 painting of Oberlin College on our cover symbolizes a radical juncture in the history of the 3,300 institutions of higher learning in the United States. The founding of Oberlin in northern Ohio during 1833, as described in Robert S. Fletcher's renowned narrative, *A History of Oberlin College* (1943), launched a crusade for the advancement of religion, abolition, and education for both sexes from all races. While Harvard College began the colonies' quest for higher learning in 1636, its curriculum and clientele constituted an English pattern of liberal education and professional study for white males of intellectual and financial ability. Harvard and other colonial institutions laid the foundation for an American mandate for higher learning. However, a new Presbyterian sentiment in the Midwest rather different from that of eastern churches and colleges inflamed the Oberlin educational reformers. Their three thousand seat campus meeting house, central dormitory and classroom building for theological students, and three other residence halls established a uniquely American institution of higher learning. Their college for *all* persons was an innovation in Western English-speaking higher education. The faculty proclaimed its values in a 1839 statement. Oberlin would assume religious, intellectual, and social obligations in its mandate for higher learning, including:

> the hearty recognition of equal human rights as belonging to all whom God has made in his own image; a deep sympathy with the oppressed of every color, in every clime; and a consecration of life to the well-being of suffering humanity—& finally this paramount principle, that the cultivation of moral feelings is the first object in education, Gospel love to God & man, the first of all acquisitions and more precious than all other disciplines.

The Oberlin faculty started the movement to democratize our colleges and universities. Such a mandate has continued for over a century and a half through rational persuasion, litigation, lobbying, and institutional diversity. The democratization of higher education thus began some fifty-seven years after the signing of the Declaration of Independence and comprised one of the distinguishing features of the incipient American system.

In their classic work, *Higher Education in Transition: A History of American Colleges and Universities, 1636-1976* (1976), John S. Brubacher and Willis Rudy draw our attention to this developing characteristic of our colleges and universities. They also identify other distinctive features: the extensive opportunities for all persons, young and old, to enroll in diverse institutions of higher learning; the broad scope of courses offered at colleges and universities; the institutional commitment to service local communities and American society; the voluntary cooperation among colleges and universities in setting standards through accrediting associations; the corporate structure of postsecondary governance; as well as the extracurriculum. Each of these attributes arose out of a unique interplay between higher education and American life, as will be noted shortly.

The Organization of the *Reader*

The *Association for the Study of Higher Education Reader on the History of Higher Education* offers the student of higher education: (1) an introductory essay on American higher education historiography; (2) overviews of each chronological period of higher education; (3) in-depth scholarly analyses from journal articles, chapters of books, and essays for each period; and (4) primary readings to capture the flavor and meaning of important issues for each period. The *Reader* replaces virtually all comprehensive histories and documentaries of American higher education suitable for a course on this subject, because these works, such as Frederick Rudolph's *The American College and University: A History* (1962), John S. Brubacher and Willis Rudy's *Higher Education in Transition* (1976), or Richard Hofstadter and Wilson Smith's *American Higher Education Documentary History* (1961), are no longer in print. While many historical analyses of particular periods within higher education or certain issues exist, suitable comprehensive texts for higher education are now lacking.

Four principles of selection guided our editorial choices. First, the text is organized chronologically. After presenting a general history of higher education, the *Reader* offers a short discussion of Central and South American higher education from 1538 to 1850 and then explores five periods within North American higher education. Second, for each period, the readings lay out the history of higher education by covering four major research topics within this field of study: (1) the organizational development of institutions, (2) faculty life, (3) curricular considerations, and (4) student life. The *Reader* thus introduces students to the themes of the other ASHE readers on organizational theory, curriculum, faculty, student life, community colleges, and finance. Our third organizational principle consisted of making available the most recent research. We deemphasized an elitist history of higher education which has centered on the rise of American research universities. Conversely, we included regional developments within higher education, especially southern and midwestern perspectives—concise histories of western, especially Californian, higher education are not yet available. Furthermore, we accentuated public colleges and universities which now enroll seventy-five percent of postsecondary students. The *Reader* also includes recent research on the education of female students, women's colleges, and coeducation as well as some analysis of colleges and universities that serve different clienteles, such as Catholics, Afro-Americans, Indians, and Hispanics. Finally our fourth principle involved listening to historians of education in making our selections. The resulting collaborative process provides a rich compendium of source materials for the history of higher education courses in the over 120 programs across the country as well as for other classes in American studies or intellectual history.

An Overview of the *Reader*'s Selections

A commentary on the *Reader*'s selections offers an opportunity to identify the historical themes for each period of American higher education and the conceptual framework underlying its organization. The study of higher education as a degree program is only thirty years old, although early courses and administrative concentrations may be traced back to the turn of the century. Yet, the quest to achieve higher learning originated in the early fabric of human culture. In our first reading, Domonkos's expansive survey of the history of higher education begins at the dawn of civilization in Mesopotamia and ancient Egypt and ends with contemporary postsecondary systems. With the rise of universities at Bologna, Salerno, and Paris in the twelfth and thirteenth centuries, Western civilization created institutions of higher learning to preserve, to transmit, and eventually to discover knowledge. This evolutionary and comparative perspective thus enables us to place the development and growth of American colleges and universities within a world context.

Colonial Education in the Americas

Soon after the discovery of the New World in the fifteenth century, European settlers established institutions of higher learning. Colonial higher education in the Americas began with the papal chartering of Santo Domingo's University of St. Thomas Aquinas in 1538, following Spanish Catholic patterns as Harold Benjamin's short essay describes. Almost one hundred years later, English colonists founded Harvard College to advance Puritan Christianity, following Cambridge and Oxonian ideals of higher learning. Lawrence Cremin's chapter from his *American Education: The Colonial Experience, 1607-1783* (1970) gives us a complete picture of the first colonial college and its curriculum. It was soon followed by the founding and chartering of eight colleges before the American revolution: the College of William and Mary, 1693; the Collegiate School at New Haven, 1701 (renamed Yale College); the College of Philadelphia, 1740 (renamed the University of Pennsylvania); the College of New Jersey, 1746 (renamed Princeton College); King's College, 1754 (renamed Columbia University); the College of Rhode Island, 1764 (renamed Brown University); Queen's College, 1766 (renamed Rutger's College); and Dartmouth College, 1769. Meanwhile to the north of the colonies, New France established a theological seminary in Quebec in the 1660s that later became Laval University. Colonial higher education, which embodied characteristics of both secondary and higher learning as may be seen at the Jesuit school established in Newton, Maryland in 1677, brought European liberal and professional knowledge to this hemisphere.

The English colonists established their nine colleges to satisfy local educational needs which arose from pastoral and missionary demands within various Christian denominations. Unlike the state church of European countries, several religious communities lived within the same province. As their numbers grew, pleas for toleration became more pressing. President Clap at Yale was forced to accept student requests for freedom of worship. When Queen's College was founded as the second collegiate institution in New Jersey, its Anglican president admitted men of all religious persuasions. Such changes in policy and governance began the process of Americanization as old world structures were tailored to meet new demands within the colonies. Herbst's article chronicles and comments on these changes as the colleges slipped from their religious moorings to be left tied mainly to colonial governments. In this shift, the original mission of these institutions waned. Bobby Wright scrutinizes how these transformations eclipsed the Indian missionary goals of the colleges. As the first of our revisionist articles, following the lead of James Axtell in his *The European and the Indian* (1981) and *The Invasion Within* (1985), he contends that the proselytizing and educating of indigenous populations was used mainly to garner financial support from English churches and benefactors rather than to be truly apostolic.

As collegiate religious aims lessened in importance by the mid-1770s, presidents turned fully toward pedagogical objectives. Here Martin Finkelstein delineates the colonial and antebellum faculty transformation from the models of English tutor to the teaching scholar. Presidential authority was also not well received among rebellious students who rejected strict guardianship, as Kathryn Moore's insightful analysis shows. Yet the social function of these colleges grew as they provided the means to acquire stature within the colonies. Phyllis Vine shows how these institutions enabled students to assume leadership roles, marry into the best families, and make social contacts that assisted their future career success. This function became even more important during the nineteenth century. The primary readings in this section explore Harvard's early student rules and charter. Such mandates established the mission of these colonial institutions and the means to control their inmates, as students were called in the eighteenth century.

These colleges embraced a different *raison d'etre* after the American revolution. Now their mandate centered on providing religious and lay leaders for a new nation. The effects of this profound transition may be learned from David Robson's *Educating Republicans: The College in the Era of the American Revolution, 1750-1800* (1985) and John Roche's *The Colonial Colleges in the War for American Independence* (1985). This epic event resulted in a new westward focus for American higher education as the next seventy years saw a tremendous growth in collegiate institutions on the frontier.

Antebellum Higher Education

The historiography of antebellum colleges and universities is controversial. Scholars disagree on the number of institutions founded, the reason for their establishment, the meaning and the pattern of their curricula, the type of student enrolled, and the effect of these institutions and their graduates on society. Robert Church and Michael Sedlak's overview, "The Antebellum College and Academy," adopts the Tewksbury thesis of collegiate proliferation, describes the differences between colleges and academies, stresses the importance of the 1819 Dartmouth Case for understanding collegiate privatization, offers a positive interpretation of the 1828 Yale Report, and notes the revival of denominationalism among the colleges after the Civil War. Church and Sedlak derived their conclusions from the revisionist historical scholarship done in the 1970s. James Axtell's "The Death of the Liberal Arts College" challenged the classic interpretations of Tewksbury, Hofstadter, and Rudolph as being Whiggish. Further support came from David Potts's argument that local boosterism explains the rash of collegiate foundations in the first half of the nineteenth century. Natalie Naylor, James McLachlin, James Findlay, and Jack Lane elaborate on these themes (see bibliography). One of the crucial developments in this period is the Dartmouth College case of 1819. Yet, the role which it played in collegiate foundings remains far from being resolved, as the John Whitehead and Jurgen Herbst debate in 1986 demonstrates. Understanding the curricular development of antebellum institutions beyond Church, Sedlak, and Potts analyses may be gained by reading Douglas Sloan's excellent treatment in his article, "Harmony, Chaos, and Consensus: The American College Curriculum" (1971), which is reprinted in Clifton Conrad's *ASHE Reader on Academic Programs in Colleges and Universities* (1987) or Rudolph's *Curriculum* (1977).

Furthermore, Axtell (1971) points to the culture of academic life as a means to understand antebellum colleges. Adhering to his insight, we chose to include other institutional perspectives, such as the founding of state universities, student life, southern higher education, and the beginning of women's higher learning, to fill out this period. Jennings Wagoner's study of the University of Virginia depicts the secular development of the American university ideal of teaching and research, and early nineteenth century student life in the South. During the first two centuries of American higher education, higher learning was for men. However, the foundings of Troy Female Seminary in 1822 and Mount Holyoke College in 1837 and the actual enrollment of women at Oberlin College opened the door to baccalaureate education for women. Patricia Palmieri's analysis provides a perspective on the development of women's higher education from 1820 to 1920. Linda Perkins discusses the origins of Black women's education with a particular emphasis on Oberlin's role and developments in the South after the Civil War. To bring closure to this period we found Robert Blackburn and Clifton Conrad's summary and analysis of the revisionist critiques particularly helpful. As a primary reading, no more important document than the 1828 Yale Report could be suggested because of its pervasive effect on the undergraduate curriculum for the rest of the century. By the Civil War, some of the distinguishing features of American higher education had begun to appear: service to local communities, collegiate governance structures which were separate from the state, and the access of persons from both sexes and all races to higher learning. These nascent developments as evidenced at Oberlin College and the University of Virginia constituted the first steps in Americanization of higher education, as Continental patterns gave way to local practices.

American Universities

After the Civil War, the societal demands on higher education in the East and Midwest created new missions for institutions of higher learning. The rise of American universities as described by Carol Gruber in her introductory chapter of *Mars and Minerva* (1975) captures the institutional differentiation which occurred during the nineteenth century as state, land-grant, and research universities were founded. She accepts the standard "consensus" argument of Laurence Veysey in his *The Emergence of the American University* (1965) that these universities arose out of a reform movement against the antebellum college. This view has been challenged by Axtell (1971) and other revisionists—as well as recent research on the scientific schools at Harvard and Yale,—see Robert Bruce's *The Launching of Modern American Science,*

1846-1876 (1987)—who perceive a gradual development of these institutional ideals. Yet, the desire for practical scientific knowledge as opposed to classical education led to the founding of the University of Virginia and land-grant universities after 1862, such as Iowa State, Kansas State, and Michigan State. Moreover, the desire for scientific inquiry particularly espoused by American graduates of German universities since 1810 encouraged early efforts to launch research-oriented institutions of higher learning. Not until the founding of Johns Hopkins University in 1876, the establishment of graduate Clark University in 1889, and the reestablishment of the University of Chicago in 1892 did a new university type begin. Both new American institutional missions encouraged the professionalization of knowledge through the rise of national disciplinary associations and faculty professionalization through the formation of the American Association of University Professors (AAUP).

The differences between the standard and revisionist arguments have been addressed by recent reassessments of these institutional types. To begin our discussion of state and land-grant universities in the *Reader*, Lang chronicles the land-grant movement by describing the founding of People's College in 1858, the Morrill Act of 1862, and the establishment of Cornell University. Eldon Johnson's revisionist article further clarifies how these institutions fit within the developing context of American higher education. He argues that the land-grant idea and curricula developed gradually at these universities. He contends that state universities resembled antebellum colleges until the turn of the century. David Hoeveler's work on the "Wisconsin Idea" then describes how the state capital-university relationship originated, reminding us of the late nineteenth century religious underpinnings of American society—a further exploration of this theme may be found in Ross's "The Religious Influences in the Development of State Colleges and Universities" (1950). Last, Stetar discusses the higher education of southern whites during the Reconstruction period which resisted the land-grant and research ideals. These works support a gradual differentiation of institutional types during the nineteenth century. Primary materials for this period include the Morrill Act of 1862 and a list of all land-grant institutions.

The major works on American research universities, Veysey's *The Emergence of the American University* (1965), Herbst's *The German Historical School in American Scholarship: A Study in the Transfer of Culture* (1965), and Geiger's *To Advance Knowledge: The Growth of the American Research University, 1900-1940* (1986), describe the beginnings of this unique American institution. Learning new methods of scholarship from German universities and institutes, American scholars advanced the ideals of "knowledge for its own sake," that is, pure research, when they began teaching at American institutions of higher learning. At the same time they placated demands for its practical application. In the *Reader*, Hugh Hawkins describes how faculty roles of teaching and research played themselves out in the developing departmental structure which so embodied the mission of these new universities. While faculty demonstrated a strong proclivity for research, Hawkins notes the primacy of teaching. Geiger's penetrating research on faculty hours at research universities clarifies any ambiguity about the amount of research time faculty were given. This new professoriate strove to professionalize knowledge through doctoral programs as well as their research, as Merle Curti describes so well. Besides the development of graduate schools, these universities also became centers for professional learning. Similar to the Continental university pattern, American research universities developed and affiliated schools of medicine, law, theology, and eventually education. Their subsequent regulation by universities and professional associations which mandated the baccalaureate degree as an entrance requirement played a crucial role in the expansion of the undergraduate programs after World War I.

The next articles in the *Reader* fill out the configuration which became the twentieth century American research university. Veysey notes how new organizational demands would not have been accomplished without the increase of administrators who took over the bureaucratic functions of the evolving universities. However, they did little to lessen the developing chasm between faculty and students. Women played a greater role in university life as coeducation became the norm. Lynn Gordon shows that women comprised as much as forty percent of the undergraduate population at some universities. Finally, Brubacher and Rudy describe the expanding role of the extracurriculum from its origins as literary societies, debate clubs, and drama festivals in the nineteenth century college to big-time sports in American universities by the turn of the century.

The unique character of the American research university can be readily seen through our primary readings for this period. Daniel Coit Gilman presents his model for Johns Hopkins University. Harvard's president, Charles W. Eliot, then discusses the elective undergraduate curriculum, a key feature in the development of research universities. Further analysis of this important dynamic may be found in Hawkins's *Between Harvard and America: The Educational Leadership of Charles W. Eliot* (1972). Similarly, the protection of academic freedom through the AAUP encouraged the growth of the American professoriate; its principles are as important today as they were then. Finally, Veysey's chart depicting the tenure of university presidents at Johns Hopkins, Clark, Chicago, Michigan, Harvard, Wisconsin, Stanford, and others shows how longevity in office allowed for the development of a consistent institutional mission. Adding to the developing distinctive features of American higher education during this period then are extensive curricular options and courses of study available to students as well as the expansion of the extracurriculum. With the establishment of the land-grant and research universities, the Americanization of higher education had been furthered. The next period saw even more gains.

The First Half of the Twentieth Century

American society underwent significant changes at the turn of the twentieth century. Great waves of immigration and the expansion of a middle class hastened the growth of American higher education. The offspring of these groups sought higher learning as a means to enter vocational, managerial, educational, and professional careers. Yet, private colleges and universities often blocked their admission. Harold Wechsler's *The Qualified Student* (1977) explored the bias that kept undesirable groups out of higher education. His article in the *Reader* describes the difficulties poor, female, Jewish, and Black students encountered in admission during the first two decades of this century. After World War I a greater demand for higher education gave rise to alternative institutions that educated first generation students. Because of discriminatory practices and pent-up educational demands, institutional differentiation and diversity occurred. David Levine shows how junior colleges, state teacher colleges, and state universities sought to satisfy this culture of aspiration which resulted also in the record foundings of women's colleges and private religious-sponsored colleges. Patricia Graham points out the results in her overview of women's colleges, administrators, faculty, and students from this period up to the present. As representative of church-related postsecondary education, I have also shown how Catholic higher education, especially American Jesuit colleges and universities, attempted to meet student demands for baccalaureate and professional education, while at the same time adjusting to the developing standards of accrediting associations. Besides the institutions established by these groups, significant changes occurred in Black higher education. Wagoner sketches the "American Compromise" as northern educational leaders invoked the ideas of Booker T. Washington and allowed southern politicians and administrators to establish a racially separate and unequal educational system. While the establishment of Black colleges, Black land-grant universities under the second Morrill Act of 1890, and Black junior colleges created *de facto* a separate system, the loss of state revenues which primarily assisted white institutions of higher learning as well as the lack of corporate and religious philanthropy by the 1920s meant the decline of historically Black institutions. A commentary on the effects of this compromise that lasted until the *Brown* decision of 1954 is given by James Anderson whose overview takes us from the end of the Civil War until the beginning of World War II. Our primary reading also explores the problems encountered by disenfranchised groups. W. E. B. DuBois describes the predicament of Blacks and Black higher education in 1903. This new historical scholarship on higher education during the first half of the twentieth century has rectified our view of "equity" and "democracy" in American colleges and universities.

As a result of these changes in American higher education, there were now greater opportunities for individuals to begin higher learning. This educational experience gradually came under the purview of professional and regional accrediting associations which attempted to ensure its academic character. A further stage in the Americanization of higher education had occurred. While each of the distinguishing features of American higher education had appeared, their full demonstration would await the most stressful period in American higher education, the boom–to–retrenchment era after the Second World War.

Higher Education in the Contemporary Period

Given the difficulties of archival access and copious institutional documentation after 1945, few historians of education have assessed the dramatic changes that occurred at colleges and universities during this time. We are forced therefore to rely on critical commentaries and sociological studies. This section of the *Reader* mirrors this change in research orientation. Federal policies and funding as well as dramatic college-age cohort increases brought about a boom period in American higher education. Our primary readings reveal the reasons for this development. The GI Bill of Rights facilitated access to higher education for World War II, Korean War, and Vietnam War veterans. President Truman's commission on higher education encouraged the education and training of all citizens and the growth of community colleges. The Higher Education Act of 1965 enabled many institutions to build classroom buildings, residence halls, and research laboratories as well as to offer students graduate scholarships. Each of these readings signifies the growing federalism of higher education. Other federal laws, especially the earlier National Defense Student Act of 1958, enabled emerging universities to accommodate increased student demands for undergraduate, professional, and graduate education as well as to make tremendous strides in research. Federal monies also sought to satisfy the need for vocational training through the now over 1,000 community colleges. These federal enactments enabled universities and colleges to meet the extraordinary demands of society.

A concise historical overview of this era may be gained by reading John Best's "Revolution of Markets and Management." It describes the developments in higher education as waves of demographic changes, public policy shifts, faculty and student demonstrations, and retrenchment programs. The rise of the federal government's role may be understood by reading Janet Kerr's discussion of policy formulation from the Truman to the Johnson presidencies. Alexander Astin then describes how student and faculty demands for change brought about governance, administrative, professorial, and pedagogical developments unparalleled in the history of higher education. Besides these internal strides for democratization, societal pressures influenced colleges and universities to open their doors to students and faculty members of all races. Frank Bowles and Frank DeCosta discuss the desegregation of southern higher education after the *Brown* decision and the progress of historically Black institutions with the assistance of federal funding. Michael Olivas extends Bowles and DeCosta's sociological overview with his discussion of Black access to higher education under the *Adams* ruling as well as portrays the conditions of American Indian, Chicano, and Puerto Rican colleges. These sweeping institutional changes also affected the character of the professoriate as research became the *sine qua non* of advancement and tenure. This mandate had significant effects on the quality of its teaching and public service. The upshot of these developments has been the very questioning of the professional stature of the American faculty. Here Walter Metzger explores these difficulties, while Gary Sykes offers a response. The effect of these shifts in professional duties changed the character and the quality of the undergraduate curriculum. Bruce Kimball provides us with a comprehensive assessment of the national reports challenging the state of the baccalaureate and the faculty's mandate. In sum, few aspects of higher education remained unchanged during this period.

Martin Trow's critical analysis of this period in his "American Higher Education: Past, Present, and Future" places these dramatic developments in a summative perspective. Calling this period one of mass higher education as over forty percent of the college-age cohort enrolled in higher education, he reviews the shifts in clientele, markets, governance, and finance. The results of these extensive changes democratized American higher education and solidified its distinctive features. Furthermore, the research productivity of the sciences and the humanities in American colleges and universities earned universal acclaim for the quality of higher education in the United States.

From the founding of Harvard College in 1636 to contemporary multicampus state systems of California, New York, Texas, Pennsylvania, Wisconsin, Illinois, and others, the development of American higher education is a fitting tribute — despite its problems and inequities — to humanity's quest for the advancement of religion, morality, and knowledge during the past three hundred and fifty years.

July 4, 1989   Lester F. Goodchild
                                            Loyola University of Chicago

History of Higher Education

Leslie S. Domonkos

"All men by nature desire to know" said Aristotle (*Metaphysics*, Book I, Section I). Man's quest for knowledge is an integral part of the human condition, as is the desire to transmit this knowledge to subsequent generations. This transmission occurs on several levels, depending on the cultural setting, the sophistication of the transmitter, and the receptiveness of the student. The knowledge transmitted varies greatly, from elementary to a level of instruction that requires considerable intellectual preparation.

In our time most of the instruction of an advanced nature takes place in the institutionalized setting of the universities. Higher education and university-level instruction have become basically synonymous. This association of higher education and the universities is a phenomenon that has its roots in the medieval European tradition. The medieval university emerged as a legal corporation with the right to grant licenses to teachers in various disciplines. Subsequently, there developed in the Western tradition an intimate association between the transmission of higher education and the institution of the university. In the ancient and classical world, or in areas untouched by the European university tradition, education often developed to such high levels that it would be intellectually dishonest to exclude it from a discussion of higher education. Although higher education did not have the same institutionalized structure that it had after the thirteenth century A.D., it did exist in almost all major civilizations.

Traditionally, the curriculum of higher education usually had a strong humanistic element as its base, often supplemented by specific training for a learned profession.

In our century, higher education witnessed an immense expansion of its curriculum, especially in the technical fields. Technical schools, academies, and community colleges have expanded the traditional curriculum to include subjects that previously were excluded from institutions of higher education and that are basically vocational or paraprofessional in content. Thus the term higher education becomes broader in meaning with each passing decade.

Education in the Ancient World

The history of higher education in the ancient world is part of the growth of urban cultures of the Nile River Valley, Mesopotamia, Crete, the river valleys of India and China, and, to a lesser degree, part of the development of civilization in Central and South America. Large aggregations of population in these areas led to the abandonment of agriculture as the sole means of earning a living and produced a differentiation in occupations. This differentiation in occupations led to the rise of arts and crafts to meet the demands of an increasingly complex pattern of culture. Further specialization, made necessary by a demand for specific skills, led to the emergence of a class of learned professionals in a wide variety of fields. The maintenance, transmission, and refinement of these specific skills led to the establishment of various schools, where knowledge was passed on from one generation to the other. Although institutions of higher education in the modern sense were lacking in the ancient cultures, higher education was definitely present in these civilizations. The intellectual, artistic, and technological advancement of the ancient empires would have been impossible without a tradition of higher education.

The Nile River Valley. Although Egypt is probably not the oldest of the ancient urban civilizations, because of its stability the Nile River Valley deserves special consideration in the history of higher education.

A very close association between higher education and the temples existed in ancient Egypt. From the time of the Old Kingdom, the government of which can be characterized as a theocracy, the ruler depended to a large degree upon the priestly class in the administration of his land. The priests were also the major custodians of all aspects of cultural life. The temples, and to a lesser degree the royal palace, were the centers of instruction, not only in the elementary subjects of writing in the various scripts, record keeping, and rudimentary sciences but also in higher education. Although elementary forms of instruction were provided by hundreds of temples in the valley, a number of important educational centers developed in association with the great temples of Heliopolis, Karnak (el-Karnak), Memphis, and Heracleopolis (Herakleopolis). In addition to moral and literary instruction, the students were also introduced to advanced mathematics, astronomy, physics, medicine, and theology. The important temple schools were richly endowed, enabling the priest-scholars to devote themselves to the pursuit of knowledge and teaching without having to worry about the mundane problems of daily existence. Both teachers and students at these great temple schools belonged to a privileged cultural elite.

Professional education, in the fields of architecture, sculpture, irrigation, and embalming, was probably carried on outside the formal instructional framework of the great temple schools, but because religion permeated almost every phase of Egyptian life, even these professional fields were under ecclesiastical influence. The conservative nature of Egyptian civilization and the close ecclesiastical supervision of education ensured the transmission of a cultural heritage for almost 3000 years without major deviation. Although not innovative, Egyptian higher education was a stable vehicle for cultural transmission. Not until the conquest by the Persians in 525 B.C. and the spread of Hellenistic civili-

zation two hundred years later was this stability challenged.

The Fertile Crescent. The civilization of ancient Mesopotamia shows far less stability and homogeneity than its near contemporary counterpart in the Nile River Valley The rise of an urban civilization in the Tigris-Euphrates Valley preceded the Egyptians by a few hundred years and the pioneers of this development were the Sumerians. Their state, originally a loose confederation of cities, was less autocratic and less theocratic than Egypt. Although in Mesopotamia the association between schools and temples seems to have existed, as it did in Egypt, the power of the ecclesiastical element appears to be less pronounced. Elementary education in the instruction of the art of writing (cuneiform) and rudimentary mathematics was carried on in the Sumerian temples. Certain temples and the libraries attached to them provided advanced instruction to an elite student body. Training in the fields of medicine, theology, and possibly law took place at these temples and libraries. Mathematics and astronomy-astrology were also highly developed. Since Sumerian culture was highly legalistic, the question of the origins of legal training arises, but unfortunately cannot be answered with any certitude; to what degree, if any, temple schools trained individuals in legal scholarship seems to be unclear. Although specific information on the nature of higher education among the Sumerians is lacking, the growth of an important literary tradition and contributions to the sciences, engineering, and legal studies all would have been impossible without the presence of some forms of higher education. The tradition of scholarship established by the Sumerians before their fall around 1900 B.C. was preserved by subsequent cultures, including the Babylonians (nineteenth to sixteenth centuries B.C.), the Assyrians (tenth to seventh centuries B.C.), and the Chaldeans (sixth century B.C.).

The influence of both Mesopotamia and Egypt is evident on the other civilizations of the Fertile Crescent, such as the Phoenicians, the Hebrews, and possibly even the Hittites and Minoans. The educational system of the ancient Hebrews laid great emphasis on morality and the keeping of

3

the law of God. Following a long period when oral tradition was passed from generation to generation, in Israel and Judah a class of scribes (Soferim) began to set down the law and to copy and interpret it. Higher education was, therefore, restricted to legal studies and reached its culmination in the work of teachers such as Hillel (first century B.C.) and Gamaliel (first century A.D.).

India. A flourishing urban-oriented civilization also arose in India, near the Indus River Valley, by the middle of the third millennium B.C. It shows certain parallels to the civilizations of the Nile and Tigris-Euphrates Valley cultures.

By 1500 B.C. the Indus Valley civilization fell under the sway of Aryan invaders, whose presence deeply affected the subsequent development of this part of the globe. The Aryans defeated the original inhabitants and settled among them, and their presence led to the four-part division of society into distinct classes that eventually evolved into castes. Of these the most important in educational-cultural history were the Brahmins, the intellectual, priestly class. The other three groups were the Kshatriyas, warrior-nobles; the Vaishyas, the gainfully employed agricultural and trading population; and the Sudras, the serf and servant element. Each of the major classes was divided into subgroups. Since the Brahmins constituted the intellectual and priestly class, education in India was closely tied to them, although Kshatriyas and Vaishyas were not excluded from instruction. Elementary instruction was given to the three upper classes, but in time advanced instruction in religion, philosophy, and the study of the *Vedas, Brahminas, Upanishads,* and *Sutras* was reserved for the members of the Brahmin class. Originally, instruction was exclusively oral and took place at the home of a learned Brahmin, where the students were subjected to strict intellectual and moral discipline. In the seventh century B.C. the monopoly of the Brahmin instruction was challenged by the forest schools, where the study of the *Vedas* was supplemented by an ascetic life. In these schools students lived in the woods with a learned teacher and studied not only the *Vedas* but other subjects such as astronomy, etymology, and grammar.

A simple life, consisting of the performance of religious ceremonies and some manual labor, was coupled with celibacy, which was strictly enforced. When students had completed this preparatory period, higher education, including instruction in philosophy, logic, grammar, law, and possibly the sciences, was available to those Brahmins who had mastered the basic text of the Hindu tradition. An important development at this time was the emergence of *parishads,* the closest equivalent of the university in ancient Hindu India. Later, especially in the period beginning in the eighth century A.D., *tols* or *pathasalas* were established by learned teachers, where advanced students lived in small communities studying logic, law, and other advanced subjects.

Because of the increasing formalism and exclusiveness of Brahmin education, Buddhism and Jainism brought about major changes in Indian education in the sixth century B.C. This new education was characterized by two developments: democratization and institutionalization through the emergence of monastic schools. The Buddhists and Jainists removed many of the class and sex distinctions of the Brahmin schools, and their monasteries emerged as new centers of learning. Between the sixth century B.C. and the sixth century A.D., Indian intellectual life flourished, especially during the Gupta Empire. Important centers of higher education were established at Taxila, Benares, Kanchi, Valabhi, and especially Nalanda. Although the more traditional Hindu Vedic tradition eventually revived during the fourth to eighth centuries A.D. and produced a "classical" renaissance, the Buddhist influence receded, and the curriculum was vastly expanded, especially in the sciences. Astronomy, medicine, engineering, and particularly mathematics enjoyed a period of great flowering. It was Indian scholars who first developed the concept of zero and the decimal system. Indian cultural and educational influence can also be detected in all parts of Southeastern Asia and China.

China. Ancient Chinese civilization originated in the second millennium B.C. From earliest times education in China emphasized the importance of civic morality—the virtuous behavior of the citizen and the preference of the educated person in the administration of the state. Unlike India, where the transmission of knowledge remained oral for a long time, the Chinese developed script, the mastery of which was one of the basics of education. This occurred during the early Chou dynasty (twelfth to eighth centuries B.C.). Schools were established where writing, mathematics, music, and martial arts were taught. The period from the eighth to the third century B.C. was one of the most fruitful periods of Chinese intellectual history. This age saw the rise of the scholar-philosopher and the development of a number of important schools of thought, especially Confucianism, Taoism, Moism, and Legalism. The major schools competed with each other for students, and China had a large number of private institutions of higher learning, where philosophical and literary work was carried on by teachers and students. There was a marked increase of literary activity and a great freedom of intellectual inquiry.

During the Han dynasty (third century B.C. to third century A.D.), Confucianism emerged as the most important school of thought, and literary scholarship reached new heights. Confucius emphasized the reliance on the scholar-administrator as the foundation of orderly society. The scholar became the backbone of the Chinese civil service, and this tradition persisted until modern times. Higher education consisted of instruction in Confucian thought, familiarity with other major schools of philosophy, literary criticism, study of the classical writings, and history. Upon completion of the prescribed course of study, those who planned to enter government service were given state examinations; thus, an elite group of scholars assisted the rulers in the administration of the realm.

It was also during the Han dynasty that Buddhism was introduced to China. The result was the translation of Buddhist literature into Chinese and the introduction of Indian mathematics, astronomy, and certain art forms to China. The Buddhist system of monastic education also took roots in China and subsequently flourished in its new environment.

The Americas. Information on the educational systems of the ancient civilizations of the Americas—Maya, Inca, and Aztec—is vague. The level of cultural achievement of these advanced civilizations suggests some formal higher education. The transmission of oral traditions, history, and poetry was an important aspect of this education. Except in Peru, written records were kept by scribes and the priestly class. The high level of excellence achieved in astronomy, mathematics, and engineering supports the view that some form of higher education did exist in the pre-Columbian Americas.

Classical Education of Greece and Rome

When the Achaeans, Ionians, and Dorians invaded and settled in the Greek world, they were still preliterate people. In the subsequent Dark Ages (1100–800 B.C.), the intellectual accomplishments of the Greeks were exceedingly primitive, and not until the last century of this period did they make an attempt to write down their oral traditions. The Homeric epics, which are part of this heritage, depict a society that was basically aristocratic in tone and in which education was largely restricted to the cultivation of the body, military training, and the acquisition of oral traditions in the form of poetry and music. Emphasis on physical education and the glorification of athletic skills remained one of the characteristics of Hellenic education throughout its history, especially in Sparta.

The pre-Socratic period. The primitive tribal- and clan-centered organization of the Greeks gave way by 800 B.C. to the *polis*, or city-state system. The city-state developed into the political, socioeconomic, and cultural center and was the unique contribution of the Greeks to political organization. Since the *polis* was the intellectual center of activities in the Hellenic world, its rise also corresponded to the greater emphasis given to education. The evolution of the *polis* corresponded with a major socioeconomic shift, the creation of a more cosmopolitan atmosphere, the decline of aristocratic domination, and the rise of an increasingly literate society.

Changes in education were evident when, in the sixth century B.C., the first major centers of philosophical speculation developed. An important early center of philosophical inquiry was the Milesian school of Thales and his followers, who sought rational explanations for the mysteries of the universe. Pythagoras and his disciples followed a speculative life and studied the abstractions of numbers. Although these and other early schools were of importance in the growth of philosophic thought, it is difficult to gauge their direct impact on education. They do, however, attest to the development of intellectual discipline and the increased specialization of studies evident in the Greek world.

The middle of the fifth century B.C. witnessed a major intellectual revolution, which corresponded in the political area with the rise of democracy in many of the city-states (except Sparta) and the growth of increasing individualism. The first important exponents of this new intellectual trend were the teachers known as Sophists. The Sophists were itinerant professional teachers who sold their learning to all who were willing to pay and to learn. Unlike the scientific philosophers, such as the Milesians, the Sophists were not so much concerned with the study of the universe; instead, they turned their attention to subjects more intimately tied to man's ability to prosper in the *polis*. Using the rational basis of thought developed by the scientific philosophers, the Sophists developed the subjects of ethics, politics, economics, logic, and rhetoric. In the democratic city-states, especially in Athens, the Sophists found an eager audience for their teaching, which did prepare the individual for participation in the political life of the *polis* and aided him in the advancement of his private fortunes. The education of the Sophists relied increasingly on rhetoric and dialects as the main means to ensure political advancement. Their educational goals, therefore, were utilitarian, which aroused some opposition against their methods. The Sophists were also attacked for teaching moral relativism, which, in the view of the more conservative Greeks, would undermine the fabric of society and would lead to anarchy and atheism. Yet the Sophists did play an important role in Greek education. Henceforth, emphasis was increasingly on intellectual development and not on the cult of the body; the scope of intellectual inquiry was greatly enlarged by the inclusion of subjects re-

lated directly to man; and education in rhetoric and dialectic was viewed as a useful tool for political advancement. The utilitarianism, relativism, opportunism, and extreme individualism of the Sophists led to an intellectual revolt against their teachings. A number of philosophers challenged them by maintaining that valid, universally true knowledge is obtainable if man uses his reason and the right method of inquiry.

Socratic and post-Socratic teaching. The first major figure of this anti-Sophist movement was Socrates (c.470–399 B.C.). Although not the founder of a specific school, Socrates believed that through disciplined dialog knowledge is obtainable and that true education consists of the quest for wisdom—not for utilitarian but for ethical purposes. The school of Socrates attracted a number of students, among them the young aristocrat Plato (427–347 B.C.), who, unlike his great teacher, wrote extensively and described in utopian terms what he considered the ideal form of higher education. In his *Republic* Plato set forth his ideal of an intellectual elite that rules over society by virtue of its superior education. This education, on the higher level, consists of extensive study of the various branches of mathematics and finally the immersion of the individual in dialectics and metaphysics, in other words, philosophy. Plato was a very successful teacher and the founder of the Academy in Athens, a community where teacher and students congregated for the purpose of learning. To what extent Plato's ideals concerning higher education were translated into reality in the Academy is hard to determine; the Academy remained a viable entity even after the great master's death. The excellence of the intellectual preparation that Plato gave his students is attested by the greatness of his most illustrious pupil, Aristotle (384–322 B.C.). Plato's elitist views on higher education were shared by Aristotle, who emphasized the biological and physical sciences in his curriculum, as opposed to mathematics, and thus was more empirical in orientation than his master. Aristotle founded the Lyceum in Athens, which became a center of not only philosophical speculation but inquiry into the natural sciences as well.

The last major figure in the history of Hellenic higher education was Isocrates

(436–338 B.C.). Although influenced by the Sophists, Isocrates held that oratory and rhetoric should not be merely empty tools for advancement in politics. The *rhetor,* or orator, should be the ideal citizen, who, because of his extensive literary education, would be dedicated to the advancement of the common good. Isocrates viewed both the mathematical emphasis of Plato and the scientific orientation of Aristotle with skepticism. It is with Isocrates that literary culture entered into the mainstream of Western education. To sharpen the intellect and prepare an individual for a career in politics, Isocrates prescribed a literary education, consisting of the study, analysis, and imitation of the classics. This included a broad background in literature, history, music, ethics, logic, and other liberal arts, upon which the mastery of rhetoric was then based.

The Hellenistic period. Both Aristotle and Isocrates were contemporaries of Alexander the Great, whose career divides classical history into the Classical Hellenic (sixth to fourth centuries B.C.) and Hellenistic (fourth century B.C. to first century A.D.) periods. The conquests of Alexander brought about a mingling and fusion of cultural trends, in which Greek and Oriental ideas were brought into contact. Changes occurred not only in the political area, where the *polis* system declined, but also in education, where the emphasis tended to elevate the individual over the communal interest of the city state.

In the field of higher education the Hellenistic age was a period of both continuity and innovation. Formal institutionalized instruction in philosophy continued uninterrupted. The Academy of Plato and the Lyceum founded by Aristotle were still in existence; to these were added the new schools of Epicurus (founded in 306 B.C.) and of the Stoics (founded by Zeno in 294 B.C.). Instruction still consisted mainly of a teacher-student relationship, but the schools became more secular in their orientation, and the object of speculation turned more to the search for individual happiness than to the general welfare of all citizens. The tradition of Isocrates also flourished, and rhetoric became the queen of academic subjects. To be truly educated meant that the individual had studied under a *rhetor*

and learned the art of eloquence. Because rhetoric could only be based on the sound groundwork laid in the study of classical literature, history, and poetry, these subjects were studied with great care in Hellenistic times. Although philosophy and rhetoric competed with each other to attract students, both of these subjects were the basis of cultured existence as perceived by the Hellenistic educated public.

The Hellenistic period was also an age of great scientific inquiry. Unlike philosophy and rhetoric, where students sought out great teachers and entered into a formal relation with them, the teaching of the sciences remained less formal. Great teachers attracted a number of students, but no systematic institutions of instruction emerged. One of the great centers of scientific inquiry was the Museum, established by the Ptolemy rulers of Egypt in Alexandria in the third century B.C. Here the major subjects that received attention were astronomy, geometry, physics, and geography. The Museum, however, was more a center of research than of teaching, and, if any instruction was given, it was to a few advanced students, similar to modern graduate seminars. The same general characteristics apply to the study of medicine; outstanding medical men attracted eager students who learned by observation and by listening to the lectures of the teacher, but formal schools of medicine were not in evidence.

Centers of learning, both in the rhetorical-philosophical subjects as well as in the sciences and medicine, could be found in many of the major cities of the Hellenistic eastern Mediterranean world. Athens naturally continued to play an important role in the history of culture, but Alexandria, Pergamum, Rhodes, Cos, Smyrna, Beirut, Antioch, and other cities also achieved international fame for the excellence of their teachers. The Hellenistic period was a great age of cultural diffusion, and Greek ideas of education made a major impact on all the nations of the Mediterranean world. Most important, however, was its influence on the Romans.

The Romans. The Romans were great borrowers of culture, and their conquest of the Hellenistic East in the second and first centuries B.C. led to the introduction of Greek education to the Roman state. Greek teachers were taken to Italy in large numbers, and the schooling of aristocratic Roman children was almost entirely in the hands of Hellenistic Greeks. Many members of the senatorial families were bilingual and were familiar with the Greek cultural heritage. The Greek influence, however, remained very strong even after the development of Latin as a literary language. This was evident in the fields of philosophy, medicine, and the sciences. Only in the area of rhetoric was the Greek tradition thoroughly Latinized. Rhetoric emerged as a major subject of higher education in Rome under the influence of Cicero (first century B.C.) and Quintilian (first century A.D.). The oratorical skills taught by rhetoric were highly valued by the politically oriented Romans.

An area where the Romans broke new ground in higher education was in the study of law. From the beginning of the second century A.D., Roman legal education became an important discipline. A number of noted legal experts (Gaius, Ulpian, Papinian, and Paulus) made the study of law an important academic subject. The works of these authors became the texts for law professors and were systematically studied, explicated, and commented upon. Rome, and later Beirut and Constantinople, became important centers of legal studies.

Neither the senate in the late Republican period (third to first centuries B.C.), nor the emperors showed any serious interest in systematic financial assistance to schools. Many primary schools were maintained by private funds and secondary instruction was often supported by the cities (civitas). There was, however, some financial aid offered to higher education in the Roman Empire; a number of state professorships were endowed by the emperors. In the first century A.D., Vespasian established two chairs of rhetoric, one for Latin and the other for Greek, in Rome. The great philosopher-emperor Marcus Aurelius Antoninus made a similar endowment in Athens and provided funds for a chair of rhetoric as well as four chairs of philosophy, representing the major schools of speculation—Platonism, Aristotelianism, Stoicism, and Epicureanism. The school of

Athens continued to exist until 529, when Emperor Justinian I closed it, but by then the institution had declined sadly. Justinian confiscated the property of the professors of rhetoric and philosophy and prohibited "pagans" from ever teaching again. The disappearance of the school of Athens marked the last chapter in the history of classical higher education, yet the Greek heritage, as transmitted by Rome, had, and still has, a deep influence on the history of Western education, determining for centuries what constitutes an educated man.

Early Medieval Period: The West, Byzantium, and Islam

The unity of the Mediterranean world, created by the Roman Empire, was destroyed in the course of the fourth to sixth centuries, when the western portion of Europe was invaded and conquered by Germanic tribes, who established a series of successor states. A twofold division emerged in what was the Roman Empire. The eastern, Greek part of the empire continued to exist and, in fact, rose to new heights in the form of the Byzantine state. The western, Latin area was overrun by the Germanic nations and the empire ceased to exist in the fifth century.

The West. Although a fusion of Latin and Germanic cultures did eventually emerge, there was a general cultural decline in the West. Roman institutions, political and cultural, decayed or disappeared, and, with the exception of a few isolated individuals, scholarship suffered greatly. The Greco-Roman heritage, fused with Christianity, was kept alive, however, by some remarkable men, such as the Latin church fathers (Ambrose, Jerome, Augustine of Hippo, and Gregory the Great), Boethius, Cassiodorus, the Venerable Bede, Alcuin, and others. The rise of Western monasteries also played a role in the preservation of culture in those dark days. By the eighth century the darkness began slowly to lift as the Latin heritage became increasingly more evident among the Germanic peoples of the West. The first manifestation of this was the so-called Carolingian Renaissance (eighth to ninth centuries). Although education in the West remained generally on a low level until the twelfth century, the flames of knowledge were burning brighter with each generation. In other parts of the Mediterranean world, the cultural decline experienced by the West with the fall of Rome was not felt as much, and scholarship and education flourished.

The Byzantine state. The most direct inheritor of the ancient Greek traditions in culture and education was the Byzantine state, with its capital in Constantinople. The history of Byzantine higher education is an extremely difficult subject to treat because of the lack of adequate sources. Higher education in Constantinople can be traced back at least as far as the reign of Theodosius II, who in 425 endowed three chairs of Latin rhetoric, ten chairs of Latin grammar, five chairs of Greek rhetoric, and ten chairs of Greek grammar; there were also funds for one professorship of philosophy and two professorships of law. This endowment was the basis of the institution often referred to as the University of Constantinople; its existence, however, is most difficult to follow in the subsequent centuries. In the seventh century the curriculum included grammar, literature, rhetoric, dialectics, philosophy, mathematics, and astronomy. Two centuries later, in 863, Bardas, the uncle of Michael III, encouraged the study of sciences. Constantine IX (Monomachus) refounded the institution, dividing it into a School of Law and a School of Philosophy in 1045. His main objective was to ensure the imperial government an ample supply of well-trained and educated civil servants. This institution, however, must have been rather limited in its scope; for example, Michael Psellus, who was the head of the School of Philosophy, was also responsible for instruction in eleven other disciplines. The School of Philosophy was able to survive the Fourth Crusade and was still in existence in 1445. Theological instruction on an advanced level was not provided at the university, where chairs of theology did not exist, but came from the Patriarchal Schools which were founded at least as early as the eleventh century. These schools provided instruction not only in strictly religious subjects but in the classics and the arts as well. Formal institutional education was not always evident, but the high number of scholarly individuals (Leo the Philosopher, Eustachius of Thessalonica, Nicephoros Gregoras, Gemistus Plethon, Manuel Chrysoloras, John Bessarion) attests to great emphasis on intellectual training and on research carried on by both secular and ecclesiastical men, probably on an individual basis or in noninstitutionalized smaller groups.

The Islamic world. The twofold partition of the Mediterranean world between the Latin-Germanic West and the Greek-Byzantine East was changed to a three-part division with the appearance of the Muslims in the seventh century. Emerging from the Arabian peninsula, Islam spread rapidly, both east and west. The great eastern Mediterranean cultural centers, Antioch, Alexandria, Jerusalem, and Beirut, fell to the conquerors. The Muslims subdued the Persian Empire and advanced even farther east into India; at the same time, they swept across North Africa and conquered most of Spain. These extensive conquests brought the Arabs into contact with an immense variety of cultural backgrounds. The Hellenistic-Byzantine centers of learning were within the borders of Islam, as was the important Persian Academy of Gondeshapur, which under the Sassanids (third to seventh centuries) had been a great center of cultural exchange, where Persian, Indian, and Hellenic traditions met.

The influence of Islam falls into two categories. First, the Muslims supported the production of translations and thus transmitted Greek, Persian, and Hindu scholarship to a wide audience in both the East and the West. Second, they made many original contributions in a wide variety of fields, usually based on the borrowed foundations. The work of translation was often done by Syrians, Nestorian Christians, Jews, and Persians and was carried out mainly during the Abbassid caliphate of Baghdad (eighth to eleventh centuries).

Baghdad in the reign of the caliph al-Ma'mun was already an important center of study, when early in the ninth century the ruler founded the Bait al-Hikmah (House of Wisdom). Not only were the sciences and philosophy studied there, but a library and an observatory were also attached to this institution. Later caliphs continued to patronize higher education in the city, and Baghdad could boast of some of the best schools in the then-known world. Other institutions of higher education were founded in a number of the cities of the Muslim world. Important centers of learning and research were established in North Africa: al-Azhar in Cairo, Qarawiyin at Fes in Morocco, and Zaytouna in Tunis. In Muslim Spain major schools or centers of translation were located at Córdoba, Toledo, Seville, Granada, and other cities. Important schools or *madaris* were also established at Damascus, Naishapur, Isfahan, and many other Eastern cities.

The curricula of the Muslim institutions of learning was influenced by the religious division within Islam—the Shiite and Sunnite controversy. The Sunnites believed that God had revealed himself to Mohammed, and this revelation had to be applied in social and religious life. Shiites, on the other hand, believed in continued revelation in each generation. Sunnite schools tended to be more theologically and legalistically oriented; Shiite institutions studied the sciences and mathematical subjects with avid interest. There was, however, no rigid division.

Muslim scholars made notable contributions to almost every subject in the academic curriculum. Al-Razi (Latin Rhazes; 850–923) was one of the greatest medieval physicians; ibn-Sina (Latin Avicenna; 980–1037) made important contributions to both medicine and philosophy. Al-Biruni (973–1048) was a renowned physician, astronomer, and physicist. In the field of philosophy al-Kindi (801–873), al-Farabi (c. 870–950), and ibn-Rushd (Averroës; c. 1126–1198) made notable contributions in transmitting Greek thought, particularly Aristotelianism, to the West.

The intellectual renaissance of the Latin West in the twelfth and thirteenth centuries would have been impossible without the advances made by the scholars of Islam. Their translations, commentaries, and original speculation on a wide variety of subjects were among the cornerstones of the European university curriculum.

Medieval Higher Education— The Age of Universities

In the eleventh, twelfth, and thirteenth centuries Western Europe was the scene of an impressive revival. This age witnessed the trend toward urbanization, increased commerce, and renewed contacts with the Byzantine and Islamic world. There were also a corresponding growth of education and a general flowering of culture. Monastic schools, which had been established in the early Middle Ages, played an important role in the first phase of this revival. Monasteries, however, were ill equipped to become great centers of learning, with the exception of a few places, such as Cluny, Bec, and Monte Cassino. The level of education in a monastic school was, to a large degree, determined by the excellence of the individual monk-teacher, the curiosity of the students, and the availability of books.

The increased urbanization of Western Europe brought about a shift in population from rural areas, which had been the setting of monasteries, to the rising cities, where cathedral schools were founded. The need for an educated clergy to meet the demands of the dynamic medieval church resulted in the founding of a number of cathedral schools, the most famous of which were to be found in northern France—Chartres, Laon, Rheims, Orléans, and Paris. The rise of these schools corresponded with the very rapid expansion of knowledge, the renewed interest in the classics, the penetration of Muslim scientific innovations, and the revival of Roman law. Cathedral schools became important centers of instruction, and some rose to international fame. The reputation of great teachers brought students in large numbers from all parts of Europe to partake of the wisdom of their instructors. The cornerstone of medieval education was the study of the seven liberal arts, which, according to Martianus Capella (fifth century), consisted of grammar, logic, and rhetoric; and arithmetic, geometry, astronomy, and music. The first three of these subjects comprised what was known as the *trivium;* the other four made up the *quadrivium.*

The earliest universities. The crowning glory of medieval higher education was the rise of universities. The organization of higher education into its modern institutionalized form is the contribution of the Western medieval tradition to the world. Although the great ancient civilizations—

Greek, Roman, Byzantine, and Islamic—all had excellent centers of learning, higher education with prescribed curricula, formal examinations, faculties, and degrees is the result of our medieval inheritance.

The rise of the earliest universities in Western Europe was a spontaneous occurrence, which took place in the twelfth century. The earliest institutions of higher education were not founded by kings, popes, or other benefactors, but resulted from a need among teachers and students to form a protective organization. The word *university* comes from the Latin *universitas* and originally meant a corporation or guild, in other words, a union of scholars. The primary reason for the development of guilds of masters and students was the need for protection. To ensure that scholars would not be exploited by burghers in buying their food and drink, in paying the rent for lodgings, and in paying tolls and taxes, and to protect themselves against physical abuse, the members of the university community formed guilds, similar to the merchant and crafts unions present in secular society. The guild also had another important function, which was to examine candidates and grant them a license to teach (*licencia docendi*)—a degree. Eventually, specific requirements evolved, with a prescribed curriculum, examinations, and disputations that had to be completed before a degree was granted. The university—or *studium generale*, as it is also called—developed into a legal corporation with specific rights, privileges, and immunities, many of which survived into modern times. An organizational structure evolved, which provided for four areas of study, or faculties—arts, medicine, theology, and law—each headed by a dean. The medieval university was an association of learned individuals, not a collection of buildings, laboratories, and libraries; it was made of men.

Bologna and Paris. In the evolution of university education, two major prototypes of organizational structure developed, the Bologna model and the Parisian system. Other institutions for centuries to come followed in either of these two patterns. The University of Bologna was not the first institution of higher learning in Italy. A famous medical school had flourished at Salerno in the eleventh century. The Bologna *studium* developed in the eleventh century and became a great center of legal studies. A number of teachers of law who taught in the city attracted students from all parts of Europe, and this congregation of students and masters gave rise to the University of Bologna. What made Bologna unique was the fact that the students organized themselves into a guild, or university, to protect their rights from the townspeople as well as from the professors. Students were eventually able to establish a long list of privileges in which they prescribed many of the conditions under which the professors had to teach. The University of Bologna was, therefore, an association of students. They elected the chief executive officer of their university—the rector—who was himself a student. The professors also formed a guild, called the college, to protect their interests, but this organization was not as powerful as the student university.

Bologna was a cosmopolitan school and attracted students from everywhere. Students from Italy were organized into the *Cismontane,* while all others formed the *Transmontane* university. The *Cismontane* and *Transmontane* students each constituted a corporation or guild, which in essence was the university. The major emphasis in the curriculum was the study of law, civil and canon; although the other faculties developed to some degree, law was the dominant subject. Most Italian universities were secular, and law and medicine were the important subjects of the curriculum. The student-dominated prototype of Bologna became the pattern of organization for a number of other universities, particularly in Italy, Southern France, and Spain.

The greatest university of the Middle Ages was the University of Paris. This institution developed in the twelfth century, spontaneously and without formal foundation. Paris did have a famous cathedral school and was frequented by many students because of the fame of its teachers; it already had an international reputation when Abelard taught there in the first half of the twelfth century. The university that subsequently developed in this city differed from Bologna in a number of ways. In Paris the university was formed as a guild of professors and not of students; it was the masters who organized themselves into the *universitas* to protect themselves and to supervise the granting of teaching licenses. The academic orientation was also different from Bologna. Paris stressed the study of the liberal arts and also became a great center of theological studies. The international student body came to be divided into French, Picard, Norman, and English-German Nations. All students in the arts faculty had to belong to one of the Nations. Most of the universities that developed in Northern, Western, and Central Europe adopted the Parisian system of organization; they were institutions dominated by the professors.

Other institutions. Among the early universities a prominent place is given to Oxford, which developed in the twelfth century. Oxford also rose spontaneously, like Paris and Bologna, and did not have a specific founder. This English university followed the Parisian, master-dominated pattern of internal organization and became an important center of scientific scholarship in the thirteenth century. Many of the universities of the thirteenth and subsequent centuries were the result of the migration of teachers and students from one of the early foundations to a new city. Since the universities were associations of individuals and were not tied to any locality by buildings, migrations were not uncommon. Cambridge was founded by scholars who left Oxford in 1209; Orléans rose to prominence after a group of Parisian masters took up residence there in 1229; Padua owes its origin to a migration from Bologna in 1220. Other universities were founded by secular rulers or by papal decree. The most important centers of learning, other than those already mentioned, which developed prior to 1300 were Montpellier, Angers, and Toulouse in France; Naples, Vercelli, Vicenza, Perugia, Piacenza, and Siena in Italy; and Salamanca and Lisbon-Coimbra on the Iberian peninsula. The Holy Roman Empire, Scandinavia, and Central Europe did not produce universities until the fourteenth and fifteenth centuries.

Social and educational forms. Students in medieval universities had clerical status;

they were invested with at least the Minor Orders of the church, and some were ordained priests or were members of the religious orders. Clerical status gave the medieval students exemptions and privileges, among them the right to be tried in the more lenient church courts, freedom from taxes, and inviolability of person.

Upon completion of university studies, not all the students entered the services of the church. Many students, especially those with degrees in civil law and medicine, entered the lay professions. A student who entered an institution of higher learning first had to pursue his studies and receive a degree in the faculty of arts. The Bachelor of Arts degree, however, did not bestow any real distinction on the recipient. To be able to teach, students were expected to reach the Master of Arts level. Those who completed the arts course were then eligible to enter the higher faculties—law, medicine, and theology, where specialized training prepared the individual for teaching in these fields, after the acquisition of the master's or doctor's degree. The Bachelor of Arts degree took four to five years of study; a Master of Arts could be obtained with an additional three to four years. It took as long as sixteen years to earn a doctorate in theology at Paris.

The social composition of medieval university students varied greatly. Higher education was not the exclusive privilege of a select few; many of the students who entered a career of studies were poor or even destitute and received free instruction. One form that developed in the Middle Ages and facilitated the life of students was the college. A college was originally an endowed residence hall, established to provide room and board for needy students. Paris, Bologna, Oxford, Cambridge, and many of the other universities soon developed a number of colleges, often established for specific purposes by benefactors. Eventually, the colleges became more than mere residence halls and assumed an increasingly important role as places of instruction, until, as in the case of the English institutions, the university became in reality an assortment of colleges.

The universities of medieval Europe played a major role in the cultural life of their time. Popes and kings competed for their favor, and almost all major intellectual trends were associated with these great institutions. The revival of the West would have been impossible without them.

The Late Medieval, Renaissance, and Reformation Traditions

The late medieval period. The period from the beginning of the fourteenth to the middle of the seventeenth century witnessed the waning of the Middle Ages, the rise and flowering of the Renaissance, and the division of the Western Christian world into Protestant and Catholic factions. The great medieval universities, especially Paris, continued to play a major role in the intellectual and political life of Europe in the early part of this period. The universities were a major factor in the rise of conciliarism and were instrumental in the ending of the schism in the church, which had resulted in two, and at one point three, popes.

The fourteenth and fifteenth centuries were also a very fertile period for new university foundations. The Holy Roman Empire and Central Europe were the scene of the rise of new institutions that were destined to become, in most cases, important national centers of learning. First of the new foundations was the University of Prague (1348), followed by a series of other institutions: Cracow (1364), Vienna (1365), Pécs in Hungary (1367), Heidelberg (1386), Cologne (1388), Erfurt (1389), and Buda (Budapest; 1389). Most of these universities followed the organizational structure of Paris. Prebends and church benefices were increasingly used by the founders to ensure the financial stability of new institutions. The fourteenth century also witnessed the continued growth of the number of universities in France (five), Spain (four), and Italy (seven). This trend continued undiminished into the fifteenth century, when new universities emerged in Scotland (St. Andrews, Glasgow, and Aberdeen), Sweden (Uppsala), Denmark (Copenhagen), Switzerland (Basel), and Hungary (Pozsony now Bratislava). Seven new universities developed in Spain, nine in France, twelve in the Holy Roman Empire, and two in Italy.

The Renaissance. The fourteenth and fifteenth centuries saw not only the flowering of late medieval culture in Northern and Central Europe but also the rise of the Renaissance in Italy. The Italian Renaissance was more than a mere return to the study of the classics, which did not really die out in the medieval period, but represented an attempt to recapture some of the spirit of the ancient world. There was the renewed emphasis on *studia humanitatis,* the studies that made man more human. These studies were based on the Latin and Greek classics. The Italian Renaissance also produced a new interest in philology and textual criticism. This period produced a new breed of intellectual, the court scholar, who was not attached to any institution of higher learning but enjoyed the patronage of wealthy secular or ecclesiastical princes. New theories of education, reflecting the Renaissance ideal of man, were proposed by a number of important scholar-teachers, especially Pier Paulo Vergerio, Guarino da Verona, and Vittorino da Feltre, but their influence was mainly on primary and secondary education. On the level of higher education, the Italian universities were generally receptive to the new learning, and the number of professorships in the humanistic disciplines was increased. Another important new development was the establishment of chairs of Greek studies at Italian, and subsequently other universities, north of the Alps. There was also a renewed interest in Greek philosophy, especially Platonism and Neo-Platonism. As a result of this, a Platonic Academy was established in the second half of the fifteenth century at Florence, presided over by Marsilio Ficino.

The international reputation of the universities of Italy was a powerful magnet that attracted students from all parts of Europe. Italy provided excellent training not only in the professions, such as law and medicine, but also in humanistic studies. It was mainly through wandering university students, who came to Italy to study and subsequently returned to their homelands, that the ideals of the Renaissance began to penetrate the countries beyond the Alps.

At first the universities outside of Italy were not very receptive toward the new learning. Scholasticism was still the dominant philosophy of these institutions, but, by the end of the fifteenth century, humanistic centers were emerging at the universities outside of Italy. Centers of classical studies, or at least some interest in humanistic learning, were evident at many of the old universities as well as at newly founded institutions. One of the major victories for the adherents of the new learning was the establishment in 1530 of the *Collège de France* by Francis I, which provided for chairs of Latin, Greek, and Hebrew as well as mathematics. In most institutions of higher learning, such as the University of Paris, scholasticism and humanism existed side by side, with the medieval tradition still dominant.

In the movement generally referred to as the Northern, or Christian, Renaissance, a number of scholars rose to prominence who wrote extensively on the subject of education. The Dutch humanist Desiderius Erasmus, the Spaniard Juan Luis Vives, and the Englishman Sir Thomas Elyot all emphasized the necessity of extensive training in the classics as the basis for higher education. The combined influence of the Italian humanist educators and these northern scholars is evident in the curriculum of what eventually developed into the German *Gymnasium,* the French *lycée,* and the English Latin grammar school. This curriculum consisted of a strong emphasis on the study of the Greek and Roman classical authors and the Christian church fathers. There was also the study of languages, oratory, and history, plus the training of the body through physical exercise. The spread of these views, as well as the dissemination of all types of scholarly material, was given extra impetus with the invention of the printing press, which revolutionized academic life.

The Reformation period. The unity of Christendom, as well as the international character of higher education, was shattered in the sixteenth century by the Reformation, the results of which were generally not favorable for the universities. As a result of the Reformation movement, higher education suffered because the autonomy and self-regulation of the universities was greatly weakened; and the economic basis of many institutions, especially those dependent on ecclesiastical benefices and prebends, was undercut either by the secu-

larization of church properties or by the inflationary spiral of the second half of the sixteenth century. Universities suffered extensively as a result of the Wars of Religion in France and the Netherlands. The Thirty Years' War had disastrous effects on institutions of learning in Germany.

Probably the most negative result of the Reformation, in both Protestant and Catholic countries, was the fact that universities often became the instruments of sectarian and confessional propaganda. Instead of serving the common intellectual heritage of the Western world, the universities came to reflect the divisions and hatreds that plagued society in general until the middle of the seventeenth century. As Europe came to be divided into regions of Protestant and Catholic domination, in the same fashion, based upon the principle of *cuius regio, eius religio* (whoever controls the region [government], controls the religion), the universities followed suit. In Germany, the original home of the Reformation, a number of the older institutions adopted the Lutheran faith, among them Wittenberg and Heidelberg; new Lutheran universities were also organized, the most famous of which were at Marburg, Königsberg, and Jena. The Scandinavian countries became Lutheran, and so did their universities. The followers of John Calvin also showed interest in higher education. Geneva became an important center of theological studies with the establishment of the Academy in 1559 under the rectorship of Théodore Béza. As the Calvinist form of reformed theology spread to several other countries, universities reflecting Presbyterian or Reformed orientation were founded in Scotland (Edinburgh) and in the Netherlands (Leiden, Amsterdam, and Utrecht). In Germany Marburg, which had originally been Lutheran, went over to the Calvinists in 1605.

The Universities of Oxford and Cambridge did not suffer as much in this transition from Catholicism to Protestantism as some of the continental institutions. Although much of their medieval autonomy was eventually lost, they recovered quickly after an initial decline following the Anglican takeover. Puritanism was, however, viewed as a threat to Anglican hegemony. In France during the sixteenth-century

Wars of Religion, there was a severe decline in the old university foundation of the Middle Ages. The French Calvinists (Huguenots) were able to establish at least eight institutions of higher learning, which were tolerated until the reign of Louis XIV. In the sixteenth century, the "golden century" of Spain's brilliance in cultural and political affairs, Spain had the most vigorously growing institutions of higher education in all Europe. Spanish universities enjoyed unprecedented growth in numbers of institutions and students until decline set in after 1640.

With the loss of most of Northern Europe to Protestantism, the Roman Catholic church reacted with belated vigor to stem the tide and reverse the trend in those countries where the reformed faiths had gained a foothold. The most effective weapon in the arsenal of the Counter-Reformation church was the Jesuit Order, founded in 1540 by Saint Ignatius of Loyola. The Jesuits recognized early that through education they could win back souls to Catholicism as well as maintain the orthodoxy of believers. Their emphasis was on secondary and university education. The Jesuits established hundreds of colleges in Western and Eastern Europe and were able to insinuate themselves into the universities. Their superb training made them effective teachers on both the secondary and university levels, and their success made the Jesuits a source of envy to their adversaries.

Another result of the Counter-Reformation were the decrees of the Council of Trent, which established within each diocese a seminary for the training of priests. These decrees had unfortunate results. In general, the seminaries did not have the intellectual breadth and vigor of the universities of the pre-Reformation period, which had been the training ground for clergy. Both Protestant and Catholic institutions were preparing their graduates for sectarian combat and the maintenance of their particular orthodoxies; this is not the type of atmosphere that is conducive to diversity of opinion and intellectual freedom.

In their curricula the Catholic and Protestant schools showed considerable similarity, with emphasis on the study of the Greek and Latin classics and the writings of the church fathers. The main aim was to create *sapiens et eloquens pietas*—learned piety. Learning was, however, often subverted to the interests of theology, and innovations in science found little support in the universities.

The Age of Enlightenment

Europe. The general malaise that characterized the history of higher education in the sixteenth century and the first half of the seventeenth continued until the end of the eighteenth century. Although there were a few bright spots in this rather bleak picture, the period of Enlightenment was not a great age for the universities of Europe. Most of the progress in education during the 150 years prior to the French Revolution was in the area of kindergarten, primary, and secondary education. John Amos Comenius, John Milton, John Locke, Etienne Bonnot de Condillac, Jean Jacques Rousseau, Marie Jean Antoine Nicolas de Caritat Condorcet, Claude Adrien Helvétius, Johann Heinrich Pestalozzi, August Hermann Francke, Johann Salomo Semler, Julius Hecker, and others, wrote extensively on theories of pedagogy, but most of their emphasis was on preuniversity-level instruction. Although this period witnessed an increase in the number of children receiving some education in both Protestant and Catholic dominated areas, the universities were not among the vital forces of society.

The baneful effects of sectarianism still haunted institutions of higher education. The financial basis and well-being of universities were often dependent on the goodwill of territorial rulers. Professors were generally ill paid, and advancement often did not depend on intellectual excellence but on the social position of the individual. Universities were also used as a refuge by aristocratic students, whose promotion to degrees bore little relation to their academic talents. The most obvious indication that the universities of the Enlightenment era were not in the forefront of intellectual activity is the fact that most of the progress made during this period in the sciences, philosophy, and other areas of inquiry was accomplished outside the institutions of higher education. Naturally there are a few exceptions to this, but, in general, the universities were not the centers of higher learning; for example, the major French *philosophes* were not university professors.

Many of the intellectuals of the period did their research and writing at a number of important centers of scholarship that emerged parallel to and supplementing the work of the institutions of higher education. These were the academies, scientific and scholarly, which grew up in most European countries and flourished during the Enlightenment. The history of academies goes back at least as far as the sixteenth century. First among the scientific societies was the *Academia Secretorum Naturae*, founded at Naples in 1560. The *Academia de ciencias matemáticas* was established by Philip II at Madrid in 1575. The famous *Accademia nazionale dei Lincei* of Rome was founded in 1603. Other institutions followed in the seventeenth and eighteenth centuries. In 1616 an informal academy was established in Weimar, and in 1700 the Academy of Sciences was founded in Berlin under the leadership of Gottfried Wilhelm von Leibnitz. Students of Galileo Galilei brought about the establishment of the *Accademia del Cimento* in 1657 at Florence. The English Royal Society began in 1660 and was formally chartered in 1662. In France the *Académie française* was incorporated in 1635 by Cardinal Richelieu. The *Académie des sciences* was invited by Jean Baptiste Colbert, minister of Louis XIV, to hold its meetings at the Royal Library in 1666 and was later moved to the Louvre in 1699. The other nations of Europe followed suit in establishing academies of sciences and humane learning, which played an increasingly important role in the intellectual life of nations, often overshadowing the universities.

The rather bleak picture of academic life was brightened toward the end of the seventeenth century with the foundation in 1693 of the University of Halle in Germany, an institution that is often referred to as the "first modern university." Halle and later the *Georg-August-Universität zu Göttingen* (established in 1737) became the leaders of an academic revival that had far-reaching consequences, particularly in the nineteenth century. Halle broke tradition by allowing lectures in German instead of Latin, allowing the separation of theology from philosophy, permitting a larger role for mathematical and scientific investigation, and eventually (1779) establishing the first chair of pedagogy, for the training of teachers, at an institution of higher education. The most important contribution of the Universities of Halle and Göttingen was the rise of academic freedom, the freedom of the professor to teach what he considers to be the truth and the freedom of the student to study under a professor of his choice.

The Americas. The exploration and colonization of the Americas led to the establishment of institutions of higher education in the New World. The first universities in the Western Hemisphere were established by the Spanish. Authorized by both the pope and the king of Spain, the *Universidad nacional autónoma de México* and the *Universidad nacional mayor de San Marco* in Peru were founded in 1551. In the first quarter of the seventeenth century, universities were established in Chile, Argentina, and Bolivia. By the end of the century there were about ten institutions of higher education in Spanish America, but no university was founded in Brazil, colonized by the Portuguese. In French Canada the first important effort to found an institution of higher education was undertaken by Bishop Laval in 1663, when he established a *grand séminaire* at Quebec.

In the English-controlled portion of the North American continent, Harvard College was the first institution of higher education. Founded in 1636, Harvard was a Puritan (Calvinist) institution. One of the characteristics of colonial higher education in North America was the denominational affiliation of many of the institutions of learning. The Anglicans established the College of William and Mary in 1693. Yale, formerly the Collegiate School of Connecticut, was founded by Congregationalists in 1701 and Princeton, formerly the College of New Jersey, by Presbyterians in 1746. King's College (1754) in New York, which later became Columbia University, was an Anglican school; Brown University, formerly the College of Rhode Island (1764), in Providence, was a Baptist foundation. Dartmouth (1769) owed its origin to the Congregationalists, and Rutgers

(1766), formerly Queens College, was established by the Dutch Reformed church. The College and Academy of Philadelphia, later known as the University of Pennsylvania, which was chartered in 1755, was the only early colonial college in America that did not have sectarian ties. It was also the first institution to offer instruction in medicine and was in contact with the famous German University of Halle, upon which it tried to pattern itself. Harvard, on the other hand, was established following the structure of Emmanuel College in England.

The medieval English traditions continued at colonial colleges for many years. Instruction was based on the study of the classics, but the sciences slowly made their entry into the curriculum. After the American Revolution and the establishment of a new independent nation, a national university was discussed but never established. Eventually the various states that comprised the United States of America took an active role in the establishment of institutions of higher education within their boundaries, although universities with religious affiliation continued, and still continue, to exist along with state-supported colleges and universities.

The late seventeenth and the eighteenth centuries did produce some progress in the growth of higher education and, above all, laid a secure foundation upon which the next century was able to build with unprecedented vitality.

The Nineteenth Century

The nineteenth century ushered in a period of intense activity in the field of higher education. Not since the Middle Ages did the universities show such vitality or witness such proliferation as in the period between the French Revolution and the turn of the twentieth century. Although the seeds were already evident in Germany in the eighteenth century (Halle, Göttingen), intellectual activity blossomed forth with great power during this period. The major characteristics of the new trends in higher education can be summarized in the following way: There was increased recognition, especially on the continent, that education on all levels is one of the responsibilities of the state. Education became more secularized, as the churches contin-

ued to lose control over institutions of learning. Science, and the accompanying belief in progress, took hold in the universities, although it did not displace the classical-humanistic curriculum. There was also the growth of a sense of nationalism evident through the century, with the insistence that each nation had a different and unique destiny and therefore required diverse forms of national education to reflect these differences. This, to some degree, undermined the universality of knowledge and often led to national hatreds and chauvinism.

Germany. The most successful and widely copied system of national higher education was established in Germany, especially in the kingdom of Prussia. The military and political collapse precipitated by Napoleon's victory at Jena in 1806 brought about a major reform movement in Prussia. The Prussian prime minister, Heinrich Friedrich Karl Stein, placed all education under the Ministry of Interior and began an intensive reorganization of the whole system of instruction. The most impressive result of this educational reorganization in Prussia was the establishment of the University of Berlin (*Humboldt-Universität zu Berlin*) in 1809, with the support of King Fredrick William III. The university was guided by the great scholar Wilhelm von Humboldt, with assistance from the philosopher Johann Fichte and the theologian Friedrich Schleiermacher.

The University of Berlin was united with the Royal Academy in 1809 and became the foremost center of learning during the nineteenth century. Its greatness stemmed from the following characteristics: the university was not subject to the maintenance of any creed or philosophical orientation; its professors and students were free to seek truth and knowledge as they understood them; the university was dedicated to the search for truth, and its eminent teachers were world-renowned scholars in their fields; and the number of subjects within the university curriculum was immensely increased. One of the most important legacies of this view of the university is the belief that impartial investigation and research, along with teaching, are the main functions of an institution of higher learning, and that the true professor is a dedicated teacher-scholar. A number of new universities, such as Bonn (originally founded in 1717 and refounded in 1818), as well as many of the older German universities, copied the University of Berlin. The reputation of German universities became worldwide, and students from all parts of the globe flocked to Germany for studies. The basic characteristics of the German universities were not only admired by others, but were widely emulated in other parts of Europe as well as Asia and America.

France. France also moved in the direction of a national system of higher education. During the French Revolution, on September 15, 1793, all the French universities, along with their colleges and medieval privileges, were abolished. The Revolution did not have a chance to reorganize education before the establishment of the Napoleonic regime. It was left to Bonaparte to create the French national system of education. In 1806 he decreed the establishment of a number of "faculties" to teach law, medicine, mathematics, sciences, natural history, mining, and engineering. Some of these faculties were new; others were the remnants of former French universities. Napoleon continued the centralization of all education, and, finally, in 1808 he created the *Université de France*, under which all educational functions were carried out, from primary level to university. France was divided into twenty-three educational districts, called *académies*, representing certain faculties and headed by a rector. The *académies* controlled and supervised all education within their area and were under the jurisdiction of the *Université de France*. Under this reorganized system two major institutions of higher education continued to function in the capital—the University of Paris and the *Ecole pratique des hautes études*. The famous *Collège de France*, which was established as a center of humanistic studies in the sixteenth century, was also restructured, and its professors were among the most noted intellects of the century. The highly centralized national system of education of France was not as readily copied worldwide as the German model. Yet it did have a profound effect in Spain, where in 1857 the whole country was divided into ten university districts, and the system of instruction was brought under close state control.

England. England did not follow the continent in establishing national systems of education. Oxford and Cambridge continued their ties with the Church of England. A number of reforms were undertaken that weakened the independence of the colleges and widened the curriculum, especially in the sciences. An interesting development was the affiliation of twenty-two colleges and universities from all parts of the British Empire with the Universities of Cambridge and Oxford. England in the nineteenth century also saw the rise of a number of new universities, such as the Universities of Durham, Manchester, and London, with its various colleges. Although the monopoly of Oxford and Cambridge was thus broken, these two ancient foundations were still the major centers of higher education, not only for England but for the whole British Empire.

Other European and Asian countries. The number of new universities established in Europe during the course of the nineteenth century is immense. Almost every state founded or refounded institutions of higher education during this period, and most of them followed the German model. In the Scandinavian countries, in Ireland, in Eastern and Central Europe, and in the Balkans, institutions of higher learning were founded in record numbers. Some of the older universities, such as Vienna, enjoyed a great period of revival, and several of the newer foundations rose to international pominence in a relatively short time. The major centers of the British Empire—India, Canada, and Australia—all were able to establish universities during this period, institutions that often matured into important centers of learning in our century. Japan also developed its first major university during this age of expansion, the University of Tokyo, founded in 1877 (later changed to Tokyo Imperial University) and influenced by both European and American trends in higher education.

The United States. The nineteenth century also witnessed a great growth in the institutions of higher education in the United States. The handful of colleges that existed on the North American continent at the end of the American Revolution soon began to grow and proliferate. Although institutions with sectarian affiliation continued to be founded, a new type of university, supported by the states, became increasingly important. One of the first major state universities in the United States was the University of Virginia, established under the guidance of Thomas Jefferson. The University of Virginia was founded in 1803 and opened its doors in 1825. It was secular in orientation and offered a broad course of study both in the humanities and in the professional fields. As the United States expanded toward the West, the various newly added states established universities, as did some of the older original states. A great impetus to the growth of state universities was the Morrill Act, passed by Congress in 1862, which granted public lands to states for the purpose of establishing state institutions of public higher education. This law led to the founding of about seventy universities or colleges, which were designated as "land grant" institutions; some of them have become first-rate universities. The United States also developed a third major type of educational institution, namely the private college or university, which owed its existence to the generosity of a wealthy benefactor. These independent foundations, which were established mainly after the Civil War, often developed into institutions of great distinction. Among the most famous are Cornell University (in Ithaca, New York), Johns Hopkins University (Baltimore, Maryland), the University of Chicago, Tulane University of Louisiana (in New Orleans), Clark University (Worcester, Massachusetts), and Stanford University (in California).

The influence of the German universities on the intellectual growth of United States institutions was profound. Many of the noted United States professors of the nineteenth century had studied in Germany, and, upon returning to the United States, they introduced German methods of scholarly investigation, the seminar system, and what developed into graduate training. Among the first United States institutions to emphasize graduate education on the German model was Johns Hopkins University, founded in 1876. The Catholic University of America in Washington, D.C., was incorporated in 1887 and was originally established as primarily a graduate institution. Many of the older universities, such as Harvard, Yale, Columbia, and Princeton, along with some of the better state universities and private institutions, soon followed this trend.

The quality of United States institutions of higher education varied widely. Some of the small denominational colleges were provincial in outlook and limited in their curricula. Some of the other universities—church affiliated, state supported, and private—rose to the challenges of a changing world and held their own against the institutions of the Old World. In the next century they emerged as the undisputed world leaders in a number of disciplines.

South America. The nineteenth century was also a fruitful period in the growth of higher education in South America. During the century twenty-four new universities were founded. Following the European model, most universities of South America were under the direct supervision of the state and were secular in orientation. In Chile, Uruguay, and Mexico the universities were also the supervisory institutions of primary and secondary schools, similar to the French and Spanish models.

The Twentieth Century

The growth of higher education in the twentieth century has been so enormous that even a cursory survey would be almost impossible. There are, however, a number of characteristics of higher education since 1900 that deserve some elaboration. This century shows a remarkable amount of continuity from the nineteenth, as well as elaboration and change. The vitality of the previous century continued to produce new universities and expanded curricula until the disaster of World War I. Since the middle of the century the pace of growth has again increased dramatically, surpassing any previous age. This rapid growth in universities since World War II is evident in both the developed and emerging countries.

The reasons for this phenomenal expansion can be seen in several factors. There is, throughout the world, a tendency toward mass education on all levels. The expansion of scientific and technical knowledge has created a serious need for well-trained individuals able to design, operate, and maintain the sophisticated industrial machinery that has evolved in the technically advanced societies. In the less developed countries the desire to catch up and keep up with this growing industrial technology has also led to the growth of institutions of higher learning. The assumption by governments of increased responsibilities in education, medicine, welfare, energy production, trade, construction, and other areas necessitates the training of educators, physicians, engineers, technocrats, and other skilled professionals to be able to staff the increasingly large institutions and bureaucracies. The growth of mass education itself led to a large number of institutions of higher education for the training of teachers. An increasingly complex society demands institutions of education that are responsive to its needs. The already growing curriculum of the nineteenth-century universities has been increased to accommodate new developments not only in the scientific-technological fields but also in the social sciences and humanities.

The university has become the "multiversity" and now even offers courses that are basically vocational in their orientation. The need for having some training above the secondary level, but without reaching the depth offered by regular degree programs, has been met worldwide by the establishment of technical institutes and vocationally oriented junior and community colleges. At the same time, extensive professional education has not been neglected. Courses leading to specialized degrees in an immense variety of fields have become part of the offering of all major modern universities. The expansion of courses in the direction of vocational training and toward highly technical professional specialization is characteristic of our time. Governments have also entered the field of education in an unprecedented fashion. They subsidize and often direct a considerable amount of research, both peaceful and military. Another development of the twentieth century has been the use of higher education by governments of totalitarian states to attempt a rapid change in the social structure of society, to increase the growth of industrial-technological proficiency, and to control scholarship for propagandistic purposes.

The immense growth of higher education has not been accomplished without problems, crises, and considerable criticism. The pursuit of mass education at the same time as the maintenance of academic standards has not always been possible. The "multiversity" has become an impersonal institution, which has alienated students and professors; the worldwide student unrest in our time is, to some degree, a reflection of this alienation. The increasingly vocational orientation of some of the universities and colleges has resulted in an antiintellectual atmosphere, which has been severely criticized by educators, especially Robert Hutchins of the University of Chicago, who detected in this trend the erosion of the very basis of what a university should be. The use of universities by totalitarian states of both the left and the right as a vehicle for propagandistic indoctrination has been a detriment to the ideals of academic freedom.

The major changes that have occurred in higher education in various countries can be summarized in the following manner:

The history of higher education in Britain reveals a general growth of opportunities, especially since the end of World War II. Although Oxford and Cambridge still have the greatest prestige among all the institutions of education in England, the number of universities now is over forty, and several of them have achieved an excellent reputation, especially in the sciences and technical fields. Since 1900 a number of technical colleges have also been founded.

In Germany higher education suffered as a consequence of the loss of World War I, the economic problems of the 1920s, and the rise of National Socialism. The creation of the Nazi state had most unfortunate effects on the universities of Germany. The National Socialist system was not only hostile to academic freedom but the universities were purged of "non-Aryan" elements and were placed under the influence of the party bureaucracy. A large number of Jewish, Social Democratic, and Liberal professors were either dismissed or were forced to retire. Many of these intellectuals eventually left Germany as the Hitler regime became increasingly more intolerable, and either settled in other European countries or, in many instances, migrated to the United States and enriched its institutions of higher learning. After the collapse of the Third Reich, each of the federal states of the *Bundesrepublik* was given control over its own institutions of higher education. After a period of growth and expansion, the universities of the Federal Republic of Germany have faced increasing politicization and disruption.

The highly centralized national system of higher education in France is also undergoing rapid change in this century, especially in recent years. Decentralization is a major trend, as is the elimination of the elitist character of higher education imposed by the French secondary school system. The various competitive examinations that determine a student's academic future are also under attack. The student disruptions of the late 1960s were prompted both by a genuine desire to change the system and make it more responsive to the needs of students, and by political agitation.

Russia, which began founding universities in the eighteenth century, tried to break its traditional orientation, and introduced fundamental changes during the Revolution of 1917. The results of this reorientation of higher education were mixed. To create a new society, the Revolution decreed academic reforms in order to eliminate the previous elitist system. The lower classes were encouraged to seek education in large numbers at institutions of learning, and so-called workers' faculties were created. In an attempt to promote greater equality, all examinations and grades were eliminated, and students were given unprecedented authority over their professors. These changes, however, were temporary and were eliminated by 1932, when Joseph Stalin placed education under tight central control. As a result of the new economic plans, which emphasized the rapid growth of industry, the Soviet system of higher education stressed technical proficiency. The institutions of higher education produce a very large number of engineers, mathematicians, and scientists, and

secondary school curricula were adjusted to provide a good basis for scientific-technical higher education. The Russians also provide for a new type of institution, the *technikum*, which offers postsecondary training in a variety of fields. All major areas of research in the sciences, humanities, and social studies have been placed under the jurisdiction of the Academy of Sciences. Research is thus centralized and closely controlled. In the natural sciences this has produced impressive results; in the humanities and social sciences a doctrinaire Marxist-Leninist line has to be followed, which is often detrimental to scholarship. In many countries of Eastern Europe, now in the Russian sphere of influence, the Academies of Science are the major research directing organizations.

China, which had developed a Western-style higher education system early in this century and had borrowed much from European and American models, underwent a more drastic change after the Communist victory in 1949. As in Russia, technical and professional education was stressed at the expense of the more traditional areas. The Cultural Revolution, which swept over the country in recent years, had very negative results on higher education. Many of the universities were closed and research and scholarship were interrupted. Institutions of higher learning were accused of being places of reactionary thought and had to be "purged" in order to bring them more in line with the teachings of Chairman Mao Tse-tung. Although some order has been restored to the universities, higher education in China has not yet achieved normalcy.

In the United States, the twentieth century witnessed a great proliferation of institutions of higher learning. The growth of state-supported institutions is particularly impressive. The federal government has indirectly entered the field of education through large subsidies for research projects, construction, and tuition benefits. American institutions have expanded their curricula in the direction of extensive graduate training as well as in vocational-technical instruction at the community college level. Of all the countries of the world, the United States has been most successful in providing mass higher education.

Canada has also participated in this

expansion of education. Its provincial universities, as well as earlier foundations, have developed rapidly and are known for their high quality of teaching and research.

Although there has also been a great growth in the number of universities in Latin America (almost two hundred), the unfortunate instability of South American governments and the limited amount of research opportunities due to the lack of funds have had a negative effect on higher education there.

Japan has followed an educational development pattern most similar to the American and European models. In less than one hundred years it has established almost 400 institutions of higher learning and educates about 1,500,000 students in a variety of professional, technical, and humanistic fields.

In Muslim North Africa in the nineteenth and twentieth centuries new universities, influenced by European models, were added. Only after World War II did sub-Sahara Africa establish its first universities. The first black African university colleges were established in 1948 in Ghana and Nigeria. Other African institutions soon followed, to meet the demands of new nations emerging from colonialism.

Rapid growth in higher education in the second half of the twentieth century is also evident in the Arab countries, in India, and in Southeast Asia. The departure of the European colonial empires signaled the establishment of independent states and the need for national systems of education on all levels.

Conclusion

The history of higher education is an optimistic story and one that should inspire mankind in the future. From the humble beginnings of education among scribes, mankind has increased the search for knowledge and expanded its horizons. The path of growth has not always been smooth. Intolerance, dogmatism, exploitation, and poverty have slowed and still do retard progress. Yet the tools that higher education has given mankind help us to understand our past and more fully appreciate the present; it is to be hoped that they will unlock the mysteries of the universe in the future.

Bibliography

Beck, R. H. *A Social History of Education.* Englewood Cliffs, New Jersey: Prentice-Hall, 1965.

Boyd, W., and King, E. J. *The History of Western Education.* (8th ed.) New York: Barnes & Noble, 1966.

Butts, R. F. *The Education of the West: A Formative Chapter in the History of Civilization.* (3rd ed.) New York: McGraw-Hill, 1973.

Butts, R. F., and Cremin, L. A. *History of Education in American Culture.* New York: Holt, Rinehart and Winston, 1953.

Clarke, M. L. *Higher Education in the Ancient World.* London: Routledge and Kegan Paul, 1971.

Cole, L. A. *Education from Socrates to Montessori.* New York: Holt, Rinehart and Winston, 1950.

Cordasco, F. *A Brief History of Education.* Totowa, New Jersey: Littlefield, Adams, 1963.

Cramer, J. F., and Browne, G. S. *Contemporary Education: A Comparative Study of National Systems.* (2nd ed.) New York: Harcourt Brace Jovanovich, 1965.

Cubberley, E. P. *The History of Education.* (2nd ed.) Boston: Houghton Mifflin, 1948.

Daly, L. J. *The Medieval University, 1200–1400.* New York: Sheed and Ward, 1961.

Dodge, B. *Muslim Education in Medieval Times.* Washington, D.C.: Middle East Institute, 1962.

Eby, F. *The Development of Modern Education.* (2nd ed.) Englewood Cliffs, New Jersey: Prentice-Hall, 1952.

Eby, F., and Arrowood, C. F. *The History and Philosophy of Education: Ancient and Medieval.* Englewood Cliffs, New Jersey: Prentice-Hall, 1940.

Frost, S. E. *Historical and Philosophical Foundations of Western Education.* Columbus, Ohio: Merrill, 1966.

Gabriel, A. L. *Summary Bibliography of the History of Universities of Great Britain and Ireland to 1800.* Notre Dame, Indiana: Mediaeval Institute, 1974.

Galt, H. S. *A History of Chinese Educational Institutions to the End of Five Dynasties (960 A.D.).* London: Probst-Hain, 1951.

Good, H. G., and Teller, J. D. *A History of Western Education.* (3rd ed.) New York: Macmillan, 1969.

Graves, F. P. *A History of Education Before the Middle Ages.* New York: Macmillan, 1925.

Gutek, G. L. *A History of the Western Educational Experience.* New York: Random House, 1972.

Haskins, C. H. *The Rise of Universities.* Ithaca: New York: Cornell University Press, 1957. (Originally published 1923.)

Hutchins, R. M. *The Higher Learning in America.* New Haven, Connecticut: Yale University Press, 1936.

Kaigo, T. *Japanese Education: Its Past and Present.* (2nd ed.) Tokyo: Kokusai Bunka Shinkokai, 1968.

Keay, F. E. *A History of Education in India and Pakistan.* (4th ed.) London: Oxford University Press, 1964.

Kerr, A. *Universities of Europe.* Westminster, Maryland: Canterbury Press, 1962.

Kibre, P. *The Nations in the Mediaeval Universities.* Cambridge, Massachusetts: Mediaeval Academy of America, 1948.

Kibre, P. *Scholarly Privileges in the Middle Ages.* Cambridge, Massachusetts: Mediaeval Academy of America, 1962.

Laurie, S. S. *Historical Survey of Pre-Christian Education.* New York: AMS Press, 1970. (Originally published 1915.)

Lucas, C. J. *Our Western Educational Heritage.* New York: Macmillan, 1972.

Marique, P. *History of Christian Education.* (3 vols.) New York: Fordham University Press, 1924–1932.

Marrou, H. I. *A History of Education in Antiquity.* (Translated by G. Lamb.) New York: Sheed and Ward, 1956.

Mayer, F. *A History of Educational Thought.* (2nd ed.) Columbus, Ohio: Merrill, 1966.

Meyer, A. E. *The Development of Education in the Twentieth Century.* Englewood Cliffs, New Jersey: Prentice-Hall, 1949.

Meyer, A. E. *An Educational History of the Western World.* New York: McGraw-Hill, 1965.

Mookerji, R. K. *Ancient Indian Education.* (4th ed.) Delhi: Motilal Banarsidass, 1969.

Mulhern, J. *A History of Education.* (2nd ed.) New York: Ronald Press, 1959.

Nakosteen, M. *History of Islamic Origins of Western Education A.D. 800–1350: Introduction to Medieval Muslim Education.* Boulder: University of Colorado Press, 1964.

Nash, P., and others. *The Educated Man: Studies in the History of Educational Thought.* New York: Wiley, 1965.

Norton, A. O. (Ed.) *Readings in the History of Education.* Cambridge, Massachusetts: Harvard University Press, 1909.

Power, E. J. *Main Currents in the History of Education.* New York: McGraw-Hill, 1962.

Rait, R. S. *Life in the Medieval University.* Cambridge, England: Cambridge University Press, 1912.

Rashdall, H. *The Universities of Europe in the Middle Ages.* (3 vols.) (Edited by F. M. Powicke and A. B. Emden.) Oxford: Oxford University Press, 1936.

Schwickerath, R. *Jesuit Education: Its History and Principles.* St. Louis, Missouri: Herder, 1903.

Stone, L. (Ed.) *The University in Society.* (2 vols.) Princeton, New Jersey: Princeton University Press, 1974.

Thorndike, L. *University Records and Life in the Middle Ages.* New York: Columbia University Press, 1944.

Thwing, C. F. *Universities of the World.* New York: Macmillan, 1911.

Tritton, A. S. *Materials on Muslim Education in the Middle Ages.* London: Luzac, 1957.

Ulich, R. *Education in Western Culture.* New York: Harcourt Brace Jovanovich, 1965.

Ulich, R. *The Education of Nations: A Comparison in Historical Perspective.* (Rev. ed.) Cambridge, Massachusetts: Harvard University Press, 1967.

Walden, J. W. H. *The Universities of Ancient Greece.* New York: Scribner's, 1909.

Wise, J. E. *The History of Education: An Analytic Survey from the Age of Homer to the Present.* New York: Sheed and Ward, 1964.

Woodward, W. H. *Studies in Education During the Age of the Renaissance, 1400–1600.* Cambridge, England: Cambridge University Press, 1924.

Woody, T. *Life and Education in Early Societies.* New York: Macmillan, 1970. (Originally published 1949.)

Part I: Colonial Higher Education in the Americas (1538-1789)

History and Objectives

Harold R. W. Benjamin

HIGHER EDUCATION IN SPANISH AMERICA, 1538 TO 1850

Within seventy-one years of Columbus's first sighting of Watling (San Salvador) Island in the Bahamas on October 12, 1492, five universities were founded in the Spanish possessions in America. Hispaniola led the way. Discovered by Columbus on his first voyage, it had in Santo Domingo the first organized Spanish government of the New World, the first European type of city, the first cathedral, the first Royal Audiencia, and the first Christian schools.

In 1538 Pope Paul III, at the request of the Dominican friars in Hispaniola, authorized the establishment of the University of Santo Tomás de Aquino in Santo Domingo (also known as the University of Santo Domingo). The papal bull provided that the new institution should "have and enjoy each of the privileges, rights, immunities, exemptions, liberties, favors and graces, as those that the universities of Alcalá and Salamanca, or any other in the Kingdom of Spain, have and enjoy."[1]

Throughout the colonial period this pattern of authorization, whether by the Pope, the King, or the Council of the Indies, remained much the same. The Spaniards were trying to set up American copies of Salamanca, with the four traditional faculties of theology, law, arts, and medicine. The arts faculty, furthermore, taught the seven liberal arts of the trivium (grammar, rhetoric, and logic) and the quadrivium (arithmetic, geometry, music, and astronomy) in strict adherence to the medieval tradition.

Santo Domingo and various other early American universities soon had to drop their faculties of medicine. There were simply not enough physicians in the New World to teach medicine. There was an ample supply of priests and friars who could fill the teaching positions in theology, law, and the arts, but most of them lacked training in medicine or surgery. It was not until the eighteenth century that the University of Santo Domingo reestablished its Faculty of Medicine. Then it announced that medicine would be taught from the text of Avicena, anatomy from the "anatomical book," and surgery from the book of Galen.

After the conquest of New Spain and Peru, Hispaniola entered a long period of decadence. The Spanish power and cultural interests moved west and south on the mainland. By 1551 the universities now known as the National Autonomous University of Mexico and the National University of San Marcos were established, respectively, in the two viceregal capitals. The Jesuits entered the higher educational field in America in 1558 by setting up a second university in Hispaniola, that of Santiago de la Paz. The ancestor of the present National University of Colombia was founded in Bogotá in 1563.

In 1586 the University of San Fulgencio in Quito was authorized by papal bull, but it did not begin instruction until 1603. In 1786, furthermore, a royal order suppressed it, one of the few times in the history of higher education that a university has been closed for academic inefficiency.

In the seventeenth century seven more universities were founded in Spanish America—Córdoba in Argentina (1613), the Javerian University of Bogotá (1622), the University of San Gregorio Magno in Quito (1622), the University of San Francisco Javier de Chuquisaca at what is now Sucre, Bolivia (1624), the National University of San Carlos in Guatemala (1676), the University of San Cristóbal de Huamanga in Ayacucho, Peru (1677), and the University of San Antonio Abad in Cuzco, Peru (1692).

Religious orders founded practically all these colonial universities. At first the Dominicans were the most active in this respect. In the seventeenth century the Jesuits became more important in higher education, establishing the first four universities of that century.

The eighteenth century saw six more higher educational institutions founded in Spanish America. Dominicans from Hispaniola started universities at Havana and Caracas in 1721. The other four—Guanajuato (1732) and Guadalajara (1792) in Mexico, the University of San Felipe in Chile (1738), and the Central University of Ecuador (1769)—also began under religious auspices.

The most dynamic single group in higher education in the first half of the eighteenth century was the Society of Jesus. Its chief aim was to train clerical and lay leaders in furthering the religious and political aims of the Society.

In 1767, Charles III, the Spanish king, expelled the Society from all his dominions. The Kings of Portugal and France had previously expelled the Jesuits in 1759 and 1764, respectively, and Pope Clement XIV suppressed the order in 1773. By 1814, when Pope Pius VII reestablished the Society, the revolutions against Spain in the Viceroyalties of New Spain, New Granada, Peru, and Buenos Aires were already under way, and religious orders were not generally welcomed in higher education by the revolutionists.

Largely under revolutionary auspices, seventeen universities were founded in the first half of the nineteenth century. Except for the first one, the University of Antioquia at Medellín, Colombia (1803), they were established in the period 1810 to 1847. The founding of the present University of Los Andes in Mérida, Venezuela, is an example of the speed with which the revolutionists sometimes moved to set up higher educational institutions. The Rebellion of Caracas began on April 19, 1810. On September 16, 1810, the province of Mérida declared its independence, and only five days later the revolutionary Junta de Mérida established the University of San Buenaventura de Mérida de los Caballeros.

The third university to be established in the nineteenth century, the University of León in Nicaragua, was founded in 1812, well before the revolutionary movement got under way in Central America. It was based on the Seminary of San Ramón which had been founded in 1670 and given a royal license in 1683. The Seminary had given instruction in various standard university subjects, including theology, law, and medicine, but its candidates for the licentiates had to take their examinations from the Royal and Pontifical University of San Carlos of Guatemala, the only university authorized to grant degrees in the Captaincy General of Guatemala.[2] The new University of León was therefore the second to be founded in Central America.

The next Spanish-American university established in the nineteenth century, that of Buenos Aires, was more completely a revolutionary product. Although the Governor (later Viceroy), Juan José Vértiz de Salcedo, had proposed the foundation of a university in Buenos Aires as early as 1771, it was not until 1821, in the government of Martín Rodríguez under the inspiration and direction of Bernardino Rivadavia, that the Congress of the United Provinces of the Río de la Plata authorized the foundation of a "major university with academic privileges and jurisdiction."

The University of Cartagena in Colombia was founded in 1824 under similar revolutionary auspices. The Universities of Trujillo (1824) and San Agustín of Arequipa (1825) in Peru had the distinction of being established by decree of Simón Bolívar, the Liberator. The Universities of Benito Juárez de Oaxaca (1825) and San Luis Potosí (1826) in Mexico, the University of Cauca (1827) in Colombia, and those of San Andrés of La Paz (1830) and San Simón at Cochabamba (1832) in Bolivia were also founded by revolutionaries.

Universities now began to be established after the first revolutionary period was passed. New national needs for members of the liberal professions and new national prides demanded that higher education be made available within new national boundaries. The University of the Republic in Uruguay was founded in 1833 while Montevideo swarmed with Argentine professors and students in exile from the Rosas dictatorship. The three Central American countries remaining without universities, El Salvador, Costa Rica, and Honduras, founded them in 1841, 1843, and 1847, respectively. Chile established her national university in 1842, under the leadership of the great Venezuelan scholar Andrés Bello.

AIMS OF HIGHER EDUCATION IN SPANISH AMERICA, 1538 TO 1850

Like practically all universities of the time, those of the Spanish colonies in the sixteenth, seventeenth, and eighteenth centuries had in view only one main higher educational purpose: the training of members of the liberal professions, namely, theology, law, medicine, and the arts.

Until the onset of revolutionary ideas in the final two decades of the eighteenth century the training of priests was by far the most important university task. Rectors were almost always clergymen; the universities were religious foundations; and theology, canon law, and philosophy were the most prestigious disciplines. The Christianization of the large indigenous population in America alone demanded unusual effort in the training of clergymen. Furthermore, the Spanish dominions constituted a bulwark against the tide of Lutheran and Calvinist doctrines. It was no accident that the Jesuit order, a most powerful counter-Reformation force, was founded in the sixteenth century by a Spanish soldier and that the Society became a great higher educational force.

The civil functionaries of the colonial regime were commonly trained in law, the second most important faculty of the early Spanish-American universities. The students in this faculty were given a minimum of his-torical and political knowledge and a maximum of juridical theory.

The faculties of medicine were considered necessary and important; but the low state of medicine in Spain and in Europe generally, the lack of trained physicians in the colonies, and, in the sixteenth and seventeenth centuries particularly, the distrust of science by ecclesias-tical authorities depressed the academic prestige of the medical faculties. The faculty of arts or of philosophy and arts was usually built upon

an earlier secondary school. It struggled along as a preparatory insti-tution to the theological faculty and as an agency for the training of secondary school teachers.

With the coming of the revolutions against Spain, the faculties of theology were reduced in importance and often suppressed. The facul-ties of law began to rank higher, usually changing their names to faculty of jurisprudence or of juridical and political or social sciences. The faculties of medicine were strengthened and regarded more highly. The faculties of arts, philosophy, and letters now began to include mathematics and natural sciences in their courses. Sometimes new faculties were established for these latter subjects. By 1850, therefore, the second main aim of the university, scientific research, was beginning to find a place in the Spanish-American higher educational systems.

These universities were generally operated as institutions for the upper social and economic classes. In some instances racial as well as social barriers were erected. At the University of San Gregorio Magno in Quito, for example, during the seventeenth and early eighteenth centuries, applicants for entrance had to establish by a detailed legal process "the purity of their blood" and prove that none of their ancestors had engaged in trade. In most cases, however, the requirement of secondary education was sufficient to signify membership in the upper classes.

[1] Pope Paul III, *In Apostolatus Culmine*, Oct. 28, 1538; quoted in Juan Francisco Sánchez, *La Universidad de Santo Domingo*, Impresora Dominicana, Ciudad Trujillo, 1955, pp. 265–266.

[2] This Captaincy General included the present Republics of Guatemala, El Salvador, Honduras, Nicaragua, and Costa Rica. It also included the provinces of Chiapas and Soconusco, which, after the revolution, were annexed to Mexico.

College

Lawrence A. Cremin

> This year, although the estates of these pilgrim people were much wasted, yet seeing the benefit that would accrue to the churches of Christ and civil government, by the Lord's blessing, upon learning, they began to erect a college, the Lord by his provident hand giving his approbation to the work, in sending over a faithful and godly servant of his, the Reverend Mr. John Harvard, who joining with the people of Christ at Charlestown, suddenly after departed this life, and gave near a thousand pounds toward this work; wherefore the government thought it meet to call it Harvard College in remembrance of him.
>
> EDWARD JOHNSON

The origins of English higher education are shrouded in obscurity. One school of historians has located them in the general quickening of theological studies in and around Oxford during the twelfth century, notably the teaching at Beaumont Palace (a favorite of the Plantagenets), the monastery at Abingdon, the priory of St. Frideswide, and a number of the local conventual churches. Another school has associated them more specifically with the recall of English scholars from the University of Paris in 1167, during the long-simmering dispute between Thomas à Becket and Henry II. In any case, there is fairly clear evidence of the gradual emergence of a *studium generale* —a cosmopolitan center of higher learning—at Oxford toward the end of the twelfth century and of the creation of a second *studium* at nearby Cambridge in 1209, after a nasty town-gown encounter at Oxford had sent students and masters in search of more propitious surroundings.[1]

Whatever the particular circumstances of their birth—and it is well to bear in mind Sir John Adams' observation that the medieval universities were not so much founded as they founded themselves —it is clear that the two English institutions, like the University of Paris, were essentially outgrowths of that fascinating convergence of intellectual rebirth and institutional development sometimes referred to as the renaissance of the twelfth century. The story is a familiar one: the era began with only the sketchiest notion of the seven liberal arts, then witnessed the rediscovery of Aristotle, Justinian, Galen, Hippocrates, Euclid, and Ptolemy, and concluded not only with a revivified conception of the arts but also with a new law, a new philosophy, and a new science; here and there, in certain leading centers, particular masters or groups of masters began to attract unusual numbers of students, to wit, teachers of law at Bologna, or medicine at Salerno, or theology at Paris; the exigencies of medieval life compelled them to form guilds—or universities—to protect and advance their mutual interests (some, like Paris, were guilds of masters, while others, like Bologna, were guilds of students); the guilds became settled and were given privileged status by popes and princes; when a guild began to draw students from a wide radius, its site came to be designated a *studium generale*; as the guilds became institutionalized, they organized themselves into faculties of arts, medicine, law, and theology, with the work in the arts faculty seen as both preparatory to and co-ordinate with that in the others; and, finally, guild and *studium* merged to form the archetype of the modern university.[2]

In this fashion, Oxford—and later Cambridge, which patterned itself closely after Oxford—slowly emerged as a characteristic medieval university. The earliest extant statutes date from 1253, and the earliest papal authorization from 1254; but, by that time, there were customary curricula for the various degrees, quite similar to those at Paris, though perhaps more flexible. The arts course began with grammar out of Priscian and Donatus, logic out of Aristotle and Boethius, and rhetoric out of Aristotle, Cicero, and Boethius, and then went to arithmetic and music out of Boethius, geometry out of Euclid, astronomy out of Ptolemy, and the three philosophies—natural, moral, and mental—out of Aristotle. After two years of study, the student was expected to take part in disputations and, after four years, in lecturing as well. The course in medicine revolved around Galen and Hippocrates, supplemented by the *Liber febrium* (*Book of Fevers*) of Isaac and the *Antidotarium* (*Pharmacopoeia*) of Nicholas; the course in theology, around the Bible and the *Sentences* of Peter the Lombard; and the courses in civil and canon law, around the *Corpus juris civilis* (*Body of Civil Law*) of Justinian, the *Decretum* (a synthesis of church law) of Gratian, and the *Decretals* (*Decrees*) of Gregory IX and his successors.[3]

The programs of study at Oxford were quite typical; indeed, the very similarity of the medieval universities, one to another, permitted the evolution of a cosmopolitan world of learning, in which scholars and ideas passed freely from one center to another. But, in at least two realms, English higher education developed along unique lines: first, with respect to the colleges, and second, with respect to the Inns of Court. The college made its initial appearance at Paris in the twelfth century as a simple device to fill an obvious need: boys were coming to the city from all over Europe at the age of fourteen or fifteen, the university felt no obligation to furnish their housing or maintenance, and so halls or dormitories called *hospitia* grew up, where students could reside while they attended lectures and engaged in disputations. Toward the end of the century, a number of endowed *hospitia*, or *collegia*, were founded to provide lodging and board for poor scholars who were unable to provide these for themselves. There was usually a modicum of supervision in such foundations, by a master or cleric; but, at the beginning at least, the business of instruction remained outside, in the hands of the regent masters and their subordinate bachelors.

In England, groups of scholars frequently hired a hall and shared the cost of living, with one among them, known as the principal, elected to preside over the college. As on the Continent, instruction initially remained external to such establishments; but, with the passage of time, college revenues came to be seen as a prime means for supporting younger masters of arts, who could count on neither benefices nor lecture fees as dependable sources of income. In the process, colleges became teaching as well as residential institutions. One must guard against exaggerating the rapidity of the transformation: at least until the early sixteenth century, the great majority of undergraduates and teachers lived in private lodgings. But the colleges did equip a small number of able men for positions of power in the church, and there is no denying that it was the colleges rather than the universities proper that attracted the more distinguished patronage of the later medieval period.

Closely related to the evolution of the colleges was the rise of the Inns of Court, whose origin derived from a fundamental difference between the Continental and English legal systems. On the Continent, the introduction of a stable system of law coincided with the development of higher legal studies, and hence the universities became the instruments by which Roman civil law and Christian canon law were diffused throughout the principalities of Europe. In England, on the other hand, the civil courts resisted the introduction of a Roman code and proceeded to create a native common law based on indigenous Anglo-Saxon elements (admiralty law and canon law were exceptions), with the result that there was a sharp disjunction between the legal arts taught at the universities and the legal realities of the courts. Not surprisingly, an apprenticeship system grew up around the great practicing lawyers, not unlike the system of instruction that had grown up around the great practicing clerics; the students required places to live, which in this instance came to be called Inns of Court; and gradually the Inns, like the contemporary colleges, took on teaching as well as residential functions.

Sir John Fortescue described the Inns in his classic treatise on English law, written between 1468 and 1471 for the instruction of Henry VI's ill-fated son, Edward. The laws of England, he noted, were taught in a "public academy, more convenient and suitable for their apprehension than any university"; that academy consisted of some ten lesser schools, called Inns of Chancery, and four greater schools, called Inns of Court; it was situated near the king's courts, in which the laws were daily pleaded and disputed and to which legal students flocked during termtime; and it taught, in addition to law, manners, dancing, singing, "and all games proper for nobles, as those brought up in the king's household are accustomed to practice."[4]

From Fortescue's description as well as from other contemporary documents, it is obvious that the Inns were enjoying something of a golden age during the later fifteenth century, recruiting an elite class of men from noble families, providing them with an essentially practical training in pleading and advocating, and sending them into the service of the Crown. As W. S. Holdsworth concluded, it was an arrangement "eminently well suited to the needs of a youthful system of law, the literature of which was yet of a manageable size." Unfortunately, the same cannot be said of instruction at the two universities. Cambridge, which had remained "provincial" compared to Oxford, was rapidly closing the gap in size and quality during the fifteenth century; but the fact is that both institutions had suffered from suspicion and repression in the wake of the Lollard movement. Absentee chancellors neglected their responsibilities, a narrow Scholasticism suffused the curriculum, and a rapid rise in the number of graces (dispensations from degree requirements) attested to growing political domination. Yet, notwithstanding a measure of intellectual decay, there is every evidence that by the end of the medieval period the two universities and the Inns had firmly established themselves within the English institutional structure, and together constituted an effective system of recruitment and training for scholarship and the professions.[5]

The very integration of the universities and Inns into the social fabric inevitably subjected them to the sweeping transformations of the Tudor and early Stuart eras; and, indeed, the years between 1480 and 1640 witnessed profound changes in English higher education. In the first place, the universities, like the grammar schools, were gradually laicized. Having gained their independence from diocesan authorities by the end of the fifteenth century—Oxford from the bishop of Lincoln and Cambridge from the bishop of Ely—they acknowledged direct allegiance to king and pope, though in the conflicts between Oxford and Archbishop Arundel in the early fifteenth century it had become clear that royal supremacy had begun to prevail. After Henry VIII broke with Rome, the universities were subject to control by the Crown alone, which manifested its prerogative during the several Tudor reigns, first, by appointing royal visitorial groups on which prominent laymen were increasingly present, and, second, by appointing a succession of lay chancellors, beginning with Thomas Cromwell at Cambridge in 1535.

Meanwhile, Parliament in 1571 enacted legislation incorporating the universities and thereby founding their privileges, liberties, and franchises on civil rather than ecclesiastical authority, a policy that was confirmed when James I granted them representation in Parliament in 1604, choosing to treat them like the ancient boroughs, counties, and cities of the realm rather than like collegiate churches or cathedral chapters. And the same merchant and gentry families that contributed so liberally to grammar schools during the Elizabethan and early Stuart years directed substantial resources to strengthening the older colleges and endowing new ones, such as Emmanuel and Sidney Sussex, in a tide of lay generosity that reached its height during the quarter-century preceding the Revolution.[6]

A second great change of the late sixteenth and early seventeenth centuries was the transformation of the colleges from small, self-contained societies on the margins of the universities into the central units of English higher education. Even before the accession of Elizabeth I, benefactions were pouring into the older colleges and facilitating the establishment of new ones; increasingly willing to accept fee-paying students, these endowed institutions displaced the informal residential halls surrounding the universities, both physically and socially. Then, in 1570, Elizabeth confirmed the shift politically with a new set of statutes for the University of Cambridge, under which most of the authority of the regent masters was transferred to the heads of the colleges, who collectively became the chief governing body of the university. The statutes were obviously an effort by William Cecil, then chancellor of Cambridge, and John Whitgift, then master of Trinity College, to limit religious dissent, as were similar mandates for Oxford, imposed in 1631 by William Laud, then chancellor of the university. Interestingly enough, the transformation of the colleges was accompanied by a decline in the vitality (though not in the drawing power) of the Inns of Court, which were plagued throughout the sixteenth century by an emphasis on form rather than function—by canceled moots and readings, by truncated courses, and by sporadic attendance on the part of students who discovered that the law was more easily learned from books than from lectures or presence at court.[7]

A third change of the late sixteenth and early seventeenth centuries was the significant increase in both the size and diversity of the groups attending the universities and Inns of Court. Lawrence Stone has estimated that the number of students annually beginning higher education (including those few who had private instruction or attended foreign institutions) rose from approximately 780 in the 1560's to over 900 in the 1570's and 1580's, then declined at the turn of the century (for reasons that are somewhat obscure, perhaps economic, perhaps ideological), then rose again to a peak of 1,240 in the

this flexibility permitted a good deal of teaching in the new sciences and mathematics, as well as in modern foreign languages, particularly through what Mark H. Curtis has called the extrastatutory curriculum, and that the universities were therefore much more the nurseries of the new learning than critics such as Francis Bacon, Thomas Hobbes, John Milton, and John Webster allowed.[9]

Considerable insight into what tutorial instruction had become by the early decades of the seventeenth century may be gleaned from the "Directions for a Student in the Universitie," prepared by Richard Holdsworth, who was a fellow at St. John's College, Cambridge, between 1613 and 1620, a Gresham professor from 1629 to 1637, and then master of Emmanuel College between 1637 and 1643. Holdsworth lists the various books to be read and indicates the order in which they should be systematically considered, providing a host of suggestions on the way in which particular works should be approached ("Before you read Ovid's *Metamorphoses* it will be requisite to run over some book of mythology. . . . Also before you read Ovid it will be very good to get two maps one of Old Greece the other of the Roman Empire and spend one afternoon or two in acquainting yourself with them, by the assistance either of your tutor, or some friend") and on the way in which the entire curriculum should be pursued ("A commonplace book ought to be fitted to that profession you follow"; "Many lose a great deal of time in visiting, which must be avoided as much as may be"; "He that will sit tippling in a tavern, and be drunk, shall never find that respect and authority amongst those where he lives, which men of sober carriage do"). And, at one point after another, Holdsworth reveals his patent preference for individual study and conversation over formal lectures on authorized texts, in a sense the epitome of everything the humanists had propounded a century before.[10]

The outcome of these sweeping changes was a shattering of the traditional framework of *imperium-sacerdotium-studium* (state-church-university) and a reconstituting of the mutual relationships between higher education and society, which dramatically affected the commonwealth of England. One must not assume that every tutor was a Holdsworth or that the universities and Inns of Court suddenly became centers of scientific and philosophical inquiry; they remained in large measure institutions where young men of ability could prepare for careers in the church and where young men of wealth and position could acquire a veneer of civility. Yet there is no denying that careers became open to talent on an unprecedented scale, that the quality of political and ecclesiastical leadership was significantly altered, and that the tone of intellectual life was mark-

1630's, and then dropped precipitously after the Revolution. Of the 1,240, some 430 were probably headed for the church, some 160 for law, and some 30 for medicine, leaving roughly half of those with higher education to enter teaching, politics, business, and other occupations that had not formerly attracted men of learning. Moreover, the students were recruited not only from gentry, merchant, and professional families but also from yeoman, artisan, and even tenant and copyhold families, whose sons worked their way through the universities or Inns as sizars or servitors. Indeed, all but the very poor—and recall that the very poor still constituted the majority of the population—had managed to gain access to higher education.[8]

ENTRANTS TO HIGHER EDUCATION 1560-1699
(decennial averages)

Decade	Universities (estimated numbers)	Inns of Court (50% of total entry)	Private and Abroad (estimated numbers)	Estimated Total (to nearest 10)
1560-1569	c. 654	80	50	c. 780
1570-1579	c. 780	79	50	c. 910
1580-1589	770	103	40	910
1590-1599	652	106	40	800
1600-1609	706	119	40	860
1610-1619	884	140	50	1,070
1620-1629	906	120	50	1,080
1630-1639	1,055	137	50	1,240
1640-1649	557	109	100	770
1650-1659	753	118	80	950
1660-1669	740	118	110*	970
1670-1679	722	124	160*	1,010
1680-1689	558	119	170*	850
1690-1699	499	95	230*	820

* Including entrants to dissenting academies.

Finally, the curriculum, particularly the arts curriculum, changed fundamentally. In the first place, as the colleges and Inns gained prominence, the power of the nonacademic aspects of education was vastly strengthened; the influence of ceremonial; the power of day-by-day social intercourse—what Cotton Mather would later refer to as the "collegiate way of living"—grew significantly vis-à-vis that of the formal study of texts. Also strengthened was the role of the tutor, who, with libraries of printed books at his disposal, was able to provide a much more flexible and individualized program of instruction than had previously been possible—one must bear this especially in mind when perusing the prescriptions of college statutes, which often set forth a course of study agreed upon years earlier and then honored increasingly in the breach. And there is evidence that

edly heightened. And, though substantial segments of English higher education remained conservative, learning proved a two-edged sword; and in his history of the Royal Society, Thomas Sprat could with no feeling of ambivalence allude to "those magnificent seats of humane knowledge, and divine; to which the natural philosophy of our nation, cannot be injurious without horrible ingratitude; seeing in them it has been principally cherished, and revived."[11]

RICHARD HOLDSWORTH'S OUTLINE OF STUDIES

Morning Study		Afternoon Study
First Year		
A briefer system and then a more fully developed system of logic	January February March	Richard Holdsworth, "Directions for a Student in the Universitie" Thomas Godwin, *Romanae historiae anthologia* Marcus Junianus Justinus, *Historiarum Philippicarum*
Controversies in logic; another more fully developed system of logic	April May June	Cicero, *Epistles* Desiderius Erasmus, *Colloquies* Terence
Controversies and disputations in logic	July August September	Alexander Ross, *Mystagogus poeticus* Ovid, *Metamorphoses* Greek Testament
A briefer system and then a more fully developed system of ethics	October November December	Terence Cicero, *Epistles* Desiderius Erasmus, *Colloquies* Theognis
Second Year		
A briefer system and then a more fully developed system of physics	January February March	Latin grammar Lorenzo Valla, *De elegantia linguae Latinae* Greek grammar Franciscus Vigerius, *De praecipuius Graecae dictionis idiotismis*
Controversies in logic, ethics, and physics	April May June	Cicero, *De senectute, De amicitia, Tusculanae quaestiones,* and *De oratore* *Aesop's Fables*
A briefer system and then a more fully developed system of metaphysics	July August September	Florus Sallust Quintus Curtius
Third Year		
Controversies of all kinds	October November December	Virgil, *Eclogues and Georgics* Ovid, *Epistles* Horace Martial Hesiod Theocrius
Controversies of all kinds for the entire year Julius Caesar Scaliger, *De subtilitate*	January February March	Nicolas Caussin, *De eloquentia*
Aristotle, *Organon,* with commentary by Brierwood	April May June	Cicero, *Orations* Demosthenes, *Orations*
Aristotle, *Physics*	July August September	Famianus Strada, *Prolusiones academicae* Robert Turner, *Orationum* Quintilian, *Institutio oratoria*
Fourth Year		
Aristotle, *Ethics*	October November December	Juvenal Persius Claudian Virgil, *Aeneid* Homer, *Iliad*
Seneca, *Quaestiones naturales* Lucretius	January February March	Hans Cluver, *Historiarum totius mundi epitome* Suetonius
Aristotle, *De anima* and *De caelo,* with commentary	April May June	Aulus Gellius Macrobius Saturnus Plautus
Aristotle, *Meteorologica,* with commentary	July August September	Cicero, *Orations, De officiis,* and *De finibus*
Marcus Frederik Wendelin, *Christianae theologiae*	October November December	Seneca, *Tragedies* Lucanus Homer, *Iliad and Odyssey*

II

Dixon Ryan Fox once suggested that the transit of liberal and professional learning from England to America proceeded through four distinct stages: first, trained men from the metropolis settled in the colonies and practiced their arts; second, the original supply of learned men was renewed when certain of the native-born youth went to the metropolis for advanced education and then returned to America; third, institutions of higher learning sprang up in the colonies, though during their formative years they remained dependent on the metropolis for the education of their teachers; and, finally, the American establishments matured sufficiently to maintain themselves, replace their faculties, and supply the colonies with educated men. Fox's analysis is useful in tracing the transplantation of higher education to the American colonies, but it requires refinement at a number of points.[12]

Certainly there can be no quarrel with the proposition that the metropolis contributed the original supply of educated men: that is in the nature of colonization. What is especially interesting with respect to the American situation was the extraordinary concentration of educated men in the Great Migration of Puritans to New England. Franklin Bowditch Dexter and Samuel Eliot Morison have identified at least 130 university men among those who immigrated before 1646: 100 had attended Cambridge, and 32 had attended Oxford (obviously, a few had attended both institutions); 87 held the B.A. degree, and 63 held the M.A. Of the 130, 98 served in the ministry in New England, 27 became public officials, 15 taught, 5 entered business, and 3 practiced medicine (again, some practiced more than one profession, and almost all were part-time farmers). True, 43 of the 130 returned to England in the years before the Restoration, but even the remainder constitutes a remarkable number of educated men for a colonial population of around 25,000.[13]

There were far fewer university men in the other colonies, owing to the way in which they were first conceived and settled, but the contrast was not nearly so stark as Dexter and others have portrayed it. By 1646, Virginia had attracted at least twenty-eight university men to the ministry alone; and to those must be added a sprinkling of physicians, such as Walter Russell, Laurence Bohun, and John Potts, and a handful of government officials, such as Thomas West (Lord Delaware) and George Sandys, as well as a succession of public and private men who had attended one or another of the Inns of Court, for example, Gabriel Archer, William Ferrar, Richard Kemp, Roger Wingate, Sir Francis Wyatt, and Edward Digges.[14]

There is no doubt, either, that colonial families very soon began sending some of their youngsters to the metropolis for advanced study. Among Virginians, John Lee attended Oxford in 1658 and 1673 and went on to Gray's Inn the following year, and William Spencer studied at Cambridge in 1684 and proceeded to the Inner Temple a year later. A significant number of New England boys who had been to Harvard chose to cross the Atlantic for additional work in the arts, medicine, law, and theology. James Ward was the first to take advantage of the willingness of the English universities to admit Harvard

graduates to advanced standing, by matriculating at Magdalen College, Oxford, in 1648; thereafter, Sampson Eyton, Henry Saltonstall, William Stoughton, and Joshua Ambrose pursued graduate study at Oxford, and John Stone, William Knight, John Haynes, and Leonard Hoar at Cambridge. By 1660, at least a dozen Harvard men had obtained M.A. degrees from the metropolitan universities. In addition, Eyton was admitted to Gray's Inn in 1658, as was Stephen Lake a decade later, while William Wharton attended the Middle Temple in 1681. Samuel Mather and his younger brother, Increase, took M.A. degrees at Trinity College, Dublin, and Nathaniel Brewster acquired a bachelor's degree in theology there. Samuel Bradstreet, Leonard Hoar, and Thomas Oakes studied medicine in England and then returned to the colonies, unlike a number of their fellow medical students, who remained in London to practice.[15]

Thus far, Fox's paradigm explains the Anglo-American experience fairly accurately. But one must bear in mind that the trip to England was uncertain and the expenses high, and those going there for advanced education constituted a trickle at most. By far the greater number of native-born youth aspiring to careers in law or medicine stayed in the colonies and studied independently or with some practitioner, thus occasioning a kind of devolution from the theoretical and systematic education offered by institutions of higher learning to the more practical and informal education associated with apprenticeship. A colonist seeking to equip himself to practice law, for example, could attend one of the Inns of Court or he could attend Harvard, though only a few managed to do either before 1689; but he could also read law on his own and then seek clients, or he could serve a clerkship in some court (which seems principally to have involved the endless transcribing of documents), or he could serve a clerkship in a private law office, preferably one with a library, mastering the law through some combination of reading, copying, informal association, formal instruction, and practice under supervision. Much the same was true of medicine, though, since there were few if any hospitals in the colonies before 1689, apprenticeships in this field were almost always under an individual. In the realm of divinity, formal study remained a prerequisite to ministerial ordination through the middle of the seventeenth century, owing to the high standards of the Puritan congregations in New England and to the expectations of the English bishops and the Dutch synods. Whereas one could still become a surgeon or a solicitor via apprenticeship in Stuart England, it was difficult to enter the ministry without higher studies; and that difficulty persisted in the colonies—at least until the expansion of the more popular sects after the 1660's, with their emphasis on divine inspiration rather than systematic education as the primary qualification of the clergy.16

Concomitant to the devolution of professional training from an aspect of the higher learning to a form of apprenticeship was the tendency, already noted, of colonists to practice more than one pro- fession, a tendency particularly prevalent among educated men who had access to the theoretical and practical manuals of several fields. Thus, in Massachusetts, John Wilson was minister, physician, and schoolmaster at Medfield from 1651 until his death forty years later; Thomas Thacher was a minister-physician, first at Weymouth and later at Boston, and wrote A Brief Rule to Guide the Common People of New-England How to Order Themselves and Theirs in the Small Pocks, or Measels (1677), the first known contribution to medical literature in America; Leonard Hoar served as a minister-physician at Boston (where he preached for a while as assistant to Thacher) before accepting the presidency of Harvard in 1672; and John Rogers was a preacher and physician at Ipswich until he became president of Harvard in 1682. In Rhode Island, John Clark, a founder of the colony who was banished from Boston with Roger Williams, prac- ticed medicine while serving as pastor of the church at Newport. And, in Virginia, Robert Paulett was a minister-physician at Jamestown between 1619 and 1622, while Nathaniel Hill combined teaching and medicine at Henrico after 1686.

If the devolution of professional training represents one needed refinement of Fox's paradigm, another is required by the extraordi- nary rapidity with which Harvard College was established and took root. "After God had carried us safe to New England," the classic ac- count runs, "and we had builded our houses, provided necessaries for our livelihood, reared convenient places for God's worship, and settled the civil government: one of the next things we longed for, and looked after was to advance learning and perpetuate it to posterity." Accordingly, on October 28, 1636, the general court of Massachu- setts "agreed to give four hundred pounds towards a school or college, whereof two hundred pounds to be paid the next year, and two hundred pounds when the work is finished, and the next court to appoint where and what building." Thus, a college was founded by a legislative body that had been in existence less than ten. As Samuel Eliot Morison has aptly observed, there has been no comparable achievement in the history of modern colonization.17

The 1636 effort was not the first attempt to found a college in the English-speaking colonies. The ill-fated plans for the university at Henrico, in Virginia, have already been discussed: by 1622, over two thousand pounds in gifts had been collected, a standing committee of gentlemen had been formed to oversee the project, the large tract of land which the Virginia Company had contributed was being cultivated by tenants brought to the colony specifically for that purpose, a Communion service had been received for the chapel, the nucleus of a library had been gathered, and the Reverend Patrick Copland had been appointed rector; but the great Indian massacre of 1622 and the subsequent dissolution of the Company were blows from which the project never recovered. There is also evidence that John Stoughton, a promoter of the Massachusetts Bay Colony who remained in England, had sometime between 1634 and 1636 con- ceived the idea of "erecting a place where some may be maintained for learning the language and instructing heathen and our own and breeding up as many of the Indians' children as providence shall bring into our hands." It should be noted, however, that both ven- tures placed heavy, though not exclusive, emphasis on educating the Indians and that both were metropolitan attempts to plant colonial institutions.18

The founding of Harvard, on the other hand, represented an in- digenous effort to plant an institution that would exercise a bene- ficent influence not only on the colony but, like Massachusetts itself, on the metropolis as well. The college was patterned after a charac- teristically English model, which derived from the "prophesyings" that had grown up during the Elizabethan years as instruments for the education of practicing ministers. The Puritans, feeling the in- creasing pressure toward uniformity after 1570, had used these for their own purposes, converting them initially into "schools of the prophets" conducted in the homes of preachers like Richard Green- ham, who sent forth such distinguished disciples as Henry Smith, Robert Browne, and Laurence Chaderton, and later into colleges, of which Emmanuel, founded in 1584 by Sir Walter Mildmay, and Sidney Sussex, founded in 1596 by the countess of Sussex (Sir Philip Sidney's aunt), are leading examples. Mildmay intended Emmanuel to educate preachers "at once learned and zealous, instructed in all that scholars should know, but trained to use their learning in the service of the reformed faith." It is said that Elizabeth once remarked to him, "Sir Walter, I hear you have erected a Puritan foundation." To which Mildmay is reputed to have replied, "No, madam: far be it from me to countenance anything contrary to your established laws; but I have set an acorn, which, when it becomes an oak, God alone knows what will be the fruit thereof." Emmanuel, of course, provided acorns for New England, contributing far more alumni than any of the other Cambridge or Oxford colleges to the ranks of the first settlers, among them, John Harvard.19

In sum, the higher learning had been a salient feature of the Puritan experience in England, and it remained so in New England.

The Times and Order of Studies 1642

	8 A.M.	9 A.M.	10 A.M.	1 P.M.	2 P.M.	3 P.M.	4 P.M.
First Year							
Monday and Tuesday	Logic; physics						Disputations
Wednesday	Greek etymology and syntax				Greek grammar, from literature		
Thursday	Hebrew grammar				Hebrew Bible readings		
Friday	Rhetoric	Declamations	Rhetoric		R h e t o r i c		
Saturday	Catechetical divinity	Commonplaces		History; nature of plants			
Second Year							
Monday and Tuesday		Ethics; politics				Disputations	
Wednesday		Greek prosody and dialects				Greek poetry	
Thursday		"Chaldee" grammar				Practice in Chaldee: Ezra and Daniel	
Friday	Rhetoric	Declamations	Rhetoric		R h e t o r i c		
Saturday	Catechetical divinity	Commonplaces		History; nature of plants			
Third Year							
Monday and Tuesday		Arithmetic; geometry; astronomy					Disputations
Wednesday			Theory of Greek [style]		Exercise in Greek style, both in prose and verse		
Thursday	Syriac grammar						Practice in Syriac: New Testament
Friday	Rhetoric	Declamations	Rhetoric		R h e t o r i c		
Saturday	Catechetical divinity	Commonplaces		History; nature of plants			

The most educated segment of a commonwealth that may well have been the most educated in the history of the world to that point, had spawned a colony designed to be a city on a hill. The founders of that colony had themselves had widespread experience with advanced studies and considered them a prime requisite for a truly civilized society. They therefore moved quickly to establish an institution of higher learning. Viewed thus, the founding of Harvard remains extraordinary but not surprising: to quote Sir John Adams again, it grew out of the nature of things.

The legislative session following the one that authorized the establishment of Harvard convened two months later in Boston, but it was soon caught up in the antinomian controversy and paid no further heed to education. Hence, the next relevant actions were taken on November 15, 1637, when the college was ordered "to be at Newetowne" (whose name was changed to Cambridge the following May)); and on November 20, when responsibility for the college was assigned to a committee—later referred to as the board of overseers—composed of six magistrates and six elders, seven of whom were alumni of Cambridge, one an alumnus of Oxford, and the remaining four fathers or brothers of Cambridge graduates. Before the year was out, Nathaniel Eaton, who had attended Trinity College, Cambridge, and then gone on to study under the distinguished Puritan theologian William Ames at the University of Franeker in the Netherlands, was appointed "professor of the said school" and entrusted with management of the donations to date. It is likely that instruction commenced sometime during the summer of 1638. And, on September 14 of that year, the Reverend John Harvard of Charlestown died of consumption, leaving half his estate (amounting to £779 17s. 2d.) and his entire library to the college. Appropriately appreciative, the general court ordered on March 13, 1639, "that the college agreed upon formerly to be built at Cambridge shall be called Harvard College."20

The choice of Eaton proved unfortunate: a former student wrote of him that he was "fitter to have been an officer in the Inquisition, or master of a house of correction, than an instructor of Christian youth"; and, as if that were not enough, his wife served meatless meals, which featured sour bread and dry pudding. Eaton was dismissed on September 9, 1639, and the college was for all intents and purposes closed until the following August 27, when Henry Dunster, an alumnus of Magdalene College, Cambridge, was appointed president. (There is some evidence that John Winthrop, Jr., invited the Moravian educator John Amos Comenius to head the institution when both were in England in 1641, but nothing came of it.) Under Dunster, the history of Harvard began in earnest: by the

time he resigned in 1654, the college could boast seventy-four alumni (seventy-two of them still living), a charter granted by the general

Petrus Ramus, and Bartholomaüs Keckermann, the theology of William Ames, and the logic of Ramus (with considerable attention given to Aristotle as well).23

Three academic exercises—the lecture, the declamation, and the disputation—lay at the heart of the education offered at seventeenth-century Harvard; the immediate goal of that education was to enable students to systematize coherently and to contend expertly, abilities highly prized in an oral culture that placed ultimate value on the discovery of philosophical and theological truth. The lecture was the master's way of demonstrating systematic thought at its best: he would commonly cast a proposition as a question, divide and subdivide it into its various elements, dealing with each separately, and then indicate the relationships among the several parts. In a sense, the lecture was an oral textbook—frequently a series of commentaries on some classic treatise—which students often transcribed verbatim and which is exemplified in literary form by a work such as Alsted's *Encyclopedia*. The declamation was also an effort to demonstrate systematic thought at its best, though it was a student rather than a faculty exercise and placed more emphasis on rhetorical grace. Declamations were characterized by an abundance of classical allusions, and it was against the need to parade such learning that most students began early in their careers to gather in commonplace books quotations neatly arranged under such rubrics as war, peace, life, death, virtue, and evil. Finally, the disputation was a highly formalized exchange in which a student argued a position on some question introduced by the moderator, while one or more respondents raised objections to his arguments. As the disputation progressed, the participants sought flaws in each other's logic, as well as errors of fact or substance; and, given the mounting tension and excitement, an apt thrust or a clever pun or just the right axiom from Aristotle could elicit spirited applause from an interested audience. The exercise ordinarily concluded with a "dismissal speech" by the moderator, frequently favorable to one or another of the disputants. At their worst—and they are frequently portrayed at their worst in the reformist literature of the Renaissance—all of these exercises were dull, formalistic, and intellectually barren. At their best, however, they nurtured clarity of expression, grace of style, nimbleness of intellect, and sharpness of wit, all of which were invaluable to men of affairs, to say nothing of teachers in pulpit or classroom. And, in their own way and by the canons of their own time, they were liberating—that is, they provided perspectives of time, place, and the imagination from which to criticize the seventeenth-century present.

In its academic program and in other respects as well, Harvard

court in 1650, a fairly respectable library (possibly numbering over a thousand volumes), and three buildings, including a spacious turreted edifice called the "Old College," an auxiliary house known as "Goffe's College," and a president's lodging, which housed a printing press that had become Dunster's responsibility when he married the widow of Jose Glover, a clergyman who had intended to set up a printing establishment in Massachusetts but who had died during the Atlantic crossing.21

An excellent picture of Harvard under Dunster is provided in *New Englands First Fruits*, a promotional pamphlet published anonymously in London in 1643 and likely written by Thomas Weld and Hugh Peter. It is clear from the rules set forth there that collegiality was the chief educational principle: every student was to be "plainly instructed" and earnestly pressed to consider that the main end of his life and studies was "to know God and Jesus Christ which is eternal life, Joh. 17. 3. and therefore to lay Christ in the bottom, as the only foundation of all sound knowledge and learning"; everyone was to exercise himself in reading the Scriptures twice a day, so that he "shall be ready to give such an account of his proficiency therein, both in theoretical observations of the language, and logic, and in practical and spiritual truths, as his tutor shall require, according to his ability"; each pupil was to attend diligently all lectures and tutorials, obey strictly the college's rules and regulations, and eschew steadfastly profanity and association with dissolute company; and no one was to "go abroad to other towns" without the consent of his tutors, his parents, or his guardians. The formal curriculum spanned three years and assumed an understanding of Cicero, along with a fair degree of fluency in Latin and an elementary knowledge of Greek grammar. The themes for disputation were divided into philological theses, organized according to the subjects of the trivium (grammar, rhetoric, and logic), and philosophical theses, organized according to the three philosophies (physics, ethics, and metaphysics).22

The program of 1655, set forth by Dunster's successor, Charles Chauncy, was similar: it ratified the additional year Dunster had added to the undergraduate curriculum sometime before the commencement of 1652 as an extension of the first year's studies; it expanded the work in ethics, physics, and metaphysics; it provided additional detail regarding disputations and declamations; and it made explicit the arrangements for the M.A. degree. From the lists of public disputations, the evidence of textbook ownership, and such student notebooks as we have, it is clear that in other respects the curriculum remained much the same throughout the seventeenth century, emphasizing the compendia of Johann Heinrich Alsted, was similar to the colleges of contemporary Oxford and Cambridge, most notably Emmanuel. It was small in size and collegial in character, embracing at any given time the president and two or three tutors, a steward, cook, butler, and several servants, and from twenty to fifty resident scholars. During Dunster's administration, the median age of entering freshmen was about seventeen; during Chauncy's, it dropped to a little over fifteen, and it remained under sixteen for the rest of the century. While the great majority of the early students were of New England Puritan background, there were enough boys from Virginia, New Netherland, Bermuda, and England to lend a tinge of cosmopolitanism to the college, and, indeed, it was assumed from the beginning that Harvard would be an Anglo-American rather than merely an American institution. As in the English universities, the offspring of magistrates, professionals, and landed families predominated, with a sprinkling of youngsters from artisan and tradesman backgrounds; few sons of husbandmen came, and John Wise of the class of 1673 was probably the first child of an indentured servant to attend. Four years of life in such a community doubtless constituted a powerful education, over and above that provided by the formal curriculum, particularly given the range of recreation, amusements, pranks, brawls, and riots inside and outside the college yard.

Harvard had six presidents between 1640 and 1689—Henry Dunster (1640-1654), Charles Chauncy (1654-1672), Leonard Hoar (1672-1675), Urian Oakes (1675-1681), John Rogers (1682-1684), and Increase Mather (1685-1701)—and forty-three tutors, who served anywhere from a few months to eight years. Dunster and Chauncy were Cambridge men; the remaining presidents were alumni of Harvard, though Hoar held an M.D. from Cambridge and Mather an M.A. from Trinity College, Dublin. That the college was able to produce its own faculty less than a half-century after Massachusetts was settled and less than thirty-five years after its classes first met—and this while maintaining standards sufficiently high to merit an assumption of equivalence on the part of metropolitan institutions—is persuasive testimony to its vitality, and suggests the need for an additional refinement of Fox's paradigm, since Fox implied a significant passage of time before native institutions of higher learning would be capable of maintaining themselves without assistance from the metropolis.

All of Harvard's early presidents were men of ability, though admittedly Chauncy stayed in office well beyond the point at which he should have retired, and Hoar, having come to an early impasse with the students, was quickly forced to resign. Certainly Dunster's administration was the most remarkable: in fourteen years, virtually singlehandedly, he converted an infant institution of uncertain future into a thoroughly acceptable college with every prospect for survival. We know precious little of Dunster's youth in England. He was born in 1609 to a yeoman family in Bury, Lancashire, and attended Magdalene College, Cambridge, taking the M.A. degree in 1634. He returned to Bury shortly after his graduation, as schoolmaster and curate, remaining there until 1640, when he immigrated to Boston with his brother Richard. Three weeks after his arrival, and almost three months to the day before his thirty-first birthday, he was elected president of Harvard.

There is every evidence that Dunster taught the entire curriculum on his own, at least during the early years of his tenure; certainly, the program of 1642 was so arranged that the president could deliver all the lectures himself, instructing the freshmen on Mondays through Thursdays from eight to nine in the morning, the second-year scholars from nine to ten, and the third-year scholars from ten to eleven, meeting with the entire student body on Fridays and Saturdays for work in rhetoric and divinity, and spending afternoons supervising disputations, recitations, and sundry tutorial exercises. Dunster's first assistance in all this came in 1643, when the overseers ordered "that two bachelors shall be chosen for the present help of the president, to read to the junior pupils as the president shall see fit," and appointed John Bulkley and George Downing, both members of the class of 1642, to the newly created positions. Thereafter Dunster had the assistance, in fairly rapid succession, of Samuel Danforth, Samuel Mather, Jonathan Mitchell, Comfort Starr, Samuel Eaton, Urian Oakes, John Collins, and Michael Wigglesworth, all of whom went on to the ministry except Eaton, who served briefly as a magistrate in the New Haven Colony until his untimely death at the age of twenty-five. Wigglesworth left a fascinating diary covering the years of his tutorship, which, though characteristically Puritan in its overweening preoccupation with spiritual self-examination and progress, makes abundantly clear both Dunster's edifying influence on him and his own continuing regard for the piety of his charges.[24]

When Dunster assumed his post, his understanding was that he would teach, and that there would be "no further care or distraction." He could not have been more mistaken. Even though he had the co-operation of a powerful board of overseers, he found himself caught up, during the fourteen years of his presidency, in all the concerns of a latter-day university administrator. He had scarcely arrived when he became involved in the completion of the "Old College" building, which had been started under Nathaniel Eaton; he had to regather the dispersed students and recruit new ones; after

educated gentlemen for the several professions. And, in their statement offering assistance to the college in 1669, the residents of Portsmouth, New Hampshire, referred to the need "for the perpetuating of knowledge, both religious and civil, among us, and our posterity after us." In these and other contemporary documents, the three great ends of seventeenth-century Anglo-American education were so intertwined as to be inseparable—except, that is, by an anti-intellectual polemicist like William Dell, and Charles Chauncy gave New England's irrevocable reply to arguments such as his in 1655.[26]

Yet one can grant the explicit purposes of Harvard and still recognize that those who studied there put the education they received to their own uses; and there is no denying the considerable variety of those uses during the period between 1642 and 1689. Whereas just under half the alumni became ministers, the striking fact is that just over half did not, going instead into medicine, public service, business, teaching, or the management of land holdings. And, whatever the spirit in which the classics were taught, there was certainly immense diversity in the manner in which they were learned: indeed the ideas gleaned from them were doubtless discussed, disputed, and eventually acted upon in ways quite at odds with what Harvard's founders had intended. Once again, the similarity to the colleges of contemporary Oxford and Cambridge is patent.[27]

OCCUPATIONS OF HARVARD ALUMNI OF THE CLASSES 1642-1689

	1642-1658	1659-1677	1678-1689	1642-1689
Clergymen	76	62	42	180
Physicians	12	11	4	27
Public Servants*	13	17	12	42
Teachers**	1	8	4	13
Merchants	3	6	1	10
Planters, Gentlemen	4	5	2	11
Soldiers, Mariners	0	1	4	5
Miscellaneous	2	3	0	5
Died Young***	11	5	11	27
Occupation Unknown****	27	35	6	68
Total	149	153	86	388

* Governors, councilors, judges, deputies (if continuing for a term of years), and permanent officials; local offices not counted.
** Schoolmasters and college tutors who made teaching a career, or who died before doing anything else.
*** Those who died in college or within five years after graduating, without getting a job.
**** Most of these are the nongraduates before 1663, whose careers have never been investigated; some have not even been identified.

marrying comfortably in 1641, he found himself unable to collect the salary that had been promised him and forced continually to plead for support from the general court, the New England Confederation, Parliament, and private donors; and, having taken over a college established under legislation of the general court (passed initially in 1637 and re-enacted in 1642), he deemed it advisable during the Commonwealth era to seek a more permanent incorporation and became the prime mover in obtaining a formal charter from from the court in 1650. Through it all, he faced the daily necessity of developing the rules, usages, and customs that would shape the character of the college: he borrowed the practice of having commencement theses from the University of Edinburgh, he took the wording of the charter and of the various "rules and precepts" from the ancient statutes of Oxford and Cambridge, he improvised here and invented there, so that by 1654 a unique and autochthonous tradition had been created for the fledgling institution.[25]

Dunster resigned the presidency in 1654, after a series of sharp encounters with the students, the board of overseers, and the General Court, first, over the extension of the undergraduate curriculum from three to four years, then, over the financial management of the institution, and finally—and fatally—over the thorny issue of Dunster's infant baptism, the propriety and efficacy of which Dunster began to doubt in 1652 and 1653. Many prominent persons in the colony sought to dissuade him from this Baptist heresy, but to no avail. After a public disputation in Boston on February 2 and 3, 1654, in which Dunster argued that infant baptism was un-Scriptural, his position became untenable, and he resigned the following June 10, removing a year later to Scituate, in the Plymouth Colony, where he served as a pastor until his death early in 1659.

III

Harvard College was founded to advance piety, civility, and learning. New Englands First Fruits spoke of the longing "to advance learning and perpetuate it to posterity" and the dread of leaving an illiterate ministry to the church, once the initial immigrants had passed from the scene. The charter of 1650 defined the ends of the college as "the advancement of all good literature, arts and sciences" and the education of English and Indian youth "in knowledge: and godliness." The Reverend Jonathan Mitchell, in his "Modell for the Maintaining of Students & Fellows of Choise Abilities at the Colledge in Cambridge," presented to the general court in 1663, insisted not only on the importance of training a learned ministry but also on the necessity of providing masters for the grammar schools,

The conditions of the colonial environment did, however, occasion certain significant departures from the English pattern. For one thing, Harvard awarded degrees, so far as can be determined, with no explicit authority from the king, or Parliament, or the general court, or any extant *studium* or university: Dunster and the overseers simply went ahead and granted them, thereby virtually declaring independence from Charles I, as Morison appropriately suggests. Then, too, Harvard early innovated in the realm of control. Without evidence to the contrary, one must assume that the founders intended the board of overseers to bring the college into being and then transfer its prerogatives to the master and fellows, much as in the English universities; and, indeed, the charter of 1650, which created a corporation composed of the president, treasurer, and five fellows to govern the college and manage its resources, doubtless envisioned such a transfer. But the charter stipulated that the orders of the corporation would be contingent upon the approval of the overseers, in effect leaving Harvard with two governing boards, one consisting of magistrates and ministers, the other of the college's officers and faculty members. To complicate the arrangement even further, as the seventeenth century progressed a number of tutors were appointed to instruct without being made fellows of the corporation, while a number of influential citizens who had no instructional responsibilities were appointed to the corporation—with the result that the college was governed by two bodies composed primarily of ministers and laymen who did not teach. It was a development quite in keeping with the tendency toward laicization in the English universities, but it was thoroughly indigenous to the colonies.

Harvard also innovated in the realm of support, largely out of necessity. The initial effort to subsidize the institution through endowment, tuition, and the assignment of various fees, like the Boston-Charlestown ferry rent, proved inadequate, and the college shortly began to experiment with schemes such as the fund-raising mission of Hugh Peter, Thomas Weld, and William Hibbins to England in 1641; the "college corn" arrangement proposed by the Commissioners of the United Colonies, whereby "but the fourth part of a bushel of corn, or something equivalent thereunto" would be contributed by every family in New England willing and able to do so; the voluntary collection of the Piscataqua towns of New Hampshire during the 1670's; and direct grants of land and tax revenues from the general court, which agreed to pay the president's salary starting with the accession of Chauncy in 1654. During the period from 1669 to 1682, 52.7 per cent of Harvard's annual income came from the government and government-sponsored subscriptions, while endowment accounted for only 12.1 per cent and tuition for only 9.4 per cent. Once again, the departure from traditional English practice was substantial.[28]

Finally, Harvard sought to innovate in the realm of Indian education, though most of its attempts failed abysmally, largely because of the unspoken assumption that the Indians should aspire to the same social and cultural ends as the whites. Harvard's principal effort was, of course, the Indian College, built around 1654 or 1655 in response to a request from the Commissioners of the United Colonies to erect "one entire room at the college" for the instruction of a half-dozen promising young Indians. Almost as soon as it was completed, however, President Chauncy was complaining that the two-story building was insufficiently used and asking permission to accommodate some white students there, which permission was granted. Unfortunately, Chauncy's complaint became a self-fulfilling prophecy and few Indians ever studied at Harvard. There is evidence that a youngster named John Sassamon attended for a term or two around 1653, before the creation of the Indian College, as a protégé of John Eliot. But it is unlikely that more than four others entered before 1689, of whom only one, known as Caleb Cheeshahteaumuck, completed the work for the B.A.—and he unfortunately died of consumption a year after graduating. Otherwise, the most useful purpose the Indian College served with respect to the red men was to house the press that printed the Indian Bible and the other Algonquian texts prepared by Eliot and his associates.[29]

The presence of Harvard, coupled with both the return of a small number of youngsters to England and the Continent for advanced education and the increasing reliance on apprenticeship to produce physicians, lawyers, and other professionals, created an interesting tension in the colonies between the maintenance of standards commensurate with those of the metropolis and the widening of access to elite positions. The historic regulatory functions of the guilds simply could not be exercised in a land three thousand miles from the seats of power and beset with a chronic labor shortage, and this was as true for the professions as it was for the trades. Hence, there were few serious attempts to restrict entry into the legal and medical professions in the colonies, and these were more often the result of a general animus toward mercenary attorneys and physicians than of a desire to preserve standards—the outstanding exception being Maryland's effort to regulate the practice of law beginning in 1657.[30]

One obvious consequence was a sharp decline in professional standards, which might have been even more precipitous and enduring had not the graduates of Harvard, Oxford, Cambridge, Padua, and Edinburgh been present to exemplify traditional canons of competence. Another outcome, however, was a considerable broadening of access to the professions, extending, to be sure, to many who sought little more than a quick and easy shilling, but extending also to those who wanted something better for themselves and for those they served. The resulting situation was egregiously ill-defined, for traditional patterns of professional self-regulation simply failed to take root. But the very lack of definition provided a favorable context for novelty, and when Americans turned to the reconstitution of legal education and medical education in the eighteenth century, they developed these in unique ways: there would be no Inns of Court and no Royal College of Physicians, merely new schools and new faculties of old colleges, open to all who could pay the modest tuition and meet the modest entrance requirements.

1 The historiographical controversy is sketched by A. B. Emden in his introduction to the third volume of Hastings Rashdall, *The Universities of Europe in the Middle Ages*, edited by F. M. Powicke and A. B. Emden (rev. ed.; 3 vols.; Oxford: Clarendon Press, 1936), III, xv-xxvi, 5-33, 465-476.

2 James Hastings, ed., *Encyclopedia of Religion and Ethics* (13 vols.; New York: Charles Scribner's Sons, 1913-1927), V, 172.

3 Rashdall, *Universities of Europe in the Middle Ages*, III, 140-168.

4 Sir John Fortescue, *De laudibus legum Anglie*, translated and edited by S. B. Chrimes (Cambridge: Cambridge University Press, 1942), pp. 115-121.

5 W. S. Holdsworth, *A History of English Law* (12 vols.; London: Methuen & Co., 1903-1938), VI, 481.

6 An Act Concerning the Several Incorporations of the Universities, 13 Eliz. I, c. xxix, *The Statutes at Large* (9 vols.; London: printed for Mark Basket, 1763-1765), II, 603-605; and James Heywood and Thomas Wright, eds., *Cambridge University Transactions During the Puritan Controversies* (2 vols.; London: Henry G. Bohn, 1854), II, 207-211.

7 George Dyer, ed., *The Privileges of the University of Cambridge* (2 vols.; London: Longman and Co., 1824), I, 181-182; and Strickland Gibson, ed., *Statuta antiqua Universitatis Oxoniensis* (Oxford: Clarendon Press, 1931), p. 570.

8 Lawrence Stone, "The Educational Revolution in England, 1560-1640," *Past & Present*, no. 28 (July, 1964), pp. 54, 41-80; and Joan Simon, "The Social Origins of Cambridge Students, 1603-1640," *ibid.*, no. 26 (November, 1963), pp. 58-67.

9 Cotton Mather, *Magnalia Christi Americana; or, The Ecclesiastical History of New-England* 1702), edited by Thomas Robbins (2 vols.; Hartford: Silas Andrus and Son, 1853-1855), II, 10; and Mark H. Curtis, *Oxford and Cambridge in Transition, 1558-1642* (Oxford: Clarendon Press, 1959), pp. 127 ff. and passim.

10 Holdsworth's "Directions" are printed in their entirety in Harris Francis Fletcher, *The Intellectual Development of John Milton* (2 vols.; Urbana: University of Illinois Press, 1956-1961), II, 623-655. For a caution on the use of the "Directions" as a source, see Christopher Hill, *Intellectual Origins of the English Revolution* (Oxford: Clarendon Press, 1965), pp. 307-314.

11 Thomas Sprat, *The History of the Royal-Society of London, for the Improving of Natural Knowledge* (London: T. R., 1667), p. 328. The principal exceptions to the general advance seem to have been the programs in medicine. See, for example, the Laudian statutes for Oxford, which required the Regius Professor of Medicine "to lecture in Hippocrates or Galen" twice weekly, in G. R. M. Ward, trans., *Oxford University Statutes, Vol. I: Containing the Caroline Code or Laudian Statutes* (London: William Pickering, 1845), p. 25.

12 Dixon Ryan Fox, *Ideas in Motion* (New York: D. Appleton-Century Company, 1935), pp. 3-36.

13 Franklin Bowditch Dexter, "The Influence of the English Universities in the Development of New England," *A Selection from the Miscellaneous Historical Papers of Fifty Years* (New Haven: The Tuttle, Morehouse & Taylor Company, 1918), pp. 102-117; and Samuel Eliot Morison, *The Founding of Harvard College* (Cambridge, Mass.: Harvard University Press, 1935), pp. 359-410.

14 Frederick Lewis Weis, *The Colonial Clergy of Virginia, North Carolina and South Carolina* (Boston: Society of the Descendants of the Colonial Clergy, 1955), pp. 1-57; Wyndham B. Blanton, *Medicine in Virginia in the Seventeenth Century* (Richmond: The William Byrd Press, 1930), pp. 80-84; and J. G. De Roulhac Hamilton, "Southern Members of the Inns of Court," *The North Carolina Historical Review*, X (1933), 278-279.

15 Willard Connely, "Colonial Americans in Oxford and Cambridge," *The American Oxonian*, XXIX (1942), 6-17, 75-77; E. Alfred Jones, *American Members of the Inns of Court* (London: The Saint Catherine Press, 1924); and William L. Sachse, "Harvard Men in England, 1642-1714," *Publications of the Colonial Society of Massachusetts*, XXXV (1951), 119-144.

16 There is some evidence that a Giles Firmin delivered a series of lectures based on an "anatomy" (probably a skeleton) in Massachusetts during the 1640's, but Firmin is known to have returned to England in 1651. See Joseph M. Toner, *Contributions to the Annals of Medical Progress and Medical Education in the United States Before and During the War of Independence* (Washington, D.C.: Government Printing Office, 1874), p. 64.

17 *New Englands First Fruits* (London: R. O. and G. D., 1643), in Morison, *Founding of Harvard College*, p. 432; and Nathaniel B. Shurtleff, ed., *Records of the Governor and Company of the Massachusetts Bay in New England* (5 vols.; Boston: William White, 1853-1854), I, 183.

18 Morison, *Founding of Harvard College*, p. 415. The only other "collegiate" institution in the English-speaking colonies before the founding of the College of William and Mary in 1693 was the Jesuit college established at Newtown, Maryland, in 1677, though this was probably more like the Latin grammar schools in the colonies and Europe than the English colleges or the Continental universities.

19 Jonathan Mitchell, "A Modell for the Maintaining of Students & Fellows of Choise Abilities at the Colledge in Cambridge" (c. 1663), *Publications of the Colonial Society of Massachusetts*, XXXI (1935), 309; and Thomas Fuller, *The History of the University of Cambridge* (new ed.; London: printed for Thomas Tegg, 1840). p. 205.

20 Shurtleff, ed., *Records of the Governor and Company of Massachusetts*, I, 208, 217, 253; and "The Colledge Booke No. 3," *Publications of the Colonial Society of Massachusetts*, XV (1925), 173.

21 William Hubbard, *A General History of New England, from the Discovery to MDCLXXX* (2d ed.; Boston: Charles C. Little and James Brown, 1848), p. 247; and "Colledge Booke No. 3," p. 172.

22 *New Englands First Fruits*, pp. 434-436, 438-440. Some typical examples of theses are the following: Philological Theses—(1) Greek is the most copious of languages, (2) Rhetoric is different in kind from logic, (3) Universals have no existence outside the mind; Philosophical Theses—(1) Prudence is the most difficult of all the virtues, (2) Form is accidental, (3) Every being is good.

23 "The Lawes of the Colledge Published Publiquely Before the Students of Harvard College, May 4, 1655," *Publications of the Colonial Society of Massachusetts*, XXXI (1935), 327-339.

24 "College Book No. 1," *ibid.*, XV (1925), 17; and *The Diary of Michael Wigglesworth, 1653-1657*, edited by Edmund S. Morgan (New York: Harper & Row, 1965), pp. 7, 9, 11, 26-27, and passim. For lists of Harvard presidents, fellows, and tutors during the seventeenth century, see Albert Matthews' introduction to the Harvard College Records in *Publications of the Colonial Society of Massachusetts*, XV (1925), clii-clxi.

25 Henry Dunster to the Honored Commissioners for the College et al., December, 1653, in Morison, *Founding of Harvard College*, pp. 448-449.

26 "The Harvard College Charter of 1650," *Publications of the Colonial Society of Massachusetts*, XXXI (1935), 5; Mitchell, "Modell for the Maintaining of Students &

Fellows," p. 317; and Shurtleff, ed., *Records of the Governor and Company of Massachusetts*, IV, ii, 433.

27 Samuel Eliot Morison, *Harvard College in the Seventeenth Century* (2 vols.; Cambridge, Mass.: Harvard University Press, 1936), II, 562.

28 Nathaniel B. Shurtleff and David Pulsifer, eds., *Records of the Colony of New Plymouth in New England* (12 vols.; Boston: William White, 1855-1861), IX, 20-21; and Margery Somers Foster, "Out of Smalle Beginnings . . ." (Cambridge, Mass.: Harvard University Press, 1962), pp. 148-149.

29 Shurtleff and Pulsifer, eds., *Records of the Colony of New Plymouth*, X, 107.

30 *Archives of Maryland*, XLI (1922), 10-11. For the short-lived effort to confine the title "counselor-at-law" to barristers certified by the Inns of Court, see William Waller Hening, ed., *The Statutes at Large; Being a Collection of All the Laws of Virginia, from the First Session of the Legislature, in the Year 1619* (13 vols.; imprint varies, 1819-1823), I, 419, 482.

From Religion to Politics: Debates and Confrontations Over American College Governance in Mid-Eighteenth Century America

Jurgen Herbst

Growing religious diversity during the middle decades of the eighteenth century challenged traditional forms of governance at the colleges in the English colonies of North America. At the beginning of that century, the secular government and the established church jointly exercised authority over each college. In subsequent decades, the arrival of Baptists, Anglicans, and Quakers in New England, and the influx of Presbyterians and Quakers in Virginia threatened the entrenched dominance of Congregationalists at Harvard, Presbyterians at Yale, and Anglicans at the College of William and Mary and placed great strains on the working agreements between the authorities of church and state.[1]

The middle colonies' religiously and ethnically mixed populations precluded college governance on the Reformation model of *cuius regio, eius religio,* by which a sovereign's denomination determined both the ecclesiastical allegiance of his or her subjects and the religious policies of colleges. Instead, the aggressive evangelism of the supporters of the Great Awakening—that pan-Protestant arousal of enthusiastic religiosity in the late 1730s and early 1740s which swept the colonies from Massachusetts to Virginia—and the heterogeneity of the people combined to produce a colonial variant of the English policy of toleration. As understood in the colonies, toleration meant the tacit recognition that the dominant church in each province was the established ecclesiastical authority. Yet, in contrast to traditional Reformation policy, members of minority denominations were guaranteed religious liberty while attending the college of the dominant religion. Thus, a colony's college was entrusted with stewardship for all Protestants. The adoption of a policy of toleration in college governance constituted a recognition that, under conditions of pluralism, accommodation and conciliation were mandatory in order to end and avoid conflicts.

In addition to problems caused by the growth of diversity, toleration had inherent defects and weaknesses; as a policy, it did not survive into the nineteenth century. In the colonies it quickly proved to be an elusive and unattainable ideal. Its pursuit led to tension and polarization between ecclesiastical authorities and secular leaders and frequently provided convenient cover for political power struggles. Questions of college governance became indistinguishable from political debates and battles, and the alliance of secular and ecclesiastical interests ultimately broke asunder.

As the Revolution approached, new distinctions were drawn between private and denominational colleges on the one hand and public colleges on the other. The beginnings of this new alignment could be seen as early as the 1760s, when Queen's College was chartered in New Jersey as a rival to the provincial college at Princeton. The trend, however, reached its full development only in the 1780s and 1790s with the chartering of the first state universities in New York, Pennsylvania, Georgia, and Vermont and with the founding of the first private colleges in Virginia, Kentucky, and Pennsylvania.[2] Yet in the mid-eighteenth century, the major issues surrounding college development stemmed from tension between the defenders of ecclesiastical authority and proponents of secular control. Under the pressure of demographic forces, toleration became an outmoded policy by the end of the eighteenth century, and the religious disputes became transformed into political battles involving the colleges in the larger social and political issues of the colonies.

The Great Awakening and College Governance

The Great Awakening was the catalyst for breaking the mold of joint ecclesiastic-secular college governance. Its very nature as an evangelical movement welcoming students and teachers from all Protestant denominations placed it in opposition to the idea of an established-church order in colony and college. Its leaders, expecting to benefit from population growth and geographic expansion, pressed the colleges to be inclusive with regard to the religious persuasions of their students and encouraged them to accept denominational differences.3

Even though authorities in England were committed to the concept of joint establishment of state and church, their endorsement of a policy of toleration and their political consideration for the welfare of the colonial populations posed few serious obstacles to interdenominational cooperation. Thus, in 1763, when the Crown recommended an Anglican fund-raising effort for King's College and for the College of Philadelphia, it spoke of "the various denominations of other Protestants" who, in addition to the Anglicans, were jointly committed to "the support and extension of the reformed religion."4

To be sure, this statement of royal support came decades after the flood tide of the Awakening had passed. Crown authorities had been somewhat less accommodating in the 1740s when the Awakening first affected the colleges of New England. But even then the main opposition arose less from the crown than from the colonial clergy—Congregational at Harvard and Presbyterian at Yale. At the Massachusetts college the effects were comparatively mild. There was no change in the governance of the college other than an increasing influence of the magistrates on the Board of Overseers and a strengthening of the liberal ministers at the expense of their orthodox brethren.5 At Yale, however, the Awakening ushered in a grave crisis. Throughout Connecticut it pitted against each other partisans and opponents of the demand for ecclesiastic-secular college governance.

At the beginning of the 1740s, the Collegiate School (as Yale was then officially known) differed in its form of governance from other colleges in the Western world. Its administration, unlike that of Harvard or William and Mary, included no representatives of the provincial government. Yale's exclusively clerical board of trustees exercised the functions of directors of a corporate body; without having been legally established as such, it constituted a quasi-corporation. While acknowledging the Connecticut Assembly as the source of funds, the trustees were prepared to accept its direction only as a court of equity in controversial matters.

In 1745, however, under the leadership of their recently elected rector, Thomas Clap, the trustees exchanged their relative freedom from legislative supervision for the security and privilege of full incorporation as The President and Fellows of Yale College. Even then they did not count civil representatives of the colonial government among their number. But under the new charter the assembly had the right to inquire into or repeal the trustees' legislative and administrative rules "when they shall think proper." Perhaps Clap thought that the legislature's pledge of annual cash grants to the college "to continue during the pleasure of this Assembly"6 amply compensated for this unavoidable concession to the assembly. Whatever his motives, the fact remained that in 1745, only five years after his election, Clap had succeeded in formally incorporating the Collegiate School and bringing it under the authority of both Connecticut's established Presbyterian churches and its legislature. The governance of the provincial college now conformed in principle, if not in every detail, to that of other colleges founded after the Reformation.7 However inconsequential or weighty the concession to assembly oversight really was, its effects could only become apparent in the future.

Clap cherished the participation of the legislature in college affairs because he had found assembly support invaluable during the late 1730s, the tumultuous years

of the Awakening. Initially he had welcomed the arrival of such well-known revivalists as George Whitefield and Gilbert Tennent, but he changed his mind when he witnessed their effects on the Yale students. Encouraged by these visiting "New Lights," as they were called, the students began to question the piety of their "Old Side" teachers and ministers. This led the Yale trustees to decree in September 1741 "that if any student of this college shall directly or indirectly say that the rector, either of the trustees or tutors are hypocrites, carnal or unconverted men, he shall for the first offense make a public confession in the hall, and for the second offense be expelled."8

Clap soon found occasion to apply the ordinance and expelled David Brainerd for having said of his tutor that he possessed no more grace than a chair. But the turmoil persisted, split the New Haven church, and led Clap to send the student body home. In April 1742, a committee of the legislature, alarmed that students had "fallen into several errors in principle and disorders in practice," recommended that the General Court grant funds to hire a college minister.9 A month later the assembly intervened with its "Act for Regulating Abuses and Correcting Disorders in Ecclesiastical Affairs" and attempted to ban itinerant ministers from Connecticut churches.10 Clap and the college trustees were wholly in sympathy with these drastic and repressive measures against the New Lights. In their desire to uphold the Old Side establishment of state, church, and college, they perceived the legislature as their strongest and most reliable ally.

Highlighting once more the existing college-church-state nexus, the most acute crisis involving the college directly in the turmoil of the Awakening came late in 1744. Two students, the brothers John and Ebenezer Cleaveland, while on college vacation at home in Canterbury, Connecticut, had attended New Light worship services with their parents. When Clap and the tutors heard of this, they charged the brothers with having violated the rules of the Gospel as well as the laws of the colony and college. John Cleaveland apologized for his ignorance of the laws as Clap had defined them but refused to admit that the meetings he had attended were anything other than gatherings of a legally constituted church. He objected strenuously to what he considered the unwarranted application of college laws outside the confines of Yale: "For we always thought," he told Clap, "that when we were out of New Haven we had full liberty to go to what meeting we pleased without a thought of transgressing any college law." But Clap would have none of this. "All college laws," he retorted, "excepting a few little ones extend farther than New Haven bounds."11 Speaking for the tutors and himself, he added:

We conceive that it would be a contradiction in the civil government to support a college to educate students to trample upon their own laws and break up the churches which they establish and protect, especially since the General Assembly in May 1742 thought proper to give the governors of the college some special advice and direction upon that account; which was to this effect, *that all proper care should be taken to prevent the scholars from imbibing those or such like errors; and that those who would not be orderly and submissive, should not be allowed the privilege of the college.* 12

Pressed to justify punishing students for violating a law which could be said to exist only by implication, Clap accused the Cleaveland brothers of knowing that their actions were contrary to his judgment, "and if you do not go according to my judgment you can't expect to enjoy college privileges."13 With this statement Clap presumed to personify both the law of the college and the law of the colony. Only the students and a few sympathizers protested. The New York *Post-Boy* published a letter by an author who was "a little warm upon this late stretch of college power,"[14] and the Yale students printed and distributed John Locke's *Essay on Toleration*. But this had little impact on the common front of college administration, Old Side establishment, and General Court.[15]

During 1745, the Cleaveland affair and the possibilities of renewed rebellion among students and young tutors pushed Clap to seek incorporation for the college. Once incorporation was accomplished, he could rest both his own authority and that of the board of trustees on the charter rights of a corporation backed by the General Court.

The terms of the Yale charter broke new ground. This was not because of the appointment of a group of nonresident ministers to the corporation, as has been stated,[16] but because of the exclusion of any and all tutors and professors from membership. At the two colonial colleges founded prior to Yale, nonresident governors served among the overseers at Harvard and among the visitors at William and Mary. However, at Harvard one professor and some of the tutors were members of the corporation, while at the Virginia college the entire faculty and the president constituted the corporation.[17] Clap barred all teachers at Yale because he recognized that threats to the Old Side establishment were more likely to arise among young, inquisitive college tutors than among established ministers. Perhaps Clap was also reminded of the rebellion of the Harvard tutors in the 1720s or of ex-President Cutler's and tutor Samuel Johnson's defections to Anglicanism, a shock that had nearly led to the closing of the college two decades earlier.[18] Regardless of his motivation, Clap rested his faith on responsible external governors, whom he placed directly under legislative oversight, and openly demonstrated his distrust of college teachers.

The same concern for keeping the college a law unto itself, for minimizing the possibilities of internal rebellion and thereby of outside interference, is manifest in the 1745 laws of the college drawn up by Clap.[19] Under these laws students were made subjects of the college and the church of New Haven, and the president, tutors, fellows, and the General Court held disciplinary authority over them. Students were specifically prohibited from attending any religious services not approved by the president or public authority. In addition, they were denied the right to enter complaints or bring suit in civil court against other members of the college unless they first obtained permission from the president or fellows. Clap sought to ensure the autonomy of the college as a provincial institution against intervention by municipal authorities or inferior courts. Narrowly circumscribing the spheres of action assigned to teachers and students, he anchored the college firmly in the bedrock of its associated institutions of church and state.

It is supremely ironic that Clap's stormy presidency eventually terminated in strife, riots, and the near collapse of the college as a result of his decision in 1753 to desert his own guidelines. Losing sympathy with his brethren in the Connecticut churches and with the assembly, Clap himself began to loosen the connections that held the college to church and state. In 1747, he wrote proudly that his charter and laws had "reduced the college to a much more perfect state" and that the former trustees, "not so proper or usual a title for the governors of a college in a more mature and perfect state,"[20] had become corporation fellows. But pride over internal ch'n,ges could do little to prevent the outside world from challenging Clap's claim of autonomy for the college and autocracy for himself.

The challenge to Clap's authority began in 1753 with the opening of an Anglican church in New Haven. Clap abruptly terminated the relationship between Yale and New Haven's First Presbyterian Church by ordering all students to worship and receive religious instruction within the college. He obviously meant to respond

to the Anglican threat by drawing the college community ever closer upon itself, even if that meant reversing his previous policy of integrating the college into the existing establishment of Presbyterian church and state. His ban offended Connecticut Presbyterians as much as Anglicans, and both groups protested strongly. Clap's only response was to note that no community could exist without enforcing uniform rules for all of its members. He now began a "go-it-alone" policy, despite its potential for splitting the college from the church and the state.[21]

Anglican reaction to Clap's new ordinance came quickly and effectively from Samuel Johnson, newly elected president of King's College in New York. Johnson, a Yale alumnus, ex-tutor, and—after his Episcopal ordination—an influential spokesman for Connecticut's Anglicans, warned Clap:

Tell it not in Gath[much less in the ears of our dear mother-country, that any of her daughters should deny any of her children leave to attend on her worship whenever they have opportunity for it. . . . For God's sake do not be so severe to think in this manner, or to carry things to this past If so, let Dissenters never more complain of their heretofore persecutions or hardships in England, unless they have us tempted to think it their principle, that they ought to be tolerated, in order at length to be established, that they may have the sole privilege of persecuting others.[22]

Johnson was blunt. He reminded Clap that New England's Anglicans might have to complain to "our superiors at home." The English officials could conclude, in turn, that Yale College, which was incorporated by the colonial assembly rather than the crown, was "a nullity in itself."[23] Moreover, the colony's act of incorporation might have been illegal, endangering its own status in law. And as if that were not enough, Johnson added, Yale College had been funded with the aid of such Anglican donors as Elihu Yale, Bishop Berkeley, and, through the annual contributions of the Connecticut Assembly, the colony's Anglican taxpayers. As much as Clap must have resented being reminded of Connecticut's changing demography, of English law, and of his own earlier views of college-church-state relationships, he had to concede the points. Johnson's threat of appeal to the crown was too formidable a risk.[24]

Clap's concession, however, came neither gracefully nor enthusiastically. Without announcing any change in policy, he began to grant permission for Anglican students to attend services of their faith if they so requested. Clap combined his reversal with a spirited defense of his original position and a novel reading of college history. He declared that the laws of the college and the rules of peace and charity demanded preservation of the original purpose and order of the college. There was no violation of liberty of conscience involved in this, Clap told Johnson: Anglicans who entered the college did so by their own free will and, by entering, accepted the college rules.[25] In a twenty-page pamphlet especially prepared for the occasion, Clap argued that "the original end and design of colleges was to instruct, educate, and train up persons for the work of the ministry." Though colleges since the Reformation had been chartered by civil government, they were run by ecclesiastical persons for spiritual purposes and were therefore religious societies. Because their purpose was to train ministers, he argued, colleges were superior to ordinary churches, which trained the common people.[26]

Clap went on to announce that, since 1746, the trustees had been accumulating an endowment fund for a professor of divinity; in the meantime, they had asked the president to perform that role. As for Messrs. Yale and Berkeley, they surely knew, wrote Clap, that their contributions to the college were supporting the intent of the original donors and could not alter the college's foundation. He added that

Connecticut's taxpaying Anglicans were amply repaid by the education of Episcopal ministers.[27] In this interpretation of college history, Clap virtually ignored the effects of the Reformation, which had left the purpose more secular and had weakened governance by ministers. He angered the Anglicans by substituting insult for injury, and he offended Presbyterian ministers and magistrates as well with his arrogant claim for the superiority of colleges to churches. All he accomplished was to isolate himself.

Clap's sparring with the Anglicans was but a prelude to a far more serious battle in the 1760s. Building on his announcement that colleges were superior to religious societies, Clap argued that colleges could carry on religious instruction, worship, and ordinances "within their own jurisdiction, by their own officers, and under their own regulation."[28] This was his justification for withdrawing students from the New Haven church and subsequently for organizing a separate college church under his direct supervision. In March 1756, the trustees installed Naphtali Daggett as professor of divinity, and on July 3, 1757, Daggett preached his first sermon as the pastor of the newly established Church of Christ in Yale College.[29] Thus, between 1753 and 1757, Clap succeeded in redefining the society over which he had presided for sixteen years. If he could have his way, Yale College for the training of civil servants for state and church was going to become a church seminary, and its first senior professor would become its chaplain. In attempting to carry out this transformation, Clap not only affronted members of the assembly and others in Connecticut who believed in the original purpose of the college, but he also violated the Saybrook Platform, which gave the consociation of churches a voice in all matters of church separation.[30] To make matters worse, in 1757 Clap sought to oust Joseph Noyes, minister of New Haven's First Church, from the college corporation by accusing him of heresy and requesting a trial.[31] In this instance, Clap was forced to back down by a gathering storm of protest and resistance to his high-handed, arbitrary administration. As Louis Tucker, Clap's biographer, reports, the Yale controversy began as a religious issue, spilled over into politics, and "in the course of the dispute, weighty questions were raised relative to the nature and purpose of Yale, the relationship of the school to the General Assembly, and the extent of authority of the Corporation and President Clap."[32] When these questions were finally taken up in the assembly, the college entered the political arena, where Clap was to experience his greatest triumph and his ultimate defeat. I will return to these events after discussing some parallels and differences among issues of college governance in other colonies.

Toleration and the Role of the State

Clap's regime at Yale contrasted markedly in two ways with the initiatives sought in New Jersey, New York, and Pennsylvania: in its repudiation of the college's integration into the network of established institutions of state and church, and in its singular determination to reject compromise with either Anglicans or Presbyterians. In each of the three Middle Atlantic provinces, a college came into existence after the high tide of the Awakening had receded during the late 1740s. But the College of New Jersey, King's College, and the College of Philadelphia all emerged in colonies where religious diversity was the norm rather than a new development.[33] These colleges, therefore, found accommodation to various denominational groups to be in their own interest. The denomination in nominal control on each board of trustees—the Presbyterians in New Jersey, the Anglicans in New York, and both of them together in Philadelphia—emphasized its stewardship rather than

its possession of the institution. The New Jersey charter proclaimed hospitality to students "of every religious denomination" with "free and equal liberty and advantage of education . . . notwithstanding any different sentiments in religion."[34] In New York, President Samuel Johnson assured parents that he had "no intention to impose on the scholars the peculiar tenets of any particular sects of Christians, but to inculcate upon their tender minds the great principles of Christianity and morality in which true Christians of each denomination are generally agreed."[35] In Philadelphia, too, the trustees agreed in 1764 to the official adoption of a policy of nondiscrimination which was to be "perpetually declaratory of the present *wide* and excellent plan of this institution."[36] Thus, in the middle colonies the new colleges founded at mid-eighteenth century endorsed the English policy of toleration as best suited to their particular circumstances.

The origins of the College of New Jersey present a case study in toleration of and accommodation to the secular and religious desires of diverse groups. The struggle over the college's founding took the form of a contest among Presbyterian factions in the colonies of New York, New Jersey, and Pennsylvania. Members of the New York presbytery wanted to establish a provincial institution on the model of the New England colleges or European universities. In the New Brunswick presbytery—joined with the New York and New Castle presbyteries in the synod of New York—revivalist New Light ministers hoped to strengthen the so-called Log College, an evangelically oriented academy founded by William Tennent, Sr., sometime between 1728 and 1730. A third group, Old Side in inclination and centered around Philadelphia, was organized into a synod named after that city. They were suspicious of their brethren in New York and in New Brunswick. In fact, their insistence on a synodical examination of ministerial candidates led in 1745 to a formal split of the synod.[37] During this time members of the New York presbytery proceeded with their plans for the New Jersey College and hoped for an eventual reconciliation among the warring factions. Consulting with Presbyterian laypersons in New York City, they were confirmed in their belief that they must not found a seminary. What was needed was a degree-granting college incorporated by the government. They declared:

> Though our great intention was to erect a seminary for educating ministers of the gospel, yet we hope it will be a means of raising up men that will be useful in other learned professions—ornaments of the State as well as the Church. Therefore we propose to make the plan of education as extensive as our circumstances will admit.[38]

Like the colleges in Massachusetts, Connecticut, and Virginia, the projected institution was to produce graduates who could "sustain with honor the offices they may be invested with for the public service."[39] In order to attract young men of Presbyterian, Quaker, Dutch Reformed, German Reformed, and Anglican backgrounds, the curriculum had to compare favorably with those of Harvard and Yale. Finally, the planners felt that their chances for success depended heavily on ready financial support. Consequently, they began a subscription drive in New York and New Jersey, which by March 1745 netted pledges of £185 in New Jersey currency.[40] The New Lights of the New York presbytery had come to feel that they could succeed only if they avoided sectarian and exclusively religious objectives: therefore, they proposed a college that would serve all interests in the middle colonies. Events proved them right. Not only did they found their college, but by 1758 they also could participate in the reconciliation of the once-hostile Presbyterian factions.

With a parallel desire to avoid identification with particular secular interests, the

conducted outside New Jersey, and on fund-raising efforts among English dissenters and Presbyterians in Scotland and Ulster.[42] The New Jersey governor and councillors confined themselves to protecting the college's interests; they also sought to ensure that the college would serve young men of diverse Protestant denominations from New Jersey and its neighboring colonies.

In New York, arguments over the prospect of founding a college revolved around different interpretations of the principle of toleration. Could this English policy continue to grant preferential treatment to the Anglicans? Or, given the religious diversity of New York's population, should it be applied even-handedly to Protestants of all denominations? But earlier in the late 1740s, few of these kinds of questions were raised. Neither the city's Anglicans nor their secular-minded opponents had any use for the enthusiastic proponents of the Great Awakening. And yet the dour Presbyterian orthodoxy of President Clap at Yale was equally unappealing. When in 1746 and 1748 the legislature authorized lotteries for a college, most interested citizens merely hoped that such an institution would bring prestige, wealth, and political stability to the province by training future civil and ecclesiastical officers. In 1749, William Livingston, reader in the Dutch Reformed church of Albany and a 1741 graduate of Yale, wrote that a college would "demolish enthusiasm and superstition" along with vice, drunkenness, and vandalism, and would "cause a surprising alteration in the behavior of our young gentry."[43] Samuel Johnson, then an Anglican missionary in Connecticut, expected the college to revitalize the colony's political, social, and economic life.[44] To govern the college, an anonymous contributor to the *New York Evening Post* proposed a board of trustees composed, like Harvard's overseers, of magistrates and ministers but with private persons added.[45] There was agreement in the city that the new institution was to be neither an academy under denominational control nor a college with an incorporated faculty.

When in November 1751 the legislature authorized a board of trustees for the lottery funds, they appointed to its membership the colony's senior councillor, the speaker of the assembly, the judges of the supreme court, the mayor of New York City, the colony's treasurer, and Messrs. James Livingston, Benjamin Nicoll, and William Livingston.[46] All three of the named members were lawyers; all of the office holders and Benjamin Nicoll, the stepson of Samuel Johnson, were active members of the Anglican church. The board reflected accurately the realities of political life in New York, where Anglicans exerted an influence quite out of proportion to their number. For these board members to claim a strong voice in the affairs of the projected college was but to follow traditional models already in force in Massachusetts, Virginia, and Connecticut. The New York college was to be a provincial institution under the guidance of the established church and state.

Nevertheless, the Anglican preponderance among the lottery trustees created uneasiness among non-Anglicans. Their sentiments found expression in a series of letters in the spring of 1753 in William Livingston's *Independent Reflector*.[47] Livingston and three collaborators, all Yale graduates, vowed to fight any Anglican influence over the college. The four men asserted that the connection of Anglican church and crown spelled potential tyranny, and they championed the assembly as the defender of the people's liberties. Early in 1753, in a letter to another Yale friend, Livingston outlined their program and essays yet to come in the *Reflector*. If the New York college were to fall under the management of churchmen, wrote Livingston, the consequence would be "universal priestcraft and bigotry in less than half a century." He complained that all the men proposed as trustees were Anglicans "and many of them the most implicit bigots" at that. He continued:

founders also stressed their intercolonial character. When John Hamilton, the acting governor, signed the charter of the College of New Jersey on October 22, 1746, the fourth colonial college came into existence. It was incorporated under a trusteeship form of government familiar to Presbyterians from the dissenting academies in England, the academies of Scotland, and the 1701 charter of Connecticut's Collegiate School. All seven of the trustees named were Presbyterians; three of them held pastorates in New Jersey and one in New York, and three were New York laymen. These men constituted the first intercolonial governing board of an eighteenth-century college. Their number was permitted to grow to twelve, with the remaining five to be chosen by the original seven. When the choice was made in the summer of 1747, all five of the new trustees were graduates of the Log College, representing the frontier areas of Pennsylvania and New Jersey.

Even though New Light clergymen dominated the board, the institution was a college and not a religious seminary. Its charter did not refer to church, presbytery, or synod, nor did it mention the training of ministers. The college also shunned ties of the colony's government. None of the trustees served in an *ex officio* capacity, and the charter neither contained nor hinted at any promise of financial aid from the legislature. The charter, in fact, had been authorized by the governor without legislative action.

It did not take long, however, for the colony of New Jersey to assert its authority as guardian of the rights of all its inhabitants and to insist on a voice in college governance. The guiding force for reform of the college's charter was Governor Belcher, who had recently arrived from Massachusetts and was intimately acquainted with the governance of Harvard College. Anxious to strengthen the position of the College of New Jersey, his "adopted daughter," he advocated tightening the relationship between school and colony. During the early part of 1748, he negotiated with the trustees, insisting both on *ex officio* membership on their board for the governor and members of his council and on the role of board president for himself. Such an organization would have resembled that of the Harvard overseers, with four ministers and four councillors balancing the interests of church and state. The New Jersey ministers on the board, however, objected strongly to the *ex officio* membership of the magistrates. They did not object to Belcher personally, but they could not be sure of his successors. Eventually they reached a compromise which named the four councillors as individuals but placed the governor on the board *ex officio* as its presiding officer.

The new charter enlarged the board of trustees from nine ministers and three laymen to twelve ministers, ten laymen, and the governor. Compared to the first charter, the 1748 document gave greater emphasis to secular and intercolonial representation by adding the New Jersey governor, his council, and three prominent Pennsylvanians—thus more than doubling the lay membership. These men served in addition to the three New Yorkers appointed under the first charter. The inclusion of the college president on the board elevated his position from that of academy headmaster to one comparable to the presidency of other colonial colleges. In this and other ways, Belcher helped bring the new college more in line with its sister institutions.

Though there were magistrates of three colonies on the board, the designation of the New Jersey governor as presiding officer and the required presence of at least twelve New Jersey board members underlined acceptance of the institution as New Jersey's provincial college.[41] To the dismay of many of the college's backers, however, this official status brought neither legislative funding nor an authorization for a colonial lottery. The college had to rely on financial gifts from friends, on lotteries

The Church can assign no color of reason to have the direction of the affair in preference of any other sect, but I would not have it managed by any sect. For that reason I would have no charter from the Crown but an act of Assembly for the purpose. Nor, for the same reason should divinity be taught at college because whoever is in the chair will obtrude his own notions for theology. Let the students follow their own inclinations in the study of divinity and read what books they please in their own chambers or apply themselves to it after they leave the college. Their religious exercises should consist of reading the scriptures, and hearing a prayer in which all Protestants may join.[48]

Livingston's essays constituted the first sustained argument against the English policy of toleration. Toleration, he reasoned, was unworkable and unfeasible. The process of moving away from the Reformation triad of established church, state, and college should not stop halfway by assigning ownership or governance of a college to one particular church or denomination and requiring that group to "tolerate" the presence and religious rights of other Protestants. Foreshadowing arguments that would be voiced in New York in the 1840s, Livingston asserted that there could be no such thing as nondenominational or nonsectarian religious instruction. In short, neither government by a religious group nor religious instruction was a possible alternative in a college intended to serve the interests of a religiously and ethnically heterogeneous society. Only a secular college with no official religious ties would do.

The counterpart to the Reflector—at least in the eyes of New York Anglicans—was A General Idea of the College of Mirania, a small volume by William Smith, a recent immigrant from Scotland who later become provost of the College of Philadelphia. Smith agreed with Livingston that the diversity of New York's population called for public institutions to counteract splintering tendencies. He wrote: "Nothing could so much contribute to make such a mixture of people coalesce and unite in one common interest as the common education of all the youth at the same public schools under the eye of the civil authority." The government should suppress private schools and see to it "that youth, who are the property of the state . . . , be educated according to the intention of the state." But unlike Livingston, Smith assigned part of this educational task to the established church. The Anglicans, as well as the president, he thought, might well furnish the ritual and order of religious services in the college, although the president should not also serve as parish minister.[49] Smith and other Anglicans like Samuel Seabury and Samuel Johnson thought that Livingston's notion of equal toleration of all churches was preposterous. As Seabury put it, it was impossible to agree on "a scheme of public worship for our college which shall not be liable to all the confusions in the building of Babel." Only the Church of England, he declared, was disinterested enough to furnish an acceptable kind of worship.[50] Smith protested against "unbridled liberty of conscience" and proclaimed the impossibility of governing a college once the incentive of preferment or the threat of disestablishment was removed.[51]

Thus, at the heart of the issue between Livingston and Smith were their differing interpretations of the policy of toleration. Their dispute centered on whether it was possible to have nondenominational worship and religious instruction in an institution intended to serve all members of the population. For Smith there could be no such thing as equal toleration: toleration had to be wedded to preferment. For Livingston, to whom preferment was anathema, equal toleration could be achieved and guaranteed only under secular, public auspices. In 1754, Smith's Anglican point of view prevailed. King's College obtained a royal charter which provided for an Anglican president and for worship services according to the prayer book of the

Church of England.[52]

In Philadelphia, still another interpretation of the toleration policy spawned a third variant of a provincial college. The College of Philadelphia, almost entirely a product of secular initiatives and interests, was the middle-colony college that was least dependent on ecclesiastical support. While it performed the functions of a provincial college, it remained a municipal institution devoted to the prosperity of Philadelphia. In 1749, a group of prominent Philadelphians had sponsored a subscription campaign for a "public academy in the City of Philadelphia."[53] The twenty-four largest subscribers functioned as trustees. Eight were wealthy merchants, four were well-known physicians, and many of the others—among them Benjamin Franklin—were active in the political life of the city and the colony. Like the trustees of such English grammar schools as St. Paul's and Merchant Taylors, they were laypersons who served as stewards of a public trust. They insisted that, with regard to the admission of students, considerations of "sect or party" be excluded. George Whitefield, the famed English revivalist of the Great Awakening, sensed correctly that the trustees had not contemplated placing the doctrines of Christianity at the school's center. He complained to Franklin that "there wants aliquid or is in it, to make it so useful as I would desire it might be."[54] To be sure, the majority of the trustees were Anglicans and parishioners of Philadelphia's Christ Church, and Franklin preferred Anglicans to Presbyterians precisely because he did not cherish the latter's "narrow" and strife-ridden denomination. As trustees, however, these men acted as laypersons and prominent citizens, not as representatives of a religion, denomination or church. Their concern was public and secular, not private or ecclesiastical.[55]

Despite these secular credentials, the College of Philadelphia could not quite avoid being drawn into denominational controversies. The school was incorporated as a college in 1755 with a charter drawn up by William Smith and Francis Alison. The former was made the college provost and the latter vice provost and rector of the academy. The alliance of Anglican priest and Old Side Presbyterian minister was meant to underscore the nondenominational character of the college and, at the same time, to distinguish the school from the New Light College of New Jersey. But Smith was rarely reluctant to engage in denominational infighting, and in 1756 he happily confided to an Anglican correspondent in England that "the Church, by soft and easy means, daily gains ground in [the college]."[56] So much did denominational jealousies enter the picture that in 1764 the Archbishop of Canterbury, the proprietors of the colony, and a representative of English dissenters presented recommendations to the trustees for "some fundamental rule or declaration to prevent inconveniences."[57] The trustees promptly adopted the recommendation from England as their own official policy declaration. It is hard to determine whether they did so out of genuine commitment to interdenominational cooperation, or in obedience to English policy, or simply in hopes of avoiding the kind of deadlock that had bedeviled the college founders in New York. It is clear, in any case, that the Philadelphia trustees sought to give little cause for religious resentment. They were happy that they had initially avoided a clear-cut identification of the college with a particular church, and they were not eager to invite difficulties over religious questions.

The difficulties that beset the Philadelphia trustees were mainly political. They derived chiefly from the constant threat of Indian warfare at the province's frontiers, from the resulting feud between the Quaker-dominated assembly and the proprietors' allies, and from the corresponding clashes in their own organization over the provost's activities. In 1756, Smith was accused of having violated the trust of his office by partisan indoctrination of his students, but both trustees and students absolved him of the charge. The students testified that he had never introduced "any thing relating to the parties now subsisting in this province, or tending to persuade us to adopt the principles of one side more than another."[58] When, two years later, the assembly found the provost in contempt and had him jailed. the trustees again came to his support and authorized him to teach his classes in jail. At the end of the year they gave him permission to go to England, where he successfully presented his case before the crown.[59]

Late in 1758, attacks came from a different direction. Pennsylvanicus, an anonymous writer in the *Pennsylvania Journal*, attacked Smith for writing political pamphlets and also censured the trustees, ministers, and magistrates of Philadelphia for having permitted a lottery for the college. Faculty members wanted to reply in the press, but the trustees vetoed that proposal. It was undignified, they argued, to respond to "low creatures who wrote from passion and resentment."[60] Pennsylvanicus, however, returned to the attack, condemned the college charter as "narrow" and "confined," criticized the trustees for being mesmerized by unlimited power, called for a new charter "more safe and generous" than the old.[61] Just as the emotions unleashed by the Awakening had rocked the colleges of other colonies in preceding decades, the passions of political warfare came to engulf the College of Philadelphia. As the 1760s approached, religious disputes gave way to political ones.

Polarization and Secularization

The culmination of the religious and political controversies over colonial college governance occurred in the 1760s. In New York, Connecticut, and Virginia these confrontations reached crisis proportions. They led to resolutions which, with local variations, emphasized the secular nature of the colleges and the role played by provincial governments. But these confrontations also led to the founding of a new type of college: one entirely under private or ecclesiastic sponsorship, without any involvement of civil authorities other than through the act of incorporation.

In New York, the Anglican victory at King's College had sown the seeds for the first denominational college. This development had begun in October 1754, when the Dutch Reformed Church of New York petitioned the assembly for a professorship of divinity at King's College. The Dutch argued that they constituted "the greatest number of any single denomination of Christians in this province."[62] In May of the next year, Domine John Ritzema, prominent leader of the conservative wing of the Dutch church and a member of the board of governors of King's College, single-handedly moved the college board to apply to New York's governor for an additional charter containing the professorship. This charter was granted. But Ritzema's consistory repudiated it, charging that it had been "prepared incontestably without our knowledge, advice, or counsel" and did not answer "to our conception of what would be advantageous for the upbuilding of our church."[63]

Ritzema correctly felt that his opposition came from members of his church who sought a college of their own in the middle colonies. The main power behind this move was Theodore Frelinghuysen who, in attacking Ritzema, had expressed his amazement at "the astonishing imposition of the encroaching party [the Anglicans] that would monopolize our intended college" and at "our own infatuation, stupidity, and lethargy" in allowing Ritzema's project to proceed unhindered. Frelinghuysen did not believe in uniting with other denominations or churches in college efforts. He concluded: "We have no business with their colleges; they may erect as

many as they please, and must expect to maintain them too, themselves. Let every one provide for his own house."[84]

Frelinghuysen's appeal in 1756 expressed a growing number of Americans' disenchantment with the task of coping with diversity. The game, Frelinghuysen seemed to say, was not worth the candle. Perhaps the Dutch in New York could afford such sentiments since they had the numbers to build their own house; perhaps, also, Frelinghuysen was simply tired of the bickering and impatient with the slow process of seeking cooperation. No matter how approached or understood, the English policy of toleration was difficult to implement in the pluralistic society of the colonies.

Frelinghuysen's suggestion bore fruit ten years later when Queen's College, later to be known as Rutgers, was founded in New Jersey to serve the Dutch Reformed churches of the middle colonies. Breaking the tradition of a provincial college monopoly, this new collegiate model marked the transition from the provincial colleges of the seventeenth and eighteenth centuries to the private institutions of the nineteenth.

The establishment of the chair of divinity for the Dutch Reformed at King's College and the subsequent founding of Queen's College constituted one kind of collegiate model arising out of the New York struggle over toleration. Livingston's project for a public college in New York foreshadowed the emergence of a second model. Livingston's proposal, officially introduced in a bill in the New York Assembly, called for a college run entirely by the government.[85] The college's trustees would need the consent of the governor, council, and assembly for any grant or sale of college property and for the appointment of college officers. They would be required to submit to the three branches of the provincial government their annual financial reports, bylaws, plan of instruction, and their plans for providing nondenominational worship services. The assembly also reserved the right to fix the location of the college and declared that new appointments to the twenty-four-member trustee board should be made by the legislature. During recess of the assembly, a majority of the trustees might temporarily appoint a president or treasurer of the college, but such a decision would have to be confirmed by the legislature at its next session. As one might expect, the bill expressly prohibited any religious tests or discrimination against Protestants. There was to be no public instruction in divinity, but both the Anglican and the Dutch Reformed churches of New York could elect professors of divinity who might privately instruct those students who so desired. Students and officers could sue the trustees, the president, and other officers of the college "in any court of law within this colony."[86]

With this bill Livingston mounted the most radical challenge to established forms of college governance yet devised in the colonies. He brushed aside both English notions of collegiate autonomy and the Reformation concept of joint church-state-college establishment as well as the modifications of the latter in New Jersey and at King's College. By allowing appeals to civil courts he would emancipate both students and officers from their total submission to college authority, contrary to Clap's policy at Yale. Had his college seen the light of day, it would have been the first genuine state college in the American colonies. But the time was not yet ripe. However, when New York's state university was created after the Revolution in 1784, its roots led back to Livingston's bill of 1754. Together with the Queen's College charter of 1766, the 1754 bill marked the outer limits of the now polarized field into which the provincial colleges of the eighteenth century had moved.

It was in Connecticut during the 1760s that the most dramatic confrontation over the issue of college governance took place. When Clap terminated Yale's relationship to the First Church of New Haven, ordered the sons of Anglicans not to attend nearby services, and established the college church, he fueled the suspicions and ill will of the Connecticut Assembly. In 1755, the assembly refused to make the annual £100 grant to the college. One of its members, Dr. Benjamin Gale, physician and deputy from Killingworth, vigorously rejected Clap's statement that Yale had been founded "principally by the ministers." He accused the president of falsely claiming that the assembly had been "neither the founder nor visitor of that house," and he disputed the legal status of the college as a corporation. He also rejected Clap's contention, derived from canon law, that Yale College was an ecclesiastical corporation. Gale and the legislators insisted on the college's accountability to the public. In striking similarity to Livingston's arguments in New York and to the views of the antiproprietary party in Philadelphia, he also asserted the legislature's rights of oversight and visitation.[67]

By 1761, disciplinary action against some students brought forth a written protest in which Connecticut citizens urged the legislature "to turn your eyes upon the society you have founded, fed, and nourished, and for the honor of what is good, great, and noble, subject it to such like visitation as other collegiate schools in this land or devise some method of redress."[68] Again the college escaped such action; the General Court "resolved in the negative." But matters went from bad to worse. By November 1762, student rebellion engulfed the college; the corporation fought back by expelling some students and placing others on probation. In the following spring, more protest memorials reached the assembly. They spoke of the college's "deplorable state," of "notorious" facts, of the uneasiness of students and parents, and of "the resentments and prejudices the youth generally bring from thence." They charged that the college law forbidding students and faculty to sue the college in civil court violated "the natural rights of Englishmen." The college, they wrote, was "an *imperium in imperio*, as shall be rather dangerous than serviceable to the community." Their numerous and specific complaints all led to one chief demand: the legislature must appoint a commission of visitation.[69] Such action would force an answer to one key question: To what extent was a college a law unto itself, and to what degree must the college be governed by the wider body politic which had authorized and supported it?

The confrontation over the issue of college autonomy took place on Sunday, May 15, 1763. Before the General Court, Clap answered the charges against this rule and concentrated on two chief items among his accusers' demands: visitation by the General Court, and students' right to appeal the corporation's disciplinary rulings to the governor and council. In a brilliant disquisition, filled with learned references to English law, Clap maintained that though the assembly held a general supervisory authority over all institutions of the province, it did not have the right of visitation over the college. He based his conclusion on a contention—doubtful, to be sure, but not contradicted in 1763—that the ministers had founded the college before it had been chartered by the General Court.[70] On the question of appeal, Clap remained equally adamant. An appeal to authorities outside the college "would occasion a great delay in government and mispence of time." The same disadvantages of "a great expense of time and money and . . . many mischiefs and confusions" would result, Clap held, if students were allowed to sue each other or the college officers.[71] On no point, in fact, did Clap budge.

Clap's intransigence was not simply a show of strength or the result of confidence in his considerable legal knowledge. He saw correctly that visitation and appeal were issues inextricably linked to each other and that the question of appeal could

be used to put the General Court on the defensive. If the court decided on visitation or permitted students to appeal Clap's disciplinary judgments, Clap warned the legislators, the college might file a complaint with authorities in London. Do not encourage the students to appeal from my jurisdiction to the governor and council, Clap seemed to be saying, lest you suggest that I appeal the colony's court decision to king and parliament. Order a visitation of the college by the assembly and you open the door to visitors from England appearing in Connecticut "with full power in themselves to redress everything in our laws or courts which they might esteem to be abuses."[72] The risk of royal interference in Connecticut affairs might have been minor in 1763, but it was nonetheless a risk, and Clap craftily and successfully made the most of it. On May 15, 1763, the General Court conceded defeat. In his 1766 *Annals or History of Yale College*, Clap allowed himself the luxury of reporting his own triumph:

> When the arguments were considered by the Honorable the Great Assembly but very few appeared to be of the opinion that the Assembly were the founders of the College, and so they acted nothing upon the memorial. [sic] And it is generally supposed that the question never will be publicly moved again.[73]

Clap was wrong in his guess for the future, but in 1763 he was the man of the hour and the victory was his.

In the light of Yale's subsequent history, however, the confrontation of 1763 was at best a winning battle at the turning point in a war that was about to be lost. As other historians have pointed out, the students accomplished what the legislature had failed to do; a few years later they brought down Clap's administration in utter ruin.[74] But more was involved in their battle than student high jinks or adolescent rebellion against an obstinate old man. Behind the students stood their parents and the other people of Connecticut. Gale and the memorialists had expressed sentiments that enjoyed wide currency beyond the immediate vicinity of the college or even the colony. When they had criticized Clap's rule against student access to the courts and objected to paying for new college buildings, they had referred to the natural rights of Englishmen and spoken of taxation without representation. Demanding visitation by the assembly, they had echoed Livingston's call in New York for a public college under the direction of the legislature and Pennsylvanicus's quest for a broader and more generous charter for the College of Philadelphia. They had clearly indicated their belief that the Fellows' assumed rights to self-visitation were anachronistic. Clap's manner and policies did nothing to help dispel the aura of autocracy surrounding him, and it is therefore difficult to agree with those who have argued that his defiance of the memorialists constituted a victory for academic freedom.[75] On the contrary, Clap's defiance was a victory for the concepts of a college as a sectarian seminary and of college governance as paternal absolutism.

Neither of Clap's concepts blended well with the prevailing temper of 1763, and it was but a matter of a few years until his world came to grief.[76] In February 1766, students accused Clap of being in his dotage and showing arbitrariness and partiality. They demanded his ouster. When the corporation failed to act on their petition, they tore up college buildings, burned furniture, threatened the tutors with bodily harm and drove them out of the college. In July, Clap offered his resignation. This the corporation accepted, effective at commencement in September. With the college nearly in ruins, the Clap regime had come to its end.

Now matters changed quickly. The members of the assembly asserted their oversight. In October they ordered the corporation to submit its accounts annually before the General Court if it expected to receive any funds from them.[77] Benjamin

Gale and his friends had won after all. In a letter to Ezra Stiles, then a minister in Newport, Gale wrote proudly of "our gentle visitation of Yale College, in which we touch'd them so gently that till some time after the assembly, they never saw they were taken in, that we had made ourselves visitors, and subjected them to an annual visitation."[78] Gale could feel satisfied. Everything Clap had resisted, with the sole exception of the students' right of appeal to the General Court, had now been accepted. Most of the vestiges of Clap's autocratic reign had been overcome. Clap's myth of Yale as a religious seminary had been laid to rest, and the school was acknowledged again as Connecticut's provincial college.

In Virginia, too, the secular-versus-ecclesiastical controversy over college governance ended with the triumph of a secular model. The College of William and Mary, like the colleges of Oxford and Cambridge, was legally a corporation composed of the president and masters who were faculty members. Unlike its sister institutions in Massachusetts, Connecticut, New Jersey, New York, and Pennsylvania, it had a board of external governors—called the visitors—that was unincorporated. The board of visitors, however, not the corporation, dominated college governance.[79] This arrangement made a struggle between corporation and visitors unavoidable.[79] The struggle, which began in the 1750s, pitted the Oxford-educated clergymen of the corporation against the representatives of the Virginia gentry who constituted the visitors. It demonstrated once more that a body of clergymen standing on prerogative and corporate rights could not prevail against lay representatives demanding that the college serve the interests of a secular society.

On September 14, 1763, the visitors issued a statute granting themselves the right, by majority vote, to discharge the president and masters and exercise direct and final authority over the internal management of the college. The statute also prohibited faculty members from taking parish assignments while holding office in the college, required their residence at college, and ordered the president and masters to take an oath pledging support of the statute.[80] There can be little doubt that these requirements constituted a severe infringement on the charter rights of the masters. The new statute placed tenure rights of the members of the corporate body at the mercy of an outside board, and it abrogated the members' basic right to administer their own affairs. If the visitors claimed that they asked for no rights other than those enjoyed by the governing boards of other colonial colleges, they ignored the fact that these other boards were themselves the college corporations; in Virginia, the faculty was the legally incorporated body. The Virginia dispute had all the earmarks of a constitutional confrontation.

The first round came in 1764, when the visitors cited their new statute and asked Professor Camm, a faculty member at William and Mary, to choose between his professorship and his parish. Refusing to respond to the question, Camm argued that he was confronted with a charge and demanded the right to submit a written defense. After considerable hesitation, the visitors agreed, and Camm severely condemned their statute, chided President Horrocks for having taken an oath on it, and announced that he would appeal the whole affair to the crown. As in Connecticut, this threat was effective; the visitors dropped their demands.[81] Later, on May 1, 1766, they agreed to amend the statute. The day-to-day administration of the college was left to the faculty under the supervision of the visitors. Nothing was said about the visitors' power of dismissal, and the prohibition of parish employment was determined not retroactively applicable. Camm could keep both his parish and his professorship. Some observers agreed with Governor Fauquier, who complained that the visitors had allowed "Mr. Camm [to] lead them by the nose."[82] The requirement of an oath on the statute, however, and the prohibition of future outside employment remained. The visitors held fast to their claim to supervision over internal college affairs and, by continuing to demand the oath, upheld the principle of their action.

The 1766 amendment accommodated Professor Camm and tried to protect the visitors' claim to their rights of governance, but it did not resolve any of the key issues raised by the statute of 1763. So the struggle continued fruitlessly, its very lack of resolution underscoring the impotence of the masters and the *de facto* power of the visitors. In 1768, the faculty petitioned for a change in the college's charter in order to clarify the roles of professors and visitors.[83] The petition met with silence on the key issue of power to govern and discipline. Concerning their request to administer charitable scholarships, the petitioners were insulted by the response that such an administrative arrangement would be "impiety to the dead and injustice to the living."[84] Instead they were offered a crumb they had not asked for—free hot suppers in the college. President Horrocks reported to the masters that the visitors had asserted their full control over the appointment of officers and servants and on the issue of parish appointments by faculty members. The masters were understandably upset. They appealed to Bishop Terrick of London, the College Chancellor:

> It seems impossible for us ... to make any other conclusion but that the visitors mean to keep the grand points of power, on which the practical utility of a college must turn, unsettled and in confusion, and to leave us without the authority which is necessary for obtaining that discipline and regularity which the visitors are desirous should be enforced. ...[85]

They concluded that they saw no solution other than to petition the crown for a new charter or to appeal to the king as the supreme visitor of the college.[86]

Here, as in Connecticut, an appeal to London was the last ace the college party could play, but after the Stamp Act crisis even that card began to lose its value. Issues of home rule versus the prerogatives of the crown and established church were becoming less threatening. Excited by the tremors of the approaching Revolution, Virginians were ill-disposed to listen to the faculty's complaints. The visitors saw no reason to desist from their attempts to place tighter reins on the faculty. They rebuked masters for having married and moved off campus, and they interfered with student discipline and curriculum. They proposed abolishing the requirement for classical studies and wanted to permit students to take mathematics without prior work in the classics.[87] Such a plan, the masters protested, would depart from the program "hitherto approved of in the most famous universities" and would do "abundantly more injury than benefit to the public."[88] But there was little the masters could do to retain the powers due them under their college charter; the Virginia visitors were in control. These members of the colony's gentry had little patience with Oxford-educated Anglican clergymen. They wanted William and Mary to function as their provincial college, intended for the education of their young men who were to become useful citizens and professionals of a society ready to break its ties to the mother country.[89]

There can be little doubt that the political agitation of the American Revolution in the late 1760 and 1770s helped to clarify and sharpen the issues of college governance. There should also be no question that the colonies' changing social structure and increasing ethnic and religious heterogeneity were fundamental factors which had already begun to transform the Reformation pattern of college governance. College governors modified the assumptions they had inherited from the Reformation in order to accommodate young men of diverse Protestant denominations without discrimination or infringement upon religious liberties. Under the new policies of equal toleration and preferment, legislators and the public held on to the Reformation view of the college as a civil institution for the training of a province's leadership. In the colonies, where clergymen of all Protestant denominations were included among the professional elite, this view implied that no one church or denomination should claim exclusive privileges.

In Massachusetts, Connecticut, New Jersey, New York, Pennsylvania, and Virginia, each college reacted differently to its particular situation in meeting the demands of a heterogenous population. In Virginia and Connecticut, those who protested against policies of toleration in the name of academic autonomy were locked in losing battles with their legislatures. In New York and New Jersey, those who rebelled against domination by their orthodox brethren broke with the established tradition of one province, one college. Their actions laid the foundation for the nineteenth-century model of the private or church-related college.

Thus, the middle decades of the eighteenth century proved to be critical years in the shaping of colleges. The second half of the eighteenth century saw the gradual emasculation of denominational and secular schemes based on the idea of toleration. A polarization of denominational and secular concerns in the 1780s gave rise to public colleges and universities which, in turn, provoked the proliferation of private or church-related colleges in the nineteenth century. That, however, takes us far beyond the confines of the eighteenth century and is, as the phrase has it, another story altogether.

1 Jurgen Herbst, "The First Three American Colleges: Schools of the Reformation," *Perspectives in American History*, 8 (1974), 7-52.

2 Jurgen Herbst, "The Eighteenth-Century Origins of the Split between Private and Public Higher Education in the United States," *History of Education Quarterly*, 15 (1975), 273-80.

3 On the Great Awakening and its impact on education, see Lawrence A. Cremin, *American Education: The Colonial Experience, 1607-1783* (New York: Harper & Row, 1970), ch. 10; Douglas Sloan, ed., *The Great Awakening and American Education: A Documentary History* (New York: Teachers College Press, 1973); William W. Sweet, *Revivalism in America: Its Origin, Growth, and Decline* (New York: Charles Scribner's Sons, 1944); and Alan Heimert and Perry Miller, eds., *The Great Awakening: Documents Illustrating the Crisis and Its Consequences* (Indianapolis, Ind.: Bobbs-Merrill, 1967).

4 "Order in Council," rpt. in *Circular of Information*, No. 2 (Washington, D.C.: U. S. Bureau of Education, 1893), pp. 77-78.

5 On Harvard College during this period, see Samuel Eliot Morison, *Three Centuries of Harvard, 1636-1936* (Cambridge, Mass.: Harvard Univ. Press, 1936), pp. 53-100; and John Maynard Hoffmann, "Commonwealth College: The Governance of Harvard in the Puritan Period," Diss. Harvard Univ. 1972.

6 Quotations from 1745 charter of Yale in Edward C. Elliott and M. M. Chambers, eds., *Charters and Basic Laws of Selected American Universities and Colleges* (New York: Carnegie Foundation, 1934), p. 592.

7 For the 1701 and 1745 charters of Yale, see Franklin B. Dexter, ed. *Documentary History of Yale University* (New Haven, Conn.: Yale Univ. Press, 1916), pp. 20-23; and Elliott and Chambers, pp. 588-93. For Yale's early history, see Richard Warch, *School of the Prophets: Yale College, 1701-1740* (New Haven, Conn.: Yale Univ. Press, 1973), p. 310.

8 Franklin B. Dexter, ed., *Biographical Sketches of the Graduates of Yale College with Annals of the College History* (New York: H. Holt and Company, 1885), I, 663.

9 The committee report of 1742 may be found in Dexter, *Documentary History*, p. 356. For narratives of the events in Connecticut, New Haven, and the college, see Benjamin Trumbull, *A Complete History of Connecticut* (New Haven, Conn.: Maltby, Goldsmith and Co., 1818), II, 160-75; Brooks M. Kelley, *Yale: A History* (New Haven, Conn.: Yale Univ. Press, 1974), pp. 49-72; and Louis L. Tucker, *Puritan Protagonist: President Thomas Clap of Yale College* (Chapel Hill, N.C.: Univ. of North Carolina Press, 1962), pp. 123-41.

10 Rpt. in Stephen Nissenbaum, ed., *The Great Awakening at Yale College* (Belmont, Calif.: Wadsworth, 1972), pp. 136-39.

11 Nissenbaum, p. 239.

12 Nissenbaum, p. 231.

13 Nissenbaum, p. 240.

14 Nissenbaum, p. 222.

15 The Cleaveland affair is described and documented in Nissenbaum, pp. 219-50; Trumbull, II, 182-83; Richard Hofstadter and Wilson Smith, eds., *American Higher Education* (Chicago: Univ. of Chicago Press, 1961), I, 74-82; and Dexter, *Documentary History*, pp. 570-72.

16 See Richard Hofstadter, *Academic Freedom in the Age of the College* (New York: Columbia Univ. Press, 1961), pp. 134-44.

17 Clap's account of the drafting of the charter and laws is contained in his "Annals of Yale College in New Haven," 1747 ms. in the Yale Archives; the Harvard charter of 1650 is reprinted in Samuel Eliot Morison, *Harvard College in the Seventeenth Century* (Cambridge, Mass.: Harvard Univ. Press, 1936), part I, pp. 5-8; and the charter of the College of William and Mary is reprinted in Edgar W. Knight, ed., *Documentary History of Education in the South before 1860* (Chapel Hill, N.C.: Univ. of North Carolina Press, 1949), I, 400-439.

18 On the defection of Cutler and Johnson, see Warch, pp. 96-117; on the tutor rebellion at Harvard, see Morison, *Three Centuries*, pp. 69-74.

19 The laws are printed in Dexter, *Biographical Sketches*, II, 2-18.

20 Clap, p. 48.

21 Tucker, pp. 166-83.

22 Herbert Schneider and Carol Schneider, eds., *Samuel Johnson, President of King's College: His Career and Writings* (New York: Columbia Univ. Press, 1929), I, 178.

23 Schneider and Schneider, I, 178.

24 Schneider and Schneider, I, 178-82.

25 Schneider and Schneider, I, 175.

26 Thomas Clap, *The Religious Constitution of Colleges* (New London, Conn.: T. Green, 1754), pp. 1-4.

27 Schneider and Schneider, I, 190-91.

28 Clap, *Religious Constitution*, p. 4.

29 Ralph Henry Gabriel, *Religion and Learning at Yale* (New Haven, Conn.: Yale Univ. Press, 1958), pp. 3-6.

30 See Kelley, p. 66; Tucker, p. 192.

31 Tucker, p. 190.

32 Tucker, p. 199.

33 For the College of New Jersey, consult Thomas J. Wertenbaker, *Princeton, 1746-1896* (Princeton, N.J.: Princeton Univ. Press, 1946). pp. 3-46; and G. Howard Miller, "A Contracting Community," Diss. Univ. of Michigan 1970, I, 2-195. The history of King's College is best presented in David C. Humphrey, "King's College in the City of New York, 1754-1776." Diss. Northwestern Univ. 1968, pp. 2-244; a brief summary may be found in John H. Van Amringe, "King's College and Columbia College," in *A History of Columbia University, 1754-1904* (New York: Columbia Univ. Press, 1904), pp. 1-41. The most recent history of the College of Philadelphia is Ann Gordon, "The College of Philadelphia, 1749-1779: The Impact of an Institution," Diss. Univ. of Wisconsin 1975; see also Edward P. Cheyney, *History of the University of Pennsylvania 1740-1940* (Philadelphia: Univ. of Pennsylvania Press, 1940).

34 Both the 1746 and the 1748 charters of the College of New Jersey are reprinted in Wertenbaker, pp. 396-404.

35 Samuel Johnson, "Advertisement," in *Charters, Acts of the Legislature, Official Documents and Records*, ed. John B. Pine, rev. and enl. ed. (New York: 1920), pp. 32-35.

36 Neela M. Westlake, ed., *Minutes of the Trustees of the College, Academy and Charitable Schools, University of Pennsylvania, Vol. 1, 1749 to 1768* (Wilmington, Del.: Scholarly Resources, 1974), p. 262.

37 The situation among middle-colony Presbyterians is described in Archibald Alexander, *Biographical Sketches of the Founder and Principal Alumni of the Log College* (Princeton, N.J.: J. T. Robinson, 1845); Leonard J. Trinterud, *The Forming of an American Tradition* (Philadelphia: Westminster Press, 1949), pp. 53-108; Elijah R. Craven, "The Log College of Neshaminy and Princeton University," *Journal of the Presbyterian Historical Society*, 1 (1902), 308-14; and Douglas Sloan, *The Scottish Enlightenment and the American College Ideal* (New York: Teachers College Press, 1971), pp. 56-102.

38 Quoted in Wertenbaker, pp. 19-20.

39 Wertenbaker, p. 20.

40 Wertenbaker, p. 21.

41 Wertenbaker, pp. 23-27; John Maclean, *History of the College of New Jersey, 1746-1854* (1877; rpt. New York: Arno Press, 1969). I, 70-113; see also Jonathan Edwards's account of the charter negotiations in *The Works of President Edwards* (New York: G. & G. & H. Carvill, 1830), I, 266-68, 275.

42 Wertenbaker, pp. 30-35; Maclean, I, 147-54; see also Alison B. Olson, "The Founding of Princeton University: Religion and Politics in Eighteenth-Century New Jersey," *New Jersey History*, 87 (1969), 133-50.

43 Hippocrate Mithridates. Apoth. (pseud. for William Livingston), *Some Serious Thoughts on the Design of Erecting a College in the Province of New York* (New York: J. Zenger, 1749), pp. 1-7.

44 Schneider and Schneider, I, 135.

45 *New York Evening Post*, 18 May 1747, n. pag.

46 Commissioners of Statutory Revision, eds., *Colonial Laws of New York from the Year 1664 to the Revolution* (Albany, N.Y.: James B. Lyon, State Printer, 1894), III, 607-16, 679-88, 731-32, and 842-44.

47 See Milton M. Klein, ed., *The Independent Reflector* (Cambridge, Mass.: Harvard Univ. Press, 1963).

48 Klein, pp. 56-57.

49 William Smith, *A General Idea of the College of Mirania*, ed. Edward M. Griffin (1753; rpt. New York: Johnson Reprint Corp., 1969), pp. 10, 66-67, 71, 75.

50 *New York Mercury*, 30 April 1753, n. pag.

51 Leonard W. Labaree, ed., *The Papers of Benjamin Franklin* (New Haven, Conn.: Yale Univ. Press, 1962), IV, 467-70, 475; Klein, pp. 201-08.

52 Hugh Hastings, ed., *Ecclesiastical Records: State of New York* (Albany: J. B. Lyon, 1905), V, 3508-14; Schneider and Schneider, IV, 24-25.

53 See Cheyney, p. 50.

54 Labaree, III, 467.

55 See Cheyney, pp. 17-40; Labaree, III, 385-88, 397-429, 462, 467; and Westlake, I, 2-5.

56 Horace W. Smith, ed., *Life and Correspondence of the Rev. William Smith* (Philadelphia: Ferguson Brothers, 1879), I, 143.

57 Westlake, I, 260.

58 Horace W. Smith, ed., *Life and Correspondence of the Rev. William Smith* (1870; rpt. New York: Arno Press, 1972), I, 126.

59 Bruce R. Lively, "William Smith, the College and Academy of Philadelphia, and Pennsylvania Politics, 1753-1758," *Historical Magazine of the Protestant Episcopal Church*, 38 (1969), 237-58; Westlake, I, 68, 70-72, 91, 97, 99; and Labaree, VII, 12, and VIII, 416.

60 Westlake, I, 99.

61 *Pennsylvania Journal and Weekly Advertiser*, 28 Sept. and 30 Nov., 1758: 25 Jan., 8 Feb., 1 March, and 15 March, 1779.

62 Hastings, V, 3505.

63 Hastings, V, 3576.

64 Frelinghuysen's statement was published under the pseudonym David Marin Ben Jesse, *A Remark on the Disputes and Contentions in this Province* (New York: Hugh Gaine, 1755), pp. 6, 11-12. Consult also Hastings, V, 3501, 3542-45, 3554-56, 3574-77, 3605, 3611-13; Nelson R. Burr, *Education in New Jersey 1630-1871* (Princeton, N.J.: Princeton Univ. Press), pp. 19-21; William H. S. Demarest, *A History of Rutgers College, 1766-1924* (New Brunswick, N.J.: Rutgers, 1924), pp. 25-50; Richard P. McCormick, *Rutgers: A Bicentennial History* (New Brunswick, N.J.: Rutgers Univ. Press, 1966), pp. 1-8; and Pine, pp. 26-27.

65 *Journal of the Votes and Proceedings of the General Assembly of the Colony of New York*, published by order of the General Assembly (New York: Hugh Gaine, printer, 1766), II, 412-19.

66 *Journal of the Votes*; *Colonial Laws*, III, 1927; and Hastings, V, 3525-26.

67 See Dexter, *Biographical Sketches*, II, 557; Thomas Clap, *A Brief History* (New Haven, Conn.: James Parker, 1755), p. 5; and Benjamin Gale, *The Present State of the Colony of Connecticut Considered* (New London, Conn.: T. Green, 1755), pp. 7, 9-11.

68 Thomas Fuller, Moses Bartlett, and Thomas Skinner, "Letter to the Assembly, 6 Oct., 1761," ms. in Yale Univ. Archives.

69 Ebenezer Devotion, Stephen White, James Cogswell, Josiah Whitney, and Benjamin Throop, "Memorial of April, 1763," ms. in Yale Univ. Archives and in *Connecticut Archives*, pp. 67a-b; and Edward Dorr, Jedediah Elderkin, Eleazer Fitch, Hezekiah Bissell, Jonathan Marsh, Josiah Talcott,

Ebenezer Grant, Daniel Sheldon, and Titus Hosmer, "Memorial of March 10, 1763," ms. in Yale Univ. Archives and in *Connecticut Archives, Colleges and Schools*, 1st ser., II, 66a-h.

70 The story of the May 15 meeting is told by Clap himself in his "Annals of Yale College in New Haven," 1766 ms. in Yale Univ. Archives, also printed as *The Annals or History of Yale College* (New Haven, Conn.: John Hotchkiss and B. Mecom, 1766). See also Trumbull, II, 327-33; Dexter, II, 780-81; *Connecticut Archives*, p. 67b; and, for greatest detail, Tucker, pp. 224-31.

71 "Answer of President and Fellows," *Connecticut Archives*, pp. 71g, 71h, 71s.

72 Answer of President and Fellows," *Connecticut Archives*, pp. 71t, 71u.

73 Clap, *Annals* (1766), pp. 76-77.

74 Tucker, pp. 232-70.

75 See Dexter, *Biographical Sketches*, II, 790-91; and compare with Hofstadter, pp. 175-76; and Gabriel, p. 29.

76 See Trumbull, II, 333.

77 Tucker, p. 257; see also Charles J. Hoadley, ed., *The Public Records of the Colony of Connecticut from May 1762 to October 1767* (Hartford, Conn.: Case, Lockwood and Brainard, 1881), pp. 513-14.

78 Franklin B. Dexter, ed., *Itineraries of Ezra Stiles* (New Haven, Conn.: Yale Univ. Press, 1916), p. 492.

79 Knight, I, 400-439.

80 William S. Perry, ed., *Virginia*, Vol. 1 of *Historical Collections Relating to the American Colonial Church* (New York: AMS Press, 1869), p. 518; William W. Manross, ed., *The Fulham Papers in the Lambeth Library: American Colonial Section—Calendar and Indexes* (Oxford: Clarendon Press, 1965). The papers described by Manross are in the Lambeth Palace Library, American Colonial Section.

81 Perry, p. 523; Manross, XIV, 95-102.

82 Manross, XIV, 91-92.

83 "Journal," *William and Mary Quarterly*, 1st ser., 5 (1896-1897), 85-89.

84 "Journal," p. 226.

85 "Journal," p. 229.

86 See also *Fulham Papers*, XIV, 147-52, 155-60.

87 Manross, XIV, 161-96, 199-202; "Minutes of the Visitors," *William and Mary Quarterly*, 1st ser., 17 (1919), 239-40.

88 "Journal," *William and Mary Quarterly*, 1st ser., 13 (1904), 150-54.

89 For an excellent analysis of the situation at the College of William and Mary, see Robert P. Thomson, "The Reform of the College of William and Mary, 1763-1780," *Proceedings*, American Philosophical Society, 115 (1971).

* The author gratefully acknowledges support received in preparation of this paper from the National Institute of Education. The opinions expressed do not necessarily reflect the position of the Institute, and no official endorsement by the Institute should be inferred.

"For the Children of the Infidels"?: American Indian Education in the Colonial Colleges

Bobby Wright

> Wild and savage people, ... they have no Arts nor Science, yet they live under superior command such as it is, they are generally very loving and gentle, and doe entertaine and relieve our people with great kindnesse: they are easy to be brought to good, and would fayne embrace a better condition.
>
> —Robert Johnson, *Nova Britannia*, 1609

> We must let you know . . . the Indians are not inclined to give their Children Learning. We allow it to be good, and we thank you for your Invitation; but our customs differing from yours, you will be so good as to excuse us.
>
> —Canassatego (Iroquois), 1744

Schemes to deliver higher education to American Indians arose sporadically throughout the colonial period. Within a decade of the first permanent European settlement at Jamestown, plans were already underway for an Indian college, and similar designs continued periodically throughout the seventeenth and eighteenth centuries. Indians in fact offered the impetus for establishing and maintaining among the nation's most enduring and prestigious halls of higher learning—such elite institutions as Harvard College, the College of William and Mary, and Dartmouth College.

The lofty aspirations to provide higher education arose amidst conflicting interests among the stay-at-home English, the colonists, and the native people for whom the colleges were intended. The English, mindful of the Crown's desire to spread the gospel among the "heathens" of America, generously endowed the educational missions in a true spirit of piety. The colonists, eager to maintain British sanction of their struggling settlements and institutions, capitalized on the religious fervor of the English, but for the most part neglected to fulfill their professed pious mission. Meanwhile, the Indians, tenacious in their cultural persistence, were rigidly resistant to the white man's interest in their spiritual welfare. Only when war and disease had disintegrated tribal integrity and left Indian communities vulnerable to English domination did Indians embrace Christianity and European culture.

Despite the prevailing literature glorifying these efforts to convert and ''civilize'' American natives, close examination of the several schemes to establish colonial Indian colleges reveals a drama of deception and fraud, in which the major players betrayed motives that were less than honorable. Most historians of the colonial era would have us believe that piety was the moving force behind the early colleges. After all, in Virginia as in New England, the officially proclaimed purpose of English colonization of America was the conversion of native ''heathens'' to Christianity. King James I, in the 1609 charter of the Virginia Company of London, reaffirmed his mandate that ''the principal Effect, which we can desire or expect of this Action, is the Conversion and Reduction of the People in those Parts unto the true Worship of God and Christian Religion.''[1] Similarly, the 1629 Charter of the Massachusetts Bay Company proclaimed its purpose to ''wynn and incite the natives . . . to the knowledge and obedience of the onlie true God and Saviour of mankinde.''[2]

In assuming their missionary charge, colonists viewed education as a primary means not only to Christianize Indians, but also to civilize and remake them in the image of the European. As early as 1609, Robert Gray advocated this means since ''it is not the nature of men, but the education of men, which makes them barbarous and uncivill, and therefore chaunge the education of men, and you shall see that their nature will be greatly rectified and corrected.''[3] Yet, despite this avowed pious calling, the colonists either ignored their mandate or failed miserably in their meager attempts to fulfill it. The most enterprising among them, however—those who promoted the Indian colleges—were able to capitalize handsomely on this mission.

In settling Jamestown in 1607, the Virginia Company had more than devotion to religious duty in mind. It was, after all, a profit-making venture, financed by the most daring entrepreneurs. Yet in *A True and Sincere Declaration of the Purpose and Ends of the Plantation* (1609), the Company declared that its principal aim was ''to preach and baptize into the Christian Religion, and by propagation of the Gospell, to recover out of the armes of the Divell, a number of poore and miserable soules, wrapt up unto death, in almost invincible ignorance.''[4] However, a dissenting faction within the Virginia Company later declared that, despite assurances to the contrary, ''conversion of those Infidels did not happen in those first 12 years during wch time the English were allmost allso in continuall Hostilitie wth ye Infidells.''[5] Indeed, the Jamestown colonists spent much more energy in seizing Indian lands than in spreading the gospel.

Indian conversion nevertheless proved fertile ground for reaping other benefits. Duly impressed with a carefully contrived visit from Pocahantas, the first and only Jamestown Indian convert, King James ordered in 1617 a special collection in churches throughout the realm. The proceeds were to be delivered to the Virginia Company for ''the erecting of some Churches and Schooles, for the education of the children of those Barbarians.''[6] Accordingly, the Virginia Company in 1618 ordered ''that a convenient place be chosen and set out for the planting of a University . . . in time to come and that in the mean time preparation be there made for the building of the said College for the Children of the Infidels.'' The company then endowed the college with 1,000 acres of land seized from the natives at Henrico, some 50 miles upriver from Jamestown.[7]

Against this backdrop entered one of this drama's most crafty and enterprising players, Sir Edwin Sandys, treasurer of the Virginia Company. Sandys reported in 1619 that the bishops' collections had already netted 1,500 pounds. However, only about half of that sum was available in cash, since the Company had borrowed the remainder for its own financial needs. By May, 1620, augmented by considerable private donations to the college, the collections grew to 2,043 pounds.[8] Despite this substantial and growing benefaction, Sandys advised a postponement in building the college. He justified the delay by proposing to invest the funds to create an endowment for the college. Evidence suggests, however, that he planned to employ the capital to further the Virginia Company's ambitious economic plan.

To save the Company, which continually wavered on the brink of bankruptcy, Sandy's new economic policy aimed to rapidly increase the population settled on the public lands and to stimulate the production of new commodities. Accordingly, he announced his intention to use the Indian college funds to ship indentured tenants for the college lands. Sandys incidentally noted that this use of the charity ''may save the Joint stock the sending out a [supply] Shipp this yeare.''[9] Instead of reaping income for the college at Henrico, half of the tenants who arrived in 1619 were assigned to private plantations. When the scattered tenants were finally resettled on the college lands, they served another aim of the Company—the production of new staples, silk and wine. With the remaining college funds, Sandys invested not in education but in yet another economic scheme, an ironworks on a plantation owned by himself and another investor. Two years later, one significant benefactor complained about the use of his donation by private investors, "contrary to my minde."[10]

By 1620, although nearly three-fourths of the money raised in England to educate Indians had been disbursed, Treasurer Sandys had diverted the charity and thwarted all intentions to construct the college. Not a penny went toward the conversion and education of would-be native scholars. Meanwhile, a native uprising in 1622 put an end to the grandiose plan for the Indian college at Henrico. Considering this scheme, an eighteenth-century historian concluded that "we do not find that the money was employed as those Religious Persons would have had it"—an understatement indeed and a better than warranted reflection on the dubious character of Sir Edwin Sandys.[11]

The New England colonists, settling their new world with the same godly mission, learned from the Virginia experience. They learned, foremost, to manipulate and capitalize on the charitable impulses of the pious English. Their enterprising machinations resulted in the construction of the Harvard Indian College, which advantaged English scholars more than it did the natives for whom it was ostensibly intended. Also like their Virginia predecessors, the New England colonists—neglectful of their chartered mission—spent more effort in seeking funds for Indian conversion than in actually spreading the gospel. Publishing several pieces of promotional literature, which greatly exaggerated their success in converting Indians and even more their desire to do so, New England leaders embarked on a plan to link the needs of the fledgling Harvard College with the proven solicitations for Indian conversion. In fact, the first promotional tract, published in 1643, recommended that contributions for the Indian work be sent to the College president.

Under pressure from New England lobbyists, in 1648 the House of Commons began to debate a bill to charter a new philanthropic corporation for Indian missions in the Puritan colonies. One debate focused on an opportunistic amendment to alter fundamentally the character of the bill, placing Indian conversion in a position of importance secondary to that of Harvard College. In this amendment, the New England colonists advocated allocating the charity "for the maintaining of the universities of Cambridge in New-England, and other schools and nurseries of learning there, and for the preaching and propagating of the Gospel among the natives." However, this attempt to include assistance for the College was thwarted, as Parliament approved the final bill designating funds solely for "the preaching and

propagating of the Gospel of Jesus Christ amongst the natives, and also for maintaining of schools and nurseries of learning, for the better educating of the children of the natives."[12] Thus, in 1649 Parliament created the Society for the Propagation of the Gospel in New England, commonly called the New England Company, charging the London-based Society to raise and administer funds for Indian conversion.

Against this backdrop, a behind-the-scenes player, Harvard President Henry Dunster, entered center stage. Although he had provided much of the information for the 1643 tract designed to create a climate of favorable support in England, Dunster made an even more strategic move by engineering Harvard's charter in 1650. The charter provided for the "education of the English and Indian Youth of this country in knowledge: and Godlines."[13] (It is instructive that, although Harvard College was established in 1636, it had not yet professed a commitment to Indian education.) In 1651, this maneuver accomplished, he inquired of the Commissioners of the United Colonies, overseer of the New England Company's disbursements in the colonies, whether the charitable funds might in some measure benefit the College. The Commissioners responded with a letter to their London agent suggesting that "an eye may bee had in the destrebutions to the enlargement of the Colledge at Cambridge wherof there is great need and furtherance of learning not soe Imediately Respecting the Indian Designe." The interests and intentions of Dunster as well as those of the colonial commissioners were clear; foremost among them was the struggling and financially strapped Harvard College.

Whatever their motives, the solicitations were fruitful. In 1653 the trustees of the missionary fund ordered "the building of one Intyre Rome att the College for the Conveniencye of six hopfull Indians youths ... which Rome may bee two storyes high and built plaine but strong and durable." The Indian college was accordingly completed in 1656.[14]

In this use of charitable funds, several factors arouse suspicion regarding the Commissioners' intentions for the Indian college. First, the building did not cost one hundred pounds as initially proposed. Twice enlarged beyond the original design—this, to accommodate English, not additional Indian students—the total cost was some four hundred pounds. Such a sum would have supported ten missionaries for four years at the prevailing twenty-pound annual rate paid through 1656.[15] Second, there were no Indian students identified to occupy the Indian college, a situation surely known to Harvard's president and to the Commissioners. Three years after construction of the Indian college building, the New England Company wanted to know

what number of Indians there are att the university and what progresse and profisiency they make in their learning; and to what degree and measure therin they have attained; and we hope wilbee such as will give good satisfaction unto divers well affected heerunto.

Although the Commissioners encouragingly reported that "there are five Indian youthes at Cambridge in the lattin [preparatory] Schoole," they made no mention of any at the Indian college.[16] Not until 1660 did an Indian student enter Harvard for the bachelor's degree, and never did more than two occupy the Indian College at any given time. Indeed, during the nearly four decades of its existence, the college housed only four Indian scholars.

Nevertheless, the building did not stand vacant. As soon as it was completed, Harvard's next President, Charles Chauncy, proposed that its rooms be used to accommodate English students. Later, a contemporary observer described the Indian College as "large enough to receive and accommodate about twenty scholars with convenient lodgings and studies; but not hitherto hath been much improved for the ends intended. . . . It hath hitherto been principally improved for to accommodate English scholars."[17]

Despite receiving encouraging reports and testimony from the colonial Commissioners, the New England Company questioned the progress relative to expenditures, reporting that "it is wondered by some heer that in all this time there are noe more in regard it appeers by the account sent; . . . we desire therfore that . . . you would please to bee more particular in youer next accounts." They also warned that "we shalbee slow to take many more English or Indian youthes upon our charge for education till wee have some experience of those on whom soe much hath bine bestowed."[18]

If the Society was suspicious of the Puritan effort by 1660, certainly the negligible progress through the remainder of the college's life to 1693 afforded no evidence to allay their misgivings. Indeed, by 1675 there was but one Indian student at the College, and the last Indian attended in 1685. The professed interest in educating Indians at Harvard merely concealed the intention to use the Indian cause to exact English funds for the survival of the colonists' college. This was a lesson learned from the earlier Virginia enterprise at Henrico, and it was once again destined to be employed in that same colony. Ironically, when the Indian College at Harvard was demolished in 1693, the College of William and Mary in Virginia received its royal charter—once again, purportedly for the education of Indian youth.

As was the case in other missionary enterprises, the promise of funds incited greater concern for the education of Indians—again under the initiative of a cunning, enterprising individual; in this case, the Commissary of Virginia, James Blair. While soliciting contributions from the merchants of London for the founding of a college in Virginia, Blair proposed in 1690 the possibility of "perhaps" creating "a foundation for ye Conversion of our neighbouring Heathen to ye Christian Faith."[19] Since there is no evidence that the proposed college was intended for Indians, it is likely that the mention of conversion was a bid to enlist the merchants' pious impulses.

A twist of fate then forced Blair to play his hand openly. In January 1691, while Blair was in London seeking a royal charter for the College of William and Mary, the Governor of the New England Company, Robert Boyle, died, leaving 5,400 pounds for unspecified "Charitable and other pious and good uses." Boyle's will recommended "the Laying out of the greatest part of the same for the Advance or propagation of the Christian religion amongst Infidells."[20] Prevailing upon the executor of Boyle's estate to direct the fund toward the support of an Indian school at the prospective college in Virginia, Blair reported from London that "Mr. Boyle died about the beginning of last month, & left a considerable Legacy for pious uses, which, when I understood, I made my interest with his executors by means of the Bishop of Salisbury, and I am promised 200.1. [pounds] of it for our college."[21]

Ultimately, Blair's solicitations proved even more successful. From the proceeds of an investment of the Boyle bequest, the executors specified an annuity to

keep att the said Colledge soe many Indian Children in Sicknesse and health in Meat drink Washing Lodgeing Cloathes Medicines bookes and Educacon from the first beginning of Letters till they are ready to receive Orders and be thought Sufficient to be sent abroad to preach and Convert the Indians.[22]

Thus, when Blair obtained in 1693 a royal charter for the establishment of the College of William and Mary, he duly contrived that, among other ends, the College would exist so that "the Western Indians."23 Despite the semblance of a pious mission, no evidence survives of Indian enrollment at William and Mary prior to 1705. Clearly, during his fifty years as the college president, Blair made no serious attempt to fulfill the intent of the Boyle legacy. Instead, he devised other than the intended uses for the charity.

By 1716 Indian students were so few that their college master requested "the liberty of teaching such English Children as shall be put to him" and that a partition be erected to separate English students from Indians.24 By 1721 William and Mary College had no native students, and the "Indian Master" rendered his services exclusively to English scholars.25 There is no evidence that Indians attended the college in the later 1720s.

In the face of an untapped and rapidly accumulating Boyle fund, President Blair began to contrive further uses for the account which might revitalize the struggling and financially strapped William and Mary College. In 1723, reviving the appearance of commitment to Indian education, Blair constructed a building for an Indian school which did not in fact exist. Built at a cost of 500 pounds, the structure, called the Brafferton, was a handsome two-and-a-half story brick house. This accomplished, Blair devised yet another tactic to capitalize on the Boyle bequest to aid the College. Using the fund to build its severely deficient library, in 1732 he authorized a London agent to spend up to 300 pounds on books for the general use of William and Mary scholars. Blair rationalized this diversion by sarcastically noting that "as we do not live in an age of miracles, it is not to be doubted that Indian scholars will want the help of many books to qualifie them to become good Pastours and Teachers."26 Little did it matter that there would be no Indian scholars at William and Mary for over a decade.

Efforts to engage Indian students were negligible throughout the remainder of President Blair's administration. On Blair's death in 1743, William Dawson became the new president. That same year, the College enrolled perhaps half a dozen Indian students.27 From the 1750s until the Revolution, when funds from England halted and the Brafferton "Indian College" simultaneously ceased to exist, William and Mary maintained a small but steady enrollment of between three and five Indian students. But, throughout the course of James Blair's presidency, the Indian School at the College of William and Mary was, in the words

of College historian J. E. Morpurgo, "an entry in the ledgers through which charitable funds could be funneled to extraneous activities."28

The final and most lucrative scheme for the advanced training of Indians during the colonial period resulted from the machinations of Eleazar Wheelock, called—perhaps mistakenly—the founder of Dartmouth College. A Congregational minister in Lebanon, Connecticut, Wheelock in 1754 established Moor's Charity School for Indian students, unquestionably a successful venture which operated for nearly a century. In 1763, seeking a land grant of thirty to thirty-five square miles, Wheelock sent to England "A Proposal for Introducing Religion, Learning, Agriculture, and Manufacture among the Pagans in America," suggesting "a large farm of several thousand acres of and within said grant be given to this Indian school [and] that the school be an academy for all parts of useful learning: part of it a College for the Education of Missionaries, Schoolmasters, Interpreters, etc., and part of it a School for reading and writing, etc."29 This proposal reflected Wheelock's growing passion for establishing a college as well as his then waning interest in educating Indians.

The efforts of Wheelock's most successful Indian protégé provided the money needed to finance his scheme. Samson Occum, Wheelock's "black son," embarked on a fundraising mission to England and Scotland from 1765 to 1768. He thus raised over 12,000 pounds in the mistaken belief that the funds were to be employed "towards building and endowing an Indian academy for cloathing, boarding, maintaining, and educating such Indians as are designed for missionaries and schoolmasters, and for maintaining those who are, or hereafter shall be employed on this glorious errand."30 These funds represented the largest amount that any college up to that time had been able to raise by direct solicitation abroad.

Yet Wheelock had become disillusioned with his Indian students because of what he called their "Sloth," ""want of Fortitude [and] Stability," and "doleful Apostasy."31 He set into motion his plans to relocate to New Hampshire, where he had secured a substantial land grant for his college. With an ample treasury at his disposal, his next task was to obtain a royal charter for the so-called "Indian achademy." On December 13, 1769, Wheelock secured the charter for Dartmouth College. In writing the charter, Wheelock had to deal with several potentially volatile matters. One centered on defining the purpose of the school. On the one hand, he had to assure the Society in Scotland for

Propagating Christian Knowledge, trustees of Samson Occum's collections, that their funds would be employed solely for the charitable education of Indians. On the other hand, he had to deal with the expectation among the people of New Hampshire that the school would supply local ministers. Wheelock had already decided that Dartmouth would emphasize the education of English scholars, but in writing the charter, he disguised his intentions well. The first charter draft defined the school's purpose as providing "for the education & instruction of Youths of the English and also of the Indian Tribes." After carefully considering that numerous English benefactors had contributed thousands of pounds to a school for Indians—*not* white colonists—he revised the reference to English youth as if to indicate their subordinate position in his scheme. Accordingly, the final draft of the charter read that the college would exist

for the education & instruction of Youth of the Indian Tribes in this Land in reading wrighting and all parts of Learning which shall appear necessary and expedient for civilizing and christianizing Children of Pagans as well as in all liberal Arts and Sciences; and also of English Youth & any others.[32]

The business of the charter settled, Wheelock completed his move to New Hampshire in 1770. During that year the number of Indian students in Wheelock's Connecticut school had conveniently diminished to three, while the number of English scholars had grown to sixteen.[33] The school continued to admit Indians after the move to New Hampshire, although with an increasing influx of white students. During the entire decade of the 1770s, the reverend was responsible for educating some forty Indians, while during the same period he had more than 120 white students at Dartmouth College and many more at the charity school. By 1774 Wheelock had exhausted all of Occum's collections for Indian education.

While Wheelock's sophistry led to the fulfillment of his dream to establish a college, it shattered the vision of his Indian protégé. Samson Occum maintained that the English funds were raised solely for his brethren, as "we told them that we were Begging solely for poor Miserable Indians." Occum further complained that he had been duped, having previously been warned in England that "You have been a fine Tool to get Money for them, and when you get home, they won't Regard you the'll set you a Drift,—I am ready to believe it Now," he wrote.[34] A nineteenth-century critic was even more harsh in his condemnation. The charitable collection for Indian education, he wrote,

is all expended; and excepting in new lands, Dartmouth College is without funds. It was intended that only the interest should be annually spent, but the fund itself is consumed. Though this was primarily designed for Indians, yet the only Indian that has graduated there was obliged to beg elsewhere towards supporting him the last year of his college residence. . . . Such a mixture of apparent piety and eminent holiness, together with the love of riches, dominion, and family aggrandizement, is seldom seen.[35]

When the sincerity of the professed commitment to Indian education in the colonial colleges is measured by comparing announced intentions against actual effort and money expended, there is reason to seriously doubt the genuineness of pious motivation. While the presence of some measure of concern for the Indians' spiritual welfare is unquestionable, other factors clearly motivated the major figures responsible for the advancement of Indian education and conversion. Certainly the colonists played cunningly on the religious impulses of stay-at-home Englishmen, capitalizing successfully on the image of "lost heathen" souls. In doing so, they were able to further their own political, economic and educational agendas, which included Indian education as an ancillary aim at best, while all the time professing their own piety as if this were their singular motivation. The Virginia Company leaders were thus able to invest charitable funds in their new economic program, intended more to revitalize the colonial enterprises than to establish the Henrico Indian college. College presidents Henry Dunster of Harvard and William and Mary's James Blair capitalized on Christian philanthropy to enhance the growth of their floundering and financially strapped colleges. So, too, was Reverend Wheelock able to profiteer and thus fulfill his desire to found Dartmouth College. Consequently, the colonial experiments in Indian higher education were not simple expressions of unblemished piety. Rather, they characterize a drama of self-righteousness, deception and neglect enacted on a stage of failure in Indian education.

NOTES

1. Willaim MacDonald, ed., *Select Charters and Other Documents Illustrative of American History, 1660–1775* (New York: MacMillan Co., 1906), 16.

2. Nathaniel B. Shurtleff, ed., *Records of the Governor and Company of the Massachusetts Bay in New England*, 5 vols. (Boston: William White Press, 1853–84), 1:17, 384.

3. [Robert Gray], *A Good Speed to Virginia* (London: Felix Kyngston, 1609); reprinted in J. Payne Collier, ed., *Illustrations of Early English Popular Literature*, 2 vols. (London: Privately Printed, 1864), 2:18.

4. Robert Hunt Land, "Henrico and Its College," *William and Mary Quarterly*, 2nd ser. 8 (1938): 470–1.

5. Susan Myra Kingsbury, ed., *The Records of the Virginia Company of London*, 4 vols. (Washington, D.C.: Government Printing Office, 1906–35), 2:395.

6. Peter Walne, "The Collections for Henrico College, 1616–18," *Virginia Magazine of History and Biography* 80 (1972): 260.

7. Kingsbury, *Records of Virginia Company*, 3:102.

8. Ibid., 1:220, 263, 335; 3:117, 576.

9. Ibid., 1:220–21.

10. Ibid., 1:586.

11. John Oldmixon, *The British Empire in America, Containing the History of the Discovery, Settlement, Progress and State of the British Colonies on the Continent and Island of America*, 2 vols. (London: John Nicholson, Benjamin Tooke, Richard Parker, and Ralph Smith, 1708), 1:300; cited by Arlyn Mark Conard, "The Christianization of Indians in Colonial Virginia" (Th.D. diss., Union Theological Seminary, 1979), 224.

12. Leo Francis Stock, ed., *Proceedings and Debates of the British Parliament Respecting North America*, 5 vols. (Washington, D.C.: Carnegie Institution, 1924), 1:209.

13. *Harvard College Records* (Boston: Colonial Society of Massachusetts, 1925; 1935).

14. David Pulsifer, ed., *Records of the Colony of New Plymouth in New England: Acts of the Commissioners of the United Colonies of New England*, 2 vols. (Boston: n.p., 1859), 2:107, 120, 128, 168.

15. George Parker Winship, *The New England Company of 1649 and John Eliot* (Boston: The Prince Society, 1920), 17.

16. William Kellaway, *The New England Company, 1649–1776: Missionary Society to the American Indians* (1961; reprint ed., Westport: Greenwood Press, 1975), 110; Pulsifer, *Acts of the Commissioners*, 2:216–17.

17. Daniel Gookin, "Historical Collections of the Indians in New England," *Collections of the Massachusetts Historical Society*, 1 (1792): 176.

18. Pulsifer, *Acts of the Commissioners*, 2:242.

19. "Papers Relating to the Founding of the College," *William and Mary Quarterly*, 1st ser. 7 (1898–99): 161.

20. A Contemporary Copy of the Will of Robert Boyle, 18 July 1691, William and Mary College Papers (Williamsburg: College of William and Mary), folder 7.

21. Herbert Lawrence Ganter, "Some Notes on 'The Charity of the Honourable Robert Boyle, Esq., of the City of London, Deceased'" *William and Mary Quarterly*, 2nd ser. 10 (1930): 68.

22. "Supplementary Documents Giving Additional Information Concerning the Four Forms of the Oldest Building of William & Mary College," *William and Mary Quarterly*, 2nd ser. 10 (1935): 14.

23. Robert Fitzgibbon Young, *Comenius in England: The Visit of Jan Amos Komensky (Comenius) The Czech Philosopher and Educationist to London in 1641–1642; Its Bearing on the Origins of the Royal Society, on the Development of the Encyclopedia, and on Plans for the Higher Education of the Indians of New England and Virginia* (London: Oxford University Press, 1932), 267.

24. *Virginia Magazine of History and Biography* 4 (1897): 172.

25. J. E. Morpurgo, *Their Majesties' Royall Colledge: William and Mary in the Seventeenth and Eighteenth Centuries* (Washington, D.C.: Hennage Creative Printers, 1976), 69.

26. "Instructions from the President and Masters of William & Mary College in Virginia, to John Randolph Esq.," William and Mary College Papers, f. 12.

27. James Axtell, *The Invasion Within: The Contest of Cultures in Colonial North America* (New York: Oxford University Press, 1985), 194.

28. Morpurgo, *Their Majesties' Royall Colledge*, 67.

29. Wheelock Papers ([microfilm edition], Hanover: Dartmouth College Archives), 763427.2

30. Frederick Chase, *A History of Dartmouth College and the Town of Hanover*, 2 vols., ed. John K. Lord (Cambridge: John Wilson & Sons, 1891), 1:59; James Dow McCallum, ed., *The Letters of Eleazar Wheelock's Indians*, Dartmouth College Manuscript Series, no. 1 (Hanover: Dartmouth College Publications, 1932), 305; James Dow McCallum, *Eleazar Wheelock, Founder of Dartmouth College*, Dartmouth College Manuscript Series, no. 4 (Hanover: Dartmouth College Publications, 1939), 164–65.

31. Wheelock Papers 769274.2, 769255; Eleazar Wheelock, *A Continuation of the Narrative of the Indian Charity-School in Lebanon, in Connecicut; From the Year 1768, to the Incorporation of it with Dartmouth-College, and Removal and Settlement of it in Hanover, in the Province of New-Hampshire, 1771* (n.p.: n.p., 1771), 19–20.

32. Wheelock Papers 769663.2; Jere R. Daniell, "Eleazar Wheelock and the Dartmouth College Charter," *Historical New Hampshire* 24 (Winter 1969): 3.

33. Harold Blodgett, *Samson Occom*, Dartmouth College Manuscript Series, no. 3 (Hanover: Dartmouth College Publications, 1935), 121–22; Chase, *History of Dartmouth College*, 88.

34. Wheelock Papers 771424.

35. Cited by Chase, *History of Dartmouth*, 559.

Bobby Wright is director of the Center for Native American Studies at Montana State University, Bozeman. He is presently conducting postdoctoral research as the 1988–89 Katrin K. Lamon Resident Scholar at the School of American Research in Santa Fe, New Mexico.

From Tutor to Specialized Scholar: Academic Professionalization in Eighteenth and Nineteenth Century America

Martin Finkelstein

DURING THE PAST DECADE and one-half, historians have taken the first steps toward development of an evolutionary "academetrics" of the American professoriate. In the 1960s, two quantitatively oriented studies of college teachers during the seventeenth and eighteenth centuries were published. In 1966, Wilson Smith examined the transformation of the tutorship at pre-revolutionary Harvard.[1] Two years later, William Carrell analyzed the career patterns of 124 professors at nineteen colleges in the second half of the eighteenth century.[2] Together, these analyses suggested that by the turn of the nineteenth century the academic role was emerging as an increasingly viable and distinctive career alternative to the practice of the traditional professions.

The years since have seen the publication of three quantitatively oriented case studies of the evolution of academic faculties during the nineteenth century at three quite different institutions: McCaughey on Harvard, Tobias on Dartmouth, and Creutz on the University of Michigan.[3] While these studies vary considerably in their temporal parameters and the breadth of their analyses[4] and while they hardly focus on what may be considered representative cases,[5] their results collectively require some qualification of earlier interpretations that had located the emergence of the modern, professional collegiate-based scholar in the last quarter of the nineteenth century and wedded his emergence to that of the American graduate university. Specifically, they suggested that (1) the professionalization of the academic role (i.e., the development of a specialized, secular scholarly vocation within the institutional context of the American college) was a gradual process that was already well underway in the ante-bellum period and (2) that professionalization proceeded quite unevenly across institutions, beginning quite early at Harvard and much later at Dartmouth, although the fundamental process in each case seemed to be of a single piece.

In light of this preliminary, albeit pioneering work, the present essay will serve two broad functions. First, it seeks to bring together developments related to two stages of professionalization: the development of academic employment as a distinctive, long term career path beginning in the eighteenth century and the subsequent development of career college teachers into career scholar-specialists a century later. In so doing, it seeks also to fill the gap concerning developments in the first quarter of the nineteenth century which have heretofore been largely ignored.[6] Second, it will supplement published analyses of Harvard, Dartmouth, and Michigan with original analyses of three additional institutions for whom data was readily available (Bowdoin, Brown and Yale) and with the less systematic data to be gleaned from secondary sources in an effort to provide a fuller, if still preliminary, map of the evolving contours of academic professionalization from the revolutionary era through the emergence of the American university.[7]

If more ambitious than previous studies in its temporal and sampling breadth, this essay is more modest in several respects. It seeks neither to provide the definitive word on developments at individual institutions nor to provide a broad cultural or sociological interpretation of the course of academic professionalization in nineteenth century America.[8] Finally, as a preliminary analysis, it cannot provide definitive historical generalizations which would require a more systematically representative sampling of institutions of more diverse orientations outside the Northeast.

In organizing the narrative map that follows, we have been guided by Donald Light's conceptualization of the three analytically distinct, yet interrelated, strands of the modern academic career.[9] The disciplinary strand includes those events specifically connected with a discipline and its goals rather than with a particular job (e.g., specialized training, work history prior to assumption of an academic career, involvements with disciplinary organizations, and research activity). The institutional career includes those events associated with a faculty member's role at a particular institution (e.g., the promotion system). Finally, the external career includes those work-related activities undertaken outside the institution but rooted in a faculty member's disciplinary expertise (e.g., consulting, government service, and public lecturing). On this basis, it serves to examine the evolutionary unfolding of these three career strands over the course of the eighteenth and nineteenth centuries.

Emergence of an Institutional Career, 1750-1800

During the seventeenth and the first half of the eighteenth century, the disciplinary career strand was, of course, virtually non-existant, and even the institutional strand proved secondary to the external one. American colleges operated on a model not unlike the British universities after the Elizabethan Statutes of the late sixteenth century.[10] Assuming that any bright graduate was ready to teach all subjects leading to the degree, instructional staffs were composed entirely of *tutors*, young men (often no more than twenty) who had just received their baccalaureate degree and who were preparing for careers in the ministry. The responsibilities of tutors were both pedagogical and pastoral or custodial in nature. Ideally, a single tutor was assigned the sheparding of a single class through all four years of their baccalaureate program, both inside and outside the classroom. "Tutors were with their pupils almost every hour of the day (in classroom recitations, study halls, and at meals) and slept in the same chamber with some of them at night. They were responsible not only for the intellectual, but for the moral and spiritual development of their charges."[11]

In the less than ideal practice, the tutorship functioned as a "revolving door." At Harvard, prior to 1685, very seldom did a tutor see a class through all four years. Only a half dozen of the forty-one tutors during this period remained at Harvard more than three years. While the next half century saw a progressive lengthening of the tutors' tenure at Harvard, and indeed the ultimate establishment of "permanent" tutorships in the latter half of the eighteenth century,[12] the "revolving door" condition persisted through this period at Yale, Brown, Dartmouth, and Bowdoin.

It was not until the last half of the eighteenth century that the institutional career began to take shape, as a small core of "permanent" faculty, the professors, began to supplement the cadre of short-term tutors. Carrell found that in 1750 there were only ten professors in all of American higher education, the bulk of whom were either at Harvard or William and Mary. By 1795, the professorial ranks had swelled tenfold to 105 while the number of colleges had only slightly more than doubled. All in all, some 200 individuals had served as professors in nineteen American colleges during this period.[13]

How did these professorships develop? At Harvard, they came into being slowly as a result of philanthropic bequests. During the 1720s, two Hollis professorships were endowed: one in divinity, occupied by Edward Wigglesworth for forty-four years; the other in mathematics and natural philosophy, occupied initially by Isaac Greenwood for eleven years, and then by John Winthrop for forty-one years. By 1750, President Holyoke was supported by three permanent faculty members, the two Hollis professors and Henry Flynt, a permanent tutor.[14] During the rest of the eighteenth century, four additional professorships were endowed, of which three were actually filled before 1800.[15] By 1800, permanent professors had achieved near parity in numbers with tutors on the Harvard faculty.

At Yale, too, the first professorship was established by a philanthropic bequest. In 1746, the Livingston Professorship of Divinity was established, and nine years later its first occupant joined President Clap and the tutors in supervising instruction. Although Yale had established only one additional professorship by 1800, it achieved near parity between permanent and transient staff two years later with the promotion of Jerimiah Day and Benjamin Silliman from their tutorships.[16]

The pattern that developed after more than a century at Harvard and a half century at Yale was adapted quickly by several of the colleges founded during the second half of the eighteenth century. At Brown, for example, within five years of its founding a core permanent faculty was emerging with Howell's promotion from tutor to professor to join forces with President Manning. By 1800, its five tutors were supplemented by three permanent professors.[17] At Princeton, by 1767, two decades after its founding, three permanent professors had joined forces with the three tutors.[18] At Dartmouth, during the administration of John Wheelock from 1779 to 1817, several professors were appointed to supplement the single professor who together with two or three tutors constituted the faculty during the preceding administration of Eleazar Wheelock.[19]

What were the characteristics of this early core permanent faculty? How did they resemble or differ from their more transient colleagues, the tutors? With regard to similarities, both professors and tutors were drawn disproportionately from the higher socioeconomic strata of colonial and postrevolutionary society; fully one quarter came from "professional" families (with fathers engaged in the ministry, law, medicine) at a time when 1-2 percent of the labor force was "professional" and 80-90 percent were engaged in agricultural pursuits.[20] Moreover, both professors and tutors undertook very similar activities as part of their college responsibilities. Both supervised recitations and dormitories and assumed overall responsibility for student discipline and moral, as well as intellectual, development. There the similarity appears to have ended. In the first place, professors did not take charge of a class for its four years at the institution; they were appointed in a particular subject area (e.g., natural philosophy, divinity, ancient languages) and were, for the most part, engaged in the supervision of instruction within that area. In the second place, professors were, on average, at least five to ten years older than the tutors. The vast majority, unlike the tutors, had had some post-baccalaureate professional training in theology, law, or medicine. Among the eight professors at Brown during the eighteenth century, for example, seven had such training, as did all ten of the professors at Harvard.[21]

The most fundamental respect, however, in which professors differed from tutors was in their "permanence." Carrell's analysis of biographical sketches of 124 professors during the second half of the eighteenth century illuminates the peculiar meaning of a "permanent" faculty appointment during this period. First, a professorship implied an "institutional" career, often at his *alma mater.* Nearly 40 percent of Carrell's sample professors did this, ranging from just over one-third at the College of Philadelphia (later the University of Pennsylvania) to 83 percent at Harvard. Fully 88 percent taught at only one institution during their academic career, while barely 2.5 percent taught at three or more institutions. Second, a permanent professorship remained an "unexclusive" career. In analyzing the lifetime occupational commitment of his sample, Carrell found that less than 15 percent appeared to identify themselves exclusively as "professional teachers," while less than 20 percent appeared to identify themselves primarily as a professional teacher (with a secondary occupation in the ministry, medicine, or law), while over half appeared to identify themselves primarily as practitioners of one of the traditional professions and only secondarily as professional college teachers.[22]

If college teaching was hardly the exclusive career, or even the first choice career, of a majority of eighteenth century professors, Carrell's analysis suggests that it became a long term commitment for many once the move was made. In an analysis of indicators of occupational commitment of his sample professors during their teaching tenure, Carrell found strikingly different results. Nearly 45 percent identified themselves exclusively as college teachers, while about one-quarter identified themselves, respectively, as primarily or secondarily college teachers. Among the latter two categories, clergy were disproportionately represented in the first, while physicians and lawyers were disproportionately represented in the second. This suggests that clergy were more likely than the other learned professions to develop a primary commitment to the professorial role once it was assumed.[23]

That the assumption of a professorship increasingly brought with it a heightened commitment to college teaching is further supported by at least three additional pieces of evidence. First, the average length of professors' tenure increased substantially between 1750-1800. At Yale, the average tenure of professors increased from 21.5 years to 36.8 years while at Brown it increased from 30.7 years to 36.0 years.[24] Second, Carrell reports a negative zero order correlation between age at first appointment and tenure in the professorial role of −.35 suggesting shorter tenures were, at least in part, attributable to late career entry.[25] Finally, Carrell's analysis reveals that only a relatively small proportion of professors during the period pursued subsequent non-academic careers. Just over half of the population died in office. Less than 25 percent engaged in another occupation after leaving the professorship; and among this group several either retired because of "bad health" or "were retired" by their institutions.[26] It would appear safe to conclude, then, that the professorial role, once undertaken, was pursued with a considerable degree of permanency, particularly when we consider the frequency of dual occupations (e.g., medicine and agriculture, law and agriculture, religion and education) characteristic of the late eighteenth century.

One final issue concerning the relationship of the tutor to the professor remains: the relative integration or separation of the two roles in terms of the individual career track. To what extent did the tutorship function as the first step toward a professorship? And to what extent was a professorship the reward of skillful "tutoring"? The evidence suggests that at least two contrasting patterns had developed by the close of the eighteenth century. The Harvard pattern was one of separate career tracks. Not a single Harvard tutor went on to a Harvard professorship during the eighteenth century. Indeed "tutoring" became something of a permanent career option in itself.[27] The pattern at Yale and Brown, and it would appear at most other institutions, was one of a separate, transient career track, tempered by the intermittent use of the tutorship as a very "selective" feeder for the professorship. Thus, at Brown, only four of eighteen eighteenth-century tutors (22.2 percent) went on to professorial appointments and three of the eight professors appointed during that period had served as Brown tutors.[28] At Yale, tutors were less than half as likely as their Brown counterparts to achieve professorial appointments, but all six Yale professors during the period had indeed served as Yale tutors.[29]

Ascent of the Institutional Career, 1800-1820

The first quarter of the nineteenth century has been credited by historian Frederick Rudolph as the beginnings of the "college movement," the large scale founding of small colleges throughout the west stimulated by the "community building" imperative of the period as well as by increasing competition among religious denominations.[30] It may also be credited as the beginning of the "professor movement." Between 1800 and 1820, the ratio of permanent professors to tutors dramatically reversed itself at many of the "leading" institutions. By 1820, permanent professors outnumbered tutors at both Harvard and Yale by a ratio of 10 to 6 where two decades earlier there had been parity at Harvard and a 3 to 1 majority of tutors at Yale. At Brown, professors outnumbered tutors by a ratio of 3 to 1 where only decades earlier the tutors had been in the majority by a 5 to 3 ratio.[31]

The momentum of the professor movement can be seen graphically in developments at Harvard during President Kirkland's administration from 1810 to 1828. During the entire eighteenth century, six professorships had been established at Harvard. They were created when funding to support them was obtained from private donors. If the initial gift was insufficient to support an incumbent, it was allowed to accumulate over one or more decades before the professorship was filled; e.g., the Hersey and Boylston professorships. Several professorships were allowed to go unfilled for as many as ten or twenty years. In the decade preceding the Kirkland presidency, a subscription was launched by Harvard for the creation of a single professorship. During the eighteen years of Kirkland's presidency, the number of Harvard professorships fully doubled. Seven professors were appointed while the funds destined for their support were not yet available. Indeed, in his zeal to make appointments, Kirkland frequently resorted to drawing on tuition revenues to pay the newly hired incumbents.[32]

How can this ascendance of the permanent faculty in a brief two decades be explained? While it is impossible to postulate an explicit cause and effect relationship, three developments during the period appear to have set the necessary, if not sufficient, conditions for that ascendance. The first of these was growth. The Yale faculty doubled in size between 1800 and 1820, while that of Harvard and Brown increased by 50 percent.[33] Beyond size, there was an increase in the number of institutions attendant upon the "college funding movement." Allied with growth was the progressive acceptance of the professorship as a long term, if not an exclusive, career line, reflected in progressively longer average tenures throughout the eighteenth century and the indicators of increasing career commitment reported by Carrell.[34] Yet, a third factor which may help to account for that increased ascendance of the institutional career were changes underway during the first quarter of the eighteenth century in the ministerial sector. Calhoun, in a case study of the New Hampshire clergy during the late eighteenth and early nineteenth century, reported a radical shift in clerical career patterns about this time, attributable to increasing secularization and urbanization. The average terms of service in local parishes, which throughout most of the eighteenth century had been measured in lifetimes, began to resemble the average tenures of modern college and university presidents. This job insecurity and difficulties in obtaining even so insecure positions, together with the low salaries of clergy in rural and small-town churches, led many ministers to seek to enhance their careers by building organizations such as benevolent societies and colleges and by becoming professors.[35] And the correlation of these developments in the clerical career with the ascent of the professorship is supported by Carrell's finding that clergymen became significantly more likely than their fellow professionals in law and medicine to identify themselves primarily as college teachers by the end of the eighteenth century (v. supra).[36]

Academic Professionalization Circa 1820

By the end of the first quarter of the nineteenth century, the "professor movement" had produced a relatively large cohort of career college teachers. While still a thoroughly homogeneous group of upper middle class, New England-born Protestants,[37] the confluence of a number of social and intellectual forces during the course of the nineteenth century wrought some fundamental changes in the group career. The progressive secularization of American society was penetrating the classical college, subjugating the demands of piety to a "religion" of progress and materialism.[38] At the same time, the rise of science and the growth of scientific knowledge was breaking apart the classical curriculum and giving rise to the development of academic disciplines (the distinction of professional versus amateur) and of research and graduate education. By mid-century, increasingly large numbers of Americans were studying abroad in Germany and were importing their version of the German university and the German idea of research back to the United States.[39] Once graduate specialization took hold in earnest in the last quarter of the nineteenth century, it was but a short step to the establishment of the major learned societies and their sponsorship of specialized, disciplinary journals: The American Chemical Society in 1876, The Modern Language Association in 1883, The American Historical Association in 1884, The American Psychological Association in 1892, etc.[40]

These developments provided American higher education with the capability of producing graduate trained specialists and career opportunities for the specialists so produced. They shaped and reflected a fundamental restructuring, i.e., professionalization, of the academic role. Although touted by some as a veritable "academic revolution," an examination of the evolving disciplinary, institutional, and external careers of faculty at the sample institutions suggests that the restructuring process actually proceeded by gradual steps over more than a half-century as successive cohorts of professors were replaced by products of the latest graduate training.

Before turning to the evolution of these three career strands during the nineteenth century, it serves to review the status of each as manifested in college faculties in 1820.

By 1820, a disciplinary career was discernible only in the cases of a few isolated individuals at selected campuses rather than among entire faculties. While a majority of individuals continued to come to the professorship with post-baccalaureate training in the traditional professions of divinity, medicine and law (mostly divinity), with the exception of Harvard few boasted post-baccalaureate training in their academic/teaching specialty.[41] For the most part without specialized training, the majority of faculties, 50 percent at Brown and Harvard and 100 percent at Bowdoin, continued to be drawn to their initial academic appointments from non-academic jobs, primarily in school teaching and the ministry and secondarily in law and medicine.[42] Moreover, for most faculty any semblance of a disciplinary career ended with their institutional career. At Brown and Bowdoin, the modal pattern was for faculty to move into non-academic careers following their tenure as college teachers (50 percent of the full professors at Brown and 60 percent of those at Bowdoin, virtually all the junior faculty at both institutions). It should be noted, however, that those full professors who "strayed from the fold" averaged nearly two decades in their teaching positions (21.2 years at Brown and 18.5 years at Bowdoin) suggesting that even among "dropouts," college teaching still constituted a significant segment of their careers.[43]

At other institutions, most notably Harvard and Yale, patterns of career commitment appeared to be differentiated along senior/junior faculty lines. While no junior faculty at either institution persisted in an

academic career beyond their tutorship or instructorship, the majority of permanent professors did (83 percent at Yale and 70 percent at Harvard).

Whatever their career commitments, institutionally speaking, college faculties in 1820 evidenced fairly low disciplinary commitment as measured by their associational involvements and scholarly publications. Only a single faculty member at Brown, Bowdoin, Harvard, and Yale was involved   , any significant extent in the activities of the learned societies of the day (Caswell at Brown, Cleaveland at Bowdoin, Peck at Harvard, and Silliman at Yale who had the year before founded the *American Journal of Science*).[44] And it was only those same single faculty members who were at all involved in publication in their specialized field (excluding the medical faculty). Many professors at these institutions were indeed publishing, but their work consisted chiefly in collections of sermons and public addresses/orations made at commencements and other public occasions.

While many professors in 1820 were actively pursuing external careers, virtually none did so in their academic specialization. Beyond the service of a few men such as Silliman and Cleaveland on the public lecture circuit, the vast majority of professors devoted their extra-institutional service to clerical and civic activities. Fully three-quarters of the professors at Bowdoin, two-thirds of those at Dartmouth, and half of those at Brown were engaged in itinerant preaching and work with missionary societies. Somewhat lower proportions participated actively in community life, principally by holding political office, assuming leadership roles in local civic associations unrelated to education or intellectual culture (e.g., tree planting societies) or, in fewer cases, taking membership in state historical societies.[45]

By 1820, the now familiar formalized institutional career track, i.e., the progression through the junior ranks to a full professorship, had not appeared. Indeed, in many respects, the two-track system largely operative at the turn of the nineteenth century remained intact with junior faculty holding temporary, dead-end appointments and senior faculty with long-term appointments. At Harvard, fully 80 percent of the senior faculty were initially appointed to their professorships from outside the institution, and 62 percent of these claimed no previous academic experience.[46] While Harvard was alone in this period in having established the "instructorship" as distinguished from the tutorship and the professorship,[47] instructors rarely moved to Harvard professorships and tutors did not advance to instructorships.[48]

While Yale and Brown continued to reflect some departure from the Harvard pattern by promotion of tutors to professorships, the extent of that departure appeared to be decreasing. Two-thirds of Brown and Yale arts and science professors served as tutors at their employing institutions, a significant decrement from the 100 percent who had so served on the faculties of 1800. Moreover, none of the six tutors on the Yale faculty in 1820 advanced to a Yale professorship, in contrast to two of six in 1800; and only two of the thirty-two tutors on the Yale faculty during the 1820s were so advanced.[49] Even more dramatically, at Brown, none of the ten tutors appointed during the decade of the 1820s advanced to a professorship.[50] It seems fair to conclude, then, at least on the basis of the increasing convergence of practices at Harvard, Yale, Brown, that by 1820 the dual track academic career, defined along junior-senior faculty lines, was on the ascent rather than the descent.

In sum, it may be said that there were at least two "typical" faculty members by the end of the first quarter of the nineteenth century. The first "typical" faculty member was quite young and took on a temporary assignment as either a tutor or instructor before embarking on a non-academic career, usually in the ministry. He typically came to his employing institution from the ranks of its immediate past graduates and probably undertook training in some traditional profession (usually the ministry) either during or just after his short term appointment. The second "typical" faculty member was the professor who had had some post-baccalaureate training in one of the traditional professions (albeit not in his teaching specialty) and had come to a professorship at his *alma mater* perhaps from a tutorship at the same employing institution, or, more likely, from a non-academic occupation (often a pastorate). During the course of his appointment, he was engaged in itinerant preaching and a variety of community activities that were probably non-educational and non-intellectual in nature, except perhaps for membership in the state historical society. Depending on his particular employing institution, he may have moved to a non-academic occupation after a tenure of nearly two decades; or he may have continued his teaching activities for the rest of his life, most probably at his original employing institution. Together, these two types approached their role as a teaching/custodial function, oftentimes as an extension of an earlier or concurrent ministerial role.

Academic Professionalization, 1820-1880

Well before the Civil War, the disciplinary career of the American professoriate as reflected in the incidence of specialized training, publication activity, associational involvements and career commitment was undergoing significant change. The preceding discussion has already established that Harvard was at the vanguard in the area of specialized training; by 1821, 40 percent of its faculty had received such training. While isolated instances of specialty-trained faculty could be discerned during the 1830s and 1840s at Brown, Bowdoin, and Yale, these institutions did not begin replicating the Harvard pattern to any significant degree until the

1850s and 1860s. At Brown, for example, as early as 1841, John Lincoln was sent to study in Europe prior to assuming his assistant professorship. However, it was not until the mid-1850s that nearly one-quarter of the Brown faculty were to take leaves for European study (two of them returning with European doctorates).[51] At Bowdoin, as early as 1835 John Goodwin was appointed professor of modern languages and dispatched to Europe for two years to prepare for his position. Goodwin, however, remained largely alone during his thirteen-year tenure, pending several other appointments in the early 1860s.[52] At Yale, as early as 1843 Thomas Thatcher took leave to engage in European study, but it was not until 1863 that Yale appointed its first Ph.D. to the faculty.[53]

At institutions such as Dartmouth and Williams, developments began later but proceeded more rapidly. At Dartmouth, as late as the mid-1850s, nearly all of the faculty in the academical department had received training in the traditional professions but none in a specialized academic discipline. With a half dozen appointments in the late 1860s and early 1870s, however, Dartmouth had virtually reversed that condition in a single decade.[54] At Williams, the first professionally trained faculty member was not appointed until 1858 (Thomas Clark who had just received his doctorate in chemistry from the University of Gottingen) and a second did not assume professorial duties until the close of the Civil War. By 1869, however, fully five of the thirteen members of the Williams faculty could boast graduate training in their teaching specialty.[55]

As the proportion of faculty with discipline-related credentials increased, so did the proportion of those embarking on an academic career immediately following their training. At Harvard, by 1869 the proportion of faculty with no previous non-academic career had doubled since 1845 (44 percent versus 22 percent).[56] Even more dramatically, at Bowdoin, during the 1870s, nearly two-thirds of the faculty embarked on their academic careers immediately after their graduate training, compared to barely 20 percent during the preceding decade.[57]

If the pattern of increased specialized training together with assumption of an academic career immediately following that training did not take hold until the 1850s and the 1860s, other aspects of the disciplinary career (i.e., scholarly publication and participation in learned societies) were developing earlier. At Bowdoin, the largest jump in the faculty's *Professional Index* during the nineteenth century occurred during the second quarter of the century.[58] By 1845, 70 percent of the faculty were publishing in their field (although nearly half of these were primarily publishing their lectures as textbooks) and nearly 30 percent were involved in the activities of scientific associations. At Harvard, the faculty's *Professional Index* took its largest jump in the early 1840s during the Quincy presidency, nearly doubling in less than two decades.[59] The most significant jump in the

Brown faculty's *Professional Index* occurred between 1845 and the end of the Civil War. By 1845, half the Brown faculty was publishing in their field of specialization (even if in the more popular media); and by the Civil War, one-half were affiliated with major disciplinary and scientific associations.[60]

By the 1850s, one unmistakable sign of the ascendance of the disciplinary career was evident. Institutional commitments built on inbreeding were breaking down in the face of disciplinary commitments which opened up opportunities at other institutions. At Bowdoin, three faculty left for positions at other institutions where only one had done so in the previous half century.[61] At Brown, while only one professor left during the decade preceding the Civil War, several junior faculty pursued career interests by moves to other institutions.[62] And during the 1850s and 1860s, the University of Michigan, and to a lesser extent the University of Wisconsin, were both serving as "revolving doors," especially for senior faculty. At Michigan, for example, among forty-three professors appointed between 1845-1868, twenty-three left, typically after relatively short tenures. While several were clearly victims of internecine strife, at least ten left for a better academic position.[63] Thus, by the eve of the Civil War, interinstitutional mobility was progressively becoming associated with academic careers.

These evolving disciplinary commitments were also extending in the 1850s to faculty extra-institutional service. Indeed, the bare outline of an external career based more on disciplinary expertise, experience as educator, and role as proponent of culture rather than proponent of religion was becoming discernible. At Brown, for example, the immediate pre-Civil War period saw the first instance of a faculty member using their expertise in the service of state government in the appointment of a professor of chemistry to head the Rhode Island Board of Weights and Measures. By the end of the Civil War, the proportion of the Brown faculty involved in itinerant preaching and other clerical activities dropped from over a third at mid-century to one-eighth. While nearly three quarters of the faculty remained involved in civic and community affairs, the nature of that involvement had changed. Only a single faculty member was directly involved in elective politics while the majority were involved in distinctively cultural, academic, and education-related activities such as membership on boards of education, holding office in national honor societies, art and historical societies, and state and federal government commissions.[64] At Bowdoin, by the eve of the Civil War, we find a majority of faculty (57 percent) engaged in extra institutional roles as specialists, educators, and men of letters. Parker Cleveland offered public lectures on minerology and Alpheus Packard on education; President Woods and Professor Packard were engaged in commissioned writing for the Maine Historical Society; and Thomas Upham was writing pamphlets for the American Peace Association.[65]

Other institutions lagged a decade or more behind in this evolution of the external career. At Dartmouth, as late as 1851 three quarters of the faculty continued to participate actively in the community as preachers, licentiates, or ordained ministers and as civic boosters. By the late 1870s, however, the proportion of faculty engaged in clerical activities had dropped precipitously to 15 percent, while more than half were engaged significantly in their fields of specialization.[66] At Wisconsin, by the early 1870s, professors at the University were being called upon to head the state geological survey.[67]

The disciplinary and discipline-based external career also gave rise to two significant, interrelated changes in the institutional career pattern during the 1860s and 1870s. New roles as instructor and assistant professor were established and forged into a career sequence that at once gave shape to the academic career and regulated the movement through the junior ranks to a professorship. Concomitantly, the junior faculty ranks were expanded and professionalized. Together, these developments served to integrate into a single structure the dual career track system of junior and senior faculty that had characterized the early part of the nineteenth century.

The instructorship and the assistant professorship actually made their appearance quite early at some institutions. As early as 1821, one-third of the Harvard faculty were serving in instructorships.[68] The first instructors were appointed at Yale in 1824 and during the 1830s in arts and sciences, at Michigan in 1843, and at Brown in 1844. The first assistant professors were appointed at Brown in 1835, at Yale in 1842, and at Michigan in 1857.[69] Despite the early precedents, these new roles did not take hold for several decades even at these trend-setting institutions (with the exception of Harvard) and for an even longer period at the more insulated institutions such as Dartmouth, Bowdoin, and Williams. Thus, at Yale, only four instructors were appointed during the two decades following the first appointment; and only four additional assistant professors were appointed during the three decades following the first appointment.[70] Similarly, at Brown and Michigan, the instructorship languished until the 1860s and the 1870s, respectively; while the assistant professorship languished until the 1890s and the 1880s, respectively.[71] At Dartmouth, Bowdoin, and Williams, it was not until the 1860s that these roles first appeared and several decades later until they were firmly entrenched.[72]

These new roles represented a significant departure from the "tutorship" for their incumbents were appointed within a specific department of instruction and were likely to be the products of specialized training. Moreover, their appearance significantly transformed the tutorship, leading to its demise at some institutions (at Brown in the 1840s and at Williams in the early 1860s) and to its transformation into a junior instructorship at others. At Yale in the 1830s, for example, tutors began to be assigned to departments of instruction.[73] But, for at least several decades, they were not equivalent to their modern counterpart in at least one fundamental respect; they did not serve in a majority of cases as feeders to the full professorship. At both Harvard and Yale, it was not until the 1860s that a substantial proportion of junior faculty were advanced to a professorship (25 percent at Harvard and just over a third at Yale) and not until the decade of the 1870s that a bare majority of the junior faculty were advanced.[74] Similar patterns prevailed at Brown and, even more dramatically, at Michigan. Between 1845-1868, only one of eight junior faculty at Michigan had risen to a full professorship; a single decade later 80 percent were promoted.[75]

During the decade immediately following the Civil War, the junior faculty role, then, had changed from a temporary, dead-end appointment to the first step in the academic career ladder. At the very same time, the ranks of the junior faculty were undergoing their most rapid expansion and their largest increase in professionalization. By 1880, junior faculty outnumbered their senior colleagues at Harvard by a ratio of 8 to 5, compared to a ration of 3 to 2 a decade earlier, had attained full parity with senior faculty at Michigan, compared with a 2 to 8 ratio a decade earlier, and were on their way to parity at Brown, constituting 40 percent of the faculty in contrast to less than a third a decade earlier.[76] They were increasingly entering their academic careers directly from graduate training in their specialty and moving from junior appointments at other institutions. At least at Harvard and Brown, they held as highly developed a professional orientation, measured by McCaughey's *Professional Index*, as their senior colleagues.

The modern academic career had come of age.

Discussion and Implications

The foregoing analysis suggests a four stage model in the evolution of the academic role by the late nineteenth century at the sample institutions: (1) the emergence of an institutional career within the matrix of the traditional professions in the latter half of the eighteenth century; (2) the rapid expansion and consolidation of that institutional career in the first quarter of the nineteenth century, at least for the permanent senior faculty; (3) the gradual professionalization of academic faculties along specialized, disciplinary lines beginning in the second and accelerating in the third quarter of the nineteenth century; (4) the formalization of the institutional career progression through the ranks, beginning in the third and accelerating in the last quarter of the nineteenth century.

This model and the data upon which it is built suggest a number of generalizations about the historical development of the American academic professions. First, they suggest that to the extent that the epithet

"revolution" may be applied to the history of academic people, the first such revolution probably ought to be located at the turn of the nineteenth century. It was then that American college faculties were transformed from "revolving doors" to "permanent" bodies of careerists; and it was then that we find the first explosive growth in the size of permanent academic faculties. Second, they suggest a series of generalizations about professionalization in the nineteenth century. The process of professionalization of college faculties as self-conscious, disciplinary specialists was well underway for several decades preceding the Civil War and the emergence of the American university in the last quarter of the nineteenth century. The transformation was a gradual one; and in at least two respects it proceeded quite unevenly. Internally, different dimensions of "professionalization" proceeded according to somewhat different timetables, i.e., participation in learned societies and in specialized scholarly publication, and, to a lesser extent, the ascendance of disciplinary over institutional commitments (as reflected in inter-institutional mobility) temporally preceded the large scale shift to specialized disciplinary training and the direct movement from graduate training to full-time academic work. Interinstitutionally, these developments began and gathered momentum at different times at different institutions — quite early, for example, at Harvard and Bowdoin, considerably later at Williams and Dartmouth. Finally, the data clearly suggest that professionalization temporally preceded by at least several decades the formalization of the modern institutional career track.

That the academic faculties examined here were engaging in specialized, scholarly publication and in the activities of scientific associations on a significant scale *before* they were seeking and receiving specialized training on a similar scale and moving from such training directly to full-time academic posts suggests the situation of a rapidly transforming profession awaiting an institutional structure within which to express its new ideals and orientations. Similarly, that professionalization preceded by several decades the formalization of the institutional career track again suggests a newly arrived group awaiting an institutional structure within which to operate. And indeed, the evidence gleaned from McCaughey's in-depth analysis of nineteenth century Harvard,[77] as well as the accounts of faculty uprisings against the ideals and organization of the "old time" college at Williams in 1868-1872 and at Dartmouth in 1881,[78] would appear to support the proposition that the growing pressures from rapidly professionalizing academic faculties were indeed a major impetus to the transformation of American higher education in the last quarter of the nineteenth century.

Having hazarded the above generalizations, it must be emphasized that both the model presented here and the inferences drawn must, of course, remain tentative. They are based on the experiences of a half dozen of the leading, eastern institutions, with the exception of Michigan. To what extent are these experiences duplicated by the younger, western institutions such as Union compare with more classical institutions such as Yale and Williams? Questions such as these suggest that sound historical conclusions about academic professionalization must await comparable data on a more representative sample of institutional types and the internal comparisons that such representativeness will allow.

Quite beyond the issue of generalizability is that of explanation. How are we to account for the emergence of the institutional career during the first quarter of the nineteenth century? How much of it may be attributable to changes in the ministerial career in New England? How are we to account for the uneven development of professionalization both across institutions and across various dimensions of professionalization? While broad explanations can certainly be located in the major social and intellectual transformations occurring in nineteenth century America, the question remains as to how these broad changes were experienced at different types of institutions and reflected in the diverse conditions of academic employment. And answers to this latter question, too, must await the generation of comparable data sets on faculties at a greater diversity of institutional types.[79]

NOTES

1. Wilson Smith, "The Teacher in Puritan Culture," *Harvard Educational Review* 36 (1966): 394-411.

2. William Carrell, "American College Professors: 1750-1800," *History of Education Quarterly*, 8 (1968): 289-305.

3. Robert McCaughey, "The Transformation of American Academic Life: Harvard University 1821-1892," *Perspectives in American History*, 8 (1974): 239-334; Marilyn Tobias, "Old Dartmouth on Trial: The Transformation of the Academic Community in Nineteenth Century America" (Ph.D. dissertation, New York University, 1977), published by the New York University Press, 1982; and Allan Creutz, "From College Teacher to University Scholars: The Evolution and Professionalization of Academics at the University of Michigan, 1841-1900" (Ph.D. dissertation, University of Michigan, 1981).

4. They range from McCaughey's more limited focus on the timing of changes in various contemporary indicators of academic professionalization (e.g., the incidence of specialized training and publication for disciplinary audiences) between 1820-1892 to Tobias' and Creutz's broader focus on the impetus and timing of changes in faculty self concepts, ideologies and career patterns during the latter half of the nineteenth century as these both reflected and shaped the intellectual and social milieu of nineteenth century America.

5. Harvard surely had to be located at the "pinnacle" of the system. Michigan was subject to unusual internecine strife among faculty and between faculty and the Board of Regents in the early years and grew more explosively than most institutions in the last three decades of the nineteenth century. Dartmouth lingered under the paternalistic leadership of President Bartlett until 1893.

6. Both Smith, *Harvard Educational Review*, and Carrell, *History of Educational Quarterly*, limit their analysis to data for the pre-1800 period. McCaughey, *Perspectives in American History*, collected data beginning in 1821, while Tobias and Creutz collected data on faculty in the second half of the nineteenth century.

7. In the cases of Brown, Bowdoin, and Yale, historical catalogues were employed to collect data comparable to McCaughey, *Perspectives in American History*, and Tobias on faculty at five points in time: 1800, 1820, 1845, 1869, 1880. See *Historical Catalogue of Brown University, 1764-1904* (Providence, Rhode Island: Brown University, 1905), Alpheus Packard, ed., *History of Bowdoin College* (Boston: James Ripley Osgood and Company, 1882), and *Historical Register of Yale University, 1701-1937* (New Haven, Connecticut: Yale University Press, 1939). The variables for which data were collected included: geographic origin, source of baccalaureate degree, the timing and nature of post-baccalaureate training, the nature of previous non-academic employment, age and years of teaching experience at time of initial appointment and at appointment to professorships, academic rank, years at focal institution, nature and timing of any subsequent occupation, nature and extent of publication activity, nature and extent of involvement with extra-institutional organization (e.g., historical and literary societies, later disciplinary organizations and local and state government), and scores on two indices developed by McCaughey, *Perspectives in American History* (The *Outsider Index* assessing the relationship of the focal individual to the institution previous to initial appointment and a *Professional Index* assessing the extent of professionalization as reflected in post-baccalaureate training, career pattern, publication/research activity, and associational involvements). A similar analysis was also undertaken for the University of Michigan faculty in 1845, 1869, and 1880, based on *The General Catalogue of the University of Michigan, 1837-1911* (Ann Arbor, Michigan: University of Michigan, 1912).

In addition to these more systematic efforts, a variety of secondary sources, ranging from standard histories of higher education to institutional histories to memoirs, were mined for data on developments related to faculty. These included: Laurence R. Veysey, *The Emergence of The American University* (Chicago: University of Chicago Press, 1965); Merle Curti, *The University of Wisconsin: 1848-1925* (Madison, Wisconsin: University of Wisconsin Press, 1949); Samuel Eliot, *A Sketch of the History of Harvard College* (Boston: Little and Brown, 1848); Samuel E. Morison, *Harvard College in the Seventeenth Century* (Cambridge, Massachusetts: Harvard University Press, 1936); Frederick Rudolph, *Mark Hopkins and the Log* (New Haven: Yale University Press, 1956); Thomas J. Wertenbaker, *Princeton 1746-1896* (Princeton, New Jersey: Princeton University Press, 1946); and Timothy Dwight, *Memories of Yale Life and Men 1845-1899* (New York: Dodd, Mead and Company, 1903).

Given the convenient, non-representative character of the institutional sample and the consequent limitations imposed on valid historical generalizations, no attempt was made to present the actual data in tabular form. Rather, it was decided to view the data as preliminary and suggestive and introduce it as necessary into the narrative.

8. In-depth institutional developments are, of course, covered in McCaughey, *Perspectives in American History*, Tobias, "Old Dartmouth on Trial," and Creutz, "From College Teacher to University Scholar." For interpretations of the cultural/social matrix of

9. Donald Light, *et. al.*, "The Impact of the Academic Revolution on Faculty Careers," *ERIC-AAHE Research Reports*, 10 (1972).

10. W. H. Cowley, *Professors, Presidents, and Trustees*, ed., Donald T. Williams (San Francisco: Jossey-Bass, 1980), pp. 18-19. Also personal communications from Allan O. Pfnister.

11. Morison, pp. 51-53.

12. Smith, *Harvard Educational Review*, shows that during the period 1685-1701 the tenure of Harvard tutors averaged 6.4 years and increased to 9.0 years during the first half of the eighteenth century.

13. Carrell, *History of Education Quarterly*, pp. 289-290.

14. At Harvard, an institutional career was provided by the appointment of "permanent" tutors as well as professors. The tutorship became institutionalized there in a way it was not at Harvard's sister institutions, largely, it would appear, as a result of the precedent set by the fifty-five year tutorship of Henry Flynt during the first half of the eighteenth century (Smith, *Harvard Educational Review* 36, pp. 400-401).

15. When endowment funds were insufficient for the full maintenance of a professorship, the funds were allowed to accumulate for as much as one or two decades before filling the position. See Eliot, p. 107.

16. *Historical Register of Yale University*, pp. 55-56, 229 (Day), 244 (Dwight), 386 (Meigs), 477 (Silliman).

17. *Historical Catalogue of Brown University*, p. 36.

18. Wertenbaker, p. 50.

19. Cowley, p. 80.

20. Carrell, *History of Education Quarterly*, pp. 294-295.

21. *Historical Catalogue of Brown University*, pp. 36, 74 (Maxey), 77 (Messer), 518 (Howell), 528 (Fobes). Also Eliot, pp. 41-44, 61, 72, 96.

22. Carrell, *History of Education Quarterly*, pp. 296-298.

23. *Ibid.*

24. *Historical Register of Yale University*, p. 63, 202 (Clap), 223 (Daggett), 229 (Day), 244 (Dwight), 386 (Meigs), 477 (Silliman). Also *Historical Catalogue of Brown University*, p. 36.

25. Carrell, *History of Education Quarterly*, pp. 298-300.

26. *Ibid.*

27. Smith, *Harvard Educational Review*, pp. 402-405.

28. *Historical Catalogue of Brown University*, pp. 36-37.

29. *Historical Register of Yale University*, pp. 54-56.

30. Frederick Rudolph, *The American College and University* (New York: Vintage Books, 1962), pp. 51-55.

31. McCaughey, *Perspectives in American History*, pp. 316-317; *The Historical Register of Yale University*, pp. 57, 63, 229 (Day), 260-261 (Fisher, Fitch), 281 (Goodrich), 328 (Ives), 342 (Kingsley), 345 (Knight), 403 (Munson), 477 (Silliman), 484 (Smith); *The Historical Catalogue of Brown University*, pp. 36-37. Even at institutions such as Bowdoin, where the ratio of professors to tutors remained the same, appointments during the 1820s gave the permanent professors ascendance (Packard, pp. 125-136).

32. Eliot, p. 107.

33. *Ibid; Historical Register of Yale University*, pp. 56-57, 244 (Dwight), 386 (**Meigs**), 229 (Day), 260-261 (Fisher, Fitch), 281 (Goodrich), 328 (Ives), 342 (Kingsley), 345 (Knight), 403 (Munson), 477 (Silliman), 484 (Smith).

34. Carrell, *History of Education Quarterly*, pp. 296-300.

35. Daniel Calhoun, *Professional Lives in America* (Cambridge, Mass.: Harvard University Press, 1965), p. 166, cited by Tobias, "Old Dartmouth on Trial," pp. 33-34.

36. Carrell, *History of Education Quarterly*, p. 297.

37. Among faculty at the "leading" institutions, over three-fourths had been sired by old New England families. Ecclesiastical and business family backgrounds continued to predominate, although the proportion of farm families had begun to increase. And Protestantism continued as the professorial religion, although some of the "lower" Protestant denominations, e.g., Baptists and Methodists, were now rivaling the Presbyterians, the Congregationalists, and Unitarians for hegemony, (v. Veysey, pp. 300-301).

38. Calhoun, pp. 166-168; John Brubacher and Willis Rudy, *Higher Education in Transition* (New York: Harper and Row, 1968), pp. 115-118; Richard Hofstadter and Walter P. Metzger, *The Development of Academic Freedom in the United States* (New York: Columbia University Press, 1955), pp. 320-363.

39. Hofstadter and Metzger, pp. 374-378; Veysey, pp. 121-133, 158-179; Wolfe, pp. 5-14, 33-63, 85-91; and Alexandra Oleson and John Voss, eds., *The Organization of Knowledge in Modern America, 1860-1920* (Baltimore: Johns Hopkins University Press, 1979), pp. 3-18, 285-312.

40. Bernard Berelson, *Graduate Education in the United States* (New York: McGraw Hill, 1960), pp. 14-15.

41. While four out of ten Harvard professors had studied in Europe, at least three of these had done so on Harvard stipends provided after their initial appointment as a means of preparation for their professorship. See McCaughey, *Perspectives in American History*, pp. 250.

42. *Ibid; Historical Catalogue of Brown University*, p. 69 (Drowne), 77 (Messer), 83 (Burges), 85 (Park), 117 (Adams), 212 (Peck), 122 (Brooks), 126 (Mann), 518 (Howell), 541 (Ingalls); Packard, pp. 125-136.

43. *Ibid.* These mobility patterns represent no significant change from those in 1800.

academic professionalization, the reader should consult Tobias and Creutz as well as Burton J. Bledstein, *The Culture of Professionalism* (New York: W. Norton and Company, 1976) and Dale Wolfle, *The Home of Science* (New York: McGraw-Hill, 1972).

44. All of these were "professional" scientists. See McCaughey, *Perspectives in American History*, p. 254; Packard, pp. 126-129; *Historical Catalogue of Brown University*, pp. 133-134; *Historical Register of Yale University*, p. 477.

45. Packard, pp. 125-136; Tobias, pp. 29-32, 254; *Historical Catalogue of Brown University*, pp. 69 (Drowne), 77 (Messer), 83 (Burges), 85 (Park), 117 (Adams), 121 (Peck), 122 (Brooks), 126 (Mann), 518 (Howell), 541 (Ingalls).

46. McCaughey, *Perspective in American History*, pp. 250 and 330-332. While we use the term "outsiders" here and subsequently to describe these appointments, it should be noted that virtually all of these outsiders at Harvard and elsewhere were in a fundamental sense "insiders" as well: i.e., they were returning after an hiatus to their baccalaureate *alma mater*.

47. Yale di... ot appoint an instructor until 1824 and that in law. None were appointed in arts and sciences until the 1830s. At Brown, the first instructor was appointed in 1844.

48. While it is true that two of Harvard's ten professors in 1820 had served as Harvard instructors, this was clearly a notable exception rather than the rule. Indeed, none of the five instructors in 1820 went on to Harvard professorships. See McCaughey, *Perspectives in American History*, pp. 250, 317.

49. *Historical Register of Yale University*, pp. 57-58.

50. *Historical Catalogue of Brown University*, p. 38.

51. *Ibid*, p. 170 (Lincoln), 156 (Chace), 167 (Jewett), 183 (Boise), 192 (Harkness), 223 (Diman).

52. Packard, p. 431 (Goodwin), 743 (Young), 135 (Rockwood).

53. *Historical Register of Yale University*, p. 507 (Thacher), 418 (Packard).

54. Tobias, pp. 28, 53-54, 249.

55. Rudolph, *Mark Hopkins and the Log*, p. 128.

56. McCaughey, *Perspectives in American History*, p. 330.

57. Packard, pp. 125-136.

58. The *Professional Index* was developed by McCaughey, *Perspectives in American History*, pp. 125-136, in his study of the nineteenth century Harvard faculty. It taps primarily two dimensions of faculty professionalization: specialized disciplinary training and publication in a specialty.

59. McCaughey, *Perspectives in American History*, pp. 262-263, 326.

60. Included in this latter group were a founder and future president of the American Philological Association; a future vice president of the American Chemical Society; a founder and future vice president of the American Association for the Advancement of Science as well as a founder of the National Academy of Sciences. *Historical Catalogue of Brown University*, pp. 133 (Caswell), 156 (Chace), 159 (Gammell), 170 (Lincoln), 183 (Boise), 192 (Harkness), 223 (Diman), 270 (Appleton).

61. Packard, pp. 431 (Goodwin), 134 (Hitchcock), 287 (Stowe).

62. *Historical Catalogue of Brown University*, pp. 183 (Boise), 195 (Day), 207 (Jillson).

63. See Creutz, pp. 55-64, for details on faculty-Board of Regents conflicts. For mobility data, see *The General Catalogue of the University of Michigan*, pp. 6-9.

64. *Historical Catalogue of Brown University*, pp. 133 (Caswell), 156 (Chace), 159 (Gammell), 170 (Lincoln), 183 (Boise), 192 (Harkness), 223 (Diman), 270 (Appleton).

65. Packard, pp. 120-124, 126-129, 131-133, 188-190.

66. Tobias, p. 254.

67. Curti, p. 53.

68. McCaughey, *Perspectives in American History*, p. 317.

69. *The Historical Catalogue of Brown University*, pp. 54-55, 56-57; *The Historical Register of Yale University*, pp. 312 (Hitchcock), 507 (Thacher); *The General Catalogue of the University of Michigan*, pp. 19, 22.

70. *The Historical Register of Yale University*, pp. 148 (Bakewell), 514 (Townsend), 518 (Turner), 532 (Waterman), 290 (Hadley), 244 (Dwight), 418 (Packard), 446 (Richards).

71. *The Historical Catalogue of Brown University*, pp. 54-55, 56-61; *The General Catalogue of the University of Michigan*, pp. 19-20, 22-24.

72. Tobias, pp. 42-43, 246; Packard, pp. 743 (Young), 839; Rudolph, *Mark Hopkins and the Log*, pp. 52-53.

73. *The Historical Register of Yale University*, pp. 19, 54.

74. *Ibid.*, pp. 60-61; McCaughey, *Perspectives in American History*, pp. 316-321.

75. *The General Catalogue of the University of Michigan*, pp. 6-9.

76. *Ibid.*, pp. 6-12, 18-19, 22-23; McCaughey, *Perspectives in American History*, pp. 319-321; *The General Catalogue of Brown University*, pp. 52-53, 54, 57.

77. McCaughey, *Perspectives in American History*, pp. 239-332.

78. For Williams, see Rudolph, *Mark Hopkins and the Log*, pp. 221-233. For Dartmouth, see Tobias, pp. 2-3, 61-72.

79. I am grateful to an anonymous reviewer for raising some of these questions.

Freedom and Constraint in Eighteenth Century Harvard

Kathryn M. Moore

Collegiate life during the eighteenth century at Harvard was characterized by a developing consciousness of student freedom on the one hand and by an increasing elaboration of student governance procedures on the other. These countervailing forces formed the seedbed of impending change in the college. Using college records of laws, customs, and cases of student indiscipline, the analysis focuses on key elements inside and outside the college that affected the decision-making process.

Now that the campus turmoil of the 1960s is becoming historical artifact, it is possible to reflect upon the circumstances that gave rise to it and to seek commonalities in prior experience. One aspect, which an examination of the past may illuminate, is the influence of students on the collegiate decision-making process. As this paper will show, the relationship of Harvard College to its students during the eighteenth century poses a particularly interesting point of comparison. But before beginning it seems useful to point out that this essay is not attempting to show how the past is simply the present writ small; that is rank present-ism, but rather how one institution within the constraints of a particular time and set of circumstances set about to solve its problems in the governance of students. Such a "case study" has less to do with the decisions that were made and more to do with the decision-making process that ensued with the view that institutions of higher education are dynamic organizations whose responses to age-old problems are inevitably and critically keyed to the ecology of their time and place.

In order to appreciate the significance of the problems Harvard faced, some knowledge of earlier, seventeenth century student-college interaction at Harvard, as reflected in collegiate laws, customs, and records of student misconduct, is essential ([5]. See also [6, 7, 9, 10]). The system of student discipline developed as a support for the educational purpose of the college, which was to train up a select group of young men to assume leadership roles in the ministry and magistracy of the Puritan Commonwealth of Massachusetts. In order to accomplish this, every aspect of student life was subject to scrutiny and close supervision by the college officials. Those students whose behavior did not conform to college laws and customs were disciplined in a manner that was chosen deliberately to reinforce the objectives of the college.

Insofar as the college social system was designed to express an idea, that idea was the same as for the larger society: persons in superior positions to oneself were to be reverenced and obeyed. Not only was the catechism of the fifth commandment applicable, but the college laws and customs also specifically stated this policy.

Thus, disrespect or rebellion greatly compounded the seriousness of any crime because it reflected the student's adverse attitude toward the college authorities. Perverseness, stubbornness, or pride were particularly abhorrent to Puritan adults for such behavior revealed the student's sinful, wrathful inner state, the clear sign of an unregenerate soul.

Nevertheless, partly because of theological predispositions and partly because of the quasi-elect status of the students, much effort was expended in attempting to reform student offenders. Over time a fairly standardized ritual developed by which a student offender, regardless of his crime (above a certain minimum), could be examined "in all particulars," sentenced and punished. Usually the sentencing was a public event and was accompanied by the student's confession. If the confession was deemed sufficiently penitent, the original punishment was reduced or excused. Even students who were expelled could be (and were) readmitted upon petition and confession.

As far as can be determined by the records, cases of student misconduct in the seventeenth century were not numerous and were usually singular in nature in the sense that solitary students were convicted and, once punished, seldom repeated their offense or committed any other. Punishments reflected customary civil and ecclesiastic practice, which consisted largely of shaming techniques such as admonition and confession. In the case of a particularly heinous crime such as fornication, theft, or assault, the college officials resorted to corporal punishment or expulsion. Fines were used sparingly and for relatively minor offenses. In sum, student discipline was an integral part of the educative and socializing process in the college.

When John Leverett became president at the beginning of the eighteenth century, in 1708, he was fully cognizant of this system of discipline. Indeed, he had played an important role in perpetuating it during his long tenure as tutor and acting president from 1686 to 1697. Doubtless he expected the system to be carried forward virtually intact during his time as president. But as the "great riot" of 1708 quickly demonstrated [10, p. 475], "the new wine of the 18th century" was already pushing hard against the old bottles [10, pp. 86–87].

Another measurable force that began to make a difference was the increase in enrollment which had been building slowly since 1686, but which took a sudden upturn in 1713. Morison noted its source and effect:

> The increase came largely from the seaports which reaped the first harvests from land speculation and West Indian commerce, and the rum business; and where the influence of court manners was most quickly felt. The new crop of young men came to be made gentlemen, not to study [7, p. 60].

The impact of these new students and these rather different intentions was both immediate and cumulative. Characterized by one historian as "a weakening sense of sin" [8, pp. 431–52], the lawbreaking that occurred took forms rather different from what had been expressed in the previous century. First, there was an increase in the sheer numbers of misdemeanors. Second, there was more evidence of youthful high spirits such as parties and pranks. Third, there was an increase in the kinds of crimes that increasing affluence encouraged; namely, debauching and petty thefts. Finally, there was a greater incidence of group misconduct. The latter two forms are commented on below.

Affluence manifested itself among the scholars in more attention to, and expenditures for, the items of a comfortable life. This included more and better clothing, books, sports equipment, and supplementary condiments such as wine and victuals [3]. All of these items appear to have attracted the covetous eyes of college thieves. Moreover, beginning with Leverett's term, Harvard became increasingly more crowded, and as a result numerous students were obliged to live out while those who resided at the college were expected to double up. With the crowding, the affluence, and the greater numbers of students coming and going about the college residences, it was predictable that thefts would occur.

Debauchery of one sort or another was another manifestation of affluence. Students spent large amounts of time and money in drinking, eating, and entertaining with others, male and female, both at college and off the premises. Drunkenness was rampant and other crimes fed upon it including fighting, lying, swearing, and card playing. In the class of 1728, for example, twenty-two students were variously punished for "nocturnal expeditions" and "entertainments" beginning with stealing and roasting geese and ending with drunken routs [10, pp. 70, 386]. Gambling was the primary vice of the classes from 1731–40; over eighty-five students were convicted and punished for that crime alone [10, chaps. 9, 10]. Over and above the students convicted of drinking and gambling, approximately twenty-five members of the classes of 1750–60 were convicted of misconduct in chapel, profaning the Sabbath, and other impieties [10, chaps. 13, 14]. Finally, several students of the class of 1766 and 1767 were sent home to be cured of "the Itch," the result of "associating with, countenancing, [and] encouraging one or more lewd women kept by the students [10, pp. 487–88]. The students were restored after a mass confession on commencement eve.

Misconduct by groups of students was particularly unknown in the seventeenth century, in large part because the numbers of students remained so small. The largest classes before 1700 were those of 1690 and 1695, both of which numbered twenty-two. However, "in November 1718, there were a hundred and twenty-four students in residence, including *domini* studying for the M.A. and other resident graduates" [7, p. 59]. This was by far the largest number of students ever to attend Harvard at one time. Enrollments stayed high until the Revolution began when they fell away significantly and did not pick up again until the 1780s.

With the increase in enrollment came an increase in the number of students participating in illegal group activities, referred to at the time as routs or riots. Most of these eighteenth century riots were prompted by commencement revelries, Guy Fawkes' Day celebrations, or bad food (see [7, 1]). A famous one, the Bad Butter Rebellion of 1766, began as a complaint against bad food in the commons but escalated to a highly charged debate between the students, headed by the governor's son, and the board of overseers, headed by the governor, over the obligation to obey an unjust sovereign. The whole episode was shot through with obvious and ironic parallels with the rising political debates in the colony. In Harvard's case, the rebellion ended with a negotiated settlement in which the rebels signed a mass confession but received no other punishments [10, pp. 442, 486–87].

In addition to the increase in riots and routs, the records reveal that certain students repeated their crimes year after year and/or figured prominently in other misdeeds. Such repetitions and linkages indicate that from time to time cliques of students existed from whom much of the misconduct emanated. The members of these cliques often included the sons of the great families of Boston such as Winthrops, Brattles, and Saltonstalls, as well as the sons of the newly rich merchants and traders. Together they were often called by the epithet, "Boston rakes and blades" [7, 5]. Their notoriety was fostered not only by their lavish lifestyles but because they were ringleaders in many of the riots and other plots that were perpetrated during the century. For example, in 1720 a Winthrop and a Brattle were convicted with other young blades of taking part in a "great debauch" in one of the graduate's rooms [10, pp. 10–11, 446]. In 1735, the sons of a prominent colonel and a sea captain were the ringleaders of "the Gamesters at Cards" referred to earlier [10, pp. 606, 612]. While in 1766, Nathaniel Sparhawk, whose father was a merchant and member of the governor's council, was convicted on two occasions for leading his classmates in disorderly behavior and "tumultuous noise" [10, p. 234].

Not all the students participated in the general lawlessness. On occasion the more pious students banded together, "for mutual advancement in virtue and piety." These efforts were impelled in part, as Morison points out, by the need to protect themselves from the onslaughts and influence of their more licentious classmates' thievery and tormenting. As one such society stated in its preamble in 1728, "whereas Vice is Now Become Alamode and Rant Riot and Excess is Accounted the Height of Good Breeding and Learning. In Order therefore to Stem That Monstrous Tide of Impiety & Ignorance, the Philomusarian Club is formed" [10, p. 62]. Beginning in 1748 students could volunteer to inform against profanity among their fellows, and in 1767 following the Bad Butter Rebellion a number of these "volunteers" formed the Association for the Suppression of Vice [10, chaps. 12, 16]. A rough analysis of the membership of the volunteers indicates that approximately 50 percent became ministers, which is a greater percentage than in the general student body at the time (see [2, p. 554]). This is not to say these students were invariably blameless, but they did seem to confine themselves to minor offenses such as cider parties and card playing. They also tended to be older and come from less affluent families. These poor and pious students comprised about one quarter to a third of any given class and were the ballast of the student body. In addition to volunteering for certain duties, they were also appointed and paid to monitor their classmates' attendance at college functions, and it is from their ranks that many tutors were drawn. They were, in many respects, the epitome of the seventeenth century ideal of the Harvard scholar.

We must ask why Harvard officials tolerated students whose purposes were counter to their collegiate ideal and whose presence in sufficient numbers began to dominate and shift the character of the student body and thereby the college as a whole. The answer can be approached on two levels: first, from the perspective of the college vis-à-vis its external constituent environment, and second, from the perspective of its internal, educative environment.

In the face of this rising tide of lawlessness the college could have decided not to admit those who would be likely to commit such acts or, where forced to discipline students, could have made the punishments severe and permanent. Such strictness would have "purified the house" and returned it to its earlier, idealized character as a small but pious seminary much as Samuel Sewall or George Whitefield wanted and as Thomas Clap would attempt to create at Yale. The college had financial difficulties for most of the century, despite increased enrollment, but it is not clear that it had to admit everyone who applied. There is some evidence that certain families refused to send their sons because of the growing "bad reputation" [10, p. 41]. We can assume, then, that Harvard might have gained financially if it had cracked down on the licentiousness and, by implication, the Boston rakes and blades, more severely. But the college did not elect that course. For the most part there was marked willingness to accept everyone who applied, particularly the sons of notable families, and to make every effort to see that the young men received their degrees, misdeeds to the contrary notwithstanding.

Leverett was a key figure in setting this course. Intellectually enlightened and theologically liberal, he "gloried in the fact that Harvard graduated not only learned ministers, but scholars, judges, physicians, soldiers . . . , merchants, and simple farmers" [7, p. 60]. Morever, Leverett was thoroughly enmeshed in what has been called "the intercommunity of the learned," which bound the Harvard faculty and the Boston elite together with ties of friendship, intellect, and shared interest, most important of which was Harvard itself [4, p. 88].

Internally, however, matters were not so harmonious. It was one thing to associate with the refined and learned citizens of Boston but it was quite another to attempt to educate their wealthy, headstrong, and hellbent sons, particularly if the values and modes of inculcation had not changed appreciably from the time of their father's education. That is to say, although the college officials were willing to admit the "new crop" of young men, they expected to achieve their education in ways virtually unchanged from the premises of the previous century. Examples of this adherence to the old ways was evident in the cases of discipline. For example, in December 1714, Leverett recorded the following episode:

The Crimes of Moody and Gray junior sophisters were taken into Consideration . . . and after . . . Considerable debate upon what punishment Should be inflicted on the guilty Criminals, It was agreed . . . . That

> Expulsion was the least and lowest manifestation by which the Corporation could show their resentments of the Outrage Committed by the Criminals . . . Mr. Flynt and Mr. Holioke declared they did not come up to Such Severity, but Submitted. [10, p. 145].

The following day the expulsion ceremony was carried out:

> In the College Hall. The President after Morning Prayer, the Fellows Masters of Art, Bachelors of Art, and the Several Classes of the Undergraduates being present, after a full opening of the Crimes of Moody and Gray, a pathetic Admonition of them, and solemn obtestation of Expulsion against the said Moody and Gray, Order'd their Names to be rent of the Tables, and them to depart the Hall [10].

The proceeding against Moody and Gray is characteristic of previous times in two respects. First, and most important, the statement calling the expulsion "the least and lowest manifestation by which the Corporation could show their resentment of the Outrage Committed by Criminals," illustrates the continuing intimate tone of the indictments. "Resentment" and "outrage" are words which denote rather personal emotions, and such diction implies that the students had violated the rules of a personal and privileged community, while the expulsion ceremony itself is virtually identical to those conducted forty and fifty years earlier.

The tension of transition is also evident in this particular case in that it was a crime committed by more than one scholar, and there is obvious evidence of debate among the officials, some of whom, Flynt and Holyoke, desired a more lenient punishment.[1]

Another example of this desire to perpetuate earlier disciplinary forms occurred in 1761 when the board of overseers decided that the use of fines was not a sufficiently effective deterrent to crime, being primarily a tax on the parents rather than the students. They, therefore, decided to reduce the use of fines and to return to a greater use of public and private admonitions and confessions and notifications to parents [9, pp. 135–36].

As the previous case illustrates, the board of overseers was the principal policy-making body. During the eighteenth century it authorized several visitation committees from among its members to inspect all aspects of the college. Not infrequently policy (and practice) related to student discipline was affected. For example, in the summer of 1723, the board of overseers, spurred on by its more conservative members, decided "that a visitation of the College would very much serve the interests of religion and learning in that society" [9, p. 317]. Judge Sewall, Leverett's arch critic, was appointed chairman of the visitation committee, which drew up ten articles proposing the matters to be investigated. Of these ten, "three had reference to the general conduct of the College; and seven, exclusive reference to its religious and moral condition; indicating very distinctly the points on which there existed, or there was a disposition to create, suspisions" [9]. Specifically, Article 4 asked: "What is the state of the College as to the morals of the youth" [9].

The committee made its visit immediately and reported its findings on October 9, 1723. Its conclusions regarding Article 4 were:

That although there is a considerable number of virtuous and studious youth in the College, yet there has been a practice of several immoralities; particularly stealing, lying, swearing, idleness, picking of locks, and too frequent use of strong drink: which immoralities, it is feared still continue in the College, notwithstanding the faithful endeavours of the rulers of the House to suppress them [9, p. 319].

From the catalogue of "immoralities" cited by the committee it would seem that Leverett had made his records available to them; they could not have observed all that activity in one visit. Moreover, the committee was apparently unable to blame any of the college officers for failing to police the college. One wishes the committee had elaborated upon its conclusions as to the source of the immoralities. Was it imputed to the impious and unschooled background of the scholars, the temper of the times, or perhaps God's disfavor with the college and even the colony? No such claims were made. However, the overseers did appoint a new committee to undertake a revision of the college laws, doubtless in the hope that more stringent or more elaborate laws would help to remedy the situation. However, the revision was of no immediate help because it was continued intermittently for the next ten years before arriving at a final form.

The other item of interest to us here is the visitation committee's acknowledgement of the different population of students who inhabited the college. As the committee conceded, a "considerable number" of the students were "virtuous and studious," while the immoralities of the few were reasonably well constrained. Nevertheless, the committee in one of its other findings also noted that "the scholars too generally spend too much of Saturday evenings in one another's Chambers; and that the Freshmen, as well as others, are seen in great numbers going into town, on Sabbath mornings, to provide breakfasts" [9, p. 320]. What the committee undoubtedly was referring to was the enaction of one phase of the college customs, errand-running for the upperclassmen. However, it is indicative of the change in lifestyle of the entire society that the committee spoke so mildly about this custom which to their own fathers would have been a gross violation of the Sabbath.

In 1755 the overseers again appointed a committee "to examine the students" regarding "great disorders . . . lately . . . committed." The committee condemned the students involved and refused to accept their appeals for restoration because "their petitions did not express a just sense of the evil nature and pernicious tendency of the crimes" [9, pp. 90-92]. This case is also an excellent example of the propensity of the overseers to reach into the direct administration of the college. Such action was understandably the bane of the president and tutors on several occasions.

Taken from the perspective of the students, the persistent and increasing amount of illegal activity appears not to have been revolutionary in intent in the sense of being designed to overthrow the college government. Ordinarily the students did not challenge the right of the college to make laws governing their conduct, but rather acknowledged the existence of the laws by breaking them with regularity and holding the officials to their obligation to enforce the laws. Moreover, the students appear to have expected to render a certain accounting for their misconduct so long as it did not involve physical abuse or truly permanent exile and so long as their dignity was left reasonably intact. From the distance of two centuries this "silent agreement" takes on the outline of an elaborate game or ritual, the rules of which are revealed by their mockery or breach. For example, students who are expelled were customarily readmitted after a decent interval and a humble petition. The day of return was often treated with mock ceremony by the students, and the culprit became the class hero. In another instance the "rules" of a criminal proceeding are revealed by the student who presented himself at chapel to be convicted and sentenced. The student thereupon rendered a "humble confession," but when his sentence was not mitigated as was the custom, he walked out [10, pp. 389–90, 33–34, 153–54, 112–13]. Finally, there is the example of the Bad Butter Rebellion whereby a student committee and a college committee negotiated the terms of the settlement [10, pp. 442, 486–87].

Historians have long pointed out that a growing prosperity was one of the greatest forces for change in New England's Puritan society. Prosperity meant not only great wealth for a few families but also comfortable living for the many; it meant settled towns, permanent roads, bustling, growing populations, and relative security from Indians, starving times, and foreign persecutions, and by the end of the seventeenth century this time had arrived in Massachusetts. By the time of the election of John Leverett as president of Harvard in 1708, the effects of the shift to an elite, mercantile society were also manifest in the college in the form of new students and new modes of behavior.

The presence of these new elements posed a severe problem in governance for Leverett and his successors. From Harvard's founding, the president and tutors had been appointed to uphold the philosophy of the college concerning piety and right conduct as well as liberal learning. Misconduct was to be taken seriously because of the implied challenge to the purposes and authority of the college. And discipline, when it followed, was designed deliberately to right the balance toward the college goals. The increase in the number of students and acts of misconduct that struck the college in the 1720s was evidence that a sufficiently large and continuous student subculture had grown up as a counter force to the immediate government and traditional purposes. The presence of this "subculture" did much to set the tone of college life for the students who participated in it and much to set the limits of freedom and constraint in which the college and all its members shared. By the midpoint of the century these students had become a prinicpal if not predominant force. Such influence was tolerated for reasons that set Harvard apart from the general trend toward a narrowly secular and pious education.

¹Holyoke became president in 1737. He served for thirty-two years and died in office. He was noted for his leniency toward students who were even more active than Leverett's.

LITERATURE CITED

1. Bevis, A. M. *Diets and Riots: An Interpretation of the History of Harvard University.* Boston: Marshall Jones Co., 1936.

2. Cremin, L. *American Education: The Colonial Experience.* New York: Harper and Row, 1970.

3. Foster, M. S. *"Out of Smalle Beginnings . . .": An Economic History of Harvard College in the Puritan Period, 1636–1712.* Cambridge: Belknap Press, 1962.

4. Lipset, S. M. and D. Riesman. *Education and Politics at Harvard.* New York: McGraw-Hill, 1975.

5. Moore, K. M. "Old Saints and Young Sinners: A Study of Student Discipline at Harvard College, 1636–1724." Unpublished dissertation, University of Wisconsin, 1972.

6. Morison, S. E. *Harvard College in the Seventeenth Century.* Cambridge: Harvard University Press, 1936.

7. _____. *Three Centuries of Harvard.* Cambridge: Harvard University Press, 1936.

8. Parkes, H. B. "Morals and Law Enforcement in Colonial New England." *New England Quarterly.* 3, pp. 431–52.

9. Qunicy, J. *History of Harvard University.* 2 vols. Cambridge: John Owen, 1840.

10. Shipton, C. K. *Sibley's Harvard Graduates.* Vols. 1–27. Boston: Massachusetts Historical Society, 1935–1975.

*This paper was presented in a slightly different form at the National Conference of the American Educational Research Association, Division F, Washington, D.C. in April 1975.

KATHRYN MCDANIEL MOORE *is assistant professor of higher education, Cornell University.*

The Social Function of Eighteenth Century Higher Education

Phyllis Vine

SINCE the appearance of Bernard Bailyn's provocative essay, *Education in the Forming of American Society*, scholars have been acknowledging their debt to him with the most enduring form of flattery: they have heeded his call for a re-examination of the meaning of education it American society. In the years since his work appeared students have rewritten the history of different schools, of eminent educators, and of the host of goals and purposes for education. (1) Yet, in an important way some of the questions raised by Bailyn's work still have not been addressed. What new socializing roles did educational institutions perform as the family shed itself of old functions after 1700? This essay will attempt to deal with that question as it inquires into the social function of eighteenth-century college education.

The rhetoric of educators, the hopes of parents, and the behavior of students indicate that a changed social function for education emerged after the 1740s. Educators perceived a moral crisis sweeping all of society and laid the blame to improper training within the family. They pinned their hopes for social stability on a pacific, orderly generation of youth. Parents recognized the increased difficulty in transmitting to their sons the advantages of class and wealth which could then be applied to leading a heterogeneous society. The concerns of each group intersected to project the college into a new role in which it would be endowed with greater responsibilities for training youth. Gradually the college was seen and came to serve as an institution which was best suited to inculcate virtue and promote social sponsorship among the privileged.

Three colleges which were founded in the 1740s and 1750s provide the basic evidence for this discussion: The College of New Jersey, 1746; The College of Philadelphia,—1754; and King's College, 1755. (2) Taken together they represent the most viable choices for higher education for the sons of the urban wealthy and landed gentry in the middle Atlantic region. Although founded by enclaves of denominational strength, each school promoted itself as having a colony wide appeal and clientele which would transcend sectarian differences in the process of promoting public well-being.

The combined impact of geographical mobility, cultural and political squabbles, religious declension and family reorientation led to fears that social disorder was growing and virtue and morality in decline in the middle of the eighteenth century. (3) Those who spoke to these issues directly, such as Princeton's President Aaron Burr, noted what must have been obvious to those who lived during the discord between Governor Lewis Morris and the elected New Jersey Assemblies in the 1740s. Burr lamented "contention between Governors and Assemblies,"

leadership could be attributed to a deficiency in the way youth were prepared for adult responsibilities. The bluntness with which a College of Philadelphia trustee, Richard Peters, identified the problem suggests how deeply this attitude ran. For Peters the problem could be firmly affixed to the mother. Mothers were too indulgent to discipline spirited youth. When a child misbehaved, rather than being corrected "he is taken into the arms of his mother, tenderly caressed, and commended for a boy of spirit." Peters lamented that the unhappy woman had no idea "what numerous evils will flow from this ill judged [sic] indulgence." (8) Akin to Puritans who feared that too much love could interfere with preparation for sainthood, educators in the eighteenth century thought too much indulgence created a generation of weak leaders. In contrast to their Puritan forebears who shifted youth from one family to another, or other critics who found fault with the family, these men created a new institution to further their aims.

Since they doubted the mother's ability to teach the child to behave with decisiveness and authority, it became important for boys to learn how to command authority from those who claimed to know: their teachers. Part of the explanation for educators' desire to remove youth from the influence of mothers and the family may be inferred from the importance of emulation in eighteenth-century pedagogical theory. As one educational theorist noted, "Without numbers there can be no emulation. It is founded on the love of distinction. In a private family this distinction cannot be acquired." Teachers had to be of "irreproachable characters; men whose lives should be a daily comment on their precepts," noted Philadelphia's Provost William Smith in the utopian tract about education in the mythical state of Mirania. (9) In short, emulation presumed that one learned how to behave by watching the example of others, and boys could receive the wrong impressions at home.

John Witherspoon's advice on correcting misbehaving children nicely illustrates these assumptions. In *Letters on Education* (1775) Witherspoon stressed the need for fathers, or other males, to enforce discipline in the home. "The mother or any female attendant," he said, "will necessarily be obliged to do things displeasing to the child." He warned his readers that the "mother or nurse should never presume to condole with the child, or show any signs of displeasure at his being crossed." On the contrary, both ought to give "every mark of approbation of their own submission to the same person." (10) Witherspoon spoke to the possibility that women would contradict the process by which boys learned how to work within a patriarchal society and a society in which those in power might have to make hard decisions.

and instructed his listeners to put aside "all private and selfish Designs." (4) William Livingston, the New York based social reformer and critic of the proposed Anglican domination of King's College, sounded the same theme. He proclaimed himself a "reformer of public abuses," and founded the *Independent Reflector* in 1752 to reveal the villainy of those who "owe their Prosperity to the Violation of their Trust." (5) Each man devoted his life to serving the public and each helped to create institutions which would foster public order. They represent a generation of leaders who were convinced that one way to stop the erosion of stability, or perhaps to permit social change to proceed according to their own visions, was through a collegiate education. They would take it upon themselves to teach individual male youth how to "serve the Public with honor to themselves and to their Country," (6) by educating them in institutions of higher learning.

With few exceptions, those who headed the eighteenth-century colleges started their careers as ministers. Moving from the church to the school, these men began sheperding young males through a course of learning and in the process they became ministers-of-education. Also, they questioned the ability of the family to produce the training needed during such times of stress. Heaping scorn upon the family, Aaron Burr of Princeton noted in 1755 that "almost all prevailing corruptions of the times" come from a "want of proper government and instruction in families." He proposed that "parents and governors of families . . . use their authority and influence, for the reforming [of] a corrupt and wicked generation." Burr represented one set of opinion about reforming youth by purifying the family; one of his successors at Princeton, John Witherspoon, represented another. In contrast to Burr, Witherspoon asked that youth be removed from the family. During a fundraising trip to the West Indies in the 1770s, the eminent Scottish educator argued that the greatest distance from home promoted the best education. In his experience, "those who come from the greatest distance, have in general behaved with most regularity." The reason was simple. Unable to rely on the support or comfort of familial ties, students were forced to behave within the guidelines established by the college. Also, educators at a distant college received less pressure from parents who wanted special considerations granted their sons. As Witherspoon told his listeners, it was necessary for students "to support a character, as they find themselves treated by their companions, teachers, and indeed all other persons, according to their behavior." (7)

Other educators fell somewhere between Burr's attitude of trying to reform the family and Witherspoon's of extricating the student from it. Wherever they stood, educators agreed that a low quality of public

In the college and away from the influence of mothers, Mirania's boys would learn what William Smith called "a manly turn of thought." These educators were apprehensive about future leaders acquiring unmanly traits. Ebenezer Pemberton, a trustee of the College of New Jersey wrote a promotional tract in 1760 in which he announced that methods of instruction attempted to prevent "idleness, effeminacy, vanity . . ." Aaron Burr noted that of the numerous vices sweeping the land, idleness and effeminacy along with discontent and contempt of authority/ "sap the very foundation of society." It was not only educators, however, who noted the potential problem with effeminacy. Edward Antill, the wealthy New Jersey patron of King's College, made clear that the ideal parent had no "false love or effeminate fondness for children." (11) Antill's remarks further emphasized the need for schools since few parents were ideal.

When speaking of manly characteristics educators placed their concerns within the eighteenth-century context of the debate between passion and reason. Reason was that agency or faculty which allowed for calculation and prudence in solving difficult problems; it directed man to his duty to God and to society. Its antithesis, passion, encompassed ambition, envy, covetousness, pride, selfishness, vanity, and indulgence—to name but a few. Both passion and reason resided in each person, and it was the goal of education to teach youth how to use reason to harness passion, how to behave properly. (12) One of the impulses which emanated from passions, and which was frequently attributed to parents, was that of indulgence. If parents had a tendency to indulge their children, women had a greater predisposition toward indulgence since they had not been taught how to control this passion. Reverend Richard Peters, the only minister who was a trustee at the College of Philadelphia, opened the Academy in 1751 with a sermon charging that parents' partiality made them "unfit to be trusted with the sole care of their children's education." (13) The mother's passion might predominate and through emulation boys might learn to act in an unmanly fashion.

It was not enough simply to remove boys from the family and the presence of indulgent mothers. Efforts to provide male role models became an important issue and this may be seen in the living arrangements colleges established. Although in 1761 King's College allowed the families of stewards and faculty to reside in the college, in 1763 the Board of Governors abolished this practice noting that "no woman under any pretense whatever (except a cook) be allowed to reside within the college for the future, and that those who are now there be removed as conveniently as may be." At the College of New Jersey when Walter

Minto, professor of Mathematics and Natural Philosophy, married in 1789, he moved out of the college. In fact when looking for a new teacher of classics and mathematics, Samuel Johnson of King's College specified that the candidate should be "a good and eloquent preacher, with a strong voice . . . a truly exemplary person . . . well acquainted not only with all parts of polite literature, but also with Hebrew Scripture, and . . . unmarried." (14) The presence of women posed a problem for training adolescent boys, whether they remained at home or at school. In the eyes of the college officials the only way to assure that young men received the proper education away from the corrosive influence of indulgent mothers was to remove them from the family and place them in a predominantly male institution.

Why would parents consent to relinquish control over their sons as they came under this criticism? What were educators offering, in addition to their scorn, that would impel parents to bestow their confidence in the college? Some explanations seem compelling. Parents appear to have sensed their growing inability to manage adolescent sons through the traditional, weakened, dependency based on the distribution of land. (15) For them the college which promised to pay strict attention to manners and morals may have seemed like a reasonable alternative to land-discipline.

Even for those who could control their sons, evidence indicates that fathers questioned their own abilities to teach sons the skills that the heterogeneous, mobile, and secular society required. The care with which Ralph Izard solicited help in 1787 from William Samuel Johnson, President of Columbia College, illustrates parental insistance that higher education must assist elite children. Izard, who was one of South Carolina's wealthiest men and whose career included station and power, told Johnson that he was sending his sons to Columbia in the hopes that an education there would afford him the prospect of "their being useful, valuable citizens of their country." (16) Izard confirmed what educators had been saying when they asserted that wealth alone would not guarantee success. It was no secret that "those of superior talents from nature, by mere slothfulness and idle habits, or self-indulgence, have lived useless and died contemptible." (17) A parent of one student and supporter of King's College, Edward Antill noted in 1761 that "riches without wisdom to use them, without skill to direct them to their proper end . . . only become sneers to us, and prove our destruction." (18) In fact, it was even more important that those born to privilege have higher education. As John Witherspoon informed his audience in Jamaica, "the station in which they enter life requires such duties, as those of the finest talents can scarcely be supposed capable of, unless they have been improved and cultivated with the utmost care." (19)

In addition to offering vague and imprecise statements about teaching students how to use riches and talents, colleges characterized themselves as offering another advantage which might seem more compelling. "Persons of Leisure and Public spirit," wrote Benjamin Franklin about the people who founded the Academy of Philadelphia, would "zealously unite, and make all the Interest that can be made to establish [students], whether in Business, Offices, Marriages, or any other thing for their advantage." (20) Franklin stated what others keenly knew: proper connections were essential for success. He offered the hope that the right schools could provide the means through which connections could be made. Thus, the emergence of the college and its attraction for parents can be related to the emergence of a need for intra-colonial structures which would institutionalize alliances which the family was hard-put to secure. Even those as well-placed as the New York DeLancey family had difficulty in 1755 finding a good merchant with whom young Stephen could learn the trade, according to Beverly Robinson. Although Stephen was apprenticed to Mrs. Peter DeLancey, within a year the family had to go through the identical process, with similar difficulty, when trying to place John. (21)

How did the process work through which the college facilitated such associations? The life of Benjamin Rush provides one illustration. Rush was graduated from the College of New Jersey in 1760, and his one year of matriculation coincided with Richard Stockton's tenure as trustee (1757-1781). At the end of an apprenticeship the aspiring physician continued his education by attending medical lectures at the University of Edinburgh (1766-1768) during the time that the College of New Jersey was actively soliciting John Witherspoon for its president. If Rush had not met Trustee Stockton before, it is certain that they met during their simultaneous efforts to attract Witherspoon. Rush's subsequent marriage to seventeen-year old Julia Stockton occurred shortly after he visited Stockton at his New Jersey estate, Morven, on the edge of Princeton. (22) James Francis Armstrong illustrates the process again. He was prepared for college by John Blair, at Fagg's Manor, one of the academies which often sent students to the College of New Jersey. After Armstrong graduated from college in 1773, he continued to study with President John Witherspoon until he was licensed for the ministry in 1777. He married Susannah Livingston, the sister of William Smith Livingston (A.B., 1772) whc two years at Princeton coincided with his. (23)

The examples of Benjamin Rush and James Francis Armstrong illus-trate how the eighteenth-century college was providing the means through which student associations were cemented. Preliminary findings based on an investigation of a sample of 368 students from Princeton, Philadelphia, and King's indicate that about one-quarter of the students married sisters of classmates or daughters of trustees or presidents. Other examples from the College of New Jersey include the marriage of Aaron Burr (A.B., 1772), son of the president, to Esther Edwards, daughter of another president, Jonathan Edwards. Their daughter, Sarah, married Tapping Reeve (A.B., 1763), who was a student and later became the family tutor. In other instances, David English (A.B., 1789) married Lydia Scudder, daughter of trustee Nathaniel Scudder; Samuel Blair, Jr., (A.B., 1760) married Susan Shippen, sister of William Shippen, Jr., (A.B., 1754); David Rice, Jr., (A.B., 1761) married Blair's sister, Mary, making the schoolmates brothers-in-law. At the College of Philadelphia a similar pattern may be seen in the marriage of Jacob Duché (A.B., 1757) to Elizabeth Hopkinson, sister of Duché's classmate Francis Hopkinson (A.B., 1757). Hopkinson's son, Joseph (A.B., 1786), married Emily Mifflin, whose father Thomas Mifflin (A.B., 1760) entered school while Francis Hopkinson was still matriculating. The Mifflin-Hopkinson ties to the college were cemented later when their tenure as trustees overlapped during the 1770s. Finally, examples from King's College include Peter Van Schaak (A.B., 1768) who eloped with Elizabeth Cruger, daughter of King's Governor Henry Cruger. Beverly Robinson, Jr., (A.B., 1773) married the sister of his classmate, Thomas Barclay (A.B., 1772), who married into the DeLancey family. Richard Hofstadter's observation that intermarriage among the Board of Trustees of the College of Philadelphia "provides us with a microcosm of the economic and social world of the colonial elite" can be applied to the patterns among the students as well. (24)

The personal connections formed in college which led to future marriages also led to apprenticeships. Again, Benjamin Rush can serve as an illustration. President Davies, Rush's mentor at Princeton, recommended him for an apprenticeship with Dr. John Redman, one of Philadelphia's leading physicians. Rush studied with Redman for the five and a half years between graduation and going to Edinburgh in 1766. Another Princeton student, Tapping Reeve, studied law with classmate William Paterson (both A.B., 1763) who was trained by Trustee Richard Stockton. (25)

The manner in which Philip Vickers Fithian (A.B., 1772) secured a job as a tutor after leaving the College of New Jersey illustrates another aspect o e ways in which colleges were becoming important institutions where one acquired social amenities and appropriate certification in addition to contacts. When John Witherspoon received a request for a tutor from Robert Carter of Westmoreland, Virginia, the inquiry was passed on to Fithian. He took the job and served the family for two years before he became licensed by the Presbyterian church. Before he left, however, he turned the job over to another classmate. About to leave Carter Hall, the experienced tutor wrote to his successor, John Peck, about the immense social value of having attended the College of New Jersey. "With a well confirmed testimonial of your having finished with credit a course of studies at Nassau-Hall, you would be rated without any more questions asked, either about your family, your estate, your business or your intention, at £10,000." (26)

Viewing eighteenth-century colleges as institutions that served a social purpose in addition to teaching sheds light on the pervasive disdain of a foreign education after the American Revolution. Prior to Independence, students were educated and graduated from European universities. Afterward, various spokesmen insisted that an education abroad would undermine character by allowing students to emulate and perhaps acquire foreign habits. This concern speaks to "education" as the process by which one inculcates the values of society. The desire to educate students at home also speaks to another concern, one arising from the knowledge that institutional education enhanced social contacts. John Jay, for example, who wrote to Robert Morris to argue that the Morris sons ought to attend college in America, will help explain. Jay noted that "connections founded at School and College have much influence, and are to be watched at that period—If judiciously formed, they will endure and be advantageous through life." Jay emphasized that schools facilitated students getting to know "those with whom they are often engaged in the business of active life." (27)

Jay's remarks reflect an attitude which was based on his own experience of how the system operated. Some of the associations he made during his years as a student at King's College proved advantageous to him as well as others. Recommending a friend for a military post in 1776, he recalled "an opinion of his abilities" drawn from an "early acquaintance with him at College." Throughout his life Jay maintained cordial relationships with many of his schoolmates, entered into a partnership with classmate Robert R. Livingston, often saw other classmates through the Debating Society, the Social Club, and even helped those whose loyalty to Britain conflicted with his own patriotic activities. (28)

The above examples illustrate that 'the purpose of going to school extended beyond the classical authors and included a strong social component. By the middle of the eighteenth century, teachers and parents began to view the college as an institutio⁀ which would abet

weaknesses in the family's socialization of youth. As educators removed students from the immediate influence of parents, and provided opportunities for a broader range of personal and professional contacts, they established an institution that functioned to solidify an elite while training students to serve the public arena.

A final dimension of the new social function for the college may be seen in the increasing importance attached to commencement ceremonies as a public means of displaying the new baccalaureates to the larger community. Educators gradually invested commencement ceremonies with a symbolic significance that told students and the community that they were "now about to step into life." In addition to marking an important *rite-de-passage* for a select group of young men, the commencement ceremonies denoted, as Samuel Johnson told King's College students, that they would hence be "called to act a more important part of life." (29) In both respects graduation became a way of informing the world beyond the college of the new importance attached to higher education.

By the middle of the century the ritual of commencement ceremonies was systematically established as a part of the requirements for receiving a degree. This is not to suggest that previously there was no such thing as college commencement. Rather, its significance grew and its form assumed a new meaning. The commencement ceremony itself is a medieval rite. (30) An important difference between the medieval ceremony and its eighteenth-century modification involves the audience for whom the graduates performed. In the medieval university the bestowal of a degree was an event within the college. Toward the end of the eighteenth century graduation became an event for the community. In 1701 Increase Mather tried to discourage the president of Yale College from holding commencement services. As a Puritan, Mather thought they "proved very expensive' & are occasion of much sin." He suggested that commencements "may be done privately as well as publickly," [sic] as they often were in England. (31) While Harvard College sporadically entertained commencement exercises, it was not until the 1767 revision of College Laws that it became important to the institution, and then it became a criterion for receiving the degree. (32)

By the time several new schools were founded in the second half of the century the ceremony of graduation was a necessary part of the established rules for governing the college. The ritual bears striking resemblance to the owning of the covenant in the early New England churches, something which had become almost defunct by the time colleges adopted its form. (33) By the middle of the eighteenth century, those ministers who became educators turned to the college to evoke a chorus confirming the secular community. Instead of beginning one's religious rebirth and commiting oneself to God's dictates, the visible saint in the eighteenth century began his secular life in public view from the college stage.

If it were not for the communal importance of the service, the actual commencement ceremony would be perfunctory. (34) The ceremony was preceded by two different examinations. The first was a private rehearsal for the second public examination before men of learning. Just as with the confession of faith in the New England church, here the communicant was questioned by elders. After completion of these two examinations the student was permitted to prepare for his graduation oration. He deposited a copy with various officials before he delivered it. Generally the ceremony took place in September. The procession included candidates, masters, tutors, professors, the president, trustees and invited officials—in that order. Students wore a special robe, their heads remained uncovered until after the service. Nothing was left to chance, and at the College of New Jersey Samuel Finley codified it by writing *The Process of Public Commencement* in 1764.

By the middle of the century graduation was becoming a ceremony for the elite community. The 1759 Valedictorian at the College of New Jersey noted:

> The transactions of this day have been public testimonies of its beauty, influence and popularity . . . Of its influence and popularity, from the respect paid to this seat of the muses, by every rank and degree of men; to that I may venture to say, the sentiments of every one present, are in favour of learning; and should every one speak, each voice would be a testimony of its attractive excellence. Else whence this unusual concourse? Why have so many gentlemen of employment in church and state, from various parts, condescended to grace this occasion with their presence? (35)

The observation about gentlemen from high station was made frequently. John Witherspoon mentioned that commencement had become a "fixed annual" event which was "attended by a vast concourse of the politist company." (36) In 1775 the College of Philadelphia moved the date for commencement "as Delegates from the different colonies are now assembled in Congress in this city, it might be proper to invite them." The following year they cancelled public commencement "on account of the present unsettled state of public affairs." At Yale College public commencement ceased throughout the entire Revolution, even though commencement was the favorite ceremony of President Ezra Stiles. Finally, in order to attend the first ceremony at Columbia College after the American Revolution, the Continental Congress suspended business for the day. (37)

The service had to be performed on the public stage for the benefit of the college and the community. Commencement was a place to see and to be seen. The diary of the peripatetic Reverend Ebenezer Parkman (Harvard, A.B., 1721) contains accounts of the various individuals who were present, of the festivities, and of any unusual circumstances at the Harvard commencements he dutifully attended. It was also a place where employment could be secured, as in the case of John Adams. In his autobiography Adams notes: "Mr. Maccarty of Worcester . . . [who] was empowered by the Select Men of that Town to procure them a Latin Master for their Grammar School engaged me to undertake it." (38) The attention of the community, local politicians and dignitaries, and future employers served to underscore the new-found significance of the college. Had the college performed its investiture in private, it would have denied itself the opportunity to assert its role in uniting culture and its important task of presenting newly-accomplished students in their ascribed role.

The importance attached to graduation ceremonies symbolized the significance of the college as a public institution designed by ministers-of-education who sought to reform youth and correct deficient family training. Educators wanted to teach adolescents to behave in a manly fashion—something they thought only they could do. They also offered the institution as a conduit for the mixing of upper echelons, and those with aspirations to the elite, by the available connections for business and marriage opportunities. Throughout a torrent of criticism parents acquiesced as they too began to recognize that intra-colonial institutions of higher education would benefit their sons. Toward the end of the century it appeared that a new function, defined in social terms, was beginning to characterize the need for higher education.

Notes

An earlier version of this paper was presented at the meetings of the American Educational Research Association, April, 1976, San Francisco, California, where it benefitted from David Allmendinger's criticism. Also, I would like to thank friends and former colleagues at Union College, Manfred Jonas, David Potts and Robert Wells, who offered encouragement and suggestions.

1. The literature which acknowledges a debt to Bailyn since the appearance of *Education in the Formation of American Society* (New York, 1960) is legion. The most comprehensive work which expands upon a number of Bailyn's insights is Lawrence Cremin, *American Education: The Colonial Experience, 1607-1783* (New York, 1970). This work also contains an excellent and extensive bibliography. Between Cremin's bibliography, and a recent essay by David B. Potts, "Students and the Social History of American Higher Education," *History of Education Quarterly*, XV (Fall, 1975): 317-327, most of the literature is discussed. Relevant works published after Cremin, and not contained within the subject of Potts' essay include: Carl F. Kaestle, *The Evolution of an Urban School System, New York City, 1750-1850* (Mass., 1973); Joseph J. Ellis, *The New England Mind in Transition: Samuel Johnson of Connecticut*,

People: Politics and Society in Colonial New York (New York, 1971); Ruth L. Higgins, *Expansion in New York, with Especial Reference to the Eighteenth Century* (Ohio, 1931); Bernard Bailyn, *The Origin of American Politics* (New York, 1967), pp. 107-114.

6. Benjamin Franklin, "A Proposal for Promoting Useful Knowledge. Among the British Plantations in America," in L. Jesse Lemisch, ed., *Benjamin Franklin: The Autobiography and Other Writings* (New York, 1961), 210.

7. Burr, *Discourse*, 33; John Witherspoon, "An Address to the Inhabitants of Jamaica," in *Works* (Edinburgh, 1815), VIII: 311; Other examples of this attitude may be found in John Witherspoon to Nicholas Van Dyke, May 12, 1786, Mss., Firestone Library, Princeton University; Charles Nisbet to the Trustees of Dickinson College, July 9, 1799, Founders Collection, Dickinson College. At Union College, President John Blair Smith went so far as to argue that there were more immoral influences at home than at school. See "Inaugural Address, 1795," Shaffer Library, Union College.

8. Richard Peters, *A Sermon on Education, Wherein Some Account is Given of the Academy* (Philadelphia, 1751), 5, 6, 11-13, 14.

9. Samuel Harrison Smith, *Remarks on Education . . .* (1797) in Frederick Rudolph, ed., *Essays on Education in the Early Republic* (Cambridge, 1965), 207. William Smith, *A General Idea about the College of Mirania* (1752), in *Discourses on Public Occasions* (London, 1822), 80. For a discussion of the role of emulation in pedagogical practice see Phyllis Vine Erenberg, "Change and Continuity: Values in American Higher Education, 1750-1800," University of Michigan, Ph.D. Thesis, 1974, 123-141.

10. Witherspoon, "Lectures on Education," in *Lectures on Moral Philosophy* (Philadelphia, 1822), 225.

11. [Ebenezer Pemberton], "A Short Account of the rise and State of the College in the Province of NEW JERSEY, in America," *The New American Magazine* XXVII (March, 1760), 103; Burr, *Discourse*, 28; Smith, *Mirania*, 42; Edward Antill to Samuel Johnson, December 13, 1758, College Papers, Columbia University Library.

12. Eighteenth-century Enlightenment philosophy debated whether reason was an innate or an acquired faculty. Even though the basic orientation of these theories differed significantly, colonial educators betrayed an eclecticism borrowing from each school to make the point that from reason came judgment. Several works discuss the history of psychology in the eighteenth century. For an emphasis on colonial America, see I. Woodbridge Riley, *American Philosophy: The Early Schools* (New York, 1907); A. A. Roback, *History of American Psychology* (New York, 1952), 3-55. To place the colonial context in a larger perspective see George Sidney Brett, *A History of Psychology*, Vols. I and II (London, 1921).

13. Peters, *A Sermon*, 5-6.

14. Minutes of the Governors, March 1, 1763, Columbia University Library; Princeton University Trustee Minutes, September 30, 1789, Princeton University Library; Milton Halsey Thomas, "The King's College Building," *New York Historical Society Quarterly* XXXIX (1955), 429; Herbert and Carol Schneider, eds., *Samuel Johnson, President of King's College* (New York, 1929), IV: 59-60.

1696-1. 2 (New Haven, 1973); Richard Warch, *School of the Prophets, Yale College, 1701-1740* (New Haven, 1973); James Axtell, *The School Upon a Hill: Education and Society in Colonial New England* (New Haven, 1974).

2. The standard histories of these schools may be found in the following: For the College of New Jersey, see Varnum Lansing Collins, *Princeton* (New York, 1914); John Maclean, *A History of the College of New Jersey*, 2 Vols. (Philadelphia, 1877); Thomas J. Wertenbaker, *Princeton, 1746-1896* (Princeton, 1946). More recently the College of New Jersey has received attention by Howard Miller's book, *The Revolutionary College: American Presbyterian Higher Education, 1707-1837* (New York, 1976); Douglas Sloan, *The Scottish Enlightenment and the Early College Ideal* (New York, 1971). For King's College consult: Howard Van Amringe, et. al., *A History of Columbia University, 1754-1904* (New York, 1904); Clement Clarke Moore, *The Early History of Columbia College* (New York, 1940 ed); and most recently, David C. Humphrey, *From Kings College to Columbia, 1746-1800* (Columbia University Press, 1976). The history of the College of Philadelphia may be found in Edward Potts Cheney, *The University of Pennsylvania, 1740-1940* (Philadelphia, 1940); Thomas Montgomery, *A History of the University of Pennsylvania from its Founding to 1770* (Philadelphia, 1900); Thomas L. Turner, "The College, Academy and Charitable School of Philadelphia: The Development of a Colonial Institution of Learning, 1740-1770," University of Pennsylvania, Ph.D. Thesis, 1952; Ann D. Gordon, "The College of Philadelphia, 1740-1779: The Impact of an Institution," University of Wisconsin, Ph.D. Thesis, 1975.

3. For examples consult: Jack Greene, "Search for Identity: An Interpretation of the Meaning of Selected Patterns of Social Response in Eighteenth-Century America," *Journal of Social History* 3 (1970): 189-220; N. Ray Hiner, "Adolescence in 18th Century America," *History of Childhood Quarterly*, 3 (1975): 252-280; Richard Bushman, *From Puritan to Yankee: Character and the Social Order in Connecticut, 1690-1765* (Cambridge, 1967). Works which discuss these concerns after the American Revolution are: Gordon Wood, *The Creation of the American Republic* (Chapel Hill, 1969); Miller, *The Revolutionary College*; John Howe, "Republican Thought and the Political Violence of the 1790s," *American Quarterly* XIX (1967): 147-165.

4. Aaron Burr, *A Discourse Delivered at New-Ark* (New York, 1755), pp. 28-29. For background consult: Donald L. Kemmerer, *Path to Freedom: The Struggle for Self-Government in New Jersey, 1703-1776* (Princeton, 1940), chapter X; John E. Pomfret, *The New Jersey Proprietors and Their Lands, 1664-1776* (Princeton, 1964), chapter X; and, Pomfret's more recent work *Colonial New Jersey: A History* (New York, 1973), chapter 7; Alison B. Olson, "The Founding of Princeton University: Religion and Politics in Eighteenth-Century New Jersey," *New Jersey History*, LXXXVII (1969): 135-150.

5. William Livingston, et. al., *The Independent Reflector*, ed., Milton M. Klein, (Cambridge, 1963), pp. 55-59. Background on New York may be found in Dorothy R. Dillon, *The New York Triumvirate; A Study of the Legal and Political Careers of William Livingston, John Morin Scott and William Smith, Jr.* (New York, 1949); Stanley Nider Katz, *Newcastle's New York: Anglo American Politics, 1732-1753* (Mass., 1968); Patricia Bonomi, *A Factious*

and 1779, however, of the thirty-one who were appointed, twenty-three were related somehow (p. 14).

Data on students from King's College comes from Leonard F. Fuld, "King's College Alumni-II," *Columbia University Quarterly* 9 (1907), 54-60; Milton Halsey Thomas, comp., *Columbia University Officers and Alumni, 1754-1857* (Columbia University Press, 1936); Walter Barrett, *The Old Merchants of New York City* (New York, 1885), I: 67; Richard B. Morris, ed., *John Jay, The Making of a Revolutionary* (New York, 1975) 81, 331-332. Through David Humphrey's discussion of King's College another aspect of the marriage alliances emerges. Humphrey notes the high incidence of students who were related to the Governors. During the 1750s about sixty percent were related as sons or nephews; by the 1770s the figure fell to less than twenty percent. See *From King's College*, 117, 137, passim.

A final note on this point comes from work on Yale. In a recent study Richard B. Warch notes that of the 386 students who attended between 1701 and 1740, the daughters of Yale alumni married 87 other Yale graduates. See *School of the Prophets, Yale College, 1710-1740* (New Haven, 1973), 276.

25. Whitefield Bell, Jr., "A Portrait of the Colonial Physician," in Bell, Jr., ed., *The Colonial Physician & Other Essays* (New York, 1975), 31; William Paterson, *Glimpses of Colonial Society and the Life at Princeton College, 1766-1773*, W. J. Mills, ed., (Philadelphia, 1903); also see relevant Princeton sources in *ibid.*

26. Philip Vickers Fithian, *Journal and Letters, 1767-1774*, ed., John Rodgers Williams (Princeton, 1900), 287; Gordon, "The College of Philadelphia," 133-134 also discusses this point.

27. John Jay to Robert Morris, October 13, 1782, quoted in Max M. Mintz, "Morris and Jay on Education," *Pennsylvania Magazine of History and Biography*, 74 (1950), 343.

28. Quoted in David Humphrey, *From King's College*, 209. The reference is probably to Edward Nicoll (A.B. 1766). See Alexander McDougall to John Jay, 20 March, 1776, in Morris, ed. *John Jay*, 240 fn. 1, 331-332, 87, 113-114.

29. William Smith, "A Charge to the Graduates," in *Discourses*, 130-131; Samuel Johnson, "To the Graduates," in Schneider and Schneider, *Johnson*, Vol. IV: 278.

30. Samuel Eliot Morison notes that the "incorporation of a newcomer into the society of masters, and his formal entrance upon his functions by the actual performance of its duties" was a part of Roman law which was essential for all forms of investiture. By the time Harvard College was founded the original significance of the 'Act' had been forgotten." See *Harvard College* (1935), 12-13, fn. 2, 34, 72-73.

31. Increase Mather to [Rev. James Pierpont], Sept. 15, 1701, in Franklin Bowditch Dexter, ed., *Documentary History of Yale College* (New Haven, 1916), 7. Also see the early proposals for Yale College which stipulated: "Let there be no such expensive Commencements, as those in other *Universities*," in *ibid.* 3.

32. Samuel Eliot Morison, et. al., "Harvard College Records," in *Publications of the Colonial Society of Massachusetts*, XXXI (1935): 332-334, 380-383; XVI (1925): 551, 562, 722, 746, 751, 761, 772, 819.

33. Edmund Morgan, *Visible Saints* (New York, 1965 ed.), 88-89, 61, 62. Perry

15. For illustration of changing patterns of land distribution and declining patriarchalism, see Philip Greven, *Four Generations: Population, Land and Family in Colonial Andover, Mass.* (Ithaca, 1970), 222-258, 272-273. For other indications of perceptions of increasing inability to control adolescents see Daniel Scott Smith and Michael S. Hindus, "Premarital Pregnancy in America, 1640-1970: An Overview and Interpretation," *Journal of Interdisciplinary History* V (1975), 537-570; Hiner, "Adolescence in 18th Century America." I am indebted to Robert Wells for allowing me to read his forthcoming article, "Illegitimacy and Bridal Pregnancy in Colonial America," which will appear in a collection of essays edited by Peter Laslett. Also see F. Musgrave, "The Decline of the Educative Family," *Universities Quarterly* XIV (1960), 337-405.

16. Ralph Izard to William Samuel Johnson, December 20, 1787, in Schneider and Schneider, *Johnson*, IV: 196.

17. Witherspoon, "An Address to the Senior Class Preceding Commencement, September 23, 1775," in *Lectures*, 182.

18. Antill to Leonard Lispenard, February 19, 1761. Antill to Johnson, December 13, 1758. Both are located in College Papers, Columbia University Library.

19. Witherspoon, "Address to the Inhabitants of Jamaica," in *Works*, Vol. VIII (Edinburgh, 1815), 311.

20. Franklin, "Proposals," 210-211. On this point see an article by sociologist Ralph Turner, "Modes of Social Ascent through Education: Sponsored and Contest Mobility," in A. H. Halsey, J. Floud, C. A. Anderson, eds., *Education, Economy and Society* (London, 1967), 121-139. Also see Lawrence Stone, "Social Mobility in England, 1500-1700," *Past and Present* 33 (1966), 16-55.

21. This is discussed in Kaestle, *The Evolution*, 11.

22. Rush mentioned Stockton's efforts in a letter to Jonathan Bayard Smith who was Rush's classmate. *Letters of Benjamin Rush*, ed., Butterfield, I: 38-43. The efforts to attract Witherspoon may also be found in Maclean, *History*, I: 285-300; L. H. Butterfield, ed., *John Witherspoon Comes to America* (Princeton, 1953). For Rush's life see David Freeman Hawke, *Benjamin Rush, Revolutionary Gadfly* (Indianapolis, 1971), especially 139-140 for details of the courtship.

23. Information on Armstrong and the other students from the College of New Jersey comes from student files in the Princeton University Archives. I would like to thank James McLachlan for graciously allowing me to use the material which he and his staff collected in preparation of the forthcoming biographical dictionary of Princeton's early students.

24. Richard Hofstadter, *Academic Freedom in the Age of the College* (New York, 1955), 150. For students from the College of Philadelphia comes from *Dictionary of American Biography*; University of Pennsylvania, *Biographical Catalogue of the Matriculates of the College, 1749-1893* (Philadelphia, 1894); W. J. Maxwell, ed., *General Alumni Catalogue of the University of Pennsylvania, 1917* (Philadelphia, 1917); Thomas Montgomery, *The University of Pennsylvania* (Philadelphia, 1900); Gordon, "The College of Philadelphia." The network of marriage patterns among students parallels the pattern which exists among the trustees as well. Gordon's recent study indicates that when the Academy opened in 1749 only two of the trustees were related through marriage. Between 1751

Miller noted that by the end of the seventeenth century the new world ritual had become a communal chant, and the minister's role depended "not upon a scholastic definition of their place in the hierarchy of being, but upon a revived community, upon the ability to evoke from year to year an answering chorus." See *The New England Mind: From Colony to Province* (Boston, 1961 ed.), 116, 118.

34. On the significance of public behavior and communal experience see Rhys Isaac, "Dramatizing the Ideology of Revolution: Popular Mobilization in Virginia, 1774 to 1776," *William and Mary Quarterly*, 3rd. Ser., XXXIII (1976), 357-385.

35. ———, *Valedictory Oration Pronounced at the Commencement in Nassau-Hall, in New Jersey, September 26, 1759* (New York, n.d.), 4-5.

36. Witherspoon, "Address to the Inhabitants," 320.

37. College of Philadelphia Trustee Minutes, January 24, 1775, May 23, 1776; Edmund Morgan, *The Gentle Puritan, A Life of Ezra Stiles, 1727-1795* (New Haven, 1962), 361; New York Journal and Weekly Register, April 13, 1786.

38. Francis G. Walett, ed., *The Diary of Ebenezer Parkman* (Worcester, 1974), 6, 49, 38, 66, 80, 120, 179, 219, 278; L. H. Butterfield, ed., *The Adams Papers: Diary and Autobiography of John Adams* (New York, 1964), Vol. III: 263.

Ms. Vine teaches American History at Sarah Lawrence College.

Statutes of Harvard, 1646

1. When any Scholar is able to Read Tully or such like classical Latin Author *ex tempore,* and make and speak true Latin in verse and prose *suo (ut aiunt) Marte,* and decline perfectly the paradigms of Nouns and verbs in the Greek tongue, then may he be admitted into the College, nor shall any claim admission before such qualifications.

2. Every one shall consider the main End of his life and studies, to know God and Jesus Christ which is Eternal life. John 17. 3.

3. Seeing the Lord giveth wisdom, every one shall seriously by prayer in secret, seek wisdom of Him. Prov. 2. 2, 3 etc.

4. Every one shall so exercise himself in reading the Scriptures twice a day that they be ready to give an account of their proficiency therein, both in theoretical observations of Language and Logic, and in practical and spiritual truths as their tutor shall require according to their several abilities respectively, seeing the Entrance of the word giveth light etc. Psalms 119, 130.

5. In the public Church assembly they shall carefully shun all gestures that show any contempt or neglect of God's ordinances and be ready to give an account to their tutors of their profiting and to use the helps of storing themselves with knowledge, as their tutors shall direct them. And all Sophisters and Bachelors (until themselves make common place) shall publicly repeat Sermons in the Hall whenever they are called forth.

6. They shall eschew all profanation of God's holy name, attributes, word, ordinances, and times of worship, and study with reverence and love carefully to retain God and his truth in their minds.

7. They shall honor as their parents, Magistrates, Elders, tutors and aged persons, by being silent in their presence (except they be called on to answer) not gainsaying showing all those laudable expressions of honor and reverence in their presence, that are in use as bowing before them standing uncovered or the like.

8. They shall be slow to speak, and eschew not only oaths, lies, and uncertain rumors, but likewise all idle, foolish, bitter scoffing, frothy wanton words and offensive gestures.

9. None shall pragmatically intrude or intermeddle in other men's affairs.

10. During their residence, they shall studiously redeem their time, observe the general hours appointed for all the Scholars, and the special hour for their own Lecture, and then diligently attend the Lectures without any disturbance by word or gesture: And if of any thing they

doubt they shall inquire as of their fellows so in case of non-resolution modestly of their tutors.

11. None shall under any pretence whatsoever frequent the company and society of such men as lead an ungirt and dissolute life.

Neither shall any without the license of the Overseers of the College be of the Artillery or traine-Band.

Nor shall any without the license of the Overseers of the College, his tutor's leave, or in his absence the call of parents or guardians go out to another town.

12. No Scholar shall buy sell or exchange any thing to the value of six-pence without the allowance of his parents, guardians, or tutors. And whosoever is found to have sold or bought any such thing without acquainting their tutor or parents, shall forfeit the value of the commodity, or the restoring of it, according to the discretion of the President.

13. The Scholars shall never use their Mother-tongue except that in public exercises of oratory or such like, they be called to make them in English.

14. If any Scholar being in health shall be absent from prayer or Lectures, except in case of urgent necessity or by the leave of his tutor, he shall be liable to admonition (or such punishment as the President shall think meet) if he offend above once a week.

15. Every Scholar shall be called by his surname only till he be invested with his first degree; except he be fellow-commoner or a Knight's eldest son or of superior nobility.

16. No Scholars shall under any pretense of recreation or other cause whatever (unless foreshowed and allowed by the President or his tutor) be absent from his studies or appointed exercises above an hour at morning-bever, half an hour at afternoon-bever; an hour and an half at dinner and so long at supper.

17. If any Scholar shall transgress any of the Laws of God or the House out of perverseness or apparent negligence, after twice admonition he shall be liable if not adultus to correction, if adultus his name shall be given up to the Overseers of the College that he may be publicly dealt with after the desert of his fault but in grosser offenses such gradual proceeding shall not be expected.

18. Every Scholar that on proof is found able to read the original of the Old and New Testament into the Latin tongue, and to resolve them logically withal being of honest life and conversation and at any public act hath the approbation of the Overseers, and Master of the College may be invested with his first degree.

19. Every Scholar that gives up in writing a Synopsis or summa of Logic, Natural and Moral Philosophy, Arithmetic, Geometry, and Astronomy, and is ready to defend his theses or positions, withal skilled in the originals as aforesaid and still continues honest and studious, at any public act after trial he shall be capable of the second degree of Master of Arts.

The Harvard Charter, 1650

WHEREAS THROUGH THE good hand of God many well devoted persons have been and daily are moved and stirred up to give and bestow sundry gifts, legacies, lands, and revenues for the advancement of all good literature, arts and sciences in Harvard College in Cambridge in the County of Middlesex and to the maintenance of the President and Fellows and for all accomodations of buildings and all other necessary provisions that may conduce to the education of the English & Indian youth of this Country in knowledge: and godliness. IT IS therefore ordered and enacted by this Court and the authority thereof that for the furthering of so good a work and for the purposes aforesaid from henceforth that the said College in Cambridge in Middlesex in New England shall be a Corporation consisting of seven persons (to wit) a President, five Fellows, and a Treasurer or Bursar; and that Henry Dunster shall be the first President; Samuel Mather, Samuel Danford, Masters of Art; Jonathan Michell, Comfort Starre, and Samuel Eaton, Bachelors of Art; shall be the five Fellows and Thomas Danford to be present Treasurer, all of them being inhabitants in the Bay, and shall be the first seven persons of which the said Corporation shall consist. And that the said seven persons or the greater number of them procuring the presence of the Overseers of of [sic] the College and by their counsel and consent shall have power and are hereby authorized at any time or times to elect a new President, Fellows, or Treasurer so often and from time to time as any of the said person or persons shall die or be removed, which said President and Fellows for the time being shall for ever hereafter in name and fact be one body politic and corporate in Law to all intents and purposes, and shall have perpetual succession, and shall be called by the name of President and Fellows of Harvard College; and shall from time to time be eligible as aforesaid; and by that name they and their successors shall and may purchase and acquire to themselves or take and receive upon free gift and donation any lands, tenements or hereditaments within this jurisdiction of the Massachusetts not exceeding the value of five hundred pounds per annum and any goods and sums of money whatsoever to the use and behoof of the said President, Fellows, and Scholars of the said College and also may sue and plead or be sued and impleaded by the name aforesaid in all courts and places of judicature within the jurisdiction aforesaid; and that the said President with any three of the Fellows shall have power and are hereby authorized when they shall think fit to make and appoint a Common Seal for the use of the said Corporation. And the President & Fellows or the major part of them from time to time may meet and choose such Officers & Servants for the College and make such allowance to them and them also to remove and after death or removal to choose such others and to make from time to time such orders & bylaws for the better ordering & carrying on the work of the College as they shall think fit. Provided the said orders be allowed by the Overseers. And also that the President and Fellows or major part of them with the Treasurer shall have power to make conclusive bargains for lands & tenements to be purchased by the said Corporation for valuable consideration. AND for the better ordering of the government of the said College and Corporation be it enacted by the authority aforesaid that the President and three more of the Fellows shall and may from time to time upon due warning or notice given by the President to the rest hold a meeting for the debating and concluding of affairs concerning the profits and revenues of any lands and disposing of their goods. Provided that all the said disposings be according to the will of the donors. And for direction in all emergent occasions execution of all orders and bylaws and for the procuring of a general meeting of all the Overseers & society in great & difficult cases, and in cases of nonagreement, in all which cases aforesaid the conclusion shall be made by the major part, the said President having a casting voice, the Overseers consenting thereunto. And that all the aforesaid transactions shall tend to & for the use and behoof of the President, Fellows, Scholars & Officers of the said College, and for all accommodations of buildings, books and all other necessary provisions & furnitures as may be for the advancement & education of youth in all manner of good literature, arts and sciences. AND further be it ordered by this Court and the authority thereof that all the lands, tenements or hereditaments, houses or revenues within this jurisdiction to the aforesaid President or College appertaining, not exceeding the value of five hundred pounds per annum shall from henceforth be freed from all civil impositions, taxes & rates; all goods to the said corporation or to any Scholars thereof appertaining shall be exempt from all manner of toll, customs & excise whatsoever. And that the said President, Fellows & Scholars, together with the servants & other necessary Officers to the said President or College appertaining not exceeding ten, viz. three to the President and seven to the College belonging, shall be exempted from all personal, civil offices, military exercises or services, watchings and wardings, and such of their estates not exceeding one hundred pounds a man shall be free from all Country taxes or rates whatsoever and none others. IN WITNESS whereof the Court has caused the Seal of the Colony to be hereunto affixed. Dated the one & thirtieth day of the third month called May, Anno 1650.

THO: DUDLEY
Governor

Part II: Higher Education during the Antebellum Period (1790-1860)

The Antebellum College and Academy

Robert L. Church and Michael W. Sedlak

AT THE SAME TIME THAT THE TYPICAL DISTRICT SCHOOL WAS ACTING OUT ITS rituals of equality in a relatively complacent community, institutions of secondary and tertiary schooling were being rapidly founded in growing communities for the purpose of giving their students claims to superiority in a society increasingly committed, at the rhetorical level at least, to equality. The academies and colleges shared with the district schools the same localistic nature—although, because academies and colleges recruited from larger areas, their "communities" were somewhat larger than a district—in that they were very much creatures of the immediate community and prepared young people for roles in that community. But, quite unlike the district school, academies and colleges offered an education whose prime function was to distinguish certain members of the society as superior to the mass. Although the conferring of such distinction may not have been their primary announced purpose—as we shall see, they had several—it certainly seems to have been their most significant accomplishment.

In this chapter we will discuss the colleges and academies together, making little distinction between them, for in essential features and functions the two institutions were fundamentally similar. Both offered post-elementary schooling for young people between the approximate ages of 10 and 40. Most students, however, ranged in age from 14 to 25. Both offered terminal education in that they claimed to provide all the formal schooling that a young person needed for life. Tuition at these private institutions was generally minimal but the student and his family had to bear the burden of the student's refraining from wage-earning employment while he pursued additional years of schooling. These foregone earnings, rather than the cost of tuition and maintenance, generally restricted institutions of higher learning to the middle and upper classes. Additional expense, and additional restrictions, grew from the fact that most students had to live away from home in order to attend these institutions.

The colleges and academies founded after the Revolution were, unlike their predecessors in the colonial period, located in most cases in small towns far from major population centers. The colleges and academies recruited from fairly wide areas surrounding these small towns—colleges, for example, recruited students from areas within a fifty-mile radius. Students came to live in the town housing the institution but, for the most part, they did not live in the institutions themselves. The boardingschool became widespread only after the Civil War. Despite the fact that the students did not live "on campus," their lives were closely disciplined by the colleges and academies. Schools often licensed the boardinghouses in which the students lived and constantly regulated what students could eat, how they should dress, and what they could do with the very little free time that the school program—which usually began with a chapel program at dawn and went straight through a full day to a chapel service at nightfall—left them. In all cases the institutions were expected to stand in loco parentis; discipline, academic and extracurricular, was very tight. Set off in a small town with little entertainment available, faced with seemingly endless and meaningless memorizing of texts, subject to constant faculty interference with their social and religious lives, without the release of organized athletics, students no doubt sometimes found higher education a pretty grim business.

It is little wonder that the pre–Civil War college and academy experienced a series of outbreaks of student violence—outbreaks which ranged from the killing of a professor at Princeton (unpremeditated) and the firing of a cannon into a college building to the more normal harassment of authority and the throwing of food in commons. This violence gradually subsided, especially after 1830; it is not clear why. The advent of organized athletics and the broadening of the curriculum possibly had something to do with it. The rising age of the student body also contributed. Relief was also found in the relaxation of the college's commitment to a rigorous interpretation of in loco parentis—a relaxation that grew from a general softening of nineteenth-century society's view of the sinfulness of children and society's gradual renunciation of force as a means of enforcing personal morals. In the first half of the nineteenth century colleges and academies came more and more to rely, not on physical force, but on the power of religion to control their students. As Frederick Rudolph has so dramatically pointed out, the ideal college experience for every student would include the experience of one revival on the campus in which that student experienced the saving light of the Lord. Masters and students sought to encourage such revivals—and, of course, the conscious effort to do away with sinful behavior was thought one of the most effective means of encouragement. Thus, schoolmasters were able to develop a desire for religious experience among their students and to depend on that desire to make the students themselves enforce a great deal of the institution's disciplinary code. This change made the colleges and academies appear less openly oppressive than earlier when they depended on physical constraints over their students, but whether revivalistic constraints were any less restrictive from the students' point of view is unclear.

The status of women in higher education was a point of much controversy in this period. Academies were most often coeducational while the colleges—with the exception of Oberlin, which, from its establishment in 1833, admitted all comers regardless of race or sex, and a few others—resisted the admission of women well into the second half of the nineteenth century. A large number of academies were opened exclusively for women, several of which offered courses of study equivalent to that offered by most men's colleges. The most famous, perhaps, were Emma Willard's Troy Female Seminary, opened in 1821, and Mary Lyon's Mount Holyoke Seminary, opened in 1837 (it gained collegiate status only in 1893). There women studied the same advanced subjects as men. In teaching women at an equal level with men, Lyon and Willard undermined the assumption that women were intellectually inferior to men that prevailed even among educators of women. The first women's college (Vassar) was not founded until 1865, the next (Smith and Wellesley) in 1875. In most schools women were taught subjects thought likely to improve their performance as housewives, mothers, and elementary school teachers. Their work emphasized English grammar rather than the classics and higher mathematics. The practice in oratory and elocution that was part of the rhetoric course for men was dropped as women were not supposed to speak in public (Lucy Stone refused to write a commencement part at Oberlin in 1842 because a male student would have to read it to the audience). Simple arithmetic, geography, the other elementary school subjects, and work in household arts such as sewing or embroidery rounded out the English course for women. Within the co-educational schools women were often segregated both socially and in the classroom. Contact between the sexes, inside or outside of class, was minimal—or at least was supposed to be minimal.

Whatever its shortcomings, "higher education" for women in the first half of the nineteenth century marked a great improvement on the colonial finishing school for young ladies. And the broadening of women's education greatly influenced education in general in the United States. First, it hastened the day when women would be considered intellectually equal to men. Second, it gave thousands of young women destined to teach the elementary grades some post-elementary-school training. Much of higher education for women in this era grew out of a generally recognized need to recruit better educated members to the steadily feminizing teaching force.

Like the district schools, academies and colleges in this era were community oriented and controlled, but as the colleges and academies recruited from and served far wider communities, the nature of community control was somewhat different. The average man did not have the same sense of control over the academy in his area as he had over the district school (although he might take a good deal more pride in having an institution of higher learning in his community than he did from the existence of a district school). Leadership and control of these institutions generally resided with the social elite of the area—the upper and upper middle classes. Academies and colleges were privately owned by boards of self-perpetuating trustees who appointed the president or master and his subordinate teachers and who had the power to establish educational policy. This form of educational polity was at that time uniquely American, one that had developed in the early colonial era when it was found that traditional ways of governing institutions of learning did not fit the conditions of the country. European precedents suggested

mercantilist age the state was supposed to determine or plan its own economic development and virtually assign individuals to the roles necessary for accomplishing that plan. Any group that drew together to manufacture glass or build a bridge or found a school or fight fires (even voluntarily) had to petition either the local or national government for a charter which would grant them the privilege of carrying out their plans. Such a grant of privilege came only when the government had determined that the activity was in the public interest. Charters also often granted monopolies. If the government granted a group the privilege of building a toll bridge in a certain place, it was likely to promise not to allow any other group to build a competing bridge nearby. Monopolies of this kind were granted in order to insure the success of the first venturers on the assumption that, if building a bridge was in the public interest, it was also in the public interest to insure that the bridge builders found the venture profitable enough to continue. In the last half of the eighteenth and the first half of the nineteenth century—the very time when thousands of colleges and academies were receiving state charters—the chartering system and the system of economic and social control that supported it were being challenged and were breaking down in England and the United States.

This period in England saw the increasing elaboration of the laissez-faire theories of Adam Smith and David Ricardo, which held that the public and state interest is best served by allowing the maximum feasible individual freedom in economic activity. A state's economy would be strongest when every individual pursued his own economic self-interest unimpeded by the state. Thus, Smith could argue that the pursuit of self-interest was also the pursuit of public interest, and that the public interest suffered whenever the state interfered with the individual pursuit of self-interest. Smith's ideas came to dominate nineteenth-century academic thought but became only partially implemented in the economies of Western Europe in that or any other century. In the United States the story was somewhat different as the weakness of centralized government in a sparsely settled country with poor internal communications made laissez faire a governmental practice long before the classical economists developed the theory. Colonial governments and early state governments had neither the enforcement machinery to regulate effectively the economic activities of widely scattered citizens nor the foresight and financial resources to understand and serve the public interest in a new and rapidly developing country. So although governments, both colonial and state, continued to issue charters and grants of privilege, they did so largely symbolically. Few entrepreneurial ventures were stopped because the state refused to grant a charter or because it effectively regulated the venture, once established. Likewise with educational institutions. Colonial and state governments in almost all cases issued charters to all who requested them and, once having granted the privilege of establish-

either educational institutions governed closely by the church and state or educational institutions largely autonomous from any outside control and governed by the institution's faculty.

The Massachusetts colonists attempted to bring the latter arrangement over from England and established Harvard College on that basis. But the Bay Colony's leaders found that they disliked entrusting their sons and the fate of the college to the young transient "faculty" at Harvard which consisted almost exclusively of young graduates of the college awaiting a "call" from a congregation to take up their proper role as ministers. Furthermore, early American colleges had no steady sources of support like those upon which Oxford and Cambridge could depend. American colleges were from the very start dependent on the gifts of their immediate communities. Community financial involvement, especially when accompanied by the absence of permanent and mature college faculties, inevitably undermined the autonomy of the colleges and led to a system of lay governance whereby community leaders assumed financial and educational responsibility for their operations. At times these lay boards of trustees were composed of community officials and area clergymen—the idea being that those men responsible for maintaining community interests in other areas would be most capable of doing so in the case of educational institutions. At other times boards of trustees of colleges were composed simply of influentials in the community, appointed because they were instrumental in founding the college or in rendering it financial support. This system of governance, which began to emerge from the very first years of Harvard's existence, was pretty well confirmed there by the 1680s when the last Harvard faculty member to serve as trustee (with a brief exception in the 1880s) was forced off the board. The second and third American colleges—William and Mary chartered in 1693 and Yale in 1701—were established with boards of trustees totally distinct—except for the college president—from the teaching body. This pattern has persisted in virtually every American college until the late 1960s when various campus crises brought tentative efforts to give faculty (and students) more "power over their lives" by including them on college boards of trustees. This pattern of governance was, from the first, the one that controlled the development of academies in the United States.

The colleges and academies of the early national period were also similar in that, although they were "private" institutions, they had a public aspect and received a certain amount of public support. Ideally, a college or academy was to apply for a charter from the state before it opened its doors (although hundreds, perhaps thousands, of academies existed for years without a state charter). The chartering process was a hold-over from a period in which the state tightly controlled economic and social life to the extent that no man was allowed to do business until the state had determined that his efforts would help the state. In that

ing an educational institution, the governments interfered in no way with the running of the institution. Indeed, by a strange piece of irony, freedom from interference became a privilege, made famous in the Dartmouth College case of 1819, that accompanied a state charter. This complex legal case was one of several which arose when state governments, following the Revolution, had sought either to take control of or to impose new conditions, more in line with revolutionary democratic doctrine about public control, on "private" colleges originally chartered by colonial governments. In the Dartmouth College case the Supreme Court ruled that since the Constitution had explicitly guaranteed that the new government would honor all contracts made under the colonial governments and that, since a charter was a contract, it was illegal for a state or local government to interfere in any way with a chartered institution except insofar as the original charter provided for such interference. In other words, a charter was a contract in perpetuity and, except under provisions written into the original contract, the state could not abridge that contract in any way. Although the charter was originally granted in recognition of the public service nature of the institution, it was now interpreted as an assurance of the essential privateness of the institution. Thus the charter was vital because it insured the trustees and potential donors that, despite the election of new governments every few years, the college would continue as planned. In an era when democracy was new and when shifts in European governments had often meant upheavals in all institutions, this kind of assurance was significant; some historians have argued that the assurance given by the Dartmouth College case was the spark which accounts for the ever increasing rate of educational institution founding after 1820. It is doubtful that the Dartmouth College decision "sparked" this movement, but it surely gave the private sector the confidence necessary to sustain the movement.

The charter had another value for an educational institution. It symbolized the fact that the institution carried out a public function—the education of the young, which was in the interest of the society as a whole. The charter symbolized this relation of the private institution to the public interest. As often as not, the charter also brought with it a certain amount of public support for the educational institution. When it chartered a public service institution, the state government would often grant the institution some public land that the school could sell to raise revenue, or a portion of the income from a state or local tax, or sometimes, when the state was feeling especially poor, a guarantee (seldom fulfilled) that the school would have a monopoly on higher education in its region. Thus Harvard College received part of the income from tolls, first on the ferry and then on the bridge across the Charles River, many academies received land in Maine from the Massachusetts legislature upon chartering, academies in many states received money from the liquor tax or from the fines paid by those guilty of certain misdemeanors in their area.

Williams College thought the state promised it a monopoly on higher education in western Massachusetts when it was chartered in 1793, and in 1821 angrily and unsuccessfully fought the establishment of Amherst forty-four miles away as a violation of its charter. Thus the charter served both to protect the private nature of the educational institution and to establish its public service character. It is this very ambiguity that is most crucial to understanding the institutional shape of the academy and college in the early nineteenth century; this ambiguity about the publicness of private educational institutions is far from being resolved even in the present day, as we can see in the battles over state support for parochial education and over the issue of the relation of government to the "private" universities.

Another area in which the college and academy resembled each other was curricular. That they should be so similar in this respect is ironic, for the academy was first suggested in America as an alternative form of higher education that was to offer modern and practical subjects—like English, modern foreign languages, navigation, surveying—instead of the classical training of the grammar school and college. The model for the American academy, defined as a secondary institution which combined instruction in the classics with more practical, "modern" subjects, came from the ideas of the poet John Milton during the Restoration. Benjamin Franklin had those dissenting academies in mind when he published, in 1749, his *Proposals Relating to the Education of Youth in Pennsylvania*, in which he suggested that Philadelphia needed an institution with a broader curriculum than that of the classical grammar school. He proposed a school where the students would "learn those Things that are likely to be *most useful and most ornamental*, Regard being had to the several Professions for which they are intended." Franklin's suggestions for practicality were more radical than most: "While they are reading Natural History, might not a little *Gardening, Planting, Grafting, Inoculating*, &c. be taught and practised; and now and then Excursions made to the neighbouring Plantations of the best Farmers, their Methods observ'd and reason'd upon for the Information of Youth. The Improvement of Agriculture being useful to all, and Skill in it no Disparagement to any."[1] English, mathematics, history and civil government, and natural history were the most important parts of the curriculum; learning foreign languages was also necessary, but Latin and Greek were accorded only equal status with French and German. Franklin's suggestions and arguments were ignored and his planned "English academy" became nothing but a preliminary adjunct to the classically oriented University of Pennsylvania and its attached grammar school.

Franklin's experience was to be repeated time and again in the next hundred years. Proposals for more practical curricula in both colleges and academies and plans for more modern schools were ignored or scrapped in order to meet the demand from faculties and apparently from students (or their parents) for the traditional Latin and Greek. Theoretically, the academy was supposed to be more modern and more practical; in fact, it seems in general to have been about as traditional as the grammar schools and the colleges. Several things may account for this. First, as Franklin found, teachers and parents wanted Latin and Greek taught. These were the subjects of elite education and few parents wanted any less for their own children. Furthermore, it is not clear that Latin and Greek were such impractical subjects from the point of view of the personal success and mobility of the students in the academies.

The practicality of the practical curricula of those academies that did claim to offer these subjects must be questioned. In most cases the practical and modern subjects in a school's catalogue or advertisements were listed only for advanced students and often it turned out that no students were advanced enough to take them. In other academies the practical subjects received cursory treatment—not through observation and induction, as Franklin suggested, but through memorization and rote recitation from a book. In the early nineteenth century we also find little pedagogical knowledge or concern about the effective teaching of modern subjects such as natural history or trigonometry. Texts in these subjects started to appear only in the thirties and they stressed the memorizable rather than the practical. Botany became the study of the names of the classifications rather than a study of how plants grow. These problems with the "practical" subjects were compounded by the fact that few teachers were even minimally trained to teach these modern subjects. All in all, what practical instruction there was was not likely to be very practical.

So far as historians know, however, most academies made hardly any effort to teach the modern or the practical. It was too expensive. The more subjects a school taught, the more books, equipment, and teachers it needed. And modernity and practicality seemed to call especially for expensive equipment such as surveying instruments and laboratories. Latin and Greek, on the other hand, were fairly cheap to offer. Any man with some college education could teach them since he had learned them in college—and, as "teaching" was largely the hearing of recitations and the grading of papers and tests, special pedagogical training was not very relevant. Furthermore, a school with a traditional classical curriculum could get by with a single teacher as any educated man was expected to know all the classical subjects. But the modern and practical subjects, if they were to be taught at all well, needed specialists at added expense. Had there been a real demand from students and parents for modern

and practical subjects, academies would undoubtedly have passed the extra expense on to the students; that so few did so suggests how little effective demand there was. The marginal economic position of most academies prevented them from taking the time and the risk to cultivate a demand for a different curriculum among the communities they served.

These same arguments explain the colleges' experience in this era—the expense and difficulties of teaching modern and practical subjects and the lack of effective demand for that kind of training prevented almost all colleges from departing from the traditional curriculum. Indeed, the colleges argued quite effectively that the traditional curriculum was the most practical teaching that a young person could receive. In 1828 the faculty of Yale College prepared a report to justify that faculty's rejection of an alumnus' suggestion that Yale add several "practical subjects" to its curriculum. The Yale Report argued that the mental discipline that the student received while studying the classics best prepared him to think for himself about other problems that he would encounter. "First exercise the mind and then furnish it," the professors wrote. "Furnishing" would most often come later, on the job or in a special training school like a seminary. The college's function was to exercise the mind and Latin and mathematics were the supreme tools for that purpose. They were pure, abstract, and complete. If a student could master a systematic, ordered, rounded body of knowledge like Latin or mathematics, he then had mastered a system of thought applicable to other, less complete subjects. Study of these traditional and well-ordered subjects gave the student a standard of knowledge, system, and completeness which he could use in seeking knowledge in other subjects. In a sense it was advantageous that Latin was a dead language since it was no longer subject to changes brought about by usage, regional corruptions, and slang. It could safely be treated and studied as a completed, logical, internally consistent, and perfect system—a closed system. Mathematics, of course, possessed the same advantages. Furthermore, the classical languages and mathematics were difficult, and it was thought best to train people on difficult subjects, as it was easier to go from the difficult to the more simple (as the modern subjects were designated). Difficult subjects also had a greater disciplinary value; the harder the subject, the greater disciplining of will power necessary to master it. The Yale Report rested on the faculty psychology and on the assumption of transfer of training—that is, the idea that exercising the mind in the study of one subject would make the mind more adept at studying other subjects, that memorizing Latin would improve the mind's ability to memorize French should the student want to do so at some future date. Thus, according to the Yale Report, disciplines which gave the mind the most rigorous and the most general exercise were the most practical school subjects. And those subjects—happily for the professors—were the traditional Greek, Latin, and mathematics.

The Yale Report came at a critical time for the fate of the classical languages in higher education. From the founding of the universities in Western Europe in the Middle Ages, the classical languages had been recognized as the languages of communication among educated men. Treatises in medicine, law, education, theology, and even science were written in Latin; the "wisdom of the ancients" was constantly called upon and applied in everyday situations. Thus, the most practical education a would-be professional or a well-rounded gentleman could hope for would be one that taught him the language and literature of primary communication. In the eighteenth century the vernacular gradually replaced Latin as the language of communication among even the most educated men. Although scholars and professional specialists still wrote and read Latin in their work, the well-rounded educated man took his ideas and his knowledge of the world from works written in the vernacular. Men still believed in the importance of the wisdom of the ancients—note the constant parallels Americans drew between their own democratic experiment and classical forms of government—but that wisdom was generally thought to be available in translation. Thus, the obvious rationale for the emphasis on the classics in education was undermined. The classics were no longer practical, some argued, and should be replaced with more useful subjects. Had the classics continued to justify their position in the curriculum on the basis of their usefulness as languages of communication and as sources of great classical ideas and ideals, they would surely have been replaced. But the Yale Report subtly but clearly changed the rationale for keeping the curriculum classical; argued, indeed, for a higher form of practicality than did the advocates of the modern subjects.

The ideas of the Yale Report were not original with the professors at Yale, but their report, widely publicized as a statement of positive educational progress (not the reactionary defense of the old that most modern historians term it), set the tone and rationale of higher education for the greater part of the remainder of the century. Although written by college professors as a manifesto about college education, the report had as great an impact on academies as it did on colleges. Here was a report that accomplished everything: it reconciled the financial interests of the schools and the cultural pretensions of the teachers with the practical tendencies of a developing nation and reconciled, perhaps more importantly, the conflict within parents and students between the desire to share the cultural training of the elite and the desire for practical training for the business of life.

There are some exceptions to the generalizations about curriculum made in the preceding pages, just as there are to all the generalizations made in this volume. The most important exceptions were the few technical schools founded for the training of engineers in early America—the United States Military Academy (1802) and Rensselaer Polytechnic Insti-

tute (1824) being the most famous. Both, because they were established to deemphasize the classics, took the name of academy or institute in order to distinguish themselves from the colleges. Also exceptional were the normal schools or teacher training academies founded in this period. These schools offered occupationally oriented secondary education (their training was hardly of professional grade, however) and as such carried out the utilitarian mandate of the original academy model. In most cases, however, the normal school was not as advanced as the academy; its curriculum concentrated largely on reviewing the elementary subjects in order to train students to teach in elementary schools.

The colleges and academies in the period 1780–1860, then, largely shaped their curricula according to the traditional classical model. The student occupied the greatest part of his time learning Latin, Greek, and mathematics. Rhetoric and forensics—training in the writing and speaking of English—took up a smaller portion of his day. The lower the level of the school, the more time it devoted to English rather than classical languages. As the period progressed, science—natural philosophy (physics and chemistry) and natural history (geology and biology)— received more attention, especially in the wealthier institutions. Benjamin Silliman gave lectures and laboratory demonstrations in chemistry at Yale in the first decade of the nineteenth century, at least twenty years before the publication of the Yale Report. The colleges and most of the academies conducted some work in mental and moral philosophy—generally in the capstone course in the curriculum where the college president or academy principal guided the graduating class through a book like Francis Wayland's *The Elements of Moral Science* (1835), a treatise that sought to cover the ethical aspects of all phases of an educated man's life. It included discussions of how the mind was formed and how it functioned, of the sources of moral ideas and ideals, of political economy and civil government, and finally of marriage and the family. Here, more than in any other class in the school, the instructor did more than simply listen to and mark recitations. Instead, he discussed and advised his charges on the moral issues of their time.

With this exception, however, pedagogy in institutions of higher learning was not markedly better than it was in the district schools. Rote recitation—in which the student memorized a passage from the text or his translation of a passage from the text and repeated it to the teacher— was a standard practice. Only in rhetoric and forensics was there much student creativity; even the few science laboratories established in the first half of the nineteenth century were used mostly to demonstrate experiments to students, not to let them *do* them. Students' creativity and imagination were stimulated much less by the curriculum and teaching of the schools than by what Frederick Rudolph has called the "extracurriculum"—the network of literary clubs, secret societies, fraternities, debating clubs, and voluntary agencies which students established and ran with a high level of intellectual rigor. Literary and debating clubs, for example, often had larger and better libraries than the colleges or academies—with especially strong collections of modern works, including novels, a class of frivolous books excluded from most college libraries. Whereas college libraries opened perhaps only an hour or two a day and discouraged the circulation of books, the club libraries were much more accessible and consequently much more intellectually influential. As the Yale Report had insisted, the institutions of higher learning were more concerned with disciplining and training the mind than with furnishing it; students turned to the clubs and societies for information about the world around them.

Even on the criteria of grade or level of curriculum and instruction, it is difficult to distinguish the academies from the colleges. Generally, of course, colleges tended to admit a slightly older student and to teach him a bit more advanced and rigorous curriculum. But only slightly and not in all cases. The matter of the age of the students is a very complicated one. We do know that academies often admitted children as young as nine and that colleges matriculated many students under fifteen. And both kinds of institutions registered substantial numbers of students over thirty. But about averages—a statistical picture of the typical student—we know next to nothing. Some colleges kept reasonably full matriculation records from which historians have been able to discover that the average age of freshmen rose steadily from 1800 to the Civil War. The increasing age of college students has also been confirmed in studies of Baptist colleges and of the recruitment patterns of the American Education Society (a group which sent young men to college in return for their promise to become ministers in the West).[2] No similar work has been done with respect to academy matriculants. It is worth noting in this regard, however, that since the academy was not seen principally as a preparation for but as an alternative to college, academy students would not necessarily be younger than those in colleges.

Equally confusing was the college's normal practice of establishing its own secondary school within the college to prepare students for college work. Colleges often sprang up in areas in which there were no secondary schools and had to accept students directly out of district school and offer them a secondary course. Throughout the period some colleges had far more students in their precollege sections than in the colleges themselves; some had no students registered in college courses. Furthermore, less than half—probably fewer—of the students who attended the secondary portion ever went on the register in the college. These colleges were academies in everything but name, as they offered terminal secondary schooling to the majority of their students. While some schools labeled academies gave courses at a level commensurate with those at all but the best colleges, others functioned only as private elementary schools. Academies, especially those located in sparsely set-

tled rural or frontier areas, were desperate for tuition money, and if paying students needed elementary work, the academy, however reluctantly, taught it.

Thus, although we can speak in the abstract of varying levels of higher education, we cannot associate those levels firmly with institutional titles. Greek, Latin, mathematics, forensics, rhetoric, natural history, and moral philosophy could be taught at the advanced or the basic level, a distinction corresponding to the tertiary and the secondary levels of schooling. But many institutions labeled colleges taught only at the basic level and many labeled academies taught both the basic and the advanced. Thus the name "college" or "academy" did not necessarily indicate what kind of school existed under that title or what kind of instruction it provided. Specific institutions chose to title themselves as they did, apparently, more in accordance with local prejudices toward the rhetorical "practicality" of the academy or the intellectual elitism of the college than in accordance with the kind of instruction they offered. Many institutions found they had made a mistake and changed their designation—the usual change, as would be expected, from the lower to the higher, from academy to college. Firm demarcation of secondary from tertiary education, however, would not come until the beginning of the twentieth century.

II

Many more colleges and academies were established in the period between the Revolution and the Civil War than were needed to fulfill the demands for higher education among the population of the period. Only by understanding why there was more popular demand for the building of these institutions than there was demand for their educational facilities will we understand the place of higher education in the early American republic.

How many academies were there? We do not really know, for the only way to count is to find copies of academy charters among neglected state legislative records. No one has made this examination as of yet. Moreover, a charter will tell us only that an academy was contemplated; it does not tell us that it was actually founded. Further complicating the statistical picture, there were many more unincorporated (unchartered) academies than incorporated ones. Perhaps the best estimates that we have are those compiled by Henry Barnard in the 1850s.[3] Barnard found that there were over 6,000 academies enrolling more than 250,000 students. He found, on the other hand, that there were 239 colleges enrolling a little over a tenth of that number. Albert Fishlow estimates that in 1850 approximately 4 million children were enrolled in public common schools.[4] This attendance figure, according to Fishlow, is equal to approximately 56 percent of the common-school-age population. On the other hand, if we take Barnard's figure of a quarter of a million children attending academies as relatively accurate, which it probably is, and compare it to the estimated total white population in the 15–24 age group—4.1 million—we find that the academies served at any one time approximately 6 percent of the available population. The chances were that about 12 percent of the population coming of age at the time had attended academies for four years during some part of their careers. Perhaps more went to academies, for it is very probable that a majority did not complete a four-year course. These figures help us to understand that the magnitude of the academy movement, in terms of institutions and students, was not insignificant. Moreover, they point out that the academies serviced a far larger proportion of the population than did their predecessors, the Latin Grammar Schools, which were limited in number and located almost exclusively in densely populated areas and which in the colonial era required substantial intellectual achievement and social status for admission. The academy movement saw the founding of literally thousands of institutions devoted primarily to secondary schooling and the spreading of secondary education from cities to the small towns.

The pattern in the growth in numbers of colleges and in numbers of students attending college presents a somewhat different picture. Nine colleges were founded in the American colonies. Between the Revolution and the Civil War the United States saw the founding of 173 colleges that were to survive until the 1920s—when Donald Tewksbury studied and counted antebellum colleges.[5] Actually, many more than 173 were founded, for a majority of these did not survive into the twentieth century—Tewksbury estimates that, for every college that survived, three or four others died.

The figures on the founding of the more hardy institutions reveal a rapidly increasing rate of growth. Only 28 of these colleges were founded before 1820; 12 in the 1820s; 35 in the thirties, 32 in the forties (there was a steep depression in the late thirties and early forties which slowed down the rate of investment in and the survival capabilities of colleges), and 66 in the 1850s. Another historian has estimated that in 1800, 18 of every 10,000 Americans were college trained (i.e., they had spent some time at an American college but had not necessarily graduated) and that in 1830, 17 of every 10,000 were college trained.[6] Although these estimates do not account for European training that some Americans had received, it is probable that no more than two tenths of a percent of the American population was college trained in the first quarter of the century. By mid-century, as Barnard's figures for 1850 suggest, considerable expansion had occurred, yet even then the colleges enrolled less than 2 percent (1.25%) of the population in the 20–24 age group. In terms of enrollments, then, the colleges were small; but their symbolic importance, their wide dispersion over the country, and the prominence of their graduates make them significant for the historian measuring American attitudes toward education and the effects of education on American society.

All the available statistics demonstrate that institutions of higher education greatly expanded in number and enrollment in the first eighty years of nationhood.[7] The most dramatic increase, however, was in the number of institutions, an increase far greater than that necessitated by increasing enrollments. The academies and colleges were seriously overbuilt. This overbuilding—the fact that that not enough tuition-paying students existed to fill the numerous institutions to the "breakeven" point —accounts for the extremely high mortality rate among colleges and what seems, so far as we can tell, a similar mortality rate among academies. The cries of educators lamenting the pinch caused by lack of students and their tuition money are universal during the period. At the college and at the academy level, trustees and presidents contemplated desperate schemes to assemble capital to get a school established or over a financial hurdle. One such scheme provided that initial donors to the college received in return a "perpetual scholarship" for their children and *their* children. Some colleges that had financed their beginnings in this manner found in the next generation that all the original contributions had been eaten up by initial building expenditures and that most of their students were descendants of original contributors who attended without charge. Northwestern University was forced to honor such a pledge and admit a student free of charge as late as the early 1970s. Most commonly, however, faculty members were forced to bear the financial burden of overbuilding. There are scores of harrowing tales of faculty members going for years without pay or with greatly reduced pay in order to help their institution stay alive. And of course students bore a considerable burden in consequence of this overbuilding. Although tuition remained surprisingly low—competition for students dictated that—educational quality and educational facilities like libraries suffered greatly because of this underfinancing.

One evidence of the overbuilding is that colleges were often founded right on the frontier line—not a generation after the founding of a town or of a state, but at the same moment as the founding of the town or state. Thus in states like Kentucky, Kansas, and Minnesota, colleges were founded before the population of the states rose above the 100,000 mark—if the 18 in 10,000 figure for college-trained people can be said to apply uniformly across the country, each of these states established colleges before there were 200 college-trained residents in the state. At the 1850 rate of enrollment for colleges in the 20-to-24 age group—less than 2 percent—there were less than 300 students available to go to college in these states. Nor is there any reason to believe that the rate of enrollment in these frontier communities reached nearly as high a figure as 2 percent. The same pattern holds true for academy foundings

departure from the idea of centralized urban culture which had pervaded Western civilization from its beginning. The founders of colleges and academies were not even content to choose a single town to be the cultural capital of each state. Every town, they seemed to say, should be a cultural center.

The cultural leaders of the West viewed the city ambiguously. On the one hand, they wanted institutions like those located in New York or Boston; on the other, they felt urban environments to be evil. Many westerners thought of Boston and New York in much the same way that Jefferson thought of Paris and London. Noah Webster was but one of many who believed that "large cities [even those in America] are always scenes of dissipation and amusement, which have a tendency to corrupt the hearts of youth and divert their minds from their literary pursuits."[10] Urban educational entrepreneurs agreed with Webster about older large cities, but felt that their own cities—absolutely imaginary as they were—would be free of such corrupting influences and thus safe places in which boys and girls could learn and where a pure culture could be maintained (although they often acknowledged the pervasive distrust of urban influence by placing their institutions on the edge of the city, in a protected place such as on a hill that overlooked the city but was somewhat isolated from it). Henry Nash Smith has described the American vision of the West as a virgin land, a new Eden, where men could begin all over again in a state of innocence, where men could be reborn. He describes this image as a kind of pastoral vision which saw the West as an agricultural heaven.[11] But the urban boosters of the antebellum period felt that the western cities-to-be could foster this same sense of innocence and rebirth. Establishing educational institutions became one way of insuring that the new urban units would live up to the cultural, moral, and Eden-like aspirations of these boosters.

The building of institutions of higher education in these areas also served to fulfill more mundane aspirations. Among these aspirations, the quest for financial profit dominated. The unflagging preoccupation with land speculation determined educational investment. A school raised the price of nearby land. One frontiersman explained that land developers "are shrewd enough to know that one of the most successful methods to give notoriety to an embryo town, and induce New England settlers, is forthwith to put in operation some institution of learning with a high sounding name." One public elementary school administrator in Madison, Wisconsin, complained that establishment of a female academy "would do more to raise the price of village lots and secure a better class of people for the future city of Madison than any amount of money expended in building school houses and providing teachers for the public schools."[12] This complaint that academies and colleges rather than public elementary schools attracted settlers and investment explains, in part, why higher education was so overbuilt relative to elementary education.

—Iowa's first appeared in 1836, ten years before statehood and when that territory (which included part of what is now Minnesota) boasted less than 40,000 inhabitants. In 1850 Texas, with a population of only 213,-000, was reported to have 97 academies. Assuming that 6 percent of the young people 15-24 attended an academy and, adjusting for the likelihood that frontier regions would contain a larger cohort of that age group than older locales (young people tended to migrate much more frequently than older, more settled people), each Texas academy could expect about 40 students at a time and Iowa's lone academy had to recruit from a potential 720 students dispersed through the vast territory.[8] And again, as in the case of the frontier colleges, there is every reason to expect that in the frontier areas where young men were especially important in helping families begin new farms and new enterprises fewer youngsters sought higher education than in more settled regions.

The rapidity with which colleges and academies sprang up did not reflect a realistic appraisal of the educational needs of the communities they were designed to serve. Rather, this overbuilding must be seen as a product of the entrepreneurial, cultural, moral, and status aspirations of their founders and patrons. When we come to understand these reasons for overbuilding this kind of institution—there was, we must note, no similar overbuilding at the common or district school level—we will come to understand the underlying functions of higher education in the United States in the first half of the nineteenth century.

Founding of institutions of higher education was one product of the overoptimistic boosterism that characterized the American development of space in the antebellum period. Daniel Boorstin in the second volume of his trilogy, The Americans (1965), describes this booster spirit with great verve and insight.[9] Every settlement, every "wide spot in the road," "claimed the name of 'city,' " he points out. No one seems to have paid any particular attention to the real meaning of the word. "Every place that claimed the honors of a city set about justifying itself by seeking to conjure up suitably metropolitan institutions." Among these metropolitan institutions were a hotel, a newspaper, and, almost as important, an institution of higher learning—whether an academy or a college. Boston, New York, Philadelphia had colleges; why should not Georgetown, Kentucky (1829), and Galesburg, Illinois (Knox, 1837)? And each got a college—when its population had barely reached 1,000.

The efforts to build Athenian cities in the West were somewhat paradoxical. As the founders of these colleges and academies sought to upgrade the towns in which they lived into cities, they brought about a diffusion of culture which would challenge the very definition of a city as a center of culture. The scattering of colleges and similar cultural institutions among hundreds of western towns represented a significant

It also suggests that settlers were attracted less by the quality of the education offered than by the titles of institutions and their superficial claims to "culture."

The contributions educational institutions made to an area's economic health were well recognized in the antebellum period. Localities actually bid for such institutions—and the institutions chose to locate where they received the best financial guarantees. The University of Missouri was established only when Boone County—where Columbia is located—outbid five other Missouri River counties. The citizens of Boone County raised pledges of $82,000 in cash and $35,000 in land—the contributions coming "from over 900 individuals, of whom nearly a hundred gave five dollars or less."[13] Such patterns of contribution, as Boorstin points out, served to tie the college to the community very closely—the University of Missouri was Columbia's own college because the people of the town and its environs had "bought" it.

What financial advantages did an institution of higher learning offer a community? It would raise land values by attracting settlers who were interested in sending their children to school. Probably more important to the people who bid for the presence of a college or academy was the fact that these establishments, by attracting students and faculty from the outlying regions and from neighboring towns, would assemble more customers for the local merchants—would pump, in modern parlance, more buying power into the town's economy. Academies and colleges of the period were small, no doubt, but the towns were also small. Thus the influx of forty or fifty students could make a great difference in the town's economy. Before the colleges and academies learned that they could make a profit from renting dormitory rooms to students, the students from the outlying regions were forced to purchase room and board from townspeople. Some colleges deliberately refrained from building dormitories to house their students so that the student board revenue would be distributed throughout the town, convincing the townsmen of the college's importance to the town's economy.

If the overbuilding of higher educational institutions rested on an exaggerated optimism about the development of new areas of the United States, it also rested in large part on an overblown fear that the movement away from the old areas of settlement and their established ways would bring about a barbarism, a lack of community, and a breakdown of culture. Men beginning new communities in new areas felt the need for reassurance that they could maintain, in a new environment, the values and culture they had left behind. Like the erection of a church just like the one they had left behind, the building of a school on the older model served to reaffirm the community's commitment to older values and its capability of achieving traditional standards of morality and culture. This eagerness to affirm that they were still part of civilization, still capable of living up to the old morality and culture, accounts for the rapidity with which communities established institutions of learning. Like the habit of building schools in order to enhance land values, the habit of building schools as symbols of the aspiration to morality and culture and civilization was applicable at all levels. In the earliest years of community settlement, thousands of district schools were founded as just such a symbol. But just as institutions of higher education had greater economic value than the district school, so did they have greater symbolic value as commitments to culture.

While participants in the new community ventures worried about what was happening in the older communities worried about them also. The college president of the early nineteenth century was no less a slave to money-raising responsibility than is his modern counterpart, and part of his obligations included frequent trips to the east coast (and sometimes to England) to raise funds for the college. The educational institution's fund raiser was most successful at home by appealing to the economic interests and community pride of the local community; he was most successful in the East in appealing to the philanthropists' and the churches' concern with the morals and manners of the westerner and frontiersman. When citizens left one community to venture to a new frontier or a new community in a less settled region, they and more particularly those who remained behind felt that the movers were breaking, or at least severely straining, the social code which emphasized loyalty and subordination of self to the interests of the group. Some of the less trusting easterners felt that the pioneers had left "civilized and religious society for the simple purpose of getting out of its restraints." By moving to the West these people had excluded themselves from the community, from "society," and from its control. They had become different and, as such, came to seem more or less dangerous to the settled ways of those living in the traditional communities.

In response to this crisis of "outsiders," several religiously oriented organizations sprang up to supply ministers, schools and Sunday schools, Bibles, and tracts to the outsiders in the hopes of influencing their morals. As the executive committee of the Home Missionary Society, in appealing for funds in 1839, put it: "The Gospel is the most economical police on earth." The most important of these benevolent societies were the American Home Missionary Society (founded in 1826), the American Tract Society (1825), the American Bible Society (1816), the American Education Society (1824). These, plus a host of small institutions, individual churches, and individual philanthropists, similarly concerned that the movement away from a settled community effected a deleterious character change in people, provided much of the capital for the overexuberant expansion of higher education in the first half of the nineteenth century. They did so in hopes that such educational institutions would reassert the authority of religion and civilization on a population that seemed to those unfamiliar with it—as the easterners largely were—a dangerous source of disorder and political and social disruption.[14]

Religion and religious instruction were very much a part of the work carried on by most of the academies and colleges founded before the Civil War—as they were of those founded after. This religious orientation manifested the concern many of the supporters of higher education in this period felt for the morals and character of those for whom the institutions were being built. The character of this religious orientation was largely nondenominational, although distinctly Protestant and militantly anti-Catholic. But it is not particularly helpful to describe this period in the history of higher education as one of denominational rivalry in the founding of schools and to attribute the overbuilding of the era to that competition. Each denomination, the argument goes, in adjusting to the voluntarism necessitated by the separation of church and state formalized by the Bill of Rights, sought to gain and keep converts. One important device for furthering this evangelistic enterprise was the denominational school and college. Thus, the argument continues, each denomination rushed to found schools in as many areas as possible so that each school could inculcate the religious dogma of the denomination which controlled it and win for the denomination a much firmer hold on the students who passed through the school. These students, thanks to their training, would be less likely to break the voluntary bonds of denominational membership. Furthermore, it is argued, the various sects sought schools in which to train ministers.

Although this argument from denominational competition has a certain superficial logic, it does not adequately fit the facts of the first half of the nineteenth century. Denominational competition was not an important characteristic or cause of the development of institutions of higher education in that era. The historian of higher education in the antebellum period finds the typical school under a nominal denominational identification, but open to all without tests of religious faith. The school served a geographic rather than a religious community and was attended by students from the surrounding territory, no matter what their religious affiliation—if any. The school engaged in no doctrinal inculcation beyond commonly accepted tenets of Christian morality. Most of the colleges founded before the 1840s took on the denominational coloring of their backers because these backers stipulated that a majority of the institution's trustees must belong to a certain denomination. Often, however, another denomination was given perpetual minority status on the board of trustees in order to secure support for the new venture among town leaders who did not share the denominational affiliation of most of the backers. At the same time, in order to make the college as attractive as possible to all comers, the backers prohibited religious tests for either faculty or students. As Frederick Rudolph has

pointed out, the "nineteenth-century American college could not support itself on a regimen of petty sectarianism; there simply were not enough petty sectarians or, if there were, there was no way of getting them to the petty sectarian colleges in sufficient numbers."[15]

On the other hand, there was little likelihood that Americans would maintain nondenominational colleges in this era. Virtually every educational institution established in the nineteenth century set out to instill piety and virtue in students and to explain to them the power and the beauty of God. All the colleges were Christian. But such a designation was hardly enough in that era—a person was, after all, a Christian in a particular way—a Methodist or a Congregationalist or what-have-you. There was no recognized general Christian way of serving God or of worshipping Him. One served and worshipped as a member of a denomination. After all, chapel services had to take some form—a form of communion and a form of the Lord's Prayer had to be agreed upon. "Nondenominational" forms of worship had yet to be invented. Even the ostensibly nonsectarian state colleges, perhaps with the exception of the University of Virginia, were thought to have been "captured" by denominations. But the nature of this "capture" reveals how unimportant denomination affiliation was from the evangelistic point of view. A college was considered captured whenever a majority of the trustees belonged to a single denomination, but the denominational affiliation of the conquerors need not have effected any change in the operation or the personnel of the college.

Denominational identification in the years before 1830 or 1840 seems largely to have been accidental in that the new institution took whatever denominational form that most of its trustees favored. Some denominational identification was virtually necessary to the functioning of the institution, and the natural and simple thing to do was to adopt the religion of the social leaders, the boosters, of the community in which the institution was housed. These were the men who became the trustees. Between 1830 and the Civil War, events become somewhat more complicated. Some academies and colleges, desperate for money, sought to emphasize their denominational leanings in order to convince churches that they merited financial support. These solicitations met with varying success—one college changed its identification three times in as many years in hopes of appealing successfully to some denomination. Also, very gradually after 1830 regional and national administrators of the various denominations grew interested in seeking or building schools in each area with which to affiliate. They took the first steps toward building a network of schools to which members of the denomination could send their children and be sure they were receiving proper religious instruction. But only after the Civil War did the denominations begin to play a central role in organizing, locating, and supporting higher education. By then the spirit of community involvement had weakened considerably.

In explaining the overbuilding of colleges and academies in the antebellum period, however, general concern for morality and social control are much more important than denominational competition.

The fourth reason that academies and colleges were so overbuilt in the decades before the Civil War was that local social leaders and their children derived considerable social status from these institutions. Institutions of higher education had economic value for these social leaders in that they increased the wealth of the community. Just as important was the fact that those institutions confirmed (or established) the social leaders' status in that community. The social leaders were, of course, the influentials in the community. They might be like the people responsible for the founding of Phillips Andover and Phillips Exeter, in 1778 and 1783 respectively, or like the founders of Lafayette College in Pennsylvania. Samuel Phillips, Jr., was descended from a long line of Harvard-trained Puritan clergymen; his father was a prominent Massachusetts businessman and politician. Samuel was a member of the convention that framed the constitution of Massachusetts; he became a judge, a state senator, and, at the time of his death, lieutenant governor. Two other members of the family assisted Samuel in establishing the two academies which still bear the family name—one a doctor, the other a leading judge in New Hampshire. The fact that the Phillips family could afford to give the two academies an endowment estimated somewhere between $100,-000 and $150,000—a lot of money at the time—attests to the family's prominence.

Status was an important motive in the founding of the academies and colleges. The Phillipses looked on higher education as a way of maintaining the traditional social order and the traditional separation of classes in a society awash with revolutionary theory and paeans to the dignity and equality of all men. Samuel Phillips wholeheartedly supported the revolutionary impulse to secure liberty and purity for Americans, but he did not think that his sons were no better than any other men living in America. He felt that the greatest weakness of the Dummer School, which he had attended between 1765 and 1767, was that it sought to educate charity students along with paying ones.[17] Academy training would give his sons a refinement, an esprit, and a sense of moral character and social responsibility that would make manifest the separation in which he believed. For a man like James Madison Porter, ambitiously trying to carve an upper-middle-class status for himself, sending his offspring to an academy or college would lend them a refinement and a status to help set them (and him) above most of the people living in northeastern Pennsylvania.

In underdeveloped regions, the patterns of influence and leadership were somewhat different. Whereas the Phillipses had both the influence and the money to start their ventures virtually alone, leaders in new towns depended on their ability to mobilize support from others. These leaders, typically, did not have deep social and economic roots in the community. They were men who hoped to establish their wealth and their prestige by developing the communities to which they had recently moved. James Madison Porter, lawyer, canal promoter, and leading citizen-booster of Easton, Pennsylvania, is a case in point. Recently settled in that small underdeveloped community seventy miles north of Philadelphia, Porter took note of the economic stimulus that colleges provided such a small town. In 1824 he published an advertisement calling on all interested citizens to meet to discuss the founding of such a college. The meeting was a success and a board of thirty-nine men was appointed. "This number included several promoters, a number of businessmen, lawyers, a physician, two newspapermen, and two hotelkeepers. Not one of the number had been born in Easton; only one had attended college."[16] The four ministers on the board were excluded so as to prevent any appearance of clerical control. Porter and the other trustees felt that their personal success depended on Easton's growth. In 1824 the town's prospects

seemed good. The town, largest in eastern Pennsylvania north of Philadelphia, lay across wagon routes to the West at the confluence of the Lehigh and Delaware rivers upon which coal and shipbuilding materials were sent to Philadelphia. They expected Lafayette College, as it was called, to draw needed attention to their community. Easton was in an eastern locale but was a town similar in its newness, pretension, and leaders to hundreds of similar towns newly founded in undeveloped regions from Maine to Minnesota.

Noah Webster noted how differences in language abilities separated people. In one sense, this is what the academies and colleges were all about. The most characteristic feature of their instruction was its emphasis on the classical languages. American educational reformers and theorists from Benjamin Franklin on stressed the need for instruction in more practical subjects in the academies—they argued that the study of English and of the arithmetical skills necessary to the merchant and the engineer should form the core of the academy curriculum. Francis Wayland repeated these injunctions and applied them to the colleges in 1842. But Wayland's efforts at reforming the curriculum in the 1840s came to naught just as Franklin's had one hundred years earlier, and the study of Latin and Greek continued as the most important aspect of instruction in these schools.

Why? Because a knowledge of Latin and Greek, however superficial, gave its possessor something—a skill, but more important a sense of refinement—that his fellow citizens did not have. Speeches and conversations of the period were filled with gratuitous snippets of Latin or Greek that served to manifest the culture and the refinement of the speaker. Ability to include such quotations served as a kind of badge of status, just as proper pronunciation of English served to separate the classes from the masses. Thus, while the elementary schools, at least in theory, sought to break down class barriers by stressing common training in English, institutions of higher education continued to erect other linguistic separations.

A knowledge of the classics, superficial or not, became a key means of access to the professions and to positions of leadership that society felt should be restricted to educated men. Although the academies and colleges served primarily the children of social leaders, they did not restrict their admissions to these people—they could not afford to. Thus, they afforded a means of mobility to young men bent on bettering themselves. Attendance at these institutions furnished the upwardly mobile youngster with all the patina of culture and refinement that a classical education could give plus the opportunity to mix with and adopt the values of the offspring of social leaders.

A great deal of the mixing, the sharing of values, and the building of cohesion among these upper-middle-class students and those who aspired to that status occurred in the student-organized clubs that appeared in the academies and colleges soon after the turn of the century. At the colleges, Greek letter fraternities appeared in the late twenties and thirties, but literary and debating societies had appeared long before. These societies functioned much as did fraternities in later years. All these clubs, societies, and fraternities carried out some of the most important goals of higher education in this period. The constitution of Phillips Exeter proposed to prepare students for "the first and principal object of this Institution Of Living," and stressed that "the *first* and *principal* object of this Institution is the promotion of true Piety and Virtue; the *second*, instruction in the English, Latin, and Greek Languages, etc."[18] In the literary and debating clubs, the students gathered to exercise their language skills and to discuss contemporary issues of morality and government—issues affecting the "real business of living." In a curriculum that was dominated by rote memorization, these clubs served an important function by transmitting common social values to students.

Thus, where the elementary schools may have been preparing students to enter comfortably the local power structure in the middling and lower ranks, the colleges and academies were preparing students to enter the local leadership group—to become influentials themselves. They provided badges of status and a sense of cohesiveness among the leaders-to-be. These higher institutions in effect socialized the students to the leadership function and to the values of the local leadership group. They also socialized students to the spirit of local boosterism—there the students were at the very center of the issue, their schooling and their future careers often dependent on whether local promoters could assemble enough money to pay the professors and keep the school in business. They lived in the midst of fund-raising campaigns and all the inevitable huckstering connected with selling the future of the town and its institu-

tions. The schools also socialized the future leaders to the sense of separateness between themselves and others—that they stood somewhat above the common man with special privileges and special responsibilities, with opportunities and duties different from those of the common man. In the early 1840s Isaiah Boot came home from college for summer vacation to visit friends and relatives. "Here for the first time did I begin to feel how perceptibly education separated those of equal age. Tho I had been but two years at college, it seemed that my schoolmates had gone backward half a century. I saw there was a wide difference between us. I supposed that society was becoming rough and going back to heathenism as fast as possible. But the fact was that my comrades were where I left them and I had gone forward."[19] And this, of course, was for many of the students, parents, and founders of institutions of higher learning the whole point of the experience—that these institutions would foster a spirit of separateness, of leadership, and of social responsibility among those lucky enough to attend them.

The academies and colleges were not intent on forming an aristocracy in America; rather, they were contributing to the formation of a broad American middle, or upper middle, class. Their students would become the promoters, the land developers, the lawyers, doctors, ministers, and teachers, the merchants and manufacturers, and the statesmen and politicians of the future. The very diffuseness of the academy and college movement prevented those institutions from assuming aristocratic pretensions. There were too many schools and too many pupils.

Evaluation of the effects of this overbuilding on higher education is very difficult. A number of historians have lamented the fact that the overbuilding of institutions of higher education in the antebellum period caused a serious decline in the quality of education at the secondary and tertiary level. Some historians have seen the antebellum period as the nadir of higher education in which anti-intellectual evangelicals displaced qualified educators and the value of higher education became debased. Much of what these historians say is true—higher education during this period was lamentably bad, for serious overbuilding did cause educational considerations to suffer because of financial and other reasons. And it is possible to argue that, had the money spent on higher education been concentrated on a few institutions, the United States would have had colleges and secondary schools ranking with the best in the world.

On the other hand, one must note that the diffusion of cultural and educational institutions and the intertwining of local economic and cultural interests vastly increased the population's interest in cultural activity. For all the superficiality of this interest in culture, for all the interest in form and disregard of content, such diffusion and such stress on the economic and local advantages of education contributed a great deal in teaching Americans to value education. Further, it is quite possible that the diffusion of higher education—however debased—may have played a major role in encouraging the economic growth of the United States in the nineteenth century and in strengthening its institutions. What higher education may have lost in intellectual quality through diffusion of effort, it may have gained in popular support and interest.

[1] Benjamin Franklin, *Proposals Relating to the Education of Youth in Pennsylvania* (Philadelphia, 1749), quoted in Theodore Sizer, ed., *The Age of the Academies* (New York, 1964), 71, 75.

[2] David F. Allmendinger, *Paupers and Scholars: The Transformation of Student Life in Nineteenth-Century New England* (New York, 1975), and David Potts, "Baptist Colleges in the Development of American Society, 1812–1861" (Unpublished Dissertation, Harvard University, 1967).

[3] Henry Barnard, "The Educational Interest of the United States," *American Journal of Education*, I (March, 1856), 368, Table III.

[4] Albert Fishlow, "The American Common School Revival: Fact or Fancy?", in Henry Rosovsky, ed., *Industrialization in Two Systems: Essays in Honor of Alexander Gerschenkron* (New York, 1966), 40–67.

[5] Donald G. Tewksbury, *The Founding of American Colleges and Universities Before the Civil War: With Particular Reference to the Religious Influence Bearing upon the College Movement* (New York, 1932).

[6] Sydney Aronson, *Status and Kinship in the Higher Civil Service: Standards of Selection in the Administrations of John Adams, Thomas Jefferson, and Andrew Jackson* (Cambridge, Mass., 1964), 122–123.

[7] On the relative decline in college enrollment in the nineteenth-century, see Frederick Rudolph, *The American College and University: A History* (New York, 1962), 99, 118–140, and John S. Whitehead, *The Separation of College and State: Columbia, Dartmouth, Harvard, and Yale, 5–1876* (New Haven, Conn., 1973).

[8] Twenty-one percent of the national population was aged 15–24 in 1850; we have figured the frontier percentage at 30 percent (which is probably too high). We have made no adjustment for the presence of blacks in the Texas population.

[9] Daniel Boorstin, *The Americans: The National Experience* (New York, 1965), especially chapters 16, 17, 20, 21. The sentence quoted below is from p. 152.

[10] Noah Webster in Frederick Rudolph, *Essays on Education in the Early Republic* (Cambridge, Mass., 1965), 52.

[11] Henry Nash Smith, *Virgin Land* (Cambridge, Mass., 1950), passim.

[12] Lloyd Jorgenson, *The Founding of Public Education in Wisconsin* (Madison, Wis., 1956), 34.

[13] Boorstin, *National Experience*, 159.

[14] The best discussion of these societies is Clifford Griffin, *Their Brothers' Keepers: Moral Stewardship in the United States, 1800–1865* (New Brunswick, N. J., 1960); quotations are from pp. 59–60, 111. Griffin quotes on p. 111 *The Home Missionary*, XII (May, 1839), 9–10.

[15] Rudolph, *American College and University*, 69.

[16] Boorstin, *National Experience*, 156. A more detailed discussion can be found in David B. Skillman, *Biography of a College* (Easton, Pa., 1932), which confirms Boorstin's account.

[17] Andover's first president preceptor, Eliphalet Pearson, modified Phillips' stand on this issue to the extent that the academy did provide some scholarship funds for indigent students. On Samuel Phillips and his academies, see especially James McLachlan, *American Boarding Schools: A Historical Study* (New York, 1970).

[18] Quoted in Elmer E. Brown, *The Making of Our Middle Schools: An Account of the Development of Secondary Education in the United States* (New York, 1903), 195.

[19] Quoted in David Potts, "Baptist Colleges" (dissertation draft, chapter 4, p. 29).

GUIDE TO FURTHER READING

FREDERICK RUDOLPH, *The American College and University: A History* (New York, 1962), remains the most thorough analysis of the antebellum college in the United States. His bibliography of institutional histories is the best and most conveniently available. The early chapters of OSCAR and MARY HANDLIN, *The American College and American Culture: Socialization as a Function of Higher Education* (New York, 1970), and more generally their essay on *Facing Life: Youth and Family in American History* (Boston, 1971) examine, with a good deal of perception, the experience of leaving home. RICHARD HOFSTADTER and WALTER P. METZGER, *The Development of Academic Freedom in the United States* (New York, 1955), Part I (published separately by Hofstadter in 1961), is the best account of that topic and a useful introduction to the antebellum academic experience in general. RICHARD HOFSTADTER and WILSON SMITH, eds., *American Higher Education: A Documentary History*, 2 vols. (Chicago, 1961), is a model collection of primary sources. An investigation of the sources of support for antebellum institutions, and an excellent introduction to the concepts of "public" and "private," are included in JOHN S. WHITEHEAD, *The Separation of College and State: Columbia, Dartmouth, Harvard, and Yale, 1776–1876* (New Haven, Conn., 1973). In *Professors and Public Ethics: Studies of Northern Moral Philosophers before the Civil War* (Ithaca, N. Y., 1956), WILSON SMITH examines ethical theorists and public policy in several antebellum institutions. Collegiate innovations based upon student requirements are explored in DAVID F. ALLMENDINGER, *Paupers and Scholars: The Transformation of Student Life in Nineteenth-Century New England* (New York, 1975). DAVID MADSEN, *The National University: Enduring Dream of the U. S. A.* (Detroit, 1966), remains the standard survey.

DONALD G. TEWKSBURY, *The Founding of American Colleges and Universities Before the Civil War: With Particular Reference to the Religious Influence Bearing Upon the College Movement* (New York, 1932), remains the standard introduction to antebellum college founding, but should be supplemented by NATALIE A. NAYLOR's critique, "The Ante-Bellum College Movement: A Reappraisal of Tewksbury's Founding of American Colleges and Universities," *History of Education Quarterly*, XIII (Fall, 1973), 261–274. DAVID POTTS examines the impact that localism had upon the secular nature of denominational institutions before the Civil War in "Baptist Colleges in the Development of American Society, 1812–1861" (Unpublished Dissertation, Harvard University, 1967) and "American Colleges in the Nineteenth Century: From Localism to Denominationalism," *History of Education Quarterly*, XI (Winter, 1971), 363–380. DANIEL BOORSTIN, *The Americans: The National Experience* (New York, 1965), suggests the influence of local "boosterism" upon the antebellum movement to establish institutions of higher learning. GEORGE P. SCHMIDT's volumes on *The Old Time College President* (New York, 1930) and *The Liberal Arts College: A Chapter in American Cultural History* (New Brunswick, N. J., 1957) remain useful.

The American academy and other nonpublic school educational institutions are surveyed in ROBERT MIDDLEKAUFF, *Ancients and Axioms: Secondary Education in Eighteenth-Century New England* (New Haven, Conn., 1963), THEODORE R. SIZER, ed., *The Age of the Academies* (New York, 1964), ROBERT F. SEYBOLT, *The Evening School in Colonial America* (Urbana, Ill., 1925), SEYBOLT, *The Public Schools of Colonial Boston, 1635–1775* (Cambridge, Mass., 1935), and ELMER E. BROWN, *The Making of Our Middle Schools: An Account of the Development of Secondary Education in the United States* (New York, 1903)

The Death of the Liberal Arts College

James Axtell

TO EVERY THING, said the Preacher, there is a season, a time to be born and a time to die. But sometimes the students of Life misread its signs and prematurely bury one whose time has yet to come. Historians no less than journalists sometimes write obituaries when they should be appraising the tenacity of age. Over the past twenty years historians of American higher education have fallen deeply into the trap of prematurity; the obituary they wrote reads something like this:

Washington, D.C., 2 July 1862. The American Liberal Arts College died today after a prolonged illness. It was 226 years old.

Born on the salty backwashes of the Charles River in Cambridge shortly after the Massachusetts Bay Colony was founded, the scion of Puritan Reform and Renaissance Civility grew to sturdy usefulness in the colonial years by overseeing America's leaders prior to their war for independence.

When the new nation emerged, however, demanding a larger, more expert citizenry, The College was unable to overcome its aristocratic origins and shortly contracted the disease that eventually led to its demise — arteriosclerosis. In the 1820s, when Jacksonian Democracy was urging needed reforms on American Institutions, The College's role in society contracted into a stance of pugnacious conservatism with the Yale Report of 1828. Even a number of its own reform-minded members could not edge it into the American Mainstream of Technological Growth and Democratic Expansion.

Today, after a recent cardiac arrest, its heart stopped on the floor of the House of Representatives, just as the roll call for Justin Morrill's Land-Grant Act had ended.

The vote was 90-25.

In short, the liberal arts college not only died a sudden death during or shortly after the Civil War, but no one should have mourned its passing, if indeed anyone did.

For those who still doubt that truth is stranger than fiction, a glance at the conventional wisdom of the nineteenth-century colleges will secure conversion. First, the antebellum colleges, which inhabit something called "The Age of the College," are variously described as "precarious, little, denomination-ridden, poverty-stricken," plagued by "dubious standards," offering little freedom or economic reward to their faculties. In a telling word, they were simply "unprogressive." Furthermore, they were vestigial structures on the American body social. "The old-time colleges were not organically knit into the fabric of economic life," says Professor Richard Hofstadter. "Although college training was an advantage, it was not necessary in the early 19th century to go to college to become a doctor, lawyer, or even a teacher, much less a successful politician or businessman. . . . Higher education was far more a luxury, much less a utility, than it is today." This explains the morbid "state of the curriculum" and the "backward condition of the art of teaching" in the old-time college that responded "so slowly to social change." As far as the colleges were concerned, antebellum America was a place of "Great Retrogression" and slow "Death." (1)

But *après Eliot le déluge!* Under the weight of the western land-grant universities (representing Utility), German scholarship and higher criticism (representing Research), and Darwinism (representing Science), "the old-time college crumbled." According to which history you read, the new universities either "absorbed," "replaced," "modified," "invaded," or "profoundly altered the content of" the colleges. By 1900 "the old independent college had yielded precedence to the university." Colleges continued to function" — a rare admission — "they even increased in number, but henceforth they carried on their activities as units of, or in competition with, the larger many-sided universities. . . . They had to adjust to a new frame of reference." Even the historian most faithful to the liberal arts colleges is led to write that "universities, indisputably, were the movement of the future" and that "it may be true that forces secreted within the American spirit were set loose by the Civil War, making inevitable the replacement of the old-time college." In the classic statement of this view, "the age of the college had passed, and the age of the university was dawning." Clearly such history resembles nothing so much as, in George Peterson's apt phrase, "a morality play written in two acts." (2)

Unfortunately, clumsy moralism is not such history's only weakness. Fundamentally it is Whig history of the most blatant kind, written from the future where historical changes seem simply "inevitable" and the past teems with "revolutionary turning points," "watersheds," and "crises," all heralding the "dawning of new eras" and death's "transfiguration." It is short-cut history at its best, replete with winners, heroes, and historical firsts, and unencumbered with the complexities of change and continuity, flux and flow.

But it is not that this kind of history is simply outdated — despite its recent vogue in the hands of putatively "radical" historians — but that it is *bad* Whig history, as its tactics so clearly show. First, it reconstructs a model of the antebellum college largely from its critics' less-than-objective appraisals. Professor Hofstadter's chapter on "The Old-Time College" in his surprisingly influential *Development of Academic Freedom in the United States* is a perfect example of how *not* to write judicious history. Of the testimony used to characterize the antebellum colleges, one out of every four references contains the name of Francis Wayland, the reform-possessed president of Brown

University who even his champions admit was either years ahead of his time or **hopelessly** unrealistic about the possibilities of American education. The other references draw on the works of Philip Lindsley, George Ticknor, F. A. P. Barnard, Thomas Jefferson, Henry Tappan, and a whole "Convention of Literary and Scientific Gentlemen" called in part to "criticize the spirit of the Yale Report in 1828," all of whom, not surprisingly, dominate the section of Hofstadter's documentary history of *American Higher Education* called "The Quest for an Adequate Educational System." The only possible glimmer of recognition that the antebellum collegiate way might have had some saving graces comes from his inclusion of the Yale Report of 1828, admittedly "the most influential document in American higher education in the first half of the nineteenth century," though one cannot help feeling that its appearance was sponsored more by the needs of its enemies than by the praise of its friends. For the friends of the colleges are never subpoenaed to Hofstadter's kangaroo court; for all intents and purposes they did not exist. The hundreds of men and women who supported the Society for the Promotion of Collegiate and Theological Education at the West, the myriad local benevolent societies for the financial aid of indigent college students, The American Home Missionary Society, the founding of over seven hundred community colleges, and the continuation of the established Yales and Princetons of the day are irrelevant at best and fantasies of romantic delusion at worst. As Professor Hofstadter assures us, "most of the *serious* literature of college reminiscence is a literature of complaint." With a judge like that, a trial is superfluous. (3)

Second, the Whig historiography invariably compares the colleges of one period with the universities of a later one. Thus we hear only of the "old-time college" (singular) with its "old-time college president" (fossilized) or of new universities (plural) with their empire-building presidents (dynamic) who fomented something called "the university revolution," but never of comparable institutions of the same era. By the same token it often slips from a consideration of the liberal education of one era to that of research, vocational, or graduate training of the next, instead of fairly assessing the changes, not necessarily for better or worse, in the liberal education of undergraduates over time. In its characteristic haste to abridge history, it conveniently blurs distinctions and rides rough-shod over differences, both of which are essential to the judicial process.

The reason for these imbalances is not hard to find. In his last reiteration of the Whig dogma, Professor Hofstadter effectively revealed the educational presuppositions with which he approached the history of higher education in "the old regime." "Sectarian competition, compounded by local competition, had prevented the educational energies of the country from being *concentrated* in a *limited* number of institutions of adequate size and adequate sustenance. Instead, the country was dotted with tiny colleges, weakly founded; only one out of five created before the Civil War survived — it is an incredible rate of failure. Those that did survive were frequently too *small* to be educationally effective; they lacked *complexity*; they lacked *variety*." It would not be unfair, I think, to suggest that Professor Hofstadter's model of an "educationally effective" collegiate institution, a model that he does not scruple to apply to the past as well as the present, resembles nothing so much as the large, sprawling centrifuge known as Columbia University. (4)

There is, of course, another interpretation of the widespread diffusion of the educational energies of antebellum America that does not regard its subject with such transparent disdain. In his chapter on "Culture with Many Capitals: The Booster College," Daniel Boorstin argues that the booster spirit and the missionary spirit worked in harness to bring each western settlement "all the metropolitan hallmarks" — a newspaper, a hotel, and a college. This ideal of the complete community not only promoted "the diffuseness of American culture," but its vigorous boosterism secured the characteristically American marriage of the college and the community. "The distinctively American college," observes Professor Boorstin with obvious relish, "was neither public nor private, but a *community* institution." As President William Tyler of Amherst told the Society for the Promotion of Theological and Collegiate Education at the West in 1856, the genius of the American college with its local trustees was that "while the college redeems the community from the curse of ignorance, the community preserves the college from an undue tendency to monkish corruption and scholastic unprofitableness." (5)

The third weakness of the Whig dogma is that it assumes a crude and misleading functionalism — borrowed from modern sociologists — between a society's needs and the college's direct attempt to satisfy them through its curriculum. As Professor Hofstadter wrote, "the curriculum is a barometer by which we may measure the cultural pressures that operate upon the school." But as long ago as 1950 Richard Storr warned us that a common source of confusion in the writing of educational history was "the failure to separate the *need* for a specific kind of knowledge at some time and the actual *demand* for instruction in it. It is one thing to say that a society should have enlightenment in it. It is another thing to say that it includes young people

who are prepared to pay for the opportunity of acquiring such knowledge." More recently Lawrence Stone has renewed the warning. "As every historian knows, all the institutions of society are partly functional and partly antiquated, vestigial, or even frankly 'dysfunctional.' This is because they all have a history and a life of their own, and their response to outside pressure is consequently imperfect, stumbling, tardy, and even reactive." (6)

Instead of the curriculum itself, Frederick Rudolph argues that the *extracurriculum* is "the most sensitive barometer of what is going on at a college" because "it is the instrument of change . . . the agency that identifies [the students'] enthusiasms, their understanding of what a college should be, their preferences . . . [and] their attitude toward the course of study. . . . And because it is the particular province of lively, imaginative young men and women not immobilized by tradition, rank, authority, and custom, the extracurriculum is likely to respond more quickly than any other agency of the college to the fundamental, perhaps not yet even clearly expressed, movements in the world beyond the campus and to the developing expectations of society." (7)

Fourth, the Whig dogmatists almost always contrast a static, black-and-white snapshot of the antebellum college with a technicolor film of the new postwar universities. Even when they concede that the liberal arts college continued to exist after the Civil War, they deny them equal treatment. Understandably they would like to have the best of both worlds. On the one hand, they assume (incorrectly as we have shown) that the institutions of higher education in any society respond directly to pressing social needs and demands. On the other, they write as if the colleges did not respond to the same *general* configuration of social needs, inherited and imported traditions, and new ideas to which the new universities responded. At best the colleges are visible only as they capitulate to the inevitability of the "university ideal."

Fortunately this kind of myopia can be cured with the perspectives of several new (and older) studies of the liberal arts college in the so-called "age of the university," all of which clearly demonstrate that several colleges at least confronted the significant social and intellectual questions of postwar America as earnestly as any university, even though their various answers happened to differ from the universities' answers. (8) They also illustrate a simple fact about social and institutional change that Whig historians tend to forget in their rush to the narcotic generality, namely that "changes have come when particular men in a particular situation have been impressed by particular urgencies and when their thoughts or actions have been questioned by particular critics." Consequently, it is simply unreasonable to expect that hundreds of particular colleges in particular social settings would react to exactly the same configuration of social forces, much less that they would react in the same way. (9)

Finally, the Whig view assumes a one-way relationship between contemporary social institutions — the university worked its magic on the college — but it never raises the possibility that something important flowed the other way. Common sense alone should call into question the reliability of any account in which a new specialized institution does not derive at least some form and substance from the sole antecedent institution of the same specialty. From most Whig histories one gets the distinct impression that modern Harvard, Cornell, and Johns Hopkins sprang full grown from the heads of Eliot, White, and Gilman, without so much as a backward glance at the collegiate institutions in which they were all educated.

Without doubt there were conscious and definite differences between the new universities and their collegiate predecessors, but their zealous promotion by the Whig historians has obscured significant continuities from one to the other. The most apparent continuity was the often frail but persistent belief that a *college* of arts and sciences should form the heart of a true university, even the most diffuse. Another was the residential nature of "the collegiate way of living." After an initial flirtation with the uncongenial German ideal of official unconcern for the student outside the classroom, the new universities returned to the distinctly American concern for the whole collegiate experience of their students. By World War I nearly every state and private university had begun to build dormitories or college systems after the Oxbridge model in an effort to recapture the union of living and learning that had been the college's primary value in the colonial period. Of particular force in securing residential housing at the midwestern universities were the graduates of the eastern women's colleges. As they assumed the deanships of women at the new institutions, these graduates gently but firmly pushed the new universities toward the domestic sociability they had known at their alma maters. (10)

And a third continuity between the old and the new institutions was their Christian character. Though they prided themselves on their nonsectarianism, many of the new state universities turned to presidents of visible, even exaggerated, religiosity, many of them ministers, and maintained compulsory daily chapel services until the turn of the century. In more areas than we have been led to believe, the line separating the liberal arts colleges and the newer universities was non-

existent. (11)

It should be obvious by now that much more of our conventional ideas about American higher education deserves close scrutiny. Professor Hofstadter's *Development of Academic Freedom in the United States* must, like all seminal works, be taken from its pedestal and critically examined, because, as Emerson warned us long ago, "genius is always sufficiently the enemy of genius by overinfluence." (12) By its particular perspective and literary assertiveness, it should have stimulated the serious study of American higher education and engendered its own competition, but instead it has only bedazzled us into mindless combat, quiescence. Even for a man who did not relish intellectual combat, Professor Hofstadter must have looked on the supine reception of his educational works with a touch of surprise.

As a small beginning toward such a reassessment, I would like to suggest some ways in which we might go about writing the history of higher education that would be at once fair to the past and helpful to the present. The first thing we must do is to ask several new questions, seemingly simple questions perhaps, but questions to which we do not have satisfactory answers, only polemical tub-thumpings or unexamined assumptions. The one that suggests itself first is, what were the antebellum colleges really like? Were they, as David Potts asks below, the victims of a debilitating sectarianism? Were they, as David Allmendinger asks, bastions of suffocating paternalism? Were they, as Professor Hofstadter insists, luxury items in an expanding economy? And if so, what other social and cultural roles did they play? By burying it in a subordinate clause, Professor Hofstadter minimizes the extent to which "college training was an advantage" before the Civil War. For instance, in 1893 Charles Thwing published a study of American leadership, based on some fifteen thousand entries in *Appleton's Cyclopedia of American Biography*, that showed that a disproportionately high number of leaders in the major professions were college graduates. In medicine, where normally about one doctor in twenty had a college degree even as late as 1893, forty-six percent of its *leaders* were graduates, as were half of the outstanding lawyers, who normally had one degree for every five practitioners. (13) The colleges were clearly instruments of social mobility but to just what extent only career-line studies of the graduates of many individual colleges will tell. (14) If they were not, as Professor Hofstadter insinuates, it is difficult to see why America's practical-minded settlers invested so heavily in them in the years after independence.

There is also the danger that in concentrating on their economic value we are overlooking the predominately religious and cultural impulses that founded the vast majority of the colleges before the Civil War and kept an amazing 182 institutions alive into the twentieth century. Equally we must distinguish carefully between the kinds of colleges in existence at the time. Perhaps the older eastern colleges and the newer frontier colleges, distinguished more by function and founding ideal than geography, served widely different functions in different subcultures of the country.

Another question that arises after reading any survey of American higher education is, what was the "university revolution" of the nineteenth century? And when did it occur? — at President Eliot's inauguration in 1869, at the founding of the University of Berlin in 1810, or sometime after 1890? How typical were Harvard, Cornell, and Johns Hopkins of the new universities? Is it fair to contrast university mountains and college valleys? If we focus on institutions of the same period — and only for comparison, not competition — how large, low advanced, and how free were the universities as compared with the colleges?

As I have suggested, before 1885 or 1890 the differences are much smaller than we have been led to believe by the Whig champions of Harvard and Cornell. In 1881, for example, about 26 institutions had enrollments of 200 students or more; of these, 17 were colleges in fact or in name. Amherst was as large as Wisconsin and Virginia, Williams was larger than Cornell and Indiana, and Bowdoin was the near-equal of Johns Hopkins and Minnesota. Yale with 687 students was much larger than Michigan, Missouri, or the City College of New York. And if we assume that the elective system meant some sort of advancement, then library size becomes important as an indication of the scope available to unprescribed, nontextbook scholarship. Even on this scale the new universities do not fare much better. Cornell's rapidly growing collection of 41,000 volumes was the best of the new universities, but it could not match the older libraries of Yale, Dartmouth, Princeton, and Brown. Amherst and Wesleyan each had had more books than Missouri, Michigan, Indiana, Wisconsin, or Minnesota. (15)

The elective system is often said to constitute the major difference between the colleges and the new universities, but Albert Bingham's study in 1897 showed that several universities still required that their students take a number of subjects — as many as twenty-four at Rutgers — while many colleges, such as Oberlin, Amherst, and Bowdoin, required as few as Chicago, Michigan, and New York University. Since the content of the requirements was as various as the number, Bingham could only exclaim, "the disagreement of the doctors is well-nigh complete." (16) There is even reason to believe that the uni-

versities did not so much choose the elective system as a principled defense of academic freedom as they were forced into it by the poor preparation of their students. A large proportion of the students at Wisconsin and Illinois, for example, were so ill prepared for the regular college course that they were either committed to remedial "preparatory departments" or permitted to elect on a hit-and-miss basis courses in which they had some interest or hope of passing. (17) In this light the university's halo begins to tarnish a little.

A final set of questions concerns the way in which colleges responded to the social and intellectual forces that created the new universities after 1865. To what particular forces did they respond? Did they respond negatively, as some of the New England colleges seem to have, or positively? Who or what was instrumental in pushing them to change — students, faculty, alumni, poverty, wealth? I say "push" because, taking a cue from cultural anthropologists, we might well make continuity and conservatism our working assumptions about societies and the educational institutions they create to preserve and transmit their ideals and social character. (18) That way we will, like the majority of people at the time, place the burden of proof for change on the innovators and reformers, and not automatically fall into the Whig trap of assuming that "new makes right."

The second thing I think we must do to improve our history of higher education is to pay much greater attention to the person on the other end of Mark Hopkins's proverbial log — the student. The neglect of students has been so pervasive in educational history that it now enjoys the status of a veritable "historical tradition." In spite of the fact that the students have probably been the "most creative and imaginative force in the shaping of the American college and university," they "constitute the most neglected, least understood element of the academic community." (19) One of the problems, of course, has been our long-standing idea of education as basically a *teaching* process, in which the prime mover is a knowledgeable instructor and the students are passive receptacles. But our recent change of perception of education as essentially a *learning* process should give us the necessary freedom to proceed with a more sensitive kind of student-centered history.

In such a history the extracurriculum, "the most sensitive barometer of what is going on at a college," will receive as much attention as the course of study. To focus only on the student's experience in the classroom would be to seriously distort the history of his education. Oscar and Mary Handlin's recent essay on "socialization as a function of higher education" is a suggestive foray into this neglected subject. (20)

But the model for all further efforts is still Robert Fletcher's incredible *History of Oberlin College*, published almost thirty years ago. (21) Although two volumes are devoted to only thirty-some years of the college's past, there is not a bit of fat. And the main reason for that is that fully three-fourths of its pages are devoted to the full cultural and intellectual history of its students, in their relations with the faculty, the community, and the nation. If there were more individual histories of its kind, we would be in a position to write a significant history of higher education in the nineteenth century and to answer many of the questions I have posed.

Professor Fletcher's history brings me to a third suggestion, which is that we must find an important context for our essentially institutional history. Twenty years ago Richard Storr suggested that one integrative perspective for the history of higher education is the culture of academic life, the values, ideas, and practices that distinguish them from other social institutions. That is a viable perspective, as Laurence Veysey's history of *The Emergence of the American University* has shown, but it is still fundamentally "house history," the story of what goes on *inside* academia. If the history of education is to have any significance at all, it must attempt to describe the complex relationships between society and its educational processes, between what a society wants of its young and what they actually become. Accordingly, the history of higher education will have to describe academic culture as part of a larger social culture, and to place its colleges and universities in the context of the whole process of both the socialization of the young and the production and diffusion of knowledge in the society. It must consider at the very least the students who came — their socioeconomic background, expectations, career plans, maturity, and scholastic preparation; the students who graduated — where they went, where they wanted to go, what value their particular collegiate education held for their later lives; and the faculty who also came and went. We could certainly profit from studies of faculty families such as James Blackwood's engaging portrait of the Comptons of Wooster at the turn of the century; but we also need, as Lawrence Stone has urged, a quantitative analysis of whole generations of students and faculty through the methods of prosopography, if for no other reason than as an antidote to the Whig preoccupation with the unusual and the bizarre. (22)

The final suggestion I would like to make is that we must fully integrate women's education into the history of education, not in lonesome chapters called "High Seriousness in Bloomers," but as a con-tinuous, important thread. (23) Next to students in general, women have been the most neglected and certainly the least understood element of the academic community for over a hundred years. It is time we stopped repeating Lyman Beecher's poor jokes about the amalgamation of the sexes and tried to understand what social and cultural impact women have made on our colleges and universities, and vice-versa.

In the face of so many unanswered questions, perhaps we can take some comfort in the memory of our Christian predecessors who asked in times of intellectual crisis, "What must I do to be saved?" and turned to the Good Book for an answer. In my mildly evangelical way I am asking that we do the same thing, with but one difference: we have to write one first.

Notes

1. Richard Hofstadter, *The Development of Academic Freedom in the United States* (New York, 1955), pp. 209, 223; Hofstadter, *The Development and Scope of Higher Education in the United States* (New York, 1952), pp. 20-21; Ernest Earnest, "Death and Transfiguration," *Academic Procession* (Indianapolis, 1953), ch. 5.

2. George P. Schmidt, *The Liberal Arts College* (New Brunswick, 1957), p. 146; William Brickman and Stanley Lehrer, eds., *A Century of Higher Education* (New York, 1962), ch. 3; Hofstadter, *Development and Scope*, p. 48; George E. Peterson, *The New England College in the Age of the University* (Amherst, 1964), p. 3.

3. Hofstadter, *Development of Academic Freedom*, pp. 222-38; Hofstadter and Wilson Smith, eds., *American Higher Education: A Documentary History* 1 (Chicago, 1961): 251-391; Hofstadter, "The Revolution in Higher Education," in *Paths of American Thought*, ed. Arthur M. Schlesinger, Jr. and Morton White (Boston, 1963), pp. 270-71 (italics added).

4. Ibid. (italics added).

5. Daniel Boorstin, *The Americans: The National Experience* (New York, 1965), pp. 152-61.

6. Hofstadter, *Development and Scope*, p. 11; Richard Storr, "Academic Culture and the History of American Higher Education," *Journal of General Education* 5 (October 1950): 12; Lawrence Stone, "The Ninneversity," *The New York Review of Books*, January 28, 1971, p. 24. John Talbott makes a similar point in "The History of Education," *Daedalus* (Winter 1971), pp. 142-43.

7. Frederick Rudolph, "Neglect of Students as a Historical Tradition," in *The College and the Student*, ed. Lawrence E. Dennis and Joseph F. Kauffman (Washington, 1966), p. 53.

8. Thomas Le Duc, *Piety and Intellect at Amherst College, 1865-1912* (New York, 1946); George W. Pierson, *Yale College: An*

Educational History, 1871-1921 (New Haven, 1952); George E. Peterson, *The New England College in the Age of the University* (Amherst, 1964); John Barnard, *From Evangelicalism to Progressivism at Oberlin College, 1866-1917* (Columbus, Ohio, 1969); Laurence R. Veysey, *The Emergence of the American University* (Chicago, 1965). There is also the possibility that the colleges and the universities were responding to two different questions or sets of questions, in which case R. G. Collingwood's advice is pertinent. You cannot discover a man's meaning, he said, simply from his written or spoken statements, even when he is perfectly articulate and honest. "In order to find out his meaning you must also know what the question was (a question in his own mind, and presumed by him to be in yours) to which the thing he has said or written was meant as an answer." Furthermore, as Richard Storr has warned, "even when vocabulary does not change, meanings do; and where denotations are static, connotations may be fluid" (Storr, "Academic Culture and the History of American Higher Education," p. 11); Quentin Skinner, "Meaning and Understanding in the History of Ideas," *History and Theory* 8 (1969): 37-38.

9. Storr, "Academic Culture and the History of American Higher Education," p. 11. See also Robert A. Nisbet, *Social Change and History* (New York, 1969), pp. 267-304.

10. W. H. Cowley, "The History of Student Residential Housing," *School and Society*, December 1-8, 1934, pp. 705-12, 758-64.

11. A study in 1913 established that thirty-two of sixty "representative" colleges, including large state and private universities, maintained compulsory chapel (Henry T. Claus, "The Problem of College Chapel," *Educational Review* [September 1913], pp. 177-87). Of Wisconsin's three presidents after the Civil War, one was a minister and two had studied theology without entering the ministry. At Minnesota, Cyrus Northrup "sanctified" the "godless institution" left to him by his predecessor with a nonsectarian but effective "evangelical religion" (Merle Curti and Vernon Carstensen, *The University of Wisconsin, 1848-1925* 1 [Madison, 1949]; James Gray, *The University of Minnesota, 1851-1951* [Minneapolis, 1951], pp. 83-85).

12. Ralph Waldo Emerson, *An Oration, Delivered Before the Phi Beta Kappa Society, at Cambridge, August 31, 1837* (Boston, 1837).

13. Charles F. Thwing, "College Men First Among Successful Citizens," *The Forum* (June 1893), pp. 494-503. See George W. Pierson's recent study of *The Education of American Leaders* (New York, 1969) for a comparison.

14. A study of the career choices of seven Yale classes between 1860 and 1920 reveals that significant numbers of sons of fathers in lower status occupations, such as farming and the ministry, chose and were able to choose professions at graduation one or two levels higher on the current status scale, especially law and business (Sam Scovil, unpublished seminar paper, Yale University, 1970).

15. Charles F. Thwing, *American Colleges: Their Students and Work*, 2d ed. (New York, 1883), pp. 202-10.

16. Albert Perry Bingham, "Present Status of the Elective System in American Colleges," *Educational Review* (November 1897), pp. 360-69.

17. Winton U. Solberg, *The University of Illinois, 1867-1894* (Urbana, 1968), pp. 105, 130, 235; Curti and Carstensen, *Wisconsin*, 1: 399-402.

18. Nisbet, *Social Change and History*; Philip Bagby, *Culture and History* (London, 1958); A. L. Kroeber, *Anthropology* (New York, 1948); George F. Kneller, *Educational Anthropology: An Introduction* (New York, 1965).

19. Rudolph, "Neglect of Students as a Historical Tradition," pp. 47-58.

20. Oscar and Mary F. Handlin, *The American College and American Culture* (New York, 1970).

21. Robert Fletcher, *History of Oberlin College* (Oberlin, 1943).

22. James R. Blackwood, *The House on College Avenue: The Comptons at Wooster, 1891-1913* (Cambridge, 1968); Lawrence Stone, "Prosopography," *Daedalus* (Winter 1971), pp. 46-79.

23. Ernest Earnest, *Academic Procession*, ch. 6.

Mr. Axtell is Assistant Professor of History, Yale University.

"College Enthusiasm!" As Public Response: 1800-1860

David B. Potts

Standard histories of higher education typically picture the early nineteenth-century college as an institution becoming increasingly unpopular with parents, students, public officials, politicians, and businessmen. Religious leaders and their most avid followers may have been happy with a curriculum dominated by Greek and Latin, the argument goes, but few others in this early era of technological take-off could find relevance in classical studies. As a result of ignoring public needs and desires, the hundreds of antebellum colleges enrolled a dwindling portion of the population. The multitude of institutions founded is seen as proof of zealous insensitivity to the lack of individual and public interest. Many colleges never opened or were soon forced to close their doors. Only with the rise of the late nineteenth-century universities offering curricula of practical appeal, the textbook interpretation concludes, was a significant portion of the public persuaded to patronize higher education. The almost century-long love affair between middle-class America and its various alma maters presumably began with such phenomena as the steady growth of engineering enrollments in land-grant colleges during the 1870s, the strengthening of links between state universities and public high schools in that same decade and the next, and the surge in enrollments in almost all institutions beginning around 1890.[1]

More than fifteen years after Bernard Bailyn provided the first major stimulus to conceptual awareness in the history of American education,[2] we are close to the point where a very different interpretation based on substantial research can be substituted for this century-old picture of early nineteenth-century higher education. As research on antebellum colleges moves from a prolonged period of historiographical criticism into an exciting phase of monographic contributions, a clearer view of the complex relationships between colleges and their constituencies has emerged. Continued reliance on the standard account of our heritage in higher education can be shown to yield only meager and distorted understandings. The chief distortion, as this essay will emphasize, concerns the capacity of educational institutions, even in difficult times, to generate public enthusiasm for their services.

Criticism and an Alternative Overview

A major portion of the historiographical case against the predominant interpretation of antebellum colleges is contributed by scholars subjecting the standard primary and secondary sources to a close and skeptical reading. This scrutiny exposes a reformer bias in the major primary documents cited and a closely related university bias in the historians basing their conclusions on a sympathetic reading of these sources.[3] The uses of writings by Francis Wayland provide a good example. Given the large extent to which Wayland's perceptions were shaped by rigid economic doctrines, a millennial vision, and peculiar problems as president of Brown University (1827–55), one can question the use of his commentaries by Richard Hofstadter and his readers as an unquestioned source of information and insights concerning early nineteenth-century colleges.[4] Younger historians familiar with the handful of fine monographs on late nineteenth-century colleges also detect a general Whiggism in the Wayland-based picture of an earlier age of inadequacy followed by the dramatic rise of the university. They find the functionalist model employed to be simplistic, and the general interpretation at some points quite contrary to "common sense."[5] Even the data foundation for the traditional interpretation supplied by Donald G. Tewksbury in *The Founding of American Colleges and Universities Before the Civil War,* long regarded as the most useful and trustworthy monograph in the field, proves to be defective. A reappraisal of this work reveals distortions, inaccuracies, and omissions which flaw its extensive use by historians over a period of more than four decades.[6]

A second source of explicit historiographical criticism is located in the work of scholars beginning to report during the last decade that their research findings fail to support many of the most basic conclusions of the accepted interpretation. Studies of sixteen Baptist colleges, fifteen northeastern colleges, early Catholic colleges, nonreformer observations of higher education, and major education societies find little or no evidence of narrow sectarian zeal or denominational proselytizing.[7] Work on the social origins of students and on college costs produces no signs of aristrocratic dominance or tendencies.[8] Investigations of curricula yield no indications of hostility to change, resistance to science, or antagonism between religion and science.[9] Comprehensive tabulations of enrollments fail to expose colleges as institutions declining in importance and public favor.[10]

More important than these negative findings are the data and generalizations in many of the same recent studies which enable us to construct the major outlines of a new alternative interpretation. Antebellum colleges can now be seen as broadly based local enterprises, deeply rooted in the economic and cultural life of hundreds of towns, counties, and surrounding areas in states extending from the east coast westward through the Mississippi Valley.[11] Access to a college education, it appears, was relatively easy compared to the years before 1800, and an increasing number of students from humble family backgrounds were enrolling and making their presence felt.[12] The curricula of these institutions, it can be argued persuasively, was intellectually vital and responsive within the cultural context of this period.[13] Especially interesting is the discovery that a constantly increasing proportion of potential college students in the national population is found to be enrolling at these institutions during the four decades preceding the Civil War.[14] When measured along all these dimensions, colleges emerge as demonstrably popular educational enterprises.

College-Community Alliances

The key to understanding this popularity resides in the many ways in which college-community relationships developed. A study of Baptist colleges[15] illustrates the intricate alliances forged between college promoters and a particular town or county. Although many of the examples cited below are found in the histories of particular Baptist-affiliated colleges, the representativeness of these examples and the validity of generalizations they support were checked against data on more than a dozen other colleges of this type as well as available evidence in the few older studies of colleges affiliated with the Methodist, Presbyterian, and Episcopal denominations.[16] The comparison verifies that Baptist colleges were sufficiently typical to warrant their extensive use as illustrations in a brief synthesis of current scholarship on antebellum colleges.[17]

Unusually extensive information concerning close college-community cooperation in the founding years can be found in the history of Colby College, the first Baptist-affiliated institution of nineteenth-century origin to offer college-level instruction.[18] At least three non-Baptist residents of Waterville, Maine, played important roles in securing the college for their town and in providing for continued broad-based support of the institution. One, a Unitarian minister and state legislator, argued successfully for state aid to the college on the same grounds that aid was granted to common schools. Colleges, he argued in 1828, are "designed for the good of all," with "all classes of the community, rich and poor, . . . equally interested in them."[19] Another non-Baptist active in the early years of Colby was a wealthy merchant and landowner who helped secure the college for his town by personally guaranteeing a major portion of the town's bid. Joining him in this effort to persuade the predominantly Baptist board of trustees to locate their college in Waterville was a prototype of the nineteenth-century local booster, Timothy Boutelle.

Boutelle, a lawyer who became a Waterville resident in the first decade of the nineteenth century, had by 1820 acquired title to much of the future business section and adjacent water rights in this promising young town. During his fifty years in Waterville, Boutelle was a major figure in establishing the town's first bank, building the first bridge across the Kennebec River to the neighboring town of Winslow, providing land for a Baptist meetinghouse and the town academy, and extending the Androscoggin and Kennebec Railroad to his town. In raising local money to supplement his own generous subscriptions to Colby College, Boutelle argued that this institution would make important contributions to the commonweal. The college, he noted, would help improve the area's common schools by supplying competent teachers and by promoting a general respect for learning. In a growing nineteenth-century town such as Waterville, the private and public interests of a man like Timothy Boutelle were tightly interwoven. By bringing a college, a bridge, and a railroad to Waterville, Boutelle improved not only his own cultural and economic status, but also that of the town and region to which he had committed his talents and energies.[20]

With substantial assistance from non-Baptist citizens like Boutelle, college promoters in many towns established institutions that were primarily the products of local forces and circumstances. Even when a Baptist state convention founded the college, as in the cases of Wake Forest, Mercer, and Furman, local ties were sought and proved helpful in establishing a viable educational enterprise. With Bucknell, Rochester, and Mississippi Colleges the community took the initiative and then solicited denominational support for its planned or existing school. Except for George Washington and Richmond, both urban colleges, the basic element in college founding was a bargain struck between the trustees of each institution and a town or county. Usually this agreement determined the location of the college and ranged in formality from the "solemn compact" between Hamilton, New York, and the New York Baptist Education Society to the verbal understanding between Bucknell and the citizens of Lewisburg, Pennsylvania, and vicinity who contributed to it. The financial terms of these written and implied contracts ranged from the less than $2,000 bid by Franklin, Indiana, in the mid-1830s, to the $100,000 offered by Rochester, New York, little more than a decade later.[21]

These initial alliances were continuously reinforced by the subsequent policies of college trustees and presidents. In recommending that construction of additional dormitory rooms and a commons be postponed, the building committee of Bucknell's board of trustees calculated that "boarding and lodging the Students with the Citizens of the Town, will interest them in the College, by the strongest plea, self-interest."[22] College presidents frequently reminded townspeople that students and teachers injected money into the local economy and that a college improved local land values. These educational leaders were well aware of the advantages derived from being in a community small enough, as President Ransom Dunn of Hillsdale College observed, for "the people [to] appreciate such an institution" yet large enough for them to "do something handsome for it."[23] Although the financial status of individual contributors has yet to be carefully assessed, evidence on the numbers of contributors found in small towns, the many local people benefiting from a college's presence, and even the large and socially diverse attendance at commencements suggests a broad base of active support. In 1835, British visitors noted that Colby College enlisted "the sympathies of every class of the community,"[24] an observation that could probably be applied to the large majority of antebellum colleges. College agents did much of their fund raising within a forty- to sixty-mile radius of each institution, the region from which a majority of students were drawn.[25]

Removal Controversies

When denominational leaders proposed that colleges be moved to new locations outside these carefully cultivated zones of support, community responses clearly demonstrated the strength and importance of local connections with colleges.[26] Each of the six major removal controversies at Baptist-affiliated colleges in the late 1840s and 1850s produced a direct confrontation between recently developed statewide denominational plans and well-established community interests. Removalists usually argued that colleges could attain increased prominence and support within the denomination if transferred to a more convenient location and reorganized to insure a larger degree of denominational control. Communities fighting to retain colleges developed an argument stressing the local role in institutional origins. This position was fully expressed in the confrontation at Colgate in the late 1840s. Replying to the removalist argument that Colgate was "the creature and handiwork of the churches throughout the state," an editorial in the Hamilton, New York, newspaper asserted that the school was "in fact the *creature and handiwork* of a few individual Baptists *and others* in Hamilton and the surrounding country."[27] Commenting more generally on the topic, this newspaper observed in 1849:

> It is local feeling, religious and secular, that has given birth to all the institutions in our land. . . . It is seldom that even a denominational institution receives aid first from the denomination as such; by it the beginnings of such institutions are frequently regarded with indifference. A few far-sighted men lay the foundation. . . . They first look well to the "local interest"—create a nucleus, deeply imbedded in the "local feeling"—in congenial soil, where the plant can take deep root.[28]

Since Hamilton residents had not only nurtured but also successfully bid for the college in competition with other towns, it would be both immoral and illegal, the anti-removal argument concluded, for the denomination to break this "solemn contract."[29]

Important financial and cultural interests were at stake for college towns threatened by removals. Granville, Ohio, stood to lose the tens of thousands of dollars annually injected into the local economy by the students and faculty of Denison. Local leaders "clearly understood that the college was the chief factor of the prosperity in Granville,"[30] and local Baptists knew that without the college they would no longer have ministerial talents comparable to those supplied to their pulpit by Denison's president. Realizing that the removal of Colgate would "deeply and permanently" injure the "intellectual, moral, social, and pecuniary interests" of their "flourishing village,"[31] Hamilton residents estimated that "from *thirty* to *forty thousand dollars* are annually expended in our vicinity by the officers and students of the University,"[32] and that its removal would cause local property to "depreciate a fourth in value."[33] In addition, "our elegant Bookstore will hardly remain a month."[34] Local investments in the colleges would also be lost; Hamilton's citizens had contributed more than $30,000 to their college, and Granville's had contributed more than $15,000 to Denison.

With these interests threatened, community resistance took many forms. The initial reaction was sometimes a mass meeting at which the citizens organized to "fight . . . nobly, Baptist and non-Baptist alike, as a community."[35] The committee appointed at such a meeting in Hamilton to defend community interests consisted of three lawyers, two businessmen, a physician, and the editor of the local newspaper; none of them belonged to the Baptist church. Lewisburg, Pennsylvania's interests were well represented because close to a majority of Bucknell's trustees were drawn from within a twenty-mile radius of the college. Unable to control a majority of the Hillsdale College board, some residents of Spring Arbor, Michigan, attempted to seize the college records and install a new slate of trustees. When this maneuver failed, citizens even confiscated books and apparatus and threatened to tar and feather one of the professors.

The most effective tactic employed by threatened college communities was to question the legality of removal.[36] They constructed a legal argument that rested largely on the way Baptist colleges originated. It was generally contended that contributions to a college, especially those made by local residents during its early years, were given with the understanding that the school would always remain at its original site. Removal of the institution would constitute a breach of trust to contributors no longer living and a breach of contract unless it was consented to by those still alive. In the case of Colgate, an actual written contract bound six citizens representing the town of Hamilton to pay $6,000 to the Baptist Education Society of the State of New York in return for the permanent location of the school in their community. Implied contracts between denominational groups and local residents who successfully bid for a school can be identified at four of the other five colleges. These local contractual arrangements were strengthened by subsequent community contributions, and in the case of Mercer were initiated by sale of land near the campus to create a college community.

In varying forms and with divergent emphases, the basic legal argument played a major role in at least four out of six removal controversies.[37] Hamilton took its case to the courts in early 1849 and on April 23, 1850, a New York State Supreme Court judge issued the permanent injunction which prevented removal of Colgate. The decision in this case was based on technicalities but also contained the judge's observation that anti-removalists who were parties to the original contract between the town and the founders of the institution had "the right to restrain the removal of the university."[38] Removalists abandoned the possibility of further legal action at this point and proceeded to found and charter a new institution, the University of Rochester. Participants in the Denison controversy were well acquainted with the Colgate case, and the legal question pervaded this debate from start to finish. The failure of the removalists to agree on a new location and the pledge of the anti-removalists to conduct an ambitious fund drive that would begin in the immediate vicinity of the college helped to prevent removal. But the clinching argument offered by anti-removalists just prior to the denomination's final decision not to remove the college featured the legal opinion that "Granville College could not be removed."[39] Similar legal opinion also occupied a prominent place in the debate at the Georgia Baptist Convention of 1857 and the decision not to attempt a removal of Mercer. In most of these cases it was the prospect of prolonged and institutionally damaging legal controversies that ultimately discouraged the removalists.

The one removal effected during this period occurred after a Michigan circuit court judge in late 1854 dissolved an injunction preventing removal of the college at Spring Arbor to Hillsdale. Claiming that they were stockholders in the college corporation, probably by virtue of their contributions, Spring Arbor citizens had obtained a preliminary injunction in mid-1853. The judge who subsequently dissolved this injunction did so on the grounds that "there were no stockholders of the corporation to be protected by a court of equity."[40] To avoid further legal difficulties the college trustees obtained a new charter in 1855. The few thousand dollars' worth of college property and equipment in Spring Arbor was abandoned. Little more was removed than the faculty, students, records, and reputation of the college. The removal to establish Hillsdale College is therefore an exception to the general pattern of success enjoyed by antebellum college communities in retaining the Baptist-affiliated institutions so deeply rooted on the local level.

The victories of anti-removalists, however, did not mean that Baptist colleges would continue as primarily local institutions.[41] Although legal opinion in the 1850s confirmed the essentially nondenominational origins and functions of Baptist colleges up to that time, it soon recognized the changing nature of these institutions. In 1871, the United States Supreme Court ruled that state legislatures usually had the right to "amend, alter, or modify"[42] corporate charters. This was a valid procedure for effecting college removals. Anyone making a contract with a private corporation such as a college, through donations, purchase of scholarships, or other means, generally did so with tacit assent to this legislative authority being part of the contract. Citing the Colgate decision, the court held that there might be some exceptional cases involving contributions to colleges that would require "judicial discretion,"[43] but subsequent court decisions tended to acknowledge legislative powers regarding charters and were characterized by increasing leniency toward college removals. A favorable county court decision and certain compensations to Penfield, Georgia, enabled Mercer to move to Macon in 1871. Howard College encountered no local legal resistance in the mid-1880s when it relocated on the outskirts of Birmingham, Alabama.

Most removal controversies, however, concluded with Baptists deciding to transform loosely affiliated local colleges into strong state denominational schools without further efforts at changes in location. The accumulation of buildings and other facilities quickly strengthened commitment to an original site. Once a removal issue was settled and denominational interest was directed toward institutional improvement, the ironic result was a decline in the importance of local contributions when compared to the increased financial support from distant sources.[44]

Egalitarian Trends

The widely dispersed and initially local nature of early nineteenth-century colleges, illustrated by the circumstances of their founding and mid-century removal controversies, rendered antebellum higher education much more accessible than colleges had been in previous centuries. In recent studies of colonial colleges, there is substantial agreement on the elitist objectives and control of these earlier institutions and on the higher proportion of students from prominent families. These students, privileged by means of family social status achieved through politics, profession, or wealth, were joined by only very limited numbers from the lower ranges of the middle class. Some signs of increasing proportions of college students from outside the ranks of wealth, power, and prestige are detected from the mid-eighteenth century through 1800, but the picture, especially for the post-Revolutionary decades, is not yet very clear.[45] Most of the evidence for a contrast between eighteenth- and nineteenth-century college students resides in a study which uses student ages as an indicator of family background. This work suggests that the percentage of graduates from late eighteenth-century Harvard and Yale who were older and poorer than the average college graduate of that time is significantly exceeded by the percentage of such students for the early nineteenth century at a group of less prominent New England colleges.[46]

Contemporary observations and quantitative data collected during the last decade support the related argument that this increased proportion of students from the middle and lower ranges of the middle class was large enough to be a distinguishing characteristic of antebellum higher education. "Little colleges," a Southern writer noted in the mid-1840s, "are the means of affording liberal education to numerous youth . . . within forty miles of [their] walls, who would never go to Cambridge."[47] Geographical proximity and modest fees were especially advantageous for families of modest means. "Men with their thousands," commented a midwestern newspaper, "can send their sons where they please; but men with only their hundreds must have a place near home, and where expenses will be at least reasonable."[48] A pamphlet published in Boston just before mid-century contained the estimate that a "full three-fourths of the members of the country colleges are from families with small means,"[49] families described by a midwestern college president as those with "small but well cultivated farms" and "economical shops."[50]

Although direct college costs were not low enough to permit easy access for children of the poor unless they were among the considerable number aided by education societies, expenses were kept at levels which made colleges increasingly more available to an expanding middle class. During most years of the early nineteenth century, significant overall gains were made in collegiate accessibility. By the 1850s, according to a recent quantitative analysis, liberal arts colleges were subsidizing students "at a percentage level higher than the most egalitarian of college systems in the United States in the 1960s."[51]

Studies for Secular Success

Despite their major commitment of resources to maintaining low direct student costs, antebellum colleges also managed to develop curricula characterized by steady growth in breadth and diversity. The academic programs of these colleges —including preparatory departments, partial and parallel courses, and a basic bachelor-of-arts curriculum that contained a wide range of courses in addition to those usually labeled classical—were designed to attract widespread attendance and support. Even the short-lived manual-labor experiments at many colleges in the 1830s and 1840s can be viewed in this light. And courses within the basic curriculum proliferated at such a pace that educational reformers soon began to perceive need for an elective system.[52]

Of primary importance for increasing breadth in the basic curriculum was development in the area of science. A study of scientific curricula at fifteen northeastern colleges finds a dramatic "awakening" from 1820 to 1860 in contrast to the relatively limited efforts and achievements of the colonial and post-colonial eras. From the "somewhat undirected revolution" of the 1820s came a proliferation of science courses in the prescribed curriculum to the point where college students devoted "more time to science than they ever had before or would again." By 1838, four of seven professorships at Williams were in science and mathematics, with most other colleges approximating this proportion. Assuming a mutually beneficial interaction between science and religious belief, colleges established a "dynamic relationship" with science which provided a firm foundation for scholarly as well as curricular developments in the late nineteenth century.[53]

A recent study reports that "trends toward a modernized higher educational system were well established by the 1830s," except in technical-vocational subjects.[54] Another analysis finds that almost one-third of students in Baptist-affiliated colleges during the 1850s were enrolled in nonclassical degree programs.[55] Yet the most interesting and vital relationship between curriculum and a modernizing society may have as its key element the basic program for a bachelor of arts degree.

Central to understanding this program's contribution to the popularity of early nineteenth-century higher education is a new analysis of the curricular philosophy expressed by the very document historians have frequently used to demonstrate the lack of rapport between colleges and the public.[56] The Yale Report of 1828 was the most prominent and influential statement of educational philosophy in America prior to 1860. In this document the faculty defined a college's prime function as the training of mental faculties, such as reason, imagination, and communication, through emphasis on classical studies. Anachronistic readings of the Report are now yielding to interpretations that find it a thoughtful, realistic, and effective approach to pre-Civil War collegiate education.[57] Recent discussions of the Report have taken into account widespread acceptance of the psychological theory upon which the authors' argument was based, the appropriateness of basic-skills training in an era when individuals frequently changed occupations or even professions,[58] and the wide variety of educational programs already provided by other contemporary institutions. These considerations lead to conclusions that the Report, despite its emphasis on classical studies, was "comprehensive, open-minded, and liberal,"[59] or at least "a reasonably modern document by the lights of its time."[60] The link between mental discipline and secular success, a pervasive theme in the Report, is particularly important in assessing this document's impact.[61] Throughout the antebellum years college promoters stressed this success theme.[62] With "intellectual faculties properly strengthened,"[63] they argued, a graduate would find that traditional college studies "do 'pay' professional men ... a large dividend, and that immediately."[64]

Increasing Enrollments

The final and most important evidence for this reinterpretation of antebellum colleges is provided by enrollment data. Scholars critical of Whiggish interpretations of the antebellum institutions have been frustrated in their search for reliable statistics. Almost all footnote trails lead to incomplete enrollment figures[65] compiled by college president-reformers plagued with peculiar problems at their own institutions.[66] And the data available are heavily concentrated in New England, the region with least growth in student population.[67] Until very recently, the paucity of compiled data might have given further reason for skepticism but could not carry a historian very far toward claiming demographic evidence that either weakened or strengthened the traditional interpretation.

Current studies are beginning to generate data that suggest antebellum college enrollments comprised a steadily increasing proportion of the college-age group in the general population. Largely through the multiplication of institutions outside of New England, the annual growth rate for enrollments in higher education from 1800 to 1860 is estimated to exceed that for either the second half of the nineteenth century or the first half of the twentieth. The growth rate for liberal-arts enrollments alone is found to be 1.7 times that of the general population.[68] A new study limited to New England colleges found that even in this region the numbers of early nineteenth-century college graduates expanded at a faster rate than that found in the growth of the region's total population.[69] The accelerating pace of college enrollment expansion is suggested by a calculation for Baptist colleges, where the number of students in the traditional curriculum increased fourfold between 1845 and 1860.[70]

Starting from a small base in 1800, this rate of expansion did not produce totals by 1860 which are impressive by twentieth-century standards. Estimates of national college enrollments for 1860 vary from about 25,000 to a little more than 30,000.[71] While much demographic work remains to be done, it is clear that, when compared with the unchanging nature of enrollment-population ratios for the last half of the eighteenth century,[72] developments in the antebellum years can now be viewed as initiating significant growth in public esteem for higher education.

College Enthusiasm

One essential task remains if we are to formulate a comprehensive reinterpretation of early nineteenth-century higher education. We need an interpretive model to replace the mechanistic one that has dominated scholarship in the field since it was spawned by the classical economics of Francis Wayland.[73] The simple, national needs-and-demands formulation, according to which institutions merely accommodate or ignore popular opinions and the perceptions of reformers, has contributed more distortion than understanding to the analytical record. A knowledge of the "social forces" often cited in functionalist models of this type can, when extensively investigated, help to define the broad constraints influencing institutional and individual behavior.[74] But an approach limited to this level of generalization obscures some of the institutional initiatives and intricate college-community interactions crucial to the viability and vitality of antebellum colleges.

One alternative to the old approach would be for historians to explore the possibilities of viewing colleges in the manner Bernard Bailyn has indicated would be appropriate for academies—as a folk movement.[75] The sources of increasing collegiate popularity seem to reside in a variety of local and regional circumstances that suggest certain affinities between colleges and academies. A foreign observer, noting in the early 1850s the local impulses that led to the founding of both colleges and academies, found "most worthy of attention . . . the great sums which have often been accumulated by means of very small contributions."[76] Particularly important to an analysis of college founding as a folk movement would be a careful delineation of the economic and cultural benefits perceived by many college supporters who never set foot in a classroom. Research designs that once assumed the hilltop college was an early version of the ivory tower should now yield to investigation of the ways in which colleges served as symbols and sources of local pride and prosperity.

Student studies would also provide information and insights of great importance for the development and testing of a more satisfying model and persuasive interpretation of antebellum colleges. In tracing the impulses to found and nurture colleges and in assessing the consequences of efforts by college agents to create increased demand for higher education in various local and regional contexts, historians will need many more investigations of geographical distribution, family background, curricular choices, and patterns of enrollment growth within the student population.[77]

The most important element in formulating a new and more complex model may be increased attention to the ways in which local sentiments were stimulated and shaped by college promoters attempting to create sufficient demand for their nascent institutions. Even contemporaries of Wayland within his own denomination disputed the assumption that demand in education was stationary while the supply of colleges multiplied. Education is different from "mercantile affairs," they argued, because "its very diffusion creates for it an increased demand."[78] The process was described with illuminating detail in the mid-1850s:

> Denominational colleges . . . derive their existence in the first instance from efforts made among the people; and their endowments are raised, and their patronage secured and continued, by employment of just such means as must necessarily increase the number of educated men. Agents, . . . sent out from time to time to secure students, . . . talk at the public gatherings and around the firesides of the masses of people. They enlist by their explanations and persuasions men who not appreciating education themselves would never have sent [sons] to any College, but for these efforts. They raise their endowments by free will offerings, which when made, secures their interests, and to obtain which requires a discussion on the subject of education in all its bearings. Many additional minds are thus enlisted by appeals to their patriotism, their benevolence, and their interests—those perhaps who never dreamed of educating their sons before such efforts were made.[79]

Given the fluidity and dispersion reflected in the population patterns, political structure, and religious institutions of early nineteenth-century America, the local role of college agents in creating a widespread faith in general education deserves intensive investigation.

"College Enthusiasm!," the words used by Ezra Stiles when reacting in 1770 to colonial college-founding,[80] may be more aptly applied to higher education in the early nineteenth century. The scholarship currently probing antebellum college enthusiasm exposes some of the major reasons why the American public began to value collegiate institutions. Further exploration of this question within a model of multiple college-community interactions should provide us with a clearer understanding of the degree to which early nineteenth-century colleges were locally prominent, economically accessible, academically attractive, and generally popular in the eyes of a significant and increasing portion of the American public.

1 For the standard account, see Frederick Rudolph, *The American College and University: A History* (New York: Knopf, 1962) and the works cited therein, especially those of Richard Hofstadter. Portions of the standard account persist in John S. Whitehead, *The Separation of College and State: Columbia, Dartmouth, Harvard, and Yale, 1776–1876* (New Haven, Conn.: Yale Univ. Press, 1973), ch. 3; Stanley M. Guralnick, *Science and the Ante-Bellum American College* (Philadelphia: American Philosophical Society, 1975), p. 141; Robert L. Church, *Education in the United States: An Interpretive History* (New York: Free Press, 1976), p. 38; and John S. Brubacher and Willis Rudy, *Higher Education in Transition*, 3rd ed., rev. and enl. (New York: Harper & Row, 1976), pp. 35, 69–74.

2 *Education in the Forming of American Society: Needs and Opportunities for Study* (Chapel Hill: Univ. of North Carolina Press, 1960).

3 George E. Peterson, *The New England College in the Age of the University* (Amherst, Mass.: Amherst College Press, 1964), pp. 2–3; David B. Potts, "Baptist Colleges in the Development of American Society, 1812–1861," Diss. Harvard Univ. 1967, pp. 1–10; James Axtell, "The Death of the Liberal Arts College," *History of Education Quarterly*, 11 (1971), 341–42; David B. Potts, "American Colleges in the Nineteenth Century: From Localism to Denominationalism," *History of Education Quarterly*, 11 (1971), 364–66; and Colin B. Burke, "The Quiet Influence: The American Colleges and Their Students, 1800–1860," Diss. Washington Univ. 1973, pp. 1–13.

4 For data on these characteristics of Wayland and his problems at Brown, see Joseph L. Blau's introduction to Francis Wayland, *The Elements of Moral Science* (Cambridge, Mass.: Harvard Univ. Press, 1963); Theodore R. Crane's introduction to Francis Wayland, *The Education Demanded by the People of the United States* (Schenectady, N.Y.: Union College, 1973); Walter C. Bronson, *The History of Brown University, 1764–1914* (Providence, R.I.: Brown Univ., 1914), ch. 7; and Donald Fleming, *Science and Technology in Providence, 1760–1914: An Essay in the History of Brown University in the Metropolitan Community* (Providence, R.I.: Brown Univ., 1952), pp. 34–43. For an example of Wayland being used more extensively than any other single source, see Richard Hofstadter and Wilson Smith, eds., *American Higher Education: A Documentary History* (Chicago: Univ. of Chicago Press, 1961), I, II. In the introduction provided for one of the documents Wayland is identified as "one of the great figures in nineteenth-century American education" and credited with a "searching appraisal of the aims and services of American colleges" (p. 334).

5 Axtell, pp. 242–45; Douglas Sloan, "Harmony, Chaos, and Consensus: The American College Curriculum," *Teachers College Record*, 72 (1971), 225–27; and Miles Bradbury, "Colonial Colleges: The Lively Communities," paper presented at the Annual Meeting of the Organization of American Historians, Boston, 17 April 1975.

6 Donald G. Tewksbury, *The Founding of American Colleges and Universities Before the Civil War* (1932; rpt. New York: Archon, 1965). The critique is presented by Natalie A. Naylor, "The Ante-Bellum College Movement: A Reappraisal of Tewskbury's Founding of American Colleges and Universities," *History of Education Quarterly*, 13 (1973), 261–74.

7 Potts, "Baptist Colleges," chs. 2–3; Potts, "American Colleges"; Guralnick, pp. 152–53; Philip Gleason, "From an Indefinite Homogeneity: The Beginnings of Catholic Higher Education in the United States," paper presented at the Catholic History Seminar, Univ. of Notre Dame, 15 March 1975, pp. 13–20; David F. Allmendinger, Jr., "The Strangeness of the American Society: Indigent Students and the New Charity: 1815–1840," *History of Education Quarterly*, 11 (1971), 3–32; Naylor, pp. 268–70; Harvey R. Bostrom, "Contributions to Higher Education by the Society for the Promotion of Collegiate and Theological Education at the West," Diss. New York Univ. 1960; Charles E. Peterson, Jr., "Theron Baldwin and Higher Education in the Old Northwest," Diss. Johns Hopkins Univ. 1970; Travis K. Hedrick, Jr., "Julian Monson Sturtevant and the Moral Machinery of Society: The New England Struggle Against Pluralism in the Old Northwest, 1829–1877," Diss. Brown Univ. 1974; and Daniel T. Johnson, "Financing the Western Colleges, 1844–1862," *Journal of the Illinois State Historical Society*, 65 (1972), 43–53.

8 Potts, "Baptist Colleges," pp. 236–37, 240–41; Burke, pp. 50–95; David F. Allmendinger, Jr., *Paupers and Scholars: The Transformation of Student Life in Nineteenth-Century New England* (New York: St. Martins, 1975), pp. 1–27, 129–38.

9 Potts, "Baptist Colleges," pp. 162–67, 323; Sloan, pp. 240–41; Burke, pp. 56–67, 96, 167; Guralnick, chs. 7–8.

10 Potts, "Baptist Colleges," pp. 322–23; David B. Potts, "Liberal Arts Colleges, Private," *The Encyclopedia of Education* (New York: Macmillan, 1971), pp. 500–501; Burke, pp. 15–24.

11 Potts, "American Colleges," pp. 367–68.

12 Allmendinger, *Paupers*, chs. 1, 6–7; Burke, pp. 50–78.

13 Potts, "Liberal Arts Colleges," pp. 499–500; Sloan, pp. 323–47; Guralnick.

14 Potts, "Liberal Arts Colleges," pp. 500–501; Burke, pp. 18–20.

15 Colleges in this study include all but a few of the institutions of higher education affiliated with the Baptists, founded after 1800, and in operation for at least a decade prior to the Civil War. For a discussion of how accurately these colleges represent widely shared characteristics of antebellum higher education see Potts, "American Colleges," pp. 371–73.

16 Sylvanus M. Duvall, *The Methodist Episcopal Church and Education up to 1869* (New York: Teachers College, Columbia Univ., 1928); C. Harve Geiger, *The Program of Higher Education of the Presbyterian Church in the United States of America* (Cedar Rapids, Iowa: Laurance Press, 1940); Hikaru Yanagihara, "Some Attitudes of the Protestant Episcopal Church in America: A Historical Study of the Attitudes of the Church and Churchmen Toward the Founding and Maintaining of Colleges and Schools Under Their Influence Before 1800," Diss. Columbia Univ. 1958; Paul M. Lambert, *Denominational Policies in the Support and Supervision of Higher Education* (New York: Teachers College, Columbia Univ., 1929).

17 New perspectives found in the most recent studies cited throughout this essay have generally been derived from investigating a group of institutions at a common point in time. These research designs created opportunities to raise and explore interesting questions at a level of generalization usually unavailable to the historian of an individual institution and yet with a degree of precision and documentation unattainable by the author of a survey history.

18 Institutions are designated here by their current names, even though in many cases different names were in use during the early nineteenth century. Related to the interpretation presented here is the fact that original names were almost always those of the towns or counties in which the colleges were located. Thus Colgate was first known as Hamilton [New York] Literary and Theological Institution; then as Madison [County] University, and finally as Colgate University after 1890. Similarly, Colby was originally known as Waterville, Bucknell as Lewisburg, and Denison as Granville.

19 "Waterville College," *Waterville Intelligencer*, 21 Feb. 1828.

20 Potts, "Baptist Colleges," pp. 12–30.

21 Potts, "Baptist Colleges," pp. 76–77.

22 Quoted in Louis Edwin Theiss, *Centennial History of Bucknell University, 1846–1946* (Lewisburg, Pa.: Bucknell Univ., 1946), pp. 63–64.

23 Ransom Dunn, "The Story of the Planting: A Reminiscence of the Founding and Early History of Hillsdale College," *Reunion*, 6 May 1885.

24 Francis A. Cox and James Hoby, *The Baptists in America: A Narrative of the Deputation From the Baptist Union in England to the United States and Canada* (New York: Leavitt, Lord, 1836), p. 342.

25 Potts, "Baptist Colleges," ch. 3.

26 Potts, "Baptist Colleges," pp. 286–306.

27 "Baptist Education Society," *Democratic Reflector*, 28 June 1848.

28 "Provided There Are No Legal Obstacles," *Democratic Reflector*, 24 May 1849.

29 "A Fraternal Address," *New York Baptist Register*, 9 Aug. 1849.

30 Nathan S. Burton, "Granville's Indebtedness to Jeremiah Hall," *Old Northwest Genealogical Quarterly*, 8 (1905), 381.

31 State of New York, *Memorial in Relation to Madison University*, State Senate Document No. 37, 16 Feb. 1849.

32 "Madison University," *Democratic Reflector*, 2 Dec. 1847.

33 "Removal of Madison University. No. II," *Democratic Reflector*, 27 July 1848.

34 "Removal of Madison University. A Last Appeal," *Democratic Reflector*, 3 Aug. 1848.

35 George W. Eaton, "Historical Discourse Delivered at the Semi-Centenary of Madison University, Wednesday, August 25, 1869," in *The First Half Century of Madison University (1819–1869) or the Jubilee Volume* (New York: Sheldon, 1872), p. 67.

36 Potts, "Baptist Colleges," pp. 306–10.

37 The legal question appeared several times in the course of the Bucknell controversy but probably did not exert a decisive influence. No mention of legal considerations can be found in the very small amount of information available concerning the dispute at Franklin College.

38 Hascall v. Madison University, 8 Barbour (N.Y.), 174 (1850).

39 "Meetings at Cleveland," *Journal and Messenger*, 29 Oct. 1852.

40 John C. Patterson, "History of Hillsdale College," *Collections and Researches Made by the Michigan Pioneer and Historical Society*, 6 (1883), 154.

41 Potts, "Baptist Colleges," pp. 310–11.

42 Pennsylvania College Cases, 13 Wallace (U.S.), 218 (1871).

43 Id. at 219.

44 Of the more than $130,000 subscribed to Colgate's semi-centennial fund in the late 1860s, only about $6,000 came from Hamilton residents. Lewisburg citizens provided slightly more than ten percent of the $100,000 subscribed to Bucknell's endowment fund a few years earlier. A contemporary campaign at Denison raised over $100,000, with $5,000 of this coming from Granville. Potts, "Baptist Colleges," pp. 311–12.

45 Donald O. Schneider, "Education in Colonial American Colleges, 1750–1770, and the Occupations and Political Offices of Their Alumni," Diss. George Peabody Univ. 1965; Richard Warch, *School of the Prophets: Yale College, 1701–1740* (New Haven, Conn.: Yale Univ. Press, 1973); David C. Humphrey, *From Kings College to Columbia, 1746–1800* (New York: Columbia Univ. Press, 1976); Guy Howard Miller, *The Revolutionary College: American Presbyterian Higher Education, 1707–1837* (New York: New York Univ. Press, 1976); Robert Polk Thomson, "Colleges in the Revolutionary South," *History of Education Quarterly*, 10 (1970), 339–412; Robert Polk Thomson, "The

Reform of the College of William and Mary, 1763–1780," *Proceedings of the American Philosophical Society*, 115 (1971), 187–213; Margaret W. Masson, "The Premises and Purposes of Higher Education in American Society, 1745–1770," Diss. Univ. of Washington 1971; James Axtell, *The School Upon a Hill: Education and Society in Colonial New England* (New Haven, Conn.: Yale Univ. Press, 1974); Phyllis Vine [Erenberg], "Change and Continuity: Values in American Higher Education, 1750–1800," Diss. Univ. of Michigan 1974; David W. Robson, "Higher Education in the Emerging American Republic, 1750–1800," Diss. Yale Univ. 1974; and Howard Miller, "Evangelical Religion and Colonial Princeton," in *Schooling and Society*, ed. Lawrence Stone (Baltimore, Md.: Johns Hopkins Univ. Press, 1976).

[46] Allmendinger, *Paupers*.

[47] "The Columbian College, D.C.," *Christian Index*, 16 Jan. 1846.

[48] "Franklin College," *Christian Messenger*, 13 Nov. 1845.

[49] Charles Haddock, *Collegiate Education* (Boston: Press of T. R. Marvin, 1848), pp. 7–8, quoted in Guralnick, p. 139.

[50] "Franklin College."

[51] Burke, pp. 47, 78, 124, 127.

[52] Potts, "Baptist Colleges," pp. 162–67, 216–24; Burke, pp. 56–57; Guralnick, pp. 126–29; and Sloan, pp. 246–48.

[53] Guralnick, pp. vii–viii, 25, 138, 37, 116, 152–47, xii–xiii.

[54] Burke, p. 96.

[55] Potts, "Baptist Colleges," p. 323.

[56] For comments on the Yale Report as the "villain in the rape of American scholarship," see Peterson, *New England College*, pp. 213–14.

[57] Potts, "American Colleges," p. 368, and "Liberal Arts Colleges," pp. 499–500; Sloan, pp. 226, 242–46; and Guralnick, pp. 28–33. For an earlier sympathetic reading, see Ralph Henry Gabriel, *Religion and Learning at Yale: The Church of Christ in the College and University, 1757–1957* (New Haven, Conn.: Yale Univ. Press, 1958), ch. 6.

[58] Burke, pp. 145–50.

[59] Guralnick, *Science*, p. 30.

[60] Sloan, "Harmony," p. 246.

[61] *Reports on the Course of Instruction in Yale College* (New Haven, Conn.; Hezekiah Howe, 1828), pp. 15, 17, 28, 29, 36–37, 54.

[62] Potts, "Baptist Colleges," pp. 228–32.

[63] "Schools and Colleges," *Journal and Messenger*, 16 July 1858.

[64] "Shurtleff College," *Christian Times*, 23 Feb. 1859.

[65] [Francis Wayland], *Report to the Corporation of Brown University, On Changes in the System of Collegiate Education, Read March 28, 1850* (Providence, R.I.: George H. Whitney, 1850), pp. 29–30; and [F. A. P. Barnard], *Analysis of Some Statistics of Collegiate Education* (New York: printed for the use of the Trustees, 1870), pp. 6–15.

[66] Bronson, pp. 258–59; and Marvin Lazerson, "F. A. P. Barnard and Columbia College: Prologue to a University," *History of Education Quarterly*, 6 (1966), 49–64.

[67] Burke, p. 171.

[68] Burke, pp. 15–16, 88, 97.

[69] Allmendinger, *Paupers*, p. 3.

[70] Potts, "Baptist Colleges," pp. 322–23.

[71] Potts, "Liberal Arts Colleges," p. 401; and Burke, pp. 21–22.

[72] Vine [Erenberg], pp. 1–2.

[73] Some links between Wayland's economic and educational ideas are suggested by Joseph L. Blau in his introduction to Wayland, *Elements*, p. xix, and by Sloan, p. 248.

[74] Burke, ch. 1.

[75] Bernard Bailyn, "Education as a Discipline: Some Historical Notes," in *The Discipline of Education*, ed. John Walton and James L. Kuethe (Madison: Univ. of Wisconsin Press, 1963), p. 135. For an excellent beginning in the direction suggested by Bailyn, see Church, *Education*, ch. 2.

[76] P. A. Silijestrom, *Educational Institutions of the United States: Their Character and Organization*, trans. Fredrica Rowan (London: John Chapman, 1853), p. 312.

[77] For a survey of reported research and a listing of studies currently in progress, see David B. Potts, "Students and the Social History of American Higher Education," *History of Education Quarterly*, 15 (1975), 317–27.

[78] "Richmond College—No. 5," *Religious Herald*, 28 Dec. 1843.

[79] "The Comparative Advantages of Denominational and State Colleges Reviewed," *Biblical Recorder*, 12 July 1855.

[80] Franklin B. Dexter, ed., *The Literary Diary of Ezra Stiles* (New York: Scribner's, 1901), I, 45–46.

How to Think About the Dartmouth College Case

John S. Whitehead and Jurgen Herbst

When I wrote *The Separation of College and State* almost fifteen years ago my goal was to trace the origins of the distinction between "public" and "private" higher education in the United States. In the 1960s the terms were well recognized; no historian of education argued with that. But when did the distinction first become well recognized by educators and the general public alike? I was suspicious of the claims sometimes bandied about at private institutions like my own Yale that the distinction dated to the very origins of American higher education. Even a cursory review of the existing literature revealed that in the colonial and early postrevolutionary periods there was at least a quasi-public relationship in terms of support and control between such institutions as Yale, Harvard, and Columbia and the colonial and early state governments of Connecticut, Massachusetts, and New York.

I concluded in *The Separation* that "a distinction between private and public or state institutions was not commonly recognized before the Civil War." After the war, particularly in the 1870s, people such as Harvard's Charles Eliot advocated that "private" colleges should be totally separate from any connection with state government. Dependence on the state, Eliot asserted, was "a most insidious and irresistible enemy of republicanism." About the same time university presidents in states such as Wisconsin and Michigan finally convinced their legislatures to make annual appropriations to the "state university" and accept some type of permanent responsibility for these institutions.

To make my case that the public/private distinction was a *postwar* phenomenon, I had a major obstacle to overcome—the Dartmouth College case of 1819. Almost every previous historian of higher education from Merle Curti to Frederick Rudolph to Lawrence Cremin had asserted in one form or another that the Supreme Court's decision in that case encouraged the development of "private" colleges by protecting them from state encroachment. Private donors were thus stimulated to found colleges. Public universities would have to be direct creations of the state, not state transformations of existing colleges. Most historians saw the spread of "private" or denominational colleges after 1819 as proof of the encouraging effects of the Dartmouth decision. They were, however, somewhat undecided whether or not public or state universities were retarded by the decision. These institutions did not appear to spring up with the same vigor as their private counterparts. The traditional interpretation portrayed the Dartmouth College case as a major watershed in educational history; it clearly affirmed the existence of the public/private distinction by 1819.

After a close observation of the available documents on the case, I revised the traditional interpretation. The case, I concluded, was not a watershed; it did not affirm a widely accepted public/private distinction. In fact, I could find few people except Justices Joseph Story and John Marshall who were particularly interested in such a distinction. Shortly after winning the case the Dartmouth trustees asked the New Hampshire legislature to pay for the legal fees they incurred in fighting the state. Throughout the 1820s Dartmouth continued to seek an alliance with New Hampshire, offering state representation on its board of trustees in exchange for financial support.

Looking beyond Dartmouth, I observed that the Supreme Court decision received scant attention after it was issued. I discovered no private college promoters who cited the case in sponsoring new institutions. In fact, some denominational colleges quite eagerly sought state aid and often received it. There was little evidence that the states paid any more attention or accepted any greater responsibility for the so-called state universities than for the denominational colleges in their boundaries. In many states, particularly in the West, the state legislature performed no other function in the prewar period than to transfer federal land grants designated for higher education to a group of state university trustees. Only in South Carolina and Virginia did I find a continuous state sponsorship of one university. In my revisionist view neither educators nor the general public saw denominational colleges and state universities in a particularly different light before the war. This is not to say that all institutions were viewed identically. It is to say that the public/private distinction so well known in the twentieth century was simply not on the minds of antebellum Americans.

Since the publication of *The Separation* in 1973, several historians have supported or accepted my revision, even while seeing further ramifications to the case. In 1974 the Dartmouth literature expanded with Steven Novak's article, "The College in the Dartmouth College Case: A Reinterpretation" in *The New England Quarterly*, Vol. 47, Novak noted that I offered "an elevated discussion of the implications of the case on the concepts of 'private' and 'public' education." However, he argued that the trustees were not really concerned with legislative control of the college. Their real concern was the religious direction of the institution. Would it be controlled by the evangelical, revivalist faith of the majority of the trustees or the liberal, Arminian-like theology of John Wheelock and his supporters? Novak concluded:

> To the participants in the college and the community, then, the significance of the Dartmouth College Case was not the political battle between Federalists and Republicans or the contest between the state legislature and the United States Supreme Court. It was, rather, the question who would control the religious future of Dartmouth and Hanover. The Supreme Court's 1819 decision in favor of the trustees was thus a major victory for the cause of evangelical education (p. 563).

Novak did not say whether Chief Justice Marshall or others outside the Dartmouth community shared the same religious, rather than political, concerns. Nor did he specifically confirm or refute my interpretation. However, his reinterpretation indicates that a public/private distinction was *not* on the minds of the Dartmouth trustees. This helps to explain

why the trustees so readily interacted with the state after the case. They had never really objected to the state; only to its support of John Wheelock in their religious feud.

Further direct acceptance of my Dartmouth interpretation came in 1980 with the publication of Lawrence Cremin's masterful *American Education: The National Experience*. Here Cremin abandoned the traditional view he and Freeman Butts had espoused a quarter century earlier in their *History of Education in American Culture*. Instead he accepted my revision by name and concluded, "it is unlikely that it [Marshall's decision] had any significant effect one way or another upon the image of colleges as community institutions in the public mind." Throughout the same volume Cremin made repeated mention of the difficulty of defining private and public education at all levels, primary and collegiate, in the nineteenth century. "The distinctions," he noted, "were in process of becoming and therefore unclear and inconsistent."

With the imprimatur of Cremin it looked as if my revision was becoming the accepted view as *The Separation* approached its tenth birthday. Such was not to be the case. In 1982 Jurgen Herbst's *From Crisis to Crisis* appeared. With it the traditional version of the Dartmouth case reemerged along with a challenge to my postwar dating of the private/public distinction. "The Dartmouth College decision," proclaimed Herbst, "was the stimulus for American higher education as we have known it since 1819."

Herbst found in *From Crisis to Crisis* that America's colonial colleges, with one exception, were even more public than I had asserted in *The Separation*. He called them "provincial" colleges, public in nature not merely because of various evidences of public control and support, but also for the acknowledged monopoly function of training leaders in each of the respective colonies. The publicness started to break down in 1766 with the founding of Queen's College (Rutgers). By ending Princeton's monopoly as the provincial college of New Jersey, Queen's led the way for the creation of "private" colleges. Over the next half century the vast multiplication of colleges nationwide effectively de-monopolized higher education in most of the states. Herbst saw the Dartmouth decision as the Supreme Court's sanction of the de-monopolizing trend, hence affirming the privatizing movement in higher education that had been taking place since 1766.

In a review of *From Crisis to Crisis* for the Summer 1984 *History of Education Quarterly* I challenged Herbst's use of the term "private" in describing both Queen's and the host of local colleges that emerged prior to 1819 and said, "His definition rests on function and clientele rather than on the presence or absence of state officials on the governing boards. . . . Private now equals local; public equals statewide." It even seemed to me ironic that Queen's, Herbst's first private college, was the only colonial college to emerge as a state university in the twentieth century. I found no new evidence in *Crisis* suggesting that "private" was a stimulus for their colleges and held to my revision that the decision at best "gave guidelines for and limits to the college-state relationship; it did not separate the two."

Since the appearance of my review, Jurgen Herbst and I have had a lively correspondence on these issues. Herbst now concedes that the term "private" may not be the best denominator for the local colleges, but he holds fast to the importance of the Dartmouth decision—particularly as it related to the numerous quarrels between legislatures and colleges that took place before 1819. I too have taken a long look at my previous work.

On dating the emergence of the private/public distinction I still hold that it was a postwar phenomenon. But Jurgen Herbst has convinced me that the de-monopolization or localizing of higher education which began with the founding of Queen's and which signaled the death of the provincial college requires even more study by historians of education. Clearly something of great consequence was happening here. But exactly what? How were colleges defining their educational function to the student bodies and communities they served? In this localizing phenomenon lie the origins of the diverse, pluralistic system that characterizes twentieth-century American higher education as much, if not more so, than the public/private distinction. What should we call this localizing process? We need a name for it.

Finding that name has caused considerable consternation for many historians. According to Herbst, "The appearance of *private* colleges thus came to signal the effectiveness of *local* efforts at development." Lawrence Cremin discovered the same colleges in *American Education*, but said, "They were essentially *local* institutions ... seen primarily as community—and in that sense *public*—institutions." Daniel Boorstin disliked both terms and concluded in the second volume of *The Americans*, "The distinctly American college was *neither public nor private*, but a *community* institution." Public, private, neither public nor private—what is the real definition of the local or community college? Possibly we should abandon the terms public and private until we can define the local college without them. (The italics are mine.)

In searching for this elusive name we must also pay greater attention to the antebellum state universities. Most of the recent literature that I have read focuses on the prewar denominational colleges, probably because there were so many more of them. It has been my observation that the same localizing forces shaped the state universities of the period. If a distinction between public and private was emerging before the Civil War, we would expect to see the state universities developing differently. I don't see that they did. As Cremin claims in *American Education*, "Most state universities during the pre-Civil War period were no more public, or enlightened, or university-like in character than the dozens of denominational colleges that surrounded them and competed with them for students." So what should we call all these institutions that seem so

indistinguishable? I intend to suggest a name. But first I want to look again at the Dartmouth decision in light of Jurgen Herbst's steadfast position.

The Dartmouth decision seems to mesmerize most historians of higher education. Even those who agree with my interpretation of the impact of the decision seem compelled to see the case as a milestone in American educational history. In 1983 Eldon Johnson expanded the Dartmouth literature once again with "The Dartmouth College Case: The Neglected Educational Meaning" in the *Journal of the Early Republic*. Writing a year after *Crisis* appeared, he still affirmed that I had shown with "convincing documentation" that the case had nor "immediately severed the college-state alliance." Nonetheless, he concluded that the "Dartmouth episode ... was an event in the formative years of American higher education which helped shape the future." The existence of a Supreme Court decision in antebellum college development must be too irresistible to dismiss. Possibly I de-emphasized it too much. Having reviewed the decision and the ever-growing literature on it, I am prepared to offer a slightly different interpretation. The decision still should be approached from two angles: (1) its effect on Dartmouth and (2) its wider implications for the development of American higher education.

Looking at the decision in terms of Dartmouth, I now find the issue even stranger than before. Jurgen Herbst and I both agree that Dartmouth was a quasi-public or provincial college when it was founded in 1769. It had not surrendered its monopoly role in New Hampshire higher education by 1819, nor did it lose it after 1819. Not only did the Dartmouth trustees seek new alliances with the New Hampshire legislature in the 1820s, they also successfully defeated an attempt in the same legislature to charter a competing state university. Dartmouth retained its monopoly role in New Hampshire, in contrast to neighboring Vermont and to every other state except Rhode Island in which a provincial college existed. If the Dartmouth decision allowed state and private institutions to exist side by side, it did so almost everywhere except in the state directly addressed in the case! I am inclined to agree with Steven Novak that the significance of the case for Dartmouth was a victory for piety rather than for privateness.

Still we must look beyond Dartmouth. To say that the case was not important because it did not directly affect New Hampshire would be like saying the Dred Scott decision was unimportant because Scott was manumitted the next year. In the wider arena I think there is a greater significance to the decision than I have previously acknowledged.

My previous contention has been that a public/private distinction was not *commonly recognized* before the Civil War. However, I must now make it clear that the public/private distinction had obviously been made. After all, that is what the Supreme Court's decision was all about. The court clearly declared there were two kinds of institutions—public and private. It made the distinction, placed Dartmouth in the private category, and indicated that the two kinds of colleges were entitled to different kinds of immunities. Clearly in the minds of *some* people the distinction existed.

What is puzzling to me about the decision, and in my mind unfortunate and downright pernicious, is the fact that the distinction bore little if any resemblance to the existing form and function of American colleges. No college in 1819, or I would assert in 1986, was or wanted to be a *public* institution in the Court's sense of an agency or branch of government. How quickly those of us who teach in state universities rise up today to beat off any assertion by governors and legislatures that our institutions are state agencies and should be so administered. Nor did any college want to be merely a *private* eleemosynary foundation whose primary function was to hold, safeguard, and distribute the *funds* of a donor. Such private institutions are more akin to today's Ford, Rockefeller, and Carnegie Foundations. They aid education by distributing funds, but they do not educate. Several historians have noted the exaggerations in the Court's decision. Eldon Johnson observed that the Dartmouth decision "went too far." But why was the Court willing to issue an opinion that was so at odds with reality?[1]

I would assert that even the justices of the Court were not really interested in making a public/private distinction. They wanted to protect educational institutions from legislative tampering. It is clear that men like Justices Marshall and Story along with other prominent Federalists found legislative influence, particularly by Republicans, dangerous to an orderly society. Story clearly stated in his concurring opinion that all educational institutions, public and private, should be immune from legislative interference. But the Court would have had difficulty in providing such blanket protection. The New Hampshire Supreme Court had upheld the legislature's action on the ground that Dartmouth was a public institution. The trustees had not challenged the right of the state to tamper with a public college. To overturn the New Hampshire decision the Court merely had to place Dartmouth in the private category.

If neither the Dartmouth trustees nor the U.S. Supreme Court were really interested in the public/private distinction, but only in the use that could be made of these terms to achieve a victory for piety or against the Republicans, then it is not surprising that little mention was made of the decision by college sponsors in the prewar period. Why should other people cite a decision that did not fit their specific needs? Nonetheless, the deed had been done. After 1819 things would never be the same. Even if for all the wrong reasons, the terms public and private, and the immunities that each implied, had now been proclaimed and sanctioned as the law of the land. If Americans ever felt a need to differentiate the vast multiplicity of institutions that surrounded them, the Court had pointed the way. It was just a matter of time.

By the 1860s the college scene was simply too confusing. The old clarity of the function of the provincial college was slipping out of anyone's memory, and the headiness of the college boom was no longer new. College leaders needed a distinguishing tool to create a new order. Public and private now had a use. Eliot and others could easily make their institutions private simply by reaching for the terms the Court had offered. The Dartmouth decision had not been challenged for almost a half-century. It provided a truly *ancient* precedent for postwar Americans.

If the terms private and public were not really appropriate to the form of American colleges in 1819, I would argue that they were equally unfortunate choices after the Civil War. Private or public—is that really what Americans wanted their colleges to be? Is that the order they wanted to place on the diversity? Americans have long claimed that the coexistence of such institutions distinguishes their university system from Europe where dependence on the state is the rule. But is that a distinction to be proud of? In some European countries (Denmark is the example I know best) the state supports so-called private schools because the people believe that everyone is entitled to a fair portion of the public wealth, not merely those who conform to majority views. Yet in America, in both schools and colleges, the public/private distinction has forced us to say that only those students who attend institutions attached to the state are entitled to an education supported by the common funds to which all have contributed. Is that a distinction Americans wanted to make or a cul-de-sac they backed themselves into by insisting that private and public are the terms that define their system?

---

[1] One article in the recent literature on the Dartmouth College case clearly challenges my position that the Court's decision was at odds with reality. Bruce A. Campbell revives the traditional interpretation of the beneficent effects of the decision with added emphasis in "Dartmouth College as a Civil Liberties Case: The Formation of Constitutional Policy," *Kentucky Law Journal* 70 (1981–82): 643-706.

Campbell claims that the case was beneficial because it dealt with the reality of the "negative American experience with relations between colleges and governments from the late colonial into the early national periods." Looking at the college-state relation from 1740 to the Dartmouth case, Campbell asserts, "legislative threats to or attacks on colleges had produced at least stagnation in and often serious injury to the institutions and never any substantial permanent gain for education or government. In light of this record, the benign 'public' to whom Chief Justice Richardson thought colleges ought to be responsible was simply an unreal abstraction."

With this background of college-state relations, Campbell argues that the Court stretched and imaginatively adapted the English common law on private eleemosynary corporations to protect Dartmouth from state encroachment because the English law "did not fit the American situation." To Campbell, John Marshall shaped constitutional policy to fit a real need to protect American colleges.

Campbell's factual basis for the "negative experience" is highly questionable. He claims, "Functionally, Dartmouth had always been private, with only limited, sporadic contact with the state." This is at odds with both my work and Jurgen Herbst's. He calls the New Hampshire legislature's action an "attack." This is contrary to Eldon Johnson's perceptive analysis of the educational goals of New Hampshire governor William Plumer. He ignores the substantial financial aid given to such colleges as Yale and Harvard during this period.

Given this problem with the facts of the issue, I do not see that the inclusion of Campbell's article in the text would advance the dialogue between Herbst and me. Herbst does not take issue with Campbell as strongly as I do but agrees that it is difficult to know exactly what Campbell means by "negative experience" and the injury that the colleges sustained. The article does deserve to be noted as a part of the recent Dartmouth literature.

At the same time that Eliot advocated privateness at Harvard and state universities began to receive annual appropriations, another kind of institution emerged which has tended to go by the wayside as an American norm. In *The Separation* I called it a hybrid institution; the prime example was Cornell. In founding Cornell, Andrew D. White blended the individual gifts of Ezra Cornell with the Morrill land grant for New York. Cornell was thus the manifestation of multiple forms of philanthropy—private and public. White thought he was doing the natural, the American thing in blending these gifts. I suggest that the Cornell example, which was duplicated in the West at Purdue, provides a clue to unraveling the localizing phenomenon in the antebellum period. Cornell was founded as an object of philanthropy. Possibly the one word that best describes the American college or university is philanthropic—not public or private. (Cornell has obviously not gone by the wayside. But one may well think what we try to call Cornell today. Is it public or private? Do we feel compelled to fit Cornell into terms that do not really describe it?)

American colleges and universities have been founded and sustained by multiple philanthropies ever since the blending of the funds of John Harvard and the Massachusetts General Court. Herbst's provincial colleges were philanthropic as were the multitude of denominational and civic colleges that took away the older institutions' monopoly. Colonial and early state support took on a philanthropic character with occasional gifts, land grants, bank bonuses, and refunds from the revolutionary war. The federal land grants in the Northwest Ordinance and the 1862 Morrill Act were also philanthropic in nature. Today state universities strive to receive "lump sum" legislative appropriations as much as private colleges long for unrestricted donations. Private and public universities receive generous contributions in their annual alumni appeals. Clearly the graduates see both kinds of institutions as philanthropic. Despite the IRS's willingness to accept voluntary contributions to reduce the national debt, how many of us want to direct our philanthropy to a branch of government—a truly public institution in John Marshall's view? Possibly the truly American quality of our colleges and universities has been the availability of vast, multiple sources of philanthropy in the United States and the ability of American institutions to blend those diverse contributions—in the same way that the American university blends so many diverse studies and disciplines in contrast to its European counterpart.

Private, public, philanthropic—where do these words now leave my discussion with Jurgen Herbst on the Dartmouth College case? I hope my meandering has been with some purpose. Both Herbst and I agree that the terms public and private may not be the best to describe the multiplicity of colleges emerging in the first two decades of the nineteenth century, or for the ensuing decades up to the Civil War. We also agree that the Dartmouth College decision sanctioned a distinction between public and private, though we may differ on when that sanction became

important and why.

What is even more significant is the fact that we both agree that the words or terms we call American institutions are crucial, though Herbst is more concerned with the legal implications of the words while I place the emphasis on their descriptive use. The words we choose, be they *provincial, public, private,* or *philanthropic,* tend to shape our conception of the form, function, and even the Americanness of our colleges and universities. Educators have at times, I believe, even changed the function of their institutions to fit the meaning of the words rather than the educational desires of their clientele. It seems to me that educators have let the lawyers and the judges tell them what their institutions really are. And that may well be a reality I have trouble accepting. Once an institution is defined in law, its function may well change over time to fit that legal category. But that could be the topic for another paper!

Jurgen Herbst and I agree that the name game is serious business. Choosing the wrong word is more than a simple case of mislabeling. As historians we need to find the right words to describe our antebellum colleges if we are to understand their function in American society and in American law. This choice of words calls for the best thought and exchange of ideas we can give it.

Jurgen Herbst

In *From Crisis to Crisis* I questioned John Whitehead's denial that the significance of the Dartmouth College case lay in its legal implications for the separation of college and state. Instead, I reaffirmed that traditional interpretation, basing my case on a comprehensive survey of the college-state relations throughout the entire preceding period from the founding of Harvard in 1636 to the Dartmouth decision in 1819.

What had prompted me to take another look at the circumstances and significance of the Dartmouth College case? As I stated in the preface to *From Crisis to Crisis*, it was the unrest of the 1960s on college campuses and the request I received in 1967 to prepare a statement on the relationship between civil and academic jurisdiction for use in federal court that started me off on my inquiries into the legal history of American higher education. In that history, the Dartmouth College case loomed large as the first instance of a college dispute reaching the United States Supreme Court. That fact persuaded me to take the case as the closing point for my investigation. Consequently—and this will help to underline the difference in approach and conclusions between John Whitehead and me—I saw many of the major legal events concerning the American colonial college as stepping stones on the way to the Dartmouth decision. The decision itself, though of great significance for the establishment in this country of fairly unique traditions of both public and private higher education, appeared in my view as the capstone of a series of similar legal cases concerning the long-standing disputes over the relative rights of college corporations vis-à-vis the overriding powers of public government.

The decision to wend my way along the major points of crisis in colonial college history while trying to look at them, as it were, from the standpoint of contemporaries, yet, at the same time, explaining much of what I found in the language of our own day, led to some of the issues under dispute between Whitehead and me. The changing definitions of public and private is a case in point.

Whitehead quite rightly observes that the usual definitions of public and private rest on the presence or absence of state officials on governing boards or on the acceptance or rejection of state support and influence in the colleges. But for the years I considered in *Crisis*, these definitions, I contend, do not adequately fit the situation.

At Queen's College, the one "private" college of the colonial period, the governor, council president, chief justice, and attorney general of New Jersey served on the board of trustees. In some private colleges founded after the Revolution, such as Blount in Tennessee, public officials also served on governing boards; in others, such as Transylvania in Kentucky and Dickinson in Pennsylvania, they merely served in their private capacities, not representing their public office. Still other private colleges—Washington College, Jefferson College, and Allegheny College in Pennsylvania—received legislative appropriations. On the other hand, throughout the colonial period Yale, Connecticut's provincial college, was governed by a board of trustees made up entirely of ministers.

The difficulty stems from the fact that during the colonial period the terms "public" and "private" were not used with reference to colleges. Colleges were chartered by either crown or colony to serve the people of a province. Before Queen's College opened in New Jersey, there had never been more than one college in a colony. The colonists regarded this college as their provincial institution, granted it a monopoly over higher education, and subjected it to public oversight by the colony's authorities. It was the colony's public or provincial college. But as far as terminology was concerned, it was simply a college.

Things changed when, with the chartering of Queen's College, the provincial college monopoly was breached for the first time. Then an opportunity was given to regard a college as something other than a provincial, i.e. public, institution. To make that distinction evident I wrote of Queen's as a forerunner of our private colleges. That choice of term, it seems, has not been very felicitous.

As a parenthetical remark I should add that I do not use the term "provincial college" in the colloquial sense as an institution of low repute in the hinterlands, but in its technical or legal sense as a colony's or province's one chief institution of higher education. During the colonial period the provincial college enjoyed and jealously guarded its monopoly on higher education in the province. The 1762 fight of the Harvard overseers against the incorporation of Queen's College in western Massachusetts is a prime example.

When I moved into the early nineteenth century, matters got more complicated yet. I then spoke of the new degree-granting institutions sponsored by localities, churches, denominations, promotional settlement associations, and professional groups as private colleges. This raises the legitimate question why a college sponsored by a locality, whether city or region, should be a private rather than public institution? So Whitehead asks quite justifiably: Were all these institutions private "in the way we think of the term today?"

The answer, of course, is no. They were not private in the way we think of that term today. They were nonpublic or nonprovincial in the way the antebellum generation thought of them. That is to say, they neither belonged among the newly founded state universities, nor were they older institutions officially founded or taken over by a state legislature, nor could they be considered in any sense as descendants of the old provincial colleges. They were something different, something new.

How to explain the newness? Working on the book I became impressed with European and American tradition that, for generations, had seen colleges and universities as attributes of territorial or provincial sovereignty or establishment. That tradition came to be questioned toward the end of the eighteenth century. Ethnic and denominational diversity provided the first impulse for this questioning, the expansion of settlement after the Revolution the second. Thus something new came into being—colleges whose sponsors no longer desired that territorial, provincial, or public connection that would make them agencies of the state. As a group, no official name existed for these institutions. Thus they could not then have been known as private colleges in the way the later nineteenth century would use that term. I wrote of them as private because, whether their governors knew it or not, they were on their way toward just that destination.

Whitehead has persuaded me that for the colonial as well as for the early national period my choice of the term "private" college was not a happy one. He has told me that, working his way back from the present, he found the modern public/private distinction emerging in the late 1860s and 1870s. That makes good sense to me. The "privatization" of Harvard and David Pott's thesis of the emergence of the denominational college after the Civil War fit into this picture. So what, then, do we call the nonprovincial colleges that came into their own during the one hundred years following the 1766 founding of Queen's?

Various suggestions have been made. As Whitehead shows, the terms local and community college have been used. It is clear, however, that not all nonpublic colleges were local institutions. Those sponsored by denominational groups, settlement or proprietary professional associations, though always to be found in a given locality, were nonetheless not sponsored or supported by their locality. To refer to them as community institutions imparts to the term community so wide a meaning that I see no reason not to include state-sponsored colleges under that term as well. It then becomes impossible to distinguish public from nonpublic institutions altogether.

Now Whitehead recommends that we view these nonpublic institutions as philanthropic foundations. As he at the same time extends the use of the term philanthropic to colonial and early state support of the provincial colleges and to the Northwest Ordinance and the Morrill Act I do not see how that definition helps us. It brings us back to the dilemma I encountered in the use of the term community: both designations prevent us from distinguishing between public and nonpublic institutions.

Whitehead claims that that precisely is the advantage of the term philanthropic: it is closer to reality. His prime examples are Cornell and Purdue where public and private philanthropy exist side by side and do not permit the use of either an unqualified public or nonpublic designation.

Quite apart from the fact that we do not normally find it very difficult to distinguish the public and the nonpublic parts of the two institutions cited, Whitehead's suggestion does not address itself to the problem I encountered: is there a term we can use to distinguish the nonprovincial, nonstate institutions that in the one hundred years after the founding of Queen's College appeared as a historically new phenomenon in the United States? If, in our concern for descriptive accuracy we hesitate to employ the term used by the Supreme Court in 1819, then, I am afraid, we may have to settle for the not very elegant, but nonetheless descriptively more accurate "nonprovincial" or "nonstate."

Another observation of Whitehead's in his review of my book refers to the place of irony and logic in historical presentation. As I mentioned before, Whitehead wonders about my definitions of public and private and seems to think that the presence or absence of state officials on governing boards or the acceptance or rejection of state support and influence in the colleges might have made for a tighter, a more logical argument. Perhaps, but, as I pointed out above, it would not have worked. We may well find this inconvenient, ironic, or illogical, but it is a fact we cannot well ignore. Somehow we have to cope with the illogicality of history and incorporate it into our interpretive structures without straining the logic of our presentation. For example, Whitehead finds it ironic that after the 1819 decision the Dartmouth trustees would again turn to the legislature for help. They even had the chutzpah to ask for state payment of the legal expenses incurred in their suit. He also finds it ironic that Queen's College, New Jersey, the institution to which I point as the first to demonstrate to us the beginnings of what became the private college in America, is today Rutgers, The State University. He could have added that it is ironic also that Harvard, our first provincial

college, a little more than two centuries after its founding became a private university.

There is more that can be said on this point. It is, indeed, not logical that governing boards of nonstate colleges have again and again asked for state support. But, we should ask ourselves, what might have prevented them from doing so? Only the fear, I submit, that state support might carry with it certain obligations. As the case of Bowdoin College in 1820 shows, that fear was outweighed by the desire for cash and other privileges. Aren't we familiar with similar instances in the twentieth century as well? Colleges do not want legislative interference in their affairs, but they look for all sorts of government grants.

I find all this ironic, too, but I guess it disturbs me less than it bothers Whitehead. I tend to think that irony and illogicality are the stuff of history. As I tell my undergraduates in class, the history out there is not logic. Our history books and lectures, to be sure, had better be written and presented with excruciating care for logic if we expect anyone to read and comprehend them. But that's not the same as saying that history happens according to our rules of logic.

And finally, the meaning of the Dartmouth College case decision of the United States Supreme Court: Whitehead wrote in his book and repeats in his review that the Dartmouth decision did no more than give "guidelines for and limits to the college-state relationship...." In the present discussion he says that the case was not a watershed and "did not affirm a widely accepted public-private distinction." I present the decision as the magna carta of the American system of higher education in which private and public institutions develop side by side, and the private colleges are protected against state violation of their charter without their consent.

Why do Whitehead and I differ? The reasons have much to do with our approaches to history. While Whitehead judges the major significance of the case to lie in what did or did not happen in the decades following the Supreme Court decision, I see it in the issues the decision had laid to rest in 1819 and in the avenues it had thereby opened for college development. As Whitehead fails to turn up any antebellum college sponsor who viewed or used the Dartmouth decision as a stimulus to private college development, he reports that he cannot find a "widely accepted" public/private distinction. I, on the other hand, see the decision as the terminus of a debate that had begun with Yale President Thomas Clap's dispute with the Connecticut Assembly, had found its climax in the struggles of the College of Philadelphia trustees with the Pennsylvania legislature, had then been revived again by the governors of Liberty Hall and Davidson academies, and had reached its definitive end in the Dartmouth decision. Thus, I evaluate that decision for its importance as a basis for the subsequent legal history of American higher education.

While Whitehead focuses on events and popular perceptions in the antebellum decades I, having traced legal antecedents in the colonial and early national period, write of long-range legal developments. From Whitehead's angle of vision, the Dartmouth decision revealed its *full* significance for the history of American higher education only after the Civil War; from my point of view it constituted a decisive *legal* turning point already in 1819.

Whitehead thinks it "unfortunate and downright pernicious" that the public/private distinction made by the Supreme Court in 1819 "bore little if any resemblance to the existing form and function of American colleges," that not even the justices of the Court "were really interested in making a public/private distinction," and that their purpose was "to protect educational institutions from legislative tampering." Admittedly, these are speculations, but I disagree with all three of them. I can see nothing unfortunate or pernicious in contemporary reality not then corresponding to a judicial view. Why should it? The Court's purpose was to set guidelines for the future, not to describe things as they then were. Given the long and technically highly complex history of the English law of corporations, the transformation of the legal distinction between English civil and charitable corporations into American public and private corporations was for the justices a challenging task. John Marshall and Joseph Story, as Whitehead himself writes, were indeed particularly interested in this subject. And, I submit, it may be doubted that the justices were any more interested in protecting educational institutions from government interference than they were in a far more important matter: to protect American business corporations under the contract clause of the Constitution from arbitrary legislative amendments or repeals of their charters.

How crucial is Whitehead's observation that few college founders referred to the Dartmouth decision as having encouraged the growth of private colleges? In a paper given at the April 1985 American Educational Research Association meeting in Chicago I countered with a question of my own: How often in the nineteenth century did the founders of turnpike and bridge companies, the entrepreneurs of railroads and canals, of iron smelters and lumber mills refer to the Dartmouth decision when they applied for charters for their enterprises? Whitehead responded that they did indeed quote from that decision, but not before the 1870s.

I have no quarrel with Whitehead on that point. I believe he is correct. But I was thinking of the decades between 1819 and 1870 when, due to Marshall's decision, the private corporation became *the* American way of doing business. That railroads and other private businesses prospered

by happily accepting, even demanding, generous public subsidies may be illogical and ironic, indeed, but it did nothing to weaken the faith in free enterprise and private business as the nation's guardian angels.

As to whether there was a difference in the enthusiasm or lack of it shown by state legislatures in the chartering of public vis-à-vis private colleges in the period from 1829 to 1850, I am not prepared to go beyond impressions I gained from an admittedly cursory overview. I found that the chartering of private colleges in the state legislatures more often than not was routine business, done without much debate, unless the issue of denominational rivalry happened to be involved. It was otherwise with the promoters of public universities and colleges. They, like the promoters of public business corporations—public utilities, for example—required special pleading and extended legislative argument. In antebellum America it was cumbersome and frustrating to get support for chartering or maintaining a state university. It is hard to forget Philip Lindsley's poignant complaint when he, as president of the University of Nashville, found that he had no private sect or party "to praise, puff, glorify, and fight" for his institution. So why should college sponsors trot out the Dartmouth decision? At best they would have wasted their time; at worst they might have called a legislature's attention to the decision's reserve clause. So they were well advised to leave well enough alone.

The point I wanted to make is that after the Dartmouth decision we encounter no further serious challenge to the side-by-side existence of public and private colleges. The real significance of that arrangement—the essence of the American system of higher education—appears when one adopts a comparative perspective and looks to other countries. Almost everywhere else, public institutions are the rule, private the exception.

So, as I said, I'll stick to my guns and will say it once more: the Dartmouth decision laid the legal foundations on which our present public and private institutions and systems of higher education have been built. If the decision was not cited every time a new institution of higher education appeared in the United States, it only shows, I believe, how firmly entrenched the notion of the side-by-side existence of private and public institutions had become. In Whitehead's words, there may not have been a need for a *magna carta*. "College fever" could have spread without the decision. But, as we often say, it sure helped, and it remains the key to understanding that which is "American" about American higher education.

Honor and Dishonor at Mr. Jefferson's University: The Antebellum Years

Jennings L. Wagoner, Jr.

It is a gracious and trusting tradition that allows the president of this Society considerable latitude in selecting a subject for this annual address. I hope I have not violated that trust by proposing to discuss a topic that, by its title, may convey marks of a parochial and narrowly conceived (if not contrived) theme. For a southerner to talk on the southern past is perhaps bad enough; but for one who teaches at the University of Virginia to dare focus on that same institution runs the risk of exceeding all bounds of courtesy and custom, to say nothing of decent historical conventions and canons of scholarship. Still, begging your indulgence, I shall seek to explore with you some possible linkages between cultural ideals and youthful conduct that gave a special cast to student life and identity in antebellum Virginia.

I

My interest in the topic of "Honor and Dishonor at Mr. Jefferson's University"—which could well be subtitled "Saints, Sinners, and Scoundrels"—stems only in part from my current association with the University of Virginia. Indeed, all students of the history of higher education in the United States are challenged to give special consideration to Thomas Jefferson's bold experiment in Charlottesville. At a time when the dominant currents in American higher education were flowing along channels most publicly charted by Jeremiah Day and his colleagues at Yale, Thomas Jefferson proposed an institution novel in many respects. Jefferson, of course, was not alone in his efforts to introduce changes or reforms in American higher education in the first quarter of the nineteenth century. In contrast to Richard Hofstadter's depiction of the antebellum period as the "age of the great retrogression," Frederick Rudolph a quarter of a century ago (and Freeman Butts even earlier) noted that "in the 1820s dissatisfaction became a movement," if indeed in many cases only an abortive one.[1] Current scholarship rejects the stereotypical view of the period as recent studies have underscored the minor chords of diversity and innovation that were sounded amidst the major themes of conformity and conservatism that characterized many collegiate institutions in the antebellum era.

Even so, we are compelled to recognize the University of Virginia as an exceptional venture in higher education reform in the 1820s. The University of Virginia, referred to paternalistically by Jefferson as "the hobby of my old age" and "the last act of usefulness I can render my country," was indeed a maverick institution.[2] John Brubacher and Willis Rudy may have exaggerated only a little when they asserted that the University of Virginia was "America's first real state university."[3] In terms of chronology, of course, Virginia, chartered in 1819, was a later creation than the state universities of Georgia, North Carolina, Vermont, and some other institutions like Blount College in Tennessee that in time evolved into state universities. But Virginia, although later in time of founding, was truly in advance of the others in terms of institutional characteristics that gave it a distinctive flavor. Jefferson, apostle of the Enlightenment as he was, dedicated the institution to the pursuit of truth, wherever it may lead, and to the toleration of any error, "so long as reason is left free to combat it."[4] The University of Virginia was to maintain a wall of separation between church and state by having no professor of divinity and by having no affiliation with any religious body. Compulsory chapel and required attendance at Sunday services, customary practices at other colleges and even state universities, had no sanction at Virginia. Moreover, Jefferson's commitment to freedom led him to design a curriculum that encompassed not only the classics but "all the branches of science deemed useful at this day and in this country. . . . "[5] Students were to be allowed choice in the selection of studies, and professors, with partial restraints on the professor of law and government, were given complete freedom in the selection of texts and the direction of their lectures.[6]

To pursue the working out in practice of any one of these novel designs in collegiate education is a fascinating journey into the mind of Jefferson and the problems inherent in the institutionalization of ideas. However, in this essay, I would direct our attention to one specific ideal, the gentleman's code of honor, and the fusion—and confusion—of that ideal with the realities of adolescent life and the special dynamics of an agrarian social order marked by class and caste distinctions. Until recent years, the concept of "the Southern Gentleman" has been too easily caricatured and shrouded with the romance of the Cavalier legend to be taken seriously by scholars. But recent studies by Bertram Wyatt-Brown and Edward L. Ayers, among others, have persuasively demonstrated that attention to the ethics sanctioned by the concept of honor can add significantly not only to our understanding of genteel behavior but can serve as well to illuminate the darker and cruder side of life in the antebellum South.[7]

Honor is a term not easily defined and one more easily misunderstood than understood in our urban, industrialized, atomistic society. Modern psychology as well as the pressures of existence and achievement in a capitalistic society emphasize individualism, not community, "doing your own thing," not respect for traditions and custom. In traditional societies, however—and the antebellum South must be approached in that context—ethics and behavior are determined by and circumscribed by community mores. In a general sense, then, honor refers essentially to an accepted code of conduct by which judgments of behavior are ratified by community consensus. Honor is characterized by "an over-weening concern with the opinions of others"; one's sense of self-worth and identity are inseparable from one's reputation in a culture of honor.[8] The anthropologist Pierre Bourdieu asserts that for those within the circle of honor, "the being and truth about a person are identical with the

being and truth that others acknowledge in him."[9]

My colleague Edward Ayers has emphasized in his recent study of crime and punishment in the nineteenth-century American South that honor did not reside only within the planter class; "Southern white men among all classes believed themselves 'honorable' men and acted on that belief." Yet, as Ayers and others have also noted, the demands of the southern honor culture did not create one temperament, one personality, or a single mode of response to real or imagined affronts to one's honor. Among the more established families of the gentry ranks, a sense of noblesse oblige and disciplined rectitude might mark the path of honor. Among that same class, as well as within the lower orders, however, violence and insolence could also be spawned by the presumed dictates of honor.[10]

Bertram Wyatt-Brown has helped to sharpen our understanding of southern honor by distinguishing between two closely related, symbiotic manifestations of the ethic. Wyatt-Brown has argued that while a general culture of "primal" honor encircled all white classes in the antebellum South, some members of the southern aristocracy adhered to a more specialized and refined concept of honor, that of "gentility." Gentility coupled moral uprightness with high social position. Among the slave-holding gentry of colonial and antebellum Virginia, there existed a sustained and self-conscious effort to perpetuate the culture of the English aristocracy." Subtle marks of status—manners, proper forms and topics of speech, tastes in clothing styles and home furnishings—were among evidences of class and social standing that mattered enough to be consciously passed on from one generation to the next in the "better" southern families and to be sought after hungrily by new claimants to gentry status.[12]

However subtle and artificial some characteristics of gentility were, three components demand special note. In the first instance, sociability reigned as the supreme grace of the southern gentry. Sociability encompassed much more than the accustomed demands of southern hospitality. It included skill in conversation and games, an affable and gregarious spirit, and the display of masculinity. Northern men of culture, whose ideal of gentility emphasized dignity, reason, sobriety, and caution, were on occasion both repelled by and attracted to the more generous and expressive life-style of Southern planters.[13] Henry Adams's description of his Virginia classmates at Harvard in the 1850s pointedly captured the ambivalent attitude of northern gentry toward their southern counterparts. Adams thought the Virginians "as little fitted" for the demands of intellectual rigor "as Sioux Indians to a treadmill," but admitted that they enlivened campus life. His description of William Henry Fitzhugh Lee ("Rooney") emphasized several dimensions of the image of sociability that were marks of planter gentility. Saying that Rooney Lee "had no mind; he had temperament," Adams also described him as "tall, largely built, handsome, genial, with liberal Virginian openness towards all he liked."[14] The *arete* of the southern man of honor rested upon his agreeable appearance as well as his pleasant and manly personality.

Inherent in Adams's description of Rooney Lee was a commentary on a second ingredient of southern gentility, education or learning. Rooney Lee notwithstanding, members of the southern gentry valued learning, especially classical literature. Few, however, either in Jefferson's generation or especially in those that followed, were as dedicated and sincere in their pursuit of knowledge as was the Sage of Monticello. As Wyatt-Brown commented when describing the formidable list of authors Jefferson recommended to his nephew, Peter Carr, the young Virginian probably found the advice "more depressing than inspirational."[15] Jefferson may well have represented an ideal unattainable by most, but still the lure of learning formed a part of gentry culture.

For most southern gentry, however, a veneer of learning would suffice. The South Carolina essayist William J. Grayson had his priorities straight in southern terms when he wrote that "The end of education is to improve the manners, morals, and the mind of the Student."[16] 'Those southerners of the antebellum period who attempted to put improvement of the mind first could easily find themselves removed and isolated from even their peers in the planter class. Still, southern romance with traditional ethics and virtue, fondness for classical allusions in social as well as political discourse, and respect for learning when balanced with other traits of honor all attest to its importance as a mark of gentility.

Southern gentry shared a third element of honor with their northern brethren, but here again the order of priorities between northern and southern gentry differed significantly. Christian piety, with its associated moral barometer driven by a sense of conscience and guilt, became fixed in the minds and souls of the Yankee gentry much earlier and much more deeply than in those of the inhabitants of the South. Not until late in the antebellum period did evangelical Christianity severely alter the dominant characteristics that defined the ideal southern gentleman. The anticlerical tradition associated with Jefferson and other southern gentry under the spell of the rationalism of the Enlightenment, coupled with planter resistance to church power and patronage, served to limit the status of ministers and diminish the appeal of the church in much of southern society. According to Wyatt-Brown, only a fifth to a third of all southern whites before the Civil War were churchgoers.[17]

Patterns of church attendance and gentry suspicion of Anglican and later evangelical ministers should not be taken to imply that religion played no part in the shaping of the southern concept of honor. As Elizabeth and Eugene Genovese have stressed, in the lives of common and rural folk especially, Christianity and Christian institutions (which included old field schools, academies, and Sunday Schools as well as congregational worship) played an important role in disseminating social and religious values among antebellum southerners. In contrast to north-

ern practice, christenings, weddings, and funerals were more commonly performed in southern homes than in churches; thus in the South "the household and the church divided institutional responsibility for Christian practices and ceremonies."[18] Christian precepts were deemed important, and there did exist pious gentry as well as yeomen (and slaves) who were guided in their conduct by scriptural advice and promptings of conscience. But in terms of the southern gentry code throughout most of the antebellum period, the secular components of honor tended to weigh more heavily than did the teachings of the New Testament.

Here again Jefferson serves as a model, however elevated, of the gentry attitude toward ethics. Referring to Jesus as perhaps the greatest teacher of morals the world has known, Jefferson again advised his nephew, Peter Carr, to study the classics as well as the scriptures as guides to right living. Jefferson counseled further:

> Give up money, give up fame, give up science, give [up] the earth itself and all it contains rather than do an immoral act. And never suppose that in any possible situation or under any circumstances that it is best for you to do a dishonourable thing however slightly so it may appear to you. Whenever you are to do a thing tho' it can never be known but to yourself, ask yourself how you would act were all the world looking at you, and act accordingly."[19]

As with his uncle's advice regarding disciplined study of the classics, Carr no doubt felt Jefferson's prescription much too demanding, yet it is significant to note in this instance that Jefferson's measure for good conduct was the voice of community approval, not God's judgment. To Jefferson and later southern gentry, "quiet conscience" and "private esteem" could not be dissassociated from "public honour."[20]

Sociability, learning, and piety—in descending order of importance—thus formed the framework for judging "honorableness" among the southern gentry. But, as suggested earlier, the bounds of honor went beyond the gentry class. Self-respect to the descendants of Yankee Puritans may have rested upon conscience or conformity to an inner voice, but to antebellum southerners of all ranks, self-respect was inseparable from reputation or the judgment of others. Those who lacked honor lacked reputation. Their penalty was shame, not a guilty conscience, for "to those whose god is honor, disgrace alone is a sin."[21]

In a perceptive essay detailing patterns of discipline in five mid-Atlantic colleges, Phyllis Vine emphasized that in the eighteenth century, honor and shame were the prevailing modes of maintaining order and encouraging genteel behavior in that region of the country. Vine, along with David Allmendinger and others, points out, however, that by the close of the eighteenth century discipline sanctioned by the concepts of honor and shame was giving way in northern colleges to appeals to self-control.[22] Public censure or praise was becoming victim of an increasingly diversified student population and to wider acceptance of legal and Christian (that is to say restrained, inward-looking, and conscience-driven) reinforcers of conduct. That shift in public as well as collegiate sensibilities in the North would not find its parallel in the South until much later in the century. If once there had been a moral perspective that embraced both North and South, a culture of honor that rested upon public approval or disapproval, then by the early antebellum period that regional kinship was broken. While northern conventions changed, southern mores remained imbedded in traditions earlier transplanted and nurtured by English and northern European forebearers.[21]

With these perspectives in mind, we can now turn our attention to the role of honor and dishonor in the scenarios sketched by the saints, sinners, and scoundrels at the University of Virginia during the antebellum period. Perhaps this deeper examination of student conduct in relation to the concept of honor will enable us to move beyond some of the more conventional assumptions that currently exist in the literature and, more importantly, will underscore the institutional diversity that existed in the antebellum era. It may well be, as one observer noted, that Virginia students were "a set of pretty wild fellows," but perhaps there is more to be said than that.[24]

II

Honor as understood by Jefferson and as it became manifested in the actions of students at his university grew from the same southern soil. However, the concept of honor bore fruit of a different variety in the mind of the aged founder of the University of Virginia from that in the minds of many of the young sons of "Southern gentlemen" who ventured there, some to study, others perhaps less inclined toward that collegiate purpose.

In creating his university, Jefferson had hoped to provide an intellectual and moral environment that would bring out the best, not the worst, habits and conduct on the part of the students. His plan for an academical village in which professors and students would live and study in close proximity was a deliberate effort to encourage rapport and respect among the members of the university community. His insistence that only the ablest professors should fill the chairs at his university led him beyond the borders of the United States in engaging his initial corps of professors. Five of the original eight professors were European. George Long, a fellow at Trinity College, Cambridge, was only twenty-five when he was chosen to be the first professor of ancient languages at the university. Thomas H. Key, a Master of Arts from Trinity College, was engaged to teach mathematics. Dr. Robley Dunglison, who had studied medicine in London and Germany, filled the chair of anatomy and medicine. Key and Dunglison were both twenty-six. Charles Bonnycastle, who became the first professor of natural philosophy at the age of thirty-three had studied at the Royal Military

Academy, where his father was a member of the faculty. George Blaetterman, of German descent, was hired to teach modern languages. His more advanced age, thirty-seven, earned him the not always affectionately applied nickname of "Old Blaet." Along with a trio of Americans—John Emmet in chemistry, George Tucker in moral philosophy, and John T. Lomax in law—Jefferson's corps of professors, "full of youth, talent, and energy," set out to give students the capacity to be ethical, moral, and democratic rather than to instill in them the dictates of Christian piety and morals.[25] However, the youthfulness of some of the professors and their apparent lack of solicitude for the personal bearing and society of the students rather quickly provoked friction not unlike that which fueled the wars between the students and the tutors at colonial colleges.[26] Equally significant, the professors' position of authority, their more serious and scholarly orientation, and the ethical code they embraced generated numerous "clashes of honor" between the faculty and the students.

Jefferson had established the university upon the principle of freedom, for students as well as the faculty. In doing so, Jefferson was aware of the risks involved, especially in the realm of student conduct. In a letter to Thomas Cooper, several years before the university opened, Jefferson voiced his concern in this manner:

The article of discipline is the most difficult in American education. Premature ideas of independence, too little repressed by parents, beget a spirit of insubordination, which is the great obstacle to science with us, and a principle cause of its decay since the revolution. I look to it with dismay in our institution, as a breaker ahead, which I am far from being confident we shall be able to weather.[27]

Jefferson endeavored to gather information from colleges and universities in both Europe and America regarding their policies toward student discipline. He studied the rules of Harvard and numerous other colleges in an effort to learn how other institutions weathered the seas of student rowdiness. As much as he was concerned about the deportment of any large body of young men brought together over an extended period of time, he nonetheless decided to chart a liberal course. The long lists of rules and regulations and specified fines and penalties so common at other colleges were not allowed to set the tone for the University of Virginia. Adopting a posture in some ways more in keeping with changing northern attitudes than with traditional southern "honor" values, Jefferson rejected fear as a way of dealing with the young. Jefferson stated in the report detailing his plans for the university:

The human character is susceptible of other incitements to correct conduct, more worthy of employ, and of better effect [than fear]. Pride of character, laudable ambition, and moral dispositions are innate correctives of the indiscretions of that lively age; and when strengthened by habitual appeal and exercise, have a happier effect on future character than the degrading motive of *fear*. Hardening them to disgrace, to corporal punishments, and servile humiliations cannot be the best process for producing erect character. The affectionate deportment between father and son offers in truth the best example for that of tutor and pupil. . . .[28]

Jefferson was still reaching for this ideal familial relationship when he informed his granddaughter in the summer of 1825 that the university officials "studiously avoid too much government" and treat the students "as men and gentlemen, under the guidance mainly of their own discretion. They so consider themselves," he added, "and make it their pride to acquire that character for their institution."[29]

Such sentiments cannot be easily discounted. After all, Jefferson and his peers on the Board of Visitors—James Madison, James Monroe, and Senator Joseph Cabell, among other notables—were men of high ideals and noble purpose and expected the same from students supposedly drawn from the finest southern families. In an effort to encourage Virginia students to assume a sense of responsibility and maturity in matters of conduct, the Visitors had placed the reins of discipline in the students' own hands. Not the Board of Visitors or the faculty, but a student-run Board of Censors was to exist as the principal judicial body. Should sin or scandal dare emerge, this student court was to sit in judgment in all but extreme cases of misconduct.[30]

In addition to establishing a form of student self-government and minimizing regulations, Jefferson and the Visitors institutionalized a principle jealously respected by men of honor, that is, that a gentleman's word is to be taken as his bond, and further, that no man should be compelled to inform on another. The 1825 *Enactments of the University* thus stated: "When testimony is required from a student, it shall be voluntary, and not on oath. And the obligation to give it shall be left to his own sense of right."[31] Jefferson's belief in the inalienable rights of man was paralleled by his faith in man's innate moral sense. The sanctity of a gentleman's word was certainly a fundamental precept in the southern code of honor. However, equally certain is the fact that many who laid claim to the title of "gentleman," at the University of Virginia as elsewhere in the South, were much more in tune with the dispositions and prejudices of their culture than with the rationalistic or theistic stirrings of an inner voice.

In many respects, the students who enrolled at the University of Virginia were not measurably different from what Jefferson had expected. Unlike their counterparts at Harvard, Princeton, and many other northern colleges, antebellum students at Virginia were remarkably homogeneous in terms of geographic origin, social class, and age. From the opening of the university in 1825 through the end of the Civil War, virtually every student came from Virginia or other southern states. Many non-Virginians who attended the university were sons of families that had emigrated from the Old Dominion to other southern states in the 1830 to 1860 period. While only 8 percent of the students at South Carolina College came from outside that state in the period from 1805 to 1862, 41 percent of those attending the University of Virginia from 1826 to 1847 were from southern states other than Virginia.[32]

Also in contrast with profiles of northern college students in the antebellum era, students at Virginia were typically sons of fairly well-established planters or of professional men or merchants living in cities. The University of Virginia was the most expensive as well as the most prominent college in the South and its students were drawn from the upper class of the region.[33] Recent research by Charles Wall has documented the fact that the overwhelming majority of Virginia students, both in-state and out-of-state and from urban as well as rural homes, came from the slave-owning class.[34] Thus, at a time when many young men from middle and lower economic classes were joining the student ranks at many northern colleges, the Virginia student population more closely resembled that of Oxford, described by Lawrence Stone as consisting of "sons of well-to-do gentry, clergy, professionals, and businessmen."[35] Predominant in numbers and influence, these sons of privilege set the tone that determined the prevailing attitudes and life-style of the student culture at the university. Students of more humble origins or more pietistic demeanor apparently were responsive to warnings that they should stay clear of the "godless university" that catered to "rich men's sons."[36]

The age distribution of Virginia students further identifies them as a wealthy and privileged group. Since the University of Virginia was designed to serve as a graduate or professional school (as well as a college) and students were expected to have attended or graduated from other colleges before entering Virginia, the average age at matriculation was several years higher than at other colleges of the period. However, research by Wall has shown that Virginia students were remarkably homogeneous in age, indicating a steady progression through the preparatory schools, academies, and colleges before entering the university. Unlike a significant percentage of New England students of the same period, it was a rare student at Virginia who postponed or interrupted his collegiate studies to tend school or engage in some other occupation in order to earn money for college expenses. Although after the mid-1840s state scholarships were created for deserving students from each of the state's thirty-two senatorial districts, the established character of the institution remained essentially constant during the antebellum period.[37]

Certainly some of the gentry students who attended the University of Virginia were serious and scholarly in disposition. Student letters, diaries, and autobiographies reveal that some students pursued their studies with resolve and commitment. For those who aspired to a diploma, demanding examinations had to be passed with distinction. Apparently typical of those students who took their studies seriously was Albert Howell of Tennessee, who, reflecting upon the previous session's law examinations in which only thirteen out of over sixty aspirants passed, commented that "It is reduced to a certainty that if a fellow graduates, he is compelled to study, even then his case is rather doubtful if his luck be bad." Another diligent student in the 1850s observed with no hint of irony: "I think it is the last place in the world for a lazy man to try to enjoy himself."[38]

Not all students, however, were prepared by temperament or prior education to accept the academic demands and the associated freedom of the university. The majority of students in the antebellum period attended the university for only one session and only a small percentage earned the title of "Graduate" from one of the schools, let alone the demanding Master of Arts degree that was instituted in 1832.[39] Between 1825 and 1874, 55 percent of the students lasted only one session; only 11 percent enrolled for three years.[40] While the elective system and the rigorous examinations motivated serious students, the emphasis on self-discipline discouraged those not so inclined. Many, perhaps most of the students at the University of Virginia during the antebellum period came to the institution less out of a desire to advance in scholarly terms than to advance or secure their position in social terms. Merely attending the University of Virginia in the company of other southern gentlemen improved one's standing as a member of the elite of southern society. As a consequence, "men of leisure" constituted a very real and markedly disruptive segment of the university population.[41]

III

Both in spite of and because of the idealistic—and honorable—plane on which the University of Virginia was established, disorder marked the university almost from the very beginning. Just as God found that He had little time to relax after His great act of creation, so too did Jefferson find serpents in his Eden. Virginia students, most of whom were accustomed to the free country life of the plantation, were disdainful of restraints or restrictions not imposed by parental right. Impressed by a code of honor that, when distorted, exalted privilege over responsibility and haughtiness over humility, some students rather quickly turned the university into what one officer described as a state of "insubordination, lawlessness, and riot."[42]

Jefferson himself soon lamented what he termed a few "vicious irregularities" that occurred during the first few months after the university opened.[43] The students, whose own sense of honor compelled them to reject complicity with authorities against members of their own community, were not pressed to serve on the student court, the Board of Censors, to judge the troublemakers. The professors, lacking authority and out of respect for Jefferson's wishes, were reluctant to act, although probably all agreed with Professor Dunglison who later called Jefferson's

scheme for student self-government a "fanciful" idea.[44] Within six months, however, even Jefferson was moved to confess that "stricter provisions are necessary for the preservation of order . . . [and] coercion must be resorted to, where confidence has been disappointed."[45] With the collapse of Jefferson's plan for student self-government crumbled also one of his most cherished convictions. Disillusioned, he encouraged the Board of Visitors to appeal to the General Assembly for authority to tighten regulations within the university. In the years that followed, the faculty and Visitors multiplied the rules as the students multiplied their offenses.

Disorder at the University of Virginia during its early years took many forms. Most occurrences were of the minor sort and perhaps could be excused or at least explained by the youthfulness of the students, their understandable boredom with the tedium of study, the large degree of freedom that continued to exist within the bounds of the university's elective system and policies that left students' academic progress up to their own initiative, and perhaps even as a reflection of the Biblical adage that, on occasion, "All have sinned and fall short of the glory of God."

To many self-styled Virginia gentlemen, however, neither God's glory nor His precepts seemed as compelling as the requirements of southern honor. Products of a culture that emphasized forms of entertainment and festivities that were frowned upon in more religious or moral quarters, students at Virginia pursued pastimes at home and at the university that included partying, drinking, dancing, smoking, card playing and gambling, horse riding and racing, and occasionally cock fighting. Jefferson recognized and appreciated some of the attributes of sociability inherent in the gentry life-style, and had made provision for lessons in music and dancing, as well as instruction in such manly arts as fencing, boxing, gymnastics, and military training. However, in pursuing these and some other amusements not provided for in the university regulations, Virginia students on occasion turned the Grounds into a distorted replica of plantation social life, thus creating an environment quite at odds with the scholarly and culturally ennobling aspirations of the founder.

Commentaries on student life and gentlemanly conduct in such southern periodicals as the *Southern Quarterly Review* and the *Southern Literary Messenger* sometimes condoned or winked at many of the social pleasures that competed with academic values. For example, Benjamin Blake Minor, editor of the *Southern Literary Messenger* and former Virginia student in the 1830s, expressed smug amusement upon printing an essay by another former Virginia student that extolled the fun and excitement of a drinking party.[46]

Student letters and diaries provide ample evidence of the students' attitude that drinking was a normal and expected social ingredient of the collegiate experience.[47] Even so, Professor William B. Rogers was probably correct when he noted in 1842 that "ninety-nine hundredths of our troubles spring from drink."[48]

While Jefferson and other officers of the university would not likely

142

have expressed great displeasure at temperate or moderate drinking, the excessive drinking and partying of Virginia students often led to more serious incidents. The *Minutes of the Faculty* are sprinkled liberally with notations of misconduct that often originated in drinking or partying episodes. "Noisemaking," apparently a favorite nocturnal student pastime, was often fueled by an earlier round of drinking. Students at Virginia as at virtually every college found that ringing the college bell and blowing tin horns proved to be surefire ways to torment professors and their families, especially when such serenades were conducted late at night and were accompanied by boisterous singing and yelling. At Virginia the students soon discovered that the covered arcades produced magnificent echoes and when horns and yelling did not prove sufficiently irritating to the professors, the dragging of iron wagon fenders down the brick pavement was certain to bring results. Firecrackers and homemade bombs placed on door stoops and windowsills also caused faculty families to spend many sleepless nights in their chambers.

Virginia students were fond of guns, and although university regulations prohibited guns in the precincts, students smuggled them in regularly. The pop of a firecracker was a puny disturbance compared to the report of pistols and rifles, and the calm of many nights was broken by gunshots from various corners of the Lawn. In October, 1831, the *Faculty Minutes* contain entries such as: "Last night, there were several pistol shots on the Lawn"; "Last night about eleven o'clock two guns were fired off on the Eastern Range"; "Last night, a pistol was fired out of a dormitory window."[49] Such entries continued to appear in the *Minutes* for many years and in some instances, as in November, 1836, the shooting episodes were well orchestrated. On that occasion, the reports of as many as eight muskets were simultaneously heard coming from the Lawn, and when the chairman of the faculty ran toward that group, they scattered and another group situated at another position picked up the action. The discouraged chairman of the faculty reported in the *Minutes* in 1836, "nothing can enable us to detect offenses of this kind committed by a combination of students but a system of espionage, to which no gentleman can submit."[50]

If Virginia professors felt restrained by their concept of gentlemanly conduct, students often tended to be more selective in their affirmation of the gentleman's code, especially in their dealings with professors and other adults. Students were quick to invoke the gentleman's code of honor when it suited *their* purposes. Not only did they refuse to inform on their classmates, they quickly took offense if servants, professors, townspeople, or fellow students were perceived to have offended their honor. Some carried concealed pistols, others knives, and challenges to duels were sometimes rashly issued and foolishly accepted, university regulations and state law notwithstanding. In 1838, a few months after one student received a dangerous stab wound, another was found to be concealing a bowie knife. When a member of the faculty asked why he felt it nec-

essary to carry such a weapon, the student replied that it might be needed "if a man insults me and refuses to give me honorable satisfaction."[51]

"Honorable satisfaction" was the excuse given in 1830 by a student who struck a professor when the latter refused to offer an apology for what the student considered an insulting rebuke. The student was promptly expelled, but his friends assembled in the Rotunda and passed a resolution justifying the assault as a matter of honor. Several years later this same professor, then serving as chairman of the faculty, was confronted by two other students, one of whom had just been expelled and the other suspended for actions the chairman allegedly had labeled as "disgraceful." In defense not of their earlier actions but rather in response to the affront to their reputation, the students challenged the professor to fight, an offer the professor refused on religious grounds. In frustration over damaged honor unreclaimed, the students "collared" and shook the professor and called him a coward. When the professor then called this act "disgraceful," one held him while the other began flogging him with a horsewhip. According to another professor's testimony, at least a hundred students had gathered round, but no serious attempt was made to interfere until the professor was whipped from behind while being held—a dishonorable act that could not be ignored.[52]

If we began this excursion into the early annals of student conduct at the University of Virginia in search of a few sinners, we have now clearly moved into the realm of what might appear to be the actions of scoundrels. Jefferson was spared most of the scenes just described, but he lived long enough to see his idealistic theory of student honor badly tarnished. Before he died in the summer of 1826, he had witnessed not only the eruption of some "vicious irregularities," but had to face the consequences of the first of what proved to be a series of riots or rebellions at the university.

The first student rebellion was sparked in the fall of 1825. After dark a band of fourteen students, some of whom were intoxicated, gathered on the Lawn disguised as Indians. Their nighttime revelry took on a more serious tone when one shouted out, "Damn the European professors." That all was not well between the students and some of the European professors had been made abundantly clear the night before when some unknown scoundrel had tossed a bottle of foul liquid, apparently of human origin, through the window of Professor Long's sitting room while guests were present.[53]

The intervention of two professors this second evening turned what might have ended as just another night of noisemaking into an honor clash between students and faculty. Anxious to put an end to the "rioting," Professors Emmet and Tucker seized a student in an attempt to identify him. Responding to his cry for help, other students poured from their rooms to save their comrade who, as they latter contended, had been dishonorably attacked by two men at once. The professors managed to reach safety from the sticks and stones but not the verbal abuses hurled at them by the supposedly outraged students. The next day, instead of showing contrition for their scandalous conduct, a student delegation presented the faculty with a resolution signed by sixty-five students that blamed the professors for starting the incident and that flatly rejected a faculty directive calling upon the students to identify the major offenders.

Two of the European professors, Long and Key, immediately offered their resignations in disgust, even before completing a full year of service on the Virginia faculty. "We have lost all confidence in the signers of this remonstrance," they said, "and we cannot and will not meet them again."[54] The remainder of the faculty adopted a resolution informing the Board of Visitors that if order were not restored, they too would resign en masse. The board, at the time meeting at Monticello, came down to the university in hopes of averting a crisis.

In one of the most dramatic moments in University of Virginia history, three former presidents of the United States—Jefferson, Madison, and Monroe—along with other distinguished members of the Board of Visitors, convened a special session of the board, faculty, and students in the Rotunda. Then eighty-two years old, Jefferson opened the meeting by declaring that it was one of the most painful events of his life. Soon overcome with emotion, the rector had to yield the floor to another Visitor, Chapman Johnson, who persuaded the guilty students to spare innocent students and the university itself by confessing their guilt. In this instance, the students did respond. Among those who came forward was a nephew of Jefferson, whose appearance in that situation agitated the elder statesman in a way he could not disguise. One witness recorded in his diary, "the shock which Mr. Jefferson felt when he, for the first time, discovered that the efforts of the last ten years of his life had been foiled by one of his family, was more than his own patience could endure, and he could not forebear using, for the first time, the language of indignation and reproach."[55] The ringleaders in this episode, including the student who had thrown the bottle of urine through Professor Long's window, were expelled, and others involved were given lesser punishments. Although the Visitors did not revoke their earlier promise of not compelling students to testify against others involuntarily, Jefferson later urged students to abandon the practice of protecting those who stirred disorder within the university.[56] The university, he said, should be made safe for "those it is preparing for virtue and usefulness."[57]

For two decades following Jefferson's death in 1826, "virtuous" students and university authorities had to contend with recurring rounds of disorder, riot, and open rebellion.[58] The specific events that sparked direct challenges of honor between the students and university authorities are of less importance than the posture often assumed by the "offended" students. Although not infrequently exaggerated, student declarations that their honor as gentlemen had been called into question or their rights

as citizens abridged by the faculty on several occasions turned minor episodes into affairs that threatened to close the university. In 1836 and again in 1845 order was restored at the university only after the militia was called in. In this last major antebellum rebellion, classes were suspended for a week before two hundred militiamen brought calm to the university. Forty students were expelled or suspended following the restoration of order, but over eighty others voluntarily withdrew, apparently in a sincere "sanctuary" of the university and as an expression of their disfavor with the Visitors for not accepting their belated pledge to end the riot if the military invasion were called off.[59]

In spite of the seriousness of the 1845 rebellion, student conduct at Virginia actually had begun to improve by the mid-1840s, but only after matters had gotten worse. One of the darkest episodes in the annals of the University of Virginia occurred in November of 1840 when, attempting to unmask one of several students who were stalking about the Grounds firing pistols, Professor John Davis was shot. Professor Davis lingered for several days before dying. The student body, shocked by the gravity of this fateful act, readily assisted in identifying the guilty student, who, after his arrest, was granted bail and escaped from the state.[60]

The murder of Professor Davis was one of several events that introduced a new, but certainly not consistent, mood of seriousness into the university community. Perhaps most significant in terms of improved student-faculty relations at the university was the adoption in 1842 of the honor system. The honor system was an outgrowth of a minor incident in 1841 in which students who had been arrested for drunk and disorderly conduct in a tavern were allowed to remain as students upon their written pledge, cosigned by three fellow students, that they would henceforth abide by university regulations. The three sureties for each student promised that they would report any violations committed by the reinstated students. The written pledges of the offending students and their sureties fashioned a subtle and ingenious use of the students' belief in honor. The integrity of their vow now made it honorable, not dishonorable, to report on the misbehavior of those who had pledged their word. The honor system and written pledge adopted the following year, which applied at first only to honesty in examinations but was later expanded to cover lying and stealing as well, institutionalized this refurbished approach to the gentleman's code of honor.[61]

The faculty as well as the students reflected a change in attitude in the university community in the 1840s. Several of the more vexing disciplinary rules that had been instituted following Jefferson's death were removed. Notable also is the fact that several new appointments to the faculty were instrumental in forming improved relationships with the students. Five of six new professors who joined the faculty in the early years of the 1840s were Americans; two, John Minor and Henry St.

144

[3] Thomas Jefferson to Judge Spencer Roane, 9 Mar. 1821, *The Writings of Thomas Jefferson*, ed. Paul L. Ford, 10 vols. (New York, 1892-1899), 10:189.

[4] John S. Brubacher and Willis Rudy, *Higher Education in Transition: A History of American Colleges and Universities, 1636-1976* (New York, 1976), 142.

[5] Jefferson to William Roscoe, 27 Dec. 1820, *The Writings of Thomas Jefferson*, ed. Andrew A. Lipscomb and Albert Ellery Bergh, 20 vols. (Washington, D.C., 1903-1904), 15:303.

[6] Jefferson to Littleton Waller Tazewell, 5 Jan. 1805, *Thomas Jefferson, Writings*, ed. Merrill D. Peterson (New York, 1984), 1151.

[7] Jefferson's antipathy to the doctrines of Federalism and his lingering bitterness from earlier struggles with Alexander Hamilton and John Marshall culminated in a resolve to keep Federalist political views from contaminating the minds of Virginia students. In an effort to insure that students of law and government at Virginia would be exposed to "proper" political ideas, the Visitors of the university agreed to prescribe certain texts, i.e., John Locke's *Second Treatise on Government*, Algernon Sydney's *Discourses on Government*, the Federalist papers, the Declaration of Independence, and James Madison's Virginia Resolutions of 1798. At Madison's suggestion, George Washington's "Farewell Address" was added to the list. See Leonard W. Levy, *Jefferson and Civil Liberties: The Darker Side* (Cambridge, Mass., 1963), 151-57.

Standard sources on Jefferson's ideas concerning the University of Virginia include Philip A. Bruce, *History of the University of Virginia, 1819-1919: The Lengthened Shadow of One Man* (New York, 1920); Herbert Baxter Adams, *Thomas Jefferson and the University of Virginia* (Washington, D.C., 1888); and John S. Patton, *Jefferson, Cabell, and the University of Virginia* (New York, 1906). See also Dumas Malone, *Jefferson and His Time* (Boston, 1981), vol. 6, *The Sage of Monticello*, 417-18.

[8] See Bertram Wyatt-Brown, *Southern Honor: Ethics and Behavior in the Old South* (New York, 1982); and Edward L. Ayers, *Vengeance and Justice: Crime and Punishment in the 19th-Century American South* (New York, 1984).

[9] Ayers, *Vengeance and Justice*, 19.

[10] Pierre Bourdieu, "The Sentiment of Honor in Kabyle Society," in *Honor and Shame: The Values of Mediterranean Society*, ed. Jean G. Peristiany (London, 1966), 212.

[11] Ayers, *Vengeance and Justice*, 19; Wyatt-Brown, *Southern Honor*, 61, 114.

[12] See, for example, Bernard Bailyn, "Politics and Social Structure in Virginia," *Shaping Southern Society: The Colonial Experience*, ed. T. H. Breen (New York, 1976), 200-201.

[13] See Wyatt-Brown, *Southern Honor*, chap. 4.

[14] Ibid., 96 and passim; see also Stow Persons, *The Decline of Gentility* (New York, 1973).

[15] Henry Adams, *The Education of Henry Adams: An Autobiography* (Boston, 1918), 56-59.

[16] Wyatt-Brown, *Southern Honor*, 94.

[17] William J. Grayson as quoted in ibid., 92.

[18] Ibid., xviii.

[19] Elizabeth Fox-Genovese and Eugene D. Genovese, "The Old South Considered as a Religious Society," National Humanities Center Newsletter, 6 (Summer 1985): 1-6.

[20] Jefferson to Peter Carr, 19 Aug. 1785, *The Papers of Thomas Jefferson*, ed. Julian P. Boyd, 21 vols. (Princeton, N.J., 1950-), 8:406. Cf. Wyatt-Brown, *Southern Honor*, 99.

[21] Jefferson to Carr, 6 Aug. 1788, *Papers of Jefferson*, ed. Boyd, 13:470. Cf. Wyatt-Brown, *Southern Honor*, 100. That Jefferson could indeed feel the pangs of conscience and contemplate God's judgment is pointedly suggested in his musings on the injustice of slavery and his statement: "Indeed I tremble for my country when I reflect that God is just: that his justice cannot sleep for ever. . . ." *Thomas Jefferson, Notes on the State of Virginia*, ed. William Peden (Chapel Hill, N.C., 1954), 163.

[22] Daniel J. Boorstin, *The Americans: The National Experience* (New York, 1965), 211.

[23] See Phyllis Vine, "Preparation for Republicanism: Honor and Shame in the Eighteenth-Century College," in *Regulated Children/Liberated Children: Education in Psychohistorical Perspective*, ed. Barbara Finkelstein (New York, 1979), 44-62; David F. Allmendinger, Jr., *Paupers and Scholars: The Transformation of Student Life in Nineteenth-Century New England* (New York, 1975), esp. chap. 7; and Steven J. Novak, *The Rights of Youth: American Colleges and Student Revolt, 1798-1815* (Cambridge, Mass., 1977).

[24] Cf. Wyatt-Brown, *Southern Honor*, 19; and Ayers, *Vengeance and Justice*, 19-20.

George Tucker, were Virginians well versed in the reciprocity of manners expected between gentlemen. The appointment in 1845 of William Holmes McGuffey to the faculty as professor of moral philosophy brought to the university one who proved to be quite successful in advancing the temperance movement and religious sentiment within the university community.

More difficult to document but also at work was a process in which the ideal of gentility itself was being modified by the growth of evangelical Christianity in the South as well as within the University of Virginia proper. Although one contributor to a southern literary magazine in the 1840s charged that Jefferson had "done more to injure religion than any person who ever lived in [the United States]," there had always been students and professors at the university who were professing and practicing Christians (and at least a few Jews).[62] During the 1830s students voluntarily contributed toward the support of a university chaplain, and a Bible society was active on the Grounds during the same period. By the 1840s and 1850s, however, religious interest appeared to quicken at the university. Soon after the arrival of Professor McGuffey, voluntary early morning prayers were instituted and became a regular feature of university life. In 1858 University of Virginia students organized the first collegiate chapter of the Young Men's Christian Association. While it is impossible to determine with any degree of precision the influence of Christianity on the attitudes and values of Virginia students, the revival enthusiasm at work among Baptists, Methodists, Presbyterians, and other denominations in the South, the growth of the temperance movement, and the increasingly vocal condemnation by ministers and others of dueling and related evils of the honor culture appear to have had an effect in encouraging moderation of the exuberant and often exaggerated requirements of the southern code of honor among students at the University of Virginia as well as at other colleges in the region.[63]

These concluding comments should not be taken to imply that after the 1840s saintly students imbued with the principles of Christian gentility overcame the sinners and scoundrels who exaggerated the honor precepts of the planter gentry. Discord and disorder continued to surface within the university, albeit with less frequency and drama, in the decades that followed. Indeed, looking beyond the boundaries of the university and the state, it might well be argued that it was the region's abiding faith in the traditional demands of honor, rooted in a society whose values were determined by the realities of class and caste, that compelled thousands of southern students and alumni finally to engage in the most horrible honor clash of all, the Civil War.

[1] Richard Hofstadter and Walter P. Metzger, *The Development of Academic Freedom in the United States* (New York, 1961), 209-21; Frederick Rudolph, *The American College and University: A History* (New York, 1962), 113; R. Freeman Butts, *The College Charts Its Course: Historical Conceptions and Current Proposals* (New York, 1939).

24 Henry Barnard as quoted by Joseph F. Kett, *Rites of Passage: Adolescence in America 1790 to the Present* (New York, 1977), 54. Kett provides a succinct review and critique of major historical explanations for student disorder, 54-59.

25 [Thomas Jefferson], "Report of the Rockfish Gap Commission Appointed to Fix the Site of the University of Virginia," 4 Aug. 1818, in *Theories of Education in Early America, 1655-1819*, ed. Wilson Smith (Indianapolis, 1973), 334.

26 Jefferson to Ellen Randolph Coolidge, 27 Aug. 1825, *The Writings of Thomas Jefferson*, ed. Lipscomb and Bergh (Washington, D.C., 1903), 18:341.

27 "Riotous, disorderly, intemperate, or indecent conduct," "fighting, or giving or accepting a challenge to a duel were among offenses that could warrant immediate suspension or expulsion by action of the faculty. *Enactments by the Rector and Visitors of the University of Virginia* (Charlottesville, 1825), 8-9.

28 Joseph C. Cabell to Jefferson, 25 May 1825, *Early History of the University of Virginia as Contained in the Letters of Thomas Jefferson and Joseph C. Cabell*, ed. Nathaniel F. Cabell (Richmond, 1856), 354; Charles Coleman Wall, Jr., "Students and Student Life at the University of Virginia, 1825 to 1861" (Ph.D. diss., University of Virginia, 1978), 6.

29 See, for example, Kathryn McDaniel Moore, "The War with the Tutors: Student-Faculty Conflict at Harvard and Yale, 1745-1771," *History of Education Quarterly* 18 (Summer 1978): 115-27.

30 Jefferson to Thomas Cooper, 2 Nov. 1822, *Crusade against Ignorance: Thomas Jefferson on Education*, ed. Gordon C. Lee (New York, 1961), 79-80.

31 Ibid., 10.

32 Wall, "Student Life at U. Va.," 44.

33 Throughout the 1825 to 1860 period Virginia students paid $75 a session for tuition. Comparable figures for other colleges in the 1830s and 1840s include Harvard, $71; South Carolina, $50; and Yale, Princeton, and Alabama, $40. Total expenses for Virginia students (including room, board, supplies, and personal expenses as well as tuition) reached into and above the $400 level, roughly twice the amount estimated to be the annual cost of an education in the 1840s at Yale, Princeton, and Harvard. See Wall, "Student Life at U. Va.," 66-67; and Ernest P. Earnest, *Academic Procession: An Informal History of the American College, 1636 to 1953* (Indianapolis, 1953); and Allmendinger, *Paupers and Scholars*, 50-51.

34 Wall, "Student Life at U. Va.," 44-49.

35 See ibid., 35; and Lawrence Stone, "The Size and Composition of the Oxford Student Body, 1850-1910," in *The University in Society*, ed. Lawrence Stone, 2 vols. (Princeton, N.J., 1974), 1:74.

36 On the infidel image of Jefferson and the University of Virginia see Merrill D. Peterson, *The Jeffersonian Image in the American Mind* (New York, 1962), 127-29.

37 Wall, "Student Life at U. Va.," 49-54. Apparently without exaggeration a student wrote his father in 1853 that "many state [scholarship] students here are *heirs to estates of considerable value*." Wall contends that a number of the scholarship students were sons of Virginia gentry who had met with financial setbacks or failures or were temporarily short of available cash for college expenses. See ibid., 64; and Edward St. George Cooke to John R. Cooke, 11 Dec. 1853, Edward St. George Cooke Collection, Accession no. 2974, Manuscripts Department, University of Virginia Library.

38 Albert Howell to George W. Keesee, 13 Nov. 1851, and Albert H. Snead to Howell, 30 Nov. 1856, as quoted in Wall, "Student Life at U. Va.," 57.

39 The University of Virginia did not offer customary academic degrees at the time of its founding except for the degree of Doctor of Medicine. Rather, a student who could pass a rigorous examination in one or more of the schools of the university could qualify for a diploma that declared him to be a "Graduate of the University of Virginia." Jefferson intended that the diploma signify advanced or graduate level accomplishment. The Master of Arts degree was instituted in 1832 and was bestowed upon any student who earned diplomas in ancient languages, mathematics, natural philosophy, chemistry, and moral philosophy. The Bachelor of Laws degree was introduced in 1840 and by 1848 the university admitted to the necessity of establishing the Bachelor of Arts degree. See Bruce, *History*, 2:135-40; and Patton, *Jefferson, Cabell, and the University*, 326-31.

23 Wall, "Student Life at U. Va.," 55.

24 "The University of Virginia's social appeal as a "finishing school" was noted by its description as "the *ne plus ultra*—the overtopping climacteric of a polite education," in "The University: Its Character and Wants," *Southern Literary Messenger*, 23 (Sept. 1856): 241.

25 The description is that of librarian William Wertenbaker as quoted in Bruce, *History*, 2:263.

26 Ibid., 317.

27 Robley Dunglison, "The Autobiographical Ana of Robley Dunglison, M.D.," in *Transactions of the American Philosophical Society*, ed. Samuel X. Radbill, vol. 53, part 8 (1963), 29-30; cf. Wall, "Student Life at U. Va.," 149.

28 Jefferson as quoted in Bruce, *History*, 2:264-65.

29 Jo of Mississippi (pseud.), "My First Frolic in College," *Southern Literary Messenger*, 11 (Feb. 1845): 109-12; see Wall, "Student Life at U. Va.," 76-77.

30 See, for example, Ronald B. Head, ed., "The Student Diary of Charles Ellis, Jr., Mar. 10-June 25, 1835," *The Magazine of Albemarle County History* 35 and 36 (1978): 30 and passim.

31 William B. Rogers to Henry Rogers, 5 Feb. 1842, as quoted in Wall, "Student Life at U. Va.," 78.

32 Bruce, *History*, 2:270.

33 Ibid.

34 Ibid., 295; see also Wall, "Student Life at U. Va.," 91-95.

35 Bruce, *History*, 2:293; Wall, "Student Life at U. Va.," 104-7.

36 *Faculty Minutes*, I, Oct. 1-5, 1825; Henry Tutwiler, *Early Years of the University of Virginia* (Charlottesville, 1882), 3-14; Bruce, *History*, 2:298-301; Wall, "Student Life at U. Va.," 155-58.

37 Bruce, *History*, 2:144-49, 299. Professors Long and Key did not in fact resign in this instance, but their action did signal a decided strain between them and the other professors as well as the students. Key left the University of Virginia after two years and Long after three, both to become professors in the newly established University of London. See also Malone, *The Sage of Monticello*, 485.

38 Robley Dunglison, "Diary," as quoted in Novak, *The Rights of Youth*, 127.

39 Except for a brief period of deviation during the 1832-33 session, this principle remained inviolate, thus making the detection and disciplining of offenders a trying task. Wall, "Student Life at U. Va.," 187.

40 Jefferson as quoted in Bruce, *History*, 2:300-301.

41 In addition to countless minor disturbances and clashes, serious rebellions occurred in 1825, 1832, 1833, 1836, and 1845. See Wall, "Student Life at U. Va.," chap. 6.

42 Ibid., 213-14.

43 The accused student, Joseph Semmes, is reported by Bruce to have later "perished miserably in Texas." However, the *Semi-Centennial Catalogue* lists Semmes as a suicide in his home state of Georgia. Bruce, *History*, 2:311; *Students of the University of Virginia: A Semi-Centennial Catalogue with Brief Biographical Sketches*, ed. Schele de Vere (Baltimore, 1878).

44 Wall, "Student Life at U. Va.," 248-65.

45 J.T.C., "Mr. Rives Address," *Southern Literary Messenger* 9 (Sept. 1847): 575.

46 See Wyatt-Brown, *Southern Honor*, 100-105.

Jennings L. Wagoner, Jr., is professor of the history of education and chairman of the Department of Educational Leadership and Policy Studies at the University of Virginia. This essay is the presidential address which was presented at the annual meeting of the History of Education Society, held at Atlanta, Georgia, in November, 1985.

From Republican Motherhood to Race Suicide: Arguments on the Higher Education of Women in the United States, 1820-1920

Patricia A. Palmieri

> Why is it, that, whenever anything is done for women in the way of education it is called "an experiment,"—something that is to be long considered, stoutly opposed, grudgingly yielded, and dubiously watched,—while, if the same thing is done for men, its desireableness is assumed as a matter of course, and the thing is done? Thus, when Harvard College was founded, it was not regarded as an experiment, but as an institution. . . . Every subsequent step in the expanding of educational opportunities for young men has gone in the same way. But, when there seems a chance of extending . . . the same collegiate advances to women, I observe that . . . the measure [is spoken of] as an "experiment."
>
> Thomas Wentworth Higginson

Scholars studying American social and intellectual history are just beginning to address the question of why women's higher education has perennially been conceptualized as a revolutionary experiment, as the social critic and reformer Thomas Wentworth Higginson observed in 1881.[1] Before the last decade, American educational history was peripheral to the study of American history. Moreover, educational history was dominated by booster portraits of elite male institutions, usually seen through the eyes of their presidents. The exceptions to the male bias of educational history, Thomas Woody's two-volume *A History of Women's Education in the United States*, written in the late 1920s, and Mabel Newcomer's *A Century of Higher Education for American Women*, issued in the 1950s, stood alone for many years, although they too demonstrated the conceptual difficulty of studying American women's higher education.[2]

A progressive historian, Woody was interested in "out-groups," in this case women, and chronicled their struggle to gain access to institutions of education created mainly for men. For Woody, access meant success and progress; women, by virtue of being admitted to a formerly male educational bastion, would ultimately achieve intellectual, social, and even political liberation.

Newcomer, a professor of economics at Vassar College, sustained this liberal outlook. Focusing on the women's colleges, she cited their propensity for innovation and noted the high proportion of notable women achievers they produced. For Newcomer, as for Woody, women's entry into higher education was a significant positive marker.

The social and political events of the 1960s, the concomitant rise of a new social history, and the emergence of many more educated, articulate women interested in the status of women gave birth to a revisionist school of women's higher educational history. Aggrieved by the documented discrimination against educated women and angered by the meager victories of even the most educated women in the professions, these social and intellectual historians saw the history of women's education darkly. They began to question the equation of access with progress, arguing that coeducation and even the separate women's colleges reinforced patterns of women's subordination in academe.[3]

At the same time, a vocal chorus of disaffected graduates of the Seven Sisters also lambasted women's education. They wrote popular books like *Peculiar Institutions* and *I'm Radcliffe! Fly Me! The Seven Sisters and the Failure of Women's Education*, books whose titles testify to their authors' disgruntlement.[4]

Beginning in the 1970s, post-revisionist scholars have struggled to shed both booster arguments and dark diatribes. Their concern with women's experiences as students and faculty and their analysis of the development of women's culture within coeducational and single-sex colleges display a new appreciation for the complexity of their subject.[5] To these approaches historians must add another: a focus on arguments for and against women's higher education. Only then can we better understand the interaction between the historical context and real changes in the lives of educated women. Such an examination of the ongoing discussion and its social and intellectual setting will make clear the need to reevaluate the periodization of the history of American women's education in the nineteenth and early twentieth centuries. Moreover, exploration of this realm reveals that in the complex history of women's education there is a central paradox: that success, overwhelming success, triggered as many problems (within the movement and without) as would have total failure.

In what follows I will briefly discuss the arguments covering women's higher education in three significant periods:

1. The Romantic period (1820–90) or, to use Linda Kerber's term, the era of "Republican Motherhood."

2. The Reform era (1860–90), which saw the opening of the women's colleges and a vigorous debate about women's higher education. In this period I find the rise of Respectable Spinsterhood.

3. The Progressive era (1890–1920), in which the first generation of college women began entering the professions, triggering a conservative reaction that I term the "Race Suicide Syndrome."

THE ROMANTIC PERIOD: 1820–60

Historians have documented that Puritan culture was suspicious of women; it classified women as evil. Woman's intellect was also considered inferior to man's, and extensive learning for women was deemed inexpedient and dangerous. In a religiously oriented society, higher education meant the production of ministers; thus males could immediately attend Harvard and Yale with a view toward assuming ministerial roles. Women, locked in a private sphere, were barred from all formal education.[6]

By the 1820s a major shift had occurred in women's roles in American culture. Post-revolutionary American society was permeated with an optimism about individuals derived from two sources: liberal enlightenment thinking and romanticism. Rather than stressing women's evil nature, the new ideology elevated and idealized women's capacity to be pure, moral, and sentimental. What impact did this new cultural definition of women have on women's education? In "The Cult of True Womanhood" and other essays, the historian Barbara Welter argues that the romantic image of woman was anti-intellectual. A woman was supposed to be passive, to indulge in domesticity, and to lead a circumscribed intellectual life. Innocence and emotionalism reigned to the detriment of intellect. The virtuous female was thought to be threatened by too much education.[7]

However, it is clear that this same romantic image could work on women's behalf. Romanticism put an emphasis on perfectionism. Educational reformers began to pit romantic images of women against the frivolous "ornamental" woman who lacked education and was nothing other than a dilettante.

In *Women of the Republic*, Linda Kerber notes that the new republic, anxiously seeking to produce a virtuous citizenry, assigned women roles as influential caretakers. Although women were not expected to participate in the public domain, they were given access to education and drawn, if only indirectly, into the new republican experiment by their responsibility to educate their sons. In this period, seminaries like Emma Willard's Troy and Mary Lyon's Mount Holyoke opened; the historian Anne Firor Scott finds that Willard's Troy was a seedbed of feminism rather than a citadel of domesticity.[8]

The new romanticism operated on women's behalf in other ways. Romantic ideology, a phenomenon discussed by Susan Conrad in *Perish* the Thought, equated genius with such qualities as intuition, emotional empathy, and insight, qualities preeminently associated with women. By laying claim to special emotional and moral traits, women could cultivate intellectual roles as teachers, translators, and social reformers.[9] Concomitant with these cultural changes, economic factors were also operating to provide a rationale for women's education. By the 1820s, America was becoming increasingly industrialized, and factory work was beginning to replace family production. In New England, at least, young women were not needed as much as before to tend farms; neither were they expected to busy themselves in home crafts or to devote themselves to domestic chores. As men moved into the urban economy or ventured West, they delayed marriage. Sensing these changes, families in the 1840s seem to have engaged in what David Allmendinger calls a "life-planning" strategy which promoted the education of daughters. A seminary education would allow women to teach, add to the family income, and support themselves until they entered marriage.[10] The common-school movement, with its demand for a cheap labor pool, dovetailed nicely with other social and economic changes that encouraged, indeed forced, women to become educated for teaching roles in the public sphere.[11]

THE ERA OF REFORM: 1860–90

Thus far historians studying women's history in general and educational history in particular have concentrated their attention on the pre-Civil War era. Our understanding of the links between the Civil War and the growing demand for women's higher education are thus minimal. In general we know that war causes disruption in social values and also allows some crossover in sex roles. Moreover, in wartime women often are allowed access to careers because their skills are in demand. During the Civil War, for example, women figured more prominently in public activities such as nursing. We also know that contemporaries believed that a superfluity of single women existed in New England as a result of the war. Addressing Mount Holyoke graduates in 1873, William Tyler claimed that there were 30,000 more young women than men in the region; he thus welcomed the opening of colleges for women. Vassar's president, John Raymond, spoke in 1870 on the "Demand of the Age for the Liberal Education of Women and How It Should Be Met." He declared that "statistics in our time place it beyond a peradventure that multitudes of women must remain unmarried." Moreover, Raymond

sounded a new cultural note. He coupled the statistical reality with the conclusion that it would be an "insult to woman" if she had to sit and wait for a man. As he noted, "Under certain circumstances it is good *not* to marry." According to Raymond, it was one of woman's unquestionable rights to serve her country. Hence women, no less than men, should be provided with the kind of education that promoted independent activity and prepared them for work. The Vassar curriculum with its innovations in science training reflected his concern that women be capable of taking their place in an increasingly professionalized society. While Raymond often envisioned women as helpmates in science, rather than as leaders, he still broke with a tradition in stressing that single women had a right to their autonomy and to education.[12] By the 1870s, then, "respectable spinsterhood," not "republican motherhood," was seen as the raison d'être of women's higher education.[13]

Beyond a demographic shift, what had caused such a tremendous transition in arguments for women's higher education? Historians have not pursued this question sufficiently. In 1870, John Raymond astutely connected the movement for women's higher education with the pre–Civil War women's rights movement. He admitted that a vanguard had awakened the public's attention to women's quest for autonomy. While he personally found some of the women's rights leaders to be "vixens and viragos," he noted that "extremists always precede and herald a true reform." Those who followed in the wake of the original agitation might "gather whatever fruit it may have shaken from the tree of truth."[14] To what extent was the opening of women's colleges an attempt to forestall more radical social change? To what extent was this movement part of a larger social reform history? These questions have yet to be sufficiently explored.

In 1868, John M. Greene, in encouraging Sophia Smith to endow a women's college in Massachusetts, stated: "The subject of women's education, woman's rights and privileges, is to be the great step in the progress of our state."[15] In the late nineteenth century, the desire for women's higher education took on the quality of a millennial-like reform movement, not unlike other communitarian reforms that dotted the American landscape in the pre–Civil War era.[16] Conventionally, most social historians conclude that the post–Civil War era was a kind of dark ages, bereft of social reform or behavior. Ronald Walters, for example, concludes that the reform impulse had entirely spent itself by the 1870s. Moreover, to many the Gilded Age has been, in the words of Geoffrey

Blodgett, "a vast gray zone of American history, monotonous and inconclusive, an era of evasion, avoidance and postponement, . . . one sterile of purposes."[17]

This standard interpretation is based on a tainted vision of politics in the post–Civil War era and on a paucity of studies in cultural and social history. Women's history and social history are just beginning to challenge this stereotype. The movement for women's higher education must be seen as an extension of the romantic and evangelical reform tradition. It was also an effort to achieve women's equality. Hence, those historians who have focused narrowly upon the history of the organized suffrage movement and view the 1870s and 1880s as the doldrums also miss the import of the social movement for women's higher education.[18]

Indeed, by the 1870s the debate about women's educability had become, at least in middle-class American society, what the abolitionist debate was before it and the suffrage debate after it—a large-scale movement, amorphous, with different intellectual strands, involving the energies of many middle-class women and men. Vassar president John Raymond alluded to this movement when asserting that "the whole world is astir with a sense of the coming change."[19]

Like those other organized movements, the movement for women's higher education had its "antis," in particular a set of doctors and educators who continuously unleashed fears about the deleterious effects on women's biological and social roles. The ideology of the anti-movement, like the ideology of the movement for women's higher education, deserves serious attention, which it has not received from scholars as yet. Most historians cite as the chief malefactor Dr. Edward Clarke of Harvard University, who in 1873 published *Sex in Education: A Fair Chance for the Girls*, in which he argued that higher education would damage women's health and ultimately inhibit their reproductive capacity. Clarke's book caused quite a stir; within a year it went through twelve printings.[20]

Clarke's book and the ensuing controversy are commonly cited by historians of higher education as illustrative of the negative climate surrounding the founding of the women's colleges in the 1870s and 1880s. Historians suggest that as a result, many of these women's institutions became defensive; they compromised their lofty educational ideals and succumbed to genteel domesticity, health regimes, and upholding rather than revolutionizing the cultural norms of "true womanhood."[21] This is, I think, misleading. Clarke's book stimulated a

debate which if anything only heightened the revolutionary quality of the struggle for women's higher education. M. Carey Thomas recalled that as a young girl she was "haunted by the clanging chains of that gloomy little specter, Dr. Edward Clarke's *Sex in Education*." Alarmed by his rhetoric, the adolescent Thomas encouraged her mother to read his book and was relieved to learn from her that broken-down invalids like those described by Clarke did not really exist. That her mother scorned Clarke's dire predictions and encouraged Thomas in her quest for collegiate training demonstrates important information about women's ambitions in the late nineteenth century and the intergenerational context of women's higher education, and introduces the historical questions of family strategies—the relationship between family culture and women's higher education.[22]

It also made the first generation of women students extraordinarily conscious of their pivotal role in proving to the world that women were men's intellectual equals. As one alumna of Wellesley's class of 1879 recalled: "We were pioneers in the adventure—voyagers in the crusade for the higher education of women—that perilous experiment of the 1870s which all the world was breathlessly watching and which the prophets were declaring to be so inevitably fatal to the American girls."[23] Here we return to Higginson's theme of "experiment," for the first generation of college women confronted the experimental, revolutionary, and adventuresome quality of women's higher education. While Higginson noted its negative implications—that women always had to prove themselves to a suspicious male world—there is of course another aspect to experiment: that daring, bravado, and adventure, that sense of being a pioneer and of course that desire to uphold extraordinarily high norms. Subsequent generations of women lost that excitement, and the nature of women's higher education changed. Clarke's dire predictions did not dampen the women's college movement. Wellesley and Smith opened in 1875, and others followed soon after.

THE PROGRESSIVE ERA AND THE BACKLASH—THE "RACE SUICIDE SYNDROME": 1890–1920

Most historians view the Progressive era as a period of advance when college women entered the professions of medicine, law, social work, and academe. But it was also a period of reaction. This reaction took different forms and emanated from a variety of groups. In 1908, boasting of the remarkable success of women's higher education, Bryn Mawr's president, M. Carey Thomas, took note of the changing public perception of college women: "Our highest hopes are all coming gloriously true. It is like reading a page of Grimm's fairy tales. The fearsome toads of those early prophecies are turning into pearls of radiance before our very eyes. Now women who have been to college are as plentiful as blackberries on summer hedges."[24] Whereas her generation had been ignominiously labeled fearsome toads, the new college woman was rapidly becoming a prized pearl. The pioneer band of college women had been so successful in weathering the dangerous experiment that in the twentieth century college attendance for women was not a sacerdotal or strange experience, but a socially sanctioned endeavor. Vassar professor Elizabeth Hazelton Haight commented on this success in 1917, stressing that unlike the "stern pioneer" many women now "wear their learning lightly like a flower."[25]

But herein lay a paradox and a dilemma. Soon the staunch pioneers, especially the first generation of academic women at the women's colleges, would be as troubled by their amazing success as they might have been over their failure. As early as 1900 many of them viewed the rising tide of more socially acceptable college girls as a grim fairy tale indeed—one that spelled death to the dedication they deemed requisite for the intellectual life and the spread of a disease they termed dilettantism.

If women faculty winced at the price of success within the internal college climate, they would soon find themselves confronted by an even thornier set of problems stemming from the growing popularity of college life. In the words of Mary Cheyney, secretary of the Western Association of Collegiate Alumnae, the "very success of the movement, which amounts to a great revolution affecting one-half the human race, has roused men to resist its progress."[26] Not so surprisingly, the 1900s saw a backlash against the women's colleges. Many male educators and doctors viewed the lengthening lines of candidates in the secondary schools with alarm. They believed the women's colleges were "institutions for the promotion of celibacy," producing a disappearing class of intellectual women who were not marrying and hence were committing race suicide.[27]

In 1908, coincident with Thomas's speech about formerly fearsome toads turning into pearls, G. Stanley Hall, a professor of psychology at Clark University, published an article entitled "The Kind of Women Colleges Produce." In it he lambasted Thomas and other "spinster" presidents and faculty who called upon women to be self-supporting and to uphold in high regard the ideal of scholarship and to train for a definite career. Hall railed: "The ideal of our colleges for young women, especially those whose regimentation is chiefly feminine, is not primarily wifehood and motherhood, but glorified spinsterhood." Women's colleges were, according to Hall, in the hands of misguided feminists."[28]

By 1905, a diffuse but increasingly outspoken group of educators, psychologists, doctors, and journalists had registered their alarm at the low marriage rates of women's college alumnae. Even President Theodore Roosevelt was concerned about celibacy. In a 1905 speech before Congress in which he condemned low marriage rates and the equally scandalous practice of birth control, he popularized the term "race suicide." The incapacity or unwillingness of the Anglo-Saxon race and particularly its highly educated members to marry and reproduce unleashed fears that within a generation or two they would die out. Presumably the leadership of the nation would then be left in the hands of immigrants from Central and Eastern Europe whose fertility was quite high, but whose intellect was deemed inferior.[29]

Viewed from this angle, M. Carey Thomas's statement about toads turning into jewels takes on another meaning: no doubt she hoped to assuage the fears of opponents who continued to relish and rely on the image of the college woman as a peculiar creature. In effect, then, from the very beginning the women faculty at the women's colleges had been battling a psychological war on two fronts: they hoped to challenge the larger culture and to change women's role in society, and in so doing they were engaging in a subversive, radical act. At the same time they wished to maintain the image of women's colleges as reputable and respectable institutions, a difficult task given that they were functioning within an inhospitable social climate for women's higher education and professionalization.

In this tangled conversation about women's education it is extremely significant that often the first generation of college-educated women who became academics wound up fueling their enemies' arguments. They had built their identities on the ideology of the select few: so long as there were only a token handful of women seeking intellectual careers, a system of special patronage and fatherly advising favorable to their careers had operated. Moreover, the tolerance for the select few meant that only someone like Madame Curie might succeed; faculty women

the ultimate feminization of American culture. Any success he attained would be devalued because women had demonstrated equal achievement. "The triumph in . . . competition is no honour if it consists in bidding under the market price. In fact, it is not merely a question of the division of labour, but a fundamental change in the character of the labour."[31] Such fears confirm the argument made by Margaret Rossiter in *Women Scientists in America*: that the growing numbers of women in the professions threatened many academic men who were caught up in defining their career paths as professional rather than amateur.[32] Like other professional men, Munsterberg was anxious to divorce himself from the cheapening effect that feminization has on the status of any profession.

Ultimately, the pioneers would discover that there was a price to be paid for an explanation of college generations that revolved around the fact that a first generation of staunch scholars were, happily or unhappily, passing from the scene. Defenders of the women's colleges were giving their opponents some potent psychological weapons. By 1920, critics and advocates agreed that the experience of the first cohort of college-educated women who went into the professions and who remained single was not representative of normal womanhood. This kind of defense was at one level useful in soothing fears and dismissing doubts about the future status of women's higher education, but it also helped to mythologize the select few, and worse, it labeled them as deviant. Of course the ideology of the select few had always had this vulnerable underbelly—one was intellectually select and prized, but one stood apart and was different from ordinary women.

The negative implications of this "extraordinary woman" approach can be clearly seen in a defense of women's higher education entitled "Education and Fecundity," written by Nellie Seeds Nearing and published in 1914 by the American Statistical Association. She argued that the "average woman . . . who went to college in the early days . . . was not the type who would have been apt to marry in any case." Just who were the pioneers? They "consisted largely of the woman who had some special talent which she wished to develop and practice, the woman of strong intellectual proclivities, who preferred not to engage in the domestic occupations usually relegated to women, and the woman who, because of personal unattractiveness, knew or feared her lack of popularity among men." The contemporary college woman, somehow, was irrefutably different. "Today it is the normal, not the unusual girl who goes to college. . . . It has become a common comfort. . . ." Nearing also believed

could never settle for being average. They set appallingly high standards for themselves and for their students.

Shocked and dismayed by how few women wanted to follow the scholarly path, some faculty balked at what they called the universalization of collegiate norms. Average women were getting the B. A. and coming to symbolize the "College Type." But as Margaret Deland astutely noted in 1910: "[The] occasional women who did so-called unwomanly things, that is, unusual things generally left to men . . . who have distinguished themselves . . . were conspicuous, because they were strays. Achieving women are not very conspicuous now, simply because there are more of them."[30]

Ironically, then, on one level, proponents and detractors of women's higher education had a mutual investment in the ideology of the select few. For the faculty at the women's colleges, any dilution of the norms or shift from the high standards threatened their status. So long as a raison d'être for college attendance was scholarship and was wrapped up in vows of renunciation, successful academic women appeared irrefutably to be geniuses and would be tolerated. Wary opponents of women's higher education were also satisfied with this equation; they could always explain away or dismiss (even while they praised) the remarkable rare exceptions. But the popularization of collegiate life caused them alarm. They were distraught because more women than they had expected were earning Phi Beta Kappa keys and seeking entry into the professions. However, only rarely did these antifeminists focus directly on their fears of feminization of colleges and professions. In 1901 Hugo Munsterberg, a professor of philosophy at Harvard, voiced his alarm: "In the colleges and universities men still dominate, but soon will not if things are not changed; the great numbers of young women who pass their doctoral examinations and become specialists in science will have more and more to seek university professorships, or else they will have studied in vain. And here, as in the school, the economic conditions strongly favour the woman; since she has no family to support, she can accept a position so much smaller that the man is more and more crowded from the field. And it may be clearly foreseen that, if other social factors do not change, women will enter as competitors in every field where the labour does not require specifically masculine strength. So it has been in the factories, so in the schools and so, in a few decades, it may be in the universities. . . ."

While in 1904 Munsterberg could acknowledge with relief that "professional chairs for the most part belong to men," he still worried over that a college education had become desirable because it polished off a woman's cultural education.[33]

Mollifying the opponents of women's colleges by emphasizing the conventionality of the collegiate experience for women drew attention away from the fact that marriage rates for college-educated women remained lower than those for the rest of the eligible population. In 1923, Vassar economics professor Mabel Newcomer found that as of the summer of 1922, of 4,424 alumnae surveyed, only 55.6 percent had married. Although Vassar women, she noted, were marrying more, and marrying at younger ages, the total picture was one of deviation from the national averages of marriage rates, which usually hovered around 90 percent.[34] Nellie Nearing had understood this, but she took pains to explain the tremendous disparity by factors other than education. She was led back to economic arguments that noted that educated people were expected a high standard of family living and that it was difficult for women to find husbands who could meet this elevated standard.

The constant need to explain away such potent statistics highlights as well the culturally charged climate of the first quarter of the twentieth century, in which marriage and family were deemed by Freudian dicta to be universally desirable experiences craved by all normal women. World War I temporarily masked the shifting social scene that produced hostility toward professional women. Writing in 1938, Marjorie Nicholson, a professor at Columbia University who had received her B. A. in 1914, commented: "We of the pre-war generation used to pride ourselves sentimentally on being the 'lost generation,' used to think that because war cut across the stable path on which our feet were set we were an unfortunate generation. But as I look back upon the records, I find myself wondering whether our generation was not the only generation of women which ever really found itself. We came late enough to escape the self-consciousness and belligerence of the pioneers, to take education and training for granted. We came early enough to take equally for granted professional positions in which we could make full use of our training. This was our double glory. Positions were everywhere open to us; it never occurred to us at that time that we were taken only because men were not available. . . . The millennium had come; it did not occur to us that life could be different. *Within a decade shades of the prison house began to close, not upon the growing boy, but upon the emancipated girls* [emphasis added]."[35]

By the end of the 1920s, renunciation of marriage in favor of professional life was equated with a race of "warped, dry creatures."[36]

Reconciliation of marriage and career became the watchword of the 1920s. Educated women "wearing their learning lightly like a flower" attempted to combine career and marriage. But lacking the support of institutions and bereft of a feminist movement, such attempts were often thwarted.

In the 1920s and continuing into the 1930s and 1940s, critics still questioned the value of women's higher education. Detractors insisted that college attendance posed innumerable dilemmas for modern American women. Thus, at some level, higher education for women was still being discussed as an experiment, the view that Higginson had castigated some forty years before. Unwilling to accept the permanency of women's entrance into academia as students or as scholars and unable to accept professional advancement of women in a wide range of careers, critics still dubbed such advances by women as "revolutionary," their worth still to be proved. But despite doubts, American women's entry into and success within higher education permanently altered their life courses and changed as well the social and intellectual course of the nation.

NOTES

1. Thomas Wentworth Higginson, "Experiments," *Common Sense about Women* (Boston: Lee and Shepard, 1882), p. 199.

2. Thomas Woody, *A History of Women's Education in the United States* (New York: Farrar, Straus and Giroux, 1980; originally published by Science Press, 1929); Mabel Newcomer, *A Century of Higher Education for American Women* (New York: Harper and Brothers, 1959).

3. See, for example, Jill Conway, "Perspectives on the History of Women's Education in the United States," *History of Education Quarterly* 14 (Spring 1974): 1–12; P. A. Graham, "So Much to Do: Guides for Historical Research on Women in Higher Education," *Teachers College Record* 75 (February 1975): 421–29; P. A. Graham, "Expansion and Exclusion: A History of Women in American Higher Education," *Signs* 3 (Summer 1978): 759–73.

4. Elizabeth Kendall, *Peculiar Institutions* (New York: G. P. Putnam's Sons, 1975); Liva Baker, *I'm Radcliffe! Fly Me! The Seven Sisters and the Failure of Women's Education* (New York: Macmillan, 1976).

5. For example, see Lynn Gordon, "Coeducation on Two Campuses: Berkeley and Chicago, 1890–1912," in *Women's Being, Woman's Place: Female Identity and Vocation in American History*, ed. Mary Kelly (Boston: G. K. Hall, 1979), 171–94; Patricia Foster Haines, "For Honor and Alma Mater: Perspectives on Coeducation at Cornell University, 1868–1885," *Journal of Education* 159 (August 1977): 25–37; Patricia Ann Palmieri, "Here Was a Fellowship:

20. Edward Clarke, *Sex in Education or A Fair Chance for the Girls* (Boston J. R. Osgood, 1874).

21. Sheila Rothman, *Woman's Proper Place* (New York: Basic Books, 1978)

22. M. Carey Thomas, "Present Tendencies in Women's College and University Education," *Educational Review* 25 (1908): 64–85, reprinted in *The Educated Woman in America*, ed. Barbara Cross (New York: Teachers College Press 1965), p. 162.

23. Louise McCoy North, "Speech for '79 and the Trustees at Semi Centennial" (Wellesley, Mass.: North Unprocessed Papers, Wellesley College Archives, 1979).

24. Thomas, "Present Tendencies," p. 162; See also Julia Ward Howe, ed. *Sex and Education: A Reply to Dr. E. H. Clarke's "Sex in Education"* (Boston: Roberts Brothers, 1874).

25. Elizabeth Hazelton Haight, "Pleasant Possibles in Lady Professors," *Journal of the Association of Collegiate Alumnae*, 11 (September 1917): 10–17.

26. Mary Cheyney, "Will Nature Eliminate the College Woman?" *Association of Collegiate Alumnae*, 3rd ser., 10 (January 1905): 1–9.

27. William L. Felter, "The Education of Women," *Educational Review* 31 (1906): 360.

28. G. Stanley Hall, "The Kind of Women Colleges Produce," *Appleton's Magazine*, September 1908, p. 314.

29. On race suicide and its relationship to immigration and other cultural issues, see Linda Gordon, *Woman's Body, Woman's Right: A Social History of Birth Control in America* (New York: Grossman, 1976).

30. Margaret Deland, "The Change in the Feminine Ideal," *Atlantic Monthly* 105 (March 1910): 289.

31. Hugo Munsterberg, *The Americans* (New York: McClure, Phillips, 1904), p. 5.

32. Margaret Rossiter, *Women Scientists in America* (Baltimore: Johns Hopkins University Press, 1982) pp. 73–100.

33. Nellie Seeds Nearing, "Education and Fecundity," *American Statistical Association* 14 (June 1914): 156.

34. Mabel Newcomer, "Vital Statistics from Vassar College," *American Journal of Sociology* 29 (July 1923–May 1924): 430–42.

35. Marjorie Hope Nicholson, "The Rights and Privileges Pertaining Thereto," *Journal of the American Association of University Women* 31 (April 1938): 136.

36. Ethel Puffer Howes, "Accepting the Universe," *Atlantic Monthly*, 129 (April 1922): 453.

A Social Portrait of the Academic Community at Wellesley College, 1890–1920," *History of Education Quarterly* 23 (Summer 1983): 195–214.

6. Laurel Thatcher Ulrich, "Vertuous Woman Found: New England Ministerial Literature, 1668–1735," *American Quarterly* 28 (Spring 1976): 19–40.

7. Barbara Welter, "The Cult of True Womanhood" in *Dimity Convictions: The American Woman in the Nineteenth Century* (Athens: Ohio University Press, 1976), pp. 21–41.

8. Linda Kerber, *Women of the Republic: Intellect and Ideology in Revolutionary America* (Chapel Hill: University of North Carolina Press, 1980).

9. Susan Conrad, *Perish the Thought: Intellectual Women in Romantic America, 1830–1860* (Secaucus, N.J.: Citadel Press, 1978).

10. David Allmendiger, "Mount Holyoke Students Encounter the Need for Life Planning, 1837–1850," *History of Education Quarterly* 19 (1979): 27–47

11. On the common school movement, see Carl F. Kaestle, *Pillars of the Republic: Common Schools and American Society, 1780–1860* (New York: Hill and Wang, 1983). Also see Nancy Hoffman, *Women's True Profession* (New York: Feminist Press, 1981).

12. John Raymond, "The Demand of the Age for the Liberal Education of Women and How It Should Be Met," in *The Liberal Education of Women*, ed James Orton (New York: A. S. Barnes, 1873), pp. 27–58.

13. For a discussion of the culture of spinsterhood before the Civil War, see Lee Chambers-Schiller, *Liberty, A Better Husband: Single Women in America. The Generations of 1780–1840* (New Haven, Conn.: Yale University Press, 1984); Patricia Ann Palmieri, " 'This Single Life': Respectable Spinsterhood" *American Quarterly* forthcoming (review of Chambers-Schiller, 1984).

14. Raymond, "Demand for Liberal Education," p. 50.

15. John M. Greene to Sophia Smith, January 7, 1868, Smith College Archives.

16. On the reform spirit, see John L. Thomas, "Romantic Reform in America 1815–1865," *American Quarterly* 17 (Winter 1965): 656–681.

17. Ronald G. Walters, *American Reformers, 1815–1860* (New York: Hill and Wang, 1978). Geoffrey Blodgett, "A New Look at the Gilded Age: Politics in a Cultural Context," in *Victorian America*, ed. Daniel Walker Howe (Philadelphia: University of Pennsylvania Press, 1976).

18. The traditional interpretation that views the 1870s and 1880s as a quiet era can be found in Aileen Kraditor, *The Ideas of the Woman Suffrage Movement, 1880–1920* (Garden City, N.Y.: Doubleday, 1971), p. 4. Recently, some scholars studying women's higher educational history have challenged this conclusion. See Sally Gregory Kohlstedt, "Maria Mitchell: The Advancement of Women in Sciences," *New England Quarterly* 51 (March 1978): 39–63.

19. Raymond, "Demand for Liberal Education," pp. 50–51.

The Impact of the "Cult of True Womanhood" on the Education of Black Women

Linda M. Perkins

This paper compares the primary purposes and functions of educating black and white women in the 19th century. For white women, education served as a vehicle for developing homemaker skills, for reinforcing the role of wife and mother, and a milieu for finding a potential husband. For black women education served as an avenue for the improvement of their race or "race uplift." The economic, political and social conditions which contributed to these purposes are discussed within a historical context.

To better understand the education of black women vis-a-vis the education of women of the larger society, it is important to place black women within a social and historical context. This essay examines the impact of the "true womanhood" philosophy on the education of white women, and the black philosophy of "race uplift" on the education and development of black women in the nineteenth century. Although blacks considered the women of their race "women" in the early and mid-nineteenth century, by the end of the century they began to place more emphasis on them being "ladies". This shift in attitudes toward women by many educated male blacks will also be discussed.

THE NINETEENTH CENTURY CONTEXT: THE ANTEBELLUM PERIOD

Observers of the early nineteenth century frequently cite the emergence of the 'cult of true womanhood' as significantly shaping women's education during this period. This concept of the "true woman" emphasized innocence, modesty, piety, purity, submissiveness and domesticity. Female education was necessary for the molding of the "ideal woman". Such education reinforced the idea of women's natural position of subordination and focused upon women being loving wives and good mothers. Literacy was deemed important for the reading of the Bible and other religious materials. And needlepoint, painting, music, art, and French dominated the curriculum of "female" education (see Cott, 1977, Rosenberg, 1982, Rothman, 1978; Welter, 1966).

This "true womanhood" model was designed for the upper and middle-class white woman, although poorer white women could aspire to this status. However, since most blacks had been enslaved prior to the Civil War and the debate as to whether they were human beings was a popular topic, black women were not perceived as women in the same sense as women of the larger (i.e., white) society. The emphasis upon women's purity, submissiveness and natural fragility was the antithesis of the reality of most black women's lives during slavery and for many years thereafter.

Not surprisingly whites of the early nineteenth century developed an educational philosophy to correspond with their attitudes towards women. At the same time, blacks espoused a philosophy of education for "race uplift". This education was for the entire race and its purpose was to assist in the economical, educational and social improvement of their enslaved and later emancipated race (For a detailed discussion see Perkins, 1981). Unlike their white counterparts, blacks established coeducational schools and similar curricula for both males and females.

The early decades of the nineteenth century witnessed a dramatic shift in the social and economic fabric of the nation. The growth of factories and increased industry provided employment outside homes and altered the colonial self-sustaining family. With the coming of urbanization and industrialization a new role for women emerged. Unlike the colonial period, when single and married white women worked without stigma, the early nineteenth century emphasized women's "proper sphere" as being within the home (See Rothman, 1978). Throughout the antebellum years, white women were deluged with sermons and speeches which stressed the "duty" of a "true woman". These speeches and sermons were reinforced by a proliferation of magazines, journals and other printed materials that focused upon instructing women of their proper sphere (Cott, 1977).

During the period of the development of the norm of "true womanhood", antebellum blacks struggled to abolish slavery and obtain equality in the nation. The theme of "race uplift" became the motto within the black communities of the nation. It was expected that blacks who were able to assist, i.e. "uplift", other members of their race, would do so (Perkins, 1981).

Although white society did not acknowledge the black women as female, the black race did. During the first half of the nineteenth century, black women's educational, civic and religious organizations in the north bore the word "ladies" in their titles, clearly indicating their perceptions of self. One of the earliest black female educational societies, the Female Literary Association of Philadelphia, combined educational and civic objectives for the group's purposes. The Preamble of the organization's constitution reflected the women's commitment to the philosophy of race "uplift". They wrote, it was their "duty . . . as daughters of a despised race, to use our utmost endeavors to enlighten the understanding, to cultivate the talents entrusted to our keeping, that by so doing, we may in a great measure, break down the strong barrier of prejudice, and raise ourselves to an equality with those of our fellow beings, who differ from us in complexion." (reported in the *Liberator*, December 3, 1931.).

Unlike women of the white society, black women were encouraged to become educated to aid in the improvement of their race. An 1837 article entitled "To the Females of Colour" in the New York black newspaper, *The Weekly Advocate*, (Jan. 7, 1837) urged black women to obtain an education. The article stated, "in any enterprise for the improvement of our people, either moral or mental, our hands would be palsied without woman's influence." Thus, the article continued, "let our beloved female friends, then, rouse up, and exert all their power, in encouraging, and sustaining this effort (educational) which we have made to disabuse the public mind of the misrepresentations made of our character; and to show the world, that there is virtue among us, though concealed; talent, though buried; intelligence, though overlooked." (To the Females of Colour, 1837). In other words, black females and males would demonstrate the race's intelligence, morality, and ingenuity.

It should be understood that during the antebellum period, free blacks lived primarily in an occupational caste. The men were relegated to menial positions while women were primarily domestic workers. Although blacks perceived education as "uplifting", most whites viewed education of blacks as threatening to their position of dominance.

By the time of emancipation in 1863, every southern state had laws that prohibited the education of slaves, and in many instances free blacks as well (Woodson, 1919/1968). There were scattered opportunities for both free blacks and slaves to become literate prior to the 1830s in the nation. However, education for blacks was viewed as dangerous after the fiery *Appeal* of David Walker in 1829 and the 1830 slave revolt of Nat Turner—both literate men. After the 1830s, all southern states instituted laws prohibiting the education of blacks, and such activities were thereby forced underground (Woodson, 1919/1968).

The decades of the 1830s and 1840s in which free blacks sought access to educational institutions in the North paralleled the founding of seminaries for white women. Historian Ann Firor Scott (1979) points out in her study of Troy Female Seminary, the first such institution to open, that the school combined the "true womanhood" ideal with feminist values from its opening in 1822. Under the direction of Emma Willard, the institution sought to preserve the traditional social and political status of women while challenging the notion of women's inferior intellectual status. Despite this challenge to society's view of the intellectual inferiority of women, Troy instilled within its students that "feminine delicacy . . . was a primary and indispensable virtue."

Other such seminaries proliferated in the nation prior to the Civil War. These institutions began the professional training of female teachers. However, few opened their doors to black women on a continuous basis. The lone exception was Oberlin College, which received notoriety in 1833 when it decided to admit both women and blacks on an equal basis with white men. As a result, most of the earliest black college graduates, male and female, were Oberlin graduates (DuBois, 1900). It was not atypical for black families to relocate to Oberlin for the education of their daughters. For example, when Blanche V. Harris was denied admission to a white female seminary in Michigan in the 1850's, her entire family moved to Oberlin (Henle & Merrill, 1979). Similarly, Mary Jane Patterson, who in 1862 became the first black woman to earn a college degree in the United States, moved from North Carolina in the 1850s to Oberlin with her family because of the educational opportunities at the College. Three Patterson females and one male graduated from Oberlin. Fanny Jackson

For several thousand New England white women who journeyed South to teach after the Civil War, it appears that the "cult of true womanhood" was a significant impetus. The women were overwhelmingly single, upper and middle-class, unemployed and educated in New England seminaries and Oberlin College (McPherson, 1975). Their letters of application to the missionary societies sponsoring teachers to the South often reflected a deep need to escape idleness and boredom. A letter stating, "my circumstances are such that it is necessary for me to be doing something" was the common theme (Jones, 1980). In contrast, black women who applied were overwhelmingly employed and financially supported families. Their letters of application consistently reflected a theme of "duty" and "race uplift". While the tenure of the white female educator in the South was normally two to three years, the black female expressed a desire to devote their entire lives to their work and most did (Perkins, in press).

Although conscious of their gender, the earliest black female college graduates repeatedly stated their desire for an education was directly linked to aiding their race. Fanny Jackson Coppin expressed in her autobiography of 1913 that, from girlhood, her greatest ambition was "to get an education and to help [her] people." Anna J. Cooper (1882), an Oberlin graduate of 1884 whose papers are housed at Howard University, stated she decided to attend college while in kindergarten and devoted her entire life to the education of her race. Affluent Mary Church Terrell, also an Oberlin graduate of '84, jeopardized her inheritance when her father, who wished her to model her life on the upper-class white "true womanhood" ideal, threatened to disinherit her if she worked after graduating from Oberlin. Terrell wrote years later (1968) of this dilemma: "I have conscientiously availed myself of opportunities for preparing myself for a life of usefulness as only four other colored (women) had been able to do . . . All during my college course I had dreamed of the day when I could promote the welfare of my race." -Although she was forced by law to forfeit her public school teaching post after marriage, she taught voluntarily in an evening school and became a widely known lecturer and women's club leader.

"Race uplift" was the expected objective of all educated blacks; however, after the Civil War, the implementation of this philosophy was placed primarily on the shoulders of black women. Women were prominent among the many educated blacks who migrated or returned south after emancipation to aid in the transition of emancipated blacks from slavery to freedom. For example, Louise DeMontie, a noted lecturer who migrated from Virginia to Boston in the 1850's, moved to New Orleans in 1865 to open the city's first orphanage for black youth. Mary Shadd Cary, who migrated to Canada in the 1850's, returned to the United States after the outbreak of the War to serve as a scout for the Union army. Scores of other black women went South to engage in the massive effort to

Coppin, the second black woman to earn a college degree in the nation, was sent from Washington, D.C. to Newport, Rhode Island, where her educational opportunities were greater. After completing the Rhode Island State Normal School, she also went to Oberlin and graduated in 1865. Bishop Daniel Payne of the African Methodist Episcopal Church was so impressed with the ambition of Fanny Jackson Coppin that he aided her with a scholarship to Oberlin (see Coppin, 1913). This financial assistance is not insignificant when one remembers that when Fanny Jackson Coppin entered Oberlin in 1860, no black women in the nation had a college degree and very few black men attempted higher education. Bishop Payne's enthusiasm and support for Coppin's education contrasts with the debates on the danger of higher education that surrounded the question of education for white women. These arguments stated that higher education not only reduced a woman's chance of marriage but also resulted in physical and psychological damage (Woody, 1929).

As early as 1787 Benjamin Rush in his publication, *Thoughts on Female Education*, stated that women should be educated to become "stewards, and guardians" of the family assets. And Noah Webster warned that "education is always wrong which raises a woman above her station." Even as high schools for women became available after the Civil War, historian Thomas Woody, in his seminal history of women's education (1929) notes that the primary purposes of such institutions were to (1) extend the scope of "female education", (2) increase the social usefulness of women, and (3) train teachers for the lower grades as opposed to the preparation for college which was the primary aim of the male high school.

Studies of the students and graduates of white female high schools and seminaries confirm that marriage usually terminated employment of the women. Teaching, the predominant profession of these women, was merely a way-station until matrimony. Scott's work on Troy women students and graduates during the period 1822–1872 indicates that only 6 percent worked during marriage and only 26 percent worked at any time during their life. David Allmendinger's (1979) research on Mt. Holyoke students from 1837–1850 is consistent with Scott's data. Although the majority of the student population taught at some point in their lives, most did so for less than five years. Only 6 percent made teaching a lifetime profession. Although data on black women for these periods are inconclusive, the literature on black attitudes towards education strongly takes the view that educated black women and marriage were not incompatible. W. E. B. DuBois' study of 1900 of the black college graduates indicates that 50 percent of the black women college graduates from 1860–1899 were married. Similarly, census statistics in 1900 report that ten times as many married black women than married white women were employed. (DuBois, 1900) This disproportionate ratio is no doubt a reflection of the economic necessity of black women to their families.

educate the newly emancipated blacks (Blassingame, 1973; Williams, 1883).

Throughout the War and afterwards, northern black women raised money and collected clothes to send South. On one occasion the Colored Ladies Sanitary Commission of Boston sent $500 to blacks in Savannah. Similarly, in Washington, D.C., Elizabeth Keckley, the mulatto seamstress of First Lady Mary Lincoln organized the Contraband Relief Association of Washington in 1862. With forty other black women, in its first two years of existence, the group sent nearly one hundred boxes and barrels of clothing to southern blacks and spent in excess of $1600 (McPherson, 1965).

Perhaps more impressive were the efforts of black women in the South to aid themselves. Viewing charity primarily as an activity for the fortunate to aid the unfortunate, white missionaries frequently recorded with astonishment the establishment of black self-help groups. One such report in *The National Freedmen* in 1865 (May 1, 1865, Number 4) cited a group of poor black women in Charleston who formed an organization to aid the sick. After working all day, members of the group devoted several hours to duty in the hospitals. In fact, *The National Freedmen*, the organ of the National Freedmen Relief Society, often reported the general charity among blacks in general and black women in particular. One such missionary report stated:

I have been greatly struck with the charity of these colored people. There are few of them even comfortably situated for this world's goods. Yet, their charity is the most extensive, hearty, genuine thing imaginable. They have innumerable organizations for the relief of the aged, the helpless or needy from whatever (*The National Freedmen*, December 15, 1865, Number 11).

The observer was greatly impressed by the work of black women. He wrote that he witnessed black women "past the prime of life and with no visible means of support" who took in whole families of orphaned children. These stories were found repeatedly in missionary letters.

Despite the significant contributions of black women to the economic, civic, religious, and educational improvement of the race, after emancipation there was a noticeable shift in the attitudes towards the role of women by many members of the race.

Schools for blacks in the South proliferated after the close of the Civil War and, by the 1870's, those founded by northern missionaries and the federal Freedmen's Bureau became the backbone of the public schools for blacks (Bullock, 1970). DuBois, in his 1900 study of the *Negro Common School*, reports that in 1890 there were over 25,000 black teachers. Half of this number were women. With education being placed at the top of the race's agenda for progress, a huge number of black teachers was necessary. By 1899, more than 28,500 black teachers were employed in the nation.

While public schools for blacks were overwhelmingly coeducational, and girls received primarily the same instruction as boys, the black men greatly

outnumbered black women in higher education. By 1890, only 30 black women held baccalaureate degrees, compared to over 300 black men and 2,500 white women. In this same year, white women constituted 35 percent of the undergraduate collegiate student bodies (Cooper, 1892; Graham, 1975). Whereas prior to the Civil War education was viewed as important for all members of the race, during and after Reconstruction, those black women who were educated were trained almost exclusively to become elementary and secondary school teachers. In contrast, the small number of educated black men had more encouragement and access to institutions of higher education. Further, employment options of black men were greater than those of black women (Johnson, 1938).

The issues of sexism and racism were confronted head on in 1892 by Anna Julia Cooper in her book, *A Voice from the South*. Citing all of the well known arguments against higher education of women promulgated by whites in the past, Cooper stated that most black men had accepted these arguments and also believed women to be inferior to men. Cooper wrote, on the women question: "[Black] men drop back into sixteenth century logic." These men, according to Cooper ascribed to the view that "women may stand on pedestals or live in doll houses . . . but not seek intellectual growth." Cooper continued, "I fear the majority of colored men do not yet think it worth while that women aspire to higher education." (Cooper, 1892, p. 75).

Cooper's observations were correct concerning the view of many educated black men. The passage of the fourteenth amendment in 1870 which granted black men the right to vote, signaled the first major gender distinction acknowledged by society towards them. As a result, black men during the latter decades of the nineteenth century moved temporarily into high political offices. Twenty-two black men served in the nation's Congress by 1900 and scores of others held local and state political positions (Franklin, 1969). As black men sought to obtain education and positions similar to that of white men in society, many adopted the prevailing notion of white society, of the natural subordination of women.

SEXISM AND THE EDUCATION OF BLACK WOMEN

Given the unique history of black women in their race, to view them as less than men was not only retrogressive but absurd. Even though the prevailing economic deprivation of blacks at the end of the nineteenth and early twentieth centuries demanded that black women work, many elite blacks nevertheless embraced the Victorian "true womanhood" ideal of the 1820's and 1830's (see Williamson, 1971). As were New England white women of the antebellum period, black women were expected to be self-sacrificing and dutiful. (Prior to emancipation, *all* blacks were expected to do so.). Speeches and articles abound citing black women as the nurturers and the guardians of—not the thinkers or leaders of the race. Most black women educators accepted that charge. (See Laney, 1899)

By the end of the nineteenth century, sexism had increased significantly among educated blacks. When the first major black American Learned Society was founded in 1897, by a group of well known black men, the constitution of the organization limited membership to "men of African descent". The issue of female membership was debated by the group and they resolved that the male stipulation would be rescinded; however, this was never done (Moss, 1981). It was clear by the end of the nineteenth century that many black men viewed women as their intellectual subordinates and not capable of leadership positions. When Fanny Jackson Coppin eulogized Frederick Douglass in 1896 (included in *In Memoriam: Frederick Douglass*) she praised him for "his good opinion of the rights of women . . . that women were not only capable of governing the household but also of elective franchise." The fact that she made this the point of her praise for Douglass indicates that his view of women was the exception rather than the rule.

Fanny Coppin headed the prestigious Institute for Colored Youth in Philadelphia, the oldest black private high school in the nation from 1869–1901. After she was forced to retire in 1901, the school was henceforth headed by black men. (For details on Coppin's years at the Institute for Colored Youth, see Perkins, Note 1.) Likewise, the prestigious, oldest black public high school in the nation, M Street School in Washington, D.C. was initially headed by a black woman, Mary Jane Patterson. Patterson served as Assistant Principal to Coppin at the Institute for Colored Youth from 1865–1869 and was appointed principal of M Street in 1869 (Perkins, Note 1). She was removed several years later so that a male could head the institution. Anna Julia Cooper also served briefly as Principal of M Street from 1901–1906 but was dismissed for her refusal to adhere to the inferior curriculum prescribed for black students. Like the Institute for Colored Youth, by the turn of the century, and thereafter M Street was headed by black men (Anna J. Cooper Papers, Howard University).

As the century came to a close, "race uplift" was synonymous with black women. With the formation of the National Association of Colored Women in 1896, educated black women focused their activities on community development. Reflecting the century old race philosophy, the group chose as their motto "lifting as we climb". Throughout the South, the organization founded orphanages, homes for the elderly and educational institutions, and supported religious programs. The crusade against lynching of this period was also spearheaded by a black woman, the fearless Ida B. Wells-Barnett.

In 1894, the black Senator John Mercer Langston from Virginia recalled his visits in the South after Emancipation and noted:

> They (black women) were foremost in designs and efforts for school, church and general industrial work for the race, always self-sacrificing and laborious . . . Through all phases of his advancement from his Emancipation to his present position of social, political, educational, moral, religious and material status, the colored American is greatly indebted to the women of his race. (Langston, 1894, p. 236)

Later, black scholar W. E. B. DuBois (1969) would also write, "after the war the sacrifice of Negro women for freedom and black uplift is one of the finest chapters in their history." Yet, today this chapter is rarely found in black, women's or educational histories.

Even into the twentieth century, the focus on educating black women to "uplift" and primarily to educate the race continued. In 1933, dean of women at Howard University, Lucy D. Slowe wrote a piece entitled "Higher Education of Negro Women," which addressed many of the same issues raised by Anna J. Cooper in 1892. Slowe voiced concern for the lack of opportunity for college educated black women to get leadership training within black colleges. Noting that while black men college graduates were found in the fields of ministry, law, medicine and other professions, teaching constituted the largest occupation of black women college graduates. After surveying the responses of forty-four black women college graduates, Slowe found that black women received little in courses, activities or role-models to aid them in leadership development. Slowe conceded that many black families were conservative when it came to the issue of independent and assertive women; however, black colleges aided in fostering this paternalistic and conservative view of women. She wrote: "The absence of women or the presence of very few on the policy-making bodies of colleges is also indicative of the attitude of college administrators toward women as responsible individuals, and toward the special needs of women (Slowe, 1933, p. 357).

Despite the feminist writings of Anna J. Cooper and Lucy Slowe, the education of black women into the twentieth century continued to be focused towards teaching and "uplifting" the race. In a 1956 study of the collegiate education of black women, Jeanne L. Noble observed that the education of black women continued to be basically utilitarian- to provide teachers for the race. One of the 412 women in her study commented on this professional isolation.

> There are entirely too many fine Negro women in the teaching profession. There should be vocational guidance to encourage them into new fields. Around this part of the country middle-class women go into teaching because this is the highest type of position for them (Noble, 1956, p. 87).

Unlike black women of the mid and late nineteenth century who consciously prepared themselves for leadership positions, as Lucy Laney stated in 1899, to many black women in the twentieth century such a role had become a burden. Rhetaugh Graves Dumas indicates in her (1980) essay "Dilemmas of Black Females in Leadership," that their leadership has been 'restricted to primarily female and youth organizations most often surrounding the black community. Recent work by sociologist Cheryl Townsend Gilkes also confirms that the education of black women leaders has been focused to meet the black community needs (Gilkes, 1980).

The shift in attitude towards women in the black community and the role they were expected to assume vis-a-vis men paralleled the acceptance by black men of the dominance of man after Emancipation. Although black women have worked far out of proportion to their white counterpart, out of economic necessity, sexism and paternalism among the men of their race have resulted in relegation of black women to the roles of nurturer and "helpmate." The recognition of sexism within the black community has been slow. Recently (Summer, 1982, Volume 51) the *Journal of Negro Education* devoted a special issue to the Impact of Black women in Education—the first such issue in the journal's fifty-one year history.

Although the shift from egalitarian to sexist views of black women can be explained historically, sociologically, and psychologically, the continued depressed economic and educational status of blacks demands that race "uplift" return to its original meaning to include both men and women.

REFERENCE NOTES

1. Perkins, L. M. *Fanny Jackson Copping and the Institute for Colored Youth: A model of nineteenth century black female educational and community leadership, 1837–1902.* Unpublished dissertation, University of Illinois, Champaign-Urbana, 1978.

REFERENCES

Blassingame, J. W. *Black New Orleans, 1860–80.* Chicago, IL: University of Chicago, 1978.
Bullock, H. A. *A history of negro education in the South From 1619 to the present.* Cambridge, MA: Harvard University Press, 1970.
Cooper, A. J. *A voice from the South.* Xenia, OH: Aldine, 1892.
Coppin, F. J. *Reminiscences of school life and hints on teaching.* Philadelphia, PA: African Methodist Episcopal Church, 1913.
Cott, N. *The bonds of womanhood: "Woman's sphere" in New England, 1780–1835.* New Haven, NJ: Yale University Press, 1977.
DuBois W. E. B. The college bred Negro. In *Proceedings of the fifth conference for the study of the negro problems.* Atlanta, GA: Atlanta University Press, 1900.
Dubois, W. E. B. *Darkwater: Voices from within the veil* (1920). New York: Schocken, 1969.
Dumas, R. G. Dilemmas of black females in leadership. In L. F. Rodgers-Rose. (Ed.), *The black woman.* Beverly Hills, CA: Sage, 1980, 203–215.
Franklin, J.H. *From slavery to freedom.* New York: Vintage, 1969.
Gilkes, C. T. Holding back the ocean with a broom: Black women and community work. In L. F. Rodgers-Rose (Ed.) *The black woman.* Beverly Hills, CA: Sage, 1980. 217–231
Graham, P. A. Expansion and exclusion: A history of women in American higher education. *Signs,* 1978, *3,* 766.

Henle, E., & Merrill, M. Antebellum black coeds at Oberlin College. *Women's Studies Newsletter,* 1979, 7, 10.
In memoriam: Fredick Douglass. Philadelphia, PA: John C. Yorston, 1895.
Johnson, C. S. *The negro college graduate.* College Park, MD: McGrath, 1938.
Jones, J. *Soldiers of light and love: Northern teachers and Georgia blacks, 1865–1873.* Chapel Hill, NC: University of North Carolina Press, 1980.
Journal of Negro Education. Special Issue on the Impact of black women in education. Vol. 51, Summer, 1982.
Laney, L. The burden of the educated colored woman. In *Hampton Negro conference.* No. 3 Hampton, VA: Hampton Institute Press, 1899.
Langston, J. M. *From the Virginia plantation to the national capital.* Hartford, MA: Hartford, 1894.
McPherson, J. M. *The negro's Civil War: How American negroes felt and acted during the war for the Union.* New York, NY: Vintage, 1965.
Moss, A. A. *The American negro academy: Voice of the talented tenth.* Baton Rouge, LA: Louisiana State University Press, 1981.
Noble, J. L. *The negro woman's college education.* New York: Teachers College, Columbia University, Bureau of Publications, 1956.
Perkins, L. M. Black women and racial "uplift" prior to emancipation. In F. C. Steady (Ed.), *The black woman cross-culturally.* Cambridge, MA: Schenkman, 1981, 317, 334.
Perkins, L. M. The black female American missionary association teacher in the South, 1860–70. In *The history of blacks in the South.* Chapel Hill, NC: The University of North Carolina Press, in press.
Rosenberg, R. *Beyond separate spheres: Intellectual roots of modern feminism.* New Haven, CT: Yale University Press, 1982.
Rothman, S. M. *Woman's proper place: A history of changing ideals and practices, 1870 to the present.* New York: Basic Books, 1978.
Rush, B. *Thoughts upon female education, accommodated to the present state of society, manners and government in the United States of America.* Philadelphia, PA: Prichard & Hall, 1787.
Scott, A. F. The ever widening circle: The diffusion of feminist values from the Troy female seminary, 1822–1872. *History of Education Quarterly,* Spring, 1979, 2, 3–25
Slowe, L. Higher education of negro women. *Journal of Negro Education,* 1933, 2, 352–358.
Terrell, M. C. *A colored woman in a white world.* Washington, DC: National Association of Colored Women's Clubs, 1968.
Welter, B. The cult of true womanhood: 1820–1860. *American Quarterly,* 1966, *18,* 151–174.
Williams, G. W. *A history of the negro race in America.* New York: Bergman, 1883.
Williamson, J. Black self-assertion before and after emancipation. In N. I. Huggins, M. Kilson, & D. M. Fox (Eds.), *Key issues in the Afro-American experience.* New York: Harcourt Brace & Jovanovich, 1971.
Woodson, C. G. *The education of the negro prior to 1861 (1919).* New York: Arnon, 1968.
Woody, T. *A history of women's education in the United States.* New York: Science Press, 1929.

This paper depends on two collections of papers at Howard University's Moorland-Springarn Research Center: the *Mary Shadd Cary Papers* and the *Anna J. Cooper Papers.*

Correspondence regarding this issue should be addressed to Dr. Linda M. Perkins, The Mary Ingraham Bunting Institute, Radcliffe College, 10 Garden Street, Cambridge, MA 02138.

The New Revisionists and the History of U.S. Higher Education

Robert T. Blackburn and Clifton F. Conrad

Abstract. This paper presents the traditional history of the development of higher education in the United States, especially during the nineteenth century, and then examines at the findings of the new revisionist historians regarding the content of the curriculum, the mode of instruction, the believed theory of learning, the quality of college leadership, and their egalitarianism. While the revisionists' evidence discredits some of the traditional interpretation of events, some of their data are questionable and some of their methods are found wanting. This paper focuses on the implications of the disparities and advances a thesis.

Over the past decade a number of historical pieces have contained evidence and explanations contrary to those found in the traditional histories of U.S. higher education. More often in articles and dissertations than in books, vital issues have been broached about the rigidity of the curriculum in the 19th century and its lack of responsiveness to societal needs; about whether recitation as the standard mode of instruction stifled learning; about the soundness of the psychology of learning on which the curriculum and pedagogy were based; about the quality of institutional leadership; and even about the non-democratic nature of the entire enterprise. As yet, the traditionalists have not responded to the questions that revisionist historians have raised.

However, no revisionist has yet produced a comprehensive history based on new evidence. At the same time, with the exception of some brief reviews, there have been no systematic critiques of the revisionists' evidence and explanations. This hiatus is most unfortunate. The present condition of higher education has been shaped on the anvil of the past just as the future will be determined by actions taken today. Today, especially, shortfalls of students and dollars precipitate critical decisions that shape the long-term futures of our college and universities. Historians can provide us with the understandings which increases the likelihood of informed action.

Of course, for historians to be successful in their inquiries, a dependable knowledge base must be established. Consequently, it is important to examine dispassionately both traditionalists' and revisionists' works. They cannot both be correct. However, both can both be in error. Higher education needs to know its development in the United States and to understand the factors which explain its evolution.

This paper begins this task. First we look at the traditional argument for the failure of the antebellum college and the data on which these historians build their case. Then we examine the counter evidence the revisionists have advanced — its reliability, validity, and representativeness — and critique selections of two revisionists.[1] The paper closes with a discussion of the current state of the debate and the advancement of an hypothesis.

equipped both in physical plant and in endowments. Libraries were small, and the librarian's duty seemed more to preserve the books than to make them accessible to the students. Technical training was as yet little known, laboratories did not exist, and the whole field of science except on the theoretical side had hardly been touched. Much of the teaching in all branches was done dogmatically and with generalizations which in many cases rested on a lack of extensive investigation or careful scholarship.

Schmidt also addressed the rigidity of the curriculum and the mode of instruction. Speaking of their deleterious consequences, he wrote (1957:44):

> Such a course [moral philosophy, the senior required course and most often taught by the president, a minister] and such a lecturer made up for years of dull recitation and routine translation of the dead languages.
>
> Whatever appeal the moral philosophy course may have had for the average undergraduate, a deeper though perhaps more unpleasant impression was left by another subject of instruction. By far the largest amount of his time and effort was devoted to the ancient languages, Greek and Latin. After practically monopolizing the student's time in the freshman and sophomore years, these "classics" continued as an important part of his program almost up to graduation. Along with mathematics they were the "core curriculum," the subjects that mattered. Other things were taught, but with the exception of the senior philosophy course they were fringe subjects.
>
> The sciences received lip service and little more. Laboratory instruction was unheard of, but the demonstrating equipment of the better institutions was probably as good as could be had at the time.

Schmidt, while noting some exceptions, viz., the University of Pennsylvania and the University of Virginia (1957:54), continues by emphasizing the stranglehold the classical curriculum had on U.S. higher education. He has the New England curriculum trailing the frontier:

> From its strongholds in the east the standard classical curriculum spread west and south, keeping with the building of new colleges and marking the advance of the cultural frontier. This frontier, by the way, showed little independence of judgment when it came to choosing a form of higher education adapted to its needs. Whatever originality it may have displayed in fashioning economic and political institutions – a point which the successors of Frederick J. Turner are still debating – in matters of higher education, the frontier was docile and receptive to eastern ideas.

The traditionalist view

In brief, the traditionalist position with respect to higher education in the United States holds that the colleges before the Civil War were failures, even those that survived. They failed to respond to the contemporary needs of individuals and of society. Colleges exist to develop people intellectually so they become creators of knowledge and solvers of problems both natural and social. Colleges exist to prepare people for vocations that society needs. Antebellum colleges failed to accomplish these purposes for several reasons: they adhered to an inappropriate curriculum (the classical curriculum), used an ineffective mode of instruction, subscribed to a false psychology of learning, suffered under poor leadership (presidents), and remained elitist. That is why, in the main, colleges failed to flourish and attracted but a very small percent age of the population. Moreover, according to the traditionists, this is why large numbers of them eventually closed their doors.

Curriculum and instruction

More than one historian claims the curriculum was all but invariant across the nation, at least through the antebellum period. At the turn of the 20th century, Flexner wrote (1908:30–31):

> Forty years ago [in 1867] the Bachelor's degree conveyed a specific and practically invariable meaning. There was one narrow path to academic confirmation; every candidate had to traverse it. Perhaps the college graduate did not expect to be a lawyer or a clergyman; he had, however, to be content with an education strictly relevant only to these two learned callings. A cultivated man was one who, whatever ignorance or limitations in other directions, had enjoyed a liberal education of this description. The classics were the backbone of the college curriculum; they were supplemented by the cut and dried philosophy and rhetoric then current, some mathematics and bookish science, and an occasional dip into modern literature.

In his biography of Cornell University's founding president, Andrew D. White, Rogers quotes White's letters voicing deep dismay at how faculty were mistreated by students. He says White felt that it was the rigidity of the classical curriculum and the way that it was taught that prompted unruly student behavior. According to Rogers (1942:44):

The American college which White dreamed of reforming was poorly

Besides promoting tedious instruction, the classical curriculum *was* the cause of low enrollments and serious financial straits and hence the consequent demise of many institutions. As Rudolph (1962:198) quotes Brown University's reform-minded president Francis Wayland:

I doubt whether anyone could attract a respectable number of pupils... did it charge for tuition the fees which would be requisite to remunerate its officers [faculty] at the rate ordinarily received by other professional men.

And later:

Can [a liberal education] not be made to recommend itself; so that he who wishes to obtain it shall also be willing to pay for it?

Rudolph answers this rhetorical question:

Wayland himself knew that the answer to his question was necessarily a resounding "no" as long as the American college insisted on holding rigidly to the prescribed classical course of study. Until the curriculum changed, the colleges, if they were to have students, would have to buy them.

In short, the high failure rate of institutions which has been claimed by Tewksbury derived from a sterile curriculum and a stultifying pedagogy. The classical curriculum and the recitations of ancient works met neither personal nor societal needs. And, according to traditional historians, potential students know it.

Theory of learning

Consonant with their emphasis on a rigid curriculum and a single mode of instruction, traditionalists have called attention to "faculty psychology." Proponents of the classical curriculum are said to subscribe to this theory of learning and thereby legitimize the classical curriculum. Butts and Cremin (1953:178) succinctly capture the essence of this theory:

Faculty psychology was especially important as providing the basic justification for mental discipline as the supreme method in college education and for giving first place to the classics, mathematics, and philosophy as the essential content of a liberal education. It was used as a bulwark against admitting new and useful studies to the college curriculum. Of all the educational statements of the time the one that most clearly illustrates the operation of the faculty psychology as the basis for mental discipline and

the prescribed curriculum of intellectual studies was the Yale faculty report of 1828 which stated in the words of President Jeremiah Day: "The two great points to be gained in intellectual culture, are the *discipline* and *furniture* of the mind; expanding its powers, and storing it with knowledge."

Invoking faculty psychology as *the* theory of learning left no alternative to the classical curriculum and the recitation method. Veysey (1965:337ff) supports this interpretation and argues that it took the demise and replacement of faculty psychology before the university could emerge. That is, only after this "mental discipline" aim of learning was discredited, could specialization and an elective curriculum emerge. Such is the traditionalist view.

The failure of leadership

According to the traditionalists, a fourth factor contributing to the inefficacy of antebellum colleges – including the demise of some institutions and the poor health of numerous others – was inept leadership. Simply, missionary zeal proved no substitute for educational savvy. Hofstader and Metzger (1955:209–210) remark how "this multiplying and scattering of colleges was primarily the result of denominational sponsorship and sectarian competition." The title of Chapter V of their work – "The Great Retrogression" – amply captures their theme. Colleges lacked leadership based on sound notions of what higher education should be. As a result, failure was less surprising than inevitable.

Nor was such ineptitude confined to the expanding West. Institutions in New England – at Hanover and New Haven – evinced the same lack of vision. Peterson (1964:81) describes the 1881 trial of Dartmouth's president.

It was a strange way for the old college to die... in the sickly phosphorescence of an alumnus's cross-examination of his president, a mathematics professor's testimony that his president was dishonest and insolent without the traces of manliness, while out in the audience the reporters scribbled their dispatches for the front pages of the Boston and New York newspapers. It was a strange death for the college and its noble ideal of harmony.

In the case of Yale, Peterson writes:

One day in 1884 William Graham Sumner and his faculty committee marched into President Noah Porter's office and informed him that they were not leaving until Yale had an elective system. Three exhausting hours

lengthy obituary column. A fixed curriculum inappropriate to a changing society, an incorrect psychology of learning, an ineffective mode of instruction, and inept leadership — these factors stubbornly maintained colleges for an aristocratic elite that the masses largely shunned. Small wonder that the college death toll was a large one, about 81 percent according to Tewksbury (1932).

Let us now turn to the revisionist interpretation of these same developments.

The revisionists' evidence

To begin with, colleges did not die at anywhere near the rate Tewksbury claimed, especially if we disqualify "still births" and "infant deaths" — that is, "colleges" which obtained charters (which was easy to do) but never built an institution, and others that made a brief, but futile appearances. Naylor has clearly shown not only that there are errors of omission and commission in Tewksbury; there are also questionable definitions regarding the birth, survival, and death of colleges. For example, when Sack updated the census of colleges in Pennsylvania, he found the survival rate to be close to 50%. In addition, if one confines the analysis to four-year colleges and does not define a two-year academy as a college, then the fatality rate drops to about 25 percent (Naylor, 1973:265–266).

Assuming Naylor's data as true (and Tewksbury's as false and misleading) and for the moment overlooking how Tewksbury's error might be derived from the cases built by traditionalists, we must next examine the perspective of the new revisionist historians.[2] We now turn to the writings revisionist historians have entered into the scholarly record that address the five components of the traditionalists' case.

The curriculum

One of the principal laments of the traditional historian with respect to the dysfunctional nature of the classical curriculum was the absence of course work in science. An examination of what was actually being taught in the colleges, however, reveals there was appreciable science content in the curriculum. As Guralnick (1974:48) writes:

It is a matter of demonstrable fact that science and the antebellum American college enjoyed an amicable, even a mutually profitable, relationship: the intellectual demands of science introduced to the college problems and subsequent changes which in turn led to further scientific expansion.

later, the professors marched out with their electives. "It was a brutal procedure," one of them said, "but it was effective."

The traditionalists link the factor of poor leadership to both the curriculum and to learning theory. By holding to the irrelevant classical curriculum and subscribing to a faulty "faculty psychology" which held that exercising the mind with classical subjects was the essence of an education, presidents were destroying their own institutions.

Exclusiveness

In Rudolph's (1962:199) interpretation, another cause for the failure of the antebellum colleges lay in the *elitist*, undemocratic label attached to the classical curriculum. In order to obtain enough students, colleges reduced and/or waived tuition for two reasons:

One, the desire to project a more democratic image in a society that had interpreted the strength of the classical curriculum as a sign of aristocratic attachments; the other, the necessity of competing among an almost unlimited number of colleges for the rather limited number of students who could afford and who wished to avail themselves of the classical course of study.

Brubacher and Rudy (1968:155) supplement Rudolph's explanation for sparse enrollments by claiming there "was an anti-intellectualism which was rife through the New West." The hard-working pioneer was unwilling to pay taxes to support higher education.

From his perspective as an advocate of the land grant movement, Ross (1942:13) echoes this notion of exclusiveness:

It appears, then, that by the forties [1840s] the nation's chief educational need was for an adequate provision for vocational training which awaited mainly the course of economic and social evolution. Only when the limitations of primitive exploitation were sufficiently manifested could there arise class-conscious interests and movements which would compel the creation of institutions at the higher as at the lower levels adopted to popular needs and desires, people's colleges as the crowning feature of a democratic school system.

In summary, the traditionalists have built a case to support Tewksbury's

As for equipment, he (1974:50) reports:

> Scientific apparatus at the average college increased in value from a few hundred thousands by mid-century, and there was the building of laboratories and astronomical observatories to house the new acquisitions.

As far as faculty are concerned, as Wesleyan Guralnick found:

> The School's first catalogue outlined a "partial course" for science-oriented students, and by 1836 Wesleyan had spent over $6,000 on scientific equipment. By 1840 the faculty consisted of the president and six professors, three of them in mathematics and science. Most telling is the fact that there was no provision for formal theological training, as indeed there was not any college in the East.

Contemporary science was clearly being taught and practiced on the established campuses as well. While the initial attempts for laboratory sciences at Princeton essentially had failed by 1810, they did revive when Joseph Henry was appointed in 1831. Benjamin Silliman gave his first scientific lectures at Yale in 1804 and Asa Gray was a contemporary at Harvard. It is true these two universities had their principal science activity in separate schools (Sheffield and Lawrence, respectively), and that Gray apparently had little interaction with students. However, it is also clear that science instruction – at least lectures and demonstrations – was taking place, and, in pedagogical modes other than recitation. In addition, the faculty were doing research in the manner that is understood today (Chisolm, 1984:183–265).

Relying on works on the history of science by Cohen, Struik, Daniels, Meier, Van Tassel and Hall, Sloan (1971) builds a strong case for the presence of science in the antebellum curriculum:

> *Scientific instruction.* Revivalism was not universal in all colleges, but science, the second major subject area of the curriculum, was. Throughout the colonial period science had not been one of the basic components of the curriculum, but the colleges had attempted to keep abreast of latest advances in scientific discoveries and methods. By the end of the eighteenth century the college scientific curriculum had expanded immensely, new teaching methods, such as the experimental lecture, had been introduced, and the utility of science was a generally recognized and lauded ideal.
>
> After the War of 1812, both the opportunities and the difficulties of scientific instruction increased rapidly. Expansion of higher education and the increase in numbers of institutions placed heavy burdens on the teaching capacities of the colleges, and the quality of scientific instruction undoubtedly suffered accordingly, or, at least, probably varied greatly from institution to institution. Nevertheless, as we shall see, there is reason to suppose that the achievements of the older institutions in maintaining high standards of science instruction and research may not have been adequately appreciated by historians of education. Demands for science instruction in the new nation, and the difficulties of providing it, were further heightened by the scientific and technical problems involved in exploration, transportation, communication, industry, agriculture, and public health. Finally, national pride, popular desire for practical knowledge, and notions of national progress and technological advance all helped to build enthusiasm for science in its many forms. And all increased the pressures on higher education.

Furthermore, science in the 19th century curriculum was not limited to men's colleges. Haddad (1980:249–261) displays the full four year curricula for New England's Mount Holyoke for 1837–1955, and for Midwestern's Oberlin in 1838, Lake Erie in 1847–48, and Western Reserve University's College for Women in 1889. While components of the classical curriculum are visible, including required mathematics and astronomy, women at single-sex Mount Holyoke were required to take botany and human physiology in their junior year and chemistry and geology in their senior year. At co-educational Oberlin, women had to take chemistry in their junior year. (Men did also, as well as anatomy and physics as freshmen.) Lake Erie was identical to Mount Holyoke (the model it selected upon opening). At the coordinate colleges at Western Reserve, men and women took physics in the second year, chemistry and physics in the third, and geology in the fourth. If they wished, they could take French and German instead of the classical languages.

At the same time, there were midwestern colleges that remained faithful to the 1828 Yale report until after the Morril Act. This 1862 federal legislation founded the agricultural and mechanical arts institutions. Until then, however, the seven evangelical colleges Findlay (1982) studied in Illinois and Indiana offered no science. Founded by ministers from Yale, their presidents were more dedicated to the classical curriculum than was the case at Yale.

In addition to science in the curriculum, Burke (1973:56–57) found the waiving of proficiency in Latin and the substitution of English as an entrance requirement:

> By the 1830s the vast majority of colleges had instituted partial, English, and science courses, as well as waiving requirements for Latin proficiency. The short courses and the reduced academic requirements decreased the dis-

tance between those without a classical background and the liberal arts college. The professional schools followed the same path of reduced requirements and reduction of the level of necessary previous training. In order to make the educational system more accessible, the schools responded to the growing heterogeneity of cultural and technical backgrounds.

In summary, an appreciable body of evidence shows that the 19th century curriculum did not universally exclude the sciences or "modern" languages.[3] In fact, just the opposite appears to have been the case. Many colleges were adjusting their curriculum to serve the needs and wishes of students and society.

Instruction

Turning to pedagogy, the evidence concerning instruction is less direct. Nonetheless, a sufficient amount exists to permit the inference that the mode of instruction had changed from the single recitation format the traditionalists claim. Three extensive studies of faculty backgrounds at different points in the 19th century show a dramatic shift from the original cleric to the 20th century academic professional. McCaughey (1974) displays the changes at Harvard at decade intervals from 1821 to 1892. Tobias (1981) shows the Dartmouth faculty in 1851 and in 1881. And Creutz (1980) reports all faculty for every year to 1900 at the University of Michigan. In each of the cases one sees that those who were being hired were anything but ministers, persons capable of teaching only the classical curriculum. Tappan at Michigan was hiring researchers long before Veysey dates the emergence of the university in this country. These were scientists in laboratories who focused their instruction on research and often lectured to large numbers of students.

In the women's domain, Palmer's (1981) study of New York's and New England's Elmira, Vassar, Smith, and Wellesley colleges shows an acquisition of the professional faculty member that paralleled and rivaled the changing composition of their male counterparts. As was seen above with respect to the addition of science to the curriculum in Haddads' institutions, the new breed of professor was not likely to utilize only recitation as the mode of instruction, if ever.

Kennedy (1961) surveyed changes in the professoriate from 1800 to 1900. She concluded that over this time span the professor had changed from a clergyman to a layman, a despot to a benevolent parent surrogate, an institutional member to a member of a department, a dilettante to a scientific scholar, a pedagogue to a subject matter specialist, a drill master to a lecturer, a classicist

to a scientist, a user of single text to one who employed a wide assortment of resources, an oral examiner to a preparer of written examinations. Kennedy does not document the precise times of these changes, and no doubt they differed from place to place. More recently, Chisolm (1982) has thoroughly documented the existence of a variety of teaching methods – lecture, laboratory, and seminar – in addition to recitation in the antebellum period for five institutions (Princeton, Yale, Harvard, Amherst, and Columbia). The inference that instruction was something more and different from what the traditionalists assert is strong.

Theory of learning

The revisionists have not dealt directly with theories of learning. To what extent beliefs about how people learned affected either the curriculum or the method of teaching is not known. Barnes (1960:339) suggests that when science was introduced into the curriculum of Ohio colleges in the last half of the century, an argument used to justify its inclusion was that learning science was good for the training of the mind. His claim supports a belief in faculty psychology persisting after the Civil War.

We need to keep in mind, however, that psychology as a scientific discipline is a 20th century phenomenon. (Psychology was not even a separate department at the University of Michigan until the 1920's. Professors working in that area were members of the philosophy department.) Inquiry into how people learn was not systematically pursued as were other sciences and hence it is unlikely that views on learning theory carried the same weight as did, say, what specialties deserved addition to a course of study or to a degree sequence.

If these curriculum and pedagogical changes that were taking place disturbed some administrators because of conflicts with faculty psychology, they do not seem to have stood in the way of the majority. We suspect, but do not know, that theories of learning (then as now) were invented to fit a desired curriculum rather than vice versa. In any event, the revisionists have yet to discredit the traditionalists' claim of the negative consequences of subscribing to faculty psychology.

Leadership

Even if some of the leadership in the antebellum period was weak, even poor – and no doubt there are cases – the overall evidence suggests there must

dents from the middle and lower ranges of the middle class was large enough to be a distinguishing characteristic of antebellum higher education. "Little colleges," a Southern writer noted in the mid-1840's, "are the means of affording liberal education to numerous youth... within forty miles of [their] walls, who would never go to Cambridge [Massachusetts]." Geographical proximity and modest fees were especially advantageous for families of modest means. "Men with their thousands," commented a midwestern newspaper, "can send their sons where they please; but men with only their hundreds must have a place near home, and where expenses will be at least reasonable. A pamphlet published in Boston just before mid-century contained the estimate that a "full three-fourths of the members of the country colleges are from families with small means," families described by a midwestern college president as those with "small but well cultivated farms" and "economical shops."

Allmendinger, Angelo, and Burke support this contention. For example, Allmendinger's (1975) inspection of the 1800–1860 graduates of a set of New England colleges (Amherst, Dartmouth, and six others) finds a large number of youths from poor families (from the one community he studied in detail). Large families and shrinking farms simply produced a "glut of young men" who had nothing to do at home. The alternatives were going to the city, west, or to college, aristocratic classical curriculum or not.[4]

As for the latter part of the century, Angelo's (1983) data on the social background of students at the University of Pennsylvania and at Temple University reveal anything but a homogeneous slice of upper class society. The numbers of low white-collar and blue-collar students were appreciable. Despite some questionable comparisons that are made, it is clear that Penn was hardly the homogeneous Ivy League elitist institution that Veysey claims. Burke (1982), as well, presents extensive data showing a student social mix far greater than the traditionalists have claimed.

Whether the revisionists data of student backgrounds proves that the colleges were aristocratic or not is another matter. The less privileged may have attended college for any of a number of reasons, in spite of discrimination they may have suffered. (Like blacks today going to northern universities which still have racist practices, they may have wanted the education, or the degree, or social mobility. The reasons can be many, and multiple.) In any event, many institutions had a heterogeneous student body.

In short, the un-/anti-democratic nature of the classical curriculum is an inadequate, and probably erroneous, explanation for college failures and for accounting for the course of higher education in the 19th century. However, before considering the implications of this new evidence, let us examine the

have been many agile, entrepreneurial presidents who were genuine success stories. Potts (1979:368) writes of institutions utilizing what we today call admissions counselors, persons hired to go out to potential clients and secure their application forms. Axtell (1971) considers the extensive and expanding library holdings of small colleges as evidence of an extended, research-based curriculum. In addition, there are many examples of antebellum leaders judged to be distinguished. Before Philip Lindsley at Nashville, Tennessee succumbed to the plethora of sectarian colleges built in his neighborhood that eventually drained off the student supply, his vision of the forthcoming university in the United States was clearly articulated and widely distributed (Rudolph, (1962:117–118). Horace Holley at Transylvania in Lexington, Kentucky enjoyed an international reputation (Borrowman, 1961). And Eliphat Nott's innovations of parallel course of study in the sciences, and his leadership on the decent treatment of students led Union College in New York to become the third largest institution in the country by 1829 and the second largest by 1839 (Rudolph, 1962:107–108, 114).

Also, there are instances of colleges that were founded in one location and then moved to another town where that city would provide land and money to have the college in its midst – local boosterism (Dominick, 1986). The presence of a college in town was good for status and good for business. (The process is not too different in kind from a city today building a sports arena with the aim of having a champion professional team within its boundaries.)

These may not all be examples of good educational leadership in the sense of presidents issuing thoughtful philosophical commentaries on the condition of higher education in the United States and what needed to be done next – but then there have never been an abundant supply of such presidents at any time in history. These activities are, however, instances that support the inference that there were presidents building colleges – acquiring resources, recruiting students, and expanding their operation – all indicators of effective leadership.

Exclusiveness

That the colleges only took in the elite is the position of the traditionalists. The evidence, however, fails to support this claim, especially after 1800. In a section on "Egalitarian Trends," Potts (1977, 1981) examines work by Haddock and data on Franklin College. His judgment is expressed below:

Contemporary observations and quantitative data collected during the last decade support the related argument that this increased proportion of stu-

quality of the evidence of two major revisionists.

The work of the revisionists

The revisionists have assembled an impressive array of evidence that seriously challenges the traditional story of the development of higher education in the United States. The traditionalists have not as yet responded to the critique of their works. In fact, there has been scant critical attention given to the revisionists' manuscripts by anyone (in or out of their camp). This section looks at two authors – Angelo and Burke – and examines parts of their publications. These two include more quantitative analysis than do most others.

With regard to the issue of access for youth outside the social elite, Angelo deals with alumni from two universities in Philadelphia – Penn and Temple – during the last quarter of the 19th century and the first third of this one. Samples are drawn, but we are not told either why (to reduce the labor required?) or, and more seriously, how (random?). If not randomly drawn, then was the sample random within specified strata (by curriculum, since this becomes an important variable for the author)?[5] The reader does not know.

Besides failing to inform the reader of these critical matters which affect the validity of any inference made, for some unstated reason the groups of years (the time intervals) are not divided into equal lengths but rather run 6, 7, 7, 6, 6, 5, 6, 4, 5, 5 years each between 1873 and 1935. Despite their unequal spans, these intervals are plotted on the graphs with equal distances between each set, as if the temporal distance between successive points was constant. While the time span differences are not great numerically, they are on a percentage basis. Would there have been differences in the findings if the expected constant intervals had been used? There is no way for the reader to answer this question and hence doubts about the findings are raised.

Next, the author has plotted the data on semi-log paper with the number of degrees reflected on the log (y-axis) scale. This choice would be a proper one for testing an hypothesis of an exponential relationship between y (number of graduates) and x (the passage of time). However, such a test is not the purpose here. What Angelo provides is a series of points connected by lines which produce peaks and valleys. On log paper, neither have absolute nor percentage equivalences except in rare instances when the number of graduates are identical. At the same time, the author spends a considerable portion of his effort accounting for rises and falls, ones that are of not equal magnitude, and, supposedly, equal social significance.

This questionable display of data is aggravated by the author's failure to test for the statistical significance of the differences between successive peri-ods. Each is treated as if the differences were consequential. Yet in many instances, if not all, the interval changes could be nothing more than random fluctuations about some (unknown) mean, i.e., the differences could have occurred by chance sampling errors (at some accepted level of significance, say, $p < 0.05$).

Such methodological deficiencies cast doubt on any and all inferences drawn from the data. We may wish to believe the author's conclusions. They may well be true. However, they are not based on accepted research canons and hence have not been properly supported.

Different but related problems surface in Burke's work.[6] To begin with, the accuracy of his counting of institutions has not been established. (The same reservation holds for Naylor's calculations.) In fact, Herbst (1983:484–485) has already found inconsistencies between some of his historical records of institutional existence and Burke's.[7] The number of discrepancies and the reasons for them are unknown but need to be dealt with before causal inferences are introduced.

Second, in dealing with enrollments in the antebellum period (pp. 53–63), numerical data are presented for the onset of successive decades in order to prove that, contrary to the claims of Wayland that enrollments in liberal arts colleges had declined in the antebellum period, enrollments had in fact increased. "The percentage of the young white males of the country who entered colleges more than doubled [between 1800 and 1860]", Burke (1982:54) claims. It is a fact that 1.18% is twice 0.59% (Table 2.1), assuming no error in either number. However, (1) exactly twice is "not more than doubled" (pp. 54) and (2) the increase is 100%, not "at least 200%" as Burke summarizes.[8] These kinds of simple arithmetical errors lessen the reader's confidence in the author's ability to handle complex data, especially when other claims he makes are advanced without providing the means to check them.

Third, Burke does not acknowledge that when one is dealing with small numbers, even small errors produce large percentage changes. Burke speaks of a fourteenfold increase in actual enrollments between 1800 and 1860, a very large expansion. That level of increase is possible in part because the base N is only 1156 students. Halve that number and the increase would be 28-fold; double the number and the increase drops to 7 fold. Such are the dramatics of percentage change when dealing with small numbers, even when the error is small. Choose an earlier decade, say 1790, and the percent increase probably would be even larger. (After all, "1800" is no more a magical year than "1790.")

A related, major flaw occurs in the discussion of Table 2.1 (and 2.2, 2.3, and many others). Burke fails to report possible errors in both of the critical measures – the enrollment and the census data (white males of age 15–20). Even if they are not large, they are not zero. When one is dealing with small numbers (low of 0.38% to high of 1.90%), small errors produce large variations and make comparisons between values questionable at best. Had mid-points (or any other points) instead of onset of decades been used, would the shifts remained be the same? We do not know.

Like Angelo, Burke has introduced many social factors to explain numerical differences that may be nothing more than random fluctuations within a reasonable margin of error. In addition, he has done so without recognizing and/or telling his reader that such is the case. We consequently lose faith in the hypotheses, even if there may have been important forces for explaining what was happening to enrollments.[9]

In summary, these two revisionists are building their cases on the analysis of quantifiable information. It appears as if they should attend more carefully to the treatment of their data, especially with regard to sampling and the consideration of error terms. They also could benefit all of us if they would use more of the readily available sophisticated statistical techniques. For example, it seems clear that Angelo had access to adequate data to treat one curriculum (say medicine) continuously over time. By time series analysis he could determine if there were eras that could be set by statistically significant differences in student populations rather than by selecting them as he did, by eyeballing of improperly plotted graphs.[10]

Discussion

Although there are flaws in data and in analysis by some of the revisionists, it appears the traditionalists, too, have patched together bits of dubious evidence to support an invalid conclusion, namely, that there was an epidemic of college failures. They write with unquestioned authority and convincingly. If there are any doubts in their minds about their explanations, they do not let the reader in on their reservations. Seldom do they entertain alternative hypotheses.

The revisionists, on the other hand, seem somewhat more attentive to the validity of evidence. They write with a bit more caution, with a "perhaps" or a "maybe" prefacing or qualifying their interpretations of the data. We worry, however, that they have rushed to explain before verifying data and completing analyses that could be made, ones that might significantly affect key relationships. Like Katz (1968) and his classical work on the vote for the Beverly high school in Massachusetts and his analysis based on a couple of bivariate relationships, nearly two decades passed before Vinovskis (1985) employed a multivariate technique on the same data. He found Katz seriously in error. Katz had prematurely halted the analysis.

In the same way that the revisionists charge the traditionalists with looking at the historical record from a biased perspective and finding only what they need to support their case, so too are the revisionists open to the identical charge, one that has already been leveled by Metzger (1984). The argument for both sides depends heavily on how one defines a surviving institution. No doubt this decision is also affected by the relative ease or difficulty that existed for a group to acquire a charter to found a college, a process that could well differ both over time and from state to state. The situation is more complex than either side seems to recognize. In this instance the burden of proof for establishing the facts falls heavier on the revisionists. In their desire to set the record "right," we fear they too may be advancing questionable "truths." The revisionists need to refine their skills for verifying and treating data. We do not need to replace old errors with new ones.

Other work, of course, remains to be done. This article is not the place or the occasion to enumerate the kinds of investigations that deserve the highest priority. Many are suggested by the chapter authors in a recent AERA monograph (Best, 1983). Questions like those raised by Mattingly (1983) regarding Vesey's history is a good case in point. In addition, there are debatable questions of what writers of either pursuasion have proved. For example, when Kimball (1986a; 1986b) weighs the evidence, he finds the revisionists not only come up short; he also believes they are documenting the traditionalist position that what transformed the American college into its contemporary university essentially took place after 1865, not before.

Finally, with respect to the evolution of higher education in the United States, it was anything but monolithic. There were not a handful of leaders whom all strived to imitate, the Riesman serpentine metaphor of the long body (of colleges) wiggling in response to every shift of a small head. Also, it does not look as if there was a rational, education decision to abandon the faculty psychology based on any scientific evidence or an alternative, demonstrated theory of learning.

In the history of U.S. higher education, it appears as if there were some good leaders and some poor ones. No doubt all wanted success and status, survival and growth. Some colleges were better located than others, in communities that became towns and cities of sufficient population to support a college. It seems as if it was the rule rather than the exception for a college to respond to the needs of potential clients and society. The classical curriculum was chipped away, and changes were justified afterwards on "educational grounds."

In the nineteenth century the world's body of knowledge was increasing at an exponential rate, and nothing could stop its growth. Disciplines split by meiosis, inevitably. Specializations spawned subspecializations. No one could unify knowledge anymore, even supposing that knowledge is actually one, a debatable assumption. With the division of knowledge and the need for specialized expertise, an elective system was inevitable, not because of a new psychology of learning (student interest being necessary). Rather, scholarly experts had to have students. Hence students had to be able to choose and not simply comply with a nonalterable set of sourses. Ergo, an elective system emerges, one which has existed ever since, indeed with variations and rises and falls, but never a disappearance. (There is always an exception or two, e.g., St. John's College in Annapolis.)

The concluding paragraphs, of course, contain only an hypothesis. Our view is that what happened and why are still open questions. Neither the traditionalist nor the revisionists have a clear case. There is exciting work awaiting historians of higher education.

Notes

1. In order to highlight the differences between the traditionalists and the revisionists in a restricted space, we have selected quotations which draw starker contrasts between the opposing points of view than one typically finds. There are authors on both sides of the controversy who have tempered the sharp reliefs we have sketched.

2. It may be that the traditionalists have created explanations for an erroneous outcome. Any evidence, no matter how incomplete and inaccurate, that would support their explanations then takes on the status of truth. If this has happened, we have before use a fair amount of history whose truth value is suspect or, at best, unknown.

3. What kind of a case could be made for other disciplines is not known. The branches of the social sciences (economics, anthropology, political science) form professional organizations later in the century.

4. This explanation for a wider social mix of students than the traditional historians have claimed, of course, would not be adequate for western colleges, for: few young males there suffered from no opportunity to work. At the same time, there could hardly have been an appreciable frontier "leisure class" and hence the student bodies are likely to have been socially mixed in these colleges.

5. Apparently not, for footnote 2 (p. 262) states that "the Penn sample was assembled by drawing names from the [annual commencement] programs on a fixed percentage basis across all curricula for groups of consecutive years.

6. Burke has given us more quantitative data than all historians and sociologists of higher education combined. We are indebted to his ingenuity, his doggedness, and the countless hours he has labored.

7. On the other hand, Luker (1983) proceeds in his interpretation of problems besetting mid-western religious based colleges on a complete acceptance of Tewksbury's claims. ("Tewksbury Revisited: The Second Great Awakening, Evangelism, Revivalism and Denominationalism in the Founding of Western Colleges, 1790–1860." Symposium paper, annual AERA meeting, Montreal, April, 1983).

8. Angelo's and Burke's errors are different. The former is from sampling (although there is no doubt that there are measurement errors in his as well); the latter is from measurement. These errors, as well as others, exist in both papers.

9. Burke also did not directly address Wayland's claim. Larger numbers of 15–20 year white males in college do not mean higher enrollments *per college* unless the number of colleges increases at a lower rate than the number of persons, a critical matter Burke does not discuss. Also, what may be true "on the average" is not likely to be true for every college. Some could be shrinking, and were, as Burke himself reports.

10. The non-quantitative revisionists also need to have their data validated. We have not undertaken such critiques.

References

Allmendinger, David F. (1975). *Paupers and Scholars: The Transformation of Student Life in 19th Century New England.* New York: St. Martin's Press.

Angelo, Richard. (1983). "The Social Transformation of American Higher Education." Jarausch, K. H. (ed.), (1983). *The Transformation of Higher Learning, 1860–1930.* Chicago: University of Chicago Press, pp. 261–292.

Axtell, James. (1971). "The Death of the Liberal Arts College." *History of Education Quarterly,* vol. 11, Winter, pp. 339–352.

Barnes, Sherman B. (1960). "Learning and Piety in Ohio Colleges, 1865–1900." *Ohio Historical Quarterly,* vol. 69, no. 4, October, pp. 327–352.

Best, John H. (ed.) (1983). *Historical Inquiry in Education: A Research Agenda.* Washington. D.C.: American Educational Research Association.

Boyer, Ernest L. and Levine, Arthur. (1981). *A Quest for Common Learning: The Aims of General Education.* Washington, D.C.: The Carnegie Foundation for the Advancement of Teaching, n.d.

Bonowman, Merle. (1961). "The False Dawn of The State University." *History of Education Quarterly,* 1 (#2): 6–22.

Burke, Colin B. (1973). "The Quiet Influence: The American Colleges and Their Students, 1800–1960." Unpublished Ph.D. dissertation, Washington University.

Burke, Colin. (1982). *American Collegiate Population: A Test of the Traditional View.* New York: New York University Press.

Butts, Freeman A. and Cremin, Lawrence A. (1953). *A History of Education in American Culture.* New York: Henry Holt.

Chisolm, Linda A. (1982). "The Art of Undergraduate Teaching in the Age of the Emerging University." Unpublished Ph.D. dissertation, Columbia University.

Creutz, Alan. (1980). "From College to University Scholar: The Evolution of the Faculty at the University of Michigan, 1850–1900." Unpublished Ph.D. dissertation, University of Michigan.

Dominick, Charles A. "A History of Selected Private Colleges in Ohio," Ph.D. dissertation (in progress), University of Michigan.

Findlay, James (1982). "Western Colleges, 1830–1870: Education Institution in Transition." *History of Higher Education Annual,* 2: 35–64.

Flexner, Abraham. (1908). "The American College: A Criticism." New York: Arno Press.

Guralnick, Stanley, M. (1974). "Sources of Misconception on the Role of Science in the Nineteenth Century American College." *Isis,* vol. 65, pp. 48–62.

Haddad, Gladys Marylin. (1980). "Social Roles and Advanced Education for Women in Nineteenth Century America: A Study of Three Western Reserve Institutions." Unpublished Ph.D.

170

dissertation, Case Western Reserve University.

Herbst, Jurgen. (1968). Review of Burke, *Higher Education* 12 (August, 1983): 484–485.

Katz, Michael. (1980). *The Irony of Early School Reform: Educational Innovation in Mid-Nineteenth Century Massachusets*, Cambridge. Maris A. Vinovskis, "The Politics of Education Reform in Nineteenth Century Massachusetts: The Controversy over the Beverly High School in 1860." ERIC (ED 200495).

Kennedy, Sister M. St. Mel., O.S.F. (1961). "The Changing Academic Characteristics of the Nineteenth Century American College Teacher." Unpublished Ph.D. dissertation, St. Louis University.

Kimball, Bruce A. (1986a). "Essay Review: History of Higher Education Annual: vols. 1–4, 1981–1984." *History of Higher Education Annual*. 5.

Kimball, Bruce A. (1986b). "Paradoxes of Inclusivism in Retelling the History of the American College." *Minerva*.

Mattingly, Paul H. (1983). "Structures Over Time: Institutional History." In: Best, John H. (ed.). *Historical Inquiry in Education: A Research Agenda*. Washington, D.C.: American Educational Research Association, pp. 34–55.

McCaughey, Robert A. (1974). "The Transformation of American Academic Life: Harvard University, 1821–1892." *Perspectives in American History*, Vol. 8, pp. 239–332.

Metzger, Walter P. (1984). Review of Burke, *Journal of Higher Education* (55): 421.

Naylor, Natalie. (1973). "The Ante-Bellum College Movement: A Reappraisal of Tewksbury's *Founding of American Colleges and Universities*." *History of Education Quarterly*. Vol. 260, Fall, pp. 261–274.

Palmer, Barbara Heslan. (1980). "Lace Bonnets and Academic Gowns: Faculty Development in Four Women's Colleges, 1875–1915." Unpublished Ph.D. dissertation, Boston College.

Peterson, George E. (1964). *The New England College in the Age of the University*. Amherst, Mass.: Amherst College Press.

Potts, David B. (1971). "American Colleges in the Nineteenth Century: From Localism to Denominationalism." *History of Education Quarterly*, vol. 11, Winter, pp. 363–380.

Potts, David B. (1977). "'College Enthusiasm!' As Public Response, 1800–1860." *Harvard Educational Review*, vol. 47, no. 1, February, pp. 28–42.

Rogers, Walter P. (1942). *Andrew White and the Modern University*. Ithica, New York: Cornell University Press.

Rudolph, Frederick. (1962). *The American College and University*. New York: Knopf.

Schmidt, George P. (1957). *The Liberal Arts College: A Chapter in American Cultural History*. New Brunswick, N.J.: Rutgers University Press.

Sloan, Douglas. (1971). "Harmony, Chaos, and Consensus: The American College Curriculum." *Teachers College Record*, vol. 73, no. 2, December, pp. 221–257.

Tewksbury, Donald G. (1932). *The Founding of American Colleges and Universities*. New York: Teachers College Press.

Tobias, Marilyn. (1982). *Old Dartmouth on Trial: The Transformation of the Academic Community in Nineteenth Century America*. New York: New York University Press.

Veysey, Laurence R. (1965). *The Emergence of the American University*. Chicago: University of Chicago Press.

Vinovskis, Maris A. (1985). *The Origins of Public High Schools: A Re-Examination of the Beverly High School Controversy*. Madison: University of Wisconsin Press.

The Yale Report of 1828

REMARKS BY THE EDITOR [BENJAMIN SILLIMAN]

The following papers relate to an important subject, respecting which there is at present some diversity of opinion. As the interests of sound learning, in relation both to literature and science, and to professional and active life, are intimately connected with the views developed in the subjoined reports, they are therefore inserted in this Journal, in the belief that they will be deemed both important and interesting by its readers.

AT A MEETING OF THE PRESIDENT AND FELLOWS OF YALE COLLEGE, SEPT IITH, 1827, THE FOLLOWING RESOLUTION WAS PASSED

That His Excellency Governor Tomlinson, Rev. President Day, Rev. Dr. Chapin, Hon. Noyes Darling, and Rev. Abel McEwen, be a committee to inquire into the expediency of so altering the regular course of instruction in this college, as to leave out of said course the study of the *dead languages,* substituting other studies therefor; and either requiring a competent knowledge of said languages, as a condition of admittance into the college, or providing instruction in the same, for such as shall choose to study them after admittance; and that the said committee be requested to report at the next annual meeting of this corporation.

This committee, at their first meeting in April, 1828, after taking into consideration the case referred to them, requested the Faculty of the college to express their views on the subject of the resolution.

The expediency of retaining the ancient languages, as an essential part of our course of instruction, is so obviously connected with the object and plan of education in the college, that justice could not be done to the particular subject of inquiry in the resolution, without a brief statement of the nature and arrangement of the various branches of the whole system. The report of the faculty was accordingly made out in *two parts;* one containing a summary view of the plan of education in the college; the other, an inquiry into the expediency of insisting on the study of the ancient languages. . . .

REPORT OF THE FACULTY, PART I

. . . We are decidedly of the opinion, that our present plan of education admits of improvement. We are aware that the system is imperfect: and we cherish the hope, that some of its defects may ere long be remedied. We believe that changes may, from time to time be made with advantage, to meet the varying demands of the community, to accommodate the course of instruction to the rapid advance of the country, in population, refinement, and opulence. We have no doubt that important improvements may be suggested, by attentive observa-

172

a subject proposed for investigation; following, with accurate discrimination, the course of argument; balancing nicely the evidence presented to the judgment; awakening, elevating, and controlling the imagination; arranging, with skill, the treasures which memory gathers; rousing and guiding the powers of genius. All this is not to be effected by a light and hasty course of study; by reading a few books, hearing a few lectures, and spending some months at a literary institution. The habits of thinking are to be formed, by long continued and close application. The mines of science must be penetrated far below the surface, before they will disclose their treasures. If a dexterous performance of the manual operations, in many of the mechanical arts, requires an apprenticeship, with diligent attention for years; much more does the training of the powers of the mind demand vigorous, and steady, and systematic effort.

In laying the foundation of a thorough education, it is necessary that *all* the important mental faculties be brought into exercise. . . . In the course of instruction in this college, it has been an object to maintain such a proportion between the different branches of literature and science, as to form in the student a proper *balance* of character. From the pure mathematics, he learns the art of demonstrative reasoning. In attending to the physical sciences, he becomes familiar with facts, with the process of induction, and the varieties of probable evidence. In ancient literature, he finds some of the most finished models of taste. By English reading, he learns the powers of the language in which he is to speak and write. By logic and mental philosophy, he is taught the art of thinking; by rhetoric and oratory, the art of speaking. By frequent exercise on written composition, he acquires copiousness and accuracy of expression. By extemporaneous discussion, he becomes prompt, and fluent, and animated. It is a point of high importance, that eloquence and solid learning should go together; that he who has accumulated the richest treasures of thought, should possess the highest powers of oratory. To what purpose has a man become deeply learned, if he has no faculty of communicating his knowledge? And of what use is a display of rhetorical elegance, from one who knows little or nothing which is worth communicating? . . .

No one feature in a system of intellectual education, is of greater moment than such an arrangement of duties and motives, as will most effectually throw the student upon the *resources of his own mind.* Without this, the whole apparatus of libraries, and instruments, and specimens, and lectures, and teachers, will be insufficient to secure distinguished excellence. The scholar must form himself, by his own exertions. The advantages furnished by a residence at a college, can do little more than stimulate and aid his personal efforts. The *inventive* powers are especially to be called into vigorous exercise. . . .

tion of the literary institutions in Europe; and by the earnest spirit of inquiry which is now so prevalent, on the subject of education.

The guardians of the college appear to have ever acted upon the principle, that it ought not to be stationary, but continually advancing. Some alteration has accordingly been proposed, almost every year, from its first establishment. . . .

Not only the course of studies, and the modes of instruction, have been greatly varied; but whole sciences have, for the first time, been introduced; chemistry, mineralogy, geology, political economy, &c. By raising the qualifications for admission, the standard of attainment has been elevated. Alterations so extensive and frequent, satisfactorily prove, that if those who are intrusted with the superintendence of the institution, still firmly adhere to some of its original features, it is from a higher principle, than a blind opposition to salutary reform. Improvements, we trust, will continue to be made, as rapidly as they can be, without hazarding the loss of what has been already attained.

But perhaps the time has come, when we ought to pause, and inquire, whether it will be sufficient to make *gradual* changes, as heretofore; and whether the whole system is not rather to be broken up, and a better one substituted in its stead. From different quarters, we have heard the suggestion, that our colleges must be *new-modelled*; that they are not adapted to the spirit and wants of the age; that they will soon be deserted, unless they are better accommodated to the business character of the nation. As this point may have an important bearing upon the question immediately before the committee, we would ask their indulgence, while we attempt to explain, at some length, the nature and object of the present plan of education at the college. . . .

What then is the appropriate object of a college? It is not necessary here to determine what it is which, in every case, entitles an institution to the *name* of a college. But if we have not greatly misapprehended the design of the patrons and guardians of this college, its object is to *lay the foundation of a superior education:* and this is to be done, at a period of life when a substitute must be provided for *parental superintendence.* The ground work of a thorough education, must be broad, and deep, and solid. For a partial or superficial education, the support may be of looser materials, and more hastily laid.

The two great points to be gained in intellectual culture, are the *discipline* and the *furniture* of the mind; expanding its powers, and storing it with knowledge. The former of these is, perhaps, the more important of the two. A commanding object, therefore, in a collegiate course, should be, to call into daily and vigorous exercise the faculties of the student. Those branches of study should be prescribed, and those modes of instruction adopted, which are best calculated to teach the art of fixing the attention, directing the train of thought, analyzing

necessary in this advanced stage of education, as in the course at college, where the time allotted to each branch is rarely more than sufficient for the learner to become familiar with its elementary principles...

We deem it to be indispensable to a proper adjustment of our collegiate system, that there should be in it both Professors and Tutors. There is wanted, on the one hand, the experience of those who have been long resident at the institution, and on the other, the fresh and minute information of those who, having more recently mingled with the students, have a distinct recollection of their peculiar feelings, prejudices, and habits of thinking. At the head of each great division of science, it is necessary that there should be a Professor, to superintend the department, to arrange the plan or instruction to regulate the mode of conducting it, and to teach the more important and difficult parts or the subject. But students in a college, who have just entered on the first elements of science, are not principally occupied with the more abstruse and disputable points. Their attention ought not to be solely or mainly directed to the latest discoveries. They have first to learn the principles which have been in a course of investigation, through the successive ages; and have now become simplified and settled. Before arriving at regions hitherto unexplored, they must pass over the intervening cultivated ground. The Professor at the head of a department may, therefore, be greatly aided, in some parts of the course of instruction, by those who are not as deeply versed as himself in all the intricacies of the science. Indeed we doubt, whether elementary principles are always taught to the best advantage, by those whose researches have carried them so far beyond these simpler truths, that they come back to them with reluctance and distaste....

In the internal police of the institution, as the students are gathered into one family, it is deemed an essential provision, that some of the officers should constitute a portion of this family; being always present with them, not only at their meals, and during the business of the day; but in the hours allotted to rest. The arrangement is such, that in our college buildings, there is no room occupied by students, which is not near to the chamber of one of the officers.

But the feature in our system which renders a considerable number of tutors indispensable, is the subdivision of our classes, and the assignment of each portion to the particular charge of one man....

The course of instruction which is given to the undergraduates in the college, is not designed to include *professional* studies. Our object is not to teach that which is peculiar to any one of the professions; but to lay the foundation which is common to them all. There are separate schools for medicine, law, and theology, connected with the college, as well as in various parts of the country; which are open for the reception of all who are prepared to enter upon the appropriate studies of

In our arrangements for the communication of knowledge, as well as in intellectual discipline, such branches are to be taught as will produce a proper symmetry and balance of character. We doubt whether the powers of the mind can be developed, in their fairest proportions, by studying languages alone, or mathematics alone, or natural or political science alone. As the bodily frame is brought to its highest perfection, not by one simple and uniform motion, but by a variety of exercises; so the mental faculties are expanded, and invigorated, and adapted to each other, by familiarity with different departments of science.

A most important feature in the colleges of this country is, that the students are generally of an age which requires, that a substitute be provided for *parental superintendence*. When removed from under the roof of their parents, and exposed to the untried scenes of temptation, it is necessary that some faithful and affectionate guardian take them by the hand, and guide their steps. This consideration determines the *kind* of government which ought to be maintained in our colleges. As it is a substitute for the regulations of a family, it should approach as near to the character of parental control as the circumstances of the case will admit. It should aim to effect its purpose, principally by kind and persuasive influence; not wholly or chiefly by restraint and terror. Still, punishment may sometimes be necessary. There may be perverse members of a college, as well as of a family. There may be those whom nothing but the arm of law can reach....

Having now stated what we understand to be the proper *object* of an education at this college, viz. to lay a solid *foundation* in literature and science; we would ask permission to add a few observations on the *means* which are employed to effect this object.

In giving the course of instruction, it is intended that a due proportion be observed between *lectures*, and the exercises which are familiarly termed *recitations*; that is, examinations in a text book. The great advantage of lectures is, that while they call forth the highest efforts of the lecturer, and accelerate his advance to professional eminence; they give that light and spirit to the subject, which awaken the interest and ardor of the student.... Still it is important, that the student should have opportunities of retiring by himself, and giving a more commanding direction to his thoughts, than when listening to oral instruction. To secure his steady and earnest efforts, is the great object of the daily examinations or recitations. In these exercises, a text-book is commonly the guide. ... When he comes to be engaged in the study of his *profession*, he may find his way through the maze, and firmly establish his own opinions, by taking days or weeks for the reexamination of each separate point. Text-books are, therefore, not as

their several professions. With these, the academical course is not intended to interfere.

But why, it may be asked, should a student waste his time upon studies which have no immediate connection with his future profession? . . . In answer to this, it may be observed, that there is no science which does not contribute its aid to professional skill. "Every thing throws light upon every thing." The great object of a collegiate education, preparatory to the study of a profession, is to give that expansion and balance of the mental powers, those liberal and comprehensive views, and those fine proportions of character, which are always confined to one particular channel. When a man has entered upon the practice of his profession, the energies of his mind must be given, principally, to its appropriate duties. But if his thoughts never range on other subjects, if he never looks abroad on the ample domains of literature and science, there will be a narrowness in his habits of thinking, a peculiarity of character, which will be sure to mark him as a man of limited views and attainments. Should he be distinguished in his profession, his ignorance on other subjects, and the defects of his education, will be the more exposed to public observation. On the other hand, he who is not only eminent in professional life, but has also a mind richly stored with general knowledge, has an elevation and dignity of character, which gives him a commanding influence in society, and a widely extended sphere of usefulness. His situation enables him to diffuse the light of science among all classes of the community. Is a man to have no other object, than to obtain a *living* by professional pursuits? Has he not duties to perform to his family, to his fellow citizens, to his country; duties which require various and extensive intellectual furniture? . . .

As our course of instruction is not intended to complete an education, in theological, medical, or legal science; neither does it include all the minute details of *mercantile, mechanical, or agricultural* concerns. These can never be effectually learned except in the very circumstances in which they are to be practised. The young merchant must be trained in the counting room, the mechanic, in the workshop, the farmer, in the field. But we have, on our premises, no experimental farm or retail shop; no cotton or iron manufactory; no hatter's, or silver-smith's, or coach-maker's establishment. For what purpose, then, it will be asked, are young men who are destined to these occupations, ever sent to a college? They should not be sent, as we think, with an expectation of *finishing* their education at the college; but with a view of laying a thorough foundation in the principles of science, preparatory to the study of the practical arts. . . .

We are far from believing that theory *alone*, should be taught in a college. It cannot be effectually taught, except in connection with prac-

tical illustrations. . . . To bring down the principles of science to their practical application by the laboring classes, is the office of men of superior education. It is the separation of theory and practice, which has brought reproach upon both. Their union alone can elevate them to their true dignity and value. The man of science is often disposed to assume an air of superiority, when he looks upon the narrow and partial views of the mere artisan. The latter in return laughs at the practical blunders of the former. The defects in the education of both classes would be remedied, by giving them a knowledge of scientific principles, preparatory to practice.

We are aware that a thorough education is not within the reach of all. Many, for want of time and pecuniary resources, must be content with a partial course. A defective education is better than none. If a youth can afford to devote only two or three years, to a scientific and professional education, it will be proper for him to make a selection of a few of the most important branches, and give his attention exclusively to these. But this is an imperfection, arising from the necessity of the case. A partial course of study, must inevitably give a partial education. . . .

A partial education is often expedient; a superficial one, never. . . .

But why, it is asked, should *all* the students in a college be required to tread in the *same steps?* Why should not each one be allowed to select those branches of study which are most to his taste, which are best adapted to his peculiar talents, and which are most nearly connected with his intended profession? To this we answer, that our prescribed course contains those subjects only which ought to be understood, as we think, by every one who aims at a thorough education. They are not the peculiarities of any profession or art. These are to be learned in the professional and practical schools. But the principles of sciences, are the common foundation of all high intellectual attainments. As in our primary schools, reading, writing, and arithmetic are taught to all, however different their prospects; so in a college, all should be instructed in those branches of knowledge, of which no one destined to the higher walks of life ought to be ignorant. What subject which is now studied here, could be set aside, without evidently marring the system[?] Not to speak particularly, in this place, of the ancient languages; who that aims at a well proportioned and superior education will remain ignorant of the elements of the various branches of the mathematics, or of history and antiquities, or of rhetoric and oratory, or natural philosophy, or astronomy, or chemistry, or mineralogy, or geology, or political economy, or mental and moral philosophy?

It is sometimes thought that a student ought not to be urged to the study of that for which he has *no taste or capacity.* But how is he to

faultless models, to be exactly copied by our American colleges; yet we would be far from condemning every feature, in systems of instruction which have had an origin more ancient than our republican seminaries. We do not suppose that the world has learned absolutely nothing, by the experience of ages; that a branch of science, or a mode of teaching, is to be abandoned, precisely because it has stood its ground, after a trial by various nations, and through successive centuries. We believe that our colleges may derive important improvements from the universities and schools in Europe; not by blindly adopting all their measures without discrimination; but by cautiously introducing, with proper modifications, such parts of their plans as are suited to our peculiar situation and character. The first and great improvement which we wish to see made, is an elevation in the standard of attainment for admission. Until this is effected, we shall only expose ourselves to inevitable failure and ridicule, by attempting a general imitation of foreign universities....

It is said that the public now demand, that the doors should be thrown open to all; that education ought to be so modified, and varied, as to adapt it to the exigencies of the country, and the prospects of different individuals; that the instruction given to those who are destined to be merchants, or manufacturers, or agriculturalists, should have a special reference to their respective professional pursuits.

The public are undoubtedly right, in demanding that there should be appropriate courses of education, accessible to all classes of youth. And we rejoice at the prospect of ample provision for this purpose, in the improvement of our academies, and the establishment of commercial high-schools, gymnasia, lycea, agricultural seminaries, &c. But do the public insist, that every college shall become a high-school, gymnasium, lyceum, and academy? Why should we interfere with these valuable institutions? Why wish to take their business out of their hands? The college has its appropriate object, and they have theirs.... What is the characteristic difference between a college and an academy? Not that the former teaches more branches than the latter. There are many academies in the country, whose scheme of studies, at least upon paper, is more various than that of the colleges. But while an academy teaches a little of every thing, the college, by directing its efforts to one uniform course, aims at doing its work with greater precision, and economy of time; just as the merchant who deals in a single class of commodities, or a manufacturer who produces but one kind of fabrics, executes his business more perfectly, than he whose attention and skill are divided among a multitude of objects....

But might we not, by making the college more accessible to different descriptions of persons, enlarge our *numbers*, and in that way, increase our income? This might be the operation of the measure, for a very know, whether he has a taste or capacity for a science, before he has even entered upon its elementary truths? If he is really destitute of talent sufficient for these common departments of education, he is destined for some narrow sphere of action. But we are well persuaded, that our students are not so deficient in intellectual powers, as they sometimes profess to be; though they are easily made to believe, that they have no capacity for the study of that which they are told is almost wholly useless.

When a class have become familiar with the common elements of the several sciences, then is the proper time for them to *divide off* to their favorite studies. They can then make their choice from actual trial. This is now done here, to some extent, in our Junior year. The division might be commenced at an earlier period, and extended farther, provided the qualifications for admission into the college, were brought to a higher standard.

If the view which we have thus far taken of the subject is correct, it will be seen, that the object of the system of instruction at this college, is not to give a *partial* education, consisting of a few branches only; nor, on the other hand, to give a *superficial* education, containing a smattering of almost every thing; nor to *finish* the details of either a professional or practical education; but to *commence a thorough* course, and to carry it as far as the time of residence here will allow. It is intended to occupy, to the best advantage, the four years immediately preceding the study of a profession, or of the operations which are peculiar to the higher mercantile, manufacturing, or agricultural establishments....

Our institution is not modelled exactly after the pattern of *European* universities. Difference of circumstances has rendered a different arrangement expedient. It has been the policy of most monarchical governments, to concentrate the advantages of a superior education in a few privileged places. In England, for instance, each of the ancient universities of Oxford and Cambridge, is not so much a single institution, as a large number of distinct, though contiguous colleges. But in this country, our republican habits and feelings will never allow a monopoly of literature in any one place. There must be, in the union, as many colleges, at least, as states. Nor would we complain of this arrangement as inexpedient, provided that starvation is not the consequence of a patronage so minutely divided. We anticipate no disastrous results from the multiplication of colleges, if they can only be adequately endowed. We are not without apprehensions, however, that a feeble and stinted growth of our national literature, will be the consequence of the very scanty supply of means to most of our public seminaries....

Although we do not consider the literary institutions of Europe as

short time, while a degree from the college should retain its present value in public estimation; a value depending entirely upon the character of the education which we give. But the moment it is understood that the institution has descended to an inferior standard of attainment, its reputation will sink to a corresponding level. After we shall have become a college in *name only*, and in reality nothing more than an academy; or half college, and half academy; what will induce parents in various and distant parts of the country, to send us their sons, when they have academies enough in their own neighborhood? There is no magical influence in an act of incorporation, to give celebrity to a literary institution, which does not command respect for itself, by the elevated rank of its education. When the college has lost its hold on the public confidence, by depressing its standard of merit, by substituting a partial, for a thorough education, we may expect that it will be deserted by that class of persons who have hitherto been drawn here by high expectations and purposes. Even if we should *not* immediately suffer in point of *numbers*, yet we shall exchange the best portion of our students, for others of inferior aims and attainments.

As long as we can maintain an elevated character, we need be under no apprehension with respect to numbers. Without character, it will be in vain to think of retaining them. It is a hazardous experiment, to act upon the plan of gaining numbers first, and character afterwards. . . .

The difficulties with which we are now struggling, we fear would be increased, rather than diminished, by attempting to unite different plans of education. It is far from being our intention to dictate to *other* colleges a system to be adopted by them. There may be good and sufficient reasons why some of them should introduce a partial course of instruction. We are not sure, that the demand for thorough education is, at present, sufficient to fill all the colleges in the United States, with students who will be satisfied with nothing short of high and solid attainments. But it is to be hoped that, at no very distant period, they will be able to come up to this elevated ground, and leave the business of second-rate education to the inferior seminaries.

The competition of colleges may advance the interests of literature: if it is a competition for *excellence*, rather than for numbers; if each aims to surpass the others, not in an imposing display, but in the substantial value of its education. . . .

Our republican form of government renders it highly important, that great numbers should enjoy the advantage of a thorough education. On the Eastern continent, the *few* who are destined to particular departments in political life, may be educated for the purpose; while the mass of the people are left in comparative ignorance. But in this country, where offices are accessible to all who are qualified for them, superior intellectual attainments ought not to be confined to any de-

scription of persons. *Merchants, manufacturers, and farmers,* as well as professional gentlemen, take their places in our public councils. A thorough education ought therefore to be extended to all these classes. It is not sufficient that they be men of sound judgment, who can decide correctly, and give a silent vote, on great national questions. Their influence upon the minds of others is needed; an influence to be produced by extent of knowledge, and the force of eloquence. Ought the speaking in our deliberative assemblies to be confined to a single profession? If it is knowledge, which gives us the command of physical agents and instruments, much more is it that which enables us to control the combinations of moral and political machinery. . . .

Can merchants, manufacturers, and agriculturists, derive no benefit from high intellectual culture? They are the very classes which, from their situation and business, have the best opportunities for reducing the principles of science to their practical applications. The large estates which the tide of prosperity in our country is so rapidly accumulating, will fall mostly into their hands. Is it not desirable that they should be men of superior education, of large and liberal views, of those solid and elegant attainments, which will raise them to a higher distinction, than the mere possession of property; which will not allow them to hoard their treasures, or waste them in senseless extravagance; which will enable them to adorn society by their learning, to move in the more intelligent circles with dignity, and to make such an application of their wealth, as will be most honorable to themselves, and most beneficial to their country?

The active, enterprising character of our population, renders it highly important, that this bustle and energy should be directed by sound intelligence, the result of deep thought and early discipline. The greater the impulse to action, the greater is the need of wise and skilful guidance. When nearly all the ship's crew are aloft, setting the topsails, and catching the breezes, it is necessary there should be a steady hand at helm. Light and moderate learning is but poorly fitted to direct the energies of a nation, so widely extended, so intelligent, so powerful in resources, so rapidly advancing in population, strength, and opulence. Where a free government gives full liberty to the human intellect to expand and operate, education should be proportionably liberal and ample. When even our mountains, and rivers, and lakes, are upon a scale which seems to denote, that we are destined to be a great and mighty nation, shall our literature be feeble, and scanty, and superficial?

REPORT OF THE FACULTY, PART II

. . . The subject of inquiry now presented, is, whether the plan of instruction pursued in Yale College, is sufficiently accommodated to the present state of literature and science; and, especially, whether such

rope, is chiefly an effort of memory. The general structure of these languages is much the same as that of our own. The few idiomatical differences, are made familiar with little labor; nor is there the same necessity of accurate comparison and discrimination, as in studying the classic writers of Greece and Rome. To establish this truth, let a page of Voltaire be compared with a page of Tacitus....

Modern languages, with most of our students, are studied, and will continue to be studied, as an accomplishment, rather than as a necessary acquisition.... To suppose the modern languages more practical than the ancient, to the great body of our students, because the former are now spoken in some parts of the world, is an obvious fallacy. The proper question is,—what course of discipline affords the best mental culture, leads to the most thorough knowledge of our own literature, and lays the best foundation for professional study. The ancient languages have here a decided advantage. If the elements of modern languages are acquired by our students in connection with the established collegiate course, and abundant facilities for this purpose, have for a long time, been afforded, further acquisitions will be easily made, where circumstances render them important and useful. From the graduates of this college, who have visited Europe, complaints have sometimes been heard, that their classical attainments were too small for the literature of the old world; but none are recollected to have expressed regret, that they had cultivated ancient learning while here, however much time they might have devoted to this subject. On the contrary, those who have excelled in classical literature, and have likewise acquired a competent knowledge of some one modern European language besides the English, have found themselves the best qualified to make a full use of their new advantages. Deficiencies in modern literature are easily and rapidly supplied, where the mind has had a proper previous discipline; deficiencies in ancient literature are supplied tardily, and in most instances, imperfectly....

Such, then, being the value of ancient literature, both as respects the general estimation in which it is held in the literary world, and its intrinsic merits,—if the college should confer degrees upon students for their attainments in modern literature only, it would be to declare *that* to be a liberal education, which the world will not acknowledge to deserve the name;—and which those who shall receive degrees in this way, will soon find, is not what it is called. A liberal education, whatever course the college should adopt, would without doubt continue to be, what it long has been. Ancient literature is too deeply inwrought into the whole system of the modern literature of Europe to be so easily laid aside. The college ought not to presume upon its influence, nor to set itself up in any manner as a dictator. If it should pursue a course very different from that which the present state of

a change is demanded as would leave out of this plan the study of the Greek and Roman classics, and make an acquaintance with ancient literature no longer necessary for a degree in the liberal arts....

Whoever ... without a preparation in classical literature, engages in any literary investigation, or undertakes to discuss any literary topic, or associates with those who in any country of Europe, or in this country, are acknowledged to be men of liberal acquirements, immediately feels a deficiency in his education, and is convinced that he is destitute of an important part of practical learning. If scholars, then, are to be prepared to act in the literary world as it in fact exists, classical literature, from considerations purely practical, should form an important part of their early discipline.

But the claims of classical learning are not limited to this single view. It may be defended not only as a necessary branch of education, in the present state of the world, but on the ground of its distinct and independent merits. Familiarity with the Greek and Roman writers is especially adapted to form the taste, and to discipline the mind, both in thought and diction, to the relish of what is elevated, chaste, and simple....

But the study of the classics is useful, not only as it lays the foundations of a correct taste, and furnishes the student with those elementary ideas which are found in the literature of modern times, and which he no where so well acquires as in their original sources;—but also as the study itself forms the most effectual discipline of the mental faculties. This is a topic so often insisted on, that little need be said of it here. It must be obvious to the most cursory observer, that the classics afford materials to exercise talent of every degree, from the first opening of the youthful intellect to the period of its highest maturity. The range of classical study extends from the elements of language, to the most difficult questions arising from literary research and criticism. Every faculty of the mind is employed; not only the memory, judgment, and reasoning powers, but the taste and fancy are occupied and improved.

Classical discipline, likewise, forms the best preparation for professional study. The interpretation of language, and its correct use, are no where more important, than in the professions of divinity and law....

In the profession of medicine, the knowledge of the Greek and Latin languages is less necessary now than formerly; but even at the present time it may be doubted, whether the facilities which classical learning affords for understanding and rendering familiar the terms of science, do not more than counterbalance the time and labor requisite for obtaining this learning....

To acquire the knowledge of any of the modern languages of Eu-

literature demands; if it should confer its honors according to a rule which is not sanctioned by literary men, the faculty see nothing to expect for favoring such innovations, but that they will be considered visionaries in education, ignorant of its true design and objects, and unfit for their places. The ultimate consequence, it is not difficult to predict. The college would be distrusted by the public, and its reputation would be irrecoverably lost. . . .

No question has engaged the attention of the faculty more constantly, than how the course of education in the college might be improved, and rendered more practically useful. Free communications have at all times been held between the faculty and the corporation, on subjects connected with the instruction of the college. When the aid of the corporation has been thought necessary, it has been asked; and by this course of proceeding, the interests of the institution have been regularly advanced. No remark is more frequently made by those, who visit the college after the absence of some years, than that changes have been made for the better; and those who make the fullest investigation, are the most ready to approve what they find. The charge, therefore, that the college is stationary, that no efforts are made to accommodate it to the wants of the age, that all exertions are for the purpose of perpetuating abuses, and that the college is much the same as it was at the time of its foundation, are wholly gratuitous. The changes in the country, during the last century, have not been greater than the changes in the college. These remarks have been limited to Yale College, as its history is here best known; no doubt, other colleges alluded to in the above quotations, might defend themselves with equal success.

Part III: The Rise of American Universities During the Nineteenth and Twentieth Centuries

Backdrop

Carol S. Gruber

IT IS COMMONPLACE to describe the emergence of the modern university in post–Civil War America as a phenomenon of revolutionary proportions, marked not only by the erection of great new institutions of higher learning but by the thorough transformation of the existing liberal arts college as well. The decades from the late 1860s to the turn of the century saw the rise of new universities, the construction of universities on the base of existing colleges, the founding of centers of professional, technical, and graduate training, and the invasion and profound alteration of the curriculum of the college itself.[1] "By contrast with England and the Continent, the problem [in America] was one of creation, not capture or redirection."[2] To be sure, the ideas and institutional devices were imported from abroad, but not before the social and material preconditions were established in the United States, and the product that resulted was stamped with the unmistakable imprint of the American environment.

The old liberal arts college that dated from colonial times was an adaptation of the English model. Its inspiration came from Oxbridge; but, because the American land was so vast and financial resources were so few and because of local and sectarian rivalries, the English pattern of great universities composed of clusters of independent, autonomous colleges never was duplicated. Instead, the American college assumed its own character, which it retained, not unchallenged but essentially unchanged, until the university revolution of the late nineteenth century.

The American liberal arts college was a sectarian institution designed to perpetuate a class of educated gentlemen. Staff members either already wore the cloth or were in training for the ministry. Its curriculum was prescribed and reflected the view that knowledge was a fixed body of truth to be acquired by rote through the discipline of the faculties of which the human mind was held to be composed: reason, memory, imagination, judgment, and attention. It was thought that these faculties could be developed best by drill in the classics, which consequently made up the heart of the curriculum. Because the course of study was fixed and because teaching chiefly was by recitation, there was no need for teachers to be specialists, and it was not uncommon for a tutor to take his students through the whole curriculum for the year (or longer, if he remained at the institution). Discipline, also under the tutor's charge, was enforced rigorously; attendance in class and chapel was compulsory and a tight rein was held on the students' behavior. The college, with its rigidly prescribed general education, its tone of moral piety, and its exclusive constituency, was isolated from the world around it. There was little, if any, articulation between college and career, school and society. Richard Shryock has observed that, in their educational level, their isolation from each other, and their pattern of lay government, pre–Civil War American colleges resembled the public schools (preparatory schools) of England more than its universities. "For more than two centuries," he concluded, "there was nothing 'higher' about American higher education."[3]

Beginning in the early nineteenth century there were serious attempts to reform the American college in conformity with the expansion of knowledge and changing social conditions and needs, but the attempts met with enormous resistance and were brought to an end by the Civil War. The commitment to general education was too firm, the colleges were too poor to restructure even if they had had the will to do so, and the business community, which might have supplied some of the necessary funds, saw no relationship between higher education and its own interests. College still was viewed as a luxury for a minority, whose needs were met by traditional liberal education.

Following the Civil War, several material and social factors converged to produce a change in conditions and convictions sufficient to precipitate the restructuring of American higher education. The acceleration of urbanization and industrialization and the settlement of the continent created a demand for scientific and technical knowledge by both business and the federal and state governments. The accumulation of great fortunes made private capital available just at the time that the business community was beginning to identify education with material success. The increasing recognition by federal and state authorities of the social value of higher education made public funds available as well. The level of original and experimental work in science and engineering began to be sufficiently high to command respect in comparison with the limitations of that curriculum to increasingly critical view. The challenge to the classical curriculum and the intellectual foundations on which it rested further was facilitated by an erosion of religious influence and an advancing secularism to which the impact of Darwinism contributed. All of these factors made American educational theorists receptive to the influence and example of university developments in Europe, particularly in Germany.

We have been cautioned against viewing the modern university of the 1870s, 1880s, and 1890s as a totally new type of institution established on foreign models. Laurence Veysey reminds us of the important legacies left by the old-time college, and Arthur Bestor insists that the university revolution essentially was a process of assimilation and integration of already present ingredients.[4] Granting the legitimacy of these caveats, it nevertheless is true that the modern university fundamentally was different in character and purpose from the college it superseded. The small, residential, closely regulated undergraduate colleges were supplanted by educational centers comprised of professional schools in law, medicine, theology, and higher arts and sciences, whose ideal intellectual climate was one of free inquiry. These centers were dedicated to the education of a mass society, to the expansion rather than mere perpetuation and transmission of knowledge, and to the teaching of technical and vocational skills. Their curricula were diversified and specialized, with scientific, technical, and vocational subjects assuming equal rank with liberal humanistic studies. The new objectives in higher education gave rise to new teaching techniques and special facilities, such as laboratories and research libraries. The universities recruited specialists in the new branches of knowledge, and the faculties were organized into departments along the lines of the various scholarly disciplines and technical and vocational subjects.

These developments were not confined to the university; they spilled over into the college itself, which was transformed in the process. Beginning with the reforms of Charles W. Eliot at Harvard in the 1870s, the new and higher studies were gradually introduced into the college curriculum. By the turn of the century, and after considerable controversy, the required classical curriculum had been invaded even in the most conservative colleges; it gave way to a program of varied studies from which the student could choose his courses. Adopting the elective system brought about the modernization of the undergraduate college along the lines laid down by the university revolution.

By 1900 the great changes had been accomplished. New university centers had been built across the country—Cornell in 1869, Johns Hopkins in 1876, Clark in 1889, Chicago in 1890, and Stanford in 1891; established institutions like California, Michigan, Minnesota, Wisconsin, Columbia, Harvard, Yale, and Princeton had been turned into modern universities; and the character of the undergraduate college had been transformed. Within these institutional changes and in reciprocal relationship to them, equally profound changes had taken place in the various branches of knowledge and in the profession of their practitioners. Two distinct but inseparable processes of professionalization had occurred: the professionalization of knowledge characterized by the emergence of discrete scholarly disciplines and the development of an academic profession characterized by the definition of standards of preparation, performance, protection, and rewards.

The professionalization of knowledge in part reflected the impact of science on American thought. The grip of theology and ethics on all branches of knowledge was weakened by the belief in rational causation, discoverable by induction from data accumulated by observation and experimentation. As knowledge expanded, it became defined and specialized into discrete subject areas. The process began with the professionalization of science itself in the second half of the nineteenth century; simultaneously, philosophy sloughed off its allegiances to theology; psychology was grounded on an experimental basis; the hodgepodge curriculum in moral philosophy broke up into the new disciplines of economics, political science, and sociology; and history, moving away from literature and philosophy, attempted to establish itself on a scientific basis.[5]

Specialists in the disciplines were trained in the new graduate schools of arts and sciences, where they were imbued with the ideal of research and instructed in its techniques. University presses and scholarly journals were founded to provide outlets for the results of their investigations. Finally, an institutional framework for the newly professionalized disciplines was provided by the establishment of associations to define standards and goals in the various fields of learning. Supplanting the pre–Civil War learned societies that were local in membership, generally open to anyone who wished to join, comprehensive in scope, and sometimes confused between scientific and humanitarian aims, the new professional associations functioned like guilds, setting standards for admission and performance on a national scale and giving the scholar a new persona as a practitioner of his discipline.[6] Organizations such as the Modern Language Association, American Historical Association, American Economic Association, American Psychological Association, and American Sociological Society, established between the last decades of the nineteenth century and the first years of the twentieth century, were indications of the professionalization of scholarship. The founding of the American Association of University Professors in 1915 signified a pro-

fessional consciousness that transcended discipline boundaries to define the academic occupation.

As the academic setting changed with the emergence of the modern university, so did the character and vocation of the faculty. The academic career previously had been relatively unstructured and accessible; it was available to cultivated men of letters who did not need to give evidence of special training or competence in scholarly subjects. The professionalization of knowledge and diversification of the curriculum created the need for a specially trained and certified faculty, which led to the establishment of standards for entry into the profession, itself becoming increasingly structured and defined. Specialized training was provided by the graduate schools of arts and sciences and the Ph.D degree became the certificate of entry into the profession, whose division into ranks provided a structure for measured advance. Finally, reflecting these changes, the general character of the calling also was changed. A vocation that previously had been confined to the teaching function was infused with the ideal of research and scholarship. The teacher no longer was an isolated instructor of immature minds; he was a member of a community of scholars dedicated to the expansion of learning as well as to its preservation and transmission.[7]

The uncertainties in the new profession, as well as its clearly emerging outlines, created a need to define its relationship with the constituent members of its own community and with the outside world. The AAUP was founded in 1915 to satisfy this need. When John Dewey defended the new association against charges of "trade unionism" and "sordid economic self-interest" by likening it to the American Medical Association and the American Bar Association,[8] he was voicing the emergent professional consciousness of the academic community. By the second decade of the twentieth century, professors had overcome their habitual individualism sufficiently to organize into a pressure group to protect their professional status. They were acknowledging that the revolution in higher learning had turned their vocation into a profession. The president of the AAUP announced at the second annual meeting:

> The truth is that we are a single profession—the most responsible branch of that profession which Fichte forever exalted with his inspired essay on 'The Nature of the Scholar.' And, to adapt a phrase of his from 'The Vocation of Man,' 'It is the vocation of our profession to unite itself into one single body, all the parts of which shall be thoroughly known to each

other and all possessed of similar intellectual standards.'. . . Separated as we have been by the distinctions of our several sciences, and sundered as we still are and will be by distances of space and by independence of institutions, the professional bond of the University Scholar and Teacher must become more and remain the strongest; for it is the one common and fundamental element in our careers. We need no charter to unite us; this bond is stronger and freer than a chartered law. Circumstances, and the ripeness of the times, have destined us to this union.'

Any description of the sources and contours of the university revolution that omits the German influence must be incomplete. To be sure, change could not occur before the ground was prepared at home; nevertheless, there was no single influence on the direction that change would take as great as that provided by the example from Germany. The influence was exerted directly on American students who, beginning in the early nineteenth century, went to the universities of Germany to acquire the professional and advanced education that was not yet available at home.

Between 1820 and 1920 almost nine thousand Americans studied in German universities—the majority during the last decades of the nineteenth century—either receiving advanced training as part of an American doctoral program or, more typically, taking a German Ph.D. degree. Among them were men who would become architects of the modern university in America, including Andrew Dickson White, Daniel Coit Gilman, and G. Stanley Hall. They returned to America inspired by the idea of the university as a community of students and scholars engaged in the free transmission and expansion of knowledge, and they proceeded to translate the idea into institutions modeled after the German example. The erection of the graduate school of arts and sciences reflected the Germanization of American higher education, as did the introduction of such teaching techniques and research devices as lectures, seminars, libraries, and laboratories. The establishment of knowledge on a scientific basis also reflected the influence of Germany, for it was there that the pioneering work was done in the various scholarly disciplines, and it was there that Americans learned to apply the methods of science to the accumulation and analysis of data. It was there, too, that they were introduced to the concept, which would become a foundation of their profession, that knowledge can be advanced only in a climate of absolute intellectual freedom. Finally, Americans who earned German

Ph.D. degrees returned home as fully trained professionals in their disciplines. Their view of the vocation of scholarship contributed to the establishment of an academic profession, with precise standards and goals and with a high sense of social value.[10]

The German influence was particularly great on the American social sciences. It promoted not only a scientific methodology but also a conviction that knowledge has a social function, and it impressed upon scholars in the new disciplines a keen sense of responsibility to the public welfare.[11] Many of the pioneering American social scientists of the late nineteenth and early twentieth century—including the economists Richard T. Ely, Henry W. Farnam, and E. R. A. Seligman, the sociologists Albion W. Small and E. A. Ross, and the historians Herbert Baxter Adams, John W. Burgess, and James Harvey Robinson—did graduate work in Germany. German-trained social scientists were in the vanguard of those who developed graduate departments in their disciplines and founded professional associations and publications. They dominated the faculties of the social sciences departments of the new universities.

That Germany was the nation to vitally influence the emergence of the modern American university is not difficult to explain. From the early nineteenth century until the advent of Nazism, the excellence of the German universities and their high level of achievement made them "model academic institutions."[12] The prestige of a German doctorate was very high, and the degree was relatively easy to acquire. Americans were drawn by the intellectual vitality of nineteenth-century German university scholarship and by the reputation of individual scholars. Furthermore, the cost of living in Germany was attractively low. By comparison, the universities of France and Britain had little to offer.[13] Indeed, although British universities were emerging from a period of "torpor and ossification" and were beginning to improve in the early twentieth century and to attract American attention,[14] the advances they made were influenced by the German example.[15] Josiah Royce beautifully described the centrality of the German experience during the formative years of university building in America. Speaking of the late 1870s, he recalled a professor at Johns Hopkins telling him that "when he dealt with young American scholars he found them feeling as if not England, but Germany, were their mother-country. . . . One went to Germany," he continued, "still a doubter as to the possibility of the theoretic life; one returned an idealist, devoted for the time to pure learning for learnings' sake determined to contribute his *Scherflein* to the massive store of human knowledge, burning for a chance to help build the American University."[16]

Americans did not hesitate to acknowledge the influence of German higher education and scholarship. For example, in 1904 the University of Chicago for its fiftieth convocation chose the theme "Recognition of the Indebtedness of American Universities to the Ideals of German Scholarship." The principal address of the occasion, delivered by Professor John M. Coulter, held up the German university as "a model to other nations." The great principles on which the German university rests, Coulter said, must be the basic principles of universities everywhere.[17] In his letter of greeting to the assemblage, President Theodore Roosevelt hailed Germany as "the mother of modern science and learning."[18] The following year, an annual exchange professorship between German and American universities was established, expressing a mutual desire to preserve and promote the affinities between the higher educational world in the two countries.

In 1914 German representatives in the United States counted on these affinities to make American university scholars sympathetic to Germany's cause in the war. These representatives founded the German University League, with the purpose of uniting "those who have enjoyed the privilege of a German university education" in efforts "to strengthen the regard for the Germans and for their aims and ideals, and to secure for them ... fair play and proper appreciation."[19] A letter from the philosophers Rudolf Eucken and Ernst Haeckel to the universities of America was distributed with the league's first announcement, expressing confidence in "the friendly feeling of the American universities," whose members, as a result of their training in Germany, the exchange of scholars, and the bonds created by scholarly research, "know what German culture means to the world." Eucken and Haeckel concluded with the expectation that American scholars would reject the Allied interpretation of the war and accept that of the Central Powers.[20]

This expectation, aside from overlooking the influence of the war's political and diplomatic issues on American scholars, was based on a mistakenly simple view of the influence of Germany on American higher education. What had been involved was a complicated process of interpretation, even misinterpretation, selection, and alteration to adapt the German example to the American environment. Americans transported the organizational structure of German scholarship—the graduate school and the instructional techniques and research devices associated with it, the professional association, and professional publications—and the new scientific methodology almost intact; but they eschewed the idealist context in which these operated in Germany. Walter P. Metzger observes, "Most Americans who went to study in Germany ... took home the methods of her seminars and laboratories, but left the *Anschauung* of idealism behind."[21] According to Veysey, Americans who, under the influence of Germany, became dedicated to scientific research missed "the larger, almost contemplative implications of *Wissenschaft*" and transformed the German ideal of "pure learning," unaffected by utilitarian demands, into an American version, "pure science," assuming that "investigation meant something specifically scientific." The Germans' lofty evocation of underlying spiritual unity was ignored by research-minded Americans, who found the inspiration for their academic theorizing on the level of German practice and became deeply inspired by the rigorous and precise examination of phenomena. "An insufficiently differentiated Germany, partly real and partly imaginary," Veysey concludes, "became the symbol for all scientific claims upon American education."[22]

Furthermore, the process of cultural transfer was ambivalent, particularly in the social sciences. Jurgen Herbst demonstrates that it was largely the influence of German methods of empirical research and inductive generalization that professionalized history in late nineteenth-century America. But, he continues, the philosophic assumptions and political ideas that were central to German historical writing at the time were incompatible with American tradition and values. Consequently, the attempt to transfer to the United States a German science of history and politics failed in the long run.[23] The writings of the first generation of German-trained historians, chief among them Herbert Baxter Adams and John W. Burgess, applied German ideas and values—statism, rejection of natural rights and the social contract, Aryan superiority—to the history of the United States. In order for the next generation of American historians to understand the dynamics of a democratic society, they had to reject the approach of Adams and his followers. Herbst declares that Adams himself came to realize the incompatibility of German ideas with American history and ended his contacts with his German mentors, drawing closer to "democratic" colleagues in England. Herbst quotes W. Stull Holt's conclusion from this fact that "the orthodox account of the dominant influence of German scholarship in America during this period [1876–1901] may need revision."[24]

Herbst maintains that it was easier to accomplish cultural transfer in the fields of economics and sociology, where the object of inquiry was society and not the state and where, consequently, the problem of antagonism between the individual and the state did not necessarily have to be confronted.[25] But even in these disciplines Americans responded with discrimination to the influence of German scholarship. For example, Joseph Dorfman points out that, although the German historical school had a seminal influence on modern economics in America, the Germans' political philosophy of centralized authority was rejected by Americans, who substituted ideas more congenial to a pluralistic society.[26]

Finally, the manner in which Americans simultaneously adopted the German principle of academic freedom and adapted it to the American environment illustrates the selectivity of the process of cultural transfer. The German ideal of the free pursuit of knowledge, without religious, political, or administrative control, exacted both praise and envy from Americans from the time they first began to study in German universities.[27] By the time they organized the AAUP, professors in America had concluded that academic freedom was the prerequisite of the profession. But their application of the principle was vastly different from that of the Germans. For one thing, unlike the Germans, they were relatively unconcerned with the issue of student freedom (*Lernfreiheit*) and restricted their efforts to the definition and protection of the freedom of the faculty (*Lehrfreiheit*). Furthermore, the Americans restricted a professor's freedom within the classroom, insisting that he confine his subject matter to his field of competence and that he maintain a "neutral" posture in presenting it. At the same time they extended the definition of academic freedom to protect freedom of expression outside university walls, insisting that a professor should no more be penalized for exercising his constitutional right of free speech than any other citizen. In this fashion, academic freedom in the United States became associated with civil liberty.[28]

One aspect of the experience of American students in Germany should at least be mentioned in connection with any evaluation of the German impact on American scholars. It was not uncommon for Americans who received their professional training in Germany and who were enormously impressed by German scholarship and culture to be at the same time disturbed, even repelled, by other traits of German society, particularly the high esteem accorded to the military establishment and

the authoritarianism that characterized German political and social life. A high regard for German learning and culture, in other words, could go hand in hand with a rejection of other German values and institutions.[29]

Taken together, the increasing discrimination with which Americans came to view German education and scholarship and the simultaneous improvement in American graduate education led to a waning of German influence on American higher education after the 1890s. Veysey concludes that, "despite the inauguration of exchange professorships between the two countries, American and German academic circles increasingly lost contact with each other well before the advent of the First World War."[30] Nevertheless, by this time an acknowledged prior debt to Germany was part of the record of American higher education and, in the case of individual American professors, there were warm professional and personal relationships with German scholars and their families that had been established when the Americans had studied abroad and that endured during the early years of the twentieth century.

Professors Eucken and Haeckel and the founders of the German University League erred not only in viewing the influence of Germany on American higher education with an undiscriminating eye, but also in failing to consider other influences on American higher education and other deep and enduring influences on American culture that would help determine American sympathies in the war. Although the erection of the modern university in America was a process of Germanization, the base on which it was imposed derived from England, and the traces of the English college and the values it represented never disappeared from the American system. Historically, from the time of its inception in the seventeenth century, the American college had belonged to the English type. In its dedication to education rather than training and to the cultivation of moral and social as well as intellectual attributes, the American college exemplified the English ideal of liberal education.[31] It was this ideal that had to be combated by the proponents of the modern university. A French observer of the American educational scene in the late nineteenth century described it as a great battlefield on which English (liberal education) and German (laboratory science) influences fought.[32] Richard Hofstädter demonstrates that, although the German ideals of scholarship and academic freedom were at the heart of the university revolution, English influences persisted even after the revolution had been accomplished. He describes these influences as follows: concern with the development of character in undergraduates and with "atmosphere" in the institutions; a passion for imposing buildings, separated if possible from the urban community; an emphasis on teaching as opposed to research; a commitment to the centrality of the college among the various parts of the university; an aim of creating a broadly educated leadership as opposed to a body of specialists; and a zeal for undergraduate sports. These influences, he concludes, remained "especially strong in the better colleges and in some universities, like Yale and Princeton."[33] The regular attendance of American Rhodes Scholars at Oxford University beginning in 1902 suggests that British ideals of higher education continued to be relevant for Americans even after they had revamped their universities largely along German lines.

The cultural and intellectual affinities between America and Britain stretched far beyond the area of educational influences and interchange and present an even more complicated picture of cultural transfer than that already described between Germany and America. Only the broad outlines of that picture can be sketched here. In his study *The American Image of the Old World*, Cushing Strout demonstrates that Americans traditionally experienced acute ambivalence toward England. From the time of the Revolution, he argues, England provoked a kind of schizophrenic response from America; it was both America's antipathy toward the detested enemy, the prime target of America's antipathy toward the Old World, and the mother country, the source of America's language, culture, and many of its most cherished institutions.[34] Throughout the nineteenth century, Anglophobia lay at the heart of American patriotism; its persistence was demonstrated every Fourth of July and was revealed in virtually every school text in American history. This Anglophobia was reinforced by the fact that it was England with whom America was engaged in the most frequent and most dangerous diplomatic controversies. But there also was a strong strain of Anglophilia in nineteenth-century American culture, which was shared by those who recognized America's profound cultural debt to Britain and by trading and financial interests that had close economic ties with England.

Toward the end of the century, as a result of developments in both countries, relations between America and England began perceptibly to improve. Anglophilia in America was strengthened considerably as white Protestant Americans became increasingly fearful of the effects of the new immigration and as popularizers of Anglo-Saxonism played on the racial and cultural affinities of the English and American peoples.

When the United States joined the ranks of imperialist powers, with its own overseas possessions and expanding interests in Latin America and the Far East, Americans grew increasingly aware of the necessity to cement the relationship with Great Britain, potentially the country's most dangerous foe. Britain was interested in improved relations because of its own imperial problems, particularly the threat of an expanding Germany. The possibilities of mutual benefit were demonstrated when Britain's benevolent neutrality in the Spanish-American War forestalled intervention by hostile European powers and Secretary of State John Hay reciprocated during the Boer War by making sure that America would take no action that would hurt the British cause.[35]

Bradford Perkins concludes that, in spite of the persistence of antipathy to England in the American popular imagination, during the years 1895–1914 a "great rapprochement" had taken place between America and Britain. With most of the concessions being made by Britain in response to challenges it faced elsewhere and with the American political elite in advance of American public opinion, the slate of more than a century of antagonism and conflict was wiped clean after the Spanish-American War, and a new spirit of understanding and accommodation between the two countries came to prevail.[36] A recent study of the intellectual roots of this Anglo-American "alliance" demonstrates that the turn-of-the-century accord reflected more than the political, economic, and strategic considerations from which it originated. Concentrating on the ideas of Theodore Roosevelt and some of his English correspondents, David H. Burton portrays a shared conviction that, despite superficial differences between England and the United States, there were deep, underlying political and cultural similarities between the two countries. The accord, these Anglo-Saxonists believed, was a "natural" response to the threats of the alien culture and polity of the dynamic, new German Empire, the uncertain future direction of the Russian state, and the chaotic conditions in China. St. Loe Strachey spoke for Anglo-Saxonists in both countries when he said: "We speak the same language, recognize the same common law principles in our law and administration, and are inspired by the same political and moral ideals."[37]

American Anglo-Saxons were in a good position to combat continuing popular tendencies in their country to twist the lion's tail, for they were well represented in the sectors of society that influenced foreign policy opinions and decisions—in presidential administrations, in the army and navy, in the leadership of Congress, and among the intelligentsia.[38] Anglophilia flourished in America's pressrooms and publishing houses and on American campuses. Among professors the close intellectual tie with England exerted great sway, "stretching in memory," as Veysey observes, "all the way back to the first importation of 'liberal education' from Cambridge to Harvard in colonial times."[39] It was the persistence of the English gentlemanly social ideal among professors that ultimately intertwined with the newer impulse toward professionalization. Finally, the concept of "civilization," which was so important to American professors' interpretation of the war, meant to them the political, legal, economic, and cultural accomplishments of the English-speaking peoples and the prospective benefits to the rest of the world from the spread of their influence.

After the influences from Germany and England have been acknowledged, the fact remains that the character of American universities from the time of their origin has been unique and has stemmed from the special circumstances of the American environment. Compared to universities elsewhere in the Western world, American institutions of higher learning have been exceptionally responsive to conditions in the surrounding community. This is partly a result of the American departure from the pattern of national universities. The concomitant decentralization of decision making in American institutions of higher learning (that is, their freedom from central planning) and the extreme heterogeneity of their quality and character have made them responsive to social and economic forces in their local environments.[40] Furthermore, American universities, Allan Nevins points out, always have been peculiarly regional, in the sense of having "relevance to a special community." The idea that universities in America should have a regional function took root from the beginning, Nevins observes, as Harvard was planted for the special inspiration of Massachusetts Bay and William and Mary for the Old Dominion. The country was so large that as higher education spread westward it had to find a state or regional pattern. This pattern was most characteristic of state universities, but not confined to them alone.[41] Finally, American universities have been particularly responsive to outside influence because of their pattern of lay government and their dependence for funds on donors in the case of private institutions and on legislative bodies in the case of public institutions.

Because the emergence of the modern university in America was associated so closely with the needs of a democratic, industrializing society, it is not surprising that its function should be defined largely in terms of serving those needs. The singularity of American institutions of higher learning stems more from the ideal of service with which they are permeated than from any other factor in their history. Although there never has been agreement about goals within the academic community, the ideal of service was pervasive in educational circles at the time of the university revolution and afterwards; it continues to be a distinguishing feature of American higher education. Indeed, Veysey makes it clear that the initial impetus toward the modern university came from those—like Charles W. Eliot of Harvard and Andrew Dickson White of Cornell—who viewed its function as serving the surrounding community. The concept of service sprang in part from the recognition by administrators of their need for support from public and private sources, from prevailing theories about the nature and function of knowledge, and from moral idealism in the faculty.[42]

The service-oriented educators made the primary assumption "that the patterns of behavior which flourished outside the campus were more 'real' than those which most often prevailed within it." "Reality" increasingly was defined as "democratic" and given a vocational tinge, and the university was to mirror that democratic reality in several ways: by establishing all fields of learning on an equal basis; by treating all students as equals; by providing easy admission; by portraying itself as an agency for individual success; by emphasizing its function to widely diffuse knowledge throughout society; and by embracing the idea that it should take its orders directly from the citizenry.[43] The commitment to service was reflected in student bodies drawn not from an intellectual elite seeking initiation into the mysteries of pure science, arts, and letters, but from those among the general population interested in acquiring an increasingly functional degree; in curricula that were highly differentiated and offered a wide range of practical training (extending downward in the education hierarchy from training for the professions of medicine, law, and engineering to training in the "science" of business administration and the "economics" of homemaking); and in faculties whose members freely donated their talents as expert advisers to municipal, state, and federal agencies.

The articulation of interest between the university and society was both appreciated and promoted by the federal government. Beginning in 1862 with the passage of the first Morrill Act and continuing with the Hatch Act of 1887 and the second Morrill Act of 1890, the federal government pledged its support to the promotion of education in the useful—agricultural and mechanical—arts, for the common man. The first Morrill Act was designed to provide improved techniques and trained operatives for the industry and agriculture upon which the northern national economy rested.[44] Grants of land under the act went both to existing institutions (in Wisconsin, for example, the state university was the beneficiary) and to newly established agricultural and technical colleges, and it was these land-grant colleges and other state institutions that came particularly to stand for the "all-purpose" curriculum and for service to the community.[45] Clark Kerr describes the Morrill Act as "one of the most seminal pieces of legislation ever enacted" and states, "Nowhere before had universities been so closely linked with the daily life of so much of their societies."[46]

The "Wisconsin Idea" was one of the earliest, most fully developed, and best publicized expressions of the service ideal and has come to stand as its archetype.[47] To be sure, the Wisconsin Idea neither significantly affected state politics nor ensured harmonious relations between the university and the legislature, educational authorities, and other officials in the state.[48] But the wide-ranging extension program and the substantial faculty advisory service to the many branches of the state government testified to the university's highly developed commitment to an organic relationship between itself and its surrounding community. However, the service ideal should not be associated exclusively with land-grant and state institutions or with universities, like Wisconsin, that established carefully planned and executed programs to put the ideal into practice. Even private institutions and those that had a more traditional focus on undergraduate liberal education or research-oriented graduate work in the pure sciences and in arts and letters appeared before the public in a garb of social service. It was not uncommon to use the idea of "service," loosely defined, to legitimize the American university.[49]

Since the revolution in higher learning was a process and not an event, it is not possible to say precisely when it was completed. But we can safely say that by 1910 the period of greatest change in the world of higher learning had taken place. By then the period of new university building had passed its peak, as had the influence of the elective principle on the undergraduate curriculum, and a professional outlook had come to characterize the scholarly disciplines and the academic vocation. That a great transformation had been accomplished, however, is not to say that a uniform product had emerged capable of clear defini-

tion or characterized by inner harmony and tranquillity. The opposite, in fact, was true. The modern university in America did not have clear goals or a common sense of purpose; aspects of the university revolution stood in contradictory relationship to each other and resulted in dysfunctional tension and antagonism; and, although the professional disciplines and a professional consciousness had been born, they were in their infancy and their future direction was unclear.

To speak at all of "the college" or "the university" in America at the time of the great transformation and down to the present can be misleading. In a country so vast, where there came to be such a great emphasis on skill and where education became identified with success, there was room for an apparently unlimited number of higher educational institutions of very uneven character and quality. The world of higher education presented a varied face. In addition to the new and reformed private universities, the reformed liberal arts colleges, and the state institutions and their far-flung extension divisions, there were various vocational and technical schools, municipal colleges, separate schools for Negroes and for women, and the old-style denominational colleges, which, no longer in the mainstream, continued to exist. Higher educational institutions were, and remain, so heterogeneous in character and quality that a contemporary observer has concluded that "there is a college somewhere in America for everybody."[50] Too, the rate of development in the period of growth, particularly among the state institutions, was uneven, reflecting the uneven material and cultural progress of their states and the particular political and social circumstances in their environments.[51] Within this decentralized and continually expanding world of higher education, and particularly among the "successful" institutions, a state of keen competition came to prevail for financial support, students, faculty, and prestige.[52]

A salient fact emerges from the history of the university revolution: it failed to replace the unified pattern of the old-time college, which it shattered, with a clear pattern of its own. Veysey's work is a massive elaboration precisely of this point. It demonstrates the competing goals that characterized the early period of the university revolution, when the proponents of liberal culture, of research, and of utility struggled to stamp their vision on the face of the new institution. The debate over goals had quieted by about 1890, he concludes, but never was settled; rather than a clear sense of purpose, only "unacknowledged confusion," "hazy generalities," and an accommodation of conflicting purposes under the general rubric of social service had resulted. To this day the university remains in a state of "uneasy balance" from its embodiment of conflicting ideals: the German ideal of research and graduate and professional education; the English ideal of liberal culture and undergraduate education; and the American ideal of "lesser professional" (other than legal and medical) education and public service.[53] "The university is so many things to so many people," concludes Kerr, "that it must, of necessity, be partially at war with itself."[54]

Tensions that sprang from the internal development of the university as a social system were as significant as those that resulted from the lack of a unified sense of purpose within and between the institutions of higher learning. The chief tensions resulted from the bureaucratization of the university in the last decades of the nineteenth century. As the university grew in size and complexity, the old "familial" pattern of management was replaced by a bureaucratic structure embodied in an elaborate administrative hierarchy.[55] By the early 1900s the universities had come to look like business corporations, with their directors (trustees), executives (administrators), and employees (faculty).[56] Within this process of bureaucratization the changing role of the president had the most dramatic consequences. Although the president's legal rights had not expanded since 1870 (legally he still was the chief executive of the trustees), his stature had grown enormously with the expansion of the institutions and their administrative personnel. So, too, had the nature of the office changed, from the president being "first among equals," who shared with his faculty a religious purpose, a teaching function, a common intellectual background, and an intimacy of daily contact, to his becoming managerial overlord of a complex organization.[57]

The change in the presidential office destroyed the homogeneity of academic society by dividing it into two vocations—administration and teaching—with clearly demarcated spheres of influence. The faculty was given hegemony over the classroom, but vital policy decisions affecting the functioning and future development of the institution were the province of the administration, even though it might assign the faculty an advisory role in these areas. During the first decades of reform, the innovative presidents and the faculty often were allies against resistant conservative forces; but significant faculty resistance to presidential authority had developed by the early twentieth century, when a new generation of managerial consolidators occupied the presidential office.[58]

Tensions between the faculty and the president reflected more than

competition for power over decision making; they reflected the deep-lying and often subtle tensions that grew out of the peculiar position of the faculty member as both professional and employee. The concept of professionalism resists easy definition, but sociologists seem to agree that autonomy—control by professionals themselves of the development and application of their field of special competence—is its essential condition. Because authority in an organization is enforced through "superordinate control," tension inevitably arises when professional roles confront organizational necessities.[59] These confrontations occurred frequently in academia; not only were subtle forms of rendering the faculty subservient involved, but head-on collisions as well.[60] The dual professional-employee position of the faculty has implications beyond the confines of the institution of higher learning. When he discusses the relative social status of university professors and other professional men like physicians and lawyers, Shryock observes that the general prestige of professors is lowered by their "quasi-employee" status.[61]

The simultaneous emergence of the modern university and professionalization of scholarship and the academic vocation offers a clue to internal tensions in the system. In many respects the two revolutions, in university structure and professionalism, were complementary, even interdependent. The new disciplines and their practitioners needed the resources of the new universities to become established, gain recognition, and extend their influence. They were enormously strengthened by being recognized in the expanding curriculum, being given departmental status (with separate budgets and considerable control over standards and staffing), and having laboratory and library resources at their command. So, too, did the universities depend on the professionals for their advance. A faculty with a high professional reputation commanded students, financial support, and prestige for its institution. In another respect, however, the two revolutions were contradictory. For, as the university revolution climaxed in the triumph of administrative bureaucracy, with its descending lines of command, this bureaucracy conflicted with the increasing professional consciousness of the faculty. Indeed, the more accomplished and professionally distinguished the faculty, the more it would resist the enlarged powers of the president, insist on a voice in university management, and demand greater freedom. The tensions created by the dual professional-employee status of the faculty were an important factor in the academic freedom cases of the late nineteenth and early twentieth centuries.

It should not be concluded from the above observations that by the early twentieth century the academic vocation was characterized by a fully developed sense of group solidarity and professional élan or that there were no tensions and strains within the academic profession itself. The division of the vocation into ranks was one index of professionalism,[62] but the establishment of a rank hierarchy introduced considerable differences of status and outlook between individuals in the lower and higher positions. The individuals on the lower rung of the occupational ladder, instructors and assistant professors, were in a precarious occupational position characterized by uncertainty and insecurity.[63] Their number among the nation's professoriate had undergone a marked proportional increase between the late nineteenth and early twentieth centuries.[64] Their lot, according to a 1910 study of a selected group of assistant professors, was one of retarded advancement and exploitation, which benefited their seniors.[65] And it was the small core of senior professors who exercised whatever influence and power the faculty had.[66]

The history of the founding of their professional association itself reveals the problematic professional solidarity of university scholars, which persists to this day. Discussing the origins of the AAUP, Metzger points out that, although there was an enormous variety of proposals for the direction the new association should take, there was consensus about what the association should *not* do: deal with the question of salaries. "Collective bargaining was unthinkable," he says; "even a collective statement was presumed to suggest trade union tactics."[67] Although this response may, in part, suggest the presence of a professional self-image, the opposition to a united front on remuneration also suggests an absence of professional solidarity. Logan Wilson quotes a study that explains this opposition as a product of the preprofessional "tradition of dignity" inherited from the professor's previous ecclesiastical function, with its resulting notions that a gentleman does not bargain, that learning is its own reward, and that the life of a scholar necessarily is one of poverty and sacrifice. The study attributes the opposition further to a spirit of individualism among professors that indicates, it says, little conception of cooperative or unified welfare. This spirit was encouraged by rank cleavages, which produced a different occupational outlook between individuals in the lower and higher ranks, and by the departmental structure, which resulted in each department seeking to advance its own interests. That the AAUP operates under much heavier odds than the American Medical Association or the American Bar As-

sociation, Wilson observes, can be attributed to the absence of an over-riding commitment to broad, professional interests among university scholars. Typically, a scholar's primary professional interest is his own discipline.[68] The limited resources and facilities of the AAUP, Shryock concludes, reflect "the fact that the first interest of professors is usually in their special fields, while their concern for the academic profession as a whole is secondary. The academic guild is, in a sense, a collection of a score or more of distinct professions." He contrasts this situation with "the solidarity of medical men who are physicians first and specialists thereafter."[69]

The scholarly disciplines themselves were in an inchoate condition in the early years of the twentieth century. Only recently established on a scientific basis and in a rudimentary state, they were characterized not only by a lack of clear definition of the substance and nature of the disciplines, but also by a lack of certainty about their limits and the lines of demarcation between them. The problems of definition and demarcation were most apparent in the social sciences, the "new body of moral philosophy studies" as Dewey called them, that emerged out of the moral philosophy curriculum in the late nineteenth century. John Higham locates the origin of the ill-conceived, post–World War I "schism in American scholarship" between the humanities and the social sciences partly in the fluidity of categories in the subjects of the human studies and in the embryonic organization of scholarship during the early years of the century. The division between the modern humanists and social scientists, he argues, began in the effort of the new disciplines to define themselves as the classical curriculum broke down in the late nineteenth century. A student of the new science of sociology has described "the whole atmosphere of social science" between about 1885 and 1915 as "one of struggle for legitimacy against adversaries."[70]

In the attempts during the late nineteenth and early twentieth centuries to define and delimit the disciplines, historians found themselves in an ambiguous position: on the defensive against assaults on their legitimacy by the new social scientists and divided among themselves about the nature of their discipline and its proper relationship to the social sciences. Higham attributes considerable significance to the prewar quarrel among historians about the extent to which they should ally themselves with social scientists, seeing in the disagreement a premonition of the larger schism in American scholarship that would develop after the war.[71]

History in America became professionalized by differentiating itself from philosophy and literature and establishing itself on a scientific basis. The first generation of professional historians adopted not only the methods of science—empirical research, a critical approach to evidence, and inductive generalization—but its spirit as well: the repudiation of romantic idealism and its search for ultimate meaning. Misreading Leopold von Ranke, they drew a sharp distinction between the science and the philosophy of history, eschewed an interpretive approach and a search for laws to explain historical development, and confined themselves to a rigid factualism in an effort to recreate the past as it actually was.[72] Scientific history soon drew fire from the social sciences on the grounds that it was, in fact, highly unscientific, if not thoroughly meaningless. For example, at a session of the American Historical Association (AHA) annual meeting in 1903 devoted to the relation of history to the social sciences, Albion Small "contended that the historians ... spend all their time in indexing dreary, profitless details about inconsequential folk, in developing their technical skill for the discovery of insignificant objects, in learning so much about how to investigate that they have forgotten what is worth investigating." Continuing the assault, Lester Ward charged that history was not a science because it was not concerned with causation, only with facts. Delivering the coup de grâce, "he declared [history] to be an agreeable occupation and a pleasant pastime."[73]

Considering the severity of the attack, it is not difficult to understand the heated tone in which George Burton Adams defended orthodox scientific history in his presidential address to the AHA in 1908. Using the language of conflict, he characterized the approach to history of political scientists, geographers, economic determinists, sociologists, and social psychologists as "a hostile movement," an "aggressive and vigorous school of thought" that threatened to drive the traditional historian from the field. This "disturbance in our province," he declared, represented a passing from the age of investigation to the perilous age of speculation (from which, he might have added, the first generation of professional historians had labored so assiduously to emerge). "What should the historian do," Adams asked, "in view of the threatened invasion of his domain by ideals and methods not quite his own?" He answered, in essence, that the historian must stick to his task of scientifically gathering the facts because, in the final analysis, if ever a philosophy of history was to emerge it could do so only on a firm foundation of

fact. "At the beginning of all conquest of the unknown," he declared, "lies the fact. ... The field of the historian is, and must long remain, the discovery and recording of what actually happened."[74]

The assault on scientific history came not only from hostile outsiders; by the early twentieth century there was defection within the ranks, as historians themselves divided along the lines suggested by the social scientists. A comparison of the address of Adams with those of his fellow historians at the International Congress of Arts and Science in St. Louis in 1904 offers evidence of this division. The remarks of Woodrow Wilson, James Harvey Robinson, and Frederick Jackson Turner at the congress were collectively a plea for interpretive history, for a rejection of narrative political history in favor of the study of history as a never-ending process of social development, which could be understood only by studying all aspects of human life and relying on all the allied sciences of human behavior. In contrast, Adams' paper amounted to an argument that history is fixed, there to be discovered by the historian, who mines the facts and from them constructs a narrative good for all time.[75]

The sources of the challenge by historians to scientific history, dubbed "the new history" by Robinson in 1912, were varied. Nurtured in the Progressive era and reflecting its spirit of democratic reform, infused with a "softened," nonideological version of Marxism, which was apparent not only in its emphasis of economic factors but in its view of causation and law in history, the new history was responding also to the prospect of the desertion of history by the social scientists. In its main outlines the new history comprised a deliberate subordination of the past to the present by selecting and emphasizing those aspects of the past most relevant to present needs; a widening of the scope of history away from the institutional focus of scientific history to embrace all aspects of human affairs; and an enthusiastic alliance with the social sciences, with a view toward discovering laws of human development.[76] Particularly in their emphasis on the present, the new historians were expressing their conviction that the discipline derived its legitimacy from being a "useful" science. This conviction was expressed perfectly in a frequently quoted sentence from the introduction to James Harvey Robinson and Charles Beard's *The Development of Modern Europe.* Admitting that they "consistently subordinated the past to the present," the authors averred that it had been their "ever-conscious aim to enable the reader to catch up with his own times; to read intelligently the foreign news in the morning paper; to know what was the attitude of Leo XIII toward the Social Democrats even if he has forgotten that of Innocent III toward the Albigenses."[77] The new historians self-consciously emphasized the practical utility of their discipline; they "wanted history to prove itself."[78]

The orthodox and reform historians shared the field before World War I and frequently were united in "the common cause of superseding amateur scholarship." Furthermore, in many areas the reformers accepted the basic principles of orthodoxy.[79] Nevertheless, their attack on scientific history was sharp, even belligerent, and the discipline clearly was divided. In the emerging split between the humanities and the social sciences, history stood somewhere in the middle, unsure of its essential character. Paradoxically, those who opposed the "adulteration" of history with social science were speaking in the name of "scientific" history; those who argued in favor of an alliance with the social sciences were speaking of introducing meaning (*i.e.*, value) into history; all the while, the social sciences themselves deliberately were moving away from the realm of value into that of empiricism.

The issue of the relationship between fact and value was a large one in early twentieth-century American thought; in almost all its branches there was a quest for a means to unite science and ethics in the interest of social reform. To be sure, the "new" social theorists in economics, sociology, philosophy, political science, history, and jurisprudence sought first to divorce science from morality, to make science "objective," because the two united traditionally had been an instrument of conservatism. But their objective was to establish morality on a scientific foundation by making science the arbiter of ethical problems. As nonrevolutionary critics of "the glaring evils of capitalism," the "new" scholars sought to apply the scientific method to social problems and thus to formulate a science of reform.[80]

Similar concerns about the nature and function of knowledge were reflected in efforts to reestablish the unity of knowledge after the great fragmentation and specialization of the late nineteenth century. The urgency of the problem of unification was suggested by the attempts in nearly every field of thought to reconcile factual and normative knowledge and to consider the significance of rapidly accumulating "facts," their relationship to each other, and their place in the whole realm of knowledge and experience. The 1904 International Congress of Arts and Science, which brought together leading scholars in all fields of thought to consider the problem, approached it from an idealist perspective: reconciliation was to be accomplished by recognizing the "inner unity" of all branches of learning and acknowledging the human intellect and "psychical" causes as the chief social determinants.[81]

Theorists who rejected the idealist view were equally committed to the quest for unity, as Jean Quandt's study, *From the Small Town to the Great Community*, makes clear. Quandt demonstrates the dedication of Progressive intellectuals to offset the individual isolation and fragmentation of life in urban, industrial America and to restore a sense of community, purpose, and shared value; she points out that they saw in the restoration of the unity of knowledge a means to this end. Their commitment to the new scholarship was not a random pursuit of truth for its own sake; they firmly believed that free inquiry would reveal the essential unity of knowledge and the oneness of man, nature, and society. Using Dewey as a prime example of this point of view, Quandt shows how he opposed the split between the cultural and the useful and the overspecialization of knowledge. Knowledge was power, according to Dewey; therefore its expansion certainly was not to be halted. But it was to be tied to action and available for use, rather than compartmentalized and separated from the totality of experience.[82] The "new" theorists became the ideologists of Progressivism; they provided the intellectual foundation for attacks on laissez-faire capitalism and contributed to the prevailing faith in knowledge as an instrument of social change.[83] As individuals, they participated in reform movements of all sorts, exulting in action to such an extent that "active participation in politics, economics, and social reform became a professorial hallmark."[84]

According to Hofstadter, the Progressive era was a high-water mark of rapprochement between the intellectual and American society. The new complexity of government and administration that was a consequence of the need to control the economy, he argues, resulted in a widely acknowledged dependence on expertise. The interests of democracy itself led to an abatement of the suspicion of the expert that had originated in the democratic ethos of Jacksonian America. In the Progressive era, Hofstadter affirms, "partly as expert, partly as social critic, the intellectual now came back to a central position such as he had not held in American politics for a century." The ferment in ideas, although it did not bring a social revolution, created a widespread confidence among intellectuals that the gulf between the world of thought and the world of action finally had been bridged, affecting the morale even of

World War. There is every indication that they were well aware of the correlation between their "usefulness" and their legitimacy in the eyes of American society.

In this respect and in many others, the response of American professors to the challenge of World War I provides a valuable test case for the subjects covered in this chapter and can be understood only in reference to them. When the war came upon America, the modern university in this country only recently had been established and lacked a clear identity and sense of purpose. It drew heavily on English and particularly on German influences but derived its special character and claim to legitimacy from a commitment to the ideal of service. Within the university the position of the faculty was insecure; its dual professional-employee status created tensions that could and did lead to confrontations and conflict. The scholarly disciplines themselves were in a rudimentary state and were seeking to define their character and limits. Professional consciousness too was rudimentary; the AAUP had just been founded in 1915 and commanded neither widespread support in the profession nor influence in the infrastructure of university politics. The social status of the newly professionalized professoriate was uncertain, reflecting the ambivalence of American society to the life of the mind. The challenge of war both exposed and sharpened many of the tensions, contradictions, and uncertainties in the academic community. Furthermore, it confronted professors with a challenge to their loyalties. They found that loyalties that could be maintained simultaneously during normal times—to one's country, institution, professional standards and ideals, to the cause of peace, and to friends and colleagues—suddenly came into conflict in the crucible of war, and choices were forced on the basis of priorities that were not necessarily acknowledged or even recognized. The challenge of war brought into sharp focus questions concerning the uses of knowledge and the uses of the university in modern America.

1. The indispensable source for the subject is Laurence R. Veysey, *The Emergence of the American University* (Chicago, 1965). See also Richard Hofstadter, "The Revolution in Higher Education," in Arthur M. Schlesinger, Jr., and Morton White (eds.), *Paths of American Thought* (Boston, 1963), 269–90; Frederick Rudolph, *The American College and University: A History* (New York, 1962); John S. Brubacher and Willis Rudy, *Higher Education in Transition: A History of American Colleges and Universities, 1636–1968* (New York, 1958); George W. Pierson, "American Universities in the Nineteenth Century: The Formative Period," in Margaret Clapp (ed.), *The Modern University* (Ithaca, 1950), 59–94; and Richard J. Storr, *The Beginnings of Graduate Edu-*

those scholars whose work was far removed from the bustle of everyday life. Hofstadter concludes that "the most abstracted of scholars could derive a sense of importance from belonging to a learned community which the larger world was compelled to consult in its quest for adequate means of social control."[85] Higham, noting the relative decline in status of humanistic scholars during the early years of the twentieth century, considers Hofstadter's characterization "too simple [a] picture." Although the new type of professor, the practical man, the expert, was winning public approval, he argues, "the humanistic scholar more often felt elbowed aside" and by the time of World War I was being dramatized as a self-denigrator in the new academic novels and had become the prime butt of popular jokes about absentmindedness.[86]

The differences between Hofstadter and Higham suggest some of the difficulties in dealing with the subject of the academic intellectual's status in American society. In their social origins, the World War I generation of professors still represented a fairly homogeneous group. Existing evidence suggests that the chief breeding ground for the first and second generations of professional university scholars (those reaching maturity between the 1870s and the First World War), as for their professional predecessors, still was the New England Protestant middle class.[87] But there was no single professorial "class" in America, no cultural elite with recognized social status and authority, no equivalent of the German "mandarinate."[88] Writing in 1906, William Graham Sumner pointed to the ambivalence of American attitudes toward intellect. On the one hand, he noted, Americans laud education and the multiplication of educational institutions; on the other hand they reserve their admiration for the "common man," with his supposedly superior store of native wisdom.[89] Merle Curti has dubbed this simultaneous faith in the rational and suspicion of the life of reason, which he sees continuing to our own time, an "American paradox."[90] Without probing the question of the sources of the paradox, a clue to the status of professors during the time of this study—the period of America's involvement in the First World War—may be found in Shryock's observation that the prestige of professors has risen during periods of involvement by them in the affairs of the "real" world. If professorial prestige periodically has risen, he argues, it is "not because Americans have ceased to prize action above thought, but rather that more academicians have qualified for recognition by becoming men of action."[91] Academicians in large numbers became "men of action" during United States involvement in the First

cation in America (Chicago, 1953). The following account is based largely on these sources; citations will be given only in the case of quotations or if otherwise indicated.

2. Pierson, "American Universities in the Nineteenth Century," 62–63.

3. Richard Shryock, "The Academic Profession in the United States," American Association of University Professors Bulletin, XXXVIII (Spring, 1952), 38.

4. See Veysey, American University, 55, and Arthur E. Bestor, Jr., "The Transformation of American Scholarship, 1875–1917," Library Quarterly, XXIII (1953), 164–79.

5. See Edward Lurie, "Science in American Thought," Journal of World History, VIII (1964–65), 638–65, and "An Interpretation of Science in the Nineteenth Century," Journal of World History, VIII (1964–65), 681–705; Dorothy Ross, G. Stanley Hall: The Psychologist as Prophet (Chicago, 1972); Geraldine Joncich, The Sane Positivist: A Biography of Edward L. Thorndike (Middletown, Conn., 1968); Jurgen Herbst, The German Historical School in American Scholarship: A Study in the Transfer of Culture (Ithaca, 1965); John Higham et al., History (Englewood Cliffs, 1965); and Merle Curti (ed.), American Scholarship in the Twentieth Century (Cambridge, Mass., 1953).

6. For the pre-Civil War learned societies see Merle Curti, The Growth of American Thought (New York, 1943), 570–71; for the guildlike character of the professional associations see Herbst, German Historical School, 40.

7. For the emergence of the academic profession see Walter P. Metzger, "Expansion and Profession" (Paper delivered before the Committee on the Role of Education in American History, Symposium on the Role of Education in Nineteenth-Century America, Chatham, Mass., June, 1964).

8. See Robert P. Ludlom, "Academic Freedom and Tenure: A History," Antioch Review, X (March, 1950), 18–19.

9. John H. Wigmore, "Presidential Address," American Association of University Professors Bulletin, II (March, 1916), 8–9.

10. See Herbst, German Historical School; Charles F. Thwing, The American and the German University: One Hundred Years of History (New York, 1928); and Walter P. Metzger, "The German Contribution to the American Theory of Academic Freedom," American Association of University Professors Bulletin, XLI (Summer, 1955), 214–30.

11. See Herbst, German Historical School, and Ernest Becker, The Lost Science of Man (New York, 1971).

12. Joseph Ben-David and Awraham Zloczower, "Universities and Academic Systems in Modern Societies," European Journal of Sociology, III (1962), 47. The authors argue that the unique success of the German university sprang less from the "idea of the university" in Germany than from circumstances that historically had shaped it, particularly the decentralization of the higher educational system.

13. See Herbst, German Historical School, Chap. 1.

14. Veysey, American University, 196.

15. See George H. Haines IV, Essays on German Influence Upon English Education and Science, 1850–1919 (Hamden, Conn., 1969).

16. Josiah Royce, "Present Ideals of American University life," Scribner's, X (1891), 383.

17. John M. Coulter, "The Contribution of Germany to Higher Education," Chicago University Record, VIII (March, 1904), 348.

18. Ibid., 354.

19. Hugo Kirbach to "Dear Sir," January, 1915, in Richard T. Ely Papers, State Historical Society of Wisconsin.

20. Rudolf Eucken and Ernst Haeckel to the universities of America, August 31, 1914, sent with O. J. Merkel to A. Lawrence Lowell, December 26, 1914, both in A. Lawrence Lowell Papers, Harvard University Archives.

21. Metzger, "German Contribution to Academic Freedom," 227.

22. Veysey, American University, 128.

23. Herbst, German Historical School, Chap. 5. He concludes that the failure was a direct consequence of the Americans' misunderstanding of Ideengeschichte. Had they correctly read Wilhelm von Humboldt and Leopold von Ranke, he maintains, "they would have realized that not only the facts but the ideas of American history had to come from American sources." (p. 128).

24. Ibid., 126.

25. Ibid., Chap. 6.

26. Joseph Dorfman, "The Role of the German Historical School in American Economic Thought," American Economic Review: Papers and Proceedings, XLV (May, 1955), 17–28.

27. See Metzger, "German Contribution to Academic Freedom," 220. For an interesting development of the observation that academic freedom always was severely limited in Germany, see Ben-David and Zloczower, "Universities and Academic Systems," 56–61.

28. See "Report of the Committee on Academic Freedom and Academic Tenure," American Association of University Professors Bulletin, I (December, 1915), 20–43. Metzger's "German Contribution to Academic Freedom" provides a detailed exposition of the reasons for the modifications of the German model in America.

29. See Melvin Small, "The American Image of Germany, 1906–1914" (Ph.D. dissertation, University of Michigan, 1965), 118.

30. Veysey, American University, 131.

31. For a description of English higher education in the nineteenth and twentieth centuries see Charles C. Gillispie, "English Ideas of the University in the Nineteenth Century," in Clapp (ed.), The Modern University, 27–55, and Albert H. Halsey, "British Universities," European Journal of Sociology, III (1962), 85–101.

32. See Veysey, American University, 196–97n.

33. Hofstadter, "The Revolution in Higher Education," 565n.

34. Cushing Strout, The American Image of the Old World (New York, 1963), 134.

35. See ibid., Chap. 8, and Harry C. Allen, Conflict and Concord: The Anglo-American Relationship Since 1783 (New York, 1959), 221–24.

36. Bradford Perkins, The Great Rapprochement: England and the United States, 1895–1914 (New York, 1968).

37. See David H. Burton, "Theodore Roosevelt and His English Correspondents: The Intellectual Roots of the Anglo-American Alliance," Mid-America, LIII (January, 1971), 12–34.

38. See Small, "American Image of Germany."

39. Veysey, American University, 196.

40. See Martin Trow, "The Democratization of Higher Education in America," European Journal of Sociology, III (1962), 232–34.

41. Allan Nevins, The State Universities and Democracy (Urbana, 1962), 18, 19.

42. See Veysey, American University, Chap. 2. Although Veysey prefers the term "utility" to "service," I choose to retain the latter because it was the term used by the professors with whom I deal. The very ambiguities in the concept of "service" are a clue to understanding the role of the academic community during the war.

43. Ibid., 61–64.

44. See Curti, "The American Scholar in Three Wars," 260.

45. See Brubacher and Rudy, Higher Education in Transition, 158.

46. Clark Kerr, The Uses of the University (Cambridge, Mass., 1963), 46–47.

47. For a detailed description of the Wisconsin Idea by one of the participants

72. Higham et al., *History*, 92–103.

73. "What Is History?" *American Historical Review*, IX (1904), 449, 450.

74. George Burton Adams, "History and the Philosophy of History," *American Historical Review*, XIV (January, 1909), 224, 227, 229, 235, 236.

75. Cf. Woodrow Wilson, "The Variety and Unity of History," James Harvey Robinson, "The Conception and Methods of History," and George Burton Adams, "Problems in American History," and Frederick Jackson Turner, "The Present Problems of Medieval History," all in Howard J. Rogers (ed.), *Congress of Arts and Science, Universal Exposition, St. Louis, 1904* (Boston and New York, 1905 1907), II, 3–20, 40–51, 183–94, 125–38.

76. Higham et al., *History*, 104–16, 171–82.

77. James Harvey Robinson and Charles Beard, *The Development of Modern Europe* (New York, 1907–1908), I, iii.

78. Higham et al., *History*, 112.

79. *Ibid.*, 183, 104, 114–15.

80. Morton G. White, *Social Thought in America: The Revolt Against Formalism* (New York, 1949), 28–29, 46. In *The Lost Science of Man*, Becker locates the central problem of the emergent discipline of sociology in efforts to make the "indignant ethical man" compatible with the "detached scientist" and thus to end the glaring disproportion between science and ethics. See pp. 20, 22,

81. George H. Haines IV and Frederick H. Jackson, "A Neglected Landmark in the History of Ideas," *Mississippi Valley Historical Review*, XXXIV (September, 1947), 201–20. The authors point out that, in fact, the contributors to the congress delved into their own fields of specialization, giving lip service only to the grand theme of unity.

82. Jean B. Quandt, *From the Small Town to the Great Community: The Social Thought of Progressive Intellectuals* (New Brunswick, 1970), especially Chap. 8. The book includes an intellectual who did not reject the idealist view; Josiah Royce plays a large part in the study.

83. Sidney Fine, *Laissez-Faire and the General Welfare State* (Ann Arbor, 1956), 169–288, and White, *Social Thought in America*.

84. Herbst, *German Historical School*, 162.

85. Richard Hofstadter, *Anti-Intellectualism in American Life* (New York, 1963), 198, 205.

86. Higham et al., *History*, 65n, 65. Higham attributes this status decline in large part to social and professional changes attendant on the breakup of the aristocracy of culture.

87. Metzger, "Expansion and Profession," 54n.

88. See Veysey, *American University*, 301, and Shryock, "Academic Profession," 33. A penetrating portrait of the "mandarinate" in Germany may be found in Fritz K. Ringer, *The Decline of the German Mandarins: The German Academic Community, 1890–1933* (Cambridge, Mass., 1969).

89. Curti, *American Paradox*. The theme is treated in greater depth in his essay "Intellectuals and Other People."

90. William Graham Sumner, *Folkways* (Boston, 1906), 205–206.

91. Shryock, "Academic Profession," 53.

in its development, see Charles R. McCarthy, *The Wisconsin idea* (New York, 1912).

48. See Merle Curti and Vernon L. Carstensen, *The University of Wisconsin* (Madison, 1949), II, 99–104. See also Veysey, *American University*, 108.

49. See, for example, Woodrow Wilson, "Princeton in the Nation's Service," *Forum*, XXII (December, 1896), 450–66, and "Public Service of University Offices," *Columbia University Quarterly*, XVI (March, 1914), 169–82.

50. Trow, "Democratization of Higher Education," 234.

51. See Nevins, *The State Universities and Democracy*, 78–79.

52. See Veysey, *American University*, 317–32.

53. See Kerr, *The Uses of the University*, 17–18, and Trow, "Democratization of Higher Education," 234.

54. Kerr, *The Uses of the University*, 8–9.

55. For a description of the rise of administration, see Veysey, *American University*, 305–17; Metzger, "Expansion and Profession," 27–31; and Shryock, "Academic Profession," 43–50.

56. Shryock, "Academic Profession," 45. Thorstein Veblen's *The Higher Learning in America* (New York, 1957) is the classic contemporary discussion of this development.

57. Metzger, "Expansion and Profession," 27.

58. *Ibid*, 29–30.

59. Bernard Barber, "Some Problems in the Sociology of the Professions," *Daedalus*, XCII (Fall, 1963), 679. That the academic profession possesses the common attributes of the major professions is demonstrated in Logan Wilson, *The Academic Man: A Study in the Sociology of a Profession* (London, 1942), 114.

60. For an excellent treatment of the theme of subserviency and dependency see James McKeen Cattell, "Academic Slavery," *School and Society*, VI (October, 13, 1917), 421–26.

61. Shryock, "Academic Profession," 54.

62. Metzger, "Expansion and Profession," 52n.

63. For a description of the occupational implications and psychological consequences of rank divisions see Wilson, *The Academic Man*, 60–70.

64. Metzger, "Expansion and Profession," 17.

65. Guido Marx, "The Problem of the Assistant Professor," *Association of American Universities Journal of Proceedings and Addresses*, XI (1910), 18–32.

66. Veysey, *American University*, 304.

67. Metzger, "Expansion and Profession," 19.

68. Wilson, *The Academic Man*, 140, 132–33.

69. Shryock, "Academic Profession," 68. It remains to be seen whether the present financial crisis in the colleges and universities and the tensions it spawns will be sufficiently threatening for professors to overcome their resistance to professional solidarity.

70. John Higham, "The Schism in American Scholarship," *American Historical Review*, LXXII (October, 1966), 1–21, and Becker, *The Lost Science of Man*, 9n.

71. Higham, "The Schism in American Scholarship," 13.

The People's College, the Mechanics Mutual Protection and the Agricultural College Act

Daniel W. Lang

ON SEPTEMBER 2, 1858 fifteen thousand persons converged on a small village in central New York to celebrate the laying of the cornerstone of a new college. In the ceremonies at the building site the college's president, Amos Brown, explained the new institution's name.

> We call the institution The People's College, intending . . . the name shall indicate something of its purpose; and the word People's has undoubtedly a particular significance as used in this connection . . . it is meant to suggest . . . that some modification of the prevailing systems of college education in this country is demanded to enable them better to subserve the wants of the people. (1)

The "modifications" of which President Brown spoke were significant. Some, at the time, were unusual and, even, unique. The People's College's first objective was to provide an education that would prepare a student to enter a mechanical trade or to take up scientific farming immediately after graduation. In addition to offering courses in agricultural and mechanical subjects the College would operate model machine shops and a farm, in which students would work as a regular part of the courses of instruction. The College would be fully coeducational; women would not only be admitted to the College, but they would enroll in agricultural and mechanical courses with men and would be awarded the same degree. The College would be open not only to the sons and daughters of farmers and mechanics, but also to farmers and mechanics themselves. Adults would be invited to attend lectures and could defray the costs of their attendance by working on the farm or in the shops with students to whom they would impart their own first-hand knowledge of farming or a trade. By their labour in the shops or on the farm, students would be enabled by the time of graduation to accumulate enough capital to establish themselves in farming or a trade. To graduate a student would have to demonstrate practical and theoretical competence in agriculture or a specific trade; the College's diploma would expressly specify the trade that the student had mastered.

The aims of The People's College set it distinctly apart from other colleges. So did its origins. The tap root of The People's College went to organized labour. The College openly disavowed religious affiliations and for a time abjured support from government. The plan for the College called for support from farmers and mechanics alone. At the outset of the movement to found the College large benefactions actually were discouraged.

Although The People's College had a short life and did not realize all of the goals that had been promised by its founders, it was a significant experiment in higher education. The People's College was a model for other colleges, particularly those founded under the auspices of the Agricultural College Act of 1862. Some historians have described the College as the prototype of the land grant colleges, which greatly influenced American higher education. (2) Even those historians who cite other institutions on which the land grant college idea might have been modelled regard The People's College as the most influential of early experiments in mechanical and agricultural education. (3) Prior to 1862 the College was the only institution seriously devoted to mechanical education. The College was significant also because of its close association with the Agricultural College Act. Amos Brown was the primary lobbyist for the Act, and the College's prospectus was widely distributed to the Congress to promote the Act.

Despite the significance of The People's College little historical attention has been paid to it and what attention there has been is incomplete.

The Mechanics Mutual Protection and the Origins of The People's College

When The People's College was chartered in 1853 interest in higher education for farmers was not new, but for mechanics it was. Agricultural societies and journals had been promoting agricultural education since the beginning of the century and the idea of a college for farmers can be found as early as 1819.

The pattern by which the movement for mechanical education evolved was unlike that for agricultural education. Although both movements comprised similar elements, like societies, journals, and fairs, the movement to found colleges for farmers was more coalescent and homogeneous. While there was no firm curricular definition of agricultural education, there was a general understanding about what it entailed. This was not so for mechanical education, which at times was understood to mean anything from educating architects and civil engineers to training machine operators and skilled tradesmen. Sometimes the mechanic arts were combined with agriculture and taken to mean the manufacture and operation of farm machinery, as was the case at the Gardiner Lyceum, which is often identified as the first agricultural school in the United States. Even Justin Morrill and Jonathan Baldwin Turner used the term "mechanic" or "industrial" arts without precision, and their plans for higher education were seen as being designed to serve the farmer almost exclusively. Morrill's bill was named the Agricultural College Act, and, after it was passed, the states were uncertain about what the bill intended for higher education in the mechanic arts. Morrill himself was uncertain. (4)

However mechanical education was defined, the movement to found a college for mechanics was woven from three threads: scientific societies, mechanics' institutes, and organized labour.

By the second decade of the nineteenth century, seven scientific societies had been founded in the United States; in almost every case, each society had a direct counterpart in Europe. The scientific societies existed to advance knowledge and thereby to educate, but they had little interest in applying knowledge to the everyday work of the artisan or in elevating his status. Memberships of scientific societies rarely included wage earners from the working classes. The role of scientific societies in the movement for mechanical education was to challenge the intellectual climate and curriculum of the American classical college; the societies did not create pressures for wider access to higher education or for practical education to serve the needs of the wage-earning mechanic.

Instead, some of these pressures came from an institution known as the mechanics' institute. The origin of the mechanics' institutes is uncertain. Generally they are thought to have originated in England or Scotland late in the eighteenth century, but they may have been American in origin. (5) However they originated, the mechanics' institutes (and they were not all so called) were introduced to serve the skilled artisan more than the theoretician. By 1820 mechanics' institutes were organized in most cities and industrial towns. Supported by benefaction and membership fees, most institutes had libraries, reading rooms, and lecture series; some had well organized schools (usually in the evening), trade fairs and journals. But the mechanics' institutes did not serve the majority of artisians. The institutes' educational programs presupposed a sound, basic education; most wage-earning mechanics did not have even that. To the average mechanic the institutes were expensive: relatively high fees were charged for membership, schools, lectures, and libraries. Some institutes openly expressed concern about their inability to appeal to the wage-earning artisan. (6)

Whether or not the mechanics' institutes served mechanics widely or well, they did more than the existing educational institutions. Moreover, the institutes championed the proposition that mechanics needed a particular type of education and thereby made mechanical education a respectable concept.

The mechanics' institutes succeeded in identifying the mechanic and his status. Mechanic or artisan or skilled tradesman or millwright, the mechanic to the institutes was a person who manufactured or operated machinery; he used his hands in developed skills and processes. The term "mechanical engineer" was not in common use until the later half of the nineteenth century and even then was not applied to wage-earning artisans engaged in manual labour. Civil engineers, who as early as 1839 sought to organize themselves as a profession, identified themselves as gentlemen and designers; they were not, they insisted mechanics. (7) To trace the development of engineering education, then, would not lead to The People's College or to any other form of education in the mechanic arts; it would lead to the United States Military Academy, Norwich University, or Rensselaer Polytechnic Institute which, although in curricular sense more practical than the classical colleges, were not institutions for the mechanic.

The third and most influential thread of the movement for mechanical education was organized labour. While scientific societies served the more affluent mechanic and merchant, early labour organizations unquestionably served the interests of the wage-earning artisan, mechanic, and tradesman. At its inception in the late 1820's organized labour was not interested in education. In the 1830's some labour groups took strong political positions in favour of educational reform in the common schools, but there still was no interest in higher education or in mechanical education as such.

In the unpropitious times that followed the Panic of 1837 and, incidentally, as manufacturing processes became more specialized and industrial technology advanced, the educational attitudes of labour organizations that represented mechanics and skilled tradesmen began to change. Some of these organizations and the mechanics' newspapers that they sponsored took strong positions in favour of education designed specifically and exclusively to serve the needs of the mechanic. It was from one of these early labour organizations that the idea of The People's College emerged.

The Mechanics Mutual Protection was founded in Buffalo in 1843 at a convention that was held to unify mechanics in opposition to the State of New York's practice of selling the labour of convicts in its prisons. The regular sale of prison labour began in New York in 1819. By 1833 it posed such a competitive threat to mechanics that they began organized efforts to abolish or revise the prison labour system. The importance of the Mechanics' Mutual Protection's opposition to the prison labour system is that it is a major discriminant in defining the membership of the association and its interest in education.

As industry was reorganized on a more complex scale — particularly in terms of divisions of labour and subcontracting — in the mid-1830's some prosperous master mechanics expanded their production capacity by performing only highly skilled operations themselves and then letting out the remaining work to less skilled and sometimes unskilled workers. Thus some master mechanics became capitalistic middlemen who operated on a large enough scale to stockpile raw materials, invest in labour-saving machinery and employ other mechanics.

This reorganization of industry had three effects important to defining and explaining the Mechanics' Mutual Protection and its plans for The People's College. By letting out or otherwise dividing production processes individual trades were split up and their identities eroded. In responding to the threat of erosion The Mechanics' Mutual Protection was neither a trade union nor a confederation of trade unions, as were most other labour organizations before the Civil War, but was without any sub-structure based on specific crafts or trades. The Protection comprised skilled workingmen whose trades were threatened by industrial upheaval, a condition that cut across trades.

The breaking up of trades also changed the status of apprenticeship. In trades that were subdivided an apprentice no longer needed to learn the entirety of the trade; instead, he learned only parts of it. Learning part of a trade took less time than learning all of one. Consequently apprentices often broke their indentures, which had become impractically long in terms of the amount of training they either needed or received.

The third effect of the changes that occurred in the way in which industry was organized was the distinction that they made between mechanics. More affluent mechanics often were employers of convict labour. Therefore, an association formed initially to oppose the prison labour system could not have been intended to comprise the person who, although trained and skilled as a mechanic, was a beneficiary of that system. Members of the Mechanics' Mutual Protection, then, were mechanics who were neither prosperous enough nor large enough to take advantage of the prison labour system.

The Mechanics' Mutual Protection thus comprised mechanics and artisans whose livelihoods and vocations were threatened by industrial progress. Changes in apprenticeship undercut the concept of specialized training, whether provided through formal instruction or on the job, for mechanical trades, thus producing within the Protection a particular concern for vocational education. The competitive threat from convict labour marked the Protection as an organization committed to representing the interests of the less affluent mechanic who was directly involved in the production process from procurement of raw material to the sale of finished product. These are significant characteristics, for they identify the Mechanics' Mutual Protection as a conservative, rather than progressive, association.

In some ways the Protection was like a guild. Membership was strictly controlled. Only mechanics were allowed to join and members were identified by their trades. Members of commerical trades, for example, storekeepers, innkeepers and peddlers, were not admitted to the Protection nor were unskilled labourers. Meetings of the Protection were closed and their records kept secret. Unlike other labour organizations, the Protection advocated neither radical, social or economic reform nor the use of the strike to achieve reform. But the Protection acknowledged the existence of class differences and understood them to be based on wealth. The Mechanics' Mutual Protection actively campaigned for shorter working hours, land reform (particularly the Homestead Exemption Law), and a reformed lien law in addition to their special concern for abolishment of the prison labour system. At its zenith between 1847 and 1854 the Protection had about 250 chapters and 10,000 members. In 1848 the Protection took up a new cause, higher education for mechanics.

The primary promoter of the cause was Harrison Howard, a member of Mechanics' Mutual Protection Number Six in Lockport, New York. Howard was a self-employed cabinet and carriage maker with a keen interest in most of the reform ideas associated with the labour movement. Although Howard sometimes was apologetic for his own lack of formal education, he read avidly about educational ideas and plans which were reported by mechanics' newspapers and journals and frequently submitted letters stating his own opinions to the editors.

When Harrison Howard first conceived the idea for a mechanics' college, he was reluctant to discuss it widely because he feared that it might not be supported. Howard and many members of the Mechanics' Mutual Protection were realistic in recognizing that classical colleges were not entirely unpopular among mechanics. While some mechanics were disdainful and skeptical about traditional educational forms, others had some confidence in the moral benefits of the classical collegiate course and its efficacy in advancing social respectability. The ambivalence of mechanics towards higher education recurred throughout the movement to found The People's College.

Throughout 1848 Howard met with three of his friends—James Murphy, Daniel H. Burtiss, and Relay Butrick—to prepare a plan for announcement to the Protection. Like Howard, these men were artisans: Burtiss was a tinsmith; Murphy, a cabinet-maker; and Butrick, a machinist. Although the movement to found the College would later embrace reformers from all classes, at the beginning the idea was developed by mechanics alone.

Howard's friends urged him to address the Protection and introduce a plan for what they called "a school of technology." Howard made the address in December 1849. It was received well enough that Lockport Protections (individual chapters of The Mechanics' Mutual Protection were called Protections) Numbers One and Six struck a special committee which on February 26, 1850 recommended that a circular calling for the establishment of a college be drafted and sent to all Protections. The circular, written by Howard, with a drafting committee comprising Murphy, Butrick, and three other members of the Protection, was published in April, 1850.

Although most of the plan was rhetorical and idealistic, it did contain several specific proposals and definitions. The proposed college would be "peculiarly his [the mechanic's] own, controlled by mechanics and used expressly for the benefit of mechanics." The plans called for a large steam engine to be installed in the college building, both for instructional purposes and to provide power to operate the college's machine shops. The workshops were to be located in the middle stories of the building, with raw materials and manufactured wares being stored on the stories below "where they might be exposed for sale, as the sale of manufactured goods would be an important lesson for those who intended to make a mechanical profession the business of life." That students would be trained in the procurement of raw materials and in the sale of finished goods as well as in their manufacture is further evidence that the college and the Protection were designed to serve, not the middleman, but the skilled artisan who undertook manufacturing processes from start to finish.

One provision of the plan was that all students would work in the shops for a regulated number of hours each day. By 1850 the concept of the manual labour school was not a novelty. The manual labour idea, based on Philip Emanual Von Fellenberg's model schools in Switzerland, was introduced to the United States in the 1820's and in 1831 the Association of the Fellenberg System of Education had been formed. Following the ideas of Heinrich Pestalozzi, the Fellenberg schools emphasized agricultural training for moral development through manual labour. By 1850 after many experiments in colleges the manual labour school was commonly regarded as a proven failure. Although not unconcerned about the moral virtues of manual toil, the proponents of The People's College adapted the manual labour idea in two important ways. Through work in the shops students could meet the cost of their education and accumulate enough capital to set themselves up in a trade. More significant was the idea that work in the shops would be an integral part of a course of instruction in the mechanic arts. The design of the College's building is clear evidence of the seriousness of this intention.

The rest of the college's curriculum was not described in detail, but its practical orientation was apparent. The plan called for courses in chemistry, geology, mineralogy, geometry, natural philosophy, and "all sciences useful to the mechanic." The plan was expressly not intended to duplicate the curriculum of either the high school, academy, or the elementary school. Although in his address to the Protection Howard had said that the college would also offer courses normally associated with the classical collegiate curriculum, the Mechanics' Mutual Protection held classical colleges in low regard and the drafting committee decided to omit all references to other colleges.

According to the Protection's plan students were to reside in the college building. While attention was to be paid to moral development, the college would be strictly non-sectarian.

Although in the margin of the draft of his address to the Protection, Howard had noted that the college would "cost a million, but I dare not say so now," the plan estimated that the cost of establishing the college to be $100,000 and proposed that the cost be met by a contribution of one dollar from every mechanic in the state (at the time, there were about 125,000 mechanics in New York). That the college would be controlled by mechanics was a point strongly made in urging mechanics to contribute to its establishment. The drafting committee considered asking the state to assign some of the income from prison labour contracts to the college but decided finally to abjure all support from the public treasury.

The committee did not underestimate the difficulty of depending solely on contributions to establish the college. "We are aware", the committee admitted, "that to raise one hundred thousand dollars in the State of New York would require some time, much hard labour, and great perseverance." This was a sober confession amid much hortatory bravado. Although the general response to his addresses had been more encouraging than discouraging, Howard had been told frankly by some persons that he "had embarked in a good cause, but ... would never see fifty thousand raised for such an Institution." Recognizing the magnitude of the fund-raising task, the committee concluded the plan by offering the mechanic two reasons why he should support the college financially. The first was not especially sanguine: ". . . mechanics cannot make their conditions worse by trying the experiment."

The second reason was more optimistic than the first and did clarify in one respect the purpose of the college. The reason was essentially the "knowledge is power" theme, which hardly could have been unfamiliar to mechanics, since mechanics' institutes and newspapers had been promoting it for several years. What is important to note is that, as the theme was applied in the plan, the benefit of knowledge as embodied by the college was that it would enable the mechanic to become a better mechanic, and his offspring to be better mechanics than he. There was no claim or implication that the sort of education provided by the college would enable the mechanic or his children to advance to other more highly regarded professions.

The plan was definitive in proposing the steps to be taken in order to establish the college. The first of these was to "form an association to be called a Mechanical Society." Although the Mechanics' Mutual Protection would bring this society into being, membership in the society was to comprise "all respectable persons who are interested." Thus the Protection would remain closed and secret to all but mechanics, while the new society would be open and public. The new association would be organized by counties with a state-wide society to be made up of delegates from each county society. The state society would have the responsibility for promoting the college and raising funds for its establishment.

Promoting the College

Public reaction to the Protection's circular was generally favourable and almost immediate. On May 2, 1850, the *New York Daily Tribune* published most of the plan and added in an article written by Horace Greeley an effusively optimistic description and several "hints of improvement." Greeley's suggestions were understood by many persons to be acceptable parts of the Protection's plan and in a few months were incorporated into it. The most significant of Greeley's hints was that the college should serve farmers as well as mechanics.

Most Protections quickly passed formal resolutions in support of the plan, but there was some hesitation about the scheme. At the Protections's general convention in 1850 some members expressed a suspicion that the plan was motivated by financial self-interest. Although groundless at the time, the suspicion was difficult to refute and would recur throughout most of the history of the college. Later in 1850 the plan was taken up by the Industrial Legislature, a state-wide gathering of mechanics from many associations, which passed several resolutions in support of the plan. The Industrial Legislature also extended a formal invitation to the farmers of the state to join a movement for a single agricultural and mechanical college.

In August 1851 the Mechanical Society for which the Protection's plan had called was formed and with Harrison Howard as secretary named the Mechanical School Association. Membership in the Association grew rapidly to about 3,000 persons. At least one chapter of the Association was established in every county of the state and in several other states. Many eminent political figures and reformers joined among whom were: Martin Van Buren, George Clinton, Washington Hunt, Gerrit Smith, Henry Ward Beecher, and Theodore Weld. Many less eminent persons also joined. For example, among sixty persons in Havana who joined there were four grocers, five lawyers, three tinsmiths, three boot makers, four machinists, three carriage-makers, two apothecaries, three physicians, two hatmakers, three harness makers, two potters, two dentists, three blacksmiths, six hardware merchants, three lumbermen, two iron founders, a carpenter, a barber, a cabinet-maker, a watch-maker, a tailor, a railway station agent, a miller, a manufacturer of wagon hubs, the county judge, and a seed merchant. Of these persons only about one-half would have been eligible for membership in the Mechanics Mutual Protection. The Association thus significantly broadened the base of support for the college.

Two early members of the Association joined Howard in the leadership movement. They were Horace Greeley and Theodore C. Peters. Peters was editor of the *Wool Grower*, a leader of the State Agricultural Society and a long-time advocate of schools that would apply science to agriculture. In 1851 Howard, Greeley, and Peters began work on a formal prospectus for the college. The prospectus was based on the Protection's original plan with two important additions. The first, attributed to Greeley, was that the college should "afford suitable facilities for the education of Young Women, as well as Young Men; and all the sciences taught in the college being as freely imparted to the former as to the latter." The second product of collaboration of Howard, Greeley, and Peters was a name for the college. Some critics of the Protection's plan had contended that the college would be divisive and undemocratically exclusive because it would serve only one class of men. Peters at first proposed that the college should be called the Farmers' and Mechanics' University. Later, as he became particularly sensitive to the issue of whether or not colleges should exist for individual classes, Peters advised Howard that there were already "class colleges enough, and . . . we would agree upon the name of People's College . . . ." (8)

In November, 1851 the prospectus was adopted by the Mechanical School Association. The prospectus was published many times during the six years directly following its adoption; it was changed only twice and became virtually the permanent definition of The People's College. One change was a statement abjuring aid from the state's treasury on the condition that the state aid no other colleges. The statement appeared in some versions of the prospectus but not in all.

The second change was more significant and tested the Association's commitment to coeducation. As soon as the prospectus was published, several prominent members of the women's rights movement expressed interest in the College. Susan B. Anthony, John Bascom, Amelia Bloomer, Amy Post, Lucy Stone, and Elizabeth C. Stanton were early members of the Association; Anthony offered to serve as a membership agent for the Association. (9) While women's rights activists supported the College, they were not entirely in agreement with the prospectus' reference to "suitable facilities for the education of Young Women." They wanted the word "suitable" replaced by "equal." Prior to the meeting at which the prospectus was ratified by the Association several meetings had been disrupted over the issue of coeducation. Prominent clergymen regularly attended the Association's meetings to attack the immorality of coeducation and warn that the evils of carnal lust would surely be unleashed if men and women were educated together. Some leaders of the Mechanics' Mutual Protection questioned the wisdom of becoming deeply involved in the women's rights movement. Others supported the movement for women's rights but believed that the manual labour idea and coeducation were inconsistent with one another.

By supporting coeducation the Association was running serious risks, not the least of which was the possibility of alienating the Mechanics' Mutual Protection. But the Association persevered and took a strong public stance in favour of coeducation. At a meeting held in conjunction with the Women's Temperance Society the Association formally adopted a resolution amending the prospectus to read "equal" rather than "suitable" in describing the College's programs for women.

The People's College Association proposed to finance the College through the sale of shares; each shareholder would have a vote in all College business. But the Association could not expect to raise much money by selling shares in an unincorporated college. The Association therefore moved immediately to obtain a charter from the state legislature. There was some opposition. Coeducation predictably was attacked. Supporters of the state's classical colleges argued that The People's College was not needed and that approval of the charter would imply that the classical colleges had failed. Some farm leaders, while they agreed that there was a need for higher education for farmers and mechanics, did not agree that a single college could serve the needs of both. The state's Board of Regents, which was concerned about the unnecessary proliferation of colleges, urged the legislature not to charter any college that was without a sufficient endowment. While the opponents of the charter were able to slow its progress, they could not defeat it. With the help of T. C. Peters, who was a member of the legislature, and Harrison Howard, who was able to have the legislature's agenda rearranged to bring the charter forward at a time when its chief opponents were absent, the charter was granted on April 12, 1853. But the Board of Regents did succeed in persuading the legislature to stipulate that the college corporation would have to raise $50,000 before it would be permitted to choose a location,

purchase land, or erect a building. The college's trustees would not be allowed to organize a faculty and open the college until suitable accommodations for at least 100 students were available. The officers of the People's College Association became the officers of the College.

With the charter in hand the Association set out to sell $250,000 of shares in The People's College. Under the general direction of Harrison Howard subscription agents were appointed in every county of New York; there were a few agents in other states. The Association was able to raise about $15,000 before the subscription campaign was stalled by the Panic of 1854, which in New York was compounded by unusually poor harvests in 1854 and 1855. The depression that followed the Panic was extremely hard on labour organizations. The Mechanics' Mutual Protection was not immune, and with the exception of one or two local Protections it ceased to exist, although many of its members and most of its leaders remained active in the People's College Association. Fund-raising was also limited by the legislature's requirement that the trustees could not locate the College until $50,000 had been raised. Although the Association sought to rely on support from mechanics and farmers, several large pledges to purchase shares were made on the condition that the College be located in particular localities. Under the terms of the charter these pledges could not be accepted.

As the prospects of raising money grew gloomy, the trustees appealed more than they had originally intended to outright philanthropy, but they expressly refused to renege on the College's long-standing policy against accepting support from the state. The trustees were disposed to seek an amendment to the charter which would permit them to locate the College when only $25,000 had been raised. The amendment would enable the trustees to accept large pledges that were conditional on location. The charter was never amended. Before action could be taken in the legislature, a wealthy businessman in a small village in central New York offered to subscribe whatever amount was needed to reach the required goal of $50,000. The village was Havana, and the man was Charles Cook.

Building the College

Charles Cook was a rough-hewn, self-made man. Left destitute by the death of his father in the War of 1812, Cook supported himself first as a small-scale merchant and later as a successful subcontractor on canal and railway projects. In 1829 Cook contracted to build a canal that would have one terminus near the village of Havana. Cook developed the village and by 1860 owned more than a dozen businesses and several farms there. He was a harsh and unpleasant man. Even his admirers confessed that Cook's personality was abrasive. His detractors questioned his business and civic ethics. On several occasions he was publicly accused of fraud and deception.

What motivated Charles Cook to make such a generous offer to The People's College? Cook was not an educated man and none of his known interests were intellectual. He was active politically but was not associated with the many reform movements that characterized New York politics in the 1840's and 1850's. He had never been employed in a mechanical trade nor had he ever operated a farm. Throughout his entire association with The People's College Cook's only explanation of his motives was that he wanted to make Havana a "little Oxford," (10) but The People's College was the antithesis of Oxford.

If educational concerns did not motivate Charles Cook's interest in The People's College, what did? Primarily it was a desire to promote Havana and his business interests there. In 1853–1854 Cook had led a fight to create a new county from the area surrounding Havana. He won but soon discovered that other towns in the new county had aspirations to be named the county seat. Another political battle ensued in which competing towns sought to prove themselves worthy of being the county seat. Cook saw The People's College as an asset that could not be matched by other towns.

Harrison Howard believed that Cook's motives were pecuniary. Early in 1855 the trustees of the State Agricultural College (which had been chartered not long after The People's College to satisfy farm leaders who believed that a single college could not serve farmers and mechanics both) discovered an unused fund in the state treasury from which they proposed to borrow $40,000 over 20 years at no interest. Their expectation was that the loan would in effect be a grant because the legislature would not demand payment. Cook had been kept informed from the beginning about the Agricultural College's plans and had been assured that the governor would endorse a similar loan for The People's College. Even before the trustees of the College had accepted his offer and despite the College's definite policy against accepting aid from the state, Cook went to Albany to seek a loan for the College.

The trustees decided to accept Cook's proposal but not unanimously. Several openly distrusted Charles Cook, and others, particularly those whose association with the College went back to the Mechanics' Mutual Protection, doubted that Havana was a suitable location for the College; Havana was neither an industrial town nor a good area for farming. But the final decision about the location had to be made by the shareholders. The trustees and Cook avoided the problem of the charter's prohibition against naming a location by arguing that no promise had been made to locate the College in Havana. The only agreement was that the trustees would recommend to the shareholders that the College should be located there.

Despite the trustees' recommendations the shareholders were divided about whether or not the College should be located in Havana. There was a tension between those whose interests were primarily in founding a college for farmers and mechanics and those whose enthusiasm was motivated by the prospect of the commercial benefits and civic pride that a college, any college, would generate wherever it was located. Cook knew before the shareholders' meeting that other towns would challenge Havana's bid for The People's College and that some shareholders thought that Havana was a poor location for the College. To forestall the challengers Cook purchased several thousand shares in the College on behalf of other persons and then secured their proxies, thus assuring victory. Harrison Howard, who oversaw the election, knew that the vote was rigged but was unwilling to jeopardize the College, just when its future seemed most secure. The intensity of the contest for location of the College is a testament to its popular appeal and to the commercial aspirations of some of its supporters.

Under Charles Cook's patronage the trustees immediately began to make plans for a building. The design that they selected was ambitious. The building would be built in the shape of an E and would have five stories. Three figures would appear on the building's facade: the largest in the centre would represent the "Mechanic Arts," two smaller figures would represent "Agriculture" and "Theory." The People's College's main mission still was to serve the mechanic.

The trustees' next order of business after getting construction of a building underway was to select a president and appoint a faculty. The trustees' work was slowed by many disagreements with Charles Cook, who dominated the board's affairs. Cook had appointed several of his associates—some were actually his employees—who lived nearby Havana to the board. By calling meetings on short notice Cook was able to arrange meetings at which he and his associates had overwhelming majorities, since the other trustees lived throughout the state. Cook continued this practice, even after the president of the board lodged a formal complaint. By the end of 1857 three key members of the original trustees had resigned: Harrison Howard, T. C. Peters and Washington Hunt. Howard was the College's key link to organized labour, Peters was president of the State Agricultural Society, and Hunt was a major political leader. They all gave similar reasons for resigning: they did not trust Charles Cook; they doubted his competence to manage a college, particularly one for mechanics and farmers; and they questioned whether or not he had a plan for the College. Even without Cook's machinations there was a basic tension between the old and new trustees. The former wanted a college that would serve mechanics and farmers; the latter wanted a college that would benefit Havana.

Other members of the board were more trustful of Cook but were concerned that he was away from Havana too often to give the College the leadership that it needed. The selection of a strong president with educational experience, therefore, became an imperative for old and new trustees alike. The board selected Amos Brown, who was then head of the Seneca Collegiate Institute (an academy in Ovid, New York) and leader of a renascent movement to found the State Agricultural College.

Brown was a curious choice to head a college for mechanics and farmers. Trained in theology, Brown had been principal of an academy in Maine and a Congregational minister before coming to the academy in Ovid. He had no background in science; one of his friends said that Brown had "less mechanical instinct than any other intelligent man" he had ever known. (11)   William Watts Folwell, who later became president of the University of Minnesota, was a student at Brown's academy; he thought that Brown knew very little about agriculture. (12)

Why was Brown selected to lead The People's College? He was an effective promoter. He had revived two ailing academies and the movement to found the State Agricultural College, which had languished since the College received a charter in 1853. He was an excellent teacher. He was committed to coeducation, which was The People's College's major public relations problem. He also was an associate of Charles Cook, who placed Brown's name before the trustees and arranged favourable letters for his nominee.

Amos Brown became the president of The People's College, but the power and influence of Charles Cook were not diminished. Despite the slow progress of fund-raising, the College received many applications from prospective students and teachers. From these applications it is unmistakable that the public saw The People's College as being, first, what its name implied and, second, an institution unlike existing colleges. An especially interesting and representative application came from a man who described himself as a teacher and farmer "according to the seasons." He wanted to teach agriculture and carpentry. Having read and heard about The People's College, he was sure that he was the sort of teacher the college would need. "What do you say" he asked, "to my putting up my carpenter tools in my trunk, and a bundle of working clothes, and giving you a fortnight's or a month's work free by way of a trial?" (13)   Curiously, letters from prospective students and teachers were addressed as often to Charles Cook as to Amos Brown. Rather than referring these letters to Brown, Cook routinely answered them himself. Although Amos Brown was Charles Cook's man, the College's president and its principal benefactor were not always in agreement. Like several of the original trustees, Brown soon became concerned that Cook was neither competent to handle the affairs of a college nor committed to education. Brown doubted that Cook had any clear-cut objectives for the College: "Mr. Cook has been operating too much without a plan and has injured the concern, but probably not seriously. His no policy operation will have the effect to kill my efficiency . . . ." (14)   Whatever his opinion of Charles

Cook as an educational leader and administrator, Brown soon would be away from the College so often that he had to share his authority with Cook.

Amos Brown and the Agricultural College Act

At the first trustees' meeting following Amos Brown's appointment to the presidency of The People's College in the fall of 1857 the trustees passed in response to a suggestion from the president a resolution that called for Brown to go to Washington and attempt to persuade Congress to "make an appropriation of the public domain for the promotion of education . . . similar in kind to that provided for in the plan of The People's College." (15)   Before Brown could decide on an appropriate form for the bill, Justin Morrill introduced the agricultural college bill.

Despite the similarity between the legislation called for in the trustees' resolution and Morrill's bill there is no evidence of collaboration between Morrill and anyone from the College. But there soon would be much collaboration. When he learned about Morrill's bill, Amos Brown with the approval and financial support of the trustees immediately set out for Washington. Although Brown was unknown to Morrill, the College's president soon was lobbying zealously for the agricultural college bill. In New York newspapers began referring to Morrill's bill as "the People's College bill." In Washington Brown linked the College with Morrill's bill by distributing pamphlets describing the College to those persons with whom he talked about the bill, thus leaving the impression that The People's College was the model of the colleges that would be founded by dint of Morrill's land grant. Although Amos Brown's educational background and ideas were not entirely congruent with those of the Mechanics' Mutual Protection, in promoting the College in Washington he used pamphlets that had been prepared earlier by Harrison Howard, and he emphasized that the College was an institution for the industrial classes.

It took Morrill and Brown nearly fourteen months to work the agricultural college bill through the Congress. When it was passed early in 1859, the College's trustees were jubilant, as were the people in Havana. Plans were made "for planting People's Colleges . . . in all the states." (16)   But the trustees' joy was cut short. Two weeks after its passage by the Congress, Morrill's bill was vetoed by President Buchanan, primarily on the grounds that it violated constitutionally guaranteed states' rights.

The trustees had invested all of their aspirations in the Agricultural College Act. When it was vetoed, prospects for the College became discouraging. The College building was underway; teachers wanted to join the faculty; and students wanted to enroll, but there was not enough money to open the College. Most of the money that the College was able to raise through the sale of shares went to the contractors who were erecting the building. One of the persons who was profiting from the construction was Charles Cook, from whom the trustees purchased building materials. Cook gave the College no discount and charged a relatively high rate of interest for credit. Completion of the building was important, because under the terms of its charter the College could not be opened until there were accommodations for 100 students.

Although the trustees were still intent on financing the College through the sale of shares to mechanics and farmers and still were opposed to accepting aid from the state, Charles Cook decided that the College could not succeed unless it were to receive an endowment from the state. In January, 1860 he had a bill introduced which called for an appropriation of $100,000 to establish a permanent endowment for the College. Amos Brown spent most of 1860 and 1861 in Albany lobbying for the endowment but achieved little success until Cook was elected to the New York Senate in 1861. Cook and Brown managed to persuade the legislature to grant the College $10,000 annually for two years beginning in 1862.

The grant was never paid because the College was unable to meet all of the conditions of the legislation, the most significant was that the College should own the building for which its charter called. The state's comptroller refused to make the payment on the grounds that Charles Cook still held liens against the building and title to the land on which it was located. Cook made no effort to rectify the impediments that thwarted payment of the grant. Amos Brown had been prepared to appoint a faculty and enrol students with the support of the state's grant, but his efforts collapsed when it became evident to prospective faculty members that the College would not open. Students continued to apply nevertheless.

The People's College Association and the trustees continued to seek support through the sale of shares in the College, but the amounts collected were insufficient to finish the College building, which was proving to be more costly than had been anticipated. The only realistic hope remaining for The People's College was that Morrill's bill — or one like it — could be passed under a new administration. When the Congress reconvened in December 1861, Amos Brown was again on hand to lobby for Morrill's bill. Morrill himself was not enthusiastic about reintroducing the bill; instead, he thought that he should give all of his attention to coping with the tragedy of civil war. But he did decide finally to reintroduce the bill with the help of Benjamin Wade in the Senate and Amos Brown. Within two months Brown had met with every member of the House of Representatives to promote the bill and coincidentally The People's College. While the constitutional problems that had thwarted the bill in 1859 were no longer present, the bill was opposed, mainly on sectional issues. Morrill attempted to launch another lobbying compaign, but Morrill at-

tempt o dissuade him in the belief that any further efforts would be in vain. With Wade's encouragement Brown persisted. After several debates and with a few minor amendments, the Agricultural College Act was passed on June 11, 1862 and signed by President Lincoln on July 2.

The People's College and the Land-Grant

As finally passed, the Agricultural College Act provided that federally held public lands would be offered to each state at the rate of 30,000 acres for each member of the state's Congressional delegation. To receive benefit of the Act a state had to accept the bill's provisions within two years. A state accepting a grant had to sell the land (or land scrip in states where there were no federally held public lands) and place 90 per cent of the proceeds in a perpetual fund that would serve as an endowment for at least one college which would provide education in the mechanic arts and agriculture. The remaining ten per cent could be expended immediately to purchase land for a new college.

In New York there was no doubt that the state would take advantage of the Agricultural College Act. The main question was what institution would be designated to receive the benefit of the land grant. Although some consideration was given briefly to using the proceeds of the land grant to establish five new colleges throughout the state, only The People's College and the New York State Agricultural College had plausible claims to the grant.

The passage of the Agricultural College Act gave The People's College new vitality and hope. The trustees, led by Cook and Brown, began to take the steps necessary to secure the land grant for the College. The Legislature was not scheduled to meet again until the beginning of 1863, but the trustees began their campaign for the land grant in the fall of 1862. Given the state comptroller's earlier refusal to make payment of the state's grant to the College, the trustees concluded that the same conditions would apply to any subsequent award based on the land grant. The trustees, led by Brown and Horace Greeley, again attempted to gain clear title to the College's land and building from Charles Cook. Cook at first promised to comply, but finally refused. The issue was postponed.

In the meantime, the trustees sought to identify the College further with the Agricultural College Act. Amos Brown's efforts in Washington had linked the Act and the College in the eyes of the Congress, but the question about which college would receive the benefit of the grant would be decided in the state legislature. Therefore Amos Brown prepared a detailed account of his work in behalf of the Act and the board of trustees procured letters from several members of Congress who described Brown's contribution to the legislation. Senators Wade and Fessenden called Brown the "father" of the bill, (17) but the most influential letter came from Justin Morrill, who said that the bill's passage was "due to b[Brown] and the institution of which he is head" and that the legislature should acknowledge the contribution in awarding the proceeds of the land grant. (18) This was powerful testimony in the College's favour.

When the Legislature reconvened in 1863, it promptly passed legislation accepting the land grant and authorizing its sale. Brown and Cook then introduced legislation calling for The People's College to be designated New York's land grant college. The State Agricultural College also sought the land grant, but it had no officers, faculty, or liquid assets. While The People's College was not open, its trustees and president were active, an ambitious building project was underway, students and teachers had applied and about $30,000 had been raised through popular subscription. The accounts of Brown's work in behalf of the Agricultural College Act, the weakness of the State Agricultural College's case, and Cook and Brown's lobbying combined to produce a vote in favour of The People's College. But the Legislature was not unaware of Charles Cook's inconsistency towards the College and added several conditions to the bill.

The bill, which was passed on May 14, 1863, awarded the proceeds of the land grant to The People's College, on the conditions that within three years the College should have ten "competent" professors, a fully stocked farm of 200 acres, a fully equipped machine shop, a library, scientific apparatus, and a building that could accomodate 250 students. A final condition, evidently aimed directly at Cook, was that all of the College's property had "to be held by the . . . Trustees absolutely, and be fully paid for." (19)

Until the conditions of the bill were met, the College could collect not one per cent of the proceeds of the land grant. The College's victory was therefore far from complete. Of the conditions stipulated the College was unable to comply with any of them when the bill passed. Compliance depended on Charles Cook, but his behaviour was enigmatic. He had more than enough money to enable the College to comply with the conditions of the bill. He could have complied with one condition, that the College own its land and building, by simply fulfilling a promise that he had made in 1856 when he first sought the College for Havana. At least he could have honoured his own subscription pledge and, thereby , have provided the College with much needed ready cash and other subscribers with an incentive to honour their pledges. He did none of these things, yet he championed the College in the legislature.

Cook's erratic attitudes were evident even before the bill assigning the proceeds of the land grant to The People's College was passed. When he spoke before the committee of the legislature to which the bill had been referred, Cook assured the members that all of the lands, buildings and equipment necessary to enable the College to meet the terms of the

Agricultural College Act would be provided, presumably by him. When the committee had drawn up the bill in its final form, its members called Cook's attention to the conditions with which he would have to comply. Cook replied "with strong emphasis that he would do no such thing."

(20) After the bill was reported from committee and was being discussed in the Senate, Cook became ill and was unable to attend the debates. He sent a spokesman to the Senate to assure its members that he would in deed comply with the terms of the bill. The bill was thereupon approved. Shortly thereafter he told a member of the legislature that "those were conditions that never would be complied with, and that he would see the committee and the Legislature in—Heaven before he would do it." (21) In 1865 while referring to the same incident, Daniel S. Dickinson, who was a trustee of The People's College, said that "The People's College, so far as Mr. Cook is concerned, is a standing and impenetrable mystery to me. If its history were written in Sanscrit I could read it as well." (22)

Cook's position was that he would not transfer title to the land and building to the trustees, until the College had "received the property (land scrip) from the State." (23) But the state would not convey any of the proceeds of the land grant to the College, until the trustees held clear title to the land and building. Cook's stance placed The People's College in a dilemma. And the dilemma was sadly ironic for Cook must have assumed that the land scrip itself would be given to the land grant colleges. The Agricultural College Act specifically provided that the scrip had to be sold by the states and could not be held by them or the colleges. Cook's motive evidently was to speculate in the sale of land scrip. This is hardly a remote possibility: most of the persons who purchased land scrip were speculators. (24) What is also evident is a division of aspirations for the College and, indeed, for the land grant colleges. Despite the express intentions of the Agricultural College Act, the legislature felt that special provisions were needed to ensure that the college supported by the land grant would have the faculty and facilities needed to offer courses in agriculture and the mechanic arts. In contrast Charles Cook and some of the College's supporters were interested mainly in the commerical and civic advantages of having the College in Havana. To them the College's curriculum was secondary. The land grant made the College even more attractive to speculators and local boosters.

When the trustees met in June, 1863 to consider how they might comply with the terms of the bill by which The People's College could secure the proceeds of the land grant, they again raised with Cook the question about ownership of the College's building and land.

Cook at first reacted angrily. He would convey clear title to the trustees but would resign from the board and demand immediate payment of all debts due him from the College. Cook's offer was curious because the trustees' debt to him was less than his debt to the College in the form of an

could receive the benefit of the land grant. This fact was not unknown to several persons who had been closely watching the College. On February 4, 1865, a newly elected member of the New York Senate introduced a motion to require the Board of Regents to advise the Senate "whether or not . . . [The People's College] is, or within the time specified . . . is likely to be, in a condition to avail itself of the [land grant] fund." (25) The resolution was adopted, and the future of The People's College was again imperiled.

The young Senator who introduced the resolution was deeply interested in higher education. He and another freshman Senator had been keeping a close eye on The People's College and particularly on Charles Cook, on whom the College's success depended. The Senator who introduced the motion was Andrew D. White, and his colleague was Ezra Cornell.

White had grand plans for an American equivalent to Oxford and Cambridge. Cornell had a long-standing interest in agricultural education. He had been a trustee of the defunct State Agricultural College and had carefully studied the plans for The People's College. (26) Initially Cornell wanted to divide the land grant between the State Agricultural College and The People's College, but he was opposed by White, who adamantly insisted that the land grant should not be dissipated by division.

During the summer of 1864, particularly after Amos Brown was dismissed, Cornell's concern about the future of The People's College intensified. Under the terms of the Agricultural College Act New York had five years to establish a college that met the Act's requirements. If it did not, all of the proceeds of the land grant would have to be returned to the federal treasury. More than one year had passed since The People's College had been designated to receive the land grant, and no progress had been made towards the College's complying with the Act. The College had no president, and its benefactor's commitment to the College was at best confused. Ezra Cornell was worried that the land grant might be lost altogether. When the College's trustees asked the legislature for an extension of the time that they would be allowed to fulfill the terms of the bill that had named The People's College to receive the land grant, Ezra Cornell was moved to act on his concern. Cornell finally agreed with White that what was needed was a university much larger and more equipped than any then in existence, including, of course, The People's College. White believed that agricultural and mechanical education had to be provided but concluded that "education in history and literature should be the bloom of the whole growth." (27) Again it was clear that White's design for a university was far more than simply an enlarged version of either The People's College or the State Agricultural College.

By the end of January, 1865, Ezra Cornell and Andrew White were

unpaid subscription pledge. The trustees found Cook's offer unacceptable, but his anger soon subsided, and he resumed his prominence in the affairs of the College. The question of ownership remained unsettled. While Cook's commitment to the College was still uncertain, a tragedy occurred which would confuse any understanding of Charles Cook's behavior throughout the remainder of his lifetime. In September, 1863 he suffered a severe stroke which left him partially paralyzed and mentally erratic.

Cook's infirmity did not diminish his influence over the College, nor did it cause him to forget his anger at the trustees, particularly Amos Brown, whom Cook held responsible for the trustee's demands that he should relinquish title to the College's land and building. Cook wanted Brown removed from the presidency. At first he pressured Brown indirectly by demanding a full accounting of the president's expenses in Washington and later by demanding that Brown pay rent on a house that Cook owned adjacent to the College building. On his part Brown resented Cook's intrusion into the appointment of faculty and development of the curriculum, areas in which Brown thought Cook was incompetent. Brown clearly was distressed by Cook's refusal to aid the College in complying with the terms of the legislation by which it would receive the proceeds of the land grant. In August, 1864 Amos Brown and The People's College severed their relationship. The parting was not amicable.

Despite many problems and deficiencies the College was able to raise enough money to begin instruction in the spring of 1864. Twelve persons had been appointed to the faculty, the building was ready for occupancy, and 60 students were enrolled. The trustees formally requested that the state comptroller pay the grant that the Legislature had authorized in 1862. But the comptroller again refused to pay. And he had several good reasons.

Of the 12 professors named to the faculty, only three were on hand. None of the students were enrolled at the collegiate level. The College's farm was not stocked. Most significantly, the trustees still did not hold clear title to the land and buildings.

The Dissolution of The People's College and the Founding of Cornell University

Although it received aid from neither the state nor the land grant, The People's College was able to remain open. By the beginning of 1865 enrolment had more than doubled to about 150 of whom half were women. Still no students were enrolled at the collegiate level.

Although the sharp increase in enrolment indicated that there was a genuine interest in The People's College, the trustees had made no progress towards fulfilling the terms of the legislation under which the College

prepared to introduce the legislation necessary to found Cornell University and to secure for it the proceeds of the land grant.

The first step in founding Cornell University was to get the land grant away from The People's College. White's motion of February 4 that called on the Board of Regents to determine whether or not the College could meet the terms of the legislation that had granted the proceeds of the land grant to it was an effective gambit. White and Cornell were convinced that the Regents would have no choice but to conclude that The People's College could not meet these terms.

On February 7, 1865 Andrew White introduced in the Senate "an act to establish the Cornell University, and to appropriate to it the income from the sale of public lands granted to this State by Congress . . . ." (28) The act listed the names of the persons who would be trustees of the new university: among them were Horace Greeley, Erastus Brooks, Edwin B. Morgan — all members of The People's College's board of trustees. There was a hidden hand at work in gaining the support of some of The People's College's trustees. Amos Brown had gone to work for Ezra Cornell. It was Brown's idea to appoint trustees from the College to the board of the new university in order to deflate opposition of the College to the creation of the new university. (29) Like White, Amos Brown was firm in insisting that the land grant fund should not be divided, which, in effect, meant that he did not think that The People's College should have it.

Introduction of the new bill was, as Andrew White observed, "a signal for war." (30) And war it was. Every college in the state, except Columbia, came forward to claim the benefit of the land grant fund. The battle was waged in the newspapers and in the legislature, both on the floor and behind closed doors. Some factions argued positively in favour of their own interests; others simply attacked the Cornell proposal by accusing Cornell and White of desiring to found a university that would serve the sons and daughters of the upper classes while ignoring the needs of students whose parents worked in shops or on farms.

Throughout all of the debate and acrimony The People's College did not fare well. A serious blow was dealt the College on February 15, when the Board of Regents submitted its report on the ability of the College to meet the terms of the bill naming it the land grant's beneficiary. Three members of the Board had visited the College where they heard the testimony of two professors, the College's treasurer and even a carpenter who was working on the College building. They also received a deposition from Charles Cook. The Regents concluded that, with the exception of quarters to accommodate ten professors, The People's College had not complied with any of the requirements of the bill. As to the Senate's question about whether or not the College would be able to meet these requirements within the bill's deadline, the Regents refrained from making a recommendation. Instead, they presented the facts of the matter as they

saw them and suggested that the Senators should draw their own conclusions. The facts were as damaging to the College's cause as any recommendation could be. The Regents pointed out that it would cost at least $242,000 to place the College in a situation that would fulfill the terms of the bill. (31) Without Charles Cook's support, The People's College had no realistic hope of raising this amount of money. Given Cook's equivocal, if not contradictory, behavior towards the College, the legislature had no reason to be confident that he would use his fortune to aid the College.

Finally, in April, 1865 after much political maneuvering, Cornell and White succeeded in persuading the Legislature to pass the bill to create Cornell University and assign to it the proceeds of the land grant.

In its final form, the bill gave The People's College 90 days in which either to fulfill all of the terms of the bill that had assigned the proceeds of the land grant to it or to deposit a sum of money sufficient to enable it to fulfill the terms after 90 days had elapsed. What would the College do? On April 26, the trustees met in Havana to chart a course. They decided realistically that it would be impossible for them within three months to meet the requirements that would allow the College to retain the land grant. They therefore wrote to the Board of Regents and requested that the Board specify the amount of money that would have to be deposited to prevent revocation of the land grant. The trustees' request implied that Charles Cook might finally endow the College. But would he?

Cook would have to do two things: provide $185,000 and transfer clear title to the College's land and buildings to the trustees. There was little likelihood that he would do the latter. When the Regents had visited the College in February according to the Senate's request, Cook had submitted a deposition in which he promised that he was "willing and ready to release all rights" to the land and buildings, if the College were "placed on a secure and satisfactory basis." (32) But Cook also insisted on retaining a reversionary right to the College's property and on applying a lien against the building. This was not acceptable to the Regents. There was no logical reason for Cook to have assumed that it would be. Given the number of times that the trustees had discussed the question of clear title with Cook, they in April of 1865 could have held little hope that Cook would suddenly change his mind. He did not.

Would Charles Cook provide the required $185,000 deposit? The answer was soon in coming. On April 26, Amos Brown reported to Ezra Cornell:

Mr. Cook has disclosed that he has given his last cent to The People's College. The term of study in the Institution, which began only some week or ten days ago. is, as I understand, to close today, & the Professors are to be dispersed to seek their forage elsewhere. You will, as I predicted, have an open sea. (33)

It is ironic that Amos Brown, who had worked long and hard for The People's College, would be the person to signal and welcome its dissolution.

These tensions confused the College's leadership and explain, in part, its initial success and its ultimate failure. The People's College attracted popular support because it appealed to several different groups: mechanics, farmers, advocates of women's rights, trades unions, educational reformers, and civic boosters. But the educational interests of these groups could not in all cases be sufficiently defined and reconciled to form a workable concept for the College. These tensions produced some uncertainty among mechanics about whether or not a radical departure from the classical collegiate course was wholly desirable. The uncertainty, when coupled with the competition between The People's College and the founders of Cornell University, suggests that the traditional liberal arts college was popular to at least some extent among farmers and mechanics. While there are other explanations, the ambivalence between traditional educational forms and agricultural and mechanical education may explain in part why land grant colleges and universities were slow to develop agricultural and mechanical programs.

The People's College struggled on without the support of the land grant until 1869, when the heir of Charles Cook donated the building to the New York Baptist Convention for use as an academy. Several trustees of the College were active members of the board of trustees of Cornell University and pursued there some of the goals that had been set for The People's College.

Conclusion

What does the history of The People's College tell us?
The relationship between the College and the Agricultural College Act is significant. Amos Brown was instrumental in the Act's passage. Through Brown's lobby The People's College was identified with the Act and became a symbol of the type of institution envisioned by it. While agricultural education was a firm concept prior to the Agricultural College Act, mechanical education was not. The People's College was the only tangible example of higher education in "the mechanic arts" prior to 1862.

The movement to found The People's College reveals several important ideas to which further study might be usefully devoted. The College's origin in organized labour is unusual and suggests an impetus for reform of higher education which has received little attention.

The College had much popular support at a time when popular support for higher education is thought to have been waning. The competition among cities and towns to win the location of The People's College supports the thesis that there was much local support for colleges before 1860. (34) But it also reveals a tension between educators and local boosters. Many of the College's local supporters including its primary benefactor were not especially interested in agricultural and mechanical education.

But there was a greater and more important tension between the mechanics who initiated the idea of the College and the educational reformers who later joined the movement. The Mechanic's Mutual Protection, following the lead of Harrison Howard, sought a college for mechanics exclusively. Had Harrison Howard and the Protection been able to build the College according to their plans, it probably would not have been coeducational or, perhaps, agricultural. The College's program would have had omitted classical subjects completely, would have emphasized the practical application of theory and would have instructed students by demonstration and direct participation in the skills in which they were being educated.

The reformers including the College's president who later joined the movement were critical of the classical collegiate course but did not wish to abandon it altogether. Amos Brown's plans for the College called for theoretical courses in mechanical and agricultural subjects to be added to a core classical curriculum. Instruction would have relied on recitation and drill, as it did in classical colleges.

NOTES

1. *Havana [N.Y.] Journal* (September 11, 1858). Havana has since been renamed Montour Falls, N.Y.
2. Merle Curti and Vernon Carstensen, *The University of Wisconsin, 1848-1928* (Madison, 1949). p. 28.
3. Earle D. Ross, *Democracy's College: The Land Grant Movement in the Formative Stage*, (Ames, Iowa 1942). pp. 20-21. See also, Frederick Rudolph, *The American College and University* (New York, 1962), p. 248.
4. In 1867 William H. Brewer, then on the faculty of the Sheffield Scientific School, asked Morrill about the origins of his bill. Morrill agreed that the name of the bill was unfortunate, but did not contend that the land grant colleges should be mechanical schools. Instead Morrill talked about "business pursuits" rather than "industrial" education. William H. Brewer, "The Intent of the Morrill Land Grant," MS in William H. Brewer Papers, Yale University.
5. Philip R. V. Curoe, *Educational Attitudes and Policies of Organized Labor in the United States* (New York, 1926). p. 42; see also Berenice M. Fisher, *Industrial Education: American Ideals and Institutions* (Madison, 1967), pp. 22-23.
6. See, for example, *Franklin Institute Journal*, Vol 2, No. 1 (July, 1826) and *Mechanic's Apprentice*, Vol. I. No. 12 (April, 1846).
7. Monte Calvert, *The Mechanical Engineer in America, 1830-1910* (Baltimore, 1967). pp. 6-8.
8. Minutes, Mechanical School Association meeting. November 25, 1851. Harrison Howard Papers, Cornell University.
9. Susan B. Anthony to Harrison Howard, September 15, 1852, Howard Papers.
10. Quoted in Harrison Howard, "Reference Book," p. 71, Howard Papers.
11. William H. Brewer to Waterman T. Hewitt, March 11, 1894, Howard Papers.
12. "Address by W. W. Folwell," May 26, 1924, MS, Howard Papers.

13. H. H. Fisher to Messrs. Cook and Brown, November 10, 1859, Bramble Family P   s, Cornell University.

14. Amos Brown to William H. Brewer, May 9, 1861, Brewer Papers.

15. "President Brown's Report," September 15, 1862, MS, Bramble Papers.

16. Alonzo I. Wynkoop to Harrison Howard, February 10, 1859, Howard Papers.

17. Benjamin F. Wade to Edwin B. Morgan, December 1, 1862, and W. P. Fessenden to Edwin B. Morgan, December 6, 1862, Howard Papers.

18. Justin S. Morrill to Edwin B. Morgan, December 1, 1862, Brewer Papers.

19. Laws of New York, Chapter 511 (1863).

20. New York State Constitutional Convention, Vol. IV (Albany, 1868), p. 2822.

21. Ibid.

22. Daniel S. Dickinson to A. D. White, February 28, 1865, quoted in Carl Becker, Cornell University: The Founders and the Founding (Ithaca, 1944), p. 231.

23. New York State Constitutional Convention, Vol. IV, p. 2821.

24. Paul W. Gates, The Wisconsin Pine Lands of Cornell University, (Madison, Wisconsin, 1965), pp. 27-34.

25. Cornell University, Laws and Documents Relating to Cornell University, 1862-1883, (Ithaca, N.Y. 1883). p. 10.

26. A copy of The People's College Prospectus annotated in Ezra Cornell's handwriting is in the Ezra Cornell Papers, Cornell University.

27. Andrew D. White, Autobiography, Vol. I (New York, 1905). p. 298.

28. Laws of New York, 1865, Chapter 586.

29. William H. Brewer to Waterman T. Hewitt, March 11, 1894, Howard Papers.

30. White, Autobiography, Vol. I, p. 300.

31. New York Senate Document No. 45 (1865).

32. Ibid.

33. Amos Brown to Ezra Cornell, April 26, 1865, Cornell Papers.

34. David B. Potts, "'College Enthusiasm!' As Public Response, 1800-1860," Harvard Educational Review, Vol. 47, No. 1 (February 1977): 28-42.

Mr. Lang is the editor of The Canadian Journal of Higher Education, *and Director of University Planning at the University of Toronto.*

Misconceptions About the Early Land-Grant Colleges

Eldon L. Johnson

The universities called "land grant" have cut a wide swath in the history of American higher education. They deserve to be acclaimed, but they ought also to be better understood. Paradoxically, their long struggle for recognition and respectability has been so fully won that criticism has turned to unthinking acceptance. As a result, some misconceptions have arisen and flourished alongside the neglect of other matters of great significance, past and present.

What is both overestimated and underestimated really does matter if we have regard, not merely for the truth, but also for a balanced view of university development at home and of what is being imported by developing countries abroad. The misconceptions arise as we roll history back, proceeding from what we have fixed in our minds now; hence, we attribute to the early land-grant colleges the characteristics that exist today. What the colleges now *are* is merely what they *were* writ large. Far from it.

These colleges of humble origin, all derived from land grants to the states under the Morrill Act of 1862, are extremely important and do have a claim to uniqueness, but not always for the reasons assumed. They are no longer colleges. They are, in the main, full-fledged universities. They exist in every state and in most of the territories. They comprise a national system, derived from national policy. As a category, they supply eight of the ten largest undergraduate campuses in the United States and enroll more than one-seventh of all university students. They and the state universities together produce two out of every three doctoral degrees granted nationally. In other words, they are prime actors at both extremes: in mass education with its emphasis on "equal access," and in graduate training with its emphasis on research specialization. They are the bulwarks of scientific and technological education. By the terms of the enabling act, they encompass agriculture and mechanic arts; but whatever their beginnings, they now embrace a much broader curriculum—either science and technology generally, with the related professions, or the whole complement indistinguishable from the most comprehensive and traditional universities. In their original rebellion against classical instruction only, they put things scientific at the center, around which an unusually strong research orientation has developed, with an emphasis on application and problem solving. Thus was born the now famous academic trilogy: instruction, research, and service—a mission description that virtually every institution, public or private, now embraces, however different the interpretations.

These are the characteristics in which misconceptions have become embedded as history is neglected or time ignored. Concurrently, some decisive considerations have dropped almost entirely from our awareness. Four of the common misconceptions and two of the neglected considerations will be treated here. The sources used are the individual institutional histories of the early land-grant colleges, taking 1890 as the approximate terminal date. Such histories, taken together, give a composite picture that strikes the reader with insights that are not so conspicuous in the individual histories because they are understandably introspective.

Land Grant Uniqueness

It is quite erroneous, first, that use of land grants was or is the distinguishing characteristic of the so-called land-grant colleges, despite the inseparable name. Nor was the practice by any means novel. Indeed it was so well established that Senator Justin Morrill, the legislative author, and his hundreds of intellectual allies were merely making a special application in 1862. That the impact was revolutionary in the end derived from a host of other considerations, not from a new social invention.

The precedents were ancient, numerous, and of high visibility. The colonies received the heritage from the English Crown. In fact, within twelve years of the founding of Jamestown, ten thousand acres of land were set aside in an abortive attempt to establish a university [10, pp. 2-4]. As states replaced colonies, they continued the practice of giving land grants for higher education, with Harvard, Yale, William and Mary, Dartmouth, and Michigan all the beneficiaries of either colonial or state gifts. Meanwhile, the vast western lands were ceded to the new national government, and because of abundant land riches, it became the chief donor. No reader need be reminded that grants in lieu of appropriations were given for great internal improvements and that the Northwest Ordinance of 1787 led to the practice of giving to each newly admitted state (unless carved out of the original thirteen) two entire townships for a "seminary of learning." What may not be remembered is that by the Civil War, and hence two years before the Morrill Act, no less than seventeen states had received two townships each, or a total of more than 4 million acres, and had spawned almost a score of state colleges and universities [39, p. 44; 1, p. 25]. Indeed many of these institutions of pre-Morrill land-grant origin were the trunk onto which the *new* land-grant shoot was grafted, always with revitalizing and sometimes life-preserving consequences.

Therefore, it is clear that the land-granting technique had become so pervasive before 1862 that turning to the federal government for educational help, instead of to the states, had become a dominant fashion. As an alert representative and senator, Justin Morrill had only to heed his eyes and ears to become the author of the famous act that bears his name, without awaiting a blinding vision that would make him "The First," as he sometimes implied in old age and as myth-makers came to believe. Insight on the times is also shown by President Lincoln's role and attitude. He did not turn a hand for the plans of Morrill, Jonathan Baldwin Turner, Horace Greeley, and all the others. He endorsed but did not promote; he signed the act but made no recorded comment. As a product of his time and place, with his free-soil ideas, he was said to have favored land grants "for all purposes and under any available condition" [43, p. 56].

If land grants were not new as a device for educational support, neither were they resorted to for purely educational reasons. Education was often the legitimizing factor, while the real objective was something else, perhaps pioneer settlement, speculation, or economic development. Citizens in Minnesota objected to having pine and farm lands chosen for universities because there were "higher" uses possible [18, p. 56]. Likewise, the unseemly emphasis on land as mere largess produced such interinstitutional scrambles among both public and private colleges that they were variously dubbed "Ohio's great land-grant sweepstakes" and Virginia's "War of the Colleges" [26, p. 51; 25, p. 21].

None of this is to deny Senator Morrill's great contribution, but rather to point it in another direction. Instead of siring the land-grant idea, even for colleges, he put together a timely political alliance that used the tried and true support mechanism for something new in higher education, certainly new in emphasis, and often new even in the kind of institution elicited. He helped establish a national policy, permissive though it was, which offered irresistible incentive to all the states at one time, old and new, to join a country-wide system of state-based institutions that had the potential we know only today. That *was* something new.

Student Demand

Another facile misconception is that the land-grant colleges were born of student demand. "People's colleges" must have had a popular base, and when established, they must have had a popular response. On the contrary, a case could be made that the new colleges were created by reformers, not practitioners, and for an ideal, not for an established need. Reaching out to sons, and later daughters, of farmers and artisans, to indigent students, and to whomever the existing system passed by was a noble egalitarian ideal that remained just that—an ideal—for decades, with laborious progress toward its realization. Dormancy or decline in enrollments had actually set in, with surprising results in the new colleges [46, p. 486; 13, pp. 66–68]. When Ohio's land-grant college opened, its public predecessor, Miami University, was forced to close its collegiate department for want of enrollment, to resume only a dozen years later [26, pp. 54, 56].

One understandable obstacle was the inadequacy of the educational underpinnings: the land-driven reform outran the public school system. This extension of education from the top down, hastily induced by land grants, caused some sparsely settled western states to open the new colleges when few, if any, high schools existed. Arizona opened with none and Nevada with two [31, p. 38; 11, p. 52]. Other states were not too different. The University of Wisconsin was itself called "a High School for the village of Madison"; Pennsylvania State University, which began as "Farmers' High School," despite its collegiate intentions, met the student shortfall through preparatory work reaching down to the common-school level [38, p. 140; 12, pp. 21, 42]. In fact, preparatory departments became established collegiate features, and their enrollments were often merged into total student figures to assuage public hostility. When the president of the University of Arkansas boasted of the fourth largest enrollment in the nation during 1879–80, he counted 300 preparatory students in his total of 450 [42, p. 122]. Not until this nationwide problem was ameliorated did the new colleges have the student "demand" for which they were built.

The test is in their success in reaching the number and kinds of students intended. The best called for apology; the worst was appalling. In New Hampshire literally no new registrant showed up for the fall opening in 1877 [56, p. 58]. Missouri had the same experience during the first week of the opening term in 1866, although 40 did appear later [41, p. 25]. Pennsylvania's opening "capacity attendance" had dropped to 22 in 1869 and then took almost thirty years to reach 150 [12, pp. 25, 67, 135–36]. Massachusetts had drastic ups and downs, with twenty years required to get the enrollment back to the modest 1870 level [7, p. 63]. Neighboring Connecticut opened in 1881 with twelve "on the ground or on the way" [53, p. 144]. In its first twenty years, Nevada never exceeded 35 [11, pp. 33]. A decade after the Civil War, no less than five institutions in Baltimore had "an enrollment at least double that of the little farmer's College" (University of Maryland), which in eight postwar years had five presidents under whom six students actually were graduated [4, p. 174]. Florida's college had a particularly difficult time: the 38 who began in 1884 were all in the preparatory department, and only 57 were in collegiate classes as late as 1898 [37, p. 278].

Some colleges did better, indeed well by national comparisons of the time, but the best had monumental troubles. Aided by an ideal combination of beginning assets and by advertising in three hundred newspapers, Cornell got off to the best beginning with the largest entering class ever admitted in the United States—412, or twice the lodging space. But after a quick ascent to a total of 600, all classes sank back to only 312 in 1882 [22, p. 184]. Minnesota and California likewise experienced huge declines after early enrollment gains, although the latter again took off to 500 by 1883 and four times that number by 1898 [18, pp. 47, 68; 52, pp. 93, 115; 16, p. 374]. Illinois did not attract the "hundreds" its head expected, but it began with about 50 (76 by the year's end) and moved rapidly in four years to 400 [51, pp. 99, 105]. Because of special fervor specially concentrated, the separated "agricultural and mechanical arts colleges," distinct from the state university in the same state, had some special drawing power—again, often without maintenance of the auspicious beginnings. Although Kansas State never reached 125 in any of its first ten years, it progressed with remarkable steadiness to 500 in the 1878–90 period [58, pp. 22, 79]. Michigan Agricultural College enjoyed "overcrowding" for only two years, and although enrollment was parlayed into a respectable 340 in the 1880s, that was far short of the intended 500; the following decade the board was looking into "the seeming lack of popularity of our College" [27, pp. 23, 187, 188].

That there was no groundswell of student demand is shown by the many stratagems used to build enrollment. Necessity bred invention. The new college in North Carolina offered a month's free board to any student who would bring in another [29, p. 64]. Missouri relied on double-sized catalogs, five thousand circulars, and faculty forays into the country to "sell" the university [54, p. 300]. Scholarships with all degrees of financial support and equitability of selection were universally used, and, not uncommonly, available awards outran the total number of students. Only one-third of the Arkansas potential was taken up in 1873 [42, p. 74]; and before 1880, New Hampshire's enrollment never exceeded thirty-three, although thirty-four scholarships were available for in-state students [56, p. 10; 48, pp. 8, 12]. In the impoverished economy of the Reconstruction, Louisiana State did attract students by the "charity" system of full-support "beneficiaries," but, reciprocally, enrollment dropped to thirty-one when politics terminated the arrangement [17, pp. 204, 221]. Some students were made automatic recipients of enrollment inducements, such as ministers, ministry students, and maimed Confederate soldiers in Georgia [23, p. 98]. Where land-grant funds were originally entrusted in New England to existing private universities, it was common to devote a share of the proceeds (half at Dartmouth) to dragooning the necessary students under state auspices [56, p. 10].

The student yield from all this frenetic effort shows that the ideal of an open sesame for neglected students was tardy in its realization. In their avowed and ready egalitarianism, the land-grant colleges differed from the traditional, but student demand was anemic everywhere, yielding the nation's topmost enrollment of 637 at Harvard in 1872, not much more than half that at Princeton, 124 at Columbia, and 88 at the University of Pennsylvania [32, p. 109]. Nothing did more *eventually* for mass or democratized education, but the land-grant colleges did little initially. It took them thirty years, or fifty, depending on one's standard for earning entitlement to what we now honor. They were committed, they opened their doors, and they pressed fate with action. Their early contribution was the ardent conviction and the provision of opportunity, the expectation, and the ideal, not the actual achievement. They were ahead of their times, not the slaves of popular demand. When the ideal did blossom, it did so magnificently, and these new institutions were often pacesetters. Within two decades of the general take-off in both enrollment and state support, Edwin Slosson was to include Wisconsin, California, Illinois, Minnesota, and Cornell among the fourteen in his *Great American Universities* [50]. As one historian was to say, "Higher education for the masses . . . really dates from the early years of the Twentieth Century"—the tardy fruition of an early ideal [36, p. 1].

National Development Role

A third major misconception attributes to the new land-grant colleges the role of supreme force in national development after the Civil War—the prime mover in the American agricultural and industrial revolutions that became the envy of the world. If the colleges ever had that capacity, it was much later, certainly after the Hatch Act of 1887 with its emphasis on research, and probably not until well into the twentieth century. The colleges' *own* development had to precede their impact on national development. That is an oversight often found among admirers in the developing countries who are looking for importable, ready-made, time-defying instruments of progress.

Since agriculture was a "leading object," the greatest impact would presumably have been on the so-called "agricultural revolution." However, the status of agricultural education was indeed low, and the trained manpower produced was generally not distinguishable from that of other educational institutions. Agricultural colleges had birth pangs that have left us lurid descriptions: "a bundle of whimsies," an "undernourished abortion," "mere symbolic patches of hay or grass," and "an Agricultural College without Agriculture in it" [28, pp. 234, 253; 35, p. 62; 32, p. 124]. Agriculture played little part in the institutional evolution in West Virginia, Louisiana, and Nevada, and a difficult role even in some of the strongest farm states. Minnesota's trustees condoned growth within the cracks, in pieces, and against odds, with resulting "hostility between university and farm community that was to plague the administration for fifty years" [18, p. 33]. Students of that discipline never exceeded three a year and then relapsed to zero in 1880. In 1874 there were no agriculture students at Wisconsin, California, Minnesota, or Missouri—all established prior to the Morrill Act, all farm states, and all committed to doing something special for agriculture. In fact, Wisconsin graduated no agriculture student until 1878, with many years before the next. Thirty years after President Lathrop had begun urging agricultural education, one student was pursuing that field in contrast to sixty in law [9, pp. 463–64]. Where brand new institutions were founded under the Morrill Act, particularly if they were separated from the state university, agriculture generally fared better; and in some places it was clearly dominant. In Michigan, Pennsylvania, Mississippi, Massachusetts, and Kansas, agriculture was the driving force in the founding or in early emphasis, or both. In the northeastern states, where the land-grant funds (except in Maine and Massachusetts) were given to existing private universities, even if to a scientific college therein, agriculture was clearly a stepchild. But in all states, the unpromising state of agriculture as a profession or science was a serious obstacle. Professors of agriculture could not be found because the subject did not yet exist. It could be taught only in the guise of something else—botany, chemistry, or physiology. One president said it was "simply a mass of empiricism" [34, p. 57].

For potential application to national development, what kind of trained manpower did the land-grant colleges produce? The best agriculture showing by far was made at Michigan Agricultural College. By 1892, it had produced six hundred agricultural graduates, one-fifth of the national figure and exceeding the total for twenty-five other states, while other Midwestern colleges were averaging from ten to twenty-four each [27, p. 171]. Ohio State was very different; only two out of ninety-three graduates from 1870 to 1886 were in agriculture, whereas twenty-seven received engineering degrees, twenty-seven bachelors of science, and thirty-seven bachelors of arts and philosophy [26, p. 131]. Maine had only thirty-four in agriculture and allied industries out of 348 living alumni in 1892, or 10 percent as compared with 41 percent in engineering; also the professions, business, and editorial/literary work compared favorably with agriculture [15, p. 93]. Purdue University in Indiana averaged one graduate in agriculture a year until 1893, only one-sixth as many as in civil and mechanical engineering [21, p. 191].

The Wisconsin Board of Visitors in 1880 lamented "finding no students in and learning of no graduates from the agriculture department" [9, p. 465]. In the heart of the farm belt, Illinois had no enrollment in agriculture/horticulture in 1890, and its new college almost expired before being revitalized by the Hatch and Second Morrill Acts [51, pp. 239–41]. The Rutgers Science School turned out ninety-nine graduates in fifteen years, six of whom were in farming [32, p. 92]. Of seventy graduates at Maryland between 1865 and 1892, two were farmers and six engineers [4, p. 198]. At the nadir, it took Arkansas thirty years to produce the first bachelor of science in agriculture, and Nevada did little better [19, p. 37; 8, p. 16].

It must be concluded, therefore, that the manpower training done by these new colleges turned out to be, both by student choice while in college and by employment choices after graduation, much more conventional than expected—it was chiefly for liberal education and for the common professions. Even in the exceptions found in institutions that deliberately restricted their curricula to a narrow interpretation of the Morrill Act, the "related" fields often did better than the explicit specialties.

No reputable history of American agriculture or of industry bears out the assumption that the new-type colleges virtually created modern America on the material side by their applications of knowledge to agriculture and industry. The ideal of development was always held by the land-grant colleges and their most evangelistic spokesmen, but the realization had to await both the generation of knowledge to apply and the development of staff to share. The volumes of *Agricultural History* contain several articles about the nineteenth century "agricultural revolution" but none assigns a significant role to the new land-grant colleges. These articles show that significant change was already evident by 1850, the century's greatest increase in agricultural productivity per worker occurred between 1860 and 1870, and a host of nonagricultural factors were at work [6, p. 121; 49, pp. 161–62; 40, pp. 193–95]. Likewise, American economic histories give more attention to natural conditions, inventions, canals, railroads, market developments, urbanization, and land policies than to land-grant education, which gets surprisingly little attention, and sometimes none at all [5, p. 101; 2, p. 452].

Before 1890, the developmental contributions of the land-grant colleges were fortuitous and indirect. They were a boon to frontier settlement and an important ingredient in the frenzy of "internal improvements" in many states. Many were ploys in the legislative maneuvering for scattering internal improvements around the state, with "equitable" distribution of college, capitol, penitentiary, insane asylum, and normal school. They gave powerful impetus to an improved and balanced school system, uplifting high schools particularly. Most potent of all was their relevance for and attachment to a particular geographical place: they served what their place names generally implied and designated. It was no accident that Kansas State scientifically demonstrated that winter wheat, among many other crops, was an answer to a harsh environment and that Florida Agricultural College experimented with semitropical fruits and vegetables [24, p. 289; 37, pp. 204, 346].

This points to the missing link. It was the absence of tested principles and verifiable knowledge that came from research. Before 1890 the colleges did not have that capacity, or more than a minuscule amount, and the concomitant capacity for systematic diffusion lagged still further. To contend otherwise is to perpetuate a myth that impedes our understanding of the developmental process and education's role in it. The direct developmental impact of the early colleges came after the agricultural experiment stations were established, after research knowledge was given an extension mechanism, after the engineering schools were equipped and well patronized for both training and applied research, and after enrollments in the practicing professions generated thousands, not merely scores, of leaders and specialists. It was a long road from the early unrealized ideal to the contemporary interlocking of development and education. The early colleges were within the system, not outside or above it. They were in some respects the product, not the cause. That may tell us more about national development and the university role in it, both past and present, both in the United States and overseas, than anything else.

State Support and Control

A fourth misunderstanding about early land-grant colleges assumes that between the federal role and state role, the latter was dominant and determining. Why else "state" universities? It is easy to infer now that the states eagerly stepped up to the federal challenge, embraced and discharged their constitutional responsibility for education, and perforce put their tax dollars behind an accepted public remedy for the deficiencies of the traditional private colleges. That is not what happened. Starting a college did not mean supporting it, and supporting a college did not mean controlling it. Support and control both had to evolve. As the giving of land grants by the federal government was a substitute for money, so the acceptance of land grants by the states was a substitute for taxes. In fact, full college adoption and reasoned tax support by the state was a phenomenon of the early twentieth century [44, p. 184].

The federal role has been neglected and underestimated. Federal land did more than entrap the states into sometimes unwanted responsibilities; its proceeds were the lifeblood in the early decades or even the sole support. The Morrill Act made a tremendous impact. Eventually every state accepted its terms. By standards of that day, not of the present, it provided a "munificent grant," "a very handsome endowment," "a permanent fund," and "a bounty of the national government" [41, p. 23; 26, p. 21; 23, p. 12; 15, p. 361]. Indeed 17.5 million acres was a handsome bounty nationwide, even if the income did fall below expectations. That bounty was "the salvation of the University of Georgia," it "helped the Maryland Agricultural College struggle to its feet," it aided Iowa Agricultural and Mechanical Arts College "in its desperate struggle for perpetuation," and in New Jersey "the foundations were laid for the new Rutgers" [23, p. 85; 4, p. 164; 45, p. 34; 32, p. 82].

For both politicians and educators in many states, the federal land grants had another strong appeal, but of a negative kind: they were an escape from state responsibility and taxation. Bad times caused some states to propose to "sell" the new college or repeal its charter as a tax-relief measure [45, p. 33; 27, p. 49]. More moderate politicians accepted the new-type college as frugal and easy on the public purse [30, p. 11; 45, p. 74]. Much legislative effort went into the search for some self-sustaining formula for the new colleges—tuition charges, sale of produce from the college farm, piggy-backing on existing institutions, and aid from the highest bidder for the college location. Counties and cities were encouraged to compete with proffered cash, loans, buildings, or whatever other attractions human ingenuity could devise. The bids made and the deals struck were awe-inspiring—and tax-saving. Arkansas endured paroxysms of salary-cutting, legislated faculty terminations with some rehiring at lower pay, library deprivations, and appropriations in warrants with value dropping as low as 30 percent [19, pp. 35–39, 55]. Wealthy creditors or benefactors also gave saving aid: for example, John Pillsbury in Minnesota and John Purdue in Indiana [18, pp. 25–31; 21, p. 32]. Citizens of Lincoln were persuaded to advance money to keep Nebraska's main building from falling down, with the expectation of legislative repayment, but the confidence proved to be misplaced [30, p. 64]. Most of the New England states hoped to avoid start-up costs, even for buildings, by assigning the land-grant funds to existing private institutions.

Thus regarding the land grants as a federal replacement of their responsibility, the states devoted many years to evasion, temporizing, reneging, and borrowing against what was neither matched nor supplemented. Even a quarter century after his famous legislation Senator Morrill complained that his own state of Vermont was not doing its part by relying on federal proceeds solely, while Vermont's president lamented that the state had "not helped by one acre or one cent" [28, pp. 223, 236].

Having tried loans, other indebtedness, fees, and nominal salaries, Missouri reached its watershed of state support almost thirty years after its founding with legislative hands forced by the conditions set by the incoming president [57, p. 113]. Until settled as damages through the courts and a special commission, Yale received "not a dollar" from the state while it administered Connecticut's land grant [53, p. 72]. Some states, like Wisconsin, entrapped themselves into a precedent for annual appropriations by having to repay easy loans taken from the federal endowment [9, p. 127]. After having waited eleven years to open the doors of the college that the Morrill Act contemplated, Ohio took eighteen more to provide a direct state levy [36, p. 1]. Worse still, it took New Jersey thirty years [32, p. 93]. The "neglected stepchild" was the dominant country-wide image left by the states' relations with the early land-grant colleges [12, p. 111; 17, p. 304; 11, p. 22; 58, pp. 30, 35–36].

It must be concluded, therefore, that the original federal land grants were not effective in priming the state pump. The states, with few exceptions, did what they had to, minimally (i.e., erected buildings that were denied the use of federal income), thus avoiding annual outlays; but an increasingly self-conscious democratic spirit gradually came to the colleges' rescue, along with agitation and reminders from the colleges and their leaders. Some crisis or emergency or appeal to fair play usually led to an appropriation for some operational purpose, and what had thus begun could then be repeated. The spasmodic gradually became habitual. Two new extensions of federal assistance, the Hatch Act of 1887 and the Second Morrill Act of 1890 (the latter, with its money rather than land for a "more complete endowment"), pulled the colleges over the financial hump and gave the states their final reprieve while adjusting to the inescapable. A new era dawned. The take-off point had been reached in state assumption of the major role in public higher education.

State control developed more or less in tandem with state support, replacing the early practice of state chartering with essentially private control through self-perpetuating boards of trustees. This evolution, beyond the space available here, gives still more evidence that state support and state control were public tastes that had to be acquired. Whether entrapped or not by accepting the Morrill Act's conditions, all states eventually conceded, however reluctantly and tardily, that state patronage should follow, that the new institution was a child of the state, and that the full faith and credit of the state were involved; but "eventually" was the key. Torn between emerging democracy and established tax resistance, the states needed time. They took it.

In addition to these major misconceptions, two significant historical developments have been omitted or grossly underestimated. One is the obverse of the state role discussed above: the neglected significance of the *national* system of state-based colleges and the national role in the formative years. The other is the great contribution of the incremental state-by-state educational upgrading that these humble colleges left in their wake enroute to becoming strong universities.

Neglected National Role

Nowadays, when the states and localities have come to be the educational bulwarks and the Congress has gone to such lengths to deny national responsibility, it is difficult to reconstruct from an earlier era the national role and its determining impact on educational reform. Born of the wartime nationalizing spirit, the Morrill Act was a masterpiece of nondirective federal aid. It was clear enough to guarantee a state-initiated college in every state but vague enough to let the college accommodate to local reality. It wanted agriculture and mechanic arts—the neglected concerns of neglected students—targeted for attention, but it did not exclude anything, however conventional. Yet the national intent showed through: a new emphasis, a new clientele, a permanent endowment, and an expected state commitment to fit into the loosely drawn national network against the alternative of refunding the income. Using their options freely, the states created all kinds of institutions, some maximizing the "leading object" of the Morrill Act and some minimizing it. It is significant that Senator Morrill himself emphasized the national purpose and role and later sought to enhance the endowment of what he called the "national colleges for the advancement of scientific and industrial education"—both "national" and, for greater breadth, "scientific" instead of "agricultural." He perceived a national educational obligation that was not to "be avoided by the cranky plea that Government has nothing to do with education" [33, pp. 3, 7, 13].

Ample evidence shows that the new colleges were regarded by their advocates and founders as a national system or network, and were so developed. The enabling act itself gave an unmistakable clue: a little-noted section provided that an annual informational report should be made by each college to every other college and to the Secretary of the Interior—that is, to others, thus serving the country-wide system, and to a national educational office, thus symbolizing the intended scope. The colleges, in parallel development with the U.S. Department of Agriculture, became the linchpin in the national "system" concept in agricultural education, research, and extension that has won world acclaim. That concept gained further cohesion by a groundswell of sentiment that culminated in the formation of the Association of American Agricultural Colleges and Experiment Stations in 1887, which brought the pieces together in both fellowship and professional advancement. With subsequent name changes, that organization promoted a host of interinstitutional objectives country-wide and lobbied vigorously for common national interests with a potency that has long been noted by academic and governmental onlookers. An informal system or network existed, too. Nationwide correspondence and meetings provided the original impetus for the colleges, for the association, and for closer relations with U.S. government officials. College officials visited other places for ideas, plans, curricula, and faculty and presidential recruitment. Arkansas built its Old Main directly from the Illinois plans [42, p. 103]. Colorado Agricultural College was slavishly patterned after the Michigan Agricultural College and Michigan law [20, p. 25]. Clearly, the national system was also a network of common philosophy and sentiment.

There were other evidences of a national system. A curricular core was imposed nationwide—agricultural and mechanic arts education and military training, whatever the fate of classical education might be. The wartime imposition of military training best symbolized the national aspects again. There was something common beyond the required core, too: the ready-to-develop ideals that would cater to the "industrial classes" and practical professions, assure the centrality of science (since it was the base for the "leading objects"), and use both experimentation and service as the cement for mutual relations with the states in which located. If one interpretation of American educational evolution after the Civil War held that there is no "great central idea" but at bottom something "formless, chaotic, and full of contradictions," as historian S. Willis Rudy has written [47, p. 156], it could accurately be said that the new colleges came closer to a "great central idea" than any others. They also had a keen and proud awareness of what they did hold in common across the nation.

Finally, it should be noted again that the national influence took tangible form, as previously noted, in the dominant financing of the early land-grant colleges. While the state fraction of the total support steadily mounted, after a tardy start, the national dominance was not overcome until the turn of the century. At that time, the catalogs for Rhode Island still boasted that all salaries were paid wholly from federal funds, and the University of Nevada still derived approximately three-fourths of its support from the "liberal aid" of the national government [14, p. 83; 8, p. 11]. A 1903 report showed that land-grant proceeds, then including federal appropriations under the 1890 Morrill Act, came to just under $2 million, whereas the states appropriated slightly less than $2.5 million for operating purposes [55, p. 11].

However, time shifted the balance against too much "nationalizing" as the Civil War receded. Senator Morrill, overtaken by political realities, eventually dropped "national" from his legislative proposals for further aid to his colleges and contented himself with the national effect from a network of state-based, federally aided institutions. While the balance thus shifted and the state role became much stronger, the national role left indelible marks. These and their history should not be forgotten nor minimized. Some such national impetus could alone have produced such a nationwide crop of colleges in so short a time. The country-wide impact on incipient institutions, on states relating thereto, and on national opportunities and rewards coming therefrom is the enduring heritage.

Incremental Improvement

The other neglected feature of the early land-grant colleges was their pragmatic, step-by-step progress, internally driven rather than externally inspired, toward better education in all the states. As a foreign observer, Lord Bryce was more prophetic than critical when, in *The American Commonwealth*, he cited the burgeoning state universities as often "true universities rather in aspiration than in fact" but still "better than nothing" [3, vol. 2, p. 681]. If they had awaited the evolution of high schools and despaired of standards below Harvard and Oxford, higher education in the United States would have been long delayed and immeasurably impoverished. Instead, the hope of incremental educational salvation sprang eternal in the new colleges. In state after state they were not much, but better than nothing—and often better in the newer states than any alternative.

While the new colleges, like most of the older ones, were running preparatory departments to undergird some pretense of university work, they were also locked into the upgrading processes whereby public school systems came into being. As soon as possible, they cut the Gordian knot of how to elicit acceptable high schools while providing a substitute. Many of the college presidents assiduously worked to make the college the leader, teacher-supplier, and upward-pulling magnet of the whole educational system of the state and found careers wending in and out of the upper layers of the emerging public school systems and their normal schools. Nebraska's chancellor said to a state teachers' convention: "I see the common school stuck in the mud and the university suspended in the air. If we are to have a system of education, the word is 'Close up' " [30, p. 90].

The modest incremental road to higher standards was clearly envisioned by President Chadbourne of Wisconsin, who said that instead of telling students what they ought to do, "We must take them as they are and do the best we can with them" [9, p. 230]. Others, like President Minor of Virginia Agricultural and Mechanical College, agreed that the problem was to encourage students "to seek the honour of a diploma not placed so high as to be beyond their reach" [25, p. 96]. The author of Nebraska's charter said his "prime objective was to get the institution at work as early as possible with as high a grade as the finances would permit, and then improve upon the general foundation as experience warranted or indicated modification" [30, p. 15]. No statement could better portray the prevailing pragmatic incrementalism—to get to work as soon as possible, to reach as high a grade as could be afforded, and to improve by experience. That ever-upward ideal was the constant and crucial factor.

As the new colleges ratcheted forward, step-by-step, opportunity by opportunity, not only was the public school system perfected, but the collegiate work was spread into a broader curriculum; professional schools and liberal arts education were given new balance; research and nonbook learning were embraced; the material instruments of learning (buildings, libraries, laboratories) burgeoned; only the "best" faculty became "good enough"; alumni successes proved that trained intelligence was a dormant resource in every state; intercollegiate rivalry and emulation nationwide added an upward impetus—until each state had a full-fledged comprehensive university (or the components shared in two, if a separate state university already existed). That was inherent in the statutory amplitude and in the linkage with public educational aspirations and the slow-but-eventually-sure public capacity for support.

This spreading around of the educational good, this doing what could be done toward an unswerving ideal, was a monumental achievement of the initial national policy and subsequent state support that flowed from the Morrill Act of 1862. Attempts to clear up misconceptions and to understand what has been neglected in our perception of the early land-grant colleges does not detract from the overall achievements, but, rather, confirms them from another perspective. When only a glimmer of the future had yet become apparent, the committee on education of the House of Representatives reported in 1890 that the land-grant colleges "have turned out a body of men who, as teachers, investigators, and leaders of industry, rank well up with the same class of men everywhere in the world," while at the same time bringing the older institutions "more closely into harmony with the spirit and purpose of the age" [58, p. 89]. This was only a modest forerunner of what was still ahead for the step-by-step incrementalism that was to change the face of American higher education. The historical adaptation of the "new education" has been remarkable. It has left something different and enduring—and something that is no longer confined to institutions called "land grant."

References

1. Becker, C. L. *Cornell University: Founders and the Founding*. Ithaca, N. Y.: Cornell University Press, 1944.

2. Bidwell, P. W., and J. I. Falconer. *History of Agriculture in the Northern United States, 1620–1860*. Washington: Carnegie Institution, 1925.

3. Bryce, J. *The American Commonwealth*. Third edition. New York: Macmillan, 1904.

4. Callcott, G. H. *A History of the University of Maryland*. Baltimore: Maryland Historical Society, 1966.

5. Carman, H. J., and R. G. Tugwell. "The Significance of American Agricultural History." *Agricultural History*, 12 (April 1938), 99–106.

6. Carter, H. L. "Rural Indiana in Transition, 1850–1860." *Agricultural History*, 20 (April 1946), 107–21.

7. Cary, H. W. *The University of Massachusetts: A History of One Hundred Years.* Amherst: University of Massachusetts, 1962.

8. Church, J. E., Jr. (ed.). *Nevada State University Tri-Decennial Celebration, May 28 to June 2, 1904.* Reno: Barndollar and Durley, n.d.

9. Curti, M., and V. Carstensen. *The University of Wisconsin, 1848–1925.* Madison: University of Wisconsin Press, 1949.

10. Dexter, E. G. *A History of Education in the United States.* New York: Macmillan, 1904.

11. Doten, S. B. *An Illustrated History of the University of Nevada.* Reno: University of Nevada, 1924.

12. Dunaway, W. F. *History of the Pennsylvania State College.* Lancaster, Pa.: Lancaster Press, 1946.

13. Eddy, E. D., Jr. *Colleges for Our Land and Time: The Land-Grant Idea in American Education.* New York: Harper, 1956.

14. Eschenbacher, H. F. *The University of Rhode Island: A History of Land-Grant Education in Rhode Island.* New York: Appleton-Century-Crofts, 1967.

15. Fernald, M. C. *History of the Maine State College and the University of Maine.* Orono, Me.: University of Maine, 1916.

16. Ferrier, W. W. *Origin and Development of the University of California.* Berkeley: Sather Gate Book Shop, 1930.

17. Fleming, W. L. *Louisiana State University 1860–1896.* Baton Rouge: Louisiana State University, 1936.

18. Gray, J. *The University of Minnesota, 1851–1951.* Minneapolis: University of Minnesota Press, 1951.

19. Hale, H. *University of Arkansas, 1871–1948.* Fayetteville: University of Arkansas Alumni Association, 1948.

20. Hansen, J. E., II. *Democracy's College in the Centennial State: A History of Colorado State University.* Fort Collins, Colo.: Colorado State University, 1977.

21. Hepburn, W. M., and L. M. Sears. *Purdue University: Fifty Years of Progress.* Indianapolis: Hollenbeck Press, 1925.

22. Hewett, W. T. *Cornell University.* New York: University Publishing Society, 1905.

23. Hull, A. L. *A Historical Sketch of the University of Georgia.* Atlanta: Foote and Davies Company, 1894.

24. Jones, C. C. "An Agricultural College's Response to a Changing World." *Agricultural History,* 42 (October 1968), 283, 295.

25. Kinnear, D. D. *The First 100 Years: A History of Virginia Polytechnic Institute and State University.* Blacksburg, Va.: Virginia Polytechnic Institute Educational Foundation, 1972.

26. Kinnison, W. A. *Building Sullivant's Pyramid.* Columbus: Ohio State University Press, 1970.

27. Kuhn, M. *Michigan State: The First Hundred Years, 1855–1955.* East Lansing, Mich.: Michigan State University Press, 1955.

28. Lindsay, J. I. *Tradition Looks Forward, The University of Vermont: A History 1791–1904.* Burlington, Vt.: University of Vermont State Agricultural College, 1954.

29. Lockmiller, D. A. *History of the North Carolina State College of Agriculture and Engineering of the University of North Carolina, 1889–1939.* Raleigh: Edwards and Broughton Company, 1939.

30. Manley, R. N. *Centennial History of the University of Nebraska,* Vol. 1, *Frontier University (1869–1919).* Lincoln: University of Nebraska Press, 1969.

31. Martin, D. D. *The Lamp in the Desert, the Story of the University of Arizona.* Tucson: University of Arizona Press, 1960.

32. McCormick, R. P. *Rutgers: A Bicentennial History.* New Brunswick, N. J.: Rutgers University Press, 1966.

33. Morrill, J. S. "Speech of Hon. Justin S. Morrill of Vermont in the Senate of the United States." Reprint headed "Educational Fund." Washington, April 26, 1876.

34. Nevins, A. *The State Universities and Democracy*. Urbana: University of Illinois Press, 1962.

35. Perry, G. S. *The Story of Texas A and M*. New York: McGraw-Hill, 1951.

36. Pollard, J. R. *History of the Ohio State University: The Story of its First Seventy-Five Years 1873–1948*. Columbus: Ohio State University Press, 1952.

37. Proctor, S. *The University of Florida: Its Early Years, 1853–1906*. Microfilm. Gainesville: University of Florida, 1958.

38. Pyre, J. F. A. *Wisconsin*. New York: Oxford University Press, 1920.

39. Rainsford, G. N. *Congress and Higher Education in the Nineteenth Century*. Knoxville: University of Tennessee Press, 1972.

40. Rasmussen, W. D. "The Civil War: A Catalyst of Agricultural Revolution." *Agricultural History*, 39 (October 1965), 187–95.

41. Read, D. "Historical Sketches of the Universities and Colleges in the United States." In *Contributions to the History of Education*, edited by F. B. Hough, pp. 15–72. Washington: Bureau of Education, Department of Interior, 1883.

42. Reynolds, J. H., and D. Y. Thomas. *History of the University of Arkansas*. Fayetteville: University of Arkansas, 1910.

43. Ross, E. D. "Lincoln and Agriculture." *Agricultural History*, 3 (April 1929), 51–66.

44. _____. "The 'Father' of the Land-Grant College." *Agricultural History*, 12 (April 1938), 151–86.

45. _____. *A History of the Iowa State College of Agriculture and Mechanic Arts*. Ames: Iowa State College Press, 1942.

46. Rudolph, F. *The American College and University*. New York: Alfred A. Knopf, 1962.

47. Rudy, S. W. "The 'Revolution' in American Higher Education, 1865–1900." *Harvard Educational Review*, 21 (Summer 1951), 155–73.

48. Sackett, E. B. *New Hampshire's University*. Somersworth, N.H.: New Hampshire Publishing Company, 1974.

49. Saloutos, T. "The Agricultural Problem and Nineteenth-Century Industrialism." *Agricultural History*, 22 (July 1948), 156–74.

50. Slosson, E. E. *Great American Universities*. New York: Macmillan, 1910.

51. Solberg, W. U. *The University of Illinois, 1867–1894*. Urbana: University of Illinois Press, 1968.

52. Stadtman, V. A. *The University of California, 1868–1968*. New York: McGraw-Hill, 1970.

53. Stemmons, W. *Connecticut Agricultural College—A History*. Storrs, Conn.: Connecticut Agricultural College, 1931.

54. Stephens, F. F. *A History of the University of Missouri*. Columbia: University of Missouri Press, 1962.

55. True, A. C., and D. J. Crosby. *The American System of Agricultural Education*. Washington: U.S. Government Printing Office, 1904.

56. University of New Hampshire. *History of the University of New Hampshire, 1866–1941*. Rochester, N.H.: University of New Hampshire, 1941.

57. Viles, J. *The University of Missouri: A Centennial History*. Columbia: University of Missouri, 1939.

58. Walters, J. D. *History of the Kansas State Agricultural College*. Manhattan, Kans.: Kansas State Agricultural College, 1909.

Eldon L. Johnson is system-wide Vice-President Emeritus, University of Illinois, and was, during the writing, Scholar-in-Residence at the Rockefeller Foundation's Study and Conference Center, Bellagio, Italy.

The University and the Social Gospel:
The Intellectual Origins of the "Wisconsin Idea"

J. David Hoeveler, Jr.

A notable fact of American life in the late nineteenth century was the remarkable transformation of the American college and its emergence as the new university. As usually described, this metamorphosis derived from three major factors: a new concern for practicality and utility in the colleges' curricular program; a democratic effort to extend the benefits of education to a wider portion of the community and to repay the public by servicing its needs; and a new academic interest in research—that is, the advancement of knowledge instead of the mere passing-on of an acquired cultural tradition.[1] These three components were mutually reinforcing, and, as integrated aspects of the social role of the American university, they found their most famous statement in the "Wisconsin Idea," which received its fullest summarization during the administration of Charles R. Van Hise in the early twentieth century. The Wisconsin Idea pledged the University of Wisconsin to serve the state by applying its research to the solution of public problems, by training experts in the physical and social sciences and joining their academic efforts to the public, administrative functions of the state, and by extending the work of the University, through its personnel and facilities, to the boundaries of the state.[2]

Particularly with respect to the social sciences, the University of Wisconsin truly did pioneer in merging the higher learning with public life. But the concept, and indeed the rhetoric, of service to the state was at this time becoming the norm of the state universities everywhere in America, and outside Wisconsin was often more starkly utilitarian in its operations. Nonetheless, Wisconsin became the focus of national interest because it gave dramatic and concrete illustration to a new concept. Historians, like the public itself, have long been interested in the Wisconsin Idea, and particularly in its reputation as a new experiment in politics associated with the governorship of Robert M. La Follette and in its network of affiliations with "the other end of State Street"—the University—in Madison. To this extent, however, they have neglected the origins of the Wisconsin Idea as it emerged within the changing intellectual milieu of nineteenth-century America. Those origins deserve emphasis, because a study of them suggests especially that the University of Wisconsin's special contribution was the conceptual as well as the practical elucidation of ideas generated by several individuals who served the institution in a critical period.

My subject, then, is in part the intellectual history of an institution; but I also endeavor to relate that history to the context of reform thought in the late nineteenth century. I wish especially to emphasize the elements of continuity between the reform impulse of evangelical Protestantism in the antebellum period and the later Social Gospel movement. Specifically, I will endeavor to show that the three persons who best articulated the Wisconsin Idea—John Bascom, Richard T. Ely, and John R. Commons—each found in the new role of the University the logical and critical vehicle of their ideals: the perfection of the Christian state.

Because the elements of continuity loom so large in the intellectual origins of the Wisconsin Idea, it is important to keep in perspective the major characteristics, the religious and social objectives of evangelical Protestantism. As Perry Miller once suggested, evangelical Protestantism was the central cultural force in the United States in the half-century before the Civil War; it in fact provided the fullest expression of America's quest for a national identity.[3] In a nation of diverse ethnic and religious groups, evangelical Protestantism looked beyond the institutional churches, the national established churches that typified the Old World, for a common religious substance, a core of spirituality that would cement the nation. The principal vehicle for evangelical Protestantism, and the answer to its quest for religious unity, was the revival. Bypassing church creeds and sectarian divisions, the revival, through the principles of divine grace and saving personal conversion, pursued a kind of "pure Christianity," one largely indifferent to the institutional church but obsessed with the notion that personal and public morality would serve as the foundation of a religious nation. This foundation was judged critical for the defense of the nation against its greatest enemies, the spirit of Mammon and the spirit of infidelity.[4]

There were important corollaries to this consensus in the realms of politics and social reform. Because America had forsaken the idea of a national church and its ties to a national government, and because it centered its quest for a pure religion outside the institutional churches, the concept of the voluntary principle became important to it. A great variety of voluntary organizations emerged in nineteenth-century Protestant America: the American Education Society, the American Bible Society, the American Sunday-School Union, the American Tract Society, the American Home Mission Society, the Society for the Promotion of Collegiate and Theological Education in the West. Their united concern was the conversion and salvation of the country. These organizations, interdenominational in membership, had their counterparts in a host of others concerned with specific social causes—temperance and prohibition, Sabbatarianism, education, and antislavery most prominent among them. The voluntary organization was a kind of surrogate for church and state, but it was not exclusively so. When large moral issues loomed, the evangelicals quite willingly called upon the state. But whatever the situation, it was to the revival that evangelicals looked for the generating of a social energy that would ignite the community's moral resolve. Theirs was the pursuit of an energizing power that could convert a nation floundering in materialism and moral laxity. Nothing could more certainly save the drunkard than the revival's conversion of his soul. Lyman Beecher's call for "a disciplined moral militia" to confront America's spiritual and social ills was the quintessential expression of a key aspect of the evangelical mind.[5] But the concept of social and moral energy was also important to the formulators of the Wisconsin Idea.

THE antebellum college (the "old-time college" as we call it now) was a critical part of the evangelical goal of a Protestant America. The nine colleges founded in the colonial period were supplemented by hundreds more in the early nineteenth century, most of them sponsored by one of the various Protestant denominations. The old-time college has not had a good press. Undoubtedly its heavily classical curriculum was narrow and its classroom life dull, often even anti-intellectual. A strict paternalism governed student life, and the college atmosphere was restrictive and inhibiting. But in ways often unappreciated, the old-time college tried to be relevant to the society it served. Revivals were common occurrences on campuses, a fact that attains special significance when seen in relation to the pattern of moral reform activities that revivals often generated.[6] Indeed, the old-time college's moral pattern related the school directly to the community outside. The spirit of collegiate reform efforts drew partly from the extracurricular life of the schools, especially the literary societies in which students debated important contemporary events, and the special student organizations to promote abolitionism, temperance, and other causes. Not surprisingly, therefore, at Oberlin College, the institution where revivalism and other evangelical ideals were most pronounced, antislavery sentiment and abolitionist activity among the faculty and students also were more pronounced than in any other American college.[7] Then too, the moral force of the old-time college grew directly from the academic life of the college. Indeed, perhaps the oldest academic tradition in America was the one which required the college president to instruct all seniors in moral and mental philosophy. In these courses, the president outlined the doctrines of a moral universe and of innate moral ideas in the human mind. Usually a full year of instruction was devoted to this system of moral law and its applications to society. For moral philosophy—perhaps the unique aspect of higher education in the United States—was not a mere exercise in philosophical abstractions. One need only examine the index to Francis Wayland's *The Elements of Moral Science*, America's first domestic, academic best-seller, to appreciate the wide penumbra of "practical ethics" embraced by this subject. They included the Sabbath, personal property, oaths, marriage, chastity, the duties of parents, the rights and obligations of children, the nature of just government, charity and poor laws, war, and the treatment of animals.[8]

JOHN Bascom was heir to this tradition when he came to the University of Wisconsin as its fifth president in 1874. Measured against the pattern of the American university then, Wisconsin had few distinctive traits. Like most state universities, it was still little different from the old-time college. Its curriculum was largely prescribed; its moral regimentation, denoted by such requirements as attendance at chapel services, was well intact; and its statutory pledges to promote agricultural and technical training were largely unfulfilled. Nor was there anything untypical about Bascom's background. Like so many college presidents of his day, he was born in a family of New Englanders who had removed by the time of his birth in 1827 to western New York. He was only one of a remarkable number of college presidents who grew up in the "burned-over" district, so called because of the flames of revivalism which between about 1800 and 1850 frequently swept this most intensely evangelical area in the nation. Bascom was a graduate of Williams College who had pursued studies at Auburn and Andover theological seminaries. He had returned to Williams to teach rhetoric, an unsuitable academic calling; the appointment at Wisconsin gave him opportunities both for administrative leadership and for bringing the full scope of his ideas personally to a growing student body.

But, as his work at Wisconsin soon proved, John Bascom was unique among the academic moral philosophers of his day. In many ways he set the future course of the institution, and one of his students, Robert M. La Follette, credits Bascom as the true originator of the Wisconsin Idea. Determining the truth of La Follette's assertion requires a close examination of Bascom's thoughts. Here it can be said that Bascom pioneered intellectually in three directions. He was one of the first religious thinkers in America to accept the main outline of evolutionary science and to establish upon it an entirely new theology, what he himself labeled the "New Theology." Secondly, he took moral philosophy, a course he taught to every individual student in the University, in important new directions. His own moral philosophy textbook, written while he was at Wisconsin and used by Bascom in his classes,[9] accorded 117 pages, significantly more than any other similar text, to the problems of government and politics and the need for expanded public authority.[10] And he pushed moral philosophy still farther by writing the first academic sociology text, a moral treatise more than a scientific one, but embracing the causes of temperance, women's rights, and the right of labor to organize. Thirdly, Bascom used his influence at Wisconsin to outline a new philosophy of state for America, a doctrine of enhanced moral powers for government and public institutions, including the state university. He worked carefully at this philosophical labor, preserving the essential objectives of the evangelical ideology in which he believed, but reconstructing that ideology to accommodate the public sphere. John Bascom was one of the first exponents of the Social Gospel in America; his unwavering quest was for the "Kingdom of Heaven."

Undoubtedly, Bascom was one of the most difficult and complex of America's philosophers, a fact that may explain a general neglect of his work. Influenced greatly by many of the liberal religious thinkers of the nineteenth century, including Ralph Waldo Emerson, Horace Bushnell, and, in philosophy, Laurens P. Hickok, Bascom combined their influences with evolutionary ideas to become one of the leading theological liberals. *The New Theology* grew out of his teaching at Wisconsin, as did *Evolution and Religion,* published after his departure. These two works carefully articulated new means to realizing the older ends of the Christian society desired by the evangelical philosophers. Bascom certainly did make important revisions in the evangelical theology, but the pervasive themes of moral advancements and social reform remained equally prominent. Essentially, Bascom perceived that evolution gave a whole new sense to the concept of the Kingdom of God and a new means of realizing it. Rejecting Herbert Spencer and William Graham Sumner's depiction of evolution as generated by powerful material and perhaps blind physical forces, Bascom painted the evolution concept in strokes of broad cosmic dimensions. Evolution demonstrated the oneness of life, the organic unity in all things; and, more importantly, it illustrated the spiritual powers at work in the world. Divine plan, as evolution showed, called for progressive improvement in the physical qualities of all the species; and it also incorporated, in the case of the human race, the unfolding of the rational, moral, and spiritual powers. Quite properly, in fact, evolution blurred the boundaries of the natural and the supernatural, and demonstrated an immanent God whose activity in the world assured the progressive realization of the Kingdom of Heaven on earth.[11]

From this perspective, Bascom drew implications for his entire educational and social philosophy. Evolution gave a whole new scope to the human intellect. The mind, Bascom said, was the correlative of the universe, and its constant expansion alone assured human grasp of God's progressive manifestation to the world, His revelation of Himself in the evolutionary scheme of things. Evolution also sounded the death knell of stale creeds, rituals, and religious formulations of divine truth. The revelation of God was not a completed fact or past event, but an indication of expanding spiritual powers in the world. Thus, Bascom wrote, "What we call the movement of evolution is also the movement of reason. . . . The world is thus laid open to us as a dynamic, living spiritual product." Moreover, religious truth was now united with secular truth; it could no longer be compartmentalized as sacred dogma or the special prerogative of a priestly class. Truth was revealed not only by the spiritual insight of the human mind as it advanced through evolution, but by the expanded powers of the intellect in science. Science then was but one aspect of "the thought of God . . . the omnipresence of his wisdom."[12] Bascom here was elaborating one of the key ideas behind the emergence of the modern university—the concept of the dynamic, plastic nature of truth. That concept played a catalytic role in transforming the old-time college's ideal of preserving a specific intellectual heritage into the new university's objective of the open-ended pursuit of new knowledge.

B ASCOM thus saw the world, as the evangelicals had described it, in terms of its pervasive moral and spiritual character. But there was an important alteration in the perspective he took. The evangelical might have the model Christian society as his foremost objective, but he continued to see the world in terms of individual sin. Always, the path to social salvation lay along the lines of the special and separate conversion of individual souls. But as evolution illuminated the oneness of things, as it merged the spiritual and physical, and as it demonstrated the complicated matrix in which all things were imbedded, it greatly enlarged the whole sphere in which the moral sense must operate. It was necessary to view the world in terms of the "ever-growing tissue of moral relations" that embraced it. In short, the moral reformer could no longer rely upon the isolated individual as the vehicle for the perfection of the community; he needed instead to be master of all the social laws affecting society. Bascom

thus wrote that "a theology which seeks the regeneration of society in ignorance of social laws is doomed to failure."[13]

Bascom continued to employ the language of the evangelicals, and gave much attention to his own new doctrine of "conversion." Not only did conversion now have an emphatic social meaning; it also described, not a sudden and convulsive change, but slow, constant improvement wrought in the social material of the world. Conversion in this sense required not so much the skill of the gospel preacher as the expertise of the social scientist, for as the race advanced, intellectual and rational powers would continually supplant emotional ones as the critical vehicles of human progress. Bascom used the terms "reason" and "spiritual power" interchangeably, and used both as surrogates for the evangelicals' "grace." They supplied for him the source of social energy and power that the evangelicals found in the revival, and Bascom even asserted that the full application of intellectual power to the unfolding spiritual laws of the universe was the certain means for the "redemption" of the world. "We are brought by these universal facts of law, unfolding themselves progressively in evolution, in contact with the world in a new way. It is not only capable of redemption, it is being redeemed."[14] Bascom, furthermore, employed the evangelical motif of pure Christianity in his new theology. Spiritual power dispensed with ritual and creeds, and had as its business the moral improvement of the world. Moral reason, in fact, was the purest expression of the religious sentiment, and of the religious nature of man.[15] And all these ideas fit nicely into the concept of the Kingdom of Heaven. "The Kingdom of Heaven, Bascom wrote, "is a physical, intellectual, social, and spiritual product. It adjusts all things and persons to each other."[16]

John Bascom brought together many of the ideas he had developed at Wisconsin, and he published them during his last year at Madison in his work, *Sociology*. This discipline was just emerging from moral philosophy as an independent academic subject in the American university,[17] and in fact Bascom made it a direct extension of moral philosophy. It was a key transitional work, though not a sociological treatise in the modern sense. Bascom defined sociology as the study of social, civic, economic, religious, and ethical forces in their various operations. But the last aspect, the ethical, was the most important. For with the evolutionary advance of the race, ethical forces emerge in more pronounced forms. Thus, not only is sociology itself a quest for the just society, but also it must rely on the spiritual as well as the empirical faculties as its tools of analysis and perception.[18] How may society discover and use spiritual power most fully? That question summarized for Bascom the central concern of the new science he now explored. "The widest and most inclusive diffusion of power, issuing in the largest aggregate of power, is the aim of society."[19]

These reflections led Bascom to one of his most important ideas, the doctrine of state power, which he developed and impressed forcefully upon the minds of the students at Wisconsin. Bascom was literally obsessed with the problem of organizing social power as outlined in *Sociology*. Bascom described for his students an age he judged to be destructive in its use of power, a ruthlessly competitive society with aggregated power in the hands of a few individuals. Such an arrangement of forces was unethical and un-Christian in nature, and ultimately debilitating to society as a whole. When Bascom therefore called for "harmonious power" as the truest expression of "beneficent power," he turned directly to the state, the agency of public power, for its exercise. The state, Bascom wrote in *Sociology*, must create social power, surpassing the work of isolated individuals.[20] Furthermore, the state must give power to the weaker elements in its midst, a concern that suffused most of the reform measures that Bascom endorsed.[21] Bascom was in fact making an important modification of the evangelical format: he now turned to the state as a surrogate for churches and voluntary societies. Modern America could no longer rely on these institutions for the perfection of the nation (Bascom even felt they had become too much the voice of entrenched private factions) and must instead look directly to the state for moral leadership and action.[22]

THESE views had important implications for Bascom's ideas about the role of the university in modern society, but it is important to bear in mind that the university question itself was only one part of the reform ideology that he and others brought to Wisconsin. On three other specific issues, Bascom was outspoken, and he examined each through the same social perspective that anticipated the Wisconsin Idea. One of these issues, prohibition, particularly shows the continuity between the older evangelical program and Bascom's sociology. Bascom was one of the most prominent members of the national Prohibition party in Wiscon-

sin, a fact that was not a little responsible for the political embroilments that plagued his administration in Madison. He paid much attention to this problem in his sociology text, and in a pamphlet he wrote for public distribution entitled *The Philosophy of Prohibition*. Prohibition above all shows how easily the transition could be made from evangelicalism to the later reform efforts. Indeed, prohibition was the catalyst in the change from an emphasis on voluntary societies to an emphasis on government controls. Here was a large moral issue, and one that affected the whole power of society—it was by definition therefore a matter for the state. Nothing, Bascom believed, more seriously blighted the spiritual powers of contemporary America than the destructive abuses of drink. In fact, Bascom wrote, "the entire moral strength of the race must be brought to the task of lifting off this burden before mankind can resume its march." Indeed the same fallacious ideology that made individual rights sacred in economics threatened to deprive the public of its own rights in defending against the evils of liquor. But the right of the state, the public good, must prevail against these. Said Bascom: "To affirm the personal rights of an individual in a case like this is to enable him to stand across the path of public progress, to check the organic movement of society. . . . Society is under no obligation to subject . . . its own high fortunes to those morally ignorant and repellent." It must "overrule unreason with reason, unrighteousness with righteousness."[23]

Bascom's *Sociology* announced that no social issue was more critical to the theory he expounded than the rights of women.[24] Nor was this a theoretical issue for him, for, as in the case of prohibition, Bascom was active in the cause. He supported co-education at the University, and before the public and to a generation that was still skeptical he advocated woman's suffrage and other feminist causes. Bascom's stance derived directly from his New Theology. He did not pose the issue in terms of natural rights, but in terms of spiritual powers in the evolution of society. Rights merely loom larger as the world progresses and moves toward full spiritual integration. Women now must be admitted, in full standing Bascom believed, to the ongoing spiritual and social progress of the world. And in this matter too, because it was one of great moral consequence, the state must assume an active role. It must provide the proper conditions "to make ready for the free exercise of [the] intelligence and virtue" of women.

Bascom defended this issue even by calling for an end to certain sacred social customs. Old habits of chivalry, he believed, simply concealed a contempt for women and conspired against their exercising their strength.[25]

Finally on the issue of the rights of labor and unionization, John Bascom took a stand uncommon for the usual college president of his day. Indeed he was one of the first to break the stranglehold of laissez-faire doctrine on academic economics in the nineteenth century. He spoke for labor organizations because they too were vehicles of power that could redress the unfair balance in an age of industrial corporations. The greatest danger to any society was precisely this imbalance, and the consequent spiritual and physical deprivation by oppression of great numbers of the population. Here again organized spiritual force was the saving factor in an age that dangerously threatened to render much of society powerless and without influence.[26]

BASCOM was a spiritual optimist who never doubted that the improvement of the world was the ordained order of things. But he could not rest content with society's present state. Ideals, he knew, outran realities, but those who were spiritually in advance of the day must fight for the perfection of the world. It is unlikely that any other college president so bluntly and so directly attacked the corrupting spirit, the individual pursuit of wealth and power, in modern America. Bascom's last baccalaureate address at Wisconsin, entitled "A Christian State," pulled no punches. Spiritually, he said, America was far from the Christian state. "We are in the full swing of individual assertion. Unbridled enterprise is our controlling temper."[27] The same year he wrote: "The money-power vigorously asserts itself, and it easily overawes the moral and social forces which should work with it. . . ."[28] Bascom's address became an urgent plea for public control of the economic forces that operated against the public interest, for "we are in danger of falling under a new economic tyranny." The collective society must assert its own rights, and, in the same way that it must protect itself against the debilitating influence of liquor, it must be equally vigilant toward the abuses of money. Bascom's religious and social thought merged at this juncture. If society was still "The Seat of Sin" (his 1876 baccalaureate address), the state must be the seat of righteousness. "The state like the individual has the duty to be righteous. It has

the right and the duty to push to completion its own organization; to do all it can for its own highest attainments in itself and its citizens."[29]

As Bascom looked to the enlarged influence of the state for the promotion of moral power in modern society, he assigned increasing prominence to the place and function of the state university more than to any other public institution. This view directly extended his efforts to achieve evangelical objectives by new methods. As the volunteer principle yielded to the doctrine of state initiative, so also, in Bascom's mind, did the new state universities assume an importance greater than the small sectarian schools—the old-time colleges. But the same quest for greater spiritual and moral power still governed his thinking. In a baccalaureate address in 1877, Bascom explained that the small colleges, because of their wide diffusion and divided purposes and efforts, deprived the state—especially a state like Wisconsin—of the unified public purpose it needed. Religious and ethnic diversity was harmful if it dispersed efforts for moral improvement and left society to depend on "a rambling halting voluntaryism."[30] Not only was it imperative that intellectual and moral power become a concern of the state; the state university itself must also be the institutional epitome of that power. Bascom, like many other university leaders in his time, looked for the extension of public education to every corner of the state; and he believed that such an educational system naturally would culminate in academic preparation of the state's students for its university. To the people of Wisconsin, Bascom held up the example of Michigan, with its large, successful university and relatively few denominational schools. Ohio, by contrast, had small schools in profusion, and not one among them nationally recognized. Wisconsin resembled too much the latter state, he said, and the result was a tragic loss of public power within its own boundaries.[31]

Bascom thus moved significantly close to the modern conception of the state university; but his views were still governed largely by a nineteenth-century religious perspective, though one clearly more secularized than the older evangelical one. Bascom's views on the state university coincided directly with his theological and philosophical ideas. They expressed, in other words, Bascom's obsession with the spiritual and moral advancement of mankind. Quite simply, public education, and the state university as its highest expression, must strengthen society's "spiritually progressive resources." For "That system of education is alone good which builds society together under spiritual law." Bascom used the language of the old-time college president in declaring that education's most important quality was the moral. Indeed, insofar as ethical law was the underlying unity, the common denominator of all religion, then the state university itself was a surrogate for the churches. Furthermore, moral power in this age must have access to large public institutions. Moral education through the vehicle of the state university provides the means by which to make all acquired powers subservient to the interests of society.[32]

The language was familiar, to be sure, but Bascom was in fact widening its application. Because his theology so thoroughly merged the natural and the supernatural, when he spoke of moral law, and joined that to the objectives of the state university, he intended no mere abstractions. Bascom, who presided over a noticeable expansion of the curriculum at Wisconsin, saw this growth as one means of increased moral power in public life. For it was precisely the new academic concerns of the modern university—and Bascom named political science, economics, constitutional law, sociology, and others—that would best unite the university's social and academic missions. These new disciplines gave the most profound social expression to ethical law. "Here," said Bascom in his 1880 baccalaureate, "moral truths have their seat." The highest expressions of religion and spiritual force enter social life by these doors. In this way, Bascom critically reconstructed the evangelical program while actually extending it. All the new learning that was the creation and concern of the new university was now available for the redemption of the world. "We seem to see the Kingdom of Heaven coming along these very lines of union between scientific research and religious insight."[33] Here, perhaps, John Bascom most completely joined his social philosophy to the academic revolution of the late nineteenth century.

His philosophical argument that brought him to this point leads directly to the message he impressed most indelibly upon the students of the University of Wisconsin. He believed that evolutionary progress dictated the spiritual and moral improvement of the race, but required for its fulfillment the enlarged influence and activity of the state. The university was especially critical to this endeavor, for its work most successfully combined a mastery of spiritual and social laws and the means to apply them to specific prob-

lems. But if this were true, then there could be no higher calling in life than service to the state in some capacity. As La Follette later recalled about his training under Bascom at Wisconsin: "He was forever telling us what the state was doing for us and urging our return obligation not . . . for our own selfish benefit, but to return some service to the state."[34] The graduates of the state university must be the intellectual vanguard of the state; they must supply the ideas that would bring about the just state and inaugurate the new era of collective power.[35] On this point, too, the evangelical refrain echoed; for there was, Bascom believed, no higher "calling" than that of public life, "but none for which the soul needs first so thorough a cleansing in the fountain of truth."[36] The state university must find its role in dispensing this truth. Bascom was never closer to the full statement of the Wisconsin Idea than when he stated, in one of his major public addresses at Madison, "The time will come, and public education will hasten it, in which educational men will gather influence within their own field, and become the servants of the State to counsel action as well as to carry it out."[37]

I T is a remarkable fact that if one were to follow John Bascom's thought and substitute for its religious and spiritual content a strictly secular or materialistic emphasis, one would have the full outline of the Wisconsin Idea as it was presented in the early twentieth century. For as Bascom gave new content and form to the evangelical ethos, so did others—President Charles R. Van Hise, Governor La Follette, Professors Richard T. Ely and John R. Commons—give a precise academic structure and a practical character to Bascom's ideals. Admittedly Bascom never wholly articulated the Wisconsin Idea in a concrete way, though certainly he anticipated its outline. There is a largely unfulfilled promise that one senses in Bascom's writings and speeches. Often he failed to see the logical implications of his own thought. But, as La Follette and Van Hise and others recognized, he prepared the way for the course of the University of Wisconsin after his resignation in 1887; the impact of his ideas on those who influenced the later development of the institution assigns to Bascom a prominent place in its intellectual history.

The appointment of Richard T. Ely in 1892 as director of the newly established School of Economics, Political Science, and History was soon to result in Wisconsin's achieving a national reputation. Frederick Jackson Turner, brought to the University from Johns Hopkins by Bascom, foresaw the need for expanded research in the social sciences, with an eye towards its direct application to the state's needs. The new school became a major link between the University's personnel and the progressive movement in Wisconsin politics, working closely with the state bureaucracy, especially the Wisconsin Industrial Commission, on practical studies of urban problems, city administration, current economic problems, welfare, and crime. By 1907, forty-one faculty members were serving the state on one or more commissions.[38] The perfection of this arrangement owed much to Ely, and to John R. Commons, whom Ely brought to Wisconsin in 1904. But how had these two men come to envision the new role of the university that they helped put into operation? A glance at their individual backgrounds shows some remarkable parallels to Bascom, and further confirms the continuity linking the evangelical ideals, the Social Gospel, and the new university.

LIKE Bascom, Ely grew up in the burned-over district of New York, and was reared in a social and family atmosphere that he remembered mostly for its moralistic severity. His father, descended from a long line of English and American Puritans, quit his engineering job and even allowed crops to spoil lest he violate the Sabbath. Also like Bascom, Ely could not adjust to the extreme aspects of the old religion ("Try as I would I could not become converted"), but endeavored throughout his life to find a new means of applying its basic ethical program. Ely was similarly influenced by Darwinism, but he read the doctrine as a statement of progress and the potential perfectibility of human society. His studies in Germany convinced him that a scientific economics was the indispensable tool for the realization of this goal. He soon emerged as the major figure of the "New Economics," literally a new gospel of hope for the eradication of the ills wrought by laissez-faire, and one whose message Ely worked with evangelical zeal to carry to the land.[39]

The New Economics was to Ely what the New Theology was to Bascom: a new but usable means for the extension of his Christian commitments, an application, in modified form, of the evangelical ideals that shaped his early life. As Ely later wrote, "In my writings and my addresses I . . . attempted to answer the question, 'What will constitute a kingdom of righteousness?' 'What must we strive to accomplish in social reform?'" For the New Economics was essentially to be "a sound, Christian political economy."[40] Nothing in fact required more of "divine grace" than the conduct of the business and commercial life of the nation. America in the late nineteenth century faced a spiritual crisis denoted by the selfish and egotistical worship of Mammon. In 1889, shortly before coming to Wisconsin, Ely had written *Social Aspects of Christianity*, one of the major works of the Social Gospel movement. He called then for "a profound revival of religion, not in any narrow or technical sense . . . but a great religious awakening which shall shake things, going down into the depths of men's lives and modifying their character." Ely employed all the force and style of evangelical rhetoric, but he crucially shifted the focus of religious outreach. "This religious reform," he said, "must infuse a religious spirit into every department of political life."[41] Like Bascom, Ely shifted attention to the state and made it the critical vehicle of social improvement and moral power. This, in fact, was the first article in the creed of the New Economics: "We regard the state as an educational and ethical agency whose positive aid is an indispensable condition of human progress."[42] A year after his appointment at Wisconsin, Ely, with John R. Commons and others, organized the American Institute for Christian Sociology.[43]

Ely came to Madison because he foresaw a great opportunity there to put into action his ideas of social reform. Particularly at the University of Wisconsin would he and his associates have access to the state capital, the courts, the legislature, and the state's administrative bureaus. The state university in fact now loomed large in Ely's mind as a factor in both the religious and the social aspects of his concerns. For although the "theological seminaries" might help us fulfill the commandment to love God, the new social sciences will help us fulfill the commandment to love our neighbor. Ely then proposed that the religious denominations center their activity around the state universities of the country; they should form Christian associations, guild houses with libraries and dormitories. This was a significant way of joining the religious life to the public life of the country, and far more useful—for Ely too was obsessed with the phenomenon of moral power—than promoting separate denominational colleges. In fact a major advantage of this approach, as Bascom had recognized, was its aiding the "unity of Christendom." Sectarianism had been ruinous to that ideal.[44] Religious perspectives probably played a lesser role in Ely's later work at Wisconsin, yielding to more strictly political and academic matters. He supported the reforms of La Follette and, as an occasional consultant, helped make the University conspicuous in the political life of the state. But his own version of the Social Gospel was important to Ely's contribution to the Wisconsin Idea.[45]

EVEN more active in the actual reform programs of the Wisconsin progressive movement was John R. Commons, professor of economics in Ely's new school. The Social Gospel acted as a catalyst also in Commons' life, resulting in his political and academic activity. Commons leaves no doubt that the major early influence on his life was his mother, "the strictest of Presbyterian Puritans," who raised him on Fox's *Book of Martyrs*. She herself represented the spirit of antebellum Oberlin College, that outstanding expression of revivalism and reform, from which she had graduated in 1853. Active then in the institution's antislavery cause, she continued her reformist work afterwards in the movement for temperance and woman's rights. Commons himself spent his undergraduate years at Oberlin. There, joined by his mother, he established an antisaloon league, the beginnings of the Ohio Anti-Saloon League, later one of the most powerful in the country. In 1884 Commons cast his first ballot, for John P. St. John, Prohibitionist candidate for President of the United States.[46] The temperance campaign was probably the major factor in widening Commons' social perspectives and propelling him into leadership, with Ely and others, in the New Economics. A series of essays, written by Commons and collected into an 1894 publication entitled *Social Reform and the Church*, illuminates his views as they emerged in the years before he came to Wisconsin.

Commons' essay called "Temperance Reform" in this volume wholly endorses complete prohibition of the liquor traffic. Like much of the old evangelical literature, it cites the social damage charged to the abuses of drink, even the harm done to unborn children. But Commons, who had recently completed studies with Ely at Johns Hopkins,

treated intemperance as a symptom as well as a cause of social evils. It was now the duty of government, in fact, to remove the causes of intemperance. Specifically, government must enforce shorter hours for labor, preserve the Sabbath (Commons now simply said "Sunday") as protection for labor from forced work, write new factory laws for women and children, abolish sweatshops, and require better wages and greater security of employment. "When all these reforms are carried out," said Commons, "it will be possible to have universal prohibition." Temperance, therefore, still remained an end in itself, but the issue carried Commons directly from evangelicalism to progressivism.[47] And for Commons, progressivism meant the union of Christian ideals with the social sciences. Sociology, by Commons' definition, "co-ordinates all the special social sciences, such as ethics, politics and religion." Commons, who had just helped establish the American Institute for Christian Sociology, still believed that "Christianity is the only solution for social problems," but he added that sociology is "one half of religion."[48] Probably more than any other individual, Commons personified the Wisconsin Idea, for his academic work at Madison was often indistinguishable from his public reform efforts. He was a major figure behind the La Follette reforms, drafting the Civil Service Law of 1905, the Public Utility Act of 1907, and the Industrial Commission Law, among others.[49]

Bascom, Ely, and Commons each brought to the University of Wisconsin perspectives on the educational function of the university that were shaped by their own efforts to define a Social Gospel program for America. But the Wisconsin Idea was not in any strict sense a religious concept. And that it was perfectly possible to accept the social content without the gospel content of the program is quite clearly indicated by the ideas of La Follette and Van Hise. La Follette left no doubt that Bascom greatly influenced him. This was true probably in a large rather than in a specific sense. One suggestion is that Bascom's moralism was most influential,[50] and La Follette himself seems to have corroborated that idea.[51] The ethical sense of life of course bore directly on La Follette's political work, but he saw the University of Wisconsin as a partner in that work. La Follette as governor occasionally sought Bascom's counsel, and particularly when he told the state legislature that the University must justify itself to the state either by its material contributions or as "an ethical force," he employed the language of his former teacher.[52]

CHARLES R. Van Hise, also a student of Bascom, a classmate of La Follette, and president of the University of Wisconsin after 1902, best illustrates the secularization of the evangelical and Social Gospel ideals and their reformulation as the Wisconsin Idea. Van Hise's background was almost entirely in the sciences; he was one of the foremost geologists of his time.[53] Religious concerns were not prominent in his thought, but emphasis on the moral and social responsibilities of the scholar to the public interest loomed very large and, it is probable, owed much to the influence of Bascom.[54] Van Hise supported the causes of prohibition and woman's rights as his former teacher had, and his own work, *Concentration and Control*, was a significant contribution to the literature of progressivism.[55] But Van Hise's version of the Wisconsin Idea was the most materialistic in content, transforming Bascom's sense of spiritual power into a doctrine of economic growth. This dogma then defined the state university's research activity, for new knowledge must be applied directly to the improvement of the lives of the people. The service ideal meant especially the invigoration of extension—the new "missionary" work of the university to use the evangelical vocabulary—so that virtually every home or business in the state, from machine shops to model dairy farms, would feel the long outreach of the state university. But this too was a doctrine of power, one that stated in stark, secular form the essential outline of Van Hise's former teacher's philosophy. It was a new kind of gospel and a new program for social redemption, indeed a new calling for America's institutions of higher learning.

[1] The best general account of these trends is in Lawrence R. Veysey, *The Emergence of the American University* (Chicago, 1965), 57–179.

[2] *Ibid.*, 107–109.

[3] Perry Miller, *The Life of the Mind in America: From the Revolution to the Civil War* (New York, 1965), 6.

[4] *Ibid.*, 8–13; Robert T. Handy, *A Christian America: Protestant Hopes and Historical Realities* (London, 1971), 30–31, 35.

[5] Miller, *Life of the Mind*, 36–42, 47, 83; Handy, *A Christian America*, 42–43, 48–51 (Beecher quotation, p. 45); Sydney Ahlstrom, *A Religious History of the American People* (New Haven, 1972), 637–647; Timothy L. Smith, *Revivalism and Social Reform: American Protestantism on the Eve of the Civil War* (New York, 1957), *passim*. Some of the most valuable recent scholarship on American society in the nineteenth century has demonstrated two broad divisions, with stark political contrasts and allegiances, based on religious affiliation. Three works in particular confirm the existence, before and after the Civil War, of a broad evangelical (pietistic) party united on a series of political issues, such as those outlined above. They are: Paul Kleppner, *The Cross of Culture: A Social Analysis of Midwestern Politics, 1850–1900* (New York, 1970); Richard Jensen, *The Winning of the Midwest: Social and Political Conflict, 1888–1896* (Chicago, 1971); and Ronald P. Formisano, *The Birth of Mass Political Parties: Michigan, 1827–1861* (Princeton, 1971).

[6] See David Robert Huehner, "Reform and the Pre-Civil War American College" (Ph.D. dissertation, University of Illinois, Urbana-Champaign, 1972), 50–51.

[7] *Ibid.*, 87–136, 148–193, 202–250, 262–311.

[8] See Francis Wayland, *The Elements of Moral Science*, ed. by Joseph L. Blau (Cambridge, Massachusetts, 1963 ed.).

[9] University of Wisconsin, *Catalogue*, 1879–1880.

[10] See John Bascom, *Ethics: Or Science of Duty* (New York, 1879), 208–324.

[11] John Bascom, *Evolution and Religion: Or Faith as a Part of a Complete Cosmic System* (New York, 1897), 53, 103; *The New Theology* (New York, 1892), 13, 49; "The Gains and Losses from Faith in Science," in the *Journal of Christian Philosophy*, 1: 8–13 (July, 1882).

[12] Bascom, *Evolution and Religion*, 6, 72–73 (first quotation), 134; *New Theology*, 17–18, 54, 61; "Gains and Losses," 5–6 (second quotation).

[13] Bascom, *Evolution and Religion*, 8–9; *New Theology*, 118. To this extent also Bascom felt that science "gives solidity and breadth to moral questions." See "Gains and Losses," 4. In an address at Madison, Bascom employed the evangelical rhetoric, saying, "If we use words as broadly as we ought, the evangelization of the world is strictly a scientific movement." *Truth and Truthfulness* (Milwaukee, 1881), 18–19 (baccalaureate address).

[14] Bascom, *Evolution and Religion*, 80–81, 84–85, 99; *New Theology*, 171; "Gains and Losses," 6 (the quotation).

[15] Bascom, *New Theology*, 51. This is the sense in which Bascom sought to bring evangelical inspiration into modified and wider use. "The movement which we designate as the New Theology owes much of its vigor to a renewed effort to unite the pietism of religion and the virtue of morality to a higher, wider, deeper spiritualism, which shall have the mastery of ideas in their practical development." *Ibid.*, 8–9. Later, "Pietism must break camp, dismiss its camp followers, and carry the glad tidings of a salvation that waits to sweep through every kingdom, physical, economic, social." *Ibid.*, 181.

[16] Bascom, *Evolution and Religion*, 139.

[17] See Gladys Bryson, "The Comparable Interests of the Old Moral Philosophy and the Modern Social Sciences," in *Social Forces*, 11: 19–27 (1932); "Sociology Considered as Moral Philosophy," in the *American Sociological Review*, 24: 26–36 (1932).

[18] John Bascom, *Sociology* (New York, 1887), 4–5. For a more detailed summary of this idea in Bascom's sociology, see Robert A. Jones, "John Bascom, 1827–1911: Anti-Positivism and Intuitionism in American Sociology," in *The American Quarterly*, 24: 501–522 (October, 1972).

[19] Bascom, *Sociology*, 48.

[20] *Ibid.*, 34, 41. "Government," Bascom wrote, "is . . . always passing beyond the office of protection, securing the conditions of industry, and laying, in various ways, the foundations of enterprise, intelligence and virtue. This great function of government by which it combines the power of all, and makes it immediately and

236

universally available, is as natural and spontaneous a function as that of protection, and can not be dispensed with." See his pamphlet, *The Philosophy of Prohibition* (New York, 1884), 4.

21 Bascom, *Sociology*, 45.

22 *Ibid.*, 162; *The Freedom of Faith* (Madison, 1874), 11–12 (baccalaureate address).

23 Bascom, *Philosophy of Prohibition*, 3–9; *Sociology*, 197–198 (the quotation); see also "What do the Members of a State University Owe to the State?" in *The University Review*, 1: 96 (December, 1884). Bascom felt this point urgently, so concerned was he with the doctrine of moral improvement in society. Elaborating on the need for prohibition, he wrote: "The majority are compelled to endure the expense, the moral exposure, the physical and social deterioration of all sorts incident to the vice, debauchery and animalism of the intemperate, simply that the intemperate may have easy access to intoxicants. In order that the minority may spend their money for their pleasure, the majority are compelled to spend their means on what they loathe—the correction of crime, the support of pauperism, the treatment of idiots, the sustenance of the insane." See his *Sociology*, 198.

24 Bascom, *Sociology*, 184; and see the ensuing discussion, 184–194.

25 John Bascom, *Woman Suffrage* (n.p., n.d.), 3–6 (quotation, p. 3). Bascom's prominence in the women's rights movement won him the special recognition and gratitude of feminist Susan B. Anthony. See Merle Curti and Vernon Carstensen, *The University of Wisconsin: A History, 1848–1925* (2 vols., Madison, 1949), 1: 291.

26 Bascom, *Sociology*, 229–231; *Sermons and Addresses* (New York, 1913), 142–143.

27 John Bascom, *A Christian State* (Milwaukee, 1887), 10. No one more blatantly exemplified this wanton danger, in Bascom's mind, than John D. Rockefeller, who more than once was the object of the moralist's wrath. Wrote Bascom of Rockefeller: "He has turned business into unceasing and unflinching warfare. . . . He has done this with an open profession of Christian faith. . . . Herein lies the guilt of this man, and of others of the same ilk, and of all who put themselves in fellowship with them, that they confound ethical distinctions and make the world one medley of wrong-doing." *Sermons and Addresses*, 144–145.

28 Bascom, *Sociology*, 211.

29 Bascom, *A Christian State*, 16, 25; see also *The Seat of Sin* ([Madison], 1876), *passim* (baccalaureate address).

30 John Bascom, *Education and the State* ([Madison], 1877), 8–13.

31 *Ibid.*, 14–15; *The Common School* (Madison, 1878). 13 (baccalaureate address).

32 John Bascom, *Tests of a School System* (Milwaukee, 1880), 10–11, 18–22 (quotation, p. 18). To this extent Bascom wholly accepted the fact that state universities could not legally teach a specific religious doctrine. "Only the more strongly and clearly may their attention be turned to a beautiful and fruitful ethical life—the culmination of religion." See "What Do the Members of a State University Owe to the State?" 100.

33 Bascom, *Tests of a School System*, 23; *The New Theology* (Milwaukee, 1884), 22 (baccalaureate address). By no means did Bascom slight the humanities in the university curriculum. He defended philosophy as the most important study, and believed that "the entire ethical and spiritual world is open to us in the humanities." See *Sermons and Addresses*, 196.

34 Robert M. La Follette, *La Follette's Autobiography: A Personal Narrative of Political Experiences* (Madison, 1960 ed.), 13.

35 Bascom, "What do the Members of a State University Owe to the State?" 94–96.

36 Bascom, *Truth and Truthfulness*, 9.

37 Bascom, *Education and the State*, 17.

38 Curti and Carstensen, *University of Wisconsin*, 1: 631–633; 2: 88.

39 Benjamin G. Rader, *The Academic Mind and Reform: The Influence of Richard T. Ely in American Life* (Lexington, 1966), 4–5, 46–48; Richard T. Ely, *Ground Under Our Feet: An Autobiography* (New York, 1938), 1–5, 14–16 (quotation on p. 16), 41–47.

40 Ely, *Ground Under Our Feet*, 77; Rader, *The Academic Mind*, 36 (quoting Ely).

41 Richard T. Ely, *Social Aspects of Christianity* (New York, 1889), 147–148.

42 Quoted by Ely from the "Platform" of the American Economic Association in *Ground Under Our Feet*, 136.

43 Rader, *The Academic Mind*, 121.

44 Ely, *Ground Under Our Feet*, 74; "The Universities and the Churches," *31st University Convention* (Albany, 1893), 351–356 (an address).

45 If Ely's own story may be believed, La Follette was highly influenced by Ely's writings and once told him that "you have been my teacher!" See *Ground Under Our Feet*, 216.

46 John R. Commons, *Myself* (Madison, 1963 ed.), 7–8, 21, 48.

47 John R. Commons, *Social Reform and the Church* (New York, 1967 ed.), 107–114. As in Ely's case, the discovery of the New Economics and his commitment to its application allowed Commons to channel a religious concern of the old evangelical variety into modern social reform. He wrote in his autobiography that this commitment "was my tribute to [my mother's] longing that I should become a minister of the Gospel." See *Myself*, 44.

48 See his essay "The Christian Minister and Sociology," in *Social Reform and the Church*, 3–19 (quotations on pp. 3, 13, and 19).

49 Lafayette G. Harder, Jr., *John R. Commons: His Assault on Laissez-Faire* (Corvallis, Oregon, 1962), 69–86; Curti and Carstensen, *University of Wisconsin*, 2: 551–552; Belle Case and Fola La Follette, *Robert M. La Follette* (2 vols., New York, 1953), 157, 164, 190. For a corresponding statement of the theme outlined in this essay, see Jean B. Quandt, "Religion and Social Thought: The Secularization of Postmillennialism," in *The American Quarterly*, 30: 390–409 (October, 1973).

50 David Paul Thelen, *The Early Life of Robert M. La Follette, 1855–1884* (Chicago, 1966), 50.

51 La Follette, *Autobiography*, 13.

52 La Follettes, *Robert M. La Follette*, 38–39, 145–146; Curti and Carstensen, *University of Wisconsin*, 1: 607.

53 Maurice M. Vance, *Charles Richard Van Hise: Scientist Progressive* (Madison, 1960), 8–75.

54 *Ibid.*, 79–82; Curti and Carstensen, *University of Wisconsin*, 2: 18–19.

55 Vance, *Van Hise*, 81; Curti and Carstensen, *University of Wisconsin*, 2: 23–24.

NOTE: This essay is an expanded version of the Fromkin Memorial Lecture, presented at the University of Wisconsin–Milwaukee in the fall of 1975. The author expresses his appreciation to the Fromkin Research and Lectureship Committee and the University of Wisconsin–Milwaukee Library for funds to support this project.

In Search of a Direction: Southern Higher Education After the Civil War

Joseph M. Stetar

THE SOUTH did not share in the enormous expansion of American higher education in the years following the Civil War. Nationally, higher education enrollments grew over five-fold in the decades following the War. In 1870 there were 62,000 students in colleges, universities, professional, normal and teacher colleges in the United States. By 1890 the total higher education enrollment was 157,000 and by 1910 had risen to 355,000.[1] Multipurpose institutions with programs characteristic of the leading twentieth-century universities began to appear in the East, West and Midwest. No such development was evident in the nineteenth-century South where colleges struggled to remain alive. Left virtually destitute by the War and lacking students, buildings and assets, college leaders clung more to romantic dreams and were unable to share in the bold expansion experienced by other regions. The point is etched clearly when one realizes that about the time Charles W. Eliot began to chart the transition of Harvard College to Harvard University, Landon C. Garland, President of the University of Alabama, and later of Vanderbilt, wrote:

> The University buildings are all burned. Nothing was saved but the private residence of the officers. The most valuable part of my library . . . was consumed. This is a great loss to me just now.

> I do not know that the University of Alabama will be rebuilt—if at all, it will be several years hence. I cannot await the final results, but must look for some employment.[2]

Indeed an attempt to reopen the University of Alabama was made in 1865, but failed when only one student (son of the former Governor Thomas H. Watts) arrived for classes. Reconstruction compounded the political problems confronting the University of Alabama. In November of 1867, a new state constitution transferred control of the University of Alabama from its trustees to an elected board, The Board of Regents of the State University. These Regents were delegated broad powers of governance including the appointment of a president and faculty;[3] there were widespread reports of the dismissal of the ante-bellum faculty for political rather than scholarly reasons.[4]

In Oxford, Mississippi, the state University closed for a portion of the War and faced debilitating financial problems and political entanglements upon reopening. Control of the Board of Trustees had passed into the hands of Reconstructionists and there was the widespread fear that the policies of the new board would undermine the University. Alexander J. Quinche, Secretary of the Faculty and Professor of Ancient Languages, spoke for many of the faculty in his assertion that the new trustees could destroy the University if they radicalized the faculty. Support for the institution, Professor Quinche insisted, came from old line Southerners and, should these patrons be alienated to the point of withdrawing their support, the University would atrophy.[5] The situation was also quite troubled in Spartanburg, South Carolina, where Wofford College watched its endowment, invested heavily in Confederate bonds and certificates, evaporate.[6] In North Carolina, the trustees of Trinity College (antecedent of Duke University) expressed some optimism, born of sheer determination, about the future of the college while contending with the effects of a war which destroyed their financial resources and saw their 1861 student body of over 200 reduced to fifty.[7]

At the close of the War, 4,000 Union soldiers occupied the village and campus of the University of North Carolina at Chapel Hill, while the University possessed $200,000 in worthless securities and debts of over $100,000. To compound the problem, the Reconstruction government dismissed the antebellum faculty in 1868 and attempted to re-establish the University with a small group of carefully chosen professors. Nevertheless, it was unable to gain adequate financial support and the institution again officially closed its doors in 1871. In 1873 friends of the University led by Alexander McIver, then North Carolina Superintendent of Public Instruction and an honors graduate of the University, sought legislative and public support to reopen the University. Their efforts met with limited success: in September of 1875 instruction was resumed with a faculty of seven and approximately seventy students,[8] considerably reduced from the ante-bellum University's 1857–1858 enrollment of over four hundred students in nine departments.[9]

In 1866 the trustees of Wake Forest College were faced with the task of re-opening an institution which had been closed for four years. Preparatory work, phased out before the War, was reinstated, and only twenty-two of the sixty-seven enrolled in 1866 were classified as collegiate level students. The campus buildings were badly in need of repair, and all but approximately $11,000 of the $100,000 ante-bellum endowment had been lost.[10]

South Carolina College, antecedent of the University of South Carolina, found rebuilding the institution to be a herculean ordeal. Declining enrollment in the early months of 1862 had forced the College to close in the spring of that year.[11] The termination of fighting did not lessen the problems confronting the College. Reconstruction forces understandably pursuing a policy of racial integration and political intervention threatened, given the explosive social situation at that time, the very existence of the College,[12] which was forced to close or reorganize several times in the ensuing years. A report by President Frederick A.P. Barnard to the Trustees of the University of Mississippi in November of 1861 describes the changes effected by the War at the University of Mississippi, and throughout Southern higher education:

> The ambitions. . . entertained for its growth in reputation and usefulness, and for the enlargement of its scope, evaluation of its aims, and its ultimate recognition as one among the honored agencies whose function is to be, not

merely by education to diffuse knowledge among men, but by original investigation to add to the priceless mass [of knowledge]. . . . But the fond dreams of so many anxiously hopeful years have been at length rudely dissipated, and the convulsions which have shaken . . . the country to its centre, have removed afar off the prospect of that distinguished preeminence in science which seemed but recently to be opening up before the University of Mississippi.[13]

The War and its social and economic consequences had a profound influence upon Southern higher education. The region's colleges were all but destroyed, and their clientele and financial support lost. Colleges that prospered in the ante-bellum era entered the latter years of the 1860s with great apprehension and little cause for optimism. Endowments had disappeared, students and faculty were in disarray and facilities were often in ruins. The War resulted not only in the closing of colleges but in a complete reversal of the pattern of antebellum expansion and prosperity.

In their attempts to rebuild, Southern academics entered into a discussion regarding the values and philosophies which would shape their future. This debate will be examined in the context of the same general categories utilized by Laurence Veysey in his examination of the development of American universities: mental discipline and piety, utility, research, and liberal culture.[14] As in Veysey's study there are numerous subgroups and considerable overlap among the categories. Within any of these categories and on most campuses many people were speaking and not all were saying the same thing. Motivations clearly differed, and on many campuses one could find proponents of each point-of-view. Nevertheless, categories do emerge which provide a highly useful perspective for examining the development of late nineteenth-century higher education. While this debate followed the general categories developed by Veysey, the results of these discussions were in many ways unique to the South.

The distinctiveness of Southern cultural life itself contributed to the uniqueness of Southern higher education. Due to the impoverishing effects to the Civil War and the South's relative cultural isolation from the rest of the nation, changes in higher education evolved at a slower pace than was true elsewhere.[15] The shared common cultural life of the South added to the region's insularity; in the years preceding the Civil War, when collectively the North, Midwest and West were becoming more alike culturally, the South-rural, isolated and dominated by slavery—was developing a uniquely regional way of life.[16] So great was this cultural difference that Wilbur J. Cash concluded:

There exists among us . . . a profound connection that the South is another land, sharply differentiated from the rest of the American nation, and exhibiting within itself a remarkable homogeneity.

As to what its singularity may consist in, there is, of course, much conflict of opinion. . . . But that it is different and that it is solid—on these things nearly everybody is agreed.[17]

Surrender at Appomatox and Reconstruction did little to bring the region into the mainstream of American life; in many ways the military defeat coupled with the tensions of Reconstruction widened the chasm between the South and the rest of the nation.[18] The post-war South, set apart by significant "differentials in per capita wealth, income and living standards that made it unique among the regions,"[19] possessed a degree of cultural solidarity and political cohesiveness perhaps never attained in the ante-bellum years.

In summary, both Southern culture and higher education were, in the latter third of the nineteenth century, distinct from those in other sections of the nation. The development of colleges and universities in this period did not replicate the process in the rest of the nation whereby research and utility dominated higher education and relegated mental discipline, piety, and liberal culture to marginal positions. The contest was much closer and markedly idiosyncratic to the South. Discipline and piety joined with liberal culture and Christian education to create a potent, viable educational philosophy which retained its strength well into the twentieth century. Although utility made significant inroads, research did not.

I

Mental Discipline and Piety

For mental disciplinarians the mind was subdivided into faculties, each of which required systematic and balanced development. Exercising certain faculties to the neglect of others, they argued, deprived students of the qualities of wholeness and balance. In the view of James Henry Thornwell, ante-bellum president of South Carolina College, and other Southern educators, the most effective course of study was one which stimulated all the various faculties of the mind and developed habits of systemic thinking. He believed that through direct exposure to classics, the original writings of the ancient Greek and Latin authors, students developed sound habits. Few ante-bellum Southerners disagreed; the discipline of the mind, rather than the acquisition of knowledge, was the aim of education. He saw each student as the focus for this education, for in his words, it was "his perfection as a man simply, being the aim of his education." During his tenure (1852-55), undergraduate education at South Carolina consisted of a fixed course of study emphasizing the classics; the sole criterion for the inclusion of a particular subject in the curriculum was its contribution to mental discipline. Undaunted by charges that education emphasizing mental discipline failed to prepare one for a particular career, Thornwell insisted upon the efficacy of a well-disciplined intellect; colleges were not to have a vocational orientation but rather the inclusion of any subject in the curriculum was to be based on its ability to perfect the mind, nothing else.[20] The War would not alter this thinking.

Nothing more seriously violated the canons of mental discipline than the charge that higher education should respond directly to the social and economic needs of society. Significant among these challenges was utilitarian-inspired legislation passed in 1865 by the South Carolina Legislature which called for ten separate schools within the College (i.e. University of South Carolina) and supported the right of students to elect areas of study. While this forced the College to adopt a more practical curriculum, it engendered significant controversy. Fisk Brewer, Professor of Ancient Languages and Literature, chastized the Legislature for capriciously abandoning the classical curriculum and for introducing fragmented schools and electives which failed to ensure symmetrical development.[21]

Evidence suggests that Professor Brewer's discontent was not as widely shared by his colleagues as he might have preferred, for eight years later, in October of 1873, the faculty had arranged for a four-year classical course to be taught jointly by all professors. The new program included an alternative to the classical course which permitted the substitution of the modern languages for Greek and Latin. The alternative curriculum proved the more popular and its enrollment quickly eclipsed that of the classical program. Brewer's own notes indicate that of fifty-six freshmen and sophomores enrolled in the Spring of 1877, only seventeen were in the classical course on a full or conditional basis, while the remaining thirty-nine were in the modern language program.[22] However, to advocates of mental discipline student enrollment—or lack of it—was of little importance; they attached "more value to quality of instruction than to the number of students; the latter will inevitably follow the former. Let the institution lift the students up, not the students drag the institution down."[23]

This concession to modern languages was significant, and it stirred considerable opposition among mental discipline's staunchest advocates. In their view substituting modern languages for the classical permitted a student to replace the difficult and essential with the easy and unnecessary. For the true classicist, all technical and professional instruction would be confined to special institutions so as not to violate the classical course. In opposing the substitution of modern languages for the classics, the rigid mental disciplinarians actually weakened their credibility. The modern language had grown in popularity due to their literary importance, cognation with the native language, and proclaimed disciplinary value, and their advocates pressed for equal status with the ancient languages. Undaunted, mental disciplinarians remained adamant in their opposition, holding that "close mental labor . . . required in studying Latin and Greek is not found in studying the modern languages,"[24] and only mastery of the classics "develops the reasoning faculty and secures the power of careful, incisive and discriminating thought. . . ."[25] Thus mental disciplinarians fought a constant and increasingly difficult battle against any encroachment on the exclusive position of the classics.

The press for limited or free electives and the inclusion of modern languages was not limited to South Carolina. John Waddel, Chancellor of the University of Mississippi from 1865-1874 and staunch mental disciplinarian, believed the classical course of study should be rigidly and universally imposed upon students. He insisted that the curriculum ". . . be compulsory, or the majority of students will neglect it."[26] The wisdom of a fixed program was considered to be self-evident and any alteration of the litany of moral and mental discipline, mathematics and the classics was unthinkable. Not surprisingly, attempts by reform-minded professors at the University of Mississippi to broaden the curriculum were soundly denounced by mental disciplinarians. In 1884 Professor Robert B. Fulton sponsored a resolution calling for an elective system in all classes of the University and permitting students to receive a B.A. degree without studying Latin and Greek. The University of Mississippi faculty were not ready for such an abrupt change, however, and the measure was defeated by nearly two to one.[27]

The massive social, political and economic problems encountered by the post-war South did little to deter mental discipline's advocates from opposing almost any and all curricular change. Five years after President Barnard's 1861 statement that all hopes for significant educational advancement at the University of Mississippi had been destroyed by the War,[28] Chancellor Waddel reaffirmed mental discipline as the basis for higher education at Mississippi. However, in 1866 more than half of the 244 students attending the University of Mississippi were Confederate Army veterans, ill-prepared to undertake even rudimentary classical studies. These post-war students were a different breed, not the traveled sons of the country gentry but seasoned soldiers hard pressed to pay the fifty-dollar University fee and anxious to rebuild their lives and fortunes. Classical education to these students was surely rather curious and remote. However, Waddel was firm. The acquisition of knowledge was of secondary consideration to the disciplining and training of the mind.[29]

At Trinity College mental discipline was an essential element of the institutional character during the late nineteenth century. Announcements for the 1885-86 academic year reminded students that anyone deficient in the classics should not expect to receive his B.A., and William T. Gannaway, Professor of Latin and French at Trinity, averred, ". . . [since] it is believed that mental training and discipline can best be secured by a *patient* and thorough *study* of the Ancient Classics, the use of translations is strictly forbidden."[30] A concession to the realities of the times was made at Wofford, where in the postwar years the number of students unwilling or unable to master Greek and Latin increased to the extent that an alternate degree program was initiated. Although the new degree, the Bachelor of Science, was considered inferior to the Bachelor of Arts degree it proved quite popular. The B.S. students must have proved especially vexing to Wofford's President Shipp, who nonetheless continued his practice of delivering the annual commencement address in Latin; it was not until James H. Carlisle assumed the presidency of Wofford in 1873 that the graduation address was delivered in the vernacular.[31]

In Columbia, South Carolina, the Reconstruction government opened the University to blacks. While these students also lacked proper prerequisite education, they nonetheless sought the opportunity preparatory classes provided for remedial work, and substantial interest in the University developed among the black community. But even this change in student population had little impact upon mental disciplinarians such as South Carolina's Fisk Brewer, who insisted everyone had to experience the joy and discipline of reading the original Caesar's war and Xenophon's march in Latin.[32]

The 1871 graduating class of the College of Charleston was reminded that the classical curriculum should be placed at a high point of elevation, and be rigorously maintained. But there was little reason to fear the College of Charleston would abandon classical studies. Henry E. Shepherd, President of the Faculty from 1882 to 1897, vigorously supported the classical curriculum, asserting with some pride that the College of Charleston was one of the few institutions in the United States which had not caved in to the pressures for an elective or optional course of study.[33] Mental discipline also occupied a secure position at Emory College (later Emory University) in Georgia, where three of its post-war presidents conceived of education almost exclusively in terms of the classical curriculum. Luther M. Smith (1868-1871), Osborn L. Smith (1871-1875), and Atticus G. Haygood (1875-1884) made few concessions to new, emerging values and were generally committed to an education which, in the words of Luther Smith, sought the development of intellectual power through mental discipline and exercise.[34]

The classicists opposed the notion of producing merchants, lawyers, farmers or physicians as too narrow and too limited an aim for higher education. They sought instead to develop broadly cultured, symmetrical men, although the irony of attempting this by means of a rigidly fixed curriculum escaped them. In their view vocationalism threatened the essence of higher education by turning colleges into workshops, and learning into technical training. If preparation for a profession meant simple acquaintance with detail and a mastery of technicalities, the colleges could be of little help; if, however, the professions required a fine, disciplined intellect capable of infinite adaptation, then a classical education was critical. Thus, despite the massive rebuilding task ahead, classicists dismissed utilitarian programs as frivolous. In this, their singular narrowness and detachment is remarkable. Unruffled by the demands of students and society they sought to provide post-war students with the same gentlemanly education offered in the 1850s: ". . . not culture alone . . . but mental discipline added to it."[35]

Concerned with educating the whole man, advocates of mental discipline also necessarily addressed themselves to the development of character and the inculcation of Christian values, often fearing a student's mental development might outpace his moral growth. Southern mental disciplinarians generally agreed that the most rigorous classical education was useless if moral and religious stamina were lacking. A classical education leavened with rigorous moral training was believed optimal for both the individual and the larger society, and a dire future was predicted for the student whose mind, "degenerated in its aims and crippled in its powers . . . flutters, like a bird of feeble wing, over the stagnant pools of sensualism."[36] Such reasoning was wholly consistent with the pervasive religious influence in the South.[37] And while such thinking seems to parallel that occurring in other sections of the nation, the South clung to these values longer and with greater intensity than did other regions.

In their efforts to ensure a moral, Christian atmosphere advocates of mental discipline and piety sought to exercise control of the campus environment. This fusion of the academic and religious was the *raison d'etre* for Wofford College. William M. Whitman, a prominent figure in the establishment of Wofford, reminded his audience at a cornerstone-laying ceremony that a prime objective of the College was the development of moral character: "which grows out of a knowledge of Christian truth . . . [and a] cultivated understanding which is the product of thorough scholarship."[38]

The University of Mississippi prided itself on its positive "moral influences, freedom from temptation to vice, and the [exemplary] conduct of her students." Every faculty member was a professed Christian, tiny Oxford boasted five churches,[39] and an 1877 committee vigorously sought to prohibit the establishment and operation of billiard saloons or "tin pan alleys" within five miles of the University.[40] Regulating students' personal lives consumed a significant amount of the faculty's time. With students ranging in age from those fifteen or younger to those in their twenties, the rigorous enforcement of discipline was a major undertaking. The University of Mississippi's Trustees required faculty to visit student rooms at irregular hours, "with a view of seeing that students are . . . not engaged in anything improper," and faculty, of course, were expected to respond to all calls from the chancellor for assistance in the maintenance of order.[41] Intent upon protecting students from pernicious influences and anxious to insure a strong sense of morality and propriety in North Carolina, Trinity's President Craven (1872-1882) soundly denounced those institutions which tolerated misbehavior and thus arrested moral development.[42]

In retrospect it is clear that Southern mental discipline and piety did not atrophy after 1865. But the rigidity which precluded its easy adaptation to the exigencies of the post-war South, its antipathy to elective studies, and its total preoccupation with the classical curriculum increasingly isolated its proponents not only from the mainstream of society but from many of its students. Yet, it retained a substantial degree of support and proved capable, especially with its spawning of liberal culture/Christian education, of checking the development of newer, competing educational philosophies.

II

Liberal Culture and Christian Education

While the narrow and rigid mental discipline and piety of the Thornwell and Waddel genre faced rough sledding in the post Civil War era, their philosophical successors were able to draw sustenance from the literary, cultural and religious traditions of the South to forge a new philosophy for higher education: liberal culture and Christian education. Rooted in Southern literary, cultural and religious traditions,[43] liberal culture combined with Christian education in the South to foster a point of view toward the curriculum and toward teaching which is distinct from the conception of liberal culture found in the emerging universities of the North and West. In general, advocates of liberal culture and Christian education were critical of the major educational values of the era. They rejected mental discipline because of its adherence to faculty psychology and its reliance upon the classical curriculum as a means of disciplining the mind. They opposed a utilitarian brand of higher education because of its emphasis upon practical studies and an elective curriculum. Finally, they rejected research because of its advocacy of graduate study and specialization.

Throughout the South advocates of liberal culture and Christian education expressed their opposition to the other educational values. Karl P. Harrington and Henry F. Linscott of the University of North Carolina and Wofford College joined numerous other Southerners of the 1880s and 1890s in calling for a return to fixed curriculum. Rooted in a liberal education tradition, these scholars advocated the study of the great books and the classical languages for their intellectual breadth rather than mental discipline properties. They argued that students must not be permitted to choose their courses whimsically since colleges were obliged to guide students toward the accomplishments of the greatest human minds. They believed in building a foundation which enabled the undergraduate to discriminate between literary masterwork and medocrity.[44]

Despite their mutual attention to literature and the classics, liberal culture sympathizers in the South strongly differed from such university-leaders of liberal culture as Irving Babbitt, Charles Eliot Norton and Barrett Wendell— all of whom rejected the religious and moral overtones of ante-bellum educational philosophies. Inspired by Matthew Arnold, these university leaders outside the South generally accepted culture as "a wide vision of the best things which man has done or aspired after," which capsulized their concern with "breadth, taste, heritage and idealism."[45] Yet the old established Southern college had been founded on piety and, while a few of the more liberated Southern proponents of liberal culture either avowedly rejected formal religion or permitted it to slip into the background, there was no significant move in the South to downgrade Christian theology.

Thus it appears at least two versions of liberal culture existed: one, identified by Veysey, was rooted in the emerging universities of the North, West and Midwest and rejected or minimized the religious and moral influences in education; a second, centered in the South, retained a central regard for the study of humanities and development of moral and religious principles, hence the term "liberal Christian education." However, common threads united all versions of liberal culture. Its advocates were, in principle, sharply opposed to the emerging university and its alien values while they identified with the traditional commitment to a required course of study. They denounced the elective system which permitted a student to graduate without studying such areas as Latin, the modern languages, history, economics, and philosophy, and they advocated a return to a fixed curriculum.[46]

Despite the apparent detachment of some Southern colleges toward the technical and utilitarian needs of the region, there was genuine concern for its cultural life; numerous faculty viewed higher education as a vehicle for the preservation and advancement of Southern culture. As a new socio-economic system gradually replaced the old, as the vast plantations were subdivided and the slaves set free, men of learning were challenged to preserve the best of Southern culture. Thus the Southern colleges and universities of the late 1800s were called upon to serve as repositories for the region's history, mythology, and traditions.[47] As David Bertelson suggests in his study, *The Lazy South*,[48] while Southerners chafed under the stereotype of an idle and self-indulgent life-style, they successfully sought an accommodation with the economic order which emerged after the war. Clearly, the gentleman-scholar ideal (for both the planter and industrialist) remained an attractive one for the region and Southern higher education presented a means for preserving that image.[49] The notion of mental and spiritual integration and wholeness became a guiding principle in the education of cultivated, disciplined men;

narrow specialists and professionals were not considered the proper product of higher education.

The immediate post-war period witnessed little popular demand for a "new South" and rather seemed to strengthen the determination of those who sought to resurrect at least part of an era that had passed away. Moreover, the post-war period witnessed an emphasis upon preserving Southern culture and included a substantial aversion for anything "Yankee."[50] In the absence of a comprehensive school system no better vehicle existed for preserving ante-bellum culture than the Southern college; rebuilding the old South required that the traditions of ante-bellum colleges be preserved and strengthened. Southern society, militarily defeated, called upon the colleges to blunt the invasion of Northern culture. At most Southern institutions, articulate and outspoken advocates of a concept of education based on religious principles held key positions throughout the post-war era, and their philosophy was deeply rooted in Southern culture.

The position of liberal Christian education with respect to research and scholarship was straightforward and clear. In the words of John Carlisle Kilgo, President of Trinity "all truth was dependent upon ultimate religious truth, and . . . literature, science, history [are] incomplete without religion." It may have been as Kilgo and others believed, that a Christian college was inherently free because it was beyond political power,[51] but liberal Christian education also had a decidedly doctrinaire flavor as exhibited by its emphasis upon the development of character and its desire to protect students from pernicious ideas. In Kilgo's view, presenting Christian views of human nature countered the false materialism of Locke, the unhealthy idealism of Kant and the wretched agnosticism of Herbert Spencer.[52]

This tendency of liberal Christian education to declare certain fundamental intellectual questions off-limits demonstrates that the South lacked the basic orientation to the essentially non-theological frame of reference associated with the German-modeled graduate centers which were developing in other regions. While Southerners variously denounced education as too restrained or too free, as lacking practicality or as overly utilitarian, it was rarely permissible to question basic Christian assumptions. The search for truth in liberal Christian education was to a great extent confined to the theological framework of the particular sect involved. Truth was ultimately defined by the scriptures and it was generally accepted by advocates of Christian education that religious truth was ultimate truth. Thus, while the literary and cultural aspects of liberal culture appealed to the South, its long tradition of religious fervor demanded that an acceptable educational philosophy accommodate itself to and include Christian philosophy as well. Thus the concept of liberal Christian education which gained wide popularity and support throughout the region was an apparent synthesis of liberal culture and the old concept of discipline and piety which had infused Southern higher education.

Liberal Christian educational values were strong throughout the South, where it was insisted that: ". . . if both intellectual power and moral power are to be fully effective, the one must be thoroughly moralized and the other thoroughly intellectualized."[53] Neither the narrow classicist of the ante-bellum era nor the modern researcher was capable of providing the blend of scholarship and religious fervor these institutions sought: "The scholarship of the college instructor should be not only broad, but must also have refined itself into the grace and strength of that culture which is human and which humanizes. . . ."[54] Faculty were typically judged by their ability to share their knowledge and Christian principles with students rather than by external demonstrations of scholarship. Becoming an excellent teacher or role-model was generally believed to be the most important career objective in any young instructor's life.[55]

As an institution Wofford College provides an illuminating case study for what emerged as the Southern philosophy of liberal Christian education. Traditionally Wofford sought to combine both the intellectual and moral traditions of the South, for this was considered most efficacious in the development of learned Christian gentlemen. Piety and character building were the primary concern of James H. Carlisle, professor at the College from its founding and president from 1875 to 1902. Carlisle borrowed equally from discipline and piety, liberal culture, and Christian education, placing primary emphasis upon instructive personal relationships with his students, and he often wrote of the educated, disciplined mind capable of adjusting to all exigencies with an enthusiasm reminiscent of Thornwell or Waddel. Opposing premature specialization, Carlisle was more concerned with winning students to the "pure and right; and wise and good," than with erudition and scholarship.[56] Symbolic of the differences between Southern higher education and the emerging universities of other regions was the reaction of Carlisle's son to Charles W. Eliot's visit to Wofford in March of 1909:

> . . . there stood the most distinguished educator of New England, representing the very last word in the educational thought of the North . . . whose five foot book shelf had no room for the Bible, looking into the face of one of the greatest educators of the South, [James H. Carlisle] with a firm belief in the Bible as the word of God. . . .[57]

Carlisle's contribution to the cause of liberal Christian education was recognized throughout the South. In a career spanning one of the most important periods in the history of American higher education, Carlisle was able to forge an eclectic position. He effectively opposed extreme utilitarianism on the one hand, while recognizing the need for practicality on the other. He maintained a balance in the educational program at Wofford, according some legitimacy to the broad concept of utility and accommodating the scholar, but his emphasis upon teaching and the development of character left little room for research. His philosophy of education drew significantly upon the precepts of mental discipline but was more flexible than Thornwell's or Waddel's. Carlisle's emphasis upon character and piety clearly illustrates the divergence between the university-centered liberal culture of the North and liberal Christian education in the South under his influence.

Wofford's curriculum was not based solely on traditional principles of mental discipline but rather on the liberal culture premise that the classics exposed students to the most profound works of the human intellect. Still the College proved capable of accommodating the new academicians, German educated scholars Charles F. Smith, who later taught at Vanderbilt and Wisconsin, and William Baskerville, who also later taught at Vanderbilt, and who both added intellectual force to Wofford. Capable of undertaking advanced research projects and conversant with the great intellectual and academic forces of the era, these scholars earned the respect of their peers and gained regional if not national status.[58] However, their presence caused some Wofford professors to protest that the research-oriented professor, "cabined, cubbed and confined in the narrow house of his own department,"[59] would force premature specialization on students and diminish the appeal of the traditional curriculum which had served the South so well in earlier years, and Carlisle agreed to a great extent. Thus under his stewardship Wofford for the most part resisted the pressures of utility and research and remained serenely committed to literary-Christian values.

The impact of liberal Christian education was, as previously indicated, not confined to institutions with formal religious ties but was felt at state institutions as well. An excellent example is the University of Mississippi, which proclaimed its intention to educate "good scholars of industrious and frugal habits, well grounded in the principles of a high Christian morality. . . ."[60] Mississippi took pride in the moral climate of Oxford and in the fact that all members of the University faculty were active in church affairs.[61] The thrust of the University was guided by the goal of moral rather than intellectual development; a goal which permitted students to graduate who could neither spell nor write grammatically correct sentences. Edward L. Mayes, president of the University in 1889, spoke for many when he professed a desire to develop a "true manly dignity, to awaken a perception of the necessity for self-pause and self-restraint, to inculcate the nobility involved in a voluntary observance of the social and moral codes"[62] in his students.

In many ways, the University of Mississippi bore a striking resemblance to church related institutions, for while Mississippi catered more to utility than did others it was decidedly a culturally-oriented institution. Because the University of Mississippi retained the philosophy of liberal Christian education, the traditions of gentlemanly behavior, moral rectitude, and spiritual enlightenment became necessary correlatives of all intellectual endeavors there. Moreover, as at many other institutions, the faculty at University of Mississippi imposed strict codes of moral and personal conduct upon their students.

Thus across the South liberal culture/Christian education drew sustenance from its antecedent mental discipline and piety to continue as a distinct and important educational value. Its appeal was clearly due to its cultural foundation, its central acceptance of the importance of Christian doctrine, and its complementarity to mental discipline. The final decade of the nineteenth century witnessed increased attacks upon liberal Christian education in the South. The emergence of science was inhospitable to liberal Christian education, and the rapid multiplication of disciplines began to force major adjustments in higher education throughout the region. No longer unchallenged as the supreme course of study, the future of the humanities provoked widespread discussion. Questions such as "Is Science an Incentive to Poetry?"[63] and "Does the Study of Science Tend to Suppress the Spirit . . . of Romance?"[64] were debated in colleges throughout the South.

After the turn of the century the Southern tradition of the gentleman-scholar, supported by liberal Christian education, was in some jeopardy. Increasingly, students sought higher education in an effort to secure financially adequate, if not lucrative, technical or professional positions. Moreover, as the new age of science emerged, its impact, measured by the growing influence of the research and utilitarian institutions, imposed increasing pressure on liberal Christian education. Indeed, liberal Christian education began to be viewed by its opponents as a frivolous and slightly droll remnant of the ante-bellum era.

III

Utility

Outside of the South the movement toward a more practical, useful, and service-oriented education increased in the decades after 1865; according to Veysey virtually every "change in the pattern of American higher education lay in the direction of concession to the utilitarian type of demand for reform."[65] The idea of a multipurpose educational institution serving the practical interests and needs of a diverse population ran counter to that of the classical college; predictably the concept of utility evoked a good deal of controversy.

In the South, insurgent utilitarians rejected the notions of mental disciplinarians and pressed for direct societal services through more practical studies. Following the War, they forced ante-bellum classical professors to share the campus with a growing number of social and applied scientists who sought to restructure education. Many saw the "new South" as needing individuals capable of accomplishing practical tasks. Viewing classical studies as anachronistic, they sought to reshape higher education in a more meaningful and responsive form. Professor Charles W. Hutson of the University of Mississippi perhaps best captured the movement's spirit:

> Against the spirit of the ancient world, which looked down upon commercial and manufacturing industries and all mechanical pursuits, must be erected the modern spirit of material progress, with all the modern appliances for furthering the advance of trade and the trades.[66]

The strong press for a more practical education is not surprising. The War had exacted a significant economic toll upon the region; widespread poverty and desolation were clearly evident.[67] Yet from this destruction arose the push for economic development, and by 1879 conditions seemed opportune in the South for a strong effort toward attaining a diversified industrial economy characteristic of the North.[68] This effort found strong support and sustenance among progressive Southerners, who generally accepted the idea that regional progress would require rapid economic growth and development of a diversified economy.[69] However, the expectations for economic development in the late nineteenth- and early twentieth-century South exceeded the reality of what actually occurred; the region continued to lag economically behind the rest of the nation.[70] Nevertheless, the push for economic development permitted the region to reconcile the competing ideologies of agrarianism and industrialism[71] and helped create an atmosphere throughout the region which would both permit and encourage Southern colleges and universities to pursue the service ideal that characterized much of American higher education.[72]

Thus it is not surprising that in numerous instances after 1870 advocates of the classical curriculum were incrementally forced to accommodate the utilitarians. At Wofford, where mental discipline seemed especially entrenched, a course in English philology was felt to be a significant response to demands for practicality in education.[73] It was evident, however, that Wofford and other colleges would have to provide more than a course in philology to satisfy utilitarian demands. The growing influence of the utilitarian curriculum threatened to alter the course of Southern higher education.[74] In the post-war society higher education was increasingly considered a proper instrument for social and economic development in the region. Southern wealth and power were shifting from plantation owners to the businessmen who organized and directed industrial enterprises; thus while the late nineteenth-century Southern economy remained basically agrarian, it was evident to those with foresight that this was changing and education would have to change with it.[75]

In 1875, dedication speeches at the new Vanderbilt University in Nashville focused on that institution's recognition "of every department of true thought, every branch of genuine knowledge, every mode of thorough scholarship"[76] and challenged other colleges to become involved in social, cultural and economic development. Years later Vanderbilt's Chancellor Kirkland, mindful perhaps of the University of Wisconsin and its relationship with the state, suggested that, among other things, higher education ought to assist state legislatures and other governmental bodies and commissions in conducting studies on public policy matters. Kirkland saw such involvement, relating theory to practice, as enabling higher education to demonstrate its potential for public service. Moreover, he sought to increase Vanderbilt's effectiveness in dealing with external groups by cultivating ties with industry. The work of the physician, mechanic, farmer, navigator, engineer and merchant was of concern to Vanderbilt which, although neither seeking nor achieving the degree of direct service attained by some state institutions, nonetheless was clearly aware of its responsiblity to a society which lay beyond the campus.[77]

Trinity College also recognized its responsibility to offer a utilitarian education. Speaking in Orangeburg, South Carolina in 1899, President Kilgo expressed an interest in bringing to the College those who had grappled with the pressing, practical problems of the day.[78] He encouraged Trinity professors to involve themselves in state and national governmental affairs, thus making themselves available to agencies and organizations which addressed regional problems. In this, he realized that Trinity could not remain isolated from society if it was to be of service:

> Let colleges lay off their coats, defy all kinds of hardships and persecutions and toil with the banker to make his bank safer; work with the manufacturer to keep his machinery in motion; contend with the merchant to secure a fair market; burn his midnight lamp with the editor to save the government from the hurt of false doctrines and evil men; join the collier in his efforts to feed and educate his child; and stand by the laborer that his day may be full of sunshine.[79]

William H. Glasson, Professor of Economics and Social Sciences at Trinity, echoed Kilgo's views in his *South Atlantic Quarterly* article which asserted that only through direct societal involvement could the resources of higher education be fully utilized. Furthermore, he viewed public service as complimentary to the teaching function despite the problems inevitable in such an educational posture.[80]

By the late 1880s Trinity's curriculum contained clear evidence of an accommodation to the more practical orientation of utility, with such courses as Civil Government (increasing knowledge of government, courts, justice, education and taxation) and "Roads and Road Building" (dealing with the location, construction, and theory of roads) and a ten month business program appearing in the catalogue. In addition, professional schools of Civil Engineering and Mining Engineering were established, the former offering instruction in theoretical and practical areas and the latter preparing one for "work in practical engineering and the actual management of mines."[81] There was little danger, however, that Trinity would fall victim to the extreme manifestations of utilitariansim (such as Ezra Cornell's unfulfilled ambition to build campus factories operated by students), for the opposing forces were far too strong.

It was the Southern state-supported institutions, however, which faced the greatest pressures to provide a more practical education. As early as 1871 demands for utilitarian education led the University of Mississippi to issue a report outlining its resolve to meet the needs of the state's diverse population. It was recognized, however, that service to heterogeneous groups required the development of multiple educational foci which threatened mental discipline's fixed curriculum.

Two models were weighed by the faculty of the University of Mississippi in its efforts to respond to pressures for agricultural education. The first was the Sheffield School at Yale with its theoretical and laboratory orientation. The second was the practical field work emphasized by Midwestern state universities. Neither was considered entirely acceptable. The Yale model was deemed too impractical for a farm constituency, while the state university model was dismissed because of an over-emphasis on practice to the detriment of theory. The prospects of working in the fields to gain experience generated resentment among Southern students who sought the traditional classroom experiences they had come to expect of higher education. Ultimately Mississippi embarked upon a middle course. Professor Eugene W. Hilgard, whose own Ph.D. was earned from Heidelberg, stated this position when he encouraged the University:

> . . . to impart, besides a general education a thorough knowledge of the principles of agriculture, combined with such acquaintance with its practice as will enable. . . graduates . . . to know [not only] how things should be done, but to do [things] themselves in the field.[82]

In the final analysis, however, the liberal subjects were so entrenched at Mississippi that the agricultural and mechanical subjects called for by the Morrill Act could *not* readily be accommodated; it was necessary to establish the Mississippi Agricultural and Mechanical College in 1878 as an adjunct to the University.[83] In Columbia, however, South Carolina College president

John McLaren McBryde, assured the state legislature in 1883 that it had a strong school of agriculture which was effectively meeting the state's needs for improved agricultural methods. The College served the farmer, analyzing his fertilizer and feed, testing new machinery, and assisting in the development of new breeds of farm animals and varieties of plants. McBryde indicated that of the 153 students then in attendance at the College, 53 were pursuing agricultural studies. He proclaimed a balance had been struck between theory and practice: South Carolina students were engaged in laboratory, classroom and field activities.[84]

It was in his milieu that Kemp Battle, President of the University of North Carolina, affirmed that University's role as an active force for societal betterment. As early as 1866 Battle realized that industry, agriculture, and government required a work force capable of applying knowledge to practical problems and he believed the modern farmer should be acquainted with the principles of chemistry and agricultural science. Therefore, schools of agriculture similar to the land-grant agricultural schools in the Midwest and West were needed in the South. Moreover, Battle urged that the services of the University not be limited to students at Chapel Hill but extended to constituents throughout the State.[85] By the turn of the century, Battle's successor, Edwin A. Alderman, affirmed that while the South could not contemplate extensive graduate education and research, public service was a most worthy mission for a state university.[86]

In the final analysis the movement toward utility in the South was a powerful one by the turn of the century. By then Southern state universities under the spreading aegis of utility were, in the words of Alderman, seeking to reach the "public school, the factory child, the hand's hire, the village library, the home, the field . . . the shop . . . with a more practical education."[87] The utilitarian movement brought together advocates of an education centered on the agricultural and mechanical arts with those who defined reform as the development of an elective system that would provide students with greater opportunities to study history, modern languages or literature. Despite the disparate composition of the reform movement its members forged a single common objective: to remove the classical course of study from its position of preeminence. They were as we have seen moderately successful.

IV

Research

Although the emphasis of American higher education decidedly favored undergraduate studies, a trend toward research and graduate education had strong support outside the South. In the 1880s and 1890s, advocates of the German-based commitment to research and specialized knowledge loosely joined with those favoring utility to challenge effectively the position of mental discipline. By 1910, the values of research and utility exerted considerable leverage upon higher education outside of the South. Graduate studies became a major endeavor of such emerging universities as Harvard, Columbia, Stanford, Wisconsin, Chicago and California. In the wake of the pioneering effort at Johns Hopkins, research became the *sine qua non* of academic respectability. American scholars, captivated by the scientific specialization and research indigenous to the German university, returned from Europe with a dedication to recast higher education in the German mold.

In contrast to the rest of the nation, however, the concept of research met with little enthusiasm in the South. Its milieu of detachment and aloofness appeared antithetical to Southern values and needs. Instead, Southern reformers addressed themselves to the problems inherent in introducing scientific knowledge, raising the levels of basic education and cultural awareness, and improving deplorable professional standards.[88]

By almost any measure Southern colleges were poor and lacked the academic and financial capital to build the graduate research centers which were beginning to emerge in other parts of the nation. College proliferation was especially pronounced in the South, which in the 1880s could boast of more colleges than New England and the Middle Atlantic states combined.[89] Endowments were grossly inadequate or non-existent at Southern colleges, which were forced to compete among themselves and with the high schools for the only available revenue-tuition. At the turn of the century:

> None of the eighteen American institutions that had endowments of $1,500,000 . . . were [sic] in the South; and of the thirty with as much as $1,000,000 the South had only two, Vanderbilt and Tulane.[90]

Moreover, the region was badly lacking in preparatory education, as Trinity's President Kilgo suggests, one cannot readily build a university in a region where preparatory education is woefully inadequate and the bachelor degree is offered by many colleges "whose entire scientific apparatus can be hauled away in a one-horse dray."[91]

While specialization and research may have gained support in other parts of the nation, Southern colleges retained a strong bias towards teaching. Southern colleges could not harbor academics who confined themselves to a library or laboratory:

> . . . the principal function of our colleges must be to teach . . . and each [professor] is required to cover a great deal of ground. He . . . does not . . . have the leisure that is necessary for carrying on work of his own, and even less often has the library or laboratory facilities for original work. So the conditions make it inevitable that the best Southern colleges should mainly tend to develop in their teachers and students not scholars and specialists, but men of ideas and power.[92]

The fate of research at Vanderbilt University is illustrative of the difficulties its proponents faced throughout the South. Founded at approximately the same time as Johns Hopkins and less than twenty years before Chicago, Vanderbilt was more a college than a university. Generally recognized as a leader of the Southern but not national university movement, Vanderbilt, plagued with inadequately prepared undergraduates, was unable and unwilling to deploy the resources necessary to build a first-rate university. Instead of developing an extensive graduate program, Vanderbilt made plans for a high school.[93]

Preparing students profoundly influenced Vanderbilt. Substantial tutorial work was thrust upon the faculty and the boyish character of the student body made research and graduate education all but impossible.[94] In 1893, when institutions in other sections of the country were prodigiously expanding their graduate offerings, Chancellor Kirkland, himself a graduate of Leipzig, strongly reaffirmed the undergraduate mission of Vanderbilt in his inaugural address. Nevertheless, research remained an unrealized aspiration for Vanderbilt. Despite Kirkland's interest in collegiate education he did not oppose graduate training and research *per se*; indeed, he recognized the contribution of advanced scholarship to higher education in hastening conversion of the theoretical into the practical.[95] But the fact that Kirkland was compelled to wrestle with the problems of establishing a basic system of secondary and elementary schools discouraged Vanderbilt and other Southern institutions from considering anything so ambitious as basic research. It was not until the 1920s that Kirkland found conditions suitable for an advanced graduate research center.[96]

John F. Crowell, Trinity's president from 1887 to 1894, was similarly committed to providing a superior undergraduate education. He recognized the need for a more qualified faculty and appreciated the fact that professors trained at graduate institutions both in America and abroad would make significant contributions to Trinity. Crowell actively recruited professors who brought a variety of skills and perspectives to bear on the various disciplines and he deemed no instructor worthy to hold a position at Trinity who did not actually contribute to research and scholarship in his discipline.[97]

Evidence of Crowell's commitment emerges from an analysis of the academic preparation of Trinity faculty, which demonstrates a steady increase in the number of faculty members holding the Ph.D. In 1889 Trinity did not have a single Ph.D. on its faculty, while Mississippi, North Carolina and South Carolina, for example, could collectively count slightly more than ten percent in this category. By 1896 the percentage of earned Ph.D.'s at Trinity (16.7%) compared favorably with others (Mississippi, 17.6%; North Carolina, 16.1%; South Carolina, 18.2%). By 1903 a greater percentage of the faculty (36.8%) held the terminal degree at Trinity than at any of the other three institutions (Mississippi, 22.7%; North Carolina, 27.7%; South Carolina, 15.8%). While upgrading the educational level of its faculty, Trinity increasingly recruited from a broader geographic area. In contrast to prior years (1875 and 1882) when the entire faculty had received its undergraduate training in North Carolina, this number declined to less than forty percent by 1903.

Recognition of scholarly pursuits coupled with the desire to move the institution from rural Randolph County to the flourishing city of Durham are indicative of the university influence upon Trinity,[98] but these advances were merely flirtations with the university model. In plans for an envisioned (but never realized) Methodist University of North Carolina, Crowell saw Trinity, theoretically its major unit, focusing on advanced work while the schools and other colleges of the state concentrated on preparatory and collegiate work respectively.[99] In practice, Crowell sought to elevate Trinity to a first rate college but he did not envision a university patterned after Johns Hopkins or Yale.

Any attempts to divert Trinity from its undergraduate and service mission to a graduate, research oriented one would have been doomed to failure since the South lacked the social, intellectual, and economic base to sustain such an effort. An inadequate school system would frustrate plans for a graduate/ research center for years to come. In 1892–1893, for example, only ten students were enrolled in Trinity's senior class while sixteen were subfreshman.[100] Secondary schools developed so slowly after the War that little seems to have changed from the 1870s, when most students lacked suitable preparation, to the 1890s when the College was accused of an inability to enforce entrance standards. Conditions began to change after the turn of the century, however, as Trinity College, with the infusion of the Duke Family fortune, eventually became a true university. Graduate departments developed and the possibility of building a richly endowed university in the South[101] was realistically assessed. With the passing of years, both Trinity and Vanderbilt evolved into graduate universities with regional, if not national, missions, but throughout the nineteenth century the focus of their resources was almost solely on undergraduate studies.

Numerous problems also precluded substantial research and graduate study at other Southern institutions. As early as 1879 the faculty of the University of Mississippi, recognizing the value of research and the need for preparing specialists, charged a faculty committee with formulating "Requirements and courses of Study for the Post-graduate degree of Doctor of Philosophy (Ph.D.)."[102] Yet at the time the institution lacked the resources to support a substantive graduate program. Moreover, unlike their colleagues in the North, whose research led to a declining interest in undergraduate education and a greater demand for professional autonomy, Southern faculty retained a pre-eminent interest in undergraduate education and were seldom afforded comparable professional autonomy. At Mississippi the Trustees hired and fired professors capriciously, stipulating not only the courses to be taught but often the length of time for which they should meet (i.e., one semester, two years, etc.) In addition, they frequently declared all positions vacant at the end of the term in order to reorganize and recruit new staff.[103] This atmosphere, far from conducive to research, imposed many distractions; instructors at Mississippi spent a good deal of time policing the students[104] and could hardly find time to immerse themselves in a discipline. Yet, despite all obstacles, some graduate education existed at Mississippi. Prior to 1900, seventeen students enrolled in doctoral programs and three degrees were granted, one each in 1893, 1894 and 1895. Generally, however, Mississippi remained a small, localized institution, with a relatively homogeneous faculty concerned primarily with undergraduate education and harboring few pretentions of research excellence.[105]

While the experiences of Trinity and Mississippi were repeated throughout the South, there nevertheless remained a clear understanding of the importance of research as reflected in the popularity of Johns Hopkins as the primary source of Southern doctorates by 1903.[106] In 1901, 236 of the 465 advanced students at Johns Hopkins came from the South and it seemed it would be the true Southern graduate university. The freedom of students and professors and the emphasis upon research at Johns Hopkins was stimulating to the graduates of Southern colleges. A graduate of Trinity attending the Baltimore institution described a great university scattered throughout the city which actually permitted students to abstain from chapel attendance. Unlike Trinity's emphasis on a structured undergraduate experience, Johns Hopkins encouraged independent research by both professor and student. And, unlike the infamous reputation some Southern colleges had earned by lowering their standards in an effort to increase enrollment, Johns Hopkins was known because of Gildersleeve, Newcome, Remsur, Adams, and their colleagues and the work they were doing, rather than for the size of an incoming freshman class.[107]

Professors educated at Johns Hopkins held many key positions in Southern colleges at the turn of the century, and a 1921 article in the *Sewanee Review* proclaimed that:

> . . . educational history of the [South] for the past quarter of a century has been largely that of the Johns Hopkins University. It is rare, indeed, to find a the South any college of note whose faculty has not been drawn largely from Baltimore, to say nothing of the impetus given everywhere to original research and to the publication of the results of such investigations.[108]

Certainly Johns Hopkins stimulated and influenced Southern higher education; however, lacking the necessary secondary school foundation, the region found it difficult to contemplate general implementation of graduate education. The secondary school problem would have to be resolved before graduate work could be introduced on a wide scale. The absence of quality secondary schools forced Southern higher education to direct substantial resources to the preparation of students for undergraduate studies and the remaining resources were often directed to the general improvement of the undergraduate program.

In conclusion, the destruction following the War and the attendant educational and financial problems set the South back many years. It was not until the 1920s that a revitalized South witnessed real attempts to build true universities in Nashville, Chapel Hill and Durham. Research universities emerged so slowly in the South that the University of Virginia was the only Southern institution to hold membership in the prestigious Association of American Universities in the eighteen years from 1904 until 1922 when it was joined by the University of North Carolina[109] Thus, Southern higher education in the latter third of the nineteenth century did not replicate the process in the rest of the nation whereby research and utility dominated higher education and relegated mental discipline and piety, and liberal culture to marginal positions. The contest was much closer. Discipline and piety joined with liberal culture and Christian education to create a potent, viable educational philosophy which retained its strength well into the twentieth century; and utility, not research, made significant inroads.

V

Conclusion

In retrospect, the last third of the nineteenth century was a transitional period in the development of Southern higher education. The traditional collegiate emphasis upon discipline and piety peaked in the years immediately preceding and following the War and thereafter declined. The mental discipline and piety of the Thornwell or Craven genre had little chance for survival in the post-war era; narrow and rigid, it could not withstand the pressures generated by a changing South. However, the importance of mental discipline and piety can be measured in part by its progeny, liberal Christian education, that peculiar brand of liberal culture which found its roots in the South. Mental discipline and piety were thus expanded and incorporated into a philosophy more in tenor with the time and region.

Utility found a gradual, if grudging, acceptance in a South confronting the debilitating effects of the war and an agrarian economy. Drawing sustenance from a more progressive South, utility's strength was expressed by the development of substantial agricultural programs at state-supported institutions such as South Carolina and Mississippi and eventually provided the rationale for the elective system at both state and private institutions. Institutions such as Trinity, Vanderbilt, North Carolina, Mississippi and Wofford eventually accommodated utilitarian concerns in a positive if at times subdued manner.

Research, handicapped by the region's need to divert substantial resources to preparatory schools and sub-collegiate classes, failed to secure a foothold in the South during the nineteenth century. No major university was established in the region, and the history of Southern higher education in the nineteenth century is therefore one of a continued domination by the college as contrasted with the emergence of the university in other sections of the nation. In the twentieth century a vastly improved financial picture, the development of the publicly-supported high school and the increased demand for highly specialized personnel in all sectors of society finally enabled Vanderbilt, Duke and North Carolina to create strong graduate components. In the nineteenth century, however, the emphasis in Southern higher education was decidedly undergraduate.

The university-centered, secular liberal culture described by Veysey found the South inhospitable. A distinctly college-centered liberal Christian education emerged instead, and its merits were extolled throughout the South. Its strong concern for the development of religious principles and gentlemanly character suited the region; with roots in both sectarian and public institutions liberal Christian education constituted a significant force in Southern higher education.

By attempting to meet the needs of the greater society, however, Southern higher education engaged in a penetrating and potentially explosive evaluation of its goals, objectives, and methods. Furthermore regardless of size or source of support only a few institutions could be neatly placed in a single category; on most any campus one could find proponents of mental discipline and piety, liberal culture/Christian education, utility and research. This recognition of and willingness to deal with a multifarious population and diverse societal needs naturally undermined the essence of the ante-bellum classical college while creating a new sense of dynamism in higher education. Had Southern higher education unanimously elected to retreat from contemporary concerns, it is likely that mental discipline would have reigned supreme for several decades after the War. This was not the case, however, for with each outward thrust, each attempt to meet the needs of the people, came new ideas and more intensive debate over the future direction of higher education in the region. But one thing is certain. Southern higher education did not follow the pattern of university development that emerged in other regions of the nation. It ultimately moved into the mainstream of American higher education but its course was decidedly different.

NOTES

1. C.B. Burke, "The Expansion of American Higher Education," in *The Transformation of Higher Learning 1860-1930*, ed. K.H. Jarausch (Chicago, 1983), p. 111.
2. Letter, L.C. Garland to his father, May 30, 1865. Joint University Library, Vanderbilt University, John James Tiger IV Collection.
3. J.B. Sellers, *History of University of Alabama, Vol. I: 1818-1902* (University of Alabama, 1953), pp. 292-313.
4. R. Somers, *The Southern State Since the War 1870-1871* (New York, 1871) pp. 159-160. Somers, a visiting Englishman, stated "the professors at the close of the war were put under the ban of political proscription . . . and new men of inferior attainments were set down in their chairs. The consequence is that Alabama has still a University, with buildings and libraries, and professors, and expenditure, but no students. . . ."
5. Letter, A.J. Quinche to J.L. Johnson, February 1, 1873, Southern Historical Collection, University of North Carolina, John Lipscomb Johnson Papers. *Note:* John Lipscomb Johnson joined the University of Mississippi faculty in 1873.
6. D.D. Wallace, *History of Wofford College* (Nashville, 1951), p. 152.
7. N.C. Chaffin, *Trinity College, 1839-1892: The Beginnings of Duke University* (Durham, 1950), pp. 255-256.
8. K.P. Battle, *The Struggle and the Story of the Rebirth of the University* (Chapel Hill, 1901), pp. 3-11. Also see H.M. Wagstaff, *Impressions of Men and Movements at the University of North Carolina* (Chapel Hill, 1950).
9. "The curricula of the university 1857-1858 and 1897-1898," *University* [North Carolina] *Record*, January, 1898.
10. G.W. Paschal, *History of Wake Forest College, Vol. II: 1865-1905* (Wake Forest, 1943), pp. 2-22 and 419.
11. D.W. Hollis, *University of South Carolina, Vol. I: South Carolina College* (Columbia, 1951), pp. 214-222.
12. D.W. Hollis, *University of South Carolina, Vol. II: College to University* (Columbia, 1956), pp. 44-79.
13. F.A. Barnard, *Report on the organization of military schools, Made to the Trustees of the University of Mississippi* (Jackson, 1861), p. 31. University of Mississippi Library, Mississippi Collections.
14. L.R. Veysey, *The Emergence of the American University*, (Chicago, 1970). For a critique of Veysey see P. Mattingly, "Structures Over Time: Institutional History," in *Historical Inquiry in Education*, ed. J.H. Best (Washington, D.C., 1983), pp. 34-55.
15. C.V. Woodward, *Origins of the New South, 1877-1913*, (Baton Rouge, 1951), pp. 436-438.
16. C. Degler, "The Two Cultures and the Civil War," in *The Development of an American Culture*, eds. S. Cohen and L. Ratner (Englewood Cliffs, 1970), pp. 92-119.
17. W.J. Cash, *The Mind of the South*, (New York, 1941), p. vii.
18. Degler, "Two Cultures and Civil War," p. 117.
19. Woodward, *Origins of the New South*, p. x.
20. B.M. Palmer, *The Life and Letters of James Henley Thornwell*, (Richmond, 1871), p. 357. Also J.N. Waddel *Nature and Advantage of the Course of Study in Institutions of the Higher Learning* (Natchez, 1866), p. 13.
21. F. Brewer, "South Carolina University," (manuscript, 1876), South Carolinian Library, University of South Carolina, Fisk Brewer Manuscript Collection.
22. F. Brewer, "Assorted class notes and notebook," *ca.* 1877, South Carolinian Library, University of South Carolina, Fisk Brewer Manuscript Collection.
23. W.D. Porter, *College and Collegians*, (Charleston, 1871), p. 19. Porter was a Trustee of South Carolina College from 1858 to 1868.
24. W.A. Pusey, "Should the classics still be studied," *Vanderbilt Observer*, 8, October, 1885, p. 2.
25. "The study of Latin and Greek," *Trinity Archive*, VI, April, 1893, p. 283.
26. Waddel, *Nature and Advantage*, p. 1.
27. Minutes of the Faculty Meeting, University of Mississippi, April 22, 1884. *Note:* Fulton joined the University of Mississippi in 1871 as a tutor and from 1892 to 1906 served as Chancellor.
28. Barnard, *Report to Trustees of University of Mississippi*, p. 31.
29. A. Cabaniss, *The University of Mississippi: Its First Hundred Years*, (Hattiesburg, 1971), p. 64.
30. *Catalogue of Trinity College*, 1885-1886, p. 9.
31. D.D. Wallace, *History of Wofford College*, (Nashville, 1951), pp. 77-78.

32. Brewer, "South Carolina University."

33. J.H. Easterby, *A History of the College of Charleston,* (Charleston, 1935), p. 164.

34. H.M. Bullock, *A History of Emory University,* (Nashville, 1936), pp. 154-174. *Also see:* M. Bauman, "Confronting the New South Creed: The Genteel Conservative as Higher Educator," in *Education and the Rise of the New South,* eds. R.K. Goodenow and A.O. White (Boston, 1981), pp. 91-113.

35. C.W. Hutson, "The South Carolina College of the late fifties," Compiler: Yates Snowden, *Sermon and Lectures South Carolina College and University, 1830-1910,* South Carolinian Library, University of South Carolina.

36. J.W. Taylor, *The Young Men of the New South: The Education, Duties and Rewards,* (Memphis, 1869). p. 8. Mississippi Collection, University of Mississippi Library.

37. W. Cash, *Mind of the South,* p. 80.

38. W.M. Whitman, "Address of the laying of the corner-stone of Wofford College," (manuscript, July 4, 1851). Sandor Teszler Library, Wofford College Archives.

39. *Catalogue of the officers and students of the University of Mississippi, 1879-1880,* pp. 74-75. *Also see:* Trustees of the State University, *Where shall I send my son?* (Oxford, 1876), pp. 3-4. Mississippi Collection, University of Mississippi Library.

40. Minutes of the Board of Trustees Meeting, University of Mississippi, June 24, 1886.

41. Minutes of the Board of Trustees Meeting, University of Mississippi, June 23, 1879.

42. B. Craven, "Mental discipline," (eight page manuscript, n.d.). Perkins Library, Duke University, Braxton Craven Papers.

43. C.V. Woodward, *Origins of the New South,* pp. 142-174 provides an excellent analysis of Southern literary and religious values in the decades following the Civil War. For a highly relevant look at higher education and Southern culture see J.L. Wagoner, "Higher Education and Transitions in Southern Culture: An Exploratory Apolgia," *Journal of Thought,* 18, Fall, 1983, pp. 104-118.

44. D.P. Harrington, Requirements for the A. B. Degree. Contained in *Proceedings of the first annual session of the College Association of North Carolina, North Carolina Teacher,* May, 1892. H.F. Linscott, "Pure Scholarship—Its Place in Civilization." *South Atlantic Quarterly,* 1(October, 1902):341-350.

45. H. Hawkins, *Between Harvard and America,* (New York, 1972), p. 264.

46. B.J. Ramage, "The Limitations of Elective Work in School and College," *Sewanee Review,* 9 (July 1901):319.

47. T.D. Witherspoon, *The appeal of the South to its educated men.* (Memphis, 1867), pp. 8-9. Mississippi Collection, University of Mississippi Library.

48. D. Bertelson, *The Lazy South,* (New York, 1967), pp. 75 and 182-183.

49. C.N. Degler, *Place Over Time* (Baton Rouge, 1977), pp. 99-132. Degler outlines the substantial economic and cultural continuity between the pre and post war South.

50. C. Degler, "Two Cultures and Civil War," p. 119.

51. E.W. Porter, *Trinity and Duke,* (Durham, 1964), pp. 70-144.

52. J.C. Kilgo, "Christian Education: Its Aims and Superiority," *ca.* 1896. Perkins Library, Duke University, John C. Kilgo Papers.

53. J.C. Kilgo, Untitled typescript, n.d., p. 5. Perkins Library, Duke University, John Carlisle Kilgo Papers.

54. H.N. Snyder, "The Denominational College in Southern Education," *South Atlantic Quarterly,* 5(January 1906):9.

55. H.N. Snyder, "The Case of the Denominational College," *Methodist Review,* 58(January, 1909):14.

56. J.H. Carlisle, An undated clipping from the Florence, South Carolina *Centenary* (January, 1892), Sandor Teszler Library, Wofford College, James H. Carlisle Papers. *Also see:* H.N. Snyder, "James H. Carlisle—Educator," *South Atlantic Quarterly,* 9(January, 1910):10-20.

57. J.H. Carlisle, Jr., "Memories of Wofford College," (manuscript, n.d.), Sandor Teszler Library, Wofford College, Wofford College Archives.

58. J.B. Henneman, "The Late Professor Baskerville," *Sewanee Review,* 8(January, 1900):26-44.

59. H.N. Snyder, "The college literary society," *Sewanee Review,* 12(January, 1904):83.

60. *Catalogue of the Officers and Students of the University of Mississippi, 1876-1877,* p. 46.

61. *Historical and current catalogue of the officers and students of the University of Mississippi, 1886-1887,* p. 152.

62. Minutes of the Board of Trustees, University of Mississippi, August 6, 1889.

63. G.T. Pugh, "Is Science an Incentive to Poetry?" *Wofford College Journal,* 7(June, 1897):281-291.

64. J.B. Wiggins, "Does the Study of Science tend to Suppress the Spirit of Poetry and Romance?" *Wofford College Journal,* 9(June, 1898):46-52.

65. Veysey, *Emergence of American University,* p. 60.

66. C.W. Hutson, *The Southern Renaissance,* (Columbia, 1885), p. 29.

67. For a contemporary's view of the South in the decades after the Civil War see C.H. Otken, *Ills of the South.* (New York, 1894). Reprint (New York, 1973). *Also see:* Woodward, *Origins of the New South,* pp. 107-112.

68. R.N. Current, *Northernizing the South,* (Athens, 1983), p. 84.

69. D.W. Grantham, *Southern Progressivism: The Reconciliation of Progress and Traditions,* (Knoxville, 1983), p. xviii.

70. Woodward, *Origins of the New South,* pp. 139-141.

71. M. O'Brien, *The Idea of the American South, 1920-1941*, (Baltimore, 1979), p. 6.

72. Grantham, *Southern Progressivism*, p. 84. Also see pp. 268-270 for an examination of the development of utility in Southern higher education and pp. 5-8 for the impact of urbanization and industrialization upon the professions.

73. *Catalogue of Wofford College, 1876-77*, p. 18. For a relevant analysis of President Eliot and the elective system at Harvard see: E.S. Joynes, "President Eliot's inaugural address," *Educational Journal of Virginia*, 1(March, 1870):136-140.

74. J.M. McBryde, *Agricultural education*. An address before the South Carolina State Legislature, December 12, 1882. (Columbia, 1883), pp. 12-15.

75. E.S. Joynes, "Relation of the state to higher education in colleges and professional schools," a paper read before the Southern Educational Association in Chattanooga on July 9, 1891. South Carolinian Library, University of South Carolina.

76. P.P. Lipscomb, *Dedication and inauguration of Vanderbilt University* (Nashville, 1875), p. 76.

77. J.H. Kirkland, *The service of citizenship*, 1911. Joint University library, Vanderbilt University, James H. Kirkland Addresses.

78. J.C. Kilgo, "Up to date education," *State*, Columbia, South Carolina, April 14, 1899. Clipping contained in Perkins Library, Duke University, John C. Kilgo Papers.

79. J.C. Kilgo, "The mission of Trinity College," *The Trinity Archive*, 15 (November 1901):127.

80. W.H. Glasson, "The college professor in the public service," *South Atlantic Quarterly*, 1(July 1902):254.

81. *Catalogue of Trinity College*, 1887-88, pp. 31-44.

82. E.W. Hilgard, Report on Organization of the Department of Agriculture and Mechanical Arts, 1871. Mississippi Collection, University of Mississippi Library.

83. R.A. McLemore, "The Roots of Higher Education in Mississippi," *Journal of Mississippi History*, 26(August 1964) Also J.K. Betterworth, *People's College: A History of Mississippi State University* (Tuscaloosa: 1953), pp. 8-11.

84. J.M. McBryde, *Agricultural education*, (Columbia, 1883), pp. 22-23. South Carolinian Library, University of South Carolina. Also see: J.M. McBryde Papers, Southern Historical Collection, University of North Carolina Library.

85. K.P. Battle, *The head and the hand*, (June 23, 1886), pp. 5-6. Pamphlet located in the South Carolinian Library, University of South Carolina.

86. E.A. Alderman, "The university: Its work and its needs, University of North Carolina," *Record 1901-1902* (Chapel Hill, 1901), p. 51.

87. E.A. Alderman, Inaugural address, January 27, 1897. North Carolina Collection, University of North Carolina, p. 29.

88. A.E. Shepherd, "Higher education in the south," *Sewanee Review*, 1(May 1893):287.

89. J.D. Dreher, "Colleges North and Colleges South," National Educational Association, *Journal of Proceedings and Addresses 1886*, pp. 370-375.

90. Woodward, *Origins of the New South*, p. 437.

91. J.C. Kilgo "Some Phases of Southern Higher Education," *South Atlantic Quarterly*, 2(April 1903):141.

92. W.P. Few, "Trinity College and Her Present Opportunity," *Trinity Archive*, 15(November, 1901):113. Few elsewhere stated: "For the good of the country as a whole [educational] centers should be distributed over the country rather than concentrated in sections. Draw a line across the map of the United States from a point just below the latitude of Washington and Baltimore on the Atlantic coast, and all the leading centers of research in graduate studies will be north of the line. The Northeast has Harvard, Columbia, Yale, and other great centers. Johns Hopkins is near the border line. The Central West has the University of Chicago, University of Michigan, University of Wisconsin, and other centers of note. The Pacific coast has the University of California, Stanford University, and California Institute of Technology. The South is making progress in four or five places and in some of these centers the progress is apt to be notable. Even so, it will be a good while before the southern states can do their share in scientific study and research." W.P. Few, "The Beginnings of an American University." (typescript, n.d.) Perkins Library, Duke University, William Preston Few Papers.

93. Minutes of the Board of Trustees, Vanderbilt University, April 29, 1874.

94. Minutes of the Board of Trustees, Vanderbilt University, June 19, 1876.

95. J.H. Kirkland, *Proceedings and addresses at the installation and inauguration of James Hampton Kirkland, Ph.D.*, (Nashville, 1893), p. 37.

96. J.H. Kirkland, "Sketch of Vanderbilt University," unpublished paper (1926). Joint University Library, Vanderbilt University, James H. Kirkland Papers.

97. W.K. Boyd, "Trinity College before its removal to Durham," (typescript copy, n.d.). Perkins Library, Duke University, William Kenneth Boyd Papers.

98. W.K. Boyd, "Trinity and Duke," (typescript copy, n.d.). Perkins Library, Duke University, William Kenneth Boyd Papers.

99. J.F. Crowell, "Plan of a Methodist University in North Carolina," (manuscript, ca. 1890). Perkins Library, Duke University, John F. Crowell Papers.

100. *Catalogue and Announcements of Trinity College, 1892-93*.

101. W.P. Few, "Trinity College and her Present Opportunity," p. 113.
102. Minutes of the Faculty Meeting, University of Mississippi, November 25, 1879.
103. Minutes of the Board of Trustees, University of Mississippi, June 22, 1886. *Also see:* Minutes of the Board of Trustees, University of Mississippi, June 27, 1889.
104. *Minutes of the Board of Trustees, University of Mississippi, June 22, 1891.*
105. M.R. Brown, *Graduate programs in Mississippi to 1900, unpublished Master's thesis* History, University of Mississippi 1968, pp 15-16.
106. According to my research of the twenty-eight members with the Ph.D. at the University of South Carolina, University of Mississippi and University of North Carolina in 1903, seven received their doctorate from Johns Hopkins, six from German Universities, four from University of North Carolina, four from Harvard University, three from other Eastern universities, two from other Southern universities, one from a Midwestern university and one was unknown.
107. D.C. Branson, "Letter from Johns Hopkins," *Trinity Archive*, IV, March, 1891.
108. B.S. Ramage, Notes, *Sewanee Review*, 9(July, 1901):379.
109. Wagoner, "Higher Education and Transitions," p. 114.

Mr. Stelar is an Associate Professor of Education and Associate Vice-president for Academic Affairs at Seton Hall University.

The Morrill Act, 1862

Section 4. *And be it further enacted,* That all moneys derived from the sale of the lands aforesaid by the States to which the lands are apportioned, and from the sales of land scrip hereinbefore provided for, shall be invested in stocks of the United States or of the States, or some other safe stocks, yielding not less than five per centum upon the par value of said stocks; and that the moneys so invested shall constitute a perpetual fund, the capital of which shall remain forever undiminished (except so far as may be provided in section five of this act), and the interest of which shall be inviolably appropriated by each State which may take and claim the benefit of this act, to the endowment, support, and maintenance of at least one college where the leading object shall be, without excluding other scientific and classical studies, and including military tactics, to teach such branches of learning as are related to agriculture and the mechanic arts, in such manner as the legislatures of the States may respectively prescribe, in order to promote the liberal and practical education of the industrial classes in the several pursuits and professions in life. . . .

Section 5. *And be it further enacted* . . .

Third. Any State which may take and claim the benefit of the provisions of this act shall provide, within five years, at least not less than one college, as described in the fourth section of this act, or the grant to such State shall cease; and said State shall be bound to pay the United States the amount received of any lands previously sold and that the title to purchasers under the State shall be valid.

Fourth. An annual report shall be made regarding the progress of each college, recording any improvements and experiments made, with their cost and results, and such other matters, including state industrial and economical statistics, as may be supposed useful, one copy of which shall be transmitted by mail free, by each, to all the other colleges which may be endowed under the provisions of this act, and also one copy to the Secretary of the Interior. . . .

Approved, July 2, 1862.

---

12 *United States Statutes at Large,* 503-5.

The Sixty-Nine Institutions of the 1862 and 1890 Morrill Land-Grant Acts

Key: B = 1890 Morril Act black institutions; O = nine oldest land grants

ALABAMA
1. Alabama A&M, Normal (B)
2. Auburn, Auburn
ALASKA
3. U. of Alaska, Fairbanks
ARIZONA
4. U. of Arizona, Tucson
ARKANSAS
5. U. of Arkansas, Pine Bluff (B)
6. U. of Arkansas, Fayetteville
CALIFORNIA
7. U. of California, Berkeley
also Davis & Riverside
COLORADO
8. Colorado State, Fort Collins
CONNECTICUT
9. U. of Conn., Storrs
DELAWARE
10. Delaware State College, Dover
11. U. of Delaware, Newark
DISTRICT OF COLUMBIA
12. U. of the D.C., Washington
FLORIDA
13. Florida A&M, Tallahasee (B)
14. U. of Florida, Gainesville
GEORGIA
15. Fort Valley State College (B)
16. U. of Georgia, Athens
HAWAII
17. U. of Hawaii, Honolulu
IDAHO
18. U. of Idaho, Moscow
ILLINOIS
19. U. of Illinois, Urbana
INDIANA
20. Purdue, W. Lafayette
IOWA
21. Iowa State, Ames (O)
KANSAS
22. Kansas State, Manhattan (O)
KENTUCKY
23. Kentucky State, Frankfort (B)
24. U. of Kentucky, Lexington

LOUISIANA
25. Louisiana State, Baton Rouge
26. Southern U., Baton Rouge (B)
MAINE
27. U. of Maine, Orono
MARYLAND
28. U. of Maryland, E. Shore (B)
29. U. of Maryland, College Park
MASSACHUSETTS
30. M.I.T., Cambridge
31. U. of Mass., Amherst
MICHIGAN
32. Michigan State, E. Lansing (O)
MINNESOTA
33. U. of Minnesota, Twin Cities (O)
MISSISSIPPI
34. Alcorn State, Lorman (B)
35. Mississippi State U.
MISSOURI
36. Lincoln U., Jefferson City (B)
37. U. of Missouri, Columbia (O)
MONTANA
38. Montana State, Bozeman
NEBRASKA
39. U. of Nebraska, Lincoln
NEVADA
40. U. of Nevada, Reno
NEW HAMPSHIRE
41. U. of N. Hampshire, Durham
NEW JERSEY
42. Rutgers, New Brunswick (O)
NEW MEXICO
43. New Mexico State, Las Cruces
NEW YORK
44. Cornell, Ithaca
NORTH CAROLINA
45. N. C. A&T, Greensboro (B)
46. N. C. State, Raleigh
NORTH DAKOTA
47. N. Dakota State, Fargo
OHIO
48. Ohio State, Columbus

OKLAHOMA
    49. Langston University (B)
    50. Oklahoma State, Stillwater
OREGON
    51. Oregon State, Corvallis
PENNSYLVANIA
    52. Penn. State, University Park (O)
PUERTO RICO
    53. U. of Puerto Rico, Mayaguez
RHODE ISLAND
    54. U. of Rhode Island, Kingston
SOUTH CAROLINA
    55. S. C. State, Orangeburg (B)
    56. Clemson, Clemson
SOUTH DAKOTA
    57. S. Dakota State, Brookings
TENNESSEE
    58. Tennessee State, Nashville (B)
    59. U. of Tennessee, Knoxville

TEXAS
    60. Prairie View A&M (B)
    61. Texas A&M, College Station
UTAH
    62. Utah State, Logan
VERMONT
    63. U. of Vermont, Burlington (O)
VIRGINIA
    64. Virginia State, Petersburg (B)
    65. Va. Polytechnic, Blacksburg
WASHINGTON
    66. Washington State, Pullman
WEST VIRGINIA
    67. West Virginia U., Morgantown
WISCONSIN
    68. U of Wisconsin, Madison (O)
WYOMING
    69. U. of Wyoming, Laramie

University Identity: The Teaching and Research Functions

Hugh Hawkins

In defending a dictionary definition of "university" that he wrote in 1891, Charles S. Peirce argued that a university had nothing to do with instruction.[1] His negation fit the research emphasis that had spurred the university movement in the United States. Dedicated teachers sometimes approached the opposite extreme and denigrated research as an institutional irrelevancy. But those academics who labored to fulfill both roles—researcher and teacher—were truer representatives of the new and newly shaped institutions that revolutionized American higher education in the last third of the nineteenth century. Even the two universities at which the research ethos was clearly dominant—Johns Hopkins and Clark—stressed the advanced level of their students, never proposing scholarship in isolation from instruction.

This essay seeks to place universities in the context of other institutionalized efforts to preserve, increase, and apply knowledge. Above all else, what distinguishes universities among knowledge-oriented organizations is their persistent concern with forming links between other allegiances to knowledge and the function of teaching. Members of a learned academy do at times speak of educating each other, directors of libraries sometimes see themselves promoting a general process of self-education, and scientists in industrial laboratories occasionally bring in apprentices, but none of these knowledge-centered institutions approaches the schooling responsibilities of universities. Indeed, the builders of universities took pride in providing an apex for the nation's incomplete school system. They often indicated that nurturing creative scholarship made universities superior to other schools, but when speaking with other learned associations in mind (usually avowing shared purposes while denying redundancy), university spokesmen gained firmest ground by stressing the effects of university teaching. Teaching, it was said, preserved the accumulated body of learning by passing it on to successive generations, provided a seedbed for future creators of new knowledge, and enhanced the contributions students would make to society. Such intertwining of teaching with the university's other knowledge-serving functions has been both its glory and its shame. Here is a case in which institutional purposes support, but also threaten, each other. The conflicts and compromises engendered by the simultaneous presence of teaching obligations and research-mindedness in the rising American universities will form the central thread of the account that follows. Attention will also be paid to the "external" aspects of teaching-research tensions, specifically to their relationship to the social setting of universities. The ability to shift the balance between these functions was part of the flexibility that helped win support for universities in a nation that often seemed too democratic and too utilitarian to nurture the life of the mind.

Definitions of the university were often only implicit in the presidential inaugural addresses that mark the emergence of the American university. At newly founded Cornell in 1868, President Andrew D. White foresaw an institution giving equal respect to liberal and practical studies in a widely inclusive curriculum, granting unusual curricular freedom to students while remaining determinedly unattached. He directed the faculty not to the challenge of distinguished covering new truth, but to the satisfactions of helping to educate distinguished alumni. A year later, when he began his forty-year presidency of Harvard, Charles W. Eliot placed similar stress on curricular inclusiveness, student freedom to elect courses, and equal status for newer studies. Although he believed that "the strongest and most devoted professors will contribute something to the patrimony of knowledge," he reminded the faculty that except for the observatory, "the University does not hold a single fund primarily intended to secure to the men of learning the leisure and means to prosecute original researches."[2]

No one was better aware than Daniel Coit Gilman of earlier struggles to attain university ideals in America. When, as president of the new Johns Hopkins University in 1876, he referred to previous efforts, he could draw on his administrative work at Yale's scientific school in the 1850s and 1860s, his friendship with White, and his three years in California as president of a state university receiving federal land-grant aid under the Morrill Act of 1862. Academic legend, accurately reflecting the major influence of the Johns Hopkins experiment in American higher education, sees Gilman as nailing the banner of research to the mast of the new enterprise in Baltimore. But in his inaugural Gilman cited the university's teaching function as its first priority. The elevated level of students seemed the most distinctive element in his plan: "The University is a place for the advanced and special education of youth who have been prepared for its freedom by the discipline of a lower school." He spoke of the university's "freedom" to investigate, but of its "obligation" to teach.[3]

Gilman differentiated the university, where "teaching is essential, research important," from the academy or learned society, where "research is indispensable, tuition rarely thought of." He included complimentary references to two Baltimore learned institutions, the Maryland Academy of Sciences and the Peabody Institute (a unique blend of library, lyceum, and music conservatory), and for good measure cited eleven "powerful instruments for the advancement of science, literature, and art" in nearby Washington, ranging from the Smithsonian Institution to the Corcoran Art Gallery. When he chose a metaphor, however, he made the university the sun, the other learned agencies the planets.[4]

Perhaps no inaugural ever expressed the research ideal as boldly as did G. Stanley Hall's address at Clark University's first-year opening exercises in 1889. Hall had earned a Ph.D. at Eliot's Harvard and held a professorship at Johns Hopkins before being called to head the new university in Worcester, Massachusetts. His design for the institution showed the prestige of investigation at a high point, and Clark opened with provision for admission of graduate students only. Hall's pristine conception was suggested in his comment that the university "should be financially and morally able to disregard practical application as well

as numbers of students . . ., and the increase of knowledge and its diffusion among the few fit should be its ideal." Faculty members should be "absorbed in and living only for pure science and high scholarship." They could best serve those few fit students by following the example of a German professor Hall described who set a newly arrived American college graduate to work on one muscle of a frog's leg, thus giving him "the invaluable training of abandoning himself to a long experimental research upon [a] very special but happily chosen point." With a faculty of eighteen, Clark in its first year had thirty-four students, all of them seeking advanced work, and twelve already holding Ph.D.'s.[5]

The opening of Clark preceded the founding of two other new universities, Stanford (1891) and Chicago (1892) by only a few years. Whereas Clark's striking concern for advancing scholarship was symbolized by its omission of undergraduates, these two universities provided space for research in much more complex institutions. Although passages in the inaugural of David Starr Jordan, the Cornell alumnus who was Stanford's first president, raised images of character-building and kindly paternalism of the Mark Hopkins-and-the-log variety, it also reflected the importance of research. He identified the heart of a university as "personal contact of young men and young women with *scholars* and *investigators*"; indeed, "a professor to whom original investigation is unknown should have no place in a university."[6]

The University of Chicago summed up the major developments in higher education of the previous three decades. In addition to a graduate school of arts and sciences, it included an undergraduate program, professional schools, an extramural adult education division, a university press, a spate of specialized journals, and a moral-competitive athletic program in which football held the star role. More striking than their existence in a single institution was the care with which these parts were organized. William Rainey Harper, Chicago's genius president, who had earned his Yale Ph.D. at the age of eighteen, had a penchant for organization. This trait made him a fit representative of a time when specialization seemed to have created a disarray that called for institutional reordering. His elaborate plan, largely drawn up before the hiring of his faculty, revealed a compulsive structuralism that led to the establishment of twelve faculty ranks, four equal quarters, a division of undergraduate work into junior and senior colleges, and a subordinating affiliation of small colleges with the university.[7]

Concentration on structure and management was evident also at older universities, where the rise of electives and the increasing autonomy of departments had brought fears of institutional incoherence. In 1890 Harvard turned its formerly amorphous graduate program into the Graduate School of Arts and Sciences, and Columbia began a reorganization that balanced its School of Political Science with Schools of Philosophy and of Pure Science. In 1896 both Columbia and Princeton signaled a sense of expanded function by adopting the name "university," often believed to symbolize unity amid diversity.[8]

In the new concern for carefully rationalized structure during the 1890s, teaching and research were not severed. The fact that its professional knowledge-creators were teachers still distinguished the university most sharply from other learned organizations. The early stress on teaching in presidential statements was, however, moderated by assertions that other functions were equally essential. In 1891 Eliot envisioned universities as having three principal functions. ''In the first place they teach; secondly, they accumulate great stores of acquired and systematized knowledge in the form of books and collections; thirdly, they investigate.'' Research, he insisted, was ''quite as indispensable'' as the other two purposes. Gilman, abandoning the circumspection of his inaugural, could in 1896 glimpse a utopian future for universities, in which dedication to creating new knowledge overshadowed the teaching function. Other presidents, especially those at state universities, increasingly included public service as a principal university characteristic. Teaching no longer held place as uniquely essential. But even though the hierarchy might change and the lists lengthen, the persisting definitional functions of universities remained teaching and investigation, two elements that could follow each other tidily in a statement of purpose, but were daily entangled in relationships of considerable ambiguity.[9]

For the dedicated discoverers of truth, scarcely any place in America offered as good a haven as did universities. That much was admitted by even the devoutly research-minded. But universities, which in the 1880s had moved to lighten the burdens that older college patterns had placed on investigators, came gradually to pose new difficulties. Complaints varied with time and place, but it seems fairly accurate to schematize them as shifting from the unsympathetic environment set by a democratic society (1880s) to interference by business power (1890s), and from the distraction of faculty administrative duties (1900s). Accompanying these were more or less constant complaints that the teaching function itself hindered the university's ability to serve as the setting for productive scholarship.

The research-teaching conflict was matter of factly put by President Jacob Gould Schurman of Cornell in 1906: ''It must, I think, be admitted that most university teachers, at least in the scientific departments, have chosen their profession not so much from the love of teaching as from the desire to continue the study of their specialty. While the number of those who have a positive distaste for teaching is small, there are many whose interest in teaching is secondary to their interest in investigation.'' But Schurman failed to convey the passionate elevation of research above teaching in the self-images of some professors. From the highest of the twelve ranks at the University of Chicago, William Gardner Hale, a Latinist, saw the advance of civilization dependent on the research ideal. After suggesting the distress of a professor who foresaw his epitaph as recounting merely, ''He learned much that other men had discovered, and conveyed much of this to others,'' Hale declared: ''Had such a statement

been always the best that could be said of any man, our science today would still be that of the primitive cave-dweller. It is the minds that have advanced *beyond* what they have received from others that have brought us to the point where we are. It is to the *discoverers*, in far greater measure than to the transmitters, that the world is under obligation.'' But assertions of the excellence of research were not always grounded in a theory of social progress. For some, its value transcended social experience. There were professors who associated the quest for new knowledge with untainted motives and ''sacred fire.'' ''Remember the research ideal, to keep it holy!'' adjured Professor Albion Small of Chicago. Research could be imagined as transforming the individual and elevating him, not merely by its advancement of the nation or mankind, but through a merging with ultimate reality akin to that of the Emersonian Genius.[10]

Professors with an eye to their own research sometimes protested the ''democratic average'' that was increasingly welcomed into university student bodies, but even more troubling than quality were the quantity of students and the amount of time that the faculty were obliged to spend teaching them. As if regularly enrolled students were not burden enough, administrators sensitive to calls for public service began in the 1890s to urge that professors involve themselves in the newly invented snares of summer school and extension lecturing.

Faculty resentment of distractions from research had grown acute by 1906, when a survey by David Starr Jordan brought long, reflective responses. One pointed to the importance of not disrupting ''that unconscious cerebration which is one of the most important factors in working out scientific results.'' Another argued that the leisure of its greatest scholars was the university's most precious asset: ''We should count it a sin to require such a man to 'cover the ground.' We should sacrifice the catalogue, make it thin and full of holes, confine the students to a narrow range of typically good choices, and by these inconsequential sacrifices preserve for the great man his chance to do the work which he alone can do.'' When it came to respect for the professor's leisure, European models were found inadequate, although they were still cited as superior to those of the United States. ''America, it would seem,'' wrote one of Jordan's respondents, ''has combined the English way of keeping its instructors occupied all day with the German idea of extending the working year over three-quarters or more of the solar year.''[11]

A survey of assistant professors at various universities taken in 1909 found them evenly divided on the question of whether their conditions of employment reasonably favored ''carrying on advanced work and intellectual growth.'' Among the complaints of the fifty-one who were dissatisfied, excessive or elementary teaching duties overshadowed other problems (such as committee work, inadequate libraries, and low salaries). Hours of scheduled teaching ranged from occasionally below ten to as high as twenty, with fifteen being ''not uncommon.''[12]

The distractions of the teaching commitment seemed to reappear constantly in new guises. Trustees and patrons of universities sometimes sympathized with student complaints about faculty disinterest in teaching and sometimes asked for proof of direct practical results, which the seekers of new truth could not give. In a regent-faculty confrontation of 1909 at the University of Wisconsin, an ad hoc faculty committee charged the regents with placing undue emphasis on introductory courses and with belittling research outside the applied sciences. The controversy had been brought to a head by Frederick Jackson Turner's resignation. A major motive for Turner's decision had been his wish to expose what he regarded as an assault on humanistic research: the regents, after agreeing to free him from every other semester of teaching, had sided with students who complained of his inaccessibility. After an exchange of views between representatives of faculty and regents (which involved other issues beside research), the faculty won the regents' formal assent to its position.[13]

Some university insiders punctured high-minded objections to the interference of teaching by insisting that absence of creative scholarship on the part of a faculty member could be traced to either inherent incapacity or dislike of hard work.[14] But the more common counter argument presented teaching and research as mutually supportive. Both administrative officers and professors joined in this interpretation, and although it became a commonplace of discourse about universities, its interior logic is not without interest.

The subordinate part of the argument declared that teaching improved the quality of research. Gilman spoke of investigators who, being also teachers, gained from "the incitement of colleagues, the encouragement of pupils, and the observation of the public." The case was put more forcefully by his successor as president of Johns Hopkins, Ira Remsen, who had been the university's first professor of chemistry. Looking back over the experimentation during the university's formative years, Remsen recalled examples when relief from teaching had proved disastrous to men who were primarily researchers, because it had deprived them of stimulus.[15] The benefit teaching could bring to research was clearest in a setting like Johns Hopkins or Clark, where advanced students offered comradeship in investigation and enlightened appreciation of achievement. At these two universities, and in research-oriented departments elsewhere, the relationship between faculty and students often resembled not so much the tutelage of apprentice by practitioner as the bond among those in an evangelical college who had experienced salvation. But even elementary teaching was said to clarify the mind of the professor and keep him conscious of fundamentals.

The reverse proposition—that research was of benefit to teaching—was the major element in the case for linking the two functions. It became a staple of prouniversity rhetoric, though not many were as emphatic as the university man who maintained in 1906 that the teacher who was not a scholar was "likely to be a self-constituted oracle whose dilettantism is quite patent to the average undergraduate." Lecturing was best, the classicist Basil L. Gildersleeve believed, when the professor enhanced the material "by the living, plastic forces of personal research and personal communion with the sources." Evoking what has elsewhere been called the "dualistic" professor, President Charles R. Van Hise of the University of Wisconsin saw creative scholarship as essential to a university faculty member, crucial to his work with graduate students, but also enriching to undergraduate instruction. He made his position unusually explicit in 1916, when he called for each Wisconsin faculty member "to resolve that he will become a recognized scholar in his field and begin at once some piece of productive work."[16]

While assertions of the beneficial effect of research on teaching were sometimes motivated by a desire to promote research, they focused on the nature of the university as fundamentally a teaching institution and thus tended to undercut the most profound dedication to investigation. Sometimes this tendency was made explicit. President Jordan was one who could bluntly subordinate research to teaching, as when he said, "for the rank and file of our university men, teaching is the main function, and investigation receives its first value from the fact that adequate teaching is impossible without it." Occasionally warnings came from professors, including active researchers, that the teaching-research interdependency was being overstated. Harvard economist Thomas Nixon Carver recalled a faculty member whose efforts at productive scholarship were failures, but who still proved extraordinarily effective in teaching advanced students and directing their research. A classicist put the matter with surest restraint: "True, an able explorer may be an indifferent teacher; a good teacher may not have the spirit of initiative which leads to successful investigation; but the two faculties, though not always in perfect balance, are seldom wholly divorced, and a university professor should possess both."[17]

The organizational elaboration of universities can be variously explained, for instance, as simply a response to problems of size or as an expression of pervasive rationalizing tendencies of modern society. But at least some light is thrown on this complexity of design when it is seen as working out tensions between the teaching and research functions. The rise of the Ph.D. degree was one product of this functional interconnectedness. Etymologically, the Doctor of Philosophy was a teacher of the love of wisdom, and most early Ph.D.'s became professors. Yet the standards for the degree called for a rigorous devotion to investigation for its own sake and to knowledge justified by the way it extended previous learning, without regard to any pedagogical promise of the recipient. This degree, first earned in America at Yale in 1861, became the hallmark of Johns Hopkins, which awarded the highest number of Ph.D.'s in the 1880s and 1890s. In succeeding years, Harvard, Columbia, and Chicago demonstrated their eminence as universities partly by leading in the number of Ph.D.'s granted.[18]

It was primarily concern over the reputation of an American doctorate that brought about the formation of the Association of American Universities in 1900. All twelve original members had graduate schools and conferred the Ph.D. All of them were concerned that the degree be distinguished as one based on formal pursuit of nonprofessional learning beyond the bachelor's. Although there was a sympathetic response when William James in 1903 branded the Ph.D. a symptom of "the Mandarin disease," observing that it offered no guarantee that its recipient would be an effective teacher, the degree remained firmly established. Its special aura symbolized both a high standard of scholarly investigation and the identification of the university with research. Yet partly because university rhetoric had so successfully intertwined teaching and research functions, the Ph.D. was desired by those seeking careers as teachers in colleges. Efforts to restrict such candidates to the master's degree failed, as did proposals to create a higher degree, comparable to the French Doctorat d'Etat. For a time, the honorary Ph.D. threatened to become the D.D. for college professors, but by 1910 the unearned Ph.D. was little more than a bad memory from a benighted academic past. The Ph.D. was unshakeable, even though one had to admit that it "really covers a multitude of things."[19]

Faculty rank was another device sometimes used to clarify relationships between teaching and research. As late as 1830 at Yale, and later elsewhere, a tutor was associated with a particular entering class, teaching it in a variety of subjects, whereas a professor was identified with a field, in which his knowledge might lead to his making scholarly contributions. In the university era, even younger faculty members were unlikely by no less a scholar than Franz Boas. Its occupants, generally just launching their careers, were expected to give only a single advanced course of lectures annually. By 1904 Hall described the rank as distinguished by its temporary nature, its independence of departmental authority, and its lack of salary. At Chicago, where the rank of docent specifically provided for half-time research and half-time advanced instruction, with payment from student fees only, President Harper declared the position to have lost its importance by 1904, though it sometimes provided a waiting niche for an aspirant to higher rank.[20]

Various plans to enable professors to pursue research, free of teaching responsibilities, trace back to Harvard's creation of the sabbatical year in 1880, a move timed to win Sanskritist Charles R. Lanman away from Hopkins. This expensive innovation had few early imitators, although by 1900 eleven colleges and universities granted sabbaticals.[21] Proposals for a more selective granting of research time through research professorships were under lively consideration by 1906.

President Arthur Twining Hadley of Yale, predicting that research professorships would bring decay of teaching power and breed envy, suggested an alternative that kept research tied to instruction; under his plan, any faculty member would be allowed to give one course of his own choosing close to his investigative concerns. It was generally considered a "first" when Cornell established a distinct research professorship in 1909 for psychologist Edward B. Titchener, though in fact he continued to teach a few graduate students. The step was part of an invigorated concern for research on the Ithaca campus. President Schurman, who had earlier stressed undergraduate liberal education and complained of the narrowness of premature specializers, now declared that "the future of the American university is with the graduate school or department of research." The recurrence of schemes to free faculty time for research suggests how strong teaching obligations remained. When both teaching and research were supposed to be underway, teaching generally got the lion's share of the faculty member's attention.[22]

Although the origins of the department system at the University of Virginia and Harvard in the 1820s lay mostly in concern for the student's opportunity to choose and to specialize, the spread of departmental organization during the university era increasingly represented the faculty's research specialization—its loss of concern for a realm of established knowledge that all educated persons should share. Terminology remained hazy for some time. Until at least 1890, the term "academic department" was often used to designate that part of an institution where studies for the Bachelor of Arts were pursued, as compared to the medical school, for instance. In the early days of Johns Hopkins, Gilman used a qualifying phrase—"of work," or "of science"—when speaking of "departments" in the newly emerging sense. The reorganization of the Harvard catalogue in 1870–71, which arranged courses by field rather than by the class of students who were allowed to take them, helped establish departmental identity, but not until the 1890s was there the clarity of organization that gave the term "the department" the precise referent that it has today. With the opening of the University of Chicago, the view that departments were indeed a requisite organizational form for a university faculty seemed ratified. By the end of its first year, Chicago had twenty-seven departments, including neurology, elocution, and physical culture, each with its "head."[23]

The emergence of the departmental system can be used as evidence of overcompartmentalization in institutions becoming too structure-conscious. Still, in a period when intensified specialization tended to leave each faculty member isolated amid his research concerns (so narrow that one scarcely dared bore a colleague with what seemed in the isolation of the study to be a momentous breakthrough), departments helped hold together colleagues in danger of estrangement. In the enlarging faculties of universities, the alternative path of having each member identified with a fully differentiated specialty might well have led to an amorphous body of individuals deprived of the stimulation of small-group identity. One Harvard professor likened departments to "little

Faculties," reporting that they "hold many and hotly contested meetings; they issue pamphlets; they edit publications; they examine candidates for honors and higher degrees." Although departments sometimes became self-aggrandizing entities that worked against broader institutional purposes, they did more good than harm. They offered both a focus for concerns about how a student could best pursue a subject and a body of research-judging peers more accessible than fellow specialists in other places.[24]

Doubtless there were occasions when university presidents thought of departments chiefly as a way of keeping the faculty under control. But in time it became clear that departments exerted institutional power that few professors could have attained as individuals. Some presidents came to worry about dictatorial attitudes of senior professors within departments, as Eliot did. The shift at Chicago in 1911 to elected chairmen indicated reaction to this concern, and something more. What could have been little more than a functional differentiation within a large organization had become a collegial, self-governing body. In Germany, by contrast, full professors—limited to one per subject—dominated academic governance.[25]

The tendency of departments to create artificial boundaries in the pursuit of knowledge was partially countered by the appearance of other intrauniversity organizational units. "Divisions" were more likely to be curricular abstractions than functioning bodies of colleagues. More significant was the emergence of superdepartments called "schools," for which Columbia's School of Political Science (1880) early set the pattern. Such schools within the university were clearly teaching bodies. They revealed not only specialization but strivings for programmatic coherence and academic and public visibility akin to those of the older professional schools. It was not enough for Richard T. Ely in making his move to Wisconsin to be called to head a department. He had to be assured that he would be director of the "School of Economics, Political Science, and History" and that the position was equivalent to the headship of the observatory. Calling schools of political and social science a necessity, President George E. MacLean of the State University of Iowa in 1904 stressed their direct utility to the public, since they pursued studies "in connection with the men of affairs and business institutions." A later development, the university research institute, sometimes associated with interdepartmentalism, sharply diverted faculty from teaching. Although such institutes were essentially a post–World War I development, they were predicted as early as 1903.[26]

With particular aptness, graduate students symbolized the dual commitment of the university. Not only were they the objects of teaching, they were also neophyte researchers. As an early official statement from Johns Hopkins put it, "The instruction is carried on by such methods . . . as will encourage the student to become an independent and original investigator." Hopkins's first faculty member, Henry A. Rowland, satirized the usual mode of undergraduate teaching when he boasted that his scientific equipment was "for investigation and [not] for amusing children." Asked what he would do with the students who had

gathered in his laboratory at Hopkins, he responded, "I shall neglect them." But Rowland's "neglect" was part of an atmosphere of scholarly production that stimulated students as well as professors.[27]

With so much of institutional purpose focused on graduate students, there was a tendency to defend the university by idealizing them and their work. G. Stanley Hall felt that a thesis which was only "a very small brick in the great temple of human knowledge" needed no apology, and he found even more admirable the transforming effects of research on the student himself. For the young graduate student to grapple with the unknown and get "ever so tiny a result" was "an experience of epoch-making importance." Speaking on behalf of publication of theses, sociologist Albion Small was equally sanguine. What mattered, he said, was "the revolution of mental and moral attitude which publication of the results of one's first serious investigation marks. The young man discovers for himself that the thing can be done. The men who write books are no longer a superior species. They are merely elect through consecration of the same powers of which he begins to be aware. He enters their ranks feeling some of the sense of responsibility with which we like to believe other men assume holy orders."

Although some professors exploited graduate students, setting them to work on narrow topics in order to get data for their own researches, both Hall and Small emphasized how much freedom students were given in choosing the subjects of their dissertations, especially if American practices were compared to German. Even while criticizing much about modern universities, the classicist Paul Shorey attributed a transforming effect to graduate study, from which even a "littérateur" could gain "the scholar's conscience and a clear conception of the difference between first-hand and second-hand knowledge."[28]

The fellowship as an award to attract resident graduate students (rather than a way for colleges to send their graduates elsewhere—usually abroad) was probably the crucial institutional invention that brought success to the early Johns Hopkins. In spite of grumblings from President Eliot and others about "hiring students" and cautionary analogies with theological schools whose subsidies for students were said to attract those with corrupt motives, the fellowship system was widely imitated. The proper arrangement for fellowships was among the questions most often discussed by the Association of American Universities. The growing propensity to utilize fellows as teaching assistants remained controversial. In 1912 President A. Ross Hill of the University of Missouri, true to the earlier vision, condemned the label "research fellowship" as a term that would once have been a redundancy and that reflected an undesirable conception of most fellows having to render an immediate return through some form of instruction. "Is not investigation," he asked, "if it is worthwhile at all, a service to the university, the fellow students of the incumbent, and the larger purposes for which the university exists?" In 1920 Dean Alfred H. Lloyd of the University of Michigan urged similar preservation of the standard: the fellowship, like the university professorship, "should mean complete freedom as well as distinct ability of mind."[29]

As graduate programs expanded after the turn of the century, the quality of students allegedly declined, but it was partly because these programs had been so freighted with institutional ideals that complaints over inferior graduate students arose. Graduate students were branded "children," mediocrities who were working off requirements, or mere "clever intellectual artisans." The brightest undergraduates were observed to be going into professional schools rather than graduate schools. Even the aging Gilman warned of useless and repetitive work from unguided graduate students. As horrible examples were exchanged, one account described a newly minted Eastern Ph.D. who, when told he would not be retained in his instructorship at the University of Michigan, replied, "Well, anyway I can drop into the ministry." In the aftermath, it was recounted, he dropped "heavily into and rapidly even through the ministry, his end being . . . in a small mercantile clerkship."[30]

One result of this post-1900 disillusionment with graduate students and alarm at perfunctory dissertations was an effort to spread into graduate programs the spirit of liberal culture that was then reviving in the colleges. Nowhere was this movement carried further than at Princeton, where both President Woodrow Wilson and Dean Andrew F. West, although divided over the graduate school's location, did agree on the name "Graduate College" and on applying the English residential pattern to graduate students. Both the surface appeal of Princeton's approach and its underlying organizational weakness were displayed at the 1913 meeting of the AAU. Wilson's successor, John G. Hibben, cited the dangers of narrowness and pedantry in graduate work as generally pursued. He spoke of the need for a sense of proportion, for human sympathy, and for linking the student's special subject with other kinds of knowledge. He wanted to insure a "humanistic strain" even in students pursuing the natural sciences. In a sharp departure from the established meaning of the Ph.D., Hibben expressed his doubts about current notions of research:

It is not absolutely essential that in the studies of a scholar some new discovery should be made. The progress of scholarship is often along the lines of rediscovering for himself that which has been known to the world of thought. The main question . . . is this, Does a scholar's research furnish a new center of illumination to lighten the path of his progress? Is his increasing knowledge a lamp to his feet? . . . The exclusive desire to discover something new and in an original way has its dangers and may lead to purely mechanical methods of investigation. And our studies will become mechanical unless we bring to our task a richly furnished mind.[31]

Hibben's audience, including the president of the University of Wisconsin, a University of Illinois professor of chemistry, and a Johns Hopkins professor of economics, expressed high admiration for his views. But subsequent discussion of his address revealed the unlikelihood of any significant change in the epistemological narrowing that accompanied the research orientation of graduate schools. Attempting to combine continued insistence on original investigation with Hibben's humanism, his auditors focused their attention principally on alternative organizational devices to add to an already highly bureaucratized

institution. They proposed requirements that graduate students pursue a minor subject, maintain a longer period of residence, major in a division rather than a department, and—fatefully—that the degree itself be subject to "more administrative thoroughness." Predictably, graduate study at most universities would remain centered on specialized individual research, but another suggestion, participation of graduate students in actual teaching, showed the survival of older notions that teaching was innately humanistic and drew on the general belief that teaching and research were mutually enhancing.[32]

For all their pride in the institutions they were building, university leaders did not forget that universities existed among other institutions dedicated to the advancement of knowledge—at first, learned academies and government agencies, later also research foundations and business laboratories. With its almost reverential mention of the "academy," Gilman's inaugural had suggested fruitful interchange between the university and the established learned societies of Europe and America. Government bureaus were regarded as a source of financial support and ideas for research, not only at Johns Hopkins, where the staff was alert to the capital's scientific community, but also at Western state universities, where federal and state geologic surveys proved particularly important as research models. An exemplary institutional collaboration was the relationship between the University of Wisconsin and the State Historical Society, which furnished quarters for the university library for many years.[33]

Granting the frequency of mutual assistance, universities were still in competition with other learned organizations for personnel, funds, and authority. In such situations, one principal weakness of the universities was the tendency of teaching responsibilities to deflect faculty from original research. In language foreshadowing that of Adolf von Harnack three years later, Robert S. Woodward, head of the Carnegie Institution, argued in 1906 that research grantees who tried to remain in part-time teaching usually found their time consumed not only by teaching but by committee work. He implied that the university setting was appropriate for limited research efforts but that major projects belonged more properly in organizations such as his. Meanwhile, Remsen was grumbling that Woodward's Carnegie Institution and another new foundation, the Rockefeller Institute, were depriving universities of needed investigators. Worse yet, Schurman could foresee a grave threat to university autonomy posed by powerful, self-perpetuating trustees of wealthy foundations with sweeping purposes to serve "civilization."[34]

Sometimes university spokesmen directly attacked competing knowledge-producing bodies: learned academies were said to be fossilized, research foundations inexperienced, governmental bureaus given over to routine and subject to political whim, and business laboratories deflected from truth-seeking by economic motivation. But the university was on firmest ground when it stressed what was, from some vantage points, a weakness—its obligation to combine teaching with creative scholarship. This very duality gave the university a unique importance. Versions of the "mutual support" argument were brought forward, with emphasis placed on the stimulation that teaching gave researchers through a return to first principles and the process of encountering the fresh queries of the younger generation. "The big man in the university," Van Hise declared, "goes broadly over his subject, in an elementary course, thinks ahead over his special lines, and puts those additional thoughts in their relations with the older ideas, and so advances his subject in a broader way than do most men in the [government] bureau. I think, if we compare a half-dozen universities with a half-dozen scientific bureaus, we shall find that, so far as great ideas are concerned, the advantage is upon the side of the university." Examining a list of the most important contributors to the fields of electricity and radioactivity, physicist Ernest G. Merritt of Cornell found that it included only professors, evidence for his assertion that nearly all major discoveries of pure science came from universities. Not only its transforming effect on research, but teaching itself was put forward as a defense of the university's importance for the increase of knowledge. The presence of disciples was sometimes called essential for productive scholarship. Only the university was designed to guarantee transgenerational continuity, and if no new scholars were trained, the learned enterprise would founder. [35]

Coinciding with the rise of American universities was the appearance of such organizations as the American Philological Association, the American Chemical Society, and the American Economic Association. The new scholarly groups differed from earlier learned academies in their emphasis on specialized fields of knowledge. Although admission did not confer the honor accorded by membership in such bodies as the American Philosophical Society and the American Academy of Arts and Sciences, the newer organizations were powerful vehicles of professional status, stressing the value of trained expertise. Since universities gained their reputation by having a professionalized faculty, their leaders were on the whole sympathetic to the emerging specialized scholarly associations. Gilman, whose reform efforts as president of the American Social Science Association appeared to convince him of its hopeless stodginess, encouraged his faculty to take the initiative in forming such groups, and Eliot (never dreaming of the epithet "slave market") praised them for giving universities valuable opportunities to discover talented candidates for their faculties. On the grounds that the associations counteracted provincialism, President W. H. P. Faunce of Brown justified his institution's financial support of attendance at annual meetings. By offering scholars extramural visibility, the associations further helped to counter the tendency of teaching to overshadow and sometimes obliterate the value of research. If students did not flock to a professor's classes, recognition from colleagues within his specialty at other institutions might more than compensate. Rather than competing, the associations helped universities in their formative years to develop an identity as institutions defined by more than the teaching function. [36]

Knowledge-oriented organizations seemed benign colaborers compared to social groups that judged universities by bald utilitarian or ideologically puristic

standards. Practical men of the nineteenth century had often seemed to expect the work of the university to lead more or less directly to the production of tangible goods. Although there is evidence that industrial leaders were rather slow to see universities as a source of technological advance, farmers with complaints about hog cholera and businessmen who associated sound money with morality and free trade with the devil applied pressure to bring universities into line. When the Populists won power in Kansas, they proved no better than their Republican predecessors at tolerating truthseekers of another economic persuasion in the State Agricultural College. The defense of the classics in the Yale Report of 1828 found echoes a half-century later as universities sought to justify the pursuit of esoteric truth in the face of accusations of uselessness, unorthodoxy, and elitism. [37]

At Cornell, the founder believed that the dignity of labor, the reduction of expenses, and the advantages in "learning a trade" dictated a Voluntary Labor Corps for students. Obliged to cooperate, President White rationalized that the shop and farm work would prove educationally illustrative and that repetitious production could be avoided. The emphasis on the major-subject system at Stanford derived in part from founder Leland Stanford's insistence on preparing students for useful lives. As president of the University of California in the early 1870s, Gilman, who had warned against dilution of the university possibilities created by the Morrill Act, found himself the target of vitriolic attacks from farm and labor organizations when he resisted using land-grant funds to give instruction in shop mechanics and basic farming techniques. Expecting to escape such pressures in Baltimore, he found that there too proponents of bread-and-butter education could be vocal, even within the circle of the Johns Hopkins trustees. One of that body, dubious about professional abstraction, insisted that the greatest discoveries always came from those involved in matters of practical application. In many ways, the new Massachusetts Institute of Technology and technically oriented Lehigh University were truer to the mood of the Flash Age than was Johns Hopkins. Eliot brought some of the MIT ethos with him to Harvard, where he had a standing disagreement with the chemistry professors over their resistance to applied courses. In 1881 he assured the American Bell Telephone Company that professors would be allowed to use Harvard's new Jefferson Laboratory in work for private corporations. [38]

State universities, which in their earliest form had been elitist classical colleges, avoided being reduced to trade schools but were increasingly obliged to demonstrate that they not only turned out students who could get jobs but were "good for the state" in the sense of helping develop resources. Geology and engineering, with their tangible contributions to industrial advance, were favored fields in the state university expansion of the 1880s. A representative of the University of Georgia recounted to a meeting of the National Association of State Universities that, given the importance of the Georgia peach, an entomological program had been particularly effective in loosening legislative pursestrings. Increasingly, state universities were expected to keep their agriculture programs open to students who were not high school graduates. But through their preparatory departments, their power to accredit high schools, and their determination to raise admission standards for their liberal arts programs, state universities managed to counter pressures that might have adulterated their work. At the same time, they created an educational ladder that appealed to ideals of equal opportunity. Not many argued that the state university should be all-inclusive, but the public expected "sensible" results from those who did attend. The down-to-earth educational philosophy of Booker T. Washington sounded like good sense not only for freedmen's offspring, but for any young person being supported by society while extending formal education into early adulthood. It grew ever harder to recall the almost superstitious awe of elegant learning that had once kept large audiences sitting through day-long commencement exercises that included addresses in Greek and Latin.[39]

Universities that had scorned the "pork-chop" practicalism of the nineteenth century often embraced a high-brow "service" orientation that focused principally upon governmental achievement. This view, recognizable as a factor in university reform as early as the post-Civil War decade, was salient during the Progressive Era, affecting the newly professionalized social sciences more than any other part of the university. The Johns Hopkins economist Jacob Hollander, noting in 1915 that "every American university has to an increasing extent felt . . . pressure—emanating from federal, state, and municipal governments . . .—for the services of members of its staff expert in economical and social affairs," granted certain benefits in these relationships but warned themselves. Indeed, as economists found themselves able to exert direct influence on those in power through their role as experts, their concern for teaching noticeably declined.[40]

The effects of these two phases of utilitarianism—economic practicalism and government service—can be traced at the University of Wisconsin, the state's sole recipient of its Morrill funds. The biology department was early steered toward practical problems of medicine, agriculture, and fisheries, and the geology program toward mining. It seemed in the early 1890s that the state's businessmen might be similarly served by a program modeled on the Wharton School at the University of Pennsylvania, but the effort was sidetracked by the restructuring necessary to attract Richard T. Ely to head the school. Yet Ely was far from shunning social utility. He and his associates sought to make the School of Economics, Political Science, and History a "West Point for civil life." The practical bent of the new program forecast the later emergence of "the Wisconsin Idea," when the activities of professors and graduates in aiding the legislative and regulatory agencies would make the university's name an international byword for government by expert. In his inaugural in 1904, Van Hise had called for an eclectic "combination university," insisting that it must support disinterested scholarship in every field. He argued that there was no real conflict with utility: "It cannot be predicted at what distant nook of knowledge, apparently remote from any practical service, a brilliantly useful stream may spring. It is

certain that every fundamental discovery yet made by the daring student has been of service to man before a decade has passed." This interpretation was common among university presidents, though Van Hise suggested an unusually speedy rate for delivery of practical applications. Although the scholarly might find it preferable to belong to an institution whose practical bent was toward general social welfare rather than business, and whose presidents recognized the difficulties in predicting ultimate utilities, it was still true that the increasing service orientation of the university drew glamour away from nonapplied research.[41]

After hearing Van Hise in 1905 predict a future of power and wealth for state universities, President Hall was worried, and not just about the status of endowed universities. Recalling that a generation earlier the uselessness of a piece of research had placed it "a little at a premium," he gently questioned the feeling, however nonmercenary it might be, "that the usefulness of a discovery is the best and most legitimate motive for the investigator of the future." Nonetheless, programs that academic purists feared were corrupting sometimes turned out to be supportive of their ideal of knowledge for its own sake. The state universities' involvement in nonutilitarian research often derived from the status originally given research programs in applied fields under the Hatch Act of 1887. When a wealthy dairyman on the Wisconsin Board of Regents attacked the policy of granting time off from teaching in the College of Letters and Science for research that he felt led nowhere, Van Hise was able to respond with an argument for fairness, since comparable research opportunities were firmly established in the Colleges of Agriculture and Engineering. The Wisconsin Idea might deflect some professorial experts from teaching, but ideals of intrainstitutional comity kept professors of philology within the range of prerogatives granted professors of public administration.[42]

To the challenge for justification of the privileges claimed by universities in a democratic society, "we teach," was perhaps the principal response. To the inquiry as to how such teaching benefited the everyday citizen who would never set foot on university grounds, the answer sometimes was that university representatives would reach these people through extension services. The answer could also be that the university prepared the teachers of the all-inclusive public schools. In fact, that task was more often carried out by normal schools that university builders regarded as separate and inferior institutions; there was nevertheless a persistent effort by even the most research-oriented universities to reach public school teachers. Johns Hopkins appointed a professor of psychology and pedagogy in 1884, and Clark University was the home of the journal *Pedagogical Seminary*. In 1890, when Massachusetts seemed likely to raise teacher preparation to postsecondary status and to create in Boston a "Normal College" with a postgraduate course, Eliot showed surprising alacrity in creating a new faculty post that made preparation for secondary school teaching careers more readily available to students at Harvard.[43]

Alternatively, "we teach" might imply that the university taught all those young people who proved themselves capable by ascending the educational ladder to its doors. The last quarter of the nineteenth century saw sustained efforts by colleges and universities to regularize admission requirements and to establish close links with public high schools as well as private preparatory schools. The movement for upgrading high schools through inspection by state universities in the West, the creation of standardized admission examinations in the East, and the development of regional accrediting associations made up of high schools and colleges—all these lent credibility to the university's claim that its teaching stood for democratic openness. Mounting enrollment statistics in institutions of higher education—from 52,000 in 1870 to 355,000 in 1910—bespoke a trend toward greater inclusiveness.[44]

As a response to social queries about the usefulness and democracy of universities, "we teach," was not a fully satisfactory answer. The persistent critic could always point out that the vast majority of "college-age" Americans were not being taught and could quickly discover examples of impractical or abstruse subjects on which good money was being "wasted." But the public was not generally unfriendly to universities. After all, Americans had long supported the recondite fields of theology and astronomy, noted for neither utility nor democracy. Prouniversity rhetoric seems to have reached a broad public; in any case, university presidents became well-known figures through newspaper interviews and public addresses, and the five-foot bookshelf that "Dr. Eliot" recommended sold beyond the publisher's most optimistic estimates. The case for universities was laid before the country with enough success that on the whole these creations of the last third of the nineteenth century were nurtured, survived, and grew.

But to the extent that university spokesmen emphasized teaching in response to challengers, they subtly undermined those who made the creation of knowledge in defining characteristic of universities and whose primary allegiance was to research. If the university rested its case before society solely on its role as teacher, then by implication other institutions might as well control the search for new truth. To emphasize teaching was especially risky after 1900 because the goals of research itself had undergone a revitalization independent of research. The integral student mind began to be seen as a ground on which to recreate the institutional coherence undermined by increasing specialization. This renewed concern for students focused attention on undergraduates not graduates, ideals not facts, and humane wholeness rather than specialized innovation by experts. This movement for liberal culture, recognizable in the 1890s, grew increasingly vocal after 1900. Although it was strongest in small liberal arts colleges, it is only a slight exaggeration to say that it captured control of Harvard when A. Lawrence Lowell succeeded Eliot as president in 1909.[45]

Some of these counterrevolutionaries (who were, ironically, among the most effective academic innovators of the twentieth century) branded as myth the widely accepted generalization that investigation led to better teaching. To the contrary, they challenged, did not the concentration essential to original investigation deprive teaching of reach, connectedness, philosophy, and links to

humane and social concerns? To the extent that students also wanted to specialize, the investigator-professor met their need. But was it not better to protect students against any tendency toward early narrowing? More and more, it was argued, whether they liked it or not, students were being drawn toward the professional scholar's stance at its worst. Undergraduate "research papers" were said to reveal formalized pedantry as often as understanding. Research-minded professors were accused of thinking that "showing them how to be like me" was the essence of good teaching.

Andrew F. West, a power at Princeton, spoke out for the nonproductive professor who could still be "a well of knowledge for everybody." (He himself apparently never published a piece of research-based work.) In this spirit, certain professors of the humanities were calling in 1906 for the creation of specifically nonresearch professorships to be held by teachers who unembarrassedly accepted results of others' investigations and dedicated themselves to education for undergraduates. Some professors even insisted that it was impossible to teach well *if* one did research, and Professor Fred Lewis Pattee of Pennsylvania State, satirizing the decline of teaching, urged that higher education "bring back Mark Hopkins." Anyone reading Edwin Slosson's description of the lecture method as he found it operating during his explorations of 1909 could easily believe something was drastically amiss: "It would be well if the teachers did not know quite so much, if they knew how to tell what they did know better.... In many cases it has seemed to me that the instructor has come into the room without the slightest idea of how he is to present his subject. He rambles on in a more or less interesting and instructive manner, but without any apparent regard to the effect on his audience or the economy of their attention." Perhaps things went better in the laboratories.[46]

What the overspecialized, "Germanized" professors who had shaped the universities had tended to forget, it was said, was "culture." "A wide vision of the best things which man has done or aspired after" was proposed as an educational goal superior to "competence" or "expertise." Culture stood for standards, connectedness, balance, and keeping nature in its place. Although it would be a distortion to reduce this attitude to a desire for social status, it is fair to say that the new rationale for academic social ascendancy, based on specialized knowledge and expert service, had failed to satisfy either the intellectual or social aspirations of some who harked back to an older ideal, that of an aristocracy of culture. Some spokesmen for a revival of culture argued in language that included graduate students as well as undergraduates, but the younger students were the usual object of concern. Unless something was done, warned Harvard's Irving Babbitt, "the A.B. degree will mean merely that a man has expended a certain number of units of intellectual energy on a list of elective studies that may range from boiler-making to Bulgarian."[47]

Attitudes at the University of Wisconsin suggest common ambivalences toward the effect of research on undergraduates. There Frederick Jackson Turner had said in 1892 that the best seniors were quite ready to pursue original investigation, and soon the research ethos had captured the annual "joint debate" between the two literary societies. This Wisconsin tradition, with its emphasis on rhetorical skill and esprit de corps, had long seemed the essence of collegialism. Under the stimulation of Ely's applied empiricism, however, it became a major investigative venture into a selected social problem, followed by publication of the accumulated findings. In fact, the research techniques practiced became the model for the state's pioneering Legislative Reference Library. But the very legislature that gained international repute for its reliance on scholarly investigation was concerned that excessive faculty involvement in research could hurt students, especially undergraduates. In 1906 a legislative committee urged that faculty research be encouraged "only so far as that can be done without detriment to the instruction to which students are entitled." The Wisconsin Alumni Magazine echoed the concern, deprecated the attention given graduate students, who tended to be out-of-staters, and urged that teaching should be the criterion for promotion. Shortly thereafter, the regents reined in the university's research-advocating president by voting that investigative ability, if not combined with teaching skill, should not be an adequate basis for hiring or promoting faculty. It was not merely in the small colleges or the older Eastern universities that research was challenged by demands for "good teaching."[48]

Although it is easy to exaggerate the importance of wars as turning points in academic history, it is still true that World War I was a test for American universities that left their relation to the world of knowledge significantly changed. Professors eagerly sought ways to join the "real world" of the war, and service to the state in its pursuit of military victory swept other ideals aside. Only an exceptional few preserved a stance of critical independence.[49] Actions taken with passionate certitude were later recalled with shame, though the record of violations of academic freedom has never been fully traced. War disrupted customs and ideas about status that had somewhat protected the university from the rest of society. Basic research in wartime appeared almost unpatriotic. Teaching took on an immediacy that pulled it toward training and indoctrination. When there was opportunity for stock-taking, however, the wartime experience appeared to have strengthened the university's identity as a knowledge-creating institution. At the same time, the rise of other research agencies had lent new urgency to putting forward the case for the special merit of research pursued in a teaching institution.

After initial alarms over the sharp drop in enrollments early in the 1917–18 school year, universities and colleges found themselves nearly swamped with students in 1918, as the Students' Army Training Corps set up programs on 525 campuses. The American Council on Education and the Bureau of Education had propagandized to get young men into the program, and some who had never intended to go to college found themselves there as a patriotic duty. Not only were a number of students academically ill-equipped, but the course of instruction set up for the SATC was designed "to develop as a great military asset the large body of young men in the colleges." The classics, for instance, were excluded, and faculty members found themselves teaching the rudiments of fields far from their areas of specialization. After the war, enrollments did not drop back. It became increasingly common for young Americans to attend college, and complaints mounted concerning poorly prepared students, overcrowded classrooms, and overburdened teaching schedules. It was not new to hear American professors say that their heavy teaching assignments kept them from their "own work." But for some, the situation now appeared so hopeless that in fairly good conscience they could settle for perfunctory teaching and escape into studies and laboratories. Honors programs, partly justified as rescuing the gifted from the sea of ordinary students, gave the investigative ideal a new hold on undergraduates.[50]

The liberal culture critics of research-mindedness had suffered a check by the quantity, quality, and motives of the new wave of students. Yet for humanists too there had been a gain. At Columbia, the interdisciplinary "war issues" course required by the SATC quickly developed into an introductory course in contemporary civilization. It was intended, in the words of Columbia's Dean Frederick J. E. Woodbridge, to "give to the generations to come a common background of ideas and commonly understood standards of judgment." Many other institutions also continued variants of the wartime course.[51]

As the war brought students flooding in, faculty were pouring out—none in greater numbers than scientists with research backgrounds. Some in fact had left before America entered the war, to work in industries stimulated by the cut-off of German dyes, drugs, and optical glass. After April 1917, they left for a range of duties—expanding food supplies for the Allies, setting industrial allocation procedures, manufacturing poison gas. Fears that the best might never return to academic life proved ill-founded: most did return, and most were still devoted to investigation. Yet wartime experiences had modified some attitudes. Now universities often seemed rather too placid. "The ideal dedicated investigator no longer stood alone on a high pedestal," James Bryant Conant recalled of his feelings on returning to the Harvard faculty after service in the Chemical Warfare Service. "I recognized that there were other fascinating ways of using one's energies."[52]

"Pure" research in particular was undercut during the war. Wisconsin reported to the Bureau of Education that almost all scientific research had been shifted into "war channels," and at Cornell war conditions had led to dropping "twenty-seven different lines of investigation." Research work in psychology was reported to be down by seventy-five percent. Like the plowman seizing his musket, the dwellers in libraries and laboratories had proved their patriotism and their versatility. Hailed for wartime services, the universities emerged with a fund of public respect. How was this new prestige to be used? It could conceivably increase autonomy and allow reaffirmation of the goal of discovering truth without regard to utility. In this season of reassessment, antiutilitarian investigators were sometimes most forcefully represented by the humanists. Dean Woodbridge, whose own works of scholarship centered on Aristotle, urged universities to strive for ''the philosophical spirit . . . the interest, poise, and sense of power which come only from the consciousness that a particular thing which one may be engaged in doing is part of a commanding whole.'' The experimental method, in contrast (and here he resisted the flexibility praised so heavily during the Progressive Era and the war), had led to ''a readiness to attack any problem without preparation,'' a tendency found at its worst in the social sciences.53

Skepticism about the German university pattern had grown up in America well before the war. The peak decade for American students in Germany had been the 1880s, and by 1900 it was generally believed that America had created a worthy university establishment of its own. It was nevertheless a shock to American academics to have Germany emerge as the enemy in war, and many who had praised German academic achievement felt themselves contaminated. A desire to purge and purify helps explain the series of incidents of intellectual chauvinism in universities. German language courses were dropped, German-born or problem-German professors fired, and German universities bitterly identified with autocratic callousness. Yet the upshot was not a rejection of the research motive. A generally accepted interpretation among the research-minded pictured German universities as betraying or forced to violate their own ideals. Some argued that the United States had now replaced Germany as the world's most favorable setting for universities that sought truth for its own sake. In any case, German universities appeared so badly weakened by the war and subsequent economic catastrophe that American scholars imagined themselves seizing the torch from a fallen leader and taking on responsibility for the highest university ideals.54

During and immediately after the war, the American learned enterprise produced a new array of knowledge-oriented organizations. Particularly challenging to universities were industrial research programs, thriving in businesses that had witnessed the wartime effectiveness of research teams. This increased competition, sharpened by industry's larger salaries, forced universities to review their relation to utilitarian purposes. In the heady materialism of postelection 1920, President Hadley of Yale could project the happiest symbiosis of social utility and university purpose. Whereas industry sought to secure ''gainful knowledge,'' he explained, universities had as their object the promotion of ''useful knowledge,'' and given the overlap of these two aims, it was appropriate to welcome outside stimuli that could make a student learn more efficiently. Involvement in industrial programs was a justifiable ''means for giving the student a motive in the way of personal advantage to himself in the solving of a problem.'' Michigan's graduate dean saw great benefit in the fact that graduate schools now included more students planning nonacademic careers. With the intentions of students becoming so varied, he maintained, ''teaching can only gain, not lose; . . . becoming at once more vigorous and more nobly serviceable. After all, it is from teaching and the teacher that interpretation and appreciation of life and the facts of life must come. Yet these things are . . . bound to be feebly done, unless teachers meet on their own solid ground those who are making so much of science and nature in the practical exploitation of life and its facts.'' A

similar feeling for solid ground and practical exploitation underlay the remarks made at about the same time by Professor Henry P. Talbot of MIT before the American Chemical Society. To improve teaching, he suggested, ''pedagogues'' should consider spending occasional summers in industrial plants.55

All this was a far cry from the old-fashioned research purism expressed by Frank Baldwin Jewett, chief engineer of the Western Electric Company who, at the same gathering that Hadley addressed, saw the university as ''primarily concerned with the mental side of the advancement of human beings and only incidentally with the material side. Its whole organization is one designed to transmit accumulated knowledge and methods of acquiring knowledge from one generation to the next, and to explore unknown fields for the purpose of extending the stock of accumulated knowledge. Its whole being is governed by a code of ethics based on the idea that the acquisition and dissemination of exact knowledge is the central force of its existence.'' A university leader like Hadley was not going to have his institution turned into any such fortress of abstraction. Yet it was on grounds close to Jewett's position that the universities could best justify themselves in a world in which industrial leaders had decided to foster investigation. Universities were the matrix, it could be maintained, from which knowledge-makers were produced. Without universities, other research organizations would soon dwindle for lack of personnel. Rather than taking advantage of university weakness, ''raiders'' should help see to it that academic salaries and other conditions did not fall too far behind those of business research organizations. Further, industrial laboratories might support some basic research, but they would remain in the shadow of a profit-making organization. Universities could by comparison justify themselves as the home of pure, theoretical—the ''highest''—research.56

Since it was not only industry that now vied with the universities for leadership in knowledge-creation, there was good reason for university rhetoric to remain multiform. The air was full of proposals for ''exclusively research institutes,'' in addition to the older Carnegie Institution and Rockefeller Institute.57 Researchers in institutes were generally freer of external concerns than those in either industry or academic life. Against these competitors, accordingly, the logic of the universities' argument was reversed. Foundations were pictured as too selective to keep knowledge growing as it should; they were even thought to be unhealthily divorced from social concerns. The same university spokesmen who warned of the practicalist bias in the industrial laboratory could caution against the isolationism of the independent research institute.

For the universities, the new coordinating bodies that developed as a result of the war, the National Research Council and the American Council of Learned Societies, did not represent a particularly new or unwelcome phenomenon. If anything, they were viewed as too inactive.58 University leaders themselves had launched the Association of American Agricultural Colleges and Experiment Stations, the National Association of State Universities, and the Association of American Universities. The rationale for these groups fit the new councils as well: in a nation where the government was relatively unconcerned with science and education, voluntaristic organizations with institutional members could discourage redundancy and uphold standards. Similarly, the scholarly professional organizations had bred a good deal of sophistication about how other loyalties could support rather than undercut university purposes. In effect, spokesmen for universities could accept the new coordinating bodies, grant them their due, and yet insist that finally, so far as the creation of new knowledge and the developing of creators of new knowledge were concerned, "it happens here."

American universities of world importance, the dream of a few frustrated academics when the Civil War broke out, were firmly established by the onset of post–World War I normalcy. It had happened within a single human lifespan. The written history of these universities, blessed with a wealth of preserved documents, has been crippled by the institutional parochialism that has made many a centennial history a catch-all of who came and went. To what purpose did they come and go—the presidents, the professors, the students? That question should not go unasked. In the congeries of individual motives, it is possible to discern that what held them together, what made them part of an institution, was a concern for knowing. Yet the goal of helping someone else know something (or how to do something) that he or she did not know before sometimes contradicted the goal of making known something never known before. The many facile denials of such conflict did not prevent its persistence. These two versions of the pursuit of knowledge underwent manipulations that had more to do with immediate situations of institutional stress than with a genuine sense of what was involved in embracing such ideals, and both were reshaped by the demands of a democratic, industrializing society. The presence of these social pressures helped force into alliance teachers and researchers (and teaching and research tendencies within individuals). The university's flexibility and its bureaucratic elaboration made room for both functions, even when their antagonism could not be disguised or removed.

Notes

1. John Jay Chapman to Mrs. Henry Whitman, 12 August 1893, in *John Jay Chapman and His Letters*, ed. M. A. DeWolfe Howe (Boston: Houghton Mifflin, 1937), pp. 96-97.

2. Andrew Dickson White, "Inaugural Address," in *Builders of American Universities: Inaugural Addresses*, ed. David Andrew Weaver (Alton, Ill.: Shurtleff College Press, 1950), pp. 248-49, 255-56, 268; Charles William Eliot, "Inaugural Address as President of Harvard College," in *Educational Reform: Essays and Addresses* (New York: Century, 1898), esp. p. 27.

3. Daniel Coit Gilman, "The Johns Hopkins University in its Beginnings," *University Problems in the United States* (New York: Century, 1898), p. 13.

4. Ibid., pp. 14, 15, 31-32; J. Thomas Scharf, *The Chronicles of Baltimore ...* (Baltimore: Turnbull, 1874), pp. 395-96.

5. Dorothy Ross, *G. Stanley Hall: The Psychologist as Prophet* (Chicago: University of Chicago Press, 1972), chap. 11, esp. p. 202; Hall, "Address at Opening Exercises," in *Builders of American Universities*, ed. Weaver, pp. 370, 373, 375-376.

6. Jordan, "Inaugural Address," in *Builders of American Universities*, ed. Weaver, pp. 353 (italics mine), 356.

7. Laurence R. Veysey, *The Emergence of the American University* (Chicago: University of Chicago Press, 1965), pp. 371-72; Richard J. Storr, *Harper's University: ... ginnings* (Chicago: University of Chicago Press, 1966), esp. pp. 61-62. See also, Thomas Wakefield Goodspeed, *A History of the University of Chicago Founded by John D. Rockefeller: The First Quarter-Century* (Chicago: University of Chicago Press, 1916).

8. Hugh Hawkins, *Between Harvard and America: The Educational Leadership of Charles W. Eliot* (New York: Oxford University Press, 1972), pp. 72-73; Nicholas Murray Butler, *Across the Busy Years: Recollections and Reflections*, 2 vols. (New York and London: Charles Scribner's Sons, 1939-40), 1:136-46; Thomas Jefferson Wertenbaker, *Princeton, 1746-1896* (Princeton: Princeton University Press, 1946), pp. 368-69.

9. Eliot, *Educational Reform*, p. 225; Gilman, "The Future of American Colleges and Universities," *Atlantic Monthly* 78 (1896): 179; George E. MacLean, "The State University the Servant of the Whole State," *Transactions and Proceedings of the National Association of State Universities* 2 (1904): 33 (hereafter cited as *NASU Transactions*).

10. Jacob Gould Schurman, "The Reaction of Graduate Work on the Other Work of the University," *Journal of Proceedings and Addresses of the Association of American Universities* 7 (1906): 60 (hereafter cited as *AAU Journal*); William Gardner Hale, "The Doctor's Dissertation," ibid. 3 (1902): 16-17 (italics in original); Veysey, *Emergence of the American University*, p. 150; Joseph Ames's remark, quoted in "The Degree of Master of Arts," *AAU Journal* 12 (1910): 45; Small, quoted in Storr, *Harper's University*, p. 159.

11. David Starr Jordan, "To What Extent Should the University Investigator Be Relieved from Teaching?" *AAU Journal* 7 (1906): 30, 34, 42.

12. Guido Hugo Marx, "The Problem of the Assistant Professor," *AAU Journal* 11 (1910): 28. This survey of younger faculty may reflect the sort of restiveness that led in Germany to one formation of the Junior Faculty Association. See Fritz Ringer, "The German Academic Community," in this volume.

13. Merle Curti and Vernon Carstensen, *The University of Wisconsin: A History, 1848-1925*, 2 vols. (Madison, Wis.: University of Wisconsin Press, 1949), 2:59-62; Ray Allen Billington, *Frederick Jackson Turner: Historian, Scholar, Teacher* (New York: Oxford University Press, 1973), pp. 292-97, 303-5.

14. Anon. remark, quoted in Jordan, "The University Investigator," p. 41.

15. Gilman, *University Problems*, p. 19; Ira Remsen's remark, quoted in "Discussion of the Opportunities for Higher Instruction and Research in State Universities," *AAU Journal* 6 (1905): 66.

16. Anon. remark, quoted in Jordan, "The University Investigator," p. 41; Hugh Hawkins, *Pioneer: A History of the Johns Hopkins University, 1874-1889* (Ithaca, N.Y.: Cornell University Press, 1960), pp. 222-23; Curti and Carstensen, *Wisconsin*, 2:47; Steven Turner, cited by Ringer in his essay in this volume, p. 413.

17. Jordan, "The University Investigator," p. 25; Basil L. Gildersleeve, quoted in Hawkins, *Pioneer*, p. 217. Cf. Joseph Ben-David, *American Higher Education: Directions Old and New* (New York: McGraw-Hill, 1972), p. 113.

18. Frederick Rudolph, *The American College and University: A History* (New York: Alfred A. Knopf, 1962), p. 335; Henry James, *Charles W. Eliot: President of Harvard University, 1869-1909*, 2 vols. (Boston: Houghton Mifflin Company, 1930), 2:345; Hawkins, *Pioneer*, p. 122.

19. "Second Day's Proceedings," *AAU Journal* 1 (1900): 14-15; Veysey, *Emergence of the American University*, pp. 175-76; James, "The Ph.D. Octopus," *Harvard Monthly* 36 (1906): 1-9; Joseph Ames's remark, quoted in "The Degree of Master of Arts," *AAU Journal* 12 (1910): 45-46; George E. Vincent, "The Granting of Honorary Degrees," ibid. 16 (1914): 27-34; "Discussion of the Granting of Honorary Degrees," ibid., pp. 34-41; Charles H. Haskins, quoted in "The Degree of Master of Arts," p. 46. See also, Edward Delavan Perry, "The American University," in *Monographs on Education in the United States*, 2 vols., ed. Nicholas Murray Butler (Albany, N.Y.: J. B. Lyon, 1904), 1:296.

20. Rudolph, *American College and University*, pp. 162-63; Hawkins, *Pioneer*, pp. 127-28; Ross, *G. Stanley Hall*, p. 197; Hall's remark, quoted in "Discussion of the Actual and the Proper Lines of Distinction Between College and University," *AAU Journal* 5 (1904): 34-36; William Rainey Harper's remark, quoted in ibid., p. 36.

21. Hawkins, *Between Harvard and America*, pp. 67-68; John S. Brubacher and Willis Rudy, *Higher Education in Transition: A History of American Colleges and Universities, 1636-1963*, rev. ed. (New York: Harper & Row, 1968), p. 386.

22. Arthur T. Hadley, "To What Extent Should the University Investigator be Relieved from

Teaching'' AAU Journal 7 (1906): 45. Morris Bishop, A History of Cornell (Ithaca, N.Y.: Cornell University Press, 1962), p. 358. David Starr Jordan opposed a separate rank but was willing to establish research years in addition to the regular sabbatic program (Jordan, ''The University Investigator,'' p. 29).

23. Veysey, Emergence of the American University, pp. 320–24; Hawkins, Pioneer, pp. 90, 91; Storr, Harper's University, p. 75n.

24. Albert Bushnell Hart, ''University Happenings,'' Harvard Graduates' Magazine 5 (1896–97): 389; Brubacher and Rudy, Higher Education in Transition, p. 117; E. Benjamin Andrews, ''Current Criticism of Universities,'' NASU Transactions 3 (1905): 28; Josiah Royce, ''Present Ideals of American University Life,'' Scribner's Magazine 10 (1891): 386. Cf. Laurence R. Veysey, ''Stability and Experiment in the American Undergraduate Curriculum,'' in Content and Context: Essays on College Education, ed. Carl Kaysen (New York: McGraw-Hill, 1973), pp. 32–34.

25. Mark Beach, ''Professional versus Professorial Control of Higher Education,'' Educational Record 49 (1968): 267–68; Hawkins, Between Harvard and America, p. 75; Goodspeed, History of the University of Chicago, p. 151. On Germany, see Ringer, ''German Academic Community,'' in this volume, pp. 420–21.

26. Raymond M. Alden's remark, quoted in ''Discussion of the Type of Graduate Scholar,'' AAU Journal 15 (1913): 31; John W. Burgess, Reminiscences of an American Scholar: The Beginnings of Columbia University (New York: Columbia University Press, 1934), pp. 187–90; Curti and Carstensen, Wisconsin, 1:635; MacLean, ''State University the Servant,'' pp. 35–36; Veysey, Emergence of the American University, p. 177.

27. Hawkins, Pioneer, pp. 46, 90, 218.

28. Hall, ''What is Research in a University Sense, and How May it Best be Promoted?'' AAU Journal 3 (1902): 46–48; Small, ''The Doctor's Dissertation: Selection of Subject, Preparation, Acceptance, Publication,'' ibid. 9 (1908): 50, 54; William A. Noyes's remark, quoted in ''Discussion of the Type of Graduate Scholar,'' p. 29; Paul Shorey, ''American Scholarship,'' Nation 92 (1911): 467.

29. Hawkins, Pioneer, pp. 79–81 idem, Between Harvard and America, p. 57; Benjamin Ide Wheeler's remark, quoted in ''Economy of the Time in Education,'' AAU Journal 16 (1914): 70; Hill, ''The Influence of Graduate Fellowships and Scholarships upon the Quality of Graduate Study,'' ibid. 14 (1912): 31; Lloyd, ''Fellowships,'' ibid. 22 (1920): 90.

30. Franklin H. Giddings's remark, quoted in ''Discussion of the Social Environment of the Graduate Student,'' AAU Journal 22 (1920): 78; Charles H. Haskins's remark, quoted in ''Discussion of the Type of Graduate Scholar,'' p. 30; Arthur T. Hadley, quoted in ''Discussion of the Organization of Research,'' AAU Journal 21 (1919): 45–56; Veysey, Emergence of the American University, pp. 178–79; Gilman, The Launching of a University and Other Papers: A Sheaf of Remembrances (New York: Dodd, Mead & Co., 1906), p. 243; Alfred H. Lloyd, ''Fellowships,'' p. 84. Cf. Edwin E. Slosson, Great American Universities (New York: Macmillan, 1910), pp. 492–94.

31. Veysey, Emergence of the American University, pp. 244–48 (see also idem, ''The Academic Mind of Woodrow Wilson,'' Mississippi Valley Historical Review 49 [1963]: 613–34); Hibben.

32. ''Discussion of the Type of Graduate Scholar,'' pp. 27–28.

33. Gilman, University Problems, pp. 15, 31–32; Hawkins, Pioneer, pp. 99, 144; Curti and Carstensen, Wisconsin, 1:359–60; Walter Muir Whitehill, Independent Historical Societies: An Enquiry into Their Research and Publication Function and Their Financial Future (Boston and Cambridge: Boston Athenaeum, distributed by Harvard University Press, 1962), pp. 256–57.

34. Harnack founded the Kaiser-Wilhelm-Gesellschaft in 1911 (see the Ringer essay in this volume, p. 421); Woodward's remark quoted in Jordan, ''The University Investigator,'' p. 43 (cf. AAU Journal 8 [1906]: 46–47); Ira Remsen's remark quoted in ''Discussion of The University Investigator,'' p. 49; Jacob Gould Schurman, ''The Policy of Incorporating Such an Organization as the Rockefeller Foundation,'' NASU Transactions (1910) 8:287–88. See also the essay by Nathan Reingold in this volume.

35. David Prescott Barrows's remark, in ''Research Professorships,'' AAU Journal 22 (1920): 51; Charles R. Van Hise's remark, in ''Discussion of to What Extent Should The University Investigator be Relieved of Teaching,'' p. 51; Merritt's remark, in ''Discussion of the Organization of Research,'' AAU Journal 21 (1919): 48–49.

36. Charles W. Eliot, University Administration (Boston: Houghton Mifflin, 1908), pp. 91–93, 151; W. H. P. Faunce, ''Annual Report to the Corporation of Brown University for 1919–20,'' quoted in American Association of University Professors Bulletin 8 (1922): 254 (hereafter cited as AAUP Bulletin); Rudolph, American College and University, pp. 403–4. For a skillful interpretation of the rationale of these new scholarly organizations, see Thomas L. Haskell The Emergence of Professional Social Science: The American Social Science Association and the Nineteenth-Century Crisis of Authority (Urbana, Ill.: University of Illinois Press, 1977).

37. See the essay in this volume by Louis Galambos, whose general argument agrees with my impression that business pressures on universities in the nineteenth century more often sought ideological and economic orthodoxy than direct economic contributions. Allan Nevins, The State Universities and Democracy (Urbana, Ill.: University of Illinois Press, 1962), pp. 53–60; Edward Danforth Eddy, Jr., Colleges for Our Land and Time: The Land-Grant Idea in American Education (New York: Harper, 1957), p. 73; Rudolph, American College and University, p. 256; Hawkins, Between Harvard and America, pp. 216–18; Richard Hofstadter and Walter P. Metzger, The Development of Academic Freedom in the United States (New York: Columbia University Press, 1955), pp. 422–25.

38. Bishop, Cornell, pp. 126–28; Orrin Leslie Elliott, Stanford University: The First Twenty-Five Years (Stanford, Ca.: Stanford University Press, 1937), pp. 24, 512; William Carey Jones, ''California,'' in Fabian Franklin et al., The Life of Daniel Coit Gilman (New York: Dodd, Mead, 1910), passim; Hawkins, Pioneer, pp. 19, 23, 305; Rudolph, American College and University, p. 246; Hawkins, Between Harvard and America, pp. 213–15.

39. Nevins, State Universities, pp. 85–90, 46–47, 91–92; Henry C. White's remark, quoted in ''Discussions,'' NASU Transactions 2 (1904): 79.

40. John G. Sproat, ''The Best Men'': Liberal Reformers in the Gilded Age (New York: Oxford University Press, 1968), pp. 7, 17–18; John Higham, History (Englewood Cliffs, N.J.: Prentice-Hall, 1965), pp. 8–11; Daniel J. Kevles, ''On the Flaws of American Physics: A Social and Institutional Analysis,'' in Nineteenth Century American Science: A Reappraisal, ed. George H. Daniels (Evanston, Ill.: Northwestern University Press, 1972), pp. 137–38; Jacob Hollander's remark, quoted in ''Discussion on Outside Remunerative Work By Professors,'' AAU Journal 17 (1915): 64–65; Robert L. Church, ''Economists as Experts: The Rise of an Academic Profession in America, 1870–1917,'' in The University in Society, ed. Lawrence Stone (Princeton: Princeton University Press, 1974), pp. 571–609. Cf. Veysey, Emergence of the American University, pp. 124–25.

41. Curti and Carstensen, Wisconsin, 2:354–56, 1:630–32, 2:87–88; Benjamin G. Rader, The Academic Mind and Reform: The Influence of Richard T. Ely in American Life (Lexington, Ky.: University of Kentucky Press, 1966), pp. 112, 128, 162; Hawkins, Pioneer, p. 202, n. 68; Ross, G. Stanley Hall, pp. 211–12; Arthur G. Powell, ''The Education of Educators at Harvard, 1891–1912,'' in Social Sciences at Harvard, 1860–1920: From Inculcation to the Open Mind. ed. Paul Herman Buck (Cambridge: Harvard University Press, 1965), pp. 226–29. Charles R. Van Hise, ''Inaugural Address,'' Science 20 (1904): 203, 204.

42. G. Stanley Hall's remark, quoted in ''Discussion of the Opportunities for Higher Instruction and Research in State Universities,'' p. 64; Eddy, Colleges for Our Land and Time, pp. 97–100; Charles R. Van Hise, ''The Opportunities for Higher Instruction and Research in State Universities,'' pp. 52–53; Curti and Carstensen, Wisconsin, 2:38–40.

43. Eddy, Colleges for Our Land and Time, pp. 104–7; Edward Potts Cheyney, History of the University of Pennsylvania, 1740–1940 (Philadelphia: University of Pennsylvania Press, 1940), pp. 347–49; Curti and Carstensen, Wisconsin, 1:711–14, 721–28; Hawkins, Pioneer, pp. 202, 204.

44. Edward A. Krug, The Shaping of the American High School (New York: Harper & Row, 1964), pp. 151–53; Hawkins, Between Harvard and America, pp. 178–80; U.S. Bureau of the Census, Historical Statistics of the United States: Colonial Times to 1957 (Washington, D.C., 1960), p. 211. As a percentage of eighteen to twenty-one year olds in the population, these figures represent 1.68 percent in 1870 and 5.2 percent in 1910. For 1920 the enrollment was 598,000 (8.09 percent). The count includes all enrolled students, not just undergraduates. For an instructive caution against interpreting increased enrollments as democratic, see the Ringer essay in this volume, p. 418. On shifting notions of whether or not college enrollment should be maximized, see Harold S. Wechsler, The Qualified Student: A History of Selective College Admission in America (New York: Wiley, 1977).

45. Veysey, Emergence of the American University, pp. 233–59. See Ringer, ''German Academic Community,'' in this volume for an account of even stronger concern among German

academics over the disappearance of values and integrative world-views from specialized scholarship.

46. Andrew F. West's remark, quoted in "Discussion of the Opportunities for Higher Instruction and Research in State Universities," p. 67; Jacob Gould Schurman, "The Reaction of Graduate Work on the Other Work of the University," *AAU Journal* 7 (1906): 59; Herbert F. Davidson, "The Puzzled Professor," *AAUP Bulletin* 8 (1922): 399–402, reprinted from *School and Society*; Pattee, "The 'Log' Unseats 'Mark Hopkins'," ibid. 9 (1923): 309–13, reprinted from *Nation*; Slosson, *Great American Universities*, p. 517.

47. Matthew Arnold, quoted in Veysey, *Emergence of the American University*, p. 186; Hawkins, *Between Harvard and America*, pp. 264–65; Charles Eliot Norton, "Harvard University," in *Four American Universities* (New York: Harper, 1895), p. 12; Irving Babbitt, "The Humanities," *Atlantic Monthly* 89 (1902): 773.

48. Curti and Carstensen, *Wisconsin*, 1: 433–38; 2: 49–50, 98–99; Rudolph, *American College and University*, p. 451.

49. Carol S. Gruber's *Mars and Minerva: World War I and the Uses of the Higher Learning in America* (Baton Rouge, La.: Louisiana State University Press, 1975) is the fullest treatment available.

50. *Report of the Commissioner of Education* (Washington, D.C.: 1918), p. 14; ibid. (1919), pp. 6–7; Parke Rexford Kolbe, *The Colleges in War Time and After* . . . (New York: Appleton, 1919), p. 201; Swarthmore College Faculty, *An Adventure in Education: Swarthmore College under Frank Aydelotte* (New York: Macmillan, 1941), pp. 81–88; Veysey, "Stability and Experiment in American Undergraduate Curriculum," pp. 11–12.

51. *Report of the Commissioner of Education* (1919), p. 9; Gruber, *Mars and Minerva*, pp. 238–45.

52. Kolbe, *Colleges in War Time*, chap. 7; James B. Conant, *My Several Lives: Memoirs of a Social Inventor* (New York: Harper & Row, 1970), p. 52, chap. 5.

53. Kolbe, *Colleges in War Time*, pp. 203–204; *Report of the Commissioner of Education* (1918),

p. 15; Frederick J. E. Woodbridge, "The Social Environment of the Graduate Student," *AAU Journal* 22 (1920): 73–75.

54. Jurgen Herbst, *The German Historical School in American Scholarship: A Study in the Transfer of Culture* (Ithaca, N.Y.: Cornell University Press, 1965), chap. 1; Hofstadter and Metzger, *Development of Academic Freedom*, pp. 368, 495–506; Curti and Carstensen, *Wisconsin*, 2: 323–24, 114; Louis G. Geiger, *University of the Northern Plains: A History of the University of North Dakota, 1883–1958* (Grand Forks, N.D.: University of North Dakota Press, 1958), p. 286; James Gray, *The University of Minnesota, 1851–1951* (Minneapolis, Minn.: University of Minnesota Press, 1951), pp. 245–49; Carol S. Gruber, "Academic Freedom at Columbia University, 1917–1918: The Case of James McKeen Cattell," *AAUP Bulletin* 58 (1972): 297–305; Arthur O. Lovejoy, "Annual Message of the President," ibid. 5 (1919): 33–35. I also draw here on a wide range of correspondence between Americans who had studied in Germany and their German mentors, notably in the papers of Ernst Ehlers, Manuscript Division, University Library, Göttingen.

55. A. Hunter Dupree, *Science in the Federal Government: A History of Policies and Activities to 1940* (Cambridge: Belknap Press of Harvard University Press, 1957), pp. 315–25; Arthur Twining Hadley's remark, quoted in "Discussion of Co-operation in Research with Private Enterprises from the Standpoint of Industry," *AAU Journal* 22 (1920): 70; Alfred Henry Lloyd, "Fellowships—with Special Consideration of Their Relation to Teaching," ibid., p. 87; Talbot, quoted in John Johnston, "Co-operation Between Universities and Industry," ibid., p. 57.

56. Frank Baldwin Jewett, "Co-operation in Research with Private Enterprises from the Standpoint of Industry," *AAU Journal* 22 (1920): 64; David Prescott Barrows's remark, quoted in "Research Professorships," ibid., p. 51. Cf. Ben-David, *American Higher Education*, p. 103.

57. James Rowland Angell, "The Organization of Research," *AAU Journal* 21 (1919): 33.

58. James R. Angell's remark, quoted in "Discussion of the Organization of Research," ibid., p. 44; Charles H. Haskins's remark, quoted in ibid.; Haskins, "Co-operation in Research in the Humanities," ibid. 22 (1920): 37–40; William Morton Wheeler, "The Dry-Rot of Our Academic Biology," *AAUP Bulletin* 9 (1923): 119, reprinted from *Science*.

The Conditions of University Research, 1900-1920

Roger L. Geiger

DURING THE LAST QUARTER OF THE NINETEENTH CENTURY the founding of Johns Hopkins, the floodtide of influence from German universities, and the academic boom of the nineties all contributed to establishing a firm commitment to research in the leading American universities.[2] The maturation of these "research universities" early in the twentieth century increasingly brought to the fore the problem of specific support for university research. A latent inconsistency, occasionally noted by university presidents themselves, existed between the ringing endorsements of research as a general university goal and faculty time outside the classroom available to realize that goal. Furthermore, the rising costs of research after 1900, particularly in the natural sciences, placed an ever-growing strain upon the ad hoc means and informal channels of raising the needed funds. The universities responded to these pressures with a variety of innovations. Although the theoretical possibilities for accommodating research may have been numerous, they were not all consistent with the realities of the American university. In the first two decades of the century, the concrete experiences of the research universities winnowed these possible adaptations down to a few viable alternatives. This process can be seen first in the treatment of faculty, and then in the matter of material resources for research.

"The American university is emphatically a teaching university," stated David Starr Jordan in 1906.[3] And, indeed, compared with the emphasis on examinations in British and French universities, or the scope allowed for research in German institutions, this was certainly the case. American students entered the university with far less preparation than their European counterparts and were consequently far more dependent upon their mentors for basic instruction. The characteristic American form of certification that emerged in this period reflected the centrality of the teaching imperative: credit hours testified to the volume of instruction received, while letter grades signified the extent to which the material may have been learned.[4] A recurrent dream of American university builders was to jettison a major portion of this basic teaching burden in order to orient the universities more definitely toward research. During the height of German university influence it was common to equate "true" university work with the graduate level of American higher education. This spirit was evident at the founding of Johns Hopkins, and explicitly behind G. Stanley Hall's unsuccessful effort to create Clark as a graduate university. Later reformers would scheme to separate the freshman and sophomore years from the advanced work of the university, but to no avail. Undergraduate education was too essential to the overall functioning of the university to be sacrificed to the interests of research. Instead, enrollment growth was welcomed as both a sign of institutional success and a necessary means for justifying a larger and more specialized faculty. And, growth frequently involved innovations such as summer sessions and professional schools that tended to increase faculty teaching obligations. For most faculty at most universities, research was possible only after teaching responsibilities were fulfilled. As a consequence, "one of the most difficult of modern university problems" for President Eliot and other university leaders was "to determine the just relation between instruction and research."⁵

The crux of the problem was the basic teaching load of faculty at research universities. Even when these loads can be determined objectively, however, there is considerable uncertainty regarding their interpretation. A 1908 survey by the Carnegie Foundation for the Advancement of Teaching (CFAT) of hours actually spent in classroom teaching notes all the appropriate caveats: classroom hours do not reflect time spent in preparation beforehand or with students afterward; different kinds of classes require varying amounts of work; nor can classroom hours alone reveal the burden of student numbers. Nevertheless, the figures reported by CFAT still shed some light on this situation.⁶

Most striking is the pronounced disparity in teaching loads between colleges and research universities. Faculty in the latter averaged 8 to 10 hours of teaching per week (non-laboratory subjects), while their counterparts in well-established liberal arts colleges (i.e., Carnegie-accepted) were professing from 15 to 18 hours. To the survey authors this represented "a difference in kind of work" that existed by this date between the two settings.⁷ A certain amount of research time was already built into faculty positions at research universities. A second conclusion of this survey was that teaching loads tended to be fairly comparable across subjects within a given institution. Discrepancies were somewhat greater between research universities, and probably represented differences in both the composition of teaching responsibilities and attitudes toward instruction. Johns Hopkins, for example, with its predominance of graduate students, had the lowest reported load among research universities, while conservative Yale had the highest. The University of Chicago was unusual in placing an explicit limit on teaching loads. In the original general regulations of the University it was specified that each faculty member "shall lecture thirty-six weeks of the year, ten to twelve hours a week; no instructor shall be required to lecture more than this amount."⁸ When this policy was promulgated in 1892, Chicago was undoubtedly well in advance of comparable universities, but only a decade and a half later this standard was equaled or surpassed by other research universities.

Another inquiry into teaching loads revealed that by 1920 some differentiation was taking place among research universities. The most prestigious universities that attracted the greatest number of graduate students, which were by and large the wealthiest institutions as well, required faculty to teach from six to eight hours per week. In other research universities, ten to twelve hours was a more likely load. The authors concluded that, "to require no more than six to eight hours of teaching from a professor...is, therefore, already in the United States a mark of first class practice."⁹ Clearly belonging in this class were Columbia, Cornell and Harvard; California and Chicago met this standard for faculty doing graduate teaching; while Stanford, Yale and perhaps Michigan barely qualified for inclusion. By this juncture, then, these schools were permitting their faculty an amount of time for research that other universities were incapable of matching.

Student/faculty ratios offer another perspective on teaching burdens. The figures given in Table I have the advantage of being comparable across forty years of university development, but some caveats are in order here as well. First, since different institutions represent rather different mixtures of teaching responsibilities, comparisons of any single university from one decade to another may be more meaningful than those between universities for a given year. For example, the existence of large medical schools at Pennsylvania and Johns Hopkins (after 1893) certainly helped to lower their ratios; and the same is probably true for the high proportion of technical education at Illinois, Cornell, and M.I.T.

Second, enrollment surges do not necessarily coincide in the short run with conditions for faculty growth. The aftermath of World War I is a good case in point as enrollments mushroomed while universities were still enduring financial adversity. The figures for public universities appear to be somewhat more volatile, indicating that they had less control over their resources and student numbers. Finally, because teaching methods changed as class size increased, it was by no means certain that the larger classes implied by higher student/faculty ratios necessarily meant greater teaching burdens. A survey of faculty at the University of Chicago revealed that classes of 20-29 students claimed the largest share of an instructor's time, and that teaching hours were reduced in smaller or larger classes.¹⁰ Nevertheless, the overall change in student/faculty ratios seems consistent with the relatively small teaching loads at research universities.

As Table I indicates, a significant transformation took place in research universities between 1890 and 1910. Even though enrollments grew enormously during these years, the number of faculty grew even faster. The number of students per teacher was halved at Princeton and Cornell and reduced by a third at Illinois, Michigan, Harvard and M.I.T. Reductions were significant at Columbia, Yale and Hopkins as well; while at the others fairly stable ratios implied a large absolute growth in faculty numbers. It is probable that this transformation produced a reduction in the teaching burden of the average faculty member, and thus increased the time available for individual research. By 1910, however, this movement was largely completed. In the next twenty years, a certain amount of backsliding seems to have taken place, most notably at Columbia and Harvard. More significant, though, was the

TABLE 1
FACULTY AND STUDENT/FACULTY RATIOS
AT RESEARCH UNIVERSITIES, 1890-1930.

	1889-90		1899-1900		1909-10		1919-20		1929-30	
	Fac.	S/F	Fac.	S/F	Fac.	S/F	Fac.	S/F	Fac.	S/F
California	67	10.5	187	13.2	297	13	1178	10.7	1660	11.3
Illinois	32	14.7	217	8.3	548	8.7	948	9	1098	12.2
Michigan	96	22.5	207	16	317	15	454	19	827	12.5
Minnesota	103	9.7	208	12.1		12.8*	814	15	952	15.7
Wisconsin	70	11.4	161	13.5		10.4*	518	14.1	704	14.8
Chicago			211	15	334	20	413	27.4	772	19.1
Columbia	180	9.3	350	7	513	6.9	970	8.8	1656	9.6
Cornell	104	12.8	321	7.3	636	6.6	876	5.9	803	7.3
Harvard	217	9.8	448	9.2	618	6.5	783	5.9	928	10.2
Johns Hopkins	58	7	141	4.6	218	3.1	341	8	640	7.9
M.I.T.	180	10.1		8.7	223	6.6	269	10.7	397	7.7
Pennsylvania	180	8.9	260	10.3	454	9.1	827	8.3	1374	6.8
Princeton	45	17.1	80	14.8	169	8.3	192	9.6	308	8.1
Stanford			131	10.2	160	10.9	298	9.4	477	9.7
Yale	143	10.3	258	9.4	404	8.2	410	7.7	598	8.9

*1908-09.

SOURCE: Bureau of Education. *Report of the Commissioner of Education*, 1889-90 (II.2), 1899-1900 (II), 1909-10 (II), "Biennial Survey of Education." *Bulletin*, 1923 (29), 1931 (20).

growing standardization between similar institutions. The discrepancies between public research universities were smaller in 1930 than at any prior time. Among private research universities (which are more heterogeneous by nature), the 1930 differences were smaller still except for Chicago, which appeared to operate on a standard all its own. Overall, then, the evidence suggests that basic faculty responsibilities for teaching duties and potential research time were fairly well established during the first decade of the century. Still, this conclusion does not settle the underlying issue: how much teaching was too much teaching?

From the viewpoint of the scientific community the teaching burden imposed by American universities was a continual obstacle to the pursuit of research. At least six of the disciplinary advisory committees set up by the Carnegie Institution of Washington in 1902, for example, recommended measures for freeing faculty from classroom duties.[11] T. W. Richards of Harvard considered this need so acute that he prepared a minority chemistry report to stress the point. According to Richards:

. . .in a few great universities some at least of the professors are given time for research . . . .But this freedom is the exception rather than the rule. Not only are most American professors overburdened with routine work, but nearly all are obliged, by the inadequacy of their salaries, to consume time and energy in hack work . . . .[12]

An informed estimate for physics around the turn of the century suggests that professors could expect one-fifth, and assistant professors one-fourth, of their time to be spent on research. For all categories of personnel, American physicists had significantly less research time than their counterparts in Germany, France and Great Britain.[13] A sampling of the views of assistant professors in research universities in 1910 revealed a situation that was perhaps less dire than that portrayed by Richards: the respondents divided evenly over the question of whether their own conditions for research and advanced work were satisfactory.[14]

The ambiguity of these responses merely underscores the fact that the problem of adequate faculty research time was only partly resolved in the first decade of the century. Moreover, there was another side to the issue. After the pronounced emphasis on university research in the last decades of the nineteenth century, the years after 1900 saw a recrudescence of a cultural emphasis on undergraduate instruction. "The Ph.D. Octopus" by William James set the tone for a literature that scorned the pedantry and pretentiousness of the German approach to university research. At the same time the movement for liberal culture gave new purpose and stature to undergraduate education.[15] The first decade of the century, then, witnessed an intermittent debate between those who thought the university should place more emphasis on teaching, and scholars who demanded a greater accommodation of research.

The individuals most affected by this conflict were undoubtedly the small fraternity of research university presidents. As a requirement of office they were virtually compelled to embrace both research and teaching ideals. And, they further believed that the two could and should be united. In reality, however, they were being pulled in opposite directions. In the background stood the new endowed research institutes, representing total dedication to research and occasionally luring away their best scientists.[16] The institutions over which they presided, on the other hand, derived their sustenance from the teaching they supplied. In their discussions together at Association of American Universities meetings, or in the everyday tasks of administering their universities, one of the foremost problems faced by university presidents was to find ways to encourage and support faculty research in "teaching universities."

The crosscurrents of this problem were exemplified in the controversial issue of research professorships. To create such extraordinary positions amounted to a policy of specialization, although it was never actually phrased that way: have the "research man," in the parlance of the day, devote all his time to investigation; and conversely, though not necessarily, have a corps of "teaching men" fully employed in instruction. Although such an explicit division of function may sound incongruous, there were sufficient innovations in the first decades of the century for specialization to be considered an experiment performed. The results reveal much about the predicament of faculty research.

As background to this question it should be noted that teaching loads were not generally standardized within institutions, or even within departments. President Charles Van Hise of Wisconsin took pride in pointing out that teaching responsibilities were adjusted according to the personal capabilities of each faculty member:

At Wisconsin there is no fixed amount of instructional work required from a professor. The quantity of this work varies greatly. Where in the faculty there is a man who is not a productive scholar, he is likely to have a rather heavy instructional work. Where, upon the other hand, there is a man who is doing things, he has large liberty as to the amount of instructional work he carries.[17]

This undoubtedly reflected the general practice at research universities. In fact, when the subject arose, the presidents strongly opposed the substitution of standards or norms for this kind of individualized treatment.[18] Before the turn of the century, pure research positions had been created, but on those occasions they were intended for junior faculty. The rank of "docent"—an approximation of the German *Privatdocent* was tried at Hopkins, Clark and Chicago, but did not endure.[19] The post of research professor was more permanent, more conspicuous, and considerably more costly. When such appointments were discussed by the AAU in 1906, the opinion of university presidents was decidedly negative, although not for those reasons. Rather, they felt that research professorships violated the unity of teaching and research to which they were strongly committed.[20] In this light, the fact that such positions were created by some of these same men appears somewhat curious.

In general, the existence of research professorships is explained by the stature of the men who held them—scholars of considerable reknown, often sought by more than one institution. Thus, the flamboyant psychologist Edward Titchener was allowed to devote himself exclusively to research and graduate work at Cornell; when Stanford made an offer to historian Frederick Jackson Turner, Wisconsin countered by allowing him half time free for research; and biologist Jacques Loeb was lured to California by the offer of a research professorship.[21] Most such appointments, however, seem to have ended badly, and the special treatment the incumbents received appears to be the root cause. Two research chairs awarded by Chicago, and one of two at Ohio State, were abandoned by their holders. Turner's favored treatment caused such acrimony with the Wisconsin regents that it prompted his departure for Harvard only two years later (1910). The same year Loeb fled to the Rockefeller Institute because "my colleagues, and very soon the community and the newspapers, quickly resented the idea that I should receive full pay and do little teaching." Loeb's conclusion that, "in a democracy today there is as yet no room in a state university for pure research," was probably too sweeping.[22] But, research professorships were nevertheless not to be the means for promoting research in American universities. Instead, they were no more than extraordinary arrangements for exceptional individuals and unusual circumstances.[23]

The other side of this coin, specialized teaching posts, also made little headway. Periodic suggestions that pure teaching professorships be created to counter undue emphasis on research were superfluous since most universities already had numerous faculty of that type.[24] President Van Hise, whose announced policy was to require productive scholarship for appointments and promotions, found when he surveyed his faculty that more than one-third engaged in no research at all. Again, there is no reason to think Wisconsin atypical in this respect. A far more interesting application of specialization in teaching occurred at Princeton. The decision by President Woodrow Wilson and Dean Andrew F. West to enlarge the faculty with a special corps of undergraduate tutors, called preceptors, directly contradicted trends at other research universities. The intense and intimate instruction that these arrangements were intended to facilitate suited the distinctive aspirations of Princeton, but also had the potential of creating a special class of faculty virtually excluded from the professional community of scholars.[25] This was precisely the situation that most research universities wished to avoid.[26]

The decisive trend working against the specialization of faculty functions was the development of democratic university departments. As the locus of disciplinary authority in universities, the department represented a unitary system of values shared by all members concerning the advancement of knowledge. As permanent department heads were increasingly replaced by rotating chairmen, and assistant professors gained a voice in departmental matters, departments were inexorably pressured to treat all members on an equitable basis.[27] This did not imply equal treatment with respect to teaching and research, but rather that each member at least be given some opportunity to pursue research. At Princeton, for example, the preceptorial system quickly was made compatible with these imperatives by having all departmental members serve as preceptors.[28]

The fundamental problem of the American research university thus became finding the means for providing every faculty member with some chance to contribute to the advancement of knowledge, not to mention the advancement of their own professional careers. Innovations that failed this test of equity were simply not imitated, and consequently were relegated to a marginal position in the university system. Thus, research professorships attained only a toehold in universities, either in subjects remote from undergraduate teaching or supported by special endowments. On the other hand, innovations that made it possible to spread research opportunities among many faculty had widespread appeal. As these needs became more clearly recognized by the second decade of the century, such mechanisms as sabbatical leaves, revolving research funds, and graduate assistantships were increasingly adopted by the research universities. They became characteristic American adaptations to the difficulty of reconciling the demands of both teaching and research.

The origin of the modern practice of sabbatical leaves can be traced back to Harvard. In 1880, as part of an offer that enticed philologist Charles Lanman away from Johns Hopkins, Eliot promised him every seventh year off with half pay. By the turn of the century this practice had spread to Columbia, Pennsylvania, and at least eight other research universities.[29] Clearly, this was the kind of perquisite that other universities had to match to remain competitive in attracting and holding leading scholars. Sabbaticals at this juncture were thus offered only to established scholars and were not an entitlement of all faculty members. They were thus part of the deliberately unequal treatment of faculty condoned by Van Hise. The process by which sabbatical leaves spread throughout American higher education to become available to faculty in general occupies most of the twentieth century. In the research universities, however, departmental democratization soon created pressures for uniform treatment. At Yale, for example, a sabbatical policy covering all professors was announced in 1910.[30] One factor which certainly impeded the utilization of sabbaticals early in the century was the precarious economic situation of faculty. Those without independent means, particularly junior faculty, could hardly afford to sacrifice half of their annual income.[31] The widespread adoption of sabbaticals for faculty research was thus dependent upon the availability of supplemental research funds. Systematic progress in this area only began to occur near the end of this period.

President Harry Pratt Judson of Chicago advocated in 1919 that separate funds be earmarked for university research. "When funds are not set aside for special purposes they must be used for general purposes." In fact, the measures he urged were already being tried. Early in the century the formation of administratively distinct graduate schools provided one conduit for aiding research. At Illinois, for example, the graduate school began receiving its own annual appropriations in 1908, some of which was used for assistants, equipment and supplies for research.[33] A more explicit provision for research occurred at California in 1915, when $2,000 was included in the university's budget for incidental faculty expenses related to research. Even though this sum was subsequently increased, it remained miniscule in comparison with potential needs. To solve the problem of equitable distribution, a faculty committee was established to recommend grants. This appears to be an indication of growing faculty authority in research-related matters. California's research fund and the faculty committee controlling it were clearly precedents for other universities.[34] Only a few years later, August Heckscher bequeathed to Cornell a $500,000 endowment to be used specifically to provide faculty with research time. Instead of creating research professorships, an alternative apparently considered, these funds were administered in a manner similar to California's. Harvard as well preferred to utilize its research funds in this manner.[35] Nevertheless, such arrangements revolving research funds in several universities provided further potential assistance for faculty research.36

During these thirty years, the American research university evolved, through trial, error and occasional success, away from the unattainable German ideal of pure research toward a characteristically American amalgamation of university teaching and research. By 1920, the organizational mechanisms were in place for this kind of university-based research system. In certain ways the situation was similar with respect to the material resources required for university research.

The material, as opposed to the human inputs to university research, cover a broader and more diverse range of phenomena, and they too were crucial in the evolution of research universities. In order to provide a coherent account of this facet of their development it is helpful to distinguish three types of material resources. First, capital inputs to research take the form of either physical structures or special endowments. The role of these university assets was not unlike that of faculty: that is, they were generally used for both teaching and research; and, the more of them that a university had, just as the more faculty it had relative to students, the greater the capacity for university research. The second category pertains to capital as well, but capital used in a special way. University research institutes were, in sharp departure from normal university practice, devoted nearly exclusively to research. Although some of these units were long established, they became more numerous and prominent after the turn of the century. The third category is reserved for funds intended to be entirely expended in aiding research. In it would fall all of the nonrecurring forms of aid that professors utilized to cover the incremental costs of investigation. These distinctions will be useful first to explicate the system of support for university research as it existed at the close of the nineteenth century, and then to identify the forces of change impinging upon this system after 1900.

In 1880, Harvard was offered $115,000 by an anonymous donor to construct a physics laboratory, with the condition that a permanent endowment of $75,000 be raised to cover its operating expenses. The stipulated funds were soon collected, and in 1884 the Jefferson Physical Laboratory opened its doors. Harvard thus came to possess one of the country's most up-to-date facilities for experimental physics. The Jefferson Physical Laboratory, then, resulted from the initiative and the intellectual preferences of the soon-identified donor, T. Jefferson Coolidge. Similarly, he later also endowed a new chemical laboratory, despite the fact that the Wolcott Gibbs Memorial Laboratory for Chemistry was then under construction.40 Both of these structures augmented Harvard's capacity for research in the physical sciences, but both essentially were the product of the initiatives of their donor.

preSupposed that separate research funds were available, and that was clearly unusual. An AAUP survey in 1921 found just nine universities with revolving research funds.36

Finally, it appears to be an entirely natural organizational adaptation for universities to turn to their own graduate students for help with the work of the university. Graduate students had the potential of providing cheap, competent and dedicated assistants for research, and as teaching fellows they could be used to considerably lighten the most resented faculty burden, that of instruction in introductory courses. Moreover, students could staff these subordinate positions without the stigma that followed those permanently relegated to such posts.

The idea behind graduate fellowships, as they were first employed at Johns Hopkins and Clark, was to guarantee their holders the means to devote themselves exclusively to their studies. Chicago was clearly exceptional when it required its fellows to spend one-sixth of their time in various forms of "university service" which did not include teaching.37 The true teaching fellowship is essentially a twentieth-century creation. Harvard employed a large bequest to create thirty such positions in 1899, requiring their holders to teach half-time. After the turn of the century Pennsylvania and Wisconsin created similar positions with teaching obligations of about five hours per week. When the AAU considered the general issue of graduate fellowships in 1906, practices differed widely among member universities. Although G. Stanley Hall castigated the practices at Harvard as a "sweating system," opinion overall seemed to have favored the use of graduate students as teachers.38 Graduate teaching fellowships certainly had practical benefits for the universities, and these undoubtedly accounted for their rapid spread after this date. By 1914, the annual payroll of enrolled students engaged in teaching or research at the University of California exceeded $100,000.39 The utilization of graduate students soon passed from the status of an innovation to being an integral practice of research universities.

When all of the factors just discussed are taken into account, there can be little doubt that the trade-off between teaching and research for the average faculty member in a research university changed markedly from 1890 to 1920. First came a progressive lowering of both the number of students per professor and the number of hours spent in the classroom. For the purposes of research, the latter seems to have been more important. After about 1910, student/teacher ratios expanded slightly, while teaching loads appear to have continued to shrink. Larger classes and the utilization of graduate teaching fellows may have made it possible for professors simultaneously to teach more students and to have more time for research. The establishment of regular sabbaticals gave every professor an opportunity—and an implicit obligation—for intensive research. At the end of this period the appearance of

A contrasting example can be found in the early history of the University of Chicago. President William Rainey Harper failed initially to secure the funds needed to construct a biology building, and by 1894 he would describe this lacuna as the university's single "greatest need." During the same interval Harper was courting a gift from the heiress and philanthropist Helen Culver. Late in 1895, after lengthy behind-the-scenes machinations, she summoned Harper to inform him of her intention to make a substantial donation to the university. Her aim was to endow an art school and gallery at a location well removed from the campus. It apparently required all of Harper's considerable persuasive powers to dissuade her, first from giving such an art school, then from her second preference of creating a music school, and eventually to implant the idea of supporting biology at the University of Chicago. The end result was Hull Quadrangle, containing ample laboratories for anatomy, physiology, botany and zoology. In this case it was the priorities of the university. most strenuously advanced by its president, that steered the Culver donation into the service of university biological research.[41]

Private universities relied heavily upon gifts for their capital needs. Columbia may have resorted to loans to construct Morningside Heights, and Harvard in 1876 reluctantly tapped its "free capital" in order to extend its library, but such steps were exceptions, to be avoided if at all possible.[42] In general, when gifts were not forthcoming projects could be postponed: existing facilities, no matter how inadequate, could be made to suffice for the next year, the year after, and so on. The nature of the gifts that produced the Jefferson Physical Laboratory and the Hull Quadrangle stand out from the thousands of capital gifts received by American universities in the late nineteenth century chiefly because they fall near the opposite end of a continuum that might be drawn from donor to university priorities. Probably most benefactions represented a more balanced combination of the desires of both institutions and givers. Nevertheless, universities could and did take special measures to see that particular needs were met. They could, as Harvard did in gathering the stipulated endowment for the Jefferson Laboratory, create a special fund, and then solicit contributions from among the university's reliable, large donors. Later, in the twentieth century, it became common to include special capital needs within organized fund-raising drives. Such needs, however, included far more than research. The essential point, then, is that a university's capacity to raise large sums of capital for research-related purposes was tied, above all, to its commitment to its research objectives, and after that to the predilections of its donors.

When it came to building needs, the state universities had primarily a single patron, one who had limited solicitude for university research before the turn of the century. In order to build a new laboratory, public universities would typically appeal to their state legislature on the basis of teaching needs, and, if successful, construct a building that would also accommodate faculty research. State universities also appealed for private gifts, but where capital needs were concerned, an implicit division of responsibility seemed to exist. The state, in its fashion, would provide for the essential university facilities, while the university had to rely upon its own efforts and its occasional large benefactors for amenities like gymnasiums or ceremonial halls. Capital for research purposes fell somewhere between these two spheres for state universities in the late nineteenth century. The notable exception was the University of California, which by the end of the century was beginning to benefit from an unusually rich and steady stream of voluntary support for research-related ends.

Capital to assist research was not confined to buildings, but also included endowments for professorships, laboratories, departmental expenses and the purchase of books. Endowed professorships had the advantage of permitting a university to pay above-market salaries to outstanding scholars, or to support esoteric subjects that would not otherwise be offered. In these, as in nearly all forms of donations, Harvard stood ahead and apart. In 1902 President Eliot noted that Harvard had 40 endowed professorships, 10 of which had been given in the previous 6 years. Eliot called these professorships "the most fundamental and permanently valuable.... of all University endowments," and they played a significant part in maintaining America's most distinguished faculty.[43] Elsewhere, special endowments played strategic roles in the advancement of specific areas. At Cornell, for example, the gifts of Henry W. Sage made possible the creation of a school of philosophy (1890), which rapidly became a major center for graduate training, home of the *Philosophical Review* (1892-), and a center for research in experimental psychology.[44] Like the buildings just discussed, these endowments not only served research needs, but also helped to underwrite some of the basic operative expenses of the university. However, a purer form of research capital was responsible for the few examples of university institutes.

During the nineteenth century, university research institutes were created for either of two purposes. One was to establish and operate an observatory—a type of research institute centered on an instrument that is now common. The second purpose, defining a more heterogeneous category, was to preserve and utilize collections of scholarly or scientific value. Although both kinds of institutes might offer some teaching, particularly at the graduate level, they essentially existed for purposes of research. They would usually have a faculty member in the capacity of director, but there would also be assistants concentrating entirely on research. Because these institutes were wholly intended for research, universities expected them to be fully supported through special endowments and private contributions.

Harvard was far in advance of other American universities in these kinds of arrangements. The Harvard Observatory was founded in 1844 through a public subscription, "filled largely by the merchant shipowners of Boston."

By the end of the century the various endowments it had accumulated allowed it to support close to 50 staff, including 2 full, 1 associate and 2 assistant professors.[45] By this juncture it had to share the leadership in American astronomy with the 36 inch telescope at California's Lick Observatory (f. 1888) and the 40 inch refractor at Chicago's Yerkes Observatory (f. 1898). The popular mystique of astronomy allowed university astronomers to appeal to the benefactors who otherwise had little interest in science. This was certainly the case with James Lick and Charles Yerkes, but there were also exceptions. Catherine Wolfe Bruce, astronomy's most consistent and generous patron at the close of the nineteenth century, was motivated by an informed concern for the subject.[46]

The donation of collections, the buildings to house them, or endowments to care for them were more often made by individuals who were particularly concerned with their subjects. By accepting such offers universities could sometimes be enticed into unintended and unforeseen areas. Harvard pretty well represents the gamut of possibilities. Prior to 1900 it had established museums or endowed collections in anatomy, archaeology, several areas of botany, mineralogy, comparative zoology and art. The status of these institutes naturally varied widely. The well-endowed Peabody Museum of Archaeology and Ethnology became an important scientific center from its establishment in the late 1860s. The Bussy Institution, however—Harvard's agricultural college and experiment station—although founded by a bequest in 1835, was by 1890 in such parlous straits that it was forced to board livestock and sell vegetables to raise income. It nevertheless improved its fortunes toward the end of the century, and in 1908 was essentially transformed into a true research institute by being made a graduate school of applied biology.[47] The timing of this development was typical. The years around the turn of the century saw the founding of numerous institutes at research universities. At California, Phoebe Apperson Hearst established the basis for the Museum of Anthropology, Jacques Loeb set up his physiological laboratory, and a parallel lab was created in anatomy.[48] Activities near the close of the century at Pennsylvania represent both the old and the new strains of university institute work. In the prestigious field of Semitic studies the Archaeology Museum conducted its most fruitful (and ultimately controversial) Babylonian expeditions. At the same time the newly organized Wistar Institute (f. 1894) was shifting from specimen collecting to active medical research, thus foreshadowing a burgeoning field of twentieth-century institute research.[49]

The definition of a university research institute employed here has been deliberately loose in order to be faithful to the conditions of nineteenth-century science. Essentially, they were intended for the tasks of description (the "old" astronomy), classification (botany, zoology), and preservation (archaeology, paleontology). Significantly, such subjects had both academic

and non-academic followings. They were peripheral to the university curriculum, and thus were studied by only a few advanced or graduate students. Also, the interest these subjects attracted outside the university was largely responsible for the donations that made them possible. For subjects with more curricular importance, physics and chemistry for example, instruction and research were largely integrated prior to 1900. The nineteenth-century research institute, however was basically an appendage to the university, its attachment made possible by the fact that it could pay its own way. After the turn of the century changes in the conduct and the funding of university research would enlarge the role of institutes, but without fundamentally altering these conditions.

It still remains to be seen how normal university research was financed in the absence, as was generally the case, of special endowments. Investigation in many disciplines might require expeditions, special apparatus, the purchase of collections, or the hiring of assistants. By the last decades of the century most of the universities made small regular contributions to their physics and chemistry labs, for example, to pay for materials consumed and the services of a mechanic or glassblower. The projects of individuals throughout the university, however, at times encountered extraordinary needs. On these occasions an appeal was directed outside the institution to the wider university community.

Small contributions ranging from one dollar to thousands of dollars flowed into universities during these years to assist almost any imaginable university activity. While it is impossible to precisely categorize these gifts, several general purposes are prominent. At the head of the list are donations intended for student scholarships, prizes, loan funds and extracurricular activities. Also common were gifts to assist research and, closely related, donations of books or money for the library. The following were typical:

$2500 to History Professor Charles K. Adams to buy books (Michigan, 1883)
$1500 for assistants' salaries, Department of Semitic Languages (Yale, 1890)
$395 for fossil fishes (Colombia, 1893)
$1850 (4 gifts) for apparatus in electrochemistry (Pennsylvania, 1900)
$250 to Physics Professor Trowbridge for magnetism research (Harvard, 1900).[50]

While generalizations about these discrete and varied occurrences are difficult, the key to understanding this kind of support appears to lie in the relationship between the university and its surrounding community. The initiative for such gifts lay predominantly with the university. There were several means by which some special need could be made known. Publicity through the president's annual report or some other official utterance was a standard practice. Department heads often had responsibility for raising donations through their contacts in the community.[51] Subscriptions were sometimes organized so that small gifts from large numbers of people could accomplish some objective. On most subscription lists, one would find the names of university officers along with some of the regular supporters of the university. This strongly suggests that the leadership of prominent citizens acting through existing social networks was the true basis of this kind of fundraising. It follows that the size of the university-connected community was an important factor in the amount of support that might be tapped in this fashion. Harvard clearly outdid all other universities in this respect, and by the turn of the century, California was also receiving a broad array of research-related gifts. Columbia, Pennsylvania, and later Chicago capitalized on their metropolitan locations to find numerous benefactors, while the comparatively small number of gifts to Cornell and Michigan may indicate the limitations of small college towns.

Mention should be made of the voluntary support received by university libraries. They were for all practical purposes the laboratories of the humanities, and gifts to augment their collections served to enhance the university's capacity for scholarship. Although large capital gifts were occasionally made to libraries, most of this giving was of the same small, piecemeal character as the donations to research just discussed. The preferences of donors were frequently evident in library gifts: people gave collections of books that they had accumulated, acted as patrons to their special areas of interest, or memorialized the intellectual tastes of their departed kin. For those without such guidelines, a common form of giving was simply to provide a sum for the purchase of books. University libraries also organized subscriptions to purchase collections that were particularly sought. Private universities depended heavily upon donations to build their collections. For example, two-thirds of the books purchased at Columbia in 1903 were financed through eleven donated funds. In addition 319 individuals gave books or pamphlets to the library that year. The largest university library, Harvard's, was completely supported by donated funds during the first half of the 1890's, and even after that endowments and gifts managed to finance all book purchases.[52]

When the material resources funneled into university research at the end of the nineteenth century are viewed as a whole, it becomes apparent that credit should be extended far beyond those individuals whose names are emblazoned over the doors of university laboratories and institutes. The university research role in fact enjoyed widespread grass-roots support across the middle and upper classes of the communities in which they were located. Some of these benefactors were alumni; others might be acquainted with university officers or department heads through local social service organizations; and members of the university who could afford it were themselves frequent contributors. It is well beyond the scope of this study to recreate the web of social relations that lay behind this type of giving. Nevertheless, it seems safe to hypothesize that such donations were based upon informal personal suggestions or requests, rather than on the kind of organized fund-raising that developed in the twentieth century. These two forms, in fact, are essentially incompatible because organized drives tend to pre-empt the philanthropic potential of large donors for university-designated purposes. This was only one reason why the nineteenth-century pattern of individual voluntary support for research was inadequate to twentieth-century research needs. More serious was the fact that such support flowed into the universities at regular intervals and in uncertain amounts. How, then, could such a system support the growing demands of modern science and scholarship? In actuality, the answer to this question was long masked by the spectacular prosperity of the research universities.

The years around the turn of the century witnessed a subtle yet significant shift in the arrangements for the university research described above. Perhaps the principal underlying cause was the steep escalation in the cost of conducting research in the natural sciences. Through the 1880's there was relatively little disparity between the needs of science and humanities departments, but this began to change in the 1890's, and changed dramatically in the twentieth century. The sciences required greater space for laboratory instruction, numerous assistants, and increasingly expensive materials and apparatus.[53] In some cases research was conducted on a heretofore unprecedented scale. The term *Grosswissenschaft* was coined in Germany in the 1890's, and by 1900 it would certainly apply to America's three leading university observatories. The Carnegie Institution would shortly extend Big Science into geological research as well. The appearance of independent research institutes at the beginning of the century was in fact symptomatic of this shift. Their inspiration sprang from serious doubts about the scientific capacity of American universities as then organized.[54] These trends provoked an ongoing concern with the organization and finance of university research.

In 1911, President Arthur Twining Hadley reviewed the spiraling costs of science at Yale during the previous decade. Yale's scientific units, which had formerly been nearly self-supporting, now presented significant and increasing charges to general university revenues. For the Sheffield Scientific School these costs rose from zero in 1901 to $25,000 in 1911; for the Peabody Museum the increase was from $5,500 to $16,000; and for the Medical School, $1,500 to $24,000. The reasons Hadley gave for this spiral were familiar—more assistants and more costly equipment were required, while scientists were demanding higher salaries and greater relief from classroom duties. In particular, Hadley believed that "competition for the services of scientific men is more acute than it was," chiefly because the western state universities and the independent research institutes had bid up salaries. Given the mode of research support then prevalent, only one solution to this problem seemed possible: "the research of a university should be as far as possible endowed research."[55] Yale clearly would have to increase its endowments for these areas.

During the first decade of the century, the presidents of the other research universities had independently come to the same conclusion. Charles Eliot in 1901 stated suggestively, "it is clear that men of means, who reflect on the uses and results of educational endowments, are more and more inclined to endow research" (his examplar--T. Jefferson Coolidge). He then proceeded to describe the current needs of Harvard for philosophy, psychology, astronomy, Latin American research, archaeology, Semitic studies, mineralogy and the art museum.[56] This approach was by no means restricted to the private universities. President Van Hise in 1905 looked forward to private donations sustaining research in state universities. Noting that the great gifts to private universities were a phenomenon of only the past generation, and mindful of California's recent success, Van Hise felt that it was only a matter of time until state universities had a numerous and, in part wealthy body of alumni, plus large local accumulations of capital, from which to draw support.[57]

Probably the most ambitious and explicit plan for endowing research was formulated in 1910 by President Jacob Gould Schurman of Cornell. Complaining that "the demand for scientific investigators, for laboratories, and for the instrumentalities of research come to the president from all departments," he invited contemporary millionaires to contribute one to three million in endowment for each of seven departments.[58] In effect, he was asking for a sum greater than twice Cornell's existing endowment (approximating, in fact, the entire Harvard endowment of 1910) for what would substantially be support for departmental research. Schurman concluded his report by adding that Cornell also needed dormitories, a gymnasium and an auditorium. Similarly, Eliot followed his earlier plea for research endowment by specifically requesting endowments for several new buildings under construction. The research universities needed funds for more than just research, and that was the crux of their problem.

It was inevitable that the need for research capital would eventually be crowded by other university needs. Although the organizational success of the research university depended heavily upon being all things to all people, there was a point at which choices had to be made concerning which needs would be publicized in the annual report, emphasized in pleas to state legislators, or urged upon a wavering Helen Culver. University initiatives were important for channeling some research-related gifts before 1900, as has been seen, but they became more important after that as fund-raising became

increasingly organized. University presidents periodically took up the cudgel for research in their appeals, but the demands stemming from the university's paramount teaching responsibilities could hardly be ignored. The steady growth of student numbers required more faculty, facilities, and, for private universities, unrestricted endowment to support them. University presidents were more likely to appeal for campus buildings, or for general support, than they were for research per se.

The negative implications for university research were nevertheless long offset by certain trends in university finance. The first fifteen years of the century were in general a period of spectacular prosperity for the research universities. The private ones found large donors in ever-increasing numbers, even as their alumni became more numerous and more devoted to *alma mater*. The state research universities benefited from a rapidly expanding tax base, as well as relative popularity with their state legislatures. During these years research universities were consequently able to build the new laboratories demanded by their scientists, to reduce the teaching burden on their scholars, and to compete with one another, as Hadley had complained, by offering "scientific men" higher salaries and better conditions for research. As a result, the research imperative was far more irrevocably entrenched in these universities by the outbreak of World War I than it had been in 1900. It was only then that the existing system of research support began to show evidence of strain.

The first decade and a half of this century witnessed a building boom at the research universities. Moreover, much of this increase in capital consisted of laboratories, libraries and other basic university resources that increased their capacity for research. The expansion of facilities was most spectacular for the state universities, amounting to more than a quadrupling of physical assets in these fifteen years. The private universities were on the whole more fully developed in 1900, but they still increased the value of their buildings and grounds by some 200 to 350 percent. A more direct indication of research resources might be the value of books and scientific equipment. For this the state universities showed a five-fold increase from 1900-1915, while the private universities averaged a three-fold rise.[60] Although these figures are obviously imprecise, there can be no doubt about the meaning of such quantum jumps in embedded university research capital, especially during a period of relatively stable prices. The existing system of university financing clearly worked admirably in these years to augment the means for faculty research.

Even while the research universities were gaining strength and maturity in the years prior to the First World War the competition was intensifying for both research capital and current research support. Furthermore, this competition emanated from within the university itself. The research universities played a crucial role in the evolution of American medical schools by providing the academic leadership, the cadres of scientists and the means for raising necessary capital. All these factors were needed to transform medical schools from loosely affiliated proprietary institutions to academic units of the universities. The consummation of this process in the 1920s produced a new and different entity. University medical schools became perhaps the most self-contained compartments within already highly compartmentalized universities. They also maintained the highest research overhead of all teaching units. Henceforth, their insatiable needs for capital and income would have to be factored into future university fund-raising plans.

Something like the opposite seems to have occured with respect to the numerous small gifts for research-related purposes. These donations appear to have accelerated after 1900 along with other forms of university giving. If anything, the first decade of the twentieth century was probably the heyday of this kind of piecemeal support for the university research. The growing size and affluence of the greater university community, together with the prestige of the universities themselves are probably sufficient to account for this. Although evidence is difficult to interpret for this kind of phenomenon, it seems likely that the importance of grass-roots support for university science steadily declined after about 1910. The number of individual gifts seems to have decreased, even though a few of them assumed larger magnitudes. Gifts in kind to libraries and museums were somewhat less affected. And, at Harvard a significant number of donors continued to support research, along with everything else. But overall, it is safe to conclude that this kind of income failed to keep pace with university giving in general, the expansion of the greater university community, or the needs of university investigators.

Changes in the nature of the university itself probably account for this development. The increasingly organized character of university fund raising may have helped to squeeze out those ad hoc, idiosyncratic appeals. Yale, the most highly organized university in this respect, had correspondingly low contributions to research. In 1912-13, for example, none of the individual gifts to income were designated to support the university's research role, but 3,605 individuals did contribute to the Alumni Fund. This pattern clearly suited the Yale treasurer, who remarked:

> ...a comparatively small number of [graduates], perhaps, can interest themselves actively in some particular phase of the University's work or attempt to endow or finance any single project. No graduate, however, is excluded from participation in the great work of the Alumni University Fund Association...[61]

contained and more professionalized, it indeed became more difficult for outsiders to "interest themselves actively" in departmental affairs. At the same time it seems likely that the social networks linking faculty and community leaders were slowly deteriorating between the 1890s and the war. President Ray Lyman Wilbur of Stanford, addressing an entirely different matter in 1921 (faculty housing), unwittingly testified to this development:

> It is wise... that [faculty] and their children are not brought in social competition with those of a less wholesome but more florid type of living. It is well to have communities where brains and not money set the pace and win the prizes.[62]

As the social distance between faculty members and community elites widened, special departmental needs ceased to be a part of the ongoing matrix of community philanthropy. The university continued to benefit in many small ways from the diffuse support of its surrounding community, but the significance of this kind of assistance for university research was on the wane by the second decade of the century.

The National Research Council conducted a survey in 1920 of all "funds available in the U. S. for the encouragement of scientific research." The results, seen in Table 2, reveal those resources specifically designated for research among the major universities at the end of the period under discussion.[63] In general, the expectations earlier voiced by university presidents for the massive endowment of university research were only fulfilled in perhaps two respects. Charles Eliot might well be pleased that Harvard's patrons had created forty-one separate funds providing $750,000 annually for research alone. Similarly, proponents of medical research might take some comfort in the considerable sums donated to that end. Otherwise the picture seems to be one of irregularity and incompleteness. Seven of these universities had regular appropriations for the departmental research (See Budgetary Appropriations, Table 2). Five of the private universities (Cal Tech, Chicago, Cornell, Harvard and Yale) had similar amounts in endowed funds, although they were usually limited to designated departments. And, four (Michigan, Columbia, Pennsylvania and Stanford) appear to be clearly deficient in this respect.

Whether the sums in Table 2 are interpreted to be a lot or a little depends upon whether one looks for reference to the past or to the future. The primary reliance upon individual philanthropy had succeeded in the first two decades of the century in greatly augmenting the research capacity of these universities. In the midwestern state universities where this approach had less success legislators had at least partly recognized the need to support directly some university research. In 1920, however, American universities faced

The research universities were undergoing a subtle transformation of their social relations during these years. As departments became larger, more self-

TABLE 2
UNIVERSITY FUNDS AVAILABLE FOR SCIENTIFIC RESEARCH, 1920

	Budgetary Approp.	Special Funds	Institutes	Medicine	Agriculture*	Engineering	Number of Research Fellowships
California	$36,000	$19,500	$100,000	$87,870	$7,080		21
Illinois	25,000		3,000	3,500		$26,946	18
Michigan	14,420						28
Minnesota	23,000			[1,693,000]**			5
Wisconsin				19,200	1,000	3,000	10+
Caltech		18,350					9
Chicago		35,860	32,000	3,250			12
Columbia		465		97,701		2,250	32
Cornell		20,514		2,571	44,550		15
Harvard		8,343	118,644	612,603			50
Johns Hopkins	?			207,730			13
M.I.T.	100,000	2,150				330	5
Pennsylvania			?	?			37+
Princeton	21,200						54
Stanford	2,000		[700,000]**	1,185			13
Yale		88,740		960			15

*Not including state or federal funds
**Principal
? Funds indicated, but amounts not given

SOURCE: Compiled from "Funds Available in 1920 for the Encouragement of Scientific Research," *Bulletin of the National Research Council*, 9 (1921): 21-54.

considerable demands on existing resources. A near doubling of price levels since the outbreak of the war had squeezed budgets badly, and an enrollment explosion following the war greatly increased their paramount teaching responsibilities. Research by this date was no longer a discretionary expenditure for this set of universities. Given the trends just explicated, however, it seems unlikely that the existing forms of research support could expand in step with the needs of science. In the previous thirty years the American research universities had devised the basic organizational machinery to accommodate both teaching and research; yet as they entered the 1920s the funds needed to drive that machinery were by no means assured. In the following years this role would be gradually fulfilled by the major philanthropic foundations.[64]

NOTES

1. This study is substantially drawn from my larger work, *American Research Universities in*

the Twentieth Century, 1900-1940 (New York: Oxford University Press, forthcoming). The "research universities" are: California, Illinois, Michigan, Minnesota, Wisconsin, Chicago, Columbia, Cornell, Harvard, Johns Hopkins, MIT, Pennsylvania, Princeton, Stanford, Yale and after 1920 Caltech.

2. Laurence Veysey, *The Emergence of the American University* (Chicago: University of Chicago Press, 1965).

3. David Starr Jordan, "To What Extent Should the University Investigator Be Relieved from Teaching," *Journal of Proceedings And Addresses of the Seventh Annual Conference of the Association of American Universities* 7 (1906):24 (hereafter cited as *JAAU*).

4. Laurence Veysey, "Stability and Change in the American Undergraduate Curriculum," in Carl Kaysen, ed. *Content and Context* (N.Y.: McGraw-Hill, 1973), pp. 23-26.

5. Harvard University, *President's Report* (Cambridge: Harvard University, 1901) p.34. The best general discussion of this issue is provided by Hugh Hawkins, "University Identity: The Teaching and Research Functions," in *The Organization of Knowledge in Modern*

America, 1860-1920, eds. Alexandra Oleson and John Voss (Baltimore: John Hopkins University Press, 1979), p.312.

6. The Carnegie Foundation for the Advancement of Teaching, *Third Annual Report* (New York: 1908), pp. 134-43.

7. Ibid. p. 137.

8. Floyd W. Reeves et al., *The University Faculty. The University of Chicago Survey*, 12 vols. (Chicago: University of Chicago Press, 1933), 3-94. *Official Bulletin No.2* of the University (April 1891) also stipulates that classes were not to exceed 30 students. In fact, the Chicago faculty was inadequate for these standards: Richard Storr, *Harper's University* (Chicago: University of Chicago Press, 1966), pp. 61n. 353. Also see table 1.

9. "Encouragement of University Research: Report of Committee R." *Bulletin of the American Association of University Professors* 8 (April 1922): 27-39.

10. Reeves et al., *University Faculty*, pp.194-95.

11. *CIW Yearbook*, 1 (1902): 15-21, 83, 164, 168, 173, 234. Contributors to the forum in *Science* often made this same point, 16 (1902): 460-9 & passim.

12. Ibid., p. 85.

13. Paul Forman, John Heilbron, and Spencer Weart, "Physics Circa 1900: Personnel, Funding, and Productivity of the Academic Establishments,"*Historical Studies in the Physical Sciences* 5 (1975): 120-23, and Morris L. Cooke, "Academic and Industrial Efficiency," Carnegie Foundation for the Advancement of Teaching, *Bulletin No. 5* (New York: 1910).

14. Guido H. Marx, "The Problem of the Assistant Professor," *JAAU* 11 (1910):17-46. Comments ranged from, "Have ideal research position," to "Have had almost no time for past five years for research or investigation." Ibid., p. 28.

15. William James, "The Ph.D Octopus,"[*Harvard Monthly* (1903)] *Educational Review*, 55 (April 1918): 149-57; and Hawkins, "University Identity," pp. 302-5.

16. See Ira Remsen, comments, "University Investigator," *JAAU* 7 (1906): 49.

17. Charles R. Van Hise, "The Opportunities for Higher Instruction and Research in State Universities," *JAAU* 6 (1905): 55.

18. H.B Hutchins, "Should Men Bearing the Same Title in Any Institution Receive the Same Pay?," *JAAU* 8 (1906): 92-106.

19. Hawkins, "University Identity," p. 292. The position of post-docs would seem to belong to this short-lived tradition. A large gift from Pennsylvania provost Charles Harrison established post-doctoral research fellowships there in 1895, and these funds were enlarged in 1904. This kind of position does not seem to have been copied elsewhere before 1920. University of Pennsylvania, *Annual Reports of the Provost* (Philadelphia: University of Pennsylvania, 1896, 1904) 1896, pp. 99-102, 175-79; and 1904, pp. 91-94.

20. "University Investigator," discussion. *JAAU* 7 (1906): 48-51.

21. Merle Curti and Vernon Carstenson, *The University of Wisconsin: A History*. 2 vols. (Madison: University of Wisconsin Press, 1949), 2: 60-61; Morris Bishop, *A History of Cornell* (Ithica, N.Y.: Cornell University Press, 1962), p. 358; and Nathan Reingold and Ida H. Reingold, *Science in America: A Documentary History, 1900-1939* (Chicago: University of Chicago Press, 1981). pp. 144-45.

22. Reingold and Reingold, *Science in America*, p.145.

23. For example, Titchener had a personality that was certainly comfortable with special treatment, if not demanding of it. Hans Eigenmann, a research professor in ichthyology at Indiana, raised a good deal of research money for the university himself, and Illinois had a research professorship in material engineering, a subject easily justified by its practical usefulness.

24. Hawkins, "University Identity," p. 303; and Cooke, "Efficiency."

25. Edwin Slosson perceived the inherent long-term contradiction in the position of preceptor: if they seek to advance in their profession, then "they have the same faults as younger instructors elsewhere. On the other hand, if a man is contented to remain a preceptor all his life, ...will he be the most inspiring and profitable of associates for young men?" *Great American Universities* (New York: MacMillan & Co., 1910), p.85.

26. President Hadley of Yale warned, "there is nothing more fatal to the efficiency of a department than the maintenance in its teaching force of a number of reasonably good instructors who are kept because they can teach moderately well, but who have little promise of inspiring either associates or their students to work of really high grade and who keep out from the faculty men of less experience but more promise." Yale University, *President's Report* (New Haven: Yale University, 1910), p. 22.

27. Regarding trends in the development of departments, see Evarts B. Greene, "Departmental Administration in American Universities," *JAAU* 13 (1911): 17-35.

28. Hardin Craig, *Woodrow Wilson at Princeton* (Norman, Okla.: University of Oklahoma Press, 1960), pp. 90-98.

29. Hugh Hawkins, *Pioneer: A History of the Johns Hopkins University, 1874-89* (Ithaca, N.Y.: Cornell University Press, 1960). p. 156; and, "University Identity," p. 292.

30. Yale University, *Annual Report*, (New Haven: Yale University, 1910), pp. 42-43.

31. Eliot commented: "The institution called the 'sabbatical year' has been decidedly useful to the University, having indeed, but one drawback—namely, that a teacher with a family and no resources but his salary can hardly avail himself of it." Harvard University, *President's Report*, (Cambridge: Harvard University, 1901), p. 13; and Marx, "Assistant Professors," pp. 19-24.

32. *JAAU* 21 (1919): 50.

33. *JAAU* 17 (1915): 54.

49. Josua L. Chamberlain, ed., *the University of Pennsylvania* (Boston: 1901), pp. 160-61, 144-46. For the controversy over the Babylonian expedition, see Paul Ritterband & Harold Wechsler, "A Message to Lushtamer: The Hilprecht Controversy and Semitic Scholarship in America, *History of Higher Education Annual* 1 (1981): 5-41.

50. These examples are drawn from the indicated annual reports.

51. E.g. "gifts...are obtained by solicitation by the heads of departments..." University of Michigan, (1901), p. 37.

52. Columbia University, *Treasurer's Report* (New York: Columbia University, 1903): and Harvard University *Treasurer's Reports* (Cambridge: Harvard University). The Harvard Library was not self-supporting either before or after the 1890s. See Lane, "Harvard College Library," p. 621

53. Forman, Heilbron and Weart, *Physics Ca. 1900* pp. 83-89; and Carl G. Bernhard et al., eds., *Science, Technology and Society in the Time of Alfred Nobel* (New York: Pergamon, 1982).

54. See Geiger, *Research Universities*.

55. Yale University, *President's Report* (New Haven: Yale University, 1911) pp. 21-27.

56. Harvard University, *President's Report* (Cambridge: Harvard University, 1901), pp. 34-41. Substantially the same message is repeated by Eliot in his 1905 President's Report (pp. 48-49).

57. Van Hise, "Opportunities," p. 57.

58. Cornell University, *President's Report* (Ithaca, N.Y.: Cornell University, 1910), also summarized in *Science* 32 (1910): 695-701.

59. See Geiger, *Research Universities*.

60. Ibid.

61. Yale University, *Treasurer's Report*, (New Haven: Yale University, 1914), p. 25.

62. Stanford University, *President's Report* (Palo Alto, Cal.: Stanford University, 1921), p. 35.

63. National Research Council, "Funds Available in 1920 in the United States of America for the Encouragement of Scientific Research," comp. Callie Hull, *Bulletin of the National Research Council* 11, 9 (March 1921): 1-82.

64. Geiger, *Research Universities*: chap. 4.

34. Armin O. Leuschner, "The Organization of the Graduate School and Its Relation to the Other Schools of the University," *JAAU* 17 (1915): 41-43. Faculty research committees were advocated as early as 1911, and one was apparently created at Minnesota. *JAAU* (1911): 37, 42. Stanford had adopted arrangements identical to California's by 1920, but allocated only $2,000 for these purposes. Stanford University, *President' Report* (Palo Alto, Cal.: Stanford University, 1921); and see table 2 below.

35. *JAAU* 22 (1920): 49-50.

36. "Report of Committee R," *AAUP Bulletin* 8 (April 1922): 27-35.

37. *The Decennial Publications of the University of Chicago*, 10 vols. (Chicago: University of Chicago Press, 1903-4), 1:41-42.

38. G. Stanley Hall, "The Appointment and Obligations of Graduate Fellows," *JAAU* 8 (1906): 16-38.

39. Leuschner, "Graduate School," p.43.

40. Harvard University, *President's Report* (Cambridge: Harvard University, 1881, 1884) 1881, p. 38; and 1884, pp. 43-44; Edwin H. Hall, "Physics, 1869-1928," in *The Development of Harvard University, 1869-1929*, ed. Samuel Eliot Morison (Cambridge: Harvard University Press, 1930), p. 277; and Charles L. Jackson and Gregory P. Baxter, "Chemistry, 1865-1929," in *The Development of Harvard*, pp. 271-72.

41. Howard S. Miller, *Dollars for Research: Science and Its Patrons in Nineteenth-Century America* (Seattle: University of Washington Press, 1970), pp. 159-62.

42. Harvard University *President's Report* (Cambridge: Harvard University, 1881), p. 40; and William C. Lane, "The Harvard College Library, 1877-1928," in *The Development of Harvard*, pp. 623-24.

43. Harvard University *President's Report* (Cambridge: Harvard University, 1902), p.62. Columbia University, *President's Report* (New York: Columbia University, 1902), pp. 8-18.

44. Waterman T. Hewett, *Cornell University: A History*, 4 vols. (New York: The University Publishing Society, 1905), 2: 66-101.

45. Solon I. Bailey, "Astronomy, 1877-1927," in *The Development of Harvard*, pp. 292-303; and *The Harvard University Catalogue*, 1900 p. 634.

46. Miller, *Dollars for Research*, pp. 98-118

47. William M. Wheeler, "The Bussey Institution, 1871-1929," in *The Development of Harvard*, pp. 508-17.

48. Verne A. Stadtman, *University of California, 1868-1968* (New York: McGraw-Hill, 1970) pp. 206-9.

The Setting and the Problems

Merle Curti

In the first half of the twentieth century man learned many things about himself that he had never known before. Living as he did in an era of earthshaking change, he also learned much that was new about his social environment, past and present. Americans continued to share, as they always had, the important revisions and exciting developments of knowledge regardless of their place of origin. American scholars also made contributions of weight and meaning to the world's expanding knowledge of man and his social environment. No part of the national history in the last half-century is probably so little known to the majority of fairly well informed Americans as the growth of knowledge about man and the society in which he lives. Yet this story, if less sensational and revolutionary than that of the natural sciences, is no less important in terms of today and tomorrow. For it is generally agreed that man's fate now largely rests on what he does with his knowledge of the physical universe. What he does with it is in turn closely related to the status and character of the social sciences and the humanities, broadly conceived.[1]

Properly speaking, the development of knowledge in the natural sciences, the social studies, and the humanities is of one piece, for each influenced, and in turn was affected by, the others. We are here concerned, however, with the development of scholarship in the social sciences and the humanities in America in the past fifty years. Now scholarship may be defined as high competence in a delimited field of conscious and sustained inquiry for related facts, valid generalizations, and workable truths. To have full meaning, the development of scholarship must be placed within the larger context of major tendencies in every sphere of living, both in the United States and in the rest of the world. But before considering ways in which the general milieu affected such things as the support and organization of scholarship, the changing status of the scholar, and the prolonged debate about his social responsibilities, let us see what some of the major tendencies in scholarship actually were, and how they can at least in part be explained.

I

At the opening of the twentieth century both the humanities and the social sciences rested on a tradition of western scholarship in which history, political economy, philology, archaeology, and philosophy enjoyed special prestige. The succeeding fifty years witnessed a steady development in all these fields.[2] But each did not

America, and the Slavic lands. Economic, political, and cultural, as well as geographical studies and international relations, also owed much to the growing world interests of the United States. The First and Second World Wars, important factors in the consolidation of American nationalism, encouraged historians to reëxamine the American past and to help rewrite the history of the world beyond our gates. War also provided an impulse to the study of propaganda techniques and public opinion, a field that also owed something to the necessity of rethinking the meaning of democracy in a new era. These are only a few examples of the many ways in which changing emphases in scholarly pursuits reflected changing conditions in the country and in the world.

Another outstanding development of the last fifty years has been a renewal of the broad scholarly ideals of the eighteenth and early nineteenth centuries. In the last two decades many scholars have, in thinking of knowledge as a whole, reacted against its narrow compartmentalization. Buckle's contention that the chief significance of any field of knowledge lies not at its center but at its periphery has been illustrated again and again in the accomplishments of scholars who have crossed conventional boundaries. From these crossings have issued sociological jurisprudence, agricultural economics, the sociology of knowledge, social psychology, and the history of science. In addition to these crossings of fields, the second quarter of the century witnessed the integration of related elements in many fields of knowledge. The child study movement, for example, while launched much earlier by G. Stanley Hall, expanded to comprise all knowledge about infants and children. Studies of the geographic and cultural areas of the world, of the regions in the United States, and, more recently, of American civilization itself, furnished other examples of this tendency to develop interdisciplinary syntheses.[8]

Another striking feature of American scholarship during the past half-century has been the more serious and extensive application of the methods of the natural sciences to the humanities. In fact, this became a dominant tendency in these disciplines. If such applications were carried to an excessive point, as many critics in the later decades of the period argued, none could deny that they had yielded important corrections, fresh insights, and even major discoveries.[4]

The application of certain techniques of the natural sciences to the social field likewise bore fruit. As a result the emphasis shifted from the older philosophical, a priori, and abstract approach to that of observation, analysis, control, and in a few cases, to actual pre-

keep the relative position it held early in the century. Philology, for example, attracted in 1950 a smaller fraction of scholars than it once had, while literary history and criticism enlisted a greater portion. No field of inquiry could boast more thrilling developments than archaeology. Yet even so, this well-established field scarcely enjoyed the relative preëminence in the scholarly world it had had fifty years earlier. Philosophical studies, despite some brilliant contributions and displays of militant vigor as the period ended, only partly succeeded in meeting the challenge offered by developments in mathematics and the natural sciences.

New fields of study, only slightly cultivated in the United States of 1900, in later decades loomed large in the literature of scholarship. These included art history and criticism, musicology, cultural history, area studies concerned with the Slavic world, Latin America, the Far East, and Africa, and the newer social sciences, especially anthropology, sociology, and social psychology. Psychology is a special case in point. At the turn of the century its foundations as a natural science were well laid in the laboratories of the Old World and the New; but it was still tied to philosophy and subordinated to it. By 1950 psychology not only enjoyed a place as a leading discipline — it overshadowed philosophy. Psychology can best be considered as a natural science; but one of its branches, social psychology, which came to enjoy growing importance after World War I, must of course figure in any account of the social disciplines.

It is not hard to find reasons for these shifts in emphasis and for these new developments. Even after giving due credit to the influence of comparable scholarly tendencies abroad, it is plain that American conditions played an important role. Interest in music, the fine arts, and literature reflected the increasing wealth, leisure, and cultural sophistication of growing cities. The rise of musicology, art history, and belletristic studies followed. So too the social sciences developed rapidly in response to the requirements of the new industrial civilization. Banking, public finance, taxation, labor relations, race relations, social legislation, public administration — all these fields of practical adjustment posed insistent questions. In an attempt to answer them statistical methods were more and more refined and put to use, and newer branches of social science appeared or expanded. To name but a few, cultural anthropology, rural and urban sociology, economic history, and industrial and social psychology received great impetus from the needs of a quickly changing society. Expanding missionary enterprises and considerations of trade, war, and America's new role as a world power, stimulated directly or indirectly studies of peoples in the Far East, Latin

to whose initiative and labors much of the international organization of scholarship was due, has reminded us of the role of these bodies in helping to reconcile scholars of various nationalities, a necessary step if intellectuals were to learn from each other and to help build the republic of letters in a peaceful world. Such international associations, often with the help of American foundations, initiated and carried forward scores of important scholarly undertakings. Americans also worked as experts in the intellectual enterprises of the League of Nations.[8]

The totalitarian onslaught further helped to reverse the traditional American dependence on European scholarship. Many gifted scholars from the Old World sought a haven in the United States. The Emergency Committee on Aid of Displaced Foreign Scholars, organized in 1933, reported ten years later that it had helped 269 foreign scholars in finding positions.

Observers, impressed by the enriching effects of this migration on American intellectual life, recalled the impact of the fall of Constantinople and the revocation of the Edict of Nantes on the flowering of scholarship in the lands to which refugees fled in earlier centuries." With the breakdown of Europe in the midst of dislocation and war, the United States in the 1940's became the chief center of learning in the world. American universities now began to contribute, along with the foundations, to the rehabilitation of European centers of learning. If the United States is thought of as essentially European in culture, the geographical shift was perhaps of no great point. But if it is regarded as the center of a new civilization, then the widely recognized prestige of American scholarship could rightly be considered as a major factor in modern cultural history.

Wars, revolutions, dislocations, mass poverty, and totalitarianism were not, of course, the sole factors in altering the traditional relationship between American and European scholarship. The advances that were made and the current eminence of American scholarship owed much to two things. The first was the national talent for organization. The second was the wealth that flowed into our universities and other research centers.

II

The period from the First World War to the mid-century point saw the American scholar functioning more and more through

diction of future social behavior. Thanks to the case study, the life history, the community survey, the controlled interview, and the use of statistical techniques, scholarship in the social disciplines increasingly resulted in relatively objective studies of the behavior of institutions and social groups. The scientific approach also undermined the older assumption that man is separate from nature. That he is a part of the natural order itself came to be largely taken for granted.[5]

The assumption that man is part of nature led to the concept of culture, one of the most important and emancipating of all twentieth-century contributions to knowledge in the social field. The culture, or totality of institutions, adjustments, and values binding a distinctive social group together, was recognized as molding personality and explaining variants in social behavior in the many cultures of the world. Human nature was thus seen to develop only in relation to a particular culture, and to be susceptible to change as the culture changed. The relativistic and pragmatic aspects of the culture concept which resembled rising theories in the physical sciences, promised, if fully and widely appreciated, to emancipate man from many age-old superstitions and prejudices and to provide a realistic basis for improved social relations.

In exploiting new scientific methods and assumptions, scholars also occupied themselves with methodological problems in their specific disciplines. At the same time they came to question previous assumptions upon which their work had been based, and began to think anew on the relationship of their specific disciplines to the total framework of knowledge. In short, they became concerned with the general problems of a philosophy of knowledge.[6]

These and other advances in American scholarship owed much to Europe and European trained scholars. But the striking fact has been the gradual reversal in the traditional debtor-creditor relationship between American and European scholars. Early in the present century European commentators began, though grudgingly, to acknowledge the contributions of men like Willard Gibbs, William James, Franz Boas, J. H. Breasted, and G. L. Kittredge.[7] The devastating effects of the First World War provided American scholars a challenging opportunity for leadership in the international community of learning. Americans took the initiative in the postwar years in establishing international unions of scholars—the International Committee of Historical Sciences, the Permanent International Congress of Linguists, and the International Union of Academies, among many others. Waldo G. Leland, an academic statesman

organizations. The major national organizations of humanistic and social science scholars, all well organized before 1917, became increasingly important factors in initiating and planning research, in providing for the dissemination of findings, and in organizing scholarship generally. Specialization within the larger fields embraced by the national professional organizations resulted in the formation of regional and functional groups within the frame of the older national organizations. Scholars from the various disciplines, finding a common interest, organized the Medieval Academy, the Byzantine Academy, the Oriental Institute, each with its officers, committees, research programs, and organs of publication. Following the example of the natural scientists, who established in 1917 the National Research Council to facilitate the pooling of resources in the war effort, the American Council of Learned Societies and the Social Science Research Council emerged after the war. These Councils were federations of related national professional organizations. In large measure they confined themselves to research planning, to the improvement of research techniques, to stimulating and supporting new interdisciplinary investigations, and to obtaining funds from the foundations for the support of specific enterprises in the form of fellowships, grants-in-aid, and other subsidies.[10]

Perhaps of even greater import were the surveys undertaken by the learned councils. These were of many kinds and varieties. The role of research in educational institutions, the status of the research scholar, and the financing of research, all were surveyed and commented upon by the various associations. It is impossible to say how widely those responsible for research activities used these surveys, but they must have been of considerable value to scholarship in America.[11]

The foundations themselves, led by the various Carnegie and Rockefeller organizations, did not limit their functions to providing grants to the American Council of Learned Societies, the Social Science Research Council, the national professional organizations of social scientists and humanistic scholars, the several universities, and libraries actively engaged in research programs. The foundations in all cases did approve or disapprove proposals for grants-in-aid of specific researches. But they also initiated projects and sought for creative scholars with new ideas.[12]

The constructive contributions of the professional organizations and the foundations to scholarship in the humanities and the social sciences can hardly be overemphasized. They provided the initiative or support for such important projects as the comprehensive study of the Mayan culture area, the excavations in the Near and Middle East conducted by Breasted and his associates, the Indus River valley excavations, the *Dictionary of American English*, the *Linguistic Atlas*, and the *Dictionary of Middle English*, to name only a few. It would be hard to overestimate the indebtedness to the foundations, directly or indirectly, of American contributions to musicology, the history of ideas, art criticism, and studies of the Far East, Latin America, and the Slavic lands. In all these areas the advantages of long-range planned research, conducted coöperatively on a large scale, have been amply demonstrated. In addition, the Councils and foundations provided facilities for the publication of new findings and for the training of young research scholars. Concepts and approaches deemed both novel and significant resulted from American emphases on coöperation, cross-fertilization, and organization.

But it became increasingly clear that councils, committees, professional organizations, and planned coöperative research were not open sesames to prosperity in learning. Rich returns, as is well known, often followed from unexpected directions. Many scholars continued to work best alone, unencumbered by the imperatives of committees and formal coöperation. Thoughtful authorities came to wonder how effective research planning could ever be in areas of pure theory.[13]

The increasing influence of these professional organizations raised still other questions. A leading official of one of the great foundations confessed that these agencies had sometimes overstimulated certain fields, spoiled talented scholars, and contributed to an undue emphasis on scientific techniques in humanistic studies. Moreover, in the first decades of the century, leading liberals maintained that the foundations sometimes showed prejudice in failing to support investigations that in their opinion might result in weakening the prevailing economic order.[14] Liberals also argued that the assumption by the foundations of responsibility for and direction of research discouraged government from supporting investigation in needed fields. The growing tendency of the foundations to work through professional scholars and to develop wise procedures lessened in time the force of such criticisms. But the indictment of the foundations nevertheless left an uneasy feeling in many minds.[15]

The increasing interest of business itself in research also affected the organization and support of investigation. Beginning in the last decade of the nineteenth century, a few large corporations systematically sponsored research in theoretical as well as in *ad hoc* technical problems. Frederick Taylor and others provided leadership in enlarging technological studies to include investigations of workers' efficiency and labor-management relations. Increasingly business firms sponsored researches in industrial psychology and in the pertinent fields of economics.[16] In the second quarter of the century the movement for the study of business history was also well under way. Here again, as in the case of the foundations, such developments raised the problem of freedom of research. In part, business set the problems, determined conditions under which investigation was conducted, and controlled the use of findings.

No chapter in the history of the organization and support of research could be more important than one dealing with the role of government in the support of social science and the humanities as well as the natural sciences. In the nineteenth century the interest of state and federal governments in research was expressed in exploring expeditions within the United States itself and overseas, in the subsidies to the Smithsonian Institution, in the state and federal geological surveys, in the expanding activities of the Bureau of Standards and the Census Bureau, and in the undertakings of the Department of Agriculture, both in Washington and in the experimental stations established at the state and federal supported colleges of agriculture.[17] The state universities, led by Michigan and Wisconsin, also proved to be increasingly important agencies for the flow of public funds into research in many fields.[18]

But the great era of government supported and directed research belongs to the twentieth century. While much of this continued to fall within the field of the natural sciences, an increasing amount involved the social sciences and even the humanities. This expansion resulted from many influences: from the problems posed by an ever more complex industrial civilization, from the exigencies of war. It is impossible here even to suggest the range and significance of government supported research, or the many agencies and institutions concerned with it. In a sense, however, the Library of Congress symbolized the development. By 1950 it housed and serviced the greatest collection of books, microfilms, manuscripts, and documents in the world, provided scholars with all sorts of aids, and initiated and conducted far-reaching projects in many fields of knowledge.

The great depression of 1929 and subsequent years occasioned a vast program of government support for scholarly activities in the social and humanistic fields. A good proportion of the three thou-sand projects the WPA sponsored in 1937–38 at the cost of $124,000,-000 fell within the fields of economics, sociology, history, anthropology, folk art, music and literature, philology, and related subjects. The professional organizations of scholars, the universities, the libraries, and other research centers in sponsoring the WPA cultural projects provided standards for competent execution and insured a commendable degree of freedom from political and economic pressures in the actual conduct of work. Nevertheless critics, especially in the conservative camp, contended that many of the research projects spoke the New Deal idiom. While this was less true than many maintained, still the widespread government support and overall direction of research raised the problem of objectives on the policy-making level. What, after all, were the considerations that governed the acceptance and rejection of suggestions for research, how representative of the great body of scholars were those who made the decisions, and how were the projects themselves related to professional interest?[19]

Although both the First and the Second World Wars in many ways interfered with scholarly progress by deflecting support and personnel to military purposes, both wars increased the role of government in the organization and support of science. Government and in some degree the public itself recognized that research was not mere abstruse busy-work conducted in ivory towers but that it was a major source of strength deserving of more generous support than it had hitherto received. Scholars in every field of the social sciences and humanities discovered in the First World War that their services were needed. This was even more true in the Second World War. Government agencies called scholars in many fields to Washington as consultants. Never before had specialized knowledge played so large a role in the making and execution of policies on almost every level. The federal capital became the intellectual center of the nation. Both wars, and especially the second, accelerated investigations in many fields, demonstrated new uses of existing knowledge, and proved that research and scholarship were as necessary to war as to peace. Military and naval history, to cite a single example, flourished as never before, thanks to vast sums spent by the government in the writing of the history of the armed forces.[20]

However important and desirable all this government support of research was, it nevertheless again raised the question of the freedom of scholars to choose the types of investigation they deemed important. He who paid the piper called the tune. Further, the problem of control became sharply focused in the discussions at the end of the Second World War regarding the nature of the proposed National Science Foundation. Proponents of the social sciences pointed out the great need for more extensive and intensive researches in their field, in the public interest. One segment of public opinion expressed fear that such support might channel investigations into controversial fields, by which these "conservatives" meant "radical" areas. Groups left of the center on the other hand feared that government support might rule out important projects unacceptable to the directors of the prevailing order.[21]

The growing role in research of the foundations, of business, and of government, raised many other issues. In competing for gifted men and women in research and scholarship, government and business posed many problems for those interested in recruiting, training, and keeping young investigators in university work and in explorations not strictly ad hoc in character. Important research continued, of course, to be done at the universities; but more and more it moved to other centers, to government, business, libraries, and museums. Increasingly the graduate schools prepared young men and women for the practice of the professions rather than for research careers. Many believed with Howard Mumford Jones that the graduate schools in trying to train both for research and for professional practice in law, medicine, and teaching failed to do either adequately. Too often the research training program did not rise above the level of collecting data which the investigator could not evaluate and interpret with any high degree of critical imagination. Yet equipped chiefly with such techniques the young Ph.D. embarked on college teaching, unprepared to enrich youth with treasures from the great cultural tradition or to guide it to constructive roles in society by acquainting it with the new movements of thought and the current social and economic realities.[22]

Various suggestions for the solution of this problem filled the pages of educational journals.[23] Howard Mumford Jones himself proposed to gear graduate programs to general education. Chancellor Robert Hutchins, forgetting perhaps the many significant contributions to knowledge resulting from the American conjoining of theory and practice, deplored the results of the effort to combine professional training and research. In his view these functions might best be entirely separated in different institutions. The halfcentury ended with the whole discussion still active.[24]

Closely associated with the national fondness for organization so well exemplified in modern American scholarship has been the

extraordinary development of its tools—of bibliographies, catalogues, finding lists, dictionaries, encyclopedias, microfilm, and microprint. European scholars have both admired and criticized the development. Whatever the force of their varied reactions, it is perhaps no overstatement to say that in the social and humanistic fields the new techniques of microfilm and microprint, to name but two, may prove as significant in the ultimate effects on scholarship as did the invention of printing itself. The late Robert Binkley expressed the hope that the new methods of mass-collecting might democratize and decentralize scholarship by making possible mutually advantageous coöperation between amateurs and professionals. Another depression, if one comes, may test that assumption and hope.[25]

No discussion of the organization and support of scholarship can properly ignore the problem of dissemination and communication of the results of research. In advocating the responsibility of scholars to communicate their findings, writers ranged over the whole question of the status of the man of learning in society and his responsibilities to the public, a problem to be discussed subsequently in this essay. Here it may be said that the professional organizations, the Councils, and the university presses assumed major responsibility for the dissemination and communication of the findings of scholarship. After the First World War, the rapid development of the older adult education movement (Chautauqua, summer schools, university extension, and the semipopular lecture) posed new problems for scholars. A few, including James Breasted and Charles and Mary Beard, made the best-seller list with their well-informed and readable syntheses. Many more shared their scholarship with a limited audience of nonspecialists who read such periodicals as the *Yale Review*, the *South Atlantic Quarterly*, the *Virginia Quarterly*, the *Antioch Review*, the *Pacific Spectator*, and the *American Scholar*. The university presses increasingly encouraged scholars to present their findings in a sufficiently attractive literary and nontechnical form to enlist the favor of the generally well educated man and woman.[26] New agencies in the second quarter of the century—including the Foreign Policy Association, the Council of Foreign Relations, and summer seminars (such as the one held at Princeton in 1935 on Arabic and Islamic studies) also served an important function in publicizing the work of scholars. So did Colonial Williamsburg, which offered archaeological and historical knowledge to its millions of visitors.

The movement for more widespread and effective dissemination of knowledge involved certain assumptions: that the public really wanted to know the results of scholarly inquiry, that communication would enlighten the citizenry on the great issues before them, and that a more general appreciation of the nature of scholarship would strengthen its underpinnings.[27] No body of scholars made greater effort than the Americans to communicate to the public its specialized knowledge in forms comprehensible to the average man and woman.

James Harvey Robinson, who made his reputation in research in medieval history, seemed to some fellow scholars almost a traitor when he became a widely-read popularizer with an emphasis on man's ability and duty to continue to change his institutions and his thinking. Again, popularization at times proved disconcerting to the more traditional segment of the scholarly world. Newspapers and periodicals sometimes unduly sensationalized an item of scholarship and put pressure on scholars to give opinions about matters on which they could not speak competently. But only a minority succumbed to the temptation to pontificate. Another criticism of popularization — in part justified — was that it led to oversimplification and superficiality. Despite misgivings, an ever larger number followed James Harvey Robinson in seeking to humanize knowledge, aware, as Francis Bacon was, that scholarship is not "a couch, whereupon to rest a searching and restless spirit . . . or a tower of state, for a proud mind to raise itself upon; or a fort, for strife and contention," but rather "a rich storehouse for the glory of the Creator," and the relief of man's estate."[28]

The distinction that American scholarship came to enjoy in the first half of the twentieth century rested in part, then, on generous support from industry, government, and the foundations, on cross-fertilization and formal coöperation, and on the union of theory and practice which developed under American pressures and conditions. It owed much to the prevalence of an atmosphere of freedom of investigation and communication — although the new developments raised questions regarding freedom, questions to be probed in the later part of this essay. But the achievements of American scholarship must be related to criticisms that both Europeans and Americans made of it.

III

Many at home and abroad regarded American scholarship as stronger in quantitative aspects than in qualitative. To some it seemed assimilative, rather than reflective and discriminating. Insofar as they admitted the truth of this indictment, observers laid the shortcomings at the door of graduate training, where the emphasis seemed to rest too heavily on the acquisition of techniques, on turning out researchers in mass quantities, and on discouraging if not crushing the few bold and original minds.[29] To meet these defects, universities and especially foundations provided for post-doctoral fellowships. Dean Andrew West of Princeton pioneered in developing a graduate school limited to a small fellowship of scholars, in which intellectual stimulus, general culture, and broad learning were to militate against a narrow overspecialized emphasis on technical research and mere survival as hurdle after hurdle was surmounted.[30] The Harvard Society of Fellows was another experiment in this direction.

Other critics held that scholars in the humanities and social disciplines too often misapplied to their work the theories and techniques of the natural sciences. In many cases, the argument ran, these were inadequate and inappropriate. The humanities as a result were dehumanized, rendered sterile and pitifully trivial, while the social studies were bogged down with scientific methodologies which robbed them of the philosophical approach and the meaningful orientation. Such was the indictment, in the barest outline.

These convictions stimulated the appearance of a vast polemical literature which mounted in bulk during the thirties and forties. Excessive emphasis on fact-finding, on overspecialization, on trivial investigations, on antiquarianism provided the theme songs of the critics. They deplored the alleged assumption that all facts are equal, that research may be divorced from a broad cultural setting. They indicted the multitude of fact finders, with their mystical faith that if enough bricks were made, a great structure would be reared.[31] Now and again a scholar who appreciated the partial truth in the indictment struck a more balanced view. Hans Zinsser, for one, reminded the critics that a multitude must clear the underbrush if a few, possessed of great vision, were to survey the roads to new unknown areas.[32]

Other critics of American scholarship attributed its so-called inadequate concern for synthesis and larger relationships to the multitude of pressures to which the scholar was subject. He was not left alone to think through the meaning of his materials, to relate his findings to the great achievements of earlier scholars in his own and in related fields. He was bogged down with too many administrative duties, too many committees, too much teaching. All this, plus the demands his duties as a citizen and his obligations to popularize his learning to a larger public made on him, led, many believed, to fragmented, unimportant publications. At the same time critics also made their targets the inadequacies of the scholar's training, his exclusiveness, and the resulting narrowness of his output.[33]

It became increasingly common to deplore the dullness of American scholarly publications, their lack of clarity and beauty of literary expression. While most historians endeavored to make history conform more closely to the canons of social science some gallantly tried to restore it as craftsmanship to the great literary tradition. In the field of literary scholarship critics cried for grace and gaiety, for proportion and verve. Nor was this all. Jacques Barzun argued that scholars generally depended on out-of-date points of view and even discredited interpretations in the peripheral fields surrounding their own highly narrow specialties.[34] As the half-century ended both laymen and natural scientists expressed dismay at finding that the social sciences and humanities, after all that had been done, were still so unsystematized, so unsure, and so indeterminate.

Yet any such verdict must be qualified. Judged even by traditional European standards American scholarship in the first decades of the twentieth century was substantial in quantity and competent in quality. At its best, humanistic scholarship certainly ranked with the most notable in contemporary Europe. In the field of the social sciences, Americans were truly creating a vigorous, original, and significant body of knowledge. But American and European scholars alike were often misled by the tendency of American scholars to be self-critical, to belittle the emphasis on fact-finding and the frequent failure to relate new discoveries to traditional knowledge and to larger perspectives. In point of fact, one of the great strengths of American scholarship was its extraordinary capacity for self-criticism, its humility, and its appreciation of the learning of other lands. In general, Europeans failed to understand this, nor was it adequately taken into account by many Americans themselves.

Moreover, it was seldom apparent to European scholars, and rarely so to Americans, that scholarship in the second quarter of the twentieth century was experiencing a redefinition and a reorientation. Profound changes in the economy and culture invited scholars to consider the relation of their work to contemporary problems and tensions, to assume a larger and more immediate responsibility to the social order of which they were a part. The responsiveness of many to this urgent call was in part explicable in terms of the value traditionally attached to humanitarianism, to the useful, to the

pragmatic. At the same time this pressure on scholars to shape their work in terms of social needs enhanced the difficulty of approaching that disinterested objectivity and universality on which scholarship had properly set so high a value.

In relating the specific finding to an immediate problem or need, in crossing traditional barriers between fields of learning, in experimenting with new techniques and with coöperative approaches, American scholars were in truth pioneering. Many did not fully sense this fact, and deplored some of its implications. That it was possible for so many to move into a relatively new area of application, explains both the self-criticism here and the unfavorable view which Europeans took toward the American performance — a view which often obscured the increasingly important contributions made in the United States to knowledge in the more traditional sense.

IV

Recent decades have seen a marked weakening of the tradition of the scholar as a figure isolated from the society in which he lived. But even before the twentieth-century, scholars devoted their specialized knowledge and gifts to solving the pressing problems of society. Long before Fichte summoned German pundits to help free and strengthen the fatherland, New England Puritans, in the tradition of medieval scholars, used their knowledge in the fight against such enemies of Zion in the Wilderness as Catholics, Indians, and witches! Yet with some point Emerson in the early nineteenth century indicted American scholarship for its Alexandrian dependence on the books of other scholars, for its indifference to the living problems of nature and man. Toward the end of the century two other Harvard men spoke their minds. Wendell Phillips excoriated his alma mater for having aligned itself with the forces of privilege in ignoring the needs of the oppressed and the unfortunate. James Russell Lowell belittled the picayunish scholarship that divorced itself from the larger culture and the larger life.

At the very time that Phillips and Lowell were making their indictments of a "sterile" American scholarship, the western state universities were heroically, if often ineffectively, struggling with the problem of relating the higher learning to current human needs. With justification President Charles Kendall Adams of Wisconsin declared in 1897 that the indictment of the Harvard scholars could not have been fairly leveled at the state universities.[35]

The call for scholars to concern themselves with living public issues did not leave the private institutions untouched. Woodrow Wilson, David Starr Jordan, William Rainey Harper, Nicholas Murray Butler, and Charles W. Eliot all sounded the same trumpet call.[36] A growing number of scholars lent their talents to the solution of public questions; the Wisconsin Idea in the first decade of the present century was only the most striking example of the scholarly concern with current issues. In the state and federal agencies a growing number of university scientists and social scientists found opportunities to put their knowledge to work in the solution of problems associated with the new industrial economy.

In the First World War scholars in the humanities as well as in sister disciplines were called on for help. They did help, and with a new sense of exhilaration and satisfaction part compensatory for the passivity and remoteness from actualities that many scholars had felt.[37] The depression also saw a national mobilization of the scholar as a vital part of society. Scholars shouldered new responsibilities in the public interest. In those years a growing number battled in public office for the country. Charles E. Merriam, William E. Dodd, Wilbur Cross, T. V. Smith, Rexford Tugwell, Robert Morss Lovett, Edwin Witte, and Paul H. Douglas are only a few examples. And throughout the land scholars who stayed at their desks talked, wrote, and lectured differently because of a new concern for the forgotten man and for neglected areas of work that might help solve his problems.[38] The Second World War, of course, carried the tendency further.

Thus the secularization of scholarship moved rapidly ahead. The old-time scholar, dressing and behaving differently from most folk, whom more worldly friends regarded with the same pity and admiration that medieval knights and merchants must have shown the monks, gave way to a new type who dressed, talked, and acted very much as a man of the world. Like other men of affairs, he struggled for prestige and success in a highly competitive profession, fought for a greater measure of economic security, and increasingly immersed himself in the main stream of events.[39]

Yet far too often this struggle for status immeasurably hindered the fulfillment of his true function as a scholar. In addition, far too often his efforts at relative economic security were doomed to failure. Being a member of a profession which, theoretically at least, did not and could not measure its results in pecuniary gain, the scholar often found himself in a state of financial embarrassment. Like other members of the white collar classes in America he found that security in an economic sense became even more distant during de-

pression periods.[40] While the scholar was usually a member of some sort of organization he found it difficult to use that organization as an economic bargaining weapon. In some educational institutions, it is true, some faculty members joined a teachers' union which was dedicated to making the economic status of the profession more attractive. But these efforts generally were not effective at the college and university level.

Despite the recognition by the lay public that scholarship was a national resource, Americans did not give the scholar the place which classical Athens and prerevolutionary China or even contemporary Europe and England awarded him. Indeed, many looked on the scholar, especially the social scientist, as a crackpot theorist if not a downright menace. Thus, for example, Frederick Prince spoke for many fellow businessmen in declaring that "professors are one of the chief curses of the country. . . . They talk too much. Most professors are a bunch of cowards and meddlers. . . . You have only to think back over the last ten years to realize the difficulties we have been drawn into through professors. The sooner we get away from their influence, the better." [41]

V

Although at no time in any culture has the scholar's freedom been divorced from the broader aspects of freedom or the lack of it in the society as a whole, the issue has become more sharply focused in twentieth-century America than ever before. The reasons are obvious. The more general participation of the scholar in public life made him even more obviously dependent on public support and approval than he had seemed when he kept largely aloof in his ivory tower. That participation also made the public more sensitive to what the scholar said and did, especially in matters explicitly affecting the general interest. New forces and pressures sharpened the confines of the area of free discussion and action in general and academic freedom as part of this. As the old question of orthodox theology versus modern science retreated or disappeared, mounting tensions in the relations between business, labor, and agriculture set in. Associated with these were conflicts arising over the new world role America was playing, accentuated by participation in two world wars and by a grave struggle with Soviet Russia.

The 1890's had witnessed several threats to the freedom of academic scholars who questioned the economic status quo. Events in the first decade and a half of the twentieth century suggested that it was no less dangerous then for a university professor to speak and write in favor of measures deemed "socialistic" or "radical." The danger was brought home in 1914 when the University of Pennsylvania dismissed Scott Nearing, a popular professor of economics, for his socialist writings and activities. When America plunged into the First World War, the dismissal of faculty members who opposed that action and their persecution at the hands of an hysterical public, emphasized anew the importance of the whole issue of academic freedom within the larger confines of the question of the civil liberties in the society as a whole.[42] The rise of Communist Russia and the fears it aroused in conservative circles in the 1920's created a sensitive area for academicians left of center. Depression augmented the potential threat to academic freedom not only in reducing the economic security of scholars along with millions of other Americans, but in focusing attention on those who lent their talents to the attempted solution of the nation's problems. As economic distress deepened, the writings and actions of the scholar took on an added significance and became more closely scrutinized. Sometimes such scrutiny resulted in loyalty oaths and in crusades for the censorship of textbooks.[43]

Finally, the advance of totalitarianism abroad, America's entrance into World War II, and the ensuing cold war with Russia, sharpened the issue of academic freedom. It became increasingly clear that if a free society was to exist in a period of reliance on military power, then the freedom of the scholar must be maintained. At least a segment of American scholars felt a deep responsibility for preserving freedom in America.

Early in 1913 a small group of scholars representing some eight major universities responded to the call of Lovejoy, Dewey, and others to meet in Baltimore to discuss the advisability of organizing an association of university professors dedicated to the exploration in a democratic fashion of the common problems of the universities, as a means of realizing more effectively, in conjunction with officials and the public, the aims of higher education. Thus was launched the American Association of University Professors. From the start the issue of academic freedom loomed large in the discussions and activities of the new organization, although it also gave much attention to the related problem of tenure and security, to professional ethics, and to the maintenance of the highest possible standards in research, instruction, and public service.[44]

The report prepared early in the history of the AAUP by the Committee on Academic Freedom and Tenure (Committee A) reflected the basic position of the Association on academic freedom and continued to guide it in this sphere. The Committee assumed that progress toward a higher civilization would follow from the continued advancement of human knowledge, from its dissemination, and from its use by experts in the service of the public. Its position on academic freedom rested on these general assumptions. The Committee maintained that the scholar could effectively function only in an atmosphere of freedom, whether in inquiry and research, in teaching, or in extramural utterance and action. Feeling that the first phase was everywhere in a sound condition, the Committee devoted itself to the latter two aspects of academic freedom. It distinguished between private colleges created for specific purposes and those institutions which were public in nature. The latter comprised not only the state universities but all those that appealed to the public for support.

The Committee maintained that if education was the cornerstone of progress, then the scholar's peculiar social function required him to reveal the results of research to fellow specialists, to students, and to the general public "without fear or favor." If the scholar was to be useful to society, society must have confidence in his disinterestedness. Hence the scholar was in no sense comparable to an employee in a business firm. The academic family must police its own ranks, lest this be done by less competent bodies. Such policing implied a sense of responsibility on the part of the scholar to his institution and to society as well as to the truth. He must in taking account of the immaturity of his students not try to indoctrinate them; he must rather stimulate them to think. In facing the public, the scholar should try to avoid hasty, intemperate statements; but it was neither possible nor desirable "to deprive a college professor of the political rights vouchsafed to every citizen." Thus it was not proper to prohibit scholars from speaking on controversial questions outside the university even when these questions fell outside their specialties. Nor was it proper to condemn academicians for lending active support to organized movements which they believed to be in the public interest.[45]

In later years succeeding presidents of the Association and succeeding reports of Committee A restated and amplified the original report. But the Association did not content itself with mere words. It defined over the years the conditions of good tenure and of proper relations between professors, administrators, governing bodies, and interest groups beyond university campuses. It is impossible to outline or even to mention the host of investigations which Committee A conducted at various institutions where charges of violation of academic freedom were made. These have been many. Yet it should be noted that most of the violations of academic freedom and tenure concerned the teaching of undergraduates or the extramural activities of the professor.

After careful investigation the Committee recommended the censuring of administrations in which the governing body failed to respect the AAUP code of academic freedom and tenure. Whether such action really achieved the desired result has been a matter of controversy. This much can be said in regard to these investigations. Usually the violation of academic freedom was attended with publicity in which the administration side of the picture dominated, if it did not monopolize, newspaper accounts. By the time Committee A had made its investigation, written its report, and tried to disseminate its findings, the harm had been done. The sober careful analysis of the reports failed to make good headlines and were all too often ignored by the newspapers; and the public, unaware of the findings, continued to entertain the original impression created by the first headlines emanating from administration sources. Thus in actuality many censured administrations went their way largely unaffected by adverse AAUP reports.

Perhaps at no time is the difficulty in maintaining academic freedom greater than in war, for patriotism and scholarship have found themselves at opposite poles as well as close supplements. In 1916 Committee A elaborated its position regarding the problem of the professor who did not accept the war as wise and desirable and necessary. That position hardly conformed with the strong stand taken in 1915 in behalf of academic freedom.[47]

With the war clouds gathering in Europe in 1939, the Association, taking note of the abridgments to intellectual freedom in 1917 and 1918, adopted resolutions calling for a sustained effort to preserve our liberties. After the country entered the war, Committee A again called upon members of the Association not to forget their role as scholars while fulfilling patriotic duties. Only if scholars continued to maintain the critical attitude, to ask basic questions, to resist drifting with the tide, could America win the only war worth winning—the war to make peace and freedom possible in the world. "If the freedom we cherish is indeed basic to our scholarship, is it too much to ask that it inspire us to act justly in a perilous time?"[48]

As late as 1944 the Committee, seeing no reason to modify its stand, maintained that events had proved its wisdom. Linking academic freedom with freedom of thought for which the war was

being waged, the Committee stated that "it would be folly to draw a boundary line across the area of freedom."[49] Never before had there been greater necessity for unbiased information than there now was to meet the great problems of the postwar world. Committee A and the Association could look with a certain pride on the record during the second world conflict.

While the need in the postwar years for accurate information remained greater than ever, the pressures against such inquiry and dissemination exceeded anything that was felt during the war itself. The cold war with Soviet Russia resulted not only in purges of Communists and Communist sympathizers from faculties, but also in clamor for restrictions on academic freedom and in new loyalty oaths. The University of Washington attracted nation-wide publicity when three faculty members were discharged largely on the ground of political affiliations. The report of Committee A had not appeared by the last day of 1952; but many believed that in the report of this case would be found a key to future policies in the face of new pressures threatening to undermine academic freedom in America.

But there were other forces seeking to hamper the pursuit of freedom by American scholars. In the 1920's fundamentalists sought to restrict the teaching of theories of evolution. A special committee set up by AAUP on Freedom of Teaching in Science took strong ground. "We are never absolutely certain as to what constitutes truth, but if there is any method of insuring that what is taught is true better than that of giving investigators and teachers utmost freedom to discover and proclaim the truth as they see it, that method has never been discovered. If those who know most about a subject sometimes decide wrongly, matters are not likely to be mended by putting the decision into the hands of those who know less."[50] In another report two years later, the Association backed up its committee which maintained that the real issue in this question was "whether or not we wish to make an intellectual slave of every teacher in a state-supported institution and to force him to square his teaching with the dogmas of any group which succeeds in getting legislative protection for its doctrines."[51]

There were other notable stands for academic freedom. In 1928 the Federal Trade Commission revealed that numerous scholars and academicians had accepted emoluments from the large private utilities for their services in writing and teaching on the subject of power. In 1931, after long consideration, the Association went on record with a statement of principle to the effect that "no university professor who receives a fee or other compensation from any person or association interested in public discussion or testimony respecting a particular question of public importance should take part in such testimony, without making public the fact that he receives a compensation therefor, and the name of the person or association paying him said compensation."[52] The Association also viewed with disapproval the campaign of the National Association of Manufacturers in 1939 to censor school textbooks on the ground that the extracting of certain "objectionable" passages from textbooks, constituted a dangerous precedent in giving false impressions to laymen of the contents of the books.[53]

The AAUP also sharply criticized the enactment by twenty-two states of legislation requiring teachers to take oaths of loyalty. In 1936 Committee A pointedly asked: "Are teachers alone to be singled out for such treatment? . . . Loyalty is something one lives, and not something one professes, in spite of views to the contrary held by misguided patriots and owners of low-class newspapers who have no conception of what the founding fathers really meant. Laws should deal with overt acts, not with a state of mind. Intellectual honesty can only be dangerous to demagogues."[54] The Committee then restated its stand on academic freedom, pointing out that "whether we like it or not, real freedom of speech means freedom for the ideas we loathe, as well as for those we approve. The whole question of academic freedom is merely a part of the larger concept of freedom of speech in America."[55] Nor did the Association confine its interest to America alone, for it protested vigorously against the persecution of colleagues in foreign lands and coöperated with agencies designed to provide relief for persecuted scholars.[56]

But the American Association of University Professors represented only part of the academic world. An unknown number of scholars shared the position of Nicholas Murray Butler, president of Columbia, who urged that academic freedom implied the limitations imposed by a common morality, common sense, common loyalty, and decent respect for the opinions of mankind.[57] Such limitations might make a mockery of the academic freedom for which the AAUP stood, especially in times of crisis, as President Butler's position in 1917 and 1939 revealed. Others felt that the scholar should publicly express himself only in those matters on which he was qualified as a specialist to speak. But this meant the forfeiture of basic constitutional rights.

Others, for religious, racial, or political reasons, refused to subscribe to them unlicensed academic freedom: this meant that which criticized their own position or doctrine. Roman Catholics, for example, while professing to hold views on academic freedom entirely in tune with those of the AAUP, actually came far from doing so, if official statements are evidence. The Catholic position denied the right of any scholar to "impose on the immature, the uncritical, the unwary, his own untested intellectual idiosyncrasies." This meant, in other words: "Academic freedom is freedom to teach what is true and to receive instruction in what is true. When it comes to defining what is true, Catholic education seeks the guidance not only of the natural law, but of Christ, our Lord, which is interpreted for us by the Church." Thus the scholar was in effect free to teach only that which corresponded to Catholic doctrine as determined by the Church itself.[58] In the graduate field the Catholic universities favored "the winds of competent criticism which will blow away the smoke screens of prejudice and especially of the modern agnostic and atheistic theophobia. It will be to keep the air clear so as to permit a full view of truth in its correct perspective."[59] By inference, academic freedom did not include anything that might possibly blow away the revealed truths of the Church. Whether this position was followed by all Catholic scholars cannot easily be determined.

Thus it is apparent that there was no general agreement on the meaning of academic freedom. Its variant principles rested rather on the several competing assumptions of the purpose and meaning of education. Where these assumptions differed, the understanding of academic freedom differed. It was certain that the world of higher education did not in anything like its entirety subscribe to the instrumentalist position, largely exemplified in the principles and practices of the AAUP. This position meant that academic freedom can never be single and general, but that it must be specific and plural, that it represents the optimum opportunity for hearing all sides and for making a choice of all possible avenues. It meant respect for, and protection of, the right of expression of opinions, hypotheses, and theories one might abhor, on the assumption that the greater the diversity of views, the better the chance for approximate truth.

It seemed, at the mid-century point, that this view was in the process of modification, that a more restricted view leaning toward some sort of absolutism was gaining ground. But it was impossible to weigh the relative strength of the contending views of academic freedom in the larger context of conflicting educational philosophies. In other words, the nature and degree of academic freedom that was to prevail rested on the acceptance of one or another of the differing conceptions of the place of the scholar and scholarship in society. The problem was one of defining the social responsibility of the scholar and scholarship.

VI

This problem, as we have already seen, has always been present in western civilization, and came to be ever more acute with the consolidation of industrial America and with her increasingly important position on the world stage. Despite the fact that innumerable scholars had lent a hand, as we have seen, to the winning of the two world wars and in the fight against the depression, and had further spoken out against the Nazi violation of human rights and scholarly values, some felt that American academicians were still too largely neutral in the face of momentous public questions. American scholars, Archibald MacLeish eloquently proclaimed in *The Irresponsibles*, had been woefully indifferent to the ordeal European scholarship and letters had been passing through, callously unwilling to defend the great western tradition that had nurtured them no less than their Old World colleagues, and tragically blinded by a false conception of learning as a useless personal ornament.[60] On a different but related level Robert K. Lynd indicted the social scientists. In his view scholars had, in assuming impartiality and in refusing to take a stand in current controversies, actually capitulated to dominant interests and then rationalized that capitulation as an objectivity which in fact was only a mirage.[61]

Drawing in part on earlier contentions of Paul Elmer More and Irving Babbitt, critics of the MacLeish-Lynd positions insisted that the essence of scholarship is the cultivation of the long view, the sustained courageous search for truth, irrespective of immediate pressures and dictates. One rejoinder declared that MacLeish had made the fatal blunder of asking scholars to pervert the intellect in order to defend it, that he had mistakenly defined the activities of scholarship in terms of certain other activities that are not essentially related to scholarship at all.[62]

For the most extreme advocates of each of these positions there was little or no conflict: the path of duty was clear. For the unknown but large number of scholars who have shared both objectives there was a genuine dilemma. Only a few of these succeeded, perhaps, as John Dewey so notably did, in integrating the two functions and in making significant contributions to both. For Dewey

has both advanced knowledge in psychology, education, and philosophy, and fought gallantly in the forum of public opinion for the democratic values he cherished.

The implicit assumption that the man of learning is a custodian of the social conscience, of cultural and human values, has further complicated the problem of his obligations to society. This assumption was often shared both by those who advocated the application of specialized knowledge to immediate social issues and by those who emphasized the long-run search for disinterested truth. Many scholars, of course, took a much more humble and limited view of the role of the man of learning in society. But those with the ideal of custodianship failed to take into account the fact that there were other groups, vested with greater power, that similarly regarded themselves as guardians of social values: for instance, columnists, the business community, the government bureaucracy, and the church. The assumption that the scholar is in a special sense the custodian of social values further overlooked the fact that large sections of the public regarded the intellectual as peculiarly inept in decision and policy making. It is only necessary to recall the prejudice against the New Deal scholars, prejudice only partly offset by the more generally appreciated services of experts in the Second World War.[63] The problem of the scholar was thus not a conflict merely between those who felt that their chief function was to interpret, defend, and extend the cultural heritage and those who felt called on to use specialized knowledge in immediate tensions and problems. It was also a conflict between what scholars wanted to do and their ability and power to do it in view of the influence of social groups outside the realm of scholarship.

An increasingly large number came to accept a different view. They accepted the thesis that it was impossible for scholars actually to divorce themselves altogether from immediate pressures in the pursuit of learning. In their minds the scholar who believed he was entirely objective in standing apart from current controversies, only deceived himself. He was indeed in one sense taking sides, however unaware of this he might be: for in failing to take a stand, he was supporting the dominant position.

There was also a growing recognition that decision making, whether by scholars or by nonscholars, results from a kind of intuitive judgment closely related to the temperament and the values of the thinker and to fluctuations in public opinion and the pressures of effectively organized groups and interests. When scholars become practitioners, they probably rely more on such intuitive judgments than on the disinterested analysis associated with scholarship.[64] Neither the scholar who in theory divorces himself from immediate issues nor the one concerned with immediate problems has any monopoly on objectivity.

That there are differences in the degree of subjectivity is, of course, true. And none denied the supreme importance of the sustained effort to be as objective as human frailties and present techniques in knowledge-finding permit. Indeed, Charles A. Beard and Carl Becker asked whether it was not true that the scholar who faced his bias and his limitations squarely was not able to be more objective than the one who claimed for himself an unattainable disinterestedness. They urged the importance of exploring more deeply the means by which the perception of relativism might be kept from becoming mere cynicism and opportunism, and by which the intuition of values and faith might be kept from becoming a rationalized camouflage of private and group interests.[65]

A third assumption, shared alike by many scholars in both groups, was that research equals progress. In insisting on their peculiar function of guarding the great cultural heritage, the above-the-battle scholars put less emphasis than others on the idea that scholarship is the way to progress. Yet there was a widespread assumption that such was the case. On his part, the scholar concerned with service almost inevitably assumed that the application of knowledge to problems of everyday life was somehow indispensable to progress. President Van Hise of the University of Wisconsin commonly calculated the dollar and cents returns of the research the state supported at his institution and pointed to the result as progress.[66] No doubt the application of knowledge to specific life problems led to an advancing standard of living. It was also widely recognized that the solution of certain problems by the application of the results of research gave rise to new problems. To recognize this was not, however, to establish a case against science and research, as some humanistic critics insisted. But it was, as such critics insisted, an argument that the results of research did not necessarily equal progress unless applications were responsibly directed toward socially desirable and ethical ends.

The humanistic rationale included—at least in certain quarters —the contention that the scholar should also stick to his last. The scholar might as an individual take part in public conflicts, but when he did so, the tools of scholarship must not be among his weapons, for these tools were sacred to the long-range search for truth. Such spokesmen as Robert Hutchins, Theodore Greene, and Henry M. Wriston insisted that scholarship already suffered too much from an oversensitivity to current issues. This, of course, was closely related to their respective positions in the educational structure, whether humanist or neo-Thomist.[67] On the other side, instrumentalists asked how, in the battles of the day, the scholar could be separated from the pursuit of truths with the instruments of scholarship.

Dissatisfied with the relativism of the second quarter of the twentieth century, many scholars reacted against it. This they did regardless of the relativistic implications of cultural anthropology, psychology, the new physics, and the philosophy of instrumentalism. They assumed that it was possible to end the world-wide moral and intellectual confusions by imposing a new unity and a new authority.[68] In the 1920's some scholars, influenced by neohumanism, found such an authority in the classical tradition. In the 1930's a few, probably a very few, scholars saw in Marxism a new coherence and authority, but after the Nazi-Russian pact there was a tendency to lose respect at least for Communist Marxism. In the 1940's some scholars found that unifying authoritative principle or synthesis in neo-Thomism, or in the great books.

But instrumentalists and relativists accepted the challenge. They replied that the great danger in an authoritarian approach was that values related to our geographic area, our institutions, our time, would be imposed as universals, as eternal truth. In failing to recognize the subjectivity of scholarship and scholars, these critics maintained, both scholars and scholarship would in effect capitulate to the dominant interests of their age. In assuming that omnipotence and universal truth were on their side, they would stifle new research and inquiry and criticism, and end by enforcing a new orthodoxy, a given absolutism.

During and after the Second World War many signs pointed to the growing vogue of what promised to become the new orthodoxy, the new absolutism. As the tension with Soviet Russia gave way to the cold war, many scholars consciously or unconsciously found an orthodoxy and a sense of security, if not an absolute, in American nationalism. They embraced more tightly the "American way of life," which scholars had long tried to define, and the more or less free enterprise system associated with political and social democracy. Both the scholars devoted to the long-range quest for truth and those committed to immediate public service saw in "Americanism" the antithesis to communism. Both assumed that

path likely to make their ultimate goal impossible of achievement. But the instrumentalists in choosing the means of freedom could give no final assurance that these would lead to an assured and defined end. In the terms of the two positions, scholarship in the mid-century turmoil seemed a somewhat inadequate instrument. Yet it was by no means clear that there was any better one at hand. At the same time, the scholarly heritage of the past, and especially of the first half of the twentieth century, required a continued and sustained search for a scholarship — in conjunction with other forces — adequate to the needs of the new atomic age. The truly impressive achievements of the first half of the twentieth century gave promise that such a quest was in no sense hopeless.

the troubles with Russia resulted solely from Soviet aggressiveness, intransigence, ruthlessness, and Marxist dogmatism. They did not always ask whether the behavior they properly deplored might not be merely a symptom of a deeper, more complex situation within Russia itself and in the larger world caught in revolutionary crisis. At least some scholars in opposing communism did sound warnings against the danger of opposing communism with methods used by the Communists themselves.

The similarities of the two scholarly positions were sometimes overlooked in the heat of discussion. Both sought, in a general way, the same ends — a free society. But it was clear that means had become all important. The absolutists in adopting authority, discipline, and accepted criteria of orthodoxy seemed in some eyes to follow a

Professional Education

John S. Brubacher and Willis Rudy

In spite of the long liberal-arts tradition of the American college, there are many who think that the college was basically a professional school in colonial times and a professional school of theology at that. Now it is true, as a matter of fact, that the majority of college graduates in colonial times did go into the professions and that theology attracted more young men than did any other. And it is also true that a predominant purpose in the founding of colonial colleges was the rearing of an educated ministry. Yet, these facts notwithstanding, it is still probably contrary to fact that the colonial college was primarily a professional school, even for theological studies. Professional education in colonial times, in contrast to the common opinion cited, was largely by apprenticeship. Not till the nineteenth century was education for the professions to be had to any considerable extent in formal schools, and not till the latter part of this century were these schools raised to university grade.

Professional Preparation Through Apprenticeship

Preparation for one of the traditional learned professions—law, theology, or medicine—has always had the two dimensions of theory and practice. Under the apprenticeship system the chief accent fell on practice. The professional candidate placed himself under an able and mature minister, lawyer, or doctor and hoped by observation and imitation to be admitted subsequently to professional status. Sometimes, as in the case of the ministry, a candidate associated himself so closely with a practitioner that he went to live in his home. Through assisting a practitioner in the performance of his professional duties, the novice had an opportunity not only to learn professional skills himself but also to repay his benefactor in some degree for both the opportunity to learn and for the direction given to his learning. Indeed some practitioners, notably successful in their teaching of apprentices, charged them a fee in addition to using their services.

In spite of the claim to being learned, the professions under the apprenticeship system made only slight demands on the nature and extent of the apprentice's training prior to signing indenture papers, if any were signed at all. The ministry, perhaps, demanded most by usually expecting the candidate to know the classical tongues and, if he had attended college, to know some theology as well. Terms of study were not exacting either, since there was no determinate length to the apprenticeship as there had been in England, some terms running several months and others several years. Under frontier conditions it is not difficult to believe that terms ran shorter rather than longer.

There were, of course, numerous activities the performance of which at once helped the practitioner and instructed the neophyte. In making copies of papers like wills and deeds the young law clerk learned much of their legal form; in serving writs and filing actions he acquainted himself with judicial procedure; and in being a handyman about the court in term time he picked up the art of the attorney and the ethics of the bar. The would-be physician started making himself useful by washing bottles, later mixing drugs, and perhaps at a still later stage progressing to such routine matters as bloodletting. By being present in the doctor's office and accompanying him on calls he picked up much of the lore of diagnosis and therapy. Again, the prospective clergyman, through "living in" with a minister of the Gospel, became intimately acquainted with pastoral routine and duties, at the same time learning to dedicate himself to the service of God and man.

Important as was the mastery of the details of professional practice, theoretical considerations were not omitted. Theory the apprentice mastered out of books. But here he did not so much pursue a systematic course of readings as he read widely and deeply from whatever library his practitioner happened to possess. In fact one reason the future divine took up residence with an ordained clergyman was to avail himself of the latter's library. Similarly the future lawyer clerked in the office of some attorney in order to "read law" in preparation for the bar. Over and beyond books, of course, law and theology presented innumerable opportunities for master and apprentice to argue fine points of theory. Furthermore, clergymen and lawyers who were conscientious beyond the ordinary in their teaching duties often set theses or questions on which their apprentices presented papers which in turn became the basis for analysis and further discussion.

In evaluating the apprenticeship period of professional training, it must be confessed that the training was very uneven in quality. Nevertheless it developed technical competence as measured by the standards of the day. The future physician at least had the advantage of learning about disease by seeing it at first hand and observing the effect of treatment on it. In the approved pedagogical language of a later day, his was truly a learning by doing. And yet in spite of such advantages there were all too obvious limitations of the apprenticeship system. The man successful in law, medicine, or theology was not necessarily a successful teacher. Not only might he lack talent for instruction, but all too frequently a crowded professional life left all too little leisure to exercise the pedagogical talent he did possess.[1] Perhaps an even more serious limitation of the system was its empirical nature. In spite of the apprentice's reading, emphasis fell heavily on *ad hoc* procedures. The theory undergirding and giving scope and direction to practice was minimized and sometimes overlooked. The legal apprentice tended to learn local procedures and local peculiarities of the substantive law rather than general principles. In the case of medicine the pedagogical emphasis on empirical rule of thumb is probably to be explained by its coinciding with an empirical period of that discipline's development. Happily some economically more favored youth were able to make up such deficits by attending European centers of professional study such as the English Inns of Court for law or the University of Edinburgh for medicine.

Early Professional Schools

Before passing from the period of informal preparation for the professions through apprenticeship to the period of more formal training through professional schools, it will be well to note how some of the colleges had already begun establishing chairs in theology and law as part of their undergraduate offerings. Chairs of theology appeared at Harvard and Yale before the middle of the eighteenth century, and chairs of law began to make their debut at sister colleges after the Revolutionary War. Thomas Jefferson was instrumental in inaugurating the first professorship at William and Mary, a professorship to be copied before the century was out at both the University of Pennsylvania and Columbia. While no doubt students pointing for the ministry or the bar found these courses ultimately useful for professional purposes, probably none would have regarded them as the main avenue to professional life since apprenticeship still dominated the approaches to the professions in the eighteenth century. Even college graduates who planned on the ministry without apprenticing themselves to some local pastor generally stayed on at college after graduation for a period of time to put themselves under the preprofessional guidance of the president, usually a clergyman.[2]

But, professional preparation aside, it is probably true that the courses in theology often had at least as strong a liberal as a professional orientation. Whatever the vocational destination of the young bachelor of arts, there was little doubt in colonial and early national times that religion was the principal integrating factor in any sound liberal education. Much the same may be said for the courses offered in law. The men who taught them—George Wythe at William and Mary, James Wilson at the University of Pennsylvania, and James Kent at Columbia—were likely thinking at least as much in the broad liberal terms of politics and jurisprudence as they were of the immediate practice of the law. This was the spirit in which Blackstone lectured at Oxford from 1768 onward, and certainly his chair was the model for American colleges. Two famous textbooks resulted from these chairs of law: Blackstone's *Commentaries on the Laws of England* and Chancellor Kent's *Commentaries on American Law,* both long and widely read by future law clerks and students.

While chairs in medicine began to appear during this same period, the first seems to have been established in 1765 at the College of Philadelphia, as might have been expected from Benjamin Franklin's interest in the college and in science. King's College followed two years later, Harvard and Dartmouth before the century was out, but Yale and Brown did not follow suit till the first decade of the nineteenth century. It is not so clear in the case of medicine as it is of law and theology that it was studied liberally and this in spite of the fact that Yale made a point of subjecting its medical students to the same college discipline—compulsory chapel and eating at commons—as her undergraduates. Similarly, at a later date Brown insisted that its medical like its academic faculty live on campus. At neither college did such regulations succeed. Yale rescinded its requirement before any serious mischief occurred, but Brown, by persisting in the enforcement of its residence rule in the face of faculty opposition, only succeeded at the expense of driving out its medical faculty.

While the colleges were establishing chairs as initial steps in the long development of professional education, burgeoning forces latent in the apprenticeship system were expanding it into the first real professional schools. Some successful pastors, for instance, were accepting not just one, or even two, but a number of young men to study with them for the ministry. Although not formally organized as schools, these aggregations were widely known as "schools of the prophets." The evolution from apprenticeship to school, however, was even more clear in the case of the law. The first and outstanding school was that of Judge Tapping Reeve at Litchfield, Connecticut. As his law practice was disrupted by the war, the judge apparently compensated by taking on more and more apprentices. In the course of time the teaching of apprentices in his office came to predominate over the carrying on of a law practice, but so gradual was the transition that there is some doubt when in the 1780s to date the beginning of the school. Once transformed, however, from office to school, Judge Reeve's method had many imitators. Medical schools, when they started in the first decade of the next century, had a not dissimilar structure. Instead of teaching their apprentices singly, however, several physicians would band together to teach their apprentices collectively, thus allowing for some degree of specialization in the faculty of their resulting school.

It is noteworthy in both cases, law and medicine, that the schools were run for the financial profit of their proprietors and were therefore for the most part incorporated independently from institutions of higher education like the old established colleges on the eastern seaboard. Since students after completing the course often called their former teachers in as consultants, membership on one of these faculties brought added professional prestige as well as a division of tuitions.[3] This led to a rapid growth in the number of such schools and a commercial exploitation of the American public which discredited the whole system.[4]

These new professional schools tended to be didactic. Lectures replaced empirical training; telling replaced doing. The lecture hall substituted both for contact with client or patient and for presence in court or at sickbed. All this made sense in the era because it enabled the practitioner-teacher to distill his own professional experience in summary form and thus economize the student's time and effort. Moreover, with emphasis on lecturing it was possible to organize a more or less systematic course of instruction to take the place of the somewhat haphazard order in which significant learning experiences arose under the apprenticeship system.[5] Some practitioner-teachers virtually dictated as they lectured, so that at the conclusion of the course, if a student had not had a text at the beginning, he now did. But, like Chancellor Kent, teachers themselves soon began to publish their lectures and thereafter lecturing was often supplemented by recitations based on the text of published lectures. It is said that the Litchfield Law School continued its popularity longer than most proprietary schools because the lectures delivered there were longest delayed in reaching the public press.

Popular as these proprietary schools became, they by no means supplanted the apprenticeship system. Rather they paralleled and competed with it. Unfortunately, as a result, their standards tended to approximate those of apprenticeship training and hardly dared exceed them for fear of losing out in the competition for students. Entrance requirements, for example, were practically nil. Boys would be admitted to these professional schools who could not gain entrance to a college or even to its preparatory department.[6] In his inaugural address at the University of Nashville in 1829, President Lindsley declared that it was easier at the time in Tennessee to qualify for the practice of the law or medicine than to build a dray or shoe a horse.[7] Not only were standards of admission almost nonexistent, but matriculation, too, was irregular. The candidate started professional school as he did an apprenticeship, when the time suited him. The length of time he stayed was also uneven. Under such conditions rigorous examinations, if any at all, were almost out of the question. Harvard, where the standards were as high as anywhere about the time of the Civil War, awarded the medical doctor's degree to any candidate who could pass five out of nine oral examinations all taken on the same day![8] With or without examinations, however, the diplomas awarded were equally impressive. In view of all these circumstances it is small wonder that the prestige of the professional student stood low. So low was it at Bowdoin that the undergraduates there looked down on the medical students on its campus with a disdain that was not above playing pranks on them.[9]

Deplorable as early standards seem to a later day, they were not without their explanation under the influence of Jacksonian democracy. With the accession of

Andrew Jackson to the Presidency of the United States, egalitarianism spread, not only to the civil service, but to qualifications for professional training as well.[10] As the common man came to power, his confidence in pioneer versatility caused him to distrust the expert. He claimed the right for all economic classes to enjoy professional privileges as a new principle of no less far-reaching significance in a democracy than the older one that those who exercise professional privileges should be trained to discharge them.[11] Thus, the 1851 Indiana constitution provided that every person of good moral character, being a voter, shall be admitted to practice law in all the courts of the state.[12] While one might reluctantly concede this principle in the case of training for the law, which is so closely akin to training for politics, the fierce egalitarianism of the frontier seemed to know no bounds and extended it to medical education as well, even though there the difference between expert and charlatan might be the difference between life and death.

Obviously neither the professional schools nor the surviving apprenticeship system worked out altogether satisfactorily. Both tended to be too specific in their curriculums. Both needed a broader scholarship. What seemed required was a type of professional education that combined the practical merits of the apprenticeship system with the academic merits of the chairs of law, theology, and medicine in the colleges. President Kirkland of Harvard was early to cry out for something better,[13] but it was Andover Theological Seminary that was early to respond.

The Congregationalists who founded this institution in 1808 had lofty ambitions. At the outset they aimed at a faculty that would give full time to teaching, a student body that would have a college education behind it, and ahead a three-year term of instruction. By starting with a sizable library and by expanding the curriculum to include history and such languages as Hebrew, they hoped to make such demands on scholarship as more nearly to merit being a learned profession. Although these plans were applauded by most thinking persons, nevertheless there was an undercurrent of dissent. There was a fear in some quarters that such a seminary would more likely turn out scholars than sturdy soldiers of the Cross. These quarters still clung conservatively to the notion that education in the privacy and seclusion of the revered "school of the prophets" was more likely to foster humility, patience, and devotion. A pleader for founding a theological seminary at Princeton refuted these anxieties by pointing out an opposite danger in the "school of the prophets," the danger that candidates confined to the provincialisms of the clergymen with whom they lived and studied might turn out to be dogmatic if not bigoted as well.[14]

After something of a false start in the next decade Harvard, under the leadership of Justice Story, finally revamped its law school in 1829 to take in only college graduates or their equivalent and to lift its sights from the study of local to general principles of law.[15] Medical education, too, if low in achievement, was not without its elevated sights. John Morgan, in inaugurating the study of medicine at Franklin's College of Philadelphia, was prophetic in the demands he made. Men coming to the study of medicine, he insisted, should be versed not only in Latin, Greek, and French but also in mathematics and the sciences. Fresh from a sojourn in Europe, he further begged that medicine be studied and taught as a science supplemented by clinical lectures from hospital physicians.[16] Taking much the same stand, Eliphalet Nott at Union College claimed that engineering education would be stronger and more effective if combined with a liberal-arts curriculum on a liberal-arts campus.

Upgrading Professional Education

Notwithstanding the sound ideals enunciated, it was difficult to match ideals with actions in the early nineteenth century. Under existing social conditions the holding power of Andover was not great enough to retain students for the full three-year term and Justice Story too frequently had to admit men to the study of law with less than a bachelor's degree and even less than its equivalent. It must be added that Story only made the fledgling school a part-time concern since at the time he was sitting on the United States Supreme Court. But better times were ahead. Improvement occurred on a number of fronts almost simultaneously.

First, after long preoccupation with opening the doors of opportunity as wide as possible to those bent on professional careers, interest came to center more and more on selective factors. Harvard was among the first to brook the danger of decreased enrollments from raising the entrance hurdles. After the Civil War her youthful and energetic new president, Charles W. Eliot, persuaded her professional schools one by one not only to require a bachelor's degree for entrance but to raise the tuition rate to boot. Enrollments fell at once in accordance with the dire predictions of the old guard, who did not sympathize with the new president. But when the quality of this new product began to make itself felt in professional life, enrollments rose again and Eliot was more than vindicated for the risk taken.[17] Not every college or university felt strong enough to take a similar risk, not even the stronger ones, but a number followed somewhat timidly by requiring at least two years of college. Some excused their timidity in terms of protecting the interests of poor boys who could not afford so long a preparatory period.[18] By the turn of the century the percentage of professional people with no training beyond secondary school was rapidly falling. Indeed better than 10 per cent of lawyers, doctors, clergymen, and college teachers by that time had had both college and professional or graduate instruction in preparation for their careers.[19]

By the first quarter of the twentieth century the mere possession of a bachelor's degree and the tuition fee was no longer enough to command entrance to the better professional schools. When applications for admission outran the number of places available, professional schools were able to pick students with particular kinds of records. Medical schools especially showed favor to applicants who had pursued a premedical curriculum of selected courses in science, such as chemistry and biology. Law and theological schools continued to accept students from a wide variety of curriculums, though specialization of some sort latterly augured greater success than its absence.[20] Of course, all professional schools showed a preference for the college graduate with a good scholastic record. In fact, studies revealed that undergraduate scholastic success was a good prediction of success in professional school.[21]

In raising the tuition as well as the threshold of entrance requirements, it was only proper that the professional schools should offer an enriched program of studies. Here the new vitamins came principally from studying the traditional professions of law, medicine, and theology in the light of neighboring disciplines.[22] Medicine particularly benefited from being studied in conjunction with the sciences of chemistry, physics, biology, physiology, psychology, and the like. Law, too, took on new proportions when studied in the light of history, philosophy, and the social sciences. As this larger scope caught on, students came to study from books whose titles changed from *Cases on the Law of* _____ to *Cases and Materials on the Law of* _____. To promote research into the wider and deeper ramifications of the law, Harvard early in the twentieth century established a graduate department of law that awarded the S.J.D. degree. Not to be outdone, theological schools reinvigorated their traditional courses of study by drawing on the resources of psychology, sociology, and politics in order to give the ministry an informed as well as a sensitive social conscience in such matters as temperance, divorce, human exploitation, racial discrimination, and similar social problems, to say nothing of keeping it abreast of the impact of scientific discoveries on theology.[23] As in the case of the Newton Theological Seminary, there was an outcry against these innovations, a fear that the professional student would lose himself in the labyrinths of theory to the serious neglect of more practical and useful concerns, but the outcry subsided.[24]

As scholarship in professional schools spread out, it became evident that independently incorporated professional schools were at a disadvantage. It was not so easy and convenient for them to draw on closely associated academic disciplines as it was for the affiliated school. Permeated by the academic atmosphere of the university and backed by its broader financial base, professional schools as parts of universities found it easier to move away from one of the great weaknesses of the proprietary school, its part-time faculty, and toward one of full-time teachers.[25] Acutely aware of this and other facts, a number of proprietary schools in the nineteenth century surrendered their independent status and became parts of old-established seats of learning. Thus the Litchfield Law School joined the Yale family of professional schools before the middle of the century, and the College of Physicians and Surgeons in New York City affiliated with Columbia at the century's end. How strong the trend became is witnessed by the fact that out of one hundred law schools at the turn of the century seventy-one were affiliated.[26] While medical schools followed this trend, theological seminaries lagged behind, the more sectarian ones fearing to lose their narrow appeal.

Schools of technology were something else again. The first ones to be founded like Rensselaer Polytechnic Institute and Massachusetts Institute of Technology not only followed the European custom of being separate and independent from the university but have remained so in spite of the centripetal influence of the university on other professional schools. These institutes, however, together with the later land-grant colleges of agriculture and mechanical arts, compensated for their independent position by enlarging their own curricula to include many university studies. Thus M.I.T. has come to offer work in the humanities, including on its faculty a professor of philosophy. In most state universities, of course, law, medicine, and engineering have been integral parts of the university almost from the beginning. Indeed, at the University of Maryland professional schools even antedated the undergraduate college.

Contemporary with strengthening of the curriculum came corresponding innovation in methods of teaching it. Excessive lecturing in medical schools began to give way to the laboratory; the amphitheater lost some of its importance to intensive study in the outpatient department and in the hospital ward. While it had been the custom of medical students to observe diagnosis and treatment, William Osler at Johns Hopkins conceived the idea of having them assist in these activities within the limits of their training.[27] Thus apprenticeship had a rebirth and transformation in the medical internship. Schools of education and social work, like medicine, were also able to include clinical work or practicums, where the candidates came into direct contact with clients as part of their regular curricula. Usually this live contact had been reserved for the end of the professional course but in at least one instance, Case-Western medical school, it was vouchsafed to even first-year students. Similar educational procedures were more difficult to employ in law and business schools, where moot courts and business games were more in vogue.[28]

Law schools also caught the scientific spirit. In introducing the case method of legal study at Harvard, Christopher C. Langdell acted on the assumption that law was capable of scientific study. Only on this assumption was it worthy of university-grade instruction; otherwise, he claimed, it should continue to be treated as a craft and taught through apprenticeship. The case method of teaching proposed to reach legal principles, like scientific ones, by induction.[29] In place of learning principles of law ready made from lectures or texts, the student was disciplined in the art of ferreting out the principles himself from an analysis of concrete adjudicated cases. Thus, taking a page from Aristotle, the student learned the art and not just the product of legal reasoning. In doing so he had the further pedagogical advantage of learning to do precisely what he would be doing later as a counselor at law or, happily even later, as a judge.

Further upgrading of professional education occurred through self-regulation by the professions themselves. Slowly at the end of the nineteenth century, but with rapid acceleration in the twentieth, public standards were raised. A three-cornered set of forces brought it about: state examining authorities, associations of practitioners, and associations of professional schools. At first the standards of state examiners improved no more rapidly than did those of the associations of practitioners themselves.[30] Professional schools, however, impatient with this pace, tended to move well out in front of practitioners. The gap opened up caused some animosity between practitioners and professional faculties, and later on within law faculties themselves, between those who taught competence for local practice and those who taught more general legal theory.[31] The American Bar Association and the American Medical Association both had committees or councils specifically concerned with studying educational requirements for admission to professional ranks. The Association of American Law Schools, for instance, formed by the better ones of their number in 1900, grew out of a committee of the American Bar Association on legal education. By operating directly or indirectly as accrediting agencies the associations of professional schools exerted a leavening and standardizing influence both inside and outside their membership.[32] Thus by 1906 law schools set a three-year term as a minimum, by 1912 required law school libraries to possess at least 5,000 volumes, and by 1915 demanded that their members have at least three full-time professors on their faculties.

The most startling and epoch-making force for the improvement of professional education has yet to be mentioned, the Carnegie Foundation for the Advancement of Teaching. The study of medical education which it sponsored under Abraham Flexner and published in 1910 produced a veritable revolution in medical education.[33] In spite of Harvard's bold leadership, followed by Johns Hopkins medical school when it opened at the end of the nineteenth century, medical education continued to be plagued by a plethora of low-grade medical schools, low in academic standards and low in even rudimentary scientific equipment. In 1890 there were actually 160 schools awarding the M.D. degree. In the next decade this number fell to 126. This drop was largely due to some publicity given to existing conditions by the *Journal of the American Medical Association*, which had started publishing figures showing how well the graduates of the different schools did on various state medical examinations. On the basis of these results the *Journal* made a preliminary rating of schools in three categories, the highest consisting of schools with 10 per cent or fewer failures, next those with 10–20 per cent, and third those with more than 20 per cent.

The American Medical Association followed this up in the first decade of the twentieth century by making an individual visit to each of the then existing medical schools and rating them according to ten basic criteria. Schools rating 70 or better went into class A, those between 50 and 70 into class B, and those below 50 into class C.[34] This paved the way for the far more thorough study of

Flexner. During his investigation twenty schools closed on the spot rather than have the devastating evidence about them exposed to public view. The final report named each remaining school and described its circumstances in detail. By 1915 the pitiless light of public scrutiny had brought the number of medical schools down to 95—66 in class A, 17 in class B, and 12 in class C. Five years later the number had shrunk to 85—70 in class A, 7 in B, and 8 in C. Later in that decade only three schools still remained in class B and six in C, all the rest being in A. This upgrading of medical education to such a phenomenally high level in so short a while was nothing short of epoch-making.

The Flexner Report put medical training out in front of other traditional forms of professional education, if by no other means than by making it unequivocally postbaccalaureate. Some schools of law and theology set their standards correspondingly high, but by no means all of them. Study for the ministry still often occupied undergraduate years in the twentieth century. Indeed in a few of the states it was still possible to prepare for the bar through apprenticeship. Notwithstanding a Carnegie Foundation study of legal education, no such startling progress was made as in medical education.

Training for the newer and younger professions—engineering, pedagogy, business, agriculture, journalism, architecture—passed through much the same stages of development that the older ones experienced. Early training for some of these occupations was quite empirical. The teacher, for instance, learned to teach by teaching, *docendo docere*. The son learned to farm from his father. Merchants took on apprentices much as did lawyers and doctors. Johns Hopkins, who left his name and fortune to the great university in Baltimore, started his business career as such. Up to the founding of Rensselaer Polytechnic Institute engineers were largely self-taught. The founding of this institute, however, marked a turning point; it signaled the fact that American life was becoming increasingly complex. No longer would simple empirical techniques be sufficient to meet the intricacies propounded by the growing industrialization of the country. The application of science, not just to medicine, but to all phases of life, began to make demands on occupations which could only be met by more theoretical schooling.

The period of founding schools for these various occupations encountered somewhat the same problems met by the older professions when schools began to supplant apprenticeship there. For one thing there was the old confusion between theory and practice. The public expected these new schools to be practical and yet at the same time to enrich practice with new scientific insights. But where to find a faculty which had this fine balance of theoretical and practical knowledge? For the most part the men who were available for the new colleges of agriculture and mechanics were academicians; they were botanists, chemists, physicists. Although they became the first professors of "applied" science, they were able to supply in the beginning only a very meagerly practical curriculum. Similarly, the only faculty available in the early business schools such as Wharton were professors of economics and political science. If presidents had tried to staff their faculties with practical men possessed of theoretical insight, they would have been even more unsuccessful, for such men simply were not in sight as yet.[35]

Encountered again was also the problem of the academic level for technical instruction. While it was possible to pitch the engineering curriculum at a collegiate level, that of pedagogy, for instance, started as a department in secondary schools, particularly academies. Through the efforts of Horace Mann and Henry Barnard normal schools came to take over this function, but early normal schools were little more than advanced academies. Shortly after the founding of Amherst its faculty made a plea for the incorporation of pedagogy into the college curriculum,[36] but it was not till the twentieth century that teacher training reached college grade and then largely in teachers' colleges separate from academic campuses. Unaffiliated with academic institutions for the most part, they suffered the same inherent weakness as had the proprietary schools of medicine and law.[37] In spite of significant beginnings of a theory of education, the academic mind refused to regard pedagogy seriously. This was even true where at the end of the nineteenth century departments of education emerged on college campuses as offshoots from departments of philosophy and psychology. But for that matter all these junior professions at first occupied a low rung on the ladder of academic prestige, as had the older professions in their early days. No matter how much the practice of these occupations demanded more and more theory to meet the demands of a vastly more complicated America, people, and particularly academic people, ironically regarded them as utilitarian and therefore compared them unfavorably to the liberal arts.[38]

Undaunted, however, the same forces moved in to upgrade the early schools for the junior professions as operated in the more traditional ones. The demands for theory which in the beginning began to lift these professions out of the rut of empirical routine continued to compound themselves and spread over into contiguous disciplines. When Joseph Pulitzer, the great journalist, for example, offered to endow a school of journalism, Charles W. Eliot suggested a curriculum of practical details—newspaper administration, the law of journalism, journalistic ethics, and the like—but Pulitzer directed his benevolence to Columbia and a curriculum much more closely related to liberal arts.[39] Similarly, as pedagogy came to draw strength from a wide range of liberal arts, but especially philosophy, psychology, and the social sciences, it outgrew its tight-fitting skin of methodology and expanded into the broad study of education itself. Also new and better methods presented themselves for teaching these expanded curriculums. Thus, corresponding to the "block" curriculum in medicine, the "project" method in agriculture was developed. Instead of studying botany, chemistry, and economics as isolated courses, the student would undertake a "project" to raise and market a particular crop on an assigned plot of land, the successful completion of which would involve an integrated use of these academic disciplines as resources.

The deeper and broader the scholarship aimed at, the more it became evident that genuine professional competence could not be achieved short of graduate study. Consequently, although much professional study continued at the undergraduate level, leading universities began to establish graduate professional schools in rising fields like education,[40] architecture,[41] and business.[42]

The Harvard Graduate Business School particularly revealed the educational statesmanship of its founders. Even before becoming president, after Eliot's retirement in 1910, A. Lawrence Lowell thought it might "mark an era" if Harvard were to establish a school of business where college graduates, without regard to their specialities in college, might study business, not as political economy, but business as business and yet not to turn out finished administrators but rather to shorten the inevitable period of apprenticeship with the growing body of theory. Business should be flavored with theory, said A. Lawrence Lowell, himself trained in the law, just as the study of law is flavored with jurisprudence in Continental Europe and should be in the United States. How to embody this philosophy in practice was a question—whether to organize the curriculum around particular branches of industrial organization like banking and railroading, around particular jobs such as accountants and statisticians, or according to the art of administration in general.[43] In any case it became quite clear that the best balance between theory and practice was gained by borrowing the case method from the law school.[44]

Repeating the history of the older professions, these newer schools of university grade formed professional associations to accredit sister schools and upgrade their quality. The Carnegie Foundation for the Advancement of Teaching was no little help here as with earlier professional education, conducting studies of engineering[45] and education[46] which, while they did not make such epochal changes as Flexner had for medicine, nevertheless erected important milestones in the improvement of training for these occupations.

Since the Second World War, many innovations have been made in the aims, curricula, and methods of both senior and junior professional schools.[47] Medical, law, and agricultural schools, for instance, have come to state their aims more broadly, in terms of the welfare of man in relation to his environment. To achieve this larger frame of reference they often find the old curriculum too long and too congested. To remedy this situation they are starting to spend less time on required core courses and more on flexible alternatives. To achieve this end there was a strong trend to integrate professional curricula with behavioral and social sciences.[48] This trend in turn led to not only interdisciplinary courses but interprofessional ones as well. Unfortunately this larger scope of professional education had a tendency to overcrowd the curriculum. In part, some thought this overcrowding resulted from adhering to the traditional notion that a candidate should become proficient in each branch of his profession. By abandoning that notion in favor of greater and earlier specialization many thought the congestion could be relieved.[49]

Broader aims and curricula naturally demand more imaginative methods. It is no surprise, therefore, that there is a shift to problem solving techniques. Often professional students are taught to conceptualize their problems in terms of "models" and "game theory." Data processing and the computer as well as programed instruction are among the new methods. The point at which the neophyte student is immersed in the practical aspects of his profession is being advanced to the second and even the first years of professional study. Moreover the clinical or apprenticeship aspects of training are being enriched at some universities by encouraging commercial and industrial concerns to locate their research laboratories on the periphery of the campus. The mutual benefits of this policy are quite obvious.

The Higher Study of Higher Education

So far references to the evolution of the professional study of education have concerned the training of personnel to man the system of elementary and secondary schools. In a history of higher education perhaps a special indulgence may be granted for the separate mention of the preparation of personnel for the higher schools as well. Here, as in the lower schools, the early rule was *docendo docere*. Seventeenth- and eighteenth-century tutors learned to teach by teaching. The ones chosen for this trial by ordeal were those who had recently completed their studies for the bachelor's degree and were waiting call to a pulpit, for the assumption was widely and tacitly held that the only preparation needed to teach was a knowledge of the subject matter to be taught. Inasmuch as the predominant method of instruction was the recitation, wherein the tutor did little more than quiz the student to see that he had read his text,[50] it is not surprising that this assumption remained long unexamined. Unless one regards the four-year college course as an apprenticeship in the liberal arts, there was no practice of any sort under the eye of a master. Perhaps the only change in these conditions of professional training till well into the nineteenth century was one noted by Charles W. Eliot when he himself decided to become a college teacher. He counted it an advance that he unequivocally chose to make a career of teaching and not just to make it a steppingstone or interim employment to some other calling.[51]

Even before the day of Eliot a number of young men were setting a new fashion in preparing themselves for college teaching. Men like George Ticknor, George Bancroft, and Henry Wadsworth Longfellow, after graduating from Dartmouth, Harvard, and Bowdoin respectively, studied in European universities, especially German, in preparation for their later obligations at home. As has already been described, they were but the vanguard of an illustrious line of Americans who returned home to top the Anglo-American college with graduate schools devoted to German ideals of scholarly research.[52] In the course of time the Ph.D. degree, which crowned this graduate instruction, became the indispensable prerequisite to a job in college teaching. Colleges grew to count their blessings in terms of the number of Ph.D. holders on the faculty and the list of the faculty's scholarly publications.[53] By taking this stand colleges and universities assured themselves of faculties which had never before been so well qualified in their mastery of the subject matter they taught. Yet, although modern faculties were far better qualified than their predecessors of the seventeenth and eighteenth centuries, no change had occurred in the underlying theory of their training. Copying German practice confirmed rather than challenged the assumption that a knowledge of subject matter was the principal if not sole preparation needed for college teaching. Not even the gradual advance from the recitation to the lecture during the nineteenth century caused a re-examination of the assumption. Lecturing was just telling, and telling was to be learned empirically by telling.

If there were slight misgivings about this system before the nineteenth century was out, there was a positive clamor of criticism in the twentieth century. The secondary schools, long accused of sending poorly trained students to college, now turned on the colleges and accused them of poor teaching themselves.[54] But the principal criticism during the first two decades of the century came from the liberal-arts colleges themselves. David Starr Jordan, from the vantage point of the presidencies of the University of Indiana and Stanford University, corroborated the complaint of the secondary school by publicly confessing that no worse teaching was to be found than that in freshman year of large colleges.[55] Their lack of success William Rainey Harper of the University of Chicago ascribed to the failure of young Ph.D.'s to realize that a different method was required in teaching freshman and sophomores from the one used in the graduate school.[56] Men like Andrew F. West, who knew the problem at first hand as dean of the Princeton Graduate School, thought that the besetting sin of the embryo Ph.D. was his intensive knowledge of his own specialty and his extensive ignorance about the subjects which bordered on it, an overspecialization purchased at the price of research studies too often of second- and third-rate quality.[57] Going further, Charles William Eliot was saying in his inaugural at Harvard, "The actual problem to be solved is not what to teach but how to teach."[58] Even before the termination of the nineteenth century George Santayana at Harvard was pointing out that young instructors were so intent on becoming scholars that they only became teachers by "accident." A little later Woodrow Wilson was to join him in deploring how modern faculties were losing the close moral and sympathetic personal touch with students which they had formerly possessed.[59]

In spite of these warnings nothing substantial was done to redress the balance between teaching and research. Publish or perish became the code by which faculties lived. In following it faculties were but pragmatically noting which side of their bread was buttered. Advance in academic rank and salary for the most part went to those with long lists of publications rather than those successful in the classroom. Perhaps the college or university administration rewarded research activities because it thought them more worth while, or perhaps because published research was a more tangible and therefore less controversial measure of appraising professional worth.[60] President Edmund Day of Cornell declared that it was up to the faculty rather than the administration to redress this balance, for it was the faculty that resented measures to evaluate the efficiency of teaching in order to put it on a par with research.[61] Although the professional study of higher education would be difficult, he saw no reason for preferring to regard it as a mystery.

The discussion of college teaching ranged far and wide, even to a discussion of the professional prototype itself. As Dean Max McConn of Lehigh observed, training for academic life is self-selective; it attracts to itself preferably thinkers rather than doers.[62] He who can, goes from college into life as a go-getter or reformer; he who can't, goes to graduate school to become a teacher. This penchant of the academic mind for the abstract, some thought, lay at the bottom of the failure of college teaching. Two abstractions in particular were stamped on the student mind—the theoretic separation of fields of specialization from each other and the abstraction of scholarly interests from life itself. Moreover it tended to fashion an ideal of liberal education which strangely resembled the professional stereotype itself, a man who had an esoteric interest in learning on its own account and who eschewed the application of learning to the concrete and specific. It was small wonder, therefore, that the professorial manner often struck the student as impractical, absent-minded, arid, verbose, and even cantankerous.[63]

The penchant for the abstract was, of course, not only the despair but also the crowning hope of the profession. No problem can be studied seriously short of analyzing it into a series of abstractions. Unless the higher learning provides a place for long-term research and unhurried meditation which transcends immediate and utilitarian demands, not even practical concerns will prosper. The happy union of scholarship and practice was notably illustrated during the depression of the 1930's and the Second World War following, when a number of professors were called into public service. If politicians and cartoonists insisted on ridiculing the professor as a "brain-truster" in this period, it but proved the important position he had achieved.[64] In any event, criticizing the teacher with a theoretical proclivity was an old pastime, as witness the fun the dramatist Aristophanes poked at Socrates, one of the greatest teachers of them all.

Whatever the merits or demerits of the professional prototype, complaints about the preparation of college teachers continued on between the two world wars. However ideally research and teaching should supplement each other, the fact nonetheless persisted that the importance of research had grown and continued to grow out of all proportion to that of teaching. At long last a number of professional associations took the problem under study, among them the Association of American Colleges, the Association of American Universities, the American Council on Education, the North Central Association, and the American Association of University Professors, the last subsidized by a grant from the Carnegie Foundation for the Advancement of Teaching.[65]

The American Association of Colleges led off in 1926 with the appointment of a commission on the recruitment and training of college teachers.[66] The work of this commission reached its climax with its third report, in 1929, which recommended that graduate schools ascertain as early as possible which graduate students were planning careers in teaching rather than research. The commission also commended to graduate schools the relaxation of research requirements and the institution of an elective on progressive instructional and curricular movements.[67] There was no new report the next year but the previous one was raked with searing blasts from several influential graduate deans. Nor was the president of the Carnegie Corporation, Henry Suzzalo, able to save the day with his sensible observation that "it is a quite commonplace fallacy among them [college professors] to believe that presentation involving a dozen different techniques may be acquired without conscious effort and thoughtful attention. . . . Deliberate acquisition of skill is necessary.[68]

In spite of Suzzalo the graduate schools refused to relax requirements as they barricaded themselves against the introduction of education courses. Even eminent deans of schools of education like Charles H. Judd of Chicago and Melvin Haggerty of Minnesota opposed required education courses in the graduate school because they did not think there was as yet enough solid research in education to justify it. But Judd's suggestion to make improvement of college instruction a part of the improvement of instruction at lower levels as well ran cold shivers up the academic spine. Not only had professors never identified with teachers on lower rungs of the educational ladder but they feared the possible upward extension of state certification laws to college teaching.

Without trying to side-step responsibility for the avoidable shortcomings of college teaching, it was generally agreed on all sides that extenuating circumstances did account for some of the difficulties. The great expansion of college enrollments after the First World War made good teaching difficult by imposing larger classes, heavier teaching loads, and more administrative responsibilities on even the best instructors. Besides, digging deeper into the barrel of students of college age resulted in a student body of less stimulating academic ability. Teaching dunces in the elementary or secondary school is bad enough, but trying to teach a mature dunce, as Santayana ruefully remarked, is the last word.[69] The situation inspired the disquieting thought that there might be more students in college who could not learn than there were teachers who could not teach.

The rising tide of college enrollments which undercut standards of teaching after the First World War threatened to engulf them after the second. Statistics published in 1957 indicated that only 23 per cent of all new full-time college teachers held earned doctor's degrees. As this was a decline of 8 per cent from 1953 the country was becoming less and less prepared to meet the avalanche of students expected in the next decade. Conversely in the same period the number of new full-time teachers holding less than a master's degree rose from 10 per cent to 23 per cent. Private institutions were maintaining a higher average than municipal ones, and the latter were ahead of state universities, but the prospect for the future was still alarming. Little abatement of the alarm was to be found in the sampling of colleges on which the statistics were based. Of the thousand institutions invited to participate in the study over 80 per cent responded, and from their original number had been excluded junior colleges, theological seminaries, schools of pharmacy, optometry, and the like.[70]

With seeming premonitions of these dangers Howard Mumford Jones again indicted the graduate schools at the war's end for neglecting the problem of training future college teachers for careers in teaching and called on the schools to rethink the problem of graduate instruction.[71] Yet the most serious effort to rethink graduate education, an effort subsidized by the Carnegie Corporation, suggested a number of innovations but no serious ones on the professional study of education.[72] Furthermore, the Council of Graduate Schools, representing over two hundred graduate institutions, dealt an apparent *coup de grâce* in 1961 to any hope for substantial change. As spokesman for graduate study in the United States the council set standards for it along strictly traditional disciplinary lines.[73]

The prolonged student strike at the University of California in 1964–65, however, shook academic complacency on this and other issues. Tremors were felt all the way from Berkeley to New Haven and points in between. One result:

Yale proposed a two-year master of philosophy degree and California a two-year doctor of arts for "ABD's" (graduate students who had completed "all but the dissertation").[74] These degrees were reminiscent of Yale's earlier policy of a two-year M.A. for teachers and corresponded to European practice where "candidate" is a recognized title for the "ABD." A year or two later the Ford Foundation gave $40,000,000 to ten universities with leading graduate schools for the improvement of graduate instruction, one phase of which was to better apprenticeship teaching of graduate assistants.[75]

In searching for ways to improve teaching in spite of these handicaps, a number of suggestions were put forward. Some favored a more careful selection of teaching personnel both before training and before placement.[76] While few were willing to relax subject-matter requirements for those accepted, not a few recommended that the subject-matter departments should give some attention to problems of teaching in their fields. It was suggested that some member of each department who himself was an especially good teacher should distill in a few meetings or lectures the secrets of successful teaching.[77] Or, after a young Ph.D. had been added to the staff, some senior professor should take upon himself the duty of visiting and supervising his inexperienced junior colleague.

Some made the more radical proposal of dividing graduate study into two doctorates, the traditional Ph.D. for those specializing in research and a new D.A. (Doctorate of Arts) for those planning careers in teaching.[78] Some hoped that a better crop of teachers might be harvested by having them forego intensive specialization and substitute in its stead a wide course of reading so that in teaching their fields they would be able to relate them meaningfully to a wide context of life.[79] Such a program would certainly afford a corrective to Dean West's complaint.

But the foregoing were but piecemeal palliatives. They underestimated the depth of undergraduate dissatisfaction with the quality of teaching they had been receiving, as witness the students' wanting tenure abolished as academic featherbedding and the haven of the incompetent. Hence students "wanted in" on the selection, promotion, and dismissal of their teachers. If the Council of Graduate Schools did not get the message, three important private foundations did—Carnegie, Danforth, and Lilly. Together they sponsored a report, *Faculty Development in a Time of Retrenchment*, which bore down once again on pedagogy as indispensable.[80] It opposed a two-track program for the doctorate because the prestige of the D.A. would inevitably lag behind that of the Ph.D. Instead the report favored a strong teaching component occurring *within* the normal span of the Ph.D. program. A strong teaching component, it went on to say, should include not only theoretical study of education but a teaching practicum under close supervision and free from other courses.[81]

As a matter of fact, from the conclusion of the First World War onward the higher study of the problems of higher education became a special field in the graduate schools of education of the leading universities of the country. There had been some demand for formal instruction in college teaching in the first decade of the twentieth century,[82] but William H. Cowley claims that G. Stanley Hall had already started giving instruction in the higher learning at Clark University as early as 1893.[83] Yet it was not till the third decade of the new century that such courses became general. After that the policy spread so rapidly that by 1936 there were three dozen institutions offering advanced study of the higher learning.[84] This number doubled and trebled after the Second World War. Most notable, perhaps, was the Carnegie Foundation's establishment of centers for the study of higher education at the University of Michigan, Columbia, and the University of California.

There was some confusion as to what direction this study of higher education should take.[85] As might be expected of a new field of study, much of the early content was little more than descriptive of contemporary practice; it lacked theory. It also lacked research as a base for practice. Oddly enough, academic disciplines seemed to have done research on nearly everything except academe itself. But the social disturbances of the late 1960s, especially those stirred up by the students themselves, brought a reversal here. Higher education came to be seen as unresponsive to the needs of the times. The resulting unrest challenged the legitimacy of higher education's presuppositions so basically that many thought it time to examine the multiplicity of postwar changes with a view to planning the rest of the century.

A number of top universities like California and Columbia conducted self-studies as springboards to new action.[86] Offering broader scope were several nationwide commissions which addressed themselves to the reform of higher education in general. One was the Assembly on University Goals and Governance, which seemed to seek guidance in a nostalgia for older forms of higher education.[87] Another more caustically critical of the contemporary situation was the Newman Report.[88] But by far the most comprehensive and thorough study of higher education ever undertaken in this country was made by the Carnegie Commission on Higher Education appointed in 1967. In the next several years it published its results in over sixty volumes.[89] The general tone of these volumes affirmed a faith in the traditional values of American higher education—its expansion, its increasing diversity, a cautious egalitarianism, and freedom to dissent. Some found fault with it, however, because it stated no embracing or integrating theory of higher education.[90]

In any event these publications made substantial additions to a modest literature of higher education which had blossomed in the 1930s[91] and which came to full bloom in the second half of the century in such books as Bernard Berelson's *Graduate Education in the United States*, Clark Kerr's *The Uses of the University*, Christopher Jencks's and David Riesman's *The Academic Revolution*.[92] Obviously these men were leaving behind the era in which the college professor had been willing to do research on nearly every human activity except his own. It was none too soon, for, with many universities operating under multi-million-dollar budgets, the conduct of higher education was rapidly moving out of the stage where its expertise could be learned on the job or in apprenticeship fashion as in the past.[93]

Reinforcing this new professionalism in higher education was the Association for Higher Education. This association had its genesis as one of the four constitutional departments set up by the National Education Association when it was founded in 1870. The department flourished till 1910, after which it steadily declined till 1924 when it was discontinued. In part the decline can be associated with the rise of such new organizations as the American Association of University Professors and the American Council on Education. Happily the department was revived again in 1942 just in time to afford professional leadership for the postwar boom in higher education. In 1950 the department changed its name to the Association for Higher Education though it still remained federated to the National Education Association. *Issues in Higher Education* has become its annual mouthpiece.

Professional Education and the Higher Learning

It has already been seen how the various professions, the older and the newer ones alike, improved the quality of their training by moving from an empirical to a theoretical stage. As they drew more and more strength from related disciplines, they came more and more to absorb the spirit of the higher learning of the graduate school of arts and sciences. The major characteristic of this spirit was the disinterested pursuit of knowledge on its own account. To qualify as a "learned" profession, therefore, some contended that professional study must be carried on at a strictly theoretical level. While it had undoubtedly been an advance to move from a narrowly practical to a broadly theoretical stage in professional preparation, to advance farther by abandoning the practical altogether required some argument.

Two points were made. On the one hand it was argued that concern with the practical is concern with the specific and the routine. The danger with pitching professional instruction at this level is that it has so limited a range of application and so quickly gets out of date. The decline of theological education President Hutchins of the University of Chicago ascribed to its increasing concern with the pastor's parish problems rather than the problems of theology itself. Law and medicine, therefore, he claimed further, should be closer to the university than to the court and the hospital.[94] Professional study, if it is to remain worthy of the higher learning and not be anti-intellectual, must treat of general principles and fundamental propositions. The commercial milieu of the university is a particular threat to the integrity of professional instruction because through its subsidies it tempts the faculty to subordinate investigation of general laws to finding specific answers for its problems.[95] Indeed, since professional education is more prone to succumb to practical exigencies, a man like Thorstein Veblen was even prepared to separate it altogether from the university, if need be, to preserve the integrity of the graduate school as a place for pure research.[96]

On the other hand Veblen also argued that professional concern with teaching was a second deterrent to the higher learning. The only instruction he would tolerate would be that which, combined with inquiry, helped to train the next generation of scholars. That there were other kinds of teaching, like undergraduate preparation for citizenship, he did not doubt. All he insisted on was that they be kept apart from instruction at the university level. The purpose of the undergraduate college is to drill and convey knowledge. It fits for the higher learning but is distinct from the higher learning itself. Moreover, while a student's health and morals might be a concern of lower schools, it was distinctly not a responsibility of the higher learning.[97] Therefore the difference between the undergraduate and graduate schools is more one of kind than one of degree. Consequently Veblen saw their continued connection in the unitary structure of the university as a "freak of aimless survival."

There was precedent for a university without an undergraduate college, but a university without professional schools would have run counter to traditions dating back to the medieval university. The medieval university, however, Veblen discounted as having emerged out of barbarian times when people were unmitigatedly, if necessarily, pragmatic in outlook. But to insist that the modern university retain this pragmatic quality, he maintained, was but to insist that it remain barbaric. From this position he was not even moved by the advantage, historically proved, that the professional schools and the graduate schools of arts and sciences had mutual need of each other, the professional school drawing on the graduate school for theoretical inspiration and the professional schools providing a context where academic theories might be tested.[98] Hutchins, together with Flexner, though sympathetic with Veblen's polemic against the practical, saw no reason to burn the barn to roast the pig. All that had to be done to retain the professional schools in the university, as they saw it, was to exorcise them of the practical by concentrating fully on the theoretical. To the argument that the medical school at least managed to combine the practical and theoretical in successful proportions, Hutchins took the position that it was an exception because the same conditions could be produced in the university hospital as off-campus in private practice. Similar conditions in law, engineering, or business simply could not be reproduced on the campus.[99]

In spite of this theoretical development of the role of theory in professional education, the great weight of custom favored striking a balance between the theoretical and practical aspects of the higher learning. Indeed there were those who justified in principle the importance of practice. Woodrow Wilson for one, the future president of Princeton, saw an advantage in the close connection between professional and liberal education,[100] and Alfred N. Whitehead, eminent professor of philosophy at Harvard, saw the importance of mating theory with practice in the university.[101]

The Education of the Educating Professions

Lawrence A. Cremin

It is a very special honor that has been accorded me, to deliver the Charles W. Hunt Lecture this evening, and I am grateful to Henry Hermanowicz and his colleagues for the invitation that has made the opportunity possible.

I had the pleasure of knowing Charles W. Hunt during the last two decades of his life. He was a great figure in the affairs of Teachers College as well as of AACTE; and no one could serve long on Morningside Heights during the 1950s and 1960s without becoming familiar with this genial alumnus, who gave so unselfishly of his time and energy to raise fellowship money for TC students who needed it. But there was another service Charlie Hunt insisted upon performing that proved of inestimable value to my generation of young, post-World War II professors: he was always ready to take you in hand, march you up to the great men and women of the profession, and see that you became acquainted. Charlie served as an invaluable link between young and old after a time of severe discontinuity in the life of our profession; and I for one shall always be grateful for the prized friendships I was privileged to enjoy as a result of his gentle, prodding mediation.

I should like to take the opportunity this evening to consider three matters with you. First, I should like to review the origins of the present-day paradigm of professional training in education, and in particular of the problematics of education as a field of study. Second, I should like to sketch the recent history of the doctorate in education, once again, with emphasis on the developing problematics of the field. And third, I should like to advance a series of recommendations about the present-day doctorate in education, based on an analysis of what seem to me to be the central requirements of the educating professions in our time.

First, to the review of origins, which takes us back to that fascinating period between 1870 and 1910, when at least three decisive models of professional training emerged in the United States — training for law, as developed by Christopher Columbus Langdell and his colleagues at the Harvard Law School; training for medicine, as developed by William Henry Welch and his colleagues at the Johns Hopkins Medical School; and training for education, as developed by James Earl Russell and his colleagues at Teachers College, Columbia University. All three models emerged at nascent universities: Johns Hopkins had been founded in 1876 entirely as a center for graduate study, and late 19th-century Harvard and Columbia were in the process of transforming themselves into universities. All three models were created in response to widespread dissatisfaction with contemporary professional training. And all three models imposed drastically raised standards upon their respective fields. But they couldn't have been more different in the solutions to the problems of professional education they embodied.

Legal education at the time of Langdell's appointment as dean of the Harvard Law School in 1870 was a combination of apprenticeship in a law office, study of textbooks on the law by commentators such as St. George Tucker, James Kent, and Joseph Story, and formal lectures. Most aspirants to the law entered the profession via apprenticeship and self-study, assisted from time to time by lectures purchased on a course-by-course basis. The primary claim of the law schools was not that they could substitute for law office training but rather that their lectures represented a more efficient way of teaching the general principles of law than the haphazard instruction of busy practising attorneys.

The heart of Langdell's law curriculum was the case method of instruction, the doctrinal analysis of appellate court opinions. Rather than studying the commentaries of Tucker, Kent, or Story, students were presented with the cases themselves and asked to derive their own commentaries in the form of general principles. And, rather than listening to lectures on the general principles of law, students were confronted with a Socratic dialogue in which the professor sought at the same time to elicit "true" rules and to inculcate proper modes of legal reasoning. (As three generations of law professors have put it, the goal was to have students "think like lawyers.") At bottom, the case method rested on three assumptions—that lawyers are better trained in law schools than in law offices, that law schools are better established within universities than independent of them, and that for law to be worthy of a place in the universities it must become a science, the substance of which can be presented in printed books. (As President Charles W. Eliot once observed, the book became for Langdell's law school what the laboratory was for the physics department.) Once students had successfully grasped the science of law, everything else of significance to the practice of law would follow(1).

Now, Langdell instituted other reforms as well. He raised admissions requirements; he lengthened and systematized the course of study; he lobbied for educational requirements for admission to the bar; and he formed powerful alliances with Harvard Law School alumni on the bench, in legislatures, on committees of the bar, and on the faculties of other law schools. But it is the problematics of his curriculum that interests me here. Preparation for law became the study, via the case method, of a baker's dozen of core subjects—property, common law pleading, contracts, torts, and criminal law during the first year; and equity, evidence, corporations, sales, agency, persons, bills and notes, and constitutional law later on. It was an undifferentiated course of study required of all aspiring practitioners, national and cosmopolitan in outlook (one could learn something of Massachusetts and New York law at Harvard but not Nebraska or Illinois law), essentially self-contained within the professional school, and wholly lacking in any systematic study of practice itself.

Medical education at the time of Welch's appointment as professor of pathology at Johns Hopkins University in 1884 was in its own way much like legal education, a combination of apprenticeship, the study of textbooks such as Caspar Wistar's anatomy, Robley Dunglison's physiology, and George Wood's medicine, and formal lectures. If there was a difference, it lay in the fact that most aspiring physicians entered the profession via one or another of the proprietary medical schools that had sprung up by the score during the 19th century. Generally organized and staffed by local practitioners and often closely allied with local medical societies, these schools offered what were essentially didactic lectures in the principal medical subjects, that is, anatomy, physiology, chemistry, surgery, medicine, therapeutics, pharmacology, and obstetrics. The total course ordinarily ran from one to three years in length, and the degree generally carried with it the legal right to practice.

The heart of Welch's medical curriculum lay in three major reforms. First, the preclinical subjects of anatomy, physiology, pharmacology, and pathology were rooted in laboratory inquiry. Following the example of the great European investigators who had revolutionized the study of physiology and medicine—Pierre Louis and later Louis Pasteur at Paris, Carl Ludwig at Leipzig, and Robert Koch at Breslau—Welch displayed an inveterate preference for facts over theories and for inquiry over didactics. Second, the clinical subjects of medicine, surgery, and obstetrics were rooted in the ongoing life of a teaching hospital with its own laboratories, so that students learned via a combination of inquiry and practice conducted under expert supervision. Following here the tradition of British hospital instruction, the General Education Board invested in medical education in the wake of Flexner's report made an enormous difference. But Flexner did not invent a model of medical education following the study of existing practice. Instead, he used an extant model as his criterion of excellence, and found contemporary practice wanting. His report was in the end an exercise in criticism and dissemination but not in creation.

Teacher education at the time of Russell's appointment as dean of Teachers College in 1898 was, if anything, even more diverse and haphazard than legal or medical education. Many primary-school teachers had had no preparation for their work whatever beyond primary schooling itself. Most of those teachers who had obtained preparation beyond primary schooling had attended an academy or a high school for a time, and some of those had then gone on for a year or two of normal-school study, which consisted of further work in the school subjects, a course or two in pedagogy and the history of education, and practice teaching at an affiliated school or a local public school. Some high school teachers and most college teachers had been trained in the colleges and universities, primarily in the substance of what they taught. A few colleges and universities—not more than two dozen in 1898—offered formal programs of education, consisting mainly of lectures and recitations on such textbooks as Gabriel Compayre's history of education and Joseph Payne's science and art of teaching.

Russell's reformed curriculum combined four components he considered essential to success in teaching: general culture, special scholarship, professional knowledge, and technical skill. He himself explicated this quadrivium in one of his early reports:

The general culture must be liberal enough to inspire respect for knowledge, broad enough to beget a love for the truth. The special scholarship must be sufficient for the work to be done; it should give that absolute command of the subjects of instruction which frees the teacher from slavish adherence to manuals and methods. The right professional knowledge should enable the teacher to view the subjects he teaches and the entire course of instruction in its relations to the child and to the society of which the child is a part. The true educator must know the nature of mind; he must understand the process of learning, the formation of ideals, the development of will, and the growth

Welch's goal was to join the clinical to the scientific in the thought and practice of the nascent physician. As his colleague Franklin P. Mall once put it: "There has always been a great deal of discussion of the question whether a physician's training should be scientific or practical. It appears to me that it should be both; for if he is educated only in the sciences underlying medicine, he is not a physician, while if he is educated in the practical branches alone, he is likely to become a shoemaker-physician who will drift into ruts and never get out of them." Third, the teaching hospital was linked to the medical school via an appointment system whereby professors in the medical school also served as heads of their respective departments in the hospital. The arrangement not only made them responsible for the delivery of medical services and the organization of medical instruction, it also permitted them to integrate advanced medical students into the life of the hospital in such a way that they could serve with maximum effectiveness while they learned with maximum efficiency. Finally, the keystone of the entire program was Welch's own subject, pathology; for the essence of medicine was conceived to be the diagnosis and cure of disease(2).

Like Langdell, Welch instituted other reforms as well. He raised admissions requirements, lengthened and systemized the course of study, and formed powerful alliances within the worlds of medicine and philanthropy. But once again, it is the problematics of Welch's curriculum that interests me. Preparation for medicine became a combination of scientific inquiry in the laboratory, via the preclinical subjects of anatomy, pharmacology, physiology, and pathology, and supervised practice leavened by scientific inquiry in the teaching hospital, via the clinical studies of surgery, medicine, and gynecology. As in law, it was an undifferentiated course of study required of all aspiring practitioners, not only national but international in outlook. As contrasted with law, however, it was not wholly self-contained within the professional school—a solid knowledge of chemistry and biology acquired at a good undergraduate institution was required for admission. And, contrary to law, it placed great emphasis on the systematic study of practice within a carefully designed instructional environment, namely, the teaching hospital.

I might add parenthetically that it was the presence of the Johns Hopkins model in operation that permitted Abraham Flexner's 1910 report, the well-known Bulletin Number Four of the Carnegie Foundation for the Advancement of Teaching, to exert such a profound influence on medical education. To be sure, the millions of dollars that

of character. The artist in every vocation must have consummate skill in the use of his tools. The teacher must be skilled in the technique of his art; he must have the ability to impart his knowledge in a way that shall broaden his pupils' horizons, extend their interests, strengthen their characters, and inspire them to right living. And as every art is most efficient when intelligently directed, the art of teaching should be founded on the science of teaching, which takes account of the ends and means of education and the nature of the material to be taught(3).

So far, so good; only the querulous would disagree. But as Russell explicated further, the radicalism of his proposals became clear. By general culture, he meant not only what was commonly accepted as a good college education circa 1900 but also the kind of preparation that would enable the student to see the relationships among the various fields of knowledge, particularly between his own field of expertise and all the others. By special scholarship, he meant not only the further academic study but the kind of reflective inquiry that would equip an aspiring teacher to select different sequences of material and adapt them to the needs of different students. These aspirations alone would have wrought a revolution in contemporary teacher education, particularly since Russell believed that the requirements were relevant to all teachers. Beyond them, there were the requirements of professional knowledge and technical skill. By professional knowledge, he implied not the mastery of didactically conveyed lecture material but rather systematic inquiry into the theory and practice of education in the United States and abroad, during past eras as well as the present, pursued via the same controlled observation and rigorous theorizing that pertained in the natural sciences and medicine. And, by technical skill, he implied not the rote knowledge gleaned by the observant apprentice but rather expert ability in determining what to teach and by what methods, when and to whom. Technical skill would be acquired in an experimental or model school, serving as a laboratory for pedagogical inquiry and a demonstration center for excellent practice. The heads of the various departments of the college would also be the heads of the corresponding departments of the school, and the teachers in the school would be critic-teachers, capable of exemplifying first-class reflective pedagogy at the same time that they oversaw the training of novices(4).

Now, like Langdell and Welch, Russell instituted other reforms as

well. He raised admission standards, lengthened the course of study, and formed enduring alliances with state departments of education, professional associations, and faculty members in other university education departments. But, again, it is the problematics of Russell's curriculum that interests me. Preparation for teaching combined a broad general education, a solid command of one or more teaching fields, an inquirer's knowledge of educational theory and practice, gained largely via the history and psychology of education, and scientifically based technical skill, developed through practice under expert supervision. The partial similarity to the Langdell and Welch models is patent, and surely not fortuitous. It was an era in which academic leaders enjoyed a considerable acquaintance across disciplinary and professional lines, for the relentless specialization of the 20th century had not yet worked its fragmenting effect. The Teachers College trustees had been in close touch with Charles W. Eliot of Harvard and Daniel Coit Gilman of Johns Hopkins for several years prior to Russell's appointment as dean; indeed, both Eliot and Gilman had actually participated in the formal exercises marking the relocation of Teachers College from University Place to Morningside Heights in 1894. Moreover, like Welch, Russell had studied in Germany and drunk the heady wine of *Wissenschaft*, and Russell had been in correspondence with a number of Welch's colleagues in connection with the establishment of the nursing education program at Teachers College. It should not be surprising, then, that, like the Langdell and Welch models, the Russell curriculum made its obeisance to science and to cosmopolitanism—it was as difficult to learn about Nebraska's laws at Teachers College as it was to learn about Nebraska's laws at Harvard. And, like the Welch model, Russell's curriculum placed great emphasis on the systematic study of practice within a carefully designed instructional environment, in this case, the model school.

Yet, granted the similarities, there were profound differences as well. Whatever Russell's belief and aspiration concerning the relevance of his curriculum to all teachers, it was admittedly designed for those preparing for positions of professional leadership, those who would supervise and administer the burgeoning school systems of the nation and those who would staff the normal schools, teachers colleges, and university departments of education. Nor was the curriculum nearly as self-contained within the professional school as Langdell's or Welch's. General culture, though essential, was obviously to be obtained during the undergraduate years. Special scholarship would be obtained, not only in Teachers College courses in the so-called professionalized treatment of subject matter, but in the graduate departments of the university as well. Only professional knowledge and skill fell entirely within the orbit of the education faculty. Finally, and the point is crucial, at the very time Russell was developing his model for the preparation of teachers at Teachers College, the graduate faculties of Columbia University, which were equally professional, I might say, despite the fact that they referred to themselves as the "non-professional graduate schools," were developing alternative models based on a different problematics, one exclusively concerned with scholarly inquiry into the substance of the subjects to be taught. The leaders of the graduate faculties—John W. Burgess, Nicholas Murray Butler, and Henry Fairfield Osborn—preferred to use the rhetoric of public service and the advancement of learning; but the latent function of their faculties was to prepare teachers for the high schools and colleges on a model that was not only different from Russell's but that competed with it for students, for positions for its graduates, and for political and financial support.

Now, as I have already remarked, the similarities among the Langdell, Welch, and Russell models were more than fortuitous. All three partook of the late 19th-century ambience of professional aspiration and academic expansionism; all three reflected the contemporary belief in scientific scholarship and the promise of its application to the improvement of human affairs; and all three profited from an expanding economy that provided jobs for trained graduates. That said, however, the differences are at least as important. For one thing, they reveal the extent to which the prevailing paradigms of professional training and the prevailing problematics of professional fields are the result of human choices at particular moments in history. There is no reason beyond the persuasiveness and influence of Langdell's model why legal education could not have included supervised practice in the courts; and there is no reason beyond the persuasiveness and influence of Welch's model why medical education could not have concerned itself as much with the maintenance of health as with the diagnosis and cure of disease. Moreover, the differences among the models tell us a good deal about the differences in the character of the several professions. Not everything, to be sure, for the social sources of aspirants, the markets for graduates, the presence or absence of competing models, and the effectiveness with which the original models were disseminated were inevitably relevant. But patterns of professional training do have their effects and are

worthy of exploration in their own right as the sources of particular historical developments.

Permit me, if I may, to move on to my second topic, namely, the recent history of the doctorate in education. I might remark at the outset that in focusing on the doctorate I am departing from what has been fairly common practice in reviewing the education of the educating professions. Most discussions have concentrated, not on the highest level of professional preparation, but rather on the minimum preparation required for entry into these professions; as a result the history of the education of the educating professions has been essentially the story of a slowly increasing minimum, from normal-school training, to baccalaureate-level training, to the masters-level training that has become common in our own times. My interest, however, is in the problematics of professional education, in the intellectual substance and systematic experience deemed essential to first-class practice; and I believe this is better gleaned from a scrutiny of doctoral programs than from consideration of preservice preparation in general. That there is such a gap between the doctorate and the minimum level of preparation required for entry into professional service is a datum of great significance.

There are three bench marks that I should like to note before turning to the more recent history. The year 1893 was the one in which Teachers College, then newly allied with Columbia, announced this country's first formal Doctor of Philosophy program in the field of education. The year 1920 was the one in which the newly established Harvard Graduate School of Education announced the first formal Doctor of Education program. And the year 1934 was the one in which Teachers College announced a Doctor of Education program alongside its Doctor of Philosophy program. The dates and programs are significant because they allow us to glimpse the problematics of professional training in education at important turning points in the history of two influential institutions.

Let us consider the requirements for the Teachers College Ph.D. in education during the early years of Russell's administration. They included formal work in educational psychology, history of education, and philosophy of education; two practica, at least one of which had to be in a specialized field of education ("practicum" seems to have been used to refer to any advanced course in which the students were expected to produce original work); graduate study in some department of Columbia other than education; and a dissertation "showing power of independent thought and capacity to advance knowledge in the candidate's chosen field." Now, at least two observations are in order as one sets these requirements against Russell's own ideal paradigm of professional education. First, as one studies the available practica, they seem much more closely related to "professional knowledge" than to "technical skill." The description of Professor Edward L. Thorndike's practicum in educational psychology read as follows: "The course prepares advanced students to investigate such problems in education as involve accurate treatment of mental characteristics, and will provide future principals and superintendents of schools with the technical knowledge of statistics which will enable them to use conveniently and profitably the data available in any school system." Fair enough, one might say; that is precisely what Professor Thorndike should have been teaching aspiring principals and superintendents. But consider the descriptions of Professor Milo Hillegas's practicum on elementary education and Professor Julius Sachs's practicum on secondary education. The description of Hillegas's read as follows: "A preliminary study of the principles underlying the course of study will be followed by a detailed investigation of current practice in the leading American cities. A comparison of conditions in this country with the practice in England, Germany, and France will form part of the course." And the description of Sachs's read: "Students are expected to prepare during the course, in addition to assigned book reviews, papers bearing either on (1) general tendencies in American and foreign secondary school systems; or (2) the relation between the secondary school and the elementary school, as well as the college; or (3) specific problems in secondary education, with special reference to the public high school." Second, as one looks over the lists of dissertations produced, it is clear that there was an initial concentration on studies in the history and philosophy of education and then a shift to studies in the psychology of education and in the statistical analysis of survey data relating to educational institutions and programs. If there was a problematics of the Teachers College curriculum circa 1910, then, it was that of a historical and statistical approach to the institutions and processes of education(5).

Let us turn now to the requirements for the Harvard Ed.D. during the early years of the Graduate School of Education in the 1920s. Students seeking candidacy for the degree were required to show evidence of successful teaching experience and a working knowledge of biology, psychology, and the social sciences. Once admitted, their

programs revolved around formal work in at least five fields of education, with studies of the social theory of education, the history of education, and educational psychology required of all. As for the thesis, its stated purpose was to enable the student "to conduct an independent investigation, in which he handles effectively the knowledge already available upon his subject and produces a constructive result of importance and value."

Once again, two observations are in order. First, as one examines the actual curriculum at Harvard, one is struck by the paucity of course offerings in comparison with those of Teachers College. The Harvard program of study had greater focus, to be sure, but doctoral candidates were more likely to pursue this program on an independent basis, doubtless with occasional assistance from the faculty. Second, the programmatic requirements for the Ed.D. were really quite similar to those for the Ph.D. at Teachers College, with the principal difference being in the latitude permitted students in the choice of thesis topics. When one considers the topics actually chosen, however, it is clear that they were far more like contemporary dissertation topics at Teachers College than they were different. Ultimately, the difference between the Harvard Ed.D. program and the Teachers College Ph.D. program during the 1920's derived much more from the differing size and character of the two institutions than from any fundamental difference in the problematics they embodied.

Finally, given the preeminence of Teachers College in doctoral training in education before World War II—Columbia granted 1,600 doctorates in the field between 1898 and 1941—it is instructive to examine the requirements for the Doctor of Education degree at Teachers College when it was first authorized in 1934. These included three years of formal course work, at least a sixth of which would consist of courses "covering issues common to workers in the educational field"; a series of written and oral examinations intended to appraise "preparation and fitness for professional leadership in the field of specialization"; and a project report on some educational activity or service, designed to demonstrate professional competence in its widest possible personal and professional application. Initially, courses "covering issues common to workers in the educational field" were conceived to be courses in the so-called foundations of education—the history, philosophy, sociology, and psychology of education—but later the conception was broadened to include courses in educational administration, guidance, and curriculum and instruction. As for the topics of project reports, they very quickly went beyond the subjects of contemporary Ph.D. dissertations to include, among other things, syllabi for new courses, suggestions for curriculum development in particular states or localities, and plans for administrative and institutional reform. By 1941, the number of Ed.D.s granted at Columbia each year was nearly equal to the number of Ph.D.s the university was awarding in the field of education.

Now, my purpose in sketching the development of these early doctoral programs at Columbia and Harvard has been primarily to convey some sense of what actually happened to Russell's model of professional education at his own institution in the years prior to World War II. And it seems to me that the principal generalization one must draw from the data is the inescapable fact of devolution. For all Russell's high aspirations to create a profession of education comparable to the professions of law and medicine, the drift in practice was steadily away from that goal. The requirement of general culture may have been assumed, but it was not carefully insisted upon, beyond the bachelor's degree needed for admission. The requirement of special scholarship was enforced in the early years of the Ph.D. via insistence on graduate study in the university outside the field of education; but it was not included in the requirements for the Ed.D., and, as a matter of fact, it was abandoned as a requirement for the Ph.D. before too long. The requirement of professional knowledge was more resolutely honored than any other, but only a minimal core of common work in the history, philosophy, and psychology of education was insisted upon. And the requirement of technical skill was acknowledged rhetorically but neither honored nor enforced programmatically. In effect, the structural disjunction between the preservice and inservice phases of professional education wreaked havoc with the integrity and coherence of the Russell model. Student teaching became the principal practicum of the preservice phase of training; and the so-called practica of the inservice phase were in truth seminars, at best, opportunities for scientific and scholarly inquiry into professional problems, at worst, didactic lectures. Even more important, the students who came for advanced training had already learned their professional roles in the field and were returning to the university for a limited amount of specialized knowledge and for eventual credentialing. The result was a fragmentation of the professional curriculum and a loss of coherence among its parts. What emerged was, to borrow a familiar phrasing from the Teachers College catalogue on the eve of World War II, a program of advanced graduate study "developed in the light of the candidate's previous

education and experience" and emphasizing "preparation for competent professional performance(8)".

That this drift was national rather than local in scope is documented by two studies of the doctorate in education undertaken in 1958 and 1969 by the American Association of Colleges for Teacher Education (in the latter instance, in collaboration with Phi Delta Kappa). The first gathered data from 3,428 doctoral graduates of 92 institutions, who had earned their degrees between 1956 and 1958; the second, which replicated the first, gathered data from 15,140 doctoral graduates of 124 institutions, who had earned their degrees between 1965 and 1969. The two surveys covered a variety of topics, including the characteristics of the institutions, the characteristics of the students when admitted, the characteristics of the instructional programs, and the characteristic personal and professional problems associated with earning the degree. Nothing emerged more clearly from these surveys than that neither the Ph.D. nor the Ed.D. program in education had much in common from one institution to another, beyond the elemental fact that they provided advanced training. As between the Ph.D. and the Ed.D., the studies concluded that the sole distinguishing difference inhered in the foreign language requirement traditionally associated with the Ph.D. As regards any common core of subject matter generally associated with the doctorate in education, the only requirements common to as many as half the programs across the country were educational measurement and statistics, educational psychology, and philosophy of education. Beyond that, everything else connected with the doctorate, except the financial and personal difficulties attendant on earning it, could be subsumed under the rubric "diversity." For all intents and purposes, three-quarters of a century after its brave formulation in 1900, the Russell paradigm and the problematics it represented were in shambles(9).

Permit me, then, to move on to my third topic: What ought the education of educators to look like in our own time? In this connection, I should like to make a number of preliminary observations about the world of present-day education and then propose a set of recommendations based on those observations.

I have argued in my recent writings that we have been living through a revolution in education that may be as profound as the original invention of the school. It is a revolution compounded of several elements—the rapid expansion of higher education to a point where one out of every two high school graduates has been going on

334

working with clients of any age in any field and in any institution ought to be broadly cultivated individuals. And this means that they ought to receive their undergraduate education at institutions where faculty members and students think seriously together about the substance and meaning of a liberal education, and particularly, to repeat Russell's concern, about the relationships among the several fields of knowledge. This is not to suggest that every undergraduate institution ought to reach the same conclusions about these matters; it would be revolution enough in my opinion if the colleges simply began to reflect on them.

Second, special scholarship. Educators working with clients of any age ought to have at least one teaching field in which they are expert or have been expert in the past. No matter how general an educator's responsibilities, no matter how far removed from the diurnal business of teaching, he or she should ideally have mastered some field of knowledge or art sufficiently well to have been able to reflect systematically on the various ways in which it might be taught to clients at different stages of development and in different teaching situations. I myself have taught history in schools and colleges, in public libraries and over commercial television, via brightly illustrated pamphlets written for factory employees and heavy tomes written for other specialists in the field. I have taught history to second-graders, using facsimiles of the *New-England Primer;* to twelfth-graders, using their own programs of study as the point of departure; to school-board members, using their most pressing problems as grist for my mill; to other professors of history, using recent monographs in the field as the basis for my discussion. The approach, the sequence, the level, and the material for immediate consideration differed from one instance to another; in all of them, however, I was teaching the same American history.

Third, professional knowledge. Here, Russell, reflecting the period in which he wrote, tended to concentrate on the history, philosophy, and psychology of schooling, though he was patently aware of the need for trained educators in "trade schools, industrial schools, Sunday schools, reform schools, houses of refuge, and other philanthropic institutions." Given the breadth of today's educational enterprise and the explosion of scholarly knowledge in the relevant humanistic, social, and behavioral disciplines, I would propose a reformulation that would include three elements: policy studies, developmental studies, and pedagogical studies. By policy studies I refer to those studies of the humanities and social sciences that contribute to an understanding of the aims of education, of the

to college; the massive shifts in population, from east to west, from south to north, from country to city, and from city to suburb, which have created new and extraordinary clienteles to educate; the movement of women into paid employment outside the home in unprecedented numbers, with prodigious consequences for the family; the changing character of work associated with the emergence of a postindustrial society, and in particular the growth of the so-called knowledge industries; the various civil rights and liberation movements of the 1960s and 1970s, which have so radically changed the management and politics of education(10).

And beneath all of these, and inexorably affecting them, has been the educational transformation wrought by mass television. In 1950, fewer than 10 percent of American homes had television sets. Today, that figure has leveled off at around 97 percent. Moreover, so far as can be determined, at least one member of the average American household is watching television more than six hours out of every 24, with the greatest amount of viewing being done by the very young, the very old, and the very poor. Once one recognizes that television teaches—not only via channels specifically labeled educational but across the entire spectrum of public and commercial programming— the fact of television in 97 percent of American homes being viewed six hours a day itself constitutes revolution. That revolution has drastically altered familial education. It has radically altered the education of the public at large. And it has fundamentally modified the context in which all schooling proceeds.

Most important for our purposes, this complex of revolutions has transformed the traditional profession of education at the same time that it has created a variety of new educating professions—one thinks, for example, of day-care workers, scriptwriters in children's television production units, learning consultants in libraries and museums, training officers in business and industry, and gerontologists in senior citizens' centers. All these people carry on educational work of profound significance that can surely be enhanced via sound professional preparation. Moreover, to be most effective, each must pursue his or her special activities with full knowledge of what the others are doing. Their work as educators is inextricably intertwined; in fact, they are in many ways members of a single profession.

What should the education of these educators look like during the years immediately ahead? In my opinion, we can do no better than to take James Earl Russell's four components and reformulate them in present-day terms. First, general culture. Obviously, educators

situations and institutions in which education proceeds in different societies, and of the inextricable ties between educational institutions and the societies that sustain them and that are in turn affected by them. By developmental studies I refer to those studies of the humanities and behavioral sciences (including biology) that contribute to an understanding of human development over the entire life cycle and of the various ways in which different forms of education affect that development—of critical importance here would be studies of socialization, enculturation, and learning that clarify the nature and outcome of the educational process. By pedagogical studies I refer to those systematic studies of the practice of teaching and learning in a variety of situations, that unite policy and developmental studies with studies of the substantive characteristics of various fields of the curriculum and with studies of the structural characteristics of various learning environments. In Herbert Simon's terms, pedagogical studies are among the "sciences of the artificial," marked by a quest for systematic knowledge about how to design particular kinds of human environments. As such, they must be pursued in the world of practice—in schools, colleges, day-care centers, libraries, museums, work places, and community agencies, all regarded as centers for creative inquiry as well as for the demonstration of excellent performance. I believe every faculty of education worthy of the name ought to have networks of such institutions associated with it in a research and teaching capacity, in the fashion of the teaching hospitals traditionally associated with medical schools(11).

Now, policy studies and developmental studies might well call to mind the so-called preclinical studies of the medical curriculum, with pedagogy, like pathology, partly preclinical and partly clinical. But the distinction between the preclinical and the clinical has broken down in medical education in recent years and I do not believe it would be a useful one to maintain in the education of educators. Professional curricula in general require a continuing mutual relationship between preclinical and clinical instruction that renders the distinction less useful than Welch's generation thought it might be. I would also remark that a spirit of inquiry must characterize the entire range of professional studies if they are not to deteriorate rapidly into mere didacticism. During the 1950s and 1960s the common solution to the problem of reviving a spirit of inquiry in education courses was to bring them into closer relationship with cognate offerings of faculties of arts and sciences; but too often the price of the heightened spirit of inquiry was the disappearance of any relevance to the problems of education. I happen to believe that the offerings of education faculties can embody both a spirit of inquiry and the required relevance to

educational problems; but to insure that they do so will take a steadfast commitment to both on the part of those faculties that has not always been in evidence in recent years. In addition, education faculties will have to be a good deal more imaginative than they have in the past with respect to grouping and synthesizing the substance and methods of policy studies, developmental studies, and pedagogical studies. There is not enough time for the aspiring educator to study the history, philosophy, anthropology, economics, politics, sociology, psychology, and biology of education seriatim in discrete units; and the current practice of permitting students to select one or another of these studies while ignoring the rest is simply not defensible(12).

Obviously, the discussion of pedagogical studies moves us easily to Russell's fourth component, technical skill. This is the realm in which the professional preparation of educators has been weakest over the years, despite the attention that has recently been paid to so-called laboratory experience in the preservice phase and to so-called competency-based instruction throughout the program. At their best, pedagogical studies join professional knowledge and technical skill in a way that bridges the gap that has historically existed between the two. Pedagogy is not merely a science of design; it is also, in Joseph Schwab's terms, one of the eclectic arts, marked by a quest for practice based on a continually changing calculus of knowledge drawn from many relevant sciences. I believe every candidate for the doctorate in education ought to study pedagogy partly via a rotating internship through a variety of educational situations, where direct participation in the daily business of teaching and learning can be joined to systematic study of tested practice based on continuing inquiry and appraisal. The hallmark of the technically skilled educator in our time ought to be his or her profound awareness of the relationship between what goes on in any particular educational situation and what goes on in all the other educational situations in which the client participates. It is this as much as anything else that dictates both a diversified internship, involving not only schools but libraries, museums, community centers, and the like, and a common professional preparation for the educating professions(13).

A word about the thesis requirement, which has long been a touchy and controversial aspect of doctoral study. My own inclination would be to abolish it in its present form, as too much a mimicking of the Ph.D. program in the traditional academic areas (where the thesis has in any case come under increasing fire as irrelevant to subsequent responsibility and performance). Instead, I would provide ample opportunity in advanced seminars and practica for individual and collaborative scholarship and performance that can be subjected to systematic review and appraisal by faculty and student colleagues. I would prefer to see one or two solid research papers, a terse scholarly evaluation of an educational undertaking, and a first-class demonstration of teaching skill as the publicly judged fruits of doctoral study in education rather than an overly long, if competent, thesis that will sit unread in the library forever. For those who have something to say, the thesis ought to remain an option; but I do not believe we should continue to require it of every doctoral candidate.

Permit me a final thought. James Earl Russell stated his belief in 1900 that general culture, special scholarship, professional knowledge, and technical skill were essential to all educators, not merely the leaders of the profession. I would restate that belief as my own. And I would maintain further that the time has come to require the doctorate for all who would seek entry into the educating professions. Many states already require five years of preparation for a permanent school certificate—the requirement is most often satisfied by four years of undergraduate education joined to a fifth year of professional preparation. I would argue for redesigned programs, not unlike the six-year B.S.-M.D. programs at Northwestern University and Boston University, in which the B.A. and the Ed.D. could be obtained at the end of six years. Through careful planning, the studies leading to general culture would also provide a base for the policy and developmental studies, some aspects of which are surely as liberal as they are professional. Through careful planning, too, the policy and developmental studies could be made to relate to the pedagogical studies far more than has hitherto been the case; and the latter could be started early enough—perhaps in the third or fourth year—that they could enrich the work in the other professional realms. I do not think the decision to pursue a career in education would necessarily have to be made during the senior year of high school, as is the case with the six-year B.S.-M.D. programs; it could probably be made as late as the sophomore year in the right kind of undergraduate program. And, for able individuals who might decide at a later stage to enter one of the educating professions, there would remain the option of the three-year doctoral program following the award of the bachelor's degree. Finally, I am assuming that there would be postdoctoral programs in education, as there are in all the other major professional fields, through which practitioners would be able to extend, deepen, and update their special scholarship, professional knowledge, and technical skill, as well as to gain expertise in such fields as management, supervision, or administration.

As G. K. Chesterton once remarked of Christianity, it is not, after all, that James Earl Russell's ideal was ever tried and found wanting, it is rather that Russell's ideal was never really tried at all. Given the anticipated steady state of American education in the early 1980s, it is unlikely that we shall have a better time to make the attempt.

NOTES

1   The Langdell curriculum is discussed in Robert Stevens, "Two Cheers for 1870: The American Law School," *Perspectives in American History*, V (1971), 405-548; Arthur E. Sutherland, *The Law at Harvard: A History of Ideas and Men, 1817-1967* (Cambridge: Harvard University Press, 1967), Chaps. vi-vii; and Alfred Z. Reed, *Training for the Public Profession of the Law* (New York: Carnegie Foundation for the Advancement of Teaching, 1921).

2   The Welch curriculum is discussed in Donald Fleming, *William H. Welch and the Rise of Modern Medicine* (Boston: Little, Brown, 1954); and Alan M. Chesney, *The Johns Hopkins Hospital and the Johns Hopkins University School of Medicine* (3 vols.; Baltimore: Johns Hopkins University Press, 1943-1963), I-II. The Mall quotation is from Franklin P. Mall, "The Value of Research in the Medical School," *The Michigan Alumnus*, X (1903-04), 395.

3   The Russell curriculum is discussed in Kenneth H. Toepfer, "James Earl Russell and the Rise of Teachers College, 1897-1915" (unpublished doctoral thesis, Teachers College, Columbia University, 1966); and Lawrence A. Cremin, David A. Shannon, and Mary Evelyn Townsend, *A History of Teachers College, Columbia University* (New York: Columbia University Press, 1954). For the historical context of Russell's curriculum, see Merle L. Borrowman, *The Liberal and Technical in Teacher Education: A Historical Survey of American Thought* (New York: Bureau of Publications, Teachers College, Columbia University, 1956), Walter S. Monroe, *Teaching-Learning Theory and Teacher Education, 1890-1952* (Urbana: University of Illinois Press, 1952), and Geraldine Joncich, *The Sane Positivist: A Biography of Edward L. Thorndike* (Middletown: Wesleyan University Press, 1968). The Russell quotation is from his *Annual Report* to the Trustees of Teachers College for 1900, pp. 13-14.

4   James E. Russell, "The Function of the University in the Training of Teachers," *Columbia University Quarterly*, I (1898-99), 323-342.

The Hunt Lectures

1960
The Dimensions of Professional Leadership
Laurence DeFee Haskew

1961
Revolution in Instruction
Lindley P. Stiles

1962
Imperatives for Excellence in Teacher Education
J.W. Maucker

1963
Africa, Teacher Education, and the United States
Karl W. Bigelow

1964
The Certification of Teachers: The Restricted State Approved Program Approach
James B. Conant

1965
Perspective on Action in Teacher Education
Florence B. Stratemeyer

1966
Leadership for Intellectual Freedom in Higher Education
Willard B. Spalding

1967
Tradition and Innovation in Teacher Education
Rev. Charles F. Donovan, S.J.

1968
Teachers: The Need and the Task
Felix C. Robb

1969
A Consumer's Hopes and Dreams for Teacher Education
Elizabeth D. Koontz

1970
Realignments for Teacher Education
Fred. T. Wilhelms

1971
The Impossible Imperatives: Power, Authority, and Decision Making in Teacher Education
Evan R. Collins

1972
Beyond the Upheaval
Edward C. Pomeroy

1973
Time for Decision in Teacher Education
Lord James of Rusholme

1974
Ferment and Momentum in Teacher Education
Margaret Lindsey

1975
Drumbeats and Dissonance: Variations on a Theme for Teachers
Calvin Gross

1976
Now you shall be REAL TO EVERYONE
Robert B. Howsam

1977
The Real World of the Teacher Educator: A Look to the Near Future
David L. Clark

1978
The Education of the Educating Professions
Lawrence A. Cremin

5   *Teachers College Announcement* (1909-10), pp. 76, 78, 80.

6   *Harvard University Catalogue* (1920-21), pp. 474-477. For the historical context of the Harvard program, see Arthur G. Powell, "University Schools of Education in the Twentieth Century," *Peabody Journal of Education*, LIV (1976-77), 3-20.

7   *Teachers College Announcement* (1934-35), pp. 6-8.

8   *Teachers College Announcement* (1941-42), p. 15.

9   Harold E. Moore, John H. Russel, and Ronald G. Ferguson, *The Doctorate in Education: An Inquiry into Conditions Affecting Pursuit of the Doctoral Degree in the Field of Education, Volume II: The Institutions* (Washington, D.C.: American Association of Colleges for Teachers Education, 1960) and Neville Robertson and Jack K. Sistler, *The Doctorate in Education: An Inquiry into Conditions Affecting Pursuit of the Doctoral Degree in the Field of Education—The Institutions* (Bloomington, Ind.: Phi Delta Kappa, 1971). For the sociological context of contemporary teacher education, see Dan C. Lortie, *Schoolteacher: A Sociological Study* (Chicago: University of Chicago Press, 1975).

10 These ideas are developed in Lawrence A. Cremin, *Public Education* (New York: Basic Books, 1976), and *Traditions of American Education* (New York: Basic Books, 1977).

11 The Russell quotation is from his *Annual Report* for 1900, p. 20. For Simon's formulation, see Herbert A. Simon, *The Sciences of the Artificial* (Cambridge: The M.I.T. Press, 1969). For a recent discussion of the changes that would be required for schools (and, by implication, other educative agencies) to become centers for creative inquiry into the nature and processes of education, see Robert J. Schaefer, *The School as a Center of Inquiry* (New York: Harper & Row, 1967). For the classic formulation, see John Dewey, "The Relation of Theory to Practice in Education," *Third Yearbook of the National Society for the Scientific Study of Education*, Part I (Chicago: Department of Education, University of Chicago, 1904).

12 On the tendency of faculties of education to vacillate between an overconcern for relevance to practice and an overconcern for academic respectability, see Nathan Glazer, "The Schools of the Minor Professions," *Minerva*, XII (1974), 346-364.

13 For Schwab's formulation, see Joseph J. Schwab, "The Practical: A Language for Curriculum," *School Review*, LXXVIII (1969-70), 1-20, and "The Practical: Arts of Eclectic," *ibid.*, LXXIX (1970-71), 493-542. See also N. L. Gage, *The Scientific Basis of the Art of Teaching* (New York: Teachers College Press, 1978).

The Gulf Between Students and Faculty

The Rise of Administration

Laurence Veysey

Between undergraduates and their professors at the end of the nineteenth century, a gulf yawned so deep that it could appropriately be called "the awful chasm." [107] The academic experience held such different meanings for the students and instructors that their minds for the most part met only the basis of temporary, intermittent compulsion. This fact lurked beneath all the alumni nostalgia on the one side and all the earnest speeches about academic purpose on the other. Recognizing the situation, Woodrow Wilson once declared: "The work of the college, the work of its classrooms and laboratories, has become the merely formal and compulsory side of its life, and . . . a score of other things, lumped under the term 'undergraduate activities,' have become the vital, spontaneous, absorbing realities for nine out of every ten men who go to college." [108] Surveying the scene in 1909, Edwin E. Slosson affirmed that "almost every educator, if asked what was the main fault of our large colleges, would . . . [reply] that it was the loss of personal relationship between instructor and student." [109]

Neither Wilson nor Slosson seemed to realize that such a personal relationship had seldom existed in the past, and least of all in the mid-nineteenth century. The barrier between teacher and taught loomed, if anything, far higher in the era of the disciplinary college; it had then been revealed by riots, the throwing of stones at professors' houses, and in at least two cases by actual murder of a professor. [110] At Dickinson College in 1866 "students regarded the faculty as a species of necessary evil, and the faculty treated the students much as if they were an unavoidable nuisance." [111] The coming of the elective system eased some of the tension, but it did not, as its advocates hoped, fundamentally alter the problem. The separation of aims and values remained, masked now by a veneer of mannerly politeness. An academically tolerant Barrett Wendell observed that "many students seem as unable to meet us intellectually as a near-sighted eye to detect a small star, or a color-blind man to read railway signals." [112] At Stanford, despite the tie of shared hardships during the initial years, the two groups drifted apart until open defiance and mass suspensions occurred in the so-called liquor rebellion. Even at Johns Hopkins, which prided itself on an unusually collaborative atmosphere, social conviviality involving both students and faculty lasted only a decade before it began to disintegrate. And William Lyon Phelps recalled a somber scene at Yale in the early nineties, when "nearly all the members of the Faculty wore dark clothes, frock coats, high collars; in the classroom their manners had an icy formality; [and] humour was usually absent, except occasional irony at the expense of a dull student. It was quite possible to attend a class three hours a week for a year," Phelps added, "and not have even the remotest conception of the personality of the man behind the desk." [113] From the faculty's point of view, President Taylor of Vassar observed in 1893: "One is obliged to suspect, at times, that the student comes to be regarded as a mere disturber of ideal schemes, and as a disquieting element in what, without him, might be a fairly pleasant life."[114] So out of touch was the Harvard faculty with the realities of the student world that it believed the undergraduates were devoting twice as much time to their studies as actually proved to be true.[115]

The deep failure of communication between students and faculty is nowhere better revealed than in their lack of a common sense of humor. Shortly after becoming president of the University of Wisconsin, Charles R. Van Hise committed a major *faux pas*. During a public jubilee he jokingly suggested that a holiday be declared in which there would be no debts, examinations, or other customary evils. To his chagrin, the students took his offhand remarks seriously and, after Van Hise announced that of course examinations were not really suspended, the students displayed a righteous anger at having been deceived. In student eyes, tests were such obnoxious symbols of an alien academic world that it was apparently inconceivable for them to be made a laughing matter. Nor, on the other hand, did professors or administrators appreciate students' jocular views of their own serious efforts. President Harper of the University of Chicago was not amused when he learned that a comic skit mocking the seminar was being prepared.[116] In a story of Harvard, a group of devil-may-care students "pleaded" with a professor to offer them an advanced course in hieroglyphics, solely as a lark. Of course the professor was delighted, talked to them in the class all term as one scholar to others, and never understood that he was being manipulated and ridiculed.[117] Some students spoke of faculty members as if they *were* animals in a zoo: "It's so interesting to watch them." One Princetonian of the Wilson period, reproved for laughing at his instructor in the classroom, declared he did so "because the teacher used repeatedly the funniest word he had ever heard. Asked what the word was, he replied, 'Spinoza.'"[118]

Amid such conditions, college administrations were naturally loath to surrender any real power to student government, although the latter in a nominal sense was beginning to appear. As Andrew S. Draper of Illinois pungently declared: "Student government is a broken reed. If actual, it is capricious, impulsive and unreliable; if not, it is a subterfuge and pretense."[119] Recognizing at least the validity of the latter half of this equation, Harvard students declined the proffered "privilege" of self-government in 1907.[120]

Numerous remedies were introduced in an attempt to bridge the gap between the students and their mentors. At many institutions ostentatious faculty teas and "at-homes" were held; although some genuine relationships doubtless grew from them, they were far more likely to become dutiful routines. The "adviser" system for supervising the selection of courses at large universities (it was the fad of the moment at Columbia in 1906) likewise soon degenerated into a perfunctory affair involving only brief, impersonal interviews. G. Stanley Hall

naïvely hoped that the spirit of scientific research would fill the breach, but he was unaware of the difficulties of such an approach in an environment less mature than that of the graduate seminar.[121] More to the point and more spectacular were the efforts of the humanistic showmen—the Phelpses and "Copeys." Yet by meeting students on their own level, these lecturers might sacrifice the essence of what the faculty stood for: "history might be interpreted . . . in terms of the football season, Dante translated into the jargon of the Y.M.C.A., or Shakespeare and Pope denatured into nineteenth century optimism."[122] Moreover, it was admitted that a man as sympathetic to the students as Dean Briggs of Harvard failed ultimately to alter the tone of student life.[123]

The most elaborate attempt to narrow the gulf occurred during the Wilson administration at Princeton. Wilson's preceptorial system was designed to enable undergraduates to share their lives with professors on an intimate basis. Although the system gave large rewards to the few students who accepted it as more than a new means of compulsion, even Wilson was forced to admit after several years of its operation that it "accomplished no revolution in human nature." The undergraduate, Wilson confessed, still turned aside

from the things which chiefly engross him to have a brief conference with his preceptor about reading which lies remote from the ordinary courses of his thought. And his preceptor can not be his companion in the matters which constitute his life. The one lives in one world, the other in another. They are not members of the same family or of the same social organism; and the rivalry between the life and the work of the student generally results in the victory of the life.[124]

Like most innovations, the preceptorial system tended to become routine, to fall into place as "merely another class."[125]

None of the attempts to transcend the barrier between students and faculty accomplished the major change which their advocates had sought. The undergraduates could not be distracted by any voluntary means from their primary loyalty to college life as distinct from university education. Only one tactic remained at the disposal of their superiors: the compulsory classroom test in the American system of higher education, from the days of the small colleges down into the period of the new university, revealed a similar continuity of student alienation from the system of which he was supposedly the most essential part. It is noteworthy that in this central matter of procedure, neither German nor English influences made themselves felt. The basic safety of the institution was here at stake, and foreign models could not be emulated. In America the power of the university to force the fleeting attention of the students upon their academic obligations had to be demonstrated, not once a year or only before the bestowal of a degree, but again and again and again. Habitual drill for those in the ranks provided the indispensable sense of security for the men in command. The consequences of a less rigid regime must have seemed too frightful, in terms of institutional cohesion, even to be openly considered. Instead, as Thorstein Veblen pointed out, the American university continued to be partially penal in character.[126] Elaborate codes and forfeits were needed to insure obedience. One libertarian experiment clearly revealed this. When attendance requirements were relaxed at Harvard in the eighties, students at once began vanishing to New York, Montreal, Bermuda, and, in one famous case, to Havana. A stern Board of Overseers immediately gave the faculty a choice between keeping accounts in the classroom or submitting the whole assemblage to a morning roll call (after the manner of an army camp or a prison).[127]

In fact, despite all the cheering for Alma Mater, college students betrayed many of the symptoms of a deeply disloyal subject population. Why else would oaths of allegiance have seemed appropriate for the students at Yale during the sixties and seventies? Or why would the freedom of students to congregate in large groups sometimes be inhibited by regulation?[128] As time passed, growing standards of courtesy made such formal regulations seem unnecessary. Yet the widespread persistence of cheating on examinations, with little sense of personal wrongdoing, bespoke the reality of continued alienation. The black market in themes was a major industry.[129] Cheating, it need hardly be said, represents a concern for the formal appearance of completed tasks, rather than pride in their substance; its psychological affiliations are with the forced labor camp. To cheating there was added the further symptom of student malingering. Thus President Eliot had to complain: "Students are inclined to neglect their duties because of small ailments which in after life would never be allowed to interfere with their daily work.[130] Woodrow Wilson accused students of being like his notion of trade unionists; they assume, he said, "the attitude of employees and give as little as possible for what they get." Henry Seidel Canby of Yale declared that the undergraduates comprised "a faction within our college body, which constantly practised direct warfare or passive resistance against its superiors, usually with the sneaking sympathy of both parents and town."[131]

The bitterness of student alienation from the academic order was constantly checked by the pleasant qualities of the campus environment. Tests might be relatively frequent, but they did not come every day, and in between them one could be blissfully happy. College was no African colony of the conventional sort. Yet the often polite and carefree atmosphere of the American academic community should not mask its most serious structural cleavage. Here was an institution, catering to respectable Americans, which thrived on a double standard "according to which it is wrong to lie, but right to deceive a professor; according to which it is wrong to steal, but right to take aids to reflection into an Examination Hall."[132] At the very least, student-faculty tension produced the hypocrisy which guards the external reputation of a deeply divided social order. Few academic officials dared show agreement with Edwin E. Slosson when he frankly asserted: "The less personal attention they [the students] get from professors the better some of them like it."[133]

The endemic gulf between these two groups of people in the American university cannot be explained by disparities of social origin. American professors lacked any clear-cut social characteristics which would sharply distinguish them from their students. Quantitative studies of professors' backgrounds in this period indicate that the largest number had businessmen for fathers, although ministers, farmers, and the other established professions were also well represented, in about that order.[134] In the late nineteenth century, clergymen's sons were downwardly mobile (or at best static), whereas the sons of farmers and businessmen were moving upward in the social scale. Since all these backgrounds were rather evenly distributed among faculty members in the new universities, no single professorial "class," with clear social status, emerges from this picture. American professors were thus far less uniform in terms of their backgrounds than, for instance, German or English professors of the same period. Nothing like a homogeneous "mandarin" element had formed in American faculty circles. Only in that a great many of them came from New England families did American professors stand apart from the American middle class as a whole,[135] and this fact probably reflects the tendency of the better colleges and universities to be located in New England or in parts of the United States which New Englanders had later settled. The social data, in other words, do not explain why this group of men (unlike their students) chose the academic life; and there were, after all, millions of Americans in roughly similar social and economic circumstances.

The "awful chasm," then, must be explained on other grounds. In part, of course, it represented the contrast between age and youth (and, as we have seen, a particularly childish version of youth). But it also stemmed from an overriding disparity in values. If the motives which led a man to become a professor could be analyzed, they would probably often reveal a desire to withdraw from fast-paced, "materialistic" realms of activity; in other words, the choice more typically resulted from a love of books than from a quest for status.[136] But the student could not understand the professor's kind of commitment; instead he anticipated for himself an entirely different way of life, the active, non-abstractive pattern shared by most Americans outside the university. Except in a small minority of instances, nothing the professor said or did could change the student's mind, for his mind was shaped far more powerfully by his parents and peers. The miracle, indeed, was that the professor himself—for whatever intellectual and psychological reasons—had managed to escape from the cycle. All this meant that the chasm could be expected long to endure. Two world wars and a possible shift toward greater respect for intellectual training would be required before it filled into an uneven and hazardous trough.

The Rise of Administration

Below the professor yawned an intellectual abyss. Above him, in the other direction, he beheld another landscape, seemingly less formidable yet with its own disconcertingly steep barriers. An entity known as "the administration" had rapidly come into being, perhaps in part from the very need to control larger quantities of students than ever before. From the administration the professor was often to feel as isolated as he did from his undergraduates.

Reading downward, the hierarchy of the American university normally came to comprise trustee, president, dean, department chairman (or "head professor," as he was sometimes called at the turn of the century), and then faculty members of several descending ranks, alongside whom, in rough equality, there developed a business staff with its own internal gradations. Below all these were the graduate assistants, the ordinary graduate students, and then the undergraduates (the older of whom sometimes conspicuously lorded it over the younger), and the custodial staff. Generally speaking, power flowed downward throughout this entire organization. Interesting exceptions could occur, however, mainly because of unusual considerations of prestige. Prestige did not accrue solely from one's position in this academic hierarchy; it also came from one's social background and, in some cases, from one's national academic reputation, which did not always correspond with one's local position. Thus a professor pre-eminent in his field, such as Frederick Jackson Turner, might consider himself a president's equal and make demands upon rather than requests to trustees; Turner was called "the king-maker" in recognition of his major role in placing Van Hise in the Wisconsin presidency in 1903.

In practice, then, the actual exercise of power downward through the ranks of the academic hierarchy might vary considerably according to specific circumstances. Yet for each academic rank a well-defined sense of an appropriate role began to develop. Only at a few inferior universities, for example, did the trustees behave as despots; their usual function was to provide quiet reassurance to the "respectable" outside world, and they employed direct authority only at moments when basic changes were being considered (as in the adoption of a new curriculum or the election of a new president). Custom or indifference might keep trustees from interfering with strictly academic matters of policy, un-

less such concerns threatened the integrity of the institution from the layman's point of view.[137] At Illinois, however, the trustees jealously limited the presidency to a two-year term, although customarily renewing the contract, and it was noted at Wisconsin that faculty members often had greater security of tenure than did the presidents themselves.[138]

Routinely the presidents wielded pre-eminent power at most of the major universities except Yale. Unlike the trustees, they devoted their lives to the institution. Lethargy or senility could, of course, affect their power, as it did for Patton at Princeton, White at Cornell, and Angell at Michigan during his declining years. Everywhere, however, the trend was toward increased presidential vigor. At the end of the nineteenth century, university heads often personally selected the faculty, though in consultation with deans and department chairmen. William R. Harper explained: "The faculties at the University of Chicago have nothing to do with the appointments in the different chairs or with the appointment of deans. The deans," he added, "are the president's administrative cabinet and hold their offices at his pleasure." [139] Presidents more frequently behaved autocratically than did trustees. But the flagrant academic autocrats tended to be old-fashioned paternalists operating in new university settings, men who were suspicious of using organized machinery—rather than their own judgment—in settling problems. (David Starr Jordan and in some respects G. Stanley Hall were of this type.) The strong president of the new academic age more often welcomed and used bureaucratic methods.

Below the president and his appointed deans stood the rank and file of the faculty. A formal subserviency was expected of them, as well as an informal deference. Thus professors were usually barred from becoming members of boards of trustees, either at their own or at other campuses.[140] Exceptional instances of faculty leadership within an institution did exist, notably at Yale and Wisconsin, but even here real power tended to center in a small group of "senior" professors rather than in the instructional staff as a whole. The usual position of the American university faculty was revealed by the fact that whenever an insurgent movement to "democratize" the structure of an institution took place, it was described as a "revolt." At the large universities, faculty meetings were often tedious and relatively inconsequential affairs; fastidious professors either attended them for amusement or else avoided them whenever possible.[141] Faculty government, where it formally existed, served much the same function as student government. It was a useful device whereby administrative leaders could sound out opinion, detect discontent so as better to cope with it, and further the posture of official solidarity by giving everyone parliamentary "rights." Occasionally, too, faculty meetings could serve as an arena for genuine debate over academic purpose, and while such debate brought few results, it at least afforded a temporary exhilaration. The professor had his own quite real dignity, but it was apt to become most apparent when he sat in his book-lined study, not when he met for formal discussions of policy. Throughout this period the concept of permanent faculty tenure, though not entirely unknown, was forthrightly accepted by very few university presidents even of leading institutions, and professors were at the mercy of their superiors to a far greater degree than would be true at the better universities a half-century later.

The term "administration," as it came into use, referred to the president, deans, business staff, and often to a number of senior professors who regularly supported the president's wishes. More than this, however, "administration" connoted a certain state of mind; it meant those people in the university community who characteristically thought in terms of institutional management or of organizational planning. Thus although American colleges had had presidents ever since the seventeenth century, administration represented a genuinely new force after the Civil War.

Academic administration came into being in two distinct stages. The first occurred in the late sixties and early seventies, when Andrew D. White, Charles W. Eliot, and James B. Angell came to power. Eliot and Angell, especially, represented a new style of worldly sophistication so far as academic executives were concerned.[142] Their aggressiveness, their concern for budgets and public relations, their interest, for example, in the statistics of their establishments, set what was then an entirely new standard. Although weak administrators continued at Yale for decades to come and occasionally still appeared elsewhere, such men clearly ran counter to the current of the academic age. Led by Eliot and Angell, the heads of more and more institutions began to revolt against the kind of conservatism which the trustees of Columbia embodied when they refused to solicit funds from local businessmen on the grounds that such donations would taint the integrity of the college.[143] In contrast, the progressive administrator of the seventies sought eagerly to broaden the base of his institution's support. Yet throughout the seventies and eighties Eliot and Angell ruled without a large bureaucratic staff to aid them, and in this sense they were still transitional in their methods.

The second stage of administrative growth began during the early nineties; it has never stopped. These were the years when William R. Harper forged the new University of Chicago and when Nicholas Murray Butler began to influence events at Columbia; placed beside Harper and Butler, Angell and Eliot in turn seemed old-fashioned almost overnight. The trend of the nineties, however, was much more widespread than could be accounted for by one or two commanding personalities. Deans became important figures at Harvard in this period; typewriters appeared and typists began flooding the correspondence files at nearly every prominent institution. By 1900 it could

be said that administration had developed something like its full measure of force in American higher education. In that year a book appeared wholly devoted to the topic of academic managership; it claimed to be the first of its kind.[144] In 1902 college presidents were urged to undertake special training as preparation for their positions.[145] Eliot's volume on University Administration appeared in 1908, amid a flurry of articles on this topic. The suggestion was raised that certain faculty members be hired and groomed on the basis of their executive talent rather than their ability as teachers or researchers. An observer remarked in 1907: "The old type of [academic] leader, learned and temperate, fast yields to the new type,—self-confident, incisive, Rooseveltian."[146]

When Nicholas Murray Butler took the reins at Columbia in 1902, his office already functioned like a well-run bureau. Butler's clerical force in that year comprised three secretaries, five stenographers, and two office boys, although it handled the correspondence of the dean as well as that of the president himself. Separate offices of the registrar and the bursar, each with its own staff, also existed. Butler's office spent eight hundred dollars a year in postage on first-class mail alone. The principal duty of the president's staff at Columbia was described as the answering of correspondence; but other obligations included keeping the records of teaching appointments, managing university social functions, handling public lectures, fellowships, and prizes, compiling catalogues, announcements, and the annual report, and serving as an employment bureau for students.[147] Many of these services, of course, would later be split among separate university offices, but in embryo all these tasks were already being performed.

The pronounced rise of administration after 1890 brought with it an alarm in many quarters that managerial staffs were running away with the American university. In fact, the proportion of funds spent on faculty salaries as compared with those spent on administration at Harvard remained about constant between 1868 and 1903.[148] At the turn of the century, therefore, such fears seem to have lacked a concrete, quantitative justification, although the power of administrators, quite apart from the money they spent on their own activities, was of course a more and more complicated question.

The secret of success for the academic administrator of the new type was to rule firmly without being a naked autocrat. This involved the capacity to consult "democratically" with everyone whose opinion counted or who might vociferously object unless "brought in" ahead of a decision. It also called for maintaining the manner of fairness and conciliation while at the same time making the best decision in the interests, not of an abstract standard, but of the balanced progress of the institution.[149] The administrator tried also, from time to time, to present bold schemes for institutional advancement, schemes that took ordinary men's breaths away and that cast the administrator as a genuine "leader" at the same time he "consulted" with others. But boldness without consultation might produce the distasteful figure of the tyrant.¹⁵⁰ A good administrator made determined efforts to keep the peace within his own institution, since if it appeared disunited it would lose prestige and influence. This meant that quarrelsome debate, including that based upon conflicts among academic ideals, must be minimized or suppressed whenever it became threateningly serious.

In these respects the model administrator behaved judiciously. In another sense, however, he was a gambler, dealing in university "futures." If any tendency was common among academic managers of the ambitious sort, it was expansion of the institution in advance of guaranteed resources. The gamble, of course, was whether benefactors could be goaded into alleviating the consequent plight by responding to the "emergency." This kind of situation dominated the whole relationship between William R. Harper and John D. Rockefeller, to give one notable example. Such hopes also commanded the actions of G. Stanley Hall at Clark University. Harper won his gamble, while Hall lost his. This bare fact by no means describes the total difference between the two men; yet if Harper had failed to prevail upon Rockefeller (as he came close to doing on several occasions), it is likely that the onus of "failure" would have settled on his shoulders as it did on Hall's. Success, in other words, came to the man who gained the reputation of already having succeeded. In this sense, administrative success depended upon that combination of luck and daring peculiar to business success in general.

Almost from its beginning, the appearance of administration provoked divisive resentments within the academic population. In the eyes of a number of professors, who might be termed "idealists" to distinguish them from their more sanguine colleagues, the administration represented an alien and illegitimate force which had "captured" the leadership of the university. The arguments of the "idealists," which were of central importance for the new conception of academic freedom, will be examined at a later point; here one need only note the presence of such a reaction. A Stanford chemist defined the basic question which administration raised when he sketched two conflicting ideal models for higher education. The first he called "a republic of letters," or perhaps an oligarchy of learning," in which no faculty member would either expect promotion or fear dismissal, because his work would be judged by no president, committee, or executive board. The second he characterized as an academic society in which all policy was considered "from the standpoint of the efficiency of the university organism, and of the actual value of the professor to his students." Here "the element of competition" would appear, leading to an analogy between the university and the business corporation. In drawing this contrast, the chemist did not believe that either of these academic settings actually flourished in America in a pure form, but he saw them

as the logical extensions of opposed tendencies which were very much at work.¹⁵¹

The loyalties of the administrator naturally centered on the institution of which he was chief executive. He made this institution his life, and for so doing he was handsomely rewarded by praise and respect from the institution's friends. On the other hand, the loyalties of the faculty "idealist" might take one of several alternative directions, or a combination of them. They might center in his discipline, conceived as a world-wide department of knowledge; in educational principles, seen as a yardstick against which particular institutions might be critically judged; in the dignity of the professorial calling; or, surreptitiously, in the progress of his own career as an individual. Much of the time the advancement of the institution coincided with all these other aspirations; that it did not always do so was demonstrated by the appearance of perennial tension on these issues. If the administrator had confined his purview to the financial and technical aspects of the university, conflict might not have appeared. But such restraint on his part would have been inconceivable, for few financial questions lacked some academic bearing as long as departments begged for money. The normal need of deciding matters of tenure and promotion would have caused emotions to rise, had there been no other form of executive interference, for when these practical questions presented themselves the dream of a "republic of letters" retreated most abjectly into the realm of theory. As it was, many academic executives claimed the abstract right to judge the performance of professors quite comprehensively. "University authorities must . . . not fear to become respecters of persons," urged David Starr Jordan. "They should give time, freedom, appliances, where these things can be used, while refusing them to the man who would thereby merely advertise his own insignificance."¹⁵² The university president by no means believed that he was in charge merely of buildings and grounds.

During the first two or three decades after the Civil War, the head of a university had often been able to fulfill two roles: as spokesman for an educational experiment and as manager of a concrete enterprise. By the 1890's the incongruity of the dual effort became obvious to nearly everyone. While faculty researchers pursued increasingly specialized investigations, presidents admitted they had little time for reading; nor, except in the case of the almost superhuman William R. Harper, did they teach in the classroom. The result was an unavoidable isolation from faculty ways of thinking. As Richard H. Jesse, president of the University of Missouri, sorrowfully admitted in 1904: "Few men can be really effective at one time in several spheres of activity. A man profoundly intellectual, profoundly spiritual, and able in administration is exceedingly rare."¹⁵³ More than this, intellectual tastes often—though not always—led to a relish for logical consistency which affected a professor's whole outlook. The faculty "idealist" was apt to see matters

344

of policy as clear-cut choices, to be acted upon with a single-minded fidelity to higher principle. "Compromise is weakness or indecision," thundered R. M. Wenley in 1910.[154] The administrator, on the other hand, was bound to be a diplomat and a politician if he were to serve the best interests of his institution. He throve on compromise; he wanted all sorts of diverse people to go away pleased. As the secretary of the Massachusetts Institute of Technology observed in 1899, "educational systems, like governments, apparently can never be rational, never a logical and economical means to a definite end. Rather must they be always makeshifts." Their continual practical accommodations, he added, must be "the bane of both conservatives and radicals."[155]

Here, then, was a major and controversial new force in American academic life. In response to what conditions had it appeared? The most important answer lies within the institution. Both intellectually and in terms of its structure, the American university was becoming too diverse easily to define—or to control. The adherence of academic leaders to varying educational philosophies, the emergence of crystallized departments of learning, and the presence of larger number of students all contributed to this result. Often an undergraduate college basically English in conception was wedded, by loose financial ties, to a Germanic graduate school. To European eyes an American institution such as Harvard might seem "a chaos."[156] No longer did any over-all intellectual formula exist to counter (or to cloak) such fragmentation; neither the Christian religion in any of its varieties, nor positive science, nor humane culture proved *self-evidently* capable of making sense out of the entire range of knowledge and opinion. As long as argument in these terms was possible, the university could mean no one thing, Santayana despairingly commented: "Each man knows the value of his work . . . but he feels also the relativity of this work and of its value without being able to survey the whole organism of human interests and adjust himself confidently to the universal life."[157] On a more popular level of reaction, the University of Chicago with its manifold activities soon acquired the nickname "Harper's Bazaar."

Bureaucratic administration was the structural device which made possible the new epoch of institutional empire-building without recourse to specific shared values. Thus while unity of purpose disintegrated, a uniformity of standardized practices was coming into being. As an observer noted in 1897, one could observe two countertendencies at work in American higher education: fragmentation and centralization. In 1910 Edwin E. Slosson, ironically adapting Herbert Spencer's formula, asserted that American universities were "passing from a state of indefinite, incoherent homogeneity to a state of definite coherent heterogeneity."[158] Institutional aggrandizement needed predictable expectations. By

1882 arguments already attacked the "period of [hit-or-miss] empiricism" in university administration and urged that rational methods be adopted by academic management.[159] At the same time, the growing size and complexity of the university made it inexpedient for entire faculties to consider business of the sort that had previously been delegated to them (such as student discipline cases). At Harvard the first major step toward the committee system was taken in 1890.[160] Soon the faculty committee itself became too unwieldy for many general purposes, deans became powerful figures, and clerical personnel, grouped into offices independent of the faculty, proliferated.[161] By 1910 one could speak of "the Registrar: whose authority is supreme, whose methods are autocratic, whose ways are beyond the highest research."[162] Assembly-line methods of registration arrived at Harvard in the autumn of 1891, and efficient orange perforated registration cards were introduced there in 1896.[163] At most universities, courses were now rationalized into a numerical system of units for credit; the catalogue began to resemble the inventory of a well-stocked and neatly labeled general store.

While bureaucratic procedures were appearing in major institutions, universities were also growing noticeably more like each other. Johns Hopkins, for example, moved in 1894 to add a fourth year to its undergraduate curriculum. Eliot and others had long hoped to establish uniform college entrance requirements, and a general trend toward mutual consultation among heads of institutions could be observed at the end of the century. A movement to "accredit" all institutions which met minimal standards got under way around 1890 and became a major force after 1901, achieving national victory in 1913.[164] The Association of American Universities was founded in 1900 for the avowed purpose of establishing a similar uniformity of standards at the level of the graduate school. It was in 1903 that William James felt moved to write his well-known article attacking "The Ph.D. Octopus." Then, also, the long-standing campaign to establish a national university in Washington, D.C., which was ardently renewed in the late nineties, also reflected the urge for a well-defined system with a "crown" at its top. Although the national university scheme failed, supra-institutional pressures increased when the Carnegie Foundation began establishing standards in connection with a major disbursement of faculty pension funds in 1906.

The few specific explanations which exist for the rise of academic bureaucracy imply that it came about in response to practical problems. Thus the Stanford administration at first attempted to treat deficient academic performance without written rules of any kind; students then complained that they depended upon firm expectations, wishing to know in advance "when they would be stepping over the line." So bureaucratic procedures were adopted.[165] More interesting is an account which has survived telling why the Johns Hopkins University, which originally had embodied opposition to all routine, quickly developed a standardized program for the Ph.D. degree:

> At first, we thought it would be sufficient simply to let the students come together and select their courses. They were advanced—they were college graduates—they would do whatever was right, and the results would be satisfactory. We found very soon . . . that something was needed to keep them in line. There was a good deal of indefinite browsing. They would fly from one thing to another. They would find something peculiar about one teacher, and something they did not like about another teacher. There was a good deal of what I might call puttering. And those of us who were charged with the management of affairs concluded that we must take advantage of the degree. We must offer something in order to keep these students in line. The Ph.D. degree was the next thing after the A.B. degree, and we recognized that we must offer this in order to keep that body of workers in line, and that, in order to secure the results we wanted, it was also necessary to require a piece of research as a requisite for that degree. That is the machinery we used. We thought, at first, that we might avoid it, but we found that we must adopt it.[166]

These remarks by Ira Remsen imply several concurrent explanations for the result: first, the researcher's dislike for anything which connoted dilettantism, and his insistence upon hard work, enforced if necessary; second, a mistrust of the maturity even of graduate students, which again had roots in the earlier college tradition (three times in the above, Remsen spoke of wanting to keep the students "in line"); finally, a desire to alleviate faculty jealousies—that is, by means of requirements, to keep students from flocking conspicuously to just a few teachers. Thus the response to a supposedly "practical" problem can actually reveal much implied intellectual and psychological content; the rise of bureaucracy, at least, should not be left in the too-simple category of pragmatic "inevitability." Particularly can this be seen by comparing the German universities, with their far smaller non-academic staffs, to the American institutions of similar size at the turn of the century.[167]

In seeking deeper causes for the bureaucratization of the American university, it is tempting, of course, to search among so-called American cultural traits or in the still larger and less well-defined domain of "Western values." One may talk of a distinctively American, or European, penchant for organization, or of an American yearning for grandiose form. In respects too nebulous to be documented,[168] some such influences may well have affected the result. A trend toward ceremonialism manifested itself strongly in the nineties, producing an intercollegiate commission on academic dress in 1895. The dignity of the college degree was carefully enhanced by appropriate words, rituals, and emphases.[169] Formalism in American organization seemed to be

gaining new ground at the very time when formalism in American thought was losing its attractiveness. Yet the movement toward bureaucracy and the symptoms of ceremonialism which accompanied it do not really require such a far-reaching kind of explanation. Instead it can be argued that these trends had far more to do with certain specific, rather unmysterious requirements of the American academic situation. In its striking diversity of personnel the new American university was unlike the German one. Of course the peculiarly American need for effective control, at least at the level of student conduct, had also pressed upon the old-time colleges, which had long survived without bureaucracy. But now such a need was felt in terms of a different numerical scale; now, too, the faculty had itself become internally diverse (in ways never true of German faculties), and changing values also required new means. The danger was no longer so much one of riots or other forms of open rebellion as it was one of drift, laxity, and the illegitimate pursuit of personal or factional advantage. Techniques of control shifted from the sermon and the direct threat of punishment toward the more appropriate devices of conference, memorandum, and filing system. Simultaneously such techniques had to be applied, if not in quite identical ways, to everyone who was bound together on a particular campus, including the president himself. In a small college where but one basic line of internal tension existed, that between students and faculty, the only formal codes dealt with student conduct. In the expanding university "faculty conduct," so to speak, was also an issue. Or, to phrase this more delicately, the multiplicity of cleavages demanded a general submission to regulation, from top to bottom, if all vestiges of order were not to disappear. Bureaucratic modes served as a low but tolerable common denominator, linking individuals, cliques, and factions who did not think in the same terms but who, unlike the students of the 1860's, were usually too polite to require threats.

It is suggestive from this point of view to compare academic bureaucracy with industrial regulations. Seen as institutions, the university and the large manufacturing concern were similar in the diversity of their internal populations. Lacking the homogeneity even of the large metropolitan church, the university and the factory both had to harness the energies of disparate groups. Oratory might help, especially against the threat of foreign competition (European steel or the Yale football team). But sermons and ceremonies were insufficient instruments of control, just as naked coercion leaned too far in the opposite direction. Bureaucratic norms offered an appropriate middle ground for this kind of internally diverse, semicompulsory institution: a means which nearly everybody could accept as the fairest for securing a reasonably efficient flow of activity. In the American setting, there were only three alternatives to academic bureaucracy: the intense dedication of a small, informal group (as at Clark University after 1892); personal autocracy (as in the older colleges and at Stanford University); or confusion and drift (as, relatively speaking, at the later Yale and Johns

Hopkins). The first of these alternatives did not educate large numbers of people—although from some points of view this fact did not matter. The second and third tended sooner or later to produce instability and loss of momentum. It is hard to avoid the conclusion that bureaucratic procedures became essential to continuity of effort, once one grants that American universities should be of generous size. Without such procedures, American academic communities would either become eccentrically authoritarian or else fall apart.

Few people liked bureaucracy, of course, and even in America academic life displayed major differences from factory life. One chief source of difference lay in the more uniform social origins of all academic participants. Extremely few students, professors, or administrators were recruited from the families of manual laborers. This meant that academic patterns of behavior could often be left to flourish tacitly; compared with the factory, many more ways of doing things were simply understood in such categories as "basic decency." Therefore academic bureaucracy did not develop with all the fulsomeness and impersonality of the industrial version. The academic time clock functioned only during examinations and at faculty meetings. Yet just because this situation was less determinate, it bred its own tensions. For the very reason that students, faculty, and administrators were all supposedly "gentlemen," there was more chafing and protest at the "unnaturalness" of the so-called red tape that did exist. Bureaucracy continually affronted fond notions of personal dignity, especially among members of the teaching staff. What was, in some degree, universally essential also produced perpetual strains, for the consequence of not being irritated by bureaucratic demands was the willing acceptance of one's lot as an "employee."

Like many mechanisms which begin as necessary evils, academic bureaucracy soon revealed that it had uses from the faculty's point of view as well. Rules, as we shall later see, could protect the professor from autocratic superiors. And the bureaucratic apparatus also began serving the professor in a less obvious fashion. It became a buffer which protected the isolation of the individuals and the small factions on each campus. Thus if the maze of officials and committees grew sufficiently complex, the whole machinery might screen the faculty member from the administration. Surrounded by politely affirmative deans and committees, the university president gradually lost touch with what was actually going on in "his" classrooms. This could mean that the professor, as long as he avoided sensationalism, became in practice relatively free of intrusion. One speculates that a large measure of academic freedom came about in just such an unintended way.

107 R. E. Pfeiffer to Woodrow Wilson, May 11, 1910 (WWLC).
108 Woodrow Wilson, "What Is a College For?" Scribner's Magazine, XLVI (1909), 574.

109 Slosson, Great American Universities, p. 76.
110 Schmidt, The Old-Time College President, pp. 83–86.
111 C. W. Super, "Contributions to the History of American Teaching," Educational Review, XXXIX (1910), 59; see also C. F. Adams, Autobiography, p. 35; Bliss Perry, And Gladly Teach, p. 65; Jacob Cooper, "The Student in American Colleges," New Englander, XXXVII (1878), 614.
112 Howe, Wendell, p. 75.
113 Phelps, Autobiography, pp. 281–82.
114 Taylor, The Neglect of the Student, p. 1.
115 Slosson, Great American Universities, p. 19. For a vivid fictional account of the gulf between students and faculty at Harvard in 1897, see the short story, "Dead Issue," in Flandrau, Harvard Episodes, pp. 249–96.
116 Curti and Carstensen, Wisconsin, II, 77; Goodspeed, Chicago, p. 260.
117 This story was fiction, but it conveys the authentic student notion of a joke. C. M. Flandrau, The Diary of a Freshman (New York, 1907), pp. 178–84.
118 Ibid., p. 32; Hardin Craig, Woodrow Wilson at Princeton (Norman, Okla., 1960), pp. 34–35.
119 Draper, "Government in American Universities," Educational Review, XXVIII (1904), 237.
120 C. W. Eliot to W. M. Wilson, Oct. 29, 1907 (CWE). See also Edith Finch, Carey Thomas of Bryn Mawr (New York, 1947), pp. 184–85.
121 G. S. Hall, "Address," in Williams College, 1793–1893, pp. 194–95.
122 Canby, Alma Mater, p. 86.
123 R. W. Brown, Briggs, p. 124.
124 Woodrow Wilson, "The Preceptorial System at Princeton," Educational Review, XXXIX (1910), 389–90.
125 Slosson, Great American Universities, p. 84; Myers (ed.), Wilson, p. 22.
126 Veblen, The Higher Learning in America, p. 163.
127 Morison, Three Centuries of Harvard, pp. 368–69.
128 See Harvard College, Regulations of the Faculty of Harvard College, Adopted 1871 ([Cambridge, 1871]) p. 7, and, on the oaths, p. 33, above.
129 See the bold advertisement of Colchester, Roberts & Co., Tiffin, Ohio (ca. 1897), which offered college essays at $3.00 to $15.00, guaranteed to be original work. A copy is in the University of California Library, Berkeley.
130 Harvard, Annual Report, 1899–1900, p. 11; cf. ibid., 1903–4, p. 15.
131 Woodrow Wilson's "Baccalaureate Address, June 13th, 1910," p. 4 (WW); Canby, Alma Mater, p. 19; cf. p. 75, where he likens the situation to "class warfare within the nation state."
132 Patton, Religion in College, p. 10.
133 Slosson, Great American Universities, p. 386.

134. For the present study the biographies of 120 prominent professors and presidents, mainly at the leading institutions, were studied in some depth. (Unfortunately this was not a random sample.) Of the 120, the fathers' occupations of 93 were clearly known. These break down as follow: merchant, banker, or manufacturer, 28; minister, missionary, or rabbi, 24; farmer, 19; college professor or president, 6; lawyer or judge, 3; doctor, 3; diplomat or statesman, 2; southern planter, 2; schoolteacher, 2; and artist, sea captain, lecturer, and manual laborer, 1 each. These proportions are roughly confirmed in Cattell's study of 885 leading scientists in 1915 (though not all of these were professors). Of the 885, the fathers of 381 were professional men (including, however, only 89 clergymen); 188 fathers were farmers, and 316 fathers were businessmen. J. M. Cattell, "Families of American Men of Science," in Cattell, I, 478–519.

135. Of the 120 academics studied, the ancestry is clearly known in 111 cases, and these break down as follows (with fractions stemming from mixed parentages): Old New England families, 76.5; Scotch-Irish, 7.5; Anglo-Saxon from the "middle" states, 7; English (recent immigrants), 5; Anglo-Saxon from the southern states, 3; Scottish, 3; Jewish, 2.5; Scandinavian, 2; German, 1.5; Old Dutch in New York, 1; Dutch-Canadian, 1; Spanish, 1.

136. The same 120 academics whose biographies were studied in some detail produce the following categories in terms of their reasons for choosing the academic profession (some provided no information; on the other hand if more than one answer was relevant for a particular individual, each one is included below): Childhood ambition, helped by favorable home influence, 11; decision made after college, 98. Of the latter 98, reasons appear as follows: generally idealistic outlook (dislike of business, law, medicine, etc., as too materialistic, or a desire to be a "pure" scholar or to reform society), 23; discontent with or waning interest in the ministry, 21; through a religious sense of duty (the minister who is asked to head a denominational college, etc.), 6; after a period of high-school teaching, 9; after a period of scholarly, scientific, or literary work unconnected with a university, 9; largely accidental (poor health causing abandonment of other plans, etc.), 20. Only 4 men were explicitly attracted by the social prestige of the academic profession. The prominence of drift and accident is probably the most striking feature of this accounting; but this may reflect the large number of men in the sample who came of age before 1880, when an academic life had been far less attractive.

137. A full-scale analysis of academic trustees in this period is much needed. This study can only touch upon these men; see the section, "Business Models for Educational Enterprise," in chapter 6. E. J. McGrath, "The Control of Higher Education in America," *Educational Record*, XVII (1936), 259–72, provides a quantitative study of the composition of such boards of trustees from 1860 to 1930.

138. W. L. Abbott to J. B. Angell, Jan. 4, 1909 (JBA); Ely, *Ground under Our Feet*, p. 197.

139. W. R. Harper to B. L. Whitman, Dec. 24, 1897 (WRH). See also C. F. Thwing, "College Organization and Government," *Educational Review*, XII (1896), 17–24; C. W. Eliot to Horace Davis, Sept. 29, 1903 (CWE), where Eliot states: "None of our Faculties ever takes any action on the selection of a professor. . . My part in the business may, I think, be correctly described as follows: . . I accept nominations of subordinate teachers [i.e., what would now be called non-tenure positions] from the departments concerned, through the chairman of the department. In regard to higher appointments [i.e., tenure level], I practically nominate to the Corporation, after a great deal of informal conference with the professors . . . most nearly interested."

140. C. E. Norton to C. W. Eliot, Sept. 6, 1898 (CWE); D. C. Gilman to H. B. Adams, July 8, 1889 (IIBA).

141. Concerning Harvard in this respect, see Bliss Perry, *And Gladly Teach*, pp. 238–40; H. J. Coolidge and R. H. Lord, *Archibald Cary Coolidge* (Boston, 1932), pp. 54–55; Barrett Wendell to C. W. Eliot, Apr. 11, 1893 (CWE); Ernest Samuels, *The Young Henry Adams* (Cambridge, 1948), p. 213; Santayana, *Persons and Places*, II, 160–61; Adolphe Cohn to C. W. Eliot, Nov. 8, 1891 (CWE); C. E. Norton to William James, Dec. 12, 1899 (H). Concerning Chicago, see Robert Herrick, *Chimes* (New York, 1926), pp. 21–25, and J. L. Laughlin to H. E. von Holst, Mar. 22, 1902 (IIE von H).

142. With less conspicuousness, so also did Provost William Pepper of the University of Pennsylvania. White loved leisure and absenteeism too much fully to qualify for the new role. See H. A. Stimson, "The Evolution of the College President," *American Monthly Review of Reviews*, XIX (1899), 451; F. N. Thorpe, *William Pepper, M.D., LL.D. (1843–1898), Provost of the University of Pennsylvania* (Philadelphia, 1904), p. 184.

143. J. W. Burgess' speech, "Reminiscences of Columbia University in the Last Quarter of the Last Century," n.d., p. 5 (JWB).

144. C. F. Thwing, *College Administration* (New York, 1900).

145. F. P. Graves, "The Need of Training for the College Presidency," *Forum*, XXXII (1902), 680–85.

146. G. M. Stratton, "Externalism in American Universities," *Atlantic Monthly*, C (1907), 518. See also Dwight, *Memories*, pp. 379–80; C. W. Eliot, "American Universities: Their Resemblances and Their Differences," *Educational Review*, XXXI (1906), 117; University of Chicago, *The President's Report: Administration*, The Decennial Publications, First Series (Chicago, 1903), p. xlvi.

147. N. M. Butler's secretary to Ira Remsen, Dec. 4, 1902 (CUA).

148. C. F. Adams, *Three Phi Beta Kappa Addresses* (Boston, 1907), p. 163. For a comparison of these ratios at a number of institutions in 1909, see Marx, "Some Trends in Higher Education," *Science*, XXIX (1909), 784, Table IV.

149. See Thwing, *College Administration*, pp. 55, 62–63.

150. See *ibid.*, p. 65; T. C. Chamberlin to R. T. Ely, Mar. 1, 1892 (RTE); and Eliot, *University Administration*, p. 238.

151. A.A.U., *Journal*, 1907, p. 72.

152. D. S. Jordan, "To What Extent Should the University Investigator Be Freed from Teaching?" *Science*, XXIV (1906), 132.

153. Religious Education Association, *Proceedings*, 1904, p. 126.

154. Wenley, "The Classics and the Elective System," *School Review*, XVIII (1910), 518.

348

155 J. P. Munroe, "Applied Science and the University," *Technology Review,* I (1899), 153.

156 Pierre de Coubertin, *Universités transatlantiques,* p. 96.

157 Santayana, "The Spirit and Ideals of Harvard University," *Educational Review,* VII (1894), 324.

158 Thwing, *The American College in American Life,* p. 188; Slosson, *Great American Universities,* p. 347.

159 Angell, *Selected Addresses,* p. 27; Hewett, "University Administration," *Atlantic Monthly,* L (1882), 505, 516–18.

160 Harvard, *Annual Report,* 1889–90, p. 13; *ibid.,* 1890–91, p. 79.

161 E.g., see N. M. Butler to J. W. Burgess, June 6, 1906 (JWB); Harvard, *Annual Report,* 1890–91, pp. 41–43; 1902–3, pp. 7–8; 1905–6, pp. 9–10; 1906–7, pp. 6–7; Curti and Carstensen, *Wisconsin,* I, 501–3, 544, 608–10.

162 Bowden-Smith, *An English Student's Wander-Year in America,* p. 9.

163 Harvard, *Annual Report,* 1890–91, pp. 13–14; *Harvard Graduates' Magazine,* V (1896), 251–52.

164 B. E. Donaldson, "The Role of College Accreditation," Association of American Colleges, *Bulletin,* XXXIX (1953), esp. pp. 274–76.

165 Elliott, *Stanford,* p. 166.

166 Remsen, "Original Research," Association of Collegiate Alumnae, *Publications,* ser. 3, 1903, pp. 24–25.

167 See R. H. Shryock, "The Academic Profession in the United States," American Association of University Professors, *Bulletin,* XXXVIII (1952), 44–45.

168 Except perhaps at the University of Chicago, as will be seen in the next chapter.

169 For significant evidence concerning the rise of ceremony in this period, see Johns Hopkins, *Annual Report,* 1892, pp. 20–21; French, *Johns Hopkins,* pp. 363–67, 370; Goodspeed, *Chicago,* p. 251; Hill, *Harvard College, by an Oxonian,* pp. 154–55; James Bryce, *The American Commonwealth* (New York, 1910), II, 755–56; Slosson, *Great American Universities,* pp. 392–93, 411, 429–30; D. S. Jordan, *The Care and Culture of Men* (San Francisco, 1896), p. 51, on academic degrees; and G. H. Howison to the Academic Council of the University of California, Apr. 22, 1897 (GHH).

Co-Education on Two Campuses:
Berkeley and Chicago, 1890-1912

Lynn D. Gordon

Controversies surrounding women in higher education in the immediate post-Civil-War era dealt mostly with their mental and physical capacities. Could they keep up with the work? Would their health, and most important-ly, their reproductive systems, collapse under the strain of higher education? Should colleges and universities admit them as students? Since the issue of women's admission to college had not yet been settled in the public mind, fewer arguments focused upon the desirability of co-education.[1] Further-more, among the very small group of women in college in 1870 (0.7 percent of the female population aged 18–21), less than half attended co-educational institutions.[2].

The generation educated between 1870 and 1890 proved that women could withstand the rigors of college and perform creditably. And in the 1890's, on many campuses, they served as teachers, deans, and mentors for young women students. As secondary school teachers they often inspired young girls to go to college. Women philanthropists and social reformers—some college graduates and some not—also took a friendly interest in women students in the 1890's. They donated money for dormitories, club houses, and scholarships, and frequently appeared on campus as speakers. By 1890, too, a whole range of institutions admitted female students. While the total number of college women remained small (2.2 percent of the eligible population), they represented 35.9 percent of the student body, and fully 70.1 percent attended co-educational schools.[3]

Between 1890 and 1912 the two generations of college women, aided by other prominent women, made a bid for recognition and status on co-educational campuses. Their activities, along with the increased percentage of female students, led to the great turn-of-the-century debate on the social implications of co-education. Co-education caused concern largely because of nineteenth-century beliefs about the sexes. Scientists and doctors of that time offered evidence that physical distinctions led to emotional and intel-lectual differences between the sexes. Analyses of physical characteristics such as skull capacity, brain weight, facial angle, body dimension, and the percentage of muscle in the body, established males and females as almost separate species.[4]

The experts claimed that the differences meant that each sex should live according to its own separate nature. Occupations, dress, language, thoughts, pleasures, and feelings appropriate for one sex were not so for the other. Each sex had a sphere of influence, each was important to the maintenance of society, but lines separating sex-role behavior must not be crossed. Middle-class men and women in the Victorian era lived largely separate lives, surrounded by support networks of same-sex associations. Particularly after puberty, the sexes were expected to have little informal contact. And they were never to compete, for to do so would have challenged the whole notion of complementary spheres of influence and competence. Men's and women's worlds touched mostly in courtship and marriage. Even within the intimacy of marriage, however, the social distance between the sexes often prevailed.

> If men and women grew up as they did in relatively homogeneous and segregated social groups, then marriage represented a major problem in adjustment. From this perspective we could interpret much of the emotional stiffness and distance that we associate with Victorian marriage as a structural consequence of contemporary sex-role differentiation and gender-role socialization. With marriage, both men and women had to adjust to life with a person who was, in essence, a member of an alien group.[5]

Co-education, post-puberty, then, represented a major departure from the attitudes and experiences of the conventional middle class. What would happen when the sexes shared the same life style, competed for the same prizes, and were in constant association with one another? Would co-education "effeminize" men, make them less aggressive, less able and willing to function in the world? Would it coarsen or "masculinize" young women, obliterating the pure, benevolent, morally superior natures they alone possessed? Would it, by lessening the distance and mystery between the sexes, make them less attractive to each other?[6] These fears cannot be dismissed solely as the self-serving rantings of males anxious about women as competitors, because women, too, worried about the consequences of exercising new options.

By examining two universities with different styles and experiences of co-education, we can perhaps better understand how these attitudes affected the experiences of women college students in the Progressive era. Their generation came to maturity at a time when traditional sex roles were being challenged not only by co-education, but in the business and political worlds. Their female mentors were often active in reform movements, feminist causes, and the fight for suffrage. Thus, the impact of higher education for women of the Progressive era had truly revolutionary potential. They had the tools, the opportunities, and the visibility to challenge conventional sex roles had they wished to do so.

Berkeley[7]

Women had been students at the University of California since 1870, after the all-male College of California became the state university in 1869. Although they increased their representation in the student body from 9 percent in 1870 to 25 percent in 1880 and 31 percent by 1892, they continued to play an insignificant part in campus life.[8]

Between 1870 and 1890 college traditions and activities centered around class loyalties and rituals—with gender distinctions. Class officers, with rare exceptions, were male. Occasionally a vice-presidency was set aside for a woman, but men and women never competed for the same positions. The men of each class wore distinctive headgear: soft blue "pork pies" for freshmen; grey-checked caps for sophomores; "plugs" or top hats for upperclassmen with the juniors wearing grey plugs and the seniors black. Social custom decreed that women wear hats in public, but they did not adopt any form of distinctive class apparel. Other traditions reveal the same dichotomy for men and women. When the yearbooks began using photographs in the 1890's, men's pictures appeared by class, women's pictures from all four classes appeared together in a separate section. On campus, men of each class had special benches and stairs reserved for their exclusive use. Women of whatever class were supposed to avoid using those places. Men were thus encouraged to identify themselves strongly by class, while women had only the sense of being an undifferentiated group of "co-eds." Yearly rituals reinforced these patterns of identification. Each year the freshmen and sophomore classes "rushed" each other, competing to see which class could wrestle and tie up all the members of the other class. The spring burial of Bourdon and Minto, the freshman algebra and composition texts, called for another fight as sophomores sought to prevent the freshmen from burying the books and symbolically ending their new-comer status on campus. Upperclassmen acted as referees during rushes, with juniors looking out for the freshmen, and the seniors taking the sophomores' side. Needless to say, "rushing" was restricted to males. Silly as they sound, these traditions represented opportunities for men to get to know each other, display leadership, plan strategy and develop an "old-boy" network of good fellowship. In short, they conferred status and recognition, and developed a sense of community.

Women also did not participate in other areas of college life. Most college clubs had no women members, and even the academic organizations, such as the Philosophical Union, listed only a few female participants in the yearbook. Musical groups, debating societies, camera clubs, and honorary societies had only male members. Even physical education classes and athletic activities for women were sharply curtailed because they had access to the gymnasium only after 5 P.M. each day. Housing arrangements exacerbated an already difficult situation. Berkeley had no student dormitories until after World War I. Most students in the early years commuted from San Francisco or Oakland, although some families moved to Berkeley to make it easier for their children to attend the university. More men than women lived on campus—50 percent of the women students still lived at home in 1914, while after 1900 71.9 percent of the student body lived on campus.[9] Men lived in boarding houses, formed residence clubs, and organized fraternities. Kappa Alpha Theta, Berkeley's first sorority, did not appear until 1890. Naturally, since many more male students lived on campus, they had greater access to activities and were more involved in university life.

Women of this early generation at Berkeley left no organizational record and few memoirs. A few, like Milicent Shinn, '80, became famous. Shinn edited for some years the *Overland Monthly*, an important regional literary magazine, before becoming Berkeley's first female Ph.D. in 1890. As an authority on child psychology, her books were translated into several languages. About the other alumnae we know very little. Why did they attend college? Did they see themselves as pioneers? Did their exclusion from campus life concern them? What became of them, and how did their experiences at Berkeley affect the remainder of their lives? Beginning in the 1890's, a far more self-conscious generation of female students made a place for themselves at Berkeley, aided by the philanthropy of Phoebe Apperson Hearst. Hearst's influence and support led to the organization of a social life for women students, and the appointment of Berkeley's first female faculty members. Hearst herself served as the first woman Regent of the university from 1897 through 1919. The wife of wealthy Senator George Hearst, Phoebe Hearst inaugurated her philanthropy in 1891 with a gift of eight, three-hundred dollar scholarships for women. Hearst's support had a great impact on the lives of women students. While not a college graduate, she had been a teacher before her marriage, and was active in many educational causes including the kindergarten movement, and secondary schools for girls.[10] She donated a building, Hearst Hall, to the women students in 1900. The top floor became a gymnasium, finally making physical education classes possible. Athletic clubs for tennis, boating, and fencing followed, as the women now had a place to meet and store equipment. In 1901 Hearst gave money for a women's outdoor basketball court (surrounded by a twelve-foot fence with no knotholes to discourage observers). Some years later she donated a swimming pool. She set up a fund to hire Dr. Mary Bennett Ritter, the first female faculty member, who gave lectures in hygiene, and served as the women's medical examiner. In a new lunchroom at Hearst Hall, Hearst supplied free tea for all women students, encouraging them to gather there at lunchtime. The Hall became the meeting place for women's clubs, and the site of parties. She also founded the Hearst Domestic Industries to teach cooking and sewing so that women students could learn these skills and use them to find part-time jobs to finance their education. Hearst's bounty encouraged women to help themselves, and it also set an interesting pattern for their social lives. Women students gradually gained recognition, but as a separate group. Rather than share men's social and organizational life, they created their own, using Hearst Hall as a focus.

In 1894 the Associated Women Students of the University of California (AWS) called its first meeting. AWS paralleled the functions of the Associated Students of the University of California (ASUC), the male-controlled student organization. Women continued to join the ASUC, but they did so by paying dues to AWS, which turned over a portion of the money to ASUC. AWS became the umbrella organization for women's clubs and committees. It sponsored, for example, the Sports and Pastimes Association to supervise women's athletic clubs and competition with Stanford, Mills, and local high schools. Other groups under the AWS aegis included all-female debating societies, musical organizations, and a dramatics club. The university yearbook, *The Blue and Gold*, began devoting an entire section to women's organizations, including the growing number of sororities and residence clubs.[11] Some segregated academic clubs also appeared: the XYZ Club for women interested in higher mathematics, and the Chemistry Fiends. The Chemistry Fiends had a revealing practice—to make themselves feel more comfortable in the chemistry building, an all-male preserve, women practiced traditional female activities: they held evening parties there, making fudge and coffee over the Bunsen burners. AWS also issued a special handbook for incoming women students, listing all the clubs available for them, and urging them to participate in campus activities. Additionally, women active in YWCA work spent time at the West Berkeley Settlement League helping working-class and poor children.

The men students had formed all-campus honor societies for service to the university—the Skull and Keys and the Golden Bear. Membership in these societies was a highly coveted honor, awarded only to prominent upperclassmen. In 1901, students Adele Lewis and Agnes Frisius, with the help of Dr. Ritter, formed their own honor society—the Prytaneans. Junior and senior women who had served the university in some way—through work in AWS, for example—could be asked to join. The Prytaneans held festivals and masques to raise money for a student infirmary. When the infirmary opened in 1907, they continued to work for a women's dormitory, a senior women's building, and the establishment of home economics courses.

With the appointment in 1906 of young Lucy Sprague, a Radcliffe graduate, as Berkeley's first Dean of Women, female students gained another advocate. Almost immediately Sprague expressed concern about the housing situation, social life, and career choices of women students. She pointed out that many women still took no part in campus life (one-third belonged to no organizations at all); that most noncommuting women lived in boarding houses over which the university exercised no control; and that 90 percent of women students planned to be elementary and secondary school teachers in a rapidly shrinking market. Sprague complained that women took narrowly specialized and technical courses, with much work in education and thereby ignored the benefits and the broadening effects of liberal arts courses.[12] Sprague attacked these practices by promoting an expansion of social life for women. She held poetry readings for women students at her own home, and took them into the community to study industries and social institutions. She started "Critics on the Hearth," a club for women to learn parliamentary procedure. Most importantly, she proposed and helped found the Partheneia, an annual pageant written, produced, and acted by women students.

Sprague also attended meetings of sororities, AWS, the YWCA, the Prytaneans, and other women's groups, assisting them in setting social standards for women students. Neither Sprague nor the students in the early twentieth century wished to flout rules or set new standards of behavior. Together they made lists of approved boarding houses for women students, set curfews for university functions, and recommended that women students attend no more than two social functions per week.[13]. Sprague did not like functioning as a "warden of women,"[14] and could not have done so anyway considering how many students lived off campus. What social control she had came from her cooperation with the women's organizations.

When Sprague married economist Wesley Clair Mitchell and moved to New York City in 1913, Lucy Ward Stebbins became Dean. Stebbins agreed with Sprague that too many women went into teaching without investigating other careers. She also expressed concern that the university failed to provide formal training for alumnae who never worked outside their homes.[15] To promote greater awareness of possible careers for women, Stebbins sent questionnaires to the thirty-seven undergraduate academic departments asking: "To what fields of paid work for women other than teaching does training in your department lead?" "What course should be pursued by the student who wishes to equip herself for any one of these fields?" "How many years of graduate or professional work is required in each case?" "What are the opportunities for advancement and the salaries paid?"[16] Stebbins also addressed herself to the needs of those who would remain in the home. With the help of the Prytaneans and political economy professor Jessica Peixotto, she took the lead in setting up a department of home economics between 1912 and 1916.

The new interest in appropriate education and expanding career choices for women, the wealth of social activities and organizations, the athletic program, the presence of supportive female faculty, and the active philanthropy of Phoebe Hearst, had greatly improved the lives of the growing numbers of Berkeley women. Representing 37 percent of the student body, 1333 undergraduate women were enrolled in 1911–1912,[17] and *The Blue and Gold* recognized their new status in an editorial aptly titled "How the Other Half lives":

> It has taken many, many years for the University of California co-ed to "find herself." When Berkeley was first on the map, the co-ed was not. The small classes of the early days struggled along without her. Today the large classes struggle with her. The co-ed has come to stay and the classes are largely lasses. In spite of the phenomenal growth of the numbers of women students in recent years, it has been only in comparatively recent times that any unification and independence has developed among them. Today, while a part of the whole college community, the women students find it profitable to carry on a distinct line of activity.... The co-ed traditions... may be properly said to be still in the making.[18]

Women had created a separate power structure, but separate was not equal on their campus. The women students and faculty at Berkeley remained marginal in some significant ways.

Intercollegiate athletics with Stanford began to replace the class traditions of the 1890's as the focus for campus activities. In 1905 freshmen and sophomore men ended the rushes, cooperating to build a "Big C" on campus for anti-Stanford rallies. Women took as small a part in the new campus atmosphere as they had in the old. They did not participate in the pregame demonstrations, parades, and "sings" except as spectators. They sat in a separate section at the games, while the men cheered alone in theirs.[19] The campus newspaper, *The Daily Californian*, devoted most of its space to discussion of athletic events. The paper's "women's editor" contributed little more than notices about club meetings. Once a year, on Women's Day, a special female staff put out the *Daily Californian*, underscoring the fact that their participation in campus journalism was an unusual event. Class officers continued to be male. And as late as 1900 Lillian Moller Gilbreth, 1900, complained:

> There was no prejudice against women students. Consequently it was a surprise, and a painful one, to aim for a Phi Beta Kappa key, only to learn that there would be no girls on the list because when it came to finding a good job, men needed the help of this honor more than women did.[20]

Career counseling and options for women remained limited. Respondents to Stebbins' questionnaire included the following occupations in their suggestions: dietitian, physician's helper, designer of costumes, designer of decorative needlework, professional shopper, food analyst, art librarian, executive secretary, caseworker, institutional worker, or buyer for a department store.[21] Just as home economics prepared women for a traditional role, the careers cited reflected equally traditional conceptions of women as nurturing and supportive.

Female faculty at Berkeley were as effectively isolated as their student counterparts. They had little influence on the tone of campus social life and did not even attend faculty meetings. As Sprague said: "Certainly we could have gone, but I knew that it would have prejudiced the men against us, and we already had enough prejudice to live down."[22] Sprague's comment suggests a partial explanation for the cooperation of Berkeley women in maintaining a limiting separate but equal policy. Clearly, they were reacting to the hostility toward co-education exhibited by many Berkeley males. Evidence of this hostility could also be found in the college yearbook where the stereotyping of women masked prejudicial attitudes and fears at the prospect of women leaving their traditional sphere to compete with men. *The Blue and Gold* poked fun at male students stereotyping "the grind" and "the fraternity man," but all women students were still "co-eds" and all alike. An ode to "Tender Dolores" in the 1893 yearbook warned that however pretty a newly arrived female student, if she studied too hard she would make "her pretty little nose very red," her "rosy cheeks" would become jaundiced, and her hair thinned. After graduation, she would become an ugly, bespectacled schoolmarm.[23] Also in 1893 *The Blue and Gold* contained a "Farewell Address of the Seniors to the Coeds of '92":

> In your future careers as schoolmistresses, when, after a wearisome day, you push your spectacles upon your brow and dream of the past, think on us, your admirers and brothers. You never will forget us, we know full well, and believe fully that indeed, indeed we will be brothers to you. In fact we desire nothing more.

The college humor magazine, *The Pelican*, took its name from the slang term for older women students attending the university while on leave from their teaching careers. Supposedly they looked like pelicans—skinny, ugly, with long noses and (at least in cartoons) spectacles. *The Pelican* featured antisuffrage cartoons showing cigar chomping female ward bosses, women drilling as soldiers, females proposing marriage to males, and generally making social institutions ridiculous by aping men's roles. *The Pelican* promoted separate but equal practices by offering support for the activities of female students if conducted within their own sphere. For example, it encouraged women to cheer at football games as long as they stayed in their own section and did not use the same yells the men did.[24] Although it is harder to find public records of their sentiments, some male faculty and administrators shared the students' views. Responding to complaints from his faculty that women students "effeminized" liberal arts courses by driving the men students away, President Benjamin Ide Wheeler ascribed declining male enrollments in such courses to increasing interest in vocational training.[25] Yet Wheeler himself warned women students not to stray from approved feminine roles. His 1904 speech to Berkeley women is indicative:

> You are not like men and you must recognize the fact....You may have the same studies as the men, but you put them to different use. You are not here with the ambition to be school teachers or old maids; but you are here for the preparation of marriage and motherhood. This education should tend to make you more serviceable as wives and mothers.[26]

Women faculty and students seemed to share the view that male-female social separation was natural and desirable. Phoebe Hearst never suggested that men and women students share the lunchroom and other facilities she provided. Lucy Sprague recognized the problems, but tried to give Berkeley women a positive self-image by encouraging them to reach out to each other, rather than by challenging the men. Lucy Stebbins phrased her career questions in terms of what was "appropriate" for women. Female students themselves made no efforts and expressed no wishes to share control over the campus, or to take dramatically feminist positions. Between 1968 and 1970, Prytanean alumnae from 1901 to 1920 were interviewed about their college days. Inverviewees happily described the number and range of women's activities, stressing their good times and enjoyment of college life. Even allowing for poor memories and sentimentalization, the lack of feminist consciousness is astonishing.[27] Not one woman mentioned the Berkeley chapter of the College Equal Suffrage League. In fact, at the time, its activities rated only an occasional paragraph in *The Daily Californian*, and it seemed to be of more interest to townswomen than to college students.[28]

At Berkeley, then, between 1890 and 1912, advanced education and close contacts between young men and young women had not broken down old ideas about appropriate sex roles and the supposed natural, innate differences between the sexes. Berkeley alumnae seeking to challenge conventional ideas about women had to look elsewhere for their inspiration.

Chicago

John D. Rockefeller and the American Baptist Education Society wanted a "magnet college" in Chicago to draw young Baptists from the Midwest for a superior undergraduate education, but Chicago's first president, William Rainey Harper, had other ideas. Envisioning the university as a major American graduate school, he conditioned his acceptance of the presidency upon Rockefeller's endorsement of his dream. Harper hoped that the first two years of undergraduate instruction would eventually move off campus, and that only upper level students would come to the University of Chicago, after proving themselves elsewhere. Recruited in the two frantic years before the University opened in 1892, Harper's faculty reflected his view of Chicago as primarily a graduate school. Scholars with German doctorates, men from Yale, Cornell, Clark, and other important eastern and midwestern institutions agreed to come to the new university. Harper's persuasiveness was legendary, and he offered top salaries to those in the upper professorial ranks. These men very consciously modelled Chicago on the Eastern universities, and it early became known as the "western Yale."[29]

The old Baptist college at Chicago had been co-educational and the university's charter explicitly stated that women were to be admitted on the same terms as men. Later, during the 1902 "segregation" controversy, trustees, president, faculty, and students claimed they had all along doubted the wisdom of co-education, but these doubts did not surface during the first ten years. In fact, Chicago's women students enjoyed a far more respected and advantageous position than Berkeley women ever achieved.

It is not, of course, appropriate to compare the Berkeley of 1870–1890 with the Chicago of 1892. By the time Chicago opened, the first generation of college-educated women could serve as supporters and mentors for women students. Off campus, the role of women in social settlement work and other Progressive era reform movements, the revival of the suffrage cause, and endless discussions of the "new woman" gave women's needs and concerns far more prominence than in the 1870's and 1880's. But even after 1890, Berkeley failed to match women's achievements at Chicago, mostly because of Chicago's strong, active women faculty. While Berkeley's Phoebe Hearst did a great deal for the women students, no female faculty appeared until the first decade of the twentieth century. Even then, the young and inexperienced Lucy Sprague had to cope with a strongly male-oriented campus virtually on her own. And, she herself had few theories about women's education and social life.[30]

In keeping with his policy of hiring established, prominent faculty, Harper asked former Wellesley College president Alice Freeman Palmer to be Chicago's Dean of Women. Palmer could only be at Chicago twelve weeks out of the year, as her marriage to Harvard philosophy professor George Herbert Palmer, and her many educational activities necessitated her presence in the East. She chose as her assistant and successor, Marion Talbot, instructor in sanitary science at Wellesley. Both women belonged to the earlier generation of college women—Palmer graduated from the University of Michigan in 1876, and Talbot from Boston University in 1880. Both had long been involved in women's higher education at Wellesley and as founders of the Association of Collegiate Alumnae (later the American Association of University Women). Talbot in particular had a strong consciousness of Eastern traditions for women's education, as the Chicago men did for Yale. When she left Boston for Chicago in 1892 a friend gave her a small piece of Plymouth Rock to take along. "I felt the gift was rather symbolical. . . . I must be reminded that the United States, at least my part of it, was founded on a rock; I might forget that four of my ancestors landed from the little ship 'Mayflower' and be tempted to follow strange gods unless I had some. . . reminder close at hand." If Chicago would be a western Yale, Talbot and Palmer determined to make it also a western Wellesley.[31]

Palmer resigned in 1897, and Talbot became dean, remaining at Chicago in that position until her retirement in 1925. Since she was perhaps the largest single influence on Chicago women, it is important to take note of her position on women's education.

Talbot firmly believed in the intellectual capacities of young women. Women, she said

> have proved their ability to enter every realm of knowledge. They must have the right to do it. No province of the mind should be peculiarly man's. Unhampered by traditions of sex, women will naturally and without comment seek the intellectual goal which they think good and fit. The logical outcome of the present status of women's education will be intellectual freedom on an individual basis.[32]

Yet she also advocated "special education" for women. Her own field of home economics taught women to run their homes and raise their children scientifically. She urged college women to understand good chemistry, proper ventilation, textiles, wise shopping, and economics so they would have efficient, modern homes. She did not question the desirability of most college women becoming full-time homemakers and mothers. Indeed, she assured parents that college attendance need not lead to the schoolroom and spinsterhood, but to an enhanced life in the home. In 1909-1910 her correspondence with Walter De La Mater of Pecatonica, Illinois, she urged him to keep his daughter Mabel in college, promising to take a personal interest in the young woman, and assuring the anxious father:

> [M]y experience leads me to believe that if you are able to give your daughter a collegiate training, it will not of necessity result in her devoting herself to the calling of teacher. There are many women who have the intellectual satisfaction of education who find their happiness in family life and render efficient and noble service in the home.[33]

Talbot supported women's intellectual equality and yet expected them to fulfill traditional roles because she felt those roles to be crucial. Healthy families produced a healthy nation. Like other feminists of her day, Talbot thought women uniquely qualified as homemakers because of their "special" sensitivities and innately superior morality. College-trained women in particular could use these womanly attributes along with their educations to reform their communities along more humane and democratic lines. In fact, many feminists supported women's suffrage because they felt women would use their political power to make badly-needed social changes.[34] This view of women's potential power included separatism, as a technique for bringing women together, reinforcing their virtues, and influencing men. Graduates of the Eastern women's colleges had already demonstrated the power of education, feminism, and separatism in the social settlement movement.[35] Thus when Marion Talbot promoted social separatism on the Chicago campus, she did so to make women more powerful, and increase their influence over the University community. Her separatist ideals had little in common with the separatism practiced at Berkeley. The social arrangements she made as Dean of Women successfully imitated the Eastern women's colleges and created a strong women's community at Chicago.

Unlike Lucy Sprague, Talbot did not merely cooperate with existing organizations to set social policy. Instead she framed the women's social life at Chicago to fit her ideals. She and Palmer lived with the women students at the Hotel Beatrice during the year 1892-1893 before the women's dormitories opened. Freshman Demia Butler's diary recorded her arrival in Chicago on September 21, 1892, entrance examinations on September 22, and sitting on a mattress in the Hotel Beatrice while Talbot and Palmer explained what the women's halls would be like when they opened in May.[36]

The residence halls represented the heart of Talbot's plans for a coherent and strong social life for Chicago women, similar to that experienced by the students at eastern women's colleges. She wanted as many women as possible to live on campus, to consider the residence halls their home, and the other residents as family. Incoming students were assigned to a hall, but could only stay for six months. At the end of that time, other residents had the option of asking them to become full members or to leave. Each hall elected officers, held house meetings, gave its own parties, set its own rules, and ran its own social life. Women faculty frequently lived in the halls, presiding over the dining tables. Talbot herself became head first of Green Hall, then of Kelly, and lived in the halls until her retirement. Important visitors, male and female, were entertained in the women's halls at teas, dinners, and receptions.

Because the halls provided a focus for women's social life, the deans opposed the forming of national sororities at Chicago. Most eastern women's colleges did not have sororities, and boasted of their democratic style of life. By 1910 Barnard, Wellesley, and Mt. Holyoke had banned their secret societies.[37] Many felt that sororities divided women, fragmenting what should have been a close female community. As Talbot said:

> [T]he University of Chicago was to provide both these essential factors (housing and social life) in the life of its students, and in addition the city provided cultural and social opportunities usually not within the reach of students in a small town. It seemed to us important that the situation should not be complicated by the introduction of policies directed by persons outside of the University and not familiar with its aims.[38]

Between 1894 and 1896 Talbot and Palmer struggled to keep the sororities off campus. A compromise was reached with Chicago women permitting the existence of local "clubs" with no national affiliations. While the clubs—Quadranglers, Mortarboard, Esoteric, Sigma, and Kailailu—had many of the trappings of sororities, including rushing, pledging, and the wearing of ribbons and pins, Talbot kept a close watch on them. Each year she checked membership lists for failing students, and urged them to make pledging practices more democratic. Chicago's clubs were not as important as Berkeley's sororities—they did not own their own buildings, and never replaced the women's halls as the focus for social life.[39]

In addition to running the halls and supervising the social clubs, Talbot's duties included: the formation of general policies concerning women, both graduate and undergraduate; the registration and approval of all social functions; direction of the social calendar; conferences with social committees and officers of organizations; assisting fraternities in maintaining good social standards; advising the Board of Student Organizations which approved or disapproved all student clubs; supervising publicity and hospitality for women's guests and speakers; setting standards of dress, dancing, conduct, and manners; organizing women's occupational conferences; and exercising "charge of the conduct of men in the Women's Quadrangle."[40] Thus, while her duties included some that Lucy Sprague would not have performed, considering them to be those of a "warden of women," she exercised control over male students and their relations with women, which Sprague did not. Her influence spread far beyond the women's halls.

Like Sprague, Talbot encountered little resistance to the social standards she set. In one case, male students invited the women to a dance they were giving at a neighborhood public hall. Talbot was dubious, but said: "Let us find out how parties are given and invitations issued by the people who are showing interest in the University. I have no inclination to force on the community the standards to which I have been accustomed, but I do not think we are compelled to adopt the standards of Podunk."[41] After some discussion it was decided that women graduate students could go if they liked, but undergraduates would be forbidden to attend. Talbot's claim that the women students supported her decision is borne out by student Demia Butler. Butler noted in her diary that the women were disappointed, but felt better when Dean Talbot wrote notes to all their escorts, explaining the situation. Butler's escort, Mr. Stone, "took it beautifully. He talked with Miss Talbot, and then understood." Talbot suggested that the men come to the Hotel Beatrice in the evening and "dance a little" instead.[42] Social regulations at Chicago limited male callers at the halls to Friday and Saturday evenings until 10:15 P.M. Dances could not be held more often than once a week, had to take place on campus, and ended at midnight. The only complaints students voiced came from those who wanted a 1 A.M. curfew for the big dances of the year—the Washington Promenade and the Settlement Dance.[43]

Talbot took the lead in founding the Women's Union in 1901. While 20 percent of Chicago's students lived in university halls, and another 40 percent in rooms close to the campus, fully 40 percent commuted from their parents' homes in the city.[44] Because of this, Talbot wanted to provide women day students with a place where they could feel more involved with campus life. The Union took over some rooms in a neighborhood church, turning them into rest rooms, reading rooms, and lunch rooms for women students. It held regular Wednesday afternoon receptions and provided women's clubs with meeting places. Undergraduate, graduate, and faculty women all joined the Union, and Talbot herself served as its president.

Her concern for the academic achievements of women students showed in her annual statement "The Women of the University," included in the *President's Report*. She listed the home states, curricular choices, and grades of undergraduates, comparing their honors to those received by male students. Women graduate students, particularly those holding fellowships or taking their degrees, received recognition in her report. She also discussed the appointments, promotions, and resignations of women faculty, and commented extensively on all aspects of women's lives at the university.

Not only the times and the female faculty, but conditions at the university favored the development of a strong women's presence. Because of Chicago's emphasis on graduate work, undergraduate pranks and games held far less importance there than they did at other schools. Since such traditions of athletics, politics, and roughhousing commonly led, as at Berkeley, to a male-oriented campus, their lesser importance at Chicago contributed to a more favorable position for women. And since campus newspapers were not dominated by discussions of the big game or class elections, they featured articles on the scholarly work of professors, the meaning of student religion, the activities of social settlements, and literary work by students. Discussions of events on the Women's Quadrangle and the parties at the halls also became important news.

Furthermore, Chicago's large arts and sciences graduate school contained a significant number of women studying for their master's and doctoral degrees. Reformers Sophonisba Breckinridge, Grace and Edith Abbott, Katherine Bement Davis, and scholars Helen Bradford Thompson, Myra Reynolds, Elizabeth Wallace, and Madeleine Wallin all did their graduate work at Chicago. Not only did Talbot publicize their efforts in her annual report, but campus newspapers proudly reported their progress.[45] These women joined academic and social clubs with undergraduate women, and often lived in the residence halls, presiding over the dinner tables. In addition to her many other achievements, Breckinridge became the assistant dean of women, serving as a link between academic women, students, and the Hull House reformers.

Particularly during the first ten years of Chicago's existence, male students reacted to their female colleagues in proud and positive ways. In addition to devoting space to women's activities and articles in campus publications, they made many supportive statements about co-education and female achievement. In contrast to Berkeley, one does not find in Chicago publications any of the degrading comments about the supposedly negative effects of co-education on femininity. Instead, the *University Weekly* asserted that "we students at Chicago shall all our lives be better for constant association with those who may be now our sweethearts, someday our wives."[46] Chicago men reiterated this position in smug comparisons of their own attitude about co-education relative to that prevailing at less enlightened institutions.[47]

In the absence of any student or faculty poll it is difficult to assess opinion on a specific feminist issue like suffrage. Nevertheless, the student newspaper gave detailed coverage to the College Equal Suffrage League's activities and proposals. The Chicago chapter was founded in 1908 by student Harriet Grim and Dean Breckinridge upon their return from the convention of the

National Equal Suffrage Association of College Women. The newspaper gave front-page coverage to their plan to enroll every woman student at the university as a member of the League. The paper also featured stories on prominent prosuffrage speakers such as Charlotte Perkins Gilman.[48]

Unquestionably, Chicago's brand of separation did not lead to equality or to the breaking down of sex roles any more than Berkeley's did. Male students ran the publications, class politics, and the debating contests. They had more options for living on or near the campus than did women students. While Harper disapproved of undergraduate fraternities, he did not forbid them, and by 1902 twelve chapters of national fraternities owned houses on or near the campus.[49] Female faculty made up only a small fraction of the instructional staff, and generally served at the lowest levels of instruction.[50] Despite the achievements ot its graduate students, Chicago's undergraduate women had very conventional career aspirations. When Talbot and Breckinridge polled ninety-six freshmen and sophomore women in 1909, fifty-six of the women wished to become teachers, while fifteen listed no choice at all. The deans followed their poll with a vocational conference, attended by three hundred thirty-six Chicago women. One hundred eighty women attended the teaching sessions, while forty heard speakers on "household management." Talbot noted that "while only 2 out of 96 women specified homekeeping as their vocation, the conference on household management drew the largest attendance but one."[51] Quite possibly some of the women who expressed interest in "art" or "writing" or "general culture" also had homemaking interests at heart.

Nevertheless, during its first ten years, the University of Chicago developed a distinctive style of co-education far more respectful of and advantageous to women than was the case at Berkeley. In fact, the very success of co-education at Chicago alarmed some faculty and students and led to the "segregation" controversy.

Between 1900 and 1902 administrators discussed the possibility of separate instruction of the sexes in the Junior College, that is, during the freshman and sophomore years. Harper proposed a Men's Quadrangle and a Women's Quadrangle, each with its own residence halls, classrooms, and gymnasium. He noted that the Junior College was increasing in numbers anyway, necessitating new buildings. Why not use the opportunity to remove undergraduates from the center of campus, and to separate them by sex? Harper believed that co-education could destroy sex-role distinctions, harming everyone. He compared "trying to conform the college life of men and women to a common standard" to attempting "to train all their voices to a common pitch." "Is there not," he asked, "a serious loss to both men and women if the university places too much emphasis upon what they have in common and gives too much emphasis to the fact that in many respects these essential common interests may be best promoted separately?"[52]

As might be expected, Marion Talbot led the vigorous opposition to the plan. She based her objections on the grounds of the intellectual equality of the sexes.

> The atmosphere of intellectual freedom enjoyed by our students,
> through which they have exercised their mental powers as human
> beings without reference to the fact that they are either men or
> women, has been appreciated by them and admired by the world.
> Separate instruction... would affect this condition unfavorably. If
> the trustees could know how eager girls and women are to study as
> thinking beings and not as females, they would hesitate in justice to
> women to adopt this measure.[53]

Talbot also feared that the quality of instruction offered to women would inevitably suffer from the expense of maintaining dual classes. She protested to Harper that the public would not understand separate instruction, and might suspect it had been initiated because women students were immoral, or because they could not keep academic pace with the men.[54] Those joining Talbot's protest included John Dewey; James Weber Linn, associate in English and a nephew of Jane Addams; classicists William G. Hale and Charles Chandler; James Tufts, Dean of the Senior College; geologists Thomas Chamberlin and Rollin Salisbury; and virtually all the female faculty. In addition, the university's Alumnae Association took up the "antisegregation" cause.

Why, after ten years, did fears arise concerning co-education? In part, we can attribute the controversy to the successes of Chicago women and resulting male fears about their domination of campus life. In her 1902 report Marion Talbot pointed out that the Junior and Senior Colleges now had more female than male students. Furthermore, between 1892 and 1902 women took 46 percent of all bachelor's degrees awarded by the university, and represented 56.3 percent of the Phi Beta Kappa membership.

Educators believed that men would not attend schools or classes where women predominated. Because the sexes differed so greatly, what attracted one would repel the other. Berkeley President Wheeler's view that men left the liberal arts due to a lack of job opportunities, not because of a surplus of women, was ignored. Instead of offering courses, as the state universities did, in agriculture, mining, and engineering, in order to attract men, private liberal arts colleges made plans to limit the numbers and influence of their women students.[56] Harper's reply to a Chicago clubwoman who wrote to him protesting segregation showed this concern about attracting male students: "The University of Chicago... has never taken any step to discourage the attendance of women. It may fairly be criticized, on the other hand, for having done much more for women than for men."[57]

Harper's view prevailed, at least for a time. Segregation took effect at Chicago in the fall quarter, 1902. But by 1907–08 it became clear that the plan was too expensive and cumbersome. Gradually, separate sections for courses were dropped. At best, however, Chicago women won the battle and lost the war. By 1910, they represented much less of a threat to conventional sex-role definitions. Between 1902 and 1912 the enrollment of men went up, the law school opened, and the Reynolds Club was established as a focus for men students' social life. The student newspaper, the *University Weekly* folded, giving way to the *Daily Maroon*. The *Maroon* dropped literary contributions, scholarly articles, and detailed news of women's activities. Instead the paper featured exhaustive accounts of athletic events and articles on the need for "spirit." Editorials addressed themselves to "Chicago men," ignoring the existence of women students.

As the position of men improved at the expense of women, and the campus atmosphere became more traditionally collegiate, women continued to develop their separate social life. Talbot considered the dedication of Ida Noyes Hall, a women's clubhouse and gymnasium, in 1915, the pinnacle of her achievement at Chicago.[58] Since she never sought the abandonment of conventional sex roles by women, she did not consider the Chicago experience a failure when that did not happen. Even on Talbot's own terms, however, women continued to lose ground at Chicago. In 1908–1909, for example, the female faculty consisted of one professor, one associate professor, two assistant professors, five instructors, one associate, one assistant, and twenty-one women associated with the newly-affiliated College of Education.[59] By 1912 women held only 15 percent of the graduate fellowships, compared to 26 percent in 1895.[60] Talbot's reports to the president grew shorter, her analyses less numerous and pointed. One of her last actions before her retirement was to complain officially to the administration about the low numbers, pay, and status of faculty women.[61] When she retired in

1925, the reports were discontinued, and her duties divided among various committees.

Conclusion

During the Progressive era, college women, with the help of their female mentors, established themselves on co-educational campuses, building good academic records and strong social lives, but for the most part acting separately from male students. Those who had feared a challenge to the social order from co-education need not have worried. Women's higher education, and co-education in particular, did not break down the barriers between the sexes, causing each to lose its "natural" distinctiveness. Instead, higher education served more conservative ends by training young women for traditional jobs, mostly in teaching or household management, and encouraging them to think of themselves in conventional ways. The results were similar whether separation was a reaction to male domination at Berkeley or a way of expanding women's roles and influence as at Chicago.

Events at Chicago, Berkeley, and other universities reflected the ideals and experience of the off-campus feminist movement. Social feminists stressed women's specialness and separateness. They asked for rights and privileges not on the basis of equality, but because women were morally superior beings. It would be beneficial, they argued, if women attended colleges and voted. Unfortunately the separate but equal theory could function like a double-edged sword. Doubtless President Harper wondered why Marion Talbot objected so strongly to separate instruction since she actively sought separation in all other areas of university life. And sadly, feminists' hopes for a new social order incorporating womanly ideals failed to materialize.

Furthermore, even when women could attend universities freely, exercise more legal rights, and vote, their ideology prevented them from entering the mainstream of American educational and political life. As separate, special, even morally superior beings, they were thought to exercise their most important influence from the sidelines. If women wanted to challenge the conventional definitions of sex roles they would first need to develop a new ideology, find ways of making their education serve those ends, and persuade men of the need for change.

Notes

1. Thomas Woody, *A History of Women's Education in the United States* (New York and Lancaster, Pennsylvania: The Science Press, 1929), Vol. II. See also Edward Clarke, *Sex and Education* (Boston: Osgood, 1874). I should like to thank Professors Steven Schlossman and Harold Wechsler of the University of Chicago for their help in preparing this essay. Archivists J.R.K. Kantor and Marie Thornton at Berkeley and Albert Tannler at Chicago were also most generous with their time and assistance.
2. Mabel Newcomer, *A Century of Higher Education for American Women* (New York: Harper and Brothers, 1959), pp. 46, 49.
3. Ibid.
4. John S. Haller, Jr., and Robin M. Haller, *The Physician and Sexuality in Victorian America* (Urbana, Illinois: University of Illinois Press, 1974). The chapter entitled "The Lesser Man," pp. 47ff., discusses how the experts designed the tests to show what the testers already believed: woman was a separate and inferior species.
5. Carroll Smith-Rosenberg, "The Female World of Love and Ritual: Relations between Women in Nineteenth-Century America," *Signs* 1 (Autumn 1975): 28.

6. Woody, Vol. 2, p. 208, and Newcomer, p. 212, discuss lower marriage rates among college women. I found little evidence that during the Progressive era the opposite was feared—that is, that co-education would lead to sexual immorality.

7. The University of California had only one campus—at Berkeley—until 1919 when UCLA was founded. Most sources of the Progressive era refer to the school as "the University of California." To avoid confusing the modern reader I have used the term "Berkeley" in this essay.

8. Verne A. Stadtman, ed., *The Centennial Record of the University of California* (Berkeley: University of California Press, 1967), pp. 212–219.

9. *President's Report*, University of California, 1900–1902, p. 23; 1913–1914, p. 14.

10. Rodman Wilson Paul, "Phoebe Apperson Hearst," in *Notable American Women* (Cambridge, Mass.: Belknap Press of Harvard University Press), Vol. 2, pp. 171–173.

11. By 1915, one-third of the student body belonged to Greek letter societies. Eight hundred thirty male students belonged to thirty-two fraternities, while thirteen sororities had three hundred ninety-seven members. Additionally there were fifteen residential clubs for men and nine for women. Thus, while opportunities to live on campus had increased for both sexes, men still had more "places" available than did the women. Then too, some fraternity and sorority members did not live at the houses. Each year the *Blue and Gold* listed the members of Greek letter societies.

12. "Report of the Dean of Women," in *President's Report*, 1906–1908, pp. 105–109. See also "Pioneering in Education," interview with Lucy Sprague Mitchell by Irene Prescott, Menlo Park, California, 1962, available in Bancroft Library, University of California at Berkeley, p. 41 of transcript.

13. References to Lucy Sprague's work with women students appear in "Reports of the Dean of Women," contained in the *President's Reports*, 1906–1912. See also the Associated Women Students' *Handbooks* (1915–1920). The University of California Archives, The Bancroft Library, Berkeley, California.

14. Lucy Sprague Mitchell, *Two Lives: The Story of Wesley Clair Mitchell and Myself* (New York: Simon and Schuster, 1953), pp. 194–195.

15. "Report of the Dean of Women," in *President's Report*, 1913–1914, p. 197.

16. Files of the Office of the President, The University of California Archives, The Bancroft Library, Berkeley, California.

17. Stadtman, *Centernnial Record*, pp. 212–219.

18. *Blue and Gold*, 1905.

19. See Stadtman, *Centennial Record*, pp. 113–117, for a list and description of student customs.

20. Lillian Moller Gilbreth, in Irving Stone, ed. *There Was Light: Autobiography of a University, Berkeley 1868–1968* (Garden City, New York: Doubleday and Company, 1970), pp. 84–85.

21. Files of the Office of the President, The University of California Archives, The Bancroft Library, Berkeley, California.

22. "Pioneering in Education," p. 42.

23. Since *The Blue and Gold* rarely used page numbers, more specific references are not possible. The type of comment referred to usually appeared in a joke section at the back.

24. *Pelican*, November 1910, editorial page.

25. *President's Report*, University of California, 1902–1904, p. 9.

26. *The Daily Californian*, September 1, 1904.

27. *The Prytaneans: An Oral History of the Prytanean Society, Its Members and Their University* (Berkeley, California: The Prytanean Alumnae, Inc., 1970).

28. *The Daily Californian*, March 16, 1909; October 6, 1909; December 11, 1911; Frequently townswomen organized the meeting, urging college women to attend. Meeting notices often reassured the college community that the club was not necessarily prosuffrage, and would be sure to consider the

other side of the question. Apparently, suffrage aroused only antipathy or indifference at Berkeley.

29. See Richard J. Storr, *Harper's University: The Beginnings* (Chicago: University of Chicago Press, 1966), for a discussion of "the eastern question" and Harper's faculty-building between 1890 and 1892. Robert Herrick's roman à clef, *Chimes* (1926), about the early years at Chicago also deals with the preeminence of "eastern" ideas.

30. Sprague was not the first female faculty member at Berkeley: Dr. Ritter and associates in physical education preceded her. She, and her successor Lucy Ward Stebbins were Radcliffe alumnae. At the time they attended Radcliffe (around 1900) it was still very much "the Harvard Annex," and had little social life for women students. Radcliffe also lacked a female faculty to provide role models for its students. The Chicago women came from eastern women's colleges with stronger traditions concerning women's academic and social life, most notably Wellesley. Part of the reason for their stronger showing on behalf of women students might have been their participation in the Wellesley tradition. I am indebted to Sally Schwager and Patricia Palmieri of the Harvard Graduate School of Education for discussing with me their research on Radcliffe and Wellesley Colleges.

31. Marion Talbot, *More Than Lore: Reminiscences of Marion Talbot, Dean of Women, the University of Chicago 1892-1925* (Chicago: University of Chicago Press, 1936), p. 6. The memoirs contain numerous references to eastern ties, and attempts to make social life for Chicago women similar to the life at the women's colleges. When Talbot visited other colleges to study their residence systems and social activities she went to Barnard, Bryn Mawr, Smith, Vassar, and Wellesley.

32. Marion Talbot, *The Education of Women* (Chicago: The University of Chicago Press, 1910), p. 22.

33. Marion Talbot to Walter De La Mater, November 25, 1910. Talbot papers, Special Collections, University of Chicago, Box IV, folder 1.

34. See William L. O'Neill, *Everyone Was Brave: A History of Feminism in America* (Chicago: Quadrangle Books, 1969).

35. Ibid. See also John P. Rousmaniere, "Cultural Hybrid in the Slums: The College Woman and the Settlement House, 1889-1894," in Michael Katz, ed., *Education in American History* (New York: Praeger Publishers, 1973).

36. Diary of Demia Butler, Special Collections, University of Chicago (no page numbers used). Many entries also undated.

37. See Anna Mary Wells, *Miss Marks and Miss Woolley* (Boston: Houghton Mifflin Company, 1978), for a discussion of the secret societies, and administrative attempts to ban them.

38. Talbot, *More Than Lore*, p. 88.

39. See Talbot's annual reports in *The President's Report*, University of Chicago, 1898–1920. She commented extensively on social life at the university, and almost always said something about the secret societies—usually something critical. See, for example, "The Women of the University," *President's Report*, 1909–1910, p. 95.

42. Talbot papers, Box IV, folder 1.

41. Talbot, *More Than Lore*, p. 62.

42. Diary of Demia Butler, February 19, 1893.

43. "The Women of the University," in *President's Report*, University of Chicago, 1897–1898, p. 133.

44. *President's Report*, 1892–1902. This report, published in honor of the decennial, summarized the university's first ten years. The figures cited come from the section called "The Student Social Life." They are not broken down into male/female students. I suspect that, as at Berkeley, more women were commuters than men.

45. Chicago had 354 graduate women in 1899–1900, while Berkeley had only 83. The difference is even greater, if we take into account that the Chicago figures do not include Education students. At Berkeley many women took a fifth year of graduate study to be eligible to teach in a secondary

school; such students probably represent most of the 83. See "The Women of the University," *President's Report*, 1892-1902, p. 125, and Stadtman, *Centennial Record*, pp. 212-219. See also *University Weekly*, December 12, 1895.

46. *University Weekly*, December 7, 1893.

47. The student newspaper at Chicago usually carried stories about events at other colleges and universities. When these stories concerned discrimination against women students, the Chicago paper was quite critical. See, for example, *Daily Maroon*, April 30, 1908; May 1, 1908.

48. *Daily Maroon*, October 15, 1909; May 13, 1908; October 23, 1908.

49. President's Papers 1889-1925, Special Collections, University of Chicago, Box 26, folder 2. Also, *President's Report*, 1892-1902, p. 391.

50. "The Women of the University," *President's Report*, 1897-1898, p. 112, lists twelve women besides Talbot and Palmer who had been on the faculty at various times between 1892 and 1898. In 1897-1898 seven women were teaching in the departments of Greek and Latin, English, Romance Languages, Physical Culture, and History. None ranked above assistant professor. Figures for 1908-1909 are given in the text.

51. "The Women of the University," *President's Report*, 1909-1910, pp. 94-95.

52. *The President's Report*, 1892-1902, preface.

53. Marion Talbot to William Rainey Harper, January 16, 1902, President's Papers, 1889-1925, Box 60, folder 11.

54. Ibid.

55. "The Women of the University," 1892-1902, p. 139. Thomas Woody discusses the "turn of the century reaction against co-education" in volume two of his *History of Women's Education in the United States*, pp. 267-297. Stanford and other schools restricted their women students in some way.

56. See note 29, above.

57. William Rainey Harper to Miss Mary B. Harris, Chicago ACA, May 13, 1902, President's Papers 1889-1925, Box 60, folder 11.

58. See "A Dream Come True," in *More Than Lore*.

59. "The Women of the University" in the *President's Report*, 1908-1909, p. 96.

60. President's Papers, 1889-1925, Box 33, Folder 3. See also, *Daily Maroon*, April 30, 1909; April 20, 1910; May 9, 1912.

61. "The Weaker Sex" in *More Than Lore*.

[Lynn D. Gordon is a doctoral candidate in the Department of History at the University of Chicago. Her dissertation, "Women on Campus in the Progressive Era," concerns the relationship of higher education, feminism, and popular images of women.]

Big-Time Athletics

John S. Brubacher and Willis Rudy

Sharing a place of eminence with the most famous clubs and fraternities, intercollegiate athletics came, after the Civil War, to provide a stage for the winning of honors as campus "big man." It had not always been so. In the early American college physical exercise was spontaneous, unorganized, and certainly not intercollegiate. Games were planned on an informal basis entirely for recreation and enjoyment. Moreover, there existed at many denominational colleges something like a contempt for mere physical prowess, as detracting from the desired high spiritual atmosphere. As late as the 1890s there were presidents at Miami University and the College of Wooster in Ohio who opposed intercollegiate athletics on the ground that they infringed on the "holy time" which was made available to the college student to prepare for later usefulness in life.[62]

The introduction of physical training and the gymnasium movement in the middle of the nineteenth century helped to dispel some of the coolness to systematic physical activity by undergraduates. In organized team play, however, American colleges lagged behind those in England. The first intercollegiate competitions did not come in the United States until the 1850s, when an upsurge of interest in boat racing occurred.[63] During the Civil War, baseball began to attain a measure of popularity with undergraduates, as well as with the general public. After 1865, "track and field" athletics also became popular and, by 1874, intercollegiate meets were being held.[64]

More important than any of these, as later events would disclose, was the first appearance of American college football. In 1869, the first intercollegiate football game occurred between Rutgers and Princeton. This was not yet the game as known today, but soccer. During the next few years, football was played between various American colleges under a confused rules situation until, in 1876, an intercollegiate conference adopted a modified form of Rugby Union rules. These modifications came to be expanded during future years to such an extent that American football came to be differentiated markedly from English rugby, soccer, or Canadian football.[65]

The influence of the growing British interest in team and school sports may well have played an important part in the rise of American collegiate sport at this time. The "Muscular Christianity" movement in Britain and the immense popularity of the book *Tom Brown's Schooldays* seem to have been factors helping to explain the rush to organize athletic activities at American institutions paralleling the team sports of the English schools.[66]

Howard Savage, in his thorough and illuminating analysis of American college athletics, has suggested that the year 1880 be taken as the dividing line between the earlier, informal period of college sports and the rise of highly organized "big-time" intercollegiate athletics. Before that date, he points out, neither training nor coaching had become specialized. Equipment was simple. Participants in matches away from home customarily paid their own expenses. Management was entirely in the hands of undergraduates. After 1880, all this began to change. Training was intensified and elaborated. Coaching became a paid profession, and a highly technical and specialized one at that. Equipment costs mounted rapidly. Alumni came to play a large role in the management of the teams. "Because it was joyously irrational," notes one observer, "(beneath the convenient façade of its supposed rules) and because it fastened upon practical rather than abstract prowess, football asserted itself as the archetypal expression of the student temperament. . . ."67

The new situation was one in which financial demands mounted rapidly. The result was a thoroughgoing commercialization of intercollegiate sport. Money to support the expanded athletic program had to be raised on a scale such as had never been seen before. The principal sources of such financing came to be gifts from wealthy alumni (who were thus enabled to secure a dominating position in the sports program) and receipts from admission charges to football games. Because the latter revenues were so important, a winning football team was considered "good business" by many college administrations. Since the game was becoming increasingly popular with a sports-hungry public, a good team could attract "big money" at the gate. In fact, many colleges took to building vast football stadia, some of them larger than the Colosseum of imperial Rome, in order to increase gate receipts by accommodating tens of thousands of spectators. The temporary grandstands of earlier days, where a handful of spectators had watched the game either free or at nominal cost, were things of the past.68

As college sport became a big business, a number of practices arose which were, to say the least, questionable. Many of these were introduced by overzealous alumni, eager for victory and bent upon "booming" their alma mater. The "tramp athlete," and his cousin, "the ringer," made their appearance, as able players canvassed the colleges and enrolled at those institutions willing to award them the most lucrative scholarship. Graduate students, even coaches, played on some teams along with the undergraduates. Many coaches found that retention of their position depended upon winning games, whether by fair means or foul. In addition to all of the foregoing, large-scale betting on college games began to pose serious problems.69

Despite these conditions, a number of college presidents were enthusiastic supporters of big-time athletics, largely on the ground that it provided good advertising for their schools. For example, President Charles Kendall Adams of the University of Wisconsin, himself a great football fan, firmly believed that an important factor in the drawing power of any American institution of learning was the prowess of its athletic teams.70 Of a similar mind was President William Rainey Harper of the University of Chicago. Like Adams, Harper was accustomed to making stirring appeals to the university's team between the halves of football games. Harper made strenuous, and finally successful, efforts to get the famous coach Amos Alonzo Stagg to come to Chicago as athletic director. In one letter, he told Stagg: "I want you to develop teams which we can send around the country and knock out all the colleges. We will give them a palace car and a vacation too."71 David Starr Jordan of Stanford started out by being an intensely sports-minded college president while Woodrow Wilson at Princeton and Vernon L. Parrington at the University of Oklahoma combined the coaching of football teams with a career of college teaching.

Presidents of small colleges were just as anxious to gain national recognition through intercollegiate athletics as were heads of large universities. Thus President Crowell of Trinity College in North Carolina was convinced that the development of a winning football team in the late 1880s was what "carried the record of Trinity's prowess beyond state limits" and enabled the institution to "enter upon a new era of its enviable and honorable career."72

There nevertheless remained a few leaders of American higher education who earnestly wished to see reforms in the whole system of intercollegiate sport. Such men as Presidents Eliot of Harvard, Butler of Columbia, and Wilson of Princeton deplored the brutality, overemphasis on winning, commercialism, and false scale of values induced by big-time football. In these criticisms they were joined by a number of periodicals,73 particularly those of a religious or denominational nature.74

Responding to these critics were a do-or-die group of college alumni, ex-players, and pro-football faculty members, who claimed that the existing situation was not as black as it had been painted.75 In the middle stood moderates like Walter Camp of Yale, who argued for the value of intercollegiate sport but called for the rigorous observance of certain standards of sportsmanship and gentlemanliness.76

Although the Harvard faculty promulgated a detailed code regulating all undergraduate sports as early as 1882, most colleges continued to drift and follow a laissez-faire attitude.77 In 1905, however, the academic world was stirred out of its lethargy by the publication in the Chicago Tribune of statistics showing that 18 players had been killed and 159 seriously injured during the football season just past.78 Immediately, President Theodore Roosevelt, a great lover of football and as an expression of his concept of the "strenuous life," summoned athletic representatives of Harvard, Yale, and Princeton to the White House for a conference. There the President called upon them to save the game by helping to eliminate from it all brutality and foul play.79

In the wake of the White House conference, action was taken all over the country to reform intercollegiate athletics. Some institutions, like Columbia, the University of Wisconsin, abolished football outright, while others, like Northwestern and Union College, suspended it for a year. In many places, shorter schedules were adopted. On the West Coast, the experiment was tried of substituting a modified form of rugby for football. Institution after institution set up special committees, usually representing faculty, students, and alumni, to superintend and control the whole field of intercollegiate athletics. A few schools, such as the University of Missouri and the University of Chicago, raised "physical culture" to the dignity of a full-fledged department of instruction, centralizing authority over both sports and physical training in one professor.[80]

Much of this zeal for reform petered out during the next few years, but one permanent element continued to work for improvement. This was represented by various regional intercollegiate athletic associations and conferences, such as the "Big Ten" of the Middle West. In 1905, this movement reached national proportions when the National Intercollegiate Athletic Association was established.[81]

The fact remains, however, that in 1929, when Howard E. Savage made his comprehensive study of intercollegiate sports for the Carnegie Foundation, he was obliged to report that these expedients had by no means eliminated the old evils of commercialism and overemphasis. Savage recommended that the colleges set up true standards of amateur sportsmanship and more actively go about their proper business of challenging the best intellectual capabilities of undergraduates.[82] These findings corroborated an analysis made by President W. H. P. Faunce of Brown more than twenty years earlier.[83]

More than four decades later, in 1974, a report published for the American Council on Education found that many abuses still existed in intercollegiate sports. The report criticized aspects of the financing of college athletics, ethical abuses in recruitment and subsidization of team members, deleterious effects of competition with professional teams for the entertainment dollar, the pressures resulting from the costs of extensive athletic plants, and a continuing confusion over the educational role, if any, of collegiate sport.[84]

What, then, can we say about the lasting significance of intercollegiate athletics in American higher education? In all fairness, we should note both the bright and dark tones in the picture. On the darker side, we must acknowledge that sports had to some extent diverted the interests of students from the intellectual aims which were supposed to be the principal purpose of higher learning.[85] At Amherst, the famous philosophy teacher Garman noted that the students were demanding for themselves a higher standard of perfection in athletics than in studies.[86] Another observer found that "honors" in football, baseball, and rowing had come to be esteemed at least as highly as academic honors, and soon the letters A.B. in America might come to stand for "bachelor of athletics" rather than bachelor of arts.[87]

We have already spoken of the commercialization of American college sport, and of the overemphasis on certain spectacular aspects. In these respects, the situation differed markedly from that at the British universities and public schools, where the amateur spirit reigned. The American emphasis on winning games for their financial or publicity value, the mass enthusiasm of "college spirit," stimulated by bands and cheer leaders, the high degree of professional organization and specialization involved in the really "big-time" athletic contests, were in many ways unique in the world.[88]

It was generally assumed that intercollegiate athletics were a profitable business enterprise for those conducting them, but this conclusion has been challenged by at least one study. An investigator in 1934 found that college football

during the 1920s did not "pay off" in helping to raise endowment for a group of average-sized institutions emphasizing it as a promotional technique. A similar group of colleges, which made no effort to emphasize big-time football, definitely outdistanced the others in this respect.[89]

It was claimed by proponents of intercollegiate athletics that the fierce competition of the playing field furnished good training for the "game" of life. This claim was belied by the findings of A. Lawrence Lowell, who made a detailed study of the careers of students who had attended Harvard during the later decades of the nineteenth century. Lowell discovered that there was no correspondence between attainment of the status of college athletic "hero" and distinction in later life.[90] Lowell's study gave documentation for a conclusion reached a little later by George Fitch in his novel *At Good Old Siwash*: "The college athlete may discover that the only use the world has for talented shoulder muscles is for hod-carrying purposes . . . and the fishy-eyed nonentity, who never did anything more glorious in college than pay his class tax, may be doing a brokerage business in skyscrapers within ten years."[91]

On the question of health, there is no clear evidence that intercollegiate athletic competition in any way improved the physical condition of the average undergraduate, or even of the active participant in varsity play. In fact, the Carnegie Foundation discovered in the 1920s that college athletes had no better life expectancy than the general run of the college population, itself a selected group, and definitely not so good a one as college men of high scholarship rank.[92] Then, too, there was the problem of physical injuries, many of them serious, resulting from football games. From 1893 to 1902, a total of 654 known serious injuries occurred among those playing college football in the United States.[93]

Some observers argued that the vogue for intercollegiate athletics helped drain off the excess energy of undergraduates and in so doing brought to a close the era of violent college rebellions.[94] Proponents of intercollegiate sport also made the claim that it helped develop ideals of sportsmanship, of loyalty to a cause, and of team play. In so doing, they asserted, college athletics had contributed important elements to the moral development of America.[95] In this connection, some have noticed a parallel between the role of physical training and athletic contests in the life of ancient Greece and their place in modern America. The cheerleaders, the "majorettes," the rooters, the intersectional "bowls," reminded at least one Briton of the great Panhellenic festivals, which, like the modern American sports spectacles, were religious exercises of a kind and instruments of national unity.[96]

One final point. College sport tended to sound a note of democratic opportunity and individualism in a society that was becoming increasingly stratified and conformist. The accident of origin or wealth meant little on the athletic field. The colleges, and the general public, too, wanted a winner.[97] To quote our British observer again:

The sons of Czechs and Poles can score there, can break through the barriers that stand in the way of the children of "Bohunks" and "Polacks." And although Harvard may secretly rejoice when it can put a winning team on to Soldier's Field whose names suggest the Mayflower, it would rather put on a team that can beat Yale. . . ."

62. Sherman B. Barnes, "Learning and Piety in Ohio Colleges, 1865–1900," *Ohio Historical Quarterly*, Vol. 69, October, 1960, pp. 334–335; Cutting, *op. cit.*, pp. 111–113; Edward A. Ross, *Seventy Years of It* (Englewood Cliffs, N.J., Prentice-Hall, 1936), p. 14; Francis A. Walker, *Discussions in Education* (New York, Holt Rinehart & Winston, 1899), pp. 260–262; Laura H. Moseley (ed.), *Diary of James Hadley* (New Haven, Conn., Yale University Press, 1951), p. 309; William Otis Carr, *Amherst Diary, 1853–1857* (Guilford, Conn., Shore Line Times Publishing, 1940), pp. 3–4; William W. Folwell, *Autobiography and Letters of a Pioneer of Culture* (Minneapolis, University of Minnesota Press, 1933), p. 61; Richard T. Ely, *The Ground Under Our Feet* (New York, Macmillan, 1938), pp. 30–31; John W. Burgess, *Reminiscences of an American Scholar* (New York, Columbia University Press, 1934), pp. 58–59.

63. The first Harvard-Yale crew race took place in 1852.

64. Mark Hopkins, *Miscellaneous Essays and Discourses* (Boston, T.R. Marvin, 1847), pp. 244–245; Hitchcock, *op. cit.*, p. 68; Hammond, *op. cit.*, pp. 179–180; Morison, *Three Centuries of Harvard*, pp. 314–316; Howard Savage, *American College Athletics* (New York, Carnegie Foundation, 1929), pp. 13–20.

65. Amos Alonzo Stagg. *Touchdown!* (New York, McKay, 1927), pp. 50–51; Savage, *op. cit.*, p. 20.

66. Guy Lewis, "The Beginning of Organized Collegiate Sport," *American Quarterly*, Vol. 22, Summer, 1970, pp. 222–227.

67. Veysey, *op. cit.*, p. 276. See also Savage, *op. cit.*

68. One source has estimated that the athletic receipts at Yale alone in 1906 were more than five times the total income of the college seventy-five years before! Clarence F. Birdseye, *Individual Training in Our Colleges* (New York, Macmillan, 1907), pp. 158–164. On this question, see Savage, *op. cit.*, pp. 22–29; Stagg, *op. cit.*, pp. 71–82, 180–181.

69. Savage, *op. cit.*, pp. 28–29.

70. Ely, *op. cit.*, p. 202; Curti and Carstensen, *op. cit.*, Vol. I, p. 578. Adams retained on the rolls able football players of little intellectual ability, despite strenuous objections from his faculty.

71. Amos Alonzo Stagg to his family, January 20, 1891; University of Chicago Archives, as quoted in Joseph E. Gould, "William Rainey Harper and the University of Chicago" (unpublished doctoral dissertation, Syracuse University, 1951), pp. 122–123.

72. John F. Crowell, *Personal Recollections* (Durham, N.C., Duke University Press, 1939), pp. 45–46, 230–231. On one occasion, Crowell wrote that a Trinity defeat of the University of North Carolina's football team "gave notice that the little college up in Randolph had come out from under."

73. Savage, *op. cit.*, p. 24; William A. Neilson, *Charles W. Eliot, The Man and His Beliefs* (New York, Harper & Row, 1926), pp. 119–120; Edward C. Elliott, *The Rise of a University* (New York, Columbia University Press, 1937), Vol. II, pp. 442–447; Burns, *op. cit.*, pp. 169–170; James F. Kemp, "The Proper Function of Athletics in Colleges and Universities," *Educational Review*, Vol. 35, February, 1908, pp. 170–177.

74. The religious press objected to the moral relapses and excessive drinking which were reputed to accompany many of the "big games." Crowell, *op. cit.*, p. 226. The denominational attitude is illustrated by President John C. Kilgo of Trinity College, North Carolina, who reversed Crowell's big-time sports program there. Kilgo maintained that the fortunes of a denominational college should hang on faith in Christ, not the record of a football team. Paul N. Garber, *J. C. Kilgo, President of Trinity College* (Durham, N.C., Duke University Press, 1937), pp. 156–162.

75. White, *op. cit.*, Vol. I, pp. 352–353; E. Benjamin Andrews, "The General Tendencies of College Athletics," National Educational Association, *Proceedings, 1904*, pp. 549–557.

76. Walter Camp, *Book of College Sports* (Englewood Cliffs, N.J., Prentice-Hall, 1910), pp. 2–8.

77. Harvard even abolished football for a couple of years, while she studied the situation. Morison, *Three Centuries of Harvard*, pp. 409–410; Conant *et al.*, *op. cit.*, pp. 50–51; Savage, *op. cit.*, p. 22.

78. These figures included both high-school and college competition. Stagg, *op. cit.*, p. 253.

79. Savage, *op. cit.*

80. Fox, *op. cit.*, pp. 35–36; Burns, *op. cit.*, pp. 169–170, Stagg, *op. cit.*, pp. 253–255; Curti and Carstensen, *op. cit.*, Vol. II, pp. 533–547. Henry O. Severance, *Richard Henry Jesse* (Columbia, Mo., published by the author, 1937), pp. 151–152; French, *op. cit.*, pp. 293–294; Bruce, *op. cit.*, Vol. V, pp. 292–298; LeDuc, *op. cit.*, pp. 132–133; Sheldon, *op. cit.*, pp. 245–253.

81. In 1894, the Southern Intercollegiate Athletic Conference was established. The Big Ten was formed the following year, and the Northwest Conference made its debut in 1904. Stagg, *op. cit.*, pp. 114–116; Savage, *op. cit.*, pp. 26–27; Curti and Carstensen, *op. cit.*, Vol. I, pp. 693–709.

82. Savage, *op. cit.*, pp. xx–xxi, 31–32, 310–311.

83. William H. P. Faunce, "Character in Athletics," National Education Association, *Proceedings, 1904*, pp. 558–565.

84. *The Chronicle of Higher Education*, Vol. 8, July 8, 1974, p. 13.

85. Edwin E. Slosson, *Great American Universities* (New York, Macmillan, 1910), pp. 506–507; Stagg, *op. cit.*, pp. 174–175. To Thorstein Veblen, this whole business was simply an expression of the "barbarian temperament." Just as fraternities manifested the primordial heritage of clannishness, so athletics manifested the predatory instinct, pure and simple. This is why, he declared, they were so closely connected. Thorstein Veblen, *Theory of the Leisure Class* (New York, Macmillan, 1912), pp. 278–379.

86. LeDuc, *op. cit.*, pp. 132–133.

87. Walker, *op. cit.*, pp. 259–260.

88. Ernest Barker, "Universities in Great Britain," in Kotschnig (ed.), *op. cit.*, pp. 98–99.

89. Arnaud C. Marts, "College Football and College Endowment," *School and Society*, Vol. 40, July 7, 1934, pp. 14–15.

90. A. Lawrence Lowell, "College Rank and Distinction in Life," *Atlantic Monthly*, Vol. 92, October, 1903, p. 519.

91. George Fitch, *At Good Old Siwash* (Boston, Little, Brown, 1911), p. 291.

92. W. Carson Ryan, *Literature of American School and College Athletics* (New York, Carnegie Foundation, 1929), pp. xi-xii.

93. Edwin G. Dexter, "Accidents from College Football," *Educational Review*, Vol. 25, April, 1903, p. 417.

94. Crowell, *op. cit.*, pp. 226–227; Thwing, *op. cit.*, pp. 388–389; Richard Hofstadter and C. DeWitt Hardy, *The Development and Scope of Higher Education in the United States* (New York, Columbia University Press, 1952), pp. 112–113.

95. Fox, *op. cit.*, p. 35; Norton, *op. cit.*, pp. 586–587.

96. Denis W. Brogan, *The American Character* (New York, Knopf, 1944), pp. 142–143.

97. Arthur T. Hadley, "Wealth and Democracy in American Colleges," *Harper's Magazine*, Vol. 113, August, 1906, p. 452.

98. Brogan, *op. cit.*, p. 142.

The Nature and Function of a University

Daniel Coit Gilman

During the last half century American universities have grown up with surprising rapidity. It is not necessary to fix an exact date for the beginning of this progress. Some would like to say that the foundation of the Lawrence Scientific School in Harvard University, and, almost simultaneously, the foundation of the Sheffield School of Science in New Haven were initial undertakings. These events indicated that the two oldest colleges of New England were ready to introduce instruction of an advanced character, far more special than ever before, in the various branches of natural and physical science. An impulse was given by the passage of the Morrill Act, by which a large amount of scrip, representing public lands, was offered to any State that would maintain a college devoted to agriculture and the mechanic arts, without the exclusion of other scientific and literary studies. The foundation of Cornell University was of the highest significance, for it fortunately came under the guidance of one who was equally devoted to historical and scientific research, one whose plans showed an independence of thought and a power of organisation then without precedent in the field of higher education. The changes introduced in Harvard, under masterful leadership, when the modern era of progress began, had profound influence. The subsequent gifts of Johns Hopkins, of Rockefeller, of Stanford, of Tulane, promoted the establishment of new institutions, in sympathy with the older colleges, yet freer to introduce new subjects and new methods. The State universities of the Northwest and of the Pacific coast, as population and wealth increased, became an important factor. These multiform agencies must all be carefully considered when an estimate is made of the progress of the last half-century.

I was a close observer of the changes which were introduced at Yale in the fifties and sixties, the grafting of a new branch—"a wild olive," as it seemed—upon the old stock. Then I had some experience, brief but significant, in California, as the head of the State University, at a time when it was needful to answer the popular cry that it should become chiefly a school of agriculture, and when it was important to show the distinction between a university and a polytechnic institute. Then came a call to the East and a service of more than a quarter of a century in the organisation and development of a new establishment. These are three typical institutions. Yale was a colonial foundation, wedded to precedents, where an effort was made to introduce new studies and new methods. California was a State institution, benefited by the so-called agricultural grant, where it was necessary to emphasise the importance of the liberal arts, in a community where the practical arts were sure to take care of themselves. Baltimore afforded an opportunity to develop a private endowment free from ecclesiastical or political control, where from the beginning the old and the new, the humanities and the sciences, theory and practice, could be generously promoted.

In looking over this period, remarkable changes are manifest. In the first place, science receives an amount of support unknown before. This is a natural consequence of the wonderful discoveries which have been made in respect to the phenomena and laws of nature and the improvements made in scientific instruments and researches. Educational leaders perceived the importance of the work carried on in laboratories and observatories under the impulse of such men as Liebig and Faraday. With this increased attention to science, the old-fashioned curriculum disappeared, of necessity, and many combinations of studies were permitted in the most conservative institutions. Absolute freedom of choice is now allowed in many places. Historical and political science has come to the front, and it is no longer enough to learn from a text-book wearisome lists of names and dates; reference must be made to original sources of information, or, at any rate, many books must be consulted in order to understand the progress of human society. Some knowledge of German and French is required of everyone. English literature receives an amount of attention never given to it in early days. Medicine is no longer taught by lectures only, but the better schools require continued practice in biological laboratories and the subsequent observation of patients in hospitals and dispensaries. The admission of women to the advantages of higher education is also one of the most noteworthy advances of the period we are considering.

The historian who takes up these and allied indications of the progress of American universities will have a difficult and an inspiring theme. It has been a delightful and exhilarating time in which to live and to work, to observe and to try. All the obstacles have not been overcome, some mistakes have been made, much remains for improvement, but on the whole the record of the last forty or fifty years exhibits its substantial and satisfactory gains. The efforts of scholars have been sustained by the munificence of donors, and more than one institution now has an endowment larger than that of all the institutions which were in existence in 1850.

In the middle of the century the word "university" was in the air. It was cautiously used in Cambridge and New Haven, where a number of professional schools were living vigorous lives near the parental domicile, then called "the college proper," as if the junior departments were colleges improper. To speak of "our university" savoured of pretence in these old colleges. A story was told at Yale that a dignitary from a distant State introduced himself as chancellor of the university. "How large a faculty have you?" asked Dominic Day. "Not any," was the answer. "Have you any library or buildings?" "Not yet," replied the visitor. "Any endowment?" "None," came the monotonous and saddening negative. "What have you?" persisted the Yale president. The visitor brightened as he said, "We have a very good charter."

Among enlightened and well-read people, the proper significance of a university was of course understood. Students came home from Europe, and especially from Germany, with clear conceptions of its scope. Everett, Bancroft, Ticknor, Hedge, Woolsey, Thacher, Whitney, Child, Gould, Lane, Gildersleeve and others were familiar with the courses of illustrious teachers on the Continent. European scholars were added to the American faculties—Follen, Beck, Lieber, Agassiz, Guyot, and others also distinguished. But the American colleges had been based on the idea of an English college, and upon this central nucleus the limited funds and the unlimited energies of the times were concentrated, not indeed exclusively, but diligently. Any diversion of the concentrated resources of the treasury to "outside" interests, like law, medicine, and theology, was not to be thought of. Even now, one hears occasionally the question, "after all, what *is* the difference between a university and a college?" To certain persons, the university simply means the best place of instruction that the locality can secure. The country is full of praiseworthy foundations which ought to be known as high-schools or academies or possibly as colleges, but which appear to great disadvantage under the more pretentious name they have assumed. Just after the war the enthusiastic sympathy of the North for the enfranchised blacks led to the bestowal of the highest term in educational nomenclature upon the institutes where the freedmen were to be taught. Fortunately, Hampton and Tuskegee escaped this christening, but Fiske, Atlanta, and Howard foundations were thus named. It is nearer the truth to say that the complete university includes four faculties—the liberal arts or philosophy, law, medicine, and theology. Sometimes a university is regarded as the union, under one board of control, of all the highest institutions of a place or region. There is one instance,—the State of New York,—where the name "university" is given to a board which in a general way supervises all the degree-giving institutions in the State.

When the announcement was made to the public, at the end of 1873, that a wealthy merchant of Baltimore had provided by his will for the establishment of a new university, a good deal of latent regret was felt because the country seemed to have already more higher seminaries than it could supply with teachers, students, or funds. Another "college" was expected to join the crowded column, and impoverish its neighbours by its superior attractions. Fortunately, the founder was wise as well as generous. He used the simplest phrases to express his wishes; and he did not define the distinguished name that he bestowed upon his child, nor embarrass its future by needless conditions. Details were left to a sagacious body of trustees whom he charged with the duty of supervision. They travelled east and west, brought to Baltimore experienced advisers, Eliot, Angell, and White, and procured many of the latest books that discussed the problem of education. By and by they chose a president, and accepted his suggestion that they should give emphasis to the word "university" and should endeavour to build up an institution quite different from a "college," thus making an addition to American education, not introducing a rival. Young men who had already gone through that period of mental discipline which commonly leads to the baccalaureate degree were invited to come and pursue those advanced studies for which they might have been prepared, and to accept the inspiration and guidance of professors selected because of acknowledged distinction or of special aptitudes. Among the phrases that were employed to indicate the project were many which then were novel, although they are now the commonplaces of catalogues and speeches.

Opportunities for advanced, not professional, studies were then scanty in this country. In the older colleges certain graduate courses were attended by a small number of followers—but the teachers were for the most part absorbed with undergraduate instruction, and could give but little time to the few who sought their guidance....

As the day has now come when there is almost a superfluity of advanced courses, let me tell some of the conditions which brought the Johns Hopkins foundations into close relations with these upward and onward movements.

Before a university can be launched there are six requisites: An idea; capital, to make the idea feasible; a definite plan; an able staff of coadjutors; books and apparatus; students. On each of these points I shall briefly dwell, conscious of one advantage as a writer—conscious, also, of a disadvantage. I have the advantage of knowing more than anyone else of an unwritten chapter of history; the disadvantage of not being able or disposed to tell the half that I remember.

"The idea of the university" was a phrase to which Cardinal Newman had given currency in a remarkable series of letters in which he advocated the establishment of a Catholic foundation in Dublin. At a time when ecclesiastical or denominational colleges were at the front, and were considered by many people the only defensible places for the

education of young men, his utterances for academic freedom were emancipating; at a time when early specialisation was advocated, his defence of liberal culture was reassuring. The evidence elicited by the British university commissions was instructive, and the writings of Mark Pattison, Dr. Appelton, Matthew Arnold, and others were full of suggestions. Innumerable essays and pamphlets had appeared in Germany discussing the improvements which were called for in that land of research. The endeavours of the new men at Cambridge and New Haven, and the instructive success of the University of Virginia, were all brought under consideration. Under these favourable circumstances, *Zeitgeist* they may be called, the Johns Hopkins was founded upon the idea of a university as distinct from a college.

The capital was provided by a single individual. No public meeting was ever held to promote subscriptions or to advocate higher education; no speculation in land was proposed; no financial gains were expected; no religious body was involved, not even the Society of orthodox Friends, in which the founder had been trained, and from which he selected several of his confidential advisers. He gave what seemed at the time a princely gift; he supplemented it with an equal gift for a hospital. It was natural that he should also give his name. That was then the fashion....

Given the idea and the funds, the next requisite was a plan. In my first interviews with the trustees, I was strongly impressed by their desire to do the very best that was possible under the circumstances in which they were placed. We quickly reached concurrence. Without dissent, it was agreed that we were to develop, if possible, something more than a local institution, and were at least to aim at national influence; that we should try to supplement, and not supplant, existing colleges, and should endeavour to bring to Baltimore, as teachers and as students, the ablest minds that we could attract. It was understood that we should postpone all questions of building, dormitories, commons, discipline, and degrees; that we should hire or buy in the heart of the city a temporary perch, and remain on it until we could determine what wants should be revealed, and until we could decide upon future buildings. We were to await the choice of a faculty before we matured any schemes of examination, instruction, and graduation....

Liberty in Education

Charles W. Eliot

How to transform a college with one uniform curriculum into a university without any prescribed course of study at all is a problem which more and more claims the attention of all thoughtful friends of American learning and education. To-night I hope to convince you that a university of liberal arts and sciences must give its students three things:

I. Freedom in choice of studies.

II. Opportunity to win academic distinction in single subjects or special lines of study.

III. A discipline which distinctly imposes on each individual the responsibility of forming his own habits and guiding his own conduct.

These three subjects I shall take up in succession, the first of them taking the greater part of the time allotted me.

I. Of freedom in choice of studies.

Let me first present what I may call a mechanical argument on this subject. A college with a prescribed curriculum must provide, say, sixteen hours a week of instruction for each class, or sixty-four hours a week in all for the four classes, without allowing for repetitions of lectures or lessons. Six or eight teachers can easily give all the instruction needed in such a college, if no repetitions are necessary. If the classes are so large that they need to be divided into two or more sections, more teachers must be employed. If a few extra or optional studies, outside of the curriculum, are provided, a further addition to the number of teachers must be made. Twenty teachers would, however, be a liberal allowance for any college of this type; and accordingly there are hundreds of American colleges at this moment with less than twenty teachers all told. Under the prescribed system it would be impossible for such a college to find work for more teachers, if it had them. Now there are eighty teachers employed this year in Harvard College, exclusive of laboratory assistants; and these eighty teach-

Charles William Eliot, *Educational Reform: Essays and Addresses* (New York, 1898), pp. 125–48.

under a discipline suited to their age, than with younger pupils under a discipline suited to theirs—as soon, in short, as it would be better for the youth to be the youngest student in a university than the oldest boy in a school. The school might still do much for the youth; the university may as yet be somewhat too free for him: there must be a balancing of advantages against disadvantages; but the wise decision is to withdraw him betimes from a discipline which he is outgrowing, and put him under a discipline which he is to grow up to. When we think of putting a boy into college, our imaginations are apt to dwell upon the occasional and exceptional evil influences to which his new freedom will expose him, more than upon those habitual and prevailing influences of college companionship which will nourish his manliness and develop his virtue; just as we are apt to think of heredity chiefly as a means of transmitting vices and diseases, whereas it is normally the means of transmitting and accumulating infinitely various virtues and serviceable capacities.

3. A young man is much affected by the expectations which his elders entertain of him. If they expect him to behave like a child, his lingering childishness will oftener rule his actions; if they expect him to behave like a man, his incipient manhood will oftener assert itself. The pretended parental or sham monastic régime of the common American college seems to me to bring out the childishness rather than the manliness of the average student; as is evidenced by the pranks he plays, the secret societies in which he rejoices, and the barbarous or silly customs which he accepts and transmits. The conservative argument is: a college must deal with the student as he is; he will be what he has been, namely, a thoughtless, aimless, lazy, and possibly vicious boy; therefore a policy which gives him liberty is impracticable. The progressive argument is: adapt college policy to the best students, and not to the worst; improve the policy, and in time the evil fruits of a mistaken policy will disappear. I would only urge at this point that a far-seeing educational policy must be based upon potentialities as well as actualities, upon things which may be reasonably hoped for, planned, and aimed at, as well as upon things which are.

4. The condition of secondary education is an important factor in our problem. It is desirable that the young men who are to enjoy university freedom should have already received at school a substantial training, in which the four great subdivisions of elementary knowl-

ers give about four hundred and twenty-five hours of public instruction a week without any repetitions, not counting the very important instruction which many of them give in laboratories. It is impossible for any undergraduate in his four years to take more than a tenth part of the instruction given by the College; and since four fifths of this instruction is of a higher grade than any which can be given in a college with a prescribed curriculum, a diligent student would need about forty years to cover the present field; and during those years the field would enlarge quite beyond his powers of occupation. Since the student cannot take the whole of the instruction offered, it seems to be necessary to allow him to take a part. A college must either limit closely its teaching, or provide some mode of selecting studies for the individual student. The limitation of teaching is an intolerable alternative for any institution which aspires to become a university; for a university must try to teach every subject, above the grade of its admission requirements, for which there is any demand; and to teach it thoroughly enough to carry the advanced student to the confines of present knowledge, and make him capable of original research. These are the only limits which a university can properly set to its instruction—except indeed those rigorous limits which poverty imposes. The other alternative is selection or election of studies.

The elective system at Harvard has been sixty years in developing, and during fourteen of these years—from 1846 to 1860—the presidents and the majority of the faculty were not in favor of it; but they could find no way of escape from the dilemma which I have set before you. They could not deliberately reduce the amount of instruction offered, and election of studies in some degree was the inevitable alternative.

The practical question then is, At what age, and at what stage of his educational progress, can an American boy be offered free choice of studies? or, in other words, At what age can an American boy best go to a free university? Before answering this question I will ask your attention to four preliminary observations.

1. The change from school to university ought to be made as soon as it would be better for the youth to associate with older students

2. The European boy goes to free universities at various ages from seventeen to twenty; and the American boy is decidedly more mature and more capable of taking care of himself than the European boy of like age.

edge—languages, history, mathematics, and natural science—were all adequately represented; but it must be admitted that this desirable training is now given in very few schools, and that in many parts of the country there are not secondary schools enough of even tolerable quality. For this condition of secondary education the colleges are in part responsible; for they have produced few good teachers, except for the ancient languages; and they have required for admission to college hardly anything but the elements of Greek, Latin, and mathematics. But how should this condition of things affect the policy of an institution which sees its way to create a university because the condition of secondary education in the country at large is unsatisfactory? Shall we stop trying to create a university because the condition of secondary education in the country at large is unsatisfactory? The difficulty with that policy of inaction is that the reform and development of secondary education depend upon the right organization and conduct of universities. It is the old problem: Which was first created, an egg or a hen? In considering the relation of college life to school life, many people are confused by a misleading metaphor —that of building. They say to themselves: on weak foundations no strong superstructure can be built; schools lay the foundations on which the university must build; therefore, if preparatory schools fail to do good work, no proper university work can subsequently be done. The analogy seems perfect, but has this fatal defect: education is a vital process, not a mechanical one. Let us, therefore, use an illustration drawn from a vital function, that of nutrition. A child has had poor milk as an infant, and is not well developed; therefore, when its teeth are cut, and it is ready for bread, meat, and oatmeal, you are to hold back this substantial diet, and give it the sweetened milk and water, and Mellin's Food, which would have suited it when a baby. The mental food of a boy has not been as nourishing and abundant as it should have been at school; therefore when he goes to college or university his diet must be that which he should have had at school, but missed. Education involves growth or development from within in every part; and metaphors drawn from the process of laying one stone upon another are not useful in educational discussions. Harvard College now finds itself able to get nearly three hundred tolerably prepared students every year from one hundred or more schools and private tutors scattered over the country; and she is only just beginning to reap the fruit of the changes in her own policy and discipline which the past eighteen years have wrought. Schools follow universities, and will be what universities make them.

With these preliminary suggestions I proceed to answer the question. At what age can an American boy best go to a university where choice of studies is free? and to defend my answer. I believe the normal age under reasonably favorable conditions to be eighteen. In the first place, I hold that the temperament, physical constitution, mental aptitudes, and moral quality of a boy are all well determined by the time he is eighteen years old. The potential man is already revealed. His capacities and incapacities will be perfectly visible to his teacher, or to any observant and intimate friend, provided that his studies at school have been fairly representative. If his historical studies have been limited to primers of Greek, Roman, and American history, his taste and capacity for historical study will not be known either to his teacher or to himself; if he has had no opportunity to study natural science, his powers in that direction will be quite unproved; but if the school course has been reasonably comprehensive, there need be no doubt as to the most profitable direction of his subsequent studies. The boy's future will depend greatly upon the influences, happy or unhappy, to which he is subjected; but given all favorable influences, his possibilities are essentially determined. The most fortunate intellectual influences will be within his reach, if he has liberty to choose the mental food which he can best assimilate. Secondly, at eighteen the American boy has passed the age when a compulsory external discipline is useful. Motives and inducements may be set vividly before him; he may be told that he must do so and so in order to win something which he desires or values; prizes and rewards near or remote may be held out to him; but he cannot be driven to any useful exercise of his mind. *Thirdly*, a well-instructed youth of eighteen can select for himself—not for any other boy, or for the fictitious universal boy, but for himself alone—a better course of study than any college faculty, or any wise man who does not know him and his ancestors and his previous life, can possibly select for him. In choosing his course he will naturally seek aid from teachers and friends who have intimate knowledge of him, and he will act under the dominion of that intense conservatism which fortunately actuates civilized man in the whole matter of education, and under various other safeguards which nature and not arbitrary regulation provides. When a young man whom I never saw before asks me what studies he had better take in college, I am quite helpless, until he tells me what he likes and what he dislikes to study, what kinds of exertion are pleasurable to him, what sports he cares for, what reading interests him, what his parents and grandparents were in the world, and what he means to be. In short, I can only show him how to think out the problem for himself with such lights as he has and nobody else can have. The proposition that a boy of eighteen can choose his own studies, with the natural helps, more satisfactorily than anybody else can choose them for him, seems at first sight absurd; but I believe it to be founded upon the nature of things, and it is also for me a clear result of observation. I will state first the argument from the nature of things, and then describe my own observations.

Every youth of eighteen is an infinitely complex organization, the duplicate of which neither does nor ever will exist. His inherited traits are different from those of every other human being; his environment has been different from that of every other child; his passions, emotions, hopes, and desires were never before associated in any other creature just as they are in him; and his will-force is aroused, stimulated, exerted, and exhausted in ways wholly his own. The infinite variety of form and feature, which we know human bodies to be capable of, presents but a faint image of the vastly deeper diversities of the minds and characters which are lodged in these unlike shells. To discern and take due account of these diversities no human insight or wisdom is sufficient, unless the spontaneous inclinations, natural preferences, and easiest habitual activities of each individual are given play. It is for the happiness of the individual and the benefit of society alike that these mental diversities should be cultivated, not suppressed. The individual enjoys most that intellectual labor for which he is most fit; and society is best served when every man's peculiar skill, faculty, or aptitude is developed and utilized to the highest possible degree. The presumption is, therefore, against uniformity in education, and in favor of diversity at the earliest possible moment. What determines that moment? To my thinking, the limit of compulsory uniform instruction should be determined by the elementary quality and recognized universal utility of the subjects of such instruction. For instance, it is unquestionable that every child needs to know how to read, write, and, to a moderate extent, cipher. Therefore primary schools may have a uniform programme. One might naturally suppose that careful study of the mother-tongue and its literature would be considered a uniform need for all youth; but as a matter of fact there is no agreement to this

effect. The English language and literature have hardly yet won a place for themselves in American schools. Only the elements of two foreign languages and the elements of algebra and geometry can be said to be generally recognized as indispensable to the proper training of all young people who are privileged to study beyond their seventeenth year. There is no consent as to the uniform desirableness of the elements of natural science, and there is much difference of opinion about the selection of the two foreign languages, the majority of educated people supposing two dead languages to be preferable, a minority thinking that living languages are permissible. The limit of that elementary knowledge, of which by common consent all persons who are to be highly educated stand in need, is therefore a narrow one, easily to be reached and passed, under respectable instruction, by any youth of fair ability before he is eighteen years old. There, at least, ceases justifiable uniformity in education. There, at least, election of studies should begin; and the safest guides to a wise choice will be the taste, inclination, and special capacity of each individual. When it comes to the choice of a profession, everybody knows that the only wisdom is to follow inclination. In my view, the only wisdom in determining those liberal studies which may be most profitably pursued after eighteen is to follow inclination. Hence it is only the individual youth who can select that course of study which will most profit him, because it will most interest him. The very fact of choice goes far to secure the coöperation of his will.

I have already intimated that there exist certain natural guides and safeguards for every youth who is called upon in a free university to choose his own studies. Let us see what these natural aids are. In the first place, he cannot help taking up a subject which he has already studied about where he left it off, and every new subject at the beginning and not at the middle. Secondly, many subjects taught at a university involve other subjects, which must therefore be studied first. Thus, no one can get far in physics without being familiar with trigonometry and analytic geometry; chemical analysis presupposes acquaintance with general chemistry; and palæontology acquaintance with botany and zoölogy; no one can study German philosophy to advantage unless he can read German, and no student can profitably discuss practical economic problems until he has mastered the elementary principles of political economy. Every advanced course, whether in language, philosophy, history, mathematics, or science, presupposes

apparently possess more theoretical and practical merit for his case than the required curriculum of my college days. Every prescribed curriculum is necessarily elementary from beginning to end, and very heterogeneous. Such is the press of subjects that no one subject can possibly be carried beyond its elements; no teacher, however learned and enthusiastic, can have any advanced pupils; and no scholar, however competent and eager, can make serious attainments in any single subject. Under an elective system the great majority of students use their liberty to pursue some subject or subjects with a reasonable degree of thoroughness. This concentration upon single lines develops advanced teaching, and results in a general raising of the level of instruction. Students who have decided taste for any particular subject wisely devote a large part of their time to that subject and its congeners. Those who have already decided upon their profession wisely choose subjects which are related to, or underlie, their future professional studies; thus, the future physician will advantageously give a large share of his college course to French, German, chemistry, physics, and biology; while the future lawyer will study logic, ethics, history, political economy, and the use of English in argumentative writing and speaking. Among the thousands of individual college courses determined by the choice of the student in four successive years, which the records of Harvard College now preserve, it is rare to find one which does not exhibit an intelligible sequence of studies. It should be understood in this connection that all the studies which are allowed to count toward the A.B. at Harvard are liberal or pure, no technical or professional studies being admissible.

Having said thus much about the way in which an American student will use freedom in the choice of studies, I desire to point out that a young American must enjoy the privileges of university life between eighteen and twenty-two, if at all. From two thirds to three fourths of college graduates go into professions or employments which require of them elaborate special preparation. The medical student needs four years of professional training, the law student at least three, the good teacher and the skilful architect quite as much. Those who enter the service of business corporations, or go into business for themselves, have the business to learn—a process which ordinarily takes several years. If a young man takes his A.B. at twenty-two, he can hardly hope to begin the practice of his profession before he is twenty-six. That is quite late enough. It is clearly impossible, therefore, that the American

acquaintance with some elementary course or courses. Thirdly, there is a prevailing tendency on the part of every competent student to carry far any congenial subject once entered upon. To repress this most fortunate tendency is to make real scholarship impossible. So effective are these natural safeguards against fickleness and inconsecutiveness in the choice of studies, that artificial regulation is superfluous.

I give, in the next place, some results of my own observation upon the working of an elective system; and that you may have my credentials before you I will describe briefly my opportunities of observation. I had experience as an undergraduate of a college course almost wholly required; for I happened upon nearly the lowest stage to which the elective system in Harvard College ever fell, after its initiation in 1825. During the nine years from 1854 to 1863 I became intimately acquainted with the working of this mainly prescribed curriculum from the point of view of a tutor and assistant professor who had a liking for administrative details. After a separation from the University of six years, two of which were spent in Europe as a student and four at the Massachusetts Institute of Technology as a professor, I went back as president in 1869, to find a tolerably broad elective system already under way. The wishes of the governing boards and external circumstances all favoring it, the system was rapidly developed. Required studies were gradually abolished or pushed back; so that first the Senior year was made completely elective, then the Junior, then the Sophomore, and finally in June last the Freshman year was made chiefly elective. No required studies now remain except the writing of English, the elements of either French or German (one of these two languages being required for admission), and a few lectures on chemistry and physics. None of the former exclusive staples, Greek, Latin, mathematics, logic, and metaphysics, are required, and no particular combinations or selections of courses are recommended by the faculty. I have therefore had ample opportunity to observe at Harvard the working of almost complete prescription, of almost complete freedom, and of all intermediate methods. In Europe I studied the free university method; and at the Institute of Technology I saw the system—excellent for technical schools—of several well-defined courses branching from a common stock of uniformly prescribed studies.

The briefest form in which I can express the general result of my observation is this: I have never known a student of any capacity to select for himself a set of studies covering four years which did not

university should be constructed on top of the old-fashioned American college. The average Freshman at Harvard is eighteen and two thirds years old when he enters, and at the majority of colleges he is older still. For the next three or four years he must have freedom to choose among liberal studies, if he is ever to enjoy that inestimable privilege.

Two common objections to an elective system shall next have our attention. The first is often put in the form of a query. Election of studies may be all very well for conscientious or ambitious students, or for those who have a strong taste for certain studies; but what becomes, under such a system, of the careless, indifferent, lazy boys who have no bent or intellectual ambition of any sort? I answer with a similar query: What became of such boys under the uniform compulsory system? Did they get any profit to speak of under that régime? Not within my observation. It really does not make much difference what these unawakened minds dawdle with. There is, however, much more chance that such young men will get aroused from their lethargy under an elective system than under a required. When they follow such faint promptings of desire as they feel, they at least escape the sense of grievance and repugnance which an arbitrary assignment to certain teachers and certain studies often creates. An elective system does not mean liberty to do nothing. The most indifferent student must pass a certain number of examinations every year. He selects perhaps those subjects in which he thinks he can pass the best examinations with the smallest amount of labor; but in those very subjects the instruction will be on a higher plane than it can ever reach under a compulsory system, and he will get more benefit from them than he would from other subjects upon which he put the same amount of labor but attained less success. It is an important principle in education, from primary school to university, that the greater the visible attainment for a given amount of labor the better; and this rule applies quite as forcibly to a weak student as to a strong one. Feeble or inert students are considerably influenced in choosing their studies by the supposed quality of the teachers whom they will meet. As a rule they select the very teachers who are likely to have the most influence with them, being guided by traditions received from older students of their sort. It is the unanimous opinion of the teachers at Cambridge that more and better work is got from this class of students under the elective system than was under the required.

Having said thus much about the effects of free choice of studies upon the unpromising student I must add that the policy of an insti-tution of education, of whatever grade, ought never to be determined by the needs of the least capable students; and that a university should aim at meeting the wants of the best students at any rate, and the wants of inferior students only so far as it can meet them without impairing the privileges of the best. A uniform curriculum, by enacting superficiality and prohibiting thoroughness, distinctly sacrifices the best scholars to the average. Free choice of studies gives the young genius the fullest scope without impairing the chances of the drone and the dullard.

The second objection with which I wish to deal is this: free choice implies that there are no studies which are recognized as of supreme merit, so that every young man unquestionably ought to pursue them. Can this be? Is it possible that the accumulated wisdom of the race cannot prescribe with certainty the studies which will best develop the human mind in general between the ages of eighteen and twenty-two? At first it certainly seems strange that we have to answer no; but when we reflect how very brief the acquaintance of the race has been with the great majority of the subjects which are now taught in a university the negative answer seems less surprising. Out of the two hundred courses of instruction which stand on the list of Harvard University this year it would be difficult to select twenty which could have been given at the beginning of this century with the illustrations, materials, and methods now considered essential to the educational quality of the courses. One realizes more easily this absence of accumulated experience on considering that all the natural sciences, with comparative philology, political economy, and history, are practically new subjects, that all mathematics is new except the elements of arithmetic, algebra, and geometry, that the recent additions to ethics and metaphysics are of vast extent, and that the literatures of the eighteenth and nineteenth centuries have great importance in several European languages. The materials and methods of university education always have been, and always will be, changing from generation to generation. We think, perhaps with truth, that the nineteenth century has been a period of unprecedented growth and progress; but every century has probably witnessed an unprecedented advance in civilization, simply because the process is cumulative, if no catastrophes arrest it. It is one of the most important functions of universities to store up the accumulated knowledge of the race, and so to use these stores that each successive generation of youth shall start with all the advantages which their predecessors have won. Therefore a university, while not neglect-in special subjects or lines of study. The uniform curriculum led to a uniform degree, the first scholar and the last receiving the same diploma. A university cannot be developed on that plan. It must provide academic honors at graduation for distinguished attainments in single subjects. These honors encourage students to push far on single lines; whence arises a demand for advanced instruction in all departments in which honors can be won, and this demand, taken in connection with the competition which naturally springs up between different departments, stimulates the teachers, who in turn stimulate their pupils. The elaborate directions given by each department to candidates for honors are so many definite pieces of advice to students who wish to specialize their work. It is an incidental advantage of the system that the organization of departments of instruction is promoted by it. The teachers of Latin, of history, or of philosophy, find it necessary to arrange their courses in orderly sequence, to compare their methods and their results, and to enrich and diversify as much as possible the instruction which they collectively offer. Many European universities, but especially the English, offer honors, or prizes, or both of these inducements, for distinguished merit in specialities; and the highly valued degree of Ph.D. in Germany is a degree given for large attainments in one or two branches of knowledge, with mention of the specialty. The Harvard faculty announced their system of honors in 1866-67, and they certainly never passed a more effective piece of legislation. In 1879 they devised a lesser distinction at graduation called honorable mention, which has also worked very well. To get honors in any department ordinarily requires a solid year and a half's work; to get honorable mention requires about half that time. The important function of all such devices is to promote specialization of work and therefore to develop advanced instruction. It is unnecessary to point out how absolutely opposed to such a policy the uniform prescription of a considerable body of elementary studies must be.

III. A university must permit its students, in the main, to govern themselves. It must have a large body of students, else many of its numerous courses of highly specialized instruction will find no hearers, and the students themselves will not feel that very wholesome influence which comes from observation of and contact with large numbers of young men from different nations, States, schools, families, sects, parties, and conditions of life. In these days a university is best placed in or near the seat of a considerable population; so that its offi-

ing the ancient treasures of learning, has to keep a watchful eye upon the new fields of discovery, and has to invite its students to walk in new-made as well as in long-trodden paths. Concerning the direct educational influence of all these new subjects the race cannot be said to have much accumulated wisdom.

One presumption of considerable scope may, however, be said to be established by experience. In every new field of knowledge the mental powers of the adventurers and discoverers found full play and fruitful exercise. Some rare human mind or minds must have laboriously developed each new subject of study. It may fairly be presumed that the youth will find some strenuous exercise of his faculties in following the masters into any field which it taxed their utmost powers to explore and describe. To study the conquests of great minds in any field of knowledge must be good training for young minds of kindred tastes and powers. That all branches of sound knowledge are of equal dignity and equal educational value for mature students is the only hopeful and tenable view in our day. Long ago it became quite impossible for one mind to compass more than an insignificant fraction of the great sum of acquired knowledge.

Before I leave the subject of election of studies, let me point out that there is not a university of competent resources upon the continent of Europe in which complete freedom of studies has not long prevailed; and that Oxford and Cambridge have recently provided an almost complete liberty for their students. In our own country respectable colleges now offer a considerable proportion of elective studies, and as a rule the greater their resources in teachers, collections, and money, the more liberal their application of the elective principle. Many colleges, however, still seem to have but a halting faith in the efficacy of the principle, and our educated public has but just begun to appreciate its importance. So fast as American institutions acquire the resources and powers of European universities, they will adopt the methods proper to universities wherever situate. At present our best colleges fall very far short of European standards in respect to number of teachers, and consequently in respect to amplitude of teaching.

As yet we have no university in America—only aspirants to that eminence. All the more important is it that we should understand the conditions under which a university can be developed—the most indispensable of which is freedom in choice of studies.

II. A university must give its students opportunity to win distinction

cers and students can always enjoy the various refined pleasures, and feel alike the incitements and the restraints, of a highly cultivated society. The universities of Rome, Paris, Vienna, Berlin, Leipsic, Christiania, Madrid, and Edinburgh forcibly illustrate both of these advantages. These conditions make it practically impossible for a university to deal with its students on any principle of seclusion, either in a village or behind walls and bars. Fifteen hundred able-bodied young men living in buildings whose doors stand open night and day, or in scattered lodging-houses, cannot be mechanically protected from temptation at the university any more than at the homes from which they came. Their protection must be within them. They must find it in memory of home, in pure companionship, in hard work, in intellectual ambition, religious sentiment, and moral purpose. A sense of personal freedom and responsibility reinforces these protecting influences, while the existence of a supervising authority claiming large powers which it has no effective means of exercising weakens them. The *in loco parentis* theory is an ancient fiction which ought no longer to deceive anybody. No American college, wherever situated, possesses any method of discipline which avails for the suppression or exclusion of vice. The vicious student can find all means of indulgence in the smallest village, and the worst vices are the stillest. It is a distinct advantage of the genuine university method that it does not pretend to maintain any parental or monastic discipline over its students, but frankly tells them that they must govern themselves. The moral purpose of a university's policy should be to train young men to self-control and self-reliance through liberty. It is not the business of a university to train men for those functions in which implicit obedience is of the first importance. On the contrary, it should train men for those occupations in which self-government, independence, and originating power are preeminently needed. Let no one imagine that a young man is in peculiar moral danger at an active and interesting university. Far from it. Such a university is the safest place in the world for young men who have anything in them—far safer than counting-room, shop, factory, farm, barrack, forecastle, or ranch. The student lives in a bracing atmosphere; books engage him; good companionships invite him; good occupations defend him; helpful friends surround him; pure ideals are held up before him; ambition spurs him; honor beckons him.

1940 Statement of Principles

American Association of University Professors

In 1940, following a series of joint conferences begun in 1934, representatives of the American Association of University Professors and of the Association of American Colleges agreed upon a restatement of principles set forth in the 1925 Conference Statement on Academic Freedom and Tenure. This restatement is known to the profession as the 1940 Statement of Principles on Academic Freedom and Tenure.

The 1940 Statement is printed below, followed by Interpretive Comments as developed by representatives of the American Association of University Professors and the Association of American Colleges during 1969.

The purpose of this statement is to promote public understanding and support of academic freedom and tenure and agreement upon procedures to assure them in colleges and universities. Institutions of higher education are conducted for the common good and not to further the interest of either the individual teacher[1] or the institution as a whole. The common good depends upon the free search for truth and its free exposition.

Academic freedom is essential to these purposes and applies to both teaching and research. Freedom in research is fundamental to the advancement of truth. Academic freedom in its teaching aspect is fundamental for the protection of the rights of the teacher in teaching and of the student to freedom in learning. It carries with it duties correlative with rights. [1][2]

Tenure is a means to certain ends; specifically: (1) Freedom of teaching and research and of extramural activities and (2) a sufficient degree of economic security to make the profession attractive to men and women of ability. Freedom and economic security, hence, tenure, are indispensable to the success of an institution in fulfilling its obligations to its students and to society.

ACADEMIC FREEDOM

(a) The teacher is entitled to full freedom in research and in the publication of the results, subject to the adequate performance of his other academic duties; but research for pecuniary return should be based upon an understanding with the authorities of the institution.

(b) The teacher is entitled to freedom in the classroom in discussing his subject, but he should be careful not to introduce into his teaching controversial matter which has no relation to his subject. [2] Limitations of academic freedom because of religious or other aims of the institution should

be clearly stated in writing at the time of the appointment. [3]

(c) The college or university teacher is a citizen, a member of a learned profession, and an officer of an educational institution. When he speaks or writes as a citizen, he should be free from institutional censorship or discipline, but his special position in the community imposes special obligations. As a man of learning and an educational officer, he should remember that the public may judge his profession and his institution by his utterances. Hence he should at all times be accurate, should exercise appropriate restraint, should show respect for the opinions of others, and should make every effort to indicate that he is not an institutional spokesman. [4]

ACADEMIC TENURE

(a) After the expiration of a probationary period, teachers or investigators should have permanent or continuous tenure, and their service should be terminated only for adequate cause, except in the case of retirement for age, or under extraordinary circumstances because of financial exigencies.

In the interpretation of this principle it is understood that the following represents acceptable academic practice:

1. The precise terms and conditions of every appointment should be stated in writing and be in the possession of both institution and teacher before the appointment is consummated.

2. Beginning with appointment to the rank of full-time instructor or a higher rank [5], the probationary period should not exceed seven years, including within this period full-time service in all institutions of higher education; but subject to the proviso that when, after a term of probationary service of more than three years in one or more institutions, a teacher is called to another institution it may be agreed in writing that his new appointment is for a probationary period of not more than four years, even though thereby the person's total probationary period in the academic profession is extended beyond the normal maximum of seven years. [6] Notice should be given at least one year prior to the expiration of the probationary period if the teacher is not to be continued in service after the expiration of that period. [7]

3. During the probationary period a teacher should have the academic freedom that all other members of the faculty have. [8]

4. Termination for cause of a continuous appointment, or the dismissal for cause of a teacher previous to the expira-

tion of a term appointment, should, if possible, be considered by both a faculty committee and the governing board of the institution. In all cases where the facts are in dispute, the accused teacher should be informed before the hearing in writing of the charges against him and should have the opportunity to be heard in his own defense by all bodies that pass judgment upon his case. He should be permitted to have with him an adviser of his own choosing who may act as counsel. There should be a full stenographic record of the hearing available to the parties concerned. In the hearing of charges of incompetence the testimony should include that of teachers and other scholars, either from his own or from other institutions. Teachers on continuous appointment who are dismissed for reasons not involving moral turpitude should receive their salaries for at least a year from the date of notification of dismissal whether or not they are continued in their duties at the institution. [9]

5. Termination of a continuous appointment because of financial exigency should be demonstrably *bona fide*.

1940 INTERPRETATIONS

At the conference of representatives of the American Association of University Professors and of the Association of American Colleges on November 7–8, 1940, the following interpretations of the 1940 *Statement of Principles on Academic Freedom and Tenure* were agreed upon:

1. That its operation should not be retroactive.
2. That all tenure claims of teachers appointed prior to the endorsement should be determined in accordance with the principles set forth in the 1925 Conference Statement on Academic Freedom and Tenure.
3. If the administration of a college or university feels that a teacher has not observed the admonitions of Paragraph (c) of the section on Academic Freedom and believes that the extramural utterances of the teacher have been such as to raise grave doubts concerning his fitness for his position, it may proceed to file charges under Paragraph (a)(4) of the section on Academic Tenure. In pressing such charges the administration should remember that teachers are citizens and should be accorded the freedom of citizens. In such cases the administration must assume full responsibility and the American Association of University Professors and the Association of American Colleges are free to make an investigation.

1970 INTERPRETIVE COMMENTS

Following extensive discussions on the 1940 Statement of Principles on Academic Freedom and Tenure *with leading educational associations and with individual faculty members and administrators, a joint committee of the AAUP and the Association of American Colleges met during 1969 to reevaluate this key policy statement. On the basis of the comments received, and the discussions that ensued, the Joint Committee felt the preferable approach was to formulate interpretations of the* Statement *in terms of the experience gained in implementing and applying the* Statement *for over thirty years and of adapting it to current needs.*

The committee submitted to the two associations for their consideration the following Interpretive Comments. These interpretations were adopted by the Council of the American Association of University Professors in April 1970 and endorsed by the Fifty-sixth Annual Meeting as Association policy.

In the thirty years since their promulgation, the principles of the 1940 *Statement of Principles on Academic Freedom and Tenure* have undergone a substantial amount of refinement. This has evolved through a variety of processes, including customary acceptance, understandings mutually arrived at between institutions and professors or their representatives, investigations and reports by the American Association of University Professors, and formulations of statements by that Association either alone or in conjunction with the Association of American Colleges. These comments represent the attempt of the two associations, as the original sponsors of the 1940 *Statement*, to formulate the most important of these refinements. Their incorporation here as Interpretive Comments is based upon the premise that the 1940 *Statement* is not a static code but a fundamental document designed to set a framework of norms to guide adaptations to changing times and circumstances.

Also, there have been relevant developments in the law itself reflecting a growing insistence by the courts on due process within the academic community which parallels the essential concepts of the 1940 *Statement*; particularly relevant is the identification by the Supreme Court of academic freedom as a right protected by the First Amendment. As the Supreme Court said in *Keyishian v. Board of Regents* 385 U.S. 589 (1967), "Our Nation is deeply committed to safeguarding academic freedom, which is of transcendent value to all of us and not merely to the teachers concerned. That freedom is therefore a special concern of the First Amendment, which does not tolerate laws that cast a pall of orthodoxy over the classroom."

The numbers refer to the designated portion of the 1940 *Statement* on which interpretive comment is made.

1. The Association of American Colleges and the American Association of University Professors have long recognized that membership in the academic profession carries with it special responsibilities. Both associations either separately or jointly have consistently affirmed these responsibilities in major policy statements, providing guidance to the professor in his utterances as a citizen, in the exercise of his responsibilities to the institution and students, and in his conduct when resigning from his institution or when undertaking government-sponsored research. Of particular relevance is the *Statement on Professional Ethics*, adopted by the Fifty-second Annual Meeting of the AAUP as Association policy and published in the *AAUP Bulletin* (Autumn 1966, pp. 290–91).

2. The intent of this statement is not to discourage what is "controversial." Controversy is at the heart of the free academic inquiry which the entire statement is designed to foster. The passage serves to underscore the need for the teacher to avoid persistently intruding material which has no relation to his subject.

3. Most church-related institutions no longer need or desire the departure from the principle of academic freedom implied in the 1940 *Statement*, and we do not now endorse such a departure.

4. This paragraph is the subject of an Interpretation

adopted by the sponsors of the 1940 *Statement* immediately following its endorsement which reads as follows:

> If the administration of a college or university feels that a teacher has not observed the admonitions of Paragraph (c) of the section on Academic Freedom and believes that the extramural utterances of the teacher have been such as to raise grave doubts concerning his fitness for his position, it may proceed to file charges under Paragraph (a)(4) of the section on Academic Tenure. In pressing such charges the administration should remember that teachers are citizens and should be accorded the freedom of citizens. In such cases the administration must assume full responsibility and the American Association of University Professors and the Association of American Colleges are free to make an investigation.

Paragraph (c) of the 1940 *Statement* should also be interpreted in keeping with the 1964 "Committee A Statement on Extramural Utterances" (*AAUP Bulletin*, Spring, 1965, p. 29) which states inter alia: "The controlling principle is that a faculty member's expression of opinion as a citizen cannot constitute grounds for dismissal unless it clearly demonstrates the faculty member's unfitness for his position. Extramural utterances rarely bear upon the faculty member's fitness for his position. Moreover, a final decision should take into account the faculty member's entire record as a teacher and scholar."

Paragraph V of the *Statement on Professional Ethics* also deals with the nature of the "special obligations" of the teacher. The paragraph reads as follows:

> As a member of his community, the professor has the rights and obligations of any citizen. He measures the urgency of these obligations in the light of his responsibilities to his subject, to his students, to his profession, and to his institution. When he speaks or acts as a private person he avoids creating the impression that he speaks or acts for his college or university. As a citizen engaged in a profession that depends upon freedom for its health and integrity, the professor has a particular obligation to promote conditions of free inquiry and to further public understanding of academic freedom.

Both the protection of academic freedom and the requirements of academic responsibility apply not only to the full-time probationary as well as to the tenured teacher, but also to all others, such as part-time faculty and teaching assistants, who exercise teaching responsibilities.

5. The concept of "rank of full-time instructor or a higher rank" is intended to include any person who teaches a full-time load regardless of his specific title.*

6. In calling for an agreement "in writing" on the amount of credit for a faculty member's prior service at other institutions, the *Statement* furthers the general policy of full understanding by the professor of the terms and conditions of his appointment. It does not necessarily follow that a professor's tenure rights have been violated because of the absence of a written agreement on this matter. Nonetheless, especially because of the variation in permissible institutional practices, a written understanding concerning these matters at the time of appointment is particularly appropriate and advantageous to both the individual and the institution.**

7. The effect of this subparagraph is that a decision on tenure, favorable or unfavorable, must be made at least twelve months prior to the completion of the probationary period. If the decision is negative, the appointment for the following year becomes a terminal one. If the decision is affirmative, the provisions in the 1940 *Statement* with respect to the termination of services of teachers or investigators after the expiration of a probationary period should apply from the date when the favorable decision is made.

The general principle of notice contained in this paragraph is developed with greater specificity in the *Standards for Notice of Nonreappointment*, endorsed by the Fiftieth Annual Meeting of the American Association of University Professors (1964). These standards are:

> Notice of nonreappointment, or of intention not to recommend reappointment to the governing board, should be given in writing in accordance with the following standards:
>
> (1) *Not later than March 1 of the first academic year of service*, if the appointment expires at the end of that year; or, if a one-year appointment terminates during an academic year, at least three months in advance of its termination.
> (2) *Not later than December 15 of the second academic year of service*, if the appointment expires at the end of that year; or, if an initial two-year appointment terminates during an academic year, at least six months in advance of its termination.
> (3) At least twelve months before the expiration of an appointment after two or more years in the institution.

Other obligations, both of institutions and individuals, are described in the *Statement on Recruitment and Resignation of Faculty Members*, as endorsed by the Association of American Colleges and the American Association of University Professors in 1961.

8. The freedom of probationary teachers is enhanced by the establishment of a regular procedure for the periodic evaluation and assessment of the teacher's academic performance during his probationary status. Provision should be made for regularized procedures for the consideration of complaints by probationary teachers that their academic freedom has been violated. One suggested procedure to serve these purposes is contained in the *Recommended Institutional Regulations on Academic Freedom and Tenure*, prepared by the American Association of University Professors.

9. A further specification of the academic due process to which the teacher is entitled under this paragraph is contained in the *Statement on Procedural Standards in Faculty Dismissal Proceedings*, jointly approved by the American Association of University Professors and the Association of American Colleges in 1958. This interpretive document deals with the issue of suspension, about which the 1940 *Statement* is silent.

The 1958 *Statement* provides: "Suspension of the faculty member during the proceedings involving him is justified only if immediate harm to himself or others is threatened by his continuance. Unless legal considerations forbid, any such suspension should be with pay." A suspension which is not followed by either reinstatement or the opportunity for a hearing is in effect a summary dismissal in violation of academic due process.

---

*For a discussion of this question, see the "Report of the Special Committee on Academic Personnel Ineligible for Tenure," *AAUP Bulletin* 52 (Autumn 1966): 280–82.

**For a more detailed statement on this question, see "On Crediting Prior Service Elsewhere as Part of the Probationary Period," *AAUP Bulletin* 64 (September 1978): 274–75.

The concept of "moral turpitude" identifies the exceptional case in which the professor may be denied a year's teaching or pay in whole or in part. The statement applies to that kind of behavior which goes beyond simply warranting discharge and is so utterly blameworthy as to make it inappropriate to require the offering of a year's teaching or pay. The standard is not that the moral sensibilities of persons in the particular community have been affronted. The standard is behavior that would evoke condemnation by the academic community generally.

---

[1]The word "teacher" as used in this document is understood to include the investigator who is attached to an academic institution without teaching duties.

[2]Bold-face numbers in brackets refer to Interpretive Comments which follow.

Chronology of Principal University Administrations

Laurence R. Veysey

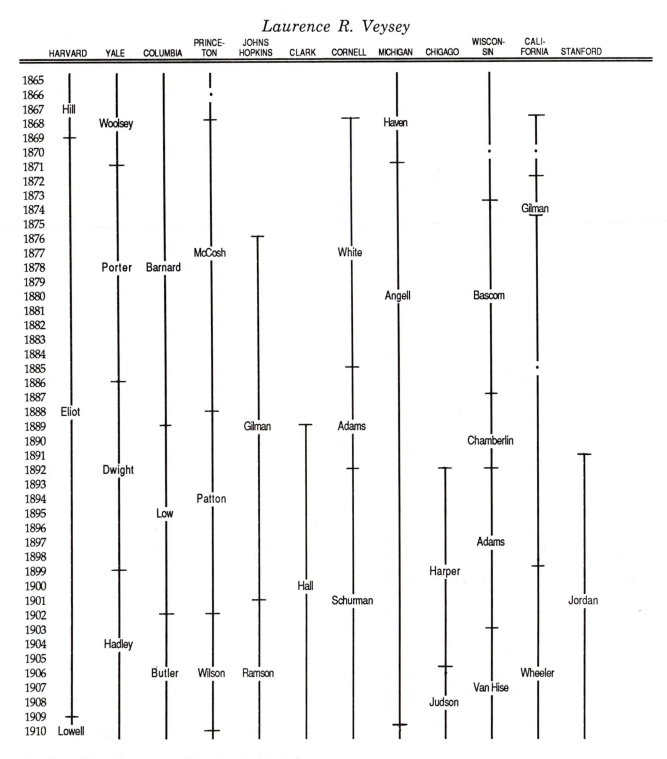

•Presidents of lesser importance to this study omitted for clarity.

Reprinted from THE EMERGENCE OF THE AMERICAN UNIVERSITY, University of Chicago Press, 1965, p.447.

Part IV: Higher Education during the First Half of the Twentieth Century and Its Legacy: Institutional Diversity and Discrimination

An Academic Gresham's Law: Group Repulsion as a Theme in American Higher Education

Harold S. Wechsler

The arrival of a new constituency on a college campus has rarely been an occasion for unmitigated joy. Perhaps such students brought with them much-needed tuition dollars. In that case, their presence was accepted and tolerated. Yet higher-education officials, and often students from traditional constituencies, usually perceived the arrival of new groups not as a time for rejoicing, but as a *problem:* a threat to an institution's stated and unstated missions (official fear) or to its social life (student fear). Most recently, America has witnessed dramas played out between black students and white students and officials, as the former attempted to obtain access to higher education, first in the South and then in the North. *Brown* v. *Board of Education* and its subsequent application to higher education have resulted in only a gradual effort at integration in the South, and then only after almost a decade of outright resistance. In the North, the existence of selective colleges and universities in or near urban ghettos produced persistent demands for the "opening up" of such institutions to a local constituency. In both cases, acquiescence to black demands was feared as inimical to the interests of the college's traditional constituencies and to its missions. The possibility that a new group might "repel" a more traditional constituency has for more than two centuries proved a persistent theme in American higher education and has not been aimed at any one new constituency in particular. Institutional officials (administrators and occasionally trustees; faculty usually played a peripheral role in these issues)[1] often feared the physical exodus of traditional students resulting in a perhaps undesirable change in the institution's status and mission. However, traditional students only infrequently lifted up stakes; more often they simply adopted a policy of segregating themselves from the insurgent group. Depending on whether the traditional group was a positive or a negative reference group, insurgent students would counter-segregate by forming structures either emulating or rejecting majority group arrangements.

In this article we will discuss four instances of this inverse Gresham's law of academic relations—real or imagined—and analyze official and student responses. In each case the entrance of a new group brought about less-than-apocalyptic changes. In the case of relatively wealthy students in nineteenth-century New England colleges, the arrival of poorer students led to a decline in activities conducted by the student body as a whole and to a rise of stratified eating and living arrangements. Ultimately, the wealthier students watched as the number of poorer brethren declined. Late in the nineteenth century the arrival of women on previously all-male campuses led to other forms of social segregation, which apprehensive administrators thought of abetting by segregating academic exercises by sex. Some years later, the arrival of a considerable number of Jewish students on east coast campuses caused concern lest gentile students seek out less "cosmopolitan" surroundings. Most recently, the arrival of significant numbers of black students at previously all-white (or almost so) institutions occasioned fears of "white flight" similar to what was perceived as happening in integrated elementary and secondary schools. In all of these cases, students adopted modest recourses—various informally segregated arrangements for living, eating, and socializing supplemented or took the place of officially sanctioned arrangements. Usually, college authorities acquiesced in or even abetted these arrangements, believing them preferable to a student exodus.

RICH AND POOR

Perhaps American college officials acquired their fear of student exodus from its perceived frequency in the medieval universities. Migrations sometimes led to the founding of rival universities. Even temporary student absences brought about local economic hardship. But in the case of the early Italian universities such migration resulted from disputes not between groups of students, but between local authorities and representatives of these student-run institutions. Early universities were quite heterogeneous, attracting students from much of Europe. By the mid-thirteenth century, the major universities had recognized the existence of "nations" that had fraternal, legal, and educational functions. Each nation contained a diversified membership, but offered cohesion and sanctuary for foreign students in a strange locality by guaranteeing the legitimacy of their members' presence. A

In American higher education, which lacked formal groupings such as nations, the questions of incorporation or rejection of an aspirant group onto a campus with a traditional constituency have had to be handled on an ad hoc basis.

During the first two centuries of higher education in America, students from increasingly diverse class backgrounds found such instruction relevant to their interests; for such institutions as reliable information exists it appears that such heterogeneity could be incorporated within the formal collegiate structure by relaxation of rules calling for continual interaction of the entire student body. Early versions of the laws of Harvard provided that no student could live or eat away from the college without the permission of the president,[2] but seventeenth-century Harvard was not a gentleman's institution. In preparing young men for the clergy and magistracy it often found that the most pious students were also the poorest.[3] Tuition charges were relatively low and meal charges varied according to quantity and quality consumed.[4] "A few resident students had board bills of less than a pound a quarter, a fourth of what their richer friends ate."[5] By the early eighteenth century, the Harvard student body's composition had significantly changed. The increase in enrollment, Samuel Eliot Morison wrote, consisted "of young men [who] came to be made gentlemen, not to study."[6] When the increase forced Harvard

to permit some students to live away from the college, a definite bifurcation in the student body ensued. Not only did the pious students domicile and board together, they formed the first student societies—early manifestations of an extracurriculum that wary college officials found themselves forced to tolerate. Thus, the first manifestation of group repulsion consisted of a self-imposed segregation of pious students in response to "the onslaughts and influence of their more licentious classmates' thievery and tormenting."[7]

At other colonial colleges, authorities permitted internal segregation from the outset. William and Mary provided in its 1729 statutes for tuition-paying and scholarship students. For the former, "we leave their parents and guardians at liberty whether they shall lodge and eat within the college or elsewhere in the town, or any country village near the town." Such students aspiring to the ministry would receive scholarship aid according to "their poverty, their ingeniousness, learning, piety, and good behavior, as to their morals." In this case, a college provided for a bifurcated student body in its statutes.[8] Yale and Kings College made provision for domicile outside the college grounds; the latter institution in fact had no dormitory during its initial years, and after its completion the enrollment rapidly exceeded the building's capacity.[9] Yale formally "ranked" its matriculants and followed these rankings when it was time to "declame." No formal ranking system existed at Kings College but President Samuel Johnson did enter each matriculant on the college's rolls in roughly the order of his social status. The children of New York's elite families readily identified each other and sought each other's company. A "few select ones" gathered regularly for conversation in John Jay's room, and those of high social standing met at a weekly "Social Club."[10] At pre-Revolutionary Princeton as at Harvard and Yale, the poorer students largely aspired to the ministry; their more wealthy classmates, however, were in one way or another also touched by evangelical religion. This, and the lack of housing alternatives to Nassau Hall, may have mitigated some social cleavages existing between rich and poor students.[11]

Thus, in the colonial college, we have evidence of mutual repulsion. The pious students who were initially attracted to each college were joined within a generation or two by students from wealthier backgrounds who attended college more as a means of elite socialization than as a means of curriculum mastery. In most cases, college officials desired attendance of both groups, although they emphatically did not desire the increase in disciplinary problems almost always attendant on the arrival of the children of the more wealthy.

During the years between the Revolution and the Civil War, the trend toward segregation by social class appears to have continued, and as the proportion of students from more modest backgrounds again increased, the fissures became more formal. Perhaps the distinctive feature in this period consisted of official acceptance of many segregated arrangements. In fact, according to one recent study, postcolonial New England colleges systematically courted poor male students. "Provincial colleges devised calendars congenial to seasons to work in nearby fields and schools, and adopted inexpensive living arrangements. Most important, they made tuition cheap, almost a charity."[12] Driven off the land by economic necessity, propelled toward the ministry by the revivals of the Second Great Awakening and attracted by recruiting efforts and special accommodations offered by the provincial colleges, students from modest backgrounds formed significant constituencies at a number of these institutions.[13]

Their absorption by the colleges required further abandonment of the ideal of community often enshrined in the college statutes. Keeping the bill of fare within range of the poorest students meant that students with fuller purses might find the menu unpalatable. Maintenance of spartanlike dormitories often led to demands by wealthier students for the privilege of domicile in more comfortable quarters. Actually, both wealthy and poorer students had motives for living and boarding off campus. The former could often locate more comfortable accommodations and food of better quality. They might move into a boarding house with students of like background, thus cementing the social contacts for which many apparently came.[14] Sometimes such arrangements formed the bases for fraternities, which received their initial impetus in the mid-nineteenth century. College officials tried at first to suppress such illiberal social organizations. "They create class and factions, and put men socially in regard to each other into an artificial and false position"[15] said Mark Hopkins, Williams's president. But the fraternities' rapid proliferation and participation by a sizable number of tuition-paying students argued against actions more drastic than an increasingly perfunctory chapel exhortation against such undemocratic institutions.[16]

The poorer students likewise found other options more attractive than commons. Many boarded in their rooms, while others founded student-run boarding clubs that often provided better and cheaper fare. Not only rich students lived in town; poorer students often found the lodgings offered by a charitable family or in a poor section more satisfactory than rooms in the college halls.

The intensity of this mutual segregation may be discerned from an account in a contemporary novel, in which two financially well-off Harvard students visit a poor classmate who resides in Divinity Hall, the traditional campus abode for poor but earnest students. When a student replied "Oh, down in Divinity," to the question "Where do you room?" the rejoinder was inevitably, "Down in Divinity? What in the name of all that is wonderful, makes you go down there among all those scrubs?" A pious atmosphere and

economy provided two answers. A resident found the theological library, located in the Hall, "a delightful place to go into and mouse around when you are tired of study, and have nothing in particular to do."[17] Evening services proved genuinely inspirational. "The music of the choir and organ rolls up through the silent halls, and sounds very beautiful," the resident commented. As for meals, the students "mostly keep themselves entirely. . . . We leave our basket and pail just outside our door over night, and in the morning take in our milk and our fresh loaf; and some of the men down here live on bread and milk for the most part, or make it answer for breakfast and tea."[18] By contrast, one visitor commented that he spent eight dollars a week for boarding out while the Divinity resident replied that he could eat satisfying meals for about a fifth of that sum.[19] Perhaps the greatest fissure between the two groups lay in their respective attitudes toward their studies. The Divinity resident professed a love for mathematics above all else. "I think it a beautiful science: it is all explained and proved so fully and exactly as you go on, and the way is made so smooth and serene, one need never make any mistakes." One visitor, who by his very willingness to visit a student in Divinity demonstrated that his attitudes were far from the most extreme, replied that he enjoyed Greek the best. "But I am afraid I should not do much work of any sort unless I were obliged to," he continued. "We come here for the most part because we do, and without even asking the reason why. . . . I think study is the last thing we come for. Of course, the work is all an imposition, and the instructors are our natural enemies. That is the way most of the fellows feel, I know."[20] The gulf between a student maintaining such an attitude and another who loved his study ("I take the purest and deepest pleasure in it, and I thought everyone else did too; and I still think you must be wrong")[21] was unfathomable, and it is highly unlikely that dialogues such as this constituted normal fare.

In the case of the relations between rich and poor students, officials demonstrated increased tolerance toward student-imposed practices of segregation. Segregation permitted a high level of enrollment, the veneer of adherence to the official goals of inculcating discipline and piety, and the acceptance of tuition from those students more prone to pranks than piety and more often in attendance for social than academic reasons. Perhaps the only time the poor but pious students attained any prestige at the institutions ostensibly founded for them occurred during the religious revivals, which occurred with less frequency as the century progressed. In this example, college authorities accepted the social arrangements devised by the students. When other distinctive groups arrived, their reaction would be less sanguine.

MALE AND FEMALE

Given the popularity of coeducational living arrangements on the modern campus, and all that such arrangements imply, one reads almost with astonishment a University of Wisconsin alumnus's 1877 statement that "the feeling of hostility [of the men students] was exceedingly intense and bitter. As I now recollect, the entire body of students were without exception opposed to the admission of the young ladies, and the anathemas heaped upon the regents were loud and deep."[22] Perhaps male resistance to coeducation can be traced to a fear that women students might outperform them in the classroom, or to a more generalized desire to retain a specific image of the American woman. The stated objections included women's purported mental incapacity and frail health, and the possibility of increased disciplinary problems. Although time dispelled these fears at the University of Wisconsin, similar concerns at Columbia led to rejection of a coeducation plan. John Burgess, dean of the political science faculty, successfully argued that women students were subject to monthly incapacities, that they would prove too distracting, and that an influx of women would repel Columbia's traditional male constituency, thus reducing the institution to a female seminary.[23] Burgess related that this argument won the day and Columbia College was thus spared coeducation.[24]

Concern persisted that women students might arrive on campus in such proportions as to pose a threat to the male students and, ultimately, to drive them out. Anxiety increased as the proportion of women among the national undergraduate population rose from 21.0 percent in 1870 to 47.3 percent in 1920.[25] Thus, early in the twentieth century authorities at a number of colleges began to reevaluate their commitment to coeducation and to suggest that some restrictive measures might be in order. A few institutions contemplated a limitation on enrollment of women students; however, the fear of tuition loss and of competitive advantage occurring to nearby colleges led most institutions to opt for less drastic measures. Several major institutions proposed, though few actually adopted, a system of academic segregation whereby course registration might be restricted to members of one sex. President Charles Van Hise of Wisconsin justified such measures as a necessary counteraction to a tendency toward "natural segregation." "With the increase in the number of women in the colleges of liberal arts of coeducational institutions, certain courses have become popular with the women, so that they greatly outnumber the men," he observed. "As soon as this situation obtains there is a tendency for the men not to elect these courses, even if otherwise they are attractive to them."[26] Similarly, he cited instances where the presence of large numbers of male students proved a disincentive for women's registration. Listing language and literature as areas of male reluctance and political economy as unattractive to women in coeducational settings, Van Hise argued that equality of result might best be obtained by segregation.

University of Chicago authorities actually established, albeit briefly, separate junior (freshman and sophomore year) colleges for men and women.

As women's enrollment increased so did the debate over the merits of coinstruction. Under President Harper's proposals social association and equal academic opportunity would continue as would the administration of the junior colleges by a single dean. However, they did provide that, when economically feasible, admission to elective and required junior college courses offered in multiple sections would be restricted to members of one sex.[27] Harper expected that the financial viability proviso would result in continued construction in about one-third of all courses[28] and that other university divisions would retain joint instruction.

Neosegregationists such as Harper or Julius Sachs also defended such arrangements on the grounds that coeducation diminished intellectual standards, or on the basis of current psychological theory. In instructional situations, wrote Harper, "the terms and tone of association are fixed too little by the essential character of the thing to be done and too much by the fact that both men and women are doing it."[29] In his widely quoted chapter "Adolescent Girls and their Education," G. Stanley Hall remarked that it was comparatively easy to educate boys since they "are less peculiarly responsive in mental tone to the physical and psychic environment, tend more strongly and early to special interests, and react more vigorously against the obnoxious elements of their surroundings." In contrast, woman, "in every fiber of her soul and body is a more generic creature than man, nearer to the race, and demands more and more with advancing age an education that is essentially liberal and humanistic." He concluded that "nature decrees that with advancing civilization the sexes shall not approximate, but differentiate, and we shall probably be obliged to carry sex distinctions, at least of method, into many if not most of the topics of the higher education."[30]

But the fear of higher education's feminization never lurked too deep beneath the surface. "Whenever the elective system permits," wrote Julius Sachs, "the young men are withdrawing from courses which are the favorite choice of the girls, the literary courses; the male students discard them as feminized, they turn by preference to subjects in which esthetic discrimination plays no part."[31]

The coeducationists were fully aware of the psychological and the "diminution of intellectual standards" arguments. "I have never chanced again upon a book that seemed to me so to degrade me in my woman hood as the seventh and seventeenth chapters on women and women's education, of President Stanley Hall's *Adolescence*," wrote President M. Carey Thomas of Bryn Mawr.[32] But the battle would be won or lost on the repulsion argument. Did peculiarly female traits lead women to favor the liberal over the practical to such an extent as to dissuade male students from following a liberal sequence?

Not so, replied University of Chicago Dean of Women Students Marion

courses in "feminized" disciplines. On the other hand, certain disciplines rapidly evolved into male preserves entered only by women students willing to pay major social and psychological costs. Outside the classroom, many colleges established administrative positions (dean of women students, etc.) that attempted to regulate students' social lives. Officials increasingly tolerated fraternities and sororities on condition that they adopt elaborate sets of rules, many specifically dealing with male-female interactions. Many colleges constructed dormitories and student centers segregated by sex.

Women administrators often supported such policies not simply as a defense—or as making a virtue of necessity—but because they believed that some social segregation would allow women undergraduates to assume leadership roles in activities that, if coeducational, would have inevitably been reserved for men. Thus, although academic practices have been emphasized here, coeducational institutions evolved elaborate social practices as well, permitting in many cases absorption of female students in significant numbers without serious redefinition of institutional missions.

Talbot. With access to other professions closed off, many college women opted for secondary-school teaching careers. With a next-to-nil chance for a woman to obtain a secondary-school position in chemistry or zoology, Talbot noted, a woman's choice of history or English in college proved to be a shrewd and practical decision—although one that might go against her personal interests. Talbot argued that despite a general belief to the contrary, "considerations of sex are rarely taken into account by women any more than by men on making a choice of studies."[33] President M. Carey Thomas, citing statistics revealing similar registration patterns for electives by male and female students at single-sex colleges, argued that the disproportionate figures reported in western coeducational institutions resulted from external circumstances, not a priori causes. "I am told," she wrote, "that economics in many western colleges is simply applied economics and deals almost exclusively with banking, railroad rates, etc., and is therefore, of course, not elected by women who are at present unable to use it practically, whereas in the eastern colleges for women theoretical economics is perhaps their favorite study."[34] Men and women alike, Thomas said, make rational choices among available subjects, and were unlikely to avoid a subject solely because of a preponderance of registration by members of the opposite sex.

The coeducationists experienced considerable success in avoiding re-segregation, but whether statistical, psychological, or economic arguments proved most persuasive is a moot question. In Wisconsin, the university regents addressed the issue in 1908 and reaffirmed their traditional pro-coeducation policy. The following year the state legislature strengthened the laws concerning university admission by adding a specific provision that "all schools and colleges of the university shall, in their respective departments and class exercises, be open without distinction to students of both sexes."[35]

But if women continued to obtain access to undergraduate education, they found few postbaccalaureate options; in fact, their ability to enter certain professions actually diminished during the early twentieth century. Mary Roth Walsh in her important book on women in the medical profession reported that institutions such as Tufts and Western Reserve, which had heretofore admitted significant numbers of women to the freshmen medical class, ceased to do so. Northwestern decided in 1902 without warning to close the women's division of its medical school. At Johns Hopkins and the University of Michigan, which remained coeducational, the percentage of females in the student body declined respectively from 33 percent in 1896 to 10 percent in 1916 and from 25 percent in 1890 to 3 percent in 1910.[36]

Just as "cheap money drives dear money out of circulation," editorialized the Boston Transcript at the time of Tufts' coeducation controversy, "the weaker sex drives out the stronger."[37] Although most authorities cite other factors as prompting a retreat from an elective system, the emergence of distribution requirements at most colleges assured that male students would attend

GENTILE AND JEW

Stephen Duggan's enthusiasm for his Jewish students at the College of the City of New York had few bounds. He admired their motivation, ambitiousness, sincerity, and intelligence; most of all he esteemed their ability to overcome the numerous hardships of life on the Lower East Side and to succeed at an institution with unfamiliar academic and social norms. "No teacher could have had a finer student body to work with," he wrote. "They were studious, keen and forthright. They did not hesitate to analyze any subject to its fundamentals regardless of tradition or age. . . . I do not hesitate to say that I learned a great deal as a result of the keen questioning of these young men. It was fatal to evade; one had always to be on the qui vive. I found these students like students everywhere, very grateful for an evident interest in their personal welfare. . . . Some of their views were quite different from those held by students in a college situated in a less cosmopolitan atmosphere. . . . They formed the most socially minded group of young people that I know."[38]

However, many college and university officials proved far less sanguine concerning the rapid influx of Jewish students into many of America's colleges and universities. "Where Jews become numerous they drive off other people and then leave themselves," wrote Harvard President Abbott Lawrence Lowell in 1922. Denying that moral character or individual qualities created the problem, Lowell attributed its cause to "the fact of segregation by groups which repel their group."[39] He refused to speculate over whether to blame Jewish "clannishness," or Gentile anti-Semitism for the Jewish tendency to "form a distinct body, and cling, or are driven, together, apart from the great

394

mass of undergraduates."[40] Lowell had observed that summer resorts, preparatory schools, and colleges, such as City College, New York University, and Columbia College, had all experienced the same phenomenon.

Lowell's solution, in the words of his biographer, "was a quota, usually called by Jewish writers a numerus clausus." Quotas, Lowell reasoned, had been employed in other social sectors with little or no objection. "Why anyone should regard himself as injured or offended by a limitation of the proportion of Jews in the student body, provided that the limitation were generous, Lowell could not understand."[41]

Others attributed the repulsion between Jew and Gentile to individual, rather than group characteristics. Frederick Paul Keppel, dean of Columbia College from 1910 to 1918, distinguished between desirable and undesirable Jewish students. His Barnard counterpart, Virginia Gildersleeve, wrote that "many of our Jewish students have been charming and cultivated human beings. On the other hand . . . the intense ambition of the Jews for education has brought to college girls from a lower social level than that of most of the non-Jewish students. Such girls have compared unfavorably in many instances with the bulk of the undergraduates."[42]

During the height of nativist sentiment immediately after World War I, many college authorities concluded that a Jewish influx threatened the character of their institutions. They proposed a variety of remedies, all aimed at limiting Jewish enrollment. Williams College, reported Harvard Philosophy Professor William Earnest Hocking, enlisted the aid of Jewish alumni in screening Jewish candidates. Other institutions employed psychological or character tests. Most devices appear to have resulted in a diminution in the number of Jewish students. At Columbia College, the percentage varied from 40 percent just after World War I to less than 20 percent by the mid-1930s. At Barnard the figure hovered around 20 percent while Radcliffe had 12 or 13 percent, Vassar had 6 percent, Bryn Mawr had 8 or 9 percent, and Wellesley had about 10 or 11 percent.[43] Most institutions that restricted Jewish access did not remove the barriers until after a change in national sentiment brought about by the events of World War II.

Other administrators proved more tolerant of the Jewish influx. Some did not believe they posed a threat to institutional missions. Others, shrewdly, cynically, or both, believed that the students could settle any difficulties among themselves and that few direct measures need be taken. When an irate constituent charged the University of Chicago with anti-Semitism because of Jewish exclusion from campus fraternities, President Henry Judson replied that no official discrimination existed and that such exclusionary practices by students were a social, not a religious problem, best left for the students to settle among themselves.

And "settle" they did, with a vengeance. "The University of Chicago," wrote the noted journalist Vincent Sheean, "one of the largest and richest institutions of learning in the world, was partly inhabited by a couple of thousand young nincompoops whose ambition was to get into the right fraternity or club, go to the right parties, and get elected to something or other."[44] Although the administration had segregated many extracurricular activities by sex, Chicago's undergraduate women demonstrated their ability to construct a social system no less rigid or more intellectually oriented than that of their male counterparts. Again Sheean, "The women undergraduates had a number of clubs to which all the 'nice' girls were supposed to belong. Four or five of these clubs were 'good' and the rest 'bad.' Their goodness or badness were absolute, past, present and future, and could not be called into question." Although no sorority houses existed, the women "maintained a rigid solidarity and succeeded in imposing upon the undergraduate society a tone of intricate, overweening snobbery."[45]

Into such a social system, Jews had no access. Sheean related his own encounter with the Chicago students. Just after World War I, he inadvertently pledged a "Jewish fraternity," although not Jewish himself. Lucy, a student with whom Sheean had conducted a flirtatious relationship, warned him to break his pledge. As she explained, "The Jews . . . could not possibly go to the 'nice' parties in the college. They could not be elected to any class office, or to office in any club, or to any fraternity except the two that they themselves had organized; they could not dance with whom they pleased or go out with the girls they wanted to go out with; they could not even walk across the quadrangles with a 'nice' girl if she could possibly escape."[46] Thus, contrary to many administrators' fears, most Gentile students had no intention of abandoning established colleges and universities in face of a Jewish influx. Perhaps it would prove necessary to tolerate their presence in class, but the student culture successfully limited all other interaction.

Jews responded predictably to such restrictions. Jacob Schiff, the financier-turned-philanthropist, anonymously endowed the Barnard Hall student center as a countermove to the self-selecting student culture. Centrally located, its facilities would be open to all. At the same time Schiff and others repeatedly urged that administrators take steps to abolish discriminatory charter provisions or to disaffiliate from national orders mandating discriminatory policies.

Jewish students responded to social exclusion either by increased emphasis on their academic work (thereby earning the reputation of "grind") or by establishment of predominantly Jewish academic and social organizations. At Harvard College in 1906, a group of Jewish undergraduates organized the first Menorah Society, which had as its purpose "the promotion in American colleges and universities of the study of Jewish history, culture and problems,

intellectual bent, **Ruth Mack** feared that banding together "would produce snobbery on both sides." A general student turnout for meetings on Jewish institutions and ideals would be unobjectionable, she explained, but "while we can say that the Menorah is not limited to Jews, we can do little to make the non-Jews come out."[52] The pressures on a woman like Ruth Mack were considerable. On the one hand her strong Jewish identity inclined her to join; on the other she feared alienation from Radcliffe's Gentiles especially because she found the parallel class among the Jewish upperclassmen "less attractive, intellectually, etc., than the parallel class among the non-Jew." Although many at the early twentieth-century college paid lip-service to "democracy"[53] on campus (by which was meant equal opportunity to succeed in the campus student culture), Jews often found themselves arbitrarily disqualified, thus producing dilemmas such as that of Ruth Mack.

By the 1920s Jewish fraternities had become virtually indistinguishable from their Gentile counterparts and Menorah Societies began to atrophy. "Between 1920 and 1930," wrote Horace Kallen, an original member of Harvard Menorah,

the tradition of a love of learning which they [Jewish students] brought to college has been dissipated. The adult responsibility which they felt for the problems of their own people and of the community at large, and which was signalized [sic] by their membership in such organizations as the Menorah Societies, the Zionist, the Liberal, or the Social Question Clubs, has been destroyed. As their numbers grew, their fields of interest and modes of behavior conformed more and more to the prevailing conditions of undergraduate life. Although excluded by expanding anti-Semitism from participation in that life, they reproduce it, heightened, in an academic ghetto of fraternities, sororities and the like. And they emulate the invidious distinctions they suffer from by projecting them upon the Jews too proud, too poor, or too Jewish to be eligible for "collegiate" secret societies of Jews.[54]

Thus, although on many private college campuses officials limited access by Jewish students, those Jewish undergraduates who obtained admission gradually arrived at an acceptable modus vivendi with their fellow students and with the authorities.

WHITE AND BLACK

During the brief tenure of Harvard President Edward Everett (1846-1848), it became known that a black student would present himself for the college's admissions examination. Although the student had tutored one of Everett's sons, and was the best scholar in his class, rumors spread that Harvard would not permit his matriculation, no matter how well he performed on the exams. The student never entered Harvard (due to "illness" according to contem-

and the advancement of Jewish ideals."[47] Far more resembling typical nineteenth-century collegiate literary societies than fraternities, Menorah societies florished on a number of colleges before and after World War I.[48]

At a typical meeting a Jewish academic from the campus or from a Menorah speakers' bureau might choose to discuss a book or topic of Jewish interest. The scope might choose to discuss a book or topic of Jewish interest. The scope included the history and culture of the Jewish people "so conceived that nothing Jewish, of whatever age or clime, shall be alien to it." Its broader purpose was to secure campus recognition of the seriousness or worthiness of its subject matter. "It must demonstrate to the whole student body that the study of Jewish history and culture is a serious and liberal pursuit; it must really afford its members a larger knowledge of the content and meaning of the Jewish tradition."[49] Deliberately eschewing a primarily social purpose (". . . a Menorah Society is not a social organization. Its activities may, indeed, partake of a sociable nature, but only so far as its real objects can thereby be the more fully carried out"), Menorah quickly found itself caught between Jewish student organizations with objectives less lofty than Menorah's academic goals, such as the Student Zionist Organization, and a quickening demand for Jewish fraternities and sororities.

The first Jewish fraternity in America was founded in New York City in 1898. Established under the watchful eye of Columbia University Semitics Professor Richard Gottheil, the Zeta Beta Tau (ZBT) fraternity originally professed ideals more ambitious than friendship and brotherhood. It aimed, wrote an early member, "to inspire the students with a sense of Jewish national pride and patriotism."[50] Although the movement's early Zionist orientation gradually diminished, it attempted to retain the intellectual and service ideals on which it was founded. Richard Gottheil repeatedly expressed concern that the fraternity's uniqueness might be lost. "For the Jew carries with him wherever he goes," Gottheil said, "the great heritage of thought and of impulse which has been handed down from father to son during the last twenty-five centuries." The organization assumed the form of a Greek letter fraternity "in order to fall in with the University habits of the community in which we live." But, he concluded, "we can have no use for those men who are Zeta Beta Tau men simply for the sake of belonging to a Greek Letter Fraternity. We wish to set an example, not to proclaim ourselves a holy people, but to live as such."[51]

Some Jews feared that creation of such groups as ZBT and Menorah might serve to enhance the Jewish stereotype. When some undergraduate Radcliffe women approached their fellow student Ruth Mack, daughter of Harvard alumnus and future Overseer Judge Julian Mack, about Menorah membership, she responded cautiously. She wondered whether the group "would tend to segregate the Jewish girls from the non-Jewish," adding that at Radcliffe "there seems to be so little of this grouping, that I think it a pity to introduce anything which encourages it." Although recognizing the organization's

porary accounts), but Everett took the occasion to announce Harvard's policy. "The admission to Harvard College depends upon examinations," he said, "and if this boy passes the examination, he will be admitted; and if the white students choose to withdraw, all the income of the College will be devoted to his education."[55] The student threat to withdraw from the college to which Everett alluded left him undaunted; however, one of his successors at Harvard, Abbott Lawrence Lowell, took a similar threat quite seriously. In 1914 Lowell closed the freshman dormitories, which supposedly had been built to reduce student social segregation, to black students, claiming, when the practice became public knowledge several years later, that he did not wish to offend the sensibilities of white students. "To maintain that compulsory residence in the Freshman Dormitories—which has proved a great benefit in breaking up the social cliques, that did much injury to the College—should not be established for 99 1/2 percent of the students because the remaining one half of one percent could not properly be included seems to me an untenable position,"[56] wrote Lowell to Roscoe Conkling Bruce, a black alumnus of Harvard seeking dormitory accommodations for his son. After a public controversy arose when Lowell denied dormitory access to the younger Bruce, the Harvard Corporation published an ambiguous rule continuing compulsory dormitory residence (exemptions permitted) and providing that "men of the white and colored races shall not be compelled to live and eat together, nor shall any man be excluded by reason of his color."[57] Whether integrated dormitories would have led to a mass exodus of white students is debatable. In practice, Harvard had few black applicants. But it did wish to attract students from the South, and did not wish to acquire a reputation for forced "race mingling" or for "social equality." As a result, Harvard's dormitories remained segregated de facto until the early 1950s.[58]

By no means was Harvard alone in confronting the housing problem. Various administrations offered different solutions ranging from outright prohibition to integration. The University of Chicago permitted the majority of residents in each dormitory to decide who should join them.[59] Apparently, at Smith, when two Southern students protested the admission of a black student to their dormitory, President William A. Neilson expressed his willingness for the protesting students to move to another dormitory, although it might prove difficult to find accommodations for them. The students replied that they had wanted the black student removed, but Neilson remained adamant. The students thereupon decided they would remain in the same dormitory.[60]

Thus in a manner reminiscent of officially sanctioned schisms among rich and poor students, a number of colleges created and/or tolerated Jim Crow dormitories, in the process sometimes undercutting claims to formal neutrality in social areas. Colleges could not at the same time argue that education provided the most effective means for overcoming intolerance while in practice facilitating social segregation. Usually hovering between

1/2 and 2 percent, the proportion of black students on northern campuses rarely if ever reached the point where officials feared a massive white exodus. Most probably they wanted to avoid a reputation for liberalism in an area surrounded with many social taboos.

As usual, the dominant student group managed social relations so as not to be inconvenienced by the presence of a distinctive minority. A black freshman enrolling at a predominantly white institution during these years arrived already knowing that he or she would lack much social life. "First of all," wrote one, "being a Negro, I was exempt from all the sororities on the campus. I knew that I would never dress for a sorority 'rush' party, or become a pledge. I knew, also, that I would never dance at the Sigma Chi or the Delta Tau houses."[61] A study published in 1942 indicated that, without underestimating the difficulties of economic or academic adjustments, almost all black students were most dissatisfied with their social lives.[62] Some suppressed their aspiration for a full social life and concentrated on their work. "My reaction was to show these people that I was a good student. . . . I cannot help feeling . . . that if I am down scholastically, and a Negro also, I might as well leave this place." But even the students with the strongest defenses could not completely escape the results of social ostracism. "There was the time when I was one among three hundred girls at a social dance, and the instructor and one other girl ventured to drag me over the floor, when all of the other girls had run frantically clutching at each other to dance with everyone else but me, simply because I was a Negro, a brown conspicuous person. That was the time I went home and fell across the bed and cried, cried until I was exhausted. That was the time I hated a white college."[63]

Conditions changed only gradually after World War II. In 1955 the Supreme Court affirmed a lower court ruling that *Brown v. Board of Education* applied to segregated institutions of higher education;[64] however, it took another decade for the first black students to gain admittance to several major southern institutions. Only with the successful prosecution of *Adams v. Richardson* in the 1970s have a number of southern states been forced to draw up comprehensive programs for the integration of their higher education systems. In the North the large in-migrations of blacks during the 1950s and 1960s produced major changes in the racial composition of elementary and secondary schools, but did not yield in due course similar changes in colleges and universities.

At first, black students experienced considerable overt hostility in newly integrated campuses. A constant barrage of insults and threats against black students at Louisiana State University (L.S.U.) was supplemented by a series of "pranks" including cross burnings and by several violent occurrences.[65] Although crude manifestations of prejudice decreased over time,[66] black students continued to report incidents, slights, and alienation. At the University of Illinois, an impersonal environment in which white students displayed few initiatives toward blacks (no blacks belonged to any white fraternity) led to disaffection and isolation.[67] As racial tension generally increased in the United States of the late 1960s, black students became less willing to overlook or accept such conditions.

During the 1950s and 1960s, many colleges had undertaken a series of reforms in an attempt to remove any vestige of discrimination against minority students. Some integrated their dormitories; others required fraternity and sorority chapters to drop restrictions against minority group access or to withdraw from national organizations that mandated retention of such restrictions. Sometimes administrators undertook such reforms vigorously; all too often changes resulted only from outside pressure. There is thus a special irony in the rise of separatist demands by black and other racial minority students, which came just when authorities had concluded that integration could not be left to "education," and that significant minority representation would not necessarily result in a majority exodus. White minority students, separatist minority students argued, would never fully accept nonwhites as social equals. Instead, they called for a series of exclusively nonwhite extracurricular activities and residential accommodations to supplement their demand for a separate academic program. "The black women [are thinking about] pushing for a Black Women's Living Center," said a junior black woman on a predominantly white campus in the early 1970s.

We want to get these pockets of black students out of these all-white dormitories and get them into a house of their own. The sororities and fraternities do it; why can't black people live together? Let's face it. Black people are just more comfortable with black people. I don't particularly like being questioned about my hair or style of life by white people. There are certain foods I like to eat which this school ignores or can't cook. Secondly, it would be a unifying device to get everyone together in a living situation. To me it's only natural. Before coming [to this school], I came from an all-black community and it's natural for me to live in one. . . . Of course, those who raise arguments against it don't say or may not realize that . . . unification is a threat.[68]

Black students quickly came to realize the necessity of significant enrollment increases as prerequisite to all such demands. Otherwise, separation would inevitably lead to increased social isolation and would restrict their ability to create an institutionalized social life. A campus with fewer than fifty black students, commented a black undergraduate, "has a vacuum of social activities for blacks."[69] Since most courtship on American campuses is intraracial, a small number of minority students implies an almost nonexistent pool of available dates, even when there are roughly equal numbers of men and women minority students. In addition, small numbers usually mean that attempts at formal social organization will rarely outlast the founders; recruitment often proves difficult even with sizable availability pools.

Unlike other groups, which confronted administrators with an "excess" number admitted by normal entrance processes, black students demanded modifications of admissions policies so as to insure inclusion of an adequate contingent. Many colleges made such commitments. Events at the City University of New York proved most spectacular. After a lengthy sit-in by black and Puerto Rican students at the university's City College, the university adopted an open admissions system in which students would be admitted either by high school grade point average (traditional method) or by high school rank in class (new method).[70]

In more "selective" institutions, that is, in colleges where subjective considerations entered into a competitive admissions process, admissions officers agreed either to take race explicitly into account or at least to make special efforts to recruit minority students who met traditional criteria. Although the absolute number of black students has increased significantly in the last decade, there have been recent signs of "slippage," and on many of the more selective predominantly white campuses the number of minority students remains 3 to 10 percent—lower than the number considered desirable by minority group members.

CONCLUSION

In many ways, the black separatists of the 1960s wanted precisely what other groups that had been victims of "repulsion" had traditionally attained: the ability to establish a set of social relationships paralleling those of the socially dominant group. However, they put forward their claims at a time when college administrators had finally overcome their fear that group repulsion would lead to an unacceptable change in institutional mission. Whether by compulsion or by volition, authorities in the 1950s and 1960s began to argue that in regulating their internal affairs, they could keep up with changes in "generally socially acceptable boundaries," and, on a number of occasions, go beyond them. Practice often fell short of ideals, and black students who directly or vicariously experienced discrimination proved less hesitant than previous groups to protest. Particularly striking on campuses with sufficient numbers of blacks was a tendency similar to that of other groups herein discussed to emulate certain aspects of the majority extracurriculum. Thus black fraternities appeared on a number of campuses that, although espousing social consciousness, retained the paraphernalia of fraternities including distinctive insignias and symbols, and various rites and "customs."

In general we may say that the initial representatives of a new campus group needed the strength to prove themselves academically while surviving socially. Although one might speculate that such pioneers were highly self-selected, we know little about dropout rates for such students. L.S.U. did show rather high attrition among its first classes of black students, but these students were subjected to crass physical abuse as well as the lesser forms of insults often experienced by other groups.[71] We might guess that pioneer

ities. And, by the third decade of the twentieth century, the prestige order among American institutions of higher education had become relatively entrenched; most institutions could "survive" even a sizable onslaught by a significant number of minority students. The more prestigious institutions could provide social and economic mobility to minority students without detracting from the status they accorded members of traditional constituencies. A Harvard or a Swarthmore, for example, could remain attractive to a student from a traditional constituency in a way that an urban high school could not. Apparently the reasoning behind magnet high schools recognizes this, at least implicitly. Such schools aim to provide sufficient educational quality and services to overcome white hesitancy over sending children to schools with a sizable minority constituency.[74] For colleges and universities, majority students usually remained on the rolls despite minority student presence so long as they and/or college officials could devise ways of avoiding undesired social intercourse. Minorities desired to attend such institutions despite expected exhibitions of prejudice not only because of the expected quality of education and the tangible rewards obtainable for acquiring such education, but also for social reasons. The ability to replicate the majority extracurriculum meant that minority students could learn the same social lessons that extracurriculum taught majority students: how to identify desirable and undesirable acquaintances, how to exercise leadership, how to function in various group settings, cooperatively and competitively, and so forth. Even if in the larger society one found discrimination similar to that existing on the campus, minority students could employ such lessons profitably within their own groups, especially since such college-educated youth usually constituted the recognized future leaders of their groups.

In short, few minority students in the periods discussed in this article found their college careers to be completely clear sailing, but most were convinced that whatever abuse they endured would in the long run be well worth the price.

Footnotes

1 See Laurence Veysey, The Emergence of the American University (Chicago: University of Chicago Press, 1965), pp. 294–302.

2 David F. Allmendinger, Jr., Paupers and Scholars: The Transformation of Student Life in New England 1760–1860 (New York: St. Martin's Press, 1975), p. 82.

3 Kathryn M. Moore, "Freedom and Constraint in Eighteenth Century Harvard," Journal of Higher Education 47 (November/December 1976): 650–51.

4 Margery Somers Foster, "Out of Smalle Beginnings . . .": An Economic History of Harvard College in the Puritan Period (1636 to 1712) (Cambridge: Belknap Press of Harvard University Press, 1962), pp. 65–68.

5 Ibid. p. 68.

6 Samuel Eliot Morison, Three Centuries of Harvard 1636–1936 (Cambridge: Harvard University Press, 1936). p. 60.

7 Moore, "Freedom and Constraint in Eighteenth Century Harvard," p. 653.

students needed rather extraordinary motivation to come to quick terms with an institution whose traditional occupants exhibited attitudes varying from indifference to hostility.

This last points to the potential significance of family in explaining motivation. Lacking numerical peer support, insurgents may have relied quite heavily on their families for needed backing. Marion Talbot's parents strongly encouraged her educational aspirations—so much so that her mother's considerable educational reform activities (she was pivotal in gaining establishment of Girls' Latin School in Boston) partly derived from obstacles faced by Marion.[72] Similarly majoritarian attitudes may well have been initially acquired off campus, and then subjected to strong peer reinforcement. Sheean at Chicago was surprised to learn that his roommate, who had also intended to pledge the "Jewish" fraternity, had learned, "from his father probably," about anti-Semitism and about "the ridicule, the complicated varieties of discrimination and prejudice, to which any Gentile who belonged to a Jewish fraternity would have to submit throughout four years of college."[73] Although many studies of campus peer groups emphasize discontinuities with the student's previous home life, it may very well be that in some areas peer groups serve to reinforce previously acquired attitudes.

There yet remains to be explored a fundamental set of questions. First, why would members of an insurgent group invade what must have almost appeared to be enemy territory? And, second, why did traditional constituencies not abandon their campuses for "safer" environs, as so many administrators feared they would? Of course, one answer to the latter question is that administrators often retained or obtained the ability to control access by "distinctive" groups. But abandonment rarely occurred even when such measures were not employed.

The fear of group repulsion bears a remarkable resemblance to the contemporary fear of "white flight" often discussed with respect to elementary and secondary education. Should the percentage of minority students in a given school exceed some subjectively sensed percentage, according to the fear, white parents will begin to move into more homogeneous neighborhoods. In due course the school will become populated almost exclusively by minorities. Current literature contains considerable speculation as to the existence and extent of white flight; a resolution of that debate goes far beyond the scope of this article. But it is very much to the point of this article to say a word about what white elementary and secondary school students are supposedly fleeing from. White parents when interviewed often claim that they withdrew their children not because of the increased presence of minority students per se, but because the quality of education and resources offered appears to deteriorate concomitant with their appearance. In contrast, the quality of most colleges' and universities' educational product remained relatively unchanged despite minority group influxes. If anything, most institutions experienced sizable expansions in endowment, faculty, and facil-

40 Abbott Lawrence Lowell to William Ernest Hocking, May 19, 1922, in ibid.

41 Henry Aaron Yeomans, *Abbott Lawrence Lowell 1856-1943* (Cambridge: Harvard University Press, 1948), p. 212.

42 Virginia Gildersleeve to Annie Nathan Meyer, March 31, 1933, Annie Nathan Meyer Papers, American Jewish Archives, "Virginia Gildersleeve" file.

43 Virginia Gildersleeve to Annie Nathan Meyer, May 6, 1929. Barnard College Archives, DO 28-29, box 1, file 1.

44 Vincent Sheean, *Personal History* (Garden City, N.Y.: Doubleday Doran, 1936). p. 9.

45 Ibid. p. 10.

46 Ibid. p. 14.

47 Henry Hurwitz and I. Leo Sharfman, eds. *The Menorah Movement for the Study and Advancement of Jewish Culture and Ideals: History, Purposes, Activities* (Ann Arbor, Mich.: Intercollegiate Menorah Association. 1914).

48 On literary societies see Rudolph. *The American College and University*, pp. 137-46; and James McLachlan. "The Choice of Hercules: American Student Societies in the Early 19th Century," in *The University in Society*, ed. Lawrence Stone (Princeton: Princeton University Press, 1974), pp. 449-94.

49 Hurwitz and Sharfman, *The Menorah Movement for the Study and Advancement of Jewish Culture and Ideals*, pp. 10-11.

50 Zeta Beta Tau, *The First Twenty Years* (New York: Zeta Beta Tau, 1924), p. 15.

51 Ibid. p. 59.

52 Ruth Mack to Julian Mack. November 26, 1914, "Letters and notes used by Harry Barnard in Researching Mack's biography," American Jewish Archives, box 1068, "Letters and notes concerning time period 1900-1929" file.

53 The most famous fictional elaboration of this theme is contained in Owen Johnson. *Stover at Yale* (New York: Collier Books, 1968 [1912]).

54 Horace Kallen. *College Prolongs Infancy* (New York: John Day, 1932). p. 24.

55 Paul Revere Frothingham. *Edward Everett: Orator and Statesman* (Boston and New York: Houghton Mifflin, 1925). My thanks to Richard Yanikoski, who is writing a thesis on Everett, for calling this incident to my attention. It is also recounted in Gordon W. Allport, *The Nature of Prejudice* (Garden City, N.Y.: Doubleday Anchor, 1958). p. 471.

56 Abbott Lawrence Lowell to Roscoe Conkling Bruce, January 6, 1923, as quoted in Neil Painter, "Jim Crow at Harvard," *New England Quarterly* 44 (1971): 629.

57 Painter. "Jim Crow at Harvard," p. 634.

58 Ibid. n. 26. See also Marcia Synnott. "A Social History of Admission Policies at Harvard, Yale and Princeton 1900-1930" (Ph.D. diss., University of Massachusetts, 1974), pp. 368-80, 396-98.

59 William Henderson to E. D. Burton. April 5, 1923. University Presidents' Papers, 1889-1925, The University of Chicago Library. "Racial Issues" file. In 1907 five white students moved out of a dormitory at the University of Chicago when university officials assigned a black student to it. Apparently this was an inadvertent breach of the university's segregationist policy. See S. Breckinridge to H. P. Judson, June 20, 1907, and S. Breckinridge to R. S. Goodspeed, June 20, 1907, University Presidents' Papers, 1889-1925, The University of Chicago Library. "Racial Issues" file.

60 B. S. Hurlbut to E. D. Burton, April 2, 1923, University Presidents' Papers, 1889-1925, The University of Chicago Library. "Racial Issues" file.

61 Edythe Hargrove, "How I Feel as a Negro at a White College." *Journal of Negro Education* 11 (October 1942): 484.

62 William H. Boone. "Problems of Adjustment of Negro Students at a White School." *Journal of Negro Education* 11 (October 1942): 481.

63 Hargrove. "How I Feel as a Negro at a White College," p. 485. The school in question was the University of Michigan.

8 "Statutes of William and Mary, 1727" in *American Higher Education: A Documentary History*, ed. Richard Hofstadter and Wilson Smith (Chicago and London: University of Chicago Press, 1961), vol. 1, pp. 47-48.

9 David C. Humphrey, *From Kings College to Columbia 1746-1800* (New York: Columbia University Press, 1976), p. 204.

10 Ibid. p. 196.

11 Howard Miller, "Evangelical Religion and Colonial Princeton," in *Schooling and Society*, ed. Lawrence Stone (Baltimore: Johns Hopkins University Press, 1976), pp. 135-39.

12 Allmendinger, *Paupers and Scholars*, pp. 9-11.

13 Ibid. Allmendinger also emphasizes the charitable support offered by the American Education Society and local groups toward meeting educational expenses—see pp. 54-78.

14 Ibid. pp. 85-86.

15 Frederick Rudolph, *The American College and University: A History* (New York: Vintage, 1962), p. 148.

16 Ibid., pp. 149-50.

17 George Henry Tripp, *Student Life at Harvard* (Boston: Lockwood, Brooks and Co., 1876), p. 317.

18 Ibid. p. 318.

19 Ibid., pp. 318-19.

20 Ibid. p. 323.

21 Ibid. p. 324.

22 Statement of James L. High, an 1864 University of Wisconsin alumnus as quoted in Helen R. Olin. *The Women of a State University, An Illustration of the Working of Coeducation in the Middle West* (New York and London: G. P. Putnam's Sons, 1909), pp. 101-02.

23 "And a Hebrew female seminary, in the character of the student body, at that," Burgess commented. John W. Burgess, *Reminiscences of an American Scholar: The Beginning of Columbia University* (New York: Columbia University Press, 1934), p. 242.

24 Ibid., pp. 241-42.

25 Mabel Newcomer. *A Century of Higher Education for American Women* (New York: Harper and Brothers, 1959), p. 46.

26 Olin, *The Women of a State University*, pp. 112-13.

27 The University of Chicago, *The President's Report: Administration*, The Decennial Publications, First Series, vol. I (Chicago: University of Chicago Press, 1903), p. cxi.

28 Ibid., p. cvi.

29 Ibid., p. cxi.

30 G. Stanley Hall, *Adolescence: Its Psychology and its Relations to Physiology, Anthropology, Sociology. Sex, Crime, Religion, and Education*, vol. 2 (New York: D. Appleton, 1908), pp. 616-17.

31 Julius Sachs, "The Intellectual Reactions of Co-education," *Educational Review* 35 (May 1908): 470.

32 M. Carey Thomas, "Present Tendencies in Women's College and University Education." *Educational Review* 35 (January 1908): 65.

33 Marion Talbot. "Report of the Dean of Women," in The University of Chicago, *The President's Report*, pp. 140, 141.

34 Thomas. "Present Tendencies in Women's College and University Education." p. 73.

35 Olin. *The Women of a State University*, pp. 139-40.

36 Mary Roth Walsh. *Doctors Wanted: No Women Need Apply* (New Haven: Yale University Press, 1977), pp. 200-06.

37 *Women's Journal*, January 1, 1910, as quoted in ibid. p. 201.

38 Stephen Duggan. *A Professor at Large* (New York: Macmillan, 1943), pp. 10-11.

39 Abbott Lawrence Lowell to Rufus S. Tucker, May 20, 1922, A. L. Lowell Papers, 1919-1922, Harvard University Archives, file 1056: "Jews."

64 Frasier v. Board of Trustees of University of North Carolina, 134 F. Supp. 589 (1955) (M.D. North Carolina); affirmed 350 U.S. 979 (1956).
65 Hansjorg Elshorst, "Two Years after Integration: Race Relations at a Deep South University," Phylon 28 (Spring 1967): 41: "A student was threatened with a knife while in his room, another was hit by acid, one was attacked with fists and a girl was hit while in the library."
66 For exceptions see Meyer Weinberg, Minority Students: A Research Appraisal (Washington, D.C.: U.S. Department of Health, Education, and Welfare–National Institute of Education, 1977), p. 199.
67 Aaron Bindman, "Participation of Negro Students in an Integrated University" (Ph.D. diss., University of Illinois, 1965), passim.
68 Charles V. Willie and Arline Sakuma McCord, Black Students at White Colleges (New York: Praeger, 1972), p. 6.
69 Ibid., p. 25.
70 See David E. Lavin, Richard D. Alba, and Richard Silberstein, "Open Admissions and Equal Access: A Study of Ethnic Groups in the City University of New York," Harvard Educational Review 49 (February 1979): 53–93; and Harold S. Wechsler, The Qualified Student: A History of Selective College Admission in America 1870–1970 (New York: Wiley-Interscience, 1977). chap. 11.
71 Elshorst, "Two Years after Integration," p. 51.
72 Richard J. Storr, "Marion Talbot," in Notable American Women 1607–1958: A Biographical Dictionary, vol. 3 (Cambridge: Belknap Press of Harvard University Press, 1971), p. 423.
73 Sheean, Personal History, p. 16.
74 For a critical study of magnet schools, see James E. Rosenbaum and Stefan Presser, "Voluntary Racial Integration in a Magnet School" School Review 86 (February 1978): 156–86.

I wish to thank Ann Breslin, Deborah Gardner, Lynn Gordon, Walter Metzger, and Paul Ritterband for their comments on this paper. I completed this work during my tenure as a Spencer Fellow of the National Academy of Education. I wish to thank the Spencer Foundation and the members of the Academy for their support.

Junior College and the Differentiation of the Public Sector

David O. Levine

Responding to the rush to the colleges between the world wars and yet wary of it, public institutions of higher education underwent a steady process of internal differentiation. Major state universities attempted to emulate the elite institutions of the private sector; despite the increasing disparity in the socioeconomic backgrounds of students at the private colleges and state universities during the interwar period, both types of institutions catered generally to young people from the middle and upper middle classes. The responsibility for offering the training sought by practical-oriented, lower-middle-class students—the new college students of the twentieth century—fell to new types of collegiate institutions expanded or created to meet the demand for mass higher education. Normal schools, for example, were transformed into four-year, access-oriented, regional teachers' colleges or state colleges. Most important, however, was the rapid development of the public junior college.

No segment of American higher education expanded so rapidly during the interwar period as the public junior college, a creation essentially of the 1920s. Although there were 85 junior colleges with 4,500 students in the country in 1918, they went unmentioned in the federal *Educational Directory* of that year. By 1940, there were 456 junior colleges scattered across the country with a total enrollment of 149,854. In 1918, only 1.9 percent of all undergraduates in the nation attended junior colleges; in 1938, 17.6 percent of the nation's college students were enrolled in two-year institutions. Nearly two-thirds of these students went to publicly controlled junior colleges.[1]

A new niche was created for the public junior college in an increasingly rigid, hierarchical educational structure: it provided mass higher education. At the outset, it was a stepping-stone for many students too young or too poor to attend four-year colleges immediately following high school. As early as the 1920s, however, educators deliberately altered the curriculum of the typical junior college from a program that prepared its students to transfer to four-year schools to one that emphasized training in semiprofessional fields that did not require additional higher learning. Just as the selective liberal arts colleges would choose the best young men, so the terminal junior colleges would produce the desired number of future semiprofessional college graduates. The junior college curriculum was designed to meet society's perceived needs, not students' expectations. During the interwar period, the junior colleges became known as the "people's colleges." But democratic equality of opportunity was a figment of educators' rhetoric, not their goal.

Public Universities and Mass Education

"None of the world's higher institutions of learning come as close to expressing the spirit of democracy as do our great state universities," education writer R. L. Duffus claimed extravagantly in 1936. Since the passage of the Morrill Act in 1863, when the federal government gave land to the states and existing territories for the promotion of agricultural and mechanical education, public higher education's future lay in the creation of institutions responsive to the growing demands for training and research. By the 1920s, finally, economic growth and social progress were attributed to the broad diffusion of education and the technical innovations and individual initiative it fostered. "In a great democracy like ours," the president of Ohio State University explained, "the State feels keenly that education and widespread intelligence are the safeguards of our perpetuity."[2] This philosophy promoted the recognition that higher education had to be viewed not merely as a privilege of the elite but as a right of all America's young people.

In the 1920s and 1930s, the public sector continued to measure its success by its service to more and more diverse segments of society. This notion of service had been firmly established initially in the state university of the Progressive Era, the heyday of the so-called Wisconsin idea. At first, with the University of Wisconsin as their model, state universities pursued agricultural and social research geared to the solution of local problems, but these efforts only laid the foundation for more extensive involvement in all spheres of society. In the next several decades, surveys of public higher education stressed that the state university should be "the state's center of inquiry and distribution of all forms of knowledge bearing on the health, material interests, the intellectual and social welfare of its citizens." "There is no intellectual service too undignified for them to perform," concluded Lotus D. Coffman, president of the University of Minnesota. Insisting that "no state university could survive in a sheer intellectual empyrean," he told a 1932 audience, "If they are faithful to their constituencies, the state universities will be dynamic institutions to which society will look with increasing frequency and pride."[3] And society did, particularly for training and research in fields only recently recognized as worthy of inclusion in an institution of higher learning.

A speaker at Massachusetts State College in 1936 echoed a well-worn theme when he claimed that public insitutions were "unhampered by any of the snobbishness, the undemocratic class-consciousness, so characteristic of private colleges. At Alabama Polytechnic Institute, as at public institutions generally, admissions criteria were affected increasingly "by political considerations and by the popular belief (not necessarily erroneous) that the State owes everyone an education—or, at least a degree." Most such universities felt obliged to enroll as many students as they could hold. Harry W. Chase, president of the University of North Carolina in the 1920s, criticized the state legislature for permitting overcrowding and warned that the state, "as a believer in equality of opportunity," should not pursue any policy that would lead to a limitation on enrollment. As David Kinley, president of the University of Illinois, put it: "No man has any right under a government like ours to undertake to determine that only a few shall be permitted to get an education of higher grade. In a democracy the only proper course is to keep proper standards and welcome all who can meet them. In saying this, of course, I am speaking of a publicly supported institution." No group in society had the right to determine how many should attend college, Kinley insisted. Anyone who spoke on behalf of the doctrine of higher education for the few had "whether consciously or not . . . aristocratic feelings and leanings."[4] Most public educators proclaimed that there could never be too many people in college, even as they pursued policies that would free their institutions from the need to bear all of the burdens of democracy.

The spirit of democracy was often expressed in ironic defenses of the social beneficence of the mass education of America's often mediocre youth. Students at the state universities came generally from upper-middle- and middle-class homes; they sought a practical higher education, hoping for careers that differed little from those pursued by their peers at the more prestigious liberal arts colleges. "There was perhaps a time when higher education could be discussed predominantly in terms of training for leadership," Harry Chase argued when he assumed the presidency of the University of Illinois in 1930, but that time had ended. "I believe in the power of leadership, but I also believe in the necessity of a high general level of intelligence and culture for the future of America."[5] Chase in essence endorsed what Coffman called "education for intelligent followership." The public university should reach beyond the traditional conception of higher education and bring many mediocre young people, as well as the best young minds of the state, to its campus. Chase, Coffman, and others hoped that the public university would continue to absorb new functions and new students.

Conservative faculty members at several public universities charged that their schools were devoting too much attention to these mediocre students. Norman Foerster, a philosopher at the University of North Carolina, wrote, "If higher education is to deserve the name, it cannot be brought within the reach of the ineducable and the passively educable." To date, he felt, the state universities "have preferred the maximum numbers, the masses, which satisfy their American zest for magnitude and grandiosity, to the smaller numbers, the more fit, which would appeal to an imagination interested in excellence and the magnanimity; and they have buttressed this preference by a pseudo-democratic idealism subversive of higher education and social stability." Foerster believed that public universities had to resist the notion that every high school graduate had a right to a university education; he proposed a return to the Jeffersonian concept of free public higher education for the few. Professor George F. Sabine of Ohio State University agreed; he called the idea that all high school graduates deserved admission to the state university "arrant sentimentality." Sabine wanted the state university to emulate the privately endowed university by emphasizing research and specialized training of high quality for talented students alone.[6] Such educators as Foerster and Sabine were offended, not seduced, by the opportunities enjoyed by public institutions to tap new markets and attract new students. As fewer intellectual-oriented students arrived at state universities, more faculty joined the ranks of those who supported the differentiation of higher education within the public sector as well as between private and public institutions.

State surveys of public higher education between the two world wars promoted the differentiation of public higher education as the most efficient means to provide higher learning. Critics of the wasteful rivalries between ambitious public institutions urged such schools to regard themselves as mere instrumentalities of a larger agency dedicated to meeting the overall educational and informational needs of society. Duplication of courses was seen as the main culprit at schools in Washington, Iowa, and at least sixteen other states. Iowa's board of education requested a survey to determine, among other questions, whether Iowa State College of Agricultural and Mechanical Arts should have an education department, a journalism program, a psychology program, or even any liberal arts at all. The competition between the University of Iowa and Iowa State produced such tension that the survey report recommended the suspension of

the annual football game between the two schools for at least five years. The experts who conducted the Iowa, Washington, and other surveys enunciated the concept of the "major-service theory," which reserved for the state university the prerogative to offer courses of study in the prestigious professions, including graduate work in education, and restricted the freedom of the land-grant college to offer nontechnical or nonagricultural courses and of teachers' colleges to offer noneducational-oriented programs.[7]

This emphasis on efficiency was motivated in large part by a desire to preserve the state university as a bastion of elitism within the public sector of higher education. Left to their own devices, public colleges and universities had pursued their individual ambitions to become self-contained units; this course struck the experts as not only wasteful but unwise. Numerous calls for the statewide coordination of higher educational institutions were heard from educators as well as from penurious state legislatures. "It is the purpose of the university to maintain itself as a school of higher training for professional work," the Board of Curators of the University of Missouri announced in 1926, "rather than as a direct competitor of the junior colleges, the teachers colleges, and the endowed colleges, for students of the freshman and sophomore ranks."[8] This approach made sense, saved money, and made conservative state university faculties happy. By the early 1930s there was a variety of institutions within the public sector, their prestige corresponding roughly to that of their major curriculum responsibilities and the socioeconomic composition of their student bodies.

Teachers' colleges, in particular, were criticized initially for putting their desire for expansion and their students' ambitions ahead of a statewide determination of the appropriate division of labor among public institutions. The remarkable growth of the high schools—in the decade after World War I the proportion of children of high school age in school more than doubled, from 20 to 50 percent—increased the demand for more and better-educated teachers. The passage of teacher certification laws by most states and the enactment of the federal Smith-Hughes Act in 1917 encouraged prospective educators to stay in college longer. Normal schools, previously little more than glorified high schools, had by the mid-1920s matured into teachers' colleges and considered themselves first-class institutions. For many of these colleges, teacher training was only the beginning; a survey team noted that the Kirksville, Missouri, State Normal School offered "a sort of educational lunch counter where everything 'the people' wish may be had in portions suited to their convenience." Studies showed that most teachers' college students came from lower-middle-class backgrounds; they could afford only a local, low-cost school and they aspired to practical training in education or in some other field of similarly low prestige. At first the expansion of these schools created tension in the public sector, but by the 1930s the distinctions between research- and professional-oriented state universities and regional-oriented teachers' colleges—some now called state colleges—were sharpened, to the satisfaction of educators at institutions of both types.[9]

Coffman's own University of Minnesota was a visible battleground between elite and democratic forces in public higher education during the 1920s and 1930s. While Coffman urged all who would seek a college education to come to the university, the dean of the school's College of Science, Literature, and the Arts, John B. Johnston, led a counterattack against open admissions. Johnston pressed successfully for the establishment of the General College, a two-year program for the general education of those students believed to be unprepared for the more rigorous four-year program. Johnston asserted that the first duty of the state university was to educate the most gifted students of the state; less talented young people must be educated also, but not at the intellectual expense of the more able. To be effective, the university must separate "the thinkers from the learners." Although he conceded it would be difficult to convince the public that it was wasteful and unwise to offer all students the same educational program, Johnston hoped that four-year curricula at state universities would be selective in the future.[10]

The General College, opened in 1932, was the solution. Its curriculum consisted of survey courses; no foreign language instruction, no laboratory courses, or advanced technical courses were offered. The new General College was designed to fill the demand for higher education among young people whose abilities or interests differed from those of the traditional university student. By 1939 it enrolled more than 1,000 students, more than one-fifth of them the children of working-class immigrants.[11] In its curriculum and in its lower-middle-class student body, the General College constituted a typical example of the public sector's efforts to broaden higher education without compromising the existent status of the capstone of its system.

Efforts to deepen the distinctions between types of institutions within the public sector accelerated during the Depression of the 1930s. Rising standards in the professions and business and the scar-

city of employment opportunities encouraged college attendance through most of the decade. Faced with the devastating financial impact of the Depression, state governments did not choose to devote increased resources to the expansion of their state universities. Instead, local teachers' colleges and public junior colleges assumed more and more responsibility for educating lower-middle-class students. The transformation of teacher's colleges into four-year state colleges, with a wider range of curricular offerings, and the continued support of public junior colleges were responses to the need for inexpensive educational opportunities within commuting distance of the homes of poorer students. Thus the growing acceptance of the idea of a right to public higher education was offset in part by the fact that such a right was exercised increasingly by privileged students at high-status institutions and by students from lower socioeconomic backgrounds at local schools of little prestige. Even within the public sector, the democratization of higher education was achieved by the expansion or creation of new types of low-status colleges rather than by the democratization of the institutions at the apex of the educational structure.

Public Higher Education in California

Nowhere was this trend more in evidence than in California. "There is more education to the square inch in California than in any other part of the United States," observed a writer in a 1902 article in *Sunset Magazine*.[12] Both the private and public sectors expanded rapidly during the first three decades of the twentieth century. Stanford University secured its place as a national institution and, during the 1920s, as the West's leading upper-class university as well. The creation of the Claremont Colleges complex constituted one of the nation's most successful efforts to recreate the atmosphere of the New England liberal arts college. In the public sector, California led the nation in the creation of junior colleges. The 1920s also witnessed the establishment of the so-called Southern Campus of the University of California, soon known as the University of California, Los Angeles.

Despite fierce opposition from Northern California legislators, a wary state Board of Control, and even the university itself, UCLA emerged gradually over a decade. In 1919 the Los Angeles Normal School became the Southern Branch of the University of California, but it continued to offer only two years of collegiate-grade work. In 1922 it was permitted to offer four years of teacher training, although it could still offer no more than two years of liberal arts. A four-year

College of Letters and Sciences was opened in the fall of 1924. It took four more years and a move to the present campus in Westwood for "the normal school that thought it could be a university" actually to become one. The demand for university-grade public higher education in the Southland had been met.[13] In the booming California of the 1920s, rather than pursue this extraordinary expansion of educational opportunity in a helter-skelter fashion, state and local governments, educators, and businessmen worked together slowly but steadily to plan the development of their state's higher education system.

In the 1930s, California developed the nation's most highly structured state system of higher education. The state legislature asked the Carnegie Foundation for the Advancement of Teaching to organize a study of California's public sector in 1932, and some of the best-known educators around the country went west to examine the plethora of public colleges and universities already formed there. The Commission of Seven was chaired by Samuel Capen, a former federal expert on higher education and now chancellor of the University of Buffalo, and included Minnesota's Coffman, George F. Zook, and the dean emeritus of Columbia University Teachers College, among others. After twenty-five years "of extensive experimentation" and confusion, the team admitted, the state had to come to grips with the financial exigencies of the Depression. More important, the report noted, there was a noticeable lack of unity in the administration of the public sector and a lack of articulation between segments of that sector. The Carnegie Foundation's 1932 report on California's public higher education stands out as the clearest statement of the philosophy of the differentiation of American higher education as originally conceived by educators between the two world wars.[14]

The study suggested that the Regents of the University of California be given the power to coordinate all public higher education above the junior college level in order to base statewide planning on "a scientific anticipation of genuine educational needs." This move would wrest control of public higher education from the ambitious hands of local educational entrepreneurs and politicians. Thus order would replace chaos, and money would be saved. Most of all, a highly organized public system of higher education would avoid the unnecessary and unwise duplication of purposes and courses among different types of institutions. The senior colleges and professional schools of the University of California should be selective because "overproduction . . . may readily become a social and professional evil, as well as an unwarranted cost to the university and the public." The new state colleges should cater to regional needs and the junior colleges should be viewed as an extension of secondary education. With the substantial increase in the number of young people seeking higher education and the increasing range of their talents and interests, this differentiation of public higher education was the most efficient, and therefore essential, response to modern educational conditions.

The report's critical message was that social efficiency should dictate the structure of higher learning in California and elsewhere in modern America. "In the past, educational careers have been too largely determined by personal whim," the experts concluded in their discussion of young people's selection of a college and a course of study. "Now that experience and psychological investigation indicate that a specific educational or vocational interest is not a good index to the possession of ability in a specific field, we are compelled to take into account both ability and interest, the first for social efficiency and the second for personal happiness. Both of these are desirable social goals." Progressive educators wanted to democratize higher education, and they did make it more accessible—the Carnegie team recommended, for example, that tuition not be charged at California junior colleges or for the first two years at the state colleges and universities—but they also believed that individual initiative should be curbed implicitly in the public interest.

This formulation for matching students with institutions is not inherently unfair, but the Carnegie team's proposal of sharp lines of demarcation between types of institutions would limit the ability of young people to move up from one segment to another. The study recommended that only the University of California at Berkeley be given the right to grant doctorates, and that the Los Angeles campus grant no degree higher than a master's. Similarly, the teachers' colleges should grant masters' degrees only in the field of education. The California Polytechnic Institute at San Luis Obispo should be abolished altogether, as its courses could be and were offered elsewhere. The four-year public colleges and universities should not provide the technical training for the minor professions, which were properly the province of the two-year junior colleges. Further, the junior colleges should restrict themselves to a semiprofessional curriculum even if historically they had provided the first two years of a standard four-year college course and continued to be popularly regarded as part of the higher or university education system. Finally, the State Council for Educational Planning and Coordination should determine the state's personnel needs in each profession and field and advise the Regents accordingly on the appropriate enrollment level at each institution and in each course of study.

In the name of social efficiency, then, young people would be channeled to certain schools and into certain fields. The state would take a census of the state's work force, with particular attention to its professional and semiprofessional occupations, and determine how many young people should go to college, and where. Local educational entrepreneurs would be held in check; similarly, ambitious students who blossomed late in life—after high school—would find it difficult to move up from their prescribed position in the educational hierarchy. Personal whim, as the experts called it, took a back seat to social planning in educational matters. As in American economic life, the free market had not proved efficient enough in education. Planning was in the best interests of everyone, students and their parents, educators, and the state alike, and it was pursued more earnestly in California than anywhere else in the 1930s.

Presiding over this system was Robert G. Sproul, president of the University of California. Sproul asserted his support for a public system of education that offered the opportunity for higher learning to all, but, equally important, he also believed that the state's educational system should and could replicate the natural distribution of talent and needs in the society. Insisting that "the university is primarily designed for one type of mind and the junior college for another," he concluded, "what we need is . . . not more colleges and universities of the traditional type . . . but altogether different institutions which will suitably train those students and get them in their lifework sooner." It was therefore the responsibility of the state to offer a variety of educational opportunities to its youth, and each segment of the public sector should cater to specific concerns. In the interest of this "natural" efficiency, the California junior colleges should restrict themselves to educating those individuals interested in postsecondary education but not equipped for the professions, which were properly the province of the state university.[15]

While the rapid development of the junior colleges was taking place, California educators were encouraging the planned growth of the state college system. In the early 1920s, several normal schools became state teachers' colleges in order to meet the demand for high school teachers in one of the nation's most rapidly growing states. But, as elsewhere, these teachers' colleges provided access and training for more than just the prospective teachers in their region. In 1935 the state designated seven of them as state colleges. The public colleges at Chico, Fresno, Humboldt, San Diego, San Francisco, San Jose, and Santa Barbara were now given permission to offer a bach-

elor's degree in any of the liberal arts. To the administrators, faculty, and students of these schools, such recognition was long overdue. After all, they pointed out, in California and elsewhere, the teachers' colleges' curriculum and the abilities of their students had differed little from those of the universities since World War I, if not earlier.[16]

Educators simply wanted to clarify and simplify the boundaries between types of institutions and to shift the emphasis in each segment by defining its functions more carefully, a statewide California administrator argued in a 1939 pamphlet. "The new challenge to Democracy and the differentiation and specialization of the democratic process" demanded no less. After their designation as state colleges, these schools faced the task "of finding their proper and permanent place in the educational life of the state." He suggested that the state colleges should not try to become universities; instead, recalling their tradition as teacher-training institutions, they should emphasize the liberal, but not the learned, professions. While universities and liberal arts colleges were interested in the "idea of 'Culture' with a capital C'"—"which carries an unconscious implication of preparation for a life of leisure and detachment from the hurly-burly of the market place"—the state colleges should remain "more sensitive to the needs of democracy."[17]

In its constituencies and its objectives, then, the state college differed from the more prestigious university; as a result, its "method will be psychological rather than logical, functional rather than structural." Preparation for teaching, middle-level government service, home economics, journalism, library work, nursing, personnel work, police work, psychiatric social work, and other social welfare work should be provided by the state college, since each of these areas was peripheral to the proper concerns of a university. Furthermore, state colleges should not be steered away from their proper functions by the growing interest in research at universities. The foundation of the state college curriculum should be an integrated study of the economic and social order which showed the organic relationships of individual personality, the scientific method, the American democratic social pattern, and the training for these liberal professions. These student-oriented institutions, as they were called, should emphasize "cooperative thinking," not the creation of new knowledge. Nor should they cultivate leadership skills, of course, since other institutions with other students logically enjoyed that privilege and responsibility. Socialization was clearly the first priority of institutions at this level. The state college had an articulated market, in theory if not always in reality, which distinguished it from the university above and the junior colleges below.

The Evolution of the Terminal Junior College

Though familiar today, the view that the predominant function of the junior college was to train its students for semiprofessional careers emerged only in the late 1920s. World War I had prompted fears that existing institutions would be overwhelmed by the crush of students. It seemed only logical to support the expansion and creation of two-year institutions in remote areas of large states, such as California, to meet the demands of people too young or impecunious to go away to college. Yet, while students and their parents continued to view the junior college as a preparatory step to university life and a university-trained career, educators began to articulate a different role for the two-year institution in an increasingly rigid educational hierarchy. Students at state universities contributed to the leadership of their generation; students at public junior colleges should contribute to social efficiency. No longer conceived of as a preparatory institution, the public junior college was altered in the late 1920s and 1930s into a terminal institution where most young people of limited means and allegedly limited abilities and aspirations concluded their education by preparing for a semi-professional occupation.

The roots of the junior college movement can be traced to American educators' interest in the German educational system in the late nineteenth century. Influential university presidents noted that secondary schools offered two more years of general education in Germany than in the United States. The graduate then went directly into the university for advanced or professional education. In the 1880s a number of private and public universities, including the universities of Michigan and Pennsylvania, made overtures to high schools in an effort to create such an arrangement. In 1892 William Rainey Harper, the "Father of the Junior College," divided the University of Chicago into the Academic College and the University College. A decade later, working with the public schools in Joliet, Illinois, Harper encouraged the establishment of the nation's first public junior college.[18]

Several top universities pursued the division of the undergraduate years into senior and junior colleges in the first two decades of the twentieth century. The lower division was separated into a distinct unit dedicated to general education. There, following the lead of Chicago's Harper and Stanford's David Starr Jordan, professional-oriented students received a general education before they specialized in the field of their choice or went directly to a professional school. The junior college was also developed to help ease the adjustment of young people who graduated from the many substandard high schools of the early twentieth century. Columbia's Nicholas Murray Butler supported the formation of Seth Low Junior College in Brooklyn, for example, because he believed it would relieve some of the pressure for admission to his college by providing the two years of collegiate education then considered necessary before entrance to schools that prepared students for the nonlearned professions.

After World War I sparked the unprecedented demand for more widely diffused, practical, and local postsecondary education, the modern junior college was born. In 1918, although there were eighty-five junior colleges in nineteen states, fifty-six of them were concentrated in the five states of California, Missouri, Virginia, Texas, and Illinois; there was no junior college east of Michigan and north of North Carolina and Kentucky. For twenty-five years before the war the number of collegiate institutions had remained fairly constant; during the 1920s, however, as the number of colleges increased sharply from 670 to 1,076, nearly half of the new institutions—196 of 406—were junior colleges. The number of junior college students climbed tenfold, to 45,000, between the war and the mid-1920s, and nearly tripled again by even the most conservative estimate between 1928 and 1938.[19]

While both private and public junior colleges experienced rapid growth between the two world wars, the public sector became predominant. Between 1922 and 1927, enrollment in public junior colleges jumped 217 percent as enrollment in private junior colleges increased (only) 102 percent. Six states had enacted laws that stipulated the conditions for state support of local junior colleges by 1926; eleven states joined them in 1927 and 1928. As late as the 1930s, well over three of every four junior colleges were still housed in high schools. In Creston, Iowa, the junior college occupied the second floor of the new high school building opened in the fall of 1926. Located, or "fortunately situated," sixty-five miles from the nearest four-year college, Creston Junior College drew 104 students from eighteen high schools to its modest offices, library, drafting room, and few classrooms. The junior college students shared the laboratory, gymnasium, and auditorium with the 570 high school students. Also typical of the explosive growth of the public junior college was Sacramento Junior College: between 1922 and 1928, enrollment skyrocketed from 198 to 1,378 regular students, the number of faculty climbed from 10 to 57, and the school's budget went from less than

$51,000 to nearly $240,000. During the Depression, no doubt in part because of their low cost (tuition was even free in eight states), public junior colleges nearly tripled their enrollment and increased their proportionate share of the junior college market.[20]

The distribution of these early junior colleges shows that they were most successful in sparsely populated regions, particularly in the Midwest, Southwest, and West. More than 40 percent of the junior college presidents surveyed after World War I gave their geographical remoteness from the state university as the primary reason for their school's creation; far fewer mentioned vocational training as the top initial priority. A 1931 proposal to establish a network of nine junior colleges in Utah demonstrated this public sentiment. The study suggested that a mining region east of Salt Lake City, for example, where only one in four high school graduates attended college, was the sort of place that needed a junior college. More rural parents than urban parents reported that their children would attend a junior college if one were nearby. Furthermore, these parents and potential students were interested in a wide variety of liberal arts and professional courses of study, particularly in commerce, but did not suggest that these studies should be terminal.[21] As far as parents and students were concerned, the public junior college was to be an all-inclusive rather than a narrowly defined institution.

Liberal arts educators were divided about whether the extraordinary growth of the junior colleges constituted a threat to their own existence in the 1920s. As late as 1929, presidents of small liberal arts schools such as Illinois's Knox College were wary of the competition. However, speaking at the National Conference of Junior Colleges in 1920, a meeting sponsored by the federal Bureau of Education, George F. Zook observed, "It is becoming increasingly apparent that universities and colleges alike are beginning to regard the junior college as an institution of great possible usefulness in the field of higher education." The dean of Carleton College insisted that most students drawn to the junior colleges were "not from the class of those who otherwise prepare themselves for larger service in the wider fields of leadership, but rather from those many of whom would have attached themselves to the artisan class a generation ago." Among the junior college's most important functions, he added, was that of freeing the liberal arts college and university from the need to educate "the throng of immature pupils who, but virtue of interest, or intellectual limitation, have no concern for a liberal education."[22] Many

of the weakest liberal arts colleges were converted to two-year schools during the 1920s, but the junior colleges' threat to the well-established schools was insignificant by the early 1930s.

President Ray L. Wilbur of Stanford University, later secretary of the interior in Herbert Hoover's cabinet, was a leading proponent of university–junior college cooperation. "Such schools become clearing-houses for the universities, culling out those unable to go further and stimulating and pointing right those for whom a university course is necessary and desirable," he wrote in 1916. With the development of the junior college, Wilbur hoped that Stanford could "see its way clear to becoming more of a university and less of a college." Until the mid-1920s, Wilbur envisioned a day in the not too distant future when Stanford could eliminate its Lower Division because it duplicated the efforts of the junior colleges and could concentrate primarily on university work.[23] Besieged by students from diverse backgrounds and with various interests, more and more four-year institutions looked to establish cooperative arrangements with junior colleges, particularly in such fields as engineering and commerce. A 1930 survey pointed out that about one-third of the graduates of these programs—sponsored by such institutions as Boston, Rutgers, and George Washington universities—transferred to a university. "From a pedagogical point of view," the federal commissioner of education concurred, "such an extension of the secondary schools is natural and justifiable."[24]

Even as more and more educators supported the concept of the terminal junior college, this so-called preparatory function remained central to the mission of the public junior college throughout the 1920s. Pushed by these educators on one side and by ambitious students on the other, many junior college presidents were concerned about the schizophrenic nature of the two-year school's identity. "Is its function to prepare boys and girls for life or to prepare them for the junior year in the A. B. college?" asked a junior college president in 1920. "I want to know whether I must build courses for the 90 percent or say 75 percent who are going no further, or the 25 percent who are going on to the junior year of the standard four-year college. Shall we take care particularly of those going out into life or those going on to college?" From his position as professor of secondary education at the University of Minnesota, Leonard V. Koos admitted in the first large-scale study of the junior college movement in the mid-1920s that the preparatory, or isthmian, function was the prima-

The vocational junior college that emerged in the 1920s flourished during the Depression. A few junior colleges were established before World War I for vocational purposes, most notably Chaffey Union Junior College in California, founded largely to assist local agricultural interests, and Chicago's Crane Junior College, which provided advanced technical training of the sort offered in the city's vocational high schools. Typically, when new junior colleges were created in the 1920s, efforts were made to incorporate local vocational interests in the curriculum. In 1923, a survey of education in Massachusetts recommended that junior colleges be formed to offer "the first two years of college work in liberal arts and sciences and such other courses of study of two years of less in length as the needs of the community seem to demand . . . [which] may include vocational, technical, commercial, and home-making courses of study." After examining the catalogues of 500 two-year colleges, G. Vernon Bennett reported in 1928 that while support for vocational junior colleges was still in its "very earliest stage," training for twenty-eight minor professions was already available, mainly at such privately controlled schools as the Wentworth Institute in Boston, the Pierce School of Business Administration in Philadelphia, the College of Industrial Arts in Denton, Texas, and even the Lewis Tea Room Institute in Washington, D.C. He predicted that more occupational fields would be included in the curricula of public junior colleges as states began to use such schools to meet the anticipated need for workers.[28]

Given these efforts, it is not surprising that surveys in the late 1920s began to indicate a rapid increase in the number of students enrolled in junior colleges for purposes other than preparation for a university education. A survey of the curricula of nineteen public junior colleges showed that while the total of credit hours offered in the ancient languages declined 18 percent between 1920–21 and 1929–30, the total number of credit hours in the social sciences rose 59 percent, and the total number of credit hours in engineering and home economics climbed 230 percent and 243 percent, respectively. A survey of more than five-thousand urban high school graduates in the San Francisco–Berkeley area who intended to go to a junior college found that nearly twice as many students were planning to take commercial and business courses as were planning to enroll in general academic courses. This 1930 study also concluded that this interest in vocational junior college education did not lead to a decline in attendance

ry thrust behind the founding of public junior colleges. A review of the statements of purpose of these schools as late as 1930 pointed out that preparation for university work was emphasized more than vocational education in nearly two-thirds of the 343 catalogues studied.[25] Most schools tried to offer both. This strategy was satisfying to students but not to those educators convinced that the junior college's function was primarily to provide semiprofessional training.

Despite the opposition of parents and students and the success of university–junior college arrangements, the public junior college was reorganized by education experts, as Southern College president Arthur Davis put it, "on a twentieth-century basis," in the 1920s and 1930s. Progressive educators, including Koos and Alexis Lange of the University of California, believed occupational training of large numbers of young people enhanced society's economic and social efficiency and secured those students' occupational, and therefore personal, happiness. Lange insisted that "the rise and progress of the Junior College needs to be looked upon as an integral phase of a country-wide movement towards a more adequate state system of education; a twentieth-century system, made in America; a system that shall function progressively so as to secure for the nation the greatest efficiency of the greatest number."[26] Businessmen eager for trained young people also boosted this concept.

The terminal junior college was viewed as an efficient and democratic solution to the problem of adjusting American youth to a modern hierarchical economic and social structure. "The problem of sifting the fit from the unfit and of selecting those who should be guided into shorter curricula on the semi-professional level would largely be solved in the junior college," Zook concluded. Consequently, when they guided certain students toward the junior college, these educators insisted they were doing those young people a favor. But most educators were actually more concerned about steering undesirable students, even if talented, away from the traditional four-year colleges; A. Lawrence Lowell of Harvard admitted, "One of the merits of these new institutions will be [the] keeping out of college, rather than leading into it, [of] young people who have no taste for higher education."[27] While parents and students still focused on the cultural aims of junior college education, educators focused the attention of the junior college on purportedly nonintellectual students. The junior college would supplement, not supplant or compete with, the four-year collegiate sector.

siastically as educators did. It proved difficult to discourage their ambitions for their children. Local access to higher education of any kind—and not just to vocational education—was the primary reason for attendance at junior colleges throughout the Depression. Parents supported the creation or expansion of junior colleges because they wanted higher education brought closer to their homes for financial or social reasons. Surveys showed that the junior colleges played a critical role in facilitating access to higher education for poor and ethnic students generally, and not just for those among them interested in the semiprofessional fields. A 1929 study showed that the proportion of lower-class students in California public junior colleges was more than three times greater than their porportion at four-year institutions in the state.[32] Junior college students were not nearly so inadequately prepared or so unintellectual as most proponents of the terminal junior college alleged they were.

The junior college students who transferred to four-year institutions did quite well there. In 1919, a study found that two-thirds of public junior college graduates continued their education at a college or university. This proportion of transfers declined throughout the 1920s, but as late as the 1930s as many as one-quarter of all junior college graduates went on to four-year schools. Even after the idea of the terminal junior college had taken hold—at a time when, for example, President Sproul of the University of California asserted that only 2 percent, or one of fifty, of the public junior college graduates were capable of university work—a substantial number of public junior college graduates moved up the educational hierarchy.[33] In addition, studies at institutions across the country pointed out that junior college transfers did as well as their peers in their junior and senior years of college, even at such prestigious universities as Minnesota, Michigan, Chicago, California, and Stanford. In the mid-1930s, for example, junior college graduates at Stanford scored slightly higher on psychological tests and graduated in greater proportions than those students who entered Stanford as freshmen.[34] Although embarrassing, the presence of these talented but poor students at public junior colleges did not deter educators from espousing the concept of terminal junior college education with increasing frequency during the 1920s and 1930s.

The history of the California public junior college movement reveals how the junior college evolved into a local, vocational-oriented institution between the two world wars. Laws passed by the legislature in 1917 and 1921 specified the rules by which local districts

at the area's four-year institutions.[29] Educators' efforts to foster the development of the vocational junior college had taken root. A new type of educational institution had been grafted successfully onto modern American higher education.

Educators and businessmen of the 1930s stressed the need for locally based schools of postsecondary education where students could be kept off the job market while they were trained for work at low cost. The number of high school graduates had doubled in each of the first three decades of the twentieth century and increased further from 667,000 to 1,210,000 a year between 1930 and 1940; this growth provided a vast reservoir of potential students ill prepared to enter the job market in the best of times, let alone during the Depression. Young people were encouraged to enroll at a junior college for vocational training in an effort to reduce the labor supply and ease the economic crisis of the 1930s a bit. "The junior college has a certain passive value that is of immeasurable importance," the editor of the *California Journal of Secondary Education* wrote, "for in this day of widespread unemployment it offers a haven where millions of unemployed youths may occupy themselves with worthwhile activities."[30] Walter C. Eells's 1941 study *Why Junior College Terminal Education?* applauded the pervasiveness of the terminal junior college. An extensive survey conducted for this report showed that 79 percent of the educators and laymen questioned believed that the terminal function of the junior college was more important than its preparatory function. Eells attributed the popularity of the public junior college to the opportunities it offered young people for "greater economic competence, social usefulness, and personal satisfaction" than they could find elsewhere, particularly during the Depression. As recently as 1937 the philosopher Norman Foerster and commented that the junior college was still "vague or inconsistent in [its] aims, awaiting some decisive definition"; but the die was soon cast. Locally based, semiprofessional, terminal junior college education became the stated goal of the American Association of Junior Colleges; similarly, sensitive to the connections between education and the labor market, W. Lloyd Warner and the Educational Policies Commission of the National Education Association endorsed the concept of semiprofessional education for those between eighteen and twenty years old. In two decades, economic and social forces had created a public junior college that trained its students for as many as 106 semiprofessional fields.[31]

Yet the public did not endorse the terminal junior college as enthu-

could receive state and county funds to set up junior college programs. One of these schools, Chaffey Junior College in Ontario, became the model vocational public junior college: it not only offered courses in commerce, home economics, and mechanical arts, it also operated an 88-acre orchard for agricultural experimental purposes. Between 1922 and 1930, the number of students in California public junior colleges increased from 2,259 to 20,641. The proportion of junior college students (both years) to high school graduates tripled in the 1920s alone, from 16 percent to 54 percent.35 For young people far from Berkeley and other well-known schools, the junior college constituted the first step up the ladder of higher education.

Yet, beginning in the 1920s, California educators saw the junior college as an extension of the high school, not as part of the university system. Sproul declared that efforts by junior colleges to expand into four-year institutions were "subversive of the best interests of democracy." Two-year schools stood simply for "further educational preparedness for the greatest number, for democratic continuity and completeness of educational opportunity," but not for university-level training and social leadership.36

The 1932 Carnegie panel of educational experts echoed these sentiments; it, too, asserted that a public junior college that emphasized its university preparatory function rather than its terminal vocational function was undemocratic. The team recited the litany of complaints against ambitious local educational entrepreneurs and parents and students. It sharply criticized local districts for their slavish imitation of "expensive, higher-type schools." The public junior college that catered to the so-called self-deceptions of local parents who wanted a college preparatory curriculum was not performing "its allotted social duty." Instead, the national panel urged that greater emphasis be put on "the proper development of completion curricula." "When junior college management looks upward to the university to discover its functions, its point of view, its procedures, and its social philosophy, it creates the largest possible gap between itself and the community high schools," the experts advised, "whereas it ought to be looking outward upon the community and its life to discover how all its unselected and different kinds of students may be educated to intelligent cooperation and useful membership in society." Labeling statistics on the significant number of junior college transfers as misleading, they urged the public junior college to grant only the Associate in Arts degree, which

was "not to be confused with the qualifying function of a junior certificate or any other title or document designed to attest fitness to enter a senior college or a professional school."37 Ironically, then, by the late 1930s, President N. H. McCollum of Lassen Junior College was speaking for the mainstream of American educational thought when he proudly proclaimed the California public junior colleges to be "the 'people's colleges,' designed and organized to provide graduates with marketable skills and knowledge that they may become self-supporting citizens of our American democracy."38

The Social Impulse behind the Junior College Movement

The emergence of the vocational-oriented public junior college bears dramatic testimony to the social influences that guided the transformation of American higher education between the two world wars. As education became more important to economic growth and social progress, the evolution of institutions of higher learning was no longer left to chance. Progressives who had sought to regulate the marketplace, however tentatively, now looked to organize higher education. Optimistically, they felt that all young people should have access to higher education in order to fulfill their personal potential. But even in a democracy, they believed, there were leaders and followers, and they set out to replicate this distinction in an equally "natural" and "efficient" differentiated system of higher learning evocative of their view of a complex modern world. Faced with a potential student body increasingly large and diverse in socioeconomic backgrounds and interests, and with a great concern for the need for an increasingly white-collar work force, educators encouraged the formation of a new type of postsecondary education devoted to semi-professional vocational training. The transmission of knowledge—as well as the aspirations and abilities of the affected students—took a back seat to the so-called public interest.

The junior college movement, then, constituted a critical stage in the dramatic explosion of educational opportunities. It resulted in the rapid and broad diffusion of higher education. At the same time, however, an increased emphasis on terminal junior college education between the two world wars circumscribed the education and training of students. Students were there to start college; educators thought they should be there to start and finish postsecondary education. Certainly, a majority of young people at the public junior colleges of this or any subsequent era were not capable of or interested in university-level work, but the interests and needs of the many who attended the junior college to prepare for the university were frustrated by educators' elitist intentions.

The social prejudices of most educators compromised their idealistic efforts to foster equality of educational opportunity. Intent on introducing order as an educational priority, they established a rigid hierarchy of institutions. Convinced of an inequitable distribution of talent in the society, and, even more important, of their ability to determine fairly those who were destined to lead and those others who were destined to follow, educators delineated distinctions be-

tween different types of institutions, and particularly between four- and two-year colleges. As a result, the public junior college evolved into an institution geared to meet society's needs for a trained work force rather than an institution of higher learning designed to accommodate the interests of worthy but not well-off students. In doing so, the public junior college did provide access to the training that was a preliminary step toward economic and social mobility for its students; yet, by leaving higher learning to four-year institutions, it also limited the opportunities available to those students. Reflective of the democratic possibilities brought about by educational expansion, the junior college movement also revealed the limitations of conservative American reform.

Expansion and Exclusion: A History of Women in American Higher Education

Patricia A. Graham

Explanations of the historical role of women in higher education in the United States between the mid-nineteenth and the mid-twentieth centuries rest upon understanding a series of related changes in both education and the status of women. In my essay I will analyze three major shifts in higher education: (1) Its movement out of the eddies and tributaries of American life into the mainstream of activity, (2) its transformation from the domain of the few to the domain of the many, and (3) the evolution of its organizational ideal from an early monolithic model through a period of diversity to a later monolithic form quite different from the first. Interacting with these were two changes that concerned women: (1) a transition of the canons of "true womanhood" or of the "ideal of true womanhood," given in the prescriptive literature of the period, from religious and social ideals to secular and social ones (this submitted women to new, more complex pressures that thwarted their professional ambitions and development); and (2) a dramatic increase in the proportion of women the prescriptive literature affected, or a universalization of social norms.

The opportunities for highly educated women were greater at the end of the nineteenth century than they were in the mid-twentieth century. Such an assertion clearly challenges the traditional American optimism about the existence of a progressive improvement in opportunities for all segments of American society. However, the democratization of higher education which occurred in the early and middle years of the twentieth century did not cut across sex lines with equal effects. Men benefited from it much more than women.

I

In the late nineteenth century, faculty members of American colleges and universities still perceived themselves and their calling as outside the mainstream of American values and mores. Not all the priestly vows of poverty, chastity, and obedience were expected of professors, but the first was required, and considerable respect for the latter two was expected as well. Professorial salaries were low, and a standard of genteel poverty prevailed in most college communities. The exceptions occurred at the prestigious institutions, where faculty members were sometimes scions of families of independent means. Everywhere, however, an academic career somehow seemed suitable for a child who could not adjust to the "real" world of business. The contrast between the "real" world of American entrepreneurial capitalism and the "ivory tower" of academe provided ample material for novelists, humorists, and dramatists. They portrayed the rumpled professor, committed to an esoteric and therefore unimportant specialty, as often forgetful, nearly incompetent in the daily routine of living, a stock figure of amusement and derision. Such characterizations reinforced the notion that colleges and universities, pleasant as they were, provided shelter for the young, as well as the aging, innocents who composed a faculty. Naiveté among adult men was not a public virtue in America in that era or this.

That colleges were separate from the mainstream of American life can be easily seen in the smallness of their size throughout the nineteenth century. In 1870 the student population included just over 1 percent of the traditional college age group.[1] Indeed, from the founding of Harvard in 1636 until as late as the end of World War II, college attendance was a rarity. The proportion of the age group attending college increased steadily, but slowly, after 1870, at the rate of 1 percentage point a decade, until 1920, when it jumped to 8 percent.[2] Such a small group represented a highly educated, if not intellectual, elite during the years between the Civil War and World War I. Their experience with formal education set them apart from the rest of the American populace, the larger society not yet altogether convinced of their necessity or importance. Their family backgrounds were probably of greater wealth and higher social status than the population at large, but the correlation between family status and college attendance was not as simple and direct as contemporary observers might guess.

During the last part of the nineteenth century, the characteristics of higher education in America began to change. Higher education, like many other facets of public life, was beginning to become a system. During these years an important shift took place in the very definition of an "educated man": In the early part of the century, he had knowledge of the classics, however it might be obtained (private study, tutors, travel, college education); by the end of the century, the educated man was seen as a person who had attended college. A goal—knowledge of the classics—was increasingly replaced by a process—studying at a college. Formal education thus began to play an ever-increasing role in American life, but its recipients were still set apart by the scarcity of their numbers.

The organizational forms and ideological commitments of prestigious colleges in America also underwent a period of rapid change in the last quarter of the nineteenth century. Before the Civil War, the liberal arts college for men possessed a prescribed curriculum and embodied the monolithic ideal of classical education. In the late nineteenth century, this ideal was increasingly abandoned for a variety of educational institutions, based on differing organizational principles and directed toward differing educational goals. For a brief period, from approximately 1875 to 1925, a strikingly heterogeneous array of acceptable and praiseworthy institutions existed in America. This coincided with a crucial period in the history of women in America and aided their advancement. For approximately fifty years, a competitive tension reigned among the various types of higher educational institutions in America. This was followed by the reemergence of a monolith, the research university, which quickly became a new ideal type. This new monolith differed markedly from the old one of fifty years before. If the old had defined itself in terms of the classics, the early twentieth-century monolith defined itself in terms of graduate research. However, the periods in which the two monoliths triumphed were similar in one characteristic: A single standard of higher education received public sanction and acclaim. A direct result was that institutions traditionally based on other standards had to choose between emulating the now almost universal model or resign themselves to providing alternatives without widespread public and professional support. An indirect result was that those categories of people, particularly women, who had not earlier won secure places for themselves in society and were now continuing to try to do so, faced a dwindling number of accepted educational pathways. This loss of variety was more serious for women as a group than men.

An example of the way in which higher educational institutions were beginning to move toward the new monolith in the early twentieth century can be seen in normal schools. The normal school, a distinctive and widespread educational institution at the turn of the century, fulfilled an important function. Then the normal school system began to feel the effects of the research infusion. By 1920 the transformation had begun, an evolution which can easily be followed by noting the changes in the names of the institutions. The "normal school" of 1890 became, often around 1920, the "state teachers college," then a few decades later the "state college," and, last, the "state university." When the institution was known as a normal school, it was still respectable to be concerned with the training of teachers and the improvement of pedagogical skills. By 1950 or 1960 a premium was being placed on "doing research," often very broadly interpreted.

Teacher training institutions were but a subset of a group of higher educational institutions with a distinctively determined curriculum. So, too, were the Roman Catholic colleges, many of which resisted the move toward the elective curriculum until World War II. Even more important were the state universities and land-grant institutions, aided by the passage of the Morrill Act in 1862. Frequently beginning as liberal arts colleges, they welcomed as students the citizens of their states, including women, and expanded their curricula to include many subjects not heretofore thought acceptable, primarily engineering, agriculture, and home economics. In addition, the best of these places defined themselves as being of service to the state, thus adding an even more disparate function to purposes of higher education. Perhaps the most characteristic American collegiate example was the historically Protestant but increasingly secular liberal arts college. An institution such as Amherst stressed teaching on the part of the faculty, not research, and envisioned the molding of students' characters rather than merely transmitting knowledge for knowledge's sake as a principal and legitimate activity of the college. This goal of character formation also was a viable educational model through World War I. Then, scholarship replaced character as the primary educational responsibility.

The overwhelming concern with scholarship, with the primacy of the institutional responsibility for generating rather than transmitting knowledge, was a direct outgrowth of the efforts of Charles William Eliot at Harvard and others to broaden the college curriculum. The move away from a prescribed curriculum that was taught by a faculty concerned more with students than with subjects led to the development of an elective system in which faculty members taught a limited number of courses, all of them in their "specialty." Such a shift meant that the faculty members had to have such specialties, which became increasingly narrow over the years. A mid-nineteenth-century professor might have thought of himself as a professor of the classics; his successor was a classicist; his successor concerned himself only with ancient Greek; his successor became a specialist in the early plays of Aeschylus. His successor, expert in Aeschylus's use of the metaphor, is unemployed.

Despite the growth of community colleges in this period, the degree to which higher education forms a pyramid with the values of research universities at the pinnacle dominating the structure is striking. All institutions discuss the need to give weight to three criteria in considering faculty for promotion (scholarship, teaching, and service), but there is little doubt anywhere that the prestige (although not necessarily the appointment) rests heavily on the first. My point is not that more good scholarship is being done by faculty members now than in the past, although that is probably true, but rather that research, preferably published and widely recognized, occupies a universal prestige and dominates other useful faculty qualities in a way that it did not in an earlier era. The institutions which have led in establishing this new value system and whose practices and institutional priorities have been widely emulated by other institutions are the old universities of the East, such as Harvard, Yale, Princeton, and Columbia, as well as the newer ones to the West, Chicago, Berkeley, and Stanford. In terms of prestige, though not necessarily in terms of remuneration or other matters, the Ivies have set the standard.

By 1920 the major changes occurring in higher education were often harbingers of even greater changes to come. Preeminent among these was the shift in faculty loyalty from their institution to their discipline and the rising professionalism attendant to that development. When one is known for one's personal qualities, rather than one's professional ones, individual idiosyncrasies can be tolerated and eccentricities enjoyed. Such characteristics often contribute to the personality of the teacher. When one is judged, however, on one's published work, as increasingly became the case for faculty members in the middle years of this century, personal characteristics that may enhance teaching but do not improve scholarship are not valued. As the society evinced greater need for the expert or specialist, tolerances have diminished for nonprofessional expertise among professors.

Gradually in the pre–World War II years and increasingly in the fifties and sixties, faculties, particularly those in universities, also came to believe that they had a responsible role in government or in the private sector. Even more important, their services were sought by government and industry, a phenomenon that rarely happened in earlier years. The faculties now tended to think of themselves as men of affairs, not as part of a remote alternative culture. While the first major figure to move from academe to the presidency, Woodrow Wilson from Princeton via the governorship of New Jersey, did not assure that such transitions would be either successful or easy, he did establish that academicians were a possible source of government servants. When Franklin Delano Roosevelt acquired his "brain trust," Columbia University was well represented. Two decades later, Columbia even donated its president to the United States, although certainly Eisenhower had not come to public notice through his educational leadership. By the fifties and sixties, however, successful professors were expected to be familiar with the routines of the market place, whether through outside grants for research or through consultantships in Washington or elsewhere.

The ideal faculty home has become indistinguishable in location or decor from that of a moderately successful paint company executive. Gone are the rattan furniture and seersucker bedspreads of the professor's bungalow near the campus of the twenties and thirties.

II

Though these changes in the colleges and universities occurred without particular concern for their effects on women, the initial consequences have been substantial. Unlike men, who were never barred from attending college on account of their sex, women were unable to enroll in any college until Oberlin permitted them entrance in 1837, ostensibly to provide ministers with intelligent, cultivated, and thoroughly schooled wives. When the shortage of male students during the Civil War made institutions willing to consider tuition-paying women as well, they became 21 percent of the total undergraduate enrollment by 1870. This figure included the students in the newly established women's colleges that began to sprout up and down the eastern seaboard as independent schools, chiefly in safe bucolic locations, or occasionally, as "coordinate colleges" adjacent to established men's colleges that refused to admit women students (Radcliffe at Harvard, Barnard at Columbia, and Evelyn at Princeton). By 1880 women constituted 32 percent of the undergraduate student body; by 1910 almost 40 percent. A decade later, 1919–20, women were 47 percent of the undergraduate enrollment, nearly as much as their proportion in the population.[3]

The decade of the twenties was critical for educated women. During that ten-year period, women achieved their highest proportion of the undergraduate population, of doctoral recipients, and of faculty members. A record 32.5 percent of college presidents, professors, and instructors were women when the decade closed in 1930.[4] That success was reflected in other professions as well. During this period, women constituted nearly 45 percent of the professional work force, a share that began declining in 1930 and reached a low point in 1960.[5] Further, from 1870 to 1930, the proportion of women in the professions was twice as high as that in the work force. By the end of the thirties, the proportion of all undergraduate women was declining, although the proportion of women receiving the A.B. was still rising slightly, and the drop had begun in the proportion of women receiving the doctorate.[6] If the percentage of women on faculties remained at the 1930 level, this was but a reflection of the professional training taken by women in the teens, twenties, and thirties who were still teaching in 1940.[7]

The women who came to maturity in the years before and immediately after World War I are probably the ones who benefited most from the flexibility of choice of the teens and early twenties. Writing in 1938, Marjorie Nicolson, who was born in 1894 and received her B.A. in 1914 from the University of Michigan, described her compatriots:

> We of the pre-war generation used to pride ourselves sentimentally on being the "lost generation," used to think that because war cut across the stable path on which our feet were set we were an unfortunate generation. But as I look back upon the records, I find myself wondering whether our generation was not the only generation of women which ever really found itself. We came late enough to escape the self-consciousness and belligerence of the pioneers, to take education and training for granted. We came early enough to take equally for granted professional positions in which we could make full use of our training. This was our double glory. Positions were everywhere open to us; it never occurred to us at that time that we were taken only because men were not available. . . . The millenium had come; it did not occur to us that life could be different. Within a decade shades of the prison house began to close, not upon the growing boy, but upon the emancipated girls.[8]

Yet, even before the decline began, all was not rosy for professional women. There was no glorious past when women professionals were ever treated equally with men. The most prestigious institutions never considered women for regular faculty positions until well after World War II. When Alice Hamilton joined the Harvard Medical School faculty in 1919 as an assistant professor (at the age of 50), with an international reputation as the leading figure in industrial toxicology, she was told that a condition of her appointment was that she must not march in the commencement procession. When women did join the faculties of institutions which would hire them, they were paid less than men. A study of fifty land-grant institutions revealed in 1927–28 that median salaries for women faculty were $860 less than for men. The higher the woman faculty member's rank, the greater the difference between her salary and that of men in corresponding posts. Women instructors received 96.6 percent of men instructors' salaries; women professors, 86.5 percent of that of men professors; women deans, 77.6 percent of that of men deans.[9] The years of the mid-twentieth century brought a decline for women's participation in an academic life whose past was itself hardly halcyon (see table 1).

The complex explanation for the limited and diminished role that highly educated women have played in American society and in the professions in the middle years of the twentieth century lies principally in the interrelationship of several major factors. First, college was not substantially at variance with society's expectations for men. If male attendance was not conventional, it was still consistent with nineteenth- and early twentieth-century expectations that men should prepare

Table 1

Year Ending	Under-graduate Students in Age Group 18–21* (%)	Women as Under-graduates* (%)	Women with Bachelor's or First Professional Degree (%)	Women as Doctorates† (%)	Women as Faculty (%)
1870	1.68‡	21‡	15	0	12
1880	2.72‡	32‡	19	6	36
1890	2.99	35‡	17	1	20
1900	3.91	35‡	19	6	20
1910	4.99	39‡	25	11	20
1920	7.88	47‡	34	15	26
1930	11.89	43‡	40	18	27
1940	14.49	40	41	13	28
1950	26.94	31	24	10	25
1960	31.27	36	35	10	22
1970	43.73	41	41	13	25
1971	45.19	42	42	14	22§
1972	45.89	42	42	16	22§
1973	45.41	43	42	18	23§
1974	41.35	45	42	19	24§
1975	42.34	45	43	21	24‖
1976	43.55	45	44	23	24‖

SOURCES.—U.S. Department of Health, Education, and Welfare, National Center for Education Statistics, *Digest of Education Statistics, 1976* (Washington, D.C.: Government Printing Office, 1976), and *Projections of Education Statistics to 1984–85* (Washington, D.C.: Government Printing Office, 1977; and estimates of the National Center for Education Studies.
*Figures for undergraduate students are degree credit and prior to 1974 include students enrolled for first professional degrees.
†Percentages should be viewed with care since the annual total of doctoral degrees conferred in 1890 and before was less than 150.
‡U.S. Department of Health, Education, and Welfare, National Center for Education Statistics, *Digest of Education Statistics, 1973* (Washington, D.C.: Government Printing Office, 1973), p. 75, tables 89, 100.
§Data are estimated and represent full-time faculty only.
‖Data represent full-time faculty only.

themselves in some way to support themselves and their families successfully as adults.[10] Gradually, college attendance became more typical for men, particularly if they were white. However, since society had quite different expectations for women, the new rationale for college attendance did not apply to them. Barbara Welter has described the quintessential female traits in the prescriptive literature for women from 1820–60, views that lingered on later in the century, as piety, purity, submissiveness, and domesticity.[11] Being an undergraduate with the independence it implied, the opportunities it afforded for subsequent employment, and the threats to purity and piety that the campus provided violated these canons. By virtue of the smallness of the original undergraduate body, this group of men and women became an elite in the classical sense of that term, a group set apart from the mass of society and potentially exempt from its strictures. As Rose Coser and others have noted, "Where the position of women is securely subordinate, a few exceptional achievers do not threaten the system and their achievement gains salience over their womanhood."[12] This was the case for undergraduate women until the base of undergraduates began to broaden in the middle years of the twentieth century.[13]

Next, except for the Roman Catholic men's colleges, the Ivy League institutions have persistently been the most resistant to admission of women, as undergraduates, graduate students, or faculty. Yale and Princeton accepted their first women undergraduates in 1969. The first woman to be appointed to a tenured professorship at Harvard was Cecelia Payne-Gaposhkin, an astronomer, in 1956; at Yale, Mary Wright in Chinese history in 1959; at Princeton, Suzanne Keller, a sociologist, in 1969; and at Columbia, Marjorie Nicolson in English in 1941.

The current absence of women from the faculties of the major research-oriented institutions is well documented. Although women constitute currently 24 percent of the college and university faculties across the nation, they make up a much smaller percentage of the faculties of the most prestigious institutions, particularly in the tenured ranks. The proportion of women in the arts and sciences faculties at Harvard is 3 percent; at Yale, 1.6 percent; at Princeton, 1 percent; at Stanford, 5 percent; at Berkeley, 5.6 percent; at Chicago, 5 percent; and at Columbia, 5 percent.[14] The point, of course, is that if these institutions became the models for higher education, then their practice of excluding women as students and markedly limiting their role on faculties and in administration was broadly noticed throughout the remaining institutions.

Though other institutions could not afford the financial luxury of limiting their undergraduates to men only, it was easy enough to follow the lead of prestigious institutions in selecting predominantly male faculties and administrations. At the faculty level, the differences between women's opportunities and men's have been most noticeable. If, as Richard Lester has told us, the merit system was working in faculty hiring (despite the absence of Jews from most faculties until the forties or Catholics from many philosophy and religion departments until later than that), the absence of women simply meant that they did not stack up against men at the best places.[15] An institution that was trying to move up the prestige ladder, then, was well advised to recognize this fact and treat its own faculty women accordingly. After World War II, several of the women's colleges made a deliberate effort to increase the number of men on their faculties, presumably in the hope that this was a sign of improved quality, or at least, status.

The reasoning, of course, became circular. If research was the way, and nearly the only way, to achieve recognition in academe, then access to the research facilities and to the time and money to utilize them, was essential. Increasingly in the last twenty-five years, the model of the solitary researcher poring over an Icelandic saga in the privacy of his or her study (an undertaking that requires much diligence but not much financial outlay for materials) has been replaced by that of a team working together on a common project with outside funds. This, particularly true in the physical and natural sciences, has even begun to permeate the social sciences. The major universities, with the best facilities for such research, are often most knowledgeable about outside sources of money. Furthermore, in these institutions, teaching loads typically have been less strenuous and more oriented toward the research interests of the faculty. Finally, these are the places that abound with graduate students, that indispensable, inexpensive, and often inventive supporting staff for researchers. Persons of either sex find it extremely difficult to do major research when isolated from proper facilities and from an environment that supports such endeavors.

In an earlier era, when teaching skills were more highly prized and when concern for students seemed more important, it was not such a disadvantage for women faculty to be concentrated in institutions which do not make major contributions to research. Women's "natural" talents seemed to make it appropriate for them to focus their energies in the instructional and nurturing activities that characterized the revered professors of past generations but that are now less important as a source of respect. Typically, women have also faithfully responded to the committee assignments that are time consuming, often dull, and sometimes necessary. Service there represents loyalty to the institution, another virtue not highly regarded today. Men who have been dedicated teachers, concerned advisers to students, and dutiful committee members have suffered the same professional disadvantages as the women who have performed these tasks.

Finally, shifts in the expectations of society for women and of women for themselves occurred during the twentieth century. A principal change in the years from 1920 to 1960 has been toward a uniform standard by which all women would be judged. The attitudes toward women are indicative of a general development in America toward a common cultural standard. The roots of such efforts lie undoubtedly in the Americanization campaigns of the early years of the century that reached their flowering during the years of World War I. By the late 1920s and 1930s, that common cultural standard was emerging. Class differences were being minimized as both the lower and upper classes gravitated toward the attitudes and beliefs associated with the middle class. Regionalism played less of a role; accents, except for southern ones, began to disappear from American speech. Even ethnic differences were reduced as Jews anglicized their names and Slavs and Scandinavians dropped syllables and unwieldy consonants from theirs.

The peak of this cultural homogenization probably came about during World War II when the common experience of military service, much more widespread for American men than World War I had been, brought together Irish-Americans from Boston and Hoosier Protestants. Even the traditional distinctions between officers and enlisted men and their distinct social class origins blurred during World War II under the pressure of mass mobilization. By 1950 listening to network radio was a national experience for Americans. Comparable adventures on television were approaching. The proportion of the rural population was dropping steadily, having fallen below 50 percent in 1920. In short, by 1970 nearly 90 percent of Americans lived in an urban setting, whether it was town, suburb, or city.[16] Information reached them via national magazines, networks, and wire services. Big purveyors of information were getting larger; the small ones were dropping by the wayside. The homogenization of American culture had become so noticeable that by the early fifties Will Herberg and others were arguing for cultural pluralism as an antidote to the monotony of American life.[17] Such a call won few listeners in that decade, and not until the sixties did it find adherents.

The feminine ideal—as opposed to the feminist one—that won such wide support in the early and middle years of the twentieth century was a constellation of virtues: youth, appearance, acquiescence, and domesticity. Every woman was supposed to enhance her youth and her appearance and foster her natural predilection for acquiescence and domesticity. The parallel between these qualities and those previously noted as the female virtues a century earlier (piety, purity, submissiveness, and domesticity) is remarkable and points to the legitimacy in many minds of the persistence of these qualities as natural or "divinely right." Yet, piety was not important for the secular twentieth-century woman. Neither was purity, particularly after the availability of effective contraception. For many Americans, the fabled emancipation of women in the twentieth century amounted to a rejection of those two nineteenth-century virtues and adoption of the twentieth-century one: acquiescence. Finally, the eternal theme of domesticity recurred. The American woman of the mid-twentieth century was to appear young, beautiful, and ardent on demand. She was also to find happiness in her home. Many found that combination difficult.

Unlike the nineteenth century's prescriptive behavior for women, the twentieth century's was not in conflict with college attendance. In fact, undergraduate study was either consistent with or irrelevant to it. To be an undergraduate became proper youthful behavior for a young woman, whose appearance was not harmed by such a step. The posture of any student should be acquiescent, not assertive. In addition, college was frequently considered the ideal place to meet the one with whom the domestic life would be shared. A woman reporter on the *New York Times* described the college girl in 1962: "After four years of studying everything from ancient art to modern psychology, the average college girl views her future through a wedding band. Despite compelling evidence that she will be working at 35, by choice or necessity, today's 21-year-old woman has difficulty looking beyond the ceremonies of her own marriage and her babies' christenings."[18] College had begun to play the role that high school had in the lives of women at the turn of the century, for many simply a pleasant interlude on the way to growing up.

Graduate school, however, was a different matter. For most women, the psychological and financial factors considered in that decision were much more serious than those for college, because graduate school was still seen as a prelude to the professions. The twentieth-century female virtues were seriously at odds with a career. It is difficult to imagine anything more hostile to professionalism than eroticism. Professionalism supposedly implies a commitment to rationality and rigorous objective standards. Eroticism, with its component of sensuality, is the antithesis of such rationality. If a woman were to be truly a woman in contemporary America, she had to have some qualities that qualified as erotic. The possession of those characteristics so necessary to her definition as a woman denied her professionalism. While it is not a bad thing for a man to be sexy or good-looking, those qualities are not as essential to his self-definition. For him to fail to be assertive or for him to place the responsibilities of his home and family over those of his job, however, would lead many to question his professional commitment. Yet these were precisely the expectations for women.

For women, then, graduate school and, even more, completion of it with the ritual of one's thesis "defense" (a nonacquiescent act certainly), placed strains on women's self-perceptions and so on society's perceptions of them. The attempted resolutions of these dilemmas varied. One common manner of handling the confusion was to adopt that final, stalwart feminine virtue, domesticity, by marrying and having children. Women graduate students began to marry, a tremendous change from an earlier era when 75 percent of the women who earned Ph.D.'s between 1875 and 1924 remained spinsters.[19] Such efforts to harmonize domestic responsibilities and those of the profession were sometimes difficult, but they represented the movement, which increased during the sixties, of women seeking full participation in society and referring less to their legitimate "spheres."

With piety and purity gone as laudable feminine qualities, another complication for some women graduate students appeared: a distinctive involvement with her professor. This encounter was sexual, either implicitly or explicitly. Probably over 90 percent of graduate school professors are men, most of whom find women attractive intellectually and, potentially, in other realms as well. For most professors, undoubtedly, the potentiality does not become an actuality. However, the proportion of women graduate students who encounter professors whose interest in them transcends the academic is high. Most women find this attention flattering but confusing, since the woman is never clear (and sometimes this is an ambiguity she compounds by her own actions) whether the interest displayed in her is a reflection of her scholarly promise or of something else. As yet, social scientists have not formally attempted to assess this factor's affect on women graduate students, but informal discussions about it among women who have been in graduate school do occur. There are no direct parallels for male graduate students, except perhaps for homosexual involvements. These, too, have not been reported in the otherwise abundant social science literature, but their absence from the literature does not confirm their absence from life.

Such complications, those of the variance between the expectations for women and the professional commitment required for completion of graduate school, are reflected in the substantially reduced proportion of women receiving doctorates in the forties and the fifties. From more than 15 percent of the doctoral recipients in the early thirties, women fell to below 10 percent in the fifties (see table 1). A study conducted by the American Historical Association of a small number of leading coeducational liberal arts college history departments showed a decline of women full professors of history from 16 percent to 0 percent in 1970.[20] In 1974, only Barnard, Wellesley, and Radcliffe, of the Seven Sisters Colleges, had women presidents, although Smith has now joined the group with the first woman president in its history, and Vassar with its second. The most recent figures from the National Center for Education Statistics reveal that, despite affirmative action programs, a decline is still evident at the senior faculty positions. The percentage of women full professors and associate professors fell between 1974 and 1975, while salary disparities between male and female professors grew.[21] The women of the forties and fifties absorbed the new values and withdrew from the professional arena. They married at very high rates at more youthful ages and had lots of babies. The birth rate reached its peak in 1957, at which time the average age for first marriage for women was just over 20. To marry young and to have several children was to insure following some of the canons of femininity. It also made it very difficult to combine a meaningful personal life with a productive professional one.

In the last several years, many women, seeming to recognize this difficulty, have taken steps to avoid it. The rate of women receiving doctorates has grown substantially since 1970, more than a percent per year, an increase unique in the last century.[22] The birth rate has fallen; the marriage age has risen; the divorce rate has increased. Women are speaking openly about their legitimate search for meaningful work, a search that a decade or two ago was often cloaked with such self-abnegating phrases as, "I'm only looking for a little something part time to help out a bit," or, more proudly, "I need work to put my husband through medical school." Although her own standards are less clear, the educated woman of the mid-seventies is less inclined to admit allegiance to the female virtues of the past several decades.

Conceivably, the monolithic ideal of the research university may also be breaking up under the pressure of new demands for higher education. In many quarters, concerns for "lifelong education" are being enthusiastically expressed. Previously, adult education programs were geared to housewives returning to school or preparing to reenter the work force. Now, however, colleges and universities may be amending their definitions to include all adults as a major part of the student body. Should this be so, opportunities for flexibility in scheduling and career, heretofore a hallmark of the life of the professional woman, may come to characterize that of the professional man as well. This may bring with it the chance to meld significant commitments to both work and family, however that family may be defined. Continuing education may then prove to be another example of innovation in which programs originally designed for women are seen to benefit men as well and thereby are permitted to enter the academic mainstream. Should my guesses about the future prove true, and it is not at all clear that they will, the educational diversity that benefited women in the late nineteenth century may reappear to do so again in the late twentieth.

1. U.S. Department of Health, Education, and Welfare, National Center for Education Statistics, *Digest of Education Statistics* (Washington, D.C.: Government Printing Office, 1973), p. 75, table 89.

2. Ibid.

3. Ibid., p. 84, table 100.

4. A jump in 1880 had brought the proportion of women faculty to 32 percent, but the numbers of faculty were then so small and so ill defined that the proportion is probably a statistical anomaly (ibid., and Rudolph C. Blitz, "Women in the Professions, 1870–1970," *Monthly Labor Review* 97, no. 5 [May 1974]: 37).

5. Blitz, p. 34.

6. Ibid.

7. U.S. Department of Health, Education, and Welfare, p. 84, table 100.

8. Marjorie Nicolson, "The Rights and Privileges Pertaining Thereto," *Journal of the American Association of University Women* 31, no. 3 (April 1938): 136.

9. Editorial, "Women in our Economy," *Journal of the American Association of University Women* 31, no. 3 (April 1938): 171.

10. Robert McCaughey has observed in his study of the Barnard College faculty that "men have been able to maximize the opportunities of academic prosperity, while women have been able to minimize the disadvantages of academic adversity" ("A Statistical Profile of the Barnard College Faculty, 1900–1974," mimeographed [New York: Department of History, Barnard College, Columbia University, 1975], p. 16).

11. Barbara Welter, "The Cult of True Womanhood: 1820–1860," *American Quarterly* 18 (Summer 1966): 151–74. For a regional revision, see Julie Ray Jeffrey, "Women in the Southern Farmers' Alliance," *Feminist Studies* 3, no. 3 (Winter 1975): 72–91.

12. Rose Coser, review of *Changing Women in Changing Society*, *Science* 182, no. 411 (November 2, 1973): 471.

13. Among the many studies which would enhance our knowledge of higher education would be one comparing the social class origins of men and women as undergraduates and faculty over the last century. I suspect, but as yet cannot document, that women students and faculty came from a higher social class than men, a finding borne out by Robert McCaughey in his previously cited study of the Barnard faculty from 1870–1970. Certainly, current data on undergraduates reveal that fewer bright daughters of poor families attend college than similarly gifted sons. If that is the case generally, it reaffirms

my principal point about the greater difficulty of a middle- or lower-class girl emancipating herself from the expectations of domesticity in adult life.

14. These figures were compiled by administrators at the named institutions and supplied to the author in the spring of 1976.

15. Richard A. Lester, *Antibias Regulation of Universities: Faculty Problems and Their Solutions* (New York: McGraw-Hill Book Co., 1974).

16. U.S. Bureau of the Census, *Statistical Abstracts of the United States: 1974*, 95th ed. (Washington, D.C.: Government Printing Office, 1974), p. 20, table 20.

17. Will Herberg, *Protestant Catholic Jew* (Garden City, N.Y.: Doubleday & Co., 1956).

18. Marilyn Bender, "College Girl Often Sees No Future But Marriage," *New York Times* (March 26, 1962).

19. William H. Chafe, *The American Woman* (New York: Oxford University Press, 1972), p. 100.

20. American Historical Association, "Report of the Ad Hoc Committee on the Status of Women in the Historical Profession" (Washington, D.C.: American Historical Association, 1973).

21. Reported in *Higher Education and National Affairs* 25, no. 4 (January 30, 1976): 1. While this article was at press, Bryn Mawr and Mt. Holyoke also appointed women presidents.

22. Betty M. Vetter, "Women, Men, and the Doctorate," *Science* 187, no. 4174 (January 31, 1975): 301.

Earlier versions of this paper have been given as talks, and I am indebted to persons who raised questions or made comments on those occasions. In particular, I have appreciated the comments of my colleagues, Marion Kilson and Hilda Kahne, and the assistance of Sally Schwager. I also wish to thank the John Simon Guggenheim Foundation for support during the period that the initial work on this project was begun.

The Turning Point in American Jesuit Higher Education: The Standardization Controversy between the Jesuits and the North Central Association, 1915-1940

Lester F. Goodchild

TO REDRESS THE ANOMALIES of the nineteenth century American college, the federal government, private associations, and philanthropic foundations devised various plans by the turn of the century to encourage greater uniformity among institutions of higher learning. During the next twenty years, the most successful approaches came from the Association of American Universities (AAU) and the North Central Association of Colleges and Secondary Schools (NCA). They introduced modern collegiate standards and certified whether member institutions conformed. Most public and private universities or colleges joined these associations or other regional accrediting bodies because they reflected or enhanced their own missions, policies, and practices.

However, Catholic university and college educators faced ideological and practical problems with these new mandates for American higher education. In particular, the Society of Jesus which enrolled 38,200 students at its 26 institutions of higher learning in 1921 confronted a perplexing dilemma.[2] To what extent, if at all, should its colleges and universities adopt these American standards? Such an accommodation threatened to alter substantially their historic governance structure, three century old *Ratio Studiorum*, and professional preparation of clerical faculty, all of which constituted the distinctive character of the Jesuit educational apostolate in the United States.

This controversy raged among American Jesuits until the Second World War, during which Jesuit universities and colleges adopted the NCA's standards and affiliated with the association. This turning point in American Jesuit higher education changed its governance structure, collegiate mission, faculty caliber, and curricular offerings. As a result, Jesuit universities and colleges embarked on an Americanization course which brought them into the mainstream of American higher education during the past twenty years.[3]

To reveal the dynamics of this controversy, this paper describes how the complex relations between the NCA and midwestern Jesuit higher education from 1915 to 1940 affected the development of Loyola University of Chicago. Chartered in 1870 as St. Ignatius College, this Jesuit men's college exemplified how the NCA influenced not only Loyola's own evolution toward American university stature but also the eight other midwestern Jesuit universities and colleges in the Missouri Province.[4] This inference is possible because of the highly centralized and coordinated structure of the Society's educational apostolates. Following the Constitutions of the Society of Jesus, the governance of higher education operated on three levels. The superior general who resided in Rome administered all Jesuit colleges and universities through regional superiors, i.e., provincials, and local superiors, i.e., rector-presidents of educational institutions.[5] Furthermore, when American Jesuit educators began national boards to coordinate their activities, their universities and colleges became a cohesive educational system. The story of Loyola University thus discloses how new American ideas, institutions, and social forces changed significantly the historic educational philosophy and practice of Jesuit higher education which comprises the largest group of private institutions in American higher education.[6]

This controversy is explored by tracing the beginnings of the accrediting associations and the initial Catholic response, by delineating the three stages of the standardization controversy and its effects on Loyola University of Chicago, and by evaluating the importance of these developments for American Jesuit higher education.

I.

During the latter part of the nineteenth century, the diverse practices of universities, colleges, academies, and high schools created great confusion about the nature of American higher education. To alleviate this problem, reform efforts arose. As early as 1870, the United States Bureau of Education published a list of collegiate institutions which conferred baccalaureate degrees.[7] By 1886, the bureau established quality rankings when it differentiated some women's colleges which were not "organized upon the usual plan of arts colleges."[8] While these listings provided a comprehensive enumeration of such institutions, the bureau's hope to improve the quality of their education never materialized. Greater strides in achieving uniformity among collegiate institutions occurred through the development of national associations, such as, the National Association of State Universities in 1896, the Association of Catholic Colleges in 1899, the Association of American Universities in 1900, and the Association of Land-Grant Colleges in 1900.[9] They intended to impose common standards on collegiate institutions by regulating their internal policies. Introducing a third approach, the Carnegie Foundation for the Advancement of Teaching offered charitable contributions to those institutions which maintained certain high standards, namely requiring students to complete at least fourteen units of high school credit for admission, employing six or more full-time professors, offering a four-year liberal arts and science course, and attaining a $200,000 endowment.[10] By 1906, it selected forty-five colleges to receive this funding; other institutions revised their policies to become similarly eligible. This foundation thus succeeded in bringing about the most immediate changes within American colleges.

However, the associations produced longer lasting results. The National

Association of State Universities met with representatives from four recently-organized regional associations, such as, the NCA, in 1906 to "present a plan ... for establishing, preserving, and interpreting in common terms standards for admission to college ..."[11] The group resolved not only this issue but also decided to create common standards for colleges during its day and a half meeting. This development launched the *standardization* movement, which later became known as *accreditation*. By 1909, the NCA formulated standards for its future affiliated colleges and universities. During the next year, the association established procedures for evaluating its member institutions. In 1911, an event determined which of the three agencies encouraging American college standards would assume the task. The AAU asked the Bureau of Education to rank colleges and universities in the United States according to their quality. After its effort leaked to the press, the bureau received such strong protests from college and university presidents that it suppressed publication of its five-tiered classification.[12] As a result, the bureau ceased its efforts to create national standards. Subsequently, the AAU began this task, although it concentrated on universities.[13] The AAU limited its focus to these institutions, because the NCA developed a viable organization for the prescription of new American collegiate standards in the Midwest.

Having established its spheres of influence, the NCA set the pace for the other three regional accrediting associations and midwestern institutions of higher learning. In 1913, it published its first list of standards for affiliated member colleges: (1) a student's admission depended upon the completion of 14 units of high school credit; (2) the conferral of the baccalaureate required 120 collegiate credits; (3) an acceptable course of studies comprised 8 departments; (4) faculty members needed a master of arts or doctor of philosophy degree, with the head of each department held by a terminally-degreed faculty member; and (5) faculty instruction should not exceed between 15 and 18 hours per semester.[14] With this adoption, NCA member institutions offered their students approved degrees which enabled them to enroll in AAU-affiliated university graduate and professional programs. Furthermore, such institutional recognition prompted philanthropic foundations to grant greater financial support. On the other hand, non-affiliated colleges jeopardized their academic reputations, limited their graduates' further study, and undermined their future development.

These events forced American Catholic higher educators to develop their own standards, since most of their institutions could not meet the NCA standards. While Georgetown College had opened as the first Catholic institution of higher learning in 1789, the state of Catholic higher education by the turn of the twentieth century found Catholic institutions struggling to differentiate their secondary and collegiate programs as they moved from their six-year Continental secondary-collegiate programs to the four-year American college pattern. Yet, significant advances had occurred in Catholic institutions, such as Georgetown, St. Louis, Notre Dame, and Fordham had been thriving colleges for more than fifty years and had been experimenting with graduate studies for at least twenty-five.[15] The Jesuits operated three of these five institutions. Furthermore, Catholic University of America, established by the American bishops as a graduate institution in 1889, represented the flagship of Catholic higher education as a charter member of the AAU. Attempting to coordinate these three levels of Catholic higher education, the Catholic Educational Association (CEA)—which had replaced the Association of Catholic Colleges in 1904—established guidelines for its members in 1915. It patterned them after the NCA standards: 16 high school units for admission, 128 credit hours for graduation (the 8 hours in addition to the NCA list allowed for religious courses during the four years), 7 departments within the college, a baccalaureate degree for the faculty, and 16 teaching hours maximum for faculty instruction per semester. The greatest disparity between these standards acknowledged the deficient Catholic faculty training which had resulted from a large preponderance of foreign clergy. In actuality, the CEA formulated these standards to demonstrate its *intention* to promote quality. Its lenient certification allowed Catholic colleges to gain CEA affiliation as most Catholic colleges could not meet its standards. There is little evidence to suggest the CEA would have done this without the NCA action. The CEA thus provided an organizational credential for Catholic universities and colleges.

On the other hand, some Catholic colleges and universities under the leadership of more modern religious educators had marshalled their resources sufficiently to meet the NCA standards. The University of Notre Dame affiliated with the NCA as a charter member in 1913 under the enlightened leadership of Provincial John Zahm, C.S.C. and President John W. Cavanaugh, C.S.C. They had little fear that NCA affiliation would compromise the Congregation of Holy Cross's governance or educational philosophy at Notre Dame. Undoubtedly, Zahm and Cavanaugh believed this association strengthened Notre Dame's academic reputation. Their action demonstrated Notre Dame's historic propensity to adopt American innovations in higher education.

However, the Jesuits failed to apply for NCA membership or institute CEA recommendations. Many factors contributed to their resistance. Concerning the NCA affiliation, the Jesuits rejected the aegis of a non-Catholic association. They believed this action jeopardized the historic mission, governance structure, *Ratio Studiorum*, and faculty preparation of the Society's educational apostolate. The Constitutions of the Society of Jesus also prohibited any external regulation of Jesuit colleges and universities. Yet, American Jesuits soon realized they had progressively less choice in this matter. There were several reasons. Other NCA-approved Catholic and non-Catholic institutions grew faster than Jesuit colleges. Notre Dame registered 360 arts and letters students within its 1,000 enrollment by 1920. Conversely, Loyola University in Chicago had only 124 such students within its 2,200 enrollment. Other midwestern non-Jesuit Catholic colleges also provided greater curricular flexibility. Notre Dame offered five baccalaureate programs with variations from the classical course to different science concentrations. On the other hand, St. Ignatius College offered only the 1832 *Ratio Studiorum* classical course—with its predominant Greek and Latin concentrations. Furthermore, students at other Catholic colleges needed only 128 hours to graduate, while the Jesuit course entailed approximately 140 hours. Catholic students also realized that admission to graduate studies at AAU-recognized universities depended upon their graduation from an NCA institution. While the Jesuits realized the seriousness of these problems, something more crucial than the issues of control, enrollments, curricular flexibility, or student access to graduate education worried them in the initial heat of this controversy: the very survival of the *Ratio Studiorum* in the United States.

II.

The first stage of the standardization controversy thus concerned whether or not midwestern Jesuit educators would revise their curriculum to accommodate the changing realities within American Catholic higher education. The Jesuits needed to reorganize their curriculum to compete more favorably with other Catholic colleges which met NCA standards. However, dismantling the historic concentrations of the *Ratio* and imposing departmental structures could not be undertaken by individual Jesuit institutions. Permission for such changes could be granted only by the Society's superior general.[16] Furthermore, these adaptations required the coordination of all Jesuit institutions throughout the four American provinces. This process took five years.

To understand the radical nature of these changes, an analysis of the turn of the century American Jesuit college and its curriculum is needed. "The Aim of College Education" in the *Catalogue of St. Ignatius College, 1902-1903* emphasized the nineteenth century concepts of religion, mental discipline, and cultural refinement. These ideas furthered the Jesuit apostolic mission to develop Christian leaders through education, Jesuit administrators contended their curriculum laid a broad and solid course for subsequent specialized or professional studies. They rejected electivism and resisted departmental structuring for they believed such practices undermined the humanistic ideals of Jesuit education.[17]

The Jesuit single baccalaureate degree program consisted of language, philosophy, and science courses, structured with Catholic content (see table 1). There were several reasons for this. First, St. Ignatius College's course continued the Counter-Reformation *pietas litterata* tradition with its Christian literature orientation, reinforced by the 1828 Yale Report and Newman's *The Idea of a University*.[18] Second, its philosophical concentration enabled students who intended to study for the priesthood to receive the necessary training before beginning theological studies at a seminary. Known as a *collegium mixtum*, this college offered specialized philosophical and classical studies for students entering clerical, professional, or commercial occupations which the Catholic bishops had approved at the Third Plenary Council in 1884.[19] Third, a central part of this curriculum entailed religion classes and moral training. Religion classes thus taught students basic Catholic dogma, doctrine, and morality twice weekly. Besides this, the Jesuits required Catholic students "to be present at the Chapel exercises, to make an annual retreat, and to approach the Sacraments at least once a month."[20] Maintaining the secondary character of Catholic education during the nineteenth century, these chapel exercises required Catholic students to attend *daily* Mass until 1917.[21] In this manner, the Jesuit educational apostolate tightly intertwined educational and religious mandates:

> ...the Jesuit System does not share the delusion of those who seem to imagine that education, understood as an enriching and stimulating part of the intellectual faculties, has of itself a morally elevating influence in human life.... Religion alone can purify the heart and guide and strengthen the will. This being the case, the Jesuit System aims at developing side by side the moral and intellectual faculties of the student, and sending forth into the world men of sound judgment, of acute and rounded intellect, of upright and manly conscience. It maintains, that, to be effective, morality is to be taught continuously; it must be the underlying base, the vital force supporting and animating the whole organic structure of education.[22]

This historic fusion soon faced multiple challenges.

Although the Chicago Jesuit community had resisted changing the college, its new leadership launched the institution on a university course during the first decade of the twentieth century. In 1904, President Henry J. Dumbach, SJ. (1858-1909) purchased land to expand St. Ignatius's collegiate program on the north side of Chicago. Partial instruction began in 1913. President Alexander J. Burrowes, SJ. (1853-1927) rechartered the college as Loyola University in 1909—just as he had done at Marquette University in 1907—after being challenged by another Chicago Catholic college which became a university, allowing Jesuit alumni to begin a law school, and receiving several requests from freestanding medical schools for university affiliation. Burrowes represented the midwestern progressive Jesuit who enabled the Society's colleges to appropriate some of the developments within American higher education. The major reason for this expansion here and at other Jesuit colleges came from the increasing demand of Catholic students who wished professional education, but found difficulty in gaining admission to non-Catholic professional schools. In this way, Burrowes hoped to establish a "Jesuit university of high rank."[23] The Jesuits thus moved away from such American collegiate models as Amherst, Oberlin, and Swarthmore.

While Loyola University with its professional schools grew, the college stagnated because Burrowes could not change the curriculum with its religious dimension. Indeed, its educational and religious curricular design and intense religious discipline made it unappealing to graduates from local Catholic academics and high schools. In the 1912-1913 school year, Loyola's undergraduate liberal arts course with its 47 students comprised less than ten percent of the 647 student body.[24]

TABLE 1

ST. IGNATIUS COLLEGE BACHELOR OF ARTS COURSE, 1907-1908

Class Year and Classes[a]	First Semester	Second Semester
Freshman:		
Latin (5)[b]	Cicero, Virgil, Horace, Christian poets	Cicero, Horace, Livy, Christian writers
Greek (4)	Basil, Homer	Homer, Lyric Poets
English (4)	Literary Analysis	Lyric and Epic Poetry
History (2)	Papacy and Empire	Rise of the Papacy
Mathematics (4)	Plane Trigonometry	Spherical Trigonometry

Subject (hours)	First	Second
Science (5)	Chemistry I	Chemistry II
Elocution (1)	Analysis/Interpretation	(same)
Religion (2)		
Elective	German, French	
Sophomore:		
Philosophy (4)	(none)	Dialects & Applied Logic
Latin (5)	Cicero, Horace, Epistles, Tacitus	Cicero, Juvenal, Tacitus
Greek (4)	Demosthenes, Chrysostom	Demosthenes, Sophocles
English (4)	Theory of Rhetoric, Rhetorical Analysis, History and Criticism	American Literature
History (2)	History of Religious Revolution	Renaissance
Mathematics (4)	Algebra	Algebra
Sciences (5)	Physics I	Physics II
Elocution (1)	Oratorical and Dramatic Selections	(same)
Religion (2)		
Elective	German, French	
Junior:		
Philosophy (5)	General Metaphysics/Cosmology	Psychology
Latin (2)	Cicero, Platus	Cicero, Terence
Greek (2)	Euripides, Hecuba or Medea	Herodotus, Thucydides
English (2)	English Literature	French Literature
History (2)	Philosophy of History, Nature and General Laws of History	Political Economy
Mathematics (5)	Astronomy	Analytical Geometry
Elocution (1)	Public Speaking and Debate	(same)
Civics (1)		
Religion (2)		
Elective		
Science (5)	Chemistry, Physics, Biology	(same)
Mathematics		
Languages	German, French	
Senior:		
Philosophy (5)	Natural Theology/Ethics	Ethics
Latin (2)	Cicero, Seneca	Church Fathers
Greek (2)	Aristophanes	Plato
English (2)	Dramatic Literature	Dramatic Literature
History (2)	History of Philosophy	History of Philosophy
Mathematics	Calculus	
Religion (2)		
Elective (5)		
Science		
Math		
Languages	German, French	

Source: *Catalogue of St. Ignatius College, 1907-1908*, pp. 13-22, LUCA.

a This course of studies began during the 1880s and continued at the institution until 1920.
b The numbers inside the parentheses indicate the numbers of hours per week that the class was held

The Jesuits took radical steps to improve collegiate enrollment at Loyola and their other colleges and universities in the Midwest. The first move came when Jesuit prefects of studies who supervised the academic affairs of these institutions met at St. Louis in July 1916 to discuss the changing conditions in American colleges and their meager enrollments. As a result, they asked Missouri Provincial Alexander J. Burrowes, who had been appointed by the general two years earlier, to form a regular committee to standardize the curriculum in their high schools and colleges.[25] In response to their request, he called a meeting of the rector-presidents of the nine Missouri universities and colleges in April 1917. The presidents focused most of their attention on declining enrollments. They suggested five causes:

(1) undue length of college course in general; (2) lack of variety in the courses offered; (3) insistence on Greek; (4) influence of professional schools in admitting students: either without preliminary college work at all or with only one or two years of such work; and (5) prevalence of the commercial and money-making spirit and diminishing esteem for college education.[26]

Four of these problems would be eliminated, if they abided by NCA standards. One of their many solutions to these problems included this mandate. The provincial wanted a greater consensus.

To obtain this, Burrowes called the prefects of studies and the presidents to a meeting at Campion College in Wisconsin during April 1919.[27] The assembly concurred with the problems identified at the 1917 meeting and proposed many recommendations for the future of Jesuit higher education. First, the Jesuits claimed their low college enrollments could be remedied by allowing greater variety and flexibility in their curriculum and by separating physically their high schools and colleges. Second, they requested all colleges to affiliate with the NCA or the AAU. Such a mandate required extensive changes in the Jesuit curriculum. Third, to accomplish this, they established a curriculum committee to suggest ways of (1) adopting major and minor concentrations, (2) revising their curricular nomenclature to follow other American public and private institutions of higher learning, and (3) shortening the length of the collegiate curriculum to 120 hours for graduation. Their fourth and fifth recommendations suggested ways to achieve this curricular reduction. They decided to eliminate a significant part of the Ratio by asking the general to drop Greek as a requirement for the baccalaureate degree. The Jesuits also wanted to reduce the number of hours in philosophy to a minimum of six semester hours, because the *collegium mixtum* college was no longer necessary with the rise of diocesan high school and collegiate seminaries. Finally, sixth, they wanted one of the Missouri province universities to establish a graduate department for Jesuit seminarians who could take specialized studies, perhaps leading to the doctorate.[28] These resolutions determined the policies at Jesuit universities and colleges for the next twenty years.

The provincial committee on curriculum developed a plan to implement the radical resolutions of the 1919 assembly. Chaired by John B. Furay, SJ. (1873-1952), the fourteenth president of Loyola University, with Albert C. Fox, S.J. (1878-1934), the rector of Campion College, as its secretary, the committee advocated a tremendous change in the American *Ratio Studiorum* by July: 128 hours for graduation similar to other Catholic colleges as suggested by the CEA and mandated by the NCA. To accomplish this, Furay and Fox made extensive course reductions in the 138 hour Jesuit collegiate curriculum to allow for a major-minor sequence and electives. They eliminated 58 required course hours by dropping Greek and reducing Latin which were crucial elements of the *pietas litterata* curriculum. On the other hand, they dropped only 10 philosophy hours rather than the 20 suggested by the assembly. Since this subject represented a traditional way of teaching Christian ideas and dogma, especially through the philosophy of Thomas Aquinas, the Jesuits retained a strong philosophy concentration as a means to promote their apostolic purpose in operating institutions of higher learning. The curriculum would change in the following way:

Subject	Hours Now Required	Hours Recommended
Latin	22	16
Greek	16	0
English	38	12
History	6	6
Mathematics	6	6
Science	16	16
Philosophy	26	16
Religion	8	8
Total	138	80[29]

Their proposal drastically revised the Jesuit *Ratio* and dismantled the philosophical concentrations endemic to the *collegium mixtum* pattern of the nineteenth century American Catholic college.

On July 31, 1919, the new Missouri provincial, Francis X. McMenamy, S.J. (1872-1949), informed the Jesuit presidents that Superior General Wlodimir Ledochowski (1886-1942) had approved their recommendations. They could confer the baccalaureate degree without Greek.[30] When McMenamy distributed the final collegiate curriculum revision a year later, his remarks pointed to a new age in Jesuit higher education which embodied elements from American higher education: "... the newly drafted collegiate curriculum, preserving, as it does, the substance of the *Ratio* while it interprets our traditional system in the terms of current educational procedure, may under God be the harbinger of a new season of prosperity and growth for the college departments of the Province."[31] The first stage of the standardization controversy thus had ended in favor of accommodation to American influences emanating from the NCA. The Jesuit *Ratio* had taken on a distinct American design.

III.

While the general had approved the Missouri province proposals, other Jesuit and Catholic presidents resisted this movement toward affiliation with the regional accrediting bodies. They hoped to use the CEA as *the* standardizing agency for Catholic higher education.[32] The second stage of the standardization controversy centered on this dilemma. Again, Albert Fox played the key role in convincing other Catholic educators to acquiesce to the accrediting agencies. Elected president of the CEA's department of colleges and secondary schools in 1920, Fox held a commanding position to promote this sentiment. He revealed his rationale for this belief in his invitation to member institutions for the spring 1920 meeting of the CEA. He stated that Catholic colleges were being assailed correctly for their poor condition. To overcome this, Fox called on Catholic educators:

...to obtain official authoritatively final recognition of the fact that ours are truly standard American colleges and universally admitted to be such not only by the Catholic, but also and especially by the non-Catholic college world in America. We owe this in strict justice to our students and their families who have continued until now to give us their time, their money and their confidence without any thought or fear of being penalized for their loyalty later on when they seek admission to professional and other advanced courses in secular institutions of learning.[33]

Fox's argument stressed the need to demonstrate the quality of Catholic higher education and the mandate of social justice.

At the next CEA conference in 1921, Fox redoubled his efforts to sway the Catholic higher education leadership. He presented a paper justifying the need of CEA member institutions to attain accreditation.

Never was the Catholic college that is as truly a college as it is Catholic, more needed than it is in this day and hour. Never was it more imperative for us to impress upon the educators and laymen of the country at large that our standards are the best and the highest, natural and supernatural, human and divine; ... Never was it more distinctly our duty to exert ourselves to the utmost that is in us, determined never to rest until we have proven conclusively to the doubters within that our institutions of higher education are not the less Catholic because they are colleges, and to the cynics without that they are none the less colleges because they are Catholic.[34]

Moreover, Fox organized a panel of speakers who presented the major forces for standardization. He invited Kendric C. Babcock who had created the Bureau of Education's 1911-1912 quality rankings and George F. Zook who was the current specialist in these matters at the bureau. Both authors presented strong justifications for accreditation with astute awareness and sensitivity to the difficulties

Catholic institutions would have in implementing these standards. Fox's efforts largely succeeded during the 1920s as more Jesuit and Catholic institutions applied and received membership within the standardizing agencies. Recognition of his work came in June 1928 when President Nicholas Murray Butler of Columbia University presented Fox with an honorary doctorate and noted his "large influence in the movement to raise the standards and improve the methods of college and university work throughout the United States, easily taking rank with the foremost educational leaders of the land."[35] Fox's efforts had broken the isolationism of Catholic higher education which had begun during the mid-nineteenth century.

Meanwhile, the 1919 Missouri province assembly had pointed the way for Jesuit higher education in the rest of the country. It was the precursor for the Inter-Province Committee on Studies which constituted the first in a series of national Jesuit governance structures to coordinate the internal policies of Jesuit educational institutions in the face of extensive external pressures during most of the twentieth century.[36] At the first meeting of the committee in June 1921, the presidents elected Fox as their chairman, discussed their enrollment crisis, and argued about the demands of the accrediting agencies. They also endorsed the resolutions of the 1917 and 1919 Missouri province committee meetings for the entire Jesuit system: (1) the creation of a committee on studies of each province, (2) the separation of the college and the high schools wherever possible, and (3) the need to standardize their collegiate and high school courses.[37] These recommendations became the new mandate for Jesuit higher education in the United States. When the Inter-Province Committee sent its recommendations which the American Jesuit provincials endorsed to General Ledochowski, he gladly approved them, since problems with the American Jesuit schools had been recognized for some time at the generalate. Furthermore, Ledochowski stipulated that the committee's role was only advisory. Following the Jesuit constitutions, he prohibited the committee or the provincials from approving "any innovation in the collegiate plan of studies without the approval of the Superior General."[38]

With these developments, the Chicago Jesuits instituted the norms from the 1919 provincial meeting of presidents and prefects. President John Furay implemented the curricular changes by the 1920-1921 school year." The introduction of the so-called Latin-English degree and its expanded course offering became the best means for Jesuit colleges to overcome their enrollment problems. In the following year, he gained NCA accreditation for Loyola.[40] Next, Furay reunited both college programs on the north side of Chicago in the 1922-1923 school year, a little over twenty years after the initial suggestion to move the college.[41] These actions produced the long-desired results. While the World War

Strategic Army Training Corps program inflated the student body between 1917 and 1919, the post-war collegiate enrollments declined to a low of only 123 students by the 1921-1922 school year. The next fall, the Reverend William H. Agnew, S.J. (1881-1931), the fifteenth president of Loyola University, saw Loyola's enrollment dramatically increase to 270, a growth of over 100 students from the previous year. Other Jesuit institutions recorded similar improvements throughout the Missouri province.

After the first two stages of the standardization controversy, the Jesuits had revised their curriculum and changed their governance structure to allow a non-Catholic agency to mandate internal policies for their universities and colleges. While the Jesuits had occasionally revised their *Ratio* during its three hundred years, they had never made such radical curricular changes nor allowed such external intervention. The price for making these historic moves would soon be realized.

IV.

As members of the NCA, Jesuit institutions now had to follow its recommendations and norms. This twenty year adjustment represented the third stage of the standardization controversy between the Missouri and Chicago province Jesuits and the NCA.[42] It involved struggles over the training of Jesuit faculties, the apostolic mission of their colleges, and the adequacy of their financial resources. The first shock came in 1923 when the NCA revised its requirements for faculty training.

> The minimum scholastic requirement of all teachers shall be graduation from a college belonging to this association, or the equivalent. The training of the members of the faculty of professorial rank shall include at least two years of study in their respective fields of teaching in a recognized graduate school, presumably including the Master's degree. For heads of departments, training should be equivalent to that required for the Ph.D. degree or should represent corresponding professional or technological training.[43]

Jesuit universities similar to other Catholic institutions had difficulty conforming with these standards, because few Jesuits had academic doctorates but rather ecclesiastical degrees, such as, a licentiate or doctorate in sacred theology.[44] Where would these faculty come from? In response, the Inter-Province Committee took steps to upgrade Jesuit training. At its 1923 meeting, the committee encouraged the provincials to allow Jesuits to study for the doctorate, which also reinforced a mandate of the *Ratio Studiorum* to develop preeminent faculty.[44] To meet the first NCA site inspections in the short-term, the 1924 meeting of the Inter-Province Committee called upon Jesuit presidents to hire lay Catholic doctoral faculty.[46] The provincials approved these recommendations.[47] Their urgency stemmed from a desire to avoid an unfavorable NCA report.

Ideally, Jesuit administrations wanted to award their own doctorates to Catholics who understood the Jesuit apostolate. Therefore, they began or revised their graduate degree requirements to meet those recommended by the standardizing agencies. In December 1925, the presidents and the prefects of study of the Missouri province established the minimum graduate standards for faculty training, the character of graduate courses, the requirements for the awarding of master of arts and doctoral degrees, the administration of graduate schools, and the necessary facilities for graduate study.[48] In this sense, the NCA requirements for faculty professionalization forced Jesuit institutions to establish graduate and doctoral programs prematurely to obtain Catholics for their faculties. Such external prescriptions changed the type of faculty which the Jesuit educational apostolate would employ in the United States. These recommendations thus laid the foundation for the most significant institutional reassessment of the American Jesuit university mission.

During the first two decades of the twentieth century, Jesuit educational leaders followed what they perceived to be the traditional European structure of a university, namely, the addition of professional schools to a strong Jesuit college. They did this to meet the needs of their Catholic clienteles and to train Catholic leaders in the professions. They eschewed the German model of graduate research with its disinterested inquiry orientation, which American universities had emulated since the 1870s. This ideal stressed the discovery of knowledge with little concern about its religious ramifications. Jesuits resisted this approach because it conflicted with their apostolic educational mission. As Jesuit institutions came under the direction of accrediting agencies composed of the most stalwart proponents of the German model, Jesuit administrations were compelled to adopt some aspects of this modern American university mission. No greater specific demarcation of this change can be noted than the recommendation of the June 1926 Inter-Province Committee meeting to follow NCA and AAU norms.

> No university is considered complete without a Graduate School, which should be organized and conducted according to approved standards. The courses offered should be of graduate caliber, and should be explicitly described in the

university catalogue. Not less than one year's work (30 semester hours) should be prescribed for a master's degree, and not less than two years additional for the doctorate.[49]

The graduate school rather than the undergraduate college thus became the new focus within the Jesuit university. This launched the research aim of Jesuit universities—and the means to train Catholic faculty.

The Jesuit plan for graduate schools did not merely replicate those of non-Catholic American private and public universities. Jesuit leaders intended to conform these new appendages to their historic apostolic purpose. The Inter-Province Committee pointed to the new Jesuit graduate focus at its 1927 New Orleans meeting.

1. Our educational aim in general being the dissemination of Catholic doctrine and in particular the development of Catholic leaders, our program of educational endeavor in the United States has always included either directly or indirectly all schools from the lowest to the highest. While recognizing that preference be given to high school and college development because of a greater spiritual good ordinarily to be obtained from undergraduate education, we cannot but recognize also that the Graduate School, particularly in our own day, has assumed special importance and therefore should be developed in proportion to its relative value in the gaining of our spiritual object.

2. It is well known that the necessity of such graduate schools is constantly on the increase, for the reason largely if not mainly that in our Catholic graduate schools alone can the false philosophies which permeate non-Catholic graduate schools and colleges be combated. The development of our high schools and colleges calls for a growing number of Catholic lay teachers, who must be equipped with a graduate degree. If they obtain these degrees from secular universities, we can never be certain of the accuracy of their knowledge or their attitude concerning mooted questions of ethics and psychology. It is therefore imperative that the training of such lay teachers be provided for and received in Catholic universities.[50]

The provincials realized the crucial importance of these graduate schools as a place "where Catholic teachers can be formed and our own scholastics and Fathers equipped for teaching, lecturing and administrative work in our

schools."[51] Without such Catholic professionals, Jesuit universities would be forced to hire terminally-degreed faculty from non-Catholic universities who could not be counted on to be sympathetic to the form and manner of Jesuit graduate instruction—as will be described shortly. In this way, the 1923 NCA mandate changed the mission and faculty caliber of American Jesuit higher education. These largely external mandates determined the developments at Loyola University.

Its Jesuit administration moved quickly to implement these policies. As early as the 1925-1926 school year, President William H. Agnew, S.J. asked Austin G. Schmidt, S.J. (1883-1960) who had earned a doctorate from the School of Education at the University of Michigan to establish Loyola's graduate school. Hoping to make Loyola a great Catholic university, Schmidt believed strengthening graduate studies *and* inaugurating the doctorate remained crucial to Loyola's future university status. Having moved beyond the president's request, Schmidt received Agnew's approval to gain the support for both efforts from significant NCA members, since the NCA has begun to evaluate the graduate education of its member institutions by the late 1920s. First, Schmidt gained the endorsement of Charles Hubbard Judd, dean of the Department of Education at the University of Chicago. Next, he received support from Joseph D. Elliff, president of the NCA, and Raymond M. Hughes, president of Miami University. With these approbations, the dean believed that he could proceed with the strengthening of Loyola's master of arts degree programs and the inauguration of the doctorate. Schmidt assumed that "we shall be certain of the sympathetic co-operation of the North Central Association.... [and] build up the Graduate School, slowly perhaps, but in a solid and substantial manner which will attract more and more students."[52]

At the meeting of the Graduate Council on January 14, 1927, Schmidt described his decision and actions to its members.[53] After much discussion, the council approved the Department of Education to award the doctorate and required departments which awarded master of arts degrees to have two doctoral and two graduate degreed faculty members.[54] These and other policies complied with NCA and AAU standards. Schmidt also created graduate courses for both degree sequences as well as policies regulating comprehensive exams, French and German proficiency exams, and a completed dissertation for the doctorate.[55] The Jesuit administration implemented these graduate degree requirements during the following year. After the first, doctoral oral examinations in May 1928, Loyola University awarded its first doctoral degrees to a Catholic layman and a Catholic religious brother.[56] This success thus helped to develop the Catholic intellectual leadership which Jesuit provincials, presidents, and deans wanted for Catholic higher education and their own universities.[57]

However, Schmidt's move provoked problems and did not provide enough Catholic terminally-degreed faculty. While the NCA informally approved Loyola's graduate school, it still lacked formal AAU approval which was the sole accrediting agency for graduate schools. Moreover, the AAU resisted expanding its membership. Yet, the Inter-Province Committee asked Jesuit universities to obtain AAU accreditation in 1929 to establish quality programs and to enable their graduates to teach "in the accredited schools of certain Regional Associations."[58] This desire had a practical urgency; the committee reminded the Jesuit presidents that no Jesuit institutions were:

> ... meeting the Standard of most Regional Associations which require every faculty member of professorial rank to have had two years of specialized graduate study at an accredited Graduate School in the branch he is teaching and the Heads of Departments to hold Ph.D. Degrees from accredited Graduate Schools. Failure to remedy this condition is endangering the membership of these colleges in their respective Regional Associations.[59]

The difficulty in meeting the NCA demands for more terminally-degreed faculty had put Jesuit higher education in a *standardizing double bind.* Jesuit presidents could not find enough qualified Catholic faculty. Nor did they have the funds to establish AAU-accredited graduate schools for training Catholic faculty or to offer scholarships to attract Catholic graduate students. This problem plagued Loyola and other Jesuit universities for another ten years until the AAU allowed the NCA to accredit doctoral programs.

Another factor made these standards even more difficult to meet. General Ledochowski called for a greater Catholic character *and* a greater academic quality within American Jesuit institutions. Responding to a Vatican charge that American Jesuit colleges were no longer Catholic, the general required Jesuit universities to strengthen their Catholic characters by hiring only Catholic faculty and by removing non-Catholics from dean and faculty positions. Moreover, he discouraged the enrollment of non-Catholic students. Thus, he wanted Jesuits to compete with other American universities and colleges but in a Catholic way.[60] Several years later, he also charged the American provincials in a letter of December 8, 1930 to "take a more influential share in determining the intellectual policy of the country."[61] He called upon Jesuit institutions of higher learning to develop a united purpose and join in a concerted action to excel beyond their completing institutions. In this way, the general required Jesuit presidents to meet or exceed the NCA standards in what became called "The Catholic Way."[62]

This triple bind hampered Jesuit universities until the worst effects of the Depression subsided.

This national economic disaster inhibited Loyola University's efforts to conform with the NCA standards and the general's instructions. Indeed, its doctoral program was in shambles only three years after Loyola granted its first degrees. By the spring of 1931, its Graduate Council charged that the Department of Education's courses lacked doctoral character; indeed, most resembled normal school classes. While some members of the council discussed abandoning the degree, they chose to strengthen the course by adding one or two additional professors, after several members informed Schmidt that Loyola University constituted the only Catholic university in the Midwest able to grant doctoral degrees in education.[63] When Schmidt informed President Robert M. Kelley, S.J. (1877-1953), the sixteenth president of Loyola University, of the graduate school's difficulties, the president endorsed his recommendations, even though they went against his own opinions.[64]

Kelley believed Loyola's graduate programs failed to maintain the primary religious and moral purposes of Jesuit education, namely, "the salvation and religious and moral perfection of students."[65] This sentiment underscored Ledochowski's recent mandates and conformed to the older notion of the Jesuit apostolate which centered on the small collegiate design. He believed this, even though Dean Schmidt had made extensive efforts to integrate Jesuit apostolic aims within Loyola's graduate and doctoral programs. In response to a 1931 questionnaire from the Roman Congregation of Seminaries and Universities, Schmidt described how the graduate school fostered Catholic beliefs:

3. What means are used to win over the non-Catholic to Catholic belief and practice? Answer: (1) The crucifix and religious pictures are on the walls of our school. (2) The library contains Catholic books. (3) There is a book-rack with pamphlets on Catholic doctrine. (4) The spirit of Catholicism in the professors manifests itself. (5) Printed material issued by the university is circulated among the students. (6) Although non-Catholics are not required to take courses in apologetics, they must take certain courses in ethics, psychology, and sociology in which the Catholic view is presented. (7) There are occasional lectures on Catholic topics. (8) Influence is exerted during the conferences between students and their advisors.[66]

Moreover, Kelley questioned the quality of Jesuit graduate programs: "we have plunged into graduate school work unprepared both academically and financially; . . . our policy in this matter has seriously injured our reputation in the United States as educators."[67] His assessment pointed to the forced origins of Catholic graduate and doctoral programs: "Graduate schools in theory had as their purpose primarily to discover new truths or to present new aspects of known truths to graduate students to make them Christian scholars. Practically speaking, the purpose was to meet the requirements of standardizing bodies particularly to qualify teachers."[68]

Nevertheless, Kelley supported the Graduate Council's recommendations to strengthen graduate programs. He approved the offering of the doctorate in the Department of History in 1932, although Loyola granted none for six years. During the following year, he instituted standard teaching loads for faculty at 15 hours per week for lower division undergraduate faculty, 12 hours per week for upper division undergraduate faculty, and 10 hours per week for graduate faculty.[69] Allowing for greater research time among graduate faculty, this standard had been implemented within graduate schools of elite American universities since the turn of the century.[70] Furthermore, he doubled the number of doctorally-degreed faculty members during his administration from nine to fourteen in 1933 (see table 2). His efforts raised the quality of Loyola's graduate school which offered the master of arts in eight disciplines and the doctor of philosophy in education and history.[71] By the end of Kelley's administration, three other education doctorates had been awarded (see table 3). Thus, Schmidt's decision to begin the doctorate had been supported by the next presidential administration. By 1933, the Jesuit administration at Loyola University had established the research aim within its institutional mission. Its experience represented the typical picture of new Jesuit universities, while the graduate and doctoral degree granting powers in 26 departments at AAU-affiliated Catholic University of America and in 44 departments at St. Louis University exemplified the strongest Catholic institutions. During the 1920s, the Jesuit administrations' adherence to the NCA regulations improved their faculties and launched their doctoral programs. All this was in response to an external agency and not the superior general of the society.

Besides meeting NCA faculty and graduate school standards, the Jesuit institutions of the Missouri province also faced new standards for their endowments and the number of doctoral granting departments necessary to be classified as a university. Each caused revisions in Loyola's governance structure and doctoral degree programs.

The movement to standardize Jesuit colleges had created new pressures within Catholic higher education. While major Catholic universities, such as the University of Notre Dame, St. Louis University, Loyola University, and DePaul University, had received NCA approval by 1925 because they had the resources to

fulfill its standards, this did not happen at many smaller Catholic colleges, especially those for religious women which educated the teachers for the growing primary and secondary Catholic school system. They lacked similar resources. Jesuit educational leaders hoped to assist these institutions so that their graduates could receive accredited degrees between 1925 and 1930 by suggesting an ingenious approach called the corporate college plan. The large Jesuit universities sought to affiliate or merge with smaller, local Catholic colleges, although there were different reasons and relationships for this development in each city. In 1925, St. Louis University signed an agreement which brought about a merger with nine other Catholic colleges. While this merger left the institutions independent corporately and financially, it established an Administrative Board consisting of the archbishop, president of St. Louis University, and two representatives from each college. This board made coordinating recommendations concerning governance, faculty, curriculum, and degrees for all the institutions to the Jesuit president of St. Louis University who had the final approval or veto. This plan enabled the corporate colleges to use the university's resources and to offer its accredited degrees. Moreover, this agreement had the NCA's approval which hoped that the Jesuit university could insure that the number, teaching, and content of the courses offered at the corporate colleges conformed to its standards.[72] A similar plan under the sponsorship of the Right Reverend Joseph Schrembs, the bishop of Cleveland, with Albert C. Fox, S.J. as its regent, linked John Carroll University with four Catholic colleges and four Catholic nursing schools in 1929. In commenting on this plan, Fox perceived this arrangement as a way to unite the scattered forces in Catholic higher education. He hoped such a plan would be considered by Catholic educators in other cities.[73]

TABLE 2

LOYOLA UNIVERSITY GRADUATE FACULTY DEGREE STATUS FOR SCHOOL YEARS 1931 TO 1937

School Year	B.A.	M.A.	M.S.	Ph.D.	S.T.D.	Total
1931-1932	3	23	1	9	1	37
1932-1933	1	4	1	14	1	21
1933-1934	1	7	1	16	1	26
1934-1935	2	27	2	19	1	51
1935-1936	5	22	2	31	1	61
1936-1937	3	26	3	38	2	72

Source: "Graduate School Statistics," Box 3, File 49: Graduate Studies, JH-LUCA.

In the meantime, the NCA encouraged these mergers when it made new demands for actual endowments at Catholic institutions after 1928 and until 1935. Initially, the NCA had allowed Catholic institutions to count the unpaid salaries of their clerical faculties as a "living endowment." However, the 1928 NCA *proposed* standard replicated the AAU's endowment guidelines.[74] This posed such an immediate threat to the status of Catholic institutions that Jesuit provincials allowed presidents to create advisory boards of lay trustees for fund raising.[75] After Loyola's commerce dean suggested establishing such a board, Kelley announced the creation of the Administrative Council in 1930, which comprised nine prominent Catholic businessmen of Chicago, such as, Stuyvesant Peabody, Edward A. Cudahy, Jr., and Samuel Insull, Jr.[76] Loyola's Council of Regents and Deans described the problem in this way:

It would appear as though the North Central Association has committed itself to a policy of reducing the number of colleges in the United States and of forcing out of existence those that do not measure up. . . . It should be borne in mind that accrediting by the North Central Association is a question of life and death [to Loyola University] . . . Conditions which may cause difficulty are the following: (1) inadequate endowment, (2) athletic scholarships, (3) sharing library and academic equipment with the academy, (4) inadequate faculty preparation, (5) excessive teaching loads, and (6) excessive size of classes.[77]

Kelley turned these problems over to his Administrative Council in June 1930.

Chairman Peabody suggested Loyola University consider consolidating the Chicago Catholic institutions of higher education. In this way, they might coordinate their efforts in raising an endowment sufficient to satisfy the NCA demands. He believed some $20 million might be raised over ten years. The members then suggested that Kelley seek Cardinal George Mundelein's approval.[78] At the next meeting of the council, Kelley reported that Mundelein endorsed the consolidation. Unlike the St. Louis and John Carroll approaches, the Chicago plan proposed actual unification of the institutions. Mundelein College, Rosary College, and St. Francis Xavier College would merge with Loyola University and DePaul University. The council agreed unanimously to approve the consolidation.

Next, Kelley sought the approval of the Vincentian Visitor of the Western Province of the Congregation of the Mission, William P. Barr, C.M., and the new president of DePaul University, Francis V. Corcoran, C.M.[79] They approved the plan by March 1931.[80] Having been the president of St. Louis University's corporate college board and having no adequate means to pay off nearly a million dollar DePaul debt, Corcoran had readily endorsed the Chicago consolidation effort as a necessary remedy to the problems brought on by the demands of the NCA and the Depression.

In April, President Kelley met with Corcoran to devise the implementation of the consolidation effort. Kelley hoped they could develop a single strategy. Kelley and Corcoran met periodically until such a plan emerged. They agreed upon the first action by October 1931: the three women's colleges would merge with Loyola University, while DePaul would retain its affiliated nursing schools and annex any other not affiliated with Loyola.[81] Everything seemed approved. Within a year, Barat College's administration asked Kelley to formalize the merger between the women's college and Loyola.[82] It became the first college to merge with Loyola on October 15, 1932.[83] Within six months, Kelley prepared documents for the incorporation of the other two women's colleges.[84] The new Catholic university of Chicago seemed at hand.

TABLE 3

LOYOLA UNIVERSITY CONFERRAL OF DOCTORAL DEGREES FOR SCHOOL YEARS 1928 TO 1940

School Year	Education	Chemistry	History	Philosophy	Total
1928-1929	2	0	0	0	2
1929-1930	1	0	0	0	1
1930-1931	1	0	0	0	1
1931-1932	1	0	0	0	1
1932-1933	0	0	0	0	0
1933-1934	0	0	0	0	0
1934-1935	1	0	0	0	1
1935-1936	1	0	0	0	1
1936-1937	2	0	0	0	2
1937-1938	0	0	0	0	0
1938-1939	0	0	1	1	2
1939-1940	0	1	3	1	5
Total	9	1	4	2	16

Source: Office of the Registrar, "Degrees Conferred by the Professional and Graduate Divisions by Year and by Curriculum, 1923-1964," Box 2: Registration and Records, LUCA.

However, by the end of the summer in 1933, the Jesuit provincial requested President Kelley to resign and assume similar responsibilities at Regis College in Denver, Samuel K. Wilson, S.J. (1882-1959) who had been the dean of the Graduate School replaced him.[85] With this presidential change, the Chicago corporate college movement stalled.

The Jesuit administration had fueled the fire of the Chicago corporate college plan since 1930 to withstand an NCA financial inspection. Kelley suggested to Peabody in August 1931 that Loyola needed an endowment of $1.5 million to meet the NCA norms.[86] The NCA visiting team inspected Loyola University in February 1932. They evaluated all components of the institution to insure its compliance with NCA standards. The much dreaded financial review proved to be unfounded: not only did Loyola have $1,487,000 in cash or bonds on hand but also $4 million worth of land assets besides its university property. Although some minor problems existed, the NCA reviewers passed the university in every category, except one. They questioned Loyola's offering of the doctorate in education and history because current faculty members held only one doctorate and one master of arts. They suggested that the administration discontinue awarding the degree until it hired adequate faculty. Finally, they stated that Loyola "should not be dropped from the Association because of its financial condition."[87]

Loyola no longer needed to compromise its Jesuit institutional structure or mission to meet the NCA demands. It abandoned the corporate college plan which ended the Chicago merger. By 1936, all Midwestern corporate college plans collapsed because North Central had "withdrawn its approval of the Corporate Colleges."[88]

The NCA inspection of other Jesuit institutions did not yield such happy results. After the NCA studied the problem of Catholic "living endowments" from 1931 to 1934, it concluded that some Catholic institutions had paid their substantial debts by skimping on educational programs and improvements, e.g., graduate and doctoral programs. The NCA thus confirmed its proposed endowment standards as the new norm. The NCA would soon rule that any Catholic college whose debt exceeded its endowment would be dropped from the accredited list. This signalled a major shift in the NCA's stance toward its colleges and universities.

In response, the Jesuit provincials prevailed upon President Wilson to convene the presidents to reassess their relationship with the NCA. Their agenda for the February 1934 meeting revealed their outrage:

... first; the implication of this recent North Central threat and our united attitude toward it; secondly; whether it is time for us to consider a united withdrawal from the North Central;

thirdly; what our united attitude shall be toward outside regulating agencies; fourthly; whether we should form our own Jesuit standardizing group.[89]

While the Jesuit presidents expressed their anger over this new NCA standard during the depths of the Depression, President Fox who chaired the meeting informed them of the major reason for the change.

... the Association has had to listen to complaints from Protestants that the Catholics were being given too much. They only think in terms of cash and cannot see our point. The committee studied the problem very carefully for three years and knows that even though we have all we say we have in regard to an endowment of men, we also have debts which must be paid in cash. They think that in order to carry on we will skimp on improvements in order to pay the debts, and as a matter of fact that is true. The non-Catholic institutions have debts too but they have no device by which they can make their books show endowments to offset them that is not in cash.[90]

Fox continued his defense by pointing out that the NCA did not desire to drop all the Catholic colleges, but only those with serious fiscal problems. Once again, he pointed out that withdrawal from the NCA jeopardized their Catholic students who wished to continue their education at AAU approved universities. Gradually, Fox won over those Jesuits wishing to leave the NCA. The presidents voted down all four motions. Instead, the Jesuits agreed to unite their forces to influence future NCA policies through various men sympathetic to their aims. For the third time in thirty years, Fox had played the instrumental role in encouraging Jesuit educators to adopt American higher education standards.

Their acquiescence would be costly. The NCA intended to pursue its new standards. In the spring of 1934, it expelled the University of Detroit and Xavier University because of their extensive debt in relationship to their endowment.[91] This NCA action jolted American Jesuit educators.

Nor did the Jesuits have long to recoup before another national disgrace occurred. The American Council on Education (ACE) made public its 1932 survey of the seventy-seven graduate schools offering the doctorate in the spring of 1934. It approved sixty-three institutions as either being distinguished or satisfactory, including Catholic University of America and the University of Notre Dame. No doctoral programs from any Jesuit institution qualified. When the *New York Times* printed the report from the *Educational Record*, the entire country

tance of the modern American university mission with its emphasis on research.

These events affected Loyola University in Chicago. The Jesuit administration improved its graduate school. With the changes in its presidential administration, Wilson decided to ask Francis J. Gerst, S.J. to replace him as graduate dean in August 1933. During the following year, Dean Gerst analyzed the graduate school and gave this assessment: "The Graduate School as at presently constituted would be classed probably as of mid-grade or even below mid-grade excellence."[99] To improve the school, the dean selected which departments would best benefit from a reallocation of resources and faculty. By 1935, he chose the departments of education, history, philosophy, and classics. Wilson concurred and moved to upgrade the graduate school.[100] Furthermore, the president affiliated the Jesuit scholasticate at Indiana, West Baden College, with the university. Having NCA approval, this move brought qualified undergraduate and graduate Jesuit students to Loyola's degree programs and increased its degreed faculty in August 1934.[101] This added about 100 to 150 undergraduate and graduate students and 12 new faculty members to the university. Next, the president added several doctoral-degreed faculty, one in classics and two in education, to complete the first important phase of the graduate rebuilding.[102] He hired 15 more doctoral-degreed faculty members by 1936 (see table 2, p. 101). Moreover, Wilson initiated new research efforts. He began the Institute of Jesuit Affairs, a research institute on Jesuit history, within the Department of History and purchased the *Illinois Catholic Historical Review* as Loyola's new history journal, *Mid-America.* The president also suggested strengthening the English department to include doctoral studies.[103] Wilson thus improved Loyola's university stature.

External influences quickly advanced his effort. In the spring of 1935, Wilson shocked Loyola's Administrative Council with new NCA internal policies for university class institutions.

It is note worthy that increasingly in the United States the term "university" is restricted to schools emphasizing graduate work. The North Central, for instance, will hereafter designate as a university only an institution offering work leading to the doctorate in at least five fields of academic interest. Even though according to the traditional definition of "university" an institution may have several professional schools and have been hitherto thus entitled to the name "university," in default of developed graduate work it will be known from now on in North Central nomenclature as a "college with professional schools."[104]

knew of the Jesuit academic embarrassment.[92]

Both the NCA and ACE actions created a furor in American Jesuit higher education. A unified response came from the Jesuit general Ledochowski faced two significant American educational bodies which questioned the academic quality of the Society's educational apostolate in the United States. His 1934 *Instructio* called on the American Jesuits to develop "a new direction and a fresh impulse of Ours [and] a systematized attempt to secure for our educational activities that due recognition and rightful standing among other groups of similar rank and grade."[93] He required Jesuit administrations to bring their institutions to the level of the best American universities. Ledochowski appointed Chicago Jesuit Daniel M. O'Connell as *commissarius* to begin this task with the supreme authority to institute the mandates of the 1934 *Instructio* within every Jesuit university and college. After his inspection of each Jesuit institution, he changed curricula, suppressed degree programs, assessed faculty, and sponsored Jesuits to undertake advanced studies at accredited universities.[94] In these undertakings, he established doctoral studies as the *sine qua non* of Jesuit preparation for university teaching and encouraged each Jesuit university to build its resources to achieve recognition by and membership in the AAU. Ledochowski's 1934 mandate represented the formal turning point in American Jesuit higher education.[95]

One of the important tasks which the 1934 *Instructio* required was the development of a national organization to direct the development of Jesuit higher education. O'Connell called for a meeting of the Interprovince Executive Committee of the Jesuit national education committee which consisted of all the prefects general of studies from the now New England, New York-Maryland, Chicago, New Orleans, California, and Oregon provinces and the Committee on Graduate Studies to begin the national Jesuit Educational Association in Chicago on April 25, 1935. This organization guided Jesuit higher education until the late 1960s. O'Connell's desire to further the 1934 *Instructio* led to the first issue on the agenda: standards for graduate education in Jesuit institutions. James B. Macelwane, S.J. (1883-1956), dean of the graduate school at St. Louis University, chaired the association for this issue.[96] He had served as chairman of the Jesuit Commission on Higher Education from 1931 to 1934 and had conducted an extensive review of Jesuit higher education in 1932. He presented his report, "Standards Proposed for Judging Graduate Schools," which outlined the requirements for graduate faculty, the organizational structure of the graduate school, the library, and graduate degree programs which incorporated the NCA and AAU norms.[97] As the first graduate standard for Catholic higher education, these norms indicated the strength of Jesuit leadership in American Catholic higher education.[98] Jesuit educators thus demonstrated their *qualified* accep-

Gerst and Wilson's actions during the previous three years enabled Loyola University to meet these requirements.

However, the NCA decision caused other Jesuit universities greater difficulty. Initially, the Jesuit administrators from the universities and colleges of the Chicago and Missouri provinces, namely, Xavier University, St. Louis University, John Carroll University, Creighton University, Marquette University, University of Detroit, Loyola University, Regis College, and Rockhurst College, met with O'Connell to discuss this problem in April 1936. They decided that each province should have only one or two universities which conformed to the new NCA norms.[105] O'Connell supported Wilson's desire to make Loyola University one of those chosen for the Chicago province. The commissioner sent Jesuit scholastics and faculty to bolster Wilson's drive to build up five departments to offer the doctorate.[106] By the end of the year, President Wilson reported to Loyola's Administrative Council that the departments of education, history, philosophy, classics, and English would offer the doctorate.[107] By the 1939-1940 school year, Loyola expanded its doctoral production to four departments (see table 3, p. 102), while anticipating graduates in the fifth department. Through the leadership of President Wilson and Dean Gerst, Loyola University had laid an adequate foundation for its research aim. This policy thus determined which Jesuit universities reached American university stature by the 1970s.

The development of Jesuit universities during the third stage of the standardization controversy had been dramatic. The increase of terminally-degreed Catholic faculty, the adoption of an American university mission with the inauguration of doctoral programs and research institutes, and the beginning of actual endowments occurred because of NCA pressure. At Loyola University, Jesuit administrations from 1920 to 1940 acted to acquire university stature. While this resulted in premature doctoral programs to maintain its NCA ranking, this action determined Loyola's university mission. Although the Chicago Jesuits may have eventually inaugurated doctoral studies, Wilson himself asserted "North Central has given us standards that we would never have labored to achieve on our own."[108]

v.

There are three main results from this investigation of the controversy between the Jesuits and the NCA. First, the need to increase collegiate enrollments to compete favorably with other NCA-affiliated Catholic institutions represented the major factor in the Jesuit presidents' and provincials' decision to have their institutions accredited by the NCA. Their classical curriculum with its Latin and Greek requirements and few electives made Jesuit institutions with their nonaccredited degrees unattractive to the growing Catholic clientele in 1920. If the Jesuits intended to have a role in American Catholic higher education in the twentieth century, they had to revise their 1832 *Ratio Studiorum* to comply with standards in American higher eduction. Second, after Jesuit institutions gained membership within the NCA, the association progressively influenced their to revise their undergraduate curriculum, professionalize their faculties, upgrade the quality of their graduate work, strengthen the fiscal condition of their institutions, and finally inaugurate doctoral studies between 1920 and 1935. The success of these developments may be attributed to three persons who encouraged the Jesuits to affiliate with the NCA. Alexander J. Burrowes encouraged and approved Missouri Jesuit colleges and universities to change their collegiate curriculum and to seek accreditation. Albert C. Fox devised the modification of the 1832 *Ratio*, promoted accreditation for all Catholic and Jesuit institutions in 1920, and succeeded in overcoming the Jesuit presidents' desire to withdraw from NCA in 1934. Wlodimir Ledochowski requested all Jesuit institutions to achieve similar rankings with other American universities in his 1930 and 1934 letters, even though he required them to maintain an intense Catholic character. The spirit of his mandates continued until the 1960s. Third, these developments led Jesuit university educators to distance themselves from the older Jesuit college model for the Society's apostolates, to eschew their European university mission with its professional studies orientation, and to adopt the modern American university mission with its research orientation.

This paper has described how the social forces within the Catholic community, the Jesuits' willingness to consider new curricular ideas, and their accommodation to the NCA changed Jesuit higher education. This turning point in American Jesuit higher education led to the full Americanization of Jesuit universities and colleges when they demonstrated their autonomy from the Catholic church by reorganizing their boards of trustees in the late 1960s and early 1970s.

NOTES

1. An earlier version of this paper was given at the 1986 American Educational Research Association Annual Meeting in Division F. The author extends his gratitude to Paul A. Fitz-Gerald, Kathryn M. Moore, Harold S. Wechsler, and two anonymous *History of Higher Education Annual* reviewers whose comments aided this revision. Further discussion of the issues raised in this article may be found in Lester F. Goodchild, "The Mission of the Catholic University in the Midwest, 1842-1980: A Comparative Case Study of the Effects of Strategic

Policy Decisions upon the Mission of the University of Notre Dame, Loyola University of Chicago, and DePaul University," 2 vols. (Ph.D. diss., University of Chicago, 1986).

2. Paul A. FitzGerald, S.J., *The Governance of Jesuit Colleges in the United States, 1920-1970,* foreword by Theodore M. Hesburgh, C.S.C. (Notre Dame, Ind.: University of Notre Dame Press, 1984), p. 3; Joseph A. Tetlow, S.J., "The Jesuits' Mission in Higher Education: Perspectives and Contexts," *Studies in the Spirituality of the Jesuits* 15-16 (November 1983-January 1984), p. 11.

3. Goodchild, "The Mission . . ." 2, pp. 701-775.

4. The Society of Jesus, a Roman Catholic religious institute founded in 1540, seeks to establish Catholic colleges to promote Christian leadership as its apostolic mission. It governs the work of its priests and brothers through a system of provinces throughout the world. By 1928, the United States was divided into four provinces, Maryland-New York (1833), Missouri (1863), New Orleans (1907), and California (1909). In the Missouri province, the Jesuits established nine universities and colleges: St. Louis University, St. Louis, Mo.; Marquette University, Milwaukee, Wisc.; Loyola University, Chicago, Ill.; Creighton University, Omaha, Neb.; University of Detroit, Detroit, Mich.; John Carroll University, Cleveland, Ohio; Xavier University, Cincinnati, Ohio; Rockhurst College, Kansas City, Mo.; and Campion College (1880-1925), Prairie du Chien, Wisc. After the closing of Campion College, Regis College, Denver, Co., which was founded in 1921, became the ninth Jesuit institution in the Midwest.

5. Ignatius of Loyola, *The Constitutions of the Society of Jesus,* trans. George E. Ganss, S.J. (St. Louis: Institute of Jesuit Sources, 1970), part IV, chapter 2, sections 1-2 [320-321], pp. 176-177. The 1949 Roman edition of the *Societatis Iesu Constitutiones et Epistomes Instituti* gave each paragraph a number rather than following the early four-partite divisions. This new standard reference system will be placed in brackets before the page numbers.

6. The Jesuits operate 28 universities and colleges in the United States, 23 of which have been classified by the Carnegie Commission as either Doctorate-Granting 1 or Comprehensive University or College I. Carnegie Council on Policy Studies in Higher Education, *A Classification of Institutions of Higher Education,* rev. ed. (Berkeley, Calif.: Carnegie Foundation for the Advancement of Teaching, 1976), pp. 1-25.

7. Frederick Rudolph, *Curriculum: A History of the American Undergraduate Course of Study Since 1636,* Carnegie Council on Policy Studies in Higher Education (San Francisco: Jossey-Bass Publishers, 1981), p. 220.

8. *Report of the Commissioner of Education for the Year 1886-87* (Washington, D.C., 1888), p. 645 cited by David S. Webster, "The Bureau of Education's Suppressed Ratings of Colleges, 1911-1912," *History of Education Quarterly* 24 (Winter 1984), p. 500.

9. Rudolph, *Curriculum* p. 220.

10. Ibid, p. 222.

11. Conference Minutes, 1906 cited by Kenneth E. Young, "Prologue: The Changing Scope of Accreditation," in *Understanding Accreditation: Contemporary Perspectives on Issues and Practices in Evaluating Educational Quality,* Jossey-Bass Higher Education Series (San Francisco: Jossey-Bass Publishers, 1983), pp. 2-3.

12. Webster, "The Bureau . . ." pp. 501-509.

13. Rudolph, *Curriculum* p. 221.

14. *Proceedings of the North Central Association of Colleges and Secondary Schools* (1913-1914). p. 61.

15. Edward J. Power, *Catholic Higher Education in America: A History* (New York: Appleton-Century-Crofts, 1972), p. 367.

16. Ignatius, part IX, chapter 3, sections 3-9 [740-749], pp. 313-315.

17. *Catalogue of St. Ignatius College, 1902-1903,* p. 11, Loyola University of Chicago Archives, Loyola University of Chicago, Chicago, Illinois (hereafter, cited as LUCA).

18. Beginning with the Italian Renaissance, the *pietas litterata* tradition integrated classical and Christian Latin and Greek authors as the basis for a Catholic curriculum of higher learning. See, James Bowen, *A History of Western Education,* vol. 2: *Civilization of Europe Sixth to Sixteenth Century* (New York: St. Martin's Press, 1975), pp. 428-432 and Allan P. Farrell, S.J., *The Jesuit Code of Liberal Education: Development and Scope of the Ratio Studiorum* (Milwaukee: Bruce Publishing Company, 1938).

19. Francis P. Cassidy, "Catholic Education and the Third Plenary Council of Baltimore, I," *Catholic Historical Review* 35 (October 1948), pp. 277-278.

20. *Catalogue of St. Ignatius College, 1907-1908,* pp. 19-20, LUCA; Robert Swickerath, S.J., "System of Education," *Bulletin of Loyola University, 1919-1920,* p. 11, LUCA.

21. *Bulletin of Loyola University, 1917-1918,* p. 18; *Bulletin of Loyola University, 1918-1919,* p. 11, LUCA.

22. Swickerath, "System of Education," pp. 8-11.

23. Cited by Thomas Q. Beesley, "Loyola University," *The St. Ignatius Collegian* 9 (November 1909), p. 3, LUCA.

24. Vice-President's Diary, October 10, 1913, 3 vols, 3: p. 242. LUCA.

25. "Report of the General Committee and Prefects of Studies, St. Louis, Missouri, July 1916," William Kane, S.J. Collection (hereafter, cited as WK). File: M1.8, LUCA.

26. Presidents Meeting of the Jesuit Colleges, April 2, 1917, p. 7, Samuel K. Wilson, S.J. Collection (hereafter, cited as SW), Box 26, File 24, LUCA.

27. Alexander J. Burrowes, S.J. to John B. Furay, S.J., February 19, 1919, Box 26, File 24, SW-LUCA.

28. Meeting of College Presidents and Prefects of Studies of the Missouri Province, Campion College, April 14 and 15, 1919, Box 26, File 24, SW-LUCA.

29. Committee on Curriculum and Administration, Report No. 1, July 10, 1919, p. 13, Box 1: Prefect of Studies, File 1, Chicago Provincial Archives of the Society of Jesus, Chicago, Illinois (hereafter, cited as CPA).

30. Francis X. McMenamy, S.J. to John B. Furay, S.J., July 31, 1919, Box 26, File 24, SW-LUCA.

31. Francis X. McMenamy to [John B. Furay], June 21, 1920, p. 1, Box 10, File: M1.1-1.9, WK-LUCA. Internal evidence points to the letter being sent to the rector of the community.

32. Hugh L. Lamb, "Discussion," in the *Report of the Proceedings and Addresses of the Eighteenth Annual Meeting, Catholic Educational Association Bulletin* 18 (November 1921), pp. 84-88.

33. Albert C. Fox, S.J. to Very Reverend Dear Father, May 24, 1920, James A. Burns Collection, Box 3: Burns Personal Correspondence, Archives of the University of Notre Dame, Notre Dame, Indiana.

34. Albert C. Fox, "The Trends of the Colleges," in the *Report of Proceedings and Addresses of the Eighteenth Annual Meeting, Catholic Educational Association Bulletin* 18 (November 1921), p. 130.

35. *Woodstock Letters*, 64, no. 2 (1935), pp. 280-281 cited by FitzGerald, *Governance*, pp. 8-9.

36. FitzGerald, *Governance*, pp. 3-4, fails to mention these meetings as being forerunners of the Inter-Province Committee. However, the next Missouri provincial, Francis X. McMenamy, S.J., also attended the June 1920 meeting in New York which called for the first inter-province meeting. It is more than coincidence that the first meeting of the Inter-Province Committee took place at Campion College, Prairie du Chien, Wisconsin.

37. Meeting of the Inter-Province Committee on Studies, March 27, 1921, File: M1.27, WK-LUCA.

38. Wlodimir Ledochowski, S.J. to Joseph Rockwell, S.J., October 20, 1921, Roman Archives of the Society of Jesus, cited by FitzGerald, *Governance*, p. 6.

39. *Bulletin of Loyola University, 1920-1921*, pp. 35-41, LUCA.

40. Vice-President's Diary, March 17, 1921, 3, p. 302, LUCA.

41. Ibid., November 23, 1921, 3, p. 311, LUCA. Minutes of the Consultors, St. Ignatius College, March 8, 1922, p. 197, LUCA. The board of trustees confirmed the separation between Loyola University and St. Ignatius Preparatory High School on August 29, 1924; Minutes of the Board of Trustees of Loyola University, August 29, 1924, Office of the President of St. Ignatius Preparatory High School, St. Ignatius Preparatory High School, Chicago, Illinois.

42. The split between the Missouri and Chicago provinces occurred in 1928 after the region became too complex to be administered by a single Jesuit provincial.

43. "Report of a Committee appointed by Reverend Father Rector in February 1926 to study ways and means of assisting our scholastics to do graduate work in the ordinary branches of the College Curriculum," p. 3, Box 1: Province Prefects, File 2: Graduate Work for Scholastics, CPA.

44. FitzGerald, *Governance*, pp. 10-11.

45. Minutes of the Inter-Province Committee on Studies, April 25, 1923, Box 10, File: M1.32, WK-LUCA.

46. Minutes of the Inter-Province Committee on Studies, June 20 to 23, 1924, Box 10, File: M1.32, WK-LUCA.

47. FitzGerald, *Governance*, p. 13.

48. Minutes of the Conference regarding Certain Suggestions of the North Central Association, December 13, 1925, pp. 4-6, File A2.16; North Central Association, WK-LUCA.

49. Minutes of the Inter-Province Committee on Studies, June 16 and 17, 1926, Box 1: JEA, File 2, CPA.

50. Minutes of the Inter-Province Committee on Studies, February 27 to March 3, 1927, p. 3, Box 1: JEA, File 2, CPA.

51. Minutes of the Provincials of the American Assistancy, April 21 and 22, 1927, pp. 3, 7, Box 1: Meetings of the Provincials of the American Assistancy, 1926-1948, File: April 21 and 22, 1927, CPA.

52. Agenda of the Meeting of the Graduate Council for January 14, 1927, Box 26, File 13: Graduate Council 1927-1933, SW-LUCA.

53. Minutes of the Graduate Council, January 14, 1927, Box 26, File 13: Graduate Council 1927-1933, SW-LUCA.

54. Ibid.

55. "History, Organization, and Purpose [of the Graduate School]," *Bulletin of Loyola University, 1926-1927*, vol 3, pp. 9-22, LUCA.

56. Memorandum, Austin G. Schmidt, S.J., May 11, 1928, Box 26, File 13: Graduate School 1927-1933, SW-LUCA.

57. Minutes of the Deans of the Missouri and Chicago Provinces, December 30, 1928, James T. Hussey, S.J. Collection (hereafter, cited as JH), Box 4, File 2, LUCA.

58. Minutes of the Inter-Province Committee on Studies, December 31 to January 3, 1929, p. 7, Box 10, File: M1.32, WK-LUCA.

59. Ibid.

60. FitzGerald, *Governance*, pp. 21-22; Wlodimir Ledochowski to Fathers and Brothers in Christ of the American Assistancy, June 7, 1928, pp. 2-4, File: A1.20, WK-LUCA.

61. Wlodimir Ledochowski to Reverend dear Father Provincial, December 8, 1930, Box 1: JEA, File 12, CPA.

62. Samuel H. Horine, S.J. to Samuel K. Wilson, June 7, 1934, Box 14, File: U1.22-1.25, WK-LUCA.

63. Minutes of the Graduate Council, April 21, 1931, Box 26, File 13, SW-LUCA; Francis J. Rooney, S.J. to Austin G. Schmidt, May 1, 1931, Box 26, File 13, SW-LUCA.

64. Austin G. Schmidt to Robert M. Kelley, S.J., May 25, 1932, File B11.28, WK-LUCA.

65. Robert M. Kelley to Provincial, November 14, 1932, "Report of the Commission on Higher Studies of the American Assistancy of the Society of Jesus, 1931-1932," p. 2, File: A1.20, WK-LUCA.

86. Kelley to Stuyvesant Peabody, August 13, 1931, File A2.24, WK-LUCA

87. Board of Review, the Commission on Higher Education of the North Central Association of Colleges and Secondary Schools to Gentlemen, March 14, 1934, pp. 1-13, File A2.31, WK-LUCA.

88. Daniel M. O'Connell, S.J. to Samuel K. Wilson, January 21, 1937, Box 3, File 44, JH-LUCA.

89. Samuel K. Wilson to Albert C. Fox, February 17, 1934, Box: NCA, File: NCA 1933-1934, WK-LUCA.

90. Minutes of the Bi-Province Committee on Outside Standardizing Agencies, February 24, 1934, p. 3, Box: NCA File: A2.31, WK-LUCA.

91. George A. Works, "Proceedings of the Commission on Institutions of Higher Education," *North Central Association Quarterly* 9 (July 1934), pp. 38, 46-47; Jesuit reaction to these actions may be found in Box 10, File: M1.43-M1.47, WK-LUCA. Both Jesuit universities were restored to the NCA accredited list the following year.

92. FitzGerald, *Governance*, pp. 36-37.

93. Wlodimir Ledochowski, "Instructio pro Assistentia Americae de Ordinandis Universitatibus, Collegiis, ac Scholis Altis et de Praeparandis Eorundem Magistris," August 15, 1934 (Woodstock, Mass.: Printed Privately, 1934).

94. FitzGerald, *Governance*, pp. 38-52.

95. Matthew J. Fitzsimmons, S.J., "The *Instructio*, 1934-1949," *Jesuit Educational Quarterly* 12 (October 1949), pp. 69-70.

96. FitzGerald, *Governance*, pp. 26-28.

97. Minutes of the Joint Meeting of the Committee on Graduate Schools and the Interprovince Executive Committee of the National Jesuit Educational Association, April 25, 1935, pp. 1-2, Box 16, File 26, SW-LUCA. The final version of these standards developed during the next two years. Edward J. Power, *A History of Catholic Higher Education in the United States* (Milwaukee: Bruce Publishing Co., 1958), pp. 354-58 reproduces this final version, "Norms Proposed by the Committee on Graduate Studies of the Jesuit Educational Association for its Guidance in Appraising Graduate Work."

98. Power, *History of Catholic Higher Education*, p. 237.

99. Samuel K. Wilson, "President's Report, 1933-1934," p. 3, File A2.71: President's Report to the Administrative Council 1933-34, WK-LUCA

100. Samuel K. Wilson to Francis J. Gerst, S.J., February 12, 1935, Box 6, File 4, SW-LUCA.

101. Wilson to Allan P. Farrell, S.J., April 1, 1935, Box 4, File 21, SW-LUCA.

102. Wilson to Daniel M. O'Connell, May 16, 1935, Box 3, File 44, JH-LUCA.

103. Wilson, "President's Report, 1934-1935," pp. 4-5, 9-11, 16-19, File A2.99: President's Report, WK-LUCA.

66. Robert M. Kelley to Ernest Ruffini, October 5, 1931, Box 27, File 28, SW-LUCA

67. Kelley to Provincial, November 14, 1932.

68. Minutes of the Annual Meeting of the Deans of the Chicago and Missouri Provinces, December 29 and 30, 1933, p. 3, Box 1: JEA, File: Central Region Dean's Conference 1928-1960, CPA

69. Robert M. Kelley, Diary, March 28, 1933, pp. 87-89, LUCA

70. Roger L. Geiger, "The Conditions of University Research, 1900-1920," *History of Higher Education Annual*, 4 (1984), pp. 4-5.

71. "Graduate School Statistics," Box 3, File 49, JH-LUCA

72. Timothy L. Bouscaren, S.J., "The 'Corporate Colleges' Plan," *America*, January 9, 1926, pp. 307-8; William B. Faherty, S.J., *Better the Dream: St. Louis University & Community, 1818-1968* (St. Louis: St. Louis University Press, 1968), p. 282.

73. Paul L. Blakeley, S.J., "The Incorporation of John Carroll University," *America*, January 25, 1930, pp. 385-386.

74. "Report of the Committee on Financial Standards for Catholic Institutions," *North Central Association Quarterly* 5 (September 1930), pp. 191-92.

75. Minutes of the Provincials of the American Assistancy, April 3 and 4, 1929, p. 8, Box 1: Minutes of the Meetings of the Provincials of the American Assistancy, 1926-1948, File: April 3 and 4, 1929, CPA.

76. Minutes of the Council of Regents and Deans, March 5, 1929 and January 7, 1930, Box 26, File 12, SW-LUCA.

77. Minutes of the Council of Regents and Deans, April 8, 1930, Box 26, File 12, SW-LUCA.

78. Minutes of the Administrative Council, June 12, 1930, p. 2, Box 27, File 11a, SW-LUCA.

79. Minutes of the Administrative Council, October 16, 1930, p. 4, Box 27, File 11a, SW-LUCA.

80. Robert M. Kelley, Diary, October 20, 1930, n.p. and March 16, 1931, p. 75, LUCA; Kelley reported the success of these meetings to the Administrative Council, Meeting of April 16, 1931, p. 2, Box 27, File 11a, SW-LUCA.

81. Robert M. Kelley, Diary, October 17, 1931, p. 290 and October 27, 1931, p. 300, LUCA

82. Minutes of the University Council, October 6, 1932, p. 2, Box 27, File 3, SW-LUCA.

83. Robert M. Kelley to Rosemary A. Gibney, R.S.C.J., October 15, 1932, File A1.26, WK-LUCA. Kelley informed Reverend Mother Gibney that Barat's corporate union with Loyola would help its enrollments and revenues to meet the NCA obligations. Their signed merger agreement is in this file.

84. Minutes of the Administrative Council, June 8, 1933, p. 2, Box 27, File 11a, SW-LUCA.

85. Robert M. Kelley, Diary, August 29, 1933, p. 241, LUCA

104. Ibid, p. 5.

105. Minutes of the Meeting of Jesuits of the Chicago and Missouri Provinces, April 23, 1936, p. 1, Box 2, File: JEA, File: Central Region Dean's Conference 1928-1960, CPA.

106. Daniel M. O'Connell to Samuel K. Wilson, n.d., Box 3, File 44, JH-LUCA.

107. Samuel K. Wilson, "President's Report, 1935-1936," p. 12, Box 27, File 16, SW-LUCA.

108. President Maguire relates a conversation which he had with Wilson in 1950; see: Memorandum, James F. Maguire, S.J. to Michael Mulligan, S.J., August 21, 1958, regarding North Central Board of Review, James F. Maguire, S.J. Collection, Box 9, File 1: Mulligan, LUCA.

The American Compromise: Charles W. Eliot, Black Education, and the New South

Jennings L. Wagoner, Jr.

It is generally accepted that by the beginning of the twentieth century, most Northerners, including many who in earlier decades had been zealously involved in Southern affairs, had turned their attention away from the plight of the Southern black. Reconstruction officially ended in 1877 and, as one Northern journal then announced, "Henceforth, the nation as a nation, will have nothing more to do with him [the black]."[1] Although lynching reached its peak in Southern states in the 1890s and Jim Crow legislation steadily relegated blacks to a position of political, economic, and social inequality,[2] many Northerners were apparently anxious to believe that the "wisest and best" men of the South could solve the Southern race problem and that indeed, a "New South" free from the legacy of racial injustice was in fact becoming a reality.[3]

The extent to which some Northern liberals abandoned the freedmen and the cause of civil rights around the turn of the century is an issue that invites further study. David W. Southern, in *The Malignant Heritage: Yankee Progressives and the Negro Question*, strongly indicts such national political leaders as Theodore Roosevelt, William H. Taft, and Woodrow Wilson for their racial attitudes and policies during this period. Southern condemns as well a number of leading liberal intellectuals and journalists for their blindness to racial injustice during the so-called "Progressive Era."[4] Other studies[5] have added credence to the argument that progressivism was for whites only and that many Northerners who were former allies of the freedmen had, with but few exceptions, become increasingly disillusioned with the slow pace of black progress by the opening years of the new century and in consequence reconstructed their notions of equality to exclude blacks and other "colored" peoples.

James Anderson and Donald Spivey, among others, have even more pointedly argued that those Northerners who did remain involved in Southern affairs, especially in the arena of black education, did so in order to help create an educational program "deliberately calculated to fit the freedmen to a new form of servitude in the caste economy of the post-war South."[6] Northern industrialists who had economic interests in the South are especially singled out by these historians for censure. Anderson's economic analysis, for example, leads him to contend that the "main end of the Southern industrialists, Northern philanthropists, and educational reformers was to force blacks into a workable scheme of social organization that would permit the structuring of a caste economy least removed from slavery. The problem of the school was to help fit blacks into that scheme."[7]

If Anderson's analysis resounds too strongly with conspiratorial tones, one must nonetheless confront the fact that, during this period of a retreat from reconstruction, widespread support was given to the philosophy of accommodation and compromise espoused by Booker T. Washington. While it has become fashionable to portray Washington as a Judas for the stand exemplified in his Atlanta address of 1895, such a simplistic view ignores the fact that many of America's most liberal spokesmen, for a wide range of reasons, orchestrating the position to which Washington gave voice. There is more than coincidence in the fact that Washington was awarded an honorary M.A. degree from Harvard University in 1896, only months after making his famous "Atlanta Compromise" speech. Harvard's gesture was symbolic of the fact that many Northerners as well as Southerners were indeed ready to lay aside the "bloody shirt" and to move toward the new century with the myopic assurance that all had been done that could or should be done for the black man. From here on, ran the conventional wisdom, the rise from slavery would largely depend upon the black man's own initiative and ability.

In the context of the paradox presented by the rising tide of progressive reform on the one hand and the capitulation of many American liberals to the concept of a racially separate and unequal society on the other, an examination of the views of selected liberal reformers can be instructive. In this study the racial attitudes and reform prescriptions of Charles W. Eliot, president of Harvard University for forty years (1869-1909), are presented as a case study in order to portray the evolving position of a widely respected educational reformer and New England liberal. Eliot, who was sometimes characterized as the nation's "first private citizen" and "our greatest moral force as an individual,"[8] was noted for his leadership in liberal causes. He was outspoken in support of "progressive" reforms in such areas as municipal government, civil service, capital-labor relations, conservation, sex hygiene, and international peace as well as in education. His direct and authoritative manner of speaking could quickly rankle those who held contrary views, but his was a voice that demanded an audience and not infrequently provoked a response. Eliot's tendency to offer judgments on issues across the spectrum of human events caused him to become, in Ralph Barton Perry's phrase, "adviser-at-large to the American people on things-in-general."[9] Although certainly Eliot cannot be said to have represented the views of all Northern whites any more than Booker T. Washington can be pictured as a spokesman for all Southern blacks, still his posture is revealing as one strand of Northern liberal thinking on the race issue. When considered in this context, the parallels between the views of Eliot and Washington as well as the paradoxes inherent in Eliot's own "liberal" attitudes take on special significance. It becomes apparent that as Eliot and other Northern liberals added their endorsement to the "Atlanta Compromise," the solution to the "Negro problem" became more than a matter of regional accommodation. The compromise, if we must call it that, took on national proportions. It became an "American compromise."

Eliot and Washington: Paradoxes and Parallels

Clearly there was little in the backgrounds of the son of a slave and the son of a mayor of Boston to cause them to reach somewhat similar conclusions regarding the place of the black man in American society.[10] When Washington was born in a crude slave hut on a Virginia plantation in 1856, Eliot had already completed his B.A. at Harvard and was serving as tutor of mathematics at his alma mater. After Emancipation young Washington struggled to obtain snatches of schooling while also working in a salt furnace and coal mine. During the same period, Eliot achieved the rank of assistant professor at Harvard and then, from 1863-1865, observed the closing years of the Civil War from newspaper accounts and letters while traveling in Europe. In 1865 Eliot returned to the states to become professor of analytical chemistry at the newly formed Massachusetts Institute of Technology. It was from this post in 1869 that Eliot was called, at the age of thirty-five, to become president of Harvard University, a position he held until 1909. Eliot was thus beginning his third year as president of Harvard when sixteen-year-old Booker T. Washington proved himself worthy of entry into Hampton Institute by sweeping the floors to the satisfaction of the matron. And it was at Hampton that Washington mastered those principles of fidelity, honesty, persistence, and a devotion to the ideals of individualism and self-help that were so highly prized by the Puritans and their descendants, men like Charles W. Eliot.

As an educational reformer, Eliot was so involved with the internal restructuring of Harvard during the first two decades of his tenure as president that he gave only passing notice to larger social currents. Strengthening the professional schools, expanding the elective system, upgrading the quality of the faculty and the student body, reforming the curriculum—these and other immediate tasks absorbed his energies and tended to divert his attention from external matters. As far as the South was concerned, Eliot's main interest during the early phase of his administration was with wooing Southern students back to Harvard. In an address before the New York Harvard Club in 1872, Eliot observed with noticeable pleasure that Harvard could number in its ranks thirty-three students from the former slave states, not counting Missouri. Noting that Yale had twenty students from the same states, Eliot held forth the olive branch by proclaiming that "we are beginning to welcome back again the South." Encouraged as he was by these signs, however, Eliot was nonetheless sensitive to the wounds of war and reconstruction and expressed his concern that among the casualties of the war was Harvard's loss of students from the leading Southern families. "We still miss," he lamented, "the old South Carolina, Virginia, and Louisiana names, and we may be sure that the wisdom of our legislators will not have perfectly solved the difficult problem of Southern reconstruction until the Pinckneys and Barnwells, the Middletons, Eustises and Lees go to colleges again with the Adamses and Lincolns, the Kents, Winthrops and Hoars."[11]

In part, at least, Eliot's strong desire to enroll more students from the "better" Southern families at Harvard eventually motivated him to concern himself with Southern conditions. There is little question but that Eliot's own Brahmin heritage predisposed him to view the plight of the South from the perspective of the former patrician class. At the same time, however, he was struck by the sluggish pace of progress in the South when compared with the tempo of growth and industrialization in the North. He despairingly observed in 1900 that the Southern situation was "depressing," and that "the backward condition of our Southern States is one of the saddest facts in all the world."[12] Eliot's specific desire to attract Southerners to Harvard and his more general but no less genuine wish to see the South enter the mainstream of national progress prompted him by the turn of the century to investigate more closely the problems and the prospects of the region in an effort to promote both ends.

Lessons From the South

Not a few Southerners saw themselves as capable of educating the president of Harvard as to the unique dimensions of the Southern race problem. Southerners of both races and all classes made their views known to Eliot on questions regarding the social and political ramifications of suffrage for blacks, on the advisability of a dual school system, on the efficacy of industrial education or any education at all for blacks, on the moral habits and inclinations of Southern blacks as compared with whites, and even on the appropriateness of Booker T. Washington dining with President Theodore Roosevelt.

Not all correspondents were as forthright as one writer from Louisiana, who identified himself as "of the 'poor white trash' of the South—that is to say I'm only a skilled workingman—owning neither a great plantation nor a newspaper" and whose only "'Harvard' was a log schoolhouse, and not since the age of 13 at that." Apologizing for thus not being able to "produce a finished essay on the subject," the writer nonetheless proceeded to advise Eliot that the workingmen of the South had "no interest whatsoever in the education of the negro" and challenged that newspapermen and politicians who said otherwise were as far from representing the correct "Southern Sentiment" on the race question as was Roosevelt from approaching greatness! Should any "Tuskegeeized" or Harvard-educated black threaten to take his job, the writer advised Eliot, his response would be to "shoot him just as

soon as dark gave the better opportunity! And never be in a moment's dread of indictment by a grand jury of my neighbors!" Convinced that social equality and miscegenation were the only outcomes of political and educational equality, the writer closed his letter by asserting: "The negro must move! So long as he is here so long will there be dissension. Let him go into Old Mexico and Central America and have done with this country for all time. Then will you and I be friends and not until then."[13]

A correspondent from Savannah, rejecting the idea that blacks possessed the ability to advance at all, informed Eliot that "those portions of Africa where the negro has full sway are as much of a wilderness as they were thousands of years ago." This Southerner took strong exception to the view that the black had made substantial progress in the forty years since slavery. "A forced, hothouse 'advance' is not true progress," he reasoned. "As well might driftwood be considered as swimming while transported downstream by the current. *No other race in history has been carried along on the back of another race as has the negro.*"[14]

Most of the letters that Eliot received from those anxious to inform him of the racial situation in the South were more moderate in tone, and in some cases the correspondence between the Harvard president and selected Southern advisers spanned a period of several years.[15] Moreover, Eliot's connections with Northern philanthropists such as Robert C. Ogden, William H. Baldwin, and John D. Rockefeller, Jr., exposed him to the perspectives and efforts of men who were themselves involved with Southern educators and upper-class paternalists in a campaign of Southern uplift.[16] Thus, when in 1904 Eliot ventured to speak on "The Problems of the Negro"[17] before a gathering of the Armstrong Association of Hampton Institute in New York and two years later when at Tuskegee he spoke to the topic "What Uplifts a Race and What Holds It Down,"[18] he was by no means uninformed as to Southern attitudes and opinions. Yet whatever the insights and sympathies some Southerners and their Northern allies may have aroused in Eliot, his clear and uncompromising assertions in private correspondence and his conciliatory yet forceful public addresses suggest that Eliot characteristically, if not always consistently, endeavored to reason from liberal principles. Responding, for example, to a Southern minister who interpreted Roosevelt's inviting Booker T. Washington to dinner as a deliberate insult to the South, Eliot firmly expressed his own position:

As a rule, I select my companions and guests, not by the color of their skins, but by their social and personal quality. It would never occur to me not to invite to my house an educated Chinaman or Japanese because their skin is yellow or brownish, or to avoid asking a negro to my table if he were an intelligent, refined and interesting person. It is the intelligence, refinement and good judgment of Mr. Booker Washington which makes him an agreable guest at any table; and to many of us Northern people, the fact that nearly half his blood is African is a matter of indifference.[19]

It may well be, as Hugh Hawkins contends, that Eliot's stance in this instance was at best only "superficially tolerant" and reveals formidable standards to which others had to conform.[20] Yet it is clear that Eliot outwardly rejected race as a criterion for social intercourse. However elitist as judged by contemporary standards Eliot may appear, he was in his own day among a liberal minority who were prone to interpret racial differences as legacies of culture as well as genetics. While Eliot understood that genetically inherited traits were not immutable (short of undesirable "amalgamation"), he contended that the possibilities of cultural assimilation were vast and believed that somehow the process of assimilation could gradually qualify and "render less visible" some racial differences. At the same time, he maintained that "the diversities of race need no more be extinguished under free institutions than the diversities between human individuals." "Freedom," he proclaimed, "should encourage diversity, not extinguish it."[21] It is hardly surprising then that Eliot, who stood fast against nativism and the clamor to restrict immigration, should be singled out by one historian as an example of the "minority with faith" during the years when restrictionism was on the rise.[22]

For all of Eliot's commitment to libertarian principles and dependence upon his inner-directed moral sense, however, he proved on more than one occasion not in the least hostile to the pragmatic temper. If he was a staunch individualist, he was also sensitive to the demands of a rising corporate state and could in time speak with conviction about the necessity of individualism yielding to collectivism and the needs of the larger society.[23] And, while he can be viewed as an exponent of fair play and equality of opportunity, and as an outspoken foe of racial discrimination, he must also be seen as one who, in assessing popular sentiment, could convince himself that there could perhaps be in some contexts racial distinctions without unjust racial discrimination.[24]

What then were the solutions offered by this liberal Northern reformer to the Southern race problem? What encouragement, what direction did he give those who searched for a way up from slavery and second-class citizenship into the promise of American life? And what assurances did he give those in the South and elsewhere who were prone to reject the idea that blacks and whites could ever live as coequal citizens, socially as well as politically? It is in searching out the answers to these questions that the dimensions of the American Compromise become clear.

Shaping the American Compromise

Sharing the platform with Andrew Carnegie, Hollis B. Frissell (the white principal of Hampton Institute), and Booker T. Washington, Eliot took the occasion of an address before the Armstrong Association meeting in New York City in 1904, to give public hearing to his views on the Southern race question. Eliot, then seventy years of age, was careful to note that there were fundamental points on which Northern and Southern sentiment was identical, foremost among these being the desire to preserve racial purity. "The Northern whites hold this opinion quite as firmly as the Southern whites," Eliot stated, "and," he continued, "inasmuch as the negroes hold the same view, this supposed danger of mutual racial impairment ought not to have much influence on practial measures." Sexual vice on the part of white men accounted for the limited degree of racial mixture which already existed, Eliot claimed, and nobody "worthy of consideration" would advocate racial intermarriage as a policy.[25]

It was against the backdrop of this assurance that racial mixture was anathema to the whole of American society—blacks as well as whites, Northerners as well as Southerners—that Eliot then proceeded to speak in more specific terms about differences in the treatment accorded blacks above and below the Mason-Dixon line. Noting that in the South separate provisions were made for blacks in schools, in public conveyances, and in public facilities, Eliot discounted the difference from practice in the North as being "socially insignificant." Indeed, Eliot observed, "with regard to coming into personal contact with negroes, the adverse feeling of the Northern whites is stronger than that of the Southern whites, who are accustomed to such contacts...."[26] Eliot noted further that while the North had not moved toward a dual school system, "in Northern towns where negro children are proportionally numerous there is just the same tendency and desire to separate them from the whites as there is in the South," a separation, he added, which if not effected by law may well result "by white parents procuring the transfer of their children to schools where negroes are few."[27] As Eliot thus evaluated the differences in practice between the North and South, he concluded that the underlying racial attitudes of the two regions appeared much the same No greater feeling of brotherhood, no deeper commitment to liberalism, no fervent devotion to ideals of liberty, equality, or justice were needed or warranted in explaining differences in practice. The fundamental explanation, Eliot contended, rested with the difference in the proportions between the races. Eliot described the situation accordingly:

> Put the prosperous Northern whites into the Southern states, in immediate contact with millions of negroes, and they would

promptly establish separate schools for the colored population, whatever the necessary cost. Transfer the Southern whites to the North, where the negroes form but an insignificant fraction of the population, and in a generation or two they would not care whether there were a few negro children in the public schools or not, and would therefore avoid the expense of providing separate schools for the few colored children.[28]

In setting forth these propositions, Eliot was speaking not in terms of what "ought" to be, or even necessarily what he wished were the case, but rather in terms of observed social realities in the North and his understanding, based on his secondhand knowledge of the South, of conditions and attitudes in that region. However much he might personally feel that race should not be the determining consideration in regard either to dinner guests or schoolmates, he judged popular sentiment to be of a different mind. And in so judging, he gave Northern liberal endorsement to the Southern system of dual schooling.

On another matter of popular sentiment, however—at least Southern sentiment—Eliot saw less national unanimity. A real difference existed, Eliot felt, between Northern and Southern views as to the supposed connection between political equality and social equality. The "Southern view" was perhaps most directly stated by Frederic Bromberg, a Mobile attorney and frequent correspondent with Eliot on the Southern problem. According to Bromberg, Southern objection to black suffrage had nothing to do with "the ignorance of the emancipated race." Rather, Bromberg asserted:

... no amount of intelligence or culture upon the part of any one with negro blood in him can overcome the objection to him as a coequal citizen.... [We] do not object to negro suffrage because of the negro's incapacity, but because he is a negro—because suffrage and the right to hold office are usually associated with each other, and holding office means possession of power, and possession of power means social equality, and social equality tends to miscegenation, and miscegenation is what we will not tolerate, and therefore oppose the beginnings....[29]

In correspondence as well as in public forums, Eliot labored to undermine what he perceived as the illogic of this Southern syllogism. Using European as well as Northern experience, Eliot argued repeatedly that possession of the ballot had never had anything to do with the social status of the individual voter. Eliot favored, as he felt most Northerners did, educational qualifications for suffrage, but he refused to accept the idea that blacks, as blacks, should be denied the ballot or right to hold office. Political rights, he main-

tained, were separable from social intercourse. "In Northern cities," he reasoned, "... the social divisions are numerous and deep; and the mere practice of political equality gives no means whatever of passing from one social set to another supposed to be higher. The social sets are determined by like education, parity of income, and similarity of occupation, and not at all by the equality of every citizen before the law."[30]

It was indeed this very logic that informed Eliot's administration of Harvard University. He frequently and fondly proclaimed that Harvard recognized among its officers and students neither class, race, caste, sect, nor political party. While in one instance denying that there was a tendency in the North "to break down the social barriers between the white race and the negro race," Eliot at the same time firmly asserted that, as far as Harvard was concerned, any person who could pass the admission examinations would be received as a student and, upon completion of his studies, would "receive the degree without the least regard to his racial quality or religious or political opinions."[31] But as far as social relations were concerned, individual preferences (indeed prejudices) superceded institutional policies. "Membership in the societies and clubs of Harvard," he wrote in 1907, "is determined entirely by social selection—this social selection being made on the basis of similar tastes, habits, and ambitions." Japanese students had been admitted to some of the desirable clubs at Harvard, Eliot noted, but he could recall no instance of blacks being invited to join a social club and thought the possibility of such "extremely unlikely."[32]

Thus, on the matter of social equality, Eliot's attitude closely paralleled the public pronouncements of Booker T. Washington. In social matters, at Harvard or elsewhere in the nation, individuals or groups were free to include or exclude according to their own preferences or prejudices. But in matters political, whether it be university admission or universal suffrage, meritocratic standards only should be invoked. There need not be, Eliot insisted, any connection between political equality and social equality.[33]

Education: Separate But Equal

Access to political equality (and the way toward gaining the tastes, habits, and ambitions that might make one socially acceptable), however, depended in part upon educational opportunity. Having acknowledged the apparent necessity of separate education in the Southern states, Eliot would not yield ground to those who argued for grossly unequal education for blacks. As Eliot interpreted Southern attitudes on the type and amount of schooling black children should receive, three different opinions seemed to emerge.

"Some Southern whites, educated and uneducated," Eliot said, "think that any education is an injury to the negro race, and that the negro should continue to multiply in the Southern States with access only to the lowest forms of labor." Another segment of the population, he continued, "holds that negro children should be educated, but only for manual occupations.... This section approves of manual training and trade schools, but takes no interest in the higher education of the negro." There was, however, a third, and to Eliot, proper attitude held by still other white Southerners, one which recognized "the obvious fact that a separate negro community must be provided with negro professional men of good quality, else neither the physical nor the moral welfare of the negro population will be thoroughly provided for."[34] Thus, to Eliot, beyond the ideal of political equality and the requirements for public safety, there existed a compelling justification for adequate provisions for higher education of blacks. "The provision of a higher education for negroes," Eliot proclaimed, "is the logical consequence of the proposition that the black and white races should both be kept pure...."[35] Separate education was thus a basic requirement for the maintenance of a segregated society.

Sympathetically recognizing the "peculiar burden upon the Southern States caused by the separation between the black and the white races in the institutions of education," Eliot closed his address before the Armstrong Association by calling for federal aid to Southern education.[36] The national government, he said, should make it possible for black schools in the South to be kept open eight months of the year instead of four. Separate colleges for agriculture and the mechanical arts should be provided throughout the South and separate professional schools for blacks should be established within existing Southern universities, all made possible by national support. "It was in the supreme interest of the whole nation that the Southern States were impoverished forty years ago by a four years' blockade and the destruction of their whole industrial system," Eliot reasoned. "It is fair that the nation should help rebuild Southern prosperity in the very best way, namely, through education."[37]

Concern with fairness—even with public security and racial purity—might have little impact on a man like Mississippi's James K. Vardaman who could ask "Why squander money on his education when the only effect is to spoil a good field hand and make an insolent cook?"[38] But Eliot's appeals, like Washington's, were primarily addressed to moderates and liberals who recognized that the problems of the blacks were also the problems of the whites. Northern as well as Southern. Yet Eliot believed, as did Washington, that provision of educational opportunities was only part of the struggle up from slavery. In the final analysis, both men maintained that the place of the black man in American society depended primarily upon the use he made of avail-

able opportunities, however limited. That their own and later generations would often twist this formulation into a cruel mechanism for "blaming the victim" was a consequence these "self-made" men could hardly appreciate.

Education and the Doctrine of Self-Help

When Eliot was invited to make an address at Tuskegee in 1906, he chose as his theme, "What Uplifts a Race and What Holds It Down." Eliot identified four essentials which must be sought after by any race which hoped, as he put it, to lift itself "out of barbarism into civilization." First among the elements necessary was a commitment to steady, productive labor. Eliot stated:

Every race that has risen from barbarism to civilization has done so by developing all grades of productive labor, beginning with agricultural labor, and rising through the fundamental mechanic arts, and mining, and quarrying, to manufacturing, elaborate transportation, trade, commerce, the fine arts, and professional labor. Respect for labor of all sorts, for the simplest as well as the most complex forms, will be manifested by every rising race. This respect is founded not only on the conviction that productive labor yields comfort, security, and progressive satisfactions, but also on the firm belief that regular labor in freedom develops the higher intellectual and moral qualities of the human being.[39]

Second to the uplift provided by honest labor, Eliot told the Tuskegee students, was devotion to Christian family life. "Respect for family life," he said, "fidelity in the marriage relation, and appreciation of the sacredness of childhood are sure signs that a race is rising."[40]

Education held third place in the scale of values Eliot sought to impress upon Tuskegee students. Observing that Americans in general seemed to place more faith in education as an agency for uplifting a race than any other avenue, Eliot contended that "habitual productive labor and family life must precede education; and the education of children cannot prevent the decline of any people whose habit of labor or family life has been impaired." Third in importance though it might be, education, especially education that would contribute to industrial efficiency, was heralded by Eliot as vital. In a line which must have warmed the heart of Washington, Eliot declared: "This effort to make education contribute immediately to industrial efficiency is thoroughly wholesome in all grades of education; and particularly it is wholesome for a race which has but lately emerged from the profound barbarism of slavery; for it unites in one uplifting process all three of the civilizing agencies I have already mentioned—productive labor, home-making, and mental and moral training."[41]

Before he proceeded into a discussion of the fourth agency of the civilizing process—respect for law—Eliot acknowledged that current educational conditions in the South were inadequate, not only for black children but for whites as well. Poorly trained teachers, short school terms, early leaving age, and limited curricula offerings all were hindrances to educational opportunity. Sounding again the theme of federal aid, Eliot declared that at least one institution like Tuskegee or Hampton should exist in every Southern state.[42]

Even though Eliot publicly praised Tuskegee and was doubtless convinced that Washington's uplift philosophy, which he endorsed, was in most respects appropriate, he observed inadequacies in the program he saw in operation. Eliot's uneasiness with the Tuskegee program was no doubt heightened by the information provided him by Roscoe C. Bruce, a Harvard graduate, then a teacher at Tuskegee, who had earlier complained to Washington that industrial activities too frequently encroached upon the academic and that "the education of the pupil is largely sacrificed to the demands of productive labor." The charges Bruce, an insider, leveled against Tuskegee—that standards of scholarship were woefully inadequate, that a student's capacity for productive labor and "goodness of heart" counted more toward promotion than intellectual attainment, that the teaching staff was inferior, that students "who plan to teach school have not one minute more for academic studies than the pupils who plan to make horseshoes or to paint houses"[43]—were not lost on Eliot. Several months after his visit to Tuskegee, Eliot was moved to inform Washington of areas in which the institute needed to improve. After questioning the ability of Tuskegee to offer adequate training in nursing and the ministry and making some recommendations regarding the use of capital outlay funds, Eliot then hit the problem of academic training. He noted his impression that the manual labor dimension of the Tuskegee program threatened to overshadow the mental labor side. "Is it not important," Eliot asked, "that the graduates of Tuskegee should have acquired not only a trade or an art, but the power to read and cipher intelligently and a taste for reading?"[44]

In responding to Eliot's concerns, Washington endeavored to justify the work being done at Tuskegee with rural ministers and defended the institute's nursing program by noting that prior to Tuskegee's efforts, "there was no trained nurse within a radius of a hundred miles." "The question is," Washington stated, "whether we should turn out people who can partially relieve suffering, or wait until we, or some other institution, are in a position to turn out those who are much better equipped than our nurses are now." Promising nonetheless to lay all of Eliot's suggestions before the board of

trustees, Washington spoke to Eliot's concern for the academic side of Tuskegee by briefly noting, "We have already reorganized our course of training so that we are spending more time in strictly academic work than was true when you were here."[45]

If in these particulars the Harvard president and Tuskegee principal differed in their emphases, on most other matters of what has been termed "accommodationist philosophy," the two found grounds for common agreement. The month before Eliot made his "Uplift" speech at Tuskegee, he had solicited Washington's advice as to the treatment of certain topics. Washington seconded Eliot's call for the creation of Tuskegees in every Southern state and felt that Eliot's "placing emphasis upon the fact that there is a difference between social intermingling and political intermingling" would prove helpful. But Washington expressed reservations regarding Eliot's suggestion that he speak in specific terms as to just and unjust examples of racial separation. "There is a class of white people in the South and in the North," Washington advised, "who are always ready to insist on unreasonable and unjust separations to the extent that I very much fear that anything you might say in this direction would be twisted into an endorsement of unjust and unreasonable separation." Washington in particular cautioned Eliot against repeating the statement made before the Armstrong Association to the effect that Northern whites might feel segregation in public schools justified in areas where the Negro population is large. "I am wondering," Washington said, "whether or not the result might not be that the colored people would receive inferior opportunities for education rather than equal opportunities?" While Washington doubted that it would "be desirable or practicable on the part of either race to attempt to bring about coeducation in the South," he did not wish to see present Southern circumstances used to excuse segregation in other regions of the country. Concluding this appeal to Eliot with a slightly different twist to the theme made famous in his Atlanta Compromise speech, Washington stated: "In all things that are purely social, the colored people do not object to separation . . . but the difficulty is in the South in many cases civil privileges are confounded with social intercourse."[46]

Apparently satisfied with the merits of Washington's observations, Eliot contented himself in his Tuskegee address with only general references to proper and improper modes of racial accommodation. "The Republic desires and believes," Eliot stated, "that all competent men within its limits should enjoy political equality, the tests of competence being the same for all races." But he felt compelled to add: "Of course the Republic does not include under political equality social equality; for social equality rests on natural or instinctive likes and dislikes, affinities and repulsions, which no political institutions have ever been able to control."[47]

Eliot as Ambassador of Accommodation and Compromise

In 1909, on the eve of Eliot's retirement from the presidency of Harvard and one year after he became a member of the General Education Board, he was prevailed upon to undertake a Southern tour. Seeing the trip as a way to further cement the growing bridge between Harvard and the South, Eliot also looked upon a period of Southern travel as an opportunity to study first-hand conditions in that region as well as an occasion to spread further the doctrines of the American Compromise. With extended stops in various cities in Tennessee, Texas, Louisiana, Alabama, Georgia, and South and North Carolina, Eliot praised Southern progress, assured Southerners that their white counterparts in the North were at one with them on the matter of social separation between the races, delivered messages of "uplift" at black churches and colleges, and counseled whites to be just in their dealings with blacks. In Montgomery Eliot was quoted as saying that "the policy of the South regarding the negro is a wise one. The white people and the negroes should be kept apart in every respect." Taking direct aim at the critics of accommodationism, Eliot reportedly added: "The work being done by Booker T. Washington, I believe to be good for his race, and that done by Professor DuBois, harmful."48

In comforting Southerners with assurances that Northerners not only understood their problem but shared it, Eliot made yet another pronouncement that sparked quite a controversy in Northern, and even a few Southern newspapers. "In the North we have our race problem," Eliot declared in Memphis and elsewhere on his trip. "I do not believe," he was quoted as saying, "in the admixture of even white races. For instance, the Irish, Jews, Italians, and other European nationalities should not intermarry with Americans of English descent."49 Newspaper accounts as to Eliot's precise wording varied, and while some publications, such as *Harper's Weekly*,50 chose to suspend judgment until confirmation of Eliot's remarks could be obtained, other papers were less patient. The *Boston Pilot* charged that Eliot was an ancestor worshipper and editorialized that he had for too many years been "talking altogether too much on every subject."51 Other papers wrote that Eliot deserved watching, one New York paper, *Town Topics*, venturing the opinion that perhaps Eliot had "reached the period of senility."52 Even the *Charleston News and Courier* expressed puzzlement, arguing that surely Eliot recognized that the "American" was the product of intermarriage among stocks differing "in minor degree." The *News and Courier* resolved the riddle by asserting: "Of course, the intermarriage of the races when the term connotes peoples of different color, as Chinese, Malays, and Negroes, ought to be prohibited and that is probably all that Dr. Eliot has said."53 A week later the same paper editorialized enthusiastically for Eliot, saying:

"He has learned a great many things in the last twenty-five years, and has displayed remarkable familiarity with the peculiar problems with which our people have had to deal all these weary years."54

If Eliot's overzealous concern for racial purity caused a temporary controversy in the Northern press, it was an episode that rather quickly faded away. What remained from Eliot's Southern tour was a testimony to the very ideals of goodwill, patience, responsibility—and accommodation—that formed the platform of the American Compromise. Eliot had laid out, as had Washington earlier in Atlanta, a program of self-help and "uplift" that gave vague promise of allowing the black to earn a "respectable" place for himself in a socially segregated American society. To blacks whose ambitions and frustrations led them to demand or expect "too much" immediately, and to those whites who doubted that progress on the part of the black man was ever possible, Eliot could paternalistically pass on the wisdom of one of America's leading educational reformers and liberal statesmen:

Why, you believe that your race problem is a new one, but it has been experienced before, only it is intensified here [in the South]. The negro cannot be expected to be ready for all phases of civilization only a few decades removed from the time when he first began to enjoy civilization as a free man. After 500 or 1000 years we may expect more substantial growth.55

Conclusion

If the tonic of self-help, educational endeavor, dependence upon white paternalism, and faith in the gradual process of cultural assimilation seemed at best an inappropriate placebo if not a near-fatal opiate, such a prescription must nonetheless be judged in the context of prevailing American liberal thought, not merely in the narrower context of black capitulation to Southern racism. Charles Eliot was but one in a long line of Northern liberals at the turn of the century who approached the race issue with counsel of compromise and accommodation. The strategies of accommodation tacitly agreed upon by Northern philanthropists and Southern reformers and endorsed by liberals such as Eliot were intended to dampen the appeal of racist demagogues and soften the demands of impatient freedmen, all for the sake of Southern progress and racial harmony. However, advocacy of accommodationist policies served in time to weaken the position of liberals as guardians of the interests of blacks and other minorities in the North as well as in the South. Eliot, for example, although a consistent champion of political equality and an opponent of racial bigotry, discounted the significance of social discrimination and came to accept as a matter of necessity the existence of a racially segregated society. While he advocated educational opportunity, he nonetheless gave his blessing to the system of dual schooling in areas where the black population was sizeable. And although he sincerely believed in the efficacy of the Puritan ethic, he preached the values of patience as well as hard work and calmly asserted that significant advance on the part of black Americans as a whole would result only after generations of effort.

Even though such strategies of accommodation and deferred commitments were condemned by those who assumed a more militant stand, the difference between "liberal-conservatives" such as Booker T. Washington and Charles W. Eliot and their more radical critics may well have been, as Eugene Genovese has argued, more a difference in emphasis, tactics, and public stance than one of fundamental ideology.[56] The goal of Washington no less than DuBois was the attainment by blacks of full rights of citizenship. As August Meier has noted, "The central theme in Washington's philosophy was that through thrift, industry, and Christian character Negroes would eventually attain their constitutional rights."[57] Thus, the accommodationist tactics of Washington were immediate means toward an ultimate end of racial equality and justice. In adopting tactics that won the approval of liberal and moderate whites, North and South, Washington was seeking allies in the struggle, recognizing that without white support, no amount of effort on the part of blacks would bring positive results. Similarly, it was W. E. B. DuBois in his celebrated critique of Washington who asserted that "While it is a great truth to say that the negro must strive and strive mightily to help himself, it is equally true that unless his striving be not simply seconded, but rather aroused and encouraged by the initiative of the richer and wiser environing group, he cannot hope for great success."[58] Certainly the encouragement and endorsements given by Charles Eliot, a respected member of the "richer and wiser environing group," were not the only directives he could have set forth, but his axioms were unquestionably representative of the major doctrines of what had become an American Compromise.

Notes

The author wishes to thank Professors Hugh Hawkins, Robert Bremner, Louis Harlan, and Ronald Goodenow for their helpful comments on earlier drafts.

1. *Nation*, April 5, 1877, as cited in Paul H. Buck, *The Road to Reunion, 1865-1900* (New York: Vintage Books, 1959), p. 294.

2. C. Vann Woodward, *The Strange Career of Jim Crow*, rev. ed., (New York: Oxford University Press, 1966). Cf. Woodward's *Origins of the New South, 1877-1913* (Baton Rouge, La.: Louisiana State University Press, 1951), p. 351, where he notes that nationally lynchings averaged 187.5 per annum between 1889 and 1899 and dropped to 92.5 during the next decade. However, the percentage of lynchings in the South increased from about 82 percent in the 1890s to about 92 percent in the 1900-1909 decade and almost 90 percent of the victims were blacks.

3. The metamorphosis from "creed" to "myth" of a "New South" based on a reconciliation of sectional differences, racial peace, and a new economic and social order based on industry and scientific, diversified agriculture is insightfully examined in Paul M. Gaston, *The New South Creed: A Study in Southern Mythmaking* (New York: Alfred A. Knopf, 1970). On the dynamics of sectional reconciliation also see Buck, *The Road to Reunion* and Stanley P. Hirshon, *Farewell to the Bloody Shirt: Northern Republicans and the Southern Negro 1877-1893* (Bloomington, Ind.: Indiana University Press, 1962).

4. David W. Southern, *The Malignant Heritage: Yankee Progressives and the Negro Question, 1901-1914* (Chicago: Loyola University Press, 1968). Southern points to the clergyman Lyman Abbott and former abolitionists Carl Schurz and Charles F. Adams, Jr., as liberals who changed their views on racial equality. Ray Stannard Baker, Herbert Baxter Adams, John R. Commons, Josiah Royce, Walter Lippmann, Herbert Croly, and Walter Weyl all in varying degrees began to consider blacks a separate caste which blighted the "promise of American life." See Chapter III, especially.

5. Charles B. Dew in "Critical Essay on Recent Works," in Woodward, *Origins*, pp. 517-628, provides an excellent survey of studies on this topic. See especially pp. 577-584. See also Arthur S. Link and Rembert W. Patrick, eds., *Writing Southern History: Essays in Historiography in Honor of Fletcher M. Green* (Baton Rouge, La.: Louisiana State University Press, 1965).

6. James Douglas Anderson, "Education for Servitude: The Social Purposes of Schooling in the Black South, 1870-1930," (Ph.D. diss., University of Illinois, 1973), p. 3; Donald Spivey, *Schooling for the New Slavery: Black Industrial Education, 1868-1915* (Westport, Conn.: Greenwood Press, 1978).

7. Anderson, "Education for Servitude," p. 4.

8. Eugen Kuehnemann, *Charles W. Eliot: President of Harvard University* (Boston: Houghton Mifflin Co., 1909), pp. 1-4, as cited in Hugh Hawkins, *Between Harvard and America: The Educational Leadership of Charles W. Eliot* (New York: Oxford University Press, 1972), p. 290.

9. Ralph Barton Perry as quoted in Hawkins, *Between Harvard and America*, p. 298.

10. Booker T. Washington, *Up From Slavery: An Autobiography* (New York: A. L. Burt, Co., 1901) is Washington's most polished account of his life. A more objective analysis is provided in Louis Harlan, *Booker T. Washington: The Making of a Black Leader* (New York:

Oxford University Press, 1972). On Washington's thought (as opposed to his biography) the standard work is still August Meier, *Negro Thought in America 1880-1915* (Ann Arbor, Mich.: University of Michigan Press, 1963). On Eliot, in addition to Hawkins cited above, see Henry James, *Charles W. Eliot: President of Harvard University, 1869-1909*, 2 vols. (New York: Houghton Mifflin, 1930).

11. Charles W. Eliot, Speech at New York Harvard Club, February 21, 1872, (Charles W. Eliot Papers, Harvard University Archives, Box 334 (hereafter cited as Eliot Papers).

12. Eliot to William G. Brown, July 26, 1900 (Eliot Papers, Letterbook 92).

13. Forrest Pope to Eliot, March 2, 1904 (Eliot Papers, Box 234).

14. Charles Kohler to Eliot, March 2, 1904 (Eliot Papers, Box 234). Emphasis in original.

15. See, for example, the series of letters from Frederick G. Bromberg to Eliot (Eliot Papers, Box 123) and William B. Watkins to Eliot (Eliot Papers, Box 234).

16. On the "Ogden Movement" and the work and racial views of the men who formed the interlocking directorate of the Southern Education Board and the General Education Board, see Charles W. Dabney, *Universal Education in the South*, 2 vols. (Chapel Hill, N.C.: University of North Carolina Press, 1936); Louis R. Harlan, *Separate and Unequal: Public School Campaigns and Racism in the Southern Seaboard States 1901-1915* (Chapel Hill, N.C.: University of North Carolina Press, 1958); and Woodward, *Origins of the New South*, especially Chapter 15, "Philanthropy and the Forgotten Man." While Eliot was not formally a part of the Southern Education Movement, he was on its fringes and after 1908 became more directly involved in Southern educational developments as a member of the General Education Board.

17. Charles W. Eliot, "The Problems of the Negro," in *The Work and Influence of Hampton*, Proceedings of a meeting held in New York City, February 12, 1904, under the direction of the Armstrong Association (Eliot Papers, Box 337).

18. Charles W. Eliot, "What Uplifts a Race and What Holds It Down," Address at Tuskegee Institute, April 1906, TS (Eliot Papers, Box 338).

19. Eliot to Rev. S. A. Steel, October 25, 1901 (Eliot Papers, Letterbook 92).

20. Hawkins, *Between Harvard and America*, p. 182.

21. Charles W. Eliot, "The Contemporary American Conception of Equality Among Men as a Social and Political Ideal," Phi Beta Kappa Oration, University of Missouri, June 2, 1909 (Eliot Papers, Box 340).

22. Barbara Miller Solomon, *Ancestors and Immigrants: A Changing New England Tradition* (Cambridge: Harvard University Press, 1956), pp. 99-102, 186-188. Cf. Hawkins, *Between Harvard and America*, pp. 182, 353. See also Eliot to Edward Lauterbach (President of National Liberal Immigration League), January 10, 1911 (Eliot Papers, Box 341).

23. See, for example, Charles W. Eliot, "Individualism vs. Collectivism," Address, New England Society in City of New York, 1905 (Eliot Papers, Box 337) and "Address at the Second Annual Conference on No-License Workers of Massachusetts," October 29, 1908, TS (Eliot Papers, Box 339).

24. Cf. Hawkins, *Between Harvard and America*, p. 191.

25. Eliot, "The Problems of the Negro," p. 9.

26. Ibid., p. 10.

27. Ibid., p. 9.

28. Ibid.

29. Frederick G. Bromberg to Eliot, October 29, 1901 (Eliot Papers, Box 123). Bromberg was a Harvard graduate of the class of 1858, a Unionist during the war, and a member of Congress during Reconstruction. While Eliot could not agree with Bromberg's position on suffrage restrictions, he nonetheless recommended him to Theodore Roosevelt as a suitable candidate for the office of district attorney for the southern district of Alabama. See Eliot to President Roosevelt, December 17, 1901 (Eliot Papers, Letterbook 92).

30. Eliot, "The Problems of the Negro," p. 10. See also Eliot to Frederick G. Bromberg, December 6, 1901 (Eliot Papers, Letterbook 92).

31. Eliot to Bruce L. Keenan, August 9, 1907 (Eliot Papers, Letterbook 96).

32. Ibid. The number of blacks at Harvard during the Eliot years was small. Eliot's secretary, Jerome Greene, when asked in 1904 about the number of "full blooded negroes at Harvard," confessed that accurate statistics were not available but that estimates placed the number at about fifteen, or one-third of one percent of the student body. He guessed that there had probably been forty or fifty black students at Harvard during the preceding ten years. See Jerome D. Greene to J. N. Hazlehurst, October 24, 1904 (Eliot Papers, Box 284). See also W. E. B. DuBois's description of his years at Harvard in *The Autobiography of W. E. B. DuBois* (New York: International Publishers, 1968), pp. 132-153.

33. Eliot, "The Problems of the Negro," p. 11.

34. Ibid., p. 13.

35. Ibid.

36. Ibid. Eliot framed a resolution to this effect for NEA consideration in 1905. See "Resolutions Suggested to Dr. Wm. H. Maxwell at his Request for the NEA Convention of 1905," TS, June 12, 1905 (Eliot Papers, Letterbook 95).

37. Ibid., p. 15.

38. As quoted in Roger M. Williams, "The Atlanta Compromise," *American History Illustrated* 3 (April 1968), p. 18. For an examination of Vardaman's several variations on this theme, see William F. Holmes, *The White Chief: James Kimble Vardaman* (Baton Rouge, La.: Louisiana University Press, 1970), especially pp. 78, 122 and passim.

39. Eliot, "What Uplifts a Race and What Holds It Down," pp. 1-2.

40. Ibid., p. 3.
41. Ibid., p. 3–4.
42. Ibid., p. 5–6.
43. Roscoe C. Bruce to Booker T. Washington, April 12, 1906, copy, (Eliot Papers, Box 234).
44. Eliot to Washington, September 7, 1906 (Eliot Papers, Letterbook 95).
45. Washington to Eliot, October 20, 1906 (Eliot Papers, Box 255). Bruce had earlier confirmed that "to my surprise and delight Principal Washington has already granted in modified form some of the things I have so long been asking for." Roscoe C. Bruce to Eliot, April 23, 1906 (Eliot Papers, Box 204).
46. Washington to Eliot, March 7, 1906. See also Jesse Max Barber to Washington, April 23, 1906 in Louis R. Harlan and Raymond W. Smock, eds., *The Booker T. Washington Papers*, vol. 8, (Urbana, Ill.: University of Illinois Press, 1979), p. 585 in which Barber states: "I am glad to have had the opportunity of reading this letter which you wrote to President Eliot. Evidently, Mr. Eliot was going to make a speech that would have done us a great deal of harm, and I am glad you influenced him not to deliver the address that he had in mind. In doing so, you have rendered the race a valuable service."
47. Eliot, "What Uplifts a Race and What Holds It Down," p. 8.
48. As quoted in *The Advertiser*, Montgomery, Alabama, March 9, 1909 (clipping, Eliot Papers, unnumbered box). DuBois's attack on Washington in *The Souls of Black Folk* (Chicago: A. C. McClurg & Co., 1904) and his leadership in the founding of the Niagara Movement

had clearly marked him as Washington's chief rival. See DuBois, *Autobiography*, pp. 236–253.
49. Ibid.
50. *Harper's Weekly*, April 3, 1909 (clipping, Eliot Papers, unnumbered box).
51. "Is He an Ancestory [sic] Worshipper?", *The Pilot*, Boston, March 6, 1909 (clipping, Eliot Papers, unnumbered box).
52. *Town Topics*, New York, March 11, 1909 (clipping, Eliot Papers, unnumbered box).
53. *News and Courier*, Charleston, S.C., March 10, 1909 (clipping, Eliot Papers, unnumbered box).
54. As quoted in ibid., March 17, 1909.
55. Ibid. In responding to a pointed letter from William Monroe Trotter, editor of *The Guardian*, Eliot similarly stated: "As to the most expedient treatment of colored people who are removed by four or five generations from Africa or slavery, I am in favor of leaving that problem to the people of a hundred years hence." Eliot to W. Monroe Trotter, May 5, 1909 (Eliot Papers, Letterbook 98).
56. See Eugene D. Genovese, *In Red and Black: Marxian Explorations in Southern and Afro-American History* (New York: Random House, 1968), pp. 143–144. Cf, however, Herbert Aptheker, "Comment," *Studies on the Left*, 6 (November/December 1966): 27–35.
57. Meier, *Negro Thought in America*, p. 103.
58. DuBois, *The Souls of Black Folk*, as quoted in Genovese, *Marxian Explorations*, p. 143.

Training the Apostles of Liberal Culture:
Black Higher Education, 1900-1935

James D. Anderson

FROM THE Reconstruction era through the Great Depression black higher education in the South existed essentially through a system of private liberal arts colleges. During this period, the federal government gave scant aid to black land-grant schools, and the southern states followed with a few funds for black normal schools and colleges. Between 1870 and 1890, nine federal black land-grant colleges were established in the South, and this number increased to sixteen by 1915. In that same year, there were also seven state-controlled black colleges in the South. These black federal land-grant and state schools, however, were colleges or normal schools in name only. According to the 1917 survey of black higher education conducted by Thomas Jesse Jones, only one of the sixteen black federal land-grant schools in the former slave states taught students at the collegiate level. The Florida Agricultural and Mechanical College enrolled 12 black college students. The seven black state colleges or normal schools had no black students enrolled in collegiate grades. Of the 7,513 students enrolled in the combined twenty-three black land-grant and state schools, 4,061 were classified as elementary level students, 3,400 were considered secondary level students and, as mentioned above, only 12 were actually enrolled in the collegiate curriculum. In 1915 there were 2,474 black students enrolled in collegiate grades in the southern states and the District of Columbia, and only 12 of them attended land-grant and state schools. Hence, as late as World War I virtually all of the black college students in the southern states were enrolled in privately owned colleges. This structure of black higher education, albeit significantly improved, persisted into the late 1920s. Arthur J. Klein's 1928 survey of black higher education demonstrated that the private black colleges were nearly all the sole promoters of higher education for Afro-American students. For the academic year 1926–27, there were 13,860 black college students in America, and approximately 75 percent of them were enrolled in private colleges. By the mid-1930s, this situation had changed and black college students in public institutions accounted for 43 percent of the total black college enrollment in the sixteen former slave states and District of Columbia. Until this time, however, private philanthropy largely determined the shape and even the survival of southern black higher education.[1]

In the South the history of black higher education from 1865 to 1935 involves largely a study of the interrelationship between philanthropy and black communities—or at least black leaders—in the development of colleges and professional schools for black youth. Three separate and distinct philanthropic groups formed the power structure in black higher education during this period. At the beginning of the Reconstruction era northern white benevolent societies and denominational bodies (missionary philanthropy) and black religious organizations (Negro philanthropy) established the beginnings of a system of higher education for black southerners. The third group of philanthropists was large corporate philanthropic foundations and wealthy individuals (industrial philanthropy). They had been involved in the development of black common schools and industrial normal schools since the Reconstruction era, but in 1914 they turned their attention to plans for the systematic development of a few select institutions of black higher education. From the late nineteenth century through the first third of the twentieth century these various groups of philanthropists debated the role of higher education in the overall scheme of black education and the relationship of classical liberal training to larger issues of black political and economic life. At the core of different educational ideologies and reform movements lay the central goal of preparing black leaders or "social guides," as they were sometimes called, for participation in the political economy of the New South. Each philanthropic group, therefore, took as its point of departure a particular view of the relationship of higher education to the "Negro's place" in the New South and shaped its educational policy and practices around that vision. The different philanthropic groups, particularly the missionary and industrial philanthropists, were in sharp disagreement over the ends and means of black education in general. Most visible were their divergent conceptions of the value and purpose of black higher education.

The northern mission societies, which were most prominent in the early crusade to establish institutions of higher education for the ex-slaves, were also largely responsible for sustaining the leading black colleges. The American Missionary Association (AMA) colleges for the freed people included Fisk University, Straight University (now Dillard), Talladega College, and Tougaloo College. The Freedmen's Aid Society of the Methodist Episcopal church founded Bennett College, Clark University, Claflin College, Meharry Medical College, Morgan College, Philander Smith College, Rust College, and Wiley College. The American Baptist Home Mission Society (ABHMS) administered Benedict College, Bishop College, Morehouse College, Shaw University, Spelman Seminary, and Virginia Union University. The Presbyterian Board of Missions for Freedmen maintained Biddle University (now Johnson C. Smith), Knoxville College, and Stillman Seminary. The major nondenominational colleges operated by independent boards of northern missionaries were Atlanta University, Howard University, and Leland University.[2]

The leading Negro philanthropic organization was the African Methodist Episcopal church, which paved the way for black religious denominations to establish and maintain colleges for black students. The leading AME colleges were Allen University, Morris Brown College, and Wilber-force College. Other AME schools were Paul Quinn College, Edward Waters College, Kittrell College, and Shorter College. The college work fostered by the African Methodist Episcopal Zion church was confined to one institution, Livingstone College. The Colored Methodist Episcopal church owned and operated four colleges: Lane, Paine, Texas, and Miles Memorial. The bulk of educational work on the college level promoted by black Baptist denominations was carried on in schools under the control of the American Baptist Home Mission Society. Still, several state conventions of black Baptists undertook to provide higher education for black youth in pressing areas not provided for by the ABHMS. Black colleges founded by the black Baptists included Arkansas Baptist College, Selma University, and Virginia College and Seminary. Most of the colleges financed by black religious organizations were small and inadequately equipped, but so were those administered by white religious organizations. According to Arthur Klein's 1928 survey of black colleges, black church organizations had been able to provide an average annual income for their colleges in excess of that for institutions operated by the northern white denominational boards. Black religious organizations owned so few of the total number of black colleges, however, that less than 15 percent of the total number of black college students were enrolled in institutions sponsored by those organizations. The black colleges supported and controlled by white missionary philanthropists enrolled a sizable majority of black college and professional students.[3]

The missionary philanthropists rallied their colleagues to support classical liberal education for black Americans as a means to achieve racial equality in civil and political life. They assumed that the newly emancipated blacks would move into mainstream national culture, largely free to do and become what they chose, limited only by their own intrinsic worth and effort. It was supposed axiomatically, in other words, that the former slaves would be active participants in the republic on an equal footing with all other citizens. Education, then, according to the more liberal and dominant segments of missionary philanthropists, was intended to prepare a college-bred black leadership to uplift the black masses from the legacy of slavery and the restraints of the postbellum caste system. The AMA's "civilizing mission" demanded permanent institutions of higher education that could educate exceptional black youth to become leaders of their people. Thus the missionary philanthropists valued the higher education of black leaders over all other forms of educational work. To these philanthropists, black leadership training meant, above all, higher classical liberal education. This view reflected, on one hand, their paternalistic tendencies to make unilateral decisions regarding the educational needs of blacks. On the other hand, such enthusiastic support for black higher education expressed—making due allowance for exceptions—the missionaries' principled liberalism, which was innocent of any inclination to doubt the intellectual potential of black Americans. As the Freedmen's Aid Society put it, "This society (in connection with similar organizations) has demonstrated to the South that the freedmen possess good intellectual abilities and are capable of becoming good scholars. Recognizing the brotherhood of mankind and knowing that intellect does not depend upon the color of the skin nor the curl of the hair, we never doubted the Negro's ability to acquire knowledge, and distinguish himself by scholarly attainments." It was the mission societies' primary duty, argued one philanthropist, "to educate . . . a number of blacks and send them forth to regenerate their own people."[4]

To be sure, missionary philanthropists were not proposing social changes that were revolutionary by national standards, but they were radical within the southern social order. Equality was carefully defined as political and legal equality. They consented to inequality in the economic structure, generally shied away from questions of racial integration, and were probably convinced that blacks' cultural and religious values were inferior to those of middle-class whites. Their liberalism on civil and political questions was matched by their conservatism on cultural, religious, and economic matters. Missionary philanthropists held that slavery had generated pathological religious and cultural practices in the black community. Slavery, not race, kept blacks from acquiring the important moral and social values of thrift, industry, frugality, and sobriety, all of which were necessary to live a sustained Christian life. In turn, these missing morals and values prevented the development of a stable family life among Afro-Americans. Therefore, missionaries argued, it was essential for education to introduce the ex-slaves to the values and rules of modern society. Without education, they concluded, blacks would rapidly degenerate and become a national menace to American civilization. In vital respects, such views are easily identified with the more conservative retrogressionist ideologies of the late nineteenth century. Generally, retrogressionist arguments, as George Fredrickson and Herbert Gutman have shown, supported the advocacy of various forms of external control over blacks, including disfranchisement and increasingly rigorous legal segregation.[5]

For the equalitarian missionaries, black economic and social conditions merely reflected the debasing effects of slavery and had nothing to do with racial characteristics. They saw no reason not to extend equal civil and political rights to black Americans. Moreover, because blacks were mentally capable and entitled to equal rights under the law, educa-

tion was viewed as a means to liberate the former slaves from the effects of enslavement. In the words of the Freedmen's Aid Society, "Let us atone for our sins, as much as possible, by furnishing schools and the means of improvement for the children, upon whose parents we have inflicted such fearful evils. Let us lend a helping hand in their escape from the degradation into which we have forced them by our complicity with oppressors. Justice, stern justice, demands this at our hands. Let us pay the debt we owe this race before we complain of weariness in the trifling sums we have given for schools and churches." Consequently, the missionary philanthropists conducted a continual criticism of the political disfranchisement, civil inequality, mob violence, and poor educational opportunities that characterized black life in the American South. From this perspective, they supported the training of a black college-bred leadership to protect the masses from "wicked and designing men."[6]

The mission societies started their educational crusade by concentrating upon schools for elementary level training, but by the early 1870s their emphasis had shifted to the establishment and maintenance of higher educational institutions. In 1870, the AMA, for example, had 157 common schools. By 1874, that number had declined to 13. In the meantime, however, the number of AMA colleges, high schools, and normal schools increased from 5 in 1867 to 29 in 1872 with the primary objective of training black youth as teachers. The AMA and other missionary philanthropists believed that common school and eventually secondary education were a state and local responsibility to be shared by private societies only until it could be assumed by state governments. Their colleges, however, were to be permanent. From the outset, the missionaries named their key institutions "colleges" and "universities," although most of their students were scarcely literate and virtually all of them were enrolled at the subcollegiate level. These labels, as Horace Mann Bond stated, "tell us that the founders took emancipation seriously, believing that the Civil War had settled, indeed, the issue of human inequality in the nation; they also tell us that the founders were applying, to the newly freed population, the ancient faith in the efficacy of higher education to elevate a people." The missionary colleges did not, as was often charged, offer their black students collegiate studies before they were ready. For instance, classes opened at the AMA's Talladega College in November 1867. All 140 students were in the elementary grades. Officials did not begin planning college work until 1878, and no such courses were outlined in the catalog until 1890. The first bachelor's degree was not granted until 1895. Generally, the missionaries developed their institutions of higher education at a reasonable and responsible pace.[7]

Negro History in 1916. But until this time black leaders and missionary philanthropists generally agreed that the transplanted New England college in southern soil was the proper way to educate the sons and daughters of ex-slaves. This shared conception of the appropriate education of black leaders was reflected in the curriculum of colleges owned and operated by black religious organizations. Languages and mathematics received greater emphasis than the other courses in these colleges. The required subjects usually included Latin, Greek, English, mathematics, elementary sciences, history, and mental and moral philosophy. The electives included Latin, French, German, chemistry, physics, and biology. Thus it was agreed that prospective black leaders could not be properly educated for teaching and leadership positions through industrial education. When the time came that white students who planned to become teachers, doctors, lawyers, ministers, and professors "should learn to hoe and plow and lay bricks rather than go to literary and classical schools," wrote President James G. Merrill of Fisk in 1901, "it will be the right policy to shut off all our literary and classical schools for negroes in the South." Consequently, despite sharp tensions between missionaries and black leaders over questions of black participation in the administration and faculty of missionary colleges, the two groups shared a common conception of the appropriate training of black leaders, and this common ground kept relations fairly harmonious. Both groups believed in the "talented tenth" theory.[9]

How did the "talented tenth" theory work out in practice? Between 1865 and 1900, the positive accomplishments of black higher education were impressive. Of all the evaluations that could be cited, the most profound and most eloquent was penned by DuBois, who praised the early missionary philanthropists as "men radical in their belief in Negro possibility." By 1900, DuBois continued, the black colleges supported by northern missionary and black religious organizations had "trained in Greek and Latin and mathematics, 2,000 men; and these men trained fully 50,000 others in morals and manners, and they in turn taught the alphabet to nine millions of men." The black colleges were far from perfect, concluded DuBois, but "above the sneers of critics" stood "one crushing rejoinder: in a single generation they put thirty thousand black teachers in the South" and "wiped out the illiteracy of the majority of the black people of the land."[10]

Yet in 1900, the mission societies and black religious organizations knew that their existing institutions had many defects, that they had nowhere near the amount of capital needed to correct those defects, and that the production of black college and professional students and graduates was minuscule compared to the number needed merely to fill the educational, medical, legal, and ministerial positions in a segregated

Consistent with their view of the need for a well-trained black leadership, the missionaries made liberal culture rather than industrial training the chief aim of their curriculum. The courses in the black colleges controlled by missionaries were similar to those in a majority of contemporary liberal arts schools. Freshmen studied Latin, Greek, and mathematics. Sophomores were taught Greek, Latin, French, mathematics, and natural science. Juniors studied the same courses with additional work in German, natural philosophy, history, English, and astronomy. Mental and moral science and political science were added for the seniors. Regular studies were supplemented at stated times with required essays, debates, declamations, and original addresses. Missionary colleges offered at least a smattering of industrial courses—mainly agriculture, building trades, and domestic science—but normally these courses were offered in the secondary or grammar grades. Some college students took manual training courses because these courses were usually connected with student work programs that allowed them to work their way through school. Industrial training, however, had no major role in the missionaries' philosophy and program of training a leadership class to guide the ex-slaves in their social, economic, and political development. In 1896 Henry L. Morehouse became the first to use the words "talented tenth" to describe this philosophy and program of black education. W. E. B. DuBois would soon make the concept central to his writings on higher education. As Morehouse put it, "In all ages the mighty impulses that have propelled a people onward in their progressive career, have proceeded from a few gifted souls." The "talented tenth" should be "trained thoroughly" by an education that would produce "thoroughly disciplined minds." From the missionaries' vantage point, this could be accomplished only through a solid grounding in the classical liberal curriculum.[8]

Between 1865 and 1900, there were tensions between the denominational missionary societies and the black leadership, but generally not over the question of curriculum. Black leaders also believed that the "Negro problem" could be solved most quickly through the training of southern black youth—mostly males—in the best traditions of New England culture and by sending such college-bred persons among the masses as scholars, ministers, doctors, lawyers, businessmen, and politicians. Colleges such as Fisk, Atlanta, and Howard were viewed as social settlements that imparted the culture of New England to black boys and girls along with the culture of the Greeks and Romans. During the first third of the twentieth century blacks would begin to modify this philosophy of education to include the scientific study of black life and culture as DuBois so successfully inaugurated at Atlanta University in 1900 and as Carter G. Woodson initiated with the founding of the *Journal of*

TABLE 7.1

Black College and Professional Students and Graduates in Southern States and the District of Columbia, by Sex, 1900

State or District of Columbia	College students		Professional students		College and professional students	College graduates		Professional graduates		College and professional graduates
	Male	Female	Male	Female	Total	Male	Female	Male	Female	Total
Alabama	23	10	206	35	274	3	1	6	7	17
Arkansas	49	21	66	0	136	3	1	0	0	4
Delaware	12	8	0	0	20	1	0	0	0	1
District of Columbia	357	125	326	32	840	3	0	47	11	61
Florida	1	0	16	0	17	0	0	0	0	0
Georgia	223	67	183	67	540	6	3	23	1	33
Kentucky	18	18	23	0	59	0	3	3	0	3
Louisiana	23	12	41	12	88	6	3	11	7	27
Maryland	10	1	19	0	30	0	0	5	0	5
Mississippi	46	6	0	0	52	13	2	0	0	15
Missouri	12	1	0	0	13	0	0	0	0	0
North Carolina	348	81	178	13	620	39	4	33	5	81
South Carolina	45	31	65	0	141	6	6	0	0	12
Tennessee	220	77	281	0	578	13	2	59	0	74
Texas	97	91	41	0	229	3	0	1	0	4
Virginia	47	6	108	0	161	9	0	18	0	27
West Virginia	0	0	0	0	0	0	0	0	0	0
Total	1,562	606	1,553	159	3,880	105	22	206	31	364

Source: U.S. Commissioner of Education, *Report, 1899–1900* (Washington, D.C.: U.S. Government Printing Office, 1901), 2:2506–7.

black community. As illustrated in Table 7.1, in 1900 there were 3,880 black students in colleges and professional schools and fewer than 400 graduates of college and professional programs. These new graduates were added to the existing pool of about 3,000 other graduates in a total black population of nearly 10 million. A decade later less than one-third of 1 percent of college-age blacks were attending college compared with more than 5 percent among whites. The ratio of black physicians to the total black population was 1 to 3,194 compared to 1 to 553 among whites; for lawyers the black ratio was 1 to 12,315 compared with 1 to 718 among whites; for college professors, 1 to 40,611 among blacks and 1 to 5,301 among whites; and in the teaching profession there was 1 black teacher for every 334 black persons compared with a ratio of 1 to 145 for whites. The small number and percentage of blacks enrolled in colleges and professional schools demonstrated clearly that nowhere near 10 percent of the college-age black population benefitted from higher education. However aggressively missionary and black religious leaders defended the wisdom of providing classical liberal education for

the "talented tenth," they admitted to themselves that they had fallen far short of their goal, and they saw no light at the end of the tunnel."

Meanwhile, beginning in the 1880s, industrial philanthropy, which had paralleled the growth of missionary and black religious philanthropy, placed its emphasis almost exclusively on industrial training. Industrial philanthropy began in the postbellum South with the educational reforms of the northern-based Peabody Educational Fund, which was founded in 1867 and was boosted by the establishment of the John F. Slater Fund in 1882. From the outset, the leaders of the industrial philanthropic foundations favored racial inequality in the American South and attached themselves early on to the Hampton Idea. Encouraged by Hampton's success, the trustees of the Slater Fund decided to concentrate their grants on industrial education. After 1890, J. L. M. Curry, former slaveholder and congressman in the antebellum South, assumed the position of field agent for both the Peabody and Slater funds and advanced further the Hampton-Tuskegee program of industrial education. With so much emphasis on Negro industrial training by such wealthy and prominent organizations and individuals, the black colleges came in for a good deal of direct and indirect criticism. Much was said of black sharecroppers who sought to learn Latin and knew nothing of farming, of pianos in cabins, and of college-bred Afro-Americans unable to obtain jobs.[12]

The industrial philanthropic foundations established in the early twentieth century followed the same pattern at least until the post–World War I period. The General Education Board, Anna T. Jeanes Foundation, Phelps-Stokes Fund, Carnegie Foundation, Laura Spelman Rockefeller Memorial Fund, and Julius Rosenwald Fund, all established between 1902 and 1917, cooperated in behalf of the Hampton-Tuskegee program of black industrial training. Moreover, industrial philanthropists viewed the missionary program of black higher education as the futile and even dangerous work of misguided romantics. In 1899 Tuskegee trustee William H. Baldwin, Jr., expressed the industrial philanthropists' general disappointment with the missionary colleges. Summarizing the missionary educational work from the Reconstruction era to the end of the nineteenth century, Baldwin commented:

> The days of reconstruction were dark for all. Their sting has not yet gone. Then appeared from the North a new army—an army of white teachers, armed with the spelling-book and the Bible; and from their attack there were many casualties on both sides, the southern whites as well as the blacks. For, although the spelling-book and the Bible were necessary for the proper education of the negro race, yet, with a false point of view, the northern white teacher educated the negro to hope that through the books he might, like the white men, learn to live from the fruits of a literary education. How false that theory was, thirty long years of experience has proved. That was not their opportunity. Their opportunity was to be taught the dignity of manual labor and how to perform it. We began at the wrong end. Instead of educating the negro in the lines which were open to him, he was educated out of his natural environment and the opportunities which lay immediately about him.

Convinced that what Afro-Americans needed most to learn was the discipline of manual labor and the boundaries of their "natural environment," Baldwin, like other industrial philanthropists, generally opposed the development of black higher education. "Except in the rarest of instances," Baldwin proclaimed, "I am bitterly opposed to the so-called higher education of Negroes." To be sure, he recognized that racial segregation of necessity required the existence of limited black higher education and professional opportunities to train needed professionals such as doctors, nurses, and social workers. Explicit in Baldwin's statements was

the philosophy that higher education ought to direct black boys and girls to places in life that were congruent with the South's racial caste system, as opposed to providing them with the knowledge and experiences that created a wide, if not unlimited, range of social and economic possibilities. Further, the needs of the South's racially segregated society were to determine the scope and purpose of black higher education, not the interests and aspirations of individual students or the collective interests of black communities. As the first chairman of the General Education Board and an influential voice among northern industrial philanthropists, Baldwin helped channel the funds of these philanthropic foundations into black industrial schools and white colleges. Yet, as demonstrated in Chapter 3, he was not alone in this effort. Industrial philanthropists in general were opposed to black higher education, except in the rarest of instances, and did not change their position until after World War I.[13]

Thus a convergence of circumstances—the lack of federal and state support for the development of black higher education, the opposition of industrial philanthropy, and the impoverishment of missionary and black religious philanthropy—combined to retard the development of black higher education during the first two decades of the twentieth century. Most important, the key promoters of black higher education, missionary and black religious societies, could not accumulate the large amounts of capital required to place black colleges on solid financial grounds. Though they plodded on persistently, preserving a modest system of black collegiate education, their nineteenth-century momentum declined sharply after 1900. By the turn of the century, the mission societies were virtually bankrupt, and their campaign to develop black higher education was rapidly diminishing in scope and activity. In looking at the future of their black colleges, the missionary philanthropists had many reasons to be downhearted. By any standard, the material and financial status of black higher education was bad. Black colleges were understaffed, meagerly equipped, and poorly financed. The combined efforts of the missionary and black organizations could not raise sufficient funds to meet annual operating expenses, increase teachers' salaries, expand the physical plant, improve libraries, or purchase new scientific and technical equipment. Indeed, almost all of the missionary black colleges lacked sufficient endowments to ensure their survival. Of the one hundred black colleges and normal schools in 1914-15, two-thirds had no endowment funds; and the remaining third had a combined total of only $8.4 million. Most of this sum belonged to Hampton and Tuskegee Institutes, which had attracted large gifts from industrial philanthropists in support of industrial education. In 1926 the total endowment of ninety-nine black colleges and normal schools had risen to $20.3 million, and more than $14 million of this belonged to Hampton and Tuskegee Institutes; the ninety-seven remaining institutions had a combined total of $6.1 million. As late as 1922, seventy-five black colleges had either a negligible endowment or none at all.[14]

The relative impoverishment of black "colleges" and "universities" made it difficult for them to increase their college-level enrollments, which were already extremely small. In the academic year 1899–1900, only fifty-eight of the ninety-nine black colleges had any collegiate students. The proportion of collegiate and professional students in these ninety-nine institutions was small in relation to their precollegiate enrollment, which amounted to 27,869. These precollegiate students constituted more than nine-tenths of the total number of students enrolled in black colleges. This pattern had not changed significantly by World War I. In 1915 only thirty-three black private institutions were "teaching any subjects of college grade." The lack of good academic elementary and secondary schools for southern black students forced the black colleges to provide training for pupils at lower levels to help meet the educational needs of local black communities. Of the 12,726 students attending these institutions in 1915, 79 percent were in the elementary and secondary grades. Many institutions were endeavoring to maintain college classes for less than 5 percent of their enrollment. Thus, lacking an adequate supply of high schoolers to enter the freshman course, the black colleges enrolled elementary and secondary students mainly as a means to feed their college departments. These enrollment patterns in black colleges differed significantly from the national pattern. In 1900 approximately one-quarter of all students enrolled in American colleges were in precollegiate programs. As late as the 1930s, the black precollegiate enrollment represented about 40 percent of the total enrollment in black institutions of higher learning.[15]

Another important development, which threatened the survival of the missionary colleges and black higher education in general, was the establishment of national and regional accrediting agencies. In the late nineteenth century regional accrediting agencies such as the Middle States Association of Colleges and Secondary Schools, the Southern Association of Colleges and Secondary Schools, and the New England Association of Colleges and Secondary Schools were formed to give more fixed meanings to the terms "high school," "college," and "university." In the early twentieth century these regional accrediting agencies were joined by national standardizing organizations such as the College Entrance Examination Board and the Carnegie Foundation for the Advancement of Teaching. Before 1913, accrediting agencies worked mainly to establish closer relations among institutions of higher learning, to standardize college admission requirements, and to improve the academic quality of college and university education. Beginning in 1913, however, the North Central Association of Colleges and Secondary Schools issued the first list of regionally accredited colleges and universities, which signaled the movement to define institutions of higher learning by specific, factual, mechanical, and uniform standards. This movement, financed by foundations like Carnegie, increased the pressures on black colleges to become full-fledged institutions of higher learning.[16]

In one sense, standardization or accrediting was a voluntary action. No institution was surveyed for the purpose of accreditation except upon application. Nevertheless, it was virtually impossible for a college or university to exist as an important institution without the approval of these rating bodies. The nonattainment or removal of accreditation, whether by a regional or national accrediting agency, was a serious detriment to the welfare of an institution. The mere publication of accredited schools had an adverse effect upon institutions that did not appear on the lists. Whether students were graduates of accredited or nonaccredited institutions figured significantly in job opportunities, acceptance to graduate and professional schools, and the acquisition of required state certificates to practice professions from teaching to medicine.[17]

Although no formal accrediting agency took black colleges seriously until 1928, when the Southern Association of Colleges and Secondary Schools decided to rate black institutions separately, there were several evaluations of black higher education from 1900 to 1928. In 1900 and 1910 W. E. B. DuBois made the first attempts to evaluate and classify the black colleges. In 1900 DuBois listed thirty-four institutions as "colleges" with a total collegiate enrollment of 726 students. He concluded, however, that these 726 students could have been accommodated by the ten institutions which he rated as first-grade colleges. In 1910 DuBois made a second and more careful evaluation of black higher education in which he attempted to classify thirty-two black colleges. Institutions like Howard, Fisk, Atlanta, Morehouse, and Virginia Union were classified as "First-Grade Colored Colleges." Lincoln, Talladega, and Wilberforce were examples of the "Second-Grade Colored Colleges," and schools such as Lane, Bishop, and Miles Memorial were included under the label "other colored colleges." DuBois's evaluation was, on balance, a friendly one designed to strengthen the black college system by concentrating college-level work in about thirty-two of the better black institutions. But in 1917, Thomas Jesse Jones, director of research for the Phelps-Stokes Fund, published a critical attack upon black higher education that questioned the legitimacy of nearly all black institutions of higher learning. From 1914 to 1916, Jones conducted a survey of black higher education for the Federal Bureau of Education that resulted in a two-volume book. In the volume on black colleges he identified only two institutions as capable of offering college-level work. These were Howard University and Fisk University. In Jones's words, "hardly a colored college meets the standards set by the Carnegie Foundation and the North Central Association." These rating agencies required, among other things, that accredited colleges maintain at least six departments or professorships with one professor giving full time to each department. The college's annual income had to be sufficient to maintain professors with advanced degrees and to supply adequate library and laboratory facilities. The rating agencies also held that the operation of a preparatory department at the high school level was undesirable, and in no case could it be under the same faculty and discipline as the college. Finally, the North Central Association of Colleges and Secondary Schools recommended that accredited colleges possess an endowment of at least $200,000. At that time, Hampton and Tuskegee were the only black institutions with substantial endowments, and these industrial normal schools did not offer collegiate courses. For Jones, his findings strongly suggested that only two or three black institutions were equipped to become accredited colleges. Hence he recommended that the remaining "colleges" convert to secondary, elementary, and normal schools. Undoubtedly his views were harsh and unwarranted, reflecting significantly his bias toward the Hampton-Tuskegee model of industrial education. Still, Jones's survey, backed by the Federal Bureau of Education and northern industrial philanthropic foundations, underscored a major crisis in black higher education. Black colleges, however segregated, could not exist apart from the power and control of white standardizing agencies. It had become apparent to missionary philanthropists and black educators that their institutions were compelled to seek admission to the society of standardized colleges and for black institutions of higher learning, rating by accrediting agencies was a primary goal in the post–World War I era.[18]

The crucial threats to the survival of black higher education could not be met effectively by missionary philanthropists or black organizations, and the black colleges were forced to seek help from industrial philanthropists. As early as 1901, Thomas J. Morgan, then corresponding secretary for the American Baptist Home Mission Society, requested fellow Baptist John D. Rockefeller to "assume the expense of fully equipping" eight of the society's leading colleges. Writing to Wallace Buttrick, Rockefeller's adviser in philanthropic affairs, Morgan suggested several ways to support black colleges: "(a) by endowing each school separately; (b) by placing in the hands of the ABHMS a lump endowment sum; (c) the creation of a fund placed in the hands of trustees especially selected for the purpose; or (d) the donation of Mr. Rockefeller annually of such a sum of money as may be essential to carry on the work." Between 1901

and 1908, the ABHMS's leading members, Morgan, Malcolm MacVicar, Henry L. Morehouse, George Sale, and George Rice Hovey, wrote to Wallace Buttrick pleading for grants to keep their black colleges financially solvent. In January 1908, George Sale made a specific request for funds to improve the ABHMS's Virginia Union University. He listed four important needs: a dormitory that would cost at least $40,000; two residences adjoining the campus for the accommodation of teachers that would cost $3,000 each; increases in the salaries of continuing instructors; and most urgently, to raise the quality of its instructional program by adding faculty positions in pedagogy, history, and social science. For these purposes, Sale asked the General Education Board to make appropriations as follows: $20,000 toward the cost of the dormitory; $3,000 toward the purchase of the two residences for teachers; and $3,000 for faculty salaries. All requests were denied. The missionaries' correspondence with Wallace Buttrick and the General Education Board reveals the growing impoverishment of their societies relative to the financial resources necessary to keep their colleges abreast of modern standards. In 1901 Morgan wrote: "Reflecting upon the future of our educational work it seems to me we have reached an actual crisis that demands very careful consideration. Suppose, for instance, that the Society is obliged to carry on the work as heretofore. What shall we do? It is exceedingly difficult to secure money to keep the schools up to their present degree of efficiency and it is uncertain whether the present interest in the schools can be kept up among the churches and individuals." In Morgan's view, black colleges simply could "not expect too much of the Society in the immediate future with reference to enlargement, improvement, and increased costs." Likewise, George Rice Hovey, president of the ABHMS's Virginia Union University, said to Buttrick: "We, I fear, can never accomplish the work that we ought to do if we rely solely on the missionary society." Hovey's assessment characterized the general state of northern missionary societies for by the turn of the century, they had become too weak financially to keep their colleges abreast of modern standards. Unfortunately, the missionaries became bankrupt at a time when black colleges depended almost exclusively upon private aid.[19]

Significantly, although some of the missionaries threw themselves upon the mercy of the General Education Board—knowing full well the board's practice of contributing funds only to industrial schools—they were unwilling to compromise their primary mission of sustaining classical liberal colleges for the training of the black "talented tenth." George Sale, though careful not to attack industrial education, informed Buttrick that "the wisest policy for Virginia Union University is to place emphasis on its college and college preparatory work." Thomas J. Morgan recalled that from the beginning the ABHMS's schools had incorporated a smattering of industrial courses. Although he was favorable to the engrafting upon missionary colleges courses in industrial training, Morgan believed it would be a great misfortune to convert them to the ABHMS trade school mission. In his letters to Buttrick, he constantly reaffirmed the ABHMS's commitment to its traditional philosophy of black education. As he wrote in January 1901,

> The one all-important function of these institutions, the work to which they must give their strength for many years to come is that of raising up a competent leadership; men and women who can think; who are independent and self-reliant; who can persuade and lead their people; they should be men and women who are themselves models and examples of what their people can and ought to become, especially should they be persons capable of teaching and preaching. No modification of their curriculum or their spirit and purpose should be allowed to interfere in any manner with this as the supreme purpose of their existence.

A day later, lest Buttrick forget, Morgan repeated the same philosophy: "I feel very keenly the sense of responsibility for using what little influence I may have in developing our schools to a high grade, so that they may offer to the ambitious and competent young Negroes the best possible opportunities for self-culture, development, training and preparation for life's duties." What worried the industrial philanthropists was the probability that such ambitious and competent young college-bred Negroes would impart their knowledge and culture to secondary and normal school students who would in turn transmit classical liberal education to the common schools, leaving no central role in the basic structure of black education for the Hampton-Tuskegee model of industrial training.[20]

On the surface it appeared that the two camps might reach a compromise because one group emphasized college training and the other preferred collegiate education. Booker T. Washington, for example, publicly supported higher education for black elites. Washington stated: "In saying what I do in regard to industrial education, I do not wish to be understood as meaning that the education of the negro should be confined to that kind alone, because we need men and women well educated in other directions; but for the masses, industrial education is the supreme need." No compromise was practical, however, because both the supporters of classical liberal and industrial education looked to the same group to spread their ideas to the masses of black citizens. They both believed that the education of black teachers was most critical to the long-term training and development of the larger black community. If the teachers were to be, as Morgan said, "models and examples of what their people can

and ought to be," there was little chance that the two camps could reach a compromise regarding the proper training of black teachers. Their conceptions of what black people could and ought to be in the American South were simply too divergent and conflicting to reach any sound agreement on the training of teachers of black southerners. In the pre-World War I period, therefore, industrial philanthropists could not bring themselves to support the expansion of black higher education because they viewed it as an infringement upon terrain they aspired to occupy and control. In 1914 Buttrick expressed a fundamental difference between the missionaries' and industrialists' view of the appropriate structure of black higher education. "I have long believed that there should be developed in the South two or three strong institutions of higher learning for the Negroes and, further, that something should be done to develop two, or possibly three, of the medical schools for Negroes," wrote Buttrick to John D. Rockefeller, Jr. "The difficulty in any attempt to promote institutions of higher learning," continued Buttrick, "is the fact that most of the Christian denominations have each founded several such schools." Indeed, altogether they had founded more than one hundred such schools. Buttrick wanted to reduce the number of black colleges and professional schools to six and thereby leave the larger field of teacher training to industrial normal and county training schools. The denominations wanted not only to maintain their more than one hundred "colleges" and professional schools but to improve and expand them. The missionaries' plans were diametrically opposed to the industrial philanthropists' conception of the proper scope and function of black higher education.[21]

Although the industrial philanthropists refused to support the missionaries' plans for the development of black higher education, they had no intentions of abandoning black collegiate and professional education. Because industrial philanthropists appropriated virtually no money for black higher education before 1920, they were often perceived as committed exclusively to the idea of Negro industrial education. This was a misperception. In 1907 Buttrick stated well his colleagues' attitude toward black higher education: "I am convinced that all members of the [General Education] Board believe that there should be a sufficient number of thoroughgoing colleges for colored people in the southern states." Further, he was inclined to agree with his fellow trustees "that the matter of collegiate education for the colored people should be taken up as a whole by this Board." In fact, as Buttrick informed George Sale, superintendent of Negro education for the ABHMS, the board had already designated one of its "School Inspectors" to make "a careful study of the whole question" of black higher education. This report, completed in May 1907 by W. T. B. Williams of Hampton Institute, set forth basic reasons to develop a small number of strong black colleges in the South. First, these institutions would produce college-bred leaders to acculturate black Americans into the values and mores of southern society. Second, it was very important that black leaders be trained in the South by institutions "in touch with the conditions to be faced by the young people in later life rather than in the North by institutions . . . out of touch with southern life." Third, and most important, the development of a few strong institutions was viewed as a strategic means to reduce the number of existing black colleges. Williams argued:

> If more strong men and good college courses, and better equipment both in the way of dormitories and apparatus could be added in a few places, and some scholarships or student aid in the college department, could be provided, as is common in the great northern universities, the mass of Negro college students would congregate in these few institutions and their numbers would steadily increase. This would render impossible many of the weaker college courses and would make for strength in organization and economy in the management of college training, for it would minimize duplication.

Williams expressed an interesting and noteworthy effect of standardization which was not so marked and known. If a few outstanding black colleges were established, industrial philanthropists could use these institutions to pressure the remaining ones into discontinuing their collegiate courses because of their inability to keep pace with the rising standards of college-level work. Buttrick regarded Williams's report as "so valuable that in my judgement all the members of the Board ought to read it just as it stands."[22]

Despite an apparent similarity in principle, there was a fundamental difference between Williams's and DuBois's proposals to reduce the number of black colleges. DuBois believed that a smaller number of financially solvent black colleges, about thirty-three, was preferable to the larger number (one hundred) of weaker schools in constant danger of folding. Further, starting from the position that the black college enrollment was much too small, he believed that a smaller number of sound institutions could both improve their academic quality and expand their physical capacity to increase the overall number and proportion of black college students. Williams's report, consistent with the philanthropists' interests, recommended the concentration of black higher education in a few institutions, about four or six, as a means to reduce dramatically the opportunities for black students to pursue higher education. This proposal reflected the philanthropists' belief that far too many black students aspired to attend college, a belief that would not change significantly until southern states began requiring all teachers to have bache-

lor's degrees. In short, DuBois recommended concentration and efficiency in black higher education to increase opportunities, whereas the Williams report to the General Education Board recommended concentration and efficiency to reduce the scope of black higher education. Though their means were similar, they envisioned very different ends.

Williams's report impressed the board's trustees and spurred them to develop a formal rationale for the support of black higher education. Wallace Buttrick and Abraham Flexner were primarily responsible for formulating the board's policy. In 1910 Flexner became nationally known for writing Carnegie Foundation Bulletin No. 4, a detailed study titled "Medical Education in the United States and Canada." This survey and the policies derived from it foreshadowed the board's approach to black higher education. Flexner inspected 155 medical schools and reported their "appalling deficiencies," which led him to conclude that all but 31 of them should discontinue. After this report appeared, the Council of Medical Education of the American Medical Association intensified its efforts to eliminate "inferior" medical colleges. Much of the financial support for the medical reform movement was provided by the General Education Board. In 1911 the board appropriated $1.5 million to Johns Hopkins Medical School for the purpose of setting standards in American medical education. Flexner was placed in charge of the board's medical reform program. His main goal was to develop a model of medical education that would force weaker institutions to shut down because of their inability to approximate the new standards. Clearly, this policy followed closely the suggestions contained in the Williams report, though there was no direct relation between the two.[23]

In 1914 Flexner became a trustee of the General Education Board and assistant secretary to Wallace Buttrick. In this capacity, he began to apply his medical model to the field of black higher education. Fortunately Flexner did not have to conduct a study of black higher education comparable to his investigation of American medical education. Both he and Buttrick were acutely aware of the survey of black higher education being conducted by Thomas Jesse Jones for the Federal Bureau of Education. They were in close contact with Jones and realized, early on, that they could rely upon his forthcoming survey as a "Flexner report" of black higher education. Buttrick informed John D. Rockefeller, Jr., in February 1914, that he was in "frequent conference" with Jones, and he assured Rockefeller that Jones's survey would "throw light" on the whole question of black education. Though Jones's survey was not published until 1917, by December 1914 Flexner was already convinced that it would sound the death knell for many black colleges as his medical report had done for the vast majority of American medical schools. Writing to Oswald Garrison Villard about the value of the Jones survey, Flexner proclaimed:

> Dr. Jones is a disinterested and competent outsider whose report will separate the wheat from the chaff. After its appearance the public will have a source of information the accuracy and impartiality of which cannot be discredited. The situation here is not different in principle from that which once existed in reference to medical schools. There was an association of American medical colleges that could enforce no standards just because it meant that the members, in order to do this, would have to legislate against one another. After, however, the Carnegie Foundation Bulletin appeared, an entirely new situation was created. Since then things have been run by the better schools and the others are rapidly disappearing.

Jones, however, was not a disinterested outsider. As a former member of Hampton's faculty, he had helped develop the Hampton-Tuskegee approach to black education and as the director of the Phelps-Stokes Fund played a critical role in adapting the Hampton-Tuskegee philosophy to Britain's African colonies. His two-volume survey of black education, published in 1917, espoused the Hampton-Tuskegee philosophy. Anticipating the impact of the Jones survey, the General Education Board held its first interracial conference on Negro education in November 1915. The invited participants represented both the major black industrial and liberal arts institutions. Presidents Fayette A. McKenzie of Fisk University and John Hope of Morehouse College represented two of the most outstanding black private colleges. Others included Principal R. R. Moton of Tuskegee Institute, Principal H. B. Frissell of Hampton Institute, Abraham Flexner of the General Education Board, Thomas Jesse Jones of the Phelps-Stokes Fund, W. T. B. Williams, field agent for the John F. Slater Fund, and James H. Dillard, president of the Anna T. Jeanes Foundation. This conference brought together the forces that represented the industrial philanthropists' overall approach to the development of black education. On one hand, Frissell, Moton, Williams, Jones, Flexner, and Dillard exemplified the movement to spread industrial education throughout the Afro-American South as the all-pervasive educational curriculum. On the other, McKenzie and Hope symbolized the industrial philanthropists' developing commitment to influence the direction of black higher education.[14]

The discussions at this conference illuminated fundamental flaws in the Hampton-Tuskegee movement that ultimately forced industrial philanthropists to reshape their approach to the promotion of industrial education for the masses of black children. The discussions also pointed to the pressing need for industrial philanthropists to become involved in the development of black colleges and professional schools if they were to be successful in redirecting the scope and function of black higher education. The original Hampton-Tuskegee Idea had run its course by 1915 and was rapidly falling behind modern educational standards. It was based largely on a program of unskilled and semiskilled agricultural and industrial training, the discouraging of college and even high-quality secondary work, and a heavy emphasis on moral development and ideological training. This program had broken down under its own weight. The extreme emphasis on routinized labor, or "learning by doing," produced graduates who found it increasingly difficult to meet state and local academic requirements for teacher certification. In certain respects, southern state and local school authorities wanted Hampton-Tuskegee graduates as teachers because they were advertised as young black men and women who "knew their place" and who were uncontaminated by the pompous ideals of classical liberal education. Yet the South, as the nation, was emphasizing and implementing certain required standards of education for teachers and even demanding college degrees to teach in public high schools and normal schools.

Such changes presented serious challenges to the traditional Hampton-Tuskegee program. Defending this tradition, Hampton principal H. B. Frissell said: "To us at Hampton the doing of the thing is the important thing, and what we might call the academic side is comparatively secondary. We have got to learn to do by doing ... the academic training is really secondary to the actual doing of the thing." The fundamental flaw in this approach was pointed out to Frissell and the other members of the conference by two of Hampton's prominent graduates, Robert R. Moton and W. T. B. Williams. Moton said: "I am a Hampton man. I went to the summer school [for teachers] two or three summers, and took gymnastics, nothing else, only on the physical side pure and simple." Williams maintained that such a poor academic program caused Hampton graduates to fall down on the job: "Even when they go to teach the elementary subjects they cannot bring any fresh information to the children." The ultimate defeat and embarrassment, as Moton recalled, was that Hampton could not find one of its own graduates sufficiently qualified to fill a teaching position at the Whittier Elementary Lab School located on Hampton's campus. In Moton's words: "We had to go to Howard University to help Miss Walter. With all our 1,200 graduates, we should have had a man we could have put in that place. We had no one with sufficient academic training for the Whittier school. That is what Miss Walter thought, and she is very loyal to us, so you see that is at our own Hampton school; after twenty-five years or so we ought to have been able to pick out some Hampton man for that work." Moton, who was in the process of leaving the Hampton staff to become principal of Tuskegee Institute, admitted that Tuskegee had similar problems. Its graduates were being kept out of the teaching profession because of poor academic training. Bruce R. Payne, president of the George Peabody College for Teachers, asked the next logical question, "What is the use of the Hampton training if we are not allowed to use it?" Hampton and Tuskegee were thus compelled to meet more modern and higher academic standards or continue producing students with insufficient academic training to pass certification standards required of entry-level teachers.[25]

The conference then shifted to the question of black higher education. H. B. Frissell asked the central question: "What is sound policy in respect to the number, scope, support, and development of higher academic institutions for Negroes?" Only John Hope questioned the relevance of engrafting vocational education on the college curriculum and stated firmly that he stood for the "modern sort of education" for black and white children. Flexner, speaking for the industrial philanthropists, insisted that black collegiate work was "very pretentious, and not calculated to get anywhere." Having tested some black college students in Latin, physics, and literature, he concluded ironically that "if it had been Greek they could not have been more puzzled." Flexner then asked for Hope's reaction to the General Education Board's thoughts about means to reduce the number of existing black colleges: "Dr. Hope, what would be the effect of selecting four or five Negro colleges and building them up, making them good, honest, sincere, effective colleges so far as they went, and letting the others alone, not try to suppress them or consolidate them, but just let them 'sweat,' would that tend in the long run, to stigmatize the inferior institutions that they would give up, the way the poor medical schools are giving up?" Hope admitted that such a policy might pressure weaker colleges to discontinue, but he did not sanction this approach.[26]

Shortly after this conference, the General Education Board formed a Committee on Negro Education to review its overall policy for the development of black education, paying particular attention to the questions of supporting schools for the training of black teachers and the shaping of black higher education. The committee's report was submitted to the board on 27 January 1916. "A crying need in Negro education," the committee reported, "is the development of state supported schools for the training of Negro teachers." The committee realized, however, "that many decades will elapse before Negro education is adequately provided for through taxation." Therefore, the committee recommended that the board use its resources to strengthen private institutions that promised to render "important educational service." "It should perhaps be ex-

plained," the committee stated, "that in making this recommendation the Committee has in mind, first, industrial schools, such as those at Fort Valley, Manassas, Calhoun, and St. Helena—schools which, on a much smaller scale, are doing for their own vicinities the valuable work which Hampton and Tuskegee have done for the country at large." Second, the committee had in mind academic institutions. It observed:

The Negro is determined to have some opportunity for higher education, and certain Negroes have made good use of such opportunities as are open to the race. Of course, there are far too many Negro colleges and universities; and of this large number, not one is well equipped and manned on a sensible, modest scale. Wise cooperation with one or two institutions would be the most effective way of bringing order out of chaos, of distinguishing the real from the imitation.

Finally, the committee recommended support for black medical education. "The Negro physician has, in our judgment, a place in the South." It was recommended that the board support one or two black medical schools. Thus, in time, with these recommendations, the committee formulated principles calling first for support of industrial normal schools, second, for assisting one or two black colleges, and, third, for aiding one or two black medical schools. The board moved immediately to provide financial support for the smaller industrial schools, but a few years passed before any major campaigns were launched to assist black colleges and professional schools.[27]

Meanwhile, a confluence of changing political and social developments in black America heightened the industrial philanthropists' interest in the scope and purpose of black higher education. Most important were the emergence of more militant post–World War I black leaders and the subsequent realization that the Hampton-Tuskegee coalition was rapidly losing political ground to the college-bred "New Negro." During the war blacks became increasingly intolerant of economic and social injustices, especially in the South, where white terrorist groups increased their brutal attacks upon black civilians while black soldiers fought on the battle front to "make the world safe for democracy." There developed in the South, and to a significant degree in other sections of the nation, a grave interracial crisis. Inflammatory rumors filled the air, suspicion and fear were rife, lynchings multiplied, race riots broke out in several northern and southern cities, and the embers of discontent smoldered in many more. The widespread racial repression in the South, coupled with labor shortages in the North, escalated the migration of blacks to northern urban areas. The white South, fearing the loss of a major proportion of its agricultural laborers, opposed the migration and used both legal and extralegal means to keep blacks from boarding the trains bound northward. Efforts to deprive blacks of even so basic a freedom as the right to migrate only served to exacerbate racial tensions. Indeed, Moton was so alarmed that he felt compelled to alert President Woodrow Wilson to the ever-present danger. In June 1918, Moton wrote a confidential letter to the president:

There is more genuine restlessness and dissatisfaction on the part of the colored people than I have before known. I have just returned from trips in Alabama, Georgia, North Carolina, and South Carolina. It seems to me something ought to be done pretty definitely to change the attitudes of these millions of black people; and this attitude, anything but satisfactory, not to use a stronger word, is due very largely to recent lynchings and burnings of colored people. The recent lynching in Georgia of six people in connection with a murder, and among them a woman, who it is reported was a prospective mother, has intensified tremendously this attitude of the colored people.

In Moton's view, blacks en masse were on the brink of becoming "indifferent or antagonistic" or "quietly hostile."[28]

After the signing of the Armistice in 1918, race relations in America deteriorated further. The South and the nation were shaken by the "Red Summer" of 1919, when a series of major riots threatened to precipitate widespread race warfare. Significantly, the Hampton-Tuskegee moderates, who traditionally served as mediators in such crises, had little influence among the post–World War I black leaders. By 1920, there was no powerful segment of the black leadership that favored the Hampton-Tuskegee accommodationist approach to race relations and political conflict. In March 1920, the NAACP's *Crisis* published a revealing article by Harry H. Jones, which argued that, except for R. R. Moton, few black leaders accepted the Hampton-Tuskegee philosophy of racial accommodation. The liberal and radical wings of the black intelligentsia were the dominant political voices in the black community, and the philanthropists understood the impact of this influence on their own political program. Philanthropist George Peabody, having read the Jones article, informed Hampton's principal, James Gregg, of its implications: "It is clear to me, with the Negro people having found themselves in a general way, during the war excitement, there is some danger of sharp definitely conscious line of division. We must, I think, give great weight in the present temper of susceptibility to the advertising influence of the

Crisis and other publications, including James Weldon Johnson and *The New York Age*." The problem, then, from the standpoint of the philanthropists, was how to secure an articulate black conservative wing with sufficient status within the race to counter the influence of such men as DuBois, Trotter, and Johnson.[29]

Peabody wanted a conservative black leader to "write the most effective reply, which I have in mind, to the article in the March issue of the *Crisis*." But he did not believe that Moton or Fred Moore, the New York *Age*'s editor, who sympathized with Moton's accommodationist philosophy, had sufficient status to challenge Johnson and DuBois. In fact, Peabody could only think of Isaac Fisher as a potentially effective ideologue of the industrial philanthropic view of black educational and social affairs. Interestingly, Fisher, a Tuskegee graduate who took his ideology from Booker T. Washington, was appointed to the Fisk University administration shortly after McKenzie became president. When McKenzie suspended the student-operated *Fisk Herald* in 1917, he established the conservative *Fisk University News* and made Fisher its editor. Following the bitter race riots of 1919, in a period of rising black militancy, Fisher called for the return of the "conservative Negro." He castigated the liberal and radical segments of the existing black leadership, claiming that they had "muzzled" the voice of the conservative Negro and taken away his "mandate to speak for his race." Fisher defined the conservative Negro leader as one who urges his people to lay a foundation in economic efficiency, submits willingly to the laws and customs of the South, and works for better race relations through the guidance of the "best white South." Toward this end, he instituted at Fisk in 1917 a seminar on race relations and later became a member of the southern-white-dominated Commission on Inter-racial Co-operation. Yet such conservatives as Fisher and Moton could not really challenge the intellectual leadership the liberals and radicals had achieved in the black community by 1919. DuBois probably expressed the dominant black view of the conservative wing when he informed the Commission on Inter-racial Co-operation that "Isaac Fisher represents nothing but his own blubbering self. Major Moton is a fine fellow, but weak in the presence of white folks." To DuBois and many other black leaders who demanded full American rights for blacks, Moton and Fisher were "the sort of Colored men that we call 'White Folks' Niggers.'" Whether they were such accommodationists was less important than their lack of influence among the postwar black leaders and especially among the masses. The black leaders of the postwar period reflected the self-determinist and militant character of the larger Afro-American society. Marcus Garvey and his Universal Negro Improvement Association epitomized some of the core values and fundamental political thoughts of the masses of Afro-Americans. Garvey

468

arrived in the United States from Jamaica in 1916 and by 1922 had several hundred thousand followers. He led the largest mass movement among Afro-Americans before the civil rights movement of the 1960s. The political thrust toward self-determination and militant demands for equality and racial justice were also manifested in the emergence of a more liberal black press and the literary tenor of the "Harlem Renaissance." Historian V. P. Franklin argues convincingly that the postwar self-determinist political and literary activities reflected values deeply embedded in black culture and tradition.[30]

These developments reaffirmed the industrial philanthropists' growing convictions of the necessity to take hold of black higher education and to influence more directly the training of black leaders. Hence, during the early 1920s they launched two national endowment campaigns that incorporated several of their major goals to shape postsecondary black education and develop the "right type" of black teachers and leaders. One campaign was to raise a million-dollar endowment for Fisk University. This campaign embodied the industrial philanthropists' plan to develop one or two black private colleges to the point that they would set new standards for black higher education and thus stigmatize the "inferior" or less fortunate ones, possibly pressuring them to discontinue or convert to secondary schools. The other endowment campaign aimed to raise at least $5 million to be split equally between Hampton and Tuskegee. This campaign reflected the industrial philanthropists' continuing commitment to the Hampton-Tuskegee Idea. They recognized, however, that Hampton and Tuskegee must meet higher educational standards if the graduates were to continue to obtain teaching jobs and other positions of leadership. Together these campaigns, conducted by the same group of industrial philanthropists, were also intended to develop sympathetic harmony between the liberal arts colleges and the industrial schools.

Not surprisingly, the industrial philanthropists selected Fisk University as the college to be developed into a model institution of black higher education. Fisk was at the financial crossroads that precipitated the transformation of the power structure in black private higher education from missionary to industrial philanthropy. President George A. Gates, who headed Fisk from 1909 to 1913, faced a drying up of the old missionary sources of revenue and, in turn, made a strong plea for southern white friendship and financial support. Booker T. Washington had been appointed to the Board of Trustees in 1909 with the hope that he would bring some of his sources of revenue to Fisk. Fisk was also selected because the industrial philanthropists regarded it as the "capstone" of black private higher education. Wallace Buttrick said: "Perhaps the most promising of the academic institutions for the higher education of the Negro is Fisk University." Outside of Howard University, Fisk had

nearly 20 percent of the private black college students enumerated in Thomas Jesse Jones's 1917 survey of black higher education. Fisk enrolled 188 of the 737 college students in private black colleges (this figure excludes the 1,050 college students enrolled in Howard University); Virginia Union University, with 51, had the next largest enrollment. Thus when the General Education Board held its 1915 conference to discuss the reorganization of black higher education, Fisk University's newly appointed white president, Fayette Avery McKenzie, was invited as a key representative of black higher education. Convinced that McKenzie was sympathetic to the board's policy, the industrial philanthropists selected him and his institution to spearhead their campaign to reshape black higher education.[31]

McKenzie, a professor of sociology at the Ohio State University before coming to Fisk in 1915, came to Nashville as a representative of industrial philanthropy. He dedicated his presidency to modernizing the curriculum (that is, emphasizing physical and social sciences) and raising a sizable endowment for the university. Industrial philanthropists regarded him as a leader who would break with the missionary or egalitarian past and lead Fisk down a path of conciliation and cooperation with conservative northern and southern whites. More than any of his predecessors, McKenzie sought to make Fisk acceptable to the white South and northern industrial philanthropists. He urged Fisk students and graduates to eschew political and social questions and concentrate on interracial cooperation and economic development. In his inaugural address, McKenzie paid homage to Fisk's liberal arts tradition but emphasized the concept of education for "service." In this context he promised that the university would help restore the South to economic prosperity: "It was the function of Fisk to increase the material wealth of the nation.... Fisk University claims the right to say that it will be one of the chief factors in achieving larger prosperity for the South. Every dollar spent here in the creation of power may mean a thousand dollars of increase in wealth of the South within a single generation." In line with these goals and priorities, McKenzie favored autocratic rule over his students and faculty, sought personal associations mainly with the teachers and administrators of the white schools in Nashville, and cultivated the goodwill of the city's white business community. These actions pleased the industrial philanthropists, and they regarded McKenzie's reign as a new and wise departure from the missionary tradition.[32]

From the outset, industrial philanthropists reinforced McKenzie's behavior by contributing their economic and political support to his regime. Julius Rosenwald, who visited Fisk at McKenzie's installation, was initially ambivalent about the possibility of transforming the college into an accommodationist institution. In revealing his "mixed feelings" about

Fisk students to Abraham Flexner, Rosenwald stated, "There seemed to be an air of superiority among them and a desire to take on the spirit of the white university rather than the spirit which has always impressed me at Tuskegee." Rosenwald and other industrial philanthropists believed that Tuskegee was training black leaders to maintain a separate and subordinate Negro society. They were primarily interested in supporting black institutions committed to this mission. Thus Flexner assured Rosenwald that McKenzie, with the help of industrial philanthropy, was working to transform Fisk into an institution more acceptable to southern white society. Toward this end, the General Education Board began appropriating in 1916 about $12,000 annually to help Fisk pay its yearly operating expenses. In 1917 the board contributed $50,000 to Fisk for endowment and building purposes and persuaded the Carnegie Foundation to give the same amount. Still, Fisk had no substantial endowment, was deeply in debt, and suffered from a deteriorating physical plant and a poorly paid faculty. According to Hollingsworth Wood, vice-chairman of the Fisk Board of Trustees, "$1,600 has been the maximum salary of a professor at Fisk University. This has meant lack of food in some cases." Fisk authorities knew that the college could not survive without a sizable endowment, and the industrial philanthropists were the only source of sufficient money. These circumstances, however, required compromise. As McKenzie put it, "Intimation has been made to me from several sources that if we continue to behave ourselves, if we are efficient in teaching and administration and continue to hold the right relationship to our environment, we can expect large and highly valuable financial aid in carrying out a great program at Fisk."[33]

The philanthropists' financial assistance to Fisk University was accompanied by a new coalition of Negro accommodationists, southern whites, and northern industrialists who took control of the university's administration from the old alliance of black educators and northern white missionaries. McKenzie and the philanthropists restructured the Fisk Board of Trustees to reflect the new power structure. In October 1915 Thomas Jesse Jones informed Flexner of the changes: "The Board of Trustees is being strengthened. Governor Brumbaugh and two influential colored men have been added in the last few weeks. With Mr. Cravath and Dr. Washington as trustees and the constant attention which I can give to the institution, we have at least a guarantee of fairly sound educational policy." By 1919, Jones was executive secretary of the Fisk Board of Trustees and one of five members on the Executive Committee. In 1920 the philanthropists, acting through the General Education Board, agreed to spearhead a campaign to obtain for Fisk a $1 million endow-

ment, and their strength on the university's Board of Trustees increased. William H. Baldwin, son of the General Education Board's first chairman, was appointed by the board to chair the endowment committee. He was immediately appointed to the Fisk Board of Trustees and became, in 1924, the chairman of the trustees' Executive Committee. Other conservatives were added as the philanthropists moved in a quiet and forceful manner to reorganize the school's administration. In May 1920, Hollingsworth Wood notified the president of the General Education Board that "Dr. Moton of Tuskegee is now on the Board; Miss Ella Sachs, daughter of Samuel Sachs, and a close friend of the Rosenwalds, is an eager new member; and Mrs. Beverly B. Mumford of Richmond, Virginia adds an excellent influence from the southern viewpoint." The traditional missionary equalitarians were gradually pushed off the Fisk Board of Trustees. They were replaced mainly by northern industrialists, southern whites, and a few Negro accommodationists who were virtually handpicked by industrial philanthropists. The philanthropists were raising an endowment for a new Fisk that was largely controlled by their agents and supporters.[34]

These philanthropists no doubt hoped that their economic and firm political hold on Fisk would squelch the school's equalitarian tradition and open the way for the development of a more conservative black leadership class. In 1923 the General Education Board generated a memorandum on the Fisk endowment campaign which emphasized the urgent need to train "the right type of colored leaders" who would help make the Negro "a capable workman and a good citizen." The industrial philanthropists, as the memorandum stated, aimed primarily at "helping the Negro to the sane and responsible leadership that the South wants him to have." To the white South, "sane" Negro leaders were those who encouraged blacks to "stay in their place." The philanthropists recognized that they were facing a new situation between the races. "How the Negro is going to get on in this country and what his relations are to be with the whites, are no longer problems of a single section; they are national," the memorandum stated. To the philanthropists, this new situation, in the context of growing racial friction, increased the necessity of training "the right kind" of black leaders. The report maintained:

Due to various experiences during and since the World War, there is a growing disposition among the Negroes to suspect all white men and their motives and therefore to break all contacts with them and go it alone. Because such a movement by ten percent of the population is obviously futile, is no reason to overlook the fact that ten percent is a large enough proportion to cause considerable harm if permitted to go off at a tangent from the general interest. This very real menace to the public welfare makes the strengthening of school facilities for Negroes a matter of national significance.

Both McKenzie and the industrial philanthropists shared the belief that the new type of black college should help curb and even extinguish the self-determinist and egalitarian character of the emergent black leadership.[35]

Toward this end McKenzie, as Raymond Wolters has shown, set out to convince the industrial philanthropists that "Fisk students were not radical egalitarians but young men and women who had learned to make peace with the reality of the caste system." Thus McKenzie disbanded the student government association, forbade student dissent, and suspended the *Fisk Herald*, the oldest student publication among black colleges. He would not allow a campus chapter of the NAACP and instructed the librarian to excise radical articles in the NAACP literature. Student discipline was rigorously enforced, special "Jim Crow" entertainments were arranged for the white benefactors of the university, and Paul D. Cravath, president of the Fisk Board of Trustees, endorsed complete racial separation as "the only solution to the Negro problem." McKenzie would not allow certain forms of social intercourse such as dancing and holding hands, and he justified his code of discipline on the grounds that black students were particularly sensuous beings who needed to be subjected to firm control. In short, McKenzie attempted to repress student initiative, undermine their egalitarian spirit, and control their thinking on race relations so as to produce a class of black intellectuals that would uncomplainingly accept the southern racial hierarchy. Historian Lester C. Lamon concluded that "McKenzie's autocratic policies took away means of self-expression, created second-class citizens, and relied upon fear instead of reason to bring societal control." Although discipline and repression of student initiative and self-expression were strict before McKenzie became president, they became harsher and more racist during his administration.[36]

By June 1924, the industrial philanthropists had successfully completed their campaign for Fisk's million-dollar endowment. The following pledges were then in hand: $500,000 from the General Education Board; $250,000 from the Carnegie Foundation; and $250,000 secured elsewhere, including sizable pledges from such philanthropists as Julius Rosenwald and George Peabody. This endowment fund was not, however, collectible until Fisk's accumulated deficits were met. The outstanding indebtedness at that time was $70,000. To solve that problem, a special campaign to raise $50,000 led by Nashville's white citizens was successfully completed by June 1924. This campaign was organized by

Nashville's Commercial Club, which included Tennessee's governor, Nashville's mayor, and many of the city's leading businessmen. From 1915 to 1924, Fisk had become so conservative that the Commercial Club was inspired to call Fisk the "key" to interracial cooperation and understanding in the South. "He came into our midst unknown," the Commercial Club said of McKenzie, "and by his wise administration and official methods won our hearty co-operation." With such backing, plans were perfected for raising the money to eliminate the school's deficits and thereby secure the endowment for Fisk's financial rehabilitation.[37]

At this juncture, however, McKenzie's conservative administration was attacked by black students, intellectuals, and community organizations. Led by W. E. B. DuBois, the Fisk alumni attacked McKenzie's Draconian code of student discipline and expressed outrage at the humiliation and insults perpetrated on the student body. DuBois openly challenged the school's administration in 1924, when he was invited to give the commencement address. He especially criticized the administration's campaign to suppress Fisk's egalitarian tradition so as to obtain economic support from industrial philanthropy. The students, long dissatisfied with McKenzie's regime, were reinforced by alumni support and escalated their protest against the school's repressive policies. In February 1925, the *New York Times* reported that Fisk's alumni were organizing in "all sections of the United States to agitate for the removal of Dr. Fayette McKenzie, the white president of the University." The following month the students went on strike against McKenzie's administration, and they were backed in their protest by the alumni, the black press, and the local black community. On the day following the student rebellion more than twenty-five hundred black citizens of Nashville convened and formally declared that McKenzie's "usefulness as president of Fisk is at an end." This protest forced McKenzie to resign in April 1925. Fisk University trustee Thomas Jesse Jones attributed McKenzie's problems to black self-determination, the very force that he and other industrial philanthropists were trying to counter. As he wrote to fellow trustee, Paul Cravath,

The present unfortunate and unfair criticism of Dr. McKenzie's policies is partly the result of misunderstandings, but largely the result of an effort on the part of a few designing Negroes to obtain control of Fisk University for a policy of Negro self-determination, so extreme in extent as to undermine all cooperation between whites and Negroes. Such an extreme attitude has appeared within the last few years in many parts of the world. While it is natural and in its more reasonable forms desirable, self-determination, as advocated by those who oppose Dr. McKenzie, is dangerous not only to the well-being of Fisk University, but to sound race-relationships throughout America.[38]

DuBois praised the students' victory over McKenzie and hailed them as a new breed of black intellectuals sorely needed to challenge the power of industrial philanthropy: "God speed the breed! Suppose we do lose Fisk; suppose we lose every cent that the entrenched millionaires have set aside to buy our freedom and stifle our complaints. They have the power, they have the wealth, but glory to God we still own our own souls and led by young men like these at Fisk, let us neither flinch nor falter, but fight, and fight and fight again." But many black intellectuals, especially those responsible for black colleges, could not easily afford to attack the policies of industrial philanthropy. After the Fisk rebellion, the General Education Board withheld the endowment pledges on the grounds that they were not collectible until Fisk eliminated all its deficits. The Nashville Commercial Club, which was expected to raise the capital to cover the deficits, withdrew from the campaign following McKenzie's resignation. Convinced that McKenzie's successor, Thomas Elsa Jones, did "not conceive himself to be a leader or an emancipator of the Negro group," the philanthropists eventually granted Fisk the endowment. Fisk, however, was still dependent on industrial philanthropy throughout the period and into the present.[39]

Although northern philanthropists sought to move Fisk and other black colleges closer to the philosophy and practice of racial accommodation throughout the first third of the twentieth century, they seemed comfortable only with Hampton, Tuskegee, and similar industrial normal schools. This attitude was revealed through their parallel involvement in the Hampton-Tuskegee endowment campaign. To be sure, they recognized that educational standards at these institutions had to change to keep abreast of minimum requirements for teacher certification, but they saw no need to modify the basic social philosophy of black accommodation to white authority. The campaign for $5 million was organized during the summer of 1924 by Clarence H. Kelsey, chairman of the Title Guarantee and Trust Company and vice-chairman of the Hampton Board of Trustees. Anson Phelps-Stokes was appointed from the Tuskegee Board of Trustees as chairman of the Special Gifts Committee. The John Price Jones Corporation was engaged to prepare the publicity for the campaign and to help with the organizational work. As a result of these efforts, the following subscriptions had been secured by the end of the first year: George Eastman, $4.3 million; General Education Board, $1 million; John D. Rockefeller, Jr., $1 million; Arthur Curtis James, $300,000; Edward H. Harkness, $250,000; Julius Rosenwald, $100,000.

Amounts equal to or greater than $25,000 were pledged by the Phelps-Stokes Fund (the largest contribution it ever made to any single object), Slater Fund, George Foster Peabody, William M. Scott, William G. Wilcox, and the Madame C. J. Walker Manufacturing Company. George Eastman, largely as a result of this campaign, became deeply impressed with the importance of the Hampton-Tuskegee Idea to the nation and on 8 December 1924 announced that in the distribution of the major portion of his estate, Hampton and Tuskegee would each obtain securities valued at $2 million. This pledge was conditional on his requirement that the Hampton-Tuskegee endowment campaign reach its $5 million goal by 31 December 1925. Eastman also contributed another $300,000 toward the goal of $5 million. Anson Phelps-Stokes believed that Eastman's gift resulted from a visit to his home by Julius Rosenwald, Clarence Kelsey, and Robert Moton in November 1924.[40]

The "Special Memorandum" to promote the Hampton-Tuskegee campaign was prepared for Kelsey by the Jones Corporation, and it detailed the reasons for the endowment campaign and the continuing importance of the Hampton-Tuskegee Idea. Part Two of the memorandum, "Our Most Grave and Perplexing Domestic Problem," was introduced with the following quotations:

"The Color line is the problem of the present century."

"The relation of Whites and Negroes in the United States is our most grave and perplexing domestic problem."

"The Negro problem is one of the greatest questions that has ever presented itself to the American people."

These quotations were attributed to J. W. Gregory, the Chicago Commission on Race Relations, and William Howard Taft, respectively. This problem, according to the memorandum, had been exacerbated because the "rise of world-wide race consciousness and ideal of self-determination has had special effect on the American Negro." Consequently, "a wide variety of leadership has sprung up to give them expression." This development was viewed largely as a crisis of leadership:

Some of this leadership, as is natural under the circumstances, is demogogical or otherwise self seeking. Some of it is patently visionary. But there are thousands of earnest, intelligent Negroes today who are fired with a belief in the possibilities within their race and with the ambition to help realize those possibilities sanely and constructively. This whole movement, in all its various forms, has taken deep root. It is not confined to the big city groups but permeates

gram for the training of black leaders remained unchanged. It was still a program of interracial harmony predicated on a social foundation of political disfranchisement, civil inequality, racial segregation, and the training of black youth for certain racially prescribed economic positions. The central question was whether this social and educational philosophy could remain intact as Hampton and Tuskegee were transformed from normal schools to secondary schools with certain forms of collegiate work. Nearly one-half, or $2 million, of the Hampton endowment was earmarked for "teacher training of collegiate grade now required by southern States." Attached to the endowment campaign's "Special Memorandum" were regulations governing certificates for teachers in North Carolina and Alabama. In 1925 North Carolina required for a high school teacher's certificate graduation from a "standard A Grade college in academic or scientific courses, embracing 120 semester hours," 18 of which had to be in professional educational subjects. Alabama required three years of standard college work approved by the State Board of Education, including nine hours of professional study. Such requirements forced Hampton and Tuskegee into the world of collegiate education. They started by offering the Bachelor of Science in agriculture and teaching, trying hard to hold closely to their traditional emphasis, but were soon compelled to expand the collegiate departments to cover a range of liberal arts fields.[43]

This very yielding to the new educational standards changed the social composition of the institution's student population, and the question of whether the Armstrong-Washington philosophy could prevail at the collegiate level was answered in part by the Hampton student strike of 1927. Traditionally, the Hampton-Tuskegee Idea rested on a denigration of academic subjects, which was easier to maintain when the institutions were composed of half-grown elementary students, regimented to strict military discipline, and overworked in simple agricultural and industrial tasks. But the new collegiate programs attracted different students. Although the total number of students enrolled at Hampton remained at about a thousand throughout the 1920s, the number of students in the college division grew steadily, from 21 in 1920 to 417 in 1927. By 1929, no new high school students were admitted. The new college-level students repeatedly insisted that academic standards be raised. In 1924 Hampton's Student Council charged that the director of the trade school had so little formal education and used such poor English that he was not qualified to teach. Similar accusations were lodged in 1925 against several teachers in the school of agriculture. There were additional complaints that white teachers were less concerned with academic subjects than with teaching manners and morals. Indeed, five of Hampton's white teachers participated in a Ku Klux Klan parade in support of a law

every part of the country. A remarkable Negro periodical and daily press has grown up within the past few years devoted, almost wholly, to advancing, directly or indirectly, these ideas.

The memorandum pointed out that it was "impossible, even if it were desirable, to stop this movement." The important thing was to assure its development in "a sound and constructive form."[41]

The industrial philanthropists believed that the right black leaders could direct the masses along "constructive" lines. "As the Negro progresses," the report stated, "the ideals of at least the sound thinking majority will be most influenced by those of advanced education and experience." Herein were the reasons to raise Hampton and Tuskegee to a level of "advanced education" and to influence the attitudes of emergent black leaders, whether they were trained in advanced industrial schools or academic colleges. From the philanthropists' standpoint, the solution to the race problem was self-evident. First, "The Negro problem has been happily and permanently solved by the application of the Hampton-Tuskegee method in many individual communities." Second, "The Hampton-Tuskegee Idea, therefore, of solving the race problem in America is to *multiply these local solutions and the national problem solves itself.*" Third, "The proposed method for doing this is to *multiply the number of Hampton and Tuskegee men and women adequately trained for present day leadership.*" Although Armstrong had died in 1893, Booker T. Washington in 1915, and H. B. Frissell in 1917, the industrial philanthropists remained steadfastly committed to the Hampton-Tuskegee methods as the fundamental solution to the race problem. Anson Phelps-Stokes said in a letter to John D. Rockefeller, Jr.: "Personally, I am increasingly convinced that Hampton and Tuskegee provide the most important contribution yet found towards the solution of the race problem in this country, and towards the development of the Negro people so as to make them fitted for the highest citizenship." Throughout the endowment campaign the industrial philanthropists reminded themselves and the larger society that the Hampton methods produced Booker T. Washington, "the outstanding Negro leader of the past," and that every president of the United States, from Grant to Calvin Coolidge, had supported the Hampton-Tuskegee Idea. President Garfield was a trustee of Hampton, President Roosevelt served for nine years as a trustee of Tuskegee, and William Howard Taft became a trustee of Tuskegee while president of the United States and was, in 1925, president of Hampton's Board of Trustees. For the industrial philanthropists, the Hampton-Tuskegee Idea had become a matter of tried and true methods, of tradition, and had congealed into a permanent policy.[42]

The basic social philosophy underlying the Hampton-Tuskegee pro-

TABLE 7.2

Black College and Professional Students in Private and Public Colleges in Southern States and the District of Columbia, by Sex, 1935

State or District of Columbia	Private college students		Public college students		Public and private college students
	Male	Female	Male	Female	Total
Alabama	793	676	325	554	2,348
Arkansas	138	203	173	172	686
Delaware	0	0	33	50	83
District of Columbia	1,069	894	148	587	2,698
Florida	132	142	267	241	782
Georgia	907	1,078	136	198	2,319
Kentucky	0	0	288	510	798
Louisiana	575	569	273	270	1,687
Maryland	163	298	66	188	715
Mississippi	184	297	127	79	687
Missouri	0	0	215	340	559
North Carolina	652	830	782	1,722	3,986
South Carolina	542	770	254	247	1,813
Tennessee	881	945	460	793	3,079
Texas	740	1,097	453	700	2,990
Virginia	960	1,103	495	523	3,081
West Virginia	0	0	464	494	958
Total	7,736	8,902	4,963	7,668	29,169

Source: Blose and Caliver, *Statistics of the Education of Negroes*, pp. 37–40.

requiring racial segregation on Hampton's campus, and other white instructors established a segregated club and openly opposed the employment of qualified black teachers. In response to Hampton's low academic standards and repressive racial policies, the students went on strike in October 1927. They demanded an end to racism and paternalism and insisted that "our educational system be so revised that we shall no longer be subjected to instructions from teachers whose apparent education is below that of the average student." The students' demands, breaking with tradition, called essentially for an abandonment of the Hampton-Tuskegee Idea. Such matters were not easily settled on a campus that had devoted more than half a century to a philosophy of racial subordination and industrial training. Student unrest and contention between the faculty and administration persisted into the spring of 1929. Confronted with this disorder, James E. Gregg, successor to H. B. Frissell, was forced to resign his office. The Hampton Board of Trustees quickly concurred. Thus both the principal of Hampton and the president of Fisk University, men who presided over the institutions' first significant endowments, were forced to resign their office because the students rejected the very policies and social philosophy that underlay the endowment campaigns.[44]

The Hampton students put the final nail in the coffin of the old Hampton-Tuskegee Idea. As Robert A. Coles, one of the leaders of the student revolt, said, Hampton's new students possessed "a DuBois ambition" that would not mix with "a Booker Washington education." Such attitudes reflected an increasing demand for collegiate education among black youth of the 1920s. Despite the industrial philanthropists' efforts to reduce the number of black colleges (through their scheme of making one or two vastly superior to the others) and their attempt to transform industrial training into a collegiate program, black youth and their parents pushed for and achieved more and better higher educational opportunities. The enrollment of college students in public colleges in the sixteen former slave states and the District of Columbia grew from 12 in 1915 to 12,631 in 1935, and, as illustrated in Table 7.2, the enrollment in private colleges in 1935 was 16,638. In 1915 there were only 2,474 students enrolled in the black private colleges. These accomplishments and the beliefs and behavior that brought them about specifically rejected the Hampton-Tuskegee Idea and its philosophy of manual training and racial subordination. The industrial philanthropists, as evidenced by their contributions of time, money, and effort during the Hampton-Tuskegee endowment campaign, did not voluntarily abandon the Hampton-Tuskegee Idea. Rather, the philosophy was decisively rejected by the black students and leaders of the 1920s, and the key institutions were compelled by changing educational requirements and student demands

to become standard institutions of higher learning. Thus was ushered in a new and different era in black higher education, and all concerned parties, blacks, missionaries, industrial philanthropists, and southern whites, had to adjust to this new departure. The battles for control and influence over the training of black leaders did not cease, but they were fought on a different terrain.[45]

The progress of black higher education during the 1930s was mixed. The northern missionaries and black educators who presided over the black colleges entered the 1920s extremely worried about the financial and material conditions of black colleges. Then, during the 1930s, northern industrial philanthropists presented black college educators with good opportunities for improving the material conditions of black higher education. To be sure, financial solvency was critical, but it was only a means to the more important and long-standing mission of black higher

ter G. Woodson argued in 1933 that the "mis-education" of black students had resulted in the creation of a highly educated bourgeois that was estranged from ordinary black people, "the very people upon whom they must eventually count for carrying out a program of progress." In 1934 writer and poet Langston Hughes denounced the "cowards from the colleges," the "meek professors and well-paid presidents," who submitted willingly to racism and the general subordination of black people. The following year, George Streator, business manager of the *Crisis*, proclaimed that black college faculty were much too conservative, "years behind the New Deal." "Further," said Streator, "Negro college students are not radical; they are reactionary." Such critics showed little sympathy for the black college educators' inability openly to protest against the system of racial caste and still expect to be well received in philanthropic circles.[47]

Some educators in black colleges, however, were also disturbed by the growing apathy and social irresponsibility of black college students. In 1937, Lafayette Harris, president of Philander Smith College in Little Rock, Arkansas, castigated black students for their general apathy and particular estrangement from common black folk: "Probably nothing gives one more concern than the frequently apparent fatalistic and nonchalant attitude of many a Negro college student and educated Negro. With him, very little seems to matter except meals, sleep, and folly. Community problems are never even recognized as existing. They know nothing of their less fortunate fellowmen and care less." The following year Randolph Edmonds, a professor at Dillard University, blamed black college educators for the attitudes of black students toward the masses. "The Negro youth is being educated to regard the race with contempt, not only by white teachers in mixed schools, but by Negro instructors in Negro colleges." The central contention of much of this criticism was that the college-bred Negroes, or "talented tenth," were not being educated to think and act in behalf of the interests of black people. Rather, they were internalizing a social ideology nearly indistinguishable from that of the philanthropists who helped finance black higher education. As one black student assessed the social consciousness of black educated leaders in 1938, "The American race problem has brought us many anomalies. But it may be some time before it equals the Negro leader, supported by workingmen's dollars, leading a working population, and yet enunciating a philosophy which would do credit to the original economic royalist or the most eloquent spokesman for America's 'sixty sinister families.'" In vital respects, the fate of black higher education during the 1930s was closely related to the attitudes and interests of the nation's wealthiest families. Only black college educators could appreciate fully the difficulty of depending on this wealth while being urged to articulate

education. For the northern missionaries and black educators, the great mission of black colleges was that of training a competent leadership, men and women who could think, who were independent and self-reliant, and who could persuade and lead the black masses. This mission was contradicted by the wonderful material improvements in endowments, physical plants, and faculty salaries because the industrial philanthropists who provided these gifts pressed continuously for the spontaneous loyalty of the college-bred Negro. As black colleges became increasingly dependent on donations from northern industrial philanthropists, the missionaries and black educators found it extremely difficult, if not impossible, to accept philanthropic gifts and assert simultaneously that many of the political and economic aims of the philanthropists were at variance with the fundamental interests of the black masses. From 1915 to 1960, the General Education Board alone expended for black higher education (exclusive of grants for medical education) over $41 million. The board disbursed over $5 million to Atlanta University; $5 million to Fisk University; $3.8 million to Tuskegee Institute; $3.5 million to Spelman College; $2.15 million to Dillard University; $1.9 million to Morehouse College; and $1.1 million to Clark College. The board symbolized the central place that northern philanthropists had come to occupy in the development of black higher education in the South. Given the industrial philanthropists' demand for a conservative black leadership that would cooperate with instead of challenge the Jim Crow system, a certain amount of compromise, indifference, apathy, and even fear developed among black college educators and students.[46]

Observers of the black colleges during the 1930s were dismayed at the apparent shift in consciousness among black college educators and students which paralleled the colleges' increasing dependence on the purse strings of northern industrial philanthropy. As early as 1930, W. E. B. DuBois, in a commencement address at Howard University, chastised the black college male students for their nihilistic behavior:

Our college man today is, on the average, a man untouched by real culture. He deliberately surrenders to selfish and even silly ideals, swarming into semiprofessional athletics and Greek letter societies, and affecting to despise scholarship and the hard grind of study and research. The greatest meetings of the Negro college year like those of the white college year have become vulgar exhibitions of liquor, extravagance, and fur coats. We have in our colleges a growing mass of stupidity and indifference.

DuBois and other prominent black intellectuals worried that black college students and educators had forsaken their obligation to become socially responsible leaders of their people. Historian and educator Car-

475

a philosophy that challenged the philanthropists' conceptions of proper race and social relations.[48]

Undoubtedly, the verbal attacks upon black college educators and students during the 1930s were engendered in part by the growing liberalism of the era. The social critics may have been excessively harsh and even off the mark in their judgments of the social consciousness of black college educators and students. Black college educators had to steer between two equally critical courses. On one hand, they were dependent on the benevolence of industrial philanthropists for the very survival of the private black colleges that formed the backbone of black higher education. On the other hand, it was their mission to represent the struggles and aspirations of black people and to articulate the very source of the masses' discomfort and oppression. One course propelled them into conflict with the other because the industrial philanthropists supported black subordination. Black college educators had no noble path out of this contradiction and sought to contain it by placating northern industrial philanthropists while training black intellectuals who would help lead black people toward greater freedom and justice. Indeed, it was a painful and difficult course to steer that frequently brought down upon black college educators the wrath of both sides. This was a moment in the history of black higher education when presidents and faculty could do little more than succeed in keeping their institutions together while maintaining themselves and their students with as great a sense of dignity as was possible. When their students helped launch the civil rights movement of the 1960s, the hard work of these educators seemed far more heroic in the hour of harvest than it did during the years of cultivation.

19. Morgan to Buttrick, 25, 29, 31 Jan. 1901, Sale to Buttrick, 23 Dec. 1909, 8 Jan. 1908, Box 716, Sale to Buttrick, 1 Jan. 1908, MacVicar to Buttrick, 7 June, 12 Aug. 1902, Buttrick to MacVicar, 18 Aug. 1902, Hovey to Buttrick, 30 Mar. 1908, Box 170, GEB Papers; Jones, *Negro Education*, 1: 7–8.

20. Sale to Buttrick, 8 Jan. 1908, Box 170, Morgan to Buttrick, 31 Jan., 1 Feb. 1901, Box 717, GEB Papers.

21. Harlan and Smock, eds., *Booker T. Washington Papers*, 3:620; Buttrick to Rockefeller, 5 Feb. 1914, Box 203, GEB Papers.

22. Buttrick to Sale, 29 May 1907, Box 59, Report of Williams to Buttrick, 22 May 1907, Buttrick to the General Education Board, 22 May 1907, Box 716, GEB Papers.

23. Fosdick, *Adventure in Giving*, pp. 151–55; Hine, "Pursuit of Professional Equality," pp. 176–77.

24. Buttrick to Rockefeller, 5 Feb. 1914, Flexner to Villard, 1 Dec. 1914, Box 203, "General Education Board's Conference on Negro Education," 19 Nov. 1915, GEB Papers; DuBois, "Thomas Jesse Jones," p. 253; Berman, "Educational Colonialism in Africa," pp. 183–94; King, *Pan-Africanism and Education*, pp. 43–57.

25. "General Education Board's Conference on Negro Education," 29 Nov. 1915, pp. 133–34.

26. Ibid., pp. 130–38, 149–52, 162–64.

27. Report of Committee on Negro Education, 24 Jan. 1916, Box 722, GEB Papers.

28. Logan, *The Negro in the United States*, pp. 74–83; Moton to Wilson, 15 June 1918, Box 303, GEB Papers.

29. Jones, "Crisis in Negro Leadership"; Peabody to Gregg, 5 Apr. 1920, Box 58, Peabody Papers.

30. Peabody to Gregg, 5 Apr. 1920, Box 58, Peabody Papers; *Fisk University News*, Sept. 1919, pp. 2–4; DuBois to Eleazer, 12 Mar. 1926, Commission on Inter-racial Co-operation Collection; Franklin, *Black Self-Determination*.

31. Jones, *Negro Education*, 1:310, 314–15; "General Education Board's Conference on Negro Education," 29 Nov. 1915, GEB Papers; Lamon, "Black Community in Nashville," p. 231.

32. McKenzie, *Ideals of Fisk*, p. 7; Aptheker, ed., *W. E. B. DuBois*, pp. 52–57; DuBois, "Fisk"; Wolters, *New Negro on Campus*, pp. 35–39.

33. Rosenwald to Flexner, 15 Jan. 1917, Flexner to Rosenwald, 17 Jan. 1917, Box 138, Flexner to Swift, 2 Apr. 1917, Appleget to Thorkelson, 12 June 1928, "Appropriations Made by the General Education Board to Fisk University"; for endowment contributions, see Baldwin to General Education Board, 6 Oct. 1924, Wood to General Education Board, 6 May 1920, Box 128, GEB Papers;

1. Logan, "Evolution of Private Colleges for Negroes," p. 216; Jones, *Negro Education*, 2:310; Klein, *Survey of Negro Colleges and Universities*; Holmes, *Evolution of the Negro College*, p. 201.

2. Holmes, *Evolution of the Negro College*, pp. 163–77.

3. Ibid., p. 216; Klein, *Survey of Negro Colleges and Universities*, pp. 5–33.

4. Richardson, *Christian Reconstruction*, p. 173; missionary philanthropists quoted from Holmes, *Evolution of the Negro College*, p. 69; Wright, "Development of Education for Blacks in Georgia," p. 31.

5. Butchart, "Educating for Freedom," p. 353; Fredrickson, *The Black Image in the White Mind*, p. 244; Gutman, *The Black Family in Slavery and Freedom*, p. 532.

6. Freedmen's Aid Society quoted from Holmes, *Evolution of the Negro College*, p. 69; Bond, "Century of Negro Higher Education," p. 187; Butchart, "Educating for Freedom," pp. 453–90; Wright, "Development of Education for Blacks in Georgia," p. 29; Logan, "Evolution of Private Colleges for Negroes," p. 216.

7. Richardson, *Christian Reconstruction*, pp. 113, 123, 128; Bond, "Century of Negro Higher Education," pp. 187–88.

8. Richardson, *Christian Reconstruction*, p. 125; McPherson, *Abolitionist Legacy*, pp. 213, 222; Morehouse quoted in ibid., p. 222.

9. Richardson, *Christian Reconstruction*, p. 125; Merrill quoted in McPherson, *Abolitionist Legacy*, p. 220.

10. DuBois quoted in McPherson, *Abolitionist Legacy*, p. 223.

11. Ibid.

12. Ibid., p. 213.

13. Baldwin, "Present Problem of Negro Education," pp. 52–60; Anderson, "Education for Servitude," pp. 208–16.

14. Weinberg, *A Chance to Learn*, p. 280.

15. Ibid., pp. 267, 280; Badger, "Negro Colleges and Universities"; Jones, *Negro Education*, 1:59.

16. Selden, *Accreditation*, pp. 32–37; Green, "Higher Standards for the Negro College"; Cozart, *History of the Association of Colleges and Secondary Schools*.

17. Selden, *Accreditation*, pp. 35–37.

18. DuBois, *College-Bred Negro*; DuBois and Dill, eds., *College-Bred Negro American*; Jones, *Negro Education*, 1:58, 64; Green, "Higher Standards for the Negro College"; Cozart, *History of the Association of Colleges and Secondary Schools*. Hampton and Tuskegee, the two black educational institutions most favored by industrial philanthropists, were excluded from consideration because they were normal schools and it was their mission to provide precollegiate education for the training of common school teachers.

Fisk University News, Dec. 1924, p. 20.

34. *Fisk University News*, Apr. 1923, p. 7; ibid., Oct. 1920, p. 21; Jones to Flexner, 4 Oct. 1915, Wood to Buttrick, 6 May 1920, Thorkelson to Wood, 5 Nov. 1926, Box 138, GEB Papers. For the philanthropists' role in actively recruiting trustees, see Flexner to Rosenwald, 8, 17 Jan. 1917, Rosenwald to Flexner, 13 Jan. 1917, Flexner to Swift, 2 Apr. 1917, Flexner to Judson, 27 Mar. 1917, Judson to Flexner, 30 Mar., 13 Apr. 1917, Box 138, GEB Papers.

35. Flexner, Memorandum on the Fisk Endowment Campaign, 25 May 1923, Box 23, GEB Papers.

36. The most thorough accounts of McKenzie's repressive educational practices are Wolters, *New Negro on Campus*, pp. 26–69; Lamon, "Fisk University Student Strike"; Richardson, *History of Fisk University*, chaps. 6 and 7.

37. "Fisk University," a 1926 memorandum, Box 138, GEB Papers; "Fisk Endowment Drive in Nashville," *Fisk University News*, May 1924, pp. 31–32; "First Million-Dollar Endowment for College Education of the Negro in the History of America," ibid., Oct. 1924, pp. 1–13; Commercial Club of Nashville to General Education Board, 24 Jan. 1920, Box 138, GEB Papers; Jones, *Negro Education*, 1:314–15, 320–21.

38. Wolters, *New Negro on Campus*, pp. 34–40; *New York Times*, 8 Feb. 1925, sec. 2, p. 1; Jones to Cravath, 20 Sept. 1924, Box 3, Folder 20, McKenzie Papers.

39. DuBois quoted in Wolters, *New Negro on Campus*, pp. 62–63; "Fisk University," a 1926 memorandum, Box 138, GEB Papers. For General Education Board contributions, see Fosdick, *Adventure in Giving*, pp. 329–32; "Fisk University," Report by Jones to the General Education Board, 27, 28 Sept. 1928, Box 138, GEB Papers.

40. Stokes to Rockefeller, 8 Jan. 1925, Box 17, Folder 8, "Special Memorandum Prepared for Clarence H. Kelsey, Esq.," 24 Oct. 1924, Box 17, Folder 5, Stokes to Rosenwald, 9 Dec. 1924, Box 17, Folder 6, Rosenwald Papers.

41. "Special Memorandum," 24 Oct. 1924, pp. 8, 23, 31–33, Box 17, Folder 5, Rosenwald Papers.

42. Ibid., pp. 10, 20; Stokes to Rockefeller, 8 Jan. 1925, Box 17, Folder 8, Rosenwald Papers.

43. "Special Memorandum," 24 Oct. 1924, p. 32, Appendix C, Box 17, Folder 5, Rosenwald Papers.

44. Wolters, *New Negro on Campus*, pp. 233, 248, 258, 273; DuBois, "The Hampton Strike," *Nation* 125 (2 Nov. 1927): 471–72.

45. Wolters, *New Negro on Campus*, p. 267.

46. Fosdick, *Adventure in Giving*, pp. 328–29.

47. Franklin, "Whatever Happened to the College-Bred Negro?" (DuBois, Woodson, and Hughes are quoted in Franklin's article); Hughes, "Cowards from the Colleges"; Streator, "Negro College Radicals."

48. Harris, "Problems before the College Negro"; Edmonds, "Education in Self-Contempt"; Allen, "Selling Out the Workers."

The Talented Tenth

W.E.B. DuBois

The Negro race, like all races, is going to be saved by its exceptional men. The problem of education, then, among Negroes must first of all deal with the Talented Tenth; it is the problem of developing the Best of this race that they may guide the Mass away from the contamination and death of the Worst, in their own and other races. Now the training of men is a difficult and intricate task. Its technique is a matter for educational experts, but its object is for the vision of seers. If we make money the object of man-training, we shall develop money-makers but not necessarily men; if we make technical skill the object of education, we may possess artisans but not, in nature, men. Men we shall have only as we make manhood the object of the work of the schools—intelligence, broad sympathy, knowledge of the world that was and is, and of the relation of men to it—this is the curriculum of that Higher Education, which must underlie true life. On this foundation we may build bread winning, skill of hand and quickness of brain, with never a fear lest the child and man mistake the means of living for the object of life.

If this be true—and who can deny it—three tasks lay before me; first to show from the past that the Talented Tenth as they have risen among American Negroes have been worthy of leadership; secondly, to show how these men may be educated and developed; and thirdly, to show their relation to the Negro problem.

You misjudge us because you do not know us. From the very first it has been the educated and intelligent of the Negro people that have led and elevated the mass, and the sole obstacles that nullified and retarded their efforts were slavery and race prejudice; for what is slavery but the legalized survival of the unfit and the nullification of the work of natural internal leadership? Negro leadership, therefore, sought from the first to rid the race of this awful incubus that it might make way for natural selection and the survival of the fittest. In colonial days came Phillis Wheatley and Paul Cuffe striving against the bars of prejudice; and Benjamin Banneker, the almanac maker, voiced their longings when he said to Thomas Jefferson, "I freely and cheerfully acknowledge that I am of the African race, and in colour which is natural to them, of the deepest dye; and it is under a sense of the most profound gratitude to the Supreme Ruler of the Universe, that I now confess to you that I am not under that state of tyrannical thraldom and inhuman captivity to which too many of my brethren are doomed, but that I have abundantly tasted of the fruition of those blessings which proceed from that free and unequalled liberty with which you are favored, and which I hope you will willingly allow, you have mercifully received from the immediate hand of that Being from whom proceedeth every good and perfect gift.

"Suffer me to recall to your mind that time, in which the arms of the British crown were exerted with every powerful effort, in order to reduce you to a state of servitude; look back, I entreat you, on the variety of dangers to which you were exposed; reflect on that period in which every human aid appeared unavailable, and in which even hope and fortitude wore the aspect of inability to the conflict, and you cannot but be led to a serious and grateful sense of your miraculous and providential preservation, you cannot but acknowledge, that the present freedom and tranquility which you enjoy, you have mercifully received, and that a peculiar blessing of heaven.

"This, sir, was a time when you clearly saw into the injustice of a state of Slavery, and in which you had just apprehensions of the horrors of its condition. It was then that your abhorrence thereof was so excited, that you publicly held forth this true and invaluable doctrine, which is worthy to be recorded and remembered in all succeeding ages: 'We hold these truths to be self evident, that all men are created equal; that they are endowed with certain inalienable rights, and that among these are life, liberty and the pursuit of happiness.'"

Then came Dr. James Derham, who could tell even the learned Dr. Rush something of medicine, and Lemuel Haynes, to whom Middlebury College gave an honorary A. M. in 1804. These and others we may call the Revolutionary group of distinguished Negroes—they were persons of marked ability, leaders of a Talented Tenth, standing conspicuously among the best of their time. They strove by word and deed to save the color line from becoming the line between the bond and free, but all they could do was nullified by Eli Whitney and the Curse of Gold.

So they passed into forgetfulness.

But their spirit did not wholly die; here and there in the early part of the century came other exceptional men. Some were natural sons of unnatural fathers and were given often a liberal training and thus a race of educated mulatoes sprang up to plead for black men's rights. There was Ira Aldridge, whom all Europe loved to honor; there was that Voice crying in the Wilderness, David Walker, and saying:

"I declare it does appear to me as though some nations think God is asleep, or that he made the Africans for nothing else but to dig their mines and work their farms, or they cannot believe history, sacred or profane. I ask every man who has a heart, and is blessed with the privilege of believing—Is not God a God of justice to all his creatures? Do you say he is? Then if he gives peace and tranquility to tyrants and permits them to keep our fathers, our mothers, ourselves and our children in eternal ignorance and wretchedness to support them and their families, would he be to us a God of Justice? I ask, O, ye Christians, who hold us and our children in the most abject ignorance and degradation that ever a people were afflicted with since the world began—I say if God gives you peace and tranquility, and suffers you thus to go on afflicting us, and our children, who have never given you the least provocation—would He be to us a God of Justice? If you will allow that we are men, who feel for each other, does not the blood of our fathers and of us, their children, cry aloud to the Lord of Sabaoth against you for the cruelties and murders with which you have and do continue to afflict us?"

This was the wild voice that first aroused Southern legislators in 1829 to the terrors of abolitionism.

In 1831 there met that first Negro convention in Philadelphia, at which the world gaped curiously but which bravely attacked the problems of race and slavery, crying out against persecution and declaring that "Laws as cruel in themselves as they were unconstitutional and unjust, have in many places been enacted against our poor, unfriended and unoffending Brethren (without a shadow of provocation on our part), at whose bare recital the very savage draws himself up for fear of contagion—looks noble and prides himself because he bears not the name of Christian." Side by side this free Negro movement, and the movement for abolition, strove until they merged into one strong stream. Too little notice has been taken of the work which the Talented Tenth among Negroes took in the great abolition crusade. From the very day that a Philadelphia colored man became the first subscriber to Garrison's "Liberator," to the day when Negro soldiers made the Emancipation Proclamation possible, black leaders worked shoulder to shoulder with white men in a movement, the success of which would have been impossible without them. There was Purvis and Remond, Pennington and Highland Garnett, Sojourner Truth and Alexander Crummel, and above all, Frederick Douglass—what would the abolition movement have been without them? They stood as living examples of the possibilities of the Negro race, their own hard experiences and well wrought culture said silently more than all the drawn periods of orators—they were the men who made American slavery impossible. As Maria Weston Chapman once said, from the school of anti-slavery agitation "a throng of authors, editors, lawyers, orators and accomplished gentlemen of color have taken their degree! It has equally implanted hopes and aspirations, noble thoughts, and sublime purposes, in the hearts of both races. It has prepared the white man for the freedom of the black man, and it has made the black man scorn the thought of enslavement, as does a white man, as far as its influence has extended. Strengthen that noble influence! Before its organization, the country only saw here and there in slavery some faithful Cudjoe or Dinah, whose strong natures blossomed even in bondage, like a fine plant beneath a heavy stone. Now, under the elevating and cherishing influence of the American Anti-slavery Society, the colored race, like the white, furnishes Corinthian capitals for the noblest temples."

Where were these black abolitionists trained? Some, like Frederick Douglass, were self-trained, but yet trained liberally; others, like Alexander Crummell and McCune Smith, graduated from famous foreign universities. Most of them rose up through the colored schools of New York and Philadelphia and Boston, taught by college-bred men like Russworm, of Dartmouth, and college-bred white men like Neau and Benezet.

After emancipation came a new group of educated and gifted leaders: Langston, Bruce and Elliot, Greener, Williams and Payne. Through political organization, historical and polemic writing and moral regeneration, these men strove to uplift their people. It is the fashion of to-day to sneer at them and to say that with freedom Negro leadership should have begun at the plow and not in the Senate—a foolish and mischievous lie; two hundred and fifty years that black serf toiled at the plow and yet that toiling was in vain till the Senate passed the war amendments; and two hundred and fifty years more the half-free serf of to-day may toil at his plow, but unless he have political rights and righteously guarded civic status, he will still remain the poverty-stricken and ignorant plaything of rascals, that he now is. This all sane men know even if they dare not say it.

And so we come to the present—a day of cowardice and vacillation, of strident wide-voiced wrong and faint hearted compromise; of double-faced dallying with Truth and Right. Who are to-day guiding the work of the Negro people? The "exceptions" of course. And yet so sure as this Talented Tenth is pointed out, the blind worshippers of the Average cry out in alarm: "These are exceptions, look here at death, disease and crime—these are the happy rule." Of course they are the rule, because a silly nation made them the rule: Because for three long centuries this people lynched Negroes who dared to be brave, raped black women who dared to be virtuous, crushed dark-hued youth who dared to be ambitious, and encouraged and made to flourish servility and lewdness and apathy. But not even this was able to crush all manhood and chastity and aspiration from black folk. A saving remnant continually survives and persists, continually aspires, continually shows itself in thrift and ability and character. Exceptional it is to be sure, but this is its chiefest promise; it shows the capability of Negro blood, the promise of black men. Do Americans ever stop to reflect that there are in this land a million men of Negro blood, well-educated, owners of homes, against the honor of whose womanhood no breath was ever raised, whose men occupy positions of trust and usefulness, and who, judged by any standard, have reached the full measure of the best type of modern European culture? Is it fair, is it decent, is it Christian to ignore these facts of the Negro problem, to belittle such aspiration, to nullify such leadership and seek to crush these people back into the mass out of which by toil and travail, they and their fathers have raised themselves?

Can the masses of the Negro people be in any possible way more quickly raised than by the effort and example of this aristocracy of talent and character? Was there ever a nation on God's fair earth civilized from the bottom upward? Never; it is, ever was and ever will be from the top downward that culture filters. The Talented Tenth rises and pulls all that are worth the saving up to their vantage ground. This is the history of human progress; and the two historic mistakes which have hindered that progress were the thinking first that no more could ever rise save the few already risen; or second, that it would better the unrisen to pull the risen down.

How then shall the leaders of a struggling people be trained and the hands of the risen few strengthened? There can be but one answer: The best and most capable of their youth must be schooled in the colleges and universities of the land. We will not quarrel as to just what the university of the Negro should teach or how it should teach it—I willingly admit that each soul and each race-soul needs its own peculiar curriculum. But this is true: A university is a human invention for the transmission of knowledge and culture from generation to generation, through the training of quick minds and pure hearts, and for this work no other human invention will suffice, not even trade and industrial schools.

All men cannot go to college but some men must; every isolated group or nation must have its yeast, must have for the talented few centers of training where men are not so mystified and befuddled by the hard and necessary toil of earning a living, as to have no aims higher than their bellies, and no God greater than Gold. This is true training, and thus in the beginning were the favored sons of the freedmen trained. Out of the colleges of the North came, after the blood of war, Ware, Cravath, Chase,

Andrews, Bumstead and Spence to build the foundations of knowledge and civilization in the black South. Where ought they to have begun to build? At the bottom, of course, quibbles the mole with his eyes in the earth. Aye! truly at the bottom, at the very bottom; at the bottom of knowledge, down in the very depths of knowledge there where the roots of justice strike into the lowest soil of Truth. And so they did begin; they founded colleges, and up from the normal schools went teachers, and around the normal teachers clustered other teachers to teach the public schools; the college trained in Greek and Latin and mathematics, 2,000 men; and these men trained full 50,000 others in morals and manners, and they in turn taught thrift and the alphabet to nine millions of men, who to-day hold $300,-000,000 of property. It was a miracle—the most wonderful peace-battle of the 19th century, and yet to-day men smile at it, and in fine superiority tell us that it was a strange mistake; that a proper way to found a system of education is first to gather the children and buy them spelling books and hoes; afterward men may look about for teachers, if haply they may find them; or again they would teach men Work, but as for Life —why, what has Work to do with Life, they ask vacantly.

Was the work of these college founders successful; did it stand the test of time? Did the college graduates, with all their fine theories of life, really live? Are they useful men helping to civilize and elevate their less fortunate fellows? Let us see. Omitting all institutions which have not actually graduated students from a college course, there are to-day in the United States thirty-four institutions giving something above high school training to Negroes and designed especially for this race.

Three of these were established in border States before the War; thirteen were planted by the Freedmen's Bureau in the years 1864-1869; nine were established between 1870 and 1880 by various church bodies; five were established after 1881 by Negro churches, and four are state institutions supported by United States' agricultural funds. In most cases the college departments are small adjuncts to high and common school work. As a matter of fact six institutions—Atlanta, Fisk, Howard, Shaw, Wilberforce and Leland, are the important Negro col-

482

leges so far as actual work and number of students are concerned. In all these institutions, seven hundred and fifty Negro college students are enrolled. In grade the best of these colleges are about a year behind the smaller New England colleges and are a typical curriculum is that of Atlanta University. Here students from the grammar grades, after a three years' high school course, take a college course of 136 weeks. One-fourth of this time is given to Latin and Greek; one-fifth, to English and modern languages; one-sixth, to history and social science; one-seventh, to natural science; one-eighth to mathematics, and one-eighth to philosophy and pedagogy.

In addition to these students in the South, Negroes have attended Northern colleges for many years. As early as 1826 one was graduated from Bowdoin College, and from that time till to-day nearly every year has seen elsewhere, other such graduates. They have, of course, met much color prejudice. Fifty years ago very few colleges would admit them at all. Even to-day no Negro has ever been admitted to Princeton, and at some other leading institutions they are rather endured than encouraged. Oberlin was the great pioneer in the work of blotting out the color line in colleges, and has more Negro graduates by far than any other Northern college.

The total number of Negro college graduates up to 1899, (several of the graduates of that year not being reported), was as follows:

	Negro Colleges.	White Colleges.
Before '76	137	75
'75–80	143	22
'80–85	250	31
'85–90	413	43
'90–95	465	66
'95–99	475	88
Class Unknown	57	64
Total	1,914	390

Of these graduates 2,079 were men and 252 were women; 50 per cent. of Northern-born college men come South to work among the masses of their people, at a sacrifice which few people realize; nearly 90 per cent. of the Southern-born graduates instead of seeking that personal freedom and broader intellectual atmosphere which their training has led them, in some degree, to conceive, stay and labor and wait in the midst of their black neighbors and relatives.

The most interesting question, and in many respects the crucial question, to be asked concerning college-bred Negroes, is: Do they earn a living? It has been intimated more than once that the higher training of Negroes has resulted in sending into the world of work, men who could find nothing to do suitable to their talents. Now and then there comes a rumor of a colored college man working at menial service, etc. Fortunately, returns as to occupations of college-bred Negroes, gathered by the Atlanta conference, are quite full—nearly sixty per cent. of the total number of graduates.

This enables us to reach fairly certain conclusions as to the occupations of all college-bred Negroes. Of 1,312 persons reported, there were:

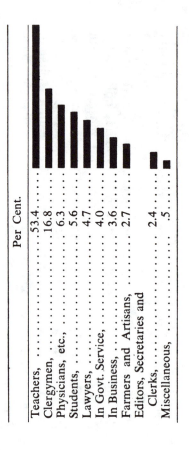

	Per Cent.
Teachers,	53.4
Clergymen,	16.8
Physicians, etc.,	6.3
Students,	5.6
Lawyers,	4.7
In Govt. Service,	4.0
In Business,	3.6
Farmers and Artisans,	2.7
Editors, Secretaries and Clerks,	2.4
Miscellaneous,	.5

Over half are teachers, a sixth are preachers, another sixth are students and professional men; over 6 per cent. are farmers, artisans and merchants, and 4 per cent. are in government service. In detail the occupations are as follows:

argued that the Negro people need social leadership more than most groups: that they have no traditions to fall back upon, no long established customs, no strong family ties, no well defined social classes. All these things must be slowly and painfully evolved. The preacher was, even before the war, the group leader of the Negroes, and the church their greatest social institution. Naturally this preacher was ignorant and often immoral, and the problem of replacing the older type by better educated men has been a difficult one. Both by direct work and by direct influence on other preachers, and on congregations, the college-bred preacher has an opportunity for reformatory work and moral inspiration, the value of which cannot be overestimated.

It has, however, been in the furnishing of teachers that the Negro college has found its peculiar function. Few persons realize how vast a work, how mighty a revolution has been thus accomplished. To furnish five millions and more of ignorant people with teachers of their own race and blood, in one generation, was not only a very difficult undertaking, but a very important one, in that, it placed before the eyes of almost every Negro child an attainable ideal. It brought the blacks in contact with modern civilization, made black men the leaders of their communities and trainers of the new generation. In this work college-bred Negroes were first teachers, and then teachers of teachers. And here it is that the broad culture of college work has been of peculiar value. Knowledge of life and its wider meaning, has been the point of the Negro's deepest ignorance, and the sending out of teachers whose training has not been simply for bread winning, but also for human culture, has been of inestimable value in the training of these men.

In earlier years the two occupations of preacher and teacher were practically the only ones open to the black college graduate. Of later years a larger diversity of life among his people, has opened new avenues of employment. Nor have these college men been paupers and spendthrifts; 557 college-bred Negroes owned in 1899, $1,342,862.50 worth of real estate, (assessed value) or $2,411 per family. The real value of the total accumulations of the whole group is perhaps about $10,000,000, or $5,000 a piece. Pitiful, is it not, beside the fortunes of oil kings and steel trusts, but after all is the fortune of the millionaire the only stamp of true and successful living? Alas! it is, with many, and there's the rub.

Occupations of College-Bred Men.

Teachers:
Presidents and Deans, ... 19
Teachers of Music, ... 7
Professors, Principals and Teachers, 675   Total 701
Clergymen:
Bishop, ... 1
Chaplains U.S. Army, ... 2
Missionaries, ... 9
Presiding Elders, ... 12
Preachers, ... 197   Total 221
Physicians,
Doctors of Medicine, ... 76
Druggists, ... 4
Dentists, ... 3   Total 83
Students, ... 74
Lawyers, ... 62
Civil Service:
U.S. Minister Plenipotentiary, ... 1
U.S. Consul, ... 1
U.S. Deputy Collector, ... 1
U.S. Gauger, ... 1
U.S. Postmasters, ... 2
U.S. Clerks, ... 44
State Civil Service 2
City Civil Service, ... 1   Total 53
Business Men:
Merchants, etc., ... 30
Managers, ... 13
Real Estate Dealers, ... 4   Total 47
Farmers, ... 26
Clerks and Secretaries:
Secretary of National Societies, ... 7
Clerks, etc., ... 15   Total 22
Artisans, ... 9
Editors, ... 9
Miscellaneous, ... 5

These figures illustrate vividly the function of the college-bred Negro. He is, as he ought to be, the group leader, the man who sets the ideals of the community where he lives, directs its thoughts and heads its social movements. It need hardly be

The problem of training the Negro is to-day immensely complicated by the fact that the whole question of the efficiency and appropriateness of our present systems of education, for any kind of child, is a matter of active debate, in which final settlement seems still afar off. Consequently it often happens that persons arguing for or against certain systems of education for Negroes, have these controversies in mind and miss the real Negro question at issue. The main question, so far as the Southern Negro is concerned, is: What under the present circumstance, must a system of education do in order to raise the Negro as quickly as possible in the scale of civilization? The answer to this question seems to me clear: It must strengthen the Negro's character, increase his knowledge and teach him to earn a living. Now it goes without saying, that it is hard to do all these things simultaneously or suddenly, and that at the same time it will not do to give all the attention to one and neglect the others: we could not give the black boys trades, but that alone will not civilize a race of ex-slaves; we might simply increase their knowledge of the world, but this would not necessarily make them wish to use this knowledge honestly; we might seek to strengthen character and purpose, but to what end if this people have nothing to eat or to wear? A system of education is not one thing, nor does it have a single definite object, nor is it a mere matter of schools. Education is that whole system of human training within and without the school house walls, which molds and develops men. If then we start out to train an ignorant and unskilled people with a heritage of bad habits, our system of training must set before itself two great aims—the one dealing with knowledge and character, the other part seeking to give the child the technical knowledge necessary for him to earn a living under the present circumstances. These objects are accomplished in part by the opening of the common schools on the one, and of industrial schools on the other. But only in part, for there must also be trained those who are to teach these schools —men and women of knowledge and culture and technical skill who understand modern civilization, and have the training and aptitude to impart it to the children under them. There must be teachers, and teachers of teachers, and to attempt to establish any sort of a system of common and industrial school training, without *first* (and I say *first* advisedly) without *first* providing

for the higher training of the very best teachers, is simply throwing your money to the winds. School houses do not teach themselves—piles of brick and mortar and machinery do not send out *men*. It is the trained, living human soul, cultivated and strengthened by long study and thought, that breathes the real breath of life into boys and girls and makes them human, whether they be black or white, Greek, Russian or American. Nothing, in these latter days, has so dampened the faith of thinking Negroes in recent educational movements, as the fact that such movements have been accompanied by ridicule and denouncement and decrying of those very institutions of higher training which made the Negro public school possible, and make Negro industrial schools thinkable. It was Fisk, Atlanta, Howard and Straight, those colleges born of the faith and sacrifice of the abolitionists, that placed in the black schools of the South the 30,000 teachers and more, which some, who depreciate the work of these higher schools, are using to teach their own new experiments. If Hampton, Tuskegee and the hundred other industrial schools prove in the future to be as successful as they deserve to be, then their success in training black artisans for the South, will be due primarily to the white colleges of the North and the black colleges of the South, which trained the teachers who to-day conduct these institutions. There was a time when the American people believed pretty devoutly that a log of wood with a boy at one end and Mark Hopkins at the other, represented the highest ideal of human training. But in these eager days it would seem that we have changed all that and think it necessary to add a couple of saw-mills and a hammer to this outfit, and, at a pinch, to dispense with the services of Mark Hopkins.

I would not deny, or for a moment seem to deny, the paramount necessity of teaching the Negro to work, and to work steadily and skillfully; or seem to depreciate in the slightest degree the important part industrial schools must play in the accomplishment of these ends, but I do say, and insist upon it, that it is industrialism drunk with its vision of success, to imagine that its own work can be accomplished without providing for the training of broadly cultured men and women to teach its own teachers, and to teach the teachers of the public schools.

But I have already said that human education is not simply a matter of schools; it is much more a matter of family and group life—the training of one's home, of one's daily companions, of one's social class. Now the black boy of the South moves in a black world—a world with its own leaders, its own thoughts, its own ideals. In this world he gets by far the larger part of his life training, and through the eyes of this dark world he peers into the veiled world beyond. Who guides and determines the education which he receives in his world? His teachers here are the group-leaders of the Negro people—the physicians and clergymen, the trained fathers and mothers, the influential and forceful men about him of all kinds; here it is, if at all, that the culture of the surrounding world trickles through and is handed on by the graduates of the higher schools. Can such culture training of group leaders be neglected? Can we afford to ignore it? Do you think that if the leaders of thought among Negroes are not trained and educated thinkers, that they will have no leaders? On the contrary a hundred half-trained demagogues will still hold the places they so largely occupy now, and hundreds of vociferous busy-bodies will multiply. You have no choice; either you must help furnish this race from within its own ranks with thoughtful men of trained leadership, or you must suffer the evil consequences of a headless misguided rabble.

I am an earnest advocate of manual training and trade teaching for black boys, and for white boys, too. I believe that next to the founding of Negro colleges the most valuable addition to Negro education since the war, has been industrial training for black boys. Nevertheless, I insist that the object of all true education is not to make men carpenters, it is to make carpenters men; there are two means of making the carpenter a man, each equally important: the first is to give the group and community in which he works, liberally trained teachers and leaders to teach him and his family what life means: the second is to give him sufficient intelligence and technical skill to make him an efficient workman; the first object demands the Negro college and college-bred men—not a quantity of such colleges, but a few of excellent quality; not too many college-bred men, but enough to leaven the lump, to inspire the masses, to raise the Talented Tenth to leadership; the second object demands a good system of common schools, well-taught, conveniently located and properly equipped.

The Sixth Atlanta Conference truly said in 1901:

"We call the attention of the Nation to the fact that less than one million of the three million Negro children of school age, are at present regularly attending school, and these attend a session which lasts only a few months.

"We are to-day deliberately rearing millions of our citizens in ignorance, and at the same time limiting the rights of citizenship by educational qualifications. This is unjust. Half the black youth of the land have no opportunities open to them for learning to read, write and cipher. In the discussion as to the proper training of Negro children after they leave the public schools, we have forgotten that they are not yet decently provided with public schools.

"Propositions are beginning to be made in the South to reduce the already meagre school facilities of Negroes. We congratulate the South on resisting, as much as it has, this pressure, and on the many millions it has spent on Negro education. But it is only fair to point out that Negro taxes and the Negroes' share of the income from indirect taxes and endowments have fully repaid this expenditure, so that the Negro public school system has not in all probability cost the white taxpayers a single cent since the war.

"This is not fair. Negro schools should be a public burden, since they are a public benefit. The Negro has a right to demand good common school training at the hands of the States and the Nation since by their fault he is not in position to pay for this himself."

What is the chief need for the building up of the Negro public school in the South? The Negro race in the South needs teachers to-day above all else. This is the concurrent testimony of all who know the situation. For the supply of this great demand two things are needed—institutions of higher education and money for school houses and salaries. It is usually assumed that a hundred or more institutions for Negro training are to-day turning out so many teachers and college-bred men that the race is threatened with an over-supply. This is sheer nonsense. There are to-day less than 3,000 living Negro college graduates in the United States, and less than 1,000 Negroes in college. Moreover, in the 164 schools for Negroes, 95 per cent. of their students are doing elementary and secondary work, work which should be done in the public schools. Over half the remaining 2,157 students are taking high school studies. The mass of so-called "normal" schools for the Negro, are simply doing elementary common school work, or, at most, high school work, with a little instruction in methods. The Negro colleges and the post-graduate courses at other institutions are the only agencies for the broader and more careful training of teachers. The work of these institutions is hampered for lack of funds. It is getting increasingly difficult to get funds for training teachers in the best modern methods, and yet all over the South, from State Superintendents, county officials, city boards and school principals comes the wail, "We need TEACHERS!" and teachers must be trained. As the fairest minded of all white Southerners, Atticus G. Haygood, once said: "The defects of colored teachers are so great as to create an urgent necessity for training better ones. Their excellencies and their successes are sufficient to justify the best hopes of success in the effort, and to vindicate the judgment of those who make large investments of money and service, to give to colored students opportunity for thoroughly preparing themselves for the work of teaching children of their people."

The truth of this has been strikingly shown in the marked improvement of white teachers in the South. Twenty years ago the rank and file of white public school teachers were not as good as the Negro teachers. But they, by scholarships and good salaries, have been encouraged to thorough normal and collegiate preparation, while the Negro teachers have been discouraged by starvation wages and the idea that any training will do for a black teacher. If carpenters are needed it is well and good to train men as carpenters. But to train men as carpenters, and then set them to teaching is wasteful and criminal; and to train men as teachers and then refuse them living wages, unless they become carpenters, is rank nonsense.

The United States Commissioner of Education says in his report for 1900: "For comparison between the white and colored enrollment in secondary and higher education, I have added together the enrollment in high schools and secondary schools, with the attendance on colleges and universities, not being sure of the actual grade of work done in the colleges and universities. The work done in the secondary schools is reported in such detail in this office, that there can be no doubt of its grade."

He then makes the following comparisons of persons in every million enrolled in secondary and higher education:

	Whole Country.	Negroes.
1880	4,362	1,289
1900	10,743	2,061

And he concludes: "While the number in colored high schools and colleges had increased somewhat faster than the population, it had not kept pace with the average of the whole country, for it had fallen from 30 per cent. to 24 per cent. of the average quota. Of all colored pupils, one (1) in one hundred was engaged in secondary and higher work, and that ratio has continued substantially for the past twenty years. If the ratio of colored population in secondary and higher education is to be equal to the average for the whole country, it must be increased to five times its present average." And if this be true of the secondary and higher education, it is safe to say that the Negro has not one-tenth his quota in college studies. How baseless, therefore, is the charge of too much training! We need Negro teachers for the Negro common schools and colleges to train them. This is the work of higher Negro education and it must be done.

Further than this, after being provided with group leaders of civilization, and a foundation of intelligence in the public schools, the carpenter, in order to be a man, needs technical skill. This calls for trade schools. Now trade schools are not nearly such simple things as people once thought. The original idea was that the "Industrial" school was to furnish education, practically free, to those willing to work for it; it was to "do" things—i.e.: become a center of productive industry, it was to be partially, if not wholly, self-supporting, and it was to teach trades. Admirable as were some of the ideas underlying this scheme, the whole thing simply would not work in practice; it was found that if you were to use time and material to teach trades thoroughly, you could not at the same time keep the industries on a commercial basis and make them pay. Many schools started out to do this on a large scale and went into virtual bankruptcy. Moreover, it was found also that it was possible to teach a boy a trade mechanically, without giving him the full educative benefit of the process, and, vice versa, that there was a distinctive educative value in teaching a boy to use his hands and eyes in carrying out certain physical processes, even though he did not actually learn a trade. It has happened, therefore, in the last decade, that a noticeable change has come over the industrial schools. In the first place the idea of commercially remunerative industry in a school is being pushed rapidly to the background. There are still schools with shops and farms that bring an income, and schools that use student labor partially for the erection of their buildings and the furnishing of equipment. It is coming to be seen, however, in the education of the Negro, as clearly as it has been seen in the education of the youths the world over, that it is the *boy* and not the material product, that is the true object of education. Consequently the object of the industrial school came to be the thorough training of boys regardless of the cost of the training, so long as it was thoroughly well done.

Even at this point, however, the difficulties were not surmounted. In the first place modern industry has taken great strides since the war, and the teaching of trades is no longer a simple matter. Machinery and long processes of work have greatly changed the work of the carpenter, the ironworker and the shoemaker. A really efficient workman must be to-day an intelligent man who has had good technical training in addition to thorough common school, and perhaps even higher training. To meet this situation the industrial schools began a further development; they established distinct Trade Schools for the thorough training of better class artisans, and at the same time they sought to preserve for the purposes of general education, such of the simpler processes of elementary trade learning as were best suited therefor. In this differentiation of the Trade School and manual training, the best of the industrial schools simply followed the plain trend of the present educational epoch. A prominent educator tells us that, in Sweden, "In the beginning the economic conception was generally adopted, and everywhere manual training was looked upon as a means of preparing the children of the common people to earn their living. But gradually it came to be recognized that manual training has a more elevated purpose, and one, indeed, more useful in the deeper meaning of the term. It came to be considered as an educative process for the complete moral, physical and intellectual development of the child."

Thus, again, in the manning of trade schools and manual training schools we are thrown back upon the higher training as its source and chief support. There was a time when any aged and wornout carpenter could teach in a trade school. But not so to-day. Indeed the demand for college-bred men by a school like Tuskegee, ought to make Mr. Booker T. Washington the firmest friend of higher training. Here he has as helpers the son of a Negro senator, trained in Greek and the humanities, and graduated at Harvard; the son of a Negro congressman and lawyer, trained in Latin and mathematics, and graduated at Oberlin; he has as his wife, a woman who read Virgil and Homer in the same class room with me; he has as college chaplain, a classical graduate of Atlanta University; as teacher of science, a graduate of Fisk; as teacher of history, a graduate of Smith, —indeed some thirty of his chief teachers are college graduates, and instead of studying French grammars in the midst of weeds, or buying pianos for dirty cabins, they are at Mr. Washington's right hand helping him in a noble work. And yet one of the effects of Mr. Washington's propaganda has been to throw doubt upon the expediency of such training for Negroes, as these persons have had.

Men of America, the problem is plain before you. Here is a race transplanted through the criminal foolishness of your fathers. Whether you like it or not the millions are here, and here they will remain. If you do not lift them up, they will pull you down. Education and work are the levers to uplift a people. Work alone will not do it unless inspired by the right ideals and guided by intelligence. Education must not simply teach work —it must teach Life. The Talented Tenth of the Negro race must be made leaders of thought and missionaries of culture among their people. No others can do this work and Negro colleges must train men for it. The Negro race, like all other races, is going to be saved by its exceptional men.

"The Talented Tenth," from *The Negro Problem: A Series of Articles by Representative Negroes of Today* (New York: James Pott & Co., 1903), pp. 33-75. Reprinted by Arno Press, 1969.

Part V: The Main Trends in Higher Education After World War II: Federalism and Democratization

The Revolution of Markets and Management: Toward a History of American Higher Education Since 1945

John Hardin Best

Revolutions are a commonplace in studies of the history of American higher education. Every decade or so seems to bring upheaval of revolutionary proportions and a literature to analyze it. Significantly, Laurence Veysey began his study of the rise of the American university with some words from Noah Porter's 1871 inaugural address as president of Yale, "college and university education are not merely agitated by reforms; they are rather convulsed by a revolution."[1] Then Veysey proceeded with his own excellent account of Porter's revolution—the forces, events, and personalities in the struggle to create the new research university at the turn of the nineteenth century. Christopher Jencks and David Riesman described quite a different sort of revolution in *The Academic Revolution*, their study of the rise of college and university faculties to preeminent professional influence in the early 1960s.[2] It was a short-lived triumph at best, for immediately followed the revolutionary upheavals of the late 1960s. At close range, but with considerable insight, Lewis B. Mayhew analyzed the causes and consequences of the troubled sixties, and more recently other studies of that revolution are beginning to appear.[3]

Now yet a new revolution in American higher education has occurred in the two decades just past. It could be aptly called the revolution of markets and management. Both elements were important in its making: first, the increasing influence of free market forces in institutional policy formation; and second, the development of new management capabilities and thereby new ways of executing policy within academe. As a result of these changes, institutions of higher education have come to behave in some very different ways. The landscape of the campus has changed; the students, the faculties, indeed many aspects of higher education institutions have changed; and there are new reflections and responses to these changes as well in American society in general.

The change created by the forces of markets and management, the rise of the American corporate college and university, is a transformation close at hand and all too familiar, and reactions to it are already beginning to come in force. There are the jeremiahs who denounce the "closing" of young minds in the intellectual bankruptcy of the university. These, the Chapter Eleven critics, see in these changes no less than the decline of civilization.[4] Even a U.S. Secretary of Education can enjoy engaging in this sort of rhetoric. Then there are the professorial reactions, generally more sullen in style, some of them merely the generational grousings of aging academics: the "what's the matter with kids today" response. But some express thoughtful concerns for the apparent inability of colleges and universities to address the serious questions of broadening responsibilities to new generations of American society.[5] This study is a beginning account, an effort to develop a history of this latest revolution in higher learning, as well as to suggest relevant considerations for the formation of institutional policy in higher education today.[6]

The Force of Markets and Management

The origins of the corporate revolution can be found in the mass expansion of higher education in the years since World War II, and further, they can be seen emerging directly from the upheavals of the late 1960s. The corporate revolution is founded on the operation of the free academic market: that system peculiar to the United States which encourages every institution of higher education, whether publicly or privately controlled and supported, to compete for enrollments of students and the tuitions they pay.[7] Given the diversity of American institutions of higher education, there are many submarkets determined by the type, nature, size, and function of differing categories of institutions—the variety of research universities, liberal arts colleges, and two-year colleges. Though the broad frame of the market is the competition to secure enrollments, any particular institution competes mainly within the realm of its own submarket to maintain its special position.[8] Success in the competition for FTEs (the quintessential Full Time Equivalents) must be attained to secure the institution's fiscal health directly or indirectly. In the case of the publicly owned institutions, a healthy record of FTE production is necessary to justify continuing levels of state appropriations. Other institutions, identifying for themselves a select position in the submarket, may not compete directly for the FTEs but for a "quality" selection of students, to establish a firm position in an elite market. It is in any event a free market model in perfect accord with American free enterprise corporate capitalism. The effect has been to create a system of higher learning that operates along business models of fiscal control and management.

In the beginning of course is the budget, essential in projecting investments in academic programs or enterprises and, with continuing cost analysis of such programs, in measuring their success. Further, the need for accountability for state and federal funds, for grants, research contracts, student loan supports, and so on, requires meticulous budgeting and record keeping. Beyond mere budgeting, however, institutions must devise broad institutional strategies to maintain their viability. "Strategic planning," in the borrowed terminology of the business world, has become an important instrument for institutions to clarify "mission," to identify their position in relevant markets, to appraise various developing societal forces in order to set institutional goals for a span of years, and to provide a base for projecting, controlling, and measuring institutional operations.[9]

Market forces within this broad frame of institutional competition operate as well in many other arenas of academe. There is the competition among disciplines and areas of study for prestige and status within the larger world of learning. Departments must search out strongholds within the university for attracting students to their particular programs, perhaps by securing a firm position in the undergraduate "general education" requirements. Others may identify a curricular position with assured connections to employment on the completion of their degree, a certification of competence to employers. Faculty may compete for security of position as individuals through tenure, for prominence within their discipline or field of study, even for recognition for effectiveness in classroom instruction. Students themselves, of course, compete from the outset with admission to the "right" college, then for grades, for recognition, for endorsement to the proper professional schools, for grants monies, and finally for placement in promising career positions.[10] Hence there are many layers of markets and competitive forces within the university.

None of this, of course, just happens: the corporate university must be carefully, precisely, and exquisitely managed. Within these several arenas of competition, as in the university's strategic plan at large, there must be managers, the cool, expert hands at the controls who insure that essential delicate balances are maintained. The management style and character of a richly bureaucratic system has come to characterize the operation of the new corporate university.

All this is not to say that academic, intellectual, or social values are not important to consider in determining policy. These values remain the very stuff of the university, the essential questions to be raised in any collegiate policy deliberations. But the overriding consideration for any institution must be, as it perhaps has always been, the continuity and vitality of the institution itself. At the turn of the century, David Starr Jordan, as the president of Stanford University, decided to lay aside the principle of academic freedom in the face of the vagaries of the university's great benefactor, revealing that above all else he would "stand by the university." Jordan acted without question to protect the university's endowment. As Veysey summarizes the case, "In a crisis only the ship mattered."[11] Today, protecting the ship has become a mode of operation that is firmly institutionalized in the university, not only to act in time of crisis but to anticipate and prepare for any threat to the university from whatever quarter. Issues of an academic, social, or political sort are routinely screened through the policy machinery of any institution with always the essential question: what are the implications for the institution's position in the competitive market, what fiscal consequences in the long and short term follow, in sum, what is the effect on the "ship"?

Given the assumption that the intent of any higher education institution is to continue to fulfill whatever mission it has defined for itself, issues of service to community and society, directions of research to be pursued, indeed every issue that impinges on the institution must be screened through the perspective of what contributes to its flourishing immediately and in the future. The screening, which is essential in institutional policy-making, moreover, far from being left to happenstance, is managed with great care. It is that deliberateness along with the management capability to create and execute policy that is the essence of this newest revolution. To illustrate at the most fundamental level, the issue of institutional survival has confronted two Pennsylvania colleges in recent years, and the responses of the two in their crises makes an interesting contrast.

Alliance College, near Pittsburgh, the only secular Polish college in the United States, announced in spring 1987 that, with too few students and too heavy a debt, the institution would be forced to close. The base of support in Polish ethnic groups for a nonreligious college is narrow, and there is no inclination on the part of the college administration or the alumni to attempt to shift or broaden the identity of the college, to search for some expanded clientele and support. Alliance accordingly closed its doors in the summer of 1987.

The trustees of Wilson College, a women's college in south central Pennsylvania, several years ago, like Alliance, announced that with small numbers of students and even less funding, the college would be forced to close. A group of faculty, alumnae, and community supporters, however, managed to prevent the immediate closing through the courts, and after two years of remarkable planning and management efforts, have made the college solvent if not flourishing once again. On the basis of market surveys, the Wilson curriculum was transformed from that of a traditional liberal arts college to a secretarial school curriculum. The college changed drastically, but it survives.

Historiographic Considerations

Americans hardly think of universities and colleges in these crude terms of markets, clients, and missions. We are much more comfortable with our images of ivied walls and tailored lawns, of benevolent deans, of kindly professors surrounded by bright young people engaged in intense intellectual discussion. Historians of higher education have given us substantial studies in years past to support these comforting views.[12] The genius of American higher learning in these accounts is its combination of the great traditions of the liberal arts college and the goals of the research university, joining to maintain traditional academic standards of learning and to create new knowledge through research and experimentation. America's universities are seen as becoming ever more firmly meritocratic in mode and increasingly democratic in spirit. Striving always to reach the intellectual heights, the higher learning is destined to continue to grow in its capacity to serve the commonwealth and the nation.

What is not so clear in this traditional framing of the history of America's colleges and universities is the point of view of the institutions themselves. Since 1945 the impulse for survival and expansion as a central

institutional perspective, and the capability to act upon it, has become increasingly important; since 1970 it has developed major significance. The fact of the academic free markets and the management expertise required to compete in this arena create circumstances that require a different grasp of the development of higher education institutions in recent years and perhaps support a revised interpretation of our past.

How did this come about, this new mode of policy-making and management, and what are the dimensions of a history of the higher learning in America in the years since 1945? There are several aspects of it that need consideration. First, there are the demographic developments—the expansion of American population since 1945 and the concurrent burgeoning of college enrollments, from the G.I. bill of the late forties through the baby boom of the sixties, and more recently in the extension of college-going to the lower middle class, to women, and minorities. Second, there is the differentiation of the students themselves: the transition from the small collegiate world of the white, male, Protestant, upper middle class to a broadened population with new interests and differing capabilities. As student populations expanded and changed, so did faculties, a third aspect of the history. Fourth, the new institutional management capabilities developed, and the bureaucracy expanded in order to effect a business mode of operation. Finally, there are the alterations in college and university curricula over the years, the changed modes of instruction and the broadened offerings of studies considered appropriate in the higher learning. The elements of curricular change since 1945 will serve to outline the history of this recent era and to indicate the influence of markets and management on the course of events.

Curriculum Transitions

From a largely uniform frame in the intellectualist tradition of the liberal arts and sciences in the years following World War II, curriculum has become today an immensely varied and flexible set of offerings reflecting many interests and open to many capabilities. There has been no less than revolutionary change in curriculum in these years. But revolutions always have their antecedents, and in fact their origins often reflect some prior revolution. And so it was in these recent transitions in the college curriculum. As early as the 1880s Charles Eliot's elective proposals at Harvard had managed to break the classical college curriculum of undergraduate studies neatly organized and framed over the four years. The elective revolution across the country coincided, of course, with faculty interests in departmentalization and with the emergence of new research interests in the universities. By the turn of the century there had been some drawing back from Eliot's full-blown elective curriculum, and a frame of the older arts and science requirements had returned. The classics, however, had collapsed; that is, no longer was a classical language required for college admission or for graduation. By the 1920s the college and university curriculum had not only abandoned the classics but was opening the door to such new and overtly vocational studies as commerce and journalism as well as expanded offerings in engineering and education."[11] Junior colleges were organized and developed during the 1920s and 1930s to offer a terminal two-year curriculum with the intent of expanding opportunity for college-going. The college curriculum however, with or without classics, junior college or otherwise, was still firmly based on the liberal arts and sciences, the traditional verbal and quantitative skills, in Mayhew's phrase, on "conceptual intellectuality."[14] And so it was to remain throughout the war years and the postwar era of the G.I. bill students, the cautious increase in enrollments in the 1950s, and the beginnings of the baby boom expansions of the 1960s.

The liberal arts and sciences were implanted at the center of undergraduate studies in the postwar curriculum. There were indeed requirements: a specified number of years of English literature and writing; a foreign language, often two; science and math; social sciences and history, all with specified levels of required attainment. Majors and minors were clearly delineated in courses and credit hours. Sequences of courses in any field were not to be violated. Registration was expected to be continuous, except in the rarest of circumstances. And of course, there was the physical education requirement (for the sound body) spanning several years, which included staying afloat in the pool, without drowning, for ten minutes. No exceptions.

There were efforts made in the post–World War II years to renew and expand the liberal curriculum, most notably the "general education movement," with its roots in the 1920s. It was an effort to preserve the values of the liberal learning by making the relevant connections of the traditional studies to contemporary social and political issues. General education was intended to clear away the aristocratic odor, the gentlemanly elitist taint of the arts and sciences. Enthusiastically current and relevant in its style, general education served the colleges well in helping to uphold the liberal intellectualist frame of the curriculum until the crack-up of the late 1960s.

By the late sixties there were other far more explosive issues than all the changes on campuses in those years, probably none were more profound than those affecting the curriculum. The hue and cry was for relevance. Students demanded that their studies focus on the problems and issues that immediately confronted them: issues of the Vietnam War, of course, of the civil rights of minorities, and of poverty, social injustice, and the problems of the "oppressed" in American society at large. Classes from freshman English to the major in microbiology were expected to

speak to the social concerns of the moment. Other issues of a more individual nature began to seem important as well: matters of social and sexual relations, the use of drugs and other substances; in fact, pressure mounted for inclusion in the curriculum of any matter that seemed to affect the lives of students significantly.

Under this pressure of the student as client, and an irate one at that, the sixties saw the dissolution of the long-held intellectualist frame of the curriculum in which the scholar/professor organized and distilled in logical style the subject matter of the course, and the student/scholar accepted and assimilated the content in the same intellectualist style. Intellectual grasp was measured in written examinations (three hours for a three-credit-hour course, etc.), and in fact the entire process was intensely competitive, requiring a high level of verbal and quantitative skill. Studies were measured precisely in time from class hours to semesters to the degree granting. The curriculum upheavals of the late 1960s not only shattered the liberal arts and science patterning of courses and requirements but also shifted the intellectual ground on which it was built.

The college and university curriculum in the 1970s began to look very different. Many if not most of the traditional requirements disappeared. A Carnegie Council survey of the nation's colleges and universities reported that "the number of institutions requiring English, a foreign language, and mathematics as part of everyone's general education declined appreciably from 1967 to 1974."[15] Only 20 percent of colleges, for example, required any mathematics by the 1970s. Further, it was largely the end of the old required breadth and depth distribution for majors and minors. Student autonomy prevailed, and the elite colleges with their highly selective admissions led the way. Such institutions as Brown and Grinnell abandoned general education requirements altogether, as well as most of the mandatory frame for majors, confident that their select students should, with complete autonomy, form their own plans for studies. Other institutions, including many public ones with little or no selection in admissions, dropped requirements as well.

The traditional liberal arts frame of instruction fell in the name of relevance, which meant at first diversity, then shortly became vocationalism. Faculties and administrators of course decried the demise of the liberal arts, but in many institutions soon discovered that by abandoning the higher learning could be opened to entire new populations of students. With the demographic threat of declining enrollments in the 1970s and projections of yet further decline in the 1980s, the new curriculum began to look good.[16] New students were attracted to the colleges for such majors as food service, police science, mortuary science, radio broadcasting, accounting, and computers and more computers. It looked good to administrators in that there seemed to be a limitless supply of new students, despite the population projections, if only more creative and aggressive efforts were made to identify and attract new clients and to utilize new markets.

During the 1970s the test of these new or nontraditional programs came to be their vocational promise.[17] The rhetoric of the relevance of the 1960s upheavals came to mean vocational value rather than the affective or the consciousness-raising side of education. On those grounds, sex and drugs were by and large moved out of curriculum into the realm of "student personnel services" on the campus. Police science and computer science flourished since they led to assured employment, whereas black studies and urban life did not. Further, there were specialized programs offered for every interest in whatever calendar or time frame and at whatever most convenient geographic location.

Age was no longer a barrier to anyone in any program. In fact, comings and goings came to be the norm even for the eighteen-to-twenty-two-year-olds. Continuous registration over four years in a bachelor's degree program almost became the exception. There were explorations on loosening the time constraints within the curriculum. For example, various institutions, junior as well as upper division colleges, developed thorough-going competency-based curricula in which students set their own pace in learning, whether in learning to repair a television set or to write a proper English paragraph. There were explorations of new ways to learn in project work of all kinds, often in group projects. Media use of varying sorts became increasingly important in creating new opportunities for independent study. Faculty could no longer use traditional methods to ensure students' competence in many curricula, in that new measures of learning put less value on the written exam and instead stressed innovative ways to demonstrate competence.

The curriculum opened up to accommodate the special interests of women who began to arrive in the mid-1970s in the universities in great numbers. The rise in enrollments of women coming into the work force, and the expanded numbers of women corresponded of course to the colleges gratefully accepted the new population. The traditional areas of childhood education, food service, and nursing were expanded, and new areas of special promise were developed within existing curricula, such as in accounting, horticulture, and parks and recreation, to accommodate the increasing numbers of newly arriving women students.

By the 1980s the curricula of many colleges and universities had little left of the "conceptual intellectuality" of the traditional liberal arts and science frame. There were still enclaves of course, entire colleges that held to the liberal arts tradition and successfully defined the college mission as such. Honors programs in the large diffuse universities, public or private, with selectivity within the academic departments, often became the intellectualist retreat on those campuses.

The position of faculty shifted considerably with the new patterns of learning and the revised expectations and capabilities of students. Many faculty members did not make the transition easily. The changes in curriculum after 1970, however, meant not so much an immediate devaluation of any particular faculty position or department, but a necessary, gradual adjustment as new curriculum areas on the campus expanded. For example, a history department marches on, but over time the history faculty may recognize a changing world as more food service majors sign for an occasional course in the department, or what may be worse, refuse to sign for a history course. Slowly, perhaps painfully, the history department may begin to adjust, to revise curriculum offerings and even style of instruction in order to maintain its market position on the campus.

In the mid-1980s a rhetoric of reaction developed with various national studies and reports calling for a return to standards of excellence and for stronger academic requirements in the college curriculum.[18] Some of this reaction can be seen as an outcome of the calls for excellence in the public schools in the Nation at Risk and other similar "crisis" studies. The threat of international economic competition appeared to demand new academic rigor in American schools as well as in the colleges. Some higher education institutions responded to the renewed press for excellence with a revival of general education requirements and more carefully defined majors and minors. And so the excellence debate continued, but the curriculum transitions of the 1970s were firmly entrenched: the shift away from the intellectualist base, the broadened range of offerings and instructional systems, the loosened time frame, and the opening to diverse interests of age and gender. This degree of democratization of the curriculum, for good or ill, had arrived to stay, and with it, an expansion of the very definition of the higher learning.

Expanded Definitions of Higher Education

As these developments of recent decades have required the broadening of the definition of higher learning, curriculum has expanded to include studies and applications of studies that had not been thought appropriate in the past, but that seem important now to new populations of college-goers. Building on the middle-class sense of urgency of the 1950s and 1960s that college was a social necessity, an urgency that by the late 1960s began to be reflected in national policy, higher education institutions acted in the 1970s to open the doors wide. Computer science offers an example of this opening. The technology was developing mightily in the 1970s, and many universities expanded the curriculum to embrace computer science as a proper undergraduate major. They might well have rejected computer science, as well as police science, food service, and other growth industry curricula, as rank vocationalism, inappropriate to the intellectual aims of the higher learning. And some institutions, in accord with a select mission, did so. But in general, institutional policy-making was in accord with the rising egalitarian spirit and with policies reflecting it that emanated from Washington. Money tends to follow policy from Washington, or did so prior to the Reagan administration, and no doubt that aided the transition. Computers were "in," and the middle-class college-going element in America became significantly broader and more inclusive. The quest for FTEs in institutional policy-making coincided with the larger policy interests of government.

A rising level of technological development in industry and business continued during the 1970s and 1980s to create more jobs and opportunities for the skilled. Management in the white collar, and particularly the service industries, continued to expand. In general, the American economic state, despite inflation, an energy crisis, and even a mild recession or two, was one of unparalleled affluence during this entire era, and the demand for the college educated continued strong throughout. The pervasive competitive spirit fed a kind of thinking among many higher education institutions that expansion, more students and bigger budgets, was always and unquestionably desirable. The colleges were opening to change, and new clients were ready to accept the new opportunities offered. A revolution was in the making.

Faculty cooperated in the transitions of the 1970s and 1980s in that the new relevant, diverse, and vocational curriculum freed them to explore various specializations of their own interests, and, further, the continuing expansion or at least stability of enrollments of the institution meant security for their appointments. Numbers of faculty, of course, had expanded greatly during the 1960s and 1970s. Graduate schools great and small had redoubled their efforts to produce new Ph.D.s, and by the late 1970s there was an overabundance of new professionals in almost every field eager for faculty appointments. Many of the new mass faculty, the so-called "lumpenprofessoriate," saw faculty membership as essentially employment, and of course as "personnel" their first interest was job security.[19] Tenure under these circumstances became a particularly prized object but was only as secure as the institution was viable. There were the chilling examples of Temple University, Southern Illinois, and others closing out academic programs of low productivity and eliminating large numbers of faculty appointments, both nontenured and tenured. Faculty support for college expansionism was thus assured for the sake of job security.

This transformation of the higher learning in the past two decades, with the universities' successful efforts continually to expand and to broaden the definition of higher education, contributed to a rising level of expectation of formal education for the American middle class. Some college attendance, preferably for the full four years, became every young person's right. Today it is said that college has become the middle-class badge of membership, in much the same way that high school became so in the early twentieth century. The causes of this transition lie in the interaction of public policy with the curious policy-making patterns of higher education institutions. The change has been effected by the interplay of market forces on several layers within and among institutions of higher education, in the context of an American society founded on these same competitive forces. In sum, it was the great postwar population expansion, the varieties of competitive forces in the academic free market system, and the creation of new, effective academic management and bureaucracy that broadened the definition of the higher learning and transformed the university and, in many ways, American society.

There are many areas to be examined in this revolution of markets and management, questions to be asked of the history of higher education, causes and consequences to be analyzed, relationships within these new forces to be explored. What are the costs, for example, of this academic free market operation? Is it a factor in the upward spiral of costs of college-going in the 1980s as institutions seem to compete not for new student markets but increasingly against each other for the same students? Who are these managers, the experts, budgetary and otherwise, who have come to have such inordinate influence in the higher learning? Can this new management capability be managed? Who are the new students who have come to college in such great numbers in recent years, the "first generation" college-goers, a euphemism it seems for the lower-middle class, for women and minorities. Have they capabilities and interests in the higher learning that are as yet unexplored? Are there new ways of instruction, following the demise of the liberal intellectualist frame, which might preserve some of the academic values that faculty in the past have honored? But what of the new generation of faculty? Does the struggle for the security of tenure mean, ironically, a waning of intellectual vitality and daring? And what of intellect itself: what does it mean in today's institution? Can colleges and universities find ways despite the market forces to address the big questions of the meaning of mind and the uses of intellect in a broadening democracy?

A history of this revolution of the 1970s and 1980s in American higher education can offer considerable clarity to issues today, issues such as the alleged "closing" of American minds. The study of institutional policy and its history can also influence the broader arena of governmental policy. A better sense of the past, in sum, can offer today's policymakers, both in higher education and in government, a better grasp of this new college and university that has emerged and is yet developing. It is essential that we inform ourselves and our publics of this latest revolution within academe.

497

[1] Laurence R. Veysey, *The Emergence of the American University* (Chicago, 1965), 1.
[2] Christopher Jencks and David Riesman, *The Academic Revolution* (New York, 1968).
[3] Lewis B. Mayhew, *Legacy of the Seventies* (San Francisco, 1977). Among recent studies see Allen J. Matusow, *The Unraveling of America: A History of Liberalism in the 1960s* (New York, 1984); and Diane Ravitch, *The Troubled Crusade: American Education 1945–1980* (New York, 1983).
[4] Allan Bloom, *The Closing of the American Mind: How Higher Education Has Failed Democracy and Impoverished the Souls of Today's Students* (New York, 1987).
[5] Mayhew, *Legacy*, 330–39.
[6] On the broad issue of the uses of history in policy-making, see Richard Neustadt and Ernest May, *Thinking in Time: The Uses of History for Decision Makers* (New York, 1986).
[7] Harry G. Judge, *American Graduate Schools of Education: A View from Abroad: A Report to the Ford Foundation* (New York, 1982), 26–28.
[8] David A. Garvin, *The Economics of University Behavior* (New York, 1980), 1–6.
[9] The basic work for such analysis is George Keller, *Academic Strategy: The Management Revolution in American Higher Education* (Baltimore, 1983).
[10] Howard S. Becker, Blanche Geer, and Everett C. Hughes, *Making the Grade: The Academic Side of College Life* (New York, 1968).
[11] Veysey, *Emergence*, 403.
[12] See for example John Brubacher and Willis Rudy, *Higher Education in Transition: A History of American Colleges and Universities, 1636–1976*, 3d ed. (New York, 1976); and Frederick Rudolph, *The American College and University* (New York, 1962).
[13] David O. Levine, *The American College and the Culture of Aspiration, 1915–1940* (Ithaca, 1986), 40. For the context of the select universities, see Roger L. Geiger, *To Advance Knowledge: The Growth of American Research Universities, 1900–1940* (New York, 1986).
[14] Mayhew, *Legacy*, 26.
[15] R. Blackburn, et al., *Changing Practices in Undergraduate Education: A Report for the Carnegie Council on Policy Studies in Higher Education* (Berkeley, 1976), 34.
[16] Kenneth P. Mortimer and Michael L. Tierney, *The Three "R's" of the Eighties: Reduction, Reallocation, and Retrenchment* (Washington, D.C., 1979).
[17] Roger L. Geiger, "The College Curriculum and the Marketplace," *Change* (Nov.–Dec. 1980): 53–54.
[18] Study Group on Conditions of Excellence in American Higher Education, *Involvement in Learning* (Washington, 1984); Ernest Boyer, *College, the Undergraduate Experience in America* (New York, 1987).
[19] Walter P. Metzger, "The Academic Profession in Hard Times," *Daedalus* 104 (Winter 1975): 25–44.

John Hardin Best is professor of education at Pennsylvania State University. This essay was delivered as the presidential address at the History of Education Society annual meeting held at Teachers College, Columbia University, October 9–11, 1987.

From Truman to Johnson: *Ad Hoc* Policy Formulation in Higher Education

Janet C. Kerr

As word spread that many of the new Frontier and Great Society programs of the 1960s had been engineered by special task forces, scholars began to realize how little of a reliable nature was known about the workings of the Presidential ad hoc advisory system. For political scientists, the Kennedy and Johnson episodes opened up the question of how ad hoc commissions and task forces function alongside the permanent cadre of Presidential advisors. For historians, the question became that of determining whether ad hoc groups have directly influenced the content of White House policy proposals over the years.

For the most part, both of these questions remain unanswered with respect to the 16 education task forces and commissions appointed since World War II. While references to the work of many of these groups are common enough in discussions of the policy advances of the period 1946-68, only two task forces have been closely analyzed using the U.S. Presidents' archives. Norman C. Thomas (1975), one of the leading students of the Johnson education task forces, completed his research on the subject before the opening of the Johnson archives (Thomas & Wolman, 1969). David Henry's (1975, pp. 69-84) discussion of the post-war commissions was also written without the benefit of archival analysis. In short, and with the exception of Robert Hawkinson's (1977) dissertation on the 1964 Gardner and 1965 Keppel Task Forces, what is known of these groups to date is derived entirely from interviews and external document review.

Using records found in the Truman, Eisenhower, Kennedy, and Johnson archives, this study reconstructs the process by which the higher education proposals of two public commissions and four "secret" task forces were formulated and then reviewed. Where the archival record was found to be incomplete or inconclusive, officials of the four Administrations supplied information through interviews and correspondence with the author. The two commissions examined in this study include the 1946 Commission on Higher Education (Zook Commission) and the 1956 Committee on Education Beyond the High School (Josephs Committee). The task forces include two groups composed of individuals from outside the Administrations, the 1960 Hovde Task Force and the 1966 Friday Task Force, and two composed of Administration officials, the 1966 Gardner-Howe Interagency Task Force and the 1967 Gardner-Howe Interagency Task Force. As the discussion will show, there were marked differences in the way which these higher education advisory groups interpreted and executed their missions, the way in which they "interfaced" with Executive Branch policy-makers, and the way in which White House, Budget Bureau, and agency officials responded to ad hoc proposals for federal aid to college students and college institutions.

The 1946 Commission on Higher Education

Plans for the Zook Commission coincided with rumblings from the academic community over the plight of the nation's colleges. Academic concern, however, was not matched by public concern until several waves of veterans had come and gone across college campuses. Like the President, the public was more interested in tackling the teacher and classroom shortages in elementary and secondary schools in early 1946 than in diverting federal resources to higher education.

Why, then, was a commission on higher education created? The answer seems to lie in a mixture of private hopes and private politics brewing within the White House. The idea for the Commission originated with Donald Kingsley and his assistant, John Thurston, both of whom worked under John Steelman when he was Director of the Office of War Mobilization and Reconversion and afterward when he became Assistant to the President. Kingsley, a former professor at Antioch and Steelman's chief staff person for manpower, had an abiding interest in higher education. Thurston had been a student of Kingsley's. As the war period came to an end, Kingsley and his staff began discussing post-war educational needs. The commission idea was borne of these discussions and then presented to Steelman for his reaction.

The proposal came at a time when Steelman, the conservative among Truman's close advisors, found himself jockeying to retain his position of influence in the face of efforts, spearheaded by Special Counsel Clark Clifford, to bring the President around to a "strong and consistent liberal position" in domestic affairs (Hartmann, 1971, p. 199; see also Anderson, 1968, pp. 93-94; Hamby, 1971, p. 295). Perhaps feeling pressure to appeal to Truman's liberal ideology while appeasing his fiscal conservatism (Flash, 1965, p. 97), Steelman welcomed the commission suggestion. He is thought to have supervised its presentation as "closely" as he could—a move probably inspired by the "intense competition" Clifford represented (J. L. Thurston, personal communication, November 30, 1982).

Kingsley and Thurston handled the selection of commission members. Sensitive to the public nature of the body, they carefully evaluated the contribution each nominee might make toward achieving a commission representative of the "major currents in educational thinking and leadership" and evenly distributed along geographical, institutional, political, and religious lines.[1] After checking names out with the Office of Education and Kingsley's own contacts in the field, Kingsley sent the membership list to Steelman for his approval (Thurston, personal communication, November 30, 1982).

Kingsley's conscientious efforts were met by praise, for the most part, when the membership was announced. However, the White House did not escape criticism for sins of commission and omission. The naming of education activist and *Washington Post* journalist Agnes Meyer, well-known for her stand against Catholic education politics, brought a flood of demands for her removal, including one from Justice Thomas Cuff of the New York Supreme Court. The appointment of the AFL's Mark Starr incensed the unrepresented CIO. Other complaints came from those upset at the seating of only one

Negro.[2]

Of those asked to serve, only Harold Dodds, President of Princeton (and later a critic of the Commission), declined. After six months of service, Eleanor Roosevelt withdrew, stating that she "found it . . . impossible to give adequate time" to the work of the Commission.[3] Her letter of resignation to the President also expressed concern at allegations by the National Education Association (NEA) that the Commission was giving "too little thought" to public education.

These charges can be traced directly to the NEA's Ralph McDonald. In no uncertain terms, McDonald threatened the White House with an NEA-wide revolt if Chairman George Zook and Executive Secretary Francis Brown, both of the American Council on Education, were not unseated. Despite several White House attempts to "calm McDonald down," he persisted in arguing that the presence of Zook and Brown on the Commission would ensure "the domination of the private and sectarian point of view."[4] A close look at the Commission's make-up (evenly divided between public and private education representatives) and its final report, however, prove McDonald's fears to have been unfounded. As Thurston and Commission member Earl McGrath have interpreted this embarrassing episode, McDonald's reaction was less a response to the appointment of Zook and Brown than a response to the fact that he was not among the chosen (Thurston, personal communication, November 30, 1982; E. J. McGrath, personal communication, November 8, 1982).

As is customary upon appointment to a public commission, each of the Zook Committee members received a letter from the President describing the Commission's mission. Though signed by Truman, the letter was drafted by Kingsley and thus represented the latter's judgment as to the issues the Commission should consider. As soon as the Commission assembled in Washington for its first meeting, it freely revised this list of issues, pruning limbs off and grafting others on as it saw fit. Kingsley, who had privately declared to Steelman his intention to "ride herd over the Commission,"[5] apparently accepted these revisions without question.

When the Commission finished negotiating its agenda, the process of collecting data began. Thurston and Brown supervised this tedious search, soliciting information as well as policy recommendations from private and government agencies.[6] Like most large advisory panels, the group divided itself into subcommittees, which met independently to digest outside documents and to hammer out positions before submitting them for debate at plenary sessions.[7] Between these meetings in Washington, members conferred over the phone and in letters.

Records of the subcommittee meetings are sparse, but those relating to the subcommittee on educational opportunity show that this topic was clearly among those over which the Commission labored long and hard. After eight months of soul-searching, the subcommittee could not yet see its way around the problems of segregation and discrimination in higher education. The crux of the dilemma was how far the Commission should go in proposing possible remedies for discriminatory and segregationist practices. As a letter from Horace Kallen of the New School for Social Research to his subcommittee fellows shows, the Commission had examined several options, none of which was wholly satisfactory. Withholding federal subventions from institutions engaging in such practices would fail to change the status quo, would penalize Negro colleges, and would never pass Congress. Creating national universities, independent of "political manipulation," would give Negroes the chance to attend integrated institutions of high quality but would not put an end to discrimination in other institutions. Federal scholarships, which the Commission ultimately endorsed but which Kallen felt to be "an evasion and postponement of the issue," could make a stab at promoting educational opportunity but fell far short of providing colleges with incentives to change.[8]

While the Commission agonized over the opportunity problem, its other subcommittees were at work on (a) a general policy statement, (b) recommendations for reorganizing higher education and for developing statewide systems of tuition-free community colleges, (c) proposals for improving the quantity and quality of college faculty, and (d) proposals for a federal role in financing one-third of the capital outlay needed to expand the public sector. Like the subcommittee on educational opportunity, the subcommittee on financing higher education found itself caught on the horns of a dilemma. Some members representing private and sectarian colleges recoiled at the prospect of limiting federal institutional aid to public colleges. As Zook wrote to Steelman in a progress report dated April 4, 1947, it took better than ten months for the subcommittee to iron "out most of the controversial issues involved."[9]

During the last several months of the Commission's life, prominent newspapers carried articles and editorials discussing the overcrowding "crisis" that had erupted as a result of veterans on the college campus and the social crisis about to erupt as a result of scientific manpower shortages. The appointment of the Zook Commission and the report of President Truman's Scientific Manpower and Research advisory committee appears to have emboldened discussion of these problems among the public and the higher education community, raising concern to a near fever pitch. The White House took notice of this change in public temper in early January of 1947, and debated whether to send Congress a special message on education that winter or to wait until the publication of the Zook report later in the year. Watson B. Miller, head of the Federal Security Agency (which then housed the Office Of Education), advised the President to go ahead with a message. Miller argued that the time was "ripe" and that a message now rather than later would capitalize on public sentiment. For reasons unclear, however, the White House decided against it.[10]

Eighteen months later (and six months after the Zook report had been published), there were no ready signs that the White House was planning to respond to the higher education crisis. Impatient with the lack of Presidential initiative, Budget Director Frank Pace pressed Truman to instruct Oscar Ewing (Miller's successor) to prepare a program for legislative clearance and presentation to the 81st Congress. Thus prompted, Truman asked Ewing in September of 1948 to submit an outline of the "principles" he would follow in developing a legislative program.[11]

Even before receiving official go-ahead from the President, the OE had started reviewing the Zook proposals for federal scholarships and fellowships. At the request of the White House, the OE also made an in-depth study of the Commission's community college recommendations and concluded that the President should appropriate funds to assist the States in exploring the creation of community college systems.[12] By and large, however, the Administration focused its attention on ways to assist college students. From mid-1948 through 1949 the new Commissioner of Education, Earl McGrath, and the Director of the OE's Division of Higher Education, John Dale Russell, took informal readings among higher education groups[13] while White House, BOB, and FSA/OE staff negotiated provisions of a student aid bill.[14] The bill, crafted along lines almost identical to the Commission's proposal, was to be submitted to Congress in early 1950.

The Commission had envisioned a federal program of undergraduate scholarships of up to $800 per year to aid 300,000 students and graduate fellowships of $1,500 per year. The program was to be administered by State commissions acting as federal agents. The state commissions would determine an applicant's eligibility and make awards to be used at the institution of the recipient's choice: public, private, in-state, or out-of-state. The Administration weighed this option against a matching grants program to the States of similar proportions, which would be administered under State control. As a supplement to federal scholarships or grants, a loan program was also proposed. The grants option, advocated by Assistant to the President David Stowe, would assist more students with given federal expenditures but would limit recipients to in-state schools—a clear disadvantage to Negro students in segregated systems. The BOB-preferred scholarship option, which would require greater federal expenditures for a given number of students, had the advantages of being more acceptable to private higher education and permitting more freedom of choice to recipients.

Stowe argued against using loans even as a supplement to grants or scholarships. The OE likewise found little reason to embrace the program. But after dogged persistence by Oscar Ewing, who proposed the loan provision, the BOB asked the OE to redraft the bill to include loans as part of a three-pronged program of scholarships, loans, and fellowships. The BOB also asked Buell Gallagher and Fred Kelly of the OE to reconsider the justification for the fellowship program. In light of existing Public Health fellowships and those which the pending National Science Foundation bill would provide, a general fellowship program might invite "duplication and competition."

Because questions relating to all three provision had yet to be settled by late December of 1949, John Thurston, now Acting FSA Administrator, and Frank Pace, Elmer Staats, and Weldon Jones, all of the BOB, agreed that any language on higher education in the President's upcoming budget message should be "very general." But unresolved details of the student aid bill's provisions were hardly the whole reason for deciding that the budget message language should be vague. The memo recording this agreement also noted that the President was worried that a higher education bill would have "adverse implications . . . upon general aid to education." Presumably, this was the reason why the higher education bill was not sent to Congress until August of 1950, even though it was ready in April.

The student aid bill, modelled on the Commission's proposals for scholarships and fellowships but also containing loans, fared no better than the Administration's fourth attempts to pass an elementary and secondary education bill. Rufus Miles, who worked with Elmer Staats and Weldon Jones in the Budget Office, has observed that the outbreak of the Korean War in June 1950 definitely dimmed the student aid bill's prospects for passage (R. E. Miles, personal communication, October 31, 1982). But to this observation John Thurston has added that neither the White House nor the Budget Bureau, acting on the President's behalf, "made any strenous effort to have the aid bill pressed in the Congress" (Thurston, personal communication, November 9, 1982). Thus while the Zook Commission was successful in convincing top Administration officials of the need for federal student aid, it fell short of changing Truman's lukewarm attitude toward the idea. As one may by now suspect, the Commission was as much intended to educate the President as to educate the public.

The 1956 Josephs Committee

After serving as President of Columbia University and as a member of the Educational Policies Commission, Dwight Eisenhower was no stranger to the problems of higher education when he entered the Oval Office. As a military man, he was keenly aware of the link between higher education's brainpower and the national defense; and, as leader of the "free world," he appreciated the importance of a citizenry well-educated in the ways of democracy. Yet throughout his term in office, Eisenhower maintained what one White House aide describes as a "healthy skepticism" toward federal aid to education—an attitude fortified, if not inspired, by what he had seen of the educational systems of Europe while commander of the Allied forces. Samuel Brownell, Commissioner of Education from 1953-56, points out that Eisenhower "had been much impressed by what he had observed" there, by "the way their national Ministries of Education had been controlled and used by their governments, a situation he strongly believed should be avoided in the U.S." (S. M. Brownell, personal communication, March 28, 1983).

Thus, when Eisenhower consented (at the suggestion of the White House Conference on Education) to appoint the Committee on Education Beyond the High School, he did so with full support for the idea (Brownell, personal communication, March 28, 1983), but with no intention of using the Commission's recommendations to launch a legislative program for higher education (White House Aide, personal communication, March 30, 1983). As a copy of the remarks he was to make at the Committee's first meeting on April 24, 1956, shows, Eisenhower was particularly interested in having the group's thoughts on issues bearing upon the nation's defense: the need to fill manpower shortages in the sciences and other professions, the need to accommodate "rapidly changing technology," and the "national security aspects" of scientific and humanistic studies. In addition to these three issues, he suggested that the Committee study ways to solve the teacher and housing shortages on American campuses.

Given the President's reserve toward federal cures for education's ailments, it is not surprising that the composition of the Josephs Committee differed from that of the Zook Commission. The Zook Commission, whose membership selection was overseen by a White House aide wholly in favor of federal aid, was overwhelmingly composed of persons with direct ties to the academic community, and its chairman was president of the chief umbrella group representing higher education interests. By contrast, only half of the 35 members of the Josephs Committee had professional ties to individual colleges or state boards of higher education. The other half was recruited from major businesses and industries, elementary and secondary school boards, labor, and politics. Moreover, neither of the Administration's two choices for the chairmanship, Roy Larsen of Time Inc. and Devereux Josephs of New York Life, was a professional educator or professional spokesman for education. Both had, however, been active in education-related affairs. Larsen had chaired a voluntary association called the National Citizens Commission for the Public Schools, and Josephs had served as President of the Carnegie Corporation.

While choosing Committee members, both Sherman Adams, The Assistant to the President, and Marion Folsom, Secretary of HEW, had agreed that the commissioners should be "politically non-partisan" and representative of business and the professions, as well as of education.[16] The major obstacle to realizing these goals was finding suitable individuals from "south of the Mason-Dixon line," a problem which HEW felt "must be solved if the Committee's work is to be a success."[17] The search for Southerners persisted over the summer months and was finally concluded with the naming of Arthur Edens of Duke University, Edgar Stern, a trustee of Tulane University, and J. Broward Culpepper of Florida's State Board of Higher Education. Like those named to the Committee in the spring, the Southern nominees were cleared through the National Republican Committee.[18] It is possible that the President's brother, Dr. Milton Eisenhower, William Russell of Columbia's Teachers College, and James Conant of Harvard also had a hand in nominating commission members (Brownell, personal communication, April 21, 1983). The President frequently called upon these three, and upon Conant and Dr. Eisenhower in particular, for advice on educational matters. It may or may not be a coincidence that both had gone on record against massive federal aid to education.

Like the Zook Commission, the Josephs Committee immediately set about adjusting its agenda to reflect its own sense of the issues that warranted consideration. By the end of its second meeting, it had expanded its list to include many of the issues that appeared in the Zook report. Among these were enlarging educational opportunity, meeting physical requirements to accommodate six million students by 1970, financing higher education for so many students, supplying qualified college teachers, and meeting manpower needs of science, industry, and government. Omitted from the agenda was consideration of the "national security aspects" of study in the sciences and humanities.[19]

In November of 1956, the Committee sent a short interim report to the President foreshadowing its priorities and positions on the questions raised during the first six months of deliberations.[20] Though the report shied away from making specific recommendations at this juncture, it did call for immediate "State by State analyses" of higher education needs and the projected costs of meeting these needs. A month later, at a meeting of legislative leaders at the White House, Secretary Folsom announced that he wanted funds and authorization to proceed with the recommended survey. Republication Congressional leaders balked at the idea, warning that such a program would be an "opening wedge for heavy federal involvement in college education." The President, however, sided with the Secretary stating that "planning for the future had to be undertaken quickly."[21]

In the late spring of 1957, the Commission finished its second interim report, which, like the first, was intended for public circulation. Josephs scheduled release of the report for June 28th. He also asked the President to write a cover letter for the report to be sent to all State

Governors pointing out the need for State and local action on some of the problems identified therein. Josephs' hope was to have the States and localities respond to the report in time for the Committee's final conclusions.[22] The White House, however, found Josephs' request and sections of the report itself importunate. Writing to Staff Secretary Andrew Goodpaster, Deputy Assistant for Intergovernmental Relations Howard Pyle recommended against releasing the report before the end of July and against a transmittal letter "from anyone in the White House" to the Governors.[23]

The problem, as Pyle saw it, was that the report "contained material for attacks on the pending school construction legislation." House debate on a school construction compromise, which was assumed by HEW and the Hill to have the President's support, was about to begin. It appears that Pyle and other White House aides had some sense of Eisenhower's ambivalence toward the bill and were worried that the Josephs Committee's recommendations for federal aid to higher education would limit the President's freedom of movement. Pyle referred obliquely to "damaging arguments" on a number of "major policy matters" set forth in the report and warned that White House transmittal would be widely regarded as an "implied endorsement" by the President. It was decided that release of the report would be best delayed, in the hope that "the legislative situation might not be so touchy" later in the summer.[24] On August 11th, the report was released—two weeks after Republican allies and HEW officials working on the school aid compromise were confounded by their inability to reach the President for his blessing.

While it is clear that the school construction issue colored the White House's initial response to the report, Presidential aides were in no hurry to endorse the report even after the school aid question had been laid to rest. When Secretary Folsom sent up a letter for the President's signature acknowledging the Committee's work in mid-August, the letter was promptly diluted.[25] Folsom's draft warmly embraced the Committee's emphasis on extending educational opportunities and the need for "cooperative endeavors at all levels of Government" to achieve this goal. It also stated that a Departmental task force was already at work following up on the report "in order that there may be brought to the problems . . . the best possible thought and action of Federal personnel concerned with education." After several days of work to correct Folsom's deviations "from the noncommittal basis" suggested by the office of Wilton Persons, Deputy Assistant to the President, a cut-and-dried letter omitting these citations was signed by the President and sent on to Josephs. Though the White House had no objection to Folsom's plans to follow up on the Committee's recommendations, it apparently wanted to avoid giving anyone, including the Committee members, reason to believe that specific actions would be forthcoming.

The Committee sent its third and final report to the President in October of 1957. The report was largely devoted to describing national response to the second report's recommendations.[26] Within three days of its receipt, HEW sent the President a critique of the Committee's recommendations and findings.[27] There is good reason to believe that the critique was written by Elliot Richardson, Assistant Secretary for Legislation, on behalf of the Departmental task force. Though Folsom had named Commissioner of Education Lawrence Derthick chairman of the task force, it was Richardson who acted in this capacity and who took the lead in reviewing the Josephs report.

The Committee identified as most pressing the following priorities: improving faculty salaries, expanding graduate education to improve and increase the supply of college teachers, expanding educational opportunity and sources of student financial aid, and expanding college facilities. It recommended federal aid in the following forms: continuing low-interest rate loans for income producing facilities, a matching grants program modelled on the Hill-Burton Act for the construction of other facilities, full overhead payment on federally-sponsored research, work-study scholarships, and greater income tax deductions to encourage private sources to create scholarship funds. Richardson agreed with most of these priorities and recommendations, except the Committee's failure to recommend a more substantial program of federal aid to students. Its preference for a "bricks and mortar" approach to federal involvement Richardson found to be somewhat inconsistent with the report's emphasis on expanding educational opportunity. He would have preferred a frontal attack on this problem, rather than reserving, as the Committee had suggested, massive federal student aid as an option to be exercised after other alternatives had been given "a fair trial." However, Richardson was quick to point out to the President "that the Committee believed that substantial Federal aid ultimately will be required" on all fronts and that the Committee had "strongly emphasize[d] [the] need for Federal leadership—pointing out that higher education is 'local in fact and national in its consequences.' "

Richardson also expressed some Departmental "disappointment in the overly logistical approach" of the Committee; i.e., its failure to take note of the fact that higher education has "become essential to economic and military strength and to ideological warfare." (This observation was made in reference to an OE study on "Education in the USSR," which was to be released on November 11, 1957.) He concluded his analysis by stating that while the Administration should avoid Congressional pressures "to adopt [a] crash program in higher education," neither "must it be shortsighted in doing what needs to be done." To this end, he told the President that the Departmental task force would deliver a program proposal "based on our analysis of the Report" before "the end of the year."

The Departmental task force, which had been working on the Josephs recommendations since July, was, in fact, well along in developing a series of proposals aimed at strengthening "excellence" in higher education by the time the HEW critique reached the President (E. L. Richardson, personal communication, March 28, 1983). During the same period that the task force began its work, Congressman Carl Elliot of Alabama announced plans to hold national hearings on the need for student aid, and, at the request of Secretary Folsom, the OE produced an exhaustive study on the subject, which was completed by Ralph Flynt of the higher education division on May 31st.[28] On October 4th, a surprise ingredient was added to this mixture of activity: the launch of the first Soviet Sputnik. As Richardson recalls of this event, Sputnik literally gave his task force "a rocket to hitch our aspirations to" (Richardson, personal communication, March 28, 1983).

The one thing that task force lacked to make its aspirations a reality was the President's approval. This he gave on November 6th at a White House meeting with Folsom, Richardson, Derthick, HEW Under Secretary John Perkins, Adams, and Persons.[29] Up until this point, the President was undecided as to whether to propose another school construction bill, which he readily admitted Congress would not pass and the budget would not accommodate. Recent discussions with scientists, who were concerned at the Russians' "tremendous emphasis on education," and assurances that the State Governors would remain firm in their resolution "that the Federal Government should stay out of school construction" were—along with the budget and the Congress—enough to push the President over the brink of indecision. He told Folsom to drop any plans for school construction and to develop a program in keeping with "the present public mood."

Now armed with the President's explicit consent, Folsom presented a general outline of an "Educational Development Act,"[30] at the November 15th meeting of the Cabinet.[31] Stating first that "much further consultation was needed in and out of Government," he described plans for a program broader than but also incorporating several of the major proposals of the Josephs Committee. The most significant differences between the Committee's and the task force's proposals were programs for undergraduate scholarship, incentives for foreign language teaching, and construction grants for technical and scientific training facilities. Some sentiment was expressed at the meeting for limiting scholarships "to fields . . . essential to our national security" and for leaving the provision of scholarships entirely to the private sector. But the President and others countered that there was "a pressing need for some Federal money" on a temporary basis.

Discussion of these plans carried over to the December 2nd Cabinet meeting.[32] Though the President's science advisor, James Killian, applauded Folsom's efforts to develop a well-rounded program, one "not confined merely to science," Eisenhower worried that the program was too broad and "might not remedy the lag in science and mathematics" or sufficiently address the need to encourage higher pay for teachers. The President was called out of the meeting at this point, and attention returned to the more fundamental issue of whether the program would "leave room for maximum effort and control by the States." Similar questions were raised at a White House meeting of Republican legislative leaders two days later,[33] with the President voicing support for restricting scholarships, though not teacher training, to national defense fields. Except for this point of disagreement, Eisenhower commended the program to the Congressmen as "something developed by the most capable groups in the country"—a comment made on the heels of Folsom's observation that there were "indications that the Congress would want something much more radical."

In the meantime, the Budget Bureau had started review of the program's cost estimates as well as review of a proposal to add $140 million to the college housing loan authority,[34] a move urged by the Josephs Committee. By late December a near final explanation of the Folsom program had been placed in the President's hands.[35] Eisenhower then asked his brother, Dr. Milton Eisenhower (who had served on the Zook Commission and was then President of Johns Hopkins), to do a confidential critique of the program.

The critique turned out to be a lengthy, hortatory document, which, while hardly adverse to the general thrust of the program, recommended several modifications.[36] For one, Dr. Eisenhower felt that Folsom's 10,000 scholarships ought to be doubled or trebled, with the difference in cost made up by dropping the matching grant proposals for testing and counseling services to high school students and the raising of science and math teachers' salaries. Neither of these suggestions, however, was adopted in the bill sent to Congress. Dr. Eisenhower also argued that fellowships should be offered to those interested in secondary as well as college teaching, but, again, the Administration decided to keep the original provision intact. Though not recommending any specific change, Dr. Eisenhower questioned the practicality of trying to distinguish between undergraduate and graduate facilities if federal funds were to be limited to the latter. In practice, he observed, facilities are used for both. The bill sent to Congress nonetheless maintained the distinction. All in all, he concluded, "politically, it seems desirable for the Administration to sponsor a bold and sizeable program."

Milton Eisenhower's review of the Folsom program signalled the final phase of White House tinkering with it, most of which resulted in shrinking the size, but not the content, of the program. Major changes thereafter were left to the Congress. The end product of nine months of deliberation, beginning in the early summer with the completion of the Josephs Committee's second report and the OE study on student financial aid alternatives, was an Administration bill incorporating some of the ideas endorsed by the Committee and many of the ideas generated by the Departmental task force. It is clear in all this that Folsom and the task force, with the help of accelerating public and Congressional support for action, were the major forces behind the development of the bill, both before and after the launching of Sputnik.

With Administration officials duly credited for their part, some specific observations are in order with respect to the contribution of the Committee itself. First, the Committee's recommendations for expanding graduate education, increasing the supply of college teachers, providing counseling and testing for high school students, and strengthening the analytical capacities of the Office of Education were included in the Administration's version of what was to become the National Defense Education Act. Of these proposals, only aid to graduate schools was eliminated after the bill was sent to Congress.

Its recommendation to continue low-interest federal loans under the college housing program was also heeded. The Committee argued the case for a Hill-Burton type of program for the construction of college facilities. While President Eisenhower refused to back Congressional proposals for direct federal loans for construction, in 1959 and 1960 he endorsed an HEW alternative—a debt-retirement plan, accompanied by federal grants that would pay up to 25% of the principal on amounts public and private colleges borrowed for construction. (His consent for the alternative was given reluctantly, but not without a genuine appreciation of "the problems of private education" and a recounting of "the dismal deficits" he ran into at Columbia.) However, the Administration's alternative was twice rebuffed.[37] In short, the only major proposal of the Josephs Committee to be overturned by the Administration was its recommendation to hold-off on federal aid to college students. Even here, the Committee had acknowleged that substantial federal aid would ultimately be necessary.

The 1960 Hovde Task Force

Unlike the Truman and Eisenhower commissions, the Kennedy Task Force on Education was not created to wrestle with the fundamental question of whether the federal government ought to change its posture toward higher education. For the Hovde Task Force, this question had already been answered in the affirmative, first by way of the steps toward change embodied in the NDEA and then by the 1960 Democratic campaign platform.

The purpose of the Kennedy Education Task Force, and of all the other task forces appointed immediately following the 1960 election, was to develop specific legislative proposals for inclusion in the President-elect's first Message to Congress. As advisor Richard Neustadt wrote to Kennedy just days before the election, the transition task forces were to do the "preliminary work of screening ideas, sharpening issues, posing choices, and then actually turning out draft-action documents."[38] Theodore Sorensen, soon to be Kennedy's Special Counsel, supervised the selection of task force members, drawing about 100 names from the professions, foundations, and universities, all of which were "considered to have some talent or some political claim or, as in most cases, both."[39] The name of Purdue University President Frederick Hovde, who had served on the Josephs Committee, was among this group. Along with Francis Keppel, Dean of the Harvard School of Education, Benjamin Willis, Superintendent of Chicago's public schools, Russell Thackrey of the Land Grant Colleges Association, Alvin Eurich, Vice President of the Ford Foundation, and John Gardner, President of the Carnegie Foundation, Hovde was asked to prepare a report for the Kennedy staff's use in developing elementary, secondary, and higher education programs.

Within weeks of receiving its marching orders, the Task Force had identified "legislative and administrative proposals of the highest priority" after sifting through "more than sixty legislative proposals put forward" in the past several years.[40] The Task Force's first priority was to provide aid to public elementary and secondary schools in the form of general per pupil aid and additional per pupil aid for low-income states and large cities. Its centerpiece higher education proposal revived the Josephs Committee's call for a Hill-Burton construction program. The Task force proposed a five-year, $500 million program of federal matching grants and low-interst loans for the construction and remodelling of academic facilities at private and public colleges and non-profit technical institutes. Of the federal funds to be allocated, 70% would go to matching grants and 30% to loans. A program combining loans and grants, the Task Force noted in an appendix only for the eyes of the Presidential staff, would "have the very substantial support of the academic community."[41] The Task Force also urged the President-elect to increase the college housing loan authority by $150 million until June of 1961 and thereafter by $350 million per year through 1964.

After examining the NDEA, the Hovde group concluded that it warranted "strengthening," beginning with a five-year extension of the Act. To expand educational opportunities the Task Force recommended a number of changes: increasing student loan funds, initiating a program of federally-guaranteed private loans, and removing the yearly ceiling on federal capital contributions to individual institutions. Major changes in federal fellowships included extending fellowships to those planning to teach in elementary or secondary schools, increasing annual fellowships to a fixed payment of $2,500, and funding more fellows to meet "the acute shortage of college teachers." Most of the other Task Force recommendations for the NDEA amounted to fine-tuning.

In the first week of January 1961, the Task Force met with Kennedy at the Carlyle Hotel in New York to present its report. Upon learning the details of the group's recommendations for construction aid, the President-elect alluded to the difficulty he might have in proposing such a program and in steering it through Congress (A. Eurich, personal communication, April 27, 1983). A decision on the proposal would have to be made soon, and for this Kennedy turned to his aides and newly-designated Cabinet and agency heads, a procedure observed with all of the transition task force reports.[42] The Hovde report was handed to Wilbur Cohen, Kennedy's choice for Assistant Secretary of HEW, along with instructions from Sorensen to begin preparing education legislation (W. J. Cohen, personal communication, January 11, 1983).

Sorenson (1965) once described Kenney's "private judgment" of the task reports as ranging from "helpful" to "terrific" (p. 237). What Kennedy thought of the Hovde report in particular is not certain; however, there is a number of reasons for believing that the President-elect's reaction was mixed. First, Kennedy was disturbed at the cool— and in Catholic quarters cold—reaction to the report when it was released (without appendices) in late January of 1961. In addition to Catholic criticism of the report's failure to recommend aid to private elementary and secondary education, hackles were raised at the report's projection that it would take $9 billion to implement all of the programs it recommended. The "undue" emphasis given to the programs' price tag frustrated the President, who felt attention should properly have been focused on the merits of the Hovde proposals (Cohen, personal communication, January 11, 1983). Second, the report was at odds with the 1960 Democratic platform's promise of scholarships (as well as loans) for college students, a cornerstone of its pledge to increase educational opportunity. The Task Force recommended more loans under the NDEA and a program of federally-guaranteed private loans, which, while not at cross-purposes with Kennedy's campaign commitment, certainly fell short of the candidate's stated goals. Third, Cohen and others assigned to develop the 1961 program were not instructed to follow the Task Force recommendations stroke for stroke. The Hovde report was but one of several sources consulted by Cohen and Keppel (Cohen, personal communication, January 11, 1983). Others included papers by education associations and BOB memos issued during the transition on items of interest to the incoming Administration.[43] In sum, the Administration was simply not wedded to the Hovde report.

The Administration's first year proposals to Congress on higher education bear this observation out.[44] Despite the Task Force's pledge of support by higher education groups for a program of grants and loans to construct non-income producing facilities, Kennedy asked only for loans, though not without giving consideration to the constitutionality of a grant program that would include sectarian colleges.[45] He did, however, include in his request, a trimmed down version of the Hovde plan for increasing authorizations to the college housing loan program.

True to his campaign promise, but contrary to the Task Force's thinking on the subject, the President proposed a scholarship program, accompanied by cost of education allowances to institutions, as an amendment to the student loan title of the NDEA. Though neither this nor other amendments to the NDEA proposed by the Administration in 1961 were to survive Congressional maneuvering, many of the Administration's changes to this Act were consistent with those recommended by the Task Force. Task Force proposals adopted by Cohen, approved by Kennedy, and sent to the Congress included establishing a permanent and expanded student loan fund, liberalizing loan forgiveness features, raising the annual ceiling on federal capital contributions, and increasing both the annual number of and annual payment to graduate fellows.[46]

In January of 1961 the President was convinced he could not propose a construction grants program that aided sectarian colleges. But by August his resolve on this matter appears to have been weakening. In March, and with his tacit consent, his college aid bill was amended by Edith Green, Chairman of the House Special Subcommittee on Education, to include construction grants. But with the sinking of the elementary and secondary school bill in July went the college aid bill (Sundquist, 1968, pp. 202-203). Anxious to pass some sort of education bill that year, the White House considered submitting "a new package on education," a package incorporating loans *and* grants. A program outline dated August 3rd and a memo from Sorensen to the President dated August 15th show tentative plans (foreshadowing Kennedy's 1963 "omnibus" strategy) for a three-titled bill to aid impacted areas, build public schools, and provide loans and grants for academic facilities.[47]

However, rather than redoubling its own efforts, the Administration let Edith Green take up the college construction issue as soon as her colleagues reconvened in 1962. Green's bill for loans and grants also included the Administration's renewed request for scholarships. Though early prospect for its passage was encouraging, the bill was later renounced on racial and religious grounds (Sundquist, 1968, pp. 203-205).

Several of the Hovde Task Force recommendations were to resurface in 1963 during the Administration's formulation of the "omnibus" bill.[48] Scholarships were retired and in their place appeared the Hovde proposals for expanding the NDEA loan program and for a new federally-insured student loan program. Graduate fellowships were to be increased dramatically to 10,000 a year, a scale even larger than that envisioned by the Task Force. Project grants to colleges for elementary and secondary teacher training programs were to be introduced under a title that contained a series of other measures for improving the quality of education. Still feeling the sting of the 1962 defeat, the Administration watered down the Task Force's recommendation for construction of academic facilities: while loans would be broadly available, grants would be limited to building and equipping facilities for technical and scientific education. Only the commuity colleges were to have unrestricted access to construction grants.

How the President's 1963 omnibus bill was to be tactically altered and then artfully navigated through the Congress to produce the Higher Education Facilities Act is a story well told by Sundquist (1968, pp. 207-209) and need not be repeated here. Of importance to this analysis is that while the Hovde Task Force identified a number of higher education proposals that would prove to be acceptable to Congress, most were not acceptable to the Administration at the time they were first proposed. The exceptions to this observation are the adjustments the Task Force recommended for titles of the NDEA, which the Administration readily approved and proposed in 1961.

The 1966 Gardner-Howe
Interagency Task Force

With the passage of the 1965 Higher Education Act, a logjam some 25 years in the making was broken (Gladieux & Wolanin, 1976, p. 12). The Act secured long-sought after programs of scholarships (grants) and federally-subsidized student loans and, in so doing, established the promotion of educational opportunity as the basic charter for federal support of higher education. The 1964 Task Force on Education, chaired by John Gardner, was instrumental in bringing this Act and charter about (Hawkinson, 1977).

Gardner's stellar performance as Task Force Chairman led to his appointment as HEW Secretary in 1965. By mid-1966, Gardner, BOB, and White House aides working on domestic program development agreed that it was time to take a look at expanding the charter created by the HEA. The vehicle for exploring this possibility would be an interagency task force under Gardner's direction and chaired by Commissioner of Education Harold Howe. Well before the Task Force was formally appointed in September of 1966, James Gaither, right-hand man to the President's Special Assistant, Joseph Califano, had begun compiling ideas for the 1967 domestic legislative program. Most of the ideas in the education section of Gaither's program binder[49] had been generated earlier in informal discussions between the White House, the BOB, Gardner, and Howe. After surveying the federal higher education landscape and finding that support for construction and students "is particularly well-covered," Gardner and the BOB concluded that new directions were in order. What was now needed was "a comprehensive plan and strategy for Federal support" and, in particular, support for "categories of institutions . . . which educate the bulk of our students," support for "the teaching function," and encouragement "of innovation and experimentation" in curricula and institutional development. One other "new departure" was identified as well: expanding educational opportunity for middle-income groups.

The Task Force's agenda had thus begun to gel by the time Califano formally charged Gardner with developing a report. Accompanying Califano's enabling memo was an abbreviated list of the ideas in Gaither's binder.[50] The list appeared again at the Task Force's first White House meeting on September 21st.[51] While Califano made clear that the Task Force was not to be limited to examining these proposals, the list made clear what the Task Force's priorities should be.

At Gardner's request, Commissioner Howe assumed supervisory responsibility for the Task Force. By early October, Howe reported to Califano that the Task Force had developed "tentative papers" along the lines suggested in the enabling memo, presumably referring to annotated outlines of four proposed acts the Task Force had drafted.[52] These included an "Education Manpower Act" (the foundation of the Educations Professions Development Act of 1967); an "Equal Educational Opportunity Act," which incorporated proposed changes to the

Elementary and Secondary Education Act of 1965 and added a title for adult education programs; vocational education amendments; and a "Higher Education Development Act" that embodied many of the ideas discussed by Gardner and others earlier in the year. Title I of this Act would provide grants to colleges for innovative academic programs. Title II would match institutional funds to introduce computers in college instruction. Title III would aid "emerging graduate schools." Title IV would raise the quality of undergraduate and graduate teacher training programs.

Califano had given Gardner and Howe a reporting deadline of October 31st, which the Task Force dutifully met. In the weeks between the September meeting at the White House and completion of the report, Califano continued to pass ideas along for the Task Force's consideration.[53] Howe responded in kind by keeping Califano abreast of the group's decisions to add, delete, or delay consideration of particular issues.[54] During this same period, the proposed Higher Education Development Act, with its duke's mixture of programs, was over-hauled to focus more upon undergraduate teaching.[55] The Task Force dropped the emerging graduate schools provision "because it would tend to encourage proliferation of lower quality graduate programs," and transferred the teacher training title to the Education Professions Development Act. The original title aimed at curricular innovations took on ambitious proportions, with a shift in emphasis from curriculum development to faculty development. All institutions above the "developing colleges" category (a category of institutions singled out for federal aid under the HEA) would be eligible for planning and project grants to upgrade and expand undergraduate teaching staff and to design and implement undergraduate curricular improvements.

In addition to these titles, the Task Force recommended another to establish up to 20 regional research and development centers for higher education, paralleling the education laboratories authorized under the ESEA. To support teaching and scholarship in the arts and humanities, the Task Force proposed institutional support grants and construction grants for special purpose facilities, both to be administered by the under-funded National Foundation on the Arts and Humanities. Only the computers title of the earlier draft was left unchanged. The now-called "Higher Education Quality Act" was estimated at $267 million for FY '68.

For reasons unclear, the Task Force submitted its report without indicating which among its broad range of proposals for elementary, secondary, vocational, adult, and higher education[56] should be accorded top priority in 1967. In his memo transmitting the report, Howe told Califano that he and Gardner had discussed the recommendations and that Gardner would convey his "priorities and qualifications" shortly.[57] Whether the undated list of priorities that appears in two of the White House aides' task force files represents the views of Gardner alone or in concert with others is open to question.[58] But there is no question that the list's author(s) believed that higher education was of lower legislative importance in 1967 than other education needs addressed by the Task Force. Of the Task Force's nine major programs, higher education ranked below innovation in vocational education, adult literacy, grants to the states elementary and secondary educational planning, improvement of the Teachers Corps, and educational TV, and ahead of Education Professions Development, improvement of economics education, and aid to rural students. How, why, and exactly when this relative ordering came about cannot be readily determined, but none of the nine programs was eliminated before detailed discussion by all parties to the White House review process.

As was customary upon White House receipt of a task force report, the BOB would independently review recommendations before they were jointly reviewed by White House aides, BOB staff, and key agency and departmental heads. William Cannon, chief of the Education, Manpower, and Science Division, conducted the budget analysis of the 1966 education report.[59] While Cannon did not flatly state that the 1968 budget could not accommodate most of the new directions recommended by the Task Force, he clearly implied that such was the case. Pointing out that new education legislation and amendments to existing legislation would total "$1.8 billion in 1968, rising to about $5 billion by 1972," he advised Budget Director Schultze that "planning in general . . . should be the principal theme for 1968 . . . [and] that major new program thrusts [sh]ould be deferred, although some 'pilot' programming may be warranted." As far as the proposed Higher Education Quality Act was concerned, Cannon concluded that the Task Force had done "a lot of good analytic work . . . on the general dimensions" of higher education problems but had done "poorly on some specific proposals." These latter included the computers proposal, which, he noted, offered "absolutely no" supporting analysis and the undergraduate teaching proposal, which, even if scaled down to provide only planning grants, would "be an open invitation to pressures for large-scale program support in future years."

With Cannon's cautions in hand, Califano convened a series of White House meetings with the Task Force, beginning in early November and ending in mid-December, to decide which proposals would go and which would stay.[60] Notes taken over the course of these meetings (apparently by Gaither) show almost step by step how and on what grounds proposals were eliminated from the 1967 legislative package. While Cannon's analysis undoubtedly set clear limits on the size and feasibility of the higher education proposals, it is important to note that *explicit* references to cost figured infrequently in the discussions (as far as can be determined from meeting notes).

The BOB's initial objections to the computer proposal were overcome when the Office of Science and Technology and the National Science Foundation, both of which had been exploring the idea, supplied the missing factual justification. OST's Donald Hornig and Commissioner Howe repeatedly argued for the program's inclusion on grounds that computers were "essential" to any "basic" education. William Gorham of HEW opposed the measure as inappropriate when there was still much to do in the realm of providing higher education opportunities for the poor. President Johnson, however, found the idea to his liking and included it in his 1967 Message on Education and Health.

Little attention was given to the Task Force's proposal to include grants for the arts and humanities until the December meetings. The question here was not whether but how much money ought to be appropriated for the program: HEW wanted double what the BOB was willing to allow. Except for this aspect of the proposal, consensus was easily reached. The same can be said of the basic concept behind the proposed regional higher education centers. Agreement was quick to come after it was decided that the path of least resistance in Congress would be to expand the mission of the elementary and secondary labs rather than seek separate authorization. However, sometime between December 10th, when draft #3 of the 1967 education program was prepared,[61] and January 12, 1967, when a copy of legislative packaging arrangements for the 1967 program was approved by HEW Under Secretary Cohen, this proposal disappeared.

The November-December hearings on the fourth title of the proposed Higher Education Quality Act stand in stark contrast to those of the other three. Opinions on the undergraduate teaching improvement program were sharply divided. On the one hand, pressing for inclusion, was White House aide Douglass Cater. On the other hand was Wilbur Cohen. Poised somewhere between were Howe, Cannon, Gardner, Hornig, and the others. While all acknowledged that the nation's middle-range colleges stood in dire need of qualitative and organizational improvements, no two could agree on how to tackle the problem without antagonizing both those the program would exclude and those the program was intended to serve. As one among the group pointed out, the program did not include community colleges, and "any higher education program *must* do so." Gardner wanted to exclude the better state universities, which he felt were not properly middle-range colleges. Even if it were possible to draw "firm" and acceptable lines of eligibility, which some doubted, there was ample evidence that the higher education community would continue to press for general aid and would oppose "another" program offering project grants.

Two alternatives to the Task Force's proposal were explored, including Cater's proposal for aid based on institutional "development plans" and on the number of federally supported students enrolled (which all readily acknowledged to be a "vehicle for getting unrestricted grants into colleges") and a Gardner-Howe proposal for categorical grants "based on institutional plans for achieving excellence." But neither of these seemed to be the solution the group was seeking. At the December 10th meeting, Cohen voiced his belief that it would be "very dangerous to go with [a middle-range college program] this year," a statement made in the context of academic opposition to project grants of any nature. Realizing that time was running out as well, the group unanimously decided to commit the middle-range college and institutional support questions to the newly appointed Friday Task Force.

On this note of deferral, the White House-Task Force deliberations on the 1967 higher education program ended. Thus, of the Task Force's four major proposals for improving the quality of higher education, only two survived the last days leading up to the preparation of the President's Message on Education and Health. To a large extent, fiscal constraints imposed by the Vietnam War were to blame for the scaling-down of the education agenda, as in other domestic areas. The decision to abandon a program to promote greater opportunity for higher education, for example, was at least partially based on budgetary considerations.[62] But it was also the thicket of dilemma confronting the Task Force and the White House—and, perhaps, the ready reason to defer decision offered by the creation of the Friday Task Force—that led to the loss of the centerpiece proposal for higher education.

The 1966 Friday Task Force and the 1967 Gardner-Howe
Interagency Task Force

Despite domestic budget constraints looming ever larger on the horizon, the White House went ahead with its plan, conceived in the summer of 1966, to have an outside task force "review formal education in the United States . . . [its] future directions . . . [and] the role the Federal Government should play in the field."[63] It was now mid-term in the Johnson Administration and time to take stock of obligations and expectations created by the Great Society's education programs. An outside task force could give the White House a reliable, private reading of the road ahead in preparation for the next half of the term—and, as it must have occurred to White House aides, for a possible second term.

As with the 1966 Interagency Task Force, the White House compiled a tentative agenda for the Friday group, an agenda containing some issues considered by the interagency group in the fall of 1966 as well as others.[64] While it is certain that a number of these program ideas were generated at the agency level, Gaither also had a hand in drafting them.[65] The agenda, which Howe presented to the Task Force at its first meeting,[66] instructed the Task Force to determine whether unrestricted grants to institutions would improve the overall quality of education, whether categorical grants could encourage innovation and diversity in programs and institutions, whether the federal government ought to do more to meet institutional needs for faculty and staff, and whether there ought to be some sort of comprehensive planning for the nation as a whole.

With the comment, "no press leaks," the President approved a list of Task Force nominees recommended by Gardner, Cater, Cannon, and Sargent Shriver on September 30, 1966.[67] The nominees included Sidney Marland, Superintendent of Pittsburgh schools, for chairman; William Friday, President of the University of North Carolina, for vice chairman (these designations were later reversed); David Bell of the Ford Foundation; Lee DuBridge, President of Cal Tech; Hugh Calkins of the Cleveland Board of Education; J.W. Edgar, Texas State Superintendent of Public Instruction; John Fischer, President of Columbia's Teachers College; Fred Harrington, President of the University of Wisconsin; Alexander Heard, Chancellor of Vanderbilt University; Edward Levi, Provost of the University of Chicago; Rev. Walter Ong, then teaching at New York University; David Reisman, Harvard University sociologist; John Goodlad of UCLA; and Leon Sullivan of the Opportunities Industrial Council in Philadelphia.

Reisman did not serve on the Task Force; Thomas Pettigrew, a "reconstructed Southerner" and also a Harvard sociologist, was selected as his replacement. Leon Sullivan's nomination sparked some controversey and his name was dropped after the Task Force's first meeting.[68] Samuel Brownell, a member of the 1956 Josephs Committee, a former Superintendent of Detroit public schools, and a consultant to Yale, was belatedly asked to serve after Marland persuaded Gardner "that another school man should be added to the Task Force" because it was "top heavy with higher education people."[69]

At its first meeting on November 22nd, the Task Force was advised "not to impose any particular political or budgetary constraints on its deliberations"—counsel which it freely heeded over the next several months. After Howe had discussed major shortcomings and oversights in federal education programs, Task Force members added their own observations, most in the form of criticism. Harrington discoursed at some length on the need for "institutional support of universities as a partner of categorical support." DuBridge argued that the federal government "talks of supporting higher education but mostly buys services." These first meeting comments foreshadowed themes that were to dominate months of debate.[70]

In early January 1967, Task Force members sent Friday and Cannon their own appraisals of federal policy and education problems.[71] General support of higher education, support of humanistic and scientific studies and scholarship, and the fate of Negro colleges were among the "absolute musts" members wanted to see the Task Force tackle. Anticipating the preeminence of the institutional support question, Cannon and Friday asked John Morse of the ACE for a memorandum discussing the pros and cons of institutional aid alternatives shortly after the November meeting.[72] Morse's paper was but the first in a long line of papers on this and other subjects that were read by the Task Force.

Predictably, the first higher education topic discussed at the January meeting was the financing of instruction, research, and general capital needs.[73] Someone raised the point that private universities, as an "instrument of national purpose," should be given "disproportionate Federal support for the sake of their maintenance." By the February meeting, this point had become principle, with the Task Force agreeing that "special attention must be focused on the need to sustain the private universities." There was no agreement, however, on "the manner" of aid to private higher education.[74]

Largely as a result of Sidney Marland's expertise and ideas, the Task Force moved quickly over elementary and secondary terrain. The institutional aid stalemate continued well into the spring. In March, the Task Force examined a number of OE financing schemes for higher education. For one reason or another, each was found inadequate.[75]

With their reporting date only two months away, the members assembled in April to review a preliminary draft of the Task Force report prepared by Cannon on April 7th.[76] During the review, commitments appeared to crystallize: the Task Force would propose no general aid to elementary and secondary education "at this time," would emphasize programs for the racial and economic integration of public schools, and would recommend "basic conditional aid for universities" along with new and conventional categorical programs.[77] However, as subsequent report drafts and other documents betray, there were still strong misgivings on the part of some Task Force members with respect to the basic aid question. On June 2nd, David Bell wrote to his colleagues arguing for a "more fully reasoned alternative" to the Harrington proposal for institutional support payments based on equal amounts per student and the DuBridge proposal to pay institutions a fixed percentage of instructional costs.[78] Bell's alternative was strictly categorical, well-argued, but not persuasive enough to deter those who wanted some form of basic institutional assistance. The debate persisted into the middle of June when a second draft of the report was circulated.[79] By June 29th, the question had been resolved by compromise. The final draft of the report recommended unrestricted grants to institutions equal to 10% of instructional costs plus

$100 per student—an approach the Task Force hoped "would satisfy the needs of both public and private universities."[80]

There is no doubt that one of the major catalysts behind the institutional support compromise was the Task Force's long-awaited receipt of William Bowen's study of "The Economics of the Major Private Universities" sometime after discussion of the April 7th draft.[81] Projecting a deficit of $20-28 million for a "typical" major private university for the year 1975-76, Bowen concluded that "serious consideration" should be given "to introducing a program of institutional grants."[82] With the final piece of evidence in, the Task Force proposed, as its first priority, a four-part program of basic aid, including (a) unrestricted grants, (b) a larger federal share of matching grants for academic facilities and increased authorizations for construction programs, (c) expanded federal support of graduate programs, creation of a Social Science Foundation, and full-cost payments for federally-supported research, and (d) raising the number of federally-supported graduate students to 50% of the total enrollment and raising cost of education allowances from $2,500 to $3,500 per student. Its second priority was improving undergraduate instruction. Many of the Task Force's recommendations followed those formulated by the 1966 Interagency Task Force, including project grants to develop better college curricula, to stimulate innovation in teaching, to allow undergraduate faculty to do research, to establish undergraduate teaching professorships, and to establish supplementary centers to encourage curricular and instructional innovation. Concern for the plight of Negro colleges was translated into a proposal to encourage developing colleges and well-established institutions to share facilities, faculty, and programs. Fourth on the Task Force's list of priorities was the expansion of student aid programs and compensatory programs for disadvantaged college youth. These proposals were followed by programs for strengthening the community service functions of universities and renovating teacher education.

By 1971, the total price tag for these proposals would be $4 billion at the funding levels recommended by the Task Force. When added to the 1971 cost of its "moon shot" programs to eliminate discrepancies in the quality of public elementary and secondary education and to the cost of proposals for planning and evaluation, the Friday recommendations would require $9 billion above 1968 outlays.[83]

Despite the obvious budget problems these staggering figures posed, Commissioner Howe found so much to commend in the report that he urged a break with the Administration's policy of task force secrecy. Within a week of receiving the report, and without first consulting Gardner, Howe wrote Cater asking him to "advise the President to make the report of the Task Force . . . a public document."[84] The report, in Howe's opinion, was "statesmanlike" and could, if released, provide the President with arms to fend off Congressional proposals for "Quie Amendments" and "tax-sharing, block-grant schemes advanced by the Republican Party." The report had utility in the next session of Congress and beyond; the President would "have some very useful options to select from . . . without buying the whole package. He could at the same time develop a position for launching a general aid program alongside major categorical efforts." Howe went on to argue that the report "for the first time puts the Federal Government in a truly responsible position in regard to higher education" and that it could be the basis for "helping" higher education rather than merely "using" it.

When Howe's proposal was advanced to the President, the decision was made to release only a modified version of the Task Force's statement on general aid to elementary and secondary education.[85] At the same time this "leak" was being engineered, requests for the Harrington and Bowen papers used by the Task Force in drawing up its basic aid proposals arrived from top foundation and association people. Cater and Gaither urged Califano to release these materials after deleting specific proposals adopted by the Task Force.[86] They reasoned that it would make little sense to refuse the requests since the "existence of these papers is widely known in academic circles" and "withholding . . . such pioneering efforts . . . is difficult to justify." Califano disagreed.

As 1968 program ideas were being assembled over the summer of 1967, Cannon, Gaither, and Califano decided that it was necessary to form a "high level Task Force to review the major recommendations of the [Friday] Task Force" and that "less important recommendations" should be staffed out to the agencies.[87] For higher education, major proposals included the four-part "basic aid" package, the proposal for compensatory services to disadvantaged college youth, and the program to foster "combinations of white and non-white institutions." Califano also decided that it was necessary to delete "all reference to the origin of the ideas and recommendations" contained in the memo chartering the 1967 follow-up Task Force,[88] a move intended either to protect the anonymity of the Friday group or to avoid raising hopes, via an agency leak, in the education community, or both. This decision, which meant that the 1967 Interagency Task Force would be restricted to a paraphrased summary of the Friday report, angered its members.[89] As Gaither reported to Califano, the early September meetings of the in-house group were characterized by "outright criticism bordering on contempt for the . . . policy." Both Gaither and White House Aide Fred Bohen asked Califano to reverse his stand, arguing that "it is indefensible to . . . hold the [Task Force] product so tightly that it has no fertilizing effect at the top of the Administration." They also warned that "the increasing hostility within the government (including Executive Office agencies) to the whole task force enterprise" would lead interagency groups to "give the ideas of outside groups very short shrift."

But there is little evidence that the 1967 Interagency Task Force gave deliberate short shrift to the Friday proposals, in spite of Howe's complaint that the Task Force needed more time than Califano would allow for review.[90] By late September, discussion papers or pricing charts had been prepared on a number of the Friday proposals, including basic institutional aid, undergraduate education, and graduate education and research. By early October, preliminary positions had been forged; and by October 23rd, the Task Force report was ready for White House review.[91]

The report itself contained no provisions for basic institutional aid, recommending instead that a Presidential commission be set up to study the question in the larger context of existing categorical aid and student aid. However, in his memo transmitting the report to Califano, Howe pointed out that a minority of the Task Force "favors having the President suggest new legislation in the next session of Congress to provide general aid to higher education" based on the Friday recommendations.[92] A week after receiving the memo and report, Califano called a meeting in his office to discuss aid to higher education. Present were Gardner, Cater, Gaither, Schultze, and Howe. A few hours after the meeting had ended, Califano sent the President a memo stating that he had instructed Howe to "devote most of his time during the next two months" to devising a "program of basic aid to higher education."[93] Such a program, he told the President, would solve "the only major educational problem which cannot be solved by legislation you have already proposed and enacted." Once in place, he added, "your record of support for education will be complete and unparalleled in human history."

Not all shared Califano's vision. When the news was announced at a November 8th meeting to discuss other recommendations of the in-house Task Force, ripples of resistance promptly surfaced at the agency level. HEW Assistant Secretary William Gorham wrote Gardner a detailed letter opposing the proposal on several grounds.[94] Speaking for Cohen as well, Gorham argued that, politically, a "program of general stringless institutional support" would be "a serious error" when "the Great Society programs of 1965-1966 are underfunded, some would say grossly underfunded." Even if funds were available, he continued, "institutional aid . . . would be a low-priority program, perhaps even an undesirable program" because its benefits would ultimately and only accrue to the middle- and upper-income groups. Moreover, institutional grants merely "give all colleges and universities a little bit more free cash," and while such a program "might save some small mediocre colleges from extinction," it would hardly provide "a base for building high-quality institutions." Having thus vented his spleen, Gorham sent a "personal and confidential" copy of his memo to Gaither,[95] presumably in the hope that Gaither would take up the issue privately with Califano.

While Howe was working behind the scenes on the basic aid question, the Task Force and White House aides continued to meet through November and into December to review other proposals.[96] The 1966 proposal to step up the Upward Bound program and enlarge its "target group," also endorsed by the Friday Task Force, was accorded high legislative priority. The outside and interagency proposals for increasing financial aid to students, and to improve R&D in undergraduate education were also deemed desirable, "but doubt [was] expressed [as to] whether the Budget would permit more than a modest expansion" of these programs. The same doubt was expressed with respect to the proposal to assist the disadvantaged to "enter and complete graduate and professional school" but, later, Califano confidentially instructed the BOB to "insure that the Budget contains sufficient funds" for this proposal.[97] Review of the Interagency Task Force proposals for graduate education also produced mixed results. The Interagency Task Force opposed the Friday recommendation for a Social Science Foundation, and the proposal was scuttled. Increased funding for the arts and humanities was approved, however. Decision on whether to have the federal government support 50% of enrolled graduate students, as the Friday Task Force had urged, was deferred until the basic aid dilemma was resolved, though it was agreed that the cost of education allowance on fellowships should be raised to $3,500. The Friday Task Force's recommendation to expand institutional support, rather than project support, of graduate schools was endorsed by the Interagency

Task Force and the White House. The BOB was instructed to determine how this shift in emphasis could be reflected in the FY '69 budget.

When Howe sent up detailed analyses of the 1968 higher education legislation package on December 5th and 6th,[98] he sent them without any proposal for basic institutional aid. In both of his transmittal memos to Califano, he reiterated his reservations, stating on the 5th that "I personally cannot see a desirable recommendation at this point," and on the 6th that "I don't think that a general aid program of the Friday type should be proposed now. Neither do John Gardner, Charlie Schultze, and Clark Kerr." He promised, nonetheless, to present his views on what might be "the most viable" approach to such a program.

Accordingly, on the 7th, and again voicing his concern, Howe sent Califano his "view of the possibilities."[99] These included the Friday proposal, a variation on the Friday proposal that would substitute faculty salary cost allowances for instructional cost allowances, a flat per capita grant proposal (i.e., without instructional or faculty salary allowances), and a variable grants per student proposal that would pay institutions $100 per freshman and sophomore, $200 per junior and senior, and $400 per graduate student enrolled. Howe threw what support he could muster behind the fourth alternative, concluding that it would be the easiest to administer and the most likely to win academic acceptance.

In an "Eyes Only" memo to Gardner a few days later, Califano asked the Secretary to review the Howe paper and a detailed plan for institutional aid based on the Friday proposal and to be ready to discuss both in Califano's office on December 13th.[100] The original Friday scheme for grants of $100 per student plus 10% of instructional costs was halved in the new plan, and while "planning" would begin in FY '69, no grants would be made until FY '71. Evidently, the only decision reached at the December 13th meeting was to narrow the field of alternatives, for at the December 20th meeting the modified Friday plan was the only alternative to appear on the agenda.[101] On that day, Gardner, Howe, and Schultze prevailed: there would be "*no* legislative proposal on general aid." Instead, the President's Message to Congress would instruct the Secretary of HEW to develop a comprehensive strategy for federal aid to higher education.[102]

Had the Administration decided to go with the Friday basic aid program, the decision would have marked a dramatic addition to the established scope of federal aid to higher education. But because of the budget, HEW resistance, and uncertainty expressed by Clark Kerr, who had been made privy to the idea, the proposal was turned over for further study to Alice Rivlin, HEW Assistant Secretary for Planning and Evaluation. By the time the Rivlin study got under way, the President had announced (in March of 1968) that he would not seek reelection. This decision, coupled with the very real prospect of a Republican successor, was to cast a pall over the tone and content of education task force recommendations for FY '69.

Rivlin's blueprint for federal support of higher education was the one exception to an otherwise perfunctory task force performance. The report concluded that federal priority should be given to promoting educational opportunity and supporting graduate education and research. It also recommended institutional cost of education allowances, but these allowances were to be based *solely* upon the number of students receiving federal Educational Opportunity Grants.[103] In effect, the report dashed cold water on the Friday Task Force's hope to shore up private higher education by more substantial means.

The Rivlin Report, made public in 1969, was not the last word heard on the matter. In 1972, higher education interest groups convinced Edith Green, still Chairman of the House Special Subcommittee on Education, to support them in their bid for institutional aid over the Senate's proposals for a Rivlin-type program of student aid accompanied by cost of instruction allowances. However, fears that institutional aid would become another "immoveable and irrational" spending program, similar to the impacted aid program, undermined Green's efforts (Gladieux & Wolanin, 1976, p. 137). When the wrangling over the 1972 Education Amendments came to an end, advocates of institutional aid had fared no better than Califano had in 1967.

Thus, the Friday Task Force was not to see its arguments for institutional aid vindicated either by the Johnson Administration or the Congress. The Task Force did see, however, positive results on a number of its other higher education proposals, which were incorporated in the Higher Education Amendments of 1968. Among the more noteworthy of these were its proposals for strengthening graduate education, for increasing the length of graduate fellowships and the size of accompanying cost of education allowances, for increased funds and new programs to aid developing colleges, for expanding the community service functions of universities, and for strengthening compensatory services for minority and low-income students.

Conclusions

Perhaps the safest generalization that can be drawn from these six episodes of ad hoc policy formulation is one borrowed from the late Stephen Bailey: they are "long on uniquities, short on ubiquities." To account for the preponderance of "uniquities" here is to confirm what others have suggested before—that the larger policy "environment" or political context, into which proposals are thrust, is what determines their fate. Two environmental ingredients or influences seem to have been the deciding factors in the success or failure of task force and commission proposals for higher education at the Executive Branch level between 1946 and 1967. One was the presence or absence of policy precedent for major proposals. Most of the incremental adjustments in, or additions to, federal policy recommended by the Zook, Josephs, Hovde, and Friday groups were quickly adopted by the White House, while many of the larger changes or new departures they recommended were not. Whether the fact that these latter changes would have directly benefited college institutions (e.g., construction grants and institutional aid) rather than college students made a difference is a question worth exploring. Both politically and constitutionally, aid to students appeared to be the path of least resistance.

Not surprisingly, agency officials concerned with education typically stood more ready than the White House to adopt new departures—up until the mid-60's, that is. By late 1966, HEW's welcome mat had worn thin. The dramatic growth of its responsibilities brought about in 1965 and the toll the Vietnam War took on domestic program funds dulled the agency's enthusiasm for new programs.

This observation points to a second important influence: the degree of White House and agency interest in the advisory group's mission. The White House tended to supply or withhold its support for ad hoc proposals in proportion to its perception of the political stakes involved. Because he felt he could not do otherwise as the nation's first Catholic President, Kennedy shied away from construction grants. President Johnson's quickly established claim to the title "Education President" made it incumbent upon his staff to seek out new policy ideas. One may presume that whatever appeal a student aid program had for President Truman (it was certainly not one of his personal priorities) lay in its compatibility with his other Fair Deal reforms. Politically speaking, there was little, if anything, to lose by proposing that the sons and daughters of those who elected him be given a chance at a college education.

In this case, and even more so in the case of Eisenhower's 1958 "Educational Development Act," agency entrepreneurs were critical influences on the outcome of ad hoc proposals. What the White House initially lacked in enthusiasm for a legislative program they supplied. While there is no doubt in the latter case that Sputnik muffled opposition to federal aid and created an unprecedented invitation for some form of federal action, there is also no doubt that HEW had plans for a higher education program in the works four months before the Soviet surprise. One, therefore, wonders whether the importance of Sputnik in bringing about an Administration program has been overdrawn and the importance of Folsom, Richardson, and his task force that followed up on the Josephs report has been overlooked.

The question of agency influence can also be raised with respect to the Friday Task Force's recommendation for institutional aid. Had agency and BOB officials, who served on the 1967 Interagency Task Force, responded differently to the idea, there is little doubt that Johnson would have proposed it to Congress. In both symbolic and real terms, the Interagency Task Force's veto pulled in the reins on the White House's pursuit of innovative aid to higher education.

[1]Memo, Donald Kingsley to John R. Steelman, 7/9/46, White House Central Files, OF 1060, Folder 1060(1945-July 1946), Harry S. Truman Library. Hereafter, the White House Central Files will be cited as WHCF, and the Truman Library will be cited as TL.

[2]Responses to the Commission announcement are contained in WHCF, OF 1060, Folder Miscellaneous, TL.

[3]Letter, Eleanor Roosevelt to the President, 2/11/47, WHCF, OF 1060, Folder 1060(Aug. 1946-53), TL.

[4]Telegram, Ralph McDonald to the President, 7/18/46, and Memo, Kingsley to Steelman, 7/18/46, both in WHCF, OF 1060, Folder 1060(1945-July 1946), TL.

[5]Memo, Kingsley to Steelman, 7/9/46, WHCF, OF 1060, Folder 1060(1945-July 1946), TL.

[6]Memo, George Zook to Steelman, 8/8/46, and Memo, Steelman to Zook, 8/15/46, both in WHCF, OF 1060, Folder 1060(Aug. 1946-53); Minutes First Meeting of the Inter-Agency Committee, 10/7/46, RG 130, Folder President's Commission on Higher Education; Progress Report attached to Memo, Zook to Steelman, 4/10/47, WHCF, OF 1060, Folder 1060(Aug. 1946-53), all in TL.

[7]Memo, Kingsley to Steelman, 11/8/46, and Memo, Zook to Steelman, 4/10/47, WHCF, OF 1060, Folder 1060(Aug. 1946-53), TL.

[8]Progress Report attached to Memo, Zook to Steelman, 4/10/47, and Letter, Horace Kallen to T. R. McConnell et al., 1/24/47, both in WHCF, OF 1060, Folder 1060(Aug. 1946-53), TL.

[9]Progress Report attached to Memo, Zook to Steelman, 4/10/47, WHCF OF 1060, Folder 1060(Aug. 1946-53), TL.

[10]Letter, Watson B. Miller to the President, 1/9/47, and Memo, Clark Clifford to Miller,

1/27/47, both in WHCF, OF 1261, Folder 419-F Message to Congress, TL.

[11]Memo to File, Frank Pace, 9/2/48, WHCF, OF 1060, Folder Miscellaneous, TL.

[12]Letter, Steelman to Seymour Smith, 4/10/48, WHCF, OF 1060, Folder Miscellaneous; Office of Education Report on the Community College, 6/30/50, Papers of Ralph M. Flynt, Box 25, Folder Office of Education Report on the Community College, TL.

[13]See 1949 Addresses, Articles, Statements, Letters, and Forewords of Earl J. McGrath, Microfilm Collection, Papers of Earl J. McGrath, 1949-53, and Speech and Article files of John Dale Russell, Papers of John Dale Russell, Boxes 9, 10, 12, 13, TL; See also "US Plan Would Aid College Students," New York Times, 10/19/49, 27:5.

[14]Formulation of the Administration's Student Aid Bill from 1948-50 is reconstructed from documents contained in the Papers of George M. Elsey, Folder Legislation-81st Congress 2nd Session-Education, TL. See in particular: Some Issues Involved in the Grant-in-aid vs Direct Federal Operation of a Scholarship Program, 11/22/49, and notes attached thereto; Memo, I. M. Labovitz and Emery Wine to Elmer Staats, 11/18/49; Memo Staats to Weldon Jones, 12/15/49; Memo with attachments, R. E. Neustadt to George Elsey, 4/21/50.

[15]Memo, Samuel Brownell to Bernard Stanley, undated but circa 4/24/56, WHCF, OF Box 900, Folder OF 236-A-2 (1) [2], Dwight D. Eisenhower Library. Hereafter, the Eisenhower Library will be cited as EL.

[16]Memo, Marion B. Folsom to Sherman Adams, 2/3/56, WHCF, OF Box 900, Folder OF 236-A-2 (1) [2], EL.

[17]Memo for Files from R. Gray, 6/11/56, WHCF, OF Box 900, Folder OF 236-A-2, EL.

[18]See memos and letters relating to clearance of nominees in WHCF, OF Box 900, Folders OF 236-A-2 (2) and OF 236-A-2 (1) [2], EL.

[19]Report on the first two meetings of the Committee on Education Beyond the High School, WHCF, OF Box 900, Folder 236-A-2, EL.

[20]First Interim Report to the President, 11/20/56, WHCF, OF Box 600, Folder 236-A-2 (2), EL.

[21]Notes of Legislative Meeting, 12/31/56, Legislative Meeting Series, Ann Whitman Files, Folder Legislative Meetings 1956 (5) December, EL. Hereafter, Ann Whitman Files will be cited as AWF.

[22]Letter, Gerald Ebers to General Andrew Goodpaster, 7/8/57, WHCF, OF Box 901, Folder 236-A-2 (3), EL.

[23]Memo, Howard Pyle to Goodpaster, 7/20/57, WHCF, OF Box 901, Folder 236-A-2 (3), EL.

[24]Memo, Wayne Warrington to Goodpaster, 7/23/57, WHCF, OF Box 901, Folder 236-A-2 (3), EL.

[25]Letter with attachments, Dwight D. Eisenhower to Devereux Josephs, 9/19/57, WHCF, OF Box 901, Folder 236-A-2, EL.

[26]Letter, Josephs to the President, 10/21/57, WHCF, OF Box 901, Folder 236-A-2 (3), EL.

[27]Memo to the President, 10/23/57, Administration Series, Box 16, Folder Folsom, Marion B. (1), EL.

[28]Financial Aid to College and University Students Report, 5/31/57, Papers of Ralph C. Flynt, Folder 2 Financial Aid to College and University Students, 5/31/57 Statement-Report, TL.

[29]Memorandum of Conference with the President, DDE Diary Series, AWF, Box 30, Folder Nov. '57 Staff Notes, EL.

[30]See draft of Educational Development Act, 11/12/57, WHCF, OF Box 545, Folder 111-C 1957, EL.

[31]Minutes of the Cabinet Meeting of November 15, 1957, Cabinet Series, AWF, Box 10, Folder Cabinet Meeting of November 15, 1957, EL.

[32]Minutes of the Cabinet Meeting of December 2, 1957, Cabinet Series, AWF, Box 10, Folder Cabinet Meeting of December 2, 1957, EL.

[33]Notes on Legislative Leadership Meeting December 4, 1957, Legislative Meeting Series, AWF, Box 2, Folder Legislative Meetings 1957 (5), EL.

[34]Memo with attachments, R. W. Jones to the Director [BOB], 11/22/57, Papers of Bryce N. Harlow, Box 12, Folder Legislative Items for 1958 and 1959, EL.

[35]Memo with attachments, Folsom to the President, 12/27/57, WHCF, OF Box 545, Folder 111-C 1957, EL.

[36]Memorandum on Education by MSE [Milton S. Eisenhower], 1/3/58, DDE Diary Series, AWF, Box 30, Folder Staff Notes, Jan. 1958, EL.

[37]Debt-retirement plan outline contained in Records of Wilton B. Persons, Box 1, Folder HEW File. For discussion of the plan, see Notes on Legislative Leadership Meeting January 20, 1959, Legislative Meetings Series, AWF, Box 3, Folder Legislative Meetings 1959 (1), EL.

[38]Memo, Richard Neustadt to JFK, 10/30/60, Papers of Theodore Sorensen, Box 18, Subject Files 1953-60, Folder Transition Correspondence and Memos 10/30/60-12/30/60, John Fitzgerald Kennedy Library. Hereafter, the Kennedy Library will be cited as KL.

[39]Memo, Lawrence O'Brien to Sorensen, 11/30/60, Papers of Sorensen, Box 18, Subject Files 1953-60, Folder Transition Correspondence and Memos 10/30/60-12/30/60, KL.

[40]Letter, Frederick Hovde to Sorensen, 1/2/61, Pre-Presidential Papers, Box 1071, Folder Education Task Force Report, KL.

[41]Appendix II of the Report of the Task Force on Education, Detailed Recommendations for Presidential Staff Use, 1/2/61, Pre-Presidential Papers, Box 1071, Folder Education Task Force Report, KL.

[42]A summary of the task force report review process is found in Memo, Special Counsel to the President-Elect, 12/13/60, Papers of Sorensen, Box 18, Folder Transition Correspondence and Memos 10/30/60-12/30/60, KL.

[43]See, for example, an ACE report sent to Sorensen by Russell Thackrey on 2/9/61 in White House Central Subject Files, Box 92, Education, Folder Education 1/1/61-2/28/61, KL. For the BOB discussion see Specific Issues Relating to Aid to Higher Education, approved by Director Stans 1/4/61, Papers of Sorensen, Box 61, Folder Education Message 11/60-1/26/61, KL.

[44]See *Congressional Quarterly Almanac: 1961*, 17:244-46, and a draft of Kennedy's bill sent by Cohen to Myer Feldman on 3/6/61 and then on to Kennedy by Feldman on 3/7/61 in White House Staff Files, Myer Feldman File, Box 27, Folder Higher Education 3/61, KL.

[45]Memo with attachments, Cohen to General Counsel Alanson Wilcox, 2/8/61, and Treatment of Church-State and Discrimination Issues in . . . Higher Education Construction Proposals, 2/8/61, both in Papers of Sorensen, Box 61, Folder Education Message 2/7/61-2/8/61, KL.

[46]Summary of Proposals for Extension and Amendment of the National Defense Education Act, undated but circa 4/61, Papers of Sorensen, Box 32, Folder Education 4/20/61, KL. See also *Congressional Quarterly Almanac: 1961*, 17:235-36.

[47]A New Package on Education, 8/3/61, and Memo, Sorensen to the President, 8/15/61, Papers of Sorensen, Box 32, Folder Education 8/9/61-11/21/61, KL.

[48]Annotated Index for the National Education Act of 1963, 1/23/61, White House Staff Files, Lee C. White File, Box 4 General File, Folder Legislation/Education 1/18/63-11/5/63, KL.

[49]1967 Legislative Program Binder, WHCF, Aides Files, Office Files of James Gaither, Box 219, Folder 1967 Legislative Program, The Lyndon Baines Johnson Library. Hereafter, Aides Files will be omitted and the particular aide's file will be designated by the aide's name. The Johnson Library will be cited as JL.

[50]Memo, Joseph Califano to John Gardner, 9/8/66, WHCF, OF James Gaither, Box 71, Folder Task Force on Education, JL.

[51]Agenda for the 9/21/66 Meeting of the 1966 Interagency Task Force on Education, WHCF, OF Douglass Cater, Box 37, Folder Material on Task Force on Education (1), JL.

[52]Memo, Harold Howe to Califano, 10/10/66, and Outlines of proposed acts, both in WHCF, OF Douglass Cater, Box 37, Folder Material on Task Force on Education (1), JL.

[53]Memo, Califano to Gardner, 10/1/66, and Memo, Califano to Gardner, 10/10/66, both in WHCF, OF James Gaither, Box 71, Folder Task Force on Education, JL.

[54]Memo, Howe to Califano, 10/10/66, WHCF, OF Douglass Cater, Box 37, Folder Material on Task Force on Education, JL.

[55]Report of the 1966 Interagency Task Force on Education, pp. 11-35, Task Force Collection, Box 13, Folder 1966 Interagency Task Force on Education, JL.

[56]The 1966 Interagency Task Force recommended programs to add flexibility and coordination to the ESEA titles; to eliminate adult illiteracy; to expand educational TV; to strengthen vocational education; to expand the Teachers Corps and consolidate education manpower programs under one act; to promote education in economics; to expand Upward Bound and Talent Search to include rural youth; and to amend and extend expiring legislation.

[57]Memo, Howe to Califano, 10/31/66, WHCF, OF James Gaither, Box 71, Folder Task Force on Education, JL.

[58]Task Force on Education (list of priorities), WHCF, OF James Gaither, Box 314, Folder Task Force on Education 1966, JL.

[59]Memo, William Cannon to Budget Director Schultze, 11/7/66, WHCF, OF James Gaither, Box 71, Folder Task Force on Education, JL.

[60]Discussion of the review of the 1966 Task Force proposals is based on notes and memos referring to four meetings between November and December. In the Task Force Collection, Box 13, Folder 1966 Interagency Task Force on Education, JL, see (1) handwritten and typed notes dated 11/14/66 for a meeting of the same date; (2) handwritten notes dated 12/5/66, referring to a meeting of 11/21/66. See WHCF, OF Ervin Duggan, Box 4, Folder 1966 Task Force on Education, JL, for handwritten notes dated 12/10/66 for a meeting of the same date.

[61]1967 Program Outline for Education, Draft #3, 12/10/66, WHCF, OF James Gaither, Box 346, Folder Education, JL; Memo with attachment, Samuel Halperin to Cater et al., 1/12/67, WHCF, Ex Le/Ed Box 35, JL.

[62]See p. 35 of the Task Force Report, Task Force Collection, Box 13, Folder 1966 Interagency Task Force on Education, JL. Other factors which may have influenced the student aid program decision were stirrings in Congress for alternative approaches to student aid, including an educational opportunity bank and tax incentives. Files examined regarding the 1966 Task Force show that the Administration explored these alternatives while trying to correct problems in the guaranteed student loan program.

[63]Letter, Califano to William Friday, 11/1/66, WHCF, OF James Gaither, Box 314, Folder Task Force on Education 1966, JL. Congress delayed all action on the 1967 higher education proposals until 1968.

[64]How the Friday Task Force' agenda was developed can be traced through the following documents: Appendix on possible directives for the Friday Task Force, sent by Gaither to Cater on 9/12/66 for a meeting on 9/13/66 attached to Memo, Cater to Gaither, 9/12/66, WHCF, OF Douglass Cater, Box 19, Folder Correspondence Sept. 1966; Issues and Questions Which Might Be Considered by the Task Force on Education, sent by Howe to Gaither on 10/17/66, WHCF, OF Douglass Cater, Box 37, Folder Materials on Task Force on Education, all in JL.

[65]Howe's memo of 10/17/66 to Gaither states that Gaither's ideas were included in the 10/17/66 list of issues and questions Howe prepared.

[66]Notes of First Meeting of the President's Task Force on Education November 22, 1966, dated 12/1/66, WHCF, OF James Gaither, Box 351, Folder Task Force on Education 1966, JL.

[67]Memo, Califano to the President, 9/30/66, WHCF, Box 363, FG 600/Task Force/E, Folder Ex FG 600/Task Force/E, JL.

[68]Memo, Gaither to Califano, 12/6/66, WHCF, OF James Gaither, Box 351, Folder Task Force on Education 1966, JL.

[69]Ibid.

[70]Notes of First Meeting of President's Task Force on Education November 22, 1966, dated 12/1/66, WHCF, OF James Gaither, Box 351, Folder Task Force on Education 1966, JL.

[71]See WHCF, OF Douglass Cater, Box 37, Folder Material on Task Force on Education (2); of James Gaither, Box 351, Folder Task Force on Education 1966; OF James Gaither, Box 315, Folder Task Force on Education, all in JL.

[72]Memo, John Morse to Friday and Cannon, 12/15/66, WHCF, OF Douglass Cater, Box 37, Folder Material on Task Force on Education (2), JL.

[73]Notes on Second Meeting of the Task Force on Education January 13 & 14, 1967, WHCF, OF Douglass Cater, Box 37, Folder Material on Task Force on Education, JL.

[74]Task Force Meeting February 10 & 11, 1967, dated 2/28/67, WHCF, OF Douglass Cater, Folder Material on Task Force on Education (4), JL.

[75]Notes on Fourth Meeting of Task Force on Education March 17-18, dated 3/29/67, WHCF, OF Douglass Cater, Box 37, Folder Material on Task Force on Education (4), JL.

[76]Summary of Task Force on Education Report, draft dated 4/7/67, WHCF, OF James Gaither, Box 315, Folder Task Force on Education 1966, JL.

[77]Notes on the Meeting of the Task Force on Education April 14 & 15, 1967, WHCF, OF Douglass Cater, Box 37, Folder Material on Task Force on Education (6), JL.

[78]Letter, David Bell to the Task Force Members, 6/2/67, WHCF, OF Douglass Cater, Box 38, Folder 9, JL.

[79]Memo, Cannon to Members of the Task Force on Education, 6/8/67, WHCF, OF Douglass Cater, Box 38, Folder 8, JL.

[80]Memo, Gaither to Califano, 8/9/67, WHCF, OF James Gaither, Box 229, Folder Education-Financial Aid to Higher Education #2, JL.

[81]The April 7, 1967 draft of the Friday report noted that the Task Force was reserving judgment on aid to private universities until receipt of the Bowen study.

[82]"The Economics of the Major Private Universities. . . ." by William Bowen, pp. 9-11, WHCF, OF James Gaither, Box 314, Folder Task Force on Education 1966 (second folder), JL.

[83]Report of the Friday Task Force, Task Force Collection, Box 4, Folder 1966 Task Force on Education (Friday Task Force), JL.

[84]Memo, Howe to Cater, 7/6/67, WHCF, OF Douglass Cater, Box 20, Folder Misc. Correspondence July-Sept. 1967, JL.

[85]Memo, Cannon to Cater, 7/13/67, and Memo with attachments, Duggan to the President, 8/21/67, WHCF, Box 363, Ex FG 600 Task Forces, Folder FG 600/Task Force/E, JL.

[86]Memo, Gaither to Califano, 8/9/67, Box 229, Folder Education-Financial Aid to Higher Education #2, and Memo, Gaither to Califano, 9/15/67, WHCF, OF James Gaither, Box 351, Folder Task Force on Education 1966, both in JL.

[87]Memo, Califano to Schultze, 8/11/67, WHCF, Box 363, Ex FG 600 Task Forces, Folder FG 600/Task Force/E, and Memo, Califano to Gardner, 8/11/67, WHCF, Box 361, Ex FG 600, Folder Ex FG 600, both in JL.

[88]Memo, Fred Bohen to Califano, 8/28/67, WHCF, OF James Gaither, Box 189, Folder 1967-68 Task Force on Education, JL.

[89]Memo, Gaither and Bohen to Califano, 8/14/67, WHCF, OF James Gaither, Box 189, Folder 1967-68 Task Force on Education, JL.

[90]Handwritten notes from 9/13/67 meeting of the 1967 Interagency Task Force, WHCF, OF James Gaither, Box 189, Folder 1967-68 Task Force on Education, JL.

[91]See working papers and pricing charts for Interagency review of Friday and other proposals in WHCF, of James Gaither, Box 190, Folder Task Force on Education 1967-68; Materials for Members of the 1968 Task Force on Education, 10/9/67, WHCF, CF Box 31, Oversize Attachments; Report of the 1967 Interagency Task Force on Education, 10/23/67, Task Force Collection, Box 21, Folder 1967 Interagency Task Force on Education, all in JL.

[92]Memo, Howe to Califano, 10/23/67, Task Force Collection, Box 21, Folder 1967 Interagency Task Force on Education, JL.

[93]Memo, Califano to the President, 11/1/67, WHCF, Ex Ed, Box 4, Folder Ed 8/25/67-11/17/67, JL.

[94]Memo, William Gorham to Gardner, 11/13/67, WHCF, Ex Ed, Box 4, Folder Ed 8/25/67-11/17/67, JL.

[95]Copy of Gorham's 11/13/67 memo sent to Gaither on 11/15/67, WHCF, OF James Gaither, Box 229, Folder Education-Financial Aid to Higher Education #2, JL.

[96]While discussion of the Task Force proposals continued well into December, decisions on most of the higher education proposals were made at the 11/8/67 meeting of the Task Force and White House aides. See Task Force on Education Meeting, November 8, 1967, WHCF, OF James Gaither, Box 189, Folder 1967-68 Task Force on Education, JL.

[97]Memo, Califano to William Carey, 11/10/67, WHCF, OF James Gaither, Box 189, Folder 1967-68 Task Force on Education, JL.

[98]Memo with attachments, Howe to Califano, 12/5/67, WHCF, OF James Gaither, Box 231, Folder Strategy for Federal Aid to Higher Education, JL.

[99]Memo with attachments, Howe to Califano, 12/7/67, WHCF, OF James Gaither, Box 227, Folder Gaither: Higher Education, JL.

[100]Memo with attachments, Califano to Gardner, 12/11/67, WHCF, CF Box 30, Folder FG 165 DHEW, JL.

[101]Agenda for 12/20/67 meeting attached to Memo, Gaither to Califano, 12/20/67, WHCF, OF James Gaither, Box 189, Folder 1967-68 Task Force on Education, JL.

[102]Memo, Howe to Califano, 12/21/67, WHCF, OF James Gaither, Box 231, Folder Strategy for Federal Aid to Higher Education, JL.

[103]See pp. 25-33, "Priorities and Recommendations" of the Rivlin Report, WHCF, OF James Gaither, Box 227, Folder Gaither: Higher Education, JL.

References

Anderson, P. O. (1968). **The Presidents' men.** New York: Doubleday.

Flash, E. S. (1965). **Economic advice and Presidential leadership: The Council of Economic Advisers.** New York: Columbia University Press.

Gladieux, L., & Wolanin, T. (1976). **Congress and the colleges.** Lexington, MA: Lexington Books.

Hamby, A. (1971). **Beyond the New Deal: Harry S Truman and American liberalism.** New York: Columbia University Press.

Hartmann, S. M. (1971). *Truman and the 80th Congress*. Columbia, MO: University of Missouri Press.

Hawkinson, R. E. (1977). *Presidential policy formulation: Lyndon Johnson and the 89th Congress*. Unpublished doctoral dissertation, University of Chicago.

Henry, D. D. (1975). *Challenges past challenges present*. San Francisco: Jossey-Bass.

Thomas, N. C. (1975). *Education in national politics*. New York: David McKay.

Thomas, N. C., & Wolman, H. (1969). The Presidency and policy formulation: The task force device. *Public Administration Review, 29*, 459-471.

Sorensen, T. (1965). *Kennedy*. New York: Harper & Row.

Sundquist, J. (1968). *Politics and policy: The Eisenhower, Kennedy, and Johnson years*. Washington, DC: Brookings Institution.

This article is condensed from a dissertation now in progress at the University of Virginia's Center for the Study of Higher Education. The author wishes to thank The Lyndon Baines Johnson Foundation and the University of Virginia School of Education for their financial support of this study.

Overview of the Unrest Era

Alexander W. Astin, Helen S. Astin, Alan E Bayer, Ann S. Bisconti

Student activism and campus unrest are nothing new in this country. Almost since their founding, American colleges and universities have gone through periods of turmoil and disruption. During the nineteenth century, discontent usually focused on such issues as poor food, inadequate housing, and excessively strict parietal rules; thus it was generally apolitical and parochial (Scranton Commission, 1970, pp. 21–22). In the early years of this century, radical and liberal student groups—usually affiliated with and dominated by adult political organizations and reflecting trends in the larger society—began to appear on college campuses. The Intercollegiate Socialist Society (ISS), founded in 1905, drew most of its members from higher education institutions on the eastern seaboard; it opposed rearmament and United States involvement in World War I and supported free speech on campus, immigration, and the World Court. The Young People's Socialist League (YPSL), organized in 1907, was closely connected with the Socialist Party and worked for the election of its candidates. The Student Christian Volunteer Movement (SCVM), which included the YMCA and YWCA, at first concentrated on foreign missionary work but later took up such domestic causes as women's rights. All these groups were primarily educational rather than activist: they invited controversial speakers to campus, distributed literature, and carried out other projects well within the scope of peaceful and nondisruptive dissent. Nevertheless, World War I diverted their energies, and the Red scare that followed the war further curbed their activities (Altbach and Peterson, 1971, p. 3).

The 1920s saw renewed student activism, grounded partly in rebellion against the conventions of society and partly in criticism of the university itself. It was accused of being too big and bureaucratic and of ignoring and alienating students—charges that again became familiar during the 1960s. Many of the groups active during this period—the National Student Federation of America, the Student League for Industrial Democracy (SLID, which in 1959 changed its name to Students for a Democratic Society), and SCVM—were pacifist; they supported disarmament and protested American military incursions into Mexico and Nicaragua. The antiwar theme persisted into the 1930s, giving rise to "the first mass student movement in American history" (Altbach and Peterson, 1971, p. 6). This movement drew most of its support from metropolitan campuses, but it involved large proportions of students (more, perhaps, than the movement of the 1960s, although a much smaller proportion of young people attended college in the earlier decade, of course).

The outbreak of World War II put an abrupt end to the radical student movement. Indeed, even before the attack on Pearl Harbor, the political left, including the Communist party, was rent by internal dissensions that vitiated its strength. Following that war, efforts to organize students on a national scale were unsuccessful. Returning veterans were more concerned with taking up their studies and making good in the working world than with pursuing political goals. Moreover, the cold war and the atmosphere of the McCarthy era frustrated the attempts of the radical left—and even of liberals—to muster widespread student support. There was some faint interest on campus in such internationalist movements as the United World Federalists, some concern over civil rights (particularly after the 1954 Supreme Court decision on school desegration), some worry about the threat of nuclear war, but the college students of the 1950s deserved the appellation "the silent generation" and the characterization "apathetic." The forties and fifties were atypical, however; radicalism and activism among students have deep historical roots. What distinguishes the past decade from earlier periods is that recent campus unrest has been student-initiated and student-centered, it has involved large numbers (if not necessarily larger proportions) of students, and it has been the subject of intensive scrutiny and widespread publicity.

Turning Points

What was it, during the early 1960s, that roused college students from their apathy? Why was the silent generation succeeded by a generation of students not merely vocal but even vociferous? While a number of underlying causes—political, economic, social, and psychological—have been proposed by many writers and theorists, our concern here is with the more immediate situational causes of extensive and dramatic campus unrest. This unrest was presaged by a number of events and undercurrents in the years immediately preceding the initial Berkeley protests. Three major issues predominated.

Early Stirrings, 1960-1964. The first—and undoubtedly the most important—issue was civil rights. In February 1960, four black students staged a sit-in at a segregated lunch counter in Greensboro, North Carolina. Their act set the pattern of nonviolent resistance that was to characterize the early stages of the civil rights movement. Soon many white students were traveling to the South to work with such organizations as the Student Nonviolent Coordinating Committee (SNCC) in freedom marches and voter registration drives. In the North, students circulated petitions, collected money, and picketed chain stores whose southern branches discriminated against blacks. Most students, whether activists or not, felt a strong sense of identity and sympathy with the cause.

The second major issue during this period was atmospheric nuclear testing. Antiwar sentiment is a recurrent theme in our history, and its manifestation in the ban-the-bomb movement of the early 1960s represents a thread of historical continuity in the student movement. These demonstrations generally ceased when atmospheric testing was ended in 1963.

The third issue that sparked student activism was the witch-hunting of the House Un-American Activities Committee (HUAC). The passive, and even craven, response of many intellectuals and academicians in the heyday of Wisconsin Senator Joseph McCarthy was changing to anger, resistance, and a reawakened concern for free speech, always a favorite campus issue. In the summer of 1960, HUAC arrived in the San Francisco Bay Area to seek out subversives, dupes, and fellow travelers. It was there confronted by loud and antagonistic crowds, among whom were students from the University of California at Berkeley and San Francisco State College. The results were the forcible removal, and subsequent arrest, of large numbers of demonstrators; the dissemination of a HUAC-sponsored film called *Operation Abolition*, which alleged that the demonstrations were Communist-inspired and that the demonstrators initiated a violent confrontation by leaping over barricades and attacking the police (the latter charge was disproved in the only case that actually came to trial); and the creation, on the Berkeley campus, of a high level of political awareness and commitment, a suitable atmosphere for the first major outbreak of campus unrest in the 1960s.

Flare-up at Berkeley, Fall 1964. The incident that touched off major unrest on the Berkeley campus was an announcement by the administration on September 16, 1964, that off-campus political groups could no longer make use of a previously "open" area—a narrow strip of university property—to hand out "advocative" literature, collect money, and solicit membership. Groups at every point on the political spectrum immediately reacted to this new stricture (actually, the revival of an old and long-unenforced rule) by forming a united front and requesting that the area be kept open. They offered to make a survey of the traffic flow (since the administration maintained that the tables manned by these off-campus groups impeded pedestrians coming to and from campus); they agreed not to solicit funds; and they volunteered to police the area to see that no group violated university regulations about posters. The administration quickly rejected the request to keep the area open. Throughout the rest of the month, students demonstrated by holding all-night vigils, staging marches, picketing the chancellor, and using other nondisruptive tactics to protest the decision. In addition, five students deliberately violated the new rules, three others supported this act of civil disobedience, and all eight were put on indefinite suspension. At this point, the Free Speech Movement (FSM) was born, with Mario Savio—one of the eight suspended students—as its spokesman.

On October 1, the most attention-getting incident in the protest took place. A nonstudent was arrested for soliciting funds for the Congress of Racial Equality (CORE), and the police car that arrived to carry him off was surrounded by hundreds of students. It remained immobilized for thirty-two hours while students gave speeches to the crowd, often climbing on the car and using it as a stage. (Eventually, students collected money to pay for damage done to the police car during this period.) October, November, and December saw continued chaos: committees were formed that issued lists of usually unheeded recommendations, the administration alternately granted concessions and imposed penalties, and students engaged in acts of protest that became more and more unruly and uncivil. A general faculty-student strike took place in December. The administration building was occupied in a sit-in, and mass arrests were made. The chancellor took a leave of absence and was later replaced. President Kerr and the acting chancellor announced, then retracted, resignations, though Kerr did indeed leave the fol-

lowing year. Mario Savio was suspended, jailed for 120 days by civil authorities, and later refused readmission to the university.

Although it is difficult to generalize out of this welter of events, certain significant tendencies emerge. First, as has been pointed out by a number of writers, the FSM was a kind of spin-off from the civil rights movement. Many Berkeley students had been involved in action groups in the South. Savio, who had worked in the Mississippi Summer Project of 1964, remarked: "The same rights are at stake in both places—the right to participate as citizens in a democratic society and the right to due process of law" (quoted by Wallerstein and Starr, 1971, p. xiii). Rightly or wrongly, many students viewed the administration decision of September 16 as directed primarily against civil rights groups. The tactic they used to counter this move by the university was the tactic employed in the South, namely civil disobedience. Moreover, they were convinced of the righteousness of their cause and thus of the repressiveness of the university.

The situation was difficult for the administration to handle because, in addition to campus issues, it involved off-campus issues over which the university had no control. The protesters' interference with the rights of others (for example, their occupation of the administration building and their "capture" of the police car) led the administration to call in the civil police, which bolstered the radicals' charge that the university was repressive and drew in large numbers of liberal or politically neutral students who might not otherwise have joined the protest.

The FSM actually accomplished very little institutional change. As Nathan Glazer said, four years later, "the world does look very different, and the FSM looks like a prophetic turning point"; but the University of California looks very much the same"; Glazer infers from this paradox that "it is rather easier to change the world than to change the university" (1970, p. 193).

The unrest at Berkeley was exploited to the fullest by the mass media—usually with the happy consent of the protesters—and probably the extensive coverage given to the FSM, particularly to the more flamboyant and disorderly incidents, helped to account for the next stage of the student movement.

Spread of the Movement, 1964–1968. It is a gross over-simplification to attribute the spread of the student movement entirely to the press and television, however. For one thing, student activists at campuses across the nation have a way of keeping in touch with one another without the help of the mass media, and this was particularly true when Students for a Democratic Society (SDS) expanded into a powerful national organization. For another, public reaction against campus unrest, repressive legislation (or the threat of it) by the federal and some state governments, and punitive civil and institutional measures taken against protesters all served to provoke students into greater rebellion. What is most important, the drift of events in the world outside the walls of academe created concern among students and, in many cases, led to disillusionment with society as a whole and with the American political and social system in particular, thus changing the tone of student protest.

In 1964 and 1965—the years when Congress passed two bills that actualized some of the goals of the civil rights movement—the Democratic National Convention refused to seat the Mississippi Freedom Democratic delegation, Malcolm X was assassinated, and the Watts riots erupted. In 1966, when Stokely Carmichael expelled the whites who had worked with SNCC in earlier years, and Huey Newton and Bobby Seale formed the Black Panther Party, the movement turned sharply from emphasis on integration and equality of opportunity to emphasis on black separatism, black pride, and black power. During these years, too, the treatment of other minority groups—Chicanos, Puerto Ricans, and Native Americans—came to be viewed by both radicals and liberals as another harsh example of the inequities permeating American society.

The bombing of North Vietnam in 1965 sparked further anger among students. O'Brien (1971) saw protest over the war as falling into two distinct periods. The first, from February 1965 to the middle of 1967, was characterized by traditional nondisruptive tactics, including teach-ins (which originated at the University of Michigan), circulation of petitions, and mass demonstrations. During this period, support of the antiwar movement increased dramatically, and the April 1967 mobilizations in New York and San Francisco attracted three hundred thousand to four hundred thousand demonstrators. Then, beginning about mid-1967, the issues expanded to the selective service system and to university involvement—through government defense contracts and military and industrial recruiters on campus—in the war. Spontaneous pro-

tests broke out on campuses around the nation. Milder forms of dissent gave way to illegal and obstructive actions, such as interference with military-industrial recruiting and burning draft cards. The moral tone of the antiwar movement changed significantly. As the Scranton Commission (1970, p. 31) put it: "From having been a 'mistake,' the war was soon interpreted by radical students as a logical outcome of the American political system. . . . The university, too, came to be seen as part of 'the system,' and therefore it became a target—as opposed as an accidental arena—of antiwar protest."

At the same time, a new counterculture had grown up. The hippies and flower children, "youthful dropouts from middle-class environments" (O'Brien, 1971, p. 21), were themselves largely apolitical, but their existence—and the marked difference between their life-style and conventional American norms—provided a supportive base for student radicals and emphasized their antagonism to the establishment.

Between 1964 and 1968, then, campus unrest increased. At first centered in large, prestigious, highly selective institutions, it gradually diffused to colleges and universities of all types. At the same time, the scope of campus unrest enlarged to cover broad social problems rather than single-campus issues, and its direction changed. Wallerstein and Starr maintained that, after the events of 1965, the movement "began to turn against liberalism and those who embodied it—the government, the Democratic Party, and eventually college professors" (1971, p. xiii). Young people had come to distrust the political system. Many had grown discouraged about the possibility of working rationally and nonviolently to bring about necessary change, a feeling later reinforced by the assassinations of Martin Luther King, Jr., and Robert Kennedy, the riots at the 1968 Democratic Convention in Chicago, and the failure of the Eugene McCarthy forces. Finally, some had come to view the university itself as an evil instrument of the system. Thus, the stage was set for Columbia.

University as Enemy: Columbia, Spring 1968. Campus unrest at Columbia University was evident as early as spring 1965, when about two hundred students participated in an antiwar protest; such demonstrations continued in 1966 and 1967, and criticism became more sharply directed at the university itself, because of its connection with the Institute for Defense Analysis (IDA), a consortium of higher education institutions that carried out research for the Department of Defense. In February 1968, ground was broken for the construction of a new gymnasium, a project that called for the displacement of black residents of the ghetto area surrounding Columbia. At that time, the campus remained quiet, though a few neighborhood groups protested. It was not until April 23 that unrest broke out on campus. A group of black students occupied Hamilton Hall (where the administration offices of the college are located), SDS quickly joined the demonstration, and a total of five buildings were occupied and held until a week later, when city police were summoned to remove the demonstrators by force. In the ensuing melee, 707 persons were arrested, and 148 were injured. During that week, classes were suspended, and the campus remained uneasy throughout the remainder of the academic year. Late in May, white students again occupied Hamilton Hall, this time in response to the suspension of SDS leaders. The police were once more called in, and, although the buildings were cleared quickly, there was subsequent violence between students and police, with injuries on both sides. According to the Scranton Commission, the underlying issues of the protest "were Columbia's relations with the surrounding black community and [its] links with American foreign policy" (1970, p. 36).

The protest at Columbia succeeded in its immediate aims: in June the IDA severed its relations with Columbia, and in February 1969 the administration announced that plans for the new gym would be suspended indefinitely. What is more important, SDS succeeded in its aim of "radicalizing" the students—an intention allegedly announced by SDS leader Mark Rudd as early as October 1967. Daniel Bell (1968, p. 80) summarized the situation as follows: "The significance . . . was not in the number of demonstrators involved—in the first three days there were not more than two hundred fifty people in the buildings, about fifty of whom were outsiders—but in the double nature of the actions: tactically, the student actions had 'leaped' five years, by adopting the latest methods of these several civil rights and peace movements, which had passed, in 'five hot summers,' from protest to confrontation to resistance and to outright obstruction; even more startling, the university as a general institution, itself, was now regarded as the enemy, the target for disruption."

The protest at Columbia had far-reaching consequences on the course of campus unrest. During the occupation of Low Library, protesters had entered President Kirk's office and ransacked his files; later, during the second occupation of Hamilton Hall, they burned the notes of a history professor. Such actions set a pattern of property destruction and vandalism; in subsequent protests on other campuses, similar acts were committed, often at the ROTC building. Violence—on the part of protesters, counterprotesters, and police—became almost commonplace. Terroristic acts—including bomb threats, planting of bombs, and attempts to intimidate administrators and unsympathetic faculty members—also grew more frequent. Ultimately, the events at Columbia resulted in fierce public and legislative reaction against campus unrest. "By mid-1970, over thirty states had enacted a total of nearly eighty laws dealing with campus unrest," most of them punitive (Scranton Commission, 1970, p. 40).

Another significant feature at Columbia was the SDS "cooptation" (to borrow one of its favorite terms) of the protest, which had been initiated by black students. During this period and shortly thereafter, SDS was at the height of its power. By the end of spring 1969, it drew support from an estimated "fifty to seventy-five thousand students at least loosely affiliated with its hundreds of campus chapters" (O'Brien, 1971, p. 23). Then, at its June convention, members of the organization quarreled over ideology and tactics and finally split into a number of factions, the most notable being the Weathermen, a group whose extremism was repudiated by most student activists and whose deeds of terrorism and violence quickly drove it underground. Though SDS retains an organizational structure and even held a convention in 1972, it is at present moribund.

Black Militancy: Cornell, Spring 1969. Beginning about 1965, many northern colleges and universities—particularly the more prestigious—initiated active recruitment programs to enroll larger proportions of blacks, many of whom came from disadvantaged family and educational backgrounds. All too often, however, these institutions failed to plan adequately for this abrupt influx of "atypical" students, who consequently felt isolated on predominantly white campuses, neglected by the administration, and

534

South, they now found themselves excluded and even reviled as interfering liberal white pigs. Many continued to give support to black demands—and, in the case of SDS, to take over protests initiated by blacks—but they suffered guilt feelings and developed an almost masochistic attitude, castigating themselves for whatever part they might have played in furthering racism while refusing to drop out of the black movement.

As early as the summer of 1966, a powerful Black Student Union (BSU) was organized at San Francisco State College, and, as a result of its efforts, a black arts and culture series was established within the framework of the experimental college at that institution. But the addition of this program was considered insufficient, and demands for the establishment of a black studies program within the regular college continued. By the end of the 1967–1968 academic year, the administration had accepted the need for such a program and appointed a special coordinator, Nathan Hare, an outspoken militant whose ideas conflicted sharply with the traditional standards of the academic community. Hare proposed drastic changes in the criteria for appointing faculty members to the program and stressed that black students should be given academic credit for field work in the black community (Bunzel, 1969).

Signs of growing militancy among black students were also evident. In November 1967, a group of blacks allegedly broke into the offices of the campus newspaper and beat up the student editor. On December 6, members of the BSU occupied the administration building; police were called in, and additional violence resulted. Indeed, the troubles at San Francisco State continued through 1969, the issues expanded to cover the demands of another group (the Third World Liberation Front), and a number of secondary issues emerged—the dismissal of a faculty member who had participated in the December takeover of the administration building, police brutality, institutional sanctions against protest participants, and a ban on all demonstrations. Other campuses around the nation experienced similar explosions. In the spring of 1968, for example, Northwestern University was the scene of turmoil that had its roots in black militancy.

It was, however, the unrest at Cornell University in the spring of 1969 that brought home most strongly to the American public the element of black militancy in campus protest. Cornell

rejected by faculty members and other students. Their frequent lack of adequate preparation in high school and their relatively poor academic records and test scores—coupled with failure on the part of the institution to provide remedial courses, special programs, tutoring, and counseling—led them to feel depression, resentment, and open hostility. These feelings expressed themselves in charges of "institutional racism" and "curricular irrelevance."

As noted, whites were no longer welcomed by such organizations as SNCC. Similarly, black students on many northern campuses, impelled by a drive for separatism, presented the administration with lists of nonnegotiable demands for black studies programs, black cultural facilities, special admissions for black students, and more black faculty and staff members.

This change in mood and direction created schisms within the black community itself. For example, writing in Newsweek (February 10, 1969), Roy Wilkins, executive director of the NAACP, argued against this separatist tendency on the part of some blacks, contending that, "in demanding a black Jim Crow studies building within a campus and exclusively black dormitories or wings of dormitories, they are opening the door to a dungeon" (quoted by Wallerstein and Starr, 1971, p. 318). On the other side, Georgia legislator Julian Bond, pointing to the "continuing failure of the white minority of peoples in the world to share power and wealth with the nonwhite majority," maintained that black demands for separate facilities were reasonable (Wallerstein and Starr, 1971, pp. 311–319). Black students themselves were divided in their feelings; many, interested primarily in the upward mobility offered by a college education, objected to being pressured into pursuing a course that might alienate them from white society but at the same time feared being called "Toms."

Certain northern institutions that had long prided themselves on being in the vanguard of the fight against racial discrimination were suddenly faced with the allegation that they themselves were prime purveyors of a deep-rooted racism in American society. White student activists were caught in an even greater dilemma. Though in large part they owed the very existence of their organizations to the civil rights movement, though they felt a strong identification with blacks and a deep conviction about the rightness of the cause, though they had often been the victims of racist persecution in the

was a hotbed of racial discontent. In 1963, President James Perkins had set up the Cornell Commission on Special Educational Projects, designed to recruit and provide scholarship aid to blacks. Unfortunately, Perkins made this decision without consulting faculty members and students. Consequently, the blacks enrolled under the program found themselves outside the mainstream of campus life, which was heavily dominated by fraternities and sororities. Because the university was far from large cities and the atmosphere of Ithaca was inhospitable, the black students were physically and psychologically isolated and could find a sense of community only among themselves. To add to the tension, a visiting professor of economics made a supposedly racist remark on the day of Martin Luther King's assassination; members of the Afro-American Society (AAS) demanded that he be forced to apologize, reprimanded, and dismissed; the administration investigated the matter (thus provoking the ire of the faculty, who felt their academic freedom threatened) but took no action against the professor in question (thus intensifying the frustration and resentment of the blacks).

Though plans were made in September 1968 for a black studies program, "the first to be established by a major American university" (Cohen, 1970, pp. 5-6), the newly elected president of the AAS considered that the administration was moving too slowly and presented a nine-point ultimatum demanding separate facilities. This was rejected by the university, and in response the blacks staged demonstrations that involved property disruption and the manhandling of university officials. Six activists were ordered to appear before the Cornell Student-Faculty Board on Student Conduct; the all-white composition of this judicial body exacerbated the hostility of the blacks. The citation of these students "was the turning-point in black-white relations at Cornell. For almost two months, since the militant demands for an autonomous college of Afro-American studies, interracial communications had almost exclusively taken the form of threats and insults" (Cohen, 1970, p. 8).

A crisis erupted on April 18, 1969, when a cross was burned in front of a black women's cooperative; the residents called on the administration for protection, and a single campus policeman was assigned to patrol the area. At six o'clock the next morning, black students took over Willard Straight Hall, the student union, and later that day issued a statement calling for dismissal of the charges

against the cited students, separate housing facilities for blacks, and a thorough investigation of the cross-burning and of what they felt to be inadequate handling of the situation by campus police. Meanwhile, someone telephoned into the student union building to say that it was going to be bombed and that armed fraternity men were on their way to expel the blacks by force. On the strength of these threats, the occupiers had guns and other weapons brought in to them by supporters outside.

The matter was temporarily settled by negotiations between AAS leaders and the administration. Shortly after four o'clock on Sunday afternoon, the blacks left Willard Straight Hall. "The sight of students wearing bandoliers and waving rifles and shotguns dramatically demonstrated that the failure to cope with student demands might result in the loss of life and the collapse of a university community" (Cohen, 1970, p. 1).

The unrest at Cornell was by no means at an end, and the issues became even more complicated, broadening to include conflict between black students (who demanded that faculty members exhibiting racist attitudes be fired) and the faculty (who charged that their academic freedom was being violated); demands by black and white students alike for more "participatory democracy" in all aspects of institutional governance; and condemnation by all sides of administrative high-handedness in making decisions and carrying out actions without consulting other members of the academic community. But it was the widely publicized photograph of the armed blacks that stamped the deepest impress on the public mind.

Reaction and Attention. As the incidence and intensity of protest at the nation's colleges and universities grew, as disruption and violence became more typical, as demonstrators became more inflammatory and radical in their criticism of American society, public alarm and hostility increased, fanned by often sensational accounts in the mass media. No doubt the visual impact of television also helped to stir anxieties. Officials viewed protests with alarm, students and faculty members gave firsthand accounts of protest events at particular campuses, pundits of varying degrees of expertise sought to analyze the events and place them in historical context. No longer was it possible to dismiss this phenomenon as an offshoot of youthful high spirits or to blame it on a handful of wild-eyed radicals or black malcontents. Serious attention had to be paid to

536

vasion of Cambodia. On May 4, the killings at Kent State University (Ohio) took place, followed ten days later by the killings at Jackson State College (Mississippi). The President's Commission on Campus Unrest (Scranton Commission) was established in June 1970 in direct response to these incidents. According to its report (Scranton Commission, 1970, pp. 17–18), issued in September, "During the six days after the president's announcement of the Cambodian incursion, but prior to the deaths at Kent State, some twenty new student strikes had begun each day. During the four days that followed the Kent killings, there were a hundred or more strikes each day. A student strike center located at Brandeis University reported that, by the tenth of May, 448 campuses were either still affected by some sort of strike or completely closed down."

The commission found (1970, p. 234) that "compared with other American universities of its size, Kent State had enjoyed relative tranquillity prior to May 1970, and its student body had generally been conservative or apolitical." There had been some protest activity in the fall of 1968 and the spring of 1969—and in both cases, SDS was involved—but neither protest was directly related to the events of May 1–4, nor is there any evidence that SDS or any other group of "agitators" was behind these events. President Nixon's announcement on Thursday was followed by an orderly antiwar rally on Friday and then by a weekend of restlessness, "trashing," and property destruction, climaxed by complete incineration of the ROTC building on Saturday. The mayor proclaimed a state of civil emergency, the governor backed him by issuing a number of hard-line statements, and the National Guard was called in on Sunday. The students, in the meantime, were confused by the imposition of ambiguous curfew regulations. In addition, both the authorities and the students were uncertain about the permissibility of peaceful assemblies in protest of the United States invasion of Cambodia and of the National Guard "invasion" of Kent State (as many students perceived it).

What happened shortly after noon on Monday, May 4 can be attributed in part to overreaction by public officials, in part to the lack of a clear direction and position by the university administration, and in part to growing antagonism between National Guardsmen and students. (Many guardsmen later reported that they

student protest; consideration had to be given to the possibility that charges made against the university might have some validity.

In June 1969, the board of directors of the American Council on Education created the Special Committee on Campus Tensions (known as the Linowitz Committee). Taking as its text an earlier ACE statement that "if colleges and universities will not govern themselves, they will be governed by others," the committee sought to describe the crisis, to analyze the complaints and desires of various collegiate constituents (students, faculty, administrators, trustees), and to make practical recommendations about what colleges and universities could do to restore order. At the same time, it recognized that "the higher education community cannot help to solve all the problems that create campus tensions. It cannot alone stop war, eliminate poverty, rebuild cities, or expunge racism" (Nichols, 1970, p. 36). As the Linowitz Committee was setting about its work, the administration in Washington predicted that there would be fewer disorders in the 1969–1970 academic year (Newsweek, September 1, 1969, p. 12). Indeed, judged solely by reports in the mass media, the fall semester was relatively calm. This "cooling down" of the campuses was more apparent than real, however, as later studies showed (for example, Bayer and Astin, 1971). Much of the protest was directed at agencies or events beyond the control of the institution rather than against institutional policies. Of particular note are the widespread observance of Earth Day (at almost two-thirds of United States institutions) and the less solid but still impressive support of the October, November, and December antiwar moratoria (discussed in detail later in this chapter). It seems obvious that students were still very much concerned not just with local campus issues but also with larger social issues—ecology and environmental pollution being relatively new themes—and, in particular, that they were still opposed to the American military presence in Southeast Asia.

Cambodia, Kent State, April–August 1970. The events of May 1970 give ample evidence of the depth of student concern and of the prematurity of predictions that "the worst of the disruption lies behind . . . or is a seasonal phenomenon" (Nichols, 1970, p. 6). On April 30, the Nixon administration announced the in-

feared for their own safety, having been the target not only of jeers and obscenities but also of stones and other missiles; many students who had previously been neutral or indifferent became resentful at having an "army" on the campus that ordered them around.) Accounts differ on the exact events that precipitated the shooting, no sniper seems to have been at work, and it is doubtful that an official order to fire was given. The outcome, however, was clear enough: at least sixty-one shots were fired, leaving four students dead, nine wounded, and a nation in shock.

The events at Jackson State College ten days later were no less shocking. Indeed, it is arguable that, because the county grand jury that later investigated the incident made every effort to whitewash the city police and highway patrolmen involved in the shootings, Jackson State represents an even greater tragedy in American life than does Kent State, and one that has deeper roots than anti-Vietnam sentiment. The Scranton Commission (1970, p. 444) noted: "Jackson State is a black school situated in a white-dominated state. This is a starting point for analyzing the causes of the student disorders of May 13 and 14, 1970. The stark fact underlying all other causes of student unrest at Jackson State is the historic pattern of racism that substantially affects daily life in Mississippi." The college had been the scene of long-standing tensions: between black students and "corner boys" (black youths who were not students but who lived in the surrounding neighborhood) and between blacks and passing white motorists (the main road connecting downtown Jackson and the white residential areas runs past the college). Rock-throwing incidents were common on the part of blacks; and harassment of blacks was common on the part of city police.

The unrest at Jackson State had no direct connection with Cambodia or with Kent State, though there had been a peaceful anti-Vietnam protest on May 7. Indeed, it is not known precisely what triggered the situation on the evening of May 13, when rock throwing began, large crowds of students gathered to jeer at law enforcement officers, two trash trailers were set afire, an attempt was made to burn down the ROTC building, and rumors abounded. On the evening of May 14, three separate law enforcement groups—each with its own perception of the situation and its own training and tactics—were on the campus: the highway patrol, the city police, and the National Guard. Soon the arena of action shifted to the area outside Alexander Hall, a women's dormitory.

As at Kent State, accounts vary on the factors that precipitated the fusillade of at least one hundred fifty rounds that was fired at both the inside and the outside of the dormitory, penetrating every floor and resulting in the death of two persons and the wounding of twelve others, all black. The size of the crowd, the threat it posed, and the possible presence of a sniper on the third floor are all in dispute, but it is evident that the law enforcement officers acted without proper precaution. Moreover, their attitude was, according to newsmen on the scene, one of levity about the shooting and of contempt for blacks. Though the killings at Jackson State did not receive the same amount of attention from the media and did not have the same shock effect on the national sensibilities as those at Kent State, they were part of a pattern that turned students—many of them innocent bystanders—into the victims of the establishment, as represented by the police and the National Guard.

That pattern suffered a reversal later that summer, when a University of Wisconsin building that housed the Army Mathematics Research Center—proclaimed by radicals to be instrumental in doing research that "has killed literally thousands of innocent people" (quoted in *Newsweek*, September 7, 1970, p. 33)—was wrecked by a bomb. Not only were the computer demolished, the physics and astronomy departments seriously damaged, and the scholarly work of both professors and graduate students destroyed, but also four persons were injured and one was killed. Though bombings and bomb threats were not new to American campuses, the incident at Madison was the most extreme act of terrorism yet carried out, and, again, the one that received the most coverage from the news media. Kenneth Keniston marks the Madison disaster as a turning point, in that it brought student activists to the realization that violence and the murder of innocents were not limited to the military-industrial establishment and its academic "lackeys"; protesters themselves were capable of perpetrating outrages. Students' reactions went beyond depression and exhaustion; the mood became one of shame and embarrassment. Keniston (1971, p. 208) commented: "The emergence of violence within the movement has in turn pushed its members to reexamine their earlier self-justifying assumption that destructiveness characterized their adversaries but not themselves." It was this reexamination, according to Keniston, that accounted for the apparent calm—or, to use Kingman Brewster's phrase, "eerie tranquillity"—on campus during the 1970–1971 and 1971–1972 academic years.

Incidence

That campus unrest was on the rise from the late 1950s through the late 1960s is evidenced by Hodgkinson's fall 1968 survey (1970a, 1970b) of all presidents of higher education institutions (with a 46-percent response rate). Hodgkinson asked them to judge retrospectively whether or not they had experienced an increase in student protests during the preceding ten years. Thus, the survey extended from a period of calm on the nation's campuses (the 1957–1958 academic year) to a period of great unrest (the 1967–1968 academic year). Only 22 percent reported that no student protests had occurred at their institutions during the decade. Another 44 percent said there had been "no change," an ambiguous response that may mean, at least in some cases, no unrest. The remaining one-third reported a change in the incidence of unrest over the decade, with fewer than 2 percent of the presidents indicating a decrease rather than an increase.

Unfortunately, precise information of the prevalence of unrest at American institutions of higher education is simply not available for the years before 1968, though data from the Educational Testing Service (ETS) surveys for the 1964–1965 and 1967–1968 academic years provide a minimum estimate. These surveys did not cover two-year colleges, nor did they report the aggregate number or proportion of institutions experiencing protest. Rather, they reported in detail the incidence of protests about twenty-seven separate issues. For instance, in 1964–1965, the most prevalent issue was civil rights, with about two-fifths (38 percent) of all institutions in the survey reporting such protests. In 1967–1968, the most prevalent issue was Vietnam; again, 38 percent of the institutions surveyed reported antiwar protests. Peterson (1968a, pp. 31–32) notes that, between these two periods, not only did the absolute number of student

protesters grow, but also the number of baccalaureate-granting institutions that experienced protest on each of the listed issues generally increased.

In the 1968–1969 academic year, Gaddy (1970), surveying the national population of junior colleges, found that two-fifths (38 percent) had experienced one or more incidents of organized student protest, a figure identical to the minimal ETS estimates for universities and four-year colleges in the earlier years.

The incidence of campus unrest continued to rise after 1968–1969. According to the ACE survey of 1969–1970, fully 45 percent of the four-year colleges experienced at least one incident of war-related protest. Four-fifths (80 percent) of the four-year institutions, and two-thirds (67 percent) of all institutions, including junior colleges, had protest incidents over some issue. That academic year—in which Earth Day, the Vietnam moratoria, the Cambodian crisis, and the Kent State and Jackson State killings took place—undoubtedly marks the zenith of protest activity on American campuses to date.

The next two years did not see a sharp drop in protest incidence and a return to a state of calm. The ACE survey for 1970–1971 shows that over a thousand campuses—43 percent of higher education institutions—experienced at least one protest incident. Though no comparable data are available for the entire 1971–1972 academic year, an ACE survey for the week of April 17 to 24, 1972, indicates that more than one-fourth (27 percent) of the entire academic community of some 2500 institutions had experienced protest incidents. By comparison, in the highly publicized "crisis" period of May 1–10, 1970, 16 percent of the institutions experienced protest after the Cambodian invasion, and 24 percent after the deaths at Kent State.

In spite of continuing unrest, "newsworthy" incidents have been rare since Cambodia. In part, the decline of news coverage can be attributed to the diffusion of campus unrest to institutions previously unaffected by it—smaller, less selective, and therefore less prestigious institutions—which held less interest for the national news media. The ACE surveys revealed that 40 percent of the institutions experiencing severe unrest in 1968–1969 received press coverage; in contrast, only 10 percent of those experiencing severe

been damaged or destroyed at fewer than 2 percent of the colleges and universities.

Comparing specific modes of protest for the 1968–1969 and the 1970–1971 academic years, some acts (such as destruction of papers, occupation of buildings, and marches resulting in violence) declined at least slightly in frequency, one mode (burning of buildings) increased slightly, and other types of property destruction were as prevalent as they had been. Protests involving injury to persons were less common, as were those involving the interruption of school functions and general campus strikes or boycotts.

Institutions where severe protests took place were more likely to experience other forms of protest as well. Threats of physical violence and bomb scares, for example, occurred much more frequently at institutions that had severe protests than at other institutions. Nevertheless, at all institutions, most protest acts were mild, taking the form of presentation of demands or grievances to an established institutional body (27 percent in 1970–1971); staging of peaceful marches, picketing, or rallies (20 percent); and circulation of petitions (19 percent). Similarly, in April 1972, the most prevalent mode of protest over the renewed bombing of North Vietnam was the staging of peaceful marches or rallies (at 394 of the 685 institutions that had protests during that week); other common protest events were teach-ins and special discussion groups or seminars (126 institutions); silent vigils (99 institutions), and distributions of antiwar literature or petitions (55 institutions).

Issues. National estimates of the proportions of student protests focusing on specific issues are available for four academic years: the ETS surveys provide information on protests at baccalaureate-granting institutions (but not two-year colleges) for 1964–1965 and 1967–1968; the ACE surveys provide information on protests at all types of institutions for 1969–1970 and for 1970–1971. Although the population bases are not the same for the different years, and although the lists of issues varied slightly, the surveys are sufficiently similar to permit the identification of broad trends and changes in the issues of protest.

Clearly, the roots of the student movement do not lie primarily in antiwar sentiment; indeed, in no single year was United States involvement in Vietnam the target of protest at the majority

unrest in 1970–1971 were covered by the press. Of the 232 relatively unselective institutions (those whose students were only average or below average in academic ability) that experienced severe protest in 1970–1971, not one was mentioned in the national media. Of the 230 institutions in the high or high-intermediate selectivity range, fully forty-eight (21 percent) were the subject of reports in the news media. Although national data on the incidence of unrest since 1972 do not exist, it is clear that an era has ended.

Severity. No systematic statistical evidence on the modes, tactics, and severity of protest is available for the period before 1968. The press accounts during this period suggest that incidents of major disruption, property destruction, and personal violence were rare. In contrast, a casual reading of press accounts for the 1968–1969 academic year seems to indicate that many colleges and universities were coming apart at the seams and that higher education in general was on the brink of chaos. The ACE survey for that year, however, indicates that the mass media gave a badly distorted picture. Violence (defined by such acts as damaging or destroying buildings, furnishings, papers, records, and files and physically injuring persons) and disruption (defined by acts such as occupying buildings, holding college officials captive, interrupting classes, speeches, meetings, and other university functions, and holding general campus strikes or boycotts) were atypical modes of protest in 1968–1969. Only 6 percent of the institutions experienced any violent incidents; an additional 16 percent suffered some kind of disruptive incident.

According to the ACE survey for the "peak year" of 1969–1970, property damage and other physical violence occurred at an estimated 9 percent of American campuses. (No comparable figures are available for disruptive acts.) By 1970–1971, violence and disruption had declined—albeit only slightly—from the levels of the preceding two years: fewer than one in five of all institutions experienced either a violent or a disruptive protest. By 1971–1972, the frequency of extreme incidents was even slighter: the ACE survey of North Vietnam indicated that no institutions had completely closed down—in contrast to the situation following Cambodia and Kent State (Scranton Commission, 1970, p. 18)—and that property had

issues, taken together, have evoked more protests in each academic year under consideration.

Academic and student life—a category that includes student power (a voice in decision-making), services to students, and parietal rules—has provided a focal point for student unrest in recent years. The two ETS studies show that, in 1964–1965, dormitory regulations 1967–1968, the Vietnam issue had become dominant, but even then only 38 percent of the universities and four-year colleges had and food services were issues of protest at one-fourth to one-third of all four-year colleges; one-fifth of these institutions experienced protests about dress regulations. In the junior colleges during 1968–1969, "situations including food service, rules on dress and appearance, student publications, and student representation in policy-making were most subject to protest activity" (Gaddy, 1970, p. 4). Moreover, accounts in the *Chronicle of Higher Education* suggest that facilities, student life, and student power have continued to be recurrent themes of protest in the academic years since 1970.

The sharpest decline over the years occurred in protests about racial issues. Civil rights (in the off-campus, local area) was the most prevalent theme of protest (at 38 percent of all baccalaureate-granting institutions) in 1964–1965; in 1967–1968, the proportion had dropped to 29 percent. On the other hand, protests about alleged racial discrimination on the part of institutions (for example, in admissions) rose from 5 percent of baccalaureate-granting institutions in 1964–1965 to 18 percent in 1967–1968. In 1969–1970, only about one in six (16 percent) of all higher education institutions had a protest about a campus issue involving race; the Jackson State killings, which occurred that same year, elicited protests at only 2 percent of the institutions. In 1970–1971, only 8 percent of the campuses experienced protest about minority group issues, usually involving special programs and special admissions policies. Of the 110 protest incidents reported in the *Chronicle of Higher Education* for 1971–1972, only 5 percent were related to racial issues.

Settings

Campus unrest was at first concentrated in a relatively small number of institutions of a particular type. An early study by Peterson (1968b) showed that such institutions tended to be large, highly

of institutions experiencing unrest, although in 1967–1968 it was the target at a plurality (38 percent) of these institutions. According to the ETS study of 1964–1965, only one in five (21 percent) of baccalaureate-granting institutions had a protest incident about United States policies in Vietnam. Protests about civil rights, parietal rules, and food services were decidedly more common. By 1967–1968, the Vietnam issue had become dominant, but even then only 38 percent of the universities and four-year colleges had protests about this issue. Comparative data for junior college protests in the following academic year (Gaddy, 1970) indicate that, while some protest incident arose on 38 percent of junior college campuses, on only 13 percent was the Vietnam War the issue.

Even in the peak year of 1969–1970—when antiwar sentiment took the form of moratoria observances and when unrest broke out following the Cambodian invasion—protests about environmental pollution were more frequent than protests about any other single issue. Earth Day was observed at close to two-fifths (39 percent) of all institutions, more than those observing the October moratorium (32 percent), protesting war-related campus issues (11 percent), protesting general United States policy in Southeast Asia (25 percent), or protesting the Cambodian invasion (16 percent). A total of 44 percent of the campuses experienced protests resulting from the combination of Cambodia, Kent State, and Jackson State, and normal institutional activities ceased for at least a day at one-fifth (21 percent) of the institutions (Peterson and Bilorusky, 1971).

In 1970–1971, only one in five institutions had a protest about a war-related issue (United States military policy, selective service policy, or such on-campus issues as ROTC, military and industrial recruiting, and defense research). Slightly more common were protests about facilities and student life (at 22 percent of the institutions) and student power (at 27 percent). However, in April 1972, the renewed bombing of North Vietnam triggered campus unrest, primarily of a nondisruptive and legal nature, at approximately one-fourth (27 percent) of American institutions (Bayer and Astin, 1972). In short, although United States military policy (particularly in Southeast Asia) and war-related issues have been a steady source of grist to the activist mill, all other categories of

selective, private, and permissive in their policies. Moreover, they attracted "protest-prone" students. What this means, as indicated in other studies (such as Astin and Bayer, 1971), is that large proportions of the students were exceptionally able academically, came from Jewish backgrounds, tended to have no current religious preference, were verbally aggressive, considered themselves political liberals, and were self-confident about their intellectual abilities. Moreover, the quality of the faculty was unusually high (as measured by the percentage who held doctoral degrees). These institutions tended to be located in the northeast or on the west coast.

Later, campus unrest became a nationwide phenomenon, spreading to various types of colleges that had not previously been affected, resulting in a "flattening out" of the relationship between institutional characteristics and protest. Nonetheless, throughout the 1960s and early 1970s, many of the same college attributes were consistently associated with the occurrence of protests on campus, particularly (in the later years) severe protests (those that involved violent incidents, such as injuries, deaths, or significant destruction of property, and those that involved nonviolent but disruptive incidents, such as the interruption of normal institutional functions and the occupation of buildings). Table 1 shows the estimated percentages of various types of institutions that experienced severe campus protest in 1968–1969 and 1970–1971, as well as the percentage that experienced protest of any kind in 1970–1971. (Data for the earlier academic year focused on violent and disruptive acts, so that no percentages are available on all types of protests.) The incidence of severe protest decreased at public universities, private universities, and four-year private nonsectarian colleges (the types of institutions that had been hardest hit in 1968–1969); it remained the same at four-year Protestant colleges; and it increased at four-year public colleges, four-year Catholic colleges, and public and private two-year colleges (the types that had previously been relatively unaffected by severe protest). Nonetheless, the rank order of institutions remained just about the same for severe protest in the years considered.

Universities, particularly private ones, were most susceptible to protests, including severe protests that often erupted in violence. Though four-year public colleges and private colleges switched their rank-order positions between 1968–1969 and 1970–1971, they too were very vulnerable to protests of all kinds. In private nonsectarian colleges, however, outbreaks of violence were rare. Protestant colleges were more likely to experience protest than were Catholic colleges, though the incidence of severe protest at the latter rose between 1968–1969 and 1970–1971, and violent incidents were proportionately more likely to occur. The two-year colleges, especially the private ones, were least susceptible to protest. These findings on the relation of educational level and type of administrative control to the occurrence of protest at an institution held fairly constant throughout the years of campus unrest.

Curricular emphasis was another characteristic found to be related to the occurrence or nonoccurrence of protest. Complex and heterogeneous institutions, such as multiversities, and (to a lesser degree) liberal arts colleges were more likely to experience protest than such specialized and single-purpose institutions as technological schools and teachers colleges. These differences are probably attributable in large part to differences in the characteristics of students and faculty members at these schools. Specialized institutions attract both students and faculty members who are more career-oriented and more conservative politically. Moreover, there is survey research evidence (see Chapter Three; Creager, 1971) that persons who major in (or teach) engineering and education are much less inclined to participate in, or even to approve of, campus demonstrations than those in the social sciences, the arts, and the humanities.

Two other institutional characteristics have been consistently related to the occurrence of unrest: size and selectivity. In general, the larger the institution, the greater the likelihood that it will experience unrest of some kind and that the unrest will involve violence and disruption. The consistent exception is the universities; those of moderate size (one thousand to five thousand students) were more protest-vulnerable than those of large size (over five thousand). This inconsistency is explained by the fact mentioned earlier that private universities, which are usually of intermediate rather than large size, were more likely to have major protests than public ones, which are larger.

Two explanations may be offered to account for the apparent causal relation between institutional size (which is closely linked to

Table 1. Incidence of Protest by Type of Institution 1968–1969 and 1970–1971

Type of Institution	Population (N)	Sample (N)		Percentage Having Severe Protest		Percentage Having Any Protest
		1968–1969	1970–1971	1968–1969	1970–1971	1970–1971
Public universities	249	54	55	43.0	35.7	73.9
Private universities	61	28	28	70.5	52.5	82.0
Four-year public colleges	343	44	45	21.7	29.4	54.8
Four-year private nonsectarian colleges	391	85	79	42.6	19.7	45.3
Four-year Protestant colleges	321	49	50	17.8	17.8	44.2
Four-year Catholic colleges	229	43	42	8.5	13.1	35.4
Two-year private colleges	230	25	22	0.0	5.2	16.1
Two-year public colleges	538	54	48	10.4	11.9	29.7
Total	2362	382	369	22.4	19.6	43.1

Sources: 1968–1969 data from Bayer and Astin, 1969, pp. 337–350; 1970–1971 data from ACE survey.

university status) and the occurrence of protest. One, labeled the "critical mass" hypothesis, was suggested by the finding (Astin and Bayer, 1971) that the *proportion* of black students at a predominantly white institution was not related to the occurrence of protests over racial policies but that the *absolute number of* black students was. The implication with respect to all students is that large institutions will be more likely to have a "critical mass" of potential activists capable of organizing a protest. A second explanation (not necessarily antithetical to the first) is that the environments of larger institutions (particularly universities) have been shown to be cold and impersonal, marked by a lack of cohesiveness and by little interaction between students and faculty members, who are often more interested in their own research or in working with graduate students than in teaching undergraduates (see Astin, 1968). Thus, students feel alienated and discontented, and these feelings may manifest themselves in protest activity.

Selectivity (the average academic ability of the student body, measured by mean scores on standardized tests) is an extremely important predictor of campus unrest, particularly severe protest (Bayer and Astin, 1969). In 1968–1969, none of the least selective universities experienced severe protest, but the incidence of protest rose sharply at each successive selectivity level; by 1970–1971, 20 percent of the least selective universities experienced severe protest, and 40 percent experienced protest of some kind, but the highly selective universities still tended to suffer protest more frequently, though the increase at each selectivity level was not as pronounced. The same was generally true for the four-year colleges. The only reversal occurred among two-year institutions in the 1970–1971 academic year: the higher the selectivity level of these institutions, the smaller the likelihood of protest. This apparent inconsistency is explained by the additional fact that protest was more likely to occur at large, public junior colleges than at small, private ones, which are usually the more selective.

The close connection between selectivity (which can be considered an aspect of student input as well as an attribute of the institution itself) has also been explained in several ways. First, the students attracted by highly selective institutions are, almost by definition, more intellectual and thus probably more aware of and concerned about political and social problems; such students may use protest to express their concern. Secondly, because it brings together a large concentration of highly able students, perhaps for the first time, the highly selective institution is likely to have an extremely competitive academic atmosphere in which students are under heavy pressure to make high grades. Their resultant feelings of stress and frustration may be channeled into activist behavior. In addition, highly selective institutions attract and recruit faculty members who may influence the protest behavior of students in two ways: their frequent neglect of teaching in favor of research may create a cold and unfriendly atmosphere (like that of large institutions) that leads students to revolt; and such faculty members may also give student activism their approval or actually join in protests, further stimulating student activism (Bayer, 1971 and Lipset, 1972).

FOR: Astin, Alexander W., and et al. "Overview of the Unrest Era." In *The Power of Protest*. San Francisco: Jossey-Bass, 1975, pp. 17-45.

Altbach, P., and Peterson, P. "Before Berkeley: Historical Perspectives on American Student Activism." *Annuals of the American Academy of Political and Social Science*, May 1971, 395, 1-14.

Astin, A.W. "A Program of Research on Student Development." *Journal of College Student Personnel*, 1968, 299-307.

Bayer, A.E. *Institutional Correlates of Faculty Support of Campus Unrest*. ACE Research Reports, Vol. 6, No. 1. Washington, D.C.: American Council on Education, 1971.

Bayer, A.E., and Astin, A.W. "Campus Unrest: Was It Really All That Quiet?" *Educational Record*, fall 1971, 52, 301-313.

Bayer, A.E., and Astin, A.W. *War Protests on U.S. Campuses during April 1972*. ACH Higher Education Panel Report No. 9. Washington, D.C.: American Council on Education, May 1972.

Bayer, A.E., and Astin, A.W. "Violence and Disruption on the U.S. Campus, 1968-1969." *Educational Record*, fall 1969, 50, 337-350.

Bell, D. "Columbia and the New Left." In D. Bell and I. Kirstol (Eds.), *Confrontation*. New York: Basic Books, 1968.

Bunzel, J.H. "Costs of Politicized Change." *Educational Record*, spring 1969, 50, 131.

Cohen, M. *Guns on Campus: Student Protest at Cornell*. Chicago: Urban Research Corporation, 1970.

Creager, J.A. *The American Graduate Student: A Normative Description*. ACE Research Reports, Vol. 6, No. 5. Washington, D.C.: American Council on Education, 1971.

Gaddy, D. *The Scope of Organized Student Protest in Junior Colleges*. Washington, D.C.: American Association of Junior Colleges, 1970.

Glazer, N. *Remembering the Answers: Essays on the American Student Revolt*. New York: Basic Books, 1970.

Hodgkinson, H.L. "Student Protest—An Institutional and National Profile." *Teachers College Record*, 1970a, 71, 537-555.

Hodgkinson, H.L. *Institutions in Transition: A Study of Change in Higher Education*. Berkeley: Carnegie Commission on Higher Education, 1970b.

Lipset, S.M. "Academia and Politics in America." In T.L. Mossiter (Ed.), *Imagination and Precision in the Social Sciences*. London: Faber and Faber, 1972.

Keniston, K. *Youth and Dissent*. New York: Harcourt Brace Jovanovich, 1971.

Nicholas, D.C. (Ed.) *Perspectives on Campus Tension: Papers Prepared for the Special Committee on Campus Tensions*. Washington, D.C.: American Council on Education, 1970.

O'Brien, J. "The Development of the New Left." *Annuals of the American Academy of Political and Social Science*, May 1971, 395, 15-25.

Peterson, R.E. *The Scope of Organized Students Protest in 1967-68*. Princeton, N.J.: Educational Testing Service, 1968a.

Peterson, R.E. "The Student Left in American Higher Education." *Deadalus*, winter 1968b.

Peterson R.E., and Bilorusky, J.A. *May 1970: The Campus Aftermath of Cambodia and Kent State*. Berkeley, Calif.: Carnegie Commission on Higher Education, 1971.

Scranton Commission. *Report of the President's Commission on Campus Unrest*. Washington, D.C.: Government Printing Office, 1970.

Wallerstein, I., and Starr, P. (eds.) *The University Crisis Reader*, Vol. I: *The Liberal University Under Attack*. New York: Random House, 1971.

1954 to the Present

Frank Bowles and Frank A. DeCosta

The higher education of Negroes in the United States from 1954 to the present has been affected by at least two new developments. First, there has been a relatively constant rate of migration of Negroes from the South to the North. Begun in 1940, it has produced a situation in which the percentage of those residing in the South has been reduced from 77 percent in 1940 to 53 percent in 1968. Obviously, if this rate continues, one may expect fewer than half the Negroes in the United States to be residents of the South in 1972 or 1973. One of the implications of this development is that the higher education of Negroes, once the major concern and responsibility of the South, has now become an equal concern and responsibility of the North.

The second development which has produced a different situation is the decisions of the United States Supreme Court on May 17 and 24, 1954, outlawing segregation in public education. These decisions changed the basic philosophy upon which the development of higher education among Negroes, particularly in the South, had been based. The philosophy changed from "separate-but-equal" to "equality within racial desegregation." Thus, the separate systems of education for whites and Negroes which had developed in the South under the separate-but-equal philosophy received a lethal blow and, consequently, had to be reoriented to the new philosophy.

Therefore, from 1954 to the present, the development of higher education among Negroes may be characterized as a period of transition. This applies not only to the historically Negro colleges but to all colleges, North and South, which have provided higher education for Negroes during the period. All have faced new problems and have attempted various solutions to the problems. At present many of the attempted solutions are buffeted about as "straws in the wind," but some will succeed.

On May 17, 1954, the U.S. Supreme Court rendered its decision in the four school segregation cases which had been undertaken by the NAACP in 1951 and 1952 (*Brown v. Board,* 347 U.S. 483). The cases involved suits against local school boards in Delaware, Kansas, South Carolina, and Virginia. The Court's decision in a similar case against the District of Columbia was rendered a week later in a separate opinion, since the District comes under federal rather than state jurisdiction (*Bolling v. Sharpe,* 347 U.S. 497).

In the four cases under state jurisdiction the Court's decision was:

We conclude that in the field of public education the doctrine of "separate but equal" has no place. Separate educational facilities are inherently unequal. Therefore, we hold that the plaintiffs and others similarly situated for whom the actions have been brought are, by reason of the segregation complained of, deprived of the equal protection of the laws guaranteed by the Fourteenth Amendment (*Brown v. Board*, 347 U.S. 483).

In the case which involved the District of Columbia and, consequently, which came under federal jurisdiction, the Court's decision was based upon the due process clause of the Fifth Amendment:

Segregation in public education is not reasonably related to any proper governmental objective, and thus it imposes on Negro children of the District of Columbia a burden that constitutes an arbitrary deprivation of their liberty in violation of the Due Process Clause (*Bolling v. Sharpe*, 347 U.S. 497).

Although these five cases were related only to public elementary and secondary school education, the Court soon let it be known that its position against racial segregation in public education would extend to higher education as well. On May 24, 1954, it rendered three more decisions against racial segregation—this time related to public higher education.[1] The fundamental position of the Court was now clear. Racial segregation in public education at all levels would be held unconstitutional.

Although the Court's decisions were rendered in May, 1954, its decree on implementation was delayed until May, 1955. The reason was the Court's opinion that insufficient emphasis had been given in the previously presented arguments and briefs to the "kind of decree or directive the Court should issue in order to require the school boards to cease the unconstitutional segregation" (Indritz, 1954, p. 358). Therefore, the Court ordered the cases to be continued on the docket for the presentation of additional arguments related to the implementation of its decisions, and it invited the Attorneys General of the United States and of several states requiring or permitting racial segregation in public education to

participate in the arguments (ibid., p. 359). The arguments were heard for four days and were presented by attorneys representing the United States, the NAACP, and 10 states and the District of Columbia. The Court rendered its implementation decree on May 31, 1955 (Thompson, 1955, pp. 161-164). It contained the following features: (1) the Court's reaffirmation of its fundamental principle that the "racial discrimination in public education is unconstitutional"; (2) recognition that the implementation of this fundamental principle may require the solution of varied local school problems; (3) remanding the cases to the lower courts which originally heard them, since these courts are close to local school problems and can best perform the judicial appraisal of whether or not the action of local school authorities "constitutes good faith implementation" of the fundamental principle; (4) directing that the lower courts "will require that the defendants make a prompt and reasonable start toward full compliance" with the fundamental principle; and (5) directing that the lower courts will "take such proceedings and enter such order and decrees . . . to admit to public schools on a racially nondiscriminatory basis with *all deliberate speed* the parties to these cases" (italics added).

In 1957, after more than a quarter-century of petitioning, discussing, and planning, the Southern Association of Colleges and Schools admitted into membership the historically Negro colleges of the South (Cozart, 1967, pp. 45-49). That year 15 of the four-year colleges and 3 of the junior colleges were admitted to the association. Among the 15 four-year colleges admitted, 5 are public and 10 are private. The 3 junior colleges admitted are private (ibid., pp. 58-59).

The admission of historically Negro colleges into membership in the Southern Association is important because it had been alleged that, under the association's prior practice of approving Negro institutions, it had employed "irregularities in inspecting schools for Negroes as compared to the uniform application of evaluative criteria applied to schools for whites" (Cozart, 1967, p. 49). Some credence for this allegation is found in the facts. Prior to consideration for membership, it was required that each Negro college be reevaluated, even though it might already have been approved by the association. Only 18 Negro colleges were initially

TABLE 3
Undergraduate enrollments and percentage change, by sex, in 51* historically Negro private four-year colleges for selected years, 1953–1968

Enrollment and percentage change	1953–54	1957–58	1961–62	1965–66	1967–68
Total enrollment	25,569	29,495	34,830	44,105	48,541
Male	10,760	13,736	15,654	19,627	21,519
Female	14,809	15,759	19,176	24,478	27,022
Total percentage change		+15.4	+18.1	+26.6	+10.1
Male		+27.7	+14.0	+25.4	+9.6
Female		+6.4	+21.7	+27.6	+10.4

*Enrollment data were not available on all 54 of the private institutions.
SOURCES: Jenkins, 1954, pp. 142–148; Poole, 1959, pp. 12–63; Huddleston and Sulkin, 1964, pp. 20–72; Chandler and Rice, 1967, pp. 52–132.

admitted to membership in 1957, whereas 59 of the colleges had previously been approved by the association (ibid., pp. 58–59; Jenkins, 1954, p. 23).

Between 1957 and the present the Southern Association has admitted to membership 59 of the 88 historically Negro colleges under its jurisdiction. They comprise 35 private four-year colleges, 21 public four-year colleges, 3 private junior colleges, and none of the 5 public junior colleges (Appendixes A through D).

Between 1954 and 1969, 54 historically Negro private four-year colleges and universities have been in existence. Three of these have enrolled only graduate or professional students: Atlanta University, Interdenominational Theological Center, and Meharry Medical College. The remaining 51 institutions have enrolled undergraduate students, and of them only 9 have enrolled graduate students. In 1967–68 the total graduate enrollment in these nine institutions was only 3,046, with 95 percent being accounted for by three institutions: Hampton Institute, Howard University, and Tuskegee Institute. Howard University enrolled 82 percent of the 3,046 graduate students in the nine institutions. Thus it may be inferred that the historically Negro private colleges and universities continued to enroll mainly undergraduate students.

Measured by undergraduate enrollment, the growth of 51 historically private four-year Negro colleges from 1954 to the present may be noted in Table 3. From this it may be observed that the total enrollment increased from 25,569 in 1953–54 to 48,541 in 1967–68, an increase of approximately 90 percent. Furthermore, it may be noted that the greatest increase in enrollment occurred between 1961–62 and 1965–66, the period during which the National Defense Education Act was passed. The act provides loans for college students and probably accounts to a considerable extent for the upsurge of enrollment. For the last two years of the period under discussion, however, it may be deduced that there was a decrease in the annual rate of growth to approximately 5 percent. This is lower than the annual rate of growth for Southern private colleges below university level. Finally, it may be observed that the historically Negro private colleges continue to enroll more female than male students, although it may be deduced that there was some reduction in the female-male ratio. Specifically, female stu-

dents accounted for 57.9 percent of the total enrollment in 1953–54 and 55.7 percent in 1967–68. This phenomenon warrants continuous study, since, as Doddy points out, the situation suggests that too few males are pursuing higher professional vocations, that much of the economic support of Negro families will continue to devolve upon Negro females, and that, if this remains unchanged, the unfortunate pattern of Negro family organization will tend to continue (Doddy, 1963, p. 489).

The growth in enrollment among the historically Negro private colleges was greater for accredited than for unaccredited colleges. This generalization is supported by the data of Table 4, in which it may be observed that the enrollment in the 38 accredited colleges increased by 98.1 percent between 1953–54 and 1967–68, whereas in 13 unaccredited colleges it increased by only 46.7 percent.[2] Obviously, this suggests to some extent the tendency of students to be attracted to accredited rather than to unaccredited colleges. Furthermore, it may be deduced from the data of Table 4 that, as accredited colleges in this group have had substantial financial support from their endowments, church bodies, the United Negro College Fund, and foundations. However, their per-student cost has been higher than that in the average accredited private Negro college (Alter, 1968, pp. 13, 42; Singletary, 1968, pp. 1463, 1464). How long the sources of their financial support will continue to believe the high cost is justifiable seems questionable. Furthermore, these four colleges are located in relatively small communities some distance from the sources of potentially large commuter student populations. Therefore, assuming that they remain in their present locations, one of the main problems they will face in increasing enrollment is providing additional campus housing.

Between 1954 and the present 35[3] historically Negro public four-year colleges have been in existence. In 1953-54, 9 offered work at the master's degree level to some 1,450 students. By 1967-68, 18 of the colleges were offering work at the master's degree level to 4,400 students. The vast majority of the graduate students were in-service teachers who pursued one or two courses a week during after-school hours or on Saturdays.

Measured by undergraduate enrollment, the growth of the historically Negro public colleges from 1954 to the present may be noted from the data in Table 5. It may be observed that the total enrollment increased from 37,764 in 1953-54 to 85,382 in 1967-68, or by about 126 percent. It seems noteworthy that, during the period, the male enrollment increased by 161 percent, so that by 1967-68 male students comprised approximately 46 percent of the total enrollment. This contrasts with the situation in 1953-54 when male students constituted only 40 percent of the total enrollment. There is some indication that the female-male ratio in these colleges will be further reduced.

An additional measure of the growth of the historically Negro public colleges during this period is the increase in the size of the individual colleges as shown in Figure 3. From these data it may be deduced that the median college had an enrollment of 820 in 1953-54 and 2,100 in 1967-68. Furthermore, it may be noted by inspection that only 4 of the colleges had enrollments below 800 in 1967-68, whereas 17 of the colleges fell into this category in 1953-54. Finally, it may be observed that 8 of the colleges had

a group, the 13 unaccredited colleges in 1967-68 were extremely small, with an average enrollment of approximately 464. In contrast, the 38 accredited colleges had an average enrollment of approximately 1,119.

During the period under review significant changes occurred in the size of the historically Negro private four-year colleges. Some of these changes may be observed in Figure 2. One which may be deduced is that the undergraduate enrollment in the median college

TABLE 4
Increases in undergraduate enrollment and percentage change of 38 accredited and 13 unaccredited historically Negro private colleges between 1953-54 and 1967-68

Enrollment and percentage change	38 accredited colleges		13 unaccredited colleges	
	1953-54	1967-68	1953-54	1967-68
Total enrollment	21,458	42,510	4,111	6,031
Male	9,213	18,750	1,547	2,769
Female	12,245	23,760	2,564	3,262
Total percentage change		98.1		46.7
Male		103.5		79.0
Female		94.0		27.2

SOURCES: Jenkins, 1954, pp. 142-148; Poole, 1959, pp. 12-63; Huddleston and Sulkin, 1964, pp. 20-72; Chandler and Rice, 1967, pp. 52-132.

increased from approximately 450 in 1953-54 to approximately 812 in 1967-68. A second change which may be noted is that 22 of the colleges had enrollments below 400 in 1953-54, whereas only 6 had enrollments that small in 1967-68. Finally, it may be observed that 8 of the colleges had enrollments above 1,200 in 1967-68 in contrast to only 3 that large in 1953-54.

One implication of these changes is that the small colleges need to become seriously concerned about their futures. Some of the

FIGURE 2 *A comparison of the 1953-54 and 1967-68 undergraduate enrollments in 51 historically Negro private four-year colleges*

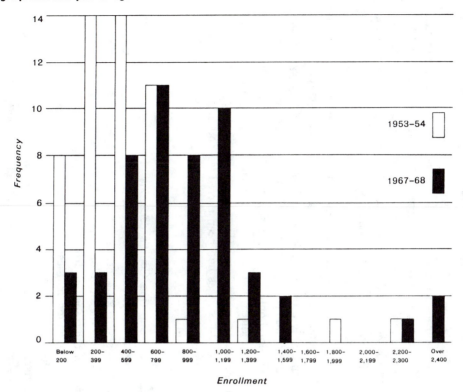

FIGURE 3 *A comparison of the 1953-54 and 1967-68 undergraduate enrollments in the 35* historically Negro public four-year colleges*

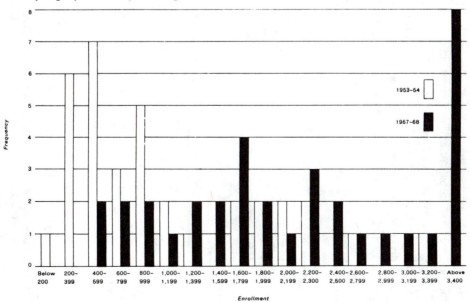

*There are 34 in 1970.

mining appropriations to state colleges is the size of enrollment.

During the period under review the Negro public colleges have shown significant development as measured by regional accreditation. They came under the jurisdiction of three regional accrediting associations in the following manner: Middle States—7; North Central—6; and Southern—22. At the beginning of the period only two of the associations—the Middle States and the North Central—accredited historically Negro colleges and admitted them to membership. At that time the six public colleges that fall under the jurisdiction of the North Central Association and four of the seven public colleges that fall under the jurisdiction of the Middle States Association had been accredited and admitted to membership (Jenkins, 1954, p. 53). The Southern Association, on the other hand, did not accredit and admit historically Negro colleges until 1957. In that year the association admitted to membership only 5 of the 22 historically Negro public colleges under its jurisdiction (Cozart, 1967, pp. 58–59). Thus, at the beginning of the period only 15 of the historically Negro public colleges had been accredited and admitted to membership by their regional accrediting associations. However, by 1968 this situation had changed; 34 colleges had been accredited and admitted, the lone exception being Mississippi Valley State College, which was not founded until 1950.

Since the Supreme Court's decisions of 1954 the admission of Negroes to historically white colleges in the South has proceeded without severe incident, except at two or three state universities. In assessing the situation in 1964, Guy Johnson summarizes: "The story of the transition from complete segregation to a high degree of desegregation in these institutions is a dramatic example of peaceful and rapid change in the structure of race relations" (G. B. Johnson, 1964, pp. 5–7). Today, six years later, the period of transition continues even more peacefully and more rapidly.

At the time of Johnson's assessment James Meredith, a Negro, had already been graduated from the University of Mississippi, and Governor Wallace had already stepped from where he "stood in the schoolhouse door" to prevent the registration of two Negro students at the University of Alabama. These were the last holdouts and really represented the only instances in which resistance to

enrollments above 3,400 in 1967–68, whereas no college had an enrollment that large in 1953–54.

Some of the small colleges need to become seriously concerned about their future. The four colleges with enrollments below 800 in 1967–68 were in the low-enrollment category in 1953–54, and their increases since then have not approached those of the other historically Negro public colleges. Obviously, problems that militate against substantial enrollment increases are faced by these colleges. Worthy of note is the fact that the four are located in two border states: three in Maryland[4] and one in West Virginia. The individual data on these colleges, however, suggest that a different set of problems is faced by each. The extent to which each

TABLE 5 Undergraduate enrollments and percentage change, by sex, in 35* historically Negro public colleges for selected years, 1953–1968

Enrollment and percentage change	1953–54	1957–58	1961–62	1965–66	1967–68
Total enrollment	37,764	44,237	58,105	75,593	85,382
Male	15,029	20,247	26,147	34,470	39,222
Female	22,735	23,990	31,958	41,123	46,160
Total percentage change		+17.1	+31.3	+30.1	+12.9
Male		+34.7	+29.1	+31.8	+13.8
Female		+5.5	+33.2	+28.7	+12.2

*By the time of publication the number of public four-year institutions had decreased to 34.

SOURCE: Compiled by the Carnegie Commission on Higher Education from various sources, including Chandler and Rice, 1967, pp. 52–134; and Chronicle of Higher Education ("White, Negro Undergraduates at Colleges . . ."), April 22, 1968, pp. 3–4.

college is able to solve its problems will determine, in a large measure, its future—especially since, as a result of racial desegregation in higher education, the basic criterion employed in deter-the admission of Negroes was so keen that it occasioned national attention and concern. The events related to the admission of Negroes to these two universities are described only as examples of the most extreme resistance that has been demonstrated in the admission of Negroes to the white colleges of the South.

In the case of the University of Alabama, Autherine Lucy registered in the University on February 1, 1956, and began attending classes on February 3. On February 6, "She was driven from the campus by rioting and the Board of Trustees later expelled her for accusing university officials of conspiring in the disorders" (Southern Education Reporting Service, 1965, p. 4). No Negroes were admitted to the University during the next seven years. In 1963 plans were laid for the registration of three Negroes in the summer session: two at the main campus in Tuscaloosa and one at the university center in Huntsville. When the two students, Miss Vivian Malone and James Hood, accompanied by officials of the U.S. Justice Department, appeared at the main campus for registration on June 11, Governor George C. Wallace, in accordance with his campaign promise, "stood in the schoolhouse door" to prevent their registration. He read a five-page statement which concluded, "I denounce and forbid this illegal act." The students and Justice Department officials withdrew from the door of Foster Auditorium where the Governor stood. However, in less than an hour, when the order of President John F. Kennedy federalizing the Alabama National Guard was read to Governor Wallace, he stepped aside, and Miss Vivian Malone and James Hood entered and were registered in the University of Alabama (ibid.). The third student registered without incident two days later at the Huntsville extension center of the university.

In the case of the University of Mississippi, Clennon King, a professor at Alcorn A. & M. College, applied in 1958 for admission to the university to work toward a doctorate. When he attempted to register in June of that year, he was arrested on a charge of disturbing the peace. Following a lunacy hearing the next day, King was committed to the state mental hospital. However, after a 12-day observation period, the hospital staff unanimously reported that it "could find no evidence of mental disorder." Thereupon, King was released from the hospital. On the day of his release Professor King left Mississippi by plane for his father's home in Georgia, stating that he had no further plans for entrance to the University (Sarratt, 1966, pp. 127-128).

In 1961 James Meredith, a student at Jackson State College, began his celebrated case which resulted in his admission as a transfer student to "Ole Miss" on October 1, 1962, and his graduation in June, 1963 (Southern Education Reporting Service, 1965, p. 14). The NAACP built Meredith's case carefully and in minute detail, and the Fifth Circuit Court of Appeals reviewed his case with understanding. In unusual maneuvers the U.S. Justice Department and the armed forces provided Meredith with physical protection upon his entrance to and throughout his enrollment at the university (Meredith, 1960). As in the case of Clennon King, the university lawyers argued that a U.S. Air Force medical report showed that Meredith suffered from a nervous stomach, that he was a psychiatric case, and that, therefore, he should be denied admission to the university. However, Federal Judge John Minor Wisdom, in rendering the appeal court's decision of June 25, 1962, shrugged off this argument with the statement, "Meredith's record shows just about the type of Negro who might be expected to crack the racial barrier of the University of Mississippi: a man with a mission and with a nervous stomach" (ibid., p. 158). Thus, on September 30, 1962, a day earlier than the date of registration, Meredith arrived on the campus of "Ole Miss" accompanied by a force of federal marshals. Riots broke out, obliging President Kennedy to send in regular troops and part of the Mississippi National Guard to restore order. Meredith, under the protection of federal marshals, registered on the following day and embarked upon his year of study which was to culminate in his graduation in June, 1963. Since Meredith's enrollment at the University of Mississippi other Negroes have followed him without serious conflict.

These two cases in the Deep South, illustrative of the most extreme resistance, suggest that the admission of Negroes to white colleges has been affected by geographic location within the South and by time. This is essentially true. Assessing the admission of Negroes to white colleges in the South in 1957, three years after the Supreme Court's decisions, Parham (1957, pp. 163-164) presents the following summary:

1 Desegregation has moved at a rapid pace in the border states; slower in Texas.

2 Desegregation has moved haltingly in Louisiana, North Carolina, Tennessee, and Virginia.

3 Segregation has been maintained in public universities and colleges in the states of the Deep South: Alabama, Georgia, Florida, Mississippi, and South Carolina.

Parham estimates that, in 1957, approximately 2,400 Negroes were enrolled in the tax-supported white colleges of the South (1957, p. 164).

With respect to the admission of Negroes to private and denominational colleges of the South in 1957, Parham remarks that, with the exception of Catholic colleges, they were reluctant to admit Negroes. Specifically, he says:

Although 51 per cent of former all-white public institutions and 77 per cent of Catholic schools were integrated as of the beginning of the 1956–57 school term, only 29 per cent of the Protestant institutions and 25 per cent of the private schools were integrated (1957, p. 166).

Seven years later, in 1964, Guy Johnson presented data which showed the effects of time and of geographic location within the South on the admission of Negroes to white colleges of the South.

His data in Table 6 show that desegregation was complete in the border states by 1961, that it was a little more than three-fourths complete in the middle states by 1964, and that it was only a little more than one-third complete in the Deep South by 1964. These data support the tendencies that were noted in 1957 by Parham.

With respect to desegregation in both public and private white colleges of the South, Johnson presents data in Table 7 from which generalizations may be drawn: (1) substantial increases in desegregation had occurred by 1964, and (2) the increases were in the same order with respect to public versus nonpublic colleges as noted earlier by Parham. Both Parham and Johnson were aware that no Negroes were enrolled in some colleges which declared an official policy of racial desegregation.

Guy Johnson (1964, p. 6) estimates that, in 1964, approximately 15,000 Negroes were enrolled in the historically white colleges of the South: 10,000 in public colleges and 5,000 in church and private colleges. Therefore, assuming the reliability of the estimates, it may be concluded that the enrollment of Negroes in these institutions increased fourfold between 1957 and 1964. These estimates included both graduate and undergraduate students.

As a result of the Civil Rights Act of 1964, which required educational institutions to sign a statement of compliance with racial desegregation in order to receive federal aid, all white public colleges of the South signed this statement by 1967 (Southern

TABLE 7
Desegregated white colleges in the South, by control, in 1964

Control	Total number of white colleges in South	Desegregated white colleges	
		Number	Percent
Public	251	182	72
Church	235	120	51
Private	114	48	42
TOTAL	600	350	58

SOURCES: G. B. Johnson, 1964, p. 6; Southern Education Reporting Service, 1967, p. 5.

TABLE 6
Percentages of white public colleges desegregated, by subregions of the South, for 1954, 1961, 1964, and 1967

Subregion	Percent desegregated			
	1954	1961	1964	1967
Border states	20	100	100	100
Middle states	8	64	79	100
Deep South	3	17	36	100

SOURCES: G. B. Johnson, 1964, p. 6; Southern Education Reporting Service, 1967, p. 3.

Education Reporting Service, 1967, p. 3). The signing by a college did not necessarily mean that the college enrolled Negro students, but it is significant to note from the data in Table 8 that only 24, or 4.8 percent, of the 495 white colleges of the South having undergraduate enrollments of 500 or more in 1967 reported no enrollment of Negro students. Thus, the enrollment situation was significantly different from that described by Parham and Guy Johnson prior to the passage of the Civil Rights Act.

The total 1967 undergraduate enrollment of Negroes in the white colleges of the South having enrollments of 500 or more, as noted in Table 8, was 38,659. No data are available on the enrollment of Negroes in graduate and professional schools or in colleges enrolling fewer than 500 students. Despite these limitations, as well as numerous errors of reporting, it seems reasonable to estimate that, in 1967, 40,000 to 50,000 Negroes were enrolled in the white colleges of the South. This estimate does not include the white part-time and summer-session graduate students.

The distribution of the 38,659 Negro undergraduates by level of offering and control of the colleges is presented in Table 9. It may be observed that fewer than 5,000 Negroes were enrolled in public colleges, and that they were almost equally divided between four-year and junior colleges. There is a positive correlation between the number of public junior colleges and Negro enrollment (rho = .61). Furthermore, it may be observed that fewer than 5,000 Negroes were enrolled in the white private colleges of the South: 4,061 in four-year and 394 in junior colleges.

As mentioned earlier, the admission of Negro students has been accepted almost universally by the white colleges in the South in the few years since 1964. The atmosphere is much different from that which surrounded Autherine Lucy's, Vivian Malone's, and James Meredith's admission to college.

Although the situation has changed to the extent that Negroes who wish to attend the white colleges in the South need no longer fear that their education must be obtained in an atmosphere of physical duress, it is still in transition. Many of the colleges enroll only one or two or a few Negroes; many continue to employ admission devices aimed at discouraging Negroes; few are earnestly concerned with the adjustment of Negro students after they are admitted; few employ their normal recruiting services for Negro students; and few, if any, have accepted the major responsibility for the college education of Negroes who reside near them. The exceptions that exist represent "straws in the wind" that point the direction for movement through this transitional period. The U.S. Department of Health, Education, and Welfare, which is charged with enforcing the compliance provision of the Civil Rights Act of 1964, has recently turned its attention to the matter of greater racial desegregation within higher institutions. Specifically, five states—Arkansas, Lousiana, Maryland, Mississippi, and Pennsylvania—have been warned that they are operating racially segregated systems of higher education and have been given deadlines for submitting definitive plans for racial desegregation (Batten, 1969, p. 28). This is just the beginning.

Assuming the reliability of earlier estimates, it may be concluded that the undergraduate enrollment of Negroes in Northern colleges has more than doubled since 1954, from almost 45,000 to almost 95,000 in 1967–68. The enrollment data for 1967–68 are presented in Table 10.

Several factors seem to be related to this marked increase in the undergraduate enrollment of Negroes in Northern colleges. The factor of greatest weight apparently is the continuing migration of Negroes to the large cities of the North and their enrollment particularly in the junior colleges. Newman points out that in 1960 five of the six cities in the United States having the largest Negro populations were located in the North and West: Los Angeles, Chicago, Detroit, New York, and Philadelphia, the sixth city being Washington, D.C. Further, she notes that San Francisco and Oakland have a combined Negro population that is larger than that of Birmingham (Newman, 1965). From the data in Table 10 it may be noted that these five cities are located in five of the six states in the North and West with the largest undergraduate enrollments of Negro students: California, Illinois, Michigan, New York, Ohio, and Pennsylvania. This concentration in the large cities of the North and West and the enrollment of Negroes in the local colleges have produced a new phenomenon in these sections of the United States; i.e., colleges in which a high percentage of the students is Negro. Some examples in 1967–68 are shown in

TABLE 8 *The 1967–68 undergraduate enrollment of Negroes in historically white colleges of the South, by state*

State	Number of white colleges in state	Number of white colleges in state with Negro enrollments	Total number of Negroes enrolled in white colleges	Control of colleges in which no Negroes were enrolled	
				Public	Private and denominational
Alabama	19	18	887	1	0
Arkansas	14	13	964	0	1
Delaware	2	2	53	0	0
District of Columbia	7	7	453	0	0
Florida	42	41	5,136	0	1
Georgia	32	28	986	1	3
Kentucky	23	23	1,656	0	0
Louisiana	14	14	2,866	0	0
Maryland	24	23	2,355	1	0
Mississippi	21	19	872	2	0
Missouri	37	36	4,430	0	1
North Carolina	51	48	2,144	0	3
Oklahoma	26	26	2,205	0	0
South Carolina	19	17	813	0	2
Tennessee	30	29	2,165	0	1
Texas	82	81	9,044	0	1
Virginia	36	30	1,007	1	5
West Virginia	16	16	623	0	0
TOTALS	495	471	38,659	6	18

SOURCES: Chandler and Rice, 1967, pp. 52–134; and *Chronicle of Higher Education* ("White, Negro Undergraduates at Colleges . . ."), April 22, 1968, pp. 3–4.

the following tabulation:

College	Location	Percent Negro
Compton	Compton, Cal.	48.9
Contra Costa	San Pablo, Cal.	26.2
Los Angeles City	Los Angeles, Cal.	26.6
Los Angeles Technical	Los Angeles, Cal.	38.0
Merritt	Oakland, Cal.	29.7
Chicago City	Chicago, Ill.	27.8
Chicago State	Chicago, Ill.	23.9
Highland Park	Highland Park, Mich.	45.7
Detroit Technical	Detroit, Mich.	24.0
Community College	Philadelphia, Pa.	25.0

A second factor which has contributed to the marked increase in the enrollment of Negroes in Northern colleges has been the activities of organized groups, such as the National Scholarship Service and Fund for Negro Students (NSSFNS) and the National Achievement Program. Established in 1948 to "increase and

TABLE 9 *The 1967–68 undergraduate enrollment of Negroes in historically white colleges of the South, by state, level of offering, and control*

State	White public 4-year colleges		White private 4-year colleges		White public junior colleges		White private junior colleges	
	No.	Negro enroll-ment	No.	Negro enroll-ment	No.	Negro enroll-ment	No.	Negro enroll-ment
Alabama	6	435	5	73	8	379	0	
Arkansas	7	600	6	326	0		1	38
Delaware	1	51	0		0		1	2
District of Columbia	0		7	453	0		0	
Florida	5	426	12	267	24	4,416	1	27
Georgia	11	550	10	135	10	301	1	0
Kentucky	6	1,302	15	311	1	39	1	4
Louisiana	8	2,171	5	181	1	514	0	
Maryland	4	1,333	12	274	8	748	0	
Mississippi	5	181	3	58	13	633	0	
Missouri	9	1,977	23	439	4	2,013	1	1
North Carolina	9	698	20	181	14	1,186	8	79
Oklahoma	10	1,589	7	211	7	331	2	74
South Carolina	5	222	7	18	4	467	3	106
Tennessee	6	1,522	20	230	2	400	2	13
Texas	18	3,114	27	728	35	5,163	2	39
Virginia	11	503	14	77	7	416	4	11
West Virginia	8	464	7	99	1	60	0	
TOTALS	129	17,138	200	4,061	139	17,066	27	394

SOURCES: Chandler and Rice, 1967, pp. 52–134; and *Chronicle of Higher Education* ("White, Negro Undergraduates at Colleges . . ."), April 22, 1968, pp. 3–4.

broaden opportunities for Negro students in interracial colleges," NSSFNS has identified competent Negro high school students and assisted them in enrolling at interracial colleges. The assistance has included supplementary financial aid, as well as scholarship aid from the colleges in which the students enroll. Plaut reports that, in 1965, NSSFNS counselees were awarded more than $1.5 million through college scholarships and other sources and that this amount was supplemented by $100,000 from NSSFNS (Plaut, 1966, pp. 393–399). Further, he reports that in 1966 the number of counselees increased to 9,000 from only 2,500 two years earlier (ibid.). The National Achievement Program also is concerned with the identification of academically able Negro high school students. Established in 1964 by a grant of $7 million from the Ford Foundation to the National Merit Scholarship Corporation, the National Achievement Program annually awards college scholarships up to $1,500 to at least 200 Negro high school graduates (ibid. p. 394). Although National Merit Scholarship selectees are free to choose their own colleges, the vast majority of them choose to attend

TABLE 10
The 1967–68
undergraduate
enrollment of
Negroes in
Northern
colleges, by
state

State	Number of white colleges in state	Number of white colleges in state with Negro enrollments	Total number of Negroes enrolled in white colleges
Alaska	2	2	30
Arizona	10	10	1,226
California	124	123	28,478
Colorado	19	19	916
Connecticut	23	23	1,266
Hawaii	4	3	172
Idaho	8	7	81
Illinois	69	65	12,082
Indiana	31	31	3,357
Iowa	42	40	1,015
Kansas	32	32	2,881
Maine	11	10	94
Massachusetts	75	70	2,203
Michigan	53	53	10,538
Minnesota	35	31	589
Montana	9	8	94
Nebraska	19	19	604
Nevada	2	2	216
New Hampshire	10	10	165
New Jersey	28	27	1,634
New Mexico	8	8	421
New York	112	111	8,720
North Dakota	9	8	79
Ohio	53	52	6,267
Oregon	24	22	1,021
Pennsylvania	90	89	5,837
Rhode Island	11	10	486
South Dakota	12	9	88
Utah	9	6	155
Vermont	12	10	88
Washington	36	34	2,312
Wisconsin	28	26	1,447
Wyoming	2	2	42
ALL STATES	1,012	972	94,604

SOURCES: Chandler and Rice, 1967, pp. 52–134; and *Chronicle of Higher Education* ("White, Negro Undergraduates at Colleges . . ."), April 22, 1968, pp. 3–4.

prestigious colleges of the North.

A third factor which has contributed to the marked increase in the enrollment of Negroes in Northern colleges has been the expanded activities of individual Northern colleges in recruitment. Institutions which have expanded their activities in recruiting Negro students include many of the well-known colleges and universities, such as Amherst, Bowdoin, Harvard, Hofstra, New York University, University of California, Los Angeles, University of Michigan, and Wesleyan. The recruitment activities of many of the colleges have been conducted on the basis that special provisions would be made for Negro students prior to or after their admission. Such provisions include summer study, reduced course loads, longer periods for graduation, and special counseling (Plaut, 1966, pp. 395 ff.).

3 Negro colleges in the South have increased their enrollment of under-graduate students (among four-year colleges, from 63,000 in 1954 to about 134,000 in 1968). Thus, it may be concluded that these colleges have continued to enroll the majority of Negro students in the South.

4 Although the historically Negro colleges have always, or recently, accepted the principle of racially desegregated education, they have not enrolled many white students. Exceptions to this generalization include Bluefield State, West Virginia State, and Lincoln University, Missouri, in which the majority of students are white; and Bowie State, Central State, Cheyney State, Kentucky State, and Lincoln University, Pennsylvania, in which the enrollment of white students ranges from 16 to 31 percent. It should be noted that all these colleges are located in border and Northern states.

A second significant change during the period under review is the continued migration of Negroes from the South to large cities of the North and West, this phenomenon producing a situation in which only a little more than half the Negroes in the United States now reside in the South. Thus, the higher education of Negroes, once the major concern and responsibility of the South, has become the equal concern and responsibility of the North and the South. In this connection, note the following developments:

1 The enrollment of Negroes in Northern colleges increased from almost 45,000 in 1954 to almost 95,000 in 1968.

2 In some of the large cities of the North and West, colleges with high percentages of Negro students are developing. This is a new phenomenon for these sections of the United States.

3 The historically white colleges of the North have begun to expand their recruiting activities to include the recruitment of Negro students.

SUMMARY

The higher education of Negroes during the period 1954 to 1968 has occurred within the framework of significant, if not revolutionary, changes in the United States. The changes are still in process; many of them are being undertaken with uncertainty, and many appear counteracting because they proceed from divergent premises. Thus, the period may be characterized as one of stark transition in the higher education of Negroes.

One of the significant changes was the United States Supreme Court's 1954 interpretation that segregation in public education is unconstitutional. This interpretation destroyed the concept of the separate-but-equal doctrine which had produced a separate system of higher education for Negroes, especially in the South, and opened the way for the new concept of "equality within the framework of racial desegregation."

There is evidence to indicate that the early stages in the development of the new concept have been entered; however, there is much uncertainty with respect to later stages and, consequently, with respect to next steps that should be taken. Note some of the evidence to support this position:

1 The white colleges in the South have increased their enrollment of under-graduate Negro students from approximately 3,000 in 1957 to approximately 39,000 in 1968. The increase, however, varies significantly among the states.

2 The white colleges in the South have accepted, almost universally, the principle that Negro students should be admitted. In 1968 only 24 of 495 of these colleges had no enrollment of Negro students. On the other hand, the small number of Negro students in so many of the colleges suggests that there has been only token acceptance of the principle.

[1] *State of Florida ex rel. Hawkins*, 347 U.S. 971; *Tureaud v. Board*, 347 U.S. 971; *Wichita Falls v. Battle*, 347 U.S. 974.

[2] Enrollment figures were not available for all 54 of the four-year private institutions.

[3] At publication the number had decreased to 34 (see Appendix B). Maryland State College became a part of the University of Maryland in 1970.

[4] One of these, Maryland State College, became a part of the University of Maryland, Easternshore, in July, 1970.

Article References

Alter, C. M. *A Profile of United Negro College Fund Members: Past, Present, and Future.* Denver: Academy for Educational Development, 1968. (Mimeographed)

Batten, J. K. "The Nixonians and School Desegregation." *Southern Education Report* 4 (No. 28, 1969).

Chandler, M.O., and Rice, M.C. *Opening Fall Enrollment in Higher Education,* 1967. Washington, D.C.: U.S. Office of Education, 1967.

Cozart, L.S. *A History of the Association of Colleges and Secondary Schools.* Charlotte, N.C.: Heritage Printers, Inc., 1967.

Doddy, H.H. "The Progress of the Negro in Higher Education." *Journal of Negro Education* 32 (No. 4, 1963): 485-492.

Huddleston, E. M., and Sulkin, N. A. *Comprehensive Report on Enrollment in Higher Education, 1961-62.* Washington, D.C.: U.S. Government Printing Office, 1964.

Indritz, Phineas. "The Meaning of the School Decisions: The Breakthrough on the Legal Front of Racial Segregation." *Journal of Negro Education* 23 (No. 3, 1954): 355-363.

Jenkins, M.D. "Enrollment in Institutions of Higher Education of Negroes." *Journal of Negro Education* 9 (1940): 268-270; *Journal of Negro Education* 19 (1950): 198-208; *Journal of Negro Education* 23 (No. 2, 1954): 139-151.

Johnson, G.B. "Desegregation in Southern Higher Education." *Higher Education* 20 (June 1964): 5-7.

Meredith, J.H. *Three Years in Mississippi.* Bloomington, Ind.: Indiana University Press, 1966.

Newman, D.K. "The Negro's Journey to the City—Part I." *Monthly Labor Review* 88 (No. 5, 1965): 502-507.

Parham, J.B. "Halls of Ivy—Southern Exposure." In *With All Deliberate Speed.* Edited by Don Shoemaker. New York: Harper & Bros., 1957.

Plaut, R.L. "Plans for Assisting Negro Students to Enter and to Remain in College." *Journal of Negro Education* 35 (No. 9, 1966): 393-399.

Poole, H.C. *Resident, Extension, and Other Enrollments in Institutions of Higher Education, 1957-1958.* Washington, D.C.: U.S. Government Printing Office, 1959.

Sarratt, R. *The Ordeal of Segregation.* New York: Harper & Row, Publisher, Inc., 1966.

Singletary, O.A., ed. *American Universities and Colleges.* 10th Ed. Washington, D.C.: American Council on Education, 1968.

Southern Education Reporting Service. *Statistical Summary, 1964-65.* Nashville, Tenn.: Southern Education Reporting Service, 1965.

Thompson, C.H. "The Desegregsation Decision—One Year Afterward." *Journal of Negro Education* 24 (No. 3, 1955): 161-164.

Indian, Chicano, and Puerto Rican Colleges: Status and Issues

Michael A. Olivas

ABSTRACT

The enormous problems facing Indian, Chicano, and Puerto Rican colleges have not been addressed by legislative efforts aimed at redressing historic exclusion nor by educational assistance designed for colleges in general. In the unique case of Indian colleges, specific legislation and program initiatives have not been effective, in part because of the fragile nature of the colleges themselves and in part because of the organizational difficulties Indian people face daily in their relationship with government agencies. Because there are only three historically Hispanic colleges, efforts to improve access for Hispanic students are not likely to be successful through minority institution initiatives.

National debates over racial inequality have historically centered upon slavery, its abolition, and its vestiges. Historical perspectives of educational inequality arise from the same memory, inevitably framing educational debates in terms of access for blacks into white institutions and school systems. Because majority Americans frequently perceive equality solely in terms of increased minority access into white institutions, adequacy of public resources for minority-controlled institutions is not often acknowledged as a corollary dimension of increased minority access. Yet, the litigation in the *Adams v. Califano* case,[1] leading to "desegregation" of black higher education institutions, has caused educators and policymakers to confront this dimension and to consider the role of black colleges in a society that perceives itself to be integrated.[2]

The Status of Historically Black Colleges

Lorenzo Morris has succinctly summarized the risk for black colleges in a search for racial balance:

> At a fundamental level of the disagreement over the Adams case(s) is a conceptual difference concerning black colleges: What are their goals, and what has been the role they fill in society? On one side, they are viewed as being just like all other colleges and universities, except for their histories of unique service to blacks under conditions in which black students and faculty have had no other educational choices. On the advocates' side, the historical conditions are similarly emphasized, but there is a rarely articulated view that black colleges are a product of the choice of black Americans and not simply a byproduct of a no-choice situation. Some imply that black institutions are an automatic outgrowth of racial inequality. Advocates, however, maintain that black institutions are the willful creations of a people seeking an opportunity that has been restricted everywhere else. Blacks attend and have attended black institutions under great constraints, but ultimately have made the choice to do so because these institutions offer them what they want and need. Through that free choice, [black colleges] are understood to have developed a special capacity to serve their communities—a capacity which will constitute an essential part of free choice in the education of blacks for a long time to come.[3]

This disagreement has profound implications for the framing of arguments and policy choices. How will white and black institutions co-exist in proximity with each other? How can both recruit a shrinking pool of qualified students? How can both draw upon state and private funds? How can historical funding patterns favoring white institutions be altered to compensate for historical underdevelopment? While no answers are proposed in this article, the questions are not rhetorical, for desegregation plans have been drafted, institutions have merged (e.g., the University of Tennessee at Nashville merged with Tennessee State University[4]), and legislation has been amended to incorporate *Adams* issues. Southern and northern states have submitted *Adams* plans to the courts for approval[5] and the Higher Education Act of 1965 reauthorized by Congress contains language requiring that federal programs comply with *Adams* mandates.[6]

The future of the 106 black colleges, particularly the 43 public black colleges,[7] remains uncertain, although recent events suggest a belated acknowledgement of federal responsibility for the network of historically black institutions. President Carter was aggressive in supporting these institutions. In January 1979, he signed a memorandum for a "Black College Initiative"; in August 1980 he signed Executive Order 12232, directing federal agencies to target money for black institutions; in September 1980 he signed another memorandum to accompany the Executive Order (see Appendix A).[8] A black college "setaside" has been incorporated into Title III of the Higher Education Act, while the College Housing Program targeted 10% of its 1980 monies for black college facilities.[9] Several federal departments have designated staff to monitor the Executive Order and Initiative and the charter of the National Advisory Committee on Black Higher Education and Black Colleges and Universities has been renewed.[10] These formal structures have increased black colleges' share of federal dollars and have provided visibility, portfolio, and support for the Black College Initiative.

The attention paid these institutions, however, has not led to comparable initiatives for other minority institutions. The memory of slavery and its present-day legacy, as well as the existence of a network of historically black colleges, have served to overshadow the more fledgling network of non-black minority institutions. Further, the larger societal perception of "minority" issues as synonymous with black civil rights derives from the larger black presence in the American minority population. Additionally, although the black colleges enroll a smaller percentage of black students than they have in the past when the colleges were the near-exclusive avenues of access (in 1976, the 106 colleges enrolled only 18% of the black students),[11] many black leaders have graduated from these colleges; this alumni network is widespread in black communities and constitutes an important minority constituency.

Non-black minorities lack such an extensive historical network, for the few Indians, Chicanos, and Puerto Ricans who hold college degrees are graduates of majority institutions. No similar network has developed for Indians, Chicanos, and Puerto Ricans, for reasons that are unclear. Although it is incontestable that these minorities have been denied educational access equal to that of majority citizens, the differences in the groups' histories of oppression may account, in part, for the lack of a college network comparable to that of blacks.

Many black colleges have been creations of official governmental segregation policies, precluding blacks from attending white colleges. A recent National Center for Education Statistics study noted of black colleges:

> They were established primarily through the efforts of missionary groups, northern-based philanthropists, and the Freedman's Bureau. More than half . . . were created during the Reconstruction period and prior to 1890. The second Morrill Land Grant Act of 1890 spurred the construction of public [black colleges] with the intention of paralleling the network of land-grant institutions which had already been established for whites, thereby legalizing "separate colleges for whites and coloreds." The remainder . . . were constructed for the most part before the outbreak of World War I, although 10 new [black colleges] emerged in the 2 decades following World War II.[12]

No similar large-scale efforts were mounted or developed for colonized American minorities: Native Americans, the first occupants; Chicanos, *mestizo* descendants of Spaniards and Indians; or Puerto Ricans, whose island was claimed by the United States following the Spanish-American War.[13] Although extensive histories of these groups are beyond the scope of this paper, a brief summary of these histories adds context to the development of non-black minority institutions.

The Development of Indian Colleges

The historical development of higher education for Indians, Chicanos, and Puerto Ricans can be characterized as a record of evangelism, majority dominance, paternalism, and neglect. Although several prestigious colleges founded during colonial times (e.g., Harvard, Dartmouth, Columbia) had missions that included instructing Indians,[14] few Indians were educated in these institutions. Indeed, the founder of Dartmouth perhaps typified the colleges' view of educating Indians when he said of one of his students, "I have taken much Pains to purge all the Indian out of him, but after all a little of it will sometimes appear."[15]

Also typical was the abrogation of education treaties signed between the U.S. government and Indian tribes. While the government issued regulations, created special funds, and sold Indian land to finance Indian education, the most common mechanism to educate Indian children before 1870 was by treaty.[16] Of these treaties, Vine Deloria has noted,

> Treaty records and related correspondence in the nation's archives relate only to a fraction of the nearly 400 treaties negotiated from 1778 to 1871. Many agreements were oral; many records have been lost. Records that do exist show conclusively, however, that Indian nations ceded their lands to the federal government with great reluctance and that they did so in the end largely on the basis of federal promises to educate their children.[17]

Appendix B lists over 100 treaties negotiated between 1804 and 1868 that had educational provisions.

Even though the treaties were patently one-sided, the government did not meet its responsibilities. A recent congressional report noted of education treaties, "Many treaty provisions for education were never effective since Congress failed to appropriate the funds to fulfill those obligations."[18] Moreover, as treaties expired, these sources of income became even less secure. The first treaty provisions for Indian higher education appear to be in a September 1830 treaty with the Choctaw Nation,[19] although the money was not used until 1841 when Indian students were given scholarships to attend white colleges; students also attended Hampton Institute, then a black normal school, under other scholarship provisions.[20]

Sheldon Jackson College was founded for Alaskan Natives in 1878 by the United Presbyterian Church.[21] Indian University was founded by the American Baptist Church in Tahlequah, Creek Nation, in February 1880; it moved in 1885 to Muskogee (later Muskogee, Oklahoma) and became known as Bacone College.[22] In 1887, North Carolina established a normal school for Indian students; it became a college in the 1930s and offered its first degree in 1940; in 1969 it became Pembroke State University, which in 1978 still enrolled over 20% Indian students.[23] No additional efforts were undertaken to establish Indian colleges until the 1960s. What federal efforts were aimed at assisting Indians to attend college consisted of establishing normal schools (including Carlisle and Haskell high schools), providing boarding or reservation schools, arranging special contracts with mission schools or black normal schools (e.g., Hampton Institute), and funding scholarships for the few Indian college students to attend majority institutions.[24]

The hodgepodge nature of support had prompted the federal Superintendent of Indian Schools to report in 1886, "The systematic organization of the educational work of the Indian [is] an impossibility."[25] The federal efforts, meager as they were, were consolidated in the Indian Reorganization Act and Johnson-O'Malley Act of 1934, although Indian affairs continued to be spread over the Bureau of Indian Affairs (BIA) of the Department of the Interior, the Office of Education, and other public agencies and departments whose policies affected Indians. It was not until 1966 that BIA officials began to plan for a federally sponsored Indian college, when studies were begun to extend Haskell Institute's high school program into a junior college, offering the first two years of a college curriculum. This effort took four years, resulting in the accreditation of Haskell Indian Junior College in 1970. Other BIA-administered colleges include the Institute for American Indian Arts, which in 1968 became the postsecondary extension of the Santa Fe Indian School, and the Southwestern Polytechnic Institute, established in Albuquerque in 1973.[26]

In addition to state-established and BIA colleges and religious-affiliated colleges, a fourth category of Indian colleges was established in 1968, when Navajo Nation began Navajo Community College. More than a dozen tribes have since established tribal colleges with Indian community boards of trustees. This has become the most fruitful method of establishing Indian colleges. Although Navajo Community College was begun as an independent tribal institution,[27] the smaller tribes have established a fifth type of institution—affiliating themselves with larger, accredited colleges, either as branch campuses or extension centers of majority institutions.

In this manner, a public institution such as Oglala Sioux Community College evolved from its original affiliated status with Black Hills State College and the Univeristy of South Dakota into a preaccredited candidate for formal accreditation on its own. Sinte Gleska College, a private institution, has also moved from its ties to Black Hills and the University of South Dakota to similar preaccredited status.[28] The Lummi tribe has an arrangement with Whatcom Community College in Bellingham, Washington, to offer a degree in aquaculture (fishery management), with technical courses taught on Lummi Island and the certificate awarded by the mainland campus.[29] Through these creative means, Indians have begun to organize and administer tribal colleges and other Indian institutions. However, these schools' relative recency and their dependency upon majority institutions for demographic and political reasons have stifled the development of Indian colleges. Sadly, the status of many of these institutions is uncertain and the list (see Table 1) is fluid. In particular the rural isolation, lack of property tax bases, and benign neglect by government have stunted the growth of Indian colleges.[30]

Historically Chicano Institutions

The development of higher education for Chicanos has had a radically different history from that for Native Americans, although the benign neglect accorded Indian education policy was similarly accorded Hispanic groups living in the Southwest and Puerto Rico once these lands became United States territory. One commentator, writing in 1914, likened Mexican American educational conditions to those of blacks:

> Just so surely as Booker T. Washington is right in saying that Tuskegee and similar institutions are the ultimate solution of the Negro problem, so surely is the same kind of education the necessary basis upon which to build a thorough and complete solution of the Mexican problem. Like the Negro, the Mexicans are a child-race without the generations of civilization and culture back of them which support the people of the United States.[31]

Not only was this commentator surely ignorant of black and Mexican history and culture, but the reference to Booker T. Washington and Tuskegee makes precisely the opposite point intended: Although many whites sought only to relegate blacks to black colleges and to prevent them from attending white institutions, blacks took the development of their own colleges seriously and developed black leadership through these institutions.[32] Chicanos, however, were not relegated to their own institutions, since racism, their economic condition, and the rural characteristics of the Southwest precluded them from completing elementary and secondary school, while no governmental or religious groups founded colleges for Mexican Americans.[33] One education historian has noted, "Mexican American children suffered not only the general inadequacies and discrimination of the rural school and castelike community social structure but also the additional handicap of migrancy."[34]

Concerning the children of migrants in California, Irving Hendrick has summarized: "Responsibility for formal schooling of migrant children was not being assumed by any agency of local, county, or state government until after 1920."[35] Even with a California state plan for migrant education begun in 1920, local school districts ignored truancy laws and failed to serve these students.[36] Complex problems of poverty, increasing urbanization of Chicano families, immigration from Mexico, deportation of Mexican-origin Americans, segregation, and English-only instruction characterized Mexican American education and precluded the development of historically Chicano colleges.[37]

In the 1960s, increasing minority political participation led to the development of Chicano Studies programs in majority colleges, the establishment of "Third World colleges" within majority universities (e.g., Oakes College at the University of California at Santa Cruz), and the establishment of alternative Chicano postsecondary institutions: Juárez-Lincoln Center (Austin, Texas); Colegio Jacinto Treviño (Mercedes, Texas); Universidad

TABLE 1

Indian Colleges

College (State) [Affiliated Institution]	Public: Private 2 yr/4yr	1979 Accred. Status	BIA/ Tribal Affiliation
Bacone College (OK)	Priv, 2	1	—
Blackfeet Community College (MT) [Flathead Valley CC]	Publ, 2	4	Blackfeet
Cheyenne River Community College (SD) [Northern State C]	Publ, 2	4	Cheyenne River Sioux
College of Ganado (AZ)	Priv, 2	1	Hopi
Dull Knife Memorial College (MT) [Miles C]	Publ, 2	4	Northern Cheyenne
Flaming Rainbow University (OK)	Priv, 2	4†	—
Fort Berthold College Center (ND) [Mary C]	Priv, 2	4	Mandan, Hidatsa, Arikara
Fort Peck Community College (MT)	Publ, 2	4	Assiniboine and Sioux
Haskell Indian Junior College (KS)	Publ, 2	1	BIA
Hehaka Sapa College at D-Q University (CA)	Priv, 2	1	Hoopa Valley, Soboba
Institute of American Indian Arts (NM)	Publ, 2	2	BIA
Inupiat University (AK)	Priv, 4	2	Inupiaq Eskimo
Little Bighorn Community College (MT) [Miles C]	Publ, 2	4	Crow
Little Hoop Community College (ND) [Lake Region JC]	Publ, 2	4	Devil's Lake Sioux
Lummi School of Aquaculture (WA) [Whatcom CC]	Publ, 2	3	Lummi
Native American Educational Services (IL)	Priv, 4	2	—
Navajo Community College (AZ)	Publ, 2	1	Navajo
Navajo Community College Branch (NM) [Navajo CC]	Publ, 2	3	
Nebraska Indian Community College (NE) [Northeast Technical C]	Publ, 2	4	Santee Sioux, Omaha, Winnebago
Nebraska Indian Satellite CC (NE) [Nebraska Indian CC]	Publ, 2	3	
Oglala Sioux Community College (SD)	Publ, 2	4†	Oglala Sioux
*Pembroke State University (NC)	Publ, 4	1	—
Salish-Kootenai Community College (MT) [Flathead Valley CC]	Publ, 2	4	Salish, Kootenai
Sheldon Jackson College (AK)	Priv, 4	1	—
Sinte Gleska College (SD)	Priv, 4	2	Rosebud Sioux
Sisseton-Wahpeton Community College (SD)	Publ, 2	4	Sisseton-Wahpeton Sioux
Southwestern Indian Polytechnic Institute (NM)	Publ, 2	1	BIA
Standing Rock Community College (ND)	Priv, 2	2	Standing Rock Sioux
Turtle Mountain Community College (ND) [North Dakota State U at Bottineau]	Publ, 2	2	Turtle Mountain Chippewa

Accreditation Key: (1) Accredited; (2) Preaccredited; (3) Branch or extension campus; (4) Unaccredited.

* Formerly Pembroke State College for Indians.

† Not listed in *Accredited Postsecondary Institutions* (September 1, 1979), but listed as having preaccredited status in *Education Directory* (May, 1980).

de Aztlán (Fresno, California); Escuela y Colegio Tlatelolco (Denver, Colorado); Colegio César Chávez (Mt. Angel, Oregon); and Deganawidah-Quetzalcoatl (D-Q) University (Davis, California), begun as a Chicano-Indian college.[38] Of the alternative institutions—all established in the late 1960s and early 1970s—only Colegio César Chávez and the Indian college of D-Q University (Hehaka Sapa) remain in 1980.[39] D-Q University (see Table 1) is accredited by the Western Association of Schools and Colleges (Accrediting Commission for Community and Junior Colleges), and Colegio César Chávez has preaccredited status with the Northwest Association of Schools and Colleges (Commission on Colleges).[40] Both institutions secured their campuses through struggles with the federal government over the land: the Davis land was a federal military base, while the Colegio campus was formerly a Catholic seminary.[41]

TABLE 2

Chicano and Puerto Rican Colleges

	Accred. status	Publ.	Priv.	2 yr.	4 yr.	UG FT Enrollment 1978	UG Total 1978
Chicano							
Colegio César Chávez Mt. Angel, Oregon	2		X		X	25	25
Puerto Rican							
Boricua College New York, NY	2		X		X	455	455
Hostos Community College New York, NY	1	X		X		2506	2634

(1) Accredited; (2) Preaccreditation status

Even with the acquisition of its campus, the establishment of a research institute (Instituto Colegial César Chávez), and preaccreditation status, Colegio César Chávez has a difficult future until it increases and stabilizes its enrollment, which in 1978-79 stood at a mere 25 full-time undergraduates in the four-year institution. Its struggles to become established and to secure its campus, its focus to serve older students and migrant farmworkers, its rural isolation, and its founding in a time when few institutions are being established all have prevented the Colegio from being recognized and supported by the larger Chicano community. Today it remains virtually unknown outside the Chicano education or alternative college communities.

This is unfortunate, for the Chicano condition in higher education is not good, and, with the exception of Colegio César Chávez, Chicano students are enrolled in historically majority schools, predominantly two-year colleges. Furthermore, in mid-1981 the status of Colegio César Chávez became even more precarious when it was denied accreditation by the Northwest Association of Schools and Colleges.[42] Without a developed, historically Chicano college, Chicano students have a diminished range of institutions from which to choose, although the demographics of some previously majority schools have changed to enroll predominantly Chicano student bodies.[43] A few of these institutions (e.g., New Mexico Highlands University, East Los Angeles College, Northern New Mexico Community College) have significant Chicano administrative leadership, while others (e.g., California State University at Los Angeles or Pan American University) have never had Chicano presidents.[44] The future of Chicanos in higher education appears to be in penetrating majority institutions, convincing policymakers that minority institution programs will not reach enough Chicano students, strengthening the network of Hispanic community-based organizations to supplement the colleges,[45] and in attracting wider community support for Colegio César Chávez.

Historically Puerto Rican Colleges

Within the Hispanic communities, Puerto Ricans in the 50 states and D.C. are the most educationally disadvantaged subgroup. For instance, although the 1976 high school non-completion rate for all Hispanic students was 25%, the figure for Puerto Ricans was 31%.[46] This appalling figure means that 3 of 10 Puerto Ricans between the ages of 14 and 30 were not in school and had not completed their high school degree. The figure for male Puerto Ricans was 35%.[47] Moreover, even the seeming progress has been illusory: "From 1950 to 1970 the median school attainment for continental Puerto Ricans advanced nearly two years. But this was due primarily to a shift from elementary school attainment to partial high school, and not to an increase in the high school completion rate, which remained proportionately the same."[48]

The colonization of Puerto Rico by the United States as a result of the Spanish-American War replaced the Island's earlier colonization by Spain; in 1899, Puerto Rico came under the jurisdiction of the U.S.[49] A series of laws since that time has not yet given autonomy to Puerto Ricans, who, since 1952, have been residents of the Commonwealth of Puerto Rico.[50] Thus, like Native Americans and Mexican Americans, Puerto Ricans share a colonial heritage. The poor condition of Puerto Rican education is, in part, the legacy of the economic exploitation of Puerto Rico, first by Spain and thereafter by the United States.

While sharing a history of colonialism with other indigenous American minority groups, the demographic and political characteristics of Puerto Ricans have resulted in a different educational history. Migration and reverse migration from the Island to the mainland and back have been major determinants of Puerto Rican educational access, including that to higher education. By 1910, Puerto Ricans in the states and D.C. numbered several thousand; by 1940, the number was approximately 70,000; by 1978, the number had grown to more than 1.8 million.[51] While most Puerto Ricans have settled in the industrial Northeast (notably New York, New Jersey, and Connecticut), large numbers of Puerto Ricans have settled in Hawaii, Florida, and California.[52]

That this massive migration occurred did not mean, however, that Puerto Ricans had increased access to mainland higher education. In 1970, for instance, New York City census data revealed that there were only 3,500 Puerto Rican college graduates in the city, an increase of only 1,000 since the 1960 census.[53] The open admissions policy of the City University of New York (CUNY), begun in 1970, substantially increased Puerto Rican enrollments, although the city's fiscal crisis has since decreased minority access.[54] In 1970, Puerto Ricans comprised 4.8% of CUNY undergraduates; by 1974 this had increased to 7.4%; Puerto Rican first-time freshmen in New York State during the same period went from 7.8% to 13.4%.[55]

It was during this time of drafting plans for an open door policy for the CUNY system that Hostos Community College was established in the South Bronx. Begun in late 1969, Hostos was the first historically Puerto Rican college to be established in the continental United States.[56] Hostos enrolls more than 2,500 students as freshmen or sophmores[57] and is accredited by the Middle States Association of Colleges and Secondary Schools, Commission on Higher Education, making it the only fully accredited Hispanic institution in the continental United States.[58]

Despite its successes, however, Hostos remains a poor relation within the CUNY system. Although it is ten years old, it has no permanent campus. Students attend classes in rooms rented in offices on the Grand Concourse in South Bronx, minutes from the spot where President Carter appeared in a "photo opportunity" to pledge his support for rebuilding the devastated slums. The fiscal crisis in New York City has prevented any construction or substantial long-term support to the college, although the students who attend are drawn from the City's poorest borough.[59] However, the college is expanding its curriculum and its status as a public institution assures a continuing base of government support.

Boricua College, the second historically Puerto Rican college, evolved from Universidad Boricua, which in turn had grown from a community group in Washington, D. C.—the Puerto Rican Research and Resources Center, Inc.[60] Boricua was established in Brooklyn in late 1973 and enrolled its first class in 1974; it opened a second facility in Manhattan in 1976.[61] A distinctive characteristic of Boricua is its network of off-campus classrooms. Its catalog boasts that "lofts, storefronts, and other easily-accessible facilities seem quite as satisfactory as ivy-covered monumental structures."[62]

Boricua's enrollment is 455 freshmen and sophmores. It has attempted to reach an extraordinarily neglected segment of the disadvantaged: older students whose situation in life prevented their having been accorded the access made available to the more traditional college-going population through CUNY's open door policies of the early 1970s. Boricua's bilingual courses and academic credits for life experiences may ameliorate to a small extent the historical exclusion of Puerto Ricans from mainland colleges.[63]

Higher education in Puerto Rico, however, has thrived. Whereas in 1940 there were only 5,000 college students on the Island, by 1970 this number had grown to 257,000.[64] By 1978, colleges in Puerto Rico enrolled one quarter of all full-time undergraduate Hispanic students in the United States and awarded over 30% of all the baccalaureate degrees.[65] [See Appendix C for selected characteristics of colleges in Puerto Rico.] In 1975, four percent (4,547) of the Puerto Rican residents enrolled in college attended school in the 50 states or D.C., while 1,300 students from the mainland enrolled in Puerto Rican colleges.[66]

Legal and Legislative Issues

As the initial sections have indicated, the survival status of Indian, Chicano, and Puerto Rican colleges is the major issue confronting these institutions. While majority institutions have serious concerns of survival in difficult economic times and while black institutions continue to face economic and legal peril, non-black minority colleges face far more serious economic futures. Their attempts at development are occurring in a time of retrenchment throughout higher education and at a time when public support of minority issues is less evident than that shown during the enactment of the 1965 Higher Education Act.[67] Moreover, several fundamental issues of a legal and legislative nature uniquely affect Indian, Chicano, and Puerto Rican colleges. Chief among these issues is identification: What is an Indian college? What is an historically Chicano or Puerto Rican college? Although these questions seem rhetorical, government programs and community support issues make the answers important. Much as black college leaders have coined new designations for institutions that serve black students but do not have "historically" or "traditionally" black missions,[68] Indian and Latino educators have insisted upon certain criteria for designation, affiliation, and program eligibility.[69]

For Indians, these criteria include a record of service to Indians or a historical Indian mission, tribal affiliation, majority Indian control or influence, a predominantly Indian student body, or a combination of these factors. Applied strictly, these criteria would include few institutions, particularly since issues of tribal identification and control fluctuate and corollary Indian legislation alters standards and even removes or restores tribal status.[70] A list of Indian institutions such as that in Table 1 necessitates as many footnotes as entries. Pembroke State University, founded for Indians, today enrolls approximately 20% Indians; in this regard, Pembroke resembles three formerly black, now predominantly white, colleges—Bluefield State College, Lincoln State University, and West Virginia State—that have been considered "traditionally black," with an asterisk.[71]

These definitional issues are not mere ethnic nitpicking, for program eligibility and political identification are important factors in minority self-determination and in educational policymaking for minority access. In the 1979 Title III (Strengthening Developing Institutions) awards, for instance, only 7 of the 25 awards to Indian Programs[72] went to the Indian colleges listed in Table 1; four of the majority institutions are affiliated with the Indian colleges in Table 1, and these arrangements had Indian participation. As Indian testimony in the Title III reauthorization noted, however, the bulk of this money designed to strengthen Indian colleges is being administered by majority institutions.[73]

More fundamental definitional issues underlie all of Indian education (indeed, all Indian affairs), and although they are beyond the scope of this article, they deserve mention to show the dilemma inherent in the need for governmental targeting of Indian programs and Indian self-definition and self-determination. Thus, for Census Bureau purposes in the 1970 questionnaire, persons identified themselves as "Indian (American)" and delineated their tribal membership and race.[74] Education eligibility for Indian programs, however, is more specific and draws upon Department of the Interior recognition and the Alaska Native Claims Settlement Act[75] for identification. In the main, these are overlapping definitions[76] incorporated into the Indian Education Act, which consist of tribal membership or enrollment, blood quantum (Indian descendancy in the first or second degree), status as an Eskimo, Aleut, or other Alaska Native, or other evidence of Indian heritage.[77] Of course, these issues have resulted in litigation, which most frequently results in inaccurate or debilitating results for Indians: confusing the Blackfeet and Sioux Blackfoot,[78] ignoring unanimous expert testimony and interpretation of treaties,[79] and deciding that the Wampanoag (Mashpees) were not a tribe and therefore had no standing in a land claim.[80]

Although it has not yet been litigated, the concept of what constitutes an Indian college is a potential conflict area, particularly if more federal programs emerge to direct assistance to minority initiatives and as more majority institutions receive federal money to serve Indian students.[81] Two examples of the ambiguity over Indian institutions or Indian eligibility will serve to illustrate the potential for conflict or confusion: What is an "Indian college" and what is an "institution of higher education"?

Recently published rules and regulations for the Indian Education Act[82] define an "Indian institution" as a "[postsecondary school] that— (1) Is established for the education of Indians; (2) Is controlled by a governing board, the majority of which is Indian; and (3) If located on an Indian reservation, operates with the sanction or by charter of the governing body of that reservation."[83] Under the terms of the Tribally Controlled Community College Assistance Act of 1978 (PL 95-471)[84] stricter definitions are drawn since only tribally controlled community colleges are targeted, except for Navajo Community College, which has its own federal legislation.[85] Any eligible institution[86] is required to be "formally controlled, or . . . formally sanctioned, or chartered, by the governing body of an Indian tribe or tribes, except that no more than one such institution shall be recognized with respect to any such tribe";[87] further, it "must be one which— (1) is governed by a board of directors or board of trustees a majority of which are Indians; (2) demonstrates adherence to stated goals, a philosophy, or a plan of operation which is directed to meet the needs of Indians; and (3) if in operation for more than a year, has students a majority of whom are Indians."[88]

While there may not need to be any clarification of these two definitions, there are curious scenarios that could occur to vitiate the purpose of either act. Taking into account the demographic characteristics of the colleges noted in Table 1, these scenarios are not far-fetched. Under the Indian Education Act, for instance, a predominantly Indian student body is not required for eligibility. It is conceivable that Indians could win election, be appointed to, or otherwise control a majority institution governing board, and by establishing an Indian mission could create an Indian institution—entitling such a non-reservation college to eligibility for a number of adult education programs under the Act.

Several colleges have altered their governance structure and have become tribal institutions. One such college is the College of Ganado, in Ganado, Arizona, on the Navajo Reservation. Previously a private college affiliated with the United Presbyterian Church,[89] the college has become a tribally controlled community college of the Hopi Tribe and is eligible for money from the Tribally Controlled Community College Assistance Act.[90] D-Q University, established as an Indian-Chicano College, is now chartered by the Hoopa Valley and Soboba tribes.[91] In both instances, institutions with predominantly Indian student enrollments reconstituted themselves and secured tribal charters. In both instances, the rural isolation and college characteristics made such transformations possible and economical.

In future cases, however, policymakers would do well to recall the distribution of resources for Indian institutional development, administered by majority institutions. While the eligibility requirements of Title III are not race-specific, many white institutions have taken Indian program initiatives in order to be eligible for Developing Institutions resources without altering their basic governance structures, which rarely include Indians.[92] Indeed, a 1976 survey of all two-year college trustees noted that fewer than .2 of 1% were Indian.[93]

A more important definitional issue than that of "Indian college" may be the definition, seemingly obvious, of "institution of higher education." The Tribally Controlled Community College Assistance Act (PL 95-471) requires that eligible colleges be "institutions of higher education" in the commonly understood and statutory meaning of the terms.[94] However, as with other provisions of law, when applied to special populations—in this case, Indian colleges—the definition becomes less obvious and may prevent the target population from being effectively served. PL 95-471 breaks down at this threshold point, for few tribally controlled community colleges can meet the definitional tests of "institutions," notably in the requirements for accreditation status. In this case, Indian colleges find themselves in a classic catch-22 situation: They are not eligible for Act money because they are not accredited, but they cannot secure accreditation without the development money and technical assistance promised in the Act.

Accreditation and Indian Colleges

The statutory definiton of "institutions of higher education" incorporates elements of post-high school admission, state authorization, degree credit, public or nonprofit status, and accreditation—all important elements for governmental and institutional quality control mechanisms. The fifth requirement, that institutions be "accredited by a nationally recognized accrediting agency or association," has become a hornets' nest as national political forces tug over accreditation authority and policy.[95] However, it is the exceptions to the accreditation requirements that have proven to be the rub for Indian colleges. The two exceptions to the accreditation requirement allow an unaccredited college to be an "institution of higher education" if it:

> (A) is an institution with respect to which the Commissioner has determined that there is satisfactory assurance, considering the resources available to the institution, the period of time, if any, during which it has operated, the effort it is making to meet accreditation standards, and the purpose for which this determination is being made, that the institution will meet the accreditation standards of such an agency or association within a reasonable time, or (B) is an institution whose credits are accepted, on transfer, by not less than three institutions which are so accredited, for credit on the same basis as if transferred from an institution so accredited... For purposes of this subsection, the Commissioner shall publish a list of nationally recognized accrediting agencies or associations which he determines to be reliable authority as to the quality of training offered.[96]

Anticipating that the unaccredited status of most Indian colleges would cause eligibility problems, the drafters of the original Tribally Controlled Community College Act bill (which had been proposed as an amendment to the Indian Self-Determination Act)[97] had incorporated the two exceptions into the bill. The legislation that emerged, however, simply incorporated the definition language, eliminating the redundant exemption references.[98]

This final language should not have been problematic, for the two waiver provisions still enabled the Commissioner (now, since the creation of the Department of Education, the Secretary) to interpret the "satisfactory assurance" generously; no regulations have been promulgated by the new Department to guide the Secretary in this regard, but in the face of larger political battles over accreditation, the Department has not chosen to interpret the colleges' status generously. Nor, inexplicably, have the colleges employed the easily available "3-letter" rule to trigger the other exemption provision. All that would be required is to enlist three accredited institutions in order to have credits accepted for transfer, but this waiver has not been widely adopted by the tribal colleges.[99]

As these issues became evident after the passage of the Tribal Act, another twist on the accreditation provisions came into play: feasibility studies. Under the terms of the Act, feasibility studies were required to "determine whether there is justification to start and maintain a tribally controlled community college."[100] These studies, to be conducted by the Secretary of the Interior, were strictly interpreted by the Office of Management and Budget (OMB) and the Bureau of Indian Affairs to require accreditation or candidacy as a measure of feasibility; the Bureau has added to the circularity of this requirement by noting that this criterion could be waived by the 3-letter rule—the accreditation waiver.[101] Thus, the accreditation requirement has an added requirement of feasibility, although accreditation standards are employed in determining feasibility. Indian educators have argued unsuccessfully that these dual requirements are redundant and that a recognized accreditation status should be prima facie evidence of any college's feasibility.[102]

Despite these difficulties, some of the tribal colleges have begun to receive money from the Act.[103] However, a coherent policy for administering Indian programs could have enabled these struggling institutions to receive the money earlier. The OMB has been inflexible in its review of feasibility criteria and has been unwilling to consider these colleges' characteristics as deserving special attention. Many Indian educators have blamed the BIA for its lukewarm support of the Tribal Act;[104] others blame the new Department of Education for its foot dragging.[105]

Both criticisms are accurate, for the BIA was not required to use accreditation as a feasibility criterion, and the Department of Education could have been more flexible in interpreting the colleges' progress toward accreditation. Indeed, the Department, in the absence of regulations governing eligibility, could have employed the discretion accorded it in Title III, where accreditation requirements for Developing Institutions eligibility can be waived in special circumstances where Indian and Spanish-speaking students will be served.[106] In either case, the bureaucratic delays have frustrated legislative attempts to create and enhance these Indian colleges.

The confusion over the Act has continued to mar its delivery of money to Indian colleges. An amendment to the Act was passed by the Senate on January 25, 1980, and was referred to the House Committee on Education and Labor on January 29; it was referred to the Subcommittee on Postsecondary Education, where it has remained since February 1.[107] The amendment clarifies the Indian eligibility requirement and increases the technical assistance authorization provisions.[108] Curiously, however, it further complicates the accreditation issue, for it restores portions of the redundant accreditation waiver provisions incorporated in the statutory definition of "institution of higher education," but gives the Secretary of the Interior (not the Secretary of Education) the authority to determine the reasonableness of the colleges' efforts toward accreditation.[109] This provision, if it were to be adopted, would further complicate the accreditation provisions, for a memorandum of agreement would have to be drafted between Interior and Education Departments to utilize the eligibility staff of the Department of Education, adding yet another layer of administration. A more reasonable approach would employ the Act's present language. Adopting accreditation or its waivers as evidence of feasibility for existing colleges would not require an amendment and would not require any renegotiation of the February 19, 1980, Memorandum of Agreement.[110] Clarifying the difference between accreditation and feasibility would give administrative guidance.

The Department of Interior has opposed passage of the increases in technical assistance authorizations contained in the amendments, predicting it would be too much money: "If all 21 [colleges] were to participate in $10 million worth of technical assistance funds, each college would average approximately $476,000 in [such] funds per year, an amount far in excess of that which can be utilized effectively."[111] That the Act could provide too much money for technical assistance to these institutions seems a curious claim and a false economy, for the money for technical assistance is prerequisite to any developmental activities necessary for accreditation or feasibility. It is not clear whether the fledgling colleges will be able to survive the legislation enacted and administered on their behalf.

Other Financial Issues

As is evident, these small institutions are plagued by rural isolation, lack of property tax bases, lack of experienced Indian personnel, lack of accreditation, and are subject to multiple jurisdictions not always helpful to the unique needs of Indian colleges. Even with special legislation, Navajo Community College, the first and largest tribal college, is in severe financial difficulty.[112] Further, the "band analysis" means of financing tribal institutions under the Indian Self-Determination Act, whereby tribes set aside their BIA funds for postsecondary programs, is being used by the BIA as a "debit" for money allocated to the tribal colleges under the Tribally Controlled Community College Assistance Act, in apparent disregard for the Tribal Act's prohibition against such substitutions: "Eligibility assistance under this title shall not, by itself, preclude the eligibility of any tribally controlled college to receive Federal financial assistance. . . ."[113] This shell game penalizes the colleges for negotiating the Tribal College Act process and punishes tribes who have assessed themselves for education programs. Analyses of these and other Indian education issues are beyond the scope of this article, but the issues clearly warrant study.

Summary and Conclusions

The enormous problems facing Indian, Chicano, and Puerto Rican colleges have not been addressed by legislative efforts aimed at redressing historic exclusion, nor by educational assistance designed for colleges in general. In the unique case of Indian colleges, specific legislation and program initiatives have not been effective, in part because of the fragile nature of the colleges themselves and in part because of the organizational difficulties Indian people face daily in their relationship with government agencies.

While the great majority of minority students will continue to receive their college education in majority institutions, increasing attention is necessary to ensure minority self-determination, particularly through historically minority colleges. The federal government has only recently recognized and acknowledged its considerable responsibility for assisting black colleges and has moved aggressively to rectify its own exclusionary practices in this regard. The Black College Initiative has given long-overdue notice to these institutions' role in educating Blacks. However, similar "Hispanic Initiatives" and "Indian Initiatives," proposing employment and program emphases for federal agencies, have languished.[114] American higher education, justifiably proud of its diversity, will be denied its most unique institutions if historically minority colleges are allowed to languish.

LULAC NATIONAL EDUCATIONAL
SERVICE CENTERS

Notes

[1]430 F. Supp. 118 (D.D.C. 1977).

[2]Haynes, *A Conceptual Examination of Desegregation in Higher Education* (Washington, DC: Institute for Services to Education, 1978); Fleming, *The Lengthening Shadow of Slavery* (Washington, DC: Howard University Press, 1976).

[3]Morris, *Elusive Equality* (Washington, DC: Howard Univeristy Press, 1979), p. 180.

[4]*Education Directory, Colleges and Universities, 1979-80* (Washington, DC: National Center for Educational Statistics [NCES], 1980), p. 468.

[5]Haynes, supra at note 2.

[6]Title III, Sec. 307 (2) prohibits payments "for an activity that is inconsistent with a State plan for desegregation of higher education applicable to such institution."

[7]Turner and Michaels, *Traditionally Black Institutions of Higher Education: Their Identification and Selected Characteristics* (Washington, DC: NCES, 1978).

[8]*Minority Higher Education Reports*, 1, No. 7 (15 August 1980), pp. 1-3.

[9]Title III, Sec. 347 (e). See also *House Conference Report to Accompany H.R. 5192*, p. 165. Under the Education Department's reorganization (PL 96-88), the College Housing Program has been transferred from Housing and Urban Development (HUD) to ED. Under the appropriations process (PL 96-103), 10% of the $85 million is to be reserved for black colleges. *Federal Register*, 1 August 1980, p. 51510.

[10]*Minority Higher Education Reports*, 1, No. 8 (12 September 1980), p. 5.

[11]Turner and Michaels, note 7, at p. 2.

[12]Turner and Michaels, note 7, at p. 1.

[13]Deloria, *Legislative Analysis of the Federal Role in Indian Education* (Washington, DC: Office of Indian Education, 1975); Thompson, ed., *The Schooling of Native America* (Washington, DC: American Association of Colleges for Teacher Education, 1978); Samora, ed., *La Raza: Forgotten Americans* (Notre Dame: University of Notre Dame Press, 1966); Carter and Segura, *Mexican Americans in School: A Decade of Change* (NY: College Board, 1979); *Puerto Ricans in the Continental United States: An Uncertain Future* (Washington, DC: U.S. Commission on Civil Rights, 1976).

[14]Van Amringe et al., *A History of Columbia University, 1754-1904* (NY: Columbia University Press, 1904), p. 32; Rudolph, *The American College and University, A History* (NY: Vintage, 1962).

[15]Rudolph, note 14, at p. 104.

[16]American Indian Policy Review Commission, *Report on Indian Education* (Washington, DC: GPO, 1976), pp. 61-73.

[17]Deloria, *A Brief History of the Federal Responsibility to the American Indian* (Washington, DC: GPO, 1979), p. 13.

[18]*Report on Indian Education*, note 16, at p. 66.

[19]7 Stat. 210; *Report on Indian Education*, note 16, at p. 268.

[20]*Report on Indian Education*, note 16, at pp. 268-69.

[21]*Education Directory*, note 4, at p. 9.

[22]Chavers, *The Feasibility of an Indian University at Bacone College* (Muskogee, OK: Bacone College, 1979).

[23]*Pembroke State University Catalog, 1980-1981*, pp. 15-16, 26-27.

[24]*Report on Indian Education*, note 16, at pp. 51-60. Chavers, "Indian Education: Failure for the Future," *American Indian Law Review*, 2 (1974), 61-84.

[25]Cited in *Report on Indian Education*, note 16, at p. 57.

[26]See, generally, *Report*, note 16, at pp. 273-75; *Southwestern Indian Polytechnic Institute Bulletin, 1975-1977*.

[27]Navajo Community College Assistance Act of 1978, 25 U.S.C. 640a.

[28]*Education Directory*, note 4 at p. 383; *Report*, note 16, at p. 351.

[29]*Report*, note 16, at p. 352.

[30]Table 1 could have included several more institutions, but adequate information was not available for Tanana Land Claims College, Ojibwa College, United Tribes Educational Technical Center, Gila River Community College.

[31]Cited in Carter and Segura, note 13, at p. 16.

[32]Fleming, note 2, at pp. 59-101.

[33]Pitt, *The Decline of the Californios: A Social History of the Spanish-Speaking Californians, 1846-1890* (Los Angeles: UCLA Press, 1966); Sánchez, *Forgotten People* (Albuquerque: University of New Mexico Press, 1940); Berger, "Education in Texas during the Spanish and Mexican Periods," *Southwestern Historical Quarterly*, 51, No. 1 (July 1947), pp. 41-53; Independent School District v. Salvatierra, 33 S.W. 2d. 790 (1930).

[34]Carter and Segura, note 13, at p. 16.

[35]Hendrick, "Early Schooling for Children of Migrant Farmworkers in California: The 1920's," *Aztlán*, 8 (1977), p. 14.

[36]Hendrick, note 35, at pp. 11-26.

[37]Berger, supra at note 33; Barrera, *Race and Class in the Southwest: A Theory of Inequality* (Notre Dame: University of Notre Dame Press, 1979).

[38]*Chicano Alternative Education* (Hayward, California: Southwest Network, 1974); Macias et al., *Educación Alternativa: On the Development of Chicano Bilingual Schools* (Hayward, CA: Southwest Network, 1975).

[39]*Education Directory*, note 4, at pp. 33, 341. Other Chicano schools do remain, but have chosen not to seek accreditation or to offer collegiate courses. Schools such as Colegio de la Tierra in California and La Academia de la Nueva Raza in New Mexico have chosen to focus on community development or folklore projects.

[40]*Accredited Postsecondary Institutions and Programs* (Washington, DC: GPO, 1979), pp. 5, 42.

[41]Discussions with officials of D-Q University and Colegio César Chávez, Summer 1980.

[42]Olivas, *The Dilemma of Access* (Washington, DC: Howard University Press, 1979). With reference to the recent denial of accreditation to Colegio César Chávez, see "Coast Hispanic College Fights to Survive," *New York Times*, 15 Nov. 1981, p. 75.

[43]Olivas and Hill, "Hispanic Participation in Postsecondary Education," in *The Condition of Education for Hispanic Americans* (Washington, DC: NCES, 1980), pp. 117-215.

[44]Arce, in Smith, ed., *Advancing Equality of Opportunity: A Matter of Justice* (Washington, DC: Howard University Press, 1978), pp. 165-75.

[45]Olivas, "Hispanics in Higher Education: Federal Barriers," *Educational Evaluation and Policy Analysis* (forthcoming).

[46]*Condition of Education for Hispanic Americans*, note 43, at p. 100.

[47]Ibid.

[48]*Social Factors in Educational Attainment Among Puerto Ricans in U.S. Metropolitan Areas, 1970* (NY: Aspira, 1976), p. 2.

[49]*Puerto Ricans in the Continental United States* (Washington, DC: U.S. Commission on Civil Rights, 1976).

[50]39 Stat. 951 (1917); 64 Stat. 319 (1950); 48 U.S.C. § 731 et seq.; De Lima v. Bidwell, 182 U.S. 1 (1901).

[51]*Puerto Ricans in the Continental United States*, note 49, at Table 7, pp. 19-35; *Condition of Education*, note 43, at Table 1.01; Hernández, "La migración puertorriqueña como factor demográfico: solución y problema," *Revista Interamericana*, 4 (1975), pp. 526-34.

[52]*Condition of Education*, note 43, at Table 1.04; *Puerto Ricans in California* (Washington, DC: U.S. Commission on Civil Rights, 1980).

[53]*Puerto Ricans in the Continental United States*, note 49, at p. 119.

[54]Lavin et al., "Open Admissions and Equal Access: A Study of Ethnic Groups in the City University of New York," *Harvard Educational Review*, 49, No. 1 (February 1979), pp. 53-92; Roosman et al., *Open Admissions at the City University of New York: An Analysis of the First Year* (Englewood Cliffs, NJ: Prentice Hall, 1975).

[55]*Puerto Ricans in the Continental United States*, note 49, at Tables 35, 36.

[56]Castro, "Hostos: Report from a Ghetto College," *Harvard Educational Review*, 44, No. 2 (May 1974), pp. 270-94.

[57]*Fall Enrollment in Higher Education, 1978* (Washington, DC: NCES, 1979), p. 132.

[58]*Accredited Postsecondary Institutions*, note 40, at p. 22.

[59]When CUNY closed early in 1976, the state appropriated a special fund to the system, including $3 million

for Hostos. *Puerto Ricans in the Continental United States*, note 49, at p. 119.

⁶⁰*Boricua College Catalog*, pp. 1-2.

⁶¹*Catalog*, note 60, at p. 19.

⁶²Ibid.

⁶³*Condition of Education*, note 43, at Table 2.32.

⁶⁴*Puerto Ricans in the Continental United States*, note 49, at Table 3.

⁶⁵Olivas and Hill, note 43, at Tables 3.10 and 3.21.

⁶⁶Olivas and Hill, note 43, at Tables 3.19 and 3.20.

⁶⁷Jones, *The Changing Mood in America* (Washington, DC: Howard University Press, 1977).

⁶⁸*Black College Primer* (Washington, DC: Institute for the Study of Educational Policy, Howard University, 1980); Turner and Michaels, note 7, at p. 1.

⁶⁹Olivas and Hill, note 43, at pp. 118-19; Olivas, "Hispanics in Higher Education," supra at note 45; Nichols, "Testimony in Hearings on Title III of the Higher Education Act," 29 March 1979; Middleton, "Indian Tribal Colleges Accuse U.S. Bureaucrats of Delaying $85 Million Congress Authorized," *Chronicle of Higher Education*, 11 February 1980, pp. 1, 12; Chavers, supra at note 22.

⁷⁰Deloria, "Legislation and Litigation Concerning American Indians," *Annals of the American Academy of Political and Social Science*, Vol. 436 (March 1978), pp. 86-96.

⁷¹Turner and Michaels, note 7, at p. 2. Another classification problem occurs when institutions mislabel their students. Alice Lloyd College reported its racial data for 1976 as if its enrollment were 90.1% American Indian, although its population is predominantly Appalachian whites (Olivas, note 42, at p. 196). Conversations with school officials, however, revealed that they considered their students "minorities," apparently "Native" Americans.

⁷²See Appendix D.

⁷³Nichols, note 69; Bad Wound, Testimony before Select Committee on Indian Affairs, U.S. Senate, 10 June 1980.

⁷⁴*American Indians, 1970 Census of Population* (Washington, DC: GPO, 1973), p. ix. For a discussion of minority census issues, including undercounts, see *Conference on Census Undercounts* (Washington, DC: GPO, 1980).

⁷⁵85 Stat. 688.

⁷⁶The recently revised Indian Education Act regulations, for instance, drew several comments and incorporated several changes to clarify Indian eligibility. See, for example, *Federal Register*, 21 May 1980, pp. 34180-34181, 34184-34185.

⁷⁷Indian Education Act, Sec. 453(a); 20 U.S.C. 1221 (h) (a). See, generally, Yinger and Simpson, "The Integration of Americans of Indian Descent", *Annals of the American Academy of Political and Social Science*, Vol. 436 (March 1978), pp. 137-51.

⁷⁸United States *ex rel.* Rollingson v. Blackfeet Tribal Court, 244 F. Supp. 474 (D. Mont. 1965).

⁷⁹United States v. Consolidated Wounded Knee Case, 389 F. Supp. 235 (D. Neb. and W.D.S.D. 1975).

⁸⁰Mashpee Tribe v. New Seabury Corp., 427 F. Supp. 899, aff'd, 592 F. 2d 575 (1st Cir. 1979). For a sample of legislative attempts to extinguish Indian claims, see S.J. Res. 86, 95th Cong. 1st Session, 123 *Congressional Record* (1977), p. 16232, concerning Mashpee claims in Massachusetts. See Newton, "At the Whim of the Sovereign: Aboriginal Title Reconsidered," *Hastings Law Journal* 31, No. 6 (1980), pp. 1215-85. See, generally, Brodeur, "The Mashpees," *New Yorker*, 6 November 1978, pp. 62-150; Deloria, "Indian Law and the Reach of History," *Journal of Contemporary Law*, 4 (1977), pp. 1-13.

⁸¹Although it is beyond the scope of this study, there is a small network of minority institution programs scattered throughout the federal government; many of these are being mobilized by the Executive Order on Black Colleges. They include, for example, the Minority Access into Research Careers (National Institutes of Health), Minority Institution Science Improvement Program (Department of Education, relocated from the National Science Foundation), and the Minority Institutions Research Support Program (Environmental Protection Agency).

⁸²86 Stat. 334 (as amended); the regulations will be recodified under 34 C.F.R., replacing the 45 C.F.R. regulations. See *Federal Register*, 21 May 1980, p. 34153.

⁸³20 U.S.C. 241 (a) (a).

⁸⁴25 U.S.C. 1801.

⁸⁵Navajo Community College Assistance Act of 1978, 25 U.S.C. 640 (a); Amendments to the Navajo Community College Act [sic], Education Amendments of 1980, Title XIV, Part F, Sec. 1451.

⁸⁶Although the institutions are community colleges, they need not be sub-baccalaureate. Higher Education Act of 1965, Title XII, Sec. 1201 (a) (3).

⁸⁷25 U.S.C. 1801.

⁸⁸25 U.S.C. 1804.

⁸⁹Locke, *A Survey of College and University Programs for American Indians* (Boulder, CO: WICHE, 1978), p. 24.

⁹⁰See Table 1.

⁹¹Supra, at note 38. See also Table 1.

⁹²See Appendix D for the distribution of Title III awards in 1979-1980 to Indian programs; Appendix E is the awards to Hispanic programs.

⁹³Grafe, *The Trustee Profile of 1976* (Washington, DC: Association of Community College Trustees, 1976), pp. 4-5. See Olivas, note 42, at pp. 86-90.

⁹⁴25 U.S.C. 1801; 20 U.S.C. 1141.

⁹⁵Higher Education Act of 1965, Title XII, Sec. 1201 (a) (5); 20 U.S.C. 1141. See, generally, Orlans et al., *Private*

Accreditation and Public Eligibility (Washington, DC: National Academy of Public Administration, 1974); *Approaches to State Licensing of Private Degree-Granting Institutions* (Washington, DC: Institute for Educational Leadership, 1975); Kaplin, *The Law of Higher Education* (San Francisco: Jossey-Bass, 1978), pp. 439-59; Finkin, "Federal Reliance and Voluntary Accreditation: The Power to Recognize as The Power to Regulate," *Journal of Law and Education,* 2, No. 3 (July 1973), pp. 339-76.

[95] Higher Education Act of 1965, Title XII, Sec. 1201 (a) (5); 20 U.S.C. 1141.

[97] S. 1215, 95th Congress, 1st Session (1 April 1977). See Senate Report 95-582, *Hearing before the United States Senate Select Committee on Indian Affairs* (28 July 1977).

[98] 25 U.S.C. 1801. In the Act, the requirement that "institutions" be "legally authorized within such State" (Higher Education Act of 1965, Title XII, Sec. 1201 (a) (2); 20 U.S.C. 1141) was deleted, recognizing that tribes were independent governmental bodies.

[99] Discussions with BIA and Indian college officials suggested that the 3-letter rule had a stigma and that senior institutions were reluctant to recognize the rule for fear it would jeopardize their own status. This subject deserves further scrutiny.

[100] 25 U.S.C. 1806. Section 105 of the Act requires an agreement between the Departments of Interior and Education (then the Office of Education, HEW); this memorandum of agreement was signed on 19 February 1980. The feasibility study form is 73 pages long, not including its required appendices.

[101] 25 C.F.R. 32b. See *Federal Register,* 21 November 1979, pp. 67040-67048. In testimony on implementation of the Act, Earl Barlow, BIA Director of Indian Education Programs, said: "One of the criteria for feasibility is that it be an accredited institution or a candidate for accreditation, or its credits must be accepted by three accredited institutions. Each of the 10 schools that have been deemed feasible has either been accredited or has been approved as a candidate for accreditation. . . . Our idea was that [technical assistance] funds would be used to assist colleges that were having some problems with either accreditation or candidacy, but the ruling was made that in order to be eligible for technical assistance grants the institution has to be feasible. It put us in a predicament. The schools that really need technical assistance are not feasible and therefore cannot get technical assistance. That is a major problem." *Hearing Before the Select Committee on Indian Affairs* (10 June 1980), Committee draft, p. 9. See also, *Guidelines for the Tribally Controlled Community Colleges.*

[102] Testimony of Leroy Clifford, American Indian Higher Education Consortium, note 101, at Committee draft, p. 17.

[103] Blackfeet Community College had received its 1979-80 check the week before the June 10, 1980, Senate hearing.

[104] Middleton, note 69, at pp. 1, 12.

[105] *Hearing,* note 101, at Committee draft, pp. 11-34; *Higher Education Daily,* 12 June 1980, pp. 5-6.

[106] Higher Education Act, Title III, Sec. 302 (a) (2). The newly reauthorized Education Amendments of 1980 have widened the waivers to include rural people, low-income individuals, and black students. Title III, Part D, Sec. 342 (b) (1-5); *Conference Report No. 96-1251,* p. 164.

[107] Senate Calendar, 24 September 1980, p. 199 [S. 1855].

[108] S. 1855, 96th Congress, 1st Session. *Senate Report.* No. 96-538, p. 6.

[109] *Senate Report,* note 108, at pp. 2-3. Congressional staffers have suggested that this reassignment was in anticipation of Higher Education Act reauthorization changes in Sec. 1201. These changes were not made in the final version of 1201.

[110] 25 U.S.C. 1808; supra, note 100.

[111] Letter from Forrest Gerard, Assistant Secretary, Department of the Interior, to Senator John Melcher, 21 November 1979. *Senate Report,* note 108, at pp. 4-5.

[112] *Hearing,* note 101, at Committee draft, p. 25. The Education Amendments of 1980 include special provisions for Navajo Community College, Title XIV, Part F, Sec. 1451; *Conference Report,* note 106, at p. 209.

[113] 25 U.S.C. 189; 20 U.S.C. 1001 *et seq.*

[114] Olivas, supra, note 45. Whereas the Black College Initiative was a Presidential Executive Order, the Hispanic and Indian Initiatives were Secretarial. Additionally, the tribal college reporting requirements of PL 95-471 have not been met by either the Department of the Interior or by NCES, despite their responsibility for an annual report to Congress [Sec. 107 (c) (2); 25 U.S.C. 1808].

* The author expresses his appreciation to Imelda Escobar, Roberta Wilson, James Koloditch, Dean Chavers, and Virginia Boylan for their assistance. The Joyce Foundation generously supported this research.

Appendix A

Executive Order

Historically Black Colleges and Universities

By the authority vested in me as President by the Constitution of the United States of America, and in order to overcome the effects of discriminatory treatment and to strengthen and expand the capacity of historically Black colleges and universities to provide quality education, it is hereby ordered as follows:

1-101. The Secretary of Education shall implement a Federal initiative designed to achieve a significant increase in the participation by historically Black colleges and universities in Federally sponsored programs. This initiative shall seek to identify, reduce, and eliminate barriers which may have unfairly resulted in reduced participation in, and reduced benefits from, Federally sponsored programs.

1-102. The Secretary of Education shall, in consultation with the Director of the Office of Management and Budget and the heads of the other Executive agencies, establish annual goals for each agency. The purpose of these goals shall be to increase the ability of historically Black colleges and universities to participate in Federally sponsored programs.

1-103. Executive agencies shall review their programs to determine the extent to which historically Black colleges and universities are unfairly precluded from participation in Federally sponsored programs.

1-104. Executive agencies shall identify the statutory authorities under which they can provide relief from specific inequities and disadvantages identified and documented in the agency programs.

1-105. Each Executive agency shall review its current programs and practices and initiate new efforts to increase the participation of historically Black colleges and universities in the programs of the agency. Particular attention should be given to identifying and eliminating unintended regulatory barriers. Procedural barriers, including those which result in such colleges and universities not receiving notice of the availability of Federally sponsored programs, should also be eliminated.

1-106. The head of each Executive agency shall designate an immediate subordinate who will be responsible for implementing the agency responsibilities set forth in this Order. In each Executive agency there shall be an agency liaison to the Secretary of Education for implementing this Order.

1-107. (a) The Secretary of Education shall ensure that an immediate subordinate is responsible for implementing the provisions of this Order.

(b) The Secretary shall ensure that each President of a historically Black college or university is given the opportunity to comment on the implementation of the initiative established by this Order.

1-108. The Secretary of Education shall submit an annual report to the President. The report shall include the levels of participation by historically Black colleges and universities in the programs of each Executive agency. The report will also include any appropriate recommendations for improving the Federal response directed by this Order.

Source: *Minority Higher Education Reports* (15 August 1980), p. 9.

Appendix B

Treaties Dealing With
Indian Education

Treaty of August 18, 1804, with Delaware Tribe, 7 Stat. 81; treaty of August 29, 1821, with Ottawa, Chippewa, and Pottawatamie, 7 Stat. 218; treaty of February 12, 1825, with Creek Nation, 7 Stat. 237; treaty of February 8, 1831, with the Menominee Indians, 7 Stat. 342; treaty of September 21, 1833, with the Otoes and Missourias, 7 Stat. 429; treaty of March 2, 1836, with the Ottawa and Chippewa, 7 Stat. 491; treaty of September 17, 1836, with the Sacs and Foxes, etc., 7 Stat. 511; treaty of October 15, 1836, with the Otoes, etc., 7 Stat. 524; treaty of January 4, 1845, with the Creeks and Seminoles, 9 Stat. 821, 822; treaty of October 13, 1846, with the Winnebago Indians, 9 Stat. 878; treaty of August 2, 1847, with the Chippewas, 9 Stat. 904; treaty of October 18, 1848, with the Menominee Tribe, 9 Stat. 952; treaty of July 23, 1851, with the Sioux, 10 Stat. 949; treaty of August 5, 1851, with the Sioux Indians, 10 Stat. 954; treaty of May 12, 1854, with the Menominee, 10 Stat. 1064; treaty of December 26, 1854, with the Nisqually, etc., Indians, 10 Stat. 1132; treaty of October 17, 1855, with the Blackfoot Indians, 11 Stat. 657; treaty of September 24, 1857, with the Pawnees, 11 Stat. 729; treaty of January 22, 1855, with The Dwamish, etc., 12 Stat. 927; treaty of January 26, 1855, with the S'Klallams, 12 Stat. 933; treaty of January 31, 1855, with Makah Tribe, 12 Stat. 939; treaty of July 1, 1855, with the Qui-nai-elt, etc., Indians, 12 Stat. 971; treaty of July 16, 1855, with the Flathead, etc., Indians, 12 Stat. 975; treaty of December 21, 1855, with the Molels, 12 Stat. 981; treaty of October 18, 1864, with the Chippewa Indians, 14 Stat. 657; treaty of June 14, 1866, with the Creek Nation, 14 Stat. 785; treaty of February 18, 1867, with the Sac and Fox Indians, 15 Stat. 495; treaty of February 19, 1867, with the Sissiton, etc., Sioux, 15 Stat. 505.

Treaty of May 6, 1828, with the Cherokee Nation, 7 Stat; treaty of New Echota, December 29, 1835, with the Cherokee, 7 Stat. 748 (provides for common schools and "a literacy institution of a higher order***"); treaty of June 5 and 17, 1846, with the Pottowautomie Nation, 9 Stat. 853; treaty of September 30, 1854, with the Chippewa Indians, 10 Stat. 1109; treaty of November 18, 1854, with the Chastas, etc., Indians, 10 Stat. 1122; treaty of April 19, 1858, with the Yancton Sioux, 11 Stat. 743; treaty of June 9, 1855, with the Walla-Wallas, etc., tribes, 12 Stat. 945;

treaty of June 11, 1855, with the Nez Perce, 12 Stat. 957; treaty of March 12, 1858, with the Poncas, 12 Stat. 997; treaty of October 14, 1865, with the Lower Brule Sioux, 14 Stat. 699; treaty of February 23, 1867, with the Senecas, etc., 15 Stat. 513; treaty of October 21, 1867, with the Kiowa and Comanche Indians, 15 Stat. 581; treaty of October 21, 1867, with the Kiowa, Comanche, and Apache Indians, 15 Stat. 589; treaty of October 28, 1867, with the Cheyenne and Arapahoe Indians, 15 Stat. 593; treaty of March 2, 1868, with the Ute Indians, 15 Stat. 619; treaty of April 29 et seq., 1868, with the Sioux Nation, 15 Stat. 635; treaty of May 7, 1868, with the Crow Indians, 15 Stat. 649; treaty of May 10, 1868, with the Northern Cheyenne and Northern Arapahoe Indians, 15 Stat. 655; treaty of June 1, 1868, with the Navajo Tribe, 15 Stat. 667; treaty of July 3, 1868, with the Eastern Band Shoshones and Bannock Tribe of Indians, 15 Stat. 673.

Treaty of November 15, 1827, with the Creek Nation, 7 Stat. 307; treaty of September 15, 1832, with the Winnebago Nation, 7 Stat. 370; treaty of May 24, 1834, with the Chickasaw Indians, 7 Stat. 450; treaty of June 9, 1863, with the Nez Perce Tribe, 14 Stat. 647; treaty of March 19, 1867, with the Chippewa of Mississippi, 16 Stat. 719.

Treaty of October 18, 1820, with the Choctaw Nation, 7 Stat. 210; treaty of June 3, 1825, with the Kansas Nation, 7 Stat. 244; treaty of August 5, 1926, with the Chippewa Tribe, 7 Stat. 290; treaty of October 21, 1837, with the Sac and Fox Indians, 7 Stat. 543; treaty of March 17, 1842, with the Wyandott Nation, 11 Stat. 581; treaty of May 15, 1846, with the Comanche, etc., Indians, 9 Stat. 844; treaty of June 5, 1854, with the Miami Indians, 10 Stat. 1093; treaty of November 15, 1854, with the Rogue Rivers, 10 Stat. 1119; treaty of November 29, 1854, with the Umpqua, etc., Indians, 10 Stat. 1125; treaty of July 31, 1855, with the Ottowas and Chippewas, 11 Stat. 621; treaty of February 5, 1856, with the Stockbridge and Munsee Tribes, 11 Stat. 663; treaty of June 9, 1855, with the Yakima Indians, 12 Stat. 951; treaty of June 25, 1855, with the Oregon Indians, 12 Stat. 963; treaty of June 19, 1858, with the Sioux bands, 12 Stat. 1031; treaty of July 16, 1859, with the Chippewa bands, 12 Stat. 1105; treaty of February 18, 1861, with the Arapahoes and Cheyenne Indians, 12 Stat. 1163; treaty of March 6, 1861, with the Sacs, Foxes and Iowas, 12 Stat. 1171; treaty of June 24, 1862, with the Ottawa Indians, 12 Stat. 1237; treaty of May 7, 1864, with the Chippewas, 13 Stat. 693; treaty of August 12, 1865, with the Snake Indians, 14 Stat. 683; treaty of March 21, 1866, with the Seminole Indians, 14 Stat. 755; treaty of April 28, 1866, with the Choctaw and Chickasaw Nation, 14 Stat. 769; treaty of August 13, 1868, with the Nez Perce Tribe, 15 Stat. 693.

Treaty of October 16, 1826, with the Potawatomie Tribe, 7 Stat. 295; treaty of September 20, 1828, Potawatamie Indians, 7 Stat. 317; treaty of July 15, 1830, with the Sacs and Foxes, etc., 7 Stat. 328; treaty of September 27, 1830, with the Choctaw Nation, 7 Stat. 333; treaty of March 24, 1832, with the Creek Tribe, 7 Stat. 366; treaty of February 14, 1833, with the Creek Nation, 7 Stat. 417; treaty of January 14, 1846, with the Kansas Indians, 9 Stat. 842; treaty of April 1, 1850, with the Wyandot Tribe, 9 Stat. 987; treaty of March 15, 1854, with the Delaware Tribe, 10 Stat. 1048; treaty of May 10, 1854, with the Shawnees, 10 Stat. 1053; treaty of May 17, 1854, with the Ioway Tribe, 10 Stat. 1165; treaty of June 22, 1855, with the Choctaw and Chickasaw Indians, 11 Stat. 611; treaty of August 2, 1855, with Williamette Bands, 10 Stat. 1143; treaty of February 22, 1855, with the Chippewa Indians of Mississippi, 10 Stat. 1165; treaty of June 22, 1855, with the Choctaw and Chicasaw Indians, 11 Stat. 611; treaty of August 2, 1855, with the Chippewa Indians of Saginaw, 11 Stat. 633; treaty of August 7, 1856, with the Creeks and Seminoles, 11 Stat. 699; treaty of June 28, 1862, with the Kickapoo Tribe, 13 Stat. 623; treaty of October 2, 1863, with the Chippewa Indians (Red Lake and Pembina Bands), 13 Stat. 667; treaty of September 29, 1865, with the Osage Indians, 14 Stat. 687.

Source: Thompson, ed., *The Schooling of Native America* (Washington, DC: American Association of Colleges for Teacher Education, 1978), pp. 183–85.

Appendix C

Selected Characteristics of Institutions of Higher Education in Puerto Rico: Fall 1978

Institution	Control		Level		Hispanic[1]
	Public	Private	2-year	4-year	enrollment
Total	10	24	16	18	123,329
American College of Puerto Rico		X	X		1,141
Antillian College		X		X	749
Bayamón Central University		X		X	2,911
Caguas City College		X	X		651
Caribbean Center for Adv. Studies		X		X	0
Caribbean University College		X		X	1,204
Catholic University of P.R.		X		X	11,380
Conservatory of Music of P.R.	X			X	249
Electronic Data Processing College	X		X		1,226
Fundación Educativa Ana E. Méndez[2]					
Colegio Universitario del Turabo		X		X	5,401
Puerto Rico Junior College		X	X		7,686
Instituto Comercial de P.R. Jr. College		X	X		1,800
Instituto Técnico Comercial Jr. College		X	X		1,256
Inter American University of P.R.					
Hato Rey Campus		X		X	8,067
San Germán Campus		X		X	6,337
7 branches[2]		X	X		13,038
Ramirez College of Business & Tech.		X	X		609
San Juan Tech. Community College	X		X		919
Universidad Politécnica de P.R.		X		X	143
Universidad de Ponce	X			X	347
University of Puerto Rico/					
Río Piedras Campus	X			X	23,535
Mayaguez Campus	X			X	8,871
Medical Sciences Campus	X			X	2,583
Cayey University College	X			X	2,601
Humacao University College	X			X	3,282
Regional Colleges Administration	X		X		7,016
University of the Sacred Heart		X		X	5,929
World University		X		X	4,398

[1] Hispanics comprised between 95 and 100 percent of total enrollment in virtually all institutions in Puerto Rico.
[2] All branches could not be listed due to space limitations.

Source: Olivas and Hill, "Hispanic Participation in Postsecondary Education," *The Condition of Education for Hispanic Americans* (Washington, DC: NCES, 1980), Table 3.17.

Appendix D

Indian Programs Funded in FY-1979

Strengthening Developing Institutions
Title III, HEA of 1965

Institution & State	Control	Amount	Project Duration	Total Multi-year Award
Alaska Pacific University, AK	4 Pvt	$150,000	1	
Bacone College, OK	2 Pvt	190,000	2	$379,000
Baker University, KS	4 Pvt	187,000	1	
Black Hills State College, SD	4 Pub	515,000	1	
Bismarck Junior College, ND	2 Pub	312,000	1	
College of Ganado, AZ	2 Pvt	315,000	2	630,000
Connors State College, OK	2 Pub	192,630	4	770,520
Flaming Rainbow University, OK	4 Pvt	75,000	1	
Flathead Valley Community College, MT	2 Pub	352,000	1	
Fort Lewis College, CO	4 Pub	144,000	1	
Huron College, SD	4 Pvt	595,000	3	595,000
Lake Region Junior College, ND	2 Pub	140,000	1	
Mary College, ND	4 Pvt	600,000	1	
Mount Senario College, WI	4 Pvt	200,000	1	
Murray State College, OK	2 Pub	100,000	1	
Navajo Community College, AZ—Consortium	2 Pub	547,000	1	
Navajo Community College, AZ—Adv. Funding	2 Pub	50,000		
Navajo Community College, AZ—Bilateral	2 Pub	147,000	1	
Northern State College, SD—Consortium	4 Pub	380,000	1	
Northland College, WI	4 Pvt	689,000	3	689,000
Pembroke State University, NC	4 Pub	800,000	4	800,000
San Juan College, NM	2 Pub	193,000	2	386,000
Seminole Junior College, OK	2 Pub	92,000	1	
Sheldon Jackson College, AK	2 Pvt	185,000	1	
Southwestern Technical Institute, NC	2 Pub	170,000	1	
Turtle Mountain Community College, ND	2 Pvt	200,000	1	
Yavapai College, AZ	2 Pub	435,000	3	1,306,000

FY-1979 Total Awards to Indian Programs $7,955,630
25 Institutions Funded

Source: Department of Education, Office for Postsecondary Education.

Appendix E

Hispanic Programs Funded in FY-1979

Strengthening Developing Institutions
Title III, HEA of 1965

Institution & State	Control	Amount	Project Duration	Total Multi-year Award
Arizona Western, AZ	2 Pub	$320,000	2	$640,000
Bayamón Central University, PR	4 Pvt	351,000	1	
Bee County College, TX	2 Pub	100,000	1	
Biscayne College, FL	4 Pvt	200,000	1	
Boricua College, NY	2 Pvt	310,000	1	
Bronx Community College, NY	2 Pub	175,000	1	
Catholic University of Puerto Rico, PR	4 Pvt	220,000	1	
Cayey University College, PR	4 Pub	200,000	1	
Central Arizona College, AZ	2 Pub	209,000	2	417,000
Colegio César Chávez, OR	4 Pvt	216,000	2	216,000
Colegio Univ. del Turabo, PR	4 Pvt	595,547	3	595,547
College of Santa Fe, NM	4 Pvt	450,000	3	450,000
Eastern Arizona College, AZ	2 Pub	125,000	1	
Eastern New Mexico University—Portales	4 Pub	1,067,000	3	1,067,000
El Paso Community College, TX—Consortium	2 Pub	276,000	1	
Fresno City College, CA	2 Pub	95,000	1	
Humacao University College, PR	4 Pub	200,000	1	
Imperial Valley College, CA	2 Pub	227,000	2	454,000
Incarnate Word College, TX	4 Pvt	900,000	3	900,000
Inter American Univ., San Juan, PR	4 Pvt	465,500	2	465,500
LaGuardia Community College, NY	2 Pub	175,000	2	350,000
Laredo Junior College, TX	2 Pub	289,000	3	866,000
Miami-Dade Community College, FL	2 Pub	300,000	3	900,000
New Mexico Highlands University, NM	4 Pub	755,000	3	755,000
Oxnard College, CA	2 Pub	69,766	1	
Puerto Rico Junior College, PR	2 Pvt	130,000	2	260,000
Saint Philips College, TX	2 Pub	97,983	2	195,966
San Juan Tech. Community College, PR	2 Pub	175,000	1	
Southwestern College, CA	2 Pub	100,000	1	
Texas Southmost College, TX	2 Pub	200,000	2	400,000
Trinidad State Junior College, CO	2 Pub	140,000	2	280,000
University of Albuquerque, NM	4 Pvt	275,000	1	
University of the Sacred Heart, PR	4 Pvt	222,000	1	
Western New Mexico University, NM	4 Pub	390,000	2	390,000
World University, PR	4 Pvt	232,000	1	

FY-1979 Total Awards to Hispanic Programs $10,252,796
35 Institutions Funded

Source: Department of Education, Office for Postsecondary Education.

A Spectre is Haunting American Scholars:
The Spectre of "Professionism"

Walter P. Metzger

Forty years ago, when I began to study the history of the academic profession in America, the words "profession," "professional," "professionalization," were charged with laudatory meanings. In public discourse, a "profession" was usually defined as an occupation that had reached the highest level of technical skill and social helpfulness; "professional," used as the antonym of both "amateur" and "commercial," showered praised upon its object by ruling out dilettantism and profiteering; "professionalization" denoted a form of progress, a series of occupational events by which humankind advanced. In the rarefied realm of social theory, these terms were given functional implications that, however varied, were almost always presented as benign. Among the leading theorists, the dominant inclination was to salute the professions as corporate guilds that protected civic morality and social solidarity from the corrosion of modern egotism (this was the backward-looking blessing conferred upon them by the Gallic Emile Durkheim) or else to laud them as pivotal institutions that enshrined the meritocratic and scientific values of advanced industrial societies (this was the less nostalgic tribute paid by the American Talcott Parsons). In the field of history, the encomiums, though less explicit, were as unrestrained. With the notable exception of A.M. Carr-Saunders, historians had not made the phenomenon of professionalism a

target of intensive study. But some had written chronicles of specific professions and these accounts had almost invariably been success stories featuring the transformation of a pursuit through a series of bootstrap feats. At that time, the contribution of historians to the study of the academic profession could be described as massive in detail and rich in color, but thin in concept and bare of theory. Still, one could easily tell, as one threaded one's way through their yarns and monographs, that they regarded the onset of academic professionalism in its modern guises—the secular training of faculty members, the departmental organization of academic work, the incorporation of specialized research into the professoriate's set of formal roles—as the gladdest of glad tidings. In various ways, they gave an attractive aura, if not a halo, to a profession they seldom treated analytically or even hailed by name.

There were, to be sure, some dissenting voices in this praising chorus. Even then, I could hear some sounds of criticism. The pettifogging lawyers in Charles Dickens' *Bleak House* and *Pickwick Papers*, the grubby medicasters in George Bernard Shaw's *Doctor's Dilemma*, the philandering minister in *Rain*, the charlatan preacher in Sinclair Lewis' *Elmer Gantry*, were already well-established stereotypes. In America, the title of "professor" was often conferred with a jocular condescension not usually evident elsewhere, and the title of "attorney-at-law" was more often associated with the native invective "shyster" than with a foreign euphemism like

Tocqueville's "aristocrat of the bar." Still it seems to me, as I look back, that the sting of these disparagements did not go deep. The plots of plays and novels showed professionals capable of human vices, but these barbed tales did not usually imply that there was something vicious about professionalism. The foibles of individual professors were pointed out but seldom painted as generic: Erskine Caldwell's rollicking short story, "The Professor", whose leading character was a lecherous snake-oil salesman, mocked the American tendency to usurp that title, but did not suggest that professors as a group were a collection of wanton quacks. And such broadsides as were aimed by literary critics at professionals as a group did not appear to stir their audiences to rethink their praise. The Shavian quip—"all professionals are conspiracies against laities"—was widely taken as a play of wit not to be taken all that seriously.

Indeed, for those who took the professions with the utmost seriousness—sociologists who made it their special business to assess the professional claims of callings—the pressing task in this period was not to redeem the label from a hostile public, but to keep it from being loved too much. It worried these arbiters of professional entitlement that all sorts of run-of-the-mill pursuits called themselves professions and presumed to wear a title above their station. They reasoned that, if *any* occupation could be thus exalted— if there could legitimately be not only a medical profession, a legal profession, and a clerical profession (the "learned" professions of hoary pedigree) and an engineering profession, an accounting profession, an architecture profession (a group of late-comers modeled on the hallowed three), but also a banking profession, an advertising profession, a real estate profession (mere businesses angling for the public's trust), and a cooking profession, a dancing profession, a baseball profession (mere skills looking for a fancy name), not to mention Mrs. Warren's profession (that unspeakable skill or business that muddied everything by being called the "first" profession)—why, then, the term would lose all eulogistic meaning and hardly make any social sense at all. Largely to save an honorific from a usage that was threatening to debase it, these sociologists took it upon themselves to compose a list of defining attributes that would distinguish the genuine article from the unworthy pretentious rest.

This proved to be a difficult undertaking. These fastidious definers generally agreed that no profession could rightly be considered a profession unless it possessed a body of complex knowledge and abided by the norms of a service ethic. Few believed, however, that these enobling stigmata would suffice. Some, in fleshing out their inventories, included such holdovers from the past as control over the admission of new members and a strong sense of collegial comraderie; others thought that the *indicia specifica* should include a university nexus, a state-supported licensing system, national associations, and other accessories with a shorter history. Nor did they agree on the stringency with which the differentia should be applied. Some insisted that an occupation, to pass muster, had to satisfy every item on the tally sheet, that a partial score meant a failing grade; others, taking their cue from the changing occupational scene, renounced the harsh canon of either-or. Dividing the universe of pursuits into a couple of winners and a host of losers had never been a stylish sport in a nation that, from its beginning, had proclaimed the moral equivalence of all honest work, and it became less so when new highly skilled pursuits emerged and refused to bow to peremptory judgments. Consequent-

ly, these self-anointed judges became increasingly disposed to scale rather than to dichotomize; to place occupations that passed only some of their litmus tests in an intermediate category—the semi-professions, the quasi-professions—where they could receive a silver medal until such time as they earned the gold. Still, though there was discord among the checklisters, all of their checklisting efforts sang out much the same tune. All presupposed that a plus mark was a sign of occupational progress, and all treated the title of "profession" as a prize for good behavior that was to be guarded, envied, and conferred with care.

Forty years later, what do we behold? On the surface, not much may seem to have changed. We still find social scientists disagreeing over the hallmarks of professionalism; indeed, within the "sociology of professions" (a subdiscipline that emerged in the intervening years), this continuing debate itself has become a hallmark—of a branch of learning forever fated to define itself. In the dictionary of ordinary speech, similar signs of continuity can be detected. Even today, when we say that a person's behavior is "unprofessional," we mean to reprove it quite severely, and when we characterize someone as a "true professional," we still intend to bestow high praise. On questionnaire surveys of public opinion, the professions continue to show up well. Asked to order a hundred or so occupations on a prestige scale, Americans are still likely to place lawyers, architects, dentists, college professors, priests, and ministers in one of the top twenty slots, and to rank physicians second only to Supreme Court justices (which, in effect, ranks them first, since sitting on the highest bench is less a type of occupation than a form of beatification). One can find other bits of evidence to support the view that the passage of time has not changed our affectional preferences: one such is the multitudes who apply to law schools, medical schools, and engineering schools and who thereby testify to the continuing popularity of professional careers.

Nevertheless, I am convinced that the moral reputation of the professions has declined during the time that has

elapsed from the "then" of my initiation to the "now" of these veteran reflections—so precipitously and so drastically that the past, recalled as prologue, may well be captioned "Before the Fall." This decline may not be evident to those who take their bearings from the residual deferences that loiter in our language, or who mistake the stimulated creation of occupational pecking-orders for spontaneous and heartfelt votes of confidence, or who believe that careers favored for their material benefits and pleasant work conditions may not also receive very mixed reviews. But it should be apparent to anyone who has taken note of the attacks on the ethics of professionals and the virtues of professionalism that were mounted several decades ago in mass media, scholarly journals, legislative bodies, and administrative agencies, and that have continued to this day unabated, albeit with varying assortments of rhetorical and legal cudgels. In my view, the buffetings the professions have received in this period have exceeded in volume and relentlessness anything they had heretofore experienced and have taken a cumulative toll that defies historical comparisons.

One of the signal novelties of these times is the public obloquy that has been visited on the profession of the medical doctor, hitherto held in lay regard as the very model of the modern *echt*-professional. The American medical profession had previously had to answer for a certain amount of deviant avariciousness—the mercenary lobbying of the American Medical Association furnishes a long-standing case in point—but never before had it been called to account for so vast an array of corruptions perceived as rife rather than aberrant: among other things, for inflating the cost of medical care by opting for the most lucrative procedures, charging exorbitant *post hoc* fees and bilking third-party payers; for violating the anti-trust laws by banning competitive advertisement and boycotting prepaid medical plans; for violating the constitutional rights of the mentally ill by failing to adhere to minimally acceptable treatment standards and by keeping them in unnecessarily prolonged detention; for violating human rights by performing surgical operations and testing experimental drugs on unknowing and unconsenting patients;

for breaking their altruistic vows by maintaining a two-tier system of hospital care where quality of service is correlated to capacity to pay; for adopting a white-coated pose of superiority so as to impress and overcharge the sick; and, lately, for joining up with for-profit hospitals that merchandise medical services at a business price. Once, American physicians were portrayed as the arch-opponents of the commercial ethos; now, judging from the string of charges, they are seen as the very incarnation of it.

Nor is it only the profession of doctors that feels the force of the public's attack. The profession of lawyers has long had its detractors, but never before has it stood accused of so much innate malfeasance and venality. In the indictments of recent years, lawyers have been charged, among other things, with setting hourly fees that would bankrupt their business clients were they not written off for tax purposes; with cornering the market in will probates, title searches, divorce proceedings, and other routine legal services that could as well be performed by laymen with a modicum of mother wit; with opposing—at least in their trial lawyer branches—such alternatives to lucrative litigation as no-fault accident insurance and ceilings on damage awards; with instructing students in their training centers how to accommodate to corporate wealth and close their eyes to institutionalized injustices; and, in the late Nixon years, with breaking the laws they were sworn to uphold so as to effect the designs of an unscrupulous client-president. Nor have the public pillories been reserved only for those professionals whose immoderate incomes, on their face, make them morally suspect. Those who belong to the "helping" professions—generally the poorest paid professions—have also been placed in the stocks, knavish heads and grasping hands exposed. Even members of the profession of social work, whose rewards seemed unimpeachably laid up in heaven because they could so rarely be found in bank accounts, have been impugned for taking "cushy" jobs in government programs designed to assist the poor. In this period of reprobation, no profession has been spared.

As a form of public entertainment, pestering professionals is hardly new. What is new about this current phase is its less genial mood, its more jugular objective. That the pastime has changed its character should be clear to anyone who, like myself, takes special note of how the academic profession fares. The double-barreled jibe that "surgeons bury their mistakes, while faculty members graduate them," or the lampoon attributed to John Galbraith that a professor is someone who "takes a sabbatical leave in the autumn so that he will be rested and ready for a winter's leave of absence to work up a course on the work ethic," do not seem to me to inflict deep wounds. But it hardly takes an over-sensitive ear to detect more than good-natured ribbing in the charge, sounded again and again in panel reports and op-ed pages, that tenure serves to secure jobs for veteran professors that should be going to their junior betters, or that students have been allowed by academic teachers to pass like so many stones through the intestinal tracts of the nation's colleges, only to emerge as unenlightened—indeed as fundamentally illiterate—as they were when they first came in. Such charges were not meant to be light or comic: When Ivar Berg entitled his book on the uselessness of prolonged teaching, *The Great Training Robbery*, that gifted sloganist was in deadly earnest, not full of fun.

One of the distinctive features of the current era has been the tendency of academic scholars to devalue their own professions and more—to deprecate the very notion that professionalism is a thing of moral beauty and a social joy. In no field has self-denigration been more conspicuous than in sociology, the field that had once made professionalism the centerpiece of a viable society and had long toiled to give the professions the right to rule the occupational roost. In the 1960s and 70s, a number of sociologists, chafing at the apologetic thrust of the reigning social theory known as *functionalism*, scornful of the efforts of their colleagues to stuff untidy occupational realities into high and low ideal-types, undertook to demythologize professionalism. Influenced by Everett C. Hughes, whose debunking study, *Men and Their Work*, cleared new paths, they advanced the argument that the benign qualities attributed to the professions are not objective descriptions, but ideological commercials, designed to promote the interests of their members. The less extreme of these idoloclasts were willing to concede that it took a more or less effective product to make these self-advertisements work. They granted that a neurologist had to be passably knowledgeable about the nervous system to vend his services at fancy prices and that an obstetrician had to have a pretty good record of safe deliveries in order to obtain a supply of docile patients and fend off the pushy midwife crowd. The extremists in this camp denied that the sales pitches of professionals needed or customarily possessed even that much substance. In their view, neurologists, obstetricians, and what have you acquired exclusive control over an area of expertise not by actually knowing more than others, but by seeming to know more than others, semblances they artfully contrived by pinning impressive but meaningless parchment testimonials to their office walls, calling alternative ways of knowing "quackish" or "unscientific," and invoking the power of the state to punish practitioners outside their fold. Doubtless most did not regard professionals as complete illusionists, but even those who did not hold that they did everything with mirrors did contend that the pre-eminence of the professions owed a great deal to symbolic hocus-pocus. Once—the more measured critics and the nullifidians both maintained—lineage had established effective claims to deference, power and good life chances; later wealth supplanted lineage; now something was replacing wealth—an ingeniously wrought and effectively argued occupational mystique.

Just how many sociologists the Eliott Freidsons, Megalo Larsons, and Joel Gerstls have converted to their unmaskings no census-taker, to my knowledge, has tried to count. But I think it can safely be said that it is very difficult nowadays to find a book or article on the meaning of professionalism written by a sociologist under 40 that does not treat it as a monopolistic stratagem put across by publicity stunts. And I have the distinct impression that those who continue to try to man the conceptual defenses of professionalism—generally they are of an older and passing generation—are seen by most rookie and a good many veteran sociologists as guardians of an empty shrine.[1]

Four decades ago, as I have indicated, the bibliography on professionalism contained comparatively few references by historians. Even today, given the reliance of social scientists on current surveys, most research on professionals is research on contemporary professionals, a monument to the living if not the quick. Nevertheless, historians have done much during the intervening years to atone for their previous absenteeism. To say that they were moved by the geist to make up for past neglects would be to underestimate their purely scholarly motivations. But there can be no doubt that the pejorative temper of the times does leave an indelible mark on what they write. A skeptical, derisive, or hostile attitude toward professionalism in particular and toward the professions in particular colors a large number of historical works of recent vintage. In American history, and especially in works that cover the post-Civil War period, this attitude has sparked revisionist interpretations of practically every intellectual movement and social trend.

Among American historians, the antiprofessional persuasion has taken a characteristics turn for which there is as yet no specific signpost, so I have invented one. In paraphrasing the first line of the *Communist Manifesto* in the title of this article, I used the term *professionism* (not, as the quick eye may read, professionalism). Professionism is my cover word for all systematic attempts to attribute historical trends— especially undesirable trends—to the rise of the professions or to the foibles of professionals. For historians of recent America, the idea that professionals are effective change-artists and that the changes they foster are for the worse has been given so many diverse applications that it has come to serve almost as an explanatory master key. Some historians hold professionals responsible for the attenuation of artisan skills and the loss of self-directing powers in the work-forces from whence they spring; others—reaching further out—regard them as prime movers behind the deterioration of the status of women, the weakening of the authority of the family, the Faustian bargains struck by scientific men of knowledge with the militaristic state; still others—those with a bent for wide-reaching accusations—see them as the principal instigators of practically every detrimental tendency in modern life. The reader of these aggregated writings might be persuaded that professionals have replaced Jesuits, Bolsheviks, Jews, and Lucifer as the omnicompetent authors of dreadful happenings, even though—at least so far—no one has recommended them for witchburnings, sedition trials, or pogroms!

Within this genre, no historical study has been more successful in attracting followers and imitators than Robert Wiebe's *Search for Order*, a seminal analysis of the American progressive movement, published in 1967. This work can be analyzed on many levels; I propose to use it as an example of what can happen, even in virtuosic writings, when the causal work-horse I call professionism comes to haunt the historical imagination.

Before Wiebe, American historians had generally regarded the period between the turn of the century and World War One as a time when social reformers called ''progressives'' sought, through the agency of the state, to curb the excesses of concentrated private enterprise, fight the corruption of political machines, and improve the condition of the urban poor. A leftist minority writing about this period had seen it as a different kind of watershed, one in which monopoly capitalism first forged the political tools that would allow it to dominate the economy, but these historians had not been able to deflect the liberal thrust of mainstream scholarship. In the standard histories of this period, it had been noted that professionals as individuals had frequently been involved in progressive causes. But it had not been generally assumed that they did so to enhance the power of their own professions, let alone that the very meaning of the progressive movement could be derived from their group ambitions. The one major study that had linked the rise of progressivism to the changing fortunes of professionals— Richard Hofstadter's *Age of Reform*— had contended that members of certain old professions, mainly lawyers, clergymen, and academics, came to feel overshadowed and demoted by the conspicuous appearance of tycoon wealth and that this ''status revolution'' induced them to make common cause with the more truly downtrodden elements in society. But Hofstadter had regarded these professionals as victims, not aggrandizers, and had continued to define progressivism as the awakening of the social conscience, even though he saw the motivations of those who contributed to it as complex.

Wiebe put matters in a different light. Impressed by the rise to public prominence in this era of economists, engineers, city planners, statisticians, public administration experts, public health officials, and other members of the so-called ''new'' professions, he thought it more sensible to stress, not what society was doing to professionals, but what professionals— energetic, ubiquitous, in command of newly developed sciences—were doing to society and for themselves. What they were doing, Wiebe concluded, was making American over in their image. In his view, these products of the new graduate and professional schools, together with like-minded corporation managers and trade union leaders, constituted a ''new middle class''—a class as conscious of itself and as filled with a sense of its saving mission as ever the industrial proletariat was destined to become in Marxist theory. True, they did not set out to expropriate the expropriators; they sought to take over the levers of culture, not the means of production. But to Wiebe, a historian inclined to put mind over matter, this did not make their bid for control any less far-reaching. As he saw it, the members of this new class were convinced that this country, with its insular communities, its weak institutions of government, its penchant for populist crusading, its deference to custom, and its indifference to trained intelligence, was incapable of solving the problems that had been heaped upon it by rapid industrialization, unplanned urbanization, and massive immigration. They were no less convinced that they, by virtue of their command of the scientific method and the art of administration, were uniquely equipped to deliver the country from its outmoded communitarianism, delusory utopianism, executive inefficiency, and economic waste. Their program of redemption consisted, first, of purging their own professions of anachronistic features that prevented them from absorbing the latest fruits of science, and then of fanning out into society to teach their gospel to backward tribes. To Wiebe, the waging by professionals (and their class allies) of a *Kulturkampf* against the prevailing folkways was the crucial story of the progressive era, and their winning of this cultural war—not the quest for greater social justice nor, alternatively, the triumph of big business—was that era's most significant and enduring legacy.

The credibility of Wiebe's thesis owed a lot to the seductiveness of his expository technique. That technique consisted of touching lightly on a wide assortment of cultural and organizational changes that came to fruition in the progressive period; of ascribing their common direction to the workings of a certain mind-set; of then assigning that mentality to a scattered legion called professionals, whose personal and situational differences are smoothed away by the homogenizing concept of social class. One of the happy consequences of the use of this technique was that it afforded the author an opportunity to weave together many intellectual and institutional strands that previous historians had left hanging. He was able to thread into an intelligible tapestry such seemingly discrete developments as the tendency to prize specialized over general knowledge, to use statistical procedures that transformed qualas into quantums and permitted the measurement of even subjective states; to redefine science as a set of verifying procedures rather than as a stack of settled truths, to picture the body politic, once conceived as a stage for implementing abstract principles, as a mechanism for easing social friction and engineering social consent. Across the warp of these new ways of thinking, he placed the woof of institutional innovations, ranging from the centralization of urban public school systems to the establishment of state purchasing and budget offices, from the integration of farmers into marketing networks to the creation of national associations for every learned discipline and business trade—all of which served to reorder human relationships on hierarchic and impersonal lines. Wiebe's vision of progressivism as a multifaceted cultural movement has much to recommend it: It offers a welcome relief from the political preoccupation of liberal historians and from the unshaded economism of the neo-Marxists. But whether professionals

were really guilty as charged—whether they formed the core of a social class that remodeled the mind of an entire nation—remains a debatable issue that even a refreshing synthesis cannot put to rest.

If Wiebe sought an encompassing term that would unite all the tendencies he was describing, he never found it: The word *bureaucratic*, which he used most often, did not do justice to the variety of his examples.[2] It is clear, however, that practically every tendency he mentioned—to value method over substance, to master everything by calculation, to depersonalize human relationships, to rid social institutions of their mystery and work patterns of their rules of thumb—had already been identified by the great German sociologist, Max Weber, as aspects of *rationalization*, a current that had arisen in western culture and that was threatening to overtake the whole of modern life. Sigmund Freud had used the same word to describe one of the defense mechanisms of the psyche (the ability of the subconscious mind to find agreeable reasons for inadmissible urges), and there were some who presumed from the sound of the word that it implied a beneficent objective (the eventual triumph of reason over passion). But Weber did not employ the word in either of these senses: For him, it denoted the growing disposition of a society to mobilize all available means for the most efficient accomplishment of ends, whether or not the ends were rational. It is in this instrumental sense that Weber's concept can be said to cover practically everything Wiebe had to say. And the American historian was in accord with his unacknowledged precursor in yet another respect: He, too, was repelled by the rationalistic world-view, although it was only the German master, soaked as he was in *fin de siecle* pessimism, who fearfully predicted its total triumph and the consequent imprisonment of mankind in an "iron cage."

Yet it is precisely when Wiebe's work is laid against a civilizational analysis of greater depth and length that one of its major failings becomes exposed. From Weber's perspective, the rationalizing impulse in western culture is as old as that culture itself. It was manifested in the science and mathematics of the ancient Greeks. It left its mark on medieval institutions—

on Catholic canon law, which routinized charismatic revelation, and on the universities, which systematized the pursuit of learning. It invaded the heart of religious belief and the deepest temple of human personality during the Protestant Reformation, when Luther decloistered monastic discipline and transformed work from a brute necessity to a calling, and when Calvin and the leaders of ascetic sects placed salvation beyond the magic of priestly intervention and the cajolery of human prayer. It informed the spirit of capitalism which, as Weber insisted, justified not acquisitive daring and sporadic plunder, but the organized pursuit of profit and ever renewed profit through unremitting enterprise—a persistent and calculative activity particularly congenial to the methodical life-style of the Protestant bourgeoisie. It reached its epitome with the advent of industrial production through which the work-discipline of the machine gained an inexorable hold on human life. However debatable it may be in its details, this sweeping *Kulturgeschichte* is compelling enough to dispute the notion that America before the progressive period was a traditionalistic society, waiting for professionals to come along and rationalize it. Protestant and capitalistic in its origins, lacking an aristocracy or a peasantry that could long arrest the spread of a market economy, abiding by a written constitution which, of all sources of authority, is furthest removed from rule by oracular decree, ever infatuated with machine technology and soon to take the lead in manufacturing, American circa 1880 was arguably the most rationalized society in the world. Doubtless some Americans believed that it had not been rationalized enough, and doubtless some of them were members of professions. But it was because their further desires went with, not against, the grain of the culture that they were able to effect them so quickly and, on the whole, with ease. The moral? It is more judicious to suppose that professionals reflect prevailing values than that they battle to overcome them. They may accelerate cultural trends in progress, but when they do, they are likely to use institutional channels that follow the lay of the land.

A second troubling issue arises when we turn to another of Wiebe's major tenets—his belief that professionals in the progressive period formed a power-seeking social class. Ever since the French Revolution, social philosophers have been predicting the rise of a new social class that would unseat the current ruling class and recreate the social order. To a large extent, these prognostications have been inspired by the constant growth in the number of brain-workers (an interstitial group that came to occupy an expanding niche between the owners of productive capital and the hand-workers), whose assets lay in their extended education and whose products consisted of uncommon knowledge and inventive skills. To be sure, the most influential of all class fortune-tellers, Karl Marx, did not predict a potent future for these *dritte personnen*. But a long line of pre-Marxists like Saint Simon and August Comte, and post-Marxists like Thorstein Veblen and Karl Mannheim, and ex-Marxists like James Burnham and Daniel Bell did contend that a third force—variously identified as intellectuals, experts, engineers, managers, and professionals—was destined to grow powerful because it possessed an essential power, the information and the prowesses on which society increasingly depends.

Although Wiebe looked backward not forward, and more with aversion than delight, his work fits into this sooth-saying tradition. And in large measure it shares its lack of realism, a lack that has perenially served to turn its foretellings into fantasies. Historians flirt with pipe-dreams when they agree with "new class" prophets that the indispensability of a social group determines its place in the scheme of power. If that were ever a valid premise, auto mechanics would be commissars and parents would be kings and queens Despite occasional flashes of skepticism, Wiebe accepted this premise and the effect was in some ways blindfolding. Among other things, it led him to lose sight of the significant fact that, while professional skills were increasingly demanded in the progressive period, professional personnel grew more dependent on the bidding of persons outside their ranks. Though Wiebe makes almost nothing of it, this was, after all, the period when professionals became salaried employees far more than free-lancers. It would be an exaggeration to say that they thereby traded complete

autonomy for abject submission. Even when self-employed, professionals had been beholden to their clients; even as employees, their educated way with words and their resilient guild complexes increased their power to bargain with those who paid their monthly checks. Realism is not served by jumping from the frying pan of professionism into the fire of an opposite form of derogation—the notion that professionals who hire out their services allow themselves to be wholly bought. But one need not denounce them as servants of power or lackeys of the owning class in order to find something anomalous in a portrayal of them, just when they were becoming prey to the vicissitudes of a payroll and the possibility of a pink-skip blow, as a group on the make and on the march.

Calling professionals members of a social class, far from rectifying this anomaly, serves to compound it. When drawn to psychological specifications, the boundaries of social class generally fail to coincide with the lines created by the power asymmetries of the workplace. By presupposing that all who think alike have a common class position, Wiebe was able to dissociate professionals from lower white-collar workers with a different mentality, such as salespeople and bookkeepers, and to align them with managers and administrators, who presumably had a similar cast of mind. If the point was to win an argument, this psychic mapping of social space served Wiebe well: It permitted him to tie professionals to the powerful coattails of Alfred Sloan and Judge Gary, while suppressing the image of Willy Loman, from whom they would not have drawn much vicarious strength. But this sorting scheme says little about who allies with whom in workaday competitive situations. No sorting scheme can capture every rift and affiliation, but it does appear that a more conventional definition of social class—say one that groups individuals on the basis of their control over the deposition of rewards—would have recognized that the middle and lower salariats of that America did have a certain community of interest when it came to allocating income and prerogatives, and that the relations between professionals and managers did at times grow acutely adversarial.

In any case, as a careful reading of

Wiebe's narrative account suggests, professionals in the progressive period did not all think alike, not even about the issue of rationalization. Few professionals were rationalizers through and through; each profession had its own way of reconciling the competing values of *Gemeinschaft* and *Gesellschaft*; many professions had vocal members who hurled the charge of "philistine" and "barbarian" at specialists who knew nothing beyond their specialties and quantiphrenics who would subject every subtlety of human existence to the crudity of a count. Wiebe's class analysis thus performed two disservices: It overrated the binding power of *mentalité* and it implied, even against the facts he was aware of, that on so complex a matter as what a country should be thinking, the members of the professions thought as one.

Warmly received by American historians and thereafter copiously cited by them, *Search for Order* was to serve as a source-book of themes that became the trademarks of professionism: The tendency to translate the high-flown rhetoric of professionals into the vocabulary of social power, to view the era called professionalism's golden age as a period of cultural impairment, to conjoin professionals and managers with the aid of a mentalist sociology. Yet it probably exerted its strongest influence, not by handing out reuseable formulas (it was too *sui generis* to lend itself to simply copying), but by opening up new vistas of historical pieties waiting to be challenged and historical narratives waiting to be redone. Its message that a large revisionist task remained unfinished may well have given the practice of professionism its strongest boost.

Taking a panoramic view of all professions, Wiebe had not dwelled on the history of any one of them. But he inspired others to do so, and the field now abounds with occupational biographies written in his spirit. One of these—Barbara Melosh's history of the nursing profession in the progressive era, *The Physician's Hand* (1982)—offers an interesting example of a follow-up that adds argumentative touches of its own. In the standard histories, it had been assumed that nursing took giant forward steps when it institutionalized Florence Nightingale's reforms and opened hospital schools for nurses, required degrees as entering cards to practice, concentrated patient care in central plants, formed national associations, and set up a system of legal licensure—in short, when it became professionalized. To Melosh, these conventional hurrahs are largely undeserved. In the name of professional reform, she argues, an elitist faction in the field destroyed the valuable work culture that had grown up in the bedrooms of the sick and in the ward infirmaries, turned nursing into an occupation beyond the reach of capable persons too poor to acquire the right credentials, created hospital bureaucracies headed by male physicians who lorded over the predominantly feminine nursing staff, and—in the end—worsened the quality of patient care. Some of this revisionist history rings true: As Melosh points out, the leaders of the professional drive were better educated and better off than the nursing rank-and-file, their efforts did meet with a good deal of internal resistance, a light did go out when hospitals, which should be oases of tender care, became stratified organizations absorbed with protocols. But the author's dalliance with professionism does not strike this reader at least as adding to the veracity of her account. I find it hard to believe that nurses did not become vastly more competent when they were taught the sciences of the body, or that employment opportunities for the disadvantaged were long choked off by the raising of admission standards, or that the gender prejudices that troubled and still trouble this profession would not have become yet more arrant if nurses had remained angels of mercy, while doctors, after the Flexner reforms, became to the nth degree credentialized.[3] And I see no reason to be scandalized by the finding that the leaders of this profession, like those in most walks of life, were a social cut above the led. No deep insight into the history of this profession is gained, it seems to me, by treating "professional" as a foul expression and "elitism" as a moral offense.

Studying the historical culture of one profession allows for pointed attacks that may yield discriminatory judgments; studying the historical culture of all professions—an ambition that springs directly from the Wiebe legacy—may result in a kitchen-sink indictment of almost anything the author happens not to like—an outcome Wiebe

did not espouse and that he in fact escaped. By way of glimpsing the mishaps that may befall when batch culturology is attempted, consider the book called *The Culture of Professionalism*, written by the historian Barton Bledstein; it caused quite a stir when it appeared in 1976. In this book, Bledstein blames professionals (whom he also sees as constituting a "new middle class" that arose after the Civil War) for practically every cultural aggravation he can think of. He blames them, *inter alia*, for the decline of artisanship (no hint that the advent of the factory might have something to do with that phenomenon), for the rise of a "vertical vision" that led Americans to vie with coworkers for the next promotion (as though careerism had never been sighted before the second half of the nineteenth century), for the childlike dependency of Americans on so-called experts (as though people had never run to conjurers and medicine men before they consulted professionals with advanced degrees), and, finally, for the widespread flummery of "professional oaths, internships, ordinations, association meetings, scholarly papers (and) awards"—a spluttering denunciation that seems to combine the notion that professionals do everything for show with the notion that doing everything for show is a relatively recent innovation. At this point, haunted by professionism, history descends into demonology.

What accounts for the vogue of this turn in scholarship? What happened in the course of the last four decades that persuaded so many historians and social scientists to nominate professionals as their black beast? No one has yet provided, perhaps no one has yet attempted, a searching answer to these questions. The roots of anti-intellectualism have been closely studied, but the roots of antiprofessionalism (the two intersect but are not identical) have not yet found their Richard Hofsadter or Jacques Barzun. All that we can do, lacking authoritative texts to turn to, is to cast our own tentative net around a number of potential causes, recognize that others may exist and each in the net may have some bearing, and then winnow the catch as best we can.

Did the professions give their true nature away by behaving scandalously

in this period? It may be that their publicized lapses from vaunted rectitude did dispel some scholarly illusions. But many of the same or worse misbehaviors had not gone unnoticed in the past, yet did not produce the same wakening effect. Lawyers had long practiced racial, religious, and sex discrimination; doctors had long dominated the medical marketplace, without either of them causing the scales to be lifted from scholars' eyes. Moreover, if later signs of professional malfeasance had the power to dispel the faith of innocents, later signs of professional repentance should have had the power to restore it. The 1960s and 70s were not a time of professional moral exhaustion; they were a time of professional moral reformation, a good part of it mounted from within. No one blew the whistle louder against the emerging "health-for-hire" order than the doughty editor of the *New England Journal of Medicine*; no one complained more about the failure of the legal system to protect the poor, or the hospital system to serve them well, than clinical professors of law and the faculties of schools of public health. And, to a large degree, the significant reforms that were accomplished in this period also owed much to internal sponsorship. Lags and resistances notwithstanding, the professional conscience did accede to hospital peer reviews to monitor surgical procedures and did contribute to the growth of public interest law. Yet these positive behaviors did not do much to alter the negative images that many scholars carried in their heads and brought to their research.

Should the new wave of scholarly writing be attributed to the rise of left-wing ideologies in this period? In some cases, the depreciation of professionals was patently an extension of the left's disparagement of liberals, a radical war carried on by other means. Of the authors mentioned in this article, Bledstein seems to be affiliated with the counter-culture, Melosh with bottom-up labor history, Larson to some degree with neo-Marxism. Of the legion of other authors smitten by professionism, some have mild anti-establishment convictions and a few have fierce ones—take Ivan Illich, that multiple nullifidian, who tried to foment a run on the moral accounts of all authorities—presidents, popes, and generals, as well as doctors, lawyers, and dons. But this is to call the roll selectively; when all believers in professionism are identified, the ideological picture becomes quite complex. Wiebe, for example, would hardly be claimed as a comrade by either Old Left or New Left doctrinists: His insertion of a *tertium quid* into the orthodox two-class struggle and his deflection of resentments from the ''power elite'' to their supposed spear-carriers, would make him ideologically incompatible with either camp. Furthermore, anyone who believes that antipathy toward professionals is a singular property of the left would have to reckon with convincing evidence that it can well up as well among conservatives, who often use it to strengthen free market arguments or to transfer amorphous popular aversions into Republican Party votes. It bears noting that it was the neo-classical economist, Milton Friedman, who led the attack on professional licensing in this period, and that it was the *Wall Street Journal* which urged the Federal Trade Commission to prosecute doctors and lawyers for engaging in illegal restraints of trade. One might more accurately say that the antiprofessional hosts owed their success to the conflation of left and right than that they gathered strength from their ideological purity. To be sure, the few defenders of the professions in this period also ranged over a broad ideological spectrum that included Paul Goodman on the left, Thomas Haskell somewhere in the center, and Robert Merton further to the right. The difference was that their voices made less of a clamor when they converged.

I would give special weight to an explanation that stresses the importance of demography. For several decades following World War Two, most of the professions in the United States underwent unprecedented expansions. The rapid numerical growth of an occupation, like a population boom in a society, is likely to have adverse as well as favorable consequences. It seems reasonable to suppose that, whatever being a professional came to signify, it ceased in this period to confer the distinction of rarity. It seems equally reasonable to suppose that as professional services became more lavishly provided they also became more widely expected, and that when these expectations were disappointed (as they were bound to be, given the rising

costs of professional training and technologies), a groundswell of hostility would result. Finally, it seems reasonable to suppose that as professionals appeared in large numbers all over the political and social landscape, they became open to attacks not specifically or initially aimed at them. So broadly and thickly did they spread that it became virtually impossible to aim a critical arrow at any social institution or public policy without piercing professional flesh.

The dramatic expansion of the academic profession, followed by its closure and contraction, may well have had a special impact on those who took the measure of professionalism in their own research. During the 1950s and 1960s, when students descended on the colleges in torrential numbers, academic planners set up huge, publicly-supported, multi-campus institutions, topped by central governing boards. They could hardly have hit on an arrangement more likely to sap the professional pride and confidence of the academic teaching corps. Faculty members who saw the locus of effective power shifting from their campuses to superboards and statehouses had reason to feel that they were beset by forces that professional manners and procedures were too weak to reach. Faculty members who found themselves in systems not sodalities, and took note of the lessening distance between themselves and government employees or other cadres of bureaucratized service help, felt fewer qualms about voting a union up even if that could be construed as voting the idea of profession down. The period of recession that set in after the period of expansion gave rise to a raft of personnel policies—not just in state systems but throughout—that would have further dispiriting effects. To ease lean budgets, institutions of higher learning saw fit to hire multitudes of part-time teachers at piece-work rates and multitudes of temporary full-time teachers who were in but never fully of the faculty and faced the prospect of going everywhere but getting nowhere. Along with these peripheral and peripatetic crowds, whose professional longings were automatically denied, came a myriad of full-time researchers who subsisted on marginal appointments and soft financing, and numerous junior professors, consigned to hopelessness by tenure quotas and

nontenure tracks, who came, served and inescapably went, like so many caterers to fancy balls—hardly the stuff of which professional devotees could be made. Then, in the late seventie and early eighties, a shattering blow to professionalism was delivered by the firing of tenured professors, not individually for proven cause, but in groups by administrative directive, allegedly on grounds of financial exigency.

Small wonder that many academics abandon the old terms of admiration when they address the subject of professionalism. ''Profession'' is a codeword for ''cartel''? This may seem a fair description to would-be and transient academics pressing their noses against window panes. Professionalism is but one of the several guises of false consciousness? This may seem no less than true to a professoriate that feels it has become declassed. Professionals are the major carriers of the rationalizing disease? This may seem a plausible hypothesis to those who work in universities that look like business corporations and who wonder how that deformation came to pass. It is probably not an accident that, among historians prone to discern the ugly faces of professionalism, the most versatile portraitists tend to be historians of higher education. In their works, one finds professionalism held responsible, in whole or in part, for such disparate misfortunes as the fragmentation of the college curriculum (Frederick Rudolph), the scientism that undermined the progressive education movement (Diane Ravitch), the replacement of vernacular and community-based science by science that was elitist and arcane (Thomas Bender), the forsaking by economists of early socialist commitments in favor of a spurious objectivity (Mary Furner), the facilitation of the birth of Nazism by German university professors in the Weimar period (Alice Gallin)—to cite only a few examples of professionism's hold in this field. Although there are historians of higher education to whom this observation does not imply, it does appear that academic students of academe tend to import their troubled professional present into their explanations of the past.

To know the reasons for a strongly-held belief is not to pronounce it sound. Before one does that one should confront a question so obvious that it almost asks itself: Why, if professionals are nothing but power-seekers, drab deceivers, purveyors of noxious thoughts and values, do we tolerate them, reward them, and let their tribe increase? The answer given by the nay-sayers is that we allow them to multiply and flourish because our dupability knows no bounds. But is there not a reason, other than such a misanthropic one, why, though we upbraid professionals, do we not cast them off?

Elsewhere I have tried to puzzle out an answer; in this space I must content myself with repeating a bare credo. I hold these truths to be self-evident but not to as many as I would wish: that as the amount of knowledge increases, so too does the relative amount of ignorance, for each person can know only a decreasing fraction of what can be known; that knowledge, as it becomes more specialized, also tends to become more potent, more capable of being used for good or ill; that the growth and specialization of knowledge produce not a *mass* society but a *lay* society—a society in which everyone is at the mercy of someone more thoroughly in the know; that this state of mutual dependency grows more dangerous as knowledge, which had once been in the hands of holy men, kin, and neighbors, passes into the hands of strangers, and as the customary means of assuring its benign uses—religious dedication, parental love, communal sanctions—tend to fall away. It is to avert a Hobbesian outcome—a war of each against each in which everyone uses the knowledge he possesses for his own advantage, and pays a terrible price for the knowledge he may lack—that societies urge those occupations that impinge on the vital concerns of human beings to tie their expertise to honorableness, to accord even ignorance moral claims.

By rehearsing this litany, I do not, I believe, return to the lullabying maxims of my scholarly youth. I do not define any profession, as it now comports itself, as a fortress against or as a perfected artifact of the modern world. I do not share the enthusiasm of the checklisters for keeping professional pretenders in their place: I believe, rather, that every desire to enoble work should be encouraged, and that it is only when that desire flags, when workers no longer give a damn whether they are or are not part of a profession, that there is cause to take

alarm. Least of all do I wish to paint the derelictions of professions with a whitening brush. By my lights, it is not necessary to believe that, in societies run on cash and often on *force majeure*, the professional ideal can make every potent knower kind; it is only necessary to believe that, without the professional ideal, the power that lodges in knowers would much more often ward off generosity. Rather than full-hearted trust, I would urge a wary appreciativeness. If I were to offer words of counsel, they would come down to these—that the next time you meet a professional, you would be well-advised to keep one hand on your wallet and, with the other, tip your hat.

---

1. Going against the tide, some sociologists of education are now urging that the training, certification, and career opportunities of the nation's school teachers be made more professional in the name of rehabilitative school reform. It is still too early to tell whether their affirmation of the redemptive power of professionalism presages a wide attack on the true unbelievers in their discipline or represents something less portentous—a limited resurgence of faith in an occupation particularly susceptible to paradisiac promises of higher status, or just another pendulum swing in the unending debate over how a mass education system may be brought to a qualitative state of grace. In any event, these sociologists confront the irony of seeking admission to a church at a time when the weight of its theology says that God is dead.

2. "The heart of progressivism" Wiebe wrote, "was the ambition of a new middle class to fullfill its destiny through bureaucratic means" (p. 166). If this one-liner means that professionals sought to bureaucratize their own relationships with authority, it is a half-truth that has a high capacity to mislead. In this period, academic professionals did seek to install such bureaucratic devices as written contracts, tenure rules, and specialized departments of instruction. But they also strove to build such bulwarks against bureaucracy as faculty senates (to preserve the idea of collegial governance), a high degree of departmental autonomy (to resist centralized domination), and a zone of immunity for teaching, research, and civic action free from institutional discipline. In this period, the mechanical engineers were arch-exponents of stricter work-norms based on time-and-motion studies of performance. But they sought to apply this system of hierarchical control to the workforce and to executives, not to themselves. Frederick Winslow Taylor, the father of the scientific management movement, collided with corporation managers when they sought to subject his stop-watch engineers to "line" authority and not grant them the independence of consulting "staff." To many professionals in this period, the growth of bureaucracy was both a heartening development and a cause for deep concern.

3. Nothing better illustrates the change in the climate of opinion represented by the vogue of professionism than the precipitous decline of Abraham Flexner's reputation among historians. During the progressive period and for three or four decades thereafter he had enjoyed an unclouded reputation among social commentators and biographers as the fearless opponent of an outmoded and abusive medical training system. As though recounting an epic story, they told how, undaunted by his own lack of medical training and with the give-away riches of the Carnegie Foundation at his side, he had conducted

a survey of American medical education in 1910 that had exposed its haphazard admissions standards, its shallow and curtailed curricula, and its indifference to research; of how his recommendations—that medical schools raise their educational requirements for admission, that the medical course of study include hospital-based clinical experience, that medical schools be affiliated with universities, and that medical diploma mills be closed—were rapidly brought into effect by a more rigorous form of licensure, and of how this heroic effort ushered in a Saturnian age of American medicine. By the early 1970s, a revisionist generation of historians was ready to cast off this encomiastic tale as myth. Flexner's Report, they argued, was a lancet that opened new abuses, a tighter grip by the AMA on the accreditation of medical schools and hospitals, a tendency on the part of the products of high-cost schooling to neglect the less remunerative practice of preventive medicine, a licensing system whose primary aim is to enhance the income of practitioners by artificially limiting their supply.

Metzger's Selected Bibliography on Anti-Professionalism

Auerbach, J. S. (1976). *Unequal justice: Lawyers and social change in modern America*. London, New York: Oxford University Press.

Bender, T. (Spring, 1976). Science and the culture of American communities: The nineteenth century. *History of Education Quarterly, 16,* 63–77.

Berlant, J. L. (1977). *Profession and monopoly: A study of medicine in the United States and Great Britain.* Berkley: University of California Press.

Bledstein, B. J. (1976). *The culture of professionalism: The middle class and the development of higher education in America.* New York: W. W. Norton.

Ehrenreich, B. & Ehrenreich, J. (1977). *The American health empire.* New York: Random House.

Friedman, M. (1962). *Capitalism and freedom.* Chicago: University of Chicago Press.

Freidson, E. (1970). *Professional dominance: The social structure of medical care.* New York: Atherton Press.

Furner, M. O. (1975). *Advocacy and objectivity: A crisis in the professionalization of American social science, 1865–1905.* Lexington, Kentucky: University of Kentucky Press.

Gallin, A. (1986). *Midwives to nazism: University professors in Weimar, Germany, 1925–1933.* Macon, Georgia: Mercer University Press.

Gerstl, J. & Jacobs, G. (Eds.) (1976). *Professions for the people: The politics of skill.* New York: J. Wiley.

Gilb, L. (1966). *Hidden hierarchies: The professions and government.* New York: Harper and Row.

Haber, S. & Gordon, M.S. (Ed.) (1974). The professions and higher education in America: A historical view. *Higher Education and the Labor Market.* New York: McGraw-Hill.

Haug, M. (1973). Deprofessionalization: An alternative hypothesis for the future. *Sociological Review.*

Hughes, E. (1958). *Men and their work.* Glencoe, Illinois: The Free Press.

Illich, I. et al. (1977). *The disabling professions.* London: Marion Boyars.

Johnson, T. J. (1972). *Professions and power.* London: Macmillan.

Kunitz, S. J. (1974, March). Progressivism and social control in the progressive era: The case of the Flexner report. *Social Problems, 22,* 16–27.

Larson, M. S. (1977). *The rise of professionalism: A sociological analysis.* Berkeley: University of California Press.

Lewis, L. S. (1975). *Scaling the ivory tower: Merit and its limits in academic careers.* Baltimore: Johns Hopkins Press.

Lieberman, J. K. (1970). *Tyranny of the expert.* New York: Walker.

Markowitz, G. & Rosnber, D. (1973, March). Doctors in crisis: A study of the use of medical education reform to establish modern professional elitism in America. *American Quarterly, 25,* 83–107.

Melosh, B. (1982). *The physicians' hand: Nurses and nursing in the twentieth century.* Philadelphia: Temple University Press.

Rader, B. G. (1966). *The academic mind and reform: The*

588

influence of Ricard T. Ely in American life. Lexington, Kentucky: University of Kentucky Press.

Ravitch, Diane (1983). *The troubled crusade*. New York: Basic Books, Inc.

Reisman, D. & Jencks, C. (1966). *The academic revolution*. New York: Doubleday.

Roth, J. A. (1974). Professionalism: The sociologist's decoy. *Sociology of Work and Occupations, 1*, 6–51.

Rothman, D. (1980). *Conscience and convenience: The asylum and its alternatives in progressive America.* Boston: Little, Brown.

Rothstein, W. G. (1972). *American physicians in the nineteenth century: from sects to science.* Baltimore: Johns Hopkins Press.

Rudolph, F. (1985, February 13). Integrity in the college curriculum. Association of American Colleges. *Chronical of Higher Education.*

Slaughter, S. (1980, March). The danger zone: Academic freedom and civil liberties. *Annals of the American Academy of Political and Social Science, 448,* 46–61.

Starr, P. (1982). *The social transformation of American medicine.* New York: Basic Books.

Stevens, R. (1971). *American medicine and the public interest.* New Haven and London: Yale University Press.

Veysey, L. (1975, December). Who's professor Who cares? *Reviews in American History.* 419–4...

Wiebe, R. H. (1967). *Search for order: 1877–1920.* New York: Hill and Wang.

WALTER P. METZGER *is at the History Department, 504 Fayerweather Hall, Columbia University, New York, New York 10027. This article is a slightly revised version of a talk given at the April, 1987 annual meeting of AERA in Washington, DC.*

Reckoning with the Spectre

Gary Sykes

Professor Metzger seeks to challenge the widespread tendency in both historical and sociological scholarship to attribute a multitude of evils to the ascendence of professions in our society. Most readers will be familiar with this profession-bashing tropism in the culture at large, itself symptomatic of a more general decline in confidence in our institutions.

Metzger's graceful, elegant critique helps illuminate two questions that are of moment in the education field: Has teaching decisively embarked on the course of professionalization, and should teaching professionalize? His essay supplies an intriguing context for these questions; some reflection on each may suggest the import of his analysis for educational policy and practice.

Professionalism in teaching is today a theme in search of specific policy initiatives and a social meaning appropriate to teaching's circumstances. Many, if not most, of the last few years' blue ribbon reports advocate teacher professionalism, but what they mean remains unclear. I would locate the significance of this policy theme in the social contract established between an occupation providing a public service and the public itself as represented by various elected and appointed officials.

One such contract involves the exchange of autonomy for obligation. A profession agrees to develop and enforce standards of good practice in exchange for the right to practice free of bureaucratic supervision and external regulation. At the policy level, this contract applies to standards for licensure, certification, and program accreditation. The state delegates substantial responsibility for such standards to the organizations that represent the occupation. At the practice level, this contract applies to the organization and management of work. Collegial norms and peer evaluation direct work that is amenable neither to administrative oversight nor to routinization.

The legitimacy of professional control at both the policy level and the organizational level rests on two kinds of trust (Barber, 1983). One is the expectation of technically competent role performance. We expect professionals to employ specialized, expert knowledge and skill in a competent manner and to stay abreast of the growth of such knowledge and skill. This form of trust is quite common and quite necessary in a society where expertise and specialization are valued and pursued.

The second form of trust is the expectation of fiduciary responsibility, the expectation that service providers demonstrate a special concern for others' interests above their own. Trust as fiduciary responsibility extends beyond technically competent performance to the moral dimension of interaction. Trust of this kind, "... is a social mechanism that makes possible the effective and just use of the power that knowledge and position give and forestalls abuses of that power" (Barber, p. 15).

There are a number of corollaries to this theory of professional control as a public trust. One is that professions recruit capable people who possess the cognitive and other capacities to acquire and apply expert knowledge in cases where judgment is necessary, where the knowledge is imperfect and the nature of the case uncertain. A second is that individuals are recruited to the occupation, not to the employing organization. Professionals must be committed primarily to the norms of their profession. They must not pander to the desires of their clients to secure a larger share of the market or develop loyalty to employers in the interest of vertical career mobility—behaviors that can weaken professional standards and the public image of professions, as Metzger's analysis indicates. A third corollary, related to the first two, is that professional practice requires a lengthy period of training, both to acquire technical competence and to become socialized to norms of the profession. Finally, the organization of work must encourage collegiality and norm enforcement together with continued growth in professional knowledge and skill.

No profession, of course, fully realizes this ideal, but one line of educational reform implicitly—often partially—advocates and pursues this model, this social contract. Initiatives in this spirit include the Holmes Group's call for postbaccalaureate teacher education, the Carnegie Task Force's recommendation and subsequent actions to establish a national board of teaching standards, the experiments with peer evaluation schemes around the country, the use of mentor teachers to induct beginners in many states, the calls for state professional standards boards controlled by teachers, the substantial state-by-state changes made in certification procedures, and the increases in teacher salaries over the past five years. The political coalition supporting such policy includes both the National Education Association and the American Federation of Teachers together with many corporate and state political leaders, especially governors.

The emerging stance of the two largest teacher

organizations who appear to be rethinking their strategy of advancement is most significant. For the past quarter century, the unions have adopted an industrial model of labor relations whose assumptions are very different from the social contract implied by professionalism. Within the industrial model, the workers' organization emphasizes rights and protections, not responsibilities. The first, legally binding obligation of the workers' organization is to protect the worker, rather than to develop standards of work or norms of practice. Management takes responsibility for enforcing work standards through close supervision. As part of the industrial bargain, the union regards issues of teacher incompetence as management's problem. The union's responsibility is to use every stratagem of the law in defending teachers in grievance and termination proceedings. Within the industrial model, the labor-management relation is adversarial. One side's win is the other's loss, breeding a zero-sum politics of confrontation and resentment.

At the state policy level, industrial model priorities are collective bargaining statutes, political action, and lobbying for higher wages and benefits. In response to this stance, state and local policymakers seek to resist demands, limit concessions, reduce the scope of bargaining, and fan the flames of backlash against militant unionism. This has been the state of affairs in recent years, exacerbated by declining enrollments, taxpayer revolts, inflation and recession.

Now emerges in both teacher organizations a leadership vanguard at national, state, and local levels committed to change. In my opinion, their appearance is the most promising development in education in the last decade. The unadulterated industrial model is losing its hold on the imagination of teacher leaders, and this opens real possibilities for the future. Without a willingness on the part of organized teachers to take risks, to experiment with new forms of agreement and cooperation, there will be no genuine reform. Teacher organizations are the key because they wield two forms of power. They can effectively veto top-down mandates at the implementation stage or, by genuinely supporting change, can help make it happen (Bachrach & Baratz, 1962).

Within both the National Education Association and the American Federation of Teachers, a struggle is underway for the soul of the organization. A powerful old guard remains committed to the agenda of hard bargaining, militant unionism, and defensive posturing. But here and there a leadership cadre willing to take risks is beginning to espouse the principles of professionalism and to consider a new service compact. Both organizations have supported the effort to set up a national standards board. The NEA is also pressing for state standards boards and encouraging mentor and master teacher programs in a number of states. AFT locals have negotiated innovative contracts featuring shared governance and re-allocation of roles and responsibilities in such communities as Miami-Dade, Florida, Pittsburgh, Pennsylvania, and Toledo, Ohio. And a number of districts in California are beginning to experiment with a new form of agreement, termed an "educational policy trust," that supplements the contract and broadens the range of issues negotiated between labor and management (for discussion, see Kerchner & Mitchell, 1985).

The movement within the teacher organizations toward professionalism is fragile and vulnerable. Conservative elements within each organization may successfully parley the politics of resentment into a return to militant unionism. Whether this happens depends in part on the disposition of public officials. If school boards, state legislatures, superintendents, and other policy influentials cannot overcome their suspicion of the unions, their adversarial posture, then the dynamics of the prisoner's dilemma will take over: trustful behavior will be punished, provoking distrustful behavior that will confirm initial suspicions of bad faith. Altering patterns of play in such games is an extremely delicate business, particularly when intra-organizational conflict compounds the difficulties of inter-organizational cooperation.

To this point it may appear that teaching is in fact professionalizing, albeit slowly and fitfully. However, counter-trends are also evident. Most notable is the continuing centralization and standardization of policy aimed at influencing practice, tendencies Arthur Wise described in *Legislated Learning* (1979). In an earlier era, the aim of educational equity supplied the rationale for regulation, prompting an explosion of federal policy. Many equity-related initiatives reached deeply into schools and classrooms. Recall, for example, the impacts of desegregation, bilingual instruction, mainstreaming, pull-out instruction for Title I students, and Title IX's sex-equity guidelines.

Today the rallying cry has shifted from equity to excellence, and the action from the federal to the state and local levels, but the regulatory impulse has not slackened. The new policy instruments include course mandates and planning requirements, detailed curricular specifications, increased student and teacher testing, and teacher evaluation systems that purport to be research-based. In many states and localities, the results have been increased paperwork, teaching to the test, and teaching to behaviors specified by the evaluation system. The emphasis, in short, is on external accountability, not professional responsibility. The consequence is to reduce teacher autonomy and to discourage development of professional judgment. The supporting social science research is used to assert administrative control over teaching rather than to encourage development of professional standards by teachers.

Some classroom observers, like McNeil (1986, 1987) and Apple (1987), note that the trend toward routinization serves to deprofessionalize teachers. Such analysis follows the footsteps of Braverman (1974), Edwards (1979), and other Marxist-oriented interpreters of work in corporate-capitalist society, echoing as well the notion that professional work in general is becoming proletarian (see Freidson, 1984 and 1985, for analysis). According to these theorists, the structure of work encourages teachers to rely on the external authority of tests, texts, and guidelines, to teach mechanically and defensively, to disengage from a professional conception of the role. These processes are not attributable solely to recent trends, but the emerging policy environment appears to abet such tendencies.

At both policy and organizational levels, then, professionalizing and deprofessionalizing trends are evident, reflecting the mixed forms of public-bureaucratic and professional control that have arisen to direct the work of teaching. These tensions are not new. Educational historians have long chronicled such "contradictions of control" (McNeil's phrase), dating at least from the progressive era—a decisive period in the minds of those chary of the benefits to laymen of the growth of professions, as Metzger notes. And Lortie (1969, 1975) framed his seminal analysis of teaching in just these terms, discerning both centralization and professionalization in teaching's future.

The question of trust recurs. The mixed forms of control, the contradictory tendencies in policy, suggest doubts in the public mind about delegating too much responsibility to teachers themselves. Both bases for trust—technical competence and fiduciary obligation—raise questions. How credible are the claims to specialized knowledge in teaching? Are teachers, collectively and individually, guardians of the best interests of children? Skepticism here raises the question of whether teaching should professionalize. The answer hinges on the values likely to be served by professionalism, and the historical record often provides the starting point for argument.

Critics of professionalism raise three value issues to which Metzger's paper makes us especially alert. First, they question whether the hunger for a technical knowledge base will erode concern for caring and compassion in the human services (see Sarason, 1985, as well as Noddings, 1984, and work that Metzger cites). Many argue, for example, that the rise of scientific medicine resulted in a loss of compassion among physicians, who came to treat diseases, not people. Teachers seeking professional status might invest in increasingly arcane knowledge to the detriment of their attentiveness to children. Teaching continues to impress many observers—and many teachers—as artistic and ethical work of a kind not amenable to analysis aimed at prescribing technique. To the extent that professionalism is associated with scientifically validated methods or a formal system of principles of practice, it will not appeal to those who perceive procedural specifications as antithetical to humane practice. There is no necessary disjunction, of course, but the divorce of technique from calling is observable in other professions.

A second criticism associates professionalism with the attempt to create social distance between the professional and the client, a move likely to undercut the democratic ideals of schooling (Koehler-Richardson & Fenstermacher, 1987). Sociologists have portrayed professionalism as a collective mobility project aimed at achieving a market shelter along with elite status (see Collins, 1979, in addition to Larson, 1977, cited below). Such motives do not comport well with the democratic ideals of schooling. The responsibility for education must be shared and inclusive. It is not the special province of a knowledge elite, because the goals of schooling include personal development and citizenship as well as academic and vocational preparation. Not simply the governance of schools but the conduct of education itself must involve a partnership of educators with parents and community members. Teachers must learn to deal sensitively with parents from the full social spectrum, rather than distance themselves as remote experts cloaked in the mysteries of technical knowledge. The history of other professions, however, illustrates the very status-seeking efforts to which teaching must not succumb. Teachers, these critics might argue, must cultivate an orientation to the *Gemeinschaft*, whereas professionalism promotes guild-loyalty, a *Gesellschaft* orientation.

Finally, professionalism may be incompatible with equity goals. Again, the historical record suggests that standard-setting in the elite professions was a conscious effort to drive women, immigrants, and minorities out of the ranks (Sykes, 1986). This motive was clearest in medicine and the law, but was undeniable as well in nursing and social work among others. A further equity consequence of raising standards for entry was to redistribute access to professional services. "Fewer and better doctors!" was Flexner's rallying cry, but an unanticipated result was that fewer and better doctors moved to well-heeled communities where practice was most lucrative, abandoning inner city and rural areas. The quality of medicine may have improved as a result, but the poor had less access to it. At a time when the shortage of minority teachers is a full-fledged crisis (Graham, 1987), many worry that standard-setting may further shrink the pool and disadvantage the black colleges that produce nearly two thirds of the supply.

Even this sketchy treatment of two questions central to teaching reform should caution against simple answers. Professionalism in teaching admits no facile judgments. To weigh the arguments requires a balanced historical appreciation, for analogies among the professions are as readily made as they are often misleading. The risks of professionalism are by now well known, and no one proposes that educators mindlessly ape the doctors and lawyers of the progressive era. As educators seek to learn the lessons of the past and to study the other professions for leads to advancement, they must attend to the basic values of their own enterprise and forge a professionalism distinctively suited to such ideals.

Apple, M. (1987). *Teachers and text: A political economy of class and gender relations in education.* New York: Routledge & Kegan Paul.
Bachrach, P. & Baratz, M. (1962). The two faces of power. *American Political Science Review.* LVII, 947-952.
Barber, B. (1983). *The logic and limits of trust.* New Brunswick, NJ: Rutgers University Press.
Braverman, H. (1974). *Labor and monopoly capital: The degradation of work in the twentieth century.* New York: Monthly Review Press.
Collins, R. (1979). *The credential society.* New York: Academic Press.
Edwards, R. (1979). *Contested terrain: The transformation of the workplace in the twentieth century.* New York: Basic Books.
Freidson, E. (1984). The changing nature of professional control. *Annual Review of Sociology, 10.* 1-20.
Freidson, E. (1985). *Professional powers: A study of the institutionalization of formal knowledge.* Chicago: University of Chicago Press.
Graham, P.A. (1987). Black teachers: A drastically scarce resource. *Phi Delta Kappan, 68*(8), 598-605.
Kerchner, C. T. & Mitchell, D. E. (1986). Teaching reform and union reform. *The Elementary School Journal, 86*(4), 449-470.
Koehler-Richardson, V. & Fenstermacher, G. D. (1987, May). *Graduate programs of teacher education: Some prior considerations.* Paper presented at the Rutgers Invitational Symposium in Education: Graduate Preparation of Teachers. New Brunswick, NJ.
Larson, M. S. (1977). *The rise of professionalism: A sociological analysis.* Berkeley: University of California Press.
Lortie, D. (1969). The balance of control and autonomy in elementary school teaching. In A. Etzioni (Ed.), *The semi-professions and their organization.* New York: Free Press, 1-53.
Lortie, D. (1975). *Schoolteacher: A sociology study.* Chicago: University of Chicago Press.
McNeil, L. (1986). *Contradictions of control: School structure and school knowledge.* New York: Routledge & Kegan Paul.
McNeil, L. (1987). Exit, voice, and community: Magnet teachers' responses to standardization. *Educational Policy, 1*(1), 93-114.
Noddings, N. (1984). *Caring: A feminist approach to ethics.* Berkeley: University of California Press.
Sarason, S. B. (1985). *Caring and compassion in clinical practice.* San Francisco: Jossey Bass.
Sykes, G. (1986). *Social consequences of standard-setting in the professions.* Paper prepared for the Carnegie Forum on Education and the Economy. Washington, DC: Carnegie Forum.
Wise, A. (1979). *Legislated learning: The bureaucratization of the American classroom.* Berkeley: University of California Press.

The Historical and Cultural Dimensions of the Recent Reports on Undergraduate Education

Bruce A. Kimball

The major points made in the recent reports on undergraduate education are analogous to the tenets of one of the two major traditions in the history of liberal education and to the central dilemmas concerning knowledge and culture now being discussed in the humanistic and social disciplines. The recent reports do not recognize these analogies, which point to the deeper implications of and important contradictions in their recommendations for undergraduate education.

After the recent blizzard of national studies addressing liberal education and the undergraduate curriculum in America, one might well wonder whether anything else needs to be said on the topic. That it will be said is certain, for blue-ribbon commissions in America have been issuing these kinds of reports and studies during every decade of the twentieth century. And many of those prior studies attracted no less attention than do the reports today. For example, the publicity concerning the 1987 study issued by Ernest Boyer, president of the Carnegie Foundation for the Advancement of Teaching,[1] scarcely exceeds the media blitz surrounding the 1943 study of the Committee on the Re-Statement of the Nature and Aims of Liberal Education. That 1943 study was reported in a news release sent to 1,894 newspapers; was summarized in a booklet distributed to over 7,000 educational organizations, journals, elected officials, and heads of colleges and universities; and was sold in unabridged form to more than 6,000 institutions of higher education.[2]

Another similarity between those older reports, particularly that 1943 study, and some of the recent ones is the tendency for such commissions, committees, and study groups to recommend everything that any member believes is important and thereby to avoid facing difficult trade-offs and choices. The 1985 report sponsored by the Association of American Colleges (AAC), the same agency that sponsored the 1943 study, exemplifies this tendency. Decrying "the decay" and "evil times" now suffered by "the bachelor's program and the bachelor's degree," the AAC study calls stridently for reform.[3] But its internal contradictions, tautologies, and distinctions without differences reveal a deep-seated ambivalence about recommending anything that would exclude or change very much of current undergraduate education.[4] This ambivalence appears to have resulted from the fact that the report presents a consensus of what all of the committee members could agree to, not what anyone thinks is the best. As with the past reports from committees that have taken this approach, the result is not very penetrating.

Contrast this eclectic approach and result with the more focused and coherent 1984 report of William J. Bennett, secretary of the Department of Education. Bennett was advised by a "study group," several of whom also served on the AAC project, but he proceeded to write his own statement and asserted that "responsibility for authorship belongs to me."[5] Like it or not, one can at least disagree with the secretary, whereas it is difficult to know exactly what the 1985 AAC report considers important.

Nevertheless, though impatient with committees that cannot discipline themselves in the very way that they expect college and university professors to discipline themselves individually and collectively, I do not share the skepticism that some have expressed about the recent reports.[6] These studies have something important to say to us, if we understand both the historical background and present intellectual context. In evaluating the reports, we have to think about the broad movements that have taken place in the history of liberal education, and we must bear in mind the profound intellectual shift that is occurring in academic culture at large. Explaining all this could, of course, fill volumes and occupy a lifetime. In this article, I can sketch only the barest outline, and I shall attempt to do so in three steps.

First, I shall identify several points that the recent reports most commonly repeat or emphasize about undergraduate education. In this effort I do not intend to be comprehensive by addressing all the reports of any individual one in detail. Rather, I shall be generalizing about the reports and some of the discussion they have stimulated. Second, I shall propose that these points, though usually presented as if they were specific responses to unrelated problems in undergraduate education, are systematically and historically related. That is to say, they imply each other conceptually, while they reexpress one of the two preeminent traditions in the history of what has been called liberal education in the past. Last, I shall argue that this coherent and historical tradition of liberal education, which the reports are distantly and unconsciously reexpressing, is part of a profound redefinition of knowledge and culture that is occurring throughout academe.

In sum, I hope to make the case that the core complaint in these recent reports echoes a persistent tradition in the history of liberal education, while it also comports closely with a broad intellectual shift that is taking place across the humanistic and social disciplines and related professional studies. The weakness of these reports, I will conclude, lies not so much in their specific recommendations, as their failure to consider the deeper causes and broader implications of what they are recommending in terms of its historical background and the current intellectual context of higher education.

I. The Recent Reports

There are five points most commonly repeated or emphasized about undergraduate education in the recent reports. First, it is said that language study deserves a great deal more attention because present college graduates cannot read, write, or speak effectively. Surely this complaint is familiar, and probably one that most professors have made at one time or another. Ernest Boyer in his new report devoted a full chapter to "Language: The First Requirement," and an entire study concerning this issue was funded by the National Endowment for the Humanities, conducted by the Department of Defense, and published in 1984 by the Association of American Universities.[7] It is important to note that when observers advocate language study they usually include within it some attention to the textual tradition of the culture, from which are to be drawn exemplary models of expression.

The second point consistently raised is the charge that colleges do not and should inculcate a sense of "values" in their graduates. With one exception, to be discussed in a moment, these missing virtues are never defined precisely except in two negative senses. A virtuous student is neither "materialistic," as the 1985 AAC report suggests, nor self-centered, as Boyer notes in arguing that students are not as egoistic as most observers have said.[8] Taken together, these two indices of an absence of values—materialism and self-centeredness—are said to be manifested in the vocationalism or "careerism" of undergraduates. A 1985 report on "careerism and intellectualism" surveyed Stanford undergraduates and found that, aside from the 25 percent of students who are "unconnected" with the college experience, some 73 percent of the rest consider career preparation their primary goal or one of two primary goals of their college education.[9]

The complement to this second point that college graduates should have acquired a sense of values is a third point: the affirmation that college graduates should become good citizens. Both the 1985 report from the president of the Education Commission of the States and a 1986 report from the commission's "Working Party on . . . Undergraduate Education" stressed as a central theme the importance of elevating individuals' commitment and service to the society and the body politic.[10] One might have expected this theme to appear in those studies, which address national and state policy concerning higher education. But the theme arises prominently even in reports on seemingly remote topics, such as that sponsored by the National Research Council on science education in college. This study stressed as its primary rationale that "nonspecialists" must acquire "the scientific and technical knowledge needed to fulfill civic responsibilities in society."[11]

This emphasis on citizenship refers not only to the nation but to all communities to which students belong. Indeed, "community" may be the most often-used word in these reports. The 1984 National Institute of Education (NIE) report advocated strongly "the creation and strengthening of communities *within* colleges," and the 1985 AAC report concluded its discussion of curriculum by citing the ideal of "a community of learning."[12] Sharon Parks in her new study calls for colleges and universities to become "communities of imagination" in order to develop a sense of faith and belief upon which meaning and value can be based.[13] Similarly, David H. Smith has spoken repeatedly on "The College as a Moral Community" to the Lilly Endowment Workshop on the Liberal Arts.[14] In such statements one can begin to see the intimate connections between these emphases on students' values, citizenship, and community, and the reports discuss the faculty in these respects as well.

However, the discussion about the values, citizenship, and community of the faculty usually pertains to a fourth major point in the reports: the call for general education, that is, a coherent and unifying purpose and structure for a curriculum that will serve all students throughout their lives. This fourth topic—coherence and unity of a general education—is causally linked by the reports to the cohesiveness and community spirit of the faculty, or lack thereof. In his 1983 comprehensive study of the entire membership of the Association of American Colleges, Jerry Gaff concluded, "I am convinced that the problem with general education is basically a problem with the faculty."[15] Two years later the Select Committee of the Association of American Colleges emphasized "the responsibility of the faculty *as a whole* for the curriculum *as a whole*."[16]

The great barrier to faculty cohesiveness, and therefore to "curricular coherence,"[17] is said to be specialization and departmentalization, about which none of the reports has anything good to say. Rather, they complain of "overspecialization,"[18] "hyper-specialization and self-isolating vocabularies,"[19] and "the autonomy" of departments, "their power to resist unwanted change and to protect their interests."[20] These institutional barriers to faculty and curricular cohesiveness are strengthened, it seems, by the desire of professors to mold their students in their own image, as MacArthur Fellow and Harvard professor Howard Gardner has suggested.[21] The 1984 NIE study points out the futility of this motive, inasmuch as the tiny fraction of entering college freshmen intending to become professors had dropped in 1982 to one-ninth of what it was in 1966, from 1.8 percent to .2 percent.[22] Meanwhile, the president of the Carnegie Foundation reported in 1981 that "very few faculty members held any convictions about what *all* students need to know."[23]

This inability of the faculty to identify and establish "coherence and . . . integrity" in the college curriculum[24] is said to be reflected in the disarray, confusion, conflict, and lack of purpose throughout the institutions themselves. In the prologue to his 1987 report, Boyer laments the "*divisions* on campus, *conflicting* priorities and *competing* interests . . . *confusion* over goals . . . *divided* loyalties and *competing* career concerns within the faculty . . . *tensions* between conformity and creativity in the classroom . . . a great *separation*, sometimes to the point of *isolation*, between academic and social life . . . *disagreement* over how the college should be governed . . . a disturbing *gap* between college and the rest of the world."[25] In analyzing this state of affairs, the reports generally admonish faculties, deans, and presidents to organize the institutions and curriculum around a unified, coherent mission and rationale. William Bennett's report on the humanities exemplifies this response. He writes:

> Many of our colleges and universities have lost a clear sense of . . . the purpose of education, allowing the thickness of their catalogues to substitute for vision and a philosophy of education. . . . The decline in learning was caused in part [he offers no other reason] by a failure of nerve and faith on the part of many college faculties and administrators, and persists because of a vacuum in educational leadership. . . . The nation's colleges and universities must reshape their undergraduate curricula based on a clear vision of what constitutes an educated person. . . . College and university presidents must take responsibility for . . . making plain what the institution stands for and what knowledge it regards as essential to good education. . . . [M]erely being exposed to a variety of subjects and points of view is not enough. Learning to think critically and skeptically is not enough.[26]

These words typify, albeit vehemently, the common view, which places responsibility for the conflict and confusion on professors, deans, and presidents.

The same groups are also held responsible for the fifth major point in the reports on undergraduate education: the well-known complaint that teaching deserves greater emphasis. Clearly, the track to professional and professorial success, notoriety, and salary increments is built upon research and publication. Teaching is relatively unrewarded and, as a result, neglected, and the various reports recommend that the reward structure be changed.[27] Not all professors agree with this recommendation, however. Daniel Bell and Stephen Jay Gould, for example, warn against "any overly romanticized notion that teaching is primary," at least "if one is thinking of a major university."[28]

To summarize, I am proposing that these five points are the topics most often repeated and emphasized about undergraduate education in the recent reports:

> Study of language and the textual tradition of the culture,
> values of students,
> citizenship and community,
> coherence and unity of general education,
> teaching.

Certainly, the reports raise other matters, and not all of the reports address all of these issues. But this constellation of points comprehends the themes most often repeated and emphasized. Indeed, one can find them brought together in the topics addressed at the national Colloquium on General Education held at the University of Chicago in 1981[29] and the national conference on undergraduate education held at Harvard this past November.[30] In the 1987 report from the Carnegie Foundation for the Advancement of Teaching, Ernest Boyer includes 16 chapters addressing the undergraduate experience. One chapter is devoted to "Language: The First Requirement"; six chapters address how "community must be built" (p. 195) on campus among students, faculty, and administration (chaps. 11, 12, 15) and off campus through the promotion of "service" and "commitment . . . to be socially and civically engaged" (pp. 278–79; chaps. 13, 14, 18); four chapters discuss the need for "a clear and vital mission" undergirding "the integrated core" of general education and the major (chaps. 3, 4, 6, 7); and three chapters discuss teachers, teaching, and evaluation (chaps. 8, 9, 16). The two other chapters are devoted to the library and computers and to student employment after graduation (chaps. 10, 17).

II. The Historical Context

Turning to consider how these points are related to each other, I wish to propose that, taken together, they constitute a reexpression of one of the two preeminent traditions in the history of liberal education. Understanding this fact will help us to see the intrinsic dilemmas and broader implications that are not explicated in the recent reports. In order to demonstrate it, I shall employ the historical framework that I have elaborated elsewhere.[31]

The history of what would come to be called liberal education begins in the Greek city-states of the sixth and fifth centuries B.C. During this period, the rise of democratic institutions of governance, especially the assembly of free citizens, undermined the Homeric tradition of noble and valorous leadership that shaped the character of the ruling elite. This change to a democratic polity coincided with the flowering of Hellenic culture, and the Greeks, especially the Athenians, devoted a great deal of effort both to understanding their cultural development and to considering how that culture could be transmitted to new generations of free citizens who were to participate in governing the city-state.

In certain respects, the problems of understanding and transmitting the culture were two different ways of asking the same question, and Heraclitus, Isocrates, and others in the fifth century argued that the answer could be found in *logos*. *Logos*, it was said, defined Greek culture, and therefore defined the nature of civilization and of a civilized human being.[32] The meaning of this important term was profoundly ambiguous, however. On the one hand, *logos* incorporated the meaning of "reason"—including its various denotations of a rationale, a faculty of thinking, and an act of thinking—and, on the other hand, *logos* denoted "speech," with all of its meanings—the pronouncement of words, the faculty of talking, and a formal act of communication.

This ambiguity was no less evident to the fifth-century Greeks than it appears to us, and the problem of resolving it assumed great importance because defining and articulating the meaning of *logos* became the core issue in the debate about understanding and transmitting culture. On one side of the debate were individuals such as the orator Isocrates, who emphasized the newly invented arts of grammar and rhetoric and the skills of composing, delivering, and analyzing a speech. These skills were paramount in a democratic city-state where persuasion determined the outcome of every question arising in the political and judicial assemblies. On the other side of the debate were those who regarded rhetoric as an imprecise and practical tool that constituted but a shadow of the true essence of *logos*. These others, including Plato and Aristotle, held the new arts of mathematics and syllogistic logic to reflect the essential nature of *logos*.

The debate between advocates of grammar and rhetoric, on one side, and mathematics and logic, on the other, extended to all issues concerning "education" or "culture." In particular, however, the debate concerned the nature of the education that was appropriate for people who were "free." This condition of being "free" was denoted by the term *eleutherios* in Greek, which corresponded to the later Latin term *liberalis*.

Now, these terms—*eleutherios, liberalis,* "free"—implied two particular kinds of freedom: first, the political freedom, which belonged to citizens, to participate in governing the city-state, and, second, the freedom, or leisure, to study, which is afforded by possessing wealth or through some fortunate set of circumstances (such as, one might observe, a technological and industrial economy that allows most workers some leisure to go to school or college). The idea of education was therefore constituent in the concept of the free, or liberal, citizen. And the debate about *logos*, culture, and transmission of culture inevitably came to focus upon the question of what kind of education was appropriate for the liberal citizen: the citizen who was free by virtue of having leisure to study. Beginning in Greece in the fifth and fourth centuries B.C., the debate commenced as to whether the arts of reason or the arts of speech and language should take precedence in this education for the liberal citizen.

The inheritance of Greek civilization passed to the Romans, who introduced the terms *ratio* and *oratio*, terminology that reflected the connection and the tension between "reason" and "speech." Nevertheless, the Romans made a choice between the two conceptions of the education and culture that had been proposed for the person who was free. Being builders, lawyers, and administrators of an emerging empire, the Romans felt most sympathetic toward the educational view that emphasized public expression, political and legal discourse, and the literary tradition that described the noble virtues and orderly society of the past. Appropriately, one can find the first recorded use of the term *artes liberales*, which is the direct antecedent in Latin of the English term "liberal arts," in the writings of Cicero, the exemplary Roman orator, who lived in the first century B.C.[33] In the first century A.D., Quintilian faithfully endorsed Cicero's approach to the liberal arts, which had become normative in Rome.

This liberal education comprised several of the disciplines that had been invented by the Greeks and taught individually by separate masters in different schools. The first liberal art was "grammar," which included the learning of literature as well as language, and therefore was studied throughout the course of education. Meanwhile, a modicum of attention was occasionally given to arithmetic, geometry, and astronomy, which were regarded as bodies of facts, useful for speeches, but not as formal or theoretical disciplines in the way that Plato and Aristotle had intended them. Music was sometimes studied as practical training for the ear and voice and as an aid to appreciating poetry, but not as a complement to the formal and theoretical sciences. Logic, or dialectic, was offered as a means of providing the skeletal arguments for public speeches, while rhetoric became the crowning art, which conveyed the methods of constructing a persuasive discourse on *any* topic, be it political, religious, military, aesthetic, or legal. This Roman preference for the rhetorical, practical, and literary over the pristine clarity of logic and mathematics is precisely what Plato, Aristotle, and many of their students found objectionable in their opponents' interpretation of the liberal arts.

From the time of Quintilian in the first century A.D., the literary and rhetorical Roman liberal arts deteriorated toward sophistry. Gradually, they were reinvigorated, but not by the philosophical descendants of Plato and Aristotle. Rather, it was Christian educators who reinforced the pagan liberal arts with a commitment to understanding and expounding the meaning of significant texts. Christians, such as Jerome and Augustine, therefore made the study of grammar and rhetoric preeminent in the liberal arts. They regarded logic as an adjunct to rhetoric and studied music primarily in its sonorous and practical dimensions. They treated mathematical and scientific disciplines as bodies of facts providing technical information useful for biblical interpretation. Specialization and advanced study were not encouraged by the Christians, or even were criticized as leading to self-indulgence—the same criticism that the orators Cicero and Isocrates had made about Plato's vision of a philosophical education extending into adulthood.

As the barbarian invasions brought an end to the period now called Antiquity, the Christian philosopher Boethius in the early sixth century tried to recover the Platonic and Aristotelian view of the liberal arts, which emphasized the study of mathematics and logic for training the mind in critical analysis and speculative thought. Boethius died at a relatively young age, however, and his influence was not as great as that of three other writers who adopted the practical, literary, and rhetorical model of liberal education: Martianus Capella, Cassiodorus, and Bishop Isidore of Seville. In the fifth and sixth centuries, these three individuals wrote handbooks, which codified liberal education into a program of seven liberal arts: grammar, logic, rhetoric, arithmetic, geometry, music, astronomy. The three handbooks served as textbooks for the Christian medieval schools throughout Western Europe.

Eventually, in the twelfth and thirteenth centuries, the rhetorical model of liberal education was challenged when the newly recovered texts of Aristotle and Islamic philosophers and mathematicians prompted a revival of critical and speculative thought on the part of the Scholastics of the newly arising medieval universities. The theoretical and rationalizing orientation of these university Scholastics, or professors, such as Thomas Aquinas, transformed the meaning and content of the liberal arts. Logic emerged supreme as a refined analytic tool, and mathematics and music increasingly addressed abstract number rather than sonorous or practical matters. Rhetoric almost dropped from sight, while grammar was transmuted into linguistic analysis and stripped of its association with literature and texts. Overall, the liberal arts became narrow and relatively brief "speculative sciences" intended to prepare the student for advanced and specialized study in the graduate faculties of the universities.

During the fourteenth and fifteenth centuries, the provocative logical disputations that provided the core of the pedagogy in the scholastic liberal arts deteriorated to sophistry. At the same time, the Ciceronian conception of liberal education was being rediscovered by the humanists of the Italian Renaissance, who early in the fifteenth century celebrated the recovery of the writings of Quintilian and Cicero, most of which had been lost in monastic libraries for centuries.

The humanist movement began outside of the universities and gradually infiltrated those institutions during the fifteenth and sixteenth centuries through the efforts of individuals such as Pier Paolo Vergerio and Desiderius Erasmus. In the course of that infiltration, the humanist model of rhetorical and literary learning was amplified with Christian ethics and with notions of courtesy derived from the medieval tradition of knighthood. These three things—the humanist model of learning, the social etiquette of courtesy, and the Christian ethics—combined to produce the ideal of the "Christian gentleman," which became the archetype of a liberally educated person in sixteenth- and seventeenth-century England. Treatises of this period proclaim the orator, the statesman, or what Sir Thomas Elyot called the "governor" as the model for a student engaged in liberal education.

That model was quite naturally endorsed by the founders of Harvard College in 1636, as well as in the eight other colleges subsequently founded in the American colonies. The bulk of the curriculum leading to the degree of Bachelor of Arts was devoted to rhetoric and grammar and to the reading, memorizing, and interpreting of literary and theological texts that defined the virtues of a citizen in God's commonwealth.

Meanwhile, leaders of the seventeenth-century Scientific Revolution and eighteenth-century Enlightenment endeavored to resurrect the philosophical tradition with its commitment to mathematical laws and Socratic criticism. These scientists and *philosophes* began to clamor for "free-thinking" and "liberating" education to replace the reading of classical texts. Such ideas entered discussion about liberal education in the late eighteenth and early nineteenth centuries, and can be seen, for example, in the writings of the Unitarian chemist Joseph Priestley and in the essays that won a contest sponsored in 1795 by the American Philosophical Society, which called for descriptions of "the best system of liberal education and literary instruction, adapted to the genius of the government of the United States."[34]

Inevitably, confrontation resulted between the rhetorical and philosophical models of liberal education, just as it had in the medieval universities and in Athens in the fifth and fourth centuries B.C. During the 1880s, the literary critic and essayist Matthew Arnold and the Darwinian scientist Thomas Henry Huxley toured the United States lecturing on diametrically opposed conceptions of liberal education. Contemporaneously, James McCosh, Presbyterian minister and president of Princeton, and Charles Eliot, chemist and president of Harvard, were engaged in the same debate.

Each of these confrontations fundamentally rehearsed the centuries-old debate as to which pole of *logos*—reason or speech—should predominate in culture and in the liberal arts. Even as Arnold and McCosh spoke, however, it seemed that Huxley, Eliot, and their allies had carried the day in America. A new generation of scholastics established a flock of universities devoted to advanced and specialized research: Cornell in 1868, Johns Hopkins in 1876, Clark University in 1889, Stanford in 1891, and Chicago in 1892. The devotion of the new university professors to the scientific method and to specialized research transformed liberal education once again into preparation for graduate study and the pursuit of truth, a truth that had come to be regarded as forever contingent and elusive, and not to be discovered in ancient texts.

The defenders of the rhetorical, practical, and textual liberal arts were not easily brushed aside, however, particularly in the small, special interest colleges that were dedicated to religious denominations, to women, or to blacks. A vigorous debate ensued in the late nineteenth and early twentieth centuries that eventually became as acrimonious as that of the thirteenth century or the fourth century B.C. The sectarian colleges and universities, particularly the Catholic institutions, clung to the humanist program of studies whose emphasis on literary and rhetorical training could be traced back through Ignatius Loyola to Cicero and Isocrates. That program was amplified by the teaching of divinity and Scholastic theology in order to form the Christian citizen. At the same time, many of the universities, encouraged by the advance of pragmatism in ethical theory and by the scientific emphasis on value-free research, abandoned the idea of training the virtuous citizen. Commensurately, they introduced the undergraduate major, a specialized preparation for the Socratic pursuit of truth that was modeled on graduate study and indicated the philosophical orientation of this liberal education.

Confusion, even chaos, resulted from the conflict of purposes. In a study of the liberal arts college published in 1908, Abraham Flexner observed: "The college is without clear-cut notions of what a liberal education is and how it is to be secured . . . and the pity of it is that this is not a local or special disability, but a paralysis affecting every college of arts in America."[35] By the year 1921, the director of the American Council on Education reported that among the "thousands of papers and not a few books giving individual interpretations of the college of liberal arts," there exists "no more agreement among the writers than among the requirements of the institutions. Moreover, it is a significant fact that nobody pays any attention to literature of this sort when it comes to defining the college of liberal arts."[36] And here we have returned at last to the topic of recent reports on the undergraduate curriculum.

What should be apparent from this brief outline of the history of liberal education is the similarity between the general contours of the liberal arts as they have been conceived in the rhetorical tradition and the constellation of five points that are repeated and emphasized in the recent reports on the undergraduate curriculum. By and large, the recent reports are, historically speaking, attempting to reassert the rhetorical tradition of liberal education against the philosophical. That is to say, these reports tend to complain (1) that college graduates have not mastered the arts of written and spoken communication and the textual tradition in which those arts are preserved and exemplified; (2) that colleges have not inculcated graduates with a sense of values and, in particular, the obligations of citizenship that are owed to the republic and other communities to which they belong; (3) that college graduates are not provided with a substantively unified and coherent general education that will prepare them to address many different kinds of problems and issues, be they political, economic, aesthetic, religious, or technological; (4) and finally that professors care less about teaching than about pursuing their own somewhat introverted, and perhaps self-indulgent, investigations.

These complaints are remarkably similar to the warnings that, for example, Isocrates and Cicero made against Plato, that John of Garland made against the medieval university Scholastics, and that Matthew Arnold made against Thomas Huxley and James McCosh made against Charles Eliot. What I am suggesting is that these concerns about language, values, citizenship, community, curricular unity and generality, and teaching are integrally related and have always been viewed as integrally related. Language implies at least two persons, or community; and community implies membership or citizenship plus shared knowledge and norms of behavior, or values, all of which must be preserved and communicated, which implies texts and language. The recent reports do not explicitly apprehend these relationships or their historicity.

One reason for this lack of apprehension is that these reports do not have a deep historical perspective of what they are examining.[37] A second reason is that this rhetorical tradition in its largest dimensions calls into question the definitions of knowledge and ideals of culture of the currently dominant intellectual tradition in higher education, which is closely allied with the natural and empirical sciences. The curricular reports are not prepared to raise fundamental questions about the scientific tradition, although such inquiries are being made in many of the academic disciplines, all of which suggests that the recent reports about undergraduate education constitute a small and unconscious expression of a much larger intellectual and cultural shift that is occurring throughout higher education.

III. The Current Intellectual Context

The most significant evidence of this shift is the massive amount of attention that scholars have recently devoted to the study of language, rhetoric, and interpretation. Since the late 1920s, when Ludwig Wittgenstein's *Tractatus Logico-Philosophico* (1921) gained attention, language has been growing as an important topic in twentieth-century discourse, and such discussion has more recently been amplified by consideration of the interpretation of texts. Indeed, John Patrick Diggins of the

University of California, Irvine, has observed: "To interpret something, a political document or a literary text, is to give meaning to it. . . . Today in intellectual circles everywhere authority is disputed, and interpretation has become the most fiercely debated subject in the humanities."[38]

Literary theory has flowered, and bibliographies have appeared to categorize the avalanche of scholarship on historical and contemporary rhetoric.[39] Books are published daily on interpretation in social theory, such as the newly released *Interpretation and Social Criticism* by Michael Walzer, professor of social science at the Institute of Advanced Study in Princeton.[40] Meanwhile, divinity schools have brought the interpretation of language and texts beyond biblical studies and into systematic theology, church history, history of religions, and ecclesiology. Similarly, at Harvard Law School this past spring Morton J. Horwitz introduced an exploratory seminar on "Theories of Statutory Interpretation" because judges in summer seminars at the Law School have said they are in great need of interpretive canons by which to read statutes.[41] Poems, novels, sutras, and historical treatises all matter, of course. But the problem of interpretation is particularly striking when considered in the legal context.

In 1919, for example, Congress passed the National Motor Vehicle Theft Act, which provided: "That whoever shall transport . . . in interstate or foreign commerce a motor vehicle, knowing the same to have been stolen, shall be punished by a fine of not more than $5,000, or by imprisonment of not more than five years or both." In 1930, William W. McBoyle was convicted under this statute "of transporting from . . . Illinois to . . . Oklahoma an airplane that he knew to have been stolen." The record does not state whether McBoyle or his lawyer had a liberal education in the rhetorical tradition. They did in any case appeal to the U.S. Supreme Court, which in 1931 considered the question of whether an airplane was comprehended under the term "motor vehicle" in the 1919 statute.[42]

How does one answer such a question? By looking to the "plain meaning" of the law? By looking to the "intent" of Congress? By considering the "purpose" of the law, however that is to be determined? And if one gives up and simply decides on the basis of some sense of fundamental right and wrong, how does one square that decision with the basic principles of the rule of law: that all statutes should be prospective, clear, and publicized, so that citizens have due warning of the prohibitions of the law?

The case of William McBoyle and his airplane demonstrates how and why judicial interpreters can be tied in knots, and the problem is equally pronounced in all forms of textual interpretation. On the one hand, professional interpreters are unable to say that there exists any absolutely true and accurate interpretation. On the other hand, they do not want to admit that any interpretation goes, for that would be to say that interpretation is ultimately arbitrary and indeterminate, which would lead to the question, among others, of why do we need professors, theologians, and lawyers?

It is significant to note that literature professor Stanley Fish of Duke University has provided one of the most prominent responses to this dilemma circulating among legal scholars. Fish argues that, even if the meaning of a text is arbitrary or indeterminate, the "interpretive community" that reads the text can agree upon authoritative canons of interpretation.[43] Though conceding a degree of indeterminancy and arbitrariness in the expertise of professional interpreters, this approach actually increases the authority of professionals because interpretation is accessible *only* to the interpretive community and not even to the occasional genius who might divine the "true" interpretive framework if it were based on natural reason, which Sir Edward Coke regarded as the basis of the common law in the seventeenth century.

Notwithstanding this increase in authority, such an appeal to "interpretive communities" amounts to a fallback position, demonstrating the concern about indeterminancy and arbitrariness that accompanies the widespread scholarly attention to language, rhetoric, and interpretation. In fact, professors in the humanistic and social disciplines, and the associated professional disciplines, are no less troubled by the disagreement, confusion, and disarray in culture generally than is William Bennett about undergraduate education.[44]

Bennett's admonitions to colleges and universities to commit themselves to something, rather than indulging in skepticism and relativism, are very similar to those of Robert M. Hutchins, the president of the University of Chicago during the 1930s. Both Hutchins and Bennett imply that the problem of curricular incoherence is one of intellectual backbone, and that the solution is a matter of willing, even wishing, the coherence to appear. Thus, Bennett writes: "We frequently hear that it is no longer possible to reach a consensus on the most significant thinkers, the most compelling ideas, and the books that all students should read. Contemporary American culture, the argument goes, has become too fragmented and too pluralistic to justify a belief in common learning. Although it is easier (and more fashionable) to doubt than to believe, it is a grave error to base a college curriculum on such doubt."[45] To this may be repeated the insightful reply that Harry D. Gideonse made in 1947 to Robert Hutchins. Hutchins had chided all of higher education with the words: "The most striking thing about the higher learning in America is the confusion that besets it."[46] And Gideonse replied: "To write volumes in support of the thesis that there *should* be a unifying philosophy, without specific indication of the type of unity or of philosophy is to miss the essential problem underlying the modern dilemma."[47]

As if responding to Gideonse, Bennett states: "I am often asked what I believe to be the most significant works in the humanities. This is an important question, too important to avoid." Here the reader assumes that Bennett is about to take on the difficult task that the faculties, deans, and presidents are shirking. But he immediately sidesteps the responsibility of prescribing what anyone should study and thereby relativizes his own judgment: "it is not my intention (nor is it my right) to dictate anyone's curriculum. My purpose is not to prescribe a course of studies but to answer, as candidly as I can, an oft-asked question."[48]

Bennett's decision to do precisely that for which he criticizes faculties, deans, and presidents can be found also in the 1984 NIE study,[49] the 1985 AAC study,[50] and Allan Bloom's recent statement on higher education.[51] Ernest Boyer's report is perhaps the most charitable in acknowledging the fundamental difficulty of the problem when he quotes Archibald MacLeish: " 'There can be no educational postulates so long as there are no generally accepted postulates of life itself.' And colleges appear to be searching for meaning in a world where diversity, not commonality, is the guiding vision." Nevertheless, even Boyer leaves the clear impression that faculties, deans, and presidents could simply decide to walk out of the wilderness if they really wanted to.[52]

The problem of instituting value and coherence in education is therefore directly connected to the problem of instituting value and coherence in society, and culture at large, and both of these problems are related to the problem of the authority of knowledge, of epistemology. This epistemological problem is an important reason for the interest in the interpretation of texts. As Jurgen Habermas has observed about neo-Aristotelians, such as Robert Hutchins, Mortimer Adler, Richard McKeon, and their fellow traveler Allan Bloom: "The ethics and politics of Aristotle are unthinkable without the connection to [his] physics and metaphysics. . . . Today it is no longer easy to render the approach of this metaphysical mode of thought plausible. It is no wonder that the neo-Aristotelian writings do not contain systematic doctrines, but are works of high interpretive art that suggest the truths of classical texts through interpretation, rather than by grounding it."[53] Here one sees why the cry for commitment to a coherent and unified curriculum and philosophy of education frequently accompanies the prescription of reading classical texts, especially those of Aristotle. Given the impossibility in the twentieth century of rationally and causally grounding systems of metaphysics and ethics, one retreats to advocating commitment and interpreting texts.

This kind of interpretation is what I venture to call the "traditional" hermeneutics. Hermeneutics is a term that is used almost as much as "community" these days. It comes from the same Greek root as Hermes, the messenger god; and in its traditional sense, it means simply the principles and method by which one interprets texts. When I attended divinity school not long ago, hermeneutics was closely linked to biblical studies, and largely conditioned by the theories of Freidrich Schleiermacher, who had proposed that interpreters might achieve a true, historical understanding of a text by recognizing and purging all prejudices and distortions arising from their own situation. This traditional sense is what I have meant by "interpretation" to this point, and its intimate connections to the desire for value and community in a skeptical and relativistic world should be evident from the foregoing observations of Stanley Fish and Jurgen Habermas.

Hermeneutics has more recently acquired a broader meaning in two senses. On the one hand, most scholars, with the telling exception of E. D. Hirsch, Jr., have rejected Schleiermacher's view that an original and true interpretation may be acquired by control of a neutral method free of contingencies of the interpreter's situation. Instead, they argue that interpretation is an active mediation or interaction between the interpreter and the text, a mediation that is both evolving and reflexive. On the other hand, certain individuals, such as Hans-Georg Gadamer, have applied this concept of interpretation to phenomena apart from texts. In speaking of "philosophical hermeneutics," Gadamer and others have proposed that all of human self-understanding and value must be seen in terms of an *interaction* between subject and object, rather than in terms of choosing between a hopelessly relativistic subjectivism or a putatively neutral objectivism.[54]

This "new" hermeneutics, along with its associated movements of poststructuralism and deconstruction, is enormously complex and changing rapidly. In fact, books have begun to appear on the topics of "Post-Structuralism" and "Superstructuralism."[55] What is important to note for purposes here is that this entire movement constitutes a challenge to scientific understanding, normally conceived, and is closely linked to the desire to identify norms and values of human endeavor. While conceding the tremendous advances that the sciences have made in understanding natural phenomena, the new hermeneutics challenges the claims of scientific knowledge to control of a neutral, objective method insofar as it applies to the study of human activities and endeavors.

In other words, this hermeneutic movement wishes to substitute interpretive method, however tentative and uncertain, for the scientific method in the analysis of social and human endeavor.[56] It thereby seeks to incorporate, rather than exclude, subjectivity and value as a dynamic in that analysis. Commensurately, the new hermeneutics attacks formalism and conceptualism. In rejecting the application of a neutral, scientific method to social and human endeavor, it questions the relationship between theorizing and the social and political reality that theorists claim to describe, understand, or predict. In this respect, the new hermeneutics attacks the very nature of formalism and theory.

To this point, we have observed that scholars in the social and humanistic disciplines are vigorously studying the topics of language, rhetoric, and interpretation. And we have seen that this investigation is closely connected in two respects with a search for values and norms of human and social endeavor. On the one hand, a more traditional understanding of hermeneutics has reinvigorated the interpretation of texts as sources of such values and norms. On the other hand, a new version of hermeneutics contends that human and social endeavor cannot be examined "objectively," apart from subjective value.

Both of these versions of hermeneutics imply a concern for community: the former, for "interpretive communities"; the latter, for the social context in which all interpretation must occur. Beyond either of these implicit concerns, however, is an explicit and pronounced concern for community that pervades the humanistic and social disciplines. This concern is manifested by Alasdair MacIntyre in philosophy, Michael J. Sandel in political theory, Roberto M. Unger in jurisprudence, and Robert Bellah and his associates in social theory, all of whom have advanced various approaches to what is sometimes called "communitarianism."[57] Even more noteworthy, but not sufficiently appreciated, is the pervasive attention being given to Republicanism in rewriting American history.

In 1967 Bernard Bailyn published a Pulitzer Prize–winning book in which he explained the derivation of "the ideology of the American revolution" from the Commonwealth Whig or Republican tradition, whose adherents emphasized the virtuous responsibility owed by each citizen to the corporate society and state, the *res publica*.[58] This tradition extends back to the Republic of Rome and to the city-states of Greece, and its importance has been traced to post-Revolutionary American political thought and legal history, as well as to "such diverse issues as the colonization movement, nullification, opposition to nullification, westward expansion, the Mexican War, the politics of both artisans and manufacturers in antebellum New York, southern politics in general and southern political culture in particular, the northern defense of the Union, and the southern drive for secession."[59]

In fact, historians have traced Republicanism into almost every aspect of American culture. Looking back through the last three years of *Reviews of American History*, I would say that nine out of 10 books reviewed address in some prominent way the theme of Republicanism, community, or isolation of the individual in American society. It is as if American historians were chronicling the origins of the "habits of the heart." Amid this historiography, Meyer Reinhold has described how the classical Republican literature dominated the curriculum of the colonial and revolutionary colleges and was gradually supplanted as the Republican tradition became muted in the course of American history.[60] Reinhold's analysis demonstrates explicitly one aspect of the general analogy that I am trying to establish between recent discussion of undergraduate education and academic culture at large.

Academicians have noted that a profound shift is taking place in definitions of knowledge and ideals of culture, at least as they appear in the humanistic and social disciplines. This transformation is yet incomplete and not at all systematic, but it clearly has to do with the study of language and rhetoric. It is concerned as well with hermeneutics, understood both as the interpretation of the textual tradition as a source of value and as an interpretive method that affirms subjectivity and value by way of supplanting the scientific method in the study of social and human endeavor. The transformation also involves an emphasis upon citizenship and community, because language and rhetoric require a community, because traditional hermeneutics implies an interpretive community, and because the new hermeneutics requires a subjective context. In addition, the transformation is encouraged by a new appreciation for the legacy of all these factors in the Republican tradition of American history.

These factors—language, rhetoric, hermeneutics, values, citizenship, and community—constitute this inchoate transformation in the disciplines as well as the constellation of points that appear in the recent reports on the undergraduate curriculum. I am proposing, therefore, that a general analogy exists between the discussion at the highest levels of academe concerning knowledge and culture and the discussion about the undergraduate curriculum.

Such an analogy will appear intuitively correct, I trust. Problems in understanding knowledge and culture should be reflected in problems of transmitting knowledge and culture. Nevertheless, even though the recent reports on undergraduate education lament the unfortunate disjunction between curricular discussion and discussion in the academic disciplines, none of them, so far as I have seen, perceives the fact that the discussions in these two different forums are strikingly similar and profoundly related. Both are about the nature and importance of language, about the problem of interpreting writing and symbols, about the significance of belonging to and sustaining communities, and about the identification of values and norms for such belonging.

In a noteworthy article, anthropologist Clifford Geertz described in 1980 how these issues pervade the academic disciplines, a fact he understood to demonstrate the "blurring" of the disciplines and "an alteration in how we think about how we think."[61] When this article was cited in curricular reports by Ernest Boyer in 1981 and Zelda Gamson in 1984, Geertz's statement was offered as testimony to the interconnections of disciplinary knowledge, and its regrettable remoteness from undergraduate education. Boyer, in particular, on the very same page on which he quoted Geertz, stated that "Faculty members who devote themselves to general education run the risk of losing touch with their disciplines."[62]

What I am proposing here and what Boyer did not see in 1981, when he appropriately misquoted, miscited, and mistitled Geertz's article, is that there is no such danger of "losing touch." In fact, the questions and issues that have appeared in the disciplines are precisely the questions being raised in regard to undergraduate education. The discussion about the undergraduate curriculum, I propose, is perplexed by the same fundamental dilemmas that are being faced at the most advanced levels in the humanistic and social disciplines. In fact, the discourse about undergraduate education is, mutatis mutandis, very much the same as that of professors about their own scholarship.

It is significant that in his new report of 1987 Boyer once more refers to the same article of Geertz. Though still applauding Geertz's statement as testimony of how "knowledge crosses intellectual boundaries," Boyer now sees this fact as complementary to and, indeed, conducive to forming an "integrated core" curriculum, in which the issues being addressed in the highest reaches of the disciplines would become central topics of general education.[63] Nevertheless, like the authors of the other recent reports, he still recommends that professors attend to the undergraduate curriculum for instrumental reasons: out of a sense of obligation to their role, to their institution, to the society, and, by extension, to themselves. Thus, professors ought to address the undergraduate curriculum for the sake of a higher end. No report that I have seen suggests that professors ought to do this because the curriculum is intrinsically part of the very same problems that occupy the disciplines.[64]

IV. Some Implications and Contradictions

If my two analogies hold—between the rhetorical tradition in the history of liberal education and the recent complaints about undergraduate education, and between those complaints and the dilemmas concerning definitions of knowledge and culture in the humanistic and social disciplines—then it becomes possible to understand the problems of undergraduate education in their deeper and broader dimensions. For example, it becomes possible to see an essential contradiction between the concern for language, citizenship, and commitment to community and the persistent, though reluctant, clinging to a "study in depth" or undergraduate major.

The historical analogy to the rhetorical tradition of liberal education suggests that it is supremely difficult for an undergraduate major, that is, a specialized study preparatory to further graduate study, to coexist with a thorough commitment to citizenship, virtues, the republic, and the appropriation of the textual tradition of the community. Indeed, the empirical fact seems to be that one almost never finds a widespread commitment to an undergraduate major reconciled with this constellation of commitments that constitutes the rhetorical tradition. The reason for this empirical fact can be found in the principled analogy between the discussion about undergraduate education and that concerning definitions of knowledge and culture in the disciplines. This second analogy suggests that the epistemology and rationale underlying the undergraduate major are fundamentally in conflict with the epistemology and purposes of this constellation of commitments that one finds in the rhetorical tradition of liberal education and the recent reports on the undergraduate curriculum. The specialized pursuit of truth through control of a putatively neutral and objective method fundamentally conflicts with the training of virtuous citizens who are committed to the historical traditions of their community.

Like the 1985 AAC Report, Ernest Boyer states in his 1987 study: "Here then is the heart of our curriculum proposal: Rather than view the major as competing with general education, we are convinced that these two essential parts of the baccalaureate program should be intertwined."[65] The two analogies proposed here indicate that historically, that is, empirically, this curriculum proposal has not worked and that in principle it cannot work. It is a nice sentiment, and being an ordained minister, I look forward to the day when the lion will lie down with the lamb. But I would not recommend to any zoo that the lions and lambs of this world be caged together, because only lions will be left. And this is precisely what has happened. All the reports complain about how the departments and specialized majors have devoured liberal education. But none of them have tried to conceive of an undergraduate education without departments and majors, which in their most recent incarnation have been with us only for the last century.

The reluctance of the reports to take note of the empirical fact that what they recommend has not worked is mirrored in their reluctance to challenge the marketplace of ideas that is enshrined in the scientific method and specialized pursuit of truth that undergirds the undergraduate major. Such challenges are being made as part of the investigation into rhetoric and hermeneutics that has led to an attack from both the Right and the Left against the Lockean and liberal tradition that underlies the American polity, economy, and society.[66] Here again, the recent reports demonstrate their own isolation and disjunction from the larger discourse in higher education. One final analogy may help to convey this point.

During the past two years as a Liberal Arts Fellow at Harvard Law School, I have spent some time reading about Critical Legal Studies, a movement that has attracted a good deal of attention.[67] The Critical Legal Scholars are a rather amorphous and diverse group, whose views have changed over time and continue to develop. By and large, these law professors have been deeply influenced by "the hermeneutical and poststructuralist perspectives" mentioned above,[68] and their approach is consonant with the broad movements in the disciplines outlined here. Epistemologically, they are challenging the liberal cornerstone of the free market of ideas; economically and politically, they are challenging the marketplace, which legitimates social policy in the absence of any absolute truths about justice and virtue; jurisprudentially, they are challenging the advocacy model of law whereby Americans resolve disputes by hiring lawyers and fighting it out until there is a winner and a loser.

In particular, the Critical Legal Scholars argue that such a model of jurisprudence is fundamentally alienating, divisive, and destructive to the community. The advocacy model of a trial, they contend, is itself a miniature free market of ideas in which disputes are usually resolved not by appeal to fundamental principles of substantive justice but by access to resources, especially to lawyers. In fact, they observe that our legal system is grounded upon the rule of law and procedural safeguards, which protect the free market of ideas without offering any substantive protections such as a right to food, shelter, or clothing. Such substantive rights would conflict with the Lockean right to property, which undergirds the free market of economic exchange.

Opposing jurists have attacked the Critical Legal Scholars as Marxists, Gramscians, or simply naive and irresponsible. Whether or not any of these charges are true and, if so, regrettable, the fact remains that this critical legal discourse is very much analogous to the criticisms of undergraduate education in the recent reports: the criticism of alienation and divisiveness, the commitment to a sense of community, the desire for secure virtues and values of citizenship, and the rejection of the skepticism and relativism of the free market of ideas. Indeed, the recent reports especially condemn "the marketplace philosophy," "marketplace demands," and the "educational garage sale,"[69] although they do not seem to realize that the source of their complaints lies in the free market of ideas.

Like the complaints about undergraduate education, much of this has been said before about the law. The Critical Legal Scholars have attracted special attention because they are eminent members of the profession who are not only restating and reformulating familiar criticism but also recommending changes that threaten the institutions and very nature of the profession. Compare this stand to the recent reports on undergraduate education. According to my reading, the reports are echoing both a historical tradition and contemporary intellectual developments that would point to sweeping and fundamental changes in undergraduate education, such as eliminating the academic departments and majors and requiring all graduating students to be able to write persuasively, to speak effectively and extemporaneously on any topic, and to offer evidence of citizenship. However, such changes would threaten a great deal in which the academic institutions and the profession have invested. The reports are reluctant to threaten, however much they bemoan and condemn. Their recommendations are, in the words of Martin Trow, "rather mild and familiar."[70]

I am not proposing here that undergraduate education ought to change in a particular direction. Neither do I condemn the free market of ideas nor express a preference between the two historical traditions of liberal education. My argument is simply that at least two distinct traditions of undergraduate education exist, and that one cannot combine or "intertwine" the different traditions and expect to harvest the benefits of both. On the other hand, whether or not undergraduate education ought to change, it seems to me that it is changing and will continue to do so, just as our conceptions of knowledge and culture are changing. My argument in this sense is not normative as much as descriptive, or, perhaps, somewhat Darwinian.

In his path-breaking book, *Strategy and Structure*, Alfred D. Chandler, Jr., the historian of business, argued that organizations, such as corporations, are governed by inertia. They change their direction, or "strategy," he maintained, only when forced to do so by competition. And a change in strategy, he concluded, will be successful only if accompanied by a decisive change in organizational structure.[71] As far as I can see, Chandler's thesis comports well with the history of institutions of undergraduate education.

If this is so, then we must proceed not with the hope that different approaches and parts of education can be "intertwined" into "a seamless web," as Ernest Boyer has it,[72] but rather with the understanding that there exist and have existed fundamental tensions between opposed conceptions of undergraduate education, which are available to us. We may decide to choose among them and restructure an entire college or university based on one conception. Or we may incorporate them dialectically into the colleges and universities by instituting opposing faculties dedicated to one or another conception. But in either case, we must be prepared to adapt the structure of our institutions and profession as our conception of education dictates. Otherwise, we will have more of the same, which, the reports all agree, is something that nobody wants and may lead, I would suggest, to the extinction of institutions of undergraduate education.

Notes

I gratefully acknowledge the support of a lectureship from the Fund for the Improvement of Postsecondary Education, a Liberal Arts Fellowship from Harvard Law School, and a Spencer Fellowship from the National Academy of Education, which aided in the preparation of this article.

1. Ernest L. Boyer, *College: The Undergraduate Experience in America* (New York: Harper & Row, for the Carnegie Foundation for the Advancement of Teaching, 1987).

2. James P. Baxter III, "Commission on Liberal Education Report," *Association of American Colleges Bulletin* 29 (1943): 269–74; "The Post-War Responsibilities of Liberal Education: Report of the Committee on the Re-Statement of the Nature and Aim of Liberal Education," ibid., pp. 275–99.

3. *Integrity in the College Curriculum: A Report to the Academic Community; The Findings and Recommendations of the Project on Redefining the Meaning and Purpose of Baccalaureate Degrees* (Washington, D.C.: Association of American Colleges, 1985), pp. 1, 3.

4. For example, the report strongly criticizes "the major as now offered" but proposes "a study in depth" comprised of "courses" in "the disciplines." Such a study, it solemnly warns, "should not be overprescribed" and "every requirement should be intellectually defensible." It welcomes "interdisciplinary studies" and "international and multicultural experiences" but dismisses "the claims . . . for bringing the new and marvelous into the course of study in dramatic and expensive ways." It criticizes the "vocational" and "professional" orientation of students and professors, but it says "education in a professional or vocational field may . . . also provide a strong, enriching form of study in depth." In recommending improvements for undergraduate teaching, it makes the radical proposal of "videotaping an actual classroom session, done unobtrusively" (*Integrity in the College Curriculum*, pp. 5–7, 14, 22, 27–32).

5. William J. Bennett, *To Reclaim a Legacy: A Report on the Humanities in Higher Education* (Washington, D.C.: National Endowment for the Humanities, 1984), p. ii.

6. For example, Martin Trow has written that the "national reports which rather casually, sweepingly, and without evidence and specificity or an appreciation of the diversity of our system, criticizes and condemns [*sic*] us for not being other than what we are . . . have done more harm than good . . . not because . . . our institutions and our forms of education are beyond criticism—far from it. But because these reports, by substituting prescription for analysis, mislead our supporters and the general public into believing that these difficult problems are simpler than they are. . . . I believe that the authors of these reports intended to strengthen the hands of those who care about the undergraduate curriculum. . . . But ironically, the form that these reports took, their sweeping criticisms and rhetoric, and especially the rather gratuitous abuse of the faculty in some, may on balance marginally reduce the public confidence in us and in our institutions on which our autonomy rests. I say marginally, because I don't think the reports will have great effect" (Martin Trow, "The National Reports on Higher Education: A Skeptical View," forthcoming in *Educational Policy* 1 [1987]).

7. Boyer, *College: The Undergraduate Experience*, chap. 5; Richard D. Lambert et al., *Beyond Growth: The Next Stage in Language and Area Studies* (Washington, D.C.: Association of American Universities, 1984).

8. *Integrity in the College Curriculum*, pp. 5, 20–21; Boyer, *College: The Undergraduate Experience*, p. 213.

9. Herant A. Katchadourian and John Boli, *Careerism and Intellectualism among College Students: Patterns of Academic and Career Choice in the Undergraduate Years* (San Francisco: Jossey-Bass, 1985).

10. Frank Newman, *Higher Education and America's Resurgence* (Princeton,

N.J.: Princeton University Press, for the Carnegie Foundation for the Advancement of Teaching, 1985); *Transforming the State Role in Undergraduate Education, Report of the Working Party on Effective State Action to Improve Undergraduate Education* (Denver: Education Commission of the States, 1986).

11. *Science for Non-Specialists: The College Years, Report of the National Research Council's Committee on a Study of the Federal Role in College Science Education of Non-Specialists* (Washington, D.C.: National Academy Press, 1982), p. 7.

12. *Involvement in Learning: Realizing the Potential of American Higher Education, Final Report of the Study Group on the Conditions of Excellence in American Higher Education* (Washington, D.C.: National Institute of Education, 1984), p. 33; *Integrity in the College Curriculum*, p. 26.

13. Sharon Parks, *The Critical Years: The Young Adult Search for a Faith to Live By* (New York: Harper & Row, 1986).

14. David H. Smith, "The College as a Moral Community" (Plenary Lecture for the Lilly Endowment Workshop on the Liberal Arts, Colorado Springs, June 1986, 1987).

15. Jerry G. Gaff, *General Education Today: A Critical Analysis of Controversies, Practices, and Reforms* (San Francisco: Jossey-Bass, 1983), p. xv. In the 1977 Carnegie study of the college curriculum, general education was described as a "disaster area" (Carnegie Foundation for the Advancement of Teaching, *Missions of the College Curriculum: A Contemporary Review with Suggestions* [San Francisco: Jossey-Bass, 1977], p. 11), and several projects were subsequently undertaken, such as the Project on General Education Models sponsored by the Society for Values in Higher Education (David L. Wee, *On General Education: Outlines for Reform* [New Haven, Conn.: Society for Values in Higher Education, 1981]) and National Project IV sponsored by the federal Fund for the Improvement of Postsecondary Education (Zelda Gamson et al., *Liberating Education* [San Francisco: Jossey-Bass, 1984]). Meanwhile, Ernest Boyer and Arthur Levine reaffirmed in a Carnegie study that general education had not improved and perhaps worsened (Boyer and Levine, *A Quest for Common Learning: The Aims of General Education* [Princeton, N.J.: Carnegie Foundation for the Advancement of Teaching, 1981], p. 33). However, Gaff in his comprehensive analysis of the membership of the AAC was optimistic, concluding that "a genuine revival of general education is now taking place as new life is being breathed into the ideal of general education" (p. 187).

16. *Integrity in the College Curriculum*, p. 9.

17. Ibid., p. 15.

18. *Involvement in Learning*, p. 23.

19. Bennett, p. 18.

20. *Integrity in the College Curriculum*, p. 9.

21. *Harvard University Gazette* 82 (March 6, 1987), p. 1; ibid. (May 1, 1987), pp. 1, 5.

22. *Involvement in Learning*, p. 11.

23. Emphasis added. Ernest L. Boyer, "The Quest for Common Learning," in *Common Learning: A Carnegie Colloquium on General Education* (Princeton, N.J.: Carnegie Foundation for the Advancement of Learning, 1981), p. 3.

24. *Integrity in the College Curriculum*, p. 5.

25. Emphasis added. Boyer, *College: The Undergraduate Experience*, pp. 2–6.

26. Bennett, pp. 1–2, 7.

27. Bennett, pp. 5–6; *Involvement in Learning*, p. 47; *Integrity in the College Curriculum*, pp. 11, 35–39.

28. Stephen Jay Gould: "To be perfectly honest, though lip service is given to teaching, I have never seriously heard teaching considered in any meeting for promotion. I do not subscribe to any overly romanticized notion that teaching is primary or that tenure should be awarded only on teaching" (p. 16). Daniel Bell: "I do not think teaching ought to be the primary criterion of tenure or scholarship at a great university. . . . I do not think that one ought to overly romanticize teaching if one is thinking of a major university which is involved in testing, challenging, and creating knowledge in the best sense of the term" (pp. 15–16), in "Balancing Teaching and Writing," *On Teaching and Writing: The Journal of the Harvard-Danforth Center*, no. 2 (January 1987), pp. 10–16.

29. The topics were: "First . . . the shared use of symbols. . . . Second . . . shared membership in groups and institutions. . . . Third . . . that . . . we are dependent on each other. . . . Fourth . . . the ordered interdependent nature

of the universe. . . . Fifth . . . our shared sense of time. . . . Finally . . . our shared values and beliefs" (Boyer, "The Quest for Common Learning," pp. 11–12).

30. The major topics were: "Teachers and Scholars," "Teaching and Learning," "College in America," ". . . Or What's a College For," "The Educated Citizen." The colloquium was sponsored by the Carnegie Foundation for the Advancement of Teaching (*Harvard University Gazette* 82 [November 14, 1987]: 1, 5).

31. Bruce A. Kimball, "The Ambiguity of *logos* and the History of the Liberal Arts," *Liberal Education*, vol. 74 (January–February 1988).

32. The orator Isocrates expressed the widespread belief about *logos* in these words from the late fifth century B.C.: "For in our other faculties we (human beings) do not excell the animals. Many of them are fleeter or stronger or otherwise better than we. But because we were endowed with the power of persuading one another and explaining [ourselves], we were not only released from bestial ways of living, but came together and founded states and established laws and invented arts. It was *logos* which enabled us to perfect almost everything we have achieved in the way of civilization. For it was this which laid down the standards of right and wrong, nobility and baseness, without which we should not be able to live together. It is through [*logos*] that we convict bad men and praise good ones. By its aid we educate the foolish and test the wise. . . . With the help of *logos* we dispute over doubtful matters and investigate the unknown. If we sum up the character of this power, we shall find that no significant thing is done anywhere without the power of *logos*, that *logos* is the leader of all actions and thoughts and that those who make most use of it are the wisest of all humanity" (Isocrates, *Antidosis* 253–57; translation adapted from Werner Jaeger, *Paideia: The Ideals of Greek Culture*, trans. Gilbert Highet, 2d ed. [Oxford: Basil Blackwell, 1944], 3:89–90).

33. Cicero, *De inventione* 1.35.

34. Frederick Rudolph, ed. *Essays on Education in the Early Republic* (Cambridge, Mass.: Harvard University Press, 1965), pp. xv, 167–224, 273–372.

35. Flexner was quoting the president of Cornell University (Abraham Flexner, *The American College: A Criticism* [New York: Century, 1908], p. 7).

36. Samuel P. Capen, "The Dilemma of the College of Arts and Sciences," *Educational Review* 61 (1921): 277–78.

37. I should mention that my interpretation of the history of liberal education in terms of two counterpoised traditions—one philosophical, the other oratorical—is at odds with that of Richard McKeon and his student and colleague, Wayne C. Booth. To put it simply, their approach would propose that there has existed only what I am calling the philosophical tradition and that rhetoric is subsumed within that tradition. As Booth recently stated at a Carnegie Foundation Colloqium on general education held at the University of Chicago in 1981: "Everyone who has thought hard about it [rhetoric] has subordinated it to some other discipline, to make sure it serves a higher good." Two things should be observed about this perfect summary statement of that view. First, it is a normative judgment disguised as a descriptive statement. The statement turns the question of historical fact into the question of who thought hard about rhetoric, and since the normative judgment is that Aristotle, by and large, thought hardest about rhetoric, the descriptive effect of the statement is to claim that only the Aristotelian view has been important historically. The second thing to be observed is that this historical fact is simply not true. To see this, we must admit a distinction between all of knowledge and that part of knowledge that is circumscribed by the term "liberal education." As far as liberal education was concerned, Cicero, Quintilian, Augustine, and their intellectual descendants recognized no higher discipline than rhetoric and grammar, which provided the capacity to interpret and reexpress the authoritative corpus of law and texts on which the Republic or City of God was founded. In contrast, Aristotle, McKeon, and Booth maintain that, within liberal education, dialectic, or logic, stands as a higher discipline and constitutes the method of inquiry whose authority is greater than any received wisdom residing in the textual tradition (Wayne C. Booth, "Mere Rhetoric, Rhetoric, and the Search for Common Learning," in *Common Learning, A Carnegie Colloquium on General Education* [Washington, D.C.: Carnegie Foundation for the Advancement of Teaching, 1981], p. 32). The corpus of writings by McKeon and Booth on rhetoric and the history of the liberal arts is voluminous, and

cannot be documented here. One might want to begin with: Richard McKeon, "Rhetoric in the Middle Ages," *Speculum* 17 (1942): 1–32.

38. John Patrick Diggins, "Dusting Off the Old Values," *New York Times Book Review* (March 15, 1987), p. 11.

39. See, e.g., Winifred B. Horner, *The Present State of Scholarship in Historical and Contemporary Rhetoric* (Columbia: University of Missouri Press, 1983).

40. Michael Walzer, *Interpretation and Social Criticism* (Cambridge, Mass.: Harvard University Press, 1987); see, too, W. J. T. Mitchell, ed., *The Politics of Interpretation* (Chicago: University of Chicago Press, 1982).

41. See William S. Blatt, "The History of Statutory Interpretation," *Cardozo Law Review* 6 (1985): 799–845.

42. McBoyle v. United States, 283 U.S. 25, 25–26, 51 S.Ct. 340, 340–41 (1931); McBoyle v. United States, 43 F.2d 273, 273 (1930).

43. Stanley Fish, *Is There a Text in This Class?* (Cambridge, Mass.: Harvard University Press, 1980), chaps. 13–16; "Working on the Chain Gang: Interpretation in Law and Literature," *Texas Law Review* 60 (1982): 551–67; and "Wrong Again," ibid. 62 (1983): 299–316; Ronald Dworkin, *Law's Empire* (Cambridge, Mass.: Harvard University Press, 1986), chaps. 2, 3; see "Symposium: Law and Literature," *Texas Law Review* 60 (1982): 373–586.

44. Bennett (n. 5 above), pp. 1–2, 7.

45. Ibid., p. 10.

46. Robert M. Hutchins, *The Higher Learning in America* (New Haven, Conn.: Yale University Press, 1936), p. 1.

47. Emphasis added. Harry D. Gideonse, *The Higher Learning in a Democracy: A Reply to President Hutchins' Critique of the American University* (New York: Farrar & Rhinehart, 1947), p. 3.

48. Bennett, p. 10.

49. *Involvement in Learning* recommends: "Faculties and chief academic officers in each institution should agree upon and disseminate a statement of the knowledge, capacities, and skills that students must develop prior to graduation" (p. 39). But: "It is not our aim to dictate particular and highly detailed sets of knowledge, capacities, skills, or attitudes that students should develop in the course of their undergraduate education. . . . [I]t would be inappropriate for us to do so. Nowhere do we mean to imply that every college graduate should have read a particular book . . . or should have taken a particular course. . . . Our reason is simple: the responsibility for defining specific standards of content and levels of student performance and college-level learning in undergraduate education must fall on academic institutions themselves, or those standards will have no credibility" (p. 16).

50. See nn. 3 and 4 above.

51. Interviewed in *Chronicle of Higher Education*, Allan Bloom insisted on the tone that pervades his recent book: that he is simply an observer and not a prescriber, though his observations have a way of implying definite prescriptions for higher education (Michael W. Hirshorn, "A Professor Decries 'Closing of the American Mind.'" *Chronicle of Higher Education* [May 6, 1987], p. 3). See Allan Bloom, *The Closing of the American Mind: How Higher Education Has Failed Democracy and Impoverished the Souls of Today's Students* (New York: Simon & Schuster, 1987), chaps. 1, 2.

52. Boyer, *College: The Undergraduate Experience*, p. 3, chaps. 3, 4.

53. Jurgen Habermas, "Legitimation Problems in the Modern State," in *Communication and the Evolution of Society*, trans. with an introduction by Thomas McCarthy (Boston: Beacon Press, 1979), Sect. V.

54. See the excellent collection of essays by Hans-Georg Gadamer, *Philosophical Hermeneutics*, trans. and ed. David E. Linge (Berkeley: University of California Press, 1976).

55. Derek Attridge, Geoff Bennington, and Robert Young, eds., *Post-Structuralism and the Question of History* (Cambridge: Cambridge University Press, 1987); Richard Harland, *Superstructuralism: The Philosophy of Structuralism and Post-Structuralism* (New York: Methuen, 1987); see, too, Hubert L. Dreyfus and Paul Rabinow, *Michel Foucault: Beyond Structuralism and Hermeneutics*, 2d ed. (Chicago: University of Chicago Press, 1983).

56. "The text analogy now taken up by social scientists is, in some ways, the broadest of the recent refigurations of social theory, the most venturesome, and the least well developed" (Clifford Geertz, "Blurred Genres: The Refiguration of Social Thought," *American Scholar* 49 [1979–80]: 175).

57　Michael J. Sandel, *Liberalism and the Limits of Justice* (Cambridge: Cambridge University Press, 1982); Alasdair MacIntyre, *After Virtue: A Study in Moral Theory*, 2d ed. (Notre Dame, Ind.: University of Notre Dame Press, 1984); Roberto M. Unger, *The Critical Legal Studies Movement* (Cambridge, Mass.: Harvard University Press, 1986); Robert N. Bellah et al., *Habits of the Heart: Individualism and Commitment in American Life* (Berkeley: University of California Press, 1985). It is noteworthy that Ernest Boyer repeatedly cites *Habits of the Heart* and echoes its language: "All parts of campus life . . . must relate to one another and contribute to a sense of wholeness. We emphasize this commitment to community . . . because our democratic way of life and perhaps our survival as a people rest on whether we can move beyond self-interest and begin to understand better the realities of our dependence on each other" (*College: The Undergraduate Experience*, pp. 8, 68, 322).

58. Bernard Bailyn, *The Ideological Origins of the American Revolution* (Cambridge, Mass.: Harvard University Press, 1967).

59. S. E. Maizlish, "Republicanism and the Whigs," *Reviews in American History* 15 (1987): 26; Gordon S. Wood, *The Creation of the American Republic 1776–1787* (Chapel Hill: University of North Carolina Press, 1969); Stanley N. Katz, "Republicanism and the Law of Inheritance in the Revolutionary Era," *Michigan Law Review* 76 (1977): 1–29.

60. Meyer Reinhold, *Classica Americana: The Greek and Roman Heritage in the United States* (Detroit: Wayne State University Press, 1984).

61. Geertz, pp. 178–79. Geertz states that this alteration appears in "philosophical inquiries looking like literary criticism (think of Stanley Cavell on Beckett or Thoreau, Sartre on Flaubert), scientific discussions looking like belles lettres *morceaux* (Lewis Thomas, Loren Eiseley), baroque fantasies presented as deadpan empirical observations (Borges, Barthelme), histories that consist of equations and tables or law court testimony (Fogel and Engerman, Le Roi Ladurie), documentaries that read like true confessions (Mailer), parables posing as ethnographies (Castenada), theoretical treatises set out as travelogues (Levi-Strauss), ideological arguments cast as historiographical inquiries (Edward Said), epistemological studies constructed like political tracts (Paul Feyerabend), methodological polemics got up as personal memoirs (James Watson)" (pp. 165–66).

62. Gamson et al. (n. 15 above), p. 101; Boyer, "The Quest for Common Learning," pp. 18–19.

63. Boyer, *College: The Undergraduate Experience*, pp. 91–92.

64. Stephen Jay Gould offers an example of how *not* to bring together discourse in these two different forums when he observes: "I have tried twice to teach a course prior to writing a book about the subject in the hope (somewhat cynical) that my task of writing the book would be easier. The courses were fine, but they were utter failures in terms of leading into the book. In order to write the book, I had to sit down for a month and think about it" ("Balancing Teaching and Writing," pp. 13–14). Gould's purpose in this case was still instrumental: the course was to serve in helping to write the book which was to serve to advance his own thinking. But why not make the course the forum for the investigation itself, rather than instrumental to the investigation: "to sit down for a month and think about it" in the course?

65. Boyer, *College: The Undergraduate Experience in America*, p. 110.

66. See Roberto M. Unger, *Knowledge and Politics* (New York: Free Press, 1975); MacIntyre; Sandel.

67. I am particularly indebted to courses in legal theory from Lewis Sargentich and legal history from Morton J. Horwitz and William W. Fisher. The best brief, disinterested description of this movement is "Note: 'Round and 'Round the Bramble Bush: From Legal Realism to Critical Legal Scholarship," *Harvard Law Review* 95 (1982): 1669–90; see, too, Unger.

68. See David C. Hoy, "Interpreting the Law: Hermeneutical and Post-structuralist Perspectives," *Southern California Law Review* 58 (1985): 136–85.

69. *Integrity in the College Curriculum*, pp. 2–3; Boyer, *College: The Undergraduate Experience in America*, pp. 3, 59; Bennett, p. 7.

70. Trow (n. 6 above), p. 19.

71. Alfred D. Chandler, Jr., *Strategy and Structure* (Cambridge, Mass.: MIT Press, 1962).

72. Boyer, *College: The Undergraduate Experience*, p. 3.

This article was the 1987 lecture in the series sponsored by the Fund for the Improvement of Postsecondary Education and was delivered to the Lilly Endowment Workshop on the Liberal Arts, Colorado Springs, June 1987.

BRUCE A. KIMBALL is assistant professor of education at the University of Rochester. His first book, *Orators and Philosophers: A History of the Idea of Liberal Education* (1986), was awarded the Frederick Ness Prize by the Association of American Colleges. His new book, *The Emergence of the Professional Ideal in America: Theology, Law, Education 1606–1907*, is forthcoming from Basil Blackwell.

American Higher Education: Past, Present, and Future

Martin Trow

American higher education differs from all others in offering access to some part of the system to almost everyone who wants to go to college or university, without their having to show evidence of academic talent or qualification. Private attitudes and public policy—so consensual across the political spectrum that they occasion hardly any comment—affirm that the more people who can be persuaded to enroll in a college or university, the better. The budgets of most American colleges and universities are directly keyed to their enrollments; the private institutions' through tuition payments, the public institutions' through a combination of tuition and funding formulas that link state support to enrollment levels. And this linkage is incentive indeed for almost every institution to seek to encourage applications and enrollments.

Enrollment levels are central to the financial health and social functions of American higher education. I begin this article by reviewing current enrollment trends and forecasts. I then explore the social and historical forces that gave rise to and sustain this unique system and conclude by examining the system's prospects for responding to change, given its peculiar and deeply rooted characteristics.

Enrollment Trends and Forecasts

American higher education is the largest and the most diverse system of postsecondary education in the world. In 1947, just after World War II, 2.3 million students were enrolled in some 1800 American colleges and universities, about half in public and half in private institutions (Andersen, 1968, p. 8009). Although both sectors have grown over the past forty years, the enormous growth of enrollments during the 1960s and 1970s was absorbed largely by public institutions, both four-year and two-year colleges. Thus, by 1986, enrollments in America's roughly 3300 colleges and universities were running at 12.4 million and holding fairly steady, with 77% enrolled in public institutions (see Table 1). No central law or authority governs or coordinates American higher education; the roughly 1800 private institutions are governed by lay boards; the 1500 public institutions (including some 900 public community colleges) are accountable to state or local authorities, but usually have a lay board of trustees as a buffer, preserving a high if variable measure of institutional autonomy.

Forecasts of future growth in higher education are almost uniformly wrong, not only in the United States but also abroad. The efforts of the British to predict the growth of their system after the *Robbins Report* in 1963 were consistently wrong, within a few years and by large amounts (Williams, 1983, p. 13). Clark Kerr has noted that the Carnegie Commission's early estimates of aggregate enrollments in the United States, of the numbers of new institutions, of

faculty salaries, and of the proportion of the gross national product spent on higher education were all too high (Kerr, 1980, pp. 6-8). And more recently, nearly everyone concerned with American higher education was predicting a marked decline in enrollments starting in 1979, a decline that was inevitable, given the decreased size of the college-age cohorts starting in that year. Indeed, the number of high school graduates did reach a peak of some 3 million in 1979 and did, in fact, decline to about 2.6 million in 1984, a drop of about 13%. The demographic projections (see Figure 1) point to a further decline in the number of high school graduates, down to a four-year trough of about 2.3 million from 1991 to 1994 (McConnell & Kaufman, 1984, p. 29). But the fall in college and university enrollments that was anticipated has simply not occurred; on the contrary, aggregate enrollments grew between 1979 and 1984 by about 6%, and "colleges and universities had close to 1.5 million more students, and $6 billion more revenues than predicted by the gloom and doomers" (Frances, 1984, p. 3).

Although the nation faces a further fall of about 10% in the numbers of high school graduates by 1991, it is unlikely that enrollments in higher education will suffer an equivalent fall. In fact, the Center for Education Statistics projects that college and university enrollments will remain fairly stable through 1991 (''Mostly stable,'' 1987). Among the reasons for not anticipating any large decline over the next decade are these:

• *First, there has been a steady growth since the early 1970s in enrollments of older students.* During the decade 1972-82, the greatest percentage increase in en-

students, and of women and minorities are all trends that are not dominated by the changing size of the college-age population. For example, relatively small proportions of Mexican American (Chicano) students in California currently go on to higher education. But the number of Chicanos in

---

TABLE 1
Higher Education Enrollment, 1947-1985

Year	Total Enrollment in thousands	Percent of Enrollments	
		Public Institutions	Private Institutions
1947	2,338	49 (1,152)	51 (1,186)
1950	2,297	50	50
1955	2,679	56	44
1960	3,789	59	41
1965	5,921	67	33
1970	8,581	75	25
1975	11,185	79	21
1980	12,097	78	22
1985	12,247	77 (9,479)	23 (2,768)
1986	12,398	77 (9,600)	23 (2,797)
		(numbers in parentheses in thousands)	

Sources compiled from:

A Fact Book on Higher Education (p. 8009) by C. J. Andersen, 1968, Washington, DC: American Council on Education.
1984-85 Fact Book (pp. 56, 59) by C. A. Ottinger, 1984, New York: American Council on Education and Macmillan Publishing Company.
''Fact-file Fall 1985 Enrollment,'' 1986, *The Chronicle of Higher Education*, p. 42.
''Mostly Stable: College and University Enrollments: 1985-1991,'' 1987, *The Chronicle of Higher Education*, p. A24.

---

rollments was among people 25-years-old and older; those 35-years and older increased by 77%, and the enrollments of 25 to 34-year-old students increased by 70%, as compared with a growth of 35% in total enrollments during that period (''Statistics,'' 1984).

• *Second, increasing numbers of students are enrolled part-time.* During the decade 1972-82, part-time enrollments increased by two-thirds, while full-time enrollments were growing by less than a fifth.

• *Third, the past decade has seen very large increases in the enrollments of women and minorities.* The number of women in colleges and universities grew by 61% in that decade, and minority enrollments grew by 85%, as compared with 15% for men, and 30% for all white students.

The growing enrollments of older students, of working and part-time

California's population, and especially among its youth, is very large. In 1981-82, they were about a quarter of all public school students, and, by the year 2000, will begin to outnumber whites in the under-20 age group (Project PACE, 1984, p. 11). Even small changes in the propensity of Chicanos to graduate from high school and go to college would have a major impact on enrollment levels in California colleges and universities. We would predict a long-term growth in the numbers of Chicanos going on to college, simply on the basis of trends among other ethnic groups throughout American history. Moreover, long-term changes in the occupational structure, such as the growth of the knowledge and information industries, increase the numbers of jobs for college-educated people. And many of our colleges and universities are more than eager to

welcome back older people who want to upgrade their skills and equip themselves for jobs in the new industries.

Enrollment levels may yet fall over the next few years. Population movements, changes in the economy, and change in the size of age cohorts will, however, affect various states and regions and their institutions differently. Not only will there be an obvious disparity in the effects for, say, Ohio and Texas, there will also be equally great differences in the effects for each region's public community colleges, minor and elite private four-year colleges, and research universities. Some private colleges will certainly close over the next decade, and perhaps some public institutions will consolidate, though recent figures show an increase in the number of private four-year colleges in recent years that one would not have predicted (Tsukada, 1986, p. 101, Figure 5.3). But the birth and death of colleges in large numbers throughout our history has been and continues to be a natural outcome of the market's great influence over our diverse and decentralized system of higher education. And although there may be closures, they will be mostly of weaker institutions and may well leave the system as a whole even stronger (Glenny, 1983).

But if it is not prediction in the sense of forecasting, the value of this exercise lies elsewhere. The effort to think about what higher education will look like in 20 or 40 years forces us to think more clearly about the historical forces that have shaped American higher education's unique qualities and character. Eric Ashby has said that we cannot know ''what the environments of tomorrow's world will be like,'' but ''we already know what its heredity will be like'' (Ashby, 1967). And, as Clark Kerr has observed, heredity in higher education is a particularly strong force. The universities of today can draw a direct line back to Bologna, Paris, Oxford, and Cambridge. Even religious institutions—those vehicles for the eternal verities—have changed more, and political and economic institutions incomparably more, than universities.

The Social and Historical Background[1]

Certain features leap out when one compares American higher education with the systems in other advanced industrial societies. American colleges

618

and universities are indeed exceptional, made so by characteristics built deeply into our history and institutions that shape their capacity to respond to unanticipatable events.

First, the market and market-related forces have a deep, pervasive influence. Second, and related to the first, the structural diversity among institutions is enormous, in their size, functions and curricula, sources of support, configurations of authority, and academic standards, a diversity their student bodies mirror in their age distributions, purposes and motivations, class, ethnic and racial origins, and much else.

Third, the internal differentiation in our comprehensive universities and many of our larger state colleges in academic standards and educational missions gives them great flexibility to respond to the markets for undergraduates, faculty, graduate students, and research support. This internal differentiation among academic departments and professional schools complements the structural differentiation between public and private, large and small, selective and open-access colleges and universities.

Fourth, a cluster of shared characteristics marks our curricula, teaching styles, and patterns of assessment: the unique role of general education as a component of nearly all American first degree courses; the considerable extent of student choice in the selection of courses; and the modular course earning *unit-credits*, an academic currency that makes a system of 3300 separate institutions.

Fifth, our mode of college and university governance is unparalleled. Lay boards and strong presidents, certainly strong by comparison with their counterparts elsewhere, command large administrative staffs located inside the institutions rather than in some central ministry or governmental agency.

The great, unique feature of American higher education is surely its diversity. It is this diversity—both resulting from and making possible the system's phenomenal growth—that has enabled our colleges and universities to appeal to so many, serve so many different functions, and insinuate themselves into so many parts of the national life. And it is through the preservation of diversity that our system will be best prepared to respond to changing demands and opportunities in the years

ahead. To see why this is so, review briefly the historical roots of this diversity and the benefits we derive from it today.

America had established nine colleges by the time of the Revolution, when two—Oxford and Cambridge—were enough for the much larger and wealthier mother country. The United States entered the Civil War with about 250 colleges, of which over 180 still survive. Even more striking is the record of failure: Between the Revolution and the Civil War perhaps as many as 700 colleges were started and failed. By 1880, England was doing very well with four universities for a population of 23 million, whereas the state of Ohio, with a population of 3 million, already boasted 37 institutions of

higher learning (Rudolph, 1962, pp. 47-48). By 1910, we had nearly a thousand colleges and universities with a third of a million students—at a time when the 16 universities of France enrolled altogether about 40,000 students, a number nearly equaled by the American faculty members at the time.

The extraordinary phenomena of high fertility and high mortality rates among institutions of higher learning are still with us. For example, between 1969 and 1975, some 800 new colleges (many of them community colleges) were created, and roughly 300 others were closed or consolidated, leaving a

net gain of nearly 500. This is a phenomenon unique to the United States—one that resembles the pattern of success and failure of small businesses in modern capitalist economies. It is in sharp contrast with the slow, deliberately planned creation of institutions of higher and further education in most advanced industrial societies or their even slower and rarer termination. And this points to the very strong link between higher education in the United States and the mechanisms of the market. This link has been a major factor in the emergence and persistence of large numbers of diverse institutions.

Two important features of markets, as compared with other forms of social action, are (a.) that their outcomes are

not the result of planning or central purposive decision, and (b.) that when producers are relatively numerous, their behaviors are marked by their competition for buyers, which strengthens the buyers' influence over the product's character and quality, indeed, over the producers' very character.

In higher education, we can see this when the buyers are students, and the producers, the colleges and universities, compete for their enrollment. We can see it also when the sellers are graduates competing for job openings. The two together translate opportunities in the job market into the size of

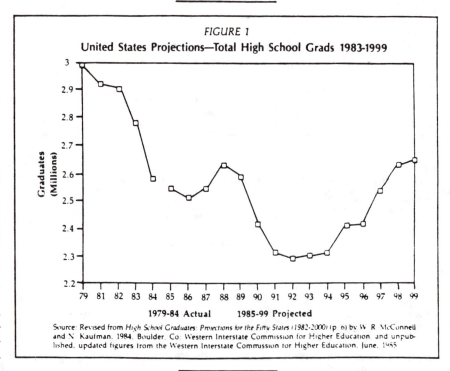

FIGURE 1

United States Projections—Total High School Grads 1983-1999

Graduates (Millions)

1979-84 Actual   1985-99 Projected

Source: Revised from *High School Graduates: Projections for the Fifty States (1982-2000)* (p. 6) by W. R. McConnell and N. Kaufman, 1984, Boulder, Co: Western Interstate Commission for Higher Education; and unpublished, updated figures from the Western Interstate Commission for Higher Education, June, 1985

academic departments and programs. The key is the considerable autonomy of American colleges and universities, which enables them to move resources between departments in response to changes in student enrollment and demand. Similarly, when research groups compete for scarce funds, funding agencies gain power over the character, direction, and quality of the research they buy. In the United States, apart from the quite unusual period of rapid growth between 1955 and 1975, the supply of places has on the whole outstripped demand; and buyers or potential buyers at both ends, students and the employers of graduates, have had a powerful influence on the behavior of the producers. This influence of buyer over seller is likely to be relatively constant in the decades ahead.

The Influence of Market Forces

We can see the emergence of strong market forces in the early history of American higher education, we can see them today in the very structure and workings of our institutions, and we can compare their strength here with the systems of other societies.

A multiplicity of forces and motives lay behind the establishment of colleges and universities throughout our history: religious motives; fears of relapse into barbarism at the frontier; the need for various kinds of professionals; state pride and local boosterism; philanthropy; idealism; educational reform; speculation in land, among others, and in all combinations. But the number and diversity of institutions, competing with one another for students, resources, teachers, bringing market considerations and market mechanisms right into the heart of this ancient cultural institution—all also required the absence of any restraining central force or authority. The states could not be that restraining force; under the pressures of competition and emulation they have tended throughout our history to create institutions and programs in the numbers and to the standards of their neighbors. Crucially important has been the absence of a federal ministry of education with the power to charter new institutions, or of a single preeminent university that could influence them in other ways.

The closest we have come as a nation to establishing such a central force was the attempt, first by George Washington, and then by the next five Presi-

dents, to found a University of the United States at the seat of government in Washington, D.C. In fact, Washington made provision for such a university in his will and mentioned it in his first and last messages to Congress. His strongest plea came in his last message to Congress, where he argued that a national university would promote national unity, a matter of deep concern at a time when the primary loyalties of many Americans were to their sovereign states, not the infant nation.

Washington saw also the possibility of creating one first-class university by concentrating money and other resources in it. As he noted in his last message to Congress: "Our Country, much to its honor, contains many Seminaries of learning highly respectable and useful; but the funds upon which they rest, are too narrow, to command the ablest Professors, in the different departments of liberal knowledge, for the Institution contemplated, though they would be excellent auxiliaries" (Hofstadter & Smith, 1961, p. 158). Here, indeed, Washington was right in his diagnosis. The many institutions that sprang up between the Revolution and the Civil War all competed for very scarce resources and all thus suffered to some degree from malnutrition. Malnutrition at the margin is still characteristic of a system of institutions influenced so heavily by market forces.

Defeat of the national university meant that American higher education would develop, to this day, without a single capstone institution. As it was, until after the Civil War, whatever the United States called its institutions of higher learning, it simply did not have a single genuine university—an institution of first-class standing that could bring its students as far or as deep into the various branches of learning as could the institutions of the old world.

A national university would have profoundly affected American higher education. As the preeminent university, it would have had an enormous influence, direct and indirect, on every other college in the country, and through them on the secondary schools as well. Its standards and educational philosophies would have been models for every institution that hoped to send some of its graduates to the university in Washington. It would, in fact, have established national academic standards for the bachelor's degree, for the undergraduate curriculum, for the

qualifications for college teachers, even for entrance to college, and thus for the secondary schools. Eventually, it would have surely constrained the growth of graduate education and research universities in the United States.

Similarly, a national university of high standard would surely have inhibited the emergence of the hundreds of small, weak, half-starved state and denominational colleges that sprang up over the next 170 years. They simply could not have offered work to the standard that the University of the United States would have set. The situation would have been familiar to Europeans, for whom the maintenance of high and, so far as possible, common academic standards has been a valued principle, almost unchallenged until recently. In the United States, after the defeat of the University of the United States, no one has challenged the principle of high academic standards across the whole system because no one has proposed it—there have been no common standards, high or otherwise. Indeed, if Europe's slogan for higher education has been "nothing, if not the best," America's has been "something is better than nothing." And in that spirit, we have created a multitude of institutions of every sort, offering academic work of every description and at every level of seriousness and standard. And, by so doing, we have offered Europeans nearly two centuries of innocent amusement at our expense.

Ironically, however, without any central model or governmental agency able to create one or more national systems, all of our 3300 institutions, public and private, modest and preeminent, religious and secular, are in some way part of a common system bound by membership in a series of markets for students, support, prestige, faculty.

Another event in the early history of the Republic that had powerful effects on the shape and character of American higher education was the 1819 Supreme Court decision in the Dartmouth College case. In 1816, the New Hampshire legislature had passed a bill giving the state government broad powers to "reform" Dartmouth. The rationale for proposed changes in its charter was the plausible argument that, as the college had been established (though as a private corporation) to benefit the people of New Hampshire, this could best be accomplished by giving the public, through the legislature, a voice in its operation. Chief Justice Marshall, ruling in favor of the college trustees, declared that state legislatures were forbidden, by the Constitution, to pass any law "impairing the obligation of contracts," and that the charter originally granted the college was a contract (Hofstadter & Smith, 1961, p. 218). This landmark decision affirmed the principle of the sanctity of contracts between governments and private institutions. In so doing, it gave expression to the Federalist belief that the government should not interfere with private property, even for the purpose of benefiting the public welfare. John Marshall, the then-Chief Justice, had written earlier: "I consider the interference of the legislature in the management of our private affairs, whether those affairs are committed to a company or remain under individual direction as equally dangerous and unwise." He and his colleagues on the Court decided, in the Dartmouth College case, that a private college or university charter was a contract that a state could not retroactively abridge. That decision of 1819 had massive repercussions both for the growth of capitalist enterprises and for the future development of higher education in the United States.

The Dartmouth College decision sustained the older, more modest role of the state in educational affairs against those who looked to the government to take a greater role in the working of society and its institutions. Marshall's decision had the practical effect of safeguarding the founding and proliferation of privately controlled colleges. Thereafter, promoters of private colleges knew that once they had obtained a state charter they were secure in the future control of the institution. By this decision, state university development was slowed or weakened, though, paradoxically, it may be that by making it more difficult to create them, state universities were ultimately strengthened.

The failure of the University of the United States and the success of Dartmouth College in its appeal to the Supreme Court were victories for local initiative and private entrepreneurship. The first set limits on the federal government's role in shaping the character of the whole of American higher education; the second set even sharper limits on the state's power over private colleges. Together, these two events constituted a kind of license for unrestrained individual and group initiative

in the creation of colleges of all sizes, shapes and creeds. As a result, colleges' and universities' behavior came to resemble living organisms' behavior in an ecological system—competitive for resources, highly sensitive to the demands of environment, and inclined, over time, through the ruthless processes of natural selection, to be adaptive to those aspects of their environment that permitted their survival. Their environment also has included other colleges, and later universities. So we see in this frog pond a set of mechanisms that we usually associate with the behavior of small entrepreneurs in a market: the anxious concern for market demands and the readiness to adapt to its apparent preferences; the effort to secure a special place in that market through the marginal differentiation of the product; and a readiness to enter into symbiotic or parasitic relationships with other producers for a portion of that market.

We are employing a language that Europeans tend to find strange and often a bit distasteful when used in connection with institutions of higher learning. But distasteful or not, an American must insist on this as a central and distinguishing characteristic of American higher education—that it has developed as a network of institutions that, in many respects, resembles in its behavior the myriad of small capitalistic enterprises that were springing up everywhere, at the same time and in the same places, and often in response to the same forces.

We are, and have been from the beginning, an acquisitive society, confronted by a continent whose ownership had not been settled by sword and custom since medieval times. In America, as Louis Hartz has noted, the market preceded society, a central and powerful fact whose ramifications can be seen in all of our institutions and throughout our national life (Hartz, 1955). We are, to put it crudely, unembarrassed by the market. By contrast, Europeans and their governments, now, as in the past, dislike market mechanisms and processes in education and do everything they can to reduce their influence. And this difference arises out of our profoundly differing feelings about culture and about cultural competence. Markets threaten the "cultural integrity" of cultural institutions by increasing the power of consumers as over against producers—that

is, as over against the people who are presumably most competent to supply some given kind of cultural entity, whether it be a performance of music or higher studies in philosophy or physics. In colleges and universities, the consumers, ordinarily students or their parents, are by definition incompetent, or at least less competent than the teachers and academic administrators who together provide instruction. Europeans try very hard to reduce the influence of the incompetent mass on high cultural matters and to preserve a realm of elite determination of cultural form and content.

We in the United States, surely the most populist society in the world, accept a larger role for the influence of consumer preference on cultural forms —even in the provision of what and how subjects are taught in colleges and universities. Europeans try to reduce the influence of consumer preference in a number of ways. Most importantly, they try to insulate their financing of institutions of higher education from student fees. By contrast, in the United States, enrollment-driven budgets in all but a few institutions, both public and private, ensure that most institutions are extremely sensitive to student preferences.

Another example of the comparative hospitality of American institutions to market forces in higher education can be seen in the ways Congress has decided to provide major public funding for colleges and universities. After sharp debate in the early 1970s, this country chose to fund colleges and universities chiefly by providing grants and loans to students, rather than through direct support to the institutions themselves; the decision was to subsidize higher education through the consumers, not the producers. The result was to strengthen the relative power of consumers over producers substantially, without increasing the power of central government over the producers.

The Character and Structure of our Institutions

We can look at broad patterns of organization and finance of higher education (for example, multiple versus single sources of support) and see the differences between market systems and those dominated by other principles of organization and political decision-making. But we can also see the influence of market mechanisms in the private life of higher education, in the very processes of teaching and learning. Our peculiar system of earned and transferable "credits," a kind of academic currency that we all take for granted in American institutions, is one example. The unit-credit system is not found in other countries, where degrees are earned by passing examinations or writing dissertations. But our credits, units that can be accumulated, banked, transferred, and, within limits, automatically accepted as legal academic tender toward an earned degree throughout the country, make possible the extraordinary mobility of our students between fields of study, and between institutions. Moreover, credits that can be accumulated and transferred also allow students to drop out, or "stop out," and return to college in ways that are increasingly familiar to us.

An inventory of the unique qualities of American higher education must include a reference to the multiplicity of subjects taught, a product of the extraordinary hospitality of our institutions to almost any subject that might have a claim to be useful or to be rooted in a body of skill and knowledge that can be studied and taught. But this range of studies, often the subject of somewhat derisive comment by Europeans, would not be possible if we had a central agency maintaining "high standards" and scrutinizing new subjects for their appropriateness as judged by traditional criteria. The openness of our institutions to new subjects is linked to the absence of a central administrative body that certifies institutions and subjects, as well as to our consequent reliance on market forces to sustain our many weak and impoverished institutions.

Or we could point to the intimate links between our colleges and universities and local industry, governments and other institutions and private organizations of all kinds, relationships that are envied and emulated elsewhere but rarely matched in scope (Eurich, 1985).

This inventory leaves us with the question of how these unique characteristics are all related, both in their origins and in their current functioning. Let us look, for example, at a cluster of phenomena embedded in American higher education: the lay board, the strong presidency, a weak professoriate, the internal administration, the absence of a central ministry of higher education. The origins of the external nonacademic board of trustees lie in the precedent set at Harvard. The founders of Harvard had intended to "carry on the English tradition of resident-faculty control" (Rudolph, 1962, p. 166). But Harvard had to be founded and not just developed. There simply was not a body of scholars to be brought together to teach and to govern themselves. A *president* could be found to take responsibility for the operation of the institution, and he might find some young men to help him with instruction as tutors. But Harvard had been established for more than 85 years before it had its first professor; Yale for more than 50. "For over a century and a half, American collegiate education relied chiefly on the college president and his young tutors." And for a very long time indeed, well into the 19th century, "The only secure and sustained professional office in American collegiate education was that of the college president himself. He alone had, in the community and before the governing boards, the full stature of a man of learning. To this situation can be traced the singular role and importance of the American college or university president" (Hofstadter & Metzger, 1955, p. 124).

The lay boards that arose to govern America's first college and the great majority of those that followed were created by groups of individuals, not by the state. These boards *had* to govern; there was no one else. They could appoint a president, and, as busy men themselves, they had to delegate to him the day-to-day running of the institution. He held his office, however, and everywhere in the U.S. still does, wholly at the pleasure of this external board; the president has no security of tenure as president (though he may hold tenure as a professor in the institution). But for a very long time there was no body of learned men making academic life a career and, thus, no challenge to the president's authority, so long as he had the support of his board of trustees.

The near absolute authority of the college president in running an institution was lost over time, especially with the rise of the great research universities and the emergence of a genuine academic profession. In this century, especially in the stronger institutions, a great deal of authority over academic affairs has been delegated to the faculty. But the American college and university president is still more powerful than his counterpart in European institutions, who faces the power held jealously by the professoriate, or by the academic staff more broadly, and by government ministries, trade unions, or student organizations (Trow, 1985a).

The relatively great power and authority of the American college and university president also insured that, when some institutions became very large and needed a big bureaucratic staff to administer them, that staff would be an extension of the president's office, rather than responsible to a faculty body or to state authorities. By keeping the administrative staff within the university, the strong presidency has helped preserve the autonomy of the public university in the face of state authority.

I have mentioned how weak, indeed for a long time nonexistent, the academic profession in America was. When professors did begin to appear, they did not command the enormous prestige and status accorded to the European professor. They were neither part of a prestigious civil service, nor were they recruited from the highest social strata. Indeed, in a society that prized action and worldly success, they were rather looked down on as men who had stepped aside from the real challenges of life. America, for the most part, has given its honors and respect chiefly to men of action rather than reflection; the very choice of an academic career for a long time suggested that a person was incapable of managing such important matters as the affairs of a university (Hofstadter, 1963, pp. 24-51; Rudolph, 1962, pp. 160-161). This tended to strengthen the hand of the president, who *may* have been a scholar, but almost certainly was also a man of affairs.

The relatively low status and weakness of the professoriate also meant that, as the academic profession grew, it was not dominated by a handful of prestigious professors. The academic ranks were established during the growth of the research universities after the Civil War, but with almost the whole teaching faculty holding the title of professor of some rank, and with remarkable independence for even young assistant professors. That is partly due to the egalitarian elements in American cultural life, which are still very strong, but partly also to the his-

622

toric weakness of the senior professor—his lack of real power, social prestige, even scholarly distinction. Academic ambition directed itself not so much to rank—that could be assumed—but to national reputation and to the distinction of the institution or department in which one gained an appointment.

Indeed, many of the most important qualities of American higher education have arisen not from design but from the weakness of its component institutions. For example, as I have suggested, the relatively egalitarian character of American academic life and the independence and authority of its junior members are products not of plan or policy, but of the slow formation of the academic profession and the professoriate and its relative poverty, low status, lack of tenure or civil service rank. But that has meant that we have avoided the bitter struggles between the professors and the other ranks of the academic profession that have marked European systems since World War II. In America, the rank of professor was no great honor and held no great reward; it was, in fact, the rank that every young instructor or assistant professor (and not just the few most talented ones) could expect to achieve in the fullness of time. That ease of access has helped to keep its status relatively low both within the university and outside it—where the title "Professor" still has slightly pejorative or comic overtones.

The connections among a weak academic profession, strong presidents, lay boards, and the power of the market in American higher education lie in the more general lack of other forces that constrain the self-interested actions of individuals and institutions. Most commonly, those constraining forces in other countries are the state authorities allied with the academic professions and its organizations or guilds. In the United States, central state power was initially weak, and in relation to higher education remained weak, in part as a result of the failure of the University of the United States and the Dartmouth College decision which guaranteed an essential role to the private sector. In addition, the weakness of the professoriate greatly reduced its constraint on the market. On the other hand, strong presidents and their administrative staffs could act in pursuit of the self-interest of individual institutions, and lay boards could ensure that those institutions would continue to be respon-

sive to the larger society, and to its markets for students and graduates, rather than to the state or professional guilds. And that certainly has been and will be a source of strength as these institutions face an uncertain future and a changing environment.

Trends in Higher Education Finance

I have been looking backward but now look at the present and near past for trends and developments that might point in the direction of larger changes in the future.

In 1985-1986 expenditures of all kinds on American colleges and universities were estimated to be over $102 billion, an increase in current dollars of 32%, and in constant dollars of 17%, over 1981-1982. This represents roughly 2.5% of the Gross National Product ("Higher education is," 1986, p. 3). One important and distinctive characteristic of American higher education is the diversity of its sources of support. This diversity of funding sources has large consequences for the autonomy of American colleges and universities and for their traditions of service to other institutions, both public and private, as well as for their finances. Taken in the aggregate, American colleges and universities get support from federal, state and local governments; from private sources such as churches, business firms, foundations, and individuals; from students, in the form of tuition and fees, living expenses in halls of residence, food services, health services, and the like; and from their own endowments, as well as from the sale of their services to others.

Government at all levels together provide nearly half of all current revenues for American higher education, and that excludes federal aid given directly to students, which shows up, for the most part, as tuition and fees from the students. The federal government provides only about 13% of the support for higher education overall, and that includes its support for research and development in the universities, but excludes the aid it provides directly to students. State and local governments (mostly state) provide a third of all support for higher education. Students themselves provide another third, including federal aid they have received. The institutions themselves contribute about 15% from their own endowments and other sources. If we count federal aid to students as

federal support to higher education, it increases the federal proportion to about 23% of total support and reduces the student contribution to about the same proportion. Another 6% is provided by individuals, foundations, and private business firms, in the form of gifts, grants, and contracts.

These proportions, of course, differ between public and private colleges and universities, though it must be stressed that all American colleges and universities are supported by a mixture of public and private funds. For example, whereas in 1981-1982 public four-year colleges and universities got over 44% of their operating budgets from their state governments, the private institutions got less than 2% from state sources. (But note, private colleges received a slightly larger proportion of their support funds from the federal government than did the public institutions.) The other big difference lies in the importance of students' fees and payments directly to the institution for services: These account for less than a quarter of the revenues to public institutions, but about a half of the support for private institutions (Plisko, 1985, p. 114, Table 2.14). These proportions differ sharply among even finer categories of colleges and universities; for example, as between public research universities and public four-year colleges.

In 1985-1986 student aid from all sources was running at over $21 billion a year, 23% higher than in 1980-1981. In real terms, however, student support from all sources had fallen by 3% since 1980-1981, and aid from federally supported programs by 10%, when adjusted for inflation ("Trends in," 1986, p. 2). The federal government in fiscal 1985 provided directly and indirectly about $23.7 billion to higher education, of which $10.2 billion was in a complex combination of student grants and loans (derived from "Higher education funds," 1986, p. 12). Student aid has widespread support in the Congress as well as in society at large. And although the Reagan administration regularly proposed cuts in that aid, many of its proposals were defeated. In 1985 Congress "blocked virtually all the cuts in aid to college students that the Reagan Administration proposed..." and was "drafting legislation to keep grants, loans and work opportunities essentially intact for five years" (Friendly, 1985, p. 15). Although pressures on the federal budget arising out of the large deficits may be reflected in further pressures on federal student aid programs, there is little likelihood of cuts so deep as to endanger the programs. Federal support for students is here to stay.

Increases in student aid at the state and the institution levels (which now comprise 22% of the total student aid reported from all sources) have helped to offset the drop in federal aid. At the federal level, the distribution of student aid has greatly shifted from grants to loans: in 1975-1976, 75% of federal student aid was awarded in the form of grants, but by 1984-1985 the share of grant aid had dropped to 29%, whereas the share of loans had tripled, from 21% in 1975 to 66% (see Table 2).

TABLE 2
Shift of Federal Student Aid
from Grants to Loans

	1975-76	1984-85
Grants	75%	29%
Loans	21%	66%
Work-Study	4%	5%

Source: "1986: Major Trends Shaping the Outlook for Higher Education" by C. Frances, 1985, *AAHE Bulletin*, p. 5.

Many states did cut their support for public colleges and universities during the severe recession of 1980-1982, but thereafter the levels of state support tended to rise about as fast as economic recovery and rising revenues permitted. State tax funds for the operation of higher education (this does not include capital costs) was nearly $31 billion for 1984-1985, up 19% over 1983-1984. "Over the last decade, [1974-1984, state] appropriations [for higher education] increased 140 per cent nationwide. Adjusted for inflation, the increase was 19 per cent" (Evangelauf, 1985, p. 1 ff.).

With regard to federal support for research, also perceived by many as endangered by the Reagan administration, between 1982 and 1985, federal obligations to universities and colleges for research and development increased by 16% in real terms, reaching $6 billion

in 1985. Moreover, in that year nearly two-thirds of all federal academic R & D support was committed to basic research projects, compared to about one-half in 1975 (National Science Foundation, 1985, p. 2; see also, "Higher education funds," 1986, p. 12).

Other Supports and Benefits of the System[2]

We need not place very great weight on recent trends in enrollments and support. We know, especially from the sad example of British higher education, how rapidly these figures can change when they are built on shallow foundations. In Britain, where the university system has few friends in industry, in the professions, in the trade unions or the political parties, its few friends in the civil service and elsewhere are unable to protect it against economic and political pressures from government.

But American higher education has many friends and, more important, many supporters in the society, not just in government. The absence of any strong central governing and standardizing authority that can control (and limit) the growth of American higher education and the concomitant responsiveness of our colleges and universities to market forces have allowed and indeed required them to find ways to serve other institutions and groups in their constant search for support. We have not been able to afford the luxury of high academic standards across all our degree-granting institutions. The result is the diversity of standards and functions in our colleges and universities that we find so familiar and that Europeans find so strange. So long as the governing assumption of a system of higher education is that only a minority of students can work at the required standard, that system is constrained both in its size and in the functions it can perform for its students and for the larger society. Such a system may perform the functions of elite selection, preparation, and certification, as most European universities have done and still do. But it cannot penetrate as deeply or broadly into the life of society as American higher education has.

Some of the effects of mass higher education on American society are not, I believe, well recognized. Economists often say that it is best to measure and assess carefully what can be measured, and leave to others—historians, sociologists, educators, politicians—the discus-

sion of higher education's larger effects on society. We cannot measure these very precisely; they are long delayed in their appearance, are "outcomes" rather than intended effects, and have sources only partly within the system and partly within the society at large. (For an economist whose views are similar to those I express below, see Bowen, 1977, pp. 359-387.)

Let me suggest some of those effects here:

• *Higher education has substantial effects on the attitudes of those exposed to it.* A large amount of research supports this assertion—and also that changes in attitudes occurring during the college years persist throughout life (Hyman, Wright, & Reed, 1975; Feldman & Newcomb, 1969). For example, higher education achieves some of what it intends by broadening the perspectives of students, giving them an appreciation of other cultures and groups, making them more tolerant of cultural differences, and weakening the prejudices characteristic of uneducated people. And those changed attitudes in a population, in turn, make possible real changes in social structures, if and when they are accompanied by changes in law and institutional behavior.

In the United States, the years after World War II saw a steady decline in hostility toward black people and a growing readiness on the part of whites to give blacks equal treatment and fair access to education, housing, and jobs. These changes can be seen in studies of attitudes both in the general population as well as among college students during the college years and after (Hyman & Wright, 1979; Stember, 1961; Stouffer, 1955; Clark, Heist, McConnell, Trow, & Yonge, 1972). I believe that the considerable progress the United States has made in race relations since World War II has been made possible by the growth of mass higher education and the marked decline in racial prejudice that accompanied it. If that is true, then it represents a very great contribution to the life of the society, one that almost never acknowledged by economists as a benefit of American higher education.

Higher education has also played visible role in this revolution by helping to expand and educate black, Hispanic, and Asian middle classes. In 1985, the University of California at Berkeley for the first time admitted freshman class made up of a majority

(52%) of those minority group members. In the next century, those students will be assuming leadership positions in every institution in our society.

• *People who have been to college or university, on the whole, view public issues in a longer time perspective than do less well-educated people.* Such perspectives are important to assessing the significance and recognizing the origins of a problem or issue, yet we do not measure them or give them value, certainly not as outcomes of higher education. Nations and industries cannot plan or develop programs without the help of people who take the long view, who can imagine the outcome of projects that may lie years in the future. And that perspective is very much a benefit of mass higher education.

In an increasingly complex society, it is not enough that a small number of elites have these longer time horizons; the successful development and implementation of plans require such people throughout the society, especially at the middle levels of the civil service in central, regional, and local governments, and in public and private enterprises. Long-range plans require continual adjustments and modifications at the levels where they are implemented; people at those levels must be able to understand the purposes of long-range programs and be able to implement and modify them within planning guidelines.

• *The capacity of citizens to learn how to learn is another skill that is gained or enhanced by exposure to higher education.* So much of what we learn in college or university is obsolescent in 10 years, obsolete in 25, that it is impossible to exaggerate the importance of the ability to continue to learn after finishing formal schooling. Wherever facilities are provided for adult education, they are now quickly filled by people with a degree or some postsecondary education, who already have, as adults, developed a desire to learn (Organization for Economic Co-operation and Development, 1977, p. 27) Modern societies need citizens with that quality of mind, which is also a product, if often a by-product, of higher education. I believe that mass higher education in the United States, especially in its generous provision of education for adults, engenders and distributes more widely the habit of "life-long learning" than is true in most other countries.

The qualities of mind (they are more than attitudes) that I have mentioned—tolerance of cultural and class differences, a longer time perspective that helps sustain initiative among middle- and lower-level administrators, the ability to learn how to learn—are all created or enhanced by exposure to postsecondary education. As I have suggested, they are usually by-products of that education, but immensely important by-products for the life and progress of any society.

• *In American political life, higher education has a familiar role as home of the cultural critic of the established political order and the nursery of radical and even revolutionary student movements. But less dramatically and visibly, the expansion and democratization of higher education may also work to legitimate the political and social order by rewarding talent and effort rather than serving merely as a cultural apparatus of the ruling classes by ensuring the passage of power and privilege across generations.*

In a time of rising expectations among all social strata around much of the world, nations must provide real opportunities for social mobility to able people from poor and modest origins. They must do so for social and political reasons, as well as for economic growth. In many countries, the armed forces have provided an avenue of mobility, and they have often gained the support of the poor even when other institutions have lost it. But, for many reasons, higher education is a better instrument for strengthening the legitimacy of a political democracy, and, where it performs that vital function, as it has in the United States, it goes unrecorded on the accounting sheets of the cost benefits analyst.

A further large benefit of American higher education, yet to be achieved, is the help and guidance extended by colleges and universities to secondary education in other ways than through teacher training and educational research. The many reports and books on public secondary education that have appeared since 1983 (e.g., National Commission on Excellence in Education, 1983; Boyer, 1983; Goodlad, 1983) have led to the creation of a large number of programs by colleges and universities that establish new links between higher and secondary education. Some of those programs are designed to strengthen the academic and college preparatory work of the high schools, not just provide remediation for ill-prepared students after they reach college (Trow, 1985b). It may be that the task is too large and that the structural characteristics of American high schools will defeat all efforts to overcome their "bias against excellence" (Clark, 1985, p. 391). But it will not be for want of trying. Already hundreds of programs that aim to correct or ameliorate deficiencies in the schools have been developed by colleges and universities. Results can already be seen in individual schools, but the larger effects will be long delayed and obscured by many other inputs and forces. My point here is to illustrate the continuing propensity of American higher education to respond to national needs of almost every kind and to try to provide some service, some program, to meet those needs.

Conclusion

I have chosen to look to the past and the present to assess characteristics of our unique system of colleges and universities that may shape the future. It is futile to make specific predictions—they all fail in a few years, even in societies that manage their systems more closely than we do. But my review of the central characteristics of American higher education leads me to believe that it is well equipped to survive major changes in the society and to respond creatively to almost any developments, short of a catastrophe. The strength of our system lies precisely in its diversity, which allows it to respond to different needs and demands on different segments of the system. Over the past forty years, enrollments have grown from about 2.3 million to 12.4 million and, along with this enormous growth, there has been further diversification and democratization of access. By the end of World War II, and perhaps much earlier, we had a system that had the capacity to grow by a factor of five without any fundamental change in its structure or functions, a system able to provide access to a broad spectrum of American society, while still providing education of the highest standard for a small fraction of our youth and research at an equally high standard in the broadest range of scholarly and scientific disciplines.

What besides this massive growth has changed significantly in American higher education over the past forty years? First, the federal government has become a major source of support, both for university-based research and through student aid. Yet it still supplies less than a quarter of all support for American higher education. Moreover, the government's influence on the system has been further muted, precisely because that support has gone to individual scientists and students rather than directly to the institutions. Of course, the federal government has become a major actor in shaping the agenda of American science. And yet science still retains a large measure of autonomy to pursue problems and issues that arise internally, rather than at the initiative of the government.

As the fifty states have increased their support for the public sector of higher education, they have demanded greater accountability from the colleges and universities for the use of these funds. Not long ago these demands by public authorities were seen as the forerunners of a dangerous shift of authority and intitiative away from the state colleges and universities to the state houses and governors' offices (Trow, 1975). Relations between public universities and state authorities vary too much for any easy generalization, yet my sense is that public authorities and university leaders in many states have been coming to a more reasoned and mutually acceptable relationship than was seen as possible or likely even ten years ago (Newman, 1987).

Higher education has expanded its relationships with industry in many ways. On the one hand, business firms provide very large and growing amounts of education and training at all levels of skill and sophistication, including degree-granting programs (Eurich, 1985). On the other hand, universities have provided the ideas and professional staffs for new science-based industries and are at the center of their physical clusterings from Boston to Silicon Valley. They also provide an organizational model and style of work for many other institutions, from consulting firms and industrial labs to legislative committees (Muir, 1982). Moreover, community colleges enroll increasing numbers of students who already hold a bachelor's degree but want further training in another specialty—new patterns of continuing education and professional development.

Certainly, the democratization of the student body has meant more mature, part-time, and working students; these kinds of students in fact have confounded the predictions of enrollment decline after 1979. There seems no limit to this development: American higher education, or at least a large segment of it, seems ready and eager to provide some useful educational service to all nontraditional students. And we have no reason to believe that this will be less true in the future, as more and more of our labor force comes to work in industries whose very survival is predicated on rapid change, new skills, and new ways of thinking.

All of this suggests that American higher education will be an even more important institution in this society in the decades to come: as a supplier of more advanced skills as well as a source of greater social equality, continuing social commentary and criticism, and the transmission of an ever-broadening cultural heritage. Higher education is, today, I believe, the key institution in American society, the source of many of its most important ideas, values, skills, and energies. That will be true, and increasingly true, as far ahead as anyone can see.

---

¹This section draws, in part, on my essay "Aspects of Diversity in American Higher Education," 1979.
²This section draws on my paper, "The State of Higher Education in the United States," 1986.

Acknowledgement: Revised from State and Welfare, USA/USSR: Contemporary Policy and Practice, *edited by Gail W. Lapidus and Guy E. Swanson, Berkeley: Institute of International Studies, University of California (forthcoming 1988). My thanks to Janet Ruyle for her help with this paper.*

Andersen, C. J. (Comp.). (1968). *A fact book on higher education* (Issue No. 1). Washington, DC: American Council on Education.

Ashby, E. (1967, November). Ivory towers in tomorrow's world. *The Journal of Higher Education,* pp. 417-427.

Bowen, H. R. (1977). *Investment in learning: The individual and social value of American higher education.* San Francisco, CA: Jossey-Bass.

Boyer, E. (1983). *High school: A report on secondary education in America.* New York: Harper & Row.

Clark, B. R. (1985, February). The high school and the university: What went wrong in America. Part I. *Phi Delta Kappan, 66,* 391-397.

Clark, B. R., Heist, P., McConnell, T. R., Trow, M. A., & Yonge, G. E. (1972). *Students and colleges: Interaction and change.* Berkeley, CA: Center for Research and Development in Higher Education, University of California.

Eurich, N. P. (1985). *Corporate classrooms: The learning business.* Princeton, NJ: Carnegie Foundation for the Advancement of Teaching.

Evangelauf, J. (1985, October 30). States' spending on colleges rises 19 pct. in 2 years, nears $31-billion for '85-86. *The Chronicle of Higher Education,* p. 1 ff.

Fact-file fall 1985 enrollment. (1986, October 15). *The Chronicle of Higher Education,* p. 42.

Feldman, K. A., & Newcomb, T. M. (1969). *The impact of college on students* (Vol. 2). San Francisco, CA: Jossey-Bass.

Frances, C. (1984, December). 1985: The economic outlook for higher education. *AAHE Bulletin,* p. 3.

Frances, C. (1985, December). 1986: Major trends shaping the outlook for higher education. *AAHE Bulletin,* p. 5.

Friendly, J. (1985, September 24). Budget ax fails to make dent in aid programs for students. *The New York Times,* p. 15.

Glenny, L. A. (1983, July). *Higher education for students: Forecasts of a golden age.* Paper delivered at a seminar sponsored by the Higher Education Steering Committee, University of California, Berkeley, CA.

Goodlad, J. I. (1983). *A place called school: Prospects for the future.* New York: McGraw-Hill.

Hartz, L. (1955). *The liberal tradition in America: An interpretation of American political thoughts since the revolution.* New York: Harcourt Brace.

Higher education funds in President Reagan's fiscal 1987 budget. (1986, February 12). *The Chronicle of Higher Education,* p. 12.

Higher education is a U.S. industry. (1986, July 28). *Higher Education & National Affairs,* p. 3.

Hofstadter, R. (1963). *Anti-intellectualism in American life.* New York: Alfred A. Knopf.

Hofstadter, R., & Metzger, W. P. (1955). *The development of academic freedom in the United States.* New York: Columbia University Press.

Hofstadter, R., & Smith, W. (Eds.). (1961). *American higher education: A documentary history* (Vol. 1). Chicago, IL: University of Chicago Press.

Hyman, H. H., & Wright, C. R. (1979). *Education's lasting influence on values.* Chicago, IL and London: University of Chicago Press.

Hyman, H. H., Wright, C. R., & Reed, J. S. (1975). *The enduring effects of education.* Chicago, IL and London: University of Chicago Press.

Kerr, C. (1980). The Carnegie policy series, 1967-1979: Consensus, approaches, reconsiderations, results. In *The Carnegie Council on policy studies in higher education.* San Francisco, CA: Jossey-Bass.

McConnell, W. R., & Kaufman, N. (1984, January). *High school graduates: Projections for the fifty states (1982-2000).* Boulder, CO: Western Interstate Commission for Higher Education.

Mostly stable: College and university enrollments: 1985-1991. (1987, November 25). *The Chronicle of Higher Education,* p. A29.

Muir, W. K. (1982). *Legislature: California's school for politics.* Chicago, IL: University of Chicago Press.

National Commission on Excellence in Education. (1983). *A nation at risk: The imperative for educational reform.* Washington, DC: U.S. Department of Education.

National Science Foundation. (1985, May 9). Federal academic R&D funds continue

626

strong growth through 1985. *Science Resources Studies Highlights.* Washington, DC: Author.

Newman, F. (1987). *Choosing quality: Reducing conflict between the state and the university.* Denver, CO: Education Commission of the States.

Organization for Economic Co-operation and Development. (1977). *Learning opportunities for adults, general report* (Vol. 1). Paris: Author.

Ottinger, C. A. (Comp.). (1984). *1984-85 fact book.* New York: American Council on Education and Macmillan Publishing Company.

Project PACE. (1984). *Conditions of education in California, 1984* (No. 84-1). Berkeley, CA: University of California.

Plisko, V. W., & Stern, J. D. (Eds.). (1985). *The condition of education, 1985 edition.* Washington, DC: National Center for Education Statistics.

Rudolph, F. (1962). *The American college and university.* New York: Alfred A. Knopf.

Statistics you can use: Growth in nontradi-tional students, 1972 to 1982. (1984, June 18). *Higher Education & National Affairs,* p. 3.

Stember, C. H. (1961). *Education and attitude change.* New York: Institute of Human Relations Press.

Stouffer, S. A. (1955). *Communism, conformity and civil liberties.* Garden City, NY: Doubleday.

Trends in student aid: 1980 to 1986. (1986). Washington, DC: The College Board.

Trow, M. (1975, Winter). The public and private lives of higher education. *Daedalus, 2,* 113-127.

Trow, M. (1979). Aspects of diversity in American higher education. In H. Gans (Ed.), *On the making of Americans: Essays in honor of David Riesman* (pp. 271-290). Philadelphia, PA: University of Pennsylvania Press.

Trow, M. (1985a). Comparative reflections on leadership in higher education. *European Journal of Education, 20,* 143-159.

Trow, M. (1985b). Underprepared students and public research universities. In J. H. Bunzel (Ed.), *Challenge to American schools* (pp. 191-215). New York and Oxford: Oxford University Press.

Trow, M. (1986). The state of higher education in the United States. In W. K. Cummings, E. R. Beauchamp, S. Ichikawa, V. N. Kobayashi, & M. Ushiogi (Eds.), *Educational policies in crisis: Japanese and American perspectives* (pp. 171-194). New York: Praeger Publishers.

Tsukada, M. (1986). A factual overview of education in Japan and the United States. In W. K. Cummings, E. R. Beauchamp, S. Ichikawa, V. N. Kobayashi, & M. Ushiogi (Eds.), *Educational policies in crisis: Japanese and American perspectives* (pp. 96-116). New York: Praeger Publishers.

Williams, G. (1983, November 18). Making sense of statistics. *The Times Higher Education Supplement,* p. 13.

MARTIN TROW *is at the Graduate School of Public Policy and the Center for Studies in Higher Education, University of California at Berkeley, Berkeley, California 94720.*

The G. I. Bill of Rights, 1944

1. Any person who served in the active military or naval service on or after September 16, 1940, and prior to the termination of the present war, and who shall have been discharged or released therefrom under conditions other than dishonorable, and who either shall have served ninety days or more, exclusive of any period he was assigned for a course of education or training under the Army specialized training program or the Navy college training program, which course was a continuation of his civilian course and was pursued to completion, or as a cadet or midshipman at one of the service academies, or shall have been discharged or released from active service by reason of an actual service-incurred injury or disability, shall be eligible for and entitled to receive education or training under this part: *Provided*, That such course shall be initiated not later than four years after either the date of his discharge or the termination of the present war, whichever is the later: *Provided further*, That no such education or training shall be afforded beyond nine years after the termination of the present war.

2. Any such eligible person shall be entitled to education or training at an approved educational or training institution for a period of one year plus the time such person was in the active service on or after September 16, 1940, and before the termination of the war, exclusive of any period he was assigned for a course of education or training under the Army specialized training program or the Navy college training program, which course was a continuation of his civilian course and was pursued to completion, or as a cadet or midshipman at one of the service academies, but in no event shall the total period of education or training exceed four years: *Provided*, That his work continues to be satisfactory throughout the period, according to the regularly prescribed standards and practices of the institution: *Provided further*, That wherever the period of eligibility ends during a quarter or semester and after a major part of such quarter or semester has expired, such period shall be extended to the termination of such unexpired quarter or semester.

3. (*a*) Such person shall be eligible for and entitled to such course of education or training, full time or the equivalent thereof in part-time training, as he may elect, and at any approved educational or training institution at which he chooses to enroll, whether or not located in the State in which he resides, which will accept or retain him as a student or trainee in any field or branch of knowledge which such institution finds him qualified to undertake or pursue: *Provided*, That, for reasons satisfactory to the Administrator, he may change a course of instruction: *And provided further*, That any such course of education or training may be discontinued at any time, if it is found by the Administrator that, according to the regularly prescribed standards and practices of the institution, the conduct or progress of such person is unsatisfactory.

(*b*) Any such eligible person may apply for a short, intensive post-graduate, or training course of less than thirty weeks: *Provided*, That the Administrator shall have the authority to contract with approved institutions for such courses if he finds that the agreed cost of such courses is reasonable and fair: *Provided further*, That (1) the limitation of paragraph 5 shall not prevent the payment of such agreed rates, but there shall be charged against the veteran's period of eligibility the proportion of an ordinary school year which the cost of the course bears to $500, and (2) not in excess of $500 shall be paid for any such course.

(c) Any such eligible person may apply for a course of instruction by correspondence without any subsistence allowance: *Provided*, That the Administrator shall have authority to contract with approved institutions for such courses if he finds that the agreed cost of such courses is reasonable and fair: *Provided further*, (1) That the provisions of paragraph 5 shall not apply to correspondence courses; (2) that one-fourth of the elapsed time in following such course shall be charged against the veteran's period of eligibility; and (3) that the total amount payable for a correspondence course or courses for any veteran shall not exceed $500; *And provided further*, That nothing herein shall be construed to preclude the use of approved correspondence courses as a part of institutional or job training, subject to regulations prescribed by the Administrator.

4. From time to time the Administrator shall secure from the appropriate agency of each State a list of the educational and training institutions (including industrial establishments), within such jurisdiction, which are qualified and equipped to furnish education or training (including apprenticeship, refresher or retraining and institutional on-farm training), which institutions, together with such additional ones as may be recognized and approved by the Administrator, shall be deemed qualified and approved to furnish education or training to such persons as shall enroll under this part: *Provided*, That wherever there are established State apprenticeship agencies expressly charged by State laws to administer apprentice training, whenever possible, the Administrator shall utilize such existing facilities and services in training on the job when such training is of one year's duration or more.

5. The Administrator shall pay to the educational or training institution (including the institution offering institutional on-farm training), for each person enrolled in full time or part time course of education or training, the customary cost of tuition, and such laboratory, library, health, infirmary, and other similar fees as are customarily charged, and may pay for books, supplies, equipment, and other necessary expenses, exclusive of board, lodging, other living expenses, and travel, as are generally required for the successful pursuit and completion of the course by other students in the institution: *Provided*, That in no event shall such payments, with respect to any person, exceed $500 for an ordinary school year unless the veteran elects to have such customary charges paid in excess of such limitation, in which event there shall be charged against his period of eligibility the proportion of an ordinary school year which such excess bears to $500: *Provided further*, That no payments shall be made to institutions, business or other establishments furnishing apprentice training on the job: *And provided further*, That any institution may apply to the Administrator for an adjustment of tuition and the Administrator, if he finds that the customary tuition charges are insufficient to permit the institution to furnish education or training to eligible veterans, or inadequate compensation therefor, may provide for the payment of such fair and reasonable compensation as will not exceed the estimated cost of teaching personnel and supplies for instruction; and may in like manner readjust such payments from time to time.

6. While enrolled in and pursuing a course under this part, (including an institutional on-farm training course) such person, upon application to the Administrator, shall be paid a subsistence allowance of $65 per month, if without a dependent or dependents, or $90 per month, if he has a dependent or dependents, including regular holidays and leave not exceeding thirty days in a calendar year: Except, That (1) while so enrolled and pursuing a course of full-time institutional training, such person, shall be paid a subsistence allowance of $75 per month, if without a dependent or dependents, or $105 per month if he has one dependent or $120 per month if he has more than one dependent, and (2) while so enrolled and pursuing a course of part-time institutional training, including a course of institutional on-farm training, or other combination course, such person shall be paid, subject to the limitations of this paragraph, additional subsistence allowance in an amount bearing the same relation to the difference between the basic rates and the increased rates provided in (1) hereof as the institutional training part of such course bears to a course of full-time institutional training. Such person attending a course on a part-time basis, and such person receiving compensation for

productive labor whether performed as part of his apprentice or other training on the job at institutions, business or other establishments, or otherwise, shall be entitled to receive such lesser sums, if any, as subsistence or dependency allowances as may be determined by the Administrator: *Provided,* That in no event shall the rate of such allowance plus the compensation received exceed $210 per month for a veteran without a dependent, or $270 per month for a veteran with one dependent, or $290 for a veteran with two or more dependents: *Provided further,* That only so much of the compensation as is derived from productive labor based on the standard work-week for the particular trade or industry, exclusive of overtime, shall be considered in computing the rate of allowances payable under this paragraph.

7. Any such person eligible for the benefits of this part, who is also eligible for the benefit of Part VII, may elect either benefit or may be provided an approved combination of such courses: *Provided,* That the total period of any such combined courses shall not exceed the maximum period or limitations under the part affording the greater period of eligibility.

Report of the President's Commision on Higher Education for Democracy, 1947

The President's Commission on Higher Education has been charged with the task of defining the responsibilities of colleges and universities in American democracy and in international affairs—and, more specifically, with reexamining the objectives, methods, and facilities of higher education in the United States in the light of the social role it has to play.

The colleges and universities themselves had begun this process of reexamination and reappraisal before the outbreak of World War II. For many years they had been healthily dissatisfied with their own accomplishments, significant though these have been. Educational leaders were troubled by an uneasy sense of shortcoming. They felt that somehow the colleges had not kept pace with changing social conditions, that the programs of higher education would have to be repatterned if they were to prepare youth to live satisfyingly and effectively in contemporary society.

One factor contributing to this sense of inadequacy has been the steadily increasing number of young people who seek a college education. As the national economy became industrialized and more complex, as production increased and national resources multiplied, the American people came in ever greater numbers to feel the need of higher education for their children. More and more American youth attended colleges and universities, but resources and equipment and curriculum did not keep pace with the growing enrollment or with the increasing diversity of needs and interests among the students.

World War II brought a temporary falling off in enrollment, but with the war's end and the enactment of Public Laws 16 and 346, the "Veterans' Rehabilitation Act," and "The G. I. Bill of Rights," the acceleration has resumed. The increase in numbers is far beyond the capacity of higher education in teachers, in buildings, and in equipment. Moreover, the number of veterans availing themselves of veterans' educational benefits falls short of the numbers that records of military personnel show could benefit from higher education. Statistics reveal that a doubling of the 1947–48 enrollment in colleges and universities will be entirely possible within 10 to 15 years, if facilities and financial means are provided.

This tendency of the American people to seek higher education in ever greater numbers has grown concurrently with an increasingly critical need for such education. To this need several developments have contributed:

(a) Science and invention have diversified natural resources, have multiplied new devices and techniques of production. These have altered in radical ways the interpersonal and intergroup relations of Americans in their work, in their play, and in their duties as citizens. As a consequence, new skills and greater maturity are required of youth as they enter upon their adult roles. And the increasing complexity that technological progress has brought to our society has made a broader understanding of social processes and problems essential for effective living.

(b) The people of America are drawn from the peoples of the entire world. They live in contrasting regions. They are of different occupations, diverse faiths, divergent cultural backgrounds, and varied interests. The American Nation is not only a union of 48 different States; it is also a union of an indefinite number of diverse groups of varying size. Of and among these diversities our free society seeks to create a dynamic unity. Where there is economic, cultural, or religious tension, we undertake to effect democratic reconciliation, so as to make of the national life one continuous process of interpersonal, intervocational, and intercultural cooperation.

(c) With World War II and its conclusion has come a fundamental shift in the orientation of American foreign policy. Owing to the inescapable pressure of events, the Nation's traditional isolationism has been displaced by a new sense of responsibility in world affairs. The need for maintaining our democracy at peace with the rest of the world has compelled our initiative in the formation of the United Nations, and America's role in this and other agencies of international cooperation requires of our citizens a knowledge of other peoples—of their political and economic systems, their social and cultural institutions—such as has not hitherto been so urgent.

(d) The coming of the atomic age, with its ambivalent promise of tremendous good or tremendous evil for mankind, has intensified the uncertainties of the future. It has deepened and broadened the responsibilities of higher education for anticipating and preparing for the social and economic changes that will come with the application of atomic energy to industrial uses. At the same time it has underscored the need for education and research for the self-protection of our democracy, for demonstrating the merits of our way of life to other peoples.

Thus American colleges and universities face the need both for improving the performance of their traditional tasks and for assuming the new tasks created for them by the new internal conditions and external relations under which the American people are striving to live and to grow as a free people.

. . .

Education for a Better Nation and a Better World

Education is an institution of every civilized society, but the purposes of education are not the same in all societies. An educational system finds its guiding principles and ultimate goals in the aims and philosophy of the social order in which it functions. The two predominant types of society in the world today are the democratic and the authoritarian, and the social role of education is very different in the two systems.

American society is a democracy: that is, its folkways and institutions, its arts and sciences and religions are based on the principle of equal freedom and equal rights for all its members, regardless of race, faith, sex, occupation, or economic status. The law of the land, providing equal justice for the poor as well as the rich, for the weak as well as the strong, is one instrument by which a democratic society establishes, maintains, and protects this equality among different persons and groups. The other instrument is education, which, as all the leaders in the making of democracy have pointed out again and again, is necessary to give effect to the equality prescribed by law.

THE ROLE OF EDUCATION

It is a commonplace of the democratic faith that education is indispensable to the maintenance and growth of freedom of thought, faith, enterprise, and association. Thus the social role of education in a democratic society is at once to insure equal liberty and equal opportunity to differing individuals and groups, and to enable the citizens to understand, appraise, and redirect forces, men, and events as these tend to strengthen or to weaken their liberties.

In performing this role, education will necessarily vary its means and methods to fit the diversity of its constituency, but it will achieve its ends more successfully if its programs and policies grow out of and are relevant to the characteristics and needs of contemporary society. Effective democratic education will deal directly with current problems.

This is not to say that education should neglect the past—only that it should not get lost in the past. No one would deny that a study of man's history can contribute immeasurably to understanding and managing the present. But to assume that all we need do is apply to present and future problems "eternal" truths revealed in earlier ages is likely to stifle creative imagination and intellectual daring. Such assumption may blind us to new problems and the possible need for new solutions. It is wisdom in education to use the past selectively and critically, in order to illumine the pressing problems of the present.

At the same time education is the making of the future. Its role in a democratic society is that of critic and leader as well as servant; its task is not merely to meet the demands of the present but to alter those demands if necessary, so as to keep them always suited to democratic ideals. Perhaps its most important role is to serve as an instrument of social transition, and its responsibilities are defined in terms of the kind of civilization society hopes to build. If its adjustments to present needs are not to be mere fortuitous improvisations, those who formulate its policies and programs must have a vision of the Nation and the world we want—to give a sense of direction to their choices among alternatives.

What America needs today, then, is "a schooling better aware of its aims." Our colleges need to see clearly what it is they are trying to accomplish. The efforts of individual institutions, local communities, the several States, the educational foundations and associations, and the Federal Government will all be more effective if they are directed toward the same general ends.

In the future as in the past, American higher education will embody the principle of diversity in unity: each institution, State, or other agency will continue to make its own contribution in its own way. But educational leaders should try to agree on certain common objectives that can serve as a stimulus and guide to individual decision and action.

A TIME OF CRISIS

It is essential today that education come decisively to grips with the world-wide crisis of mankind. This is no careless or uncritical use of words. No thinking person doubts that we are living in a decisive moment of human history.

Atomic scientists are doing their utmost to make us realize how easily and quickly a world catastrophe may come. They know the fearful power for destruction possessed by the weapons their knowledge and skill have fashioned. They know that the scientific principles on which these weapons are based are no secret to the scientists of other nations, and that America's monopoly of the engineering processes involved in the manufacture of atom bombs is not likely to last many years. And to the horror of atomic weapons, biological and chemical instruments of destruction are now being added.

But disaster is not inevitable. The release of atomic energy that has brought man within sight of world devastation has just as truly brought him the promise of a brighter future. The potentialities of atomic power are as great for human betterment as for human annihilation. Man can choose which he will have.

The possibility of this choice is the supreme fact of our day, and it will necessarily influence the ordering of educational priorities. We have a big job of reeducation to do. Nothing less than a complete reorientation of our thinking will suffice if mankind is to survive and move on to higher levels.

In a real sense the future of our civilization depends on the direction education takes, not just in the distant future, but in the days immediately ahead.

This crisis is admittedly world-wide. All nations need reeducation to meet it. But this fact does not lessen the obligation of colleges and universities to undertake the task in the United States. On the contrary, our new position in international affairs increases the obligation. We can do something about the problem in our own country and in occupied areas, and hope that by so doing we will win the friendly cooperation of other nations.

The fundamental goal of the United States in its administration of occupied areas must be the reeducation of the populations to the individual responsibilities of democracy. Such reeducation calls for the immediate removal of authoritarian barriers to democratic education, and inculcation of democratic ideals and principles through the guidance, example, and wisdom of United States occupation forces. The primacy of the objective of reeducation, however, appears too often to have been lost sight of in the press of day-to-day administrative problems. Yet every contact by Americans with Germans or Japanese either strengthens or retards the achievement of the goal. Evidence reaching this Commission indicates that while many specific existing barriers to democratic reform have been removed, new obstacles are being created daily by inadequacies of educational personnel and policy. Cognizant of the great responsibility of American education to promote democratic ideals in occupied areas, this Commission recommends the formation of a special committee to appraise progress and offer advice to the Departments of State and National Defense on educational policy and administration in occupied areas.

The schools and colleges are not solely or even mainly to blame for the situation in which we find ourselves, or that the responsibility for resolving the crisis is not or can not be entirely theirs. But the scientific knowledge and technical skills that have made atomic and bacteriological warfare possible are the products of education and research, and higher education must share proportionately in the task of forging social and political defenses against obliteration. The indirect way toward some longer view and superficial curricular tinkering can no longer serve. The measures higher education takes will have to match in boldness and vision the magnitude of the problem.

In the light of this situation, the President's Commission on Higher Education has attempted to select, from among the principal goals for higher education, those which should come first in our time. They are to bring to all the people of the Nation:

Education for a fuller realization of democracy in every phase of living.

Education directly and explicitly for international understanding and cooperation.

Education for the application of creative imagination and trained intelligence to the solution of social problems and to the administration of public affairs.

. . .

TOWARD THE SOLUTION OF SOCIAL PROBLEMS

It is essential that we apply our trained intelligence and creative imagination, our scientific methods of investigation, our skill in invention and adaptation, as fully to the problems of human association as to the extension of knowledge about the physical world. This is what is meant by the development of *social invention* and *social technology*.

Human Relations

We have worked wonders by the application of technology to the problems of our physical environment, but we have scarcely touched the fringes of its possibilities in the realm of human relations. In fact, we hardly recognize the existence of inventiveness in the social sphere. Yet the United Nations and UNESCO are inventions no less than the atom bomb, and they are just as capable of technical improvement.

As a people, Americans have come to appreciate the need for experimental research and technical training in the physical and natural sciences, but we tend still to think that good will, tolerance, and the cooperative spirit are all we need to make society function. These attitudes are vitally necessary; we shall make little progress without them; and, as has already been emphasized, education should concern itself with developing them. But alone they are not enough. Social techniques and social mechanisms must be found to express and implement them.

One often hears or reads, for example, puzzled questioning as to why man's intense desire for security and his fear of another war have produced so little actual progress toward peace in the world. But man's fear of smallpox did not eliminate that scourge until medical science and technology had invented and improved the technique of vaccination. Nor did man's desire to fly enable him to accomplish the feat until scientific ingenuity and engineering skill had produced the necessary mechanism and had trained men to use it.

In comparable fashion it will take social science and social engineering to solve the problems of human relations. Our people must learn to respect the need for special knowledge and technical training in this field as they have come to defer to the expert in physics, chemistry, medicine, and other sciences. Relieving the tensions that produce war, for example, will require methods as specific and as technical as are those of aeronautics or electronics.

The development of social technology is an imperative today because of the remarkable advances we have made in natural science. Scientific discoveries and their technological application have altered our physical environment profoundly in the space of only a few generations, but our social institutions have not kept pace with the changes—although by applying the methods of science we have achieved marked success in some forms of social organization.

Understanding of Self

Man's capacity to subdue nature to his will has raced far ahead of his ability to understand himself or to reconstruct his institutions. This is true in spite of the fact that higher education itself traditionally has followed the Socratic prescription of putting the study of man first. We have grown strong in the mastery of our physical world, but by no means equally strong in the ability to manage and direct the social forces that shape our lives.

The gap between our scientific know-how and our personal and social wisdom has been growing steadily through the years, until now with the release of atomic energy it has become too wide to be safe.

It is imperative that we find not only the will but the ways and means to reorder our lives and our institutions so as to make science and technology contribute to man's well-being rather than to his destruction. We need to experiment boldly in the whole area of human relations, seeking to modify existing institutions and to discover new workable patterns of association. We must bring our social skills quickly abreast of our skills in natural science.

The irony is that the very developments which have precipitated this critical situation seem likely to aggravate it. The spectacular achievements of natural science, especially during World War II, are certain to bring increased pressure for scientific advance. Already it is suggested that "scientific preeminence will be the keystone of national security." But will it? Can we depend solely, or even primarily, on natural science for our national safety?

In the recent war the margin of our scientific and technical superiority over our enemies was dangerously narrow at times, and the scientists themselves are warning us at every opportunity that they can provide no defense against the new weapons. It is they who are proclaiming most vigorously that this defense can be found only in the realm of social and political organization on a world-wide scale. To quote Albert Einstein for one: "Being an ingenious people, Americans find it hard to believe there is no foreseeable defense against atomic bombs. But this is a basic fact. Scientists do not even know of any field which promises us any hope of adequate defense. . . . Our defense is in international law and order."

Leadership Needed

Upon leadership in social invention, then, as much as upon superiority in natural science and engineering, rests our hope of national survival. Unfortunately, the uneasy state of the world leads us to discuss these matters in terms of national defense. The ultimate justification for progress in science, social and natural, is the contribution it can make to the welfare of people everywhere. Continued advance in natural science will give strength to democracy in the eyes of other peoples because of the improvement it makes possible in our standard of living, and the development of a more effective social science will contribute to a fuller realization of the democratic principles of justice and freedom for all.

The colleges and universities, the philanthropic foundations, and the Federal Government should not be tempted by the prestige of natural science and its immediately tangible results into giving it a disproportionate emphasis in research budgets or in teaching programs. It is the peculiar responsibility of the colleges to train personnel and inaugurate extensive programs of research in social science and technology. To the extent that they have neglected this function in the past they should concentrate upon it in the decades just ahead.

We cannot pin our faith on social drift, hoping that if each individual pursues his own ends with intelligence and good will, things will somehow right themselves. We cannot rely on the processes of automatic adjustment. We must develop a positive social policy, both within and among nations. We must plan, with intelligence and imagination, the course we are to take toward the kind of tomorrow we want.

IT CAN BE DONE

In emphasizing education for democracy, for international understanding, and for more effective social science as objectives for higher education in America today, the President's Commission has no desire to suggest limitations on progress and experimentation in other directions. Diversity in purpose is a potential source of strength in democratic institutions. From the innovative and experimental approach of today may well come the general objective of tomorrow.

These three goals are stated as the minimum essentials of the program to be developed in all institutions of higher education. And they pose a truly staggering job for the colleges and universities. But it can be done. The necessary intelligence and ability exist. What we need is awareness of the urgency of the task, the will and the courage to tackle it, and a wholehearted commitment to its successful performance.

But to delay is to fail. Colleges must accelerate the normally slow rate of social change which the educational system reflects; we need to find ways quickly or making the understanding and vision of our most farsighted and sensitive citizens the common possession of all our people.

To this end the educational task is partly a matter of the numbers to be educated and partly one of the kind of education that is to be provided. We shall have to educate more of our people at each level of the educational program, and we shall have to devise patterns of education that will prepare them more effectively than in the past for responsible roles in modern society.

These two aspects of the task ahead are the subjects of the succeeding chapters of this volume.

.   .   .

Education for All

Education is by far the biggest and the most hopeful of the Nation's enterprises. Long ago our people recognized that education for all is not only democracy's obligation but its necessity. Education is the foundation of democratic liberties. Without an educated citizenry alert to preserve and extend freedom, it would not long endure.

Accepting this truth, the United States has devoted many of its best minds and billions of its wealth to the development and maintenance of an extensive system of free public schools, and through the years the level of schooling attained by more and more of our people has steadily risen.

RECORD OF GROWTH

The expansion of the American educational enterprise since the turn of the century has been phenomenal. The 700,000 enrollment in high schools in the school year 1900 was equal to only 11 percent of the youth of usual high-school age, 14 through 17 years old. This increased in 1940 to over 7,000,000 students representing 73 percent of the youth.

Almost as spectacular has been the increase in college attendance. In 1900 fewer than 250,000 students, only 4 percent of the population 18 through 21 years of age, were enrolled in institutions of higher education. By 1940 the enrollment had risen to 1,500,000 students, equal to a little less than 16 percent of the 18–21 year olds. In 1947, enrollments jumped to the theretofore unprecedented peak of 2,354,000 although approximately 1,000,000 of the students were veterans, older than the usual college age because World War II had deferred their education. The situation in the fall of 1947 gives every indication that the school year 1948 will witness even larger enrollments. (See Chart 1, "Growth of College Population.")

This record of growth is encouraging, but we are forced to admit nonetheless that the educational attainments of the American people are still substantially below what is necessary either for effective individual living or for the welfare of our society.

According to the U. S. Bureau of the Census, almost 17,000,000 men and women over 19 years of age in 1947 had stopped their schooling at the sixth grade or less. Of these, 9,000,000 had never attended school or had stopped their schooling before completing the fifth

Chart 1

GROWTH OF COLLEGE POPULATION
IN THE UNITED STATES

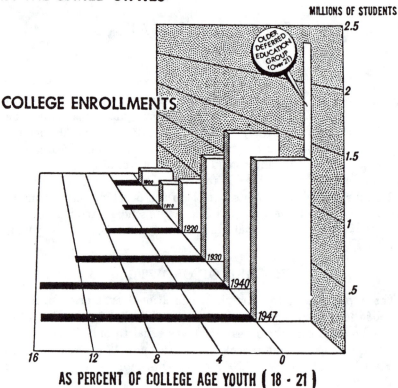

Resident enrollments from U. S. Office of Education. Population data from U. S. Bureau of the Census; that for 1947 adjusted to exclude numbers in the armed forces.

grade. In 1947, about 1,600,000 or 19 percent of our high-school-age boys and girls were not attending any kind of school, and over two-thirds of the 18- and 19-year-old youths were not in school.

These are disturbing facts. They represent a sobering failure to reach the educational goals implicit in the democratic creed, and they are indefensible in a society so richly endowed with material resources as our own. We cannot allow so many of our people to remain so ill equipped either as human beings or as citizens of a democracy.

Great as the total American expenditure for education may seem, we have not been devoting any really appreciable part of our vast wealth to higher education. As table 1 shows, even though in the last 15 years our annual budget for education has risen in number of dollars, it has actually declined in relation to our increasing economic productivity.

The $1,000,000,000 we have put into our colleges and universities in 1947 was less than one-half of 1 percent of the gross national product, which is the market value of all the goods and services produced in the country in that year.

TABLE 1.—*Direct Cost of Higher Education and Its Relation to the Gross National Product*

Fiscal year	Amount (in millions)[1]	Proportion of gross national product (percent)[2]
1932	$421	0. 63
1940	522	. 55
1947	1. 005	. 46

[1] Source: General and educational expenditures, not including capital expansion, as reported by U. S. Office of Education.
[2] Source of gross national product: U. S. Bureau of Foreign and Domestic Commerce.

BARRIERS TO EQUAL OPPORTUNITY

One of the gravest charges to which American society is subject is that of failing to provide a reasonable equality of educational opportunity for its youth. For the great majority of our boys and girls, the kind and amount of education they may hope to attain depends, not on their own abilities, but on the family or community into which they happened to be born or, worse still, on the color of their skin or the religion of their parents.

Economic Barriers

The old, comfortable idea that "any boy can get a college education who has it in him" simply is not true. Low family income, together with the rising costs of education, constitutes an almost impassable barrier to college education for many young people. For some, in fact, the barrier is raised so early in life that it prevents them from attending high school even when free public high schools exist near their homes.

Despite the upward trend in average per capita income for the past century and more, the earnings of a large part of our population are still too low to provide anything but the barest necessities of physical life. It is a distressing fact that in 1945, when the total national income was far greater than in any previous period in our history, half of the children under 18 were growing up in families which had a cash income of $2,530 or less. The educational significance of these facts is heightened by the relationship that exists between income and birth rate. Fertility is highest in the families with lowest incomes.

In the elementary and secondary schools the effects of these economic conditions are overcome to a considerable extent, though not entirely, by the fact that education is free and at certain ages is compulsory. But this does not hold true at the college level. For a number of years the tendency has been for the college student to bear an increasing share of the cost of his own education. Even in State-supported institutions we have been moving away from the principle of free education to a much greater degree than is commonly supposed.

Under the pressure of rising costs and of a relative lessening of public support, the colleges and universities are having to depend more and more on tuition fees to meet their budgets. As a result, on the average, tuition rates rose about 30 percent from 1939 to 1947.

Nor are tuition costs the whole of it. There are not enough colleges and universities in the country, and they are not distributed evenly enough to bring them within reach of all young people. Relatively few students can attend college in their home communities. So to the expense of a college education for most youth must be added transportation and living costs—by no means a small item.

This economic factor explains in large part why the father's occupation has been found in many studies to rank so high as a determining factor in a young person's college expectancy. A farm laborer earns less than a banker or a doctor, for instance, and so is less able to afford the costs of higher education for his children. The children, moreover, have less inducement to seek a college education because of their family background. In some social circles a college education is often considered a luxury which can be done without, something desirable perhaps, "but not for the likes of us."

The importance of economic barriers to post-high school education lies in the fact that there is little if any relationship between the ability to benefit from a college education and the ability to pay for it. Studies discussed in the volume of this Commission's report, "Equalizing and Expanding Individual Opportunity," show that among children of equally high ability those with fathers in higher-income occupations had greater probability of attending college.

By allowing the opportunity for higher education to depend so largely on the individual's economic status, we are not only denying to millions of young people the chance in life to which they are entitled; we are also depriving the Nation of a vast amount of potential leadership and potential social competence which it sorely needs.

. . .

Barrier of a Restricted Curriculum

We shall be denying educational opportunity to many young people as long as we maintain the present orientation of higher education toward verbal skills and intellectual interests. Many young people have abilities of a different kind, and they cannot receive "education commensurate with their native capacities" in colleges and universities that recognize only one kind of educable intelligence.

Traditionally the colleges have sifted out as their special clientele persons possessing verbal aptitudes and a capacity for grasping abstractions. But many other aptitudes—such as social sensitivity and versatility, artistic ability, motor skill and dexterity, and mechanical aptitude and ingenuity—also should be cultivated in a society depending, as ours does, on the minute division of labor and at the same time upon the orchestration of an enormous variety of talents.

If the colleges are to educate the great body of American youth, they must provide programs for the development of other abilities than those involved in academic aptitude, and they cannot continue to concentrate on students with one type of intelligence to the neglect of youth with other talents.

Racial and Religious Barriers

The outstanding example of these barriers to equal opportunity, of course, is the disadvantages suffered by our Negro citizens. The low educational attainments of Negro adults reflect the cumulative effects of a long period of unequal opportunity. In 1940 the schooling of the Negro was significantly below that of whites at every level from the first grade through college. At the college level, the difference is marked; 11 percent of the white population 20 years of age and over had completed at least 1 year of college and almost 5 percent had finished 4 years; whereas for the nonwhites (over 95 percent of whom are Negroes) only a little more than 3 percent had completed at least 1 year of college and less than 1½ percent had completed a full course.

Gains Have Been Made. Noteworthy advances have been made toward eliminating the racial inequalities which in large measure are responsible for this low level of educational achievement by the Negroes. Between 1900 and 1940 the percentage of Negroes 5 to 20 years of age attending school rose from 31.0 percent to 64.4 percent. And the percentage of Negro youth 15 to 20 years old attending school increased from 17.5 in 1900 to 33.8 in 1940. That differentials still persist, however, is shown in table 5.

TABLE 5.—*Proportion of Young Persons Attending School, by Age and Color: April 1947* [1]

Age	Attending school	
	White	Nonwhites (about 95 percent Negro)
	Percent	*Percent*
6 years of age	67.8	63.4
7 to 9 years of age	97.1	89.2
10 to 13 years of age	98.2	93.7
14 to 17 years of age	82.5	71.9
18 to 19 years of age	28.2	24.2
20 to 24 years of age	11.3	6.7

[1] Source: U. S. Bureau of the Census.

Institutions which accept both Negro and non-Negro students do not maintain separate record systems for Negroes, and so data on enrollment of Negroes are restricted to those institutions—usually located in the South—which accept only Negro students. In recent years, since 1932, these institutions have almost tripled their enrollments whereas the institutions for whites or which are unsegregated only about doubled theirs:

TABLE 6.—*Enrollment of Institutions of Higher Education and Index of Change* [1]

Year	Enrollments in institutions accepting			
	Negroes only		All other	
	Number	Index of change (1932=100)	Number	Index of change (1932=100)
1932	21,880	100	1,132,237	100
1936	32,628	149	1,175,599	104
1940	41,839	191	1,452,364	128
1947 [2]	63,500	290	2,290,500	202

[1] Source is resident enrollment as reported by U. S. Office of Education.
[2] Estimated.

Inequalities Remain. But the numbers enrolled in school do not tell the whole story. Marked as has been the progress in Negro education in recent years, it cannot obscure the very great differences which still persist in educational opportunities afforded the Negro and the non-Negro.

In 17 States and the District of Columbia, segregation of the Negroes in education is established by law.[1] In the *Gaines* decision, the U. S. Supreme Court ruled that "if a State furnishes higher education to white residents, it is bound to furnish [within the State] substantially equal advantages to Negro students". Although segregation may not legally mean discrimination as to the quality of the facilities it usually does so in fact. The schools maintained for the Negroes are commonly much inferior to those for the whites. The Negro schools are financed at a pitifully low level, they are often housed in buildings wholly inadequate for the purpose, and many of the teachers are sorely in need of more education themselves. Library facilities are generally poor or lacking altogether, and professional supervision is more a name than a reality.

These facts are supported strongly by a recent study in the District of Columbia. The District's Superintendent of Schools in his 1946–47 report to the Board of Education states that the student-teacher ratios in the schools for Negroes were significantly and consistently higher than those for non-Negroes—from the kindergartens through the teachers' colleges.

Segregation lessens the quality of education for the whites as well. To maintain two school systems side by side—duplicating even inadequately the buildings, equipment, and teaching personnel—means that neither can be of the quality that would be possible if all the available resources were devoted to one system, especially not when the States least able financially to support an adequate educational program for their youth are the very ones that are trying to carry a double load.

It must not be supposed that Negro youth living in States in which segregation is not legalized are given the same opportunities as white youth. In these areas economic and social discrimination of various sorts often operates to produce segregation in certain neighborhoods, which are frequently characterized by poorer school buildings, less equipment and less able teachers.

Equality of educational opportunity is not achieved by the mere physical existence of schools; it involves also the quality of teaching and learning that takes place in them.

The Quota System. At the college level a different form of discrimination is commonly practiced. *Many colleges and universities, especially in their professional schools, maintain a selective quota system for admission, under which the chance to learn, and thereby to become more useful citizens, is denied to certain minorities, particularly to Negroes and Jews.*

---

[1] In the case of *Mendez* v. *Westminster School District*, the segregation of students of Mexican ancestry in the Westminster, Calif., school district, on the alleged grounds that because of their ancestry such students have language difficulties, was held illegal. The U. S. district court which heard the case held that segregation is unconstitutional under the Federal Constitution. On appeal by the Westminster school district, the U. S. circuit court of appeals limited its affirmance of the district court's decision by holding that the specific statutes involved were illegal under the California law.

This practice is a violation of a major American principle and is contributing to the growing tension in one of the crucial areas of our democracy.

The quota, or *numerous clausus*, is certainly un-American. It is European in origin and application, and we have lately witnessed on that continent the horrors to which, in its logical extension, it can lead. To insist that specialists in any field shall be limited by ethnic quotas is to assume that the Nation is composed of separate and self-sufficient ethnic groups and this assumption America has never made except in the case of its Negro population, where the result is one of the plainest inconsistencies with our national ideal.

The quota system denies the basic American belief that intelligence and ability are present in all ethnic groups, that men of all religious and racial origins should have equal opportunity to fit themselves for contributing to the common life.

Moreover, since the quota system is never applied to all groups in the Nation's population, but only to certain ones, we are forced to conclude that the arguments advanced to justify it are nothing more than rationalizations to cover either convenience or the disposition to discriminate. The quota system cannot be justified on any grounds compatible with democratic principles.

Consequences of Inequalities of Opportunity

These various barriers to educational opportunity involve grave consequences both for the individual and for society.

From the viewpoint of the individual they are denying to millions of young people what the democratic creed assumes to be their birthright: an equal chance with all others to make the most of their native abilities. From the viewpoint of society the barriers mean that far too few of our young people are getting enough preparation for assuming the personal, social, and civic responsibilities of adults living in a democratic society.

It is especially serious that not more of our most talented young people continue their schooling beyond high school in this day when the complexity of life and of our social problems means that we need desperately every bit of trained intelligence we can assemble. The present state of affairs is resulting in far too great a loss of talent—our most precious natural resource in a democracy.

In a country as vast as the United States, with all its regional differences in cultural patterns and economic resources, absolute equality of educational opportunity perhaps may not be reasonably expected. But today the differences that do exist are so great as to compel immediate action.

In communities where the birth rate is low, where the burden of caring for the nurture and education of the oncoming generation is relatively light, where the level of living is high, the advantages of education are extended to youth on more nearly equal terms. But in communities where the birth rate is high, where the economic structure is weak, where the level of living is low, where community and family resources contribute least to intellectual growth, there we support education in niggardly fashion, though at great effort.

If over the years we continue to draw the population reserves of the Nation from the most underprivileged areas and families and fail to make good the deficit by adequate educational opportunities, we shall be following a course that is sure to prove disastrous to the level of our culture and to the whole fabric of our democratic institutions.

We have proclaimed our faith in education as a means of equalizing the conditions of men. But there is grave danger that our present policy will make it an instrument for creating the very inequalities it was designed to prevent. If the ladder of educational opportunity rises high at the doors of some youth and scarcely rises at all at the doors of others, while at the same time formal education is made a prerequisite to occupational and social advance, then education may become the means, not of eliminating race and class distinctions, but of deepening and solidifying them.

It is obvious, then, that free and universal access to education, in terms of the interest, ability, and need of the student, must be a major goal in American education.

TOWARD EQUALIZING OPPORTUNITY

The American people should set as their ultimate goal an educational system in which at no level—high school, college, graduate school, or professional school—will a qualified individual in any part of the country encounter an insuperable economic barrier to the attainment of the kind of education suited to his aptitudes and interests.

This means that we shall aim at making higher education equally available to all young people, as we now do education in the elementary and high schools, to the extent that their capacity warrants a further social investment in their training.

Obviously this desirable realization of our ideal of equal educational opportunity cannot be attained immediately. But if we move toward it as fast as our economic resources permit, it should not lie too far in the future. Technological advances, that are already resulting in phenomenal increases in productivity per worker, promise us a degree of economic well-being that would have seemed wholly Utopian to our fathers. With wise management of our economy, we shall almost certainly be able to support education at all levels far more adequately in the future than we could in the past.

The Commission recommends that steps be taken to reach the following objectives without delay:

1. **High school education must be improved and should be provided for all normal youth.**

This is a minimum essential. We cannot safely permit any of our citizens for any reason other than incapacity, to stop short of a high school education or its equivalent. To achieve the purpose of such education, however, it must be improved in facilities and in the diversity of its curriculum. Better high school education is essential, both to raise the caliber of students entering college and to provide the best training possible for those who end their formal education with the twelfth grade.

2. **The time has come to make education through the fourteenth grade available in the same way that high school education is now available.**

This means that tuition-free education should be available in public institutions to all youth for the traditional freshman and sophomore years or for the traditional 2-year junior college course.

To achieve this, it will be necessary to develop much more extensively than at present such opportunities as are now provided in local communities by the 2-year junior college, community institute, community college, or institute of arts and sciences. The name used does not matter, though community college seems to describe these schools best; the important thing is that the services they perform be recognized and vastly extended.

Such institutions make post-high-school education available to a much larger percentage of young people than otherwise could afford it. Indeed, as discussed in the volume of this Commission's report, "Organizing Higher Education," such community colleges probably will have to carry a large part of the responsibility for expanding opportunities in higher education.

3. The time has come to provide financial assistance to competent students in the tenth through fourteenth grades who would not be able to continue their education without such assistance.

Tuition costs are not the major economic barrier to education, especially in college. Costs of supplies, board, and room, and other living needs are great. Even many high-school students are unable to continue in school because of these costs.

Arrangements must be made, therefore, to provide additional financial assistance for worthy students who need it if they are to remain in school. Only in this way can we counteract the effect of family incomes so low that even tuition-free schooling is a financial impossibility for their children. Only in this way can we make sure that all who are to participate in democracy are adequately prepared to do so.

4. The time has come to reverse the present tendency of increasing tuition and other student fees in the senior college beyond the fourteenth year, and in both graduate and professional schools, by lowering tuition costs in publicly controlled colleges and by aiding deserving students through inaugurating a program of scholarships and fellowships.

Only in this way can we be sure that economic and social barriers will not prevent the realization of the promise that lies in our most gifted youth. Only in this way can we be certain of developing ror the common good all the potential leadership our society produces, no matter in what social or economic stratum it appears.

5. The time has come to expand considerably our program of adult education, and to make more of it the responsibility of our colleges and universities.

The crisis of the time and the rapidly changing conditions under which we live make it especially necessary that we provide a continuing and effective educational program for adults as well as youth. We can in this way, perhaps, make up some of the educational deficiencies of the past, and also in a measure counteract the pressures and distractions of adult life that all too often make the end of formal schooling the end of education too.

6. The time has come to make public education at all levels equally accessible to all, without regard to race, creed, sex or national origin.

If education is to make the attainment of a more perfect democracy one of its major goals, it is imperative that it extend its benefits to all on equal terms. It must renounce the practices of discrimination and segregation in educational institutions as contrary to the spirit of democracy. Educational leaders and institutions should take positive steps to overcome the conditions which at present obstruct free and equal access to educational opportunities. Educational programs everywhere should be aimed at undermining and eventually eliminating the attitudes that are responsible for discrimination and segregation—at creating instead attitudes that will make education freely available to all.[2]

NUMBER WHO SHOULD RECEIVE HIGHER EDUCATION

Achieving these immediate objectives necessarily will require a tremendous expansion of our educational enterprise at the college level.

It will be noted that many of the Commission's projects focus upon the year 1960. There are several important reasons why the Commission has chosen to look this far ahead. First of all, in the President's letter of appointment, the Commission was asked to direct its energies toward the investigation of long-term policy issues in American higher education. The Commission itself selected the terminal date of 1960 since it was felt that manageable data could be procured for studies up to this point. The basic consideration of population data weighed heavily in the selection. Individuals who will be enrolled in colleges in 1960 through 1964 have already been born, and thus the Commission has a tangible figure with which to make its projections.

The Commission believes that in 1960 a minimum of 4,600,000 young people should be enrolled in nonprofit institutions for education beyond the traditional twelfth grade. Of this total number, 2,500,000 should be in the thirteenth and fourteenth grades (junior college level); 1,500,000 in the fifteenth and sixteenth grades (senior college level); and 600,000 in graduate and professional schools beyond the first degree.

In thus appraising future enrollment in institutions of post-high school education, this Commission has not sought to project the future on the basis of the past nor to predict annual enrollments over the period 1948 to 1960. It frankly recognizes that such a forecast would be subject to unpredictable world-wide social and economic conditions.

. . .

Education for Free Men

American colleges and universities have assumed a huge task in the last half century. To have opened their doors for so many of our youth was difficult enough; to have done so at a time when the complexity of society was increasing rapidly and its pattern was shifting, so that the ends of education itself were subject to continual revision, was to attempt the nearly impossible. The wonder is, not that the colleges have fallen short in some respects, but that they have achieved so considerable a degree of success.

This is no cause for complacency, however. If still greater expansion in number of students is to be undertaken in a period of still greater uncertainty, higher education must act quickly to bring its policies and programs more closely into line with the social purposes it professes to serve.

THE NEED FOR GENERAL EDUCATION

Present college programs are not contributing adequately to the quality of students' adult lives either as workers or as citizens. This is true in large part because the unity of liberal education has been splintered by overspecialization.

For half a century and more the curriculum of the liberal arts college has been expanding and disintegrating to an astounding degree. The number of courses has so multiplied that no student could take all of them, or even a majority of them, in a lifetime. In one small midwestern college, for example, the number of courses offered increased from 67 in 1900 to 296 in 1930. During the same period the liberal arts college of one of the great private universities lengthened its list of courses from 960 to 1,897.

This tendency to diversify the content of what was once an integrated liberal education is in part the consequence of the expansion of the boundaries of knowledge. New advances in every direction have added more and more subjects to the liberal arts curriculum and have at the same time limited the area of knowledge a single course could cover. This development is at once the parent and the child of specialization.

Specialization is a hallmark of our society, and its advantages to mankind have been remarkable. But in the educational program it has become a source both of strength and of weakness. Filtering downward from the graduate and professional school levels, it has taken over the undergraduate years, too, and in the more extreme instances it has made of the liberal arts college little more than another vocational school, in which the aim of teaching is almost exclusively preparation for advanced study in one or another specialty.

This tendency has been fostered, if not produced, by the training of college teachers in the graduate school, where they are imbued with the single ideal of an ever-narrowing specialism.

The trend toward specialization has been reenforced by the movement toward democratization of higher education. The young people appearing in growing numbers on college campuses have brought with them widely diverse purposes, interests, capacities, and academic backgrounds. Some expect to enter one of the old-line professions; others want training in one of the numerous branches of agriculture, industry or commerce. Some consider college education a natural sequel to high school; others seek it as a road to higher social status.

The net result of the situation is that the college student is faced with a bewildering array of intensive courses from which to make up his individual program. To secure a reasonably comprehensive grasp of his major field, he must in some cases spend as much as half or more of his time in that one department. The other half he scatters among courses in other departments which, designed for future specialists in those fields, are so restricted in scope that the student can gain from them only a fragmentary view of the subject. He, therefore, leaves college unacquainted with some of the fundamental areas of human knowledge and without the integrated view of human experience that is essential both for personal balance and for social wisdom.

Today's college graduate may have gained technical or professional training in one field of work or another, but is only incidentally, if at all, made ready for performing his duties as a man. a parent, and a citizen. Too often he is "educated" in that he has acquired competence in some particular occupation, yet falls short of that human wholeness and civic conscience which the cooperative activities of citizenship require.

The failure to provide any core of unity in the essential diversity of higher education is a cause for grave concern. A society whose members lack a body of common experience and common knowledge is a society without a fundamental culture; it tends to disintegrate into a mere aggregation of individuals. Some community of values, ideas, and attitudes is essential as a cohesive force in this age of minute division of labor and intense conflict of special interests.

The crucial task of higher education today, therefore, is to provide a unified general education for American youth. Colleges must find the right relationship between specialized training on the one hand, aiming at a thousand different careers, and the transmission of a common cultural heritage toward a common citizenship on the other.

There have already been many efforts to define this relationship. Attempts to reach conclusions about the ends and means of general education have been a major part of debate and experimentation in higher education for at least two decades.

"General education" is the term that has come to be accepted for those phases of nonspecialized and nonvocational learning which should be the common experience of all educated men and women.

General education should give to the student the values, attitudes, knowledge, and skills that will equip him to live rightly and well in a free society. It should enable him to identify, intrepret, select, and build into his own life those components of his cultural heritage that contribute richly to understanding and appreciation of the world in which he lives. It should therefore embrace ethical values, scientific generalizations, and aesthetic conceptions, as well as an understanding of the purposes and character of the political, economic and social institutions that men have devised.

But the knowledge and understanding which general education aims to secure whether drawn from the past or from a living present, are not to be regarded as ends in themselves. They are means to a more abundant personal life and a stronger, freer social order.

Thus conceived, general education is not sharply distinguished from liberal education; the two differ mainly in degree, not in kind. General education undertakes to redefine liberal education in terms of life's problems as men face them, to give it human orientation and social direction, to invest it with content that is directly relevant to the demands of contemporary society. General education is liberal education with its matter and method shifted from its original aristocratic intent to the service of democracy. General education seeks to extend to all men the benefits of an education that liberates.

This purpose calls for a unity in the program of studies that a uniform system of courses cannot supply. The unity must come, instead, from a consistency of aim that will infuse and harmonize all teaching and all campus activities.

The Higher Education Act of 1965

With wide bipartisan support, Congress enacted the Higher Education Act of 1965 (HR 9567 -- PL 89-329) authorizing $804,350,000 in fiscal 1966 for a wide variety of major new programs to aid students and colleges. With passage of the measure, Congress took on important new responsibilities in the sphere of higher education. The bill contained eight titles, most of which were funded for three years.

HR 9567 was revolutionary in several aspects, particularly in its student aid provisions. For the first time in U.S. history Congress approved federal scholarships for undergraduate students. The $70 million authorized annually for first-year scholarships was estimated to provide 140,000 students of "exceptional financial need" with scholarships each year. Scholarships had been approved by the Senate in past years only to die in the House. When HR 9567 was first debated by the House, an amendment to remove scholarships from the bill was defeated on a 58-88 standing vote. No further efforts were made to delete the provision.

Another new aid program for college students was insurance on loans, with federal subsidies on interest payments. Federally insured loans had been proposed by President Johnson when he was in Congress, and were subsequently requested by President Kennedy in 1963. Insured loans and scholarships, combined with an expanded work-study program also authorized by the Act, were expected to help students from middle-income as well as low-income backgrounds. They were designed to supplement the first general student loan program, which was authorized in the National Defense Education Act of 1958 (NDEA). As of Oct. 31, 1965, this program had provided $619 million in loans to 750,000 students.

Five titles of the 1965 Act provided aid for colleges and universities. For the first time, funds were voted ($50 million a year) to buy library materials, including books. At the request of the colleges, Congress added two titles not included in the Administration's bill: (1) more funds ($290 million) for construction of classrooms under the 1963 college aid bill, and (2) a new program of grants to colleges for special equipment (including television) to improve the quality of instruction. Lower schools already received federal aid for equipment under NDEA.

Other college aid programs in the Act provided grants to develop university extension courses related to community problems and funds to raise the academic quality of impoverished small colleges. The latter program was authorized for only one year because the Senate insisted on making junior colleges eligible, and the House was opposed.

The 89th Congress continued a trend started in 1964 to make federal college aid available on a broad basis and avoid limitations on the use of funds. An amendment in the House removed categorical limitations tied to construction grants. They had originally been limited to buildings used for science, mathematics and foreign languages. NDEA programs of teacher training and equipment grants had also been earmarked for these subjects (because of the demands of national defense). In 1964 House Republicans fought unsuccessfully against adding history, English and other subjects. By 1965 the battle was over, and economics and industrial arts were added without opposition.

Teacher Corps. A new program called the National Teacher Corps, which stemmed from Congressional initiative, provoked the most controversy. The idea of a corps of skilled teachers to improve school education in slums and other impoverished areas was first proposed by Sens. Edward M. Kennedy (D Mass.) and Gaylord Nelson (D Wis.). President Johnson endorsed the proposal July 17 in a letter to Congress that also requested a graduate fellowship program for elementary and high school teachers.

The Teacher Corps was incorporated into HR 9567 by the Senate and a separate bill authorizing the Corps was reported to the House the same day by the Education and Labor Committee. But House Republican conferees refused to sign the conference report on HR 9567 because it included the Corps. They said it would enable the Government to exercise control over local schools.

During floor debate on adoption of the conference report Oct. 20, Albert H. Quie (R Minn.) moved to send the bill back to conference to delete the Teacher Corps provision. The motion was defeated by a 152-226 roll-call vote. The final bill authorized the Corps for two years. (For voting, see chart p. 1020)

Appropriations. After clearing HR 9567, Congress passed a supplemental appropriations bill (HR 11588) providing $160 million of the $274 million requested by the Administration for the new higher education programs. The Senate voted funds for the Teacher Corps, but the money was dropped in conference with the House. (See story p. 182)

Provisions

As signed by the President, the Higher Education Act carried these provisions:

Title I -- Community Service, Continuing Education. Authorized federal matching grants to the states to develop community service programs conducted by public or private non-profit colleges and universities. The programs were to give particular emphasis to urban and suburban problems, including housing, poverty, employment, transportation, health and other local problems.

Authorized $25 million in grants in fiscal 1966 and $50 million each in fiscal 1967-68, with the Federal Government paying 75 percent of each state's plan for community services in fiscal 1966-67 and 50 percent in fiscal

1968-70. (Authorizations for fiscal 1969-70 were left to future Congressional action.) Set minimum allotments for the states and territories, with the remainder allocated according to state population, and limited state administrative expenses to 5 percent of the costs of its program or $25,000, whichever was larger.

Required the states to draw up plans for comprehensive, statewide community service programs, to be approved by the U.S. Commissioner of Education. Permitted states to seek judicial review in federal courts of appeal if the Commissioner should disapprove a state plan.

Authorized the President to appoint a National Advisory Council on Extension and Continuing Education composed of the U.S. Commissioner, representatives of other federal agencies engaged in extension education, and 12 members from outside the Government. Directed the Council to review the administration and effectiveness of all federally supported extension and continuing education programs and to make annual reports to the President and Congress, beginning on March 31, 1967.

Title II -- College Library Assistance, Training and Research. Authorized (in Part A) $50 million annually in fiscal 1966-68 for grants to enable institutions of higher education to improve their library resources.

Earmarked 75 percent of each year's appropriation for matching basic grants, not to exceed $5,000 for each institution or branch. Required assurances that each institution would not reduce its average library expenditures for the preceding two years and would match on a 50-50 basis the basic grant it received. From sums not needed for basic grants or special purpose grants (below), authorized non-matching supplemental grants to needy institutions, not to exceed $10 for each full-time student.

Earmarked 25 percent of each year's appropriation for special purpose grants to institutions that demonstrated special needs for library resources, or plans for national or regional library and informational service programs, or joint-use facilities with other institutions. Required $1 in matching funds for each $3 provided in federal grants.

Directed the Commissioner of Education to establish an Advisory Council on College Library Resources to advise him on criteria for making supplemental and special purpose grants.

Specified that institutions would be deemed accredited if the library grants received under this title would bring them up to recognized standards.

Authorized (in Part B) $15 million annually in fiscal 1966-68 for grants to institutions of higher education to train librarians and information science specialists and for research and demonstration projects relating to the improvement of libraries, including the development of new techniques.

Repealed, effective July 1, 1967, a provision in the National Defense Education Act of 1958 authorizing training institutes for elementary and secondary school librarians.

Authorized (in Part C) $5 million in fiscal 1966, $6,315,000 in fiscal 1967 and $7,770,000 in fiscal 1968 to enable the Library of Congress to expand its centralized cataloguing service and its acquisition of scholarly materials.

Title III -- Strengthening Developing Institutions. Authorized $55 million in fiscal 1966 to raise the academic quality of developing institutions (colleges which "are struggling for survival and are isolated from the main currents of academic life").

Allocated 78 percent of the appropriation to colleges that award B.A. degrees and 22 percent to two-year institutions, including those that provide a semi-professional education of technicians in engineering, mathematical and scientific fields.

Waived accreditation requirements for schools that accept only high school graduates, are "making reasonable progress toward accreditation" and have been in existence for five years.

Authorized grants to developing institutions and other colleges or businesses for cooperative programs to strengthen the developing colleges' academic programs and administration, including the exchange of faculty or students, fellowships, work-study programs and joint use of libraries and laboratories.

Authorized "national teaching fellowships" to graduate students and junior faculty members who, at the request of a developing institution, would teach there for up to two years. Permitted a stipend of up to $6,500 for each fellowship, plus $400 for each dependent.

Directed the Commissioner to establish an Advisory Council on Developing Institutions to help him identify institutions qualifying for federal aid.

Title IV -- Student Assistance. Authorized federal scholarships ("educational opportunity grants"), federally insured loans and subsidies on interest for full-time college students, transferred the work-study program authorized in the 1964 Economic Opportunity Act and amended several sections of the 1958 National Defense Education Act (NDEA).

Scholarships. Authorized (in Part A) $70 million annually in fiscal 1966-68 for grants to institutions of higher education for first-year scholarships to full-time students "of exceptional financial need," plus whatever sums were necessary to continue scholarships beyond the first year. Made each year's appropriation available through the following fiscal year.

Limited the amount of each scholarship to the lesser of $800 or half the amount of financial aid provided the student by the college or a state or private scholarship program, including loans and scholarships under the Act but excluding aid under work-study programs. (To be eligible for a federal scholarship, a student must receive an equal amount of other financial aid.) Prohibited scholarships of less than $200. Authorized a $200 bonus to scholarship students who in their preceding college year placed in the upper half of their class.

Allocated scholarship funds among the states according to the ratio of the number of each state's college students to the number nationally.

Required colleges, in applying for scholarship funds, to make an agreement with the U.S. Commissioner of Education to review each applicant's financial need and to establish programs to encourage able but needy high school students to attend college and to continue their average expenditures for student aid in the preceding three years. Permitted colleges to make conditional scholarship commitments to high school students, with particular emphasis on students in the 11th grade or lower.

Permitted colleges to transfer 25 percent of their grants for scholarships under the Act to their NDEA student loan fund.

Authorized the U.S. Commissioner to make contracts totaling up to $100,000 per year with state, local or non-profit private organizations to identify and encourage needy high school students to attend post-secondary schools, to publicize existing student aid programs and to encourage high school and college dropouts of demonstrated aptitude to continue their education. Authorized appropriation of necessary funds.

Insured Loans. Authorized the Commissioner (in Part B) to make repayable advances to establish or strengthen state or private non-profit student loan insurance programs. Set a $17.5 million authorization for the advances through fiscal 1968.

Required that to be eligible for advances and federal interest subsidies, state or private loan insurance must cover 80 percent of the unpaid principal, must insure loans of $1,000 to $1,500, at no more than 6-percent interest on the unpaid principal, with repayment not to begin until two months after the student completes his study, and must cover at least six years of academic study.

Established a federal loan insurance fund for students without reasonable access to state or non-profit private insurance plans. Limited insurance on new loans in any year to $700 million in fiscal 1966, $1 billion in fiscal 1967, $1.4 billion in fiscal 1968. Authorized appropriation of $1 million to the fund plus whatever else might be necessary. Permitted 100-percent insurance at a premium of one-fourth of 1 percent of the unpaid principal.

Set as conditions for federal insurance of a loan: a loan in any year cannot exceed $1,500 for a graduate student and $1,000 for undergraduates, and the aggregate of loans for a student cannot exceed $7,500 and $5,000, respectively; students must carry at least half of a full-time workload; loans are to be repaid over a 5- to 10-year period beginning 9 to 12 months after the student ceases academic study (with exceptions for those in the armed forces or Peace Corps) and annual repayments must be at least $360; maximum interest rates are to be set by the Commissioner on a regional or national basis and cannot exceed 6 percent annually on the unpaid principal except in exceptional circumstances, where it can be 7 percent.

Interest Subsidies. For students from families with adjusted annual income of less than $15,000 who have received insured or state loans, authorized the Commissioner to pay all interest charges while the student was in college and 3 percentage points of interest on the unpaid principal thereafter. Prohibited interest subsidies on loans from NDEA college loan funds.

Made eligible for the program four-year and two-year colleges, non-profit collegiate or associate degree nursing schools and one-year post-high school non-profit vocational schools meeting accreditation standards.

Permitted federal credit unions to use 10 percent of their assets to make insured loans to student members.

Directed the Secretary of Health, Education and Welfare to establish an Advisory Council on Insured Loans to Students, including members of insurance programs, lending institutions and colleges, to advise the Commissioner.

Work-Study Program. Transferred to the Office of Education (in Part C) the work-study program for college students authorized in the Economic Opportunity Act (under which the Government currently paid 90 percent of the cost of part-time employment made available to students by their colleges). Removed the requirement that eligible students must be from low-income families but gave preference to such students. Permitted colleges to provide their matching share of the cost through services and equipment, including tuition and books. Authorized $129 million for the program in fiscal 1966

(including a transfer of $60 million from the antipoverty program's authorization), $165 million in fiscal 1967 and $200 million in fiscal 1968.

NDEA Amendments. Amended (in Part D) Title II of NDEA (which established low-interest loans for college students) by requiring repayment of loans to begin nine months after the recipient ceases to carry half a full-time workload, setting a minimum monthly repayment rate of $15, permitting institutions to pay half of their administrative costs from the loan fund and assess students for delinquent payments.

Permitted total loan "forgiveness" (cancellation) to students who teach in public or private non-profit elementary or high schools with high concentrations of children from low-income families eligible for federal aid under the Elementary and Secondary Education Act (PL 89-10). Set the forgiveness rate at 15 percent for each year of teaching. Allowed no more than 25 percent of a state's schools to qualify under this section.

Amended Title III of NDEA (which authorized aid to lower schools to purchase equipment for use in teaching certain subjects) by increasing the fiscal 1966-68 authorizations by $10 million (to a $100 million total) and adding economics as a subject for which equipment could be bought.

Amended Title XI of NDEA (which authorized funds to help colleges conduct advanced teacher training institutes) by increasing the fiscal 1966-68 authorizations by $17,250,000 (to a $50 million total) and making teachers of economics, civics and industrial arts eligible for the institutes.

Title V -- Teacher Programs. Directed the Commissioner of Education to establish an Advisory Council on Quality Teacher Preparation to review the effectiveness of the title's programs in attracting, preparing and retaining highly qualified elementary and secondary school teachers.

Teacher Corps. In Part B, established in the Office of Education a National Teacher Corps, headed by a Director.

Authorized the Commissioner of Education to recruit and select experienced teachers and inexperienced teacher-interns with B.A. degrees for enlistment in the Corps for up to two years. Authorized him to contract with colleges or public education agencies to train Corps members for up to three months. Authorized him to make arrangements with local school agencies to furnish Corps members to schools with concentrations of children from low-income families and to pay the local school agencies for the compensation of their Corps contingents, who were to be either experienced teachers or teaching teams made up of teacher-interns and an experienced teacher. Directed that teacher-interns be given time, while teaching, for graduate training leading to a graduate degree, if possible.

Directed the Commissioner, if the demand for Corps teachers exceeds the supply, to allocate 2 percent to Puerto Rico and the Virgin Islands and the remainder among the states according to their relative number of children from impoverished families.

Permitted local school districts to use Corps members to provide educational services in which private school children may participate, as authorized in the Elementary and Secondary Education Act (PL 89-10).

Specified that Corps members were not federal employees and that experienced teachers and teacher-interns were to receive the same salaries paid teachers

652

in the local district, but that the pay of teaching team leaders was to be set by consultation between the school district and the Commissioner. Authorized the Commissioner to pay Corps members their travel expenses, any employee benefits they would have had at an institution to which they planned to return, and stipends for initial training for the Corps.

Specified that Corps members would be under "the direct supervision" of the school agencies to which they were assigned and that the agencies could assign and transfer the members, determine what they should teach and discontinue their employment if desired.

Specified that Corps members were not to displace any teacher who would otherwise be employed by the school agency.

Authorized appropriation for Corps activities of $36,100,000 in fiscal 1966 and $64,715,000 in fiscal 1967.

Teacher Fellowships. Part C declared a need to improve the quality of education in elementary and secondary schools by providing fellowships for graduate study by teachers and strengthening universities' teacher education programs. Specified that the program applied not only to teachers and prospective teachers but also to supervisors, school librarians, social workers and the fields of guidance, counseling, educational media and special education for handicapped children.

Authorized the Commissioner to award 4,500 fellowships in fiscal 1966 and 10,000 annually in fiscal 1967-68. Authorized appropriations of $40 million in fiscal 1966, $160 million in fiscal 1967 and $275 million in fiscal 1968 plus funds to enable those who received fellowships before July 1, 1968, to complete their studies by June 30, 1970.

Specified that the fellowships were for study leading to an advanced degree other than Ph.D., were not to extend beyond 24 months, and were to be allocated equitably among the states unless the Advisory Council should propose allocations to meet "an urgent national need." (Although Senate provisions strictly earmarking the allocation of fellowships were dropped from the final Act, House-Senate conferees expressed a wish that up to 20 percent of the fellowships be awarded teachers who lost their jobs as a result of desegregation and consolidation of schools in accordance with the 1964 Civil Rights Act.)

Authorized the Commissioner to pay stipends and living allowances for fellowship recipients comparable to those paid under other federally supported programs and to pay the institution at which the recipient was studying $2,500 per academic year less fees charged the graduate student.

Required fellowship recipients to take a full-time course of study and to limit part-time employment to fields related to their training and approved by the Commissioner.

Specified that institutions' graduate programs must meet the approval of the Commissioner. Authorized him, in the interest of better geographical distribution of high-quality teacher training programs, to make grants to develop or strengthen graduate programs.

Title VI -- Improvement of Undergraduate Courses. Authorized (in Part A) matching federal grants to institutions of higher education to improve their classroom instruction as follows: for laboratory, audiovisual equipment and printed material, other than textbooks, for courses in science, humanities, arts and education, and for minor remodeling, $35 million in fiscal 1966, $50 million in fiscal 1967, $60 million in fiscal 1968; for

closed-circuit television receiving equipment and minor remodeling, $2.5 million in fiscal 1966 and $10 million annually in fiscal 1967-68.

Limited the federal share of each project's cost to 50 percent unless a state commission sets the share at up to 80 percent for colleges too poor to participate otherwise.

Allocated the money among the states according to a formula based on each state's number of college students and per capita income. Required the states to draw up plans and assign priorities for grants to their colleges and permitted judicial review if the Commissioner should disapprove a state's plan.

Authorized the Commissioner to make grants to the states of $1 million annually in fiscal 1966-68 for administration of state plans.

Authorized to the Commissioner (in Part B) $5 million annually in fiscal 1966-68 for grants to colleges to conduct short-term workshops or institutes for college teachers or specialists planning to use educational media equipment. Permitted stipends of $75 per week for those attending the institutes (but not the workshops), plus $15 per week for each dependent.

Title VII -- Amendments to the Higher Education Facilities Act of 1963. Amended the 1963 college classroom construction act (PL 88-204) as follows:

Increased the fiscal 1966 grant authorization for undergraduate facilities by $230 million (to a $460 million total); permitted a college to receive a grant if it would increase its capacity to carry out on-campus extension and continuing education programs; and removed the 1963 Act's categorical restrictions on the program (which permitted aid only for science, math, modern foreign language and engineering buildings or libraries).

Increased the fiscal 1966 grant authorization for graduate facilities by $60 million (to a $120 million total).

Permitted a state to transfer allotments between junior colleges and four-year colleges if not needed for the original purpose. (The 1963 Act required that 22 percent of the appropriations go to junior colleges.)

Established a 3-percent maximum rate of interest on loans for construction of academic facilities made after enactment of the bill (the 1963 Act set the rate at one-fourth of 1 percent over the average interest rate of federal securities -- currently 3-7/8 percent.)

Title VIII -- General Provisions. Defined the term institution of higher education as including non-profit four-year and two-year colleges, business schools and technical institutions. Defined state as including the District of Columbia, Puerto Rico, Guam, American Samoa and the Virgin Islands.

Specified that nothing in the bill authorized any federal control over the curriculum, administration, personnel or library resources of any institution.

Specified that nothing in the bill authorized any federal control over the membership practices or internal operations of any college fraternal organization, private club or religious organization which was financed exclusively by private funds and whose facilities were not owned by the college. Exempted the service academies and Coast Guard Academy from this section.

Specified in each title of the Act that aid to any school or department of divinity or any educational activity related to sectarian instruction or religious workshop was prohibited.

The Higher Education Act - 1966 Amendments

As signed into law, the Higher Education Amendments of 1966 (PL 89-752) contained the following major provisions:

1963 Act. Extended the first three titles of the Higher Education Facilities Act of 1963 for three years, from fiscal 1968 through fiscal 1971 (existing law provided no appropriations authorization for fiscal 1967 and 1968).

Title I. Authorized appropriations of $475 million in fiscal 1967, $728 million in fiscal 1968, $936 million in fiscal 1969 and such sums as later authorized by Congress in fiscal 1970-71 for grants to construct undergraduate facilities. Stipulated that 22 percent in fiscal 1967, 23 percent in fiscal 1968 and 24 percent in fiscal 1969 of the appropriations be allotted to two-year public community colleges and public technical institutes, with the remainder to be allotted to other four-year institutions.

Authorized the Commissioner of Education to reallot among the states the unused portion of the construction funds until the end of the fiscal year succeeding the year for which the funds were appropriated.

Authorized $7 million in each of fiscal years 1967-69 and such sums as later authorized by Congress for fiscal 1970-71 for the Commissioner to spend for: (1) the administration of state plans for construction grants under Title I and grants to improve classroom instruction under Title VI (Part A) of the Higher Education Act of 1965 and (2) grants to state commissions to conduct comprehensive planning studies to determine the construction needs of higher institutions, particularly those in regional groupings. Limited to $3 million the amount to be spent for the administration of state plans.

Title II. Authorized appropriations of $60 million in fiscal 1967 and $120 million annually in fiscal 1968-69 and such sums as later authorized by Congress in fiscal 1970-71 for construction of graduate facilities.

Title III. Authorized appropriations of $200 million in fiscal 1967 and $400 million annually in fiscal 1968-69 and such sums as later authorized by Congress in fiscal 1970-71 for loans for construction of graduate and undergraduate facilities.

Related Provisions. Provided that any amounts authorized but not appropriated in a fiscal year could be carried forward to the following year and be available for appropriation.

Provided that funds appropriated for grants for construction of graduate facilities (Title II) and for loans for construction of graduate and undergraduate facilities (Title III) remain available until spent.

Permitted spending up to 1 percent of the total cost of the facility for works of art for the facility.

Repealed the authority of the Commissioner of Education to set a fee schedule to cover the costs of inspection at the site of the projects being built with academic facilities loans.

Stipulated that construction plans were to ensure that all facilities built with federal aid would be accessible to the appropriate extent to handicapped persons.

1965 Act. Amended the Higher Education Act of 1965 as follows:

Title II. Required an applicant for college library aid to ensure that it would spend during the fiscal year for which the money was requested for library purposes, exclusive of construction, not less than its average annual expenditures during the two years prior to June 30, 1965 (as required under existing law), or not less than the average annual expenditures during the two years prior to the fiscal year for which the grant was requested -- whichever expenditure was less.

Title III. Extended the "developing institutions" assistance program for two years, authorizing $30 million in fiscal 1967 and $55 million in fiscal 1968.

Title IV. Authorized the District of Columbia Board of Commissioners to establish a student loan insurance program meeting the requirements of existing loan insurance programs and financed by such authorized appropriations deemed necessary and by private donations. Stipulated that a minor obtaining a loan under the program would be legally bound by any note or other written agreement, regardless of whether such a binding obligation was applicable under existing law.

Directed the Commissioner of Education to make a study of improving the Title IV loan insurance program -- particularly in making loans more available to students -- and required him to report the results and recommendations to the President and Congress by Jan. 1, 1968.

Title VI. Required institutions applying for college equipment grants after Dec. 30, 1966, to spend from current funds for institutional and library purposes (other than personnel costs) an amount not less than spent for the same purposes during the previous year. (Currently, an institution was required to maintain its previous fiscal year level of spending for "specific purposes" covered by the program. The amendment, in part, provided that an applicant's capitalized investment in new building equipment -- which would be included under the former "specific purposes" definition -- would no longer have to be maintained to receive a grant.

NDEA. Amended the National Defense Education Act of 1958 as follows:

Title II. Increased authorizations of funds for capital contributions to the national defense student loan program from $195 to $225 million in fiscal 1968. (The authorization for fiscal 1967 was kept at its previously authorized level of $190 million.)

Expanded the teacher loan "forgiveness" provisions to permit up to 100-percent cancellation at 15 percent per year on loans to students who become full-time teachers of handicapped children in public or nonprofit elementary or secondary schools. Also made eligible for loan "forgiveness" those who teach in a Pacific trust territory.

Title III. Added industrial arts to the list of "critical subjects" under the program to improve instruction of such subjects. Increased the fiscal 1968 authorization for the program from $100 to $110 million, retaining the existing 1967 authorization of $100 million.

Student Loan Data

Under Secretary of the Treasury Joseph W. Barr Feb. 4, 1967, said that in the fall of 1966, $160 million in loans were made to 190,000 students. For the full school year of 1966-67 the goal was $700 million in loans to 963,000 students, but Barr said estimates were that only $400 million would be made available to 480,000 students.

BIBLIOGRAPHY

Part I: General Works on the History of Higher Education

Brockliss, L. W. B. *French Higher Education in the Seventeenth and Eighteenth Centuries.* Oxford: Clarendon Press, 1987.

Brubacher, John S., and Rudy, Willis. *Higher Education in Transition: A History of the American Colleges and Universities, 1636-1976.* 3rd ed., rev. and enl. New York: Harper & Row, Publishers, 1976.

Carpenter, Joel A., and Shipps, Kenneth W. *Making Higher Education Christian: The History and Mission of Evangelical Colleges in America.* Grand Rapids, Mich.: William B. Eerdmans Publishing Co., 1986.

Chambers, M. M. *Higher Education in the Fifty States.* Danville, Ind.: Interstate Printers and Publishers, Inc., 1970.

Clarke, Burton R. *The Distinctive College: Antioch, Reed, & Swarthmore.* Chicago: Aldine Publishing Co., 1970.

Clarke, M.L. *Higher Education in the Ancient World.* London: Routledge, 1971.

Cobban, Alan. *The Medieval Universities: Oxford and Cambridge to c. 1500.* Berkeley and Los Angeles: University of California Press, 1988.

_____. *The Medieval Universities: Their Development and Organization.* London: Methuen, 1975.

Duryea, E. D. "The University and the State: A Historical Overview." In *Higher Education in American Society.* Edited by Philip Altbach and Robert Berdahl. Rev. Ed. Buffalo: Prometheus Books, 1981.

Ferruolo, Stephen C. *The Origins of the University: The Schools of Paris & Their Critics, 1100-1215* Stanford: Stanford University Press, 1985.

Good. H. G. *A History of Western Education.* 2nd ed. New York: Macmillan Co., 1960.

Hofstadter, Richard and Metzger, Walter P. *The Development of Academic Freedom in the United States.* New York: Columbia University Press, 1955.

Hofstadter, Richard, and Smith, Wilson. *American Higher Education Documentary History.* 2 vols. Chicago: University of Chicago Press, 1961.

Horowitz, Helen Lefkowitz. *Alma Mater: Design and Experience in the Women's Colleges from their 19th Century Beginnings to the 1930's.* New York: Alfred A. Knopf, Inc., 1984.

_____. *Campus Life: Undergraduate Cultures from the End of the Eighteenth Century to the Present.* New York: Alfred A. Knopf, Inc., 1987.

Karp, Alan. "John Calvin and the Geneva Academy: Roots of the Board of Trustees." *History of Higher Education Annual* 5 (1985): 3-41.

Kimball, Bruce A. *Orators & Philosophers: A History of the Idea of Liberal Education.* New York: Teachers College Press, 1986.

Lagemann, Ellen C. *Private Power for the Public Good: A History of the Carnegie Foundation for the Advancement of Teaching.* Middletown, Conn.: Wesleyan University Press, 1983.

Lanning, John Tate. *Academic Culture in the Spanish Colonies.* New York: Oxford University Press, 1940.

Ludmerer, Kenneth M. *Learning to Heal: The Development of American Medical Education.* New York: Basic Books, 1985.

Madsen, David. "History and Philosophy of Higher Education." *Encyclopedia of Educational Research.* Vol. 2: 795-803.

Makdisi, George. *The Rise of Colleges: Institutions of Learning in Islam and the West.* Edinburgh: Edinburgh University Press, 1981.

Perrin, Tom. *Football: A College History.* Jefferson, N.C.: McFarland & Co., 1988.

Power, Edward J. *Catholic Higher Education in America: A History.* New York: Appleton-Century-Crofts, Inc., 1972.

Rashdall, Hastings. *The Universities of Europe in the Middle Ages.* 3 Vols. Oxford: Clarendon Press, 1895.

Ringenberg, William C. *The Christian College: A History of Protestant Higher Education in America.* Grand Rapids, Mich.: William B. Eerdsmans Publishing Co., 1984.

Rudolph, Frederick. *The American College and University: A History.* New York: Vintage Books, 1962.

_____. *Curriculum: A History of the American Undergraduate Course of Study Since 1636.* San Francisco: Jossey-Bass Publishers, 1977.

Sloan, Douglas. *The Scottish Enlightenment and the American College Ideal.* New York: Teachers College Press, 1971.

Solberg, Richard W. *Lutheran Higher Education in North America.* Minneapolis: Augsburg Publishing House, 1985.

Solomon, Barbara M. *In the Company of Educated Women: A History of Women and Higher Education in America.* New Haven: Yale University Press, 1985.

Stone, Lawrence. *The University in Society.* Vol. 1: *Oxford and Cambridge from the 14th to the Early 19th Century.* Vol. 2, *Europe, Scotland, and the United States from the 16th Century to the 20th Century.* Princeton: Princeton University Press, 1974.

Storr, Richard J. "The Public Conscience of the University, 1775-1956." *Harvard Educational Review* 26 (Winter 1956): 71-84.

Thelin, John R. *Higher Education and Its Useful Past*. Cambridge, Mass.: Schenkman Publishing Co., 1982.

Warren, Donald R. "History of Education." *Encyclopedia of Educational Research*. Vol. 2: 809-815.

Woody, Thomas. *A History of Women's Education in the United States.* 2 vols. New York: Farrar, Straus, and Giroux, 1980. Reprint of Lancaster, Pa.: Science Press, 1929.

Part II: Colonial Higher Education in the Americas (1538-1789)

Allmendinger, David F. *Paupers and Scholars: The Transformation of Student Life in Nineteenth Century New England*. New York: St. Martin's Press, 1975.

Axtell, James. *The European and the Indian: Essays in the Ethnohistory of Colonial North America*. New York: Oxford University Press, 1981.

_____. *The Invasion Within: The Contest of Cultures in Colonial North America*. New York: Oxford University Press, 1985.

Benjamin, Harold R. W. *Higher Education in the American Republics*. New York: McGraw-Hill Book Co., 1965.

Brewer, Clifton H. *A History of Religious Education in the Episcopal Church to 1835*. New Haven: Yale University Press, 1924.

Cowley, William H. "A History of College Admissions Criteria." *Association of American Colleges Bulletin* 26 (1940): 522-557.

Cremin, Lawrence A. "College." In *American Education: The Colonial Experience, 1607-1783*. New York: Harper & Row, 1970.

Durnin, Richard G. "The Role of the Presidents in American Colleges of the Colonial Period." *History of Education Quarterly* 1 (June, 1961): 23-31.

Finkelstein, Martin. "From Tutor to Specialized Scholar: Academic Professionalization in Eighteenth and Nineteenth Century America." *History of Higher Education Annual* 3 (1983): 99-121.

Frost, S. E. "Higher Education Among the American Indians During the Colonial Period." *History of Education Journal* 9 (Spring 1958): 59-66.

Herbst, Jurgen. "From Religion to Politics: Debates and Confrontations Over American College Governance in Mid-Eighteenth Century." *Harvard Educational Review* 46 (August 1976): 397-424.

_____. *From Crisis to Crisis: American College Government 1636-1819*. Cambridge, Mass.: Harvard University Press, 1982.

Hofstadter, Richard. "The Colonial Colleges." In *Academic Freedom in the Age of the College*. New York: Columbia University Press, 1955.

Humphrey, D. C. "The King's College Medical School and the Professionalization of Medicine in Pre-revolutionary New York." *Bulletin of The History of Medicine* 49 (Summer 1975): 206-234.

McAnear, Beverly. "College Founding in the American Colonies: 1745-1775." *Mississippi Valley Historical Review* 46 (1955): 24-44.

Miller, Howard. *The Revolutionary College: American Presbyterian Higher Education, 1707-1837.* New York: New York University Press, 1976.

_____. "Evangelical Religion and Colonial Princeton." In *Schooling and Society: Studies in the History of Education.* Edited by Lawrence Stone. Baltimore: Johns Hopkins University Press, 1976.

Moore, Kathryn M. "The Dilemma of Corporal Punishment at Harvard College." *History of Education Quarterly* 14 (1974): 335-346.

_____. "Freedom and Constraint in Eighteenth Century Harvard." *Journal of Higher Education* 47 (November/December 1976): 649-659.

_____. "The War With the Tutors: Student-Faculty Conflict at Harvard and Yale, 1745-1771." *History of Education Quarterly* 18 (1978): 115-127.

Morgan, Edmund S. "Ezra Stiles and Timothy Dwight." *Massachusetts Historical Society Proceedings* 72 (1963): 101-117.

Morison, Samuel Eliot. "Origins of the Universities." In *The Founding of Harvard College.* Cambridge, Mass.: Harvard University Press, 1935.

Robson, David W. *Educating Republicans: The College in the Era of the American Revolution, 1750-1800.* Contributions to the Study of Education Series, No. 15. Westport, Conn.: Greenwood Press, 1985.

Roche, John F. *The Colonial Colleges in the War for American Independence.* Millwood, N.Y.: Association Faculty Press, 1985.

Rudolph, Frederick. "The Colonial College." In *American College and University: A History.* New York: Vintage Books, 1962.

Thomson, Robert P. "Colleges in the Revolutionary South: The Shaping of a Tradition." *History of Education Quarterly* 10 (1970): 399-412.

Vine, Phyllis. "The Social Function of Eighteenth-Century Higher Education." *History of Education Quarterly* 16 (Winter 1976): 409-424.

Wright, Bobby. "For the Children of the Infidels?: American Indian Education in the Colonial Colleges." *American Indian and Culture Research Journal* 12 (August 1989): 1-14.

Primary Readings

Benjamin Rush on a Federal University, 1788; Hofstadter, Richard, and Smith, Wilson. *American Higher Education: A Documentary History.* 2 Vols. Chicago: University of Chicago Press, 1961, pp. 1: 152-156. [Hereafter cited as Hofstadter and Smith]

Cotton Mather's History of Harvard, 1702, Hofstadter and Smith, pp. 1: 13-19.

Statutes of Harvard, 1646, Hofstadter and Smith, pp.1: 8-9.

Harvard Charter, 1650, Hofstadter and Smith, pp.1: 10-13.

Statutes of William and Mary, 1727, Hofstadter and Smith, pp. 1: 39-49.

Thomas Jefferson's Plans for the University of Virginia, 1800, Hofstadter and Smith, pp. 1: 175-176.

Yale Laws of 1745, Hofstadter and Smith, pp. 1: 54-61.

Part III: Higher Education during the Antebellum Period (1790-1860)

Allmendinger, Jr., David F. "Mount Holyoke Students Encounter the Need for Life-Planning, 1837-1850."*History of Education Quarterly* 19 (Spring 1979): 27-46.

Axtell, James. "The Death of the Liberal Arts College." *History of Education Quarterly* 11 (Winter 1971): 339-352.

Black, W. I. "Education in the South from 1820 to 1860 with Emphasis on the Growth of Teacher Education." *Louisiana Studies* 12 (Winter 1973): 617-629.

Bruce, Robert. *The Launching of Modern American Science, 1846-1876.* New York: Alfred A. Knopf, 1987.

Burke, Colin B. *American Collegiate Populations: A Test of the Traditional View.* New York: New York University Press, 1982.

Calhoun, David H. *Professional Lives in America: Structure and Aspiration, 1750-1850.* Cambridge, Mass.: Harvard University Press, 1965.

Church, Robert L., and Sedlak, Michael W. "The Antebellum College and Academy." In *Education in the United States: An Interpretive History.* New York: Free Press, 1976, pp. 23-51.

Curti, Merle. "The Education of Women." In *The Social Ideas of American Educators.* New York: Charles Scribner's Sons, 1935.

Daniels, George H. "The Process of Professionalization in American Science: The Emergent Period, 1820-1860." *ISIS* 57 (1967): 151-166.

DeMartini, Joseph. "Student Culture as a Change Agent in American Higher Education: An Example from the 19th Century." *Journal of Social History* 9 (June 1976): 526-541.

660

Engs, Robert F. "Black Hampton and Armstrong's Institute." In *Freedom's First-Generation: Black Hampton, Virginia, 1861-1890*. Philadelphia: University of Pennsylvania Press, 1979.

Findlay, James. "Agency, Denominations, and the Western Colleges, 1830-1860: Some Connections Between Evangelicalism and American Higher Education." *Church History* 50 (March 1981): 64-80.

_____. " 'Western' Colleges, 1830–1870: Educational Institutions in Transition." *History of Higher Education Annual* 2 (1982): 35–64.

Fletcher, Robert Samuel. *A History of Oberlin College: From its Foundation through the Civil War*. 2 vols. Chicago: R. R. Donnelley & Sons, Co., 1943.

Goodheart, Lawrence B. "Abolitionists As Academics: The Controversy at Western Reserve College, 1832-1833." *History of Education Quarterly* 22 (Winter 1982): 421-433.

Guralnick, Louis. *Science and the Ante-Bellum College*. Philadelphia: American Philosophical Society, 1975.

Hofstadter, Richard. "The Great Retrogression." In *Academic Freedom in the Age of the College*. New York: Columbia University Press, 1955.

Johnson, Eldon L. "The 'Other Jeffersons' and the State University Idea." *Journal of Higher Education* 58 (March/April 1987): 127-150.

Lane, Jack C. "The Yale Report of 1828 and Liberal Education: A Neorepublican Manifesto." *History of Education Quarterly* 27 (Fall 1987): 325-338.

McLachlan, James. "American Student Societies in the Early Nineteenth Century." In *The University in Society*. Vol. 2: *Europe, Scotland, and the United States from the 16th Century to the 20th Century*. Edited by Lawrence Stone. Princeton: Princeton University Press, 1974.

_____. "The American College in the Nineteenth Century: Toward a Reappraisal." *Teachers College Record* 80 (December 1978): 286-306.

Metcalf, Keyes D. "The Undergraduate and the Harvard Library, 1765-1877." *Harvard Library Bulletin* 1 (Winter 1947): 29-51.

Mohsenin, Iran Cassim. "Notes on Age Structure of College Students." *History of Education Quarterly* 23 (Winter 1983): 491-498.

Naylor, Natalie A. "The Ante-Bellum College Movement: A Reappraisal of Tewksbury's Founding of American Colleges and Universities." *History of Education Quarterly* 13 (Fall 1973): 261-274.

Palmieri, Patricia A. "From Republican Motherhood to Race Suicide: Arguments on the Higher Education of Women in the United States, 1820-1920." In *Educating Men and Women Together: Coeducation in a Changing World*. Edited by Carol Lasser. Urbana: University of Illinois Press with Oberlin College, 1987.

Pearson, Ralph L. "Reflections on Black Colleges: The Historical Perspective of Charles S. Johnson." *History of Education Quarterly* 23 (1983): 55-68.

Perkins, Linda M. "The Impact of the 'Cult of True Womanhood' on the Education of Black Women." *Journal of Social Issues* 39 (No. 3, 1983): 17-28.

Potts, David B. "American Colleges in the Nineteenth Century: From Localism to Denominationalism" *History of Education Quarterly* 11 (Winter 1971): 363-380..

_____. " 'College Enthusiasm!' As Public Response, 1800-1860." *Harvard Educational Review* 47 (February 1977): 28-42.

_____. "Curriculum and Enrollments: Some Thoughts On Assessing the Popularity of Ante-Bellum Colleges." *History of Higher Education Annual* 1 (1981): 88-109.

Robson, David W. "College Founding in the New Republic, 1776-1800." *History of Education Quarterly* 23 (Fall 1983): 323-341.

Rose, Richard M. "Diverging Paths: The Emergence of Secret Societies in Antebellum Georgia Colleges." *Comparative Studies in Society and History* 25 (January 1983): 3-25.

Rudolph, Frederick. "Neglect of Students as a Historical Tradition." In *The College and the Student*. Edited by Lawrence E. Dennis and Joseph F. Kauffman. Washington, D.C.: American Council on Education 1966.

Rury, John and Harper, Glenn. "The Trouble with Coeducation: Mann and Women at Antioch, 1853–1960." *History of Education Quarterly* 27 (1987): 481–502.

Simpson, L. "The Development and Scope of Undergraduate Literary Libraries at Columbia, Dartmouth, Princeton, and Yale 1783-1830." *Journal of Library History* 12 (Summer 1977): 206-221.

Sloan, Douglas. "Harmony, Chaos, and Consensus: The American College Curriculum." *Teachers College Record* 73 (December 1971): 221-251.

Smith, Wilson. "Francis Wayland and the Civil War." In *Professors and Public Ethics: Studies of Northern Moral Philosophers Before the Civil War*. Ithaca, N.Y.: Cornell University Press, 1956.

_____. "Apologia pro Alma Mater: The College as Community in Ante-Bellum America." In *The Hofstadter Aegis: A Memorial*. Edited by S. Elkins and E. McKitrick. New York: Alfred A. Knopf, 1974.

Story, Ronald. "Harvard Students, the Boston Elite, and the New England Preparatory System, 1800-1876." *History of Education Quarterly* 15 (1975): 281-298.

Tewksbury, Donald G. *The Founding of American Colleges and Universities before the Civil War*. New York: Teachers College Press, 1932.

Wagoner, Jr., Jennings L. "Honor and Dishonor at Mr. Jefferson's University: The Antebellum Years." *History of Education Quarterly* 26 (Summer 1986): 155-179.

Whitehead, John S., and Herbst, Jurgen. "How to Think about the Dartmouth College Case." *History of Education Quarterly* 26 (1986): 333-350.

Primary Readings

Chief Justice Marshall's Opinion in the Dartmouth College Case. In *Education in the United States: A Documentary History*. Vol. 3. Edited by Sol Cohen. New York: Random House, 1974, pp. 1437-1451. [Hereafter cited as Cohen]

Daniel Webster Argues the Dartmouth Case, 1819, Hofstadter and Smith, pp. 1: 202-213.

Emma Willard on the Education of Women (1819), Cohen. pp. 3: 1573-1580.

Frederick, A. P. Barnard. "On Improvement Practicable in American Colleges." *American Journal of Education* 1 (August 1855): 174-185; 2 (March 1856): 269-284.

Henry Adams Describes His Education at Harvard (1854-58). Cohen. pp. 3: 1460-1467.

Julian M. Sturtevant on the Quality of Teaching at Yale in the 1820's, Hofstadter and Smith, pp. 1: 274-275.

The Plan of Studies at the University of Virginia, 1824, Hofstadter and Smith, pp. 1: 230-231.

Report of the Rockfish Gap Commission on the Proposed University of Virginia, 1824, Hofstadter and Smith, pp.1: 193-199.

Wayland on the Collegiate System, 1842, Hofstadter and Smith, pp. 1: 334-375.

The Yale Report of 1828, Hofstadter and Smith, pp.1: 275-291.

Part IV: The Rise of American Universities during the Nineteenth and Twentieth Centuries—State and Land-Grant Universities

Angelo, Richard. "The Students at the University of Pennsylvania and the Temple College of Philadelphia, 1873-1906: Some Notes on Schooling, Class and Social Mobility in the Late Nineteenth Century." *History of Education Quarterly* 19 (Summer 1979): 179-205.

Barnes, Sherman B. "The Entry of Science and History in the College Curriculum, 1865-1914." *History of Education Quarterly* 4 (March 1964): 44-58.

Bowles, Frank, and DeCosta, Frank A. *Between Two Worlds: A Profile of Negro Higher Education*. New York: McGraw-Hill Book Co., 1971.

Burke, Colin B. "The Expansion of American Higher Education." In *The Transformation of Higher Learning, 1860-1930*. Edited by Konrad H. Jarausch. Chicago: University of Chicago Press, 1983.

Cowley, William H. "History of Student Residential Housing." *Social and Society* 40 (December 1934): 705-710, 758-763.

Curti, Merle, and Nash, Roderick. *Philanthropy in the Shaping of American Higher Education*. New Brunswick, N.J.: Rutgers University Press, 1965.

Gordon, Lynn D. "Annie Nathan Meyer and Barnard College: Mission and Identity in Women's Education, 1889-1950." *History of Education Quarterly* 26 (1986): 503-522.

Hawkins, Hugh. "Problems in Categorization and Generalization in the History of American Higher Education: An Approach Through the Institutional Associations." *History of Higher Education Annual* 5 (1985): 43-55.

Herbst, Jurgen. "Nineteenth Century Normal Schools in the United States." *History of Education* 9 (September 1980): 219-227.

Hoeveler Jr., J. David. "The University and the Social Gospel: The Intellectual Origins of the Wisconsin Idea." *Wisconsin Magazine of History* 59 (Summer 1976): 282-298.

Jencks, Christopher, and Reisman, David. "Class Interests and the 'Public-Private' Controversy." In *The Academic Revolution*. 2nd Ed. Chicago: University of Chicago Press, 1977.

_____. "Feminism, Masculinism, and Coeducation." In *The Academic Revolution*. 2nd ed. Chicago: University of Chicago Press, 1977.

Johnson, Eldon L. "Misconceptions About the Early Land-Grant Colleges." *Journal of Higher Education* 52 (July-August 1981): 333-351.

Johnson, William R. "Education and Professional Life Styles: Law and Medicine in the Nineteenth Century." *History of Education Quarterly* 14 (Summer 1974): 185-207.

Kousser, J. Morgan, and McPherson, James M. *Region, Race, and Reconstruction*. New York: Oxford University Press, 1982.

Lang, Daniel W. "The People's College, the Mechanics Mutual Protection and the Agricultural College Act." *History of Education Quarterly* 18 (Fall 1978): 295-321.

Leslie, W. Bruce. "The Response of Four Colleges to the Rise of Intercollegiate Athletics 1865-1915." *Journal of Sport History* 3 (Winter 1975): 213-222.

_____. "Localism, Denominationalism, and Institutional Strategies in Urbanizing America: Three Pennsylvania Colleges, 1870-1915." *History of Education Quarterly* 17 (Fall 1977): 235-256.

_____."Between Pity and Expertise: Professionalism of College Faculty in the Age of the University." *Pacific Historian* 46 (July 1979): 245-265.

McPherson, James M. "The New Puritanism: Values and Goals of Freedman's Education in America." In *The University in Society*. Vol. 2, *Europe, Scotland, and the United States from the 16th to the 20th Century*. Edited by Lawrence Stone. Princeton: Princeton University Press, 1974.

Palmieri, Patricia. "*Incipit Vita Nuova:* Founding Ideals of the Wellesley College Community." *History of Higher Education Annual* 3 (1983): 59-78.

Ratcliff, James L. "A Re-examination of the Past: Some Origins of the 'Second Best' Notion." *Community/Junior College Quarterly* 8 (1984): 273-284.

Reisner, Edward. "The Origins of Lay University Boards of Control in the United States." *Columbia University Quarterly* 23 (1931): 63-69.

Ross, Earle D. *Democracy's College: The Land-Grant Movement in the Formative State.* Ames, Iowa: Iowa State College Press, 1942.

————. "Religious Influences in the Development of State Colleges and Universities." *Indiana Magazine of History* 66 (1950): 343-362.

Rudy, Willis. "The 'Revolution' in American Higher Education—1865-1900." *Harvard Educational Review* 21 (1951): 155-174.

Shannon, Samuel H. "Land Grant College Legislation and Black Tennesseans: A Case Study in the Politics of Education." *History of Education Quarterly* 22 (Summer 1982): 139-157.

Stetar, Joseph M. "In Search of A Direction: Southern Higher Education After the Civil War." *History of Education Quarterly* 25 (Fall 1985): 341-367.

Wein, Roberta. "Women's Colleges and Domesticity, 1875-1918." *History of Education Quarterly* 14 (Spring 1974): 31-47.

Primary Readings

"Charles Kendall Adams Argues the Merits of the State University, 1875, Hofstadter and Smith, pp 667–676.

The Morrill Act, 1862, Hofstadter and Smith, pp. 2: 568-569.

"The Veto Message of President James Buchanan on the Morrill Bill, 1859." In *Readings in American Educational History.* Edited by Edgar W. Knight and Hall, Clifton L. New York: Appleton-Century-Crofts, Inc., 1951.

Washington, Booker T. "Speech at the Atlanta Exposition and What I am Trying to Do." In *Great Documents in Black American History.* New York: Praeger Publishers, 1970.

White, Andrew D. "Description of Early Days at Cornell (c. 1860)." Cohen, pp. 3: 1542-1545.

Part V: The Rise of American Universities during the Nineteenth and Twentieth Centuries—Research Universities

Ben-David, Joseph. "Universities and Growth of Knowledge in Germany and the United States." *Minerva* 7 (1968): 1-35.

Bishop, Charles C. "Teaching at Johns Hopkins: The First Generation." *History of Education Quarterly* 27 (Winter 1987): 499-515.

Brubacher, John S., and Rudy, Willis. "Professional Education." *Higher Education in Transition: A History of American Colleges and Universities, 1636-1976.* 3rd ed. rev. and enl. New York: Harper & Row, Publishers, 1976.

Brubacher, John S. "The Evolution of Professional Education." In *Sixty-First Yearbook of the National Society for the Study of Education*. Edited by G. Lester Anderson. Chicago: University of Chicago Press, 1962.

Busch, Alexander. "The Vicissitudes of the *Privatdozent*: Breakdown and Adaptation in the Recruitment of the German University Teacher." In *The State of the University: Authority and Change*. Edited by C. Kruythosch and S. Messinger. Beverly Hills, CA.: Sage Publications, 1970.

Church, Robert L. "Economists as Experts: The Rise of an Academic Profession in America, 1870-1917." In *The University in Society*. Vol. 2, *Europe, Scotland, and the United States from the 16th to the 20th Centuries*. Edited by Lawrence Stone. Princeton: Princeton University Press, 1974.

Cornford, Francis M. *Microcosmographia Academia*. Cambridge: Bowes & Bowes, 1923.

Cohen, Sheldon S. "Maroon Farewell: The Abolition of Intercollegiate Football at the University of Chicago." *Journal of the Midwest History of Education Society* 9 (1981): 42-58.

Cox, Dwayne. "The Gottschalk-Calvin Case: A Study in Academic Purpose and Command." *Register of the Kentucky Historical Society* 85 (Winter 1987): 46-68.

Cremin, Lawrence. "The Education of the Educating Professions." *Research Bulletin: Horace Mann-Lincoln Institute* 18 (March 1978): 1-8.

Curti, Merle. "The Setting and the Problems." In *American Scholarship in the 20th Century*. Cambridge, Mass.: Harvard University Press, 1953.

Eckleberry, R. H. "The History of the Municipal University in the United States." Bulletin, No. 2. Washington, D.C.: U. S. Office of Education, 1932.

Franklin, Fabian. *The Life of Daniel Coit Gilman*. New York: Dodd, Mead, and Co., 1910.

Geiger, Roger L. "The Conditions of University Research, 1900-1920." *History of Higher Education Annual* 4 (1984): 3-29.

_____."After the Emergence: Voluntary Support and the Building of American Research Universities." *History of Education Quarterly* 35 (Fall 1985): 369-381.

_____. *To Advance Knowledge: The Growth of American Research Universities, 1900-1940*. New York: Oxford University Press, 1986.

Girhard, Dietrich. "The Emergence of the Credit System in American Education." *Bulletin of American Association of University Professors* 41 (1955): 647-648.

Gordon, Lynn D. "Co-Education on Two Campuses: Berkeley and Chicago, 1890-1912." In *Women's Being, Women's Place: Female Identity and Vocation in American History*. Boston: G. K. Hall & Co., 1979.

Graham, Patricia. *Community and Class in American Education*. New York: Harper & Row, 1974.

Hawkins, Hugh. "Charles W. Eliot, University Reform and Religious Faith in America, 1869-1909." *Journal of American History* 51 (1964): 191-213.

_____. "The University-Builders Observe the Colleges." *History of Education Quarterly* 11 (Winter 1971): 353-362.

_____. "University Identity: The Teaching and Research Functions." In *The Organization of Knowledge in Modern America, 1860-1920*. Edited by Alexandra Oleson and John Voss. Baltimore: Johns Hopkins University Press, 1979.

Herbst, Jurgen. "Liberal Education and the Graduate Schools: An Historical View of College Reform." *History of Education Quarterly* 2 (December 1962): 244-258.

_____. *The German Historical School in American Scholarship: A Study in the Transfer of Culture*. New York: Cornell University Press, 1965.

Ludmerer, Kenneth. "The Flexner Report." In *Learning to Heal: The Development of American Medical Education*. New York: Basic Books, 1986.

McCaughey, Robert. "The Transition of American Academic Life: Harvard University, 1821-1892." *Perspectives in American History* 8 (1974): 239-334.

McGrath, Earl J. "The Control of Higher Education, 1860-1930." *Educational Record* 17 (1936): 259-272.

Metzger, Walter P. "The German Contribution to the American Theory of Academic Freedom." *AAUP Bulletin* 41 (Summer 1955): 214-230.

_____. "Academic Tenure in America: A Historical Essay." In *Faculty Tenure*. Edited by William R. Keast and John W. Marcy, Jr. San Francisco: Jossey-Bass, Publishers, 1973.

_____. "The Academic Profession in the United States." In *The Academic Profession.: National, Disciplinary, and Institutional Settings*. Edited by Burton R. Clark. Berkeley: University of California Press, 1987.

Mugleston, W. F. "The Press and Student Activism at the University of Georgia in the 1970's." *Georgia Historical Quarterly* 64 (Fall 1980): 241-252.

O'Boyle, Lenore. "Learning for Its Own Sake: The German University as Nineteenth Century Model." *Comparative Studies in Society and History* 25 (January 1983): 3-25.

Perry, Charles M. *Henry Philip Tappan: Philosopher and University President*. Ann Arbor: University of Michigan Press, 1933.

Rossiter, Margaret W. "Doctorates for American Women, 1868-1907." *History of Education Quarterly* 22 (Summer 1982): 159-183.

Rudy, Willis. "From Normal School to Multi-Purpose College." *History of Education Quarterly* 20 (Summer 1980): 241-246.

Rulon, P. R. "The Compress Cadets: A History of Collegiate Military Training, 1891-1951." *Chronicle of Oklahoma* 57 (Spring 1979): 67-90.

Shils, Edward. "The Order of Learning in the United States from 1865 to 1920: The Ascendancy of the Universities." In *The Organization of Knowledge in America, 1860-1920.* Edited by Alexandra Oleson and John Voss. Baltimore: Johns Hopkins University Press, 1979.

Storr, Richard J. "In the Age of the College." "Dreams of the American University." In *The Beginning of the Future: A Historical Approach to Graduate Education in the Arts and Sciences.* Carnegie Commission on Higher Education. New York: McGraw-Hill Book Co., 1973.

Synnott, Marcia Graham. *The Half-Opened Door: Discrimination and Admissions at Harvard, Yale, and Princeton, 1900-1970.* Westport, Conn.: Greenwood Press, 1979.

_____. "The Admission and Assimilation of Minority Students at Harvard, Yale, and Princeton, 1900-1970." *History of Education Quarterly* 19 (Fall 1979): 285-304.

Thelin, John R. "Cliometrics and the Colleges: The Campus Condition, 1880-1910." *Research in Higher Education* 21 (1984): 425-437.

Veblen, Thorstein. "The Governing Boards." In *The Higher Learning in America.* New York: Hill and Wang, 1957.

Veysey, Laurence R. "The Academic Mind of Woodrow Wilson." *Mississippi Valley Historical Review* 49 (1963): 613-634.

_____. *The Emergence of the American University.* Chicago: University of Chicago Press, 1965.

_____. "The Plural Organized Worlds of the Humanities." In *The Organization of Knowledge in Modern America, 1860-1920.* Edited by Alexandra Oleson and John Voss. Baltimore: Johns Hopkins University Press, 1979.

Webster, David S. "The Bureau of Education's Suppressed Rating of Colleges, 1911-1912." *History of Education Quarterly* 24 (Winter 1984): 499-511.

Wechsler, Harold S. *The Qualified Student: A History of Selective College Admission in America, 1870-1970.* New York: Wiley-Interscience, 1977.

_____. "An Academic Gresham's Law: Group Repulsion as a Theme in American Higher Education." *Teachers College Record* 82 (Summer, 1981): 567-588.

Wren, Dan. "American Business Philanthropy and Higher Education in the 19th Century." *Business History Review* 57 (Autumn 1983): 321-346.

Primary Readings

Angell, James. "Discipline in American Colleges." *North American Review* 149 (July 1889): 6.

_____. *The Reminiscences of James Burrell Angell.* New York: Longmans, Green, and Co., 1912.

Burns, C.S.C., James A. *Catholic Education: A Study of Conditions.* New York: Longmans, Green, and Co., 1917.

Eliot, Charles W. "The History of American Teaching." *Educational Review* 32 (November 1911): 362.

_____. "Inaugural Address as President at Harvard," Hofstadter and Smith, pp. 2: 601-623.

Flexner, Abraham. *Universities: American, English, and German.* New York: Oxford University Press, 1930.

Gilman, Daniel Coit. *The Launching of a University.* New York: Dodd, Mead, and Co., 1906.

_____. *University Problems in the United States.* New York: Century, 1898.

_____. "On the Business of a University (1885)." Cohen. pp. 3: 1566-1567.

_____.. "The Accomplishments of the University Era, 1861-1902," Hofstadter and Smith, pp. 2: 595-601.

Hall, G. Stanley. "Gilman's Policies at the Johns Hopkins University in the 1880s," Hofstadter and Smith, pp. 2: 648-652.

_____. "W. R. Harper's Raid Upon the Clark Faculty," 1892, Hofstadter and Smith, pp. 2: 759-760.

_____. "Co-education." *NEA Proceedings* (1904): 538-542.

Slosson, Edwin E. *Great American Universities.* New York: Arno Press, 1977. Reprint. New York: Macmillan, 1910.

Tappan, Henry P. "University Education, 1851," Hofstadter and Smith, pp. 2: 488-511.

White, Andrew D. "Description of Michigan under Tappan, ca. 1860," Hofstadter and Smith, pp. 2: 545-549.

_____. "His Achievements at Cornell, 1893," Hofstadter and Smith, pp. 2: 676-684.

Part VI: Higher Education during the First Half of the Twentieth Century and Its Legacy: Institutional Diversity and Discrimination

Altbach, Phillip. "The Thirties: A Movement Comes of Age." In *Student Politics in America: A Historical Analysis.* New York: McGraw-Hill Book Co, 1974.

Anderson, James O. "Training the Apostles of Liberal Culture: Black Higher Education, 1900-1935." In *The Education of Blacks in the South, 1860-1935.* Chapel Hill: University of North Carolina Press, 1988.

Antler, Joyce. "Culture, Service, and Work: Changing Ideals of Higher Education for Women." In *The Undergraduate Women: Issues in Educational Equity.* Edited by Pamela Perun. Lexington, Mass.: Lexington Books, 1982.

Clifford, Geraldine Joncich, and Guthrie, James W. *School: A Brief for Professional Education*. Chicago: University of Chicago Press, 1988.

Cohen, Arthur M., and Brawer, Florence B. "Background." In *The American Community College*. San Francisco: Jossey-Bass Publishers, 1982.

Crawfurd, A. "A Short History of the Public Community Junior College in the United States." *Pedagogica Historica* 10 (1970): 28-48.

Donnelly, J. B. "The Vision of Scholarship: Johns Hopkins After the War." *Maryland History Magazine* 73 (June 1978): 137-162.

Fisher, Lois A. "State Legislatures and the Autonomy of Colleges and Universities: A Comparative Study of Legislation in Four States, 1900-1979." *Journal of Higher Education*, 59 (March/April 1988): 133-162.

Fitzgerald, S.J., Paul A. *The Governance of Jesuit Colleges in the United States, 1920-1970*. Notre Dame, Ind.: University of Notre Dame Press, 1984.

Gleason, Philip W. "American Catholic Higher Education: A Historical Perspective." In *The Shape of Catholic Higher Education*. Edited by Robert Hassenger. Chicago: University of Chicago Press, 1967.

Goodchild, Lester F. "The Turning Point in American Jesuit Higher Education: The Standardization Controversy between the Jesuits and the North Central Association, 1915-1940." *History of Higher Education Annual* 6 (1986): 81-116.

_____. "American Catholic Legal Education and the Founding of DePaul's College of Law." *DePaul Law Review* 37 (Spring 1988).

Graham, Patricia. "Expansion and Exclusion: A History of Women in American Higher Education." *Signs* 3 (Summer 1978): 759-773.

Gruber, Carol S. *Mars and Minerva: World War I and the Uses of the Higher Learning in America*. Baton Rouge: Louisiana State University Press, 1975.

Hijiya, James A. "The Free Speech Movement and the Heroic Moment." *Journal of American Studies* 22 (April 1988): 43-66.

Hofstadter, Richard. *Anti-Intellectualism in American Life*. New York: Alfred A. Knopf, 1963.

Koos, Leonard V. *The Junior-College Movement*, Boston: Ginn and Co., 1925.

Levine, David O. "Junior College and the Differentiation of the Public Sector." In *The American College and the Culture of Aspiration. 1915-1940*. Ithaca, N.Y.: Cornell University Press, 1986.

McLachlan, James. "American Colleges and the Transmission of Culture: The Case of the Mugwumps." In *The Hofstadter Aegis: A Memorial*. Edited by S. Elkins and E. McKitrick. New York: Alfred A. Knopf, 1974.

Orr, Kenneth B. "Higher Education and the Great Depression: An Introduction to the Early Thirties." *Review of Higher Education* 2 (1979): 1-10.

Peterson, George E. "The University's Winnowing Breeze of Freedom." In *The New England College in the Age of the University*. Amherst, Mass.: Amherst College Press, 1964.

Pfinster, Allan O. "The Role of the Liberal Arts College: A Historical Overview of the Debates." *Journal of Higher Education* 55 (March/April 1984): 145-170.

Ratcliff, James L. " 'First' Public Junior Colleges in an Age of Reform. "*Journal of Higher Education* 58 (March/April 1987): 151-180.

Riesman, David. "Football in America: A Study in Cultural Diffusion." In *Individualism Reconsidered, and Other Essays*. Glencoe, Ill.: Free Press, 1954.

Rose, Louise Blecher. "The Secret Life of Sarah Lawrence." *Commentary* 64 (May 1983): 52-56.

Rothblatt, Sheldon. "General Education on the American Campus: A Historical Introduction in Brief." In *Cultural Literacy and the Ideas of General Education*. Edited by Ian Westbury and Alan C. Purves. NSSE Yearbook. Vol. 2. Chicago: University of Chicago Press, 1988.

Veysey, Laurence R. "Stability and Change in the American College Curriculum." In *Content and Context: Essays on College Education*. Edited by Carl Kaysen. New York: McGraw-Hill Book Company, 1973.

Wagoner, Jr., Jennings L. "The American Compromise: Charles W. Eliot, Black Education, and the New South." In *Education and the Rise of the New South*. Edited by Ronald K. Goodenow and Arthur O. White. Boston: G. K. Hall, 1981.

Wechsler, Harold S. "An Academic Gresham's Law: Group Repulsion as a Theme in American Higher Education." *Teachers College Record* 82 (Summer 1981): 567-588.

Westly, David, and Sack, Allen. "The Commercialization and Functional Rationalization of College Football: Its Origins." *Journal of Higher Education* 47 (November 1976): 625-647.

Primary Readings

A. Lawrence Lowell Justifies the Control of Universities by Laymen, 1920, Hofstadter and Smith, pp. 2: 823-840.

Abraham Flexner Criticizes the American University, 1930, Hofstadter and Smith, pp. 2: 905-921.

Harry Gideonse on Hutchins and Flexner, 1937, Hofstadter and Smith, pp. 2: 941-948.

James Wechsler, *Revolt on Campus* (New York, 1935), pp. 108-116. Cohen, pp. 5: 2791-2795.

Du Bois, W.E.B. "The Talented Tenth" [from *The Negro Problem*. 1903]. In *Writings*. New York: Literary Classics of the United States, Inc., 1986. pp. 842- 861.

Thomas, M. Carey. "On the Higher Education of Women." Cohen, pp. 5: 2791-2795.

John Dewey on Hutchins' Philosophy of Education, Hofstadter and Smith, pp. 949-954.

Robert M. Hutchins Assesses the State of the Higher Learning, 1936, Hofstadter and Smith, pp. 2: 924-940.

Meiklejohn, Alexander. "Progressive Education in the Liberal College." In *Higher Education Faces the Future*. Edited by Paul A. Schilpp. New York: Horace Liveright, 1930.

Part VII: The Main Trends in Higher Education after World War II: Federalism and Democratization

Astin, Alexander W., et al. "Overview of the Unrest Era." In *The Power of Protest*. San Francisco: Jossey-Bass, 1975, pp. 17-45.

Best, John Hardin. "The Revolution of Markets and Management: Toward a History of American Higher Education since 1945." *History of Education Quarterly* 28 (Summer 1988): 177-189.

Bowles, Frank and DeCosta, Frank A. "1954 to the Present." In *Between Two Worlds: A Profile of Negro Higher Education*. Carnegie Commission on Higher Education. New York: McGraw-Hill Book Company, 1971, pp. 61-80.

Brubacher, John S., and Rudy, Willis. "Distinguishing Features of American Higher Education." In *Higher Education in Transition: A History of American Colleges and Universities, 1636-1976*. 3rd ed., rev. and enl.. New York: Harper & Row, Publishers, 1976.

Fleming, Donald, and Bailyn, Bernard. "Introduction." In *The Intellectual Migration: Europe and America, 1930-1960*. Cambridge, Mass.: Harvard University Press, 1969.

Gitlin, Todd. *The Sixties: Years of Hope, Years of Rage*. New York: Bantam Books, 1987.

Gordon, Milton. "Enrollment of Black Students in Higher Education, 1940-1972." *Journal of Negro Education* 45 (1976): 117-149.

Graham, Hugh Davis. "Task Forcing Toward Lyndon Johnson's Great Society." In *The Uncertain Triumph: Federal Education Policy in the Kennedy and Johnson Years*. Chapel Hill, N.C.: University of North Carolina Press, 1982.

Horowitz, Helen Lefkowitz. "The 1960s and the Transformation of Campus Cultures." *History of Education Quarterly* 26 (Spring 1986): 1-38.

Jencks, Christopher, and Riesman, David. *The Academic Revolution*. Chicago: University of Chicago Press, 1968.

Keppel, Francis. "The Higher Education Acts Contrasted, 1965-1986: Has Federal Policy Come of Age?" *Harvard Educational Review* 57 (February 1987): 49-67.

Kerr, Janet C. "From Truman to Johnson: *Ad Hoc* Policy Formulation in Higher Education." *Review of Higher Education* 8 (Fall 1984): 15-54.

Kimball, Bruce A. "The Historical and Cultural Dimensions of the Recent Reports on Undergraduate Education." *American Journal of Education* 98 (May 1988): 293- 322.

672

Metzger, Walter P. "A Spectre is Haunting American Scholars: The Spectre of 'Professionism'." *Educational Researcher* 16 (August-September 1987): 10-19.

Olivas, Michael A. "Indian, Chicano, and Puerto Rican Colleges: Status and Issues." *Bilingual Review* 9 (January-April 1982): 36-58.

_____. "State Law and Postsecondary Coordination: The Birth of the Ohio Board of Regents." *Review of Higher Education* 7 (Summer 1984): 357-395.

Ravitch, Diane. "From Berkeley to Kent State." In *The Troubled Crusade: American Education, 1945 - 1980*. New York: Basic Books, Inc., Publishers, 1983.

Russ, Ann J. "American Higher Learning since World War II: Professionalism, Bureaucracy and Managerial Elites." In *History of Education*. New York: Institute for Research in History and the Haworth Press, 1984.

Schrecker, Ellen W. *No Ivory Tower: McCarthyism and the Universities*. New York: Oxford University Press, 1986.

Shils, Edward. "The University: A Backward Glance." *The American Scholar* (Spring 1982): 163-179.

Solomon, Barbara Miller. "The Promises of Liberal Education—Forgotten and Fulfilled." In *In the Company of Educated Women: A History of Women and Higher Education in America*. New Haven: Yale University Press, 1985.

Sykes, Gary. "Reckoning with the Spectre." *Educational Researcher* 16 (August-September 1987): 19-21.

Trow, Martin. "American Higher Education: Past, Present, Future." *Educational Researcher* 14 (April 1988): 13-23.

_____. "Elite and Popular Functions in American Higher Education." In *Higher Education: Demand and Response*. Edited by W. R. Niblett. San Francisco: Jossey-Bass Publishers, 1970.

Tuttle, W. M. "American Higher Education and the Nazis: The Care of James B. Conant and Harvard's University Diplomatic Relations with Germany." *American Studies* 22 (Spring 1979): 159-165.

Wright, Bobby. "Tribally-Controlled Community Colleges." *Canadian Journal of Native Education* 14 (Winter 1987): 29-36.

Primary Readings

Farker, Jerry. "Modern Slaves: The Student as Nigger." *Los Angeles Free Press* (March 3, 1967). Cohen, pp. 5: 2864-2867.

"The GI Bill of Rights" (1944) from House Committee Print No. 371, 80th Cong. 2d Session (Washington, D.C. 1948), pp. 7-10, Cohen, pp. 5: 2799-2802.

Higher Education Act of 1965. In *Federal Role in Education*. 2nd ed. Washington, D.C:
Congressional Quarterly Service, 1967, pp. 50-54.

John F. Kennedy. "Civil Rights Message from the President of the United States,"
Congressional Record — House (Washington 1963). Cohen, pp. 5: 3245-3247, 3361-3365.

Pamphlet of the Free Speech Movement at the University of California, Berkeley (1965).
Edited by Seymor M. Lipset and Sheldon S. Wolin. In *The Berkeley Student Revolt: Facts
and Interpretations* . Garden City, NY: 1965, pp. 209-215.

The President's Commission on Higher Education for Democracy, 1947, Hofstadter and Smith,
pp. 2: 970-990. A Report on General Education by the Harvard Committee (1945) from
General Education in a Free Society. Cambridge, Mass., 1945, pp. 43-47, 50, 57-58. Cohen,
pp. 5: 2802-2806.

Part VIII: Historiographic, Methodological, and Organizational Perspectives

Barzun, Jacques, and Graff, Henry F. *The Modern Researcher*. 3rd ed. New York: Harcourt,
Brace & Jovanovich, 1977.

Becher, Carl. "Everyman His Own Historian." *American Historical Review* 37 (January 1932):
221-236.

Blackburn, Robert T., and Conrad, Clifton F. "The New Revisionists and the History of U.S.
Higher Education." *Higher Education* 15 (Nos. 3-4, 1986): 211-230.

Bonnell, Victoria E. "The Uses of Theory, Concepts, and Comparison in Historical Sociology."
Comparative Studies in Society and History 22 (April 1980): 156-173.

Burstyn, Joan N. "History as Image: Changing the Lens." *History of Education Quarterly* 27
(Summer 1987): 167-180.

Clark, Burton. "Organization Saga in Higher Education." *Administrative Science Quarterly* 17
(June 1972): 172-184.

Gaffield, Chad. "Coherence and Chaos in Educational Historiography." *Interchange* 17
(Summer 1986): 112- 121.

Gawronski, Donald V. *History: Meaning and Method*. 3rd edition. Glenview, Il: Scott,
Foresman, and Company, 1975.

Gottschalk, Louis. *Understanding History: A Primer of Historical Method*. New York: Alfred
A. Knopf, 1960.

Gottschalk, Louis, ed. *Generalization in the Writing of History*. Chicago: University of
Chicago Press, 1963.

Graham, Patricia A. "Historians as Policy Makers." *Educational Researcher* 9 (No. 11, 1980):
21-24.

Hamerow, Theodore S. *Reflections on History and Historians*. Madison, Wisc.: University of
Wisconsin Press, 1987.

Hansot, Elisabeth, and Tyack, David. "A Usable Part: Using History in Educational Policy." *Policy Making in Education*. Eighty-First Yearbook of the National Society for the Study of Education. Vol. 1. Edited by Ann Lieberman and Milbrey W. McLaughlin. Chicago: University of Chicago Press, 1982.

Hodysh, Henry W. "Objectivity and History in the Study of Higher Education." *Canadian Journal of Higher Education* 17 (no. 1, 1987): 83-93.

Kent, Sherman. *Writing History*. New York: Appleton-Century-Crofts, Inc., 1941.

Mattingly, Paul H. "Structures Over Time: Institutional History." *Historical Inquiry in Education: A Research Agenda*. Edited by John Hardin Best. Washington, D.C.: American Educational Research Association, 1983.

Moore, Kathryn M. "Toward a Synthesis of Organizational Theory and Historical Analysis: The Case of Academic Women." *Review of Higher Education* 5 (Summer 1982): 213-223.

Storr, Richard J. "The Uses of History." In *The Beginning of the Future: A Historical Approach to Graduate Education in the Arts and Sciences*. Carnegie Commission on Higher Education. New York: McGraw-Hill Book Co., 1973.

Thelin, John R. "Stepping in By Looking Back: Using History to Introduce the Study of Higher Education." *Review of Higher Education* 3 (Winter 1980): 31-34.

Veysey, Laurence. "Intellectual History and the New Social History." In *New Directions in American Intellectual History*. Edited by John Higham and Paul K. Conkin. Baltimore: Johns Hopkins University Press, 1979.

PART IX: Reference Works and Bibliographies

Beach, Mark. *A Bibliographic Guide to American Colleges and Universities from Colonial Times to the Present*. Westport, Conn.: Greenwood Press, 1975.

_____. *A Subject Bibliography of the History of American Higher Education*. Westport, Conn.: Greenwood Press, 1984.

Beauchamp, Edward R. *Dissertations in the History of Education, 1970-1980*. Metuchen, N.J.: Scarecrow Press, 1985.

Best, John Hardin, ed. *Historical Inquiry in Education: A Research Agenda*. Washington, D.C.: American Educational Research Association, 1983.

Brickman, William W. "Bibliographical Introduction to History of U.S. Higher Education." In *Century of Higher Education: Classical Citadel to Collegiate Colossus*. Edited by William W. Brickman and Stanley Lehrer. New York: Society for the Advancement of Education, 1962.

_____. "*Notae*: Selected Bibliography on Church-State-School Relations in Historical, International, and Comparative Perspectives." *Paedagogica Historica* 12 (1972): 158-65.

Caldwell, John. *Histories of American Colleges and Universities: A Bibliography.* Bethesda, Md: ERIC Processing and Reference Facility, 1976.

Chambers, Frederick, ed. *Black Higher Education in the U.S.: A Selected Bibliography on Negro Higher Education and Historically Black Colleges and Universities.* Westport, Conn.: Greenwood Press, 1978.

Cordasco, Francesco, and Brickman, W. William. *The Bibliography of American Educational History.* New York: Garland Press, 1976.

Duncan, James A., et al. *The Role of Universities in Development Programs: The Land Grant Idea—Annotated Bibliography of Selected Readings.* Madison, Wisc.: Department of Agriculture Extension Education, University of Wisconsin, 1967.

Kramer, John E., ed. *The American College Novel: An Annotated Bibliography.* New York: Garland Press, 1981.

Krug, Edward A. *Salient Dates in American Education.* New York: Harper & Row, 1966.

Ohles, John F., and Ohles, Shirley M., *Biographical Dictionary of American Educators.* 3 Vols. Westport, Conn.: Greenwood Press, 1978.

_____. *Private Colleges and Universities.* 2 vols. Westport, Conn.: Greenwood Press, 1982.

_____. *Public Colleges and Universities.* Westport, Conn.: Greenwood Press, 1986.

Perkins, M. H. *American Higher Education: A Selected Bibliography on Aims and Curricula.* Evanston, Ill.: Northwestern University Library, 1950.

Porter, Dale H. *The Emergence of the Past: A Theory of Historical Explanation.* Chicago: University of Chicago Press, 1981.

Sedlack, Michael W., and Walsh, Timothy, eds. *American Educational History: A Guide to Information Sources.* New York: Garland Press, 1981.

Songe, Alice H. *American Universities and Colleges: A Dictionary of Name Changes.* Metuchen, N.J.: Scarecrow Press, Inc., 1978.

_____. *The Land-Grant Idea in American Higher Education: A Guide to Information Sources.* New York: K. G. Saur Publishing, 1980.